# WileyPLUS Learning Space

An easy way to help your students **learn**, **collaborate**, and **grow**.

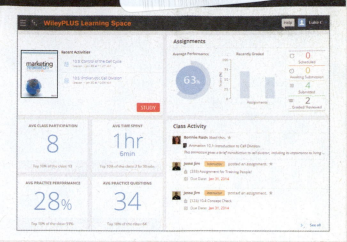

## Personalized Experience

Students create their own study guide while they interact with course content and work on learning activities.

## Flexible Course Design

Educators can quickly organize learning activities, manage student collaboration, and customize their course—giving them full control over content as well as the amount of interactivity between students.

## Clear Path to Action

With visual reports, it's easy for both students and educators to gauge problem areas and act on what's most important.

## Instructor Benefits

- Assign activities and add your own materials
- Guide students through what's important in the interactive e-textbook by easily assigning specific content
- Set up and monitor collaborative learning groups
- Assess learner engagement
- Gain immediate insights to help inform teaching

## Student Benefits

- Instantly know what you need to work on
- Create a personal study plan
- Assess progress along the way
- Participate in class discussions
- Remember what you have learned because you have made deeper connections to the content

**We are dedicated to supporting you from idea to outcome.**

WILEY

# Marketing Research

Tenth Edition

# Marketing Research

## Tenth Edition

**Carl McDaniel, Jr.**
Professor Emeritus
University of Texas at Arlington

**Roger Gates**
DSS Research

WILEY

*Dedicated to*
*Mimi Olsen*
*Abby, Will, Connor, Will, Cole, Jake, Knox*

VICE PRESIDENT & EXECUTIVE PUBLISHER George Hoffman
EXECUTIVE EDITOR Lisé Johnson
SPONSORING EDITOR Marian Provenzano
PROJECT EDITOR Brian Baker
EDITORIAL ASSISTANT Jacqueline Hughes
ASSOCIATE EDITOR Christina Volpe
CONTENT MANAGER Elle Wagner
SENIOR MARKETING MANAGER Kelly Simmons
DESIGN DIRECTOR Harry Nolan
SENIOR PHOTO EDITOR Lisa Gee
COVER PHOTO German/E+/Getty Images

This book was set in Adobe Garamond by SPiGlobal, and printed and bound by Quad Graphics/Versailles. The cover was printed by Quad Graphics/Versailles.

This book is printed on acid free paper. ⊚

Founded in 1807, John Wiley & Sons, Inc. has been a valued source of knowledge and understanding for more than 200 years, helping people around the world meet their needs and fulfill their aspirations. Our company is built on a foundation of principles that include responsibility to the communities we serve and where we live and work. In 2008, we launched a Corporate Citizenship Initiative, a global effort to address the environment, social, economic, and ethical challenges we face in our business. Among the issues we are addressing are carbon impact, paper specifications and procurement, ethical conduct within our business and among our vendors, and community and charitable support. For more information, please visit our website: www.wiley.com/go/citizenship.

ISBN-978-1118-808849

Printed in the United States of America

10 9 8 7 6 5 4 3 2 1

# Preface

## THE WORLD OF MARKETING RESEARCH HAS CHANGED

Some research pundits would say that the world of marketing research has completely changed since the last edition of this text was published in 2012. While we aren't willing to go that far, we do agree that several innovations and trends have had a substantial impact on the field of marketing research. The era of Big Data has arrived! Big data analytics can offer profound insights into customers, potential customers, and markets like never before. We introduce big data in Chapter One and discuss it, where applicable, throughout the text. Further, not isolated to big data, the area of analytics has arrived with clients demanding tools that provide more direction and insight for decision making. This trend is noted at appropriate places in the text, but particularly in Chapter Eighteen.

The trend toward mobile and social media marketing research is changing how decision making information is obtained and, in some cases, what data is gathered. This is discussed extensively in Chapter Seven. The availability of online survey tools, such as those offered by Survey Monkey, has resulted in many more firms diving into do-it-yourself (DIY) marketing research. We cover the benefits and dangers of the trend toward DIY marketing research in Chapter Twelve.

## AS IN EVERY PAST EDITION, WE OFFER: REAL DATA/REAL RESEARCH/ REAL RESEARCHERS

### Real Data – A new Nationwide Survey on Quick Service Restaurants Created Exclusively For This Text

Our new case examines how Americans 18 to 34 years old view, patronize and consume food from Quick Service Restaurant (QSR) chains such as McDonalds, Taco Bell and many more. By analyzing the data you can gain insights on what factors caused consumers to patronize a particular chain and which chains perform the best on factors such as quality of food, menu variety, atmosphere and others. The case also features a host of demographic characteristics to enable you to analyze preferences, likes and dislikes by attitudes toward health and nutrition, level of education, income, living situation, and other variables.

We have retained our three popular data cases, which are based on a nationwide sample of 2,000 college-aged students. The sample was drawn by the world leader in sampling solutions, Survey Sampling International. You can find out more about them at *www.surveysampling.com*. Each of the three cases focuses on topics of interest to college students. They include an Online Dating Service, an Online Student Travel Service, and a new chain of combination fast-food and convenience store located near college campuses. Not only do we have demographic and attitudinal data for each respondent, but working with Claritas, a leading provider of marketing databases (*www.claritas.com*), we offer students a chance to work with PRIZM NE appended to our data sets. This version of the original PRIZM is the most widely used target marketing system in the United States! PRIZM NE is a 66-segment model. These segments are arranged to make up two standard sets of groups: Social Group and Lifestage Group.

In addition to these cases, we have retained the data case, Rockingham National Bank Visa Card Survey, for the tenth edition. This was done in response to many requests from our users. We know that you will enjoy working with this student favorite!

## Real Research

What could be more real than a new nationwide study on quick service restaurants. The sample was drawn, the questionnaire created, and data gathered by marketing research professionals at DSS Research. All end-of-chapter cases are real and most are new for this tenth edition. It is part of our commitment to you to bring the student the most authentic, real-world marketing research text on the market.

## Real Market Researchers

Our world-view is that of marketing research. We are here every day, not as observers, but participants. Roger Gates, one of your co-authors is President of DSS Research, one of America's largest health-care marketing research firms. You can learn more at www.dss-research.com. Carl McDaniel was a co-founder of a marketing research company that is vibrant today. He also was a co-founder of the Master of Science in Marketing Research program at the University of Texas at Arlington. Along with Roger Gates and several others, Carl created the MSMR Advisory Board. The Advisory Board consists of leaders and shakers in the marketing research industry (go to www.uta.edu/msmr/advisory-board/advisory-board-members.com). You are holding the only text written by marketing research insiders. It is like writing about football as you witness the game from the stands or writing about the sport as a player on the field. We are not spectators viewing marketing research from afar. Unlike authors of other research texts, we are on the field and continue to offer you the global leader in marketing research texts.

# AS THE FIELD OF MARKETING RESEARCH CONTINUES TO TRANSFORM, WE ARE THERE, EVERY STEP OF THE WAY, PROVIDING THE LATEST TRENDS AND METHODOLOGY IN EVERY CHAPTER

## New Content by Chapter:

### Chapter One – The Role of Marketing Research in Management Decision Making

New section on "The Era of Big Data" and its impact on marketing research. New box on forces that are poised to change the world of marketing research. Dynamic new examples throughout.

## Chapter Two – The Marketing Research Industry and Research Ethics

New material on big data analytic firms. New list of America's largest research firms. New section on online, mobile, and Big Data analytic tracking firms. All new discussion on the state of the marketing research industry including material on research in a period of great change.

## Chapter Three – Problem Definition, Exploratory Research, and the Research Process

Completely rewritten section on research objectives as hypothesis. New Practicing Marketing Research box on making marketing research more strategic.

## Chapter Four – Secondary Data and Big Data Analytics

Completely rewritten chapter emphasizing the nature of secondary data and Big Data. New section on what advantages Big Data offers a firm and a discussion on how Big Data came about. New material on making Big Data actionable. A section on the growing importance of data visualization.

## Chapter Five – Qualitative Research

Revised material on key attributes of a good focus group moderator. Discussion of a new trend in focus groups entitled "the rotated opposed view." New discussion on getting the right respondents for focus groups. Detailed, new examples on individual depth interviews and "story telling".

## Chapter Six – Traditional Survey Research

New material on telephone refusal rates. New discussion on predictive dialing. New Practicing Marketing Research box on respondent respect. Important new data on the maximum length of interviews.

## Chapter Seven – Online Marketing Research – The Growth of Mobile and Social Media Research

Major new sections on mobile internet research and social media marketing research. New material on using blogs as a form of individual depth interviews. New discussion on online bulletin board focus groups. New section on webcam online focus groups. New section on improving virtual focus groups with telepresence. Completely revised material on online individual depth interviews and participants in a research community. New discussion on the quality of online samples.

## Chapter Eight – Primary Data Collection: Observation

Expanded discussion on ethnography. New section on neuromarketing. Completely revised section on eye tracking. New section on in-store tracking. All new material on television audience measurement and tracking. Major new sections on online tracking and social media tracking. In-depth examples of Facebook, Pinterest, and Twitter.

## Chapter Nine – Primary Data Collection: Experimentation and Test Marketing

Eliminated some sections and focused the chapter more on the practical problems of doing experiments including new material on simulated test markets. New commentary and examples are offered throughout the chapter.

## Chapter Ten – The Concept of Measurement

New material on construct equivalence. New Practicing Marketing Research box on designing a better questionnaire.

### Chapter Eleven – Using Measurement Scales to Build Marketing Effectiveness

Expanded discussion of graphic rating scales as "sliders." Major new section on Net Promoter Scores.

### Chapter Twelve – Questionnaire Design

Discussed the changing nature of data collection in marketing research. Added new coverage of issues related to designing questionnaires for mobile devices, including Practicing Marketing Research covering tips for effective mobile interviewing. New discussion on how to approach the appropriate data collection method based on the options available today. Updated discussion of online interviewing tools and options. Added information on benefits and dangers of DIY research, including best practices. New case covers mobile survey research example.

### Chapter Thirteen – Basic Sampling Issues

Major new discussion of sampling issues related to big data and social media. Updated the role of data collection methods and sampling related to mobile data collection and big data. Added Practicing Marketing Research feature discussing the blending of social media and online panels. New information on the comparability of online panel and telephone survey results is provided.

### Chapter Fourteen – Sample Size Determination

A number of new examples are given and a new end-of-chapter case.

### Chapter Fifteen – Data Processing and Fundamental Data Analysis

New section on quality assurance procedures for online data collection. Updated coding discussion with discussion of automated coding systems, text processing software and word clouds with an extended Practicing Marketing Research on text processing. Addressed the need for some type of text processing to address big data and the analysis of social media feeds. Also added a Practicing Marketing Research feature covering an application of Semantria text analytics and how this system can be utilized to improve market insights. Discussed the declining reliance on crosstabs and the reasons for this decline. Added case that asks students to compare traditional coding results with what they can get from Semantria. Data provided, access to Semantria is free.

### Chapter Sixteen – Statistical Testing of Differences and Relationships

New material on statistical testing in the context of big data. New Practicing Marketing Research feature that discusses, in simple terms, the logic behind statistical testing.

### Chapter Seventeen – Bivariate Correlation and Regression

New Practicing Marketing Research feature on regression. A second Practicing Marketing Research feature discusses using regression analysis in key driver analysis. New case provides a very realistic and current example requiring the application of regression analysis.

### Chapter Eighteen – Multivariate Data Analysis

New Practicing Marketing Research feature covers the high demand for data scientists in marketing research. Fuzzy clustering added to cluster analysis discussion, and also neural networks. Conjoint analysis section updated with recent developments. The application of multivariate techniques to big data was added. Also, material on predictive analytics, which includes a detailed discussion of the predictive analytics process and predictive analytics implications in marketing research. Interesting finding from predictive analytics ("How Target Figured Out a Teen Girl

Was Pregnant Before Her Father Did") added as a Practicing Marketing Research feature. Case added covering predictive analytics in retail.

### Chapter Nineteen – Communicating The Research Results

New Practicing Marketing Research feature added with tips for preparing a marketing research report for a contemporary audience. Also added a feature covering the importance of telling a story in the research report and a Practicing Marketing Research feature on how to give more effective research presentations.

### Chapter Twenty – Managing Marketing Research

Added more emphasis on project management and provided a new Practicing Marketing Research feature covering project management. Added discussions of the RFP process and proposal preparation. Feature added on the elevation of marketing research in the corporate hierarchy and, added feature on how the future marketing organization might look. New case added covering the process of selecting a research supplier.

# Outstanding Resources For All Teaching Needs

## WileyPlus Learning Space

What is *WileyPLUS Learning Space*? It's a place where students can learn, collaborate, and grow. Through a personalized experience, students create their own study guide while they interact with course content and work on learning activities.

*WileyPLUS Learning Space* combines adaptive learning functionality with a dynamic new e-textbook for your course—giving you tools to quickly organize learning activities, manage student collaboration, and customize your course so that you have full control over content as well as the amount of interactivity between students.

You can:

- Assign activities and add your own materials
- Guide students through what's important in the e-textbook by easily assigning specific content
- Set up and monitor collaborative learning groups
- Assess student engagement
- Benefit from a sophisticated set of reporting and diagnostic tools that give greater insight into class activity

Learn more at www.wileypluslearningspace.com. If you have questions, please contact your Wiley representative.

# Classroom-Tested Instructor's Manual

We have done everything possible to facilitate your teaching marketing research with a comprehensive instructor's manual. Each chapter contains the following:

- *Suggested Lesson Plans*. Suggestions are given on how to decide the chapter material, based on the frequency and duration of your class period.
- *Chapter Scan*. A quick synopsis highlights the core material in each chapter.
- *Learning Objectives*. The list of learning objectives found in the text is repeated here.

- *General Chapter Outline*. The main headers provide a quick snapshot of all the content areas within the chapter.
- *List of Key Terms*. The key terms introduced to the students in the text are repeated here.
- *Detailed Chapter Outline*. This outline fleshes out the general outline given previously. It also indicates where ancillary materials fit into the discussion: PowerPoint slides, exhibits from the text, learning objectives, and review questions. Boxed features are also included in this outline.
- *Summary Explaining Learning Objectives*. An explanation of how the learning objectives are satisfied by chapter material is the basis of the Instructor's Manual summary.
- *Answers to Pedagogy*. Suggested answers and approaches to the critical thinking questions, the Internet activities, the cases, the cross-functional questions, and the ethical dilemmas are offered at the end of each chapter or part.

Instructors can access the electronic files on the Instructor Companion Site at *www.Wiley.com/College/Mcdaniel*.

## Comprehensive PowerPoint Package

We have created a comprehensive, fully interactive PowerPoint presentation with roughly 400 slides in the package. You can tailor your visual presentation to include the material you choose to cover in class. This PowerPoint presentation gives you the ability to completely integrate your classroom lecture with a powerful visual statement of chapter material. Keep students engaged and stimulate classroom discussion! The entire collection of slides will be available for download from our Web site at *www.Wiley.com/College/Mcdaniel*.

## Classroom-Tested Comprehensive Test Bank

Our test bank is comprehensive and thoroughly classroom-tested. The questions range from definitions of key terms to basic problem-solving questions to creative-thinking problems. This new and improved test bank includes approximately 60 questions per chapter consisting of multiple-choice, true/false, and essay questions. Regardless of the type and level of knowledge you wish to test, we have the right questions for your students. A computerized version of this newly created test bank is also available on the book's companion Web site so that you can customize your quizzes and exams. Instructions can access the electronic files on the Instructor's Companion Site at *www.Wiley.com/College/Mcdaniel*.

## Focus Group Video and Lecture Launches

Additional *Real Research* is offered through a focus group video conducted by another one of our research partners. Jerry Thomas, president of Decision Analyst (*www.decisionanalysis.com*). Decision Analyst, Incorporated is a large international marketing research firm. The focus group subject is online dating data case. We also offer several interviews featuring Jerry Thomas and your author, Carl McDaniel, discussing key topics in marketing research. For more information on this 45-minute video, available on DVD, please contact your local Wiley representative.

## New Wiley Marketing Research Video Series

New interview-style video clips of top marketing research companies. Each video, six to eight minutes in length, presents interviews with key personnel to discuss how they apply the major concepts of marketing research to their business. The Marketing Wiley Research Video Series can be accessed on the student and Instructor's Companion site at www.Wiley.com/College/Mcdaniel.

# Acknowledgments

As with all texts, this book is a team effort that could not have been brought to print without their support. Carl McDaniel continues to marvel at the excellent job Pam Rimer does in typing his portion of the manuscript. Thanks also Pam for the many great editorial suggestions.

Roger Gates thanks Mike Foytik for his input on big data issues and analytics in general and extend special thanks to Jan Schneider for her outstanding work in keeping everything straight in his chapters. Could not have done it without her very competent assistance.

We also extend our deep appreciation to the John Wiley & Sons team for making this text a reality. In particular, a special thank you goes to the team at Wiley: Brian Baker (Project Editor), Lisé Johnson (Executive Editor), and Jacqueline Hughes (Editorial Assistant).

# Contents

**PREFACE** vii

**1 The Role of Marketing Research in Management Decision Making 1**

**Nature of Marketing 1**

The Marketing Concept 2

Opportunistic Nature of Marketing Research 2

External Marketing Environment 2

**Marketing Research and Decision Making 3**

Marketing Research Defined 3

Importance of Marketing Research to Management 4

Understanding the Ever-Changing Marketplace 6

Social Media and User-Generated Content 6

Proactive Role of Marketing Research 6

Applied Research versus Basic Research 7

Nature of Applied Research 7

Decision to Conduct Marketing Research 8

**Development of Marketing Research 11**

Inception: Pre-1900 11

Early Growth: 1900–1920 11

Adolescent Years: 1920–1950 11

Mature Years: 1950–2000 12

The Connected World: 2000–2010 13

ERA of Big Data: 2010–Present 14

**Summary 15**

**Key Terms 16**

**Questions For Review & Critical Thinking 16**

REAL-LIFE RESEARCH 1.1: Give Me a Coupon That I Can Use Online! 17

REAL-LIFE RESEARCH 1.2: Can Anyone Be a Market Researcher? 18

**2 The Marketing Research Industry and Research Ethics 19**

**Evolving Structure of the Marketing Research Industry 20**

**Organizations Involved in Marketing Research 20**

Consumer and Industrial Goods and Services Producers 20

Governments and Universities 22

Media Companies 22

Custom Research Firms 22

Syndicated Service Firms 22

Limited-Function Research Firms 23

Online and Mobile Tracking Firms 23

Big Data Analytic Firms 24

Specialized Service Suppliers 24

**Consumer and Industrial Corporate Marketing Research Departments 25**

**Research Suppliers 26**

Consumer Watch 26

Consumer Buy 27

**Using Marketing Research—A Corporate Perspective 28**

External Clients 28

Internal Clients 29

**The State of the Marketing Research Industry 31**

**Marketing Research Ethics 32**

Ethical Theories 32

Research Supplier Ethics 33

Client Ethics 36

Field Service Ethics 38

Respondents' Rights 38

Ethics and Professionalism 40

**Summary 42**

**Key Terms 42**

**Questions For Review & Critical Thinking 42**

**Working the Net 43**

REAL-LIFE RESEARCH 2.1: Respondent Recruiters— Clean Up Your Act 43

REAL-LIFE RESEARCH 2.2: Coke Juices up a Market Test 44

**3. Problem Definition, Exploratory Research, and the Research Process 46**

**Critical Importance of Correctly Defining the Problem 46**

Recognize the Problem or Opportunity 47

Find Out Why the Information Is Being Sought 48

Understand the Decision-Making Environment with Exploratory Research 48

Use the Symptoms to Clarify the Problem 50

Translate the Management Problem into a Marketing Research Problem 51

Determine Whether the Information Already Exists 51

Determine Whether the Question Can Be Answered 52

State the Research Objectives 52

**Research Objectives As Hypotheses 52**

**Marketing Research Process 53**

Creating the Research Design **54**

Choosing a Basic Method of Research **55**

Selecting the Sampling Procedure **56**

Collecting the Data **56**

Analyzing the Data **57**

Writing and Presenting the Report **57**

Following Up **58**

**Managing the Research Process 58**

The Research Request **58**

Request for Proposal **59**

**The Marketing Research Proposal 59**

What to Look for in a Marketing Research Supplier **61**

**What Motivates Decision Makers to Use Research Information? 61**

**Summary 62**

**Key Terms 63**

**Questions For Review & Critical Thinking 63**

**Working the Net 64**

REAL-LIFE RESEARCH 3.1: Let's Go Out to Eat! **64**

APPENDIX 3A: A Marketing Research Proposal **69**

**Background 70**

**Objectives 70**

**Study Design 70**

**Areas of Questioning 70**

**Data Analysis 71**

**Personnel Involved 71**

**Specifications/Assumptions 71**

**Services 71**

**Cost 72**

**Timing 72**

**4. Secondary Data and Big Data Analytics 73**

**Nature of Secondary Data 73**

Advantages of Secondary Data **74**

Limitations of Secondary Data **75**

**Internal Databases 77**

Creating an Internal Database **77**

Data Mining **77**

Behavioral Targeting **78**

**Big Data Analytics 79**

Defining Relationships **79**

The Big Data Breakthrough **79**

Making Big Data Actionable **81**

Data Visualization **81**

Battle over Privacy **81**

**Geographic Information Systems 86**

**Decision Support Systems 87**

**Summary 88**

**Key Terms & Definitions 89**

**Questions For Review & Critical Thinking 89**

**Working the Net 89**

REAL-LIFE RESEARCH 4.1: The Interesting and Curious World of Nate Silver **90**

**5. Qualitative Research 92**

**Nature of Qualitative Research 92**

Qualitative Research versus Quantitative Research **93**

Popularity of Qualitative Research **93**

Limitations of Qualitative Research **94**

**Focus Groups 95**

Popularity of Focus Groups **95**

Conducting Focus Groups **96**

Focus Group Trends **102**

Benefits and Drawbacks of Focus Groups **104**

**Other Qualitative Methodologies 106**

Individual Depth Interviews **106**

Projective Tests **110**

**Future of Qualitative Research 115**

**Summary 116**

**Key Terms 116**

**Questions for Review & Critical Thinking 117**

**Working the Net 117**

REAL-LIFE RESEARCH 5.1: McDonald's Listening Tour **117**

**6 Traditional Survey Research 119**

**Popularity of Survey Research 119**

**Types of Errors in Survey Research 120**

Sampling Error **120**

Systematic Error **121**

**Types of Surveys 125**

Door-to-Door Interviews **125**

Executive Interviews **125**

Mall-Intercept Interviews **125**

Telephone Interviews **126**

Self-Administered Questionnaires **128**

Mail Surveys **129**

**Determination of the Survey Method 131**

Sampling Precision **131**

Budget **133**

Requirements for Respondent Reactions **133**

Quality of Data **133**

Length of the Questionnaire **134**

Incidence Rate **134**

Structure of the Questionnaire **135**

Time Available to Complete the Survey **135**

**Summary 135**

**Key Terms 136**

**Questions for Review & Critical Thinking 136**

REAL-LIFE RESEARCH 6.1: Pitney Bowes Places a Premium on Satisfaction **137**

**7 Online Marketing Research—The Growth of Mobile and Social Media Research 139**

The Online World 140

Using the Internet for Secondary Data 140
Sites of Interest to Marketing Researchers 140
Newsgroups 140
Blogs 143

Online Qualitative Research 144
Webcam Online Focus Groups 144
Improving Virtual Focus Groups with Telepresence 144
Using Channel M2 to Conduct Online Focus Groups 145
Using the Web to Find Focus Group Participants 146
Online Individual Depth Interviews (IDI) 146
Marketing Research Online Communities (MROC) 147

Online Survey Research 149
Advantages of Online Surveys 149
Disadvantages of Online Surveys 150
Methods of Conducting Online Surveys 152

Commercial Online Panels 154
Panel Recruitment 154
Respondent Participation 156
Panel Management 156

Mobile Internet Research—
The Future Is Now 157
Advantages of Mobile 157
A Few Bumps at the Beginning 158
Designing a Mobile Survey 158

Social Media Marketing Research 159
Conduction a Facebook Focus Group 160
Conducting Surveys 161

Summary 161
Key Terms 162
Questions For Review & Critical Thinking 162
Woking the Net 163
REAL-LIFE RESEARCH 7.1: Procter & Gamble Uses Its Online Community to Help Develop Scents for a New Product Line 163

**8 Primary Data Collection: Observation 165**

Nature of Observation Research 165
Conditions for Using Observation 166
Approaches to Observation Research 166
Advantages of Observation Research 168
Disadvantages of Observation Research 168

Human Observation 169
Ethnographic Research 169
Mystery Shoppers 174

One-Way Mirror Observations 175
Machine Observation 176
Neuromarketing 176
Facial Action Coding Services (FACS) 179
Gender and Age Recognition Systems 180
In-Store Tracking 180
Television Audience Measurement and Tracking 181
TiVo Targeting 182
Cablevision Targeting 182
Symphony IRI Consumer Network 182

Tracking 183
Your E-Reader Is Reading You 184
Social Media Tracking 184

Observation Research and Virtual Shopping 187
Summary 188
Key Terms 189
Questions for Review & Critical Thinking 189
Working the Net 190
REAL-LIFE RESEARCH 8.1: Eating Well and Doing Good 190

**9 Primary Data Collection: Experimentation and Test Markets 193**

What Is an Experiment? 194

Demonstrating Causation 194
Concomitant Variation 194
Appropriate Time Order of Occurrence 195
Elimination of Other Possible Causal Factors 195

Experimental Setting 195
Laboratory Experiments 195
Field Experiments 196

Experimental Validity 196

Experimental Notation 196

Extraneous Variables 197
Examples of Extraneous Variables 197
Controlling Extraneous Variables 199

Experimental Design, Treatment, and Effects 200

Limitations of Experimental Research 201
High Cost of Experiments 201
Security Issues 201
Implementation Problems 202

Selected Experimental Designs 202
Pre-Experimental Designs 202
True Experimental Designs 204
Quasi-Experiments 205

Test Markets 207
Types of Test Markets 210
Costs of Test Marketing 212
Decision to Conduct Test Marketing 212
Steps in a Test Market Study 213

Other Types of Product Tests **217**
**Summary 218**
**Key Terms 218**
**Questions For Review & Critical Thinking 219**
**Working the Net 220**
REAL-LIFE RESEARCH 9.1: Texas Red Soft Drinks **220**
REAL-LIFE RESEARCH 9.2: Alcon **221**

**10 The Concept of Measurement 222**
**Measurement Process 222**
**Step One: Identify the Concept of Interest 223**
**Step Two: Develop a Construct 224**
**Step Three: Define the Concept Constitutively 224**
**Step Four: Define the Concept Operationally 224**
**Step Five: Develop a Measurement Scale 226**
Nominal Level of Measurement **226**
Ordinal Level of Measurement **227**
Interval Level of Measurement **228**
Ratio Level of Measurement **228**
**Step Six: Evaluate the Reliability
and Validity of the Measurement 229**
Reliability **232**
Validity **234**
Reliability and Validity—A Concluding Comment **238**
**Summary 238**
**Key Terms 239**
**Questions for Review & Critical Thinking 239**
**Working the Net 240**
REAL-LIFE RESEARCH 10.1: Profiles on Women
Shoppers **240**

**11 Using Measurement Scales to Build Marketing
Effectiveness 241**
**Attitudes, Behavior, and Marketing Effectiveness 241**
Link between Attitudes and Behavior **242**
Enhancing Marketing Effectiveness **243**
**Scaling Defined 243**
**Attitude Measurement Scales 244**
Graphic Rating Scales **244**
Itemized Rating Scales **245**
Traditional One-Stage Format **248**
Two-Stage Format **248**
Rank-Order Scales **248**
Paired Comparisons **250**
Constant Sum Scales **250**
Semantic Differential Scales **250**
Stapel Scales **252**
Likert Scales **253**
Purchase-Intent Scales **254**
Scale Conversions **257**
Net Promoter Score (NPS) **258**

**Considerations in Selecting a Scale 259**
The Nature of the Construct Being Measured **259**
Type of Scale **259**
Balanced versus Nonbalanced Scale **260**
Number of Scale Categories **260**
Forced versus Nonforced Choice **260**
**Attitude Measures and Management
Decision Making 261**
Direct Questioning **261**
Indirect Questioning **262**
Observation **262**
Choosing a Method for Identifying
Determinant Attitudes **262**
**Summary 264**
**Key Terms 264**
**Questions For Review & Critical Thinking 265**
**Working the Net 265**
REAL-LIFE RESEARCH 11.1: Improving the Long-Term
Prognosis of Pharmaceutical Brands **266**

**12 Questionnaire Design 271**
**Role of a Questionnaire 271**
**Criteria for a Good Questionnaire 272**
Does It Provide the Necessary
Decision-Making Information? **272**
Does It Consider the Respondent? **273**
Does It Meet Editing and Coding Requirements? **273**
**Does It Solicit Information In An Unbiased Manner:
Questionnaire Design Process 275**
Step One: Determine Survey Objectives, Resources,
and Constraints **275**
Step Two: Determine the Data-Collection
Method **276**
Step Three: Determine the Question Response
Format **281**
Step Four: Decide on the Question Wording **287**
Step Five: Establish Questionnaire Flow and
Layout **290**
Model Introduction/Opening **292**
Model Closing **292**
Step Six: Evaluate the Questionnaire **293**
Step Seven: Obtain Approval of All Relevant
Parties **293**
Step Eight: Pretest and Revise **294**
Step Nine: Prepare Final Questionnaire Copy **294**
Step Ten: Implement the Survey **295**
Field Management Companies **296**
**Impact of the Internet on Questionnaire
Development 297**
**Adapting to Mobile Device Questionnaires 300**
**Costs, Profitability, and Questionnaires 302**

Summary **304**
Key Terms **304**
Questions for Review & Critical Thinking **304**
Working the Net **305**
REAL-LIFE RESEARCH 12.1: Understanding Buyer
    Behavior **305**
REAL-LIFE RESEARCH 12.2: Sonic Goes Mobile **307**

**13 Basic Sampling Issues 308**

Concept of Sampling **308**
    Population **309**
    Sample versus Census **309**
Developing a Sampling Plan **309**
    Step One: Define the Population of Interest **310**
    Step Two: Choose a Data-Collection Method **312**
    Step Three: Identify a Sampling Frame **313**
    Step Four: Select a Sampling Method **314**
    Step Five: Determine Sample Size **316**
    Step Six: Develop Operational Procedures for Selecting
        Sample Elements **316**
    Step Seven: Execute the Operational
        Sampling Plan **317**
Sampling and Nonsampling Errors **318**
Probability Sampling Methods **318**
    Simple Random Sampling **319**
    Systematic Sampling **320**
    Stratified Sampling **321**
    Cluster Sampling **323**
Nonprobability Sampling Methods **325**
    Convenience Samples **325**
    Judgment Samples **325**
    Quota Samples **326**
    Snowball Samples **326**
Internet Sampling **326**
Summary **328**
Key Terms **328**
Questions for Review & Critical Thinking **328**
Working the Net **329**
REAL-LIFE RESEARCH 13.1: The Research Group **329**
REAL-LIFE RESEARCH 13.2: Community Bank **330**

**14 Sample Size Determination 331**

Determining Sample Size for Probability Samples **331**
    Budget Available **334**
    Rule of Thumb **334**
    Number of Subgroups Analyzed **334**
    Traditional Statistical Methods **335**
Normal Distribution **335**
    General Properties **335**
    Standard Normal Distribution **336**
Population and Sample Distributions **337**

Sampling Distribution of the Mean **337**
    Basic Concepts **338**
    Making Inferences on the Basis of a Single
        Sample **341**
    Point and Interval Estimates **341**
    Sampling Distribution of the Proportion **343**
Determining Sample Size **343**
    Problems Involving Means **343**
    Problems Involving Proportions **345**
    Determining Sample Size for Stratified
        and Cluster Samples **346**
    Sample Size for Qualitative Research **346**
    Population Size and Sample Size **346**
    Determining How Many Sample Units Are
        Needed **350**
Statistical Power **350**
Summary **351**
Key Terms **352**
Questions For Review & Critical Thinking **352**
Working the Net **353**
REAL-LIFE RESEARCH 14.1: Concomm **353**
REAL-LIFE RESEARCH 14.2: Building a Village **354**
SPSS Jump Start For Chi-Square Text **355**

**15 Data Processing and Fundamental
    Data Analysis 358**

Overview of the Data Analysis Procedure **358**
Step One: Validation and Editing **359**
    Validation **359**
    Editing **362**
Step Two: Coding **366**
    Coding Process **367**
    Automated Coding Systems and Text
        Processing **368**
Step Three: Data Entry **372**
    Intelligent Entry Systems **373**
    The Data Entry Process **373**
    Scanning **374**
Step Four: Logical Cleaning of Data **374**
Step Five: Tabulation and Statistical
Analysis **375**
    One-Way Frequency Tables **375**
    Cross Tabulations **377**
Graphic Representations of Data **379**
    Line Charts **380**
    Pie Charts **381**
    Bar Charts **381**
Descriptive Statistics **383**
    Measures of Central Tendency **383**
    Measures of Dispersion **384**
    Percentages and Statistical Tests **386**

**Summary 386**
**Key Terms 387**
**Questions For Review & Critical Thinking 387**
**Working the Net 389**
REAL-LIFE RESEARCH 15.1: Waffle World **389**
REAL-LIFE RESEARCH 15.2: Tico Taco **390**
**SPSS Exercises for Chapter 15 391**

**16 Statistical Testing of Differences and Relationships 395**
**Evaluating Differences and Changes 395**
**Statistical Significance 396**
**Hypothesis Testing 398**
Steps in Hypothesis Testing **399**
Types of Errors in Hypothesis Testing **402**
Accepting $H_0$ versus Failing to Reject (FTR) $H_0$ **403**
One-Tailed versus Two-Tailed Test **403**
Example of Performing a Statistical Test **404**
**Commonly Used Statistical Hypothesis Tests 408**
Independent versus Related Samples **408**
Degrees of Freedom **409**
**Goodness of Fit 409**
Chi-Square Test **409**
**Hypotheses about One Mean 416**
$Z$ Test **416**
$t$ Test **417**
**Hypotheses about Two Means 421**
**Hypotheses about Proportions 422**
Proportion in One Sample **422**
Two Proportions in Independent Samples **423**
**Analysis of Variance (ANOVA) 425**
**$P$ Values and Significance Testing 428**
**Summary 429**
**Key Terms 430**
**Questions For Review & Critical Thinking 430**
**Working the Net 432**
REAL-LIFE RESEARCH 16.1: Analyzing Global Bazaar Segmentation Results **432**
REAL-LIFE RESEARCH 16.2: AT &T Wireless **433**
**SPSS Exercises For Chapter 16 434**

**17 Bivariate Correlation and Regression 438**
**Bivariate Analysis of Association 438**
**Bivariate Regression 439**
Nature of the Relationship **439**
Example of Bivariate Regression **441**
**Correlation for Metric Data: Pearson's Product–Moment Correlation 452**
**Summary 458**
**Key Terms 458**
**Questions For Review & Critical Thinking 458**
**Working the Net 460**

REAL-LIFE RESEARCH 17.1: Axcis Athletic Shoes **460**
REAL-LIFE RESEARCH 17.2: Lambda Social Hotspot **461**
**SPSS Exercises For Chapter 17 462**

**18 Multivariate Data Analysis 464**
**Multivariate Analysis Procedures 464**
**Multivariate Software 466**
**Multiple Regression Analysis 468**
Applications of Multiple Regression Analysis **469**
Multiple Regression Analysis Measures **470**
Dummy Variables **470**
Potential Use and Interpretation Problems **471**
**Multiple Discriminant Analysis 472**
Applications of Multiple Discriminant Analysis **473**
**Cluster Analysis 473**
Procedures for Clustering **473**
**Factor Analysis 476**
Factor Scores **477**
Factor Loadings **478**
Naming Factors **479**
Number of Factors to Retain **479**
**Conjoint Analysis 479**
Example of Conjoint Analysis **479**
Considering Features Conjointly **480**
Estimating Utilities **481**
Simulating Buyer Choice **482**
Limitations of Conjoint Analysis **484**
**Big Data and Hadoop 484**
**Predictive Analytics 484**
Using Predictive Analytics **485**
Privacy Concerns and Ethics **487**
Commercial Predictive Modeling Software and Applications **487**
**Summary 488**
**Key Terms 488**
**Questions for Review & Critical Thinking 489**
**Working the Net 490**
REAL-LIFE RESEARCH 18.1: Satisfaction Research for Pizza Quik **491**
REAL-LIFE RESEARCH 18.2: Gibson's Uses Predictive Analytics **492**
APPENDIX: Role of Marketing Research in the Organization and Ethical Issues **494**
**SPSS Exercises For Chapter 18 496**

**19 Communicating the Research Results 499**
**The Research Report 499**
**Organizing the Report 501**
**Interpreting the Findings 502**
Format of the Report **504**
Formulating Recommendations **504**
The Presentation **505**

**Making a Presentation** **508**
   Presentations by Internet **513**
**Summary 514**
**Key Terms 514**
**Questions For Review & Critical Thinking 514**
**Working the Net 514**
REAL-LIFE RESEARCH 19.1: The United Way **515**
REAL-LIFE RESEARCH 19.2: TouchWell Storefront Concept and Naming Research **516**

**20 Managing Marketing Research 522**

**Marketing Research Supplier Management 523**
   What Do Clients Want? **523**
   Consolidating the Number of Acceptable Suppliers **525**
**Communication 525**
**The Key Role of the Project Manager 526**
**Managing the Research Process 527**
   Organizing the Supplier Firm **527**
   Data Quality Management **529**
   Time Management **530**
   Cost Management **531**
   Client Profitability Management **532**
   Staff Management and Development **533**
**Managing a Marketing Research Department 535**
   Allocating the Research Department Budget **535**
   Prioritizing Projects **536**
   Retaining Skilled Staff **537**
   Selecting the Right Marketing Research Suppliers **538**
   Moving Marketing Research into a Decision-Making Role **540**

Measuring Marketing Research's Return on Investment (ROI) **546**
**Summary 549**
**Key Terms 549**
**Questions for Review & Critical Thinking 550**
**Working the Net 550**
REAL-LIFE RESEARCH 20.1: Walther Research Deals with Managing Project Managers **550**
REAL-LIFE RESEARCH 20.2: Johnny Jets Drive-Ins **551**

**APPENDIX ONE: Statistical Tables A-1**

**APPENDIX TWO: Considerations in Creating a Marketing Plan (Online)**

**APPENDIX THREE: Comprehensive Cases (Online)**

A Biff Targets an Online Dating Service for College Students **A-14**

B Freddy Favors Fast Food and Convenience for College Students **A-17**

C Superior Online Student Travel—A Cut Above **A-21**

D Rockingham National Bank Visa Card Survey **A-25**

**ENDNOTES E-1**

**GLOSSARY G-1**

**QSR SURVEY QSR-1**

**INDEX I-1**

© Yuri/iStockphoto

# The Role of Marketing Research in Management Decision Making

## LEARNING OBJECTIVES

1. Review the marketing concept and the marketing mix.

2. Comprehend the marketing environment within which managers must make decisions.

3. Examine the history of marketing research.

Welcome to the fascinating world of marketing research! How does marketing research help managers reach their goals? How did the field of marketing research evolve? What big changes are occurring? We will explore this topic in Chapter 1.

# Nature of Marketing

**Marketing** is the activity, set of institutions, and processes for creating, communicating, delivering, and exchanging offerings that have value for customers, clients, partners, and society at large.[1] Good customer relationships often result in exchanges; that is, a good or service is exchanged for money. The potential for exchange exists when there are at least two parties and each has something of potential value to the other. When the two parties can communicate and deliver the desired goods or services, exchange can take place.

How do marketing managers attempt to stimulate exchange? They follow the "right" principle. They attempt to get the right goods or services to the right people at the right

**marketing**
The process of planning and executing the conception, pricing, promotion, and distribution of ideas, goods, and services to create exchanges that satisfy individual and organizational objectives.

place at the right time at the right price, using the right promotion techniques. The "right" principle describes how marketing managers control the many factors that ultimately determine marketing success. To make the "right" decisions, management must have timely decision-making information. Marketing research is a primary channel for providing that information.

## The Marketing Concept

**marketing concept**
A business philosophy based on consumer orientation, goal orientation, and systems orientation.

To efficiently accomplish their goals, firms today have adopted the **marketing concept**, which requires (1) a consumer orientation, (2) a goal orientation, and (3) a systems orientation. A **consumer orientation** means that firms strive to identify the people (or firms) most likely to buy their product (the target market) and to produce a good or offer a service that will meet the needs of target customers most effectively in the face of competition. The second tenet of the marketing concept is **goal orientation**; that is, a firm must be consumer-oriented only to the extent that it also accomplishes corporate goals. The goals of profit-making firms usually center on financial criteria, such as a 15 percent return on investment.

**consumer orientation**
The identification of and focus on the people or firms most likely to buy a product and the production of a good or service that will meet their needs most effectively.

The third component of the marketing concept is a **systems orientation**. A system is an organized whole—or a group of diverse units that form an integrated whole—functioning or operating in unison. It is one thing for a firm to say it is consumer-oriented and another actually to *be* consumer-oriented. First, systems must be established to find out what consumers want and to identify market opportunities. As you will see later, identifying target market needs and finding market opportunities are the tasks of marketing research. Next, this information must be fed back to the firm. Without feedback from the marketplace, a firm is not truly consumer-oriented.

**goal orientation**
A focus on the accomplishment of corporate goals; a limit set on consumer orientation.

**systems orientation**
The creation of systems to monitor the external environment and deliver the desired marketing mix to the target market.

## Opportunistic Nature of Marketing Research

Marketing research is an excellent tool for discovering opportunities in the marketplace. Midmarket hotel chains, such as Holiday Inn, (especially those with less than 150 rooms), often don't generate enough traffic to support a full-service restaurant. Holiday Inn surveyed 10,000 guests and found that its guests were mostly business people, sales people, and government employees. These people revealed that they had no desire to simply sit in their room. They wanted to be around other people.

Holiday Inn management decided that the bar should play a bigger role at the hotels. The social hub would tailor Holiday Inn's lunch and dinner menus to bar fare that can be shared, such as gourmet meatballs, sesame chicken wings, hamburgers, and a few significant entrees, such as steaks and salmon club sandwiches.

Those changes allow for more food to be served by the bar staff, which, in turn, allows Holiday Inn's franchisees to limit their labor costs by reducing restaurant staff, especially at slow times of the day.[2]

## External Marketing Environment

**marketing mix**
The unique blend of product/service, pricing, promotion, and distribution strategies designed to meet the needs of a specific target market.

Over time, the **marketing mix** must be altered because of changes in the environment in which consumers and businesses exist, work, compete, and make purchasing decisions. Some new consumers and businesses will become part of the target market, while others will drop out of the market; those who remain may have different tastes, needs, incomes, lifestyles, and purchase habits than the original target consumers.

Although managers can control the marketing mix, they cannot control elements in the external environment that continually mold and reshape the target market. Unless management understands the external environment, the firm cannot intelligently plan its future, and organizations are often unaware of the forces that influence their future.

Marketing research is a key means for understanding the environment. Knowledge of the environment helps a firm not only alter its current marketing mix but also take advantage of new opportunities. John Deal, a St. Louis resident, commissioned a marketing research study to determine the potential demand for a small (two- to three-store) chain in the local area that would feature bath and kitchen appliances and accessories. The survey results were positive and John decided to move forward. One issue that concerned John was what role the Internet should play in his stores. Fortunately, he was able to acquire a study titled "Seamless Retail" by Accenture. A few highlights were:

*Forty-nine percent of consumers believe the best thing retailers can do to improve the shopping experience is to better integrate in-store, online and mobile shopping channels. Eighty-nine percent of consumers said it is important for retailers to let them shop for products in the way that is most convenient for them, no matter which sales channel they choose.*

*The report says that consistency weighs heavily on the consumer experience: 73 percent of consumers expect a retailer's online pricing to be the same as its in-store pricing, and 61 percent expect a retailer's online promotions to be the same as it in-store promotions.*

*Asked what kind of information would be useful to have from their favorite retailers before going to a physical store, 82 percent of consumers selected having access to current product availability as their top choice.*

*Forty-nine percent of those surveyed are influenced by in-store offers (promotional displays, salespeople), 56 percent are influenced by e-mail coupons and offers, and an equal amount say they are influenced by coupons mailed to their home. Sixty-nine percent and 62 percent, respectively, said that online pop-up ads and mobile banner ads would never influence their purchasing.*[3]

After having read the report, John was then in a position to craft an effective integrated retailing strategy involving the web and a traditional store.

# Marketing Research and Decision Making

Marketing research plays two key roles in the marketing system. First, as part of the marketing intelligence feedback process, marketing research provides decision makers with data on the effectiveness of the current marketing mix and offers insights into necessary changes. Second, marketing research is the primary tool for exploring new opportunities in the marketplace. Segmentation research and new product research help identify the most lucrative opportunities for a firm.

## Marketing Research Defined

Now that you have an understanding of how marketing research fits into the overall marketing system, we can proceed with a formal definition of the term, as stated by the American Marketing Association:

*Marketing research is the function that links the consumer, customer, and public to the marketer through information—information used to identify and define marketing opportunities and problems; generate, refine, and evaluate marketing actions; monitor marketing performance; and improve understanding of marketing as a process. Marketing research specifies the information required to address these issues, designs the method for collecting information, manages and implements the data collection process, analyzes the results, and communicates the findings and their implications.*

**marketing research**
The planning, collection, and analysis of data relevant to marketing decision making and the communication of the results of this analysis to management.

We prefer another definition: **Marketing research** is the planning, collection, and analysis of data relevant to marketing decision making and the communication of the results of this analysis to management.

## Importance of Marketing Research to Management

Marketing research can be viewed as playing three functional roles: descriptive, diagnostic, and predictive. Its **descriptive function** includes gathering and presenting statements of fact. What is the historic sales trend in the industry? What are consumers' attitudes and beliefs toward a product? Opening a pack of bacon is a messy job. Bacon lovers have to reach into the package, and if they only pull out a few slices, there's no easy way to store the remainder. Oscar Mayer marketing researchers hear plenty from consumers about what they disliked about its former bacon packaging. So marketers figured the best solution would be a packaging innovation that eliminated the chore of placing the opened pack in a resealable plastic bag or wrapping it in plastic or foil. This unwanted task was done so that the last piece of bacon would be as fresh as the first.

**descriptive function**
The gathering and presentation of statements of fact.

Oscar Mayer Center Cut Bacon was introduced in a new "Stay-Fresh Reclosable Tray." The flip-top lid allows easy access to the bacon inside. The top snaps closed, making it readily resealable. The flat tray makes for simplified storage in the refrigerator.

**diagnostic function**
The explanation of data or actions.

The second role of research is the **diagnostic function**, wherein data and/or actions are explained. For example, what was the impact on sales when the Oscar Mayer package design was changed? How can product/service offerings be altered to better serve customers and potential customers? Since kids eat over 5 billion ounces of ketchup each year, Heinz decided that the heavy users (kids) should have a lot to say (via marketing research) about how to make ketchup fun. Heinz listened and watched children using ketchup, which resulted in a new bottle design and name selection. The true ketchup connoisseurs helped create Heinz EZ Squirt ketchup!

**predictive function**
Specification of how to use descriptive and diagnostic research to predict the results of a planned marketing decision.

The final role of research is the **predictive function**. How can the firm best take advantage of opportunities as they arise in the ever-changing marketplace? Bonobos is the largest apparel brand ever built on the web in the United States. They attribute customer dialogue (marketing research) for helping them create a signature line of better-fitting men's pants. Their research brings the customer into the design process to create successful product offerings. Marketing research has identified different target markets for Bonobos such as the "Sporty Guy," "Guy Next Door," and "Men Who Wear Red Pants."[4]

**The Unrelenting Drive for Quality and Customer Satisfaction** Quality and customer satisfaction are the key competitive weapons in today's marketplace. U.S. automobile manufacturers have been among the most battered in recent years but now are running side by side with the imports. The watchwords are quality and customer service. As one auto executive puts it:

*If you go back to even a very short time ago, our whole idea of a customer was that we would wholesale a car to a dealer, the dealer would then sell the car to the customers, and we hoped we never heard from the customer—because if we did, it meant something was wrong. Today, we want to establish a dialogue with the customer throughout the entire ownership experience. We want to talk to our customers every step of the way. We want to be a consumer-products and services company that just happens to be in the automotive business.[5]*

Where does marketing research come into play? The J. D. Power Awards rank cars based on the level of customer satisfaction. This, in turn, drives sales of specific companies and models. Lexus has always done well in a number of quality and customer satisfaction studies. This has helped increase sales of the IS, LS, and RX models. At some Lexus dealers, you can get a manicure and a massage while having your oil changed. Automobile manufacturers use marketing research to aid designers, determine what new features to add to specific models, and learn how their cars stack up with those of the competition.

Quality that means little to customers usually doesn't produce a payoff in improved sales, profits, or market share; it represents wasted effort and expense. Today, the new mantra is **return on quality**, which means that (1) the quality being delivered is the quality desired by the target market and (2) the added quality must have a positive impact on profitability. For example, banking giant Bank of America measures every improvement in service quality, from adding more tellers to offering new products, in terms of added profitability. REI, the Seattle-based outdoors sporting goods chain, has earned a nickname, "Return Everything Inc." Hundreds of returned items are stacked in bins, hanging on racks and lining shelves. Tags detail the customer complaints: "Suddenly not waterproof" on a frayed, blue, men's rain jacket from a previous decade; "Don't fit well" on a pair of thick, black, women's clogs so well-worn that their original design as faded.

At another REI store, a customer recently returned a pair of women's sandals, designed for hiking and wading in rivers. The problem? According to the tag, "not sexy enough." Several years ago, a customer in Washington State successfully returned an REI snowsuit he bought to climb Mount Rainier in 1970.[6]

In 2013, though, the chain announced it would henceforth take back items only within a year of purchase. In this case, over-the-top service quality was having a negative impact on the return on quality.

**return on quality**
Management objective based on the principles that (1) the quality being delivered is at a level desired by the target market and (2) the level of quality must have a positive impact on profitability.

## Paramount Importance of Keeping Existing Customers
An inextricable link exists between customer satisfaction and customer loyalty. Long-term relationships don't just happen; they are grounded in the delivery of service and value, as the REI example shows. Customer retention pays big dividends for firms. Powered by repeat sales and referrals, revenues and market share grow. Costs fall because firms spend less funds and energy attempting to replace defectors. Steady customers are easy to serve because they understand the modus operandi and make fewer demands on employees' time. A firm's ability to retain customers also drives job satisfaction and pride, which leads to higher employee retention. In turn, long-term employees acquire additional knowledge that increases productivity.

A Bain & Company study estimates that a 5 percent decrease in the customer defection rate can boost profits by 25 to 95 percent.[7] Another study found that the customer retention rate has a major impact on the value of the firm.[8]

The ability to retain customers is based on an intimate understanding of their needs. This knowledge comes primarily from marketing research. For example, British Airways recast its first-class transatlantic service based on detailed marketing research. Most airlines stress top-of-the-line service in their transatlantic first-class cabins. However, British Air research found that most first-class passengers simply want to sleep. British Air now gives premium flyers the option of dinner on the ground, before takeoff, in the first-class lounge. Then, once on board, they can slip into British Air pajamas, put their heads on real pillows, slip under blankets, and enjoy an interruption-free flight. On arrival at their destination, first-class passengers can have breakfast, use comfortable dressing rooms and showers, and even have their clothes pressed before they set off. These changes in British Air's first-class service were driven strictly by marketing research.

## Understanding the Ever-Changing Marketplace

Marketing research also helps managers to understand trends in the marketplace and to take advantage of opportunities. Marketing research has been practiced for as long as marketing has existed. The early Phoenicians carried out market demand studies as they traded in the various ports on the Mediterranean Sea. Marco Polo's diary indicates he was performing a marketing research function as he traveled to China. There is evidence that the Spanish systematically conducted marketing surveys as they explored the New World, and examples exist of marketing research conducted during the Renaissance.

## Social Media and User-Generated Content

In the past few years, the world of promotion has been turned upside down. Previously, marketers created a message and then one, or a series, of traditional media, TV, print, radio, billboards to deliver that message to a target market. Now, more people than ever participate in blogs, forums, online communities, product/service reviews—think Trip Advisor—and social media sites that created user-generated content (UGC). The opinions expressed in the venues are unsolicited, typically honest, candid, and passionate and can be extremely thoughtful. Social media such as Twitter, Facebook, and Linked-In generate millions of comments a day about products and services. About 20 percent of all Tweets are about brands.[9]

In 2003, digital media accounted for less than 10 percent of advertising spending, relative to TV and print. In 2008, its share was in the low teens. By 2013, it exceeded 20 percent, according to Zenith Optimedia and TNS Media Intelligence.[10]

Marketing researchers are tapping into these huge streams of data to determine what people think about their products and services, as well as those of the competition. Researchers are building profiles of persons online and using this data to target their promotional efforts. Other researchers tap online communities to build new products and services.

Smartphones are causing major changes in the way media are used and buying decisions are made. Add in tablets, traditional computers, and TV, and one finds that the consumer may be looking at four different screens at the same time! Researchers must now measure consumers' consumption of content and their exposure to advertising across all four screens. ESPN, the sports network, is now gathering data across five platforms: radio, television, computers, smartphones, and tablets.[11]

© David R. Frazier Photolibrary, Inc./Alamy

Asking the right questions in marketing research can be as important as getting good answers. UPS found that customers wanted more interaction with their UPS driver. Go to http://www.ups.com to find out how UPS uses marketing research to better serve its customers.

## Proactive Role of Marketing Research

Understanding the nature of the marketing system is a necessity for a successful marketing orientation. By having a thorough knowledge of factors that have an impact on the target market and the marketing mix, management can be proactive rather than reactive. Proactive management alters the marketing mix to fit newly emerging patterns in economic, social, technological, and competitive environments, whereas reactive management waits for change to have a major impact on the firm before deciding to take action. It is the difference between viewing the turbulent marketing environment as a threat (a reactive stance) and seeing it as an opportunity (a proactive stance). Apple, for example, has been very proactive about bringing cutting-edge technology products to the marketplace. This, in turn, has generated huge profits for the company.

A proactive manager not only examines emerging markets but also seeks, through strategic planning, to develop a long-run **marketing strategy** for the firm. A marketing strategy guides the long-term use of the firm's resources based on the firm's existing and projected internal capabilities and on projected changes in the external environment. A good strategic plan is based on good marketing research. It helps the firm meet long-term profit and market share goals.

"I don't *know* what I'm doing—this is pure research!"

Rex F. May

## Applied Research versus Basic Research

Virtually all marketing research is conducted to better understand the market, to find out why a strategy failed, or to reduce uncertainty in management decision making. All research conducted for these purposes is called **applied research**. For example, should the price of DiGiorno frozen pizza be raised 40 cents? What name should Toyota select for a new sedan? Which commercial has a higher level of recall: A or B? By contrast, **basic**, or **pure**, **research** attempts to expand the frontiers of knowledge; it is not aimed at a specific pragmatic problem. Basic research is conducted to validate an existing theory or learn more about a concept or phenomenon. For example, basic marketing research might test a hypothesis about high-involvement decision making or consumer information processing. In the long run, basic research helps us understand more about the world in which we live. Managers usually cannot implement the findings of basic research in the short run. Most basic marketing research is now conducted in universities; the findings are reported in such publications as *The Journal of Marketing Research* and *The Journal of Marketing*. In contrast, most research undertaken by businesses is applied research because it must be cost-effective and of demonstrable value to the decision maker.

Although basic research is still important at some firms, particularly high tech, the notion of time-to-market has changed. That is, the basic research can be fairly long term but must have a focus on ultimately solving real-world problems. Companies conducting basic research include Genentech, Cisco Systems, and Google. Google, for example, has done basic research that has led to applied research that resulted in the creation of a self-driving car.

## Nature of Applied Research

Marketing research studies can be classified into three broad categories: programmatic, selective, and evaluative. **Programmatic research** is conducted to develop marketing options through market segmentation, market opportunity analysis, or consumer attitude and product usage studies. **Selective research** is used to test decision alternatives. Some examples are testing concepts for new products, advertising copy testing, and test marketing. **Evaluative research** is done to assess program performance; it includes tracking advertising recall, doing organizational image studies, and examining customer attitudes on a firm's quality of service.

Programmatic research arises from management's need to obtain a market overview periodically. For example, product management may be concerned that the existing market information base is inadequate or outdated for present decision making, or marketing

**marketing strategy**
A plan to guide the long-term use of a firm's resources based on its existing and projected internal capabilities and on projected changes in the external environment.

**applied research**
Research aimed at solving a specific, pragmatic problem—better understanding of the marketplace, determination of why a strategy or tactic failed, or reduction of uncertainty in management decision making.

**basic, or pure, research**
Research aimed at expanding the frontiers of knowledge rather than solving a specific, pragmatic problem.

**programmatic research**
Research conducted to develop marketing options through market segmentation, market opportunity analyses, or consumer attitude and product usage studies.

**selective research**
Research used to test decision alternatives.

**evaluative research**
Research done to assess program performance.

plans may call for the introduction of new products, ad campaigns, or packaging. Whatever the specific situation, current information is needed to develop viable marketing options. Typical programmatic research questions include the following:

- Has its target market changed? How?
- Does the market exhibit any new segmentation opportunities?
- Do some segments appear to be more likely candidates than others for the firm's marketing efforts?
- What new product or service opportunities lie in the various segments?

Equidistant between Los Angeles and San Francisco in the Eastern Sierra Nevada Mountains, Mammoth Mountain has been serving the skiers and snowboarders of central California for more than 50 years. With the summit reaching above 11,000 feet and average annual snowfall hitting 400 inches, thousands of customers flock to the slopes and the lodges annually.

Yet, the resort's longstanding direct-mail program just wasn't driving the traffic. While the resort wasn't losing visitors (most resort traffic industrywide comes from existing skiers and snowboarders rather than those new to the sports), executives hoped to gain some ground in an overall stable market by injecting some life into what had become an out-of-date marketing campaign—and to increase the frequency of visits by the 900,000 customers in its database.

Resort executives used programmatic research collected from an annual survey, the National Skier and Snowboarder Opinion Survey conducted on behalf of resorts across the country, and found that 94 percent of Mammoth's users in particular acknowledge using the Internet to find information about everything from weather advisories to checking room rates at one of Mammoth's lodges.

This information led to the creation of an e-mail marketing system that reaches 18,000 subscribers. The format is chatty and informing. For example, "The weather has been beautiful here lately, and with a 12- to 14-foot base you can't go wrong anywhere on the mountain. At 1:15 p.m. the temperature is 34 degrees at Main Lodge with clear skies and moderate to gusty winds. It's extremely windy and cold on top at 17 degrees, so be sure to bundle up." Skier visit numbers have been increasing 5 percent or more annually as a result of the programmatic research![1]

Selective research typically is conducted after several viable options have been identified by programmatic research. If no one alternative is clearly superior, product management usually will wish to test several alternatives. However, selective research may be required at any stage of the marketing process, such as when advertising copy is being developed, various product formulations are being evaluated, or an entire marketing program is being assessed, as in test marketing.

The need for evaluative research arises when the effectiveness and efficiency of marketing programs must be evaluated. Evaluative research may be integrated into programmatic research when program changes or entirely new options are demanded because of current performance, such as at Mammoth Mountain.

## Decision to Conduct Marketing Research

A manager who is faced with several alternative solutions to a particular problem should not instinctively call for applied marketing research. In fact, the first decision to be made is whether to conduct marketing research at all. In a number of situations, it is best not to conduct research.

- *Resources are lacking.* There are two situations in which a lack of resources should preclude marketing research. First, an organization may lack the funds to do the research properly. If a project calls for a sample of 800 respondents but the budget allows for only 50 interviews, the quality of the information would be highly suspect. Second, funds may be available to do the research properly but insufficient to implement any decisions resulting from the research. Small organizations in particular sometimes lack the resources to create an effective marketing mix. In one case, for example, the director of a performing arts guild was in complete agreement with the recommendations that resulted from a marketing research project. However, two years after the project was completed, nothing had been done because the money was not available.

- *Research results would not be useful.* Some types of marketing research studies measure lifestyle and personality factors of steady and potential customers. Assume that a study finds that introverted men with a poor self-concept, yet a high need for achievement, are most likely to patronize a discount brokerage service. The management of Charles Schwab's discount brokerage service might be hard-pressed to use this information.

- *The opportunity has passed.* Marketing research should not be undertaken if the opportunity for successful entry into a market has already passed. If the product is in the late maturity or decline stage of the product life cycle (such as cassette recorders or black-and-white television sets), it would be foolish to do research on new product entry. The same may be true for markets rapidly approaching saturation, such as super-premium ice cream (Häagen-Dazs, Ben and Jerry's). For products already in the market, however, research is needed to modify the products as consumer tastes, competition, and other factors change.

- *The decision already has been made.* In the real world of management decision making and company politics, marketing research has sometimes been used improperly. Several years ago, a large marketing research study was conducted for a bank with over $800 million in deposits. The purpose of the research project was to guide top management in mapping a strategic direction for the bank during the next 5 years. After reading the research report, the president said, "I fully agree with your recommendations because that was what I was going to do anyway! I'm going to use your study tomorrow when I present my strategic plan to the board of directors." The researcher then asked, "What if my recommendations had been counter to your decision?" The bank president laughed and said, "They would have never known that I had conducted a marketing research study!" Not only was the project a waste of money, but it also raised a number of ethical questions in the researcher's mind.

- *Managers cannot agree on what they need to know to make a decision.* Although it may seem obvious that research should not be undertaken until objectives are specified, it sometimes happens. Preliminary or exploratory studies are commonly done to better understand the nature of the problem, but a large, major research project should not be. It is faulty logic to say, "Well, let's just go ahead and do the study and then we will better understand the problem and know what steps to take." The wrong phenomena might be studied, or key elements needed for management decision making may not be included.

- *Decision-making information already exists.* Some companies have been conducting research in certain markets for many years. They understand the characteristics of their target customers and what they like and dislike about existing products. Under these circumstances, further research would be redundant and a waste of money. Procter & Gamble, for example, has extensive knowledge of the coffee market. After it conducted initial taste tests, P&G went into national distribution with Folgers Instant

© Pictorium /Alamy

The super-premium ice cream market is reaching saturation. At this point, it might not be wise to enter this market. However, marketing research is necessary to keep products already in the market ahead of the competition.

Coffee without further research. The Sara Lee Corporation did the same thing with its frozen croissants, as did Quaker Oats with Chewy Granola Bars. This tactic, however, does not always work. P&G thought it understood the pain reliever market thoroughly, so it bypassed marketing research for Encaprin, encapsulated aspirin. The product failed because it lacked a distinct competitive advantage over existing products and was withdrawn from the market.

■ *The costs of conducting research outweigh the benefits.* Rarely does a manager have such tremendous confidence in her or his judgment that additional information relative to a pending decision would not be accepted if it were available and free. However, the manager might have sufficient confidence to be unwilling to pay very much for it or wait long to receive it. Willingness to acquire additional decision-making information depends on a manager's perception of its quality, price, and timing. The manager would be willing to pay more for perfect information (that is, data that leave no doubt as to which alternative to follow) than for information that leaves uncertainty as to what to do. Therefore, research should be undertaken only when the expected value of the information is greater than the cost of obtaining it.

Two important determinants of potential benefits are profit margins and market size. Generally speaking, new products with large profit margins are going to have greater potential benefit than products with smaller profit margins, assuming that both items have the same sales potential. Also, new product opportunities in large markets are going to offer greater potential benefits than those in smaller markets if competitive intensity is the same in both markets (see Exhibit 1.1).

| EXHIBIT 1.1 | Deciding Whether to Conduct Marketing Research | |
| --- | --- | --- |
| **Market Size** | **Small Profit Margin** | **Large Profit Margin** |
| Small | Costs likely to be greater than benefits (e.g., eyeglass replacement screw, tire valve extension). DON'T CONDUCT MARKETING RESEARCH. | Benefits possibly greater than cost (e.g., ultra-expensive Lamborghini-type sportswear, larger specialized industrial equipment such as computer-aided metal stamping machines). PERHAPS CONDUCT MARKETING RESEARCH. LEARN ALL YOU CAN FROM EXISTING INFORMATION PRIOR TO MAKING DECISION TO CONDUCT RESEARCH. |
| Large | Benefits likely to be greater than costs (e.g., Stouffers frozen entrees, Crest's teeth whitener strips). PERHAPS CONDUCT MARKETING RESEARCH. LEARN ALL YOU CAN FROM EXISTING INFORMATION PRIOR TO MAKING DECISION TO CONDUCT RESEARCH. | Benefits most likely to be greater than costs (e.g., medical equipment like CAT scanners, 3D printers). CONDUCT MARKETING RESEARCH. |

# Development of Marketing Research

The many benefits that accrue to management from using marketing research served as the initial impetus to begin conducting marketing research in the United States. In light of the competitive advantage a company can gain from engaging in marketing research, it is surprising that the industry did not move out of its embryonic stage until 1900.

## Inception: Pre-1900

The first recorded marketing research survey was taken in July 1824 by the *Harrisburg Pennsylvanian.* It was an election poll in which Andrew Jackson received 335 votes; John Quincy Adams, 169; Henry Clay, 29; and William H. Crawford, 9. Later the same year, another newspaper, the *Raleigh Star,* canvassed political meetings held in North Carolina, "at which the sense of the people was taken." Perhaps the first marketing researcher was John Jacob Astor, who in the 1790s employed an artist to sketch the hats worn by fashionable New York women so that he could keep abreast of fashion trends.[13]

The first documented use of research to make informed marketing decisions was carried out by the advertising agency N. W. Ayer in 1879. That systematic effort was a simple survey of state and local officials to determine expected levels of grain production. The purpose of the research was to develop the scheduling of advertising for a producer of farm equipment. The second documented instance of marketing research appears to have been at E. I. duPont de Nemours & Company toward the end of the nineteenth century. It involved the systematic compilation of salespersons' reports on a variety of customer characteristics. The response to this second research effort was a harbinger of things to come. The salespersons who were responsible for obtaining and reporting the data were outraged because they didn't like the extra paperwork.

Academic researchers entered into marketing research about 1895, when Harlow Gale, a professor of psychology at the University of Minnesota, introduced the use of mail surveys to study advertising. He mailed 200 questionnaires and received 20 completed questionnaires, a 10 percent response rate. Gale's work was quickly followed by the pioneering work of Walter Dill Scott at Northwestern University. Scott introduced the use of experimentation and psychological measurement to the fledgling practice of advertising.

## Early Growth: 1900–1920

It was not until after the turn of the century that consumer demand surged; the growth of mass production meant larger and more distant markets. No longer was America characterized by cottage industries where the craftsman–seller was in daily contact with the marketplace. The need arose to understand consumers' buying habits and attitudes toward manufacturers' wares. In response to this need, the first formal marketing research department was established by the Curtis Publishing Company in 1911. The research focused primarily on the automobile industry, as manufacturers had decided that everyone who had the money and inclination to buy a car had done so. The manufacturers were seeking a new group of consumers to which to target their promotions. A few years later, Daniel Starch pioneered recognition measures of advertising response, and E. K. Strong introduced recall measures and scaling to marketing research.

## Adolescent Years: 1920–1950

Percival White developed the first application of scientific research to commercial problems. White's words express his realization of the need for systematic and continual marketing research:

*Perhaps the greatest advantage of the company's having its own market analysis department is that the work then becomes a continuous process, or at least a process which is carried forward at periodic intervals, so that altered conditions in the market and in the industry at large are always kept in view. The necessity for regarding markets as constantly changing and not as fixed phenomena should not be lost sight of.*[14]

White's book bore scant resemblance to this text. For example, the book avoided the use of statistics and mathematics, only briefly mentioning the U.S. Census.

The 1930s saw widespread use of survey research. A. C. Nielsen entered the research business in 1922. He expanded on White's earlier work by developing the "share of market" concept and many other services that became the foundation for one of America's largest marketing research organizations. It was not until the late 1930s that formal courses in marketing research became common on college campuses; a substantial body of knowledge developed within both the practice and academic communities. Two events—the spread of broadcast media and World War II—helped the fledgling discipline coalesce into a well-defined profession. Social scientists found that broadcast media created interesting new phenomena and increased the variability of human behavior.

By the end of the 1930s, simple examinations of respondents' replies were becoming categorized and compared across groups classified by differences in income, gender, or family status. Simple correlation analysis came into use but was not widespread; those who would use it had to be able to go directly to the statistical sources for such techniques, using texts by some of the pioneers in the field at this time, including G. Udney Yule, Mordecai Ezekiel, and Horace Sechrist.

The requirements of World War II pressed social scientists into service on a number of fronts. Tools and methods that had been novelties before the war were adopted and adapted to study the consumer behavior of soldiers and of their families on the home front. Among those tools were experimental design, opinion polling, human factors research, and operations research techniques.

In the 1940s, focus groups developed under the leadership of Robert Merton. During the late 1940s, the importance of random selection in sampling became widely recognized, and major advances were made in sampling techniques and polling procedures. A small number of psychologists who had been assigned to work in the Army Quartermaster Corps found their way into industry, where they introduced techniques for consumer tests of products.[15]

## Mature Years: 1950–2000

The change from a seller's market to a buyer's market (resulting from post–World War II pent-up demand) necessitated better marketing intelligence. No longer could producers sell all of anything they made. The rising costs of production "tooling up," advertising, inventories, and other factors made the price of failure much higher than it had been in the past. Thus, research became much more important. Now, marketing research first determines what the market wants and then goods are crafted to meet those needs.

The mid-1950s brought the concept of market segmentation, based largely on easily identifiable demographic characteristics of customers. The same period gave rise to motivation research, with its emphasis on why consumers behave as they do. The underlying concepts of segmentation and motivation analysis, combined with the power of survey techniques, led to such innovations as psychographics and benefit segmentation. In the 1960s, mathematical models were developed for description and prediction—stochastic models, Markovian models, and linear learning models. Even more significant was the development of the computer during the early 1960s, greatly enhancing the researcher's ability to quickly analyze, store, and retrieve large amounts of data.

# The Connected World: 2000–2010

The Internet has brought profound changes to marketing research. In a global survey, 94 percent of the research firms stated that they were conducting online research.[16] Some firms are beginning to focus on mobile interviewing—mobile self-completion on a smartphone, iPhone, Blackberry, Droid, and the like. Today, 56 percent of American adults own a smartphone[17] and over 98 percent of the U.S. population has Internet access.[18]

The Internet has produced many benefits for marketing researchers:

- Provides more rapid access to business intelligence, which allows for better and faster decision making.
- Improves a firm's ability to respond quickly to customer needs and market shifts.
- Facilitates conducting follow-up studies and longitudinal research.
- Slashes labor- and time-intensive research activities (and associated costs), including mailing, telephone solicitation, data entry, data tabulation, and reporting.

Conducting surveys and analyzing mountains of user data are not the sum total of the Internet revolution in marketing research. The Internet has also greatly enhanced management of the research process and dissemination of information. Specifically, the Internet has greatly affected several key areas:

- *Libraries and various printed materials, which may be virtually replaced as sources of information.* On its website, the Bureau of Census (*http://www.census.gov*) indicates that it plans to gradually make the Internet the major means of distributing census data. The same is true for a number of other government agencies. Information from countless databases (both governmental and nongovernmental) can be called up almost instantaneously on the user's desktop, notebook, smartphone, Kindle, iPad, or other E-reader.

- *The distribution of requests for proposals (RFPs) and the proposals themselves.* Companies can now quickly and efficiently send RFPs to a select e-mail list of research suppliers. In turn, the suppliers can develop proposals and e-mail them back to clients. A process that used to take days now occurs in a matter of hours.

- *Collaboration between the client and the research supplier in the management of a research project.* Both the researcher and the client might look at a proposal, RFP, report, or some type of statistical analysis at the same time on their computer screens while discussing it over the telephone. This is very effective and efficient, as changes in sample size, quotas, and other aspects of the research plan can be discussed and changes made immediately.

- *Data management and online analysis.* Clients can access their survey via the research supplier's secure Web site and monitor the data gathering in real time. The client can use sophisticated tools to actually carry out data analysis as the survey develops. This real-time analysis may result in changes in the questionnaire, sample size, or types of respondents interviewed. The research supplier and the client become partners in "just-in-time" marketing research.

- *Publishing and distribution of reports.* Reports can be published directly to the Web from such programs as PowerPoint and all the latest versions of leading word processing, spreadsheet, and presentation software packages. This means that results are available to appropriate managers worldwide on an almost instantaneous basis. Reports can be searched for content of specific interest, with the same Web browser used to view the report.

- *Oral presentations of marketing research surveys,* which now can be viewed by widely scattered audiences. Managers throughout the world can see and hear the actual client presentation on password-protected websites. This saves firms both time and money, as managers no longer need to travel to a central meeting site.

## ERA of Big Data: 2010–Present

**Big Data**
The accumulation and analysis of massive quantities of information.

The hottest buzzword in marketing research is Big Data. Interestingly enough, most authors never bother to define the term, so it is unclear whether people are always speaking about the same thing. For our purposes, we will define **Big Data** as the accumulation and analysis of massive quantities of information. Every day, three times per second, we produce the equivalent amount of data that the Library of Congress has in its entire print collection.

Up until recently, managers were limited to analyzing structure data. Structured data consists of fixed answers and numbers that can be arranged in rows and columns. These data are easily stored, categorized, queried, analyzed, and reported. A few examples of structured data formatting are: (1) Are you (A) male, (B) female?; (2) Did you find the restaurant (A) excellent, (B) good, (C) fair or (D) poor? The data in question 2 can be crossed with the gender data to ascertain how many men and how many women found the restaurant to be "excellent." The analysis is simple, direct, and straight-forward.

The breakthrough came in 2009 when new algorithms were created to analyze unstructured and free-form data. Now, data scientists can analyze YouTube videos, social media posts, web-click behavior, GPS tracking data, satellite imagery, video streams, public surveillance videos, in-store tracking cameras, and more.

So how do marketers use Big data to improve their profitability? Here is one example.

*Chico's FAS Inc., Fort Myers, Florida-based specialty retailer of private branded women's apparel, listens to what consumers say about its brand on Facebook, Twitter and YouTube, and in discussion forums and blogs. With social media analytic tools, Chico's can find key influencers for the brand and determine how their brand-related online conversations affect business results. Such findings ultimately guide brand and communication strategies, and customer-focused efforts. Chico's works in real time to identify tweets related to its brands, and categorizes them based on their sentiment and the author's degree of influence. The company can then respond to the important comments.*[20]

McKinsey & Company, an international consulting firm, says that companies who use Big Data and the proper analytics can deliver productivity and profit gains that are 5 to 6 percent higher than the competition.[21] The tremendous value of Big Data means that big data technology and services market will grow at a 31 percent rate, with revenues reaching $24 billion by 2016.[22]

The mathematics used in analyzing Big Data goes far beyond the scope of this text. We will, however, take a more detailed look at the nature and benefits of Big Data from a managers' or users' perspective in Chapter 4.

Big Data is not the only change agent swirling around in the marketing research environment, as our *Practicing Marketing Research* box shows.

# PRACTICING MARKETING RESEARCH

## A Few Forces That May Change the World of Marketing Research

Joseph Rydholm is the editor of Quirk's Marketing Research Review, the industry's most popular and influential trade magazine. Here, Joe quotes Quartz, an online news source that focuses on the forces and factors they see shaping the global economy. (The Quartz commentary is shown in italics.) Joe then muses on what he thinks these forces may have on the marketing research world.

### The mobile Web

*Between ever-cheaper smartphones and "dumbphones," which cost as little as $10, plus the dawn of banking, messaging, and social networking services that can run on any device, the possibility that everyone on Earth could be connected is more real than ever....How will new form factors, like watches and face-based computers, change our experience of the Web?*

**Possible Impacts on Marketing Research:** It's obviously a ways down the road, but what could Google Glass or things like the Pebble watch mean for marketing research? Is "wearable computing" just an extension of the Internet or a whole new form of interaction for respondents and researchers or consumers and companies?

### Digital Money

*... the Web, mobile phones and new sales terminals are making possible payment mechanisms that improve on credit card transactions or do away with them all together. That's a lucrative business, which is why the payments sector has seen some of the highest pre-IPO valuations of any in Silicon Valley. Meanwhile, the rise of bitcoin and its imitators means that a stateless virtual currency could become a serious intermediary between other currencies or payment methods in its own right. And in emerging markets, payments via mobile phone are already turning telecoms companies into banks.*

**Possible Impacts on Marketing Research:** Could the accruing of several micropayments over time hold more appeal for survey respondents than entries in sweepstakes that "no one ever wins"? And do those payments (micro or otherwise) have to be in monetary form? Will, as Quartz terms it, a "stateless virtual currency" take over as a preferred form of payment for participation in research?

## China's Transition

*To keep growing, China must now get its 1.35 billion people to consume more, while simultaneously righting global trade imbalances, ramping up its service sector and managing the debt it has racked up. Under its latest set of leaders, how will China cope with these challenges to its economy—and how will its successes and failures affect the global economy, too?*

**Possible Impacts on Marketing Research:** Hmm...1.35 billion people, you say? That's a lot of potential research respondents. How do we get them familiar with and positively predisposed to the marketing research process? And beyond that, how do we begin understanding the psychology behind the act of consumption in a country that only a handful of decades ago actively discouraged it?

## How We Buy

*As the global middle class keeps swelling, consumer spending on everything from corn to cars to air conditioners is hitting new highs and moving online and doing so especially fast in emerging economies....What sorts of companies and products are meeting these changing demands? How is spending in developed economies shifting? What is the future of physical retail stores? Is the context between e-commerce operations and bricks-and-mortar stores really a zero-sum war? How will spending shape global trade and economics, and how do shifting political tides affect spending?*

**Possible Impacts on Marketing Research:** This one makes your head spin. I think the Quartz list of questions is sufficiently mind-boggling on its own without requiring more input from me![23]

## Questions

1. How do you think these forces will affect business and marketing research?
2. Which topic will have the greatest impact on business? Why?

## SUMMARY

Marketing is an organizational function and a set of processes for creating, communicating, and delivering value to customers and for managing customer relationships in ways that benefit the organization and its stockholders. Marketing managers attempt to get the right goods or services to the right people at the right place at the right time at the right price, using the right promotion technique. This may be accomplished by following the marketing concept, which is based on consumer orientation, goal orientation, and systems orientation.

The marketing manager must work within an internal environment of the organization and understand the external environment over which he or she has little, if any, control. The primary variables over which the marketing manager has control are distribution, price, promotion, and product/service decisions. The unique combination of these four variables is called the *marketing mix*.

Marketing research plays a key part in providing the information for managers to shape the marketing mix. Marketing research has grown in importance because of management's focus on customer satisfaction and retention. It also is a key tool in proactive management. Marketing research should be undertaken only when the perceived benefits are greater than the costs.

A marketing research study can be described as programmatic, selective, or evaluative. Programmatic research is done to develop marketing options through market segmentation, market opportunity analysis, or consumer attitude and product usage studies. Selective research is used to test decisional alternatives. Evaluative research is done to assess program performance.

Marketing research in the United States traces its roots back to 1824, when the first public poll was taken. Its early growth period, from 1900 to 1920, was characterized by the establishment of the first formal marketing research department. Its adolescent years, from 1920 until 1950, saw the widespread use of marketing research. The maturing of marketing research began in 1950 and continues through 2012.

The Internet has had a major impact on the marketing research industry. The use of Internet surveys has increased dramatically because they can be quickly deployed, cost significantly less, are readily personalized, have high response rates, and provide the ability to contact the hard-to-reach respondent. Most importantly, as Internet participation by households has increased, identical online and offline surveys have been shown to produce the same business decisions.

Marketing research has also found other uses for the Internet. It serves as a major information source, aids in the distribution of request for proposals and proposals, facilitates collaboration between the client and the research supplier in the management of a research project, provides data management and online analysis, and allows for the publication and distribution of reports and the viewing of oral presentations by a widely scattered audience.

We are now in the era of Big Data made possible by the development of new and very sophisticated means of analyzing nonstructured data. Nonstructured data include things such as Facebook posts and YouTube videos. Big Data analysis is leading to both productivity and profit gains in firms that have mastered the technology.

## KEY TERMS

| | | |
|---|---|---|
| marketing   1 | marketing research   3 | applied research   7 |
| marketing concept   2 | descriptive function   3 | basic, or pure, research   7 |
| consumer orientation   2 | diagnostic function   3 | programmatic research   7 |
| goal orientation   2 | predictive function   3 | selective research   7 |
| systems orientation   2 | return on quality   5 | evaluative research   7 |
| marketing mix   2 | marketing strategy   7 | Big Data   14 |

## QUESTIONS FOR REVIEW & CRITICAL THINKING

1. The role of marketing is to create exchanges. What role might marketing research play in facilitating the exchange process?

2. Marketing research traditionally has been associated with manufacturers of consumer goods. Today, an increasing number of organizations, both profit and nonprofit, are using marketing research. Why do you think this trend exists? Give some examples.

3. Explain the relationship between marketing research and the marketing concept.

4. Comment on the following statement by the owner of a restaurant in a downtown area: "I see customers every day whom I know on a first-name basis. I understand their likes and dislikes. If I put something on the menu and it doesn't sell, I know that they didn't like it. I also read the magazine *Modern Restaurants* to keep up with industry trends. This is all the marketing research I need to do."

5. Why is marketing research important to marketing executives? Give several reasons.

6. What differences might you note among marketing research conducted for (a) a retailer, (b) a consumer goods manufacturer, (c) an industrial goods manufacturer, and (d) a charitable organization?

7. Comment on the following: Ralph Moran is planning to invest $1.5 million in a new restaurant in Saint Louis. When he applied for a construction financing loan, the bank officer asked whether he had conducted any research. Ralph replied, "I checked on research, and a marketing research company wanted $20,000 to do the work. I decided that with all the other expenses of opening a new business, research was a luxury that I could do without."

8. What is meant by *return on quality*? Why do you think that the concept evolved? Give an example.

9. Describe three situations in which marketing research should not be undertaken. Explain why this is true.

10. Give an example of (a) the descriptive role of marketing research, (b) the diagnostic role of marketing research, and (c) the predictive function of marketing research.

11. Using the Internet and a Web browser, visit a search engine such as Google or Bing and type "marketing research." From the thousands of options you are offered, pick a website that you find interesting and report on its content to the class.

12. Divide the class into groups of four. Each team should visit a large organization (profit or nonprofit) and conduct an interview with a top marketing executive to discover how this firm is using marketing research. Each team then should report its findings in class.

13. How is the Internet changing the field of marketing research?

14. Explain the concept of Big Data.
*(Team Exercise)*

# REAL-LIFE RESEARCH • 1.1

## Give Me a Coupon That I Can Use Online!

While consumers certainly enjoy coupons, what do retailers stand to gain? Turns out, plenty. The study suggests that coupons have a significant impact on retailers' bottom lines in addition to the obvious consumer benefit, as couponers are likely to spend more, have higher satisfaction, and return to the retailer where the coupon was used, according to Online Shopper Intelligence, a study from Boston research company Compete.

More than half of the consumers who used a coupon code during their last online purchase said that if they had not received the discount, they would not have bought the item(s)—57 percent said no, 43 percent yes—and more online shoppers are using coupons now than ever. One-third of online shoppers reported that they generally use coupon sites while shopping online, and 35 million consumers visited coupon sites monthly. Coupons have a high return on investment, as the small discount consumers receive encourages them to spend money. When asked how much they spent on their most recent online purchase, consumers who use a coupon spent almost twice as much as consumers who did not use a coupon ($216 with a coupon versus $122 without).

Coupons can be an effective way for retailers to build goodwill with consumers and increase customer satisfaction. When asked about their overall shopping experience, satisfaction was higher for consumers who used a coupon than for those who did not. Ninety-two percent of coupon shoppers were extremely or very satisfied versus 88 percent of noncouponers. Consumers who used a coupon also said they are more likely to buy from the retailer again when compared to those who did not use a coupon. Of consumers with coupons, 91 percent reported being extremely or very likely to shop again at the retailer where the coupon was redeemed versus 86 percent of consumers without coupons.[19]

## Questions

1. How might a firm like The Home Depot use this information? Would Amazon.com use the same couponing strategy as The Home Depot?

2. Do you think that The Home Depot might need more research before it develops a couponing strategy? If so, what does it need to know?

3. Do you think it is necessary for online retailers to conduct marketing research? Why?

## REAL-LIFE RESEARCH • 1.2

### Can Anyone Be a Market Researcher?

Recently, Google announced that it was offering Google Consumer Surveys (www.google.com/insights/consumersurvey) to anyone wanting to do marketing research. Google says that the service is for anyone from Fortune 500 companies to "the local bike shop." It is promoted as a fast, accurate, and low-cost alternative to traditional marketing research. The Google survey website notes, "With Google Consumer Surveys, you choose your target audience, type your question, and watch the results roll in within hours. Get complete results in days; not weeks." Google notes that users can test product concepts, track brands, measure consumer satisfaction, and more.

Paul McDonald, a creator of Google Consumer Surveys, addresses several concerns from the marketing research industry about the new service. "I think your concerns about the quality of the data from self-service survey platforms are well known in the research community," McDonald wrote. "As the mantra goes, 'Garbage in, garbage out'… We try to encourage survey best practices in our help content, program policies and by providing survey templates to guide new researchers. In the end, we are providing a platform which can be used to create professional and statistically accurate surveys."[24]

## Questions

1. Go to Google's Consumer Survey website. After clicking through how it works, and examples, do you feel competent to create an Internet survey? Why or why not?

2. Do you think that the marketing research industry should be concerned about Google Consumer Surveys? Why?

3. Most traditional consumer surveys conclude with a series of demographic questions such as gender, age, location, and so forth. Google Consumer Surveys doesn't ask these questions. Instead, it infers approximate demographic and location information using the respondent's IP address and DoubleClick cookie. The respondent's nearest city can be determined from the respondent's IP address. Income and urban density can be computed by mapping the location to census tracts and using the census data to infer income and urban density. Gender and age group can be inferred from the types of pages the respondent has previously visited in the Google Display Network using the DoubleClick cookie. Google says that this information is used to ensure that each survey receives a representative sample and to enable survey researchers to see how subpopulations answered questions. Inferring this demographic data enables Consumer Surveys researchers to ask few questions in a survey, which, in turn, increases the number of consumers that respond. Do you think that this methodology is better than simply asking the demographic questions? Do you see any problems with Google's methodology?

# The Marketing Research Industry and Research Ethics

## LEARNING OBJECTIVES

1. Appreciate the structure of the marketing research industry.

2. Comprehend the nature of corporate marketing research departments.

3. Understand the types of marketing research suppliers.

4. Examine how corporations use marketing research.

5. Review the current state of the marketing research industry.

6. Appraise ethical trends and unethical practices among marketing research suppliers, clients, and marketing research field services.

The marketing research industry has undergone tremendous change in recent years. Where is the industry going and who are the key players? What is the role of each player? Ethics is one of the most important topics taught in the field of business. What are the ethical issues in marketing research? What are several key approaches to ethical decision making? We discuss each of these issues in Chapter 2.

# Evolving Structure of the Marketing Research Industry

Today, over $32 billion a year is spent on marketing/advertising/public opinion research services around the world.[1] The 25 largest marketing research firms in the world account for 58 percent of this total. Of the top global 25 firms, 16 have the United States as their corporate home country, while the balance have their home base in Japan, the United Kingdom, France, Brazil, or Germany.[2]

Within the United States, marketing research revenues of the 50 largest firms slightly exceed $17 billion. This number is expected to grow significantly as the economy continues to expand. A number of the top 50 firms are basically large database companies that have long-term contracts with their clients (package goods manufacturers, retailers, durable goods manufacturers, and high-tech firms). Firms with long-term contracts fared well during the recent recession, whereas many who specialize in custom, one-of-a-kind research projects saw sales decline.

# Organizations Involved in Marketing Research

The various types of organizations encountered in the marketing research industry are summarized in Exhibit 2.1. Exhibit 2.2 depicts the structure of the marketing research industry.

## Consumer and Industrial Goods and Services Producers

Producers of goods and services, such as Procter & Gamble and American Airlines, are the ultimate users of the research data. Their primary business is the sale of products and services. They use marketing research data on an ongoing basis in a variety of ways to support the marketing decision-making process:

- To determine how various target groups will react to alternative marketing mixes
- To evaluate the ongoing success of operational marketing strategies
- To understand what customers and noncustomers are saying about their brands and competing brands
- To assess changes in the external, or uncontrollable, environment and the implications of those changes for their product or service strategy
- To identify new target markets
- To measure the quality of customer service and level of satisfaction
- To more effectively target their promotion

We will discuss users of marketing research in greater detail later in the chapter.

**Retailers and Wholesalers** In the highly competitive retail market, understanding the customer is paramount. Walmart, The Home Depot, Saks Fifth Avenue, and Bass Pro Shop, as well as many others want to understand their customers' level of satisfaction, the reasons for the satisfaction or dissatisfaction, and what they can do to improve. Those firms that do not understand the customer are destined to failure.

| EXHIBIT 2.1 | General Categories of Organizations Involved in Marketing Research |
|---|---|
| **Organization** | **Activities, Functions, and Services** |
| Consumer and industrial goods and services producers | Firms such as Kraft General Foods, Procter & Gamble, Ford Motor, and Caterpillar are included in this category. They use marketing research data on an ongoing basis in a variety of ways to support the marketing decision-making process. |
| Governments and universities | Government agencies, university research bureaus, individual university professors, and database providers are both users and providers of data. |
| Media companies | Advertising agencies such as J. Walter Thompson, Young & Rubicam, and Draftfcb. Also included are public relations companies such as Hill and Knowlton, and sales promotion firms such as Acosta. |
| Custom research firms | Marketing research consulting firms such as Ipsos, DSS Research, and Burke, Inc., do customized marketing research projects that address specific problems for individual clients. |
| Syndicated service firms | Marketing research data gathering and reporting firms, such as The Nielsen Company, Arbitron, and Symphony IRI, collect data of general interest to many firms but for no one firm in particular. That is, anyone can buy the data they collect. These firms are prominent in the media audience field and retail sales data. |
| Limited-function research firms | Some firms specialize in one or a few activities, techniques, or industries. For example, Westat serves government agencies. |
| Online and mobile tracking firms | Companies like Nielsen, and TNS Cymfony on social media sites such as Twitter, along with blogs and discussion boards. Nielsen collects information from 130 million blogs and 8,000 message boards. Firms like Clearspring and Rap Leaf and Google's Double Click gather information about a person's online activities. These data are sold to firms to be used for targeted advertising. |
| Big ata analytic firms | Someone must make sense of the huge flow of structured and unstructured data flowing into firms and also available through data providers such as DoubleClick. Enter the big data analytic firms. The market is served by long-time players in the analytics market such as Oracle, IBM and SAS. A number of new firms have entered the market, such as Splunk and MicroStrategy. |
| Specialized service suppliers | Some firms provide specialized support services to the marketing research industry, such as Sawtooth Software, which provides sophisticated quantitative analysis or SSI, which provides samples for marketing research suppliers. Field service firms collect data only, on a subcontract basis, for corporate marketing research departments, ad agency research departments, custom research firms, or syndicated research firms. |

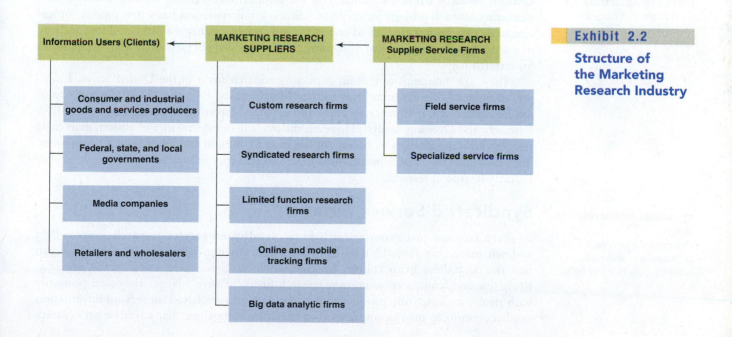

**Exhibit 2.2**

**Structure of the Marketing Research Industry**

**Manufacturers** A key to turning the American automobile industry around is producing cars that people want to buy. Ford, General Motors, and Chrysler are all moving more to marketing research to guide them in producing the right vehicles at the right price points. Even industrial goods manufacturers such as Caterpillar use marketing research to measure both dealer and customer satisfaction.

## Governments and Universities

The various branches of government are both buyers and providers of marketing research information, as are universities. This information includes everything from census data to where a new city park should be located to Americans' attitudes toward nutritional labeling.

Although no estimates are available for marketing research expenditures at the state and local levels, federal marketing research expenditures are estimated at over $5 billion annually.[3] Except for Westat, America's fourth largest market research firm, little of this money goes to traditional marketing researchers. Instead, the bulk of the work is either done in-house or conducted through academic nonprofits, such as the National Opinion Research Center (University of Chicago), Institute for Social Research (University of Michigan), or Research Triangle Institute—as well as think-tank for-profits such as Rand Corporation and Mathematica Policy Research.

## Media Companies

Media companies include advertising agencies, sales promotion companies, public relations agencies, and direct marketing firms. All are concerned with getting the right message to the right target market. Marketing research information is often required to accomplish this goal. Media companies may obtain the data from custom or syndicated research firms and in some cases may conduct the research themselves.

## Custom Research Firms

**custom research firms**
Companies that carry out customized marketing research to address specific projects for corporate clients.

**Custom research firms** are primarily in the business of executing custom, one-of-a-kind marketing research projects for corporate clients. If a corporation has a new product or service idea, a packaging idea, an ad concept, a new pricing strategy, a product reformulation, or a related marketing problem or opportunity, it typically will go to a custom research firm for research help.

There are thousands of custom marketing research firms in the United States. Examples of large custom research firms include Market Facts, Inc., the MARC Group, Opinion Research Corp. International, Elrick and Lavidge Marketing Research, Burke, Inc., DSS Research, and Decision Analyst. However, the overwhelming majority of custom marketing research firms are small, with billings of less than $1 million and fewer than 10 employees. They may limit their client base to their local area and may or may not specialize by type of industry or type of research.

## Syndicated Service Firms

**syndicated service research firms**
Companies that collect, package, and sell market research data to many firms.

In sharp contrast to custom research firms, **syndicated service research firms** collect and sell marketing research data to many firms. Anyone willing to pay the price can buy the data these firms collect, package, and sell. Syndicated service firms are relatively few and, compared to custom research firms, relatively large. They deal primarily with media audience and product movement data and are based on serving information needs common to many companies. For example, companies that advertise on network television want to select shows that reach their target customers most efficiently. They need information on the size and demographic composition of the audiences for various TV programs. It would be extremely inefficient for each company to collect these data itself.

Firms like Nielsen Holding sell standardized TV ratings to a group of clients known as a syndicate—thus, the term *syndicated data*. Some syndicated firms, like Roper Starch Worldwide, sell lifestyle data that are both syndicated and customized. The standardized process is the same to gather the data, but some members of the syndicate may want special information just for their company. This, in fact, is quite common. An additional charge is levied for each custom question added to the syndicated survey.

Exhibit 2.3 shows some syndicated service firms and the specific type of marketing research they offer.

## Limited-Function Research Firms

Some firms specialize in one or a few activities. They may, for example, serve only one industry. Westat, for example, serves various government agencies, whereas IMS Health and DSS Research focus on healthcare. Other firms use a single research technique or a special type of research technique. Mystery Shopper organizations, such as Shop 'n Check and Speedmark, engage only in mystery shopping (discussed in Chapter 7). The Pretesting Company uses devices such as the People Reader to measure how much time is spent reading an ad in a magazine or newspaper.

## Online and Mobile Tracking Firms

Online tracking is computer-based tracking of Internet activities. Mobile-based is tracking of mobile Internet and on-device activities. Many people carry their lives on their mobile devices. They use them to keep in touch with friends and business acquaintances, take and store pictures, read news and sports, play games, and use apps that make their lives easier. The mobile experience is much more intimate than the desktop experience. One survey found that 44 percent of the respondents had slept with their phone next to the bed because they wanted to make sure that they didn't miss any calls, text messages, or updates during the night.[6] Firms such as Luth Research, Tapad, and Drawbridge track mobile behavior. A major advantage to researchers is that they can track smartphone locations. A group of academic researchers gathered information using call date, time, and position of 100,000 European mobile phone users. After analyzing 16 million records of these users, the researchers could forecast someone's future location with 93 percent accuracy.[7]

| EXHIBIT 2.3 | Syndicated Service Research Firms |
| --- | --- |
| **Firm** | **Syndicated Services** |
| Nielsen Holdings, New York | Television ratings<br>Scanner-based data<br>Wholesale/retail audits<br>Internet research |
| FIND/SVP, New York | Large variety of industry/product studies |
| Maritz Marketing Research Inc., Fenton, Missouri | Customer satisfaction studies |
| GfK NOP, New York | Public opinion surveys Lifestyle data Media/advertising effectiveness data |
| Symphony IRI, Chicago | Scanner-based data |

## Big Data Analytic Firms

Some of the key players in analyzing big data were mentioned in Exhibit 2.1. A second component of understanding big data is data visualization. Most people have trouble recalling strings of numbers that are longer than their phone numbers. Then how does one comprehend billions of bits of data? The answer is pictures. Visualization acts as an engine for bringing patterns to light in even the largest data sets. Think of all of the wind currents now blowing across the United States and at various speeds. Now go to http://hint.fm/wind and you will see data visualization. Firms offering data visualization software include Gooddata, AYASDI, Gfk, Tidemark, and Platfora.

## Specialized Service Suppliers

As already discussed, custom, syndicated, and limited-function marketing research firms represent the front line of the research industry. They sell research services, design research studies, analyze the results, and make recommendations to their clients. Online tracking firms will be discussed in greater detail in Chapters 7 and 8. This section wraps up the players involved in marketing research with a quick look at specialized service suppliers. These will be further discussed later in this chapter.

**Marketing Research Supplier Service Firms**    As the heading above implies, these firms service the research industry. Services range from software providers, such as Sawtooth Software, to providers of samples, such as SSI. There are several large online panel (groups of persons willing to answer marketing surveys) providers to the marketing research industry. Harris Interactive claims to have the largest panel in the world with members from over 200 countries. Service firms will be described in more detail below.

A number of firms service marketing research suppliers. When research departments of corporations, such as Kraft General Foods, are conducting their own research, these service firms also cater to them. The two largest categories of service firms are field service organizations and sampling firms.

**Field service firms**
Companies that only collect survey data for corporate clients or research firms.

*Field Service Firms*    A true **field service firm** does nothing but collect survey data—no research design, no analysis. Field service firms are data-collection specialists, collecting data on a subcontract basis for corporate marketing research departments, custom research firms, ad agency research departments, and others.

The following description of the sequence of activities undertaken by a typical field service company provides a good idea of how these firms operate:

1. *Client contact.* Custom or syndicated research firm or corporate or ad agency research department alerts field service firm, usually by e-mail, that it wants to conduct a particular type of study (telephone interview, mall interview, focus group, taste test, etc.).

2. *Interviewer training.* The day the job is to begin, a briefing or training session is held to acquaint interviewers with the requirements of the particular job or questionnaire.

3. *Interviewing status reports.* Daily progress reports are made via e-mail to the client regarding number of interviews completed and costs incurred. These reports permit the client to determine whether the job is on schedule and within budget and allow the field service to advise the client of any problems.

4. *Quality control.* The interviews are edited; that is, specially designed software is used to verify that they were completed correctly.

5. *Ship to client.* Finally, the completed, edited interviews are shipped (typically electronically) to the client.

Most custom research firms rely on field services because it is not cost-effective for them to handle the work themselves. There are too many geographic areas to cover, and it is hard to know which areas will be needed over time. Field service firms in particular areas maintain a steady workflow by having numerous research firms and corporate and ad agency research departments as their clients.

The major field service firm of today has a permanent office. It probably has one or more permanent mall test centers, focus group facilities, a central telephone interviewing facility, as well as other specialized facilities and equipment. A recent trend among field service firms is the establishment of satellite offices in multiple cities.

***Sampling Firms*** Sampling firms provide samples (persons to interview) to marketing research suppliers and other research creators. The largest sampling firm is Survey Sampling Inc. (SSI); this firm does nothing but generate samples for mail, telephone, or Internet surveys. SSI's Survey Spot Internet panel has over 6 million members. The firm's SSI-Lite eSample is a panel categorized by lifestyles; the panel contains over 3,500 topical lists and 12 million names. Other firms, such as Harris Interactive and Decision Analyst, have huge Internet panels that they use for their own research and rent to other research suppliers.

**Software Firms** A number of companies specialize in providing software for statistical analysis and/or Internet interviewing. The most popular statistical package, used by over two-thirds of all research suppliers, is SPSS, now owned by IBM. This is the same software that we provide you when you purchase a new text. Other companies, like Perseus and Web Surveyor, sell software for online interviewing. The firms also will host surveys on their own servers.

**Other Service Companies** Other service companies provide a variety of services to research firms. For example, Sawtooth Software, offers sophisticated data analysis to marketing research suppliers. MarketingResearchCareers.com specializes, as the name implies, in careers in the marketing research field. Quirk's publishes a magazine, *Quirk's Marketing Research Review*, and directories such as directories of field service firms, international research companies, focus group facilities, and others. Quirk's also hosts an online forum for marketing researchers.

# Consumer and Industrial Corporate Marketing Research Departments

Because corporations are the final consumers and the initiators of most marketing research, they are the logical starting point in developing an understanding of how the industry operates. Most large corporations (and virtually all consumer package goods manufacturers of any size) have marketing research departments. Currently, some are melding marketing research and strategic planning, whereas others are combining marketing research and customer satisfaction departments.

The average size of marketing research departments is quite small. One study found that only 15 percent of service companies, such as Federal Express and American Airlines, had marketing research departments with more than 10 employees. Only 23 percent of manufacturers' research departments had more than 10 employees. The size of marketing research departments has been experiencing a downward trend because of mergers and reengineering. The great recession has reversed a long-running trend of more outsourcing to marketing research suppliers. Today, insourcing is the watchword. Corporations are trying to find ways to do more with less. This will mean more work for supplier service firms such as Confirmit, Marketingsight, and Vovici, who provide online survey software, and tools for analyzing and reporting survey data.

Because we cannot cover all types of marketing research departments in this text, we will focus our attention on those found in larger, more sophisticated companies, where marketing research is a staff department and the director of the department generally reports to the top marketing executive. Most of the work of the department is with product or brand managers, new product development managers, and other front-line managers. With the possible exception of various recurring studies that may be programmed into a firm's marketing information system, the marketing research department typically does not initiate studies. In fact, the research manager may control little or no actual budget. Instead, line managers have funds in their budgets earmarked for research.

When brand managers perceive that they have a problem that requires research, they go to the marketing research department for help. Working with the marketing research manager or a senior analyst, they go through a series of steps that may lead to the design and execution of a marketing research project.

# Research Suppliers

Although the marketing research industry is characterized by hundreds of small firms, there are some giants in the industry. Exhibit 2.4 shows total revenues for the 25 largest marketing research firms. The largest firm in the industry—The Nielsen Company—is largely a syndicated service firm.

Nielsen Holdings was founded in 1923. It has been America's largest research firm for over 40 years. Nielsen has offices in more than 100 countries and employs more than 33,000 people. The firm is a global information and media firm offering services in marketing and consumer information, TV and other media measurements, online intelligence, mobile measurement, trade shows, and business publications. Nielsen is divided into two divisions: Watch, which does media research, and Buy, which focuses on consumer research.

## Consumer Watch

Nielsen's Watch segment includes measurement and analytical services related to TV, online, and mobile devices, and provides viewership data and analytics primarily to the media and advertising industries. Its media clients use the data to price their advertising inventory and maximize the value of their content, and its advertising clients use the data to plan and optimize their advertising spending and to better ensure that their advertisements reach the intended audiences. Nielsen provides measurement services across three screens: TV, online, and mobile.

Nielsen provides two principal TV ratings services in the United States: measurement of national TV audiences and measurement of local TV audiences in all 210 designated local TV markets. It uses various methods to collect the data from households, including electronic meters and written diaries. The methods collect not only TV viewing data, but also the demographics of the audience from which it calculates estimates of total TV viewership.

Nielsen is a provider of Internet media and market research, audience analytics, and social media measurement of the behavior of online audiences for online publishers, Internet and media companies, marketers, and retailers. It measures and analyzes consumer-generated media, including opinions, advice, peer-to-peer discussions, and shared personal experiences on more than 100 million blogs, social networks, user groups, and chat boards.

| EXHIBIT 2.4 | Top 25 U.S. Market Research Organizations* | | | |
|---|---|---|---|---|
| **U.S. Rank 2012** | **Organization** | **Headquarters** | **Web Site www.** | **U.S. Research Revenue ($, in millions)** |
| 1 | Nielsen Holdings N.V. | New York | nielsen.com | $2,651.0 |
| 2 | Kantar | London & Fairfield, CT | kantar.com | 929.4 |
| 3 | Ipsos | New York | Ipsos-NA.com | 590.0 |
| 4 | Westat Inc. | Rockville, MD | westat.com | 491.1 |
| 5 | Information Resources Inc. (IRI) | Chicago, IL | Iriworldwide.com | 478.7 |
| 6 | Arbitron Inc. | Columbia, MD | Arbitron.com | 444.1 |
| 7 | GfK USA | Nuremberg, Germany | Gfk.com | 330.0 |
| 8 | IMS Health Inc. | Norwalk, CT | IMSHealth.com | 271.3 |
| 9 | The NPD Group Inc. | Port Washington, NY | NPD.com | 191.8 |
| 10 | ICF International Inc. | Fairfax, VA | ICFI.com | 191.2 |
| 11 | comScore Inc. | Reston, VA | comScore.com | 183.4 |
| 12 | Abt SRBI Inc. | Cambridge, MA | abtassociates.com | 157.4 |
| 13 | J.D. Powers & Associates | Westlake Village, CA | JDPower.com | 156.1 |
| 14 | Maritz Research | Fenton, MO | MaritzResearch.com | 154.0 |
| 15 | Symphony Health Solutions | Horsham, PA | SymphonyHealth.com | 153.5 |
| 16 | dunnhumbyUSA LLC | Cincinnati OH | Idunnhumby.com/us/ | 118.1 |
| 17 | Harris Interactive Inc. | New York | HarrisInteractive.com | 85.3 |
| 18 | Lieberman Research Worldwide | Los Angeles CA | LRWonline.com | 72.9 |
| 19 | National Research Corp. | Lincoln, NE | NationalResearch.com | 67.7 |
| 20 | Market Strategies International | Livonia, MI | MarketStrategies.com | 62.6 |
| 21 | Communispace Corp. | Boston, MA | Communispace.com | 59.3 |
| 22 | ORC International | Princeton, NJ | ORCInternational.com, | 56.5 |
| 23 | Vision Critical Communications Inc. | Vancouver, BC | VisionCritical.com | 51.0 |
| 24 | Market Force Information Inc. | Louisville, CO | MarketForce.com | 50.5 |
| 25 | Burke Inc. | Cincinnati, OH | Burke.com | 48.3 |

*Source:* "Honomichl Top 50", *Marketing News* (June 2013), pp. 35.
*Some large privately held firms, such as DSS Research and Decision Analyst, would be included in the list, but they do not disclose financial data.

The firm offers consumer research and independent measurement for telecom and media companies in the mobile telecommunications industry, including mobile carriers and device manufacturers. In the United States, its metrics are an indicator of market share, customer satisfaction, device share, service quality, revenue share, content audience, and other key performance measures.

## Consumer Buy

Nielsen's Buy segment provides retail transactional measurement data, consumer behavior information and analytics primarily to businesses in the consumer packaged-goods industry. Its Buy clients use the information and insights in an effort to better manage their brands, uncover new sources of demand, launch and grow new products, improve their marketing mix, and establish more effective customer relationships.[5]

# Using Marketing Research—A Corporate Perspective

Now that you are familiar with the marketing research industry, let's look in more detail at research users. There is a very good possibility that any future encounters that you, as a businessperson, will have with marketing research will be as a research user. Exhibit 2.5 shows some of the various types of marketing research clients. Despite the importance of nonmarketing, *internal* clients, such as finance or manufacturing, to the success of an organization, some firms' research departments have paid little attention to nonmarketing clients' specific marketing information needs. As you might expect, these poorly served clients have demonstrated little interest in marketing research information. It has been our experience that the most successful marketing research departments and firms are those committed to the complete satisfaction of all of their clients. Let's take a closer look at the types of information these various clients need and use.

## External Clients

Because marketing research can be a valuable source of information about new or improved competitive advantages and because such information is often very expensive to gather, data gathered by a firm's research department is rarely circulated outside of the firm. Many firms don't provide any information to outsiders, such as suppliers. However, those that do usually find that it is to their mutual benefit.

**strategic partnership**
An alliance formed by two or more firms with unique skills and resources to offer a new service for clients, provide strategic support for each firm, or in some other manner create mutual benefits.

**Vendors** Manufacturers are moving into **strategic partnerships** with their vendors in order to implement just-in-time manufacturing. These alliances are based on fully integrated manufacturer–supplier logistics systems that get the component to the assembly line just when it is needed. The result is little or no raw materials inventory and significantly reduced carrying costs. The backbone of this system is shared information. Large retailers, such as Walmart and Lowes, have such relationships with their major vendors.

Within the framework of strategic partnering, marketing research information is fed back to a manufacturer's suppliers when consumers voice opinions about a component on the manufacturer's customer satisfaction surveys. For example, if Pioneer was supplying radios for Honda automobiles and customers were complaining about how difficult a certain

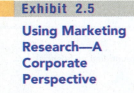

**Exhibit 2.5**

**Using Marketing Research—A Corporate Perspective**

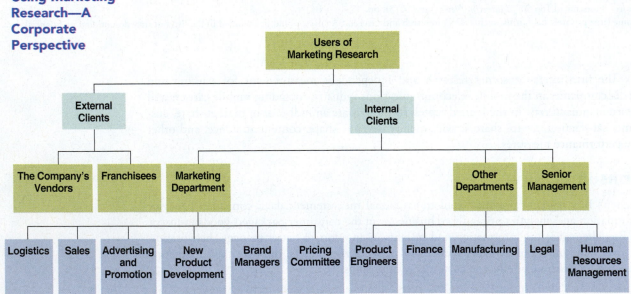

model was to program, this research information would be shared with Pioneer. In one case, a major retail chain commissioned a study on changes in customer preferences for Christmas-related items such as gift wrap, cards, artificial trees, and ornaments, to help its suppliers of production materials understand the importance of making specific product changes and to provide guidance in making those changes.

Steve Allen /Getty Images

A major retail chain commissioned a study on changes in customer preferences for Christmas-related items in order to help suppliers understand the need for product change and what product changes to make.

**Franchisees** Most major franchisors of consumer goods and services provide marketing research data to their franchisees. Perhaps the most common way of gathering data is from *mystery shoppers*. A mystery shopper, posing as a customer, observes how long it takes to be waited on and/or make a purchase, the courtesy of the clerks, the cleanliness of the operation, and whether his or her purchase or order was properly prepared. Mystery shopping is discussed in detail in Chapter 7.

Franchisors also share marketing research information with their franchisees to support certain recommendations or actions. When McDonald's suggests to a franchisee that a restaurant be remodeled in a particular style, it will show research data indicating that the building is perceived as out-of-date or old-fashioned. Other data might reveal which theme or style current customers prefer. When Burger King launches a major new promotional campaign, it may share with franchisees research data showing that customers and noncustomers preferred the selected campaign theme over alternative themes.

## Internal Clients

**Marketing Managers** Virtually every manager within an organization will, at some point, be a user of marketing research information. However, marketing managers use research data more than any other group. Recall that the marketing mix consists of decisions regarding products or services, promotion, distribution, and pricing. Marketing research helps decision makers in each of these areas make better decisions. Product managers, for example, begin by using research to define their target market. In some cases, managers use research to determine the heavy users of their product within the target market. Marketing research revealed that heavy users of Miracle Whip consume 550 servings, or 17 pounds, of the product a year. These data were used to target a $30 million promotional campaign to core users, telling them not to "skip the zip." As a result, Miracle Whip's market share went up 2.1 percent, to $305 million in annual sales.[8] The ad campaign also was thoroughly tested for effectiveness by marketing research before it was launched.

New product development managers are among the heaviest users of marketing research. From qualitative research techniques that generate product ideas to concept testing, product prototype testing, and then test marketing, marketing research is the key to creating a new product. For example, Post's research on cereals had always shown that bananas are America's favorite cereal fruit. Therefore, why not a banana-flavored cereal? Post's new product manager concocted cereals with dried banana pieces, but they failed marketing research taste tests. Further research, conducted to explain why this happened, uncovered the fact that consumers saw no reason to buy a cereal with preserved bananas, as the fresh fruit is quite cheap year-round. If consumers wanted a banana-flavored cereal, they'd peel a banana and make one on the spot. One day, the new product manager had an inspiration: Consumers had said that they liked banana nut bread; it conjured up thoughts of something delicious that grandma used to make.

Marketing research helped Gatorade position its product toward those who use it most often—men between the ages of 19 and 44. Go to *http://www .gatorade. com* to see if the company positions its website for this demographic.

NHLI via Getty Images

The manager had Post's labs create a new cereal for test marketing in consumers' homes, where it received very high consumer test scores. Thus, Great Grains' Banana Nut Crunch, one of Post's hottest cereals, was born. It is solely a product of marketing research, created from the initial concept of a new product manager.

Marketing research also plays an important role in the distribution function. It is used to choose locations for new stores and to test consumer reactions to internal store design fixtures and features. Banana Republic, for example, has relied on marketing research to create the right atmosphere in its stores.

Within larger organizations, pricing decisions are usually made by committees composed of representatives from marketing, finance, production, and perhaps other departments. A few years ago, Procter & Gamble examined the electric toothbrush market and noted that most electric toothbrushes cost over $50. The firm conducted pricing marketing research and found the demand for electric toothbrushes to be very elastic. The company brought out the Crest SpinBrush that works on batteries and sells for just $9. It is now the nation's best-selling toothbrush, manual or electric, and has helped the Crest brand of products become P&G's twelfth billion-dollar brand.

**Top Management** Procter & Gamble has brought marketing research to the forefront of the company. This, in turn, has meant rising market share, profits, and shareholder value. Top executives at DuPont, Walmart, Marriott, Carnival Cruise Lines, Pillsbury, and Amazon.com look to marketing research for strategic guidance.

**Other Internal Users** From time to time, other individuals besides marketing managers and senior management find a need for marketing research. Toyota's engineers sometimes invent new items for which demand must be assessed. Toyota's marketing research, however, feeds engineering management a steady stream of consumer desires and dislikes. Manufacturing also receives continual feedback, from customer satisfaction surveys, about loose-fitting door panels, balky sunroof openers, sudden acceleration, and the like.

Finance departments use test market data to forecast revenue streams for one to three years. Similarly, repositioning research helps financial managers forecast revenue spurts from older products. Originally, Gatorade was promoted as a drink for competitive athletes. Marketing research found that its main users were men, aged 19 to 44, who understood the product, had a good perception of what it did, and knew when to drink it. The product was repositioned toward physical activity enthusiasts as a drink that would quench their thirst and replenish the minerals lost during exercise better than other beverages did. The new positioning dramatically increased sales.

Human resource managers may call on marketing research to survey employees about a variety of topics. Quality customer service requires that employees have a positive image of the company, an attitude that they then convey to customers. Firms such as Southwest Airlines and Nations-Bank monitor employee attitudes through survey research.

Companies are increasingly turning to marketing research to win their cases in court. Schering-Plough and Pfizer went to court over physicians' perceptions about various antihistamines and sales messages used by sales reps about the products. Marketing research is also used to prove or disprove consumer perceptions regarding similar brand names.

A San Francisco jury ruled against Kendall-Jackson Winery in its case against E. & J. Gallo Winery. Kendall-Jackson claimed that Gallo copied the design of its Vintner's Reserve label, which features a grape leaf with fall colors, by using a similarly styled logo on the Gallo Turning Leaf line of varietal wines. Marketing research won the case for Gallo.

# The State of the Marketing Research Industry

More than $15.4 billion was spent within the United States on marketing research in 2013. Revenues were essentially flat from the previous year. The top 50 U.S. firms account for 91 percent of the total revenue.[9] The biggest spender on research, by far, are agencies of the federal government, which spent an estimated $6.3 billion in 2013.[10] This $9.5 billion figure does not include universities, such as the University of Michigan Survey Research Center. Also not included are many large U.S. corporations, such as Proctor & Gamble and General Motors, which do a considerable amount of research in-house. Most marketing research by large consulting firms and advertising agencies is also done internally.

One trend continues unabated in the marketing research industry. The use of online data collection for survey projects continues to grow. Data can be gathered quicker, cheaper, and from a more diverse population via online interviewing versus in-person or telephone interviewing.[11]

Gordon Wyner, vice president of Client Solutions for Millward Brown, a large, global research firm, discusses the rapid change in marketing research in the Practicing Marketing Research box below.

# PRACTICING MARKETING RESEARCH

## Marketing Research In a Period of Great Change

New capabilities are emerging that promise to remake the landscape of what research is and does. What's less clear is how these changes enable marketers to better achieve their goals.

### The Upside

Some of the biggest potential growth areas include:

1. More data: measurement of more consumer behaviors
2. More control: predictability of consumers' response to marketing initiatives
3. More depth: understanding how consumers' minds work

Some of the behaviors that we take for granted today didn't exist 10 years ago, for the most part. For example, Web search, digital media, e-commerce, and social media have become important to understanding consumers. Measuring behavior related to these activities ranks high on the marketing researcher's priority list.

The list is still expanding, thanks to new technologies, especially mobile. More new behaviors are, in principle, measurable, such as checking in with your social network from each new location.

Even behaviors that are not new can be more comprehensively measured. More points of interaction between a consumer and a brand are amenable to measurement, such as bank customers' visits to tellers, ATMs or bank websites, or their interactions with call centers and interactive advertising.

Since the new behaviors are electronically captured, the opportunity to use the information for marketing analysis is abundant. More variables and more granular measurement should lead to more predictive power, especially anticipating consumer response to marketing actions. This, in turn, should lead to better decisions about what marketing actions to take and how to allocate valuable resources.

### Gap

These new capabilities don't address all important marketing issues.

### Innovation

How will the new capabilities of marketing research assist and improve the innovation process? Surely, the availability of data will allow marketers to respond quickly to changes in the marketplace, and make product and channel modifications accordingly, but where will the new ideas for products and services come from? An intense focus on past and current behavior won't necessarily reveal insights as to what consumers will want in the future.

### Brand

Although the new techniques enable careful listening to what consumers say, they don't directly answer some important questions:

1. What does the brand stand for? (Not just to the vocal minority who express themselves online, but to the addressable market)

2. How should the brand be positioned? (Relative to competition)

3. What types of communications will best improve brand equality? (Compared with alternative themes, strategies and executions)[12]

## Questions

1. How can researchers determine what consumers want in the future? Simply ask them?

2. Do you see any privacy issues in this material? If so, what are they?

---

A discussion of the state of the art of the marketing research industry would not be complete without mentioning ethics.

# Marketing Research Ethics

**ethics**
Moral principles or values, generally governing the conduct of an individual or group.

The two most important factors for research clients in their relationships with research departments/suppliers are client confidentiality and honesty. Each is a question of ethics. **Ethics** are moral principles or values generally governing the conduct of an individual or group. Ethical behavior is not, however, a one-way relationship. Clients and suppliers, as well as field services, must also act in an ethical manner.

Ethical questions range from practical, narrowly defined issues, such as a researcher's obligation to be honest with its customers, to broader social and philosophical questions, such as a company's responsibility to preserve the environment and protect employee rights. Many ethical conflicts develop from conflicts between the differing interests of company owners and their workers, customers, and surrounding community. Managers must balance the ideal against the practical—the need to produce a reasonable profit for the company's shareholders with honesty in business practices, and larger environmental and social issues.

## Ethical Theories

People usually base their individual choice of ethical theory on their life experiences. The following are some of the ethical theories that apply to business and marketing research.[13]

**Deontology**  The deontological theory states that people should adhere to their obligations and duties when analyzing an ethical dilemma. This means that a person will follow his or her obligations to another individual or society because upholding one's duty is what is considered ethically correct. For instance, a deontologist will always keep his promises to a friend and will follow the law. People who follow this theory will produce very consistent decisions since they will be based on the individual's set duties. Note that this theory is not necessarily concerned with the welfare of others. Say, for example, a research supplier has decided that it's his ethical duty (and very practical!) to always be on time to meetings with clients. Today, he is running late. How is he supposed to drive? Is the deontologist supposed to speed, breaking his duty to society to uphold the law, or is the deontologist supposed to arrive at his meeting late, breaking his duty to be on time? This scenario of conflicting obligations does not lead us to a clear ethically correct resolution, nor does it protect the welfare of others from the deontologist's decision.

**Utilitarianism** The utilitarian ethical theory is founded on the ability to predict the consequences of an action. To a utilitarian, the choice that yields the greatest benefit to the most people is the choice that is ethically correct. One benefit of this ethical theory is that the utilitarian can compare similar predicted solutions and use a point system to determine which choice is more beneficial for more people. This point system provides a logical and rational argument for each decision and allows a person to use it on a case-by-case context.

There are two types of utilitarianism: act utilitarianism and rule utilitarianism. *Act utilitarianism* adheres exactly to the definition of utilitarianism as described in the previous section. In act utilitarianism, a person performs the acts that benefit the most people, regardless of personal feelings or the societal constraints such as laws. *Rule utilitarianism*, however, takes into account the law and is concerned with fairness. A rule utilitarian seeks to benefit the most people but through the fairest and most just means available. Therefore, added benefits of rule utilitarianism are that it values justice and doing good at the same time.

As is true of all ethical theories, however, both act and rule utilitarianism contain numerous flaws. Inherent in both are the flaws associated with predicting the future. Although people can use their life experiences to attempt to predict outcomes, no human being can be certain that his predictions will be true. This uncertainty can lead to unexpected results, making the utilitarian look unethical as time passes because his choice did not benefit the most people as he predicted.

Another assumption that a utilitarian must make is that he has the ability to compare the various types of consequences against each other on a similar scale. However, comparing material gains such as money against intangible gains such as happiness is impossible since their qualities differ so greatly.

**Casuist** The casuist ethical theory compares a current ethical dilemma with examples of similar ethical dilemmas and their outcomes. This allows one to determine the severity of the situation and to create the best possible solution according to others' experiences. Usually, one will find examples that represent the extremes of the situation so that a compromise can be reached that will hopefully include the wisdom gained from the previous situations.

One drawback to this ethical theory is that there may not be a set of similar examples for a given ethical dilemma. Perhaps that which is controversial and ethically questionable is new and unexpected. Along the same line of thinking, this theory assumes that the results of the current ethical dilemma will be similar to results in the examples. This may not be necessarily true and would greatly hinder the effectiveness of applying this ethical theory.

## Research Supplier Ethics

Understanding ethical theories will help us better decide how certain unethical practices in marketing research should be resolved.

Exhibit 2.6 details some of the unethical practices most common among the various groups involved in marketing research. This section looks at unethical research supplier practices, ranging from low-ball pricing to black-box branding. The following sections address ethical issues pertaining to research clients and field services.

**Low-Ball Pricing** A research supplier should quote a firm price based on a specific incidence rate (percentage of the respondents in the sample that will qualify to complete the survey) and questionnaire length (time to complete). If either of the latter two items changes, then the client should expect a change in the contract price. **Low-ball pricing** in any form is unethical. In essence, low-ball pricing is quoting an unrealistically low price to secure a firm's business and then using some means to substantially raise the price.

**low-ball pricing**
Quoting an unrealistically low price to secure a firm's business and then using some means to substantially raise the price.

| EXHIBIT 2.6 | Unethical Practices in Marketing Research | |
|---|---|---|
| **Research Suppliers** | **Research Clients** | **Field Services** |
| Low-ball pricing | Issuing bid requests when a supplier has been predetermined | Using professional respondents |
| Allowing subjectivity into the research | Soliciting free advice and methodology via bid requests | Not validating data |
| Abusing respondents | Making false promises | |
| Selling unnecessary research | Issuing unauthorized requests for proposal | |
| Violating client confidentiality | | |
| Black-box branding | | |

For example, quoting a price based on an unrealistically high incidence rate is a form of low-ball pricing. Offering to conduct a focus group at $8,000 a group and, after the client commits, saying, "The respondents' fees for participating in the group discussion are, of course, extra" is a form of low-balling.

**Allowing Subjectivity into the Research** Research suppliers must avoid using biased samples, misusing statistics, ignoring relevant data, and creating a research design with the goal of supporting a predetermined objective. One area of research today is so-called *advocacy studies*. These studies are commissioned by companies or industries for public relations purposes or to advocate or prove a position. For example, Burger King once used positive responses to the following question in an advocacy study in an attempt to justify the claim that its method of cooking hamburgers was preferred over that of McDonald's: "Do you prefer your hamburgers flame-broiled or fried?" When another researcher rephrased the question—"Do you prefer a hamburger that is grilled on a hot stainless-steel grill or cooked by passing the meat through an open gas flame?"—the results were reversed: McDonald's was preferred to Burger King.

Kiwi Brands, a shoe polish company, commissioned a study on the correlation between ambition and shiny shoes. The study found that 97 percent of self-described ambitious young men believe polished shoes are important. In many cases, advocacy studies simply use samples that are not representative of the population. For example, a news release for a diet products company trumpeted: "There's good news for the 65 million Americans currently on a diet." A company study had shown that people who lose weight can keep it off—the sample consisted of 20 graduates of the company's program, who also endorsed its products in commercials.

When studies are released to the news media, the methodology should be readily available to news reporters. Typically, this information is withheld, often on the ground that the material is proprietary. A survey done for Carolina Manufacturer's Service, a coupon redemption company,

When studies are released to the news media, the methodology should be readily available to news reporters. A survey done for a coupon redemption company found that "a broad cross-section of Americans find coupons to be true incentives for purchasing products." The description of the methodology, however, was available only for a price of $2,000.

found that "a broad cross-section of Americans find coupons to be true incentives for purchasing products." The description of the methodology was available only at a price: $2,000.

**Abusing Respondents** Respondent abuse can take several forms. Perhaps the most common is lengthy interviews. This problem stems in part from the "as long as you're asking questions" mentality of many product managers. It is not uncommon for clients to request additional "nice to know" questions, or even exploratory questions on an entirely separate project. This leads to lengthy questionnaires, 30-minute telephone or Internet interviews, and 40-minute mall-intercept interviews. As a result of long interviews and telephone sales pitches, more and more Americans are refusing to participate in survey research. The refusal rate for telephone surveys now averages 60-plus percent, an increase of 10 percent over 10 years. Forty-nine percent of the people who do participate say the surveys are "too personal." Fortunately, more people are willing to participate in Internet surveys than other types of research.

Interest in a product or service is often discerned during the interviewing process, and the researcher knows the interviewees' potential purchasing power from their answers to income and other pertinent financial questions. Although the introduction phase of the questionnaire usually promises confidentiality, some researchers have sold names and addresses of potential customers to firms seeking sales leads. Individuals willing to participate in the survey research process have a right to have their privacy protected.

The state of New York sued Student Marketing Group for selling information on a broad scale to direct marketers. The survey filled out by students included age, gender, religious affiliation, career interests, and grade point average. The company said that it was gathering the data for universities to help the students gain admission and financial aid. Actually, direct marketers used the information to sell credit cards, magazines, videos, cosmetics, and other products.[14]

**Selling Unnecessary Research** A research supplier dealing with a client who has little or no familiarity with marketing research often has the opportunity to "trade the client up." For example, if a project called for four focus groups and an online survey of approximately 350 consumers, the research supplier might sell eight groups and 1,000 Internet interviews, with a 400-interview telephone follow-up in six months.

It is perfectly acceptable to offer a prospective client several research designs with several alternative prices when and if the situation warrants alternative designs. The supplier should point out the pros and cons of each method, along with sample confidence intervals. The client, in consultation with the supplier, then can decide objectively which design best suits the company's needs.

**Violating Client Confidentiality** Information about a client's general business activities or the results of a client's project should not be disclosed to a third party. The supplier should not even disclose the name of a client unless permission is received in advance.

The thorniest issue in confidentiality is determining where "background knowledge" stops and conflict arises as a result of work with a previous client. One researcher put it this way:

*I get involved in a number of proprietary studies. The problem that often arises is that some studies end up covering similar subject matter as previous studies. Our code of ethics states that you cannot use data from one project in a related project for a competitor. However, since I often know some information about an area, I end up compromising my original client. Even though upper management formally states that it should not be done, they also expect it to be done to cut down on expenses. This conflict of interest situation is difficult to deal with. At least in my firm, I don't see a resolution to the issue. It is not a onetime situation, but rather a process that perpetuates itself. To make individuals redo portions of studies which have recently been done is ludicrous, and to forgo potential new business is almost impossible from a financial perspective.[15]*

**Black-Box Branding** Marketing research suppliers have discovered branding. Synovate has over 25 branded product offerings, including Brand Vision and M2M. Maritz Research offers Loyalty Maximizer, and Harris Interactive has TRBC, a scale bias correction algorithm. Go to virtually any large marketing research firm's website, and you'll see a vast array of branded research products for everything from market segmentation to customer value analysis—all topped off with a diminutive $^{SM}$, $^{TM}$, or ®.

A common denominator across some of these products is that they are proprietary, which means the firms won't disclose exactly how they work. That's why they're also known pejoratively as black boxes. A black-box method is proprietary—a company is able to protect its product development investment. And if customers perceive added value in the approach, suppliers can charge a premium price to boot. (Black boxes and brand names are not synonymous. Almost all proprietary methods have a clever brand name, but there are also brand names attached to research methods that are not proprietary.)

At least two factors have given rise to this branding frenzy. First, competitive pressures force organizations to seek new ways to differentiate their product offerings from those of their competitors. Second, many large research companies are publicly held, and publicly held companies are under constant pressure to increase sales and profits each quarter. One way to do this is to charge a premium price for services. If a company has a proprietary method for doing a marketing segmentation study, presumably it can charge more for this approach than another firm using publicly available software such as SPSS or SAS.

Clients have no objective way of determining whether the results of a proprietary method would vary significantly from those of more standard approaches, and neither have we. Go to five different companies that have five different black boxes for choice modeling, for example. Each company claims its method is superior, yet it's impossible to assess, from a psychometric perspective, which possesses the highest level of validity.

Of course, no one is forcing clients to purchase a black-box method, and they can always contact other organizations that have used a supplier's proprietary method to assess its effectiveness. Often, clients will obtain multiple bids on a project so that they can select from a variety of approaches to help them answer their research questions.[16]

## Client Ethics

Like research suppliers, clients (or users) also have a number of ethical dos and don'ts. Some of the more common client problems are requesting bids when a supplier has been predetermined, requesting bids to obtain free advice and methodology, making false promises, and issuing unauthorized RFPs.

**Requesting Bids When a Supplier Has Been Predetermined** It is not uncommon for a client to prefer one research supplier over another. Such a preference may be due to a good working relationship, cost considerations, ability to make deadlines, friendship, or quality of the research staff. Having a preference per se is not unethical. It is unethical, however, to predetermine which supplier will receive a contract and yet ask for proposals from other suppliers to satisfy corporate requirements. Requiring time, effort, and money from firms that have no opportunity to win the contract is very unfair. Why more than a single RFP? Some corporations require more than one bid.

**Requesting Bids to Obtain Free Advice and Methodology** Client companies seeking bargain-basement prices have been known to solicit detailed proposals, including complete methodology and a sample questionnaire, from a number of suppliers. After "picking the brains" of the suppliers, the client assembles a questionnaire and then contracts directly with field services to gather the data. A variation of this tactic is to go to the cheapest supplier with the client's own proposal, derived by taking the best ideas from the other proposals. The client then attempts to get the supplier to conduct the more elaborate study at the lower price.

**Making False Promises** Another technique used by unethical clients to lower their research costs is to hold out a nonexistent carrot. For example, a client might say, "I don't want to promise anything, but we are planning a major stream of research in this area, and if you will give us a good price on this first study, we will make it up to you on the next one." Unfortunately, the next one never comes—or if it does, the same line is used on another unsuspecting supplier.

**Requesting Proposals without Authorization** In each of the following situations, a client representative sought proposals without first receiving the authority to allocate the funds to implement them:

1. A client representative decided to ask for proposals and *then* go to management to find out whether she could get the funds to carry them out.

2. A highly regarded employee made a proposal to management on the need for marketing research in a given area. Although managers were not too enthused about the idea, they told the researcher to seek bids so as not to dampen his interest or miss a potentially (but, in their view, highly unlikely) good idea.

3. A client representative and her management had different ideas on what the problem was and how it should be solved. The research supplier was not informed of the management view, and even though the proposal met the representative's requirements, management rejected it out of hand.

4. Without consulting with the sales department, a client representative asked for a proposal on analyzing present sales performance. Through fear of negative feedback, corporate politics, or lack of understanding of marketing research, the sales department blocked implementation of the proposal.

**Retailer Ethics** Intense competition at the retail level has resulted in a mushrooming of customer satisfaction surveys. Perhaps this is nowhere more evident than in auto dealerships. As many auto manufacturers, particularly American, have drastically cut their number of dealerships, those remaining are under strong pressure to provide exceptional customer service. The level of service is measured by manufacturer-supplied customer relationship surveys. One survey of 1,700 new car buyers found that 45 percent of the respondents believed that the dealership tried to influence their survey responses.[17] Some buyers weren't sure when the dealer asked, "Please let us address any problems rather than reporting them." Is this an attempt to influence the buyer, or just good customer service?

Specifically, customers responded in the following ways to the question, "When you purchased your car, what did the salesperson or manager say about the survey?":

- 25 percent—They never mentioned the survey.
- 30 percent—They mentioned that I would receive a survey (but none of the following).
- 36 percent—They asked me to let them address the problems rather than reporting them.
- 28 percent—They asked me to give them perfect scores but did not beg.
- 8 percent—They begged me for perfect scores.
- 9 percent—They said they would only get a bonus if I gave them perfect scores.
- 2 percent—They asked me to bring the survey in to the dealer and fill it out while they watched.
- 2 percent—They asked me to bring the blank survey to the dealer so they would fill it out.
- 2 percent—They offered me a gift in exchange for one of the above.[18]

As you can see, responses exist on a continuum, but a number are clearly unethical. Manufacturers can help solve the problem by sending the questionnaire to the respondent's home; establishing and enforcing a strong policy against survey manipulation allows the respondents to remain anonymous.

## Field Service Ethics

Marketing research field services have been the traditional production arm of the research industry, requiring mail or face-to-face interviews. They are the link between the respondent and the research supplier. It is imperative that they properly record information and carefully follow sampling plans. Otherwise, even the best research design will produce invalid information (garbage in; garbage out). Maintaining high ethical standards will aid a field service in procuring good raw data for the research firm.

**Using Professional Respondents**  The problem of professional respondents arises most often in the recruitment of focus group participants. Virtually all field services maintain a database of people willing to participate in qualitative discussion groups, along with a list of their demographic characteristics. Maintaining such a list is good business and quite ethical. When qualifications for group participants are easy (e.g., pet owners, persons who drive SUVs), there is little temptation to use professional respondents. However, when a supplier wants, for example, persons who are heavy users of Oxydol detergent or who own a Russian Blue cat, it is not unheard of for a group recruiter to call a professional respondent and say, "I can get you into a group tomorrow with a $75 respondent fee, and all you need to say is that you own a Russian Blue cat."

In an attempt to weed out professional respondents, a research supplier may specify that the participant must not have been a member of a qualitative discussion group within the past six months. However, dishonest field services will simply tell the professional respondent to deny having participated in a group within the past six months.

## Respondents' Rights

Respondents in a marketing research project typically give their time and opinions and receive little or nothing in return. These individuals, however, do have certain rights that should be upheld by all marketing researchers. All potential participants in a research project have the right to choose, the right to safety, the right to be informed, and the right to privacy.

**Right to Choose**  Everyone has the right to determine whether or not to participate in a marketing research project. Some people, such as poorly educated individuals or children, may not fully appreciate this privilege. A person who would like to terminate an interview or experiment may give short, incomplete answers, or even false data.

The fact that a person has consented to be part of an experiment or to answer a questionnaire does not give the researcher carte blanche to do whatever she or he wants. The researcher still has an obligation to the respondent to honor other rights. For example, if a person participating in a taste test involving a test product and several existing products prefers the test product, the researcher does not have the right to use the respondent's name and address in a promotion piece, saying that "Ms. Jones prefers new Sudsies to Brand X."

**Right to Safety**  Research participants have the right to safety from physical or psychological harm. Although it is unusual for a respondent to be exposed to physical harm, there have been cases of persons becoming ill during food taste tests. Also, on a more subtle level, researchers rarely warn respondents that a test product contains, say, a high level of salt. An unwitting respondent with hypertension could be placed in physical danger if the test ran several weeks.

It is much more common for a respondent to be placed in a psychologically damaging situation. Individuals might experience stress when an interviewer presses them to participate in a study. Others might experience stress when they cannot answer questions or are given a time limit to complete a task (e.g., "You have 5 minutes to browse through this magazine, and then I will ask you a series of questions").

**Right to Be Informed**   Research participants have the right to be informed of all aspects of a research task. Knowing what is involved, how long it will take, and what will be done with the data, a person can make an intelligent choice as to whether to participate in the project.

Often, it is necessary to disguise the name of the research sponsor to avoid biasing the respondent. For example, it is poor research practice to say, "We are conducting a survey for Pepsi; which brand of soft drink do you consume most often?" In cases in which disguising the sponsor is required, a debriefing should take place following the completion of the interview. The debriefing should cover the study's purpose, the sponsor, what happens next with the data, and any other pertinent information. A debriefing can reduce respondent stress and build goodwill for the research industry. Unfortunately, taking the time to debrief a respondent is a cost that most companies are unwilling to incur.

In some business and academic research, the researcher may offer to provide the respondent with a copy of the research results as an incentive to obtain his or her participation in the project. When a commitment has been made to disseminate the findings to survey respondents, it should be fulfilled. On more than one occasion, we have participated in academic surveys where the carrot of research results was offered but never delivered.

**Right to Privacy**   All consumers have the right to privacy. All major research organizations, including the MRA, CASRO, the Internet Marketing Research Association (IMRO), the American Marketing Association (AMA), and the Advertising Research Foundation (ARF), have privacy codes. For example, with online survey research, lists of potential respondents must have one of two characteristics. Potential respondents must have either a prior opt-in for contact or they must have an existing business relationship with the sender through which an e-mail contact would not be considered a random, unsolicited e-mail (spam).

The privacy battle is most heated in the area of what online and mobile tracking companies are gathering. Tracking companies know what you do online and with mobile devices, but they either can't or won't keep your name in their databases. The industry often cites this layer of anonymity as a reason that tracking shouldn't be considered intrusive. However, some tracking companies meld a number of online and offline databases so they know your name, e-mail address, and a lot of personal offline information.

RapLeaf recently provided a conservative politician with e-mail addresses to target his election campaign. In one example, RapLeaf knew a woman's name, that she was conservative, had an interest in the Bible, and contributed to environmental and political causes. RapLeaf claims it strips out personal information like names before selling them for online advertising. However, data gathered and sold by RapLeaf can be very specific. According to documents reviewed by the *Wall Street Journal,* RapLeaf's segments included a person's household income range, age range, political leaning, and gender and age of children in the household, as well as interests in topics including religion, the Bible, gambling, tobacco, adult entertainment, and "get rich quick" offers. In all, RapLeaf segmented people into more than 400 categories.[19]

When it comes to social media listening and online privacy, consumers want it both ways. According to a survey conducted by NetBase, a Mountain View, California, research company, 51 percent of consumers want to talk about companies without being listened to but another 58 percent want companies to respond to complaints shared on social media. Forty-three percent of consumers think companies monitoring their comments intrude on privacy yet 32 percent of consumers of all ages have no idea companies are listening to what they say in social medial.[20]

We will address privacy issues throughout the text. Technology is evolving so rapidly that federal and state laws are woefully behind. More privacy legislation will be forthcoming, though no one is sure what form it will take.

# Ethics and Professionalism

Today's business ethics are actually a subset of the values held by society as a whole. The values that underlie marketing decisions have been acquired through family, educational, and religious institutions, and social movements (e.g., women's rights, environmental protection). A marketing researcher with a mature set of ethical values accepts personal responsibility for decisions that affect the community. Considerations include the following:

- Employees' needs and desires and the long-range best interests of the organization
- The long-range goodwill and best interests of people who are directly affected by company activities (a bonus: good publicity for the firm)
- The societal values and conditions that provide the basis for the social structure in which the company exists

High standards of ethics and professionalism go hand in hand. Good ethics provide a solid foundation for professionalism, and striving for a lofty level of professionalism requires ethical behavior on the part of researchers.

**Fostering Professionalism** Because of the specialized knowledge and expertise they possess, members of a profession have influence and power over those for whom they provide a particular service. The tools of a doctor or lawyer cannot easily be obtained and sold in the marketplace; these professions guard their knowledge and control who has access to it. Although marketing researchers and marketers wield power and influence over their customers and even society, the marketing industry does not have a credentialing process or high entry barriers. The argument can be made that the marketers who most need to think, believe, and behave with professionalism are those in marketing research.

**profession**
Organization whose membership is determined by objective standards, such as an examination.

The distinction between a profession and professionalism is important: a **profession** and membership in it are objectively determined (e.g., by medical board exams), whereas **professionalism** is evaluated on more personal and subjective levels. A study designed to measure the level of professionalism in marketing research found that researchers had autonomy in their jobs, were permitted to exercise judgment, and were recognized for their level of expertise and ability to work independently. These characteristics are marks of professionalism. However, most researchers did not readily identify the contribution that marketing makes to society, nor did most firms tend to reward researchers' participation in professional organizations. These characteristics do not indicate a high level of professionalism.

**professionalism**
Quality said to be possessed by a worker with a high level of expertise, the freedom to exercise judgment, and the ability to work independently.

A profession and membership in it are objectively determined; professionalism is evaluated on more personal and subjective levels.

Several steps have been taken recently to improve the level of professionalism in the marketing research industry. For example, CASRO has sponsored symposia dealing with ethical issues in survey research. CASRO also has created a code of ethics that has been widely disseminated to research professionals. The CASRO board has worked with groups such as the Marketing Research Association (MRA) to provide input to legislatures considering antimarketing research legislation. The MRA has also created its own code of ethics. Selected provisions are summarized in Exhibit 2.7.

| EXHIBIT 2.7 | A Partial Listing of the Marketing Research Association Code of Marketing Research Standards |

1. Will ensure that each study is conducted according to the agreement with the client.

2. Will never falsify or omit data for any reason at any phase of a research study or project.

3. Will protect and preserve the confidentiality of all research techniques and/or methodologies and of information considered confidential or proprietary.

4. Will report research results accurately and honestly.

5. Will protect the rights and privacy of respondents.

6. Will treat respondents in a professional manner.

7. Will take all reasonable precautions that respondents are in no way directly harmed or adversely affected as a result of their participation in a marketing research project.

8. Will not misrepresent themselves as having qualifications, experience, skills, resources or other facility locations that they do not possess.

9. Will not use research information to identify respondents without the permission of the respondent. The following are exceptions:
   a. Respondent identification information may be used in processing the data and merging data files.
   b. Respondent identification information may be used to append client or third-party data to a survey-based data file.
   c. Respondent identification information may be revealed in compliance with a court order or other legal demand from a competent and recognized legal authority (e.g., discovery phase of a pending legal case).

10. Will respect the respondent's right to withdraw or to refuse to cooperate at any stage of the study and will not use any procedure or technique to coerce or imply that cooperation is obligatory.

11. Will ensure that respondents are informed at the outset if the interview/discussion is being audio or video recorded by any means and will, if required, obtain written consent if the recorded interview/discussion will be
    - viewed by a third party
    - reproduced for outside use

12. Will consider all research materials provided by the client or generated as a result of materials provided by the client to be the property of the client. These materials will be retained or disposed of as agreed upon with the client at the time of the study.

13. For Internet research, will not use any data in any way contrary to the provider's published privacy statement without permission from the respondent. *Data shall not be captured without respondent's consent. Doing so is in direct violation of the privacy rights stated in the Code and may violate the laws of a particular jurisdiction.*

14. For Internet research, will not send unsolicited e-mail to those who have opted out.

15. Will compile, maintain and utilize Internet samples of only those individuals who have provided their permission to be contacted (opt-in) and who have a reasonable expectation that they will receive Internet invitations for opinion and marketing research purposes.

16. Will, upon request, identify the appropriateness of the sample methodology itself and its ability to accomplish research objectives.

17. Will offer respondents the choice with each survey to be removed (opt-out) for future Internet invitations.

*Source:* MRA, 2013.

**Researcher Certification** Today, it is far too easy to begin practicing marketing research. We have seen several "fast talkers" convince unwary clients that they are qualified researchers. Unfortunately, relying on poor information to make major decisions has resulted in loss of market share, reduction in profits, and, in some cases, bankruptcy.

Certification has generated a great deal of debate among members of the marketing research industry. It should be noted that certification is not licensing. *Licensing* is a mandatory procedure administered by a governmental body that allows one to practice a profession. *Certification* is a voluntary program administered by a nongovernmental body that provides a credential for differentiation in the marketplace. The issue of certification is sensitive because it directly affects marketing researchers' ability to practice their profession freely.

The MRA has launched a Professional Researcher Certification program. The objectives, according to the MRA, are "to encourage high standards within the profession in order to raise competency, establish an objective measure of an individual's knowledge and proficiency, and to encourage continued professional development."[21] The program allows for certification as a research user, supplier, or data collector. The process requires a series of continuing education credits and then passing an exam. To date, over 1,500 people have become certified.

## SUMMARY

The marketing research industry consists of (1) information users (consumer and industrial goods and services producers; federal, state, and local governments; media companies; retailers and wholesalers); (2) marketing research suppliers (custom research firms' syndicated research firms, limited-function research firms, online and mobile tracking firms, and big data analytic firms); and (3) specialized supplier service firms.

Users of marketing research can be further categorized as external or internal to the firm. External users include company vendors and franchisees. The primary internal user of marketing research is the marketing department, which seeks data for decision making in such areas as logistics, sales, promotions, new product development, brand management, and pricing. Other internal groups and departments using marketing research are senior management, product engineers, finance, manufacturing, human resources management, and legal.

Sales in the marketing research industry are around $15.4 billion. The U.S. government is the largest single spender on marketing research. An important trend in the research industry is the continued rapid growth of online data collection.

Ethics are moral principles or values generally governing the conduct of an individual or group. The deontology theory says that a person will follow his or her obligations to another individual or society because upholding one's duty is what is considered ethically correct. In contrast, utilitarian ethical theory maintains that a choice yielding the greatest benefit to the greatest number of people is the choice that is ethically correct. The casuist theory holds that a decision should be made by comparing a current ethical dilemma with examples of similar ethical dilemmas and their outcomes.

Unethical practices by some suppliers include low-ball pricing, allowing subjectivity into the research, abusing respondents, selling unnecessary research, violating client confidentiality, and using black-box branding. Unethical practices performed by some research clients include requesting bids when a supplier has been predetermined, requesting bids to gain free advice or methodology, making false promises, and issuing unauthorized requests for proposals. Marketing research field services have used professional respondents, which is unethical. The growing amounts of data collected by online tracking firms have resulted in demands by many consumers for stronger privacy laws.

Respondents have certain rights, including the right to choose whether to participate in a marketing research project, the right to safety from physical and psychological harm, and the right to be informed of all aspects of the research task. They should know what is involved, how long it will take, and what will be done with the data. Respondents also have the right to privacy.

The level of professionalism in the marketing research industry can be raised through the efforts of organizations such as CASRO and CMOR, as well as socially concerned marketing research firms. Researcher certification is available through the MRA.

## KEY TERMS

custom research firms **22**
syndicated service research firms **22**
field service firms **24**

strategic partnership **28**
ethics **32**
low-ball pricing **33**

profession **40**
professionalism **40**

## QUESTIONS FOR REVIEW & CRITICAL THINKING

1. Do you think that data collection by mobile devices will become increasingly popular?

2. What is the role of field service firms in marketing research?

3. What is Big Data, and why is it generating so much excitement?

4. List several key characteristics of corporate marketing research departments.

5. Discuss the various project offerings of syndicated service firms.

6. Divide the class into groups of five. Each group should select one section of the city in which the course is

being taught (or the closest large city) and determine the zip codes for this section of the city. Next, go to *www.claritas.com/MyBestSegments/Default.jsp* and follow the instructions for getting Prizm profiles by zip code. Each group should then discuss the marketing profile for its section of the city.

7. What do you see as the role of a code of ethics within an organization? What can be done to ensure that employees follow this code of ethics?

8. Who would you say has the greatest responsibility within the marketing research industry to raise the standards of ethics—marketing research suppliers, marketing research clients, or field services?

9. What role should the federal government play in establishing ethical standards for the marketing research industry? How might such standards be enforced?

10. If respondents consent to interviews after being told they will be paid $50 for their opinions, do they forfeit all respondent rights? If so, what rights have been forfeited?

11. What is the relationship between ethics and professionalism? What do you think can be done to raise the level of professionalism within the marketing research industry?

12. Are online and mobile tracking firms gathering too much information about people? Why or why not?

## WORKING THE NET

1. Compare the offerings of two marketing research firms, DSS Research and Burke Incorporated, by visiting their websites at *http://dssresearch.com* and *http://www.burke.com*.

2. The Kantar Group, is a major international marketing research firm, with offices in 54 countries. Go to its website at *http://www.kantar.com* and report on its global research capabilities.

3. Interviewers must take special care when interviewing children or young people. The informed consent of the parent or responsible adult first must be obtained for interviews with children. Parents or responsible adults must be told some specifics about the interview process and special tasks, such as audio or video recording, taste testing, and respondent fees before permission is obtained. All researchers must adhere to all federal and state regulations regarding the interviewing of children 13 years of age or younger. All interviews conducted online must adhere to the Children's Online Privacy Protection Act (COPPA). Use the Internet to gather more information about interviewing children and report the results to the class.

4. Go to *http://www.marketingresearch.org/agenda* for a discussion of the latest issue regarding government affairs.

## REAL-LIFE RESEARCH • 2.1

### Respondent Recruiters—Clean Up Your Act

Mark Goodin is president of Aaron-Abrams Field Services, Las Vegas. The firm specializes in delivering respondents to qualitative marketing researchers. Here he discusses problems he sees in the respondent recruitment business. When he discusses "supplies," he is referring to firms that recruit respondents. Thus, respondent suppliers may be recruiting for a research supplier, as discussed in the chapter, or a research client, such as a manufacturer like Frito-Lay, which is doing its own qualitative research.

Over the past few years, I have witnessed a couple of disturbing trends in qualitative research. And I have to believe that if this is happening to me on such a large and consistent basis, then it's happening to other research buyers in the industry as well— they're just not talking about it. These trends are not good for the future of qualitative research:

- The trend of respondent recruiters accepting projects and then forcing changes in vital aspects of the project's original design once recruiting is underway.

- The trend among recruiters to recruit unqualified respondents and then charge for the recruiting and incentive.

My belief is that many suppliers simply shut up, take the project, and let the problems unfold. I believe they have adopted the attitude that clients can ask for the moon but in the end they're going to get what they get. More often than not, that's what happens once a project goes into the field.

I've never seen so many projects that are accepted by respondent recruiters as-is— without sharing their concerns or issuing any warnings—only to say later, "We're not finding what you're looking for, you'll need to make relaxations in the qualifications of the type of person that you are looking for." Or, "We've reached our budget, and we'll need more money if you want us to continue."

What's more, it's even less palatable to accept respondent suppliers' need for relaxations or additional money when, along the way, they've delivered substandard service:

- Recruiting progress reports aren't delivered when requested.
- Recruiting progress reports contain errors and misspellings.
- Respondents don't qualify when rescreened or revalidated.
- Screeners have been incorrectly administered.
- Discrepancies in the screener have been overlooked or ignored.
- Instructions have not been followed.
- Recruiting hours have been put into the job, but not enough contacts—or calls—have been made.

## Must Stop Today

The practice of respondent suppliers charging for respondents who don't fit the qualifying criteria must stop today.

If the respondent isn't qualified and cannot be used in the research, we should not be charged for the respondent. Period. It's time for respondent suppliers to stop recruiting unqualified or marginally qualified respondents and hiding behind a myriad of excuses. Recruiters are entirely responsible for respondent accuracy. Period. If recruiters cannot stand behind the product they deliver, they should find another line of work. Our firm has a simple policy that third-party recruiting suppliers know about prior to the start of a project: We will not pay recruiting fees or the incentives for any respondents who do not qualify at rescreening or at the time of the actual research. We actively encourage all researchers to do the same.[22]

## Questions

1. Why is it important for respondents to meet the exact qualifications specified for the research project?

2. Have you ever participated in a research project where you knew that you were marginally qualified to participate? Did you tell the researcher?

3. Is it unethical for respondent suppliers to charge their clients for unqualified respondents?

4. Would it be unethical if a recruiter was seeking current cat owners and you said, "No but I had a cat when I was growing up," to which the recruiter replied, "That will work; just tell them that you still have a cat."

## *REAL-LIFE RESEARCH • 2.2*

### Coke Juices up a Market Test

For several days Dyquan Gibson and his friends had a strong incentive to study every afternoon at a neighborhood Richmond, Virginia, Boys & Girls Club. "If you finished your homework, you got a burger," says Dyquan, who is now 11 years old.

Dyquan and his friends didn't know it, but the free Whoppers came from a consultant hired by Coca-Cola Company. Officials at the Atlanta beverage company had sent the man to Richmond with $9,000. He gave cash to the clubs and other nonprofit groups and told them to treat the children to hundreds of "value meals" at Burger King.

Millions of dollars in sales were at stake for Coke. The company was trying to persuade Burger King to run a national promotion for its slushy dessert drink, Frozen Coke, which Burger King sells at all of its restaurants. But Burger King wanted to

run a test promotion before it invested in a big campaign. So the Miami-based restaurant chain ran a two-week test in Richmond, offering a coupon for a free Frozen Coke when customers bought a value meal—a sandwich, fries, and drink combo. If the meals sold well enough, and enough people redeemed the coupons, Burger King would take the promotion national.

The Coke officials embarked on the buying spree because the initial test results were dismal. In the end, their efforts added only 700 value meals to the nearly 100,000 sold during the promotion. But even that small number helped bolster Coke's case for national push. Burger King sank roughly $10 million into the campaign.

Later, Coke acknowledged that some of its employees "improperly influenced" the sales results in Richmond, and that the actions were "wrong and inconsistent with the values of the Coca-Cola Co." It issued a public apology to Burger King and agreed to pay the company and its franchisees up to $21 million to make amends.[23]

## Questions

1. Were Coke's attempts to fix the market test unethical? If so, was Coke guilty of unethical behavior, or was it just the fault of some misguided employees?

2. Burger King is Coke's second largest fountain drink customer after McDonald's. The Richmond test started out very poorly, and it was clear that unless results improved, the national Frozen Coke promotion was not going to happen. Coke was worried that without the promotion, it would not make its fountain sales objectives for the year. At that point, it was decided to stimulate value-meal sales in Richmond. Did the desired end (meeting sales goals) justify the actions taken? Why or why not?

3. Use the ethics theories described in the chapter to illustrate how Coke decision makers could have reached a different decision.

4. Should Coke fire those responsible, counsel them, or do nothing?

© fotosipsak /iStockphoto

# Problem Definition, Exploratory Research, and the Research Process

## LEARNING OBJECTIVES

1. Analyze the problem definition process.

2. Learn the steps involved in the marketing research process.

3. Understand the components of the research request.

4. Appreciate the importance of the marketing research proposal.

5. Examine what motivates decision makers to use marketing research information.

Conducting marketing research involves a series of logical steps, beginning with problem definition and research objectives. What are the steps in the marketing research process? How is the research process initiated? These are the issues we will address in this chapter.

# Critical Importance of Correctly Defining the Problem

Correctly defining the problem is the crucial first step in the marketing research process. If the research problem is defined incorrectly, the research objectives will also be wrong, and the entire marketing research process will be a waste of time and money. A large consumer packaged goods company wanted to conduct a study among a brand's heavy users in order to understand the brand's equity. More specifically, it wanted to expand that equity into new products. The brand had very low penetration, so the company needed new products to meet the upcoming fiscal year's volume goal of double-digit growth. Notice the absence of tying research learning—understanding the brand's equity—to the business objective.

The brand had a small base from which to grow, so simply investigating the brand's equity among its most loyal users wouldn't help decision makers reach a double-digit growth rate. Upon reflection, the business objective focused on identifying marketing levers that would increase brand penetration—and thus growth. Accordingly, the research objectives transformed into understanding barriers to current brand purchase and identifying bridges that would motivate category users to buy the brand.

Study results showed that the brand chiefly suffered from awareness problems. Both brand and category users liked the product, but didn't use it as often as others in the category because they simply forgot about the brand. Reminders—in the form of advertising, incentives, and new products—became the levers that could improve brand penetration and growth. Conducting an equity study among heavy users clearly wouldn't have caught this.[1]

The process for defining the problem is shown in Exhibit 3.1. Note that the ultimate goal is to develop clear, concise, and meaningful marketing research objectives. Researching such objectives will yield precise decision-making information for managers.

## Recognize the Problem or Opportunity

The marketing research process begins with the recognition of a marketing problem or opportunity. As changes occur in the firm's external environment, marketing managers are faced with the questions, "Should we change the existing marketing mix?" and, if so, "How?" Marketing research may be used to evaluate products and services, promotion, distribution, and pricing alternatives. In addition, it may be used to find and evaluate new opportunities, in a process called **opportunity identification**.

Let's look at an example of opportunity identification. Annual U.S. salsa sales are about $1.1 billion and are more than twice that of hummus. Hummus is made by blending steamed chickpeas with a paste called tahini made from shelled sesame seeds. Hummus is generally flavored with olive oil, lemon juice, and garlic. New flavors such as black olive and roasted red pepper have helped drive demand. Yet, only 18 percent of U.S. households have ever bought hummus. Western states, such as California and Arizona, usually are quick to accept new, nonmeat food items. Yet, the west has the lowest average weekly hummus sales per store ($382); followed by the south ($406); the central states ($493); and the east ($762). It seems that opportunity abounds in the hummus market. After all, hummus is just

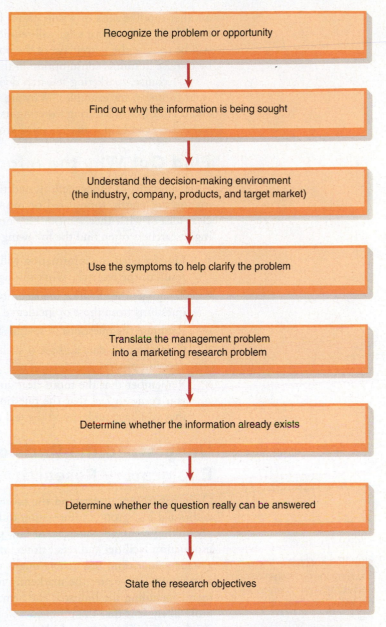

Recognize the problem or opportunity

Find out why the information is being sought

Understand the decision-making environment (the industry, company, products, and target market)

Use the symptoms to help clarify the problem

Translate the management problem into a marketing research problem

Determine whether the information already exists

Determine whether the question really can be answered

State the research objectives

**Exhibit 3.1**

**Problem Definition Process**

**opportunity identification** Using marketing research to find and evaluate new opportunities.

another dip like salsa or a sour cream based dip. To grow the hummus market to match or exceed the demand for salsa will require innovative marketing strategy. Part of that strategy will be to raise the percentage of the population that has tried the product. Another key will be to raise hummus consumption in the west and south.[2]

Of course, marketing research doesn't always deal with opportunities. Managers might want to know, for example, "Why are we losing marketing share?" or "What should we do about Ajax Manufacturing lowering its prices by 10 percent?" In these instances, marketing researchers can help managers solve problems.

## Find Out Why the Information Is Being Sought

Large amounts of money, effort, and time are wasted because requests for marketing information are poorly formulated or misunderstood. For example, managers may not have a clear idea of what they want or may not phrase their questions properly. Therefore, marketing researchers often find the following activities helpful:

- Discuss what the information will be used for and what decisions might be made as a result of the research. Work through detailed examples to help clarify the issue.
- Try to get the client or manager to prioritize their questions. This helps sort out central questions from those of incidental interest.
- Rephrase the questions in several slightly different forms and discuss the differences.
- Create sample data and ask if such data would help answer the questions. Simulate the decision process.
- Remember that the more clear-cut you think the questions are and the more quickly you come to feel that the questions are straightforward, the more you should doubt that you have understood the real need.

## Understand the Decision-Making Environment with Exploratory Research

Once researchers understand the motivation for conducting the research, often they need additional background information to fully comprehend the problem. This may mean simply talking to brand managers or new product managers, reading company reports, visiting production facilities and retail stores, and perhaps talking with suppliers. If the industry has a trade association, researchers might peruse its website for information published by the association. The better the marketing researcher understands the decision-making environment, including the industry, the firm, its products or services, and the target market, the more likely it is that the problem will be defined correctly. This step may be referred to as conducting a **situation analysis**.

Sometimes informed discussions with managers and suppliers and on-site visits aren't enough. **Exploratory research** may be conducted to obtain greater understanding of a concept or to help crystallize the definition of a problem. It is also used to identify important variables to be studied. Exploratory research is preliminary research, not the definitive research used to determine a course of action.

Exploratory research can take several forms: pilot studies, experience surveys, secondary data analysis, pilot studies case analysis, and focus groups. **Pilot studies** are surveys using a limited number of respondents and often employing less rigorous sampling techniques than are employed in large, quantitative studies.

Nickelodeon, for example, was well aware of the new baby boom and wanted to know what it meant for the network. Exploratory research found that a long-held assumption about kids' attitudes was not accurate: the belief that female images in TV programming generally work with girls but alienate boys. The exploratory research consisted of a

**situation analysis**
Studying the decision-making environment within which the marketing research will take place.

**exploratory research**
Preliminary research conducted to increase understanding of a concept, to clarify the exact nature of the problem to be solved, or to identify important variables to be studied.

**pilot studies**
Surveys using a limited number of respondents and often employing less rigorous sampling techniques than are employed in large, quantitative studies.

small-scale pilot study on the Internet and focus groups in which children were brought together to discuss their attitudes toward television. Like Nickelodeon's research, much exploratory research is highly flexible, with researchers following ideas, clues, and hunches as long as time and money constraints permit. Often, ideas are obtained from so-called experts in the field. Nickelodeon, for example, could have spoken with child psychologists.

As the researcher moves through the exploratory research process, a list of marketing research problems and subproblems should be developed. The investigator should identify all factors that seem to be related to the problem area, as these are probable research topics. This stage of problem definition requires a brainstorming-type approach, but one guided by the previous stage's findings. All possibilities should be listed without regard to the feasibility of addressing them via research. Nickelodeon ultimately decided to define the marketing research problem as determining whether a live-action show with girls as the protagonists would appeal to both sexes. Quantitative marketing research results showed that such a program would have dual appeal. Managerial action taken as a result yielded a program where the star was female, but the audience was 53 percent male.[3]

### Experience Surveys Analysis

A second form of exploratory research is **experience surveys.** Experience surveys involve talking with knowledgeable individuals, both inside and outside the organization, who may provide insights into the problem. Rarely do experience surveys include a formal questionnaire. Instead, the researcher may simply have a list of topics to be discussed. The survey, then, is much like an informal discussion. For example, if Jet Blue is redesigning the interior of its aircraft, it may use experience surveys to speak with interior designers, frequent flyers, flight attendants, and pilots.

**experience surveys**
Discussions with knowledgeable individuals, both inside and outside the organization, who may provide insights into the problem.

### Secondary Data Analysis

Secondary data analysis is another form of exploratory research. Because secondary data analysis is covered extensively in Chapter 4, we will touch on it only lightly here. *Secondary data* are data that have been gathered for some purpose other than the one at hand. Today, marketing researchers can use the Internet to access countless sources of secondary data quickly and at minimal expense. There are few subjects that have not been analyzed at one time or another. With a bit of luck, the marketing researcher can use secondary data to help precisely define the problem.

### Case Analysis

**Case analysis** represents the fourth form of exploratory research. The purpose of case analysis is to review information from a few other situations that are similar to the current research problem. For example, electric utilities across the United States are scrambling to adopt the marketing concept and to become customer-oriented; these utilities are conducting market segmentation research, customer satisfaction studies, and customer loyalty surveys. To better understand the deregulation of the electric utility industry, marketing researchers are examining case studies on the deregulation of the airline industry. Researchers, however, must always take care to determine the relevancy of any case study to the present research problem.

**case analysis**
Reviewing information from situations that are similar to the current one.

### Focus Groups

Focus groups are in-depth discussions, usually consisting of 8 to 12 participants, which are led by a moderator and are generally limited to one particular concept, idea, or theme. The general idea is to have what one person says generate thoughts and comments by others, therefore creating group dynamics. That is, the interplay of responses will yield more information than if the same number of persons had contributed in individual interviews. Focus groups are the primary topic of discussion in Chapter 5, so they will be lightly covered here. We mention them now because they are probably the most popular form of exploratory research.

Focus groups can, and do, cover just about any topic imaginable. Your authors, unlike all other marketing research text authors, have conducted over 3,000 focus group sessions.

When used in exploratory research, focus groups are used to help clarify and understand the problem and issues involved. A few examples of topics that we have covered include: what creates the Harley-Davidson mystique, what happens when you discover head lice in your children, whether having a tequila made in America is a problem, what kitchen item is most difficult to clean, and the list goes on.

**Using Intranets for Exploratory Research** The computer can be a very powerful tool for doing exploratory research. In very large organizations with intranets, the researcher has the capability of determining whether needed or relevant information is available somewhere inside the organization. The corporate marketing research department at Texas Instruments (TI), for example, has developed a powerful intranet application that permits TI managers worldwide to search for past research studies and those currently in progress on the basis of key words. They have immediate online access to a brief description of each study and can send e-mail seeking permission to view the full text of reports on old projects. Permission can be granted electronically via e-mail by the owner of the report (the person who paid for it), and the full text can be accessed online.

More and more organizations are developing similar systems to permit much more effective managerial use of information resources. In large organizations, it is not uncommon for a group in one part of the organization to conduct a research project that might have great value to managers in another part of the organization. Too often, there is no way for one group to find out what another group has already done. Intranet systems like the one at Texas Instruments will help organizations get the most mileage out of their research dollars.

While intranets provide easy access to internal data, the Internet is an invaluable resource for searching tens of millions of external sources for the information needed. At the exploratory stage, a researcher might use any one or several of the online search engines to find information needed. This type of search not only is much faster than a traditional library search but also provides access to an incredible array of information that is not available in any library. The researcher can perform an Internet search and point out or download the desired information in a matter of hours rather than the days or weeks a standard library search might require. Finally, the researcher can identify a range of discussion or special-interest groups on the Internet that may be relevant to a research project.

**Completing Exploratory Research** The end of exploratory study comes when the marketing researchers are convinced that they have found the major dimensions of the problem. They may have defined a set of questions that can be used as specific guides to a detailed research design. Or they may have developed a number of potential ideas about possible causes of a specific problem of importance to management. They may also have determined that certain other factors are such remote possibilities that they can be safely ignored in any further study. Finally, the researchers may end exploration because they feel that further research is not needed or is not presently possible due to time, money, or other constraints.

## Use the Symptoms to Clarify the Problem

Marketing researchers must be careful to distinguish between symptoms and the real problem. A symptom is a phenomenon that occurs because of the existence of something else. For example, managers often talk about the problem of poor sales, declining profits, increased customer complaints, or defecting customers. Each of these is a symptom of a deeper problem. That is, something is causing a company's customers to leave. Is it lower prices offered by the competition? Or is it better service? Focusing on the symptoms and not the true problem is often referred to as the *iceberg principle*. Approximately 10 percent of an iceberg rises out of the ocean; the remaining 90 percent is below the surface. Preoccupied with the obstacle they can see, managers may fail to comprehend and confront the deeper problem, which remains submerged.

Ensuring that the true problem has been defined is not always easy. Managers and marketing researchers must use creativity and good judgment. Cutting through to the heart of a problem is a bit like peeling an onion—you must take off one layer at a time. One approach to eliminating symptoms is to ask, "What caused this to occur?" When the researcher can no longer answer this question, the real problem is at hand. For example, when a Saint Louis manufacturer of pumps faced a 7 percent decline in sales from the previous year, managers asked, "What caused this?" A look at sales across the product line showed that sales were up or about the same on all items except large, heavy-duty submersible pumps, whose sales were down almost 60 percent. They then asked, "What caused this?" Sales of the pump in the eastern and central divisions were about the same as in the previous year. However, in the western region, sales were zero! Once again they asked, "What caused this?" Further investigation revealed that a Japanese manufacturer was dumping a similar submersible pump in Western markets at about 50 percent of the Saint Louis manufacturer's wholesale price. This was the true problem. The manufacturer lobbied the Justice Department to fine the Japanese company and to issue a cease-and-desist order.

## Translate the Management Problem into a Marketing Research Problem

Once the true management decision problem has been identified, it must be converted into a marketing research problem. The **marketing research problem** specifies what information is needed to solve the problem and how that information can be obtained efficiently and effectively. The **marketing research objective**, then, is the goal statement, defining the specific information needed to solve the marketing research problem. Managers must combine this information with their own experience and other related information to make a proper decision.

In contrast to the marketing research problem, the **management decision problem** is action-oriented. Management decision problems tend to be much broader in scope and far more general than marketing research problems, which must be narrowly defined and specific if the research effort is to be successful. Sometimes several research studies must be conducted to solve a broad management decision problem.

## Determine Whether the Information Already Exists

It often seems easier and more interesting to develop new information than to delve through old reports and data files to see whether the required information already exists. There is a tendency to assume that current data are superior to data collected in the past, as current data appear to be a "fix on today's situation." And because researchers have more control over the format and comprehensiveness of fresh data, they promise to be easier to work with. Yet, using existing data can save managers time and money if such data can answer the research question.

Research objectives must be as specific and unambiguous as possible. Remember that the entire research effort (in terms of time and money) is geared toward achieving the objectives. When the marketing researcher meets with a committee to learn the goals of a particular project, committee members may not fully agree on what is needed. We have learned from experience to go back to a committee (or the individual in charge) with a written list of research objectives. The researcher should then ask the manager, "If we accomplish the objectives on this list, will you have enough information to make informed decisions about the problem?" If the reply is yes, the manager should be asked to sign off on the objectives. The researcher should then give the manager a copy and keep a copy for the research files. Putting the agreed-on objectives in writing prevents the manager from saying later, "Hey,

**marketing research objective**
A goal statement, defining the specific information needed to solve the marketing research problem.

**marketing research problem**
A statement specifying the type of information needed by the decision maker to help solve the management decision problem and how that information can be obtained efficiently and effectively.

**management decision problem**
A statement specifying the type of managerial action required to solve the problem.

this is not the information I wanted." In a busy and hectic corporate environment, such misunderstandings happen more frequently than one might imagine.

Avoid. the *nice-to-know syndrome*. Even after conducting exploratory research, managers often tend to discuss research objectives in terms of broad areas of ignorance. They say, in effect, "Here are some things I don't know." A Starbucks executive might wonder: "You know, we already sell fresh-baked goods in our stores. . . . I wonder if people would buy frozen Starbucks pastries and rolls in supermarkets?" Maybe I'll ask this question on our out-of-home advertising media study. Unfortunately, this scenario usually leads to disappointment. There is nothing wrong with interesting findings, but they must also be *actionable*. That is, the findings must provide decision-making information. Accomplishment of a research objective has to do more than reduce management's level of ignorance. Unless all the research is exploratory, it should lead to a decision. Perhaps the best way to assure that research is actionable is to determine how the research results will be implemented. Asking a single question about purchase intent of Starbucks frozen baked goods in a grocery store is not actionable. So much more would have to be known—for example, type of goods, price points, packaging design, and so forth. Numerous taste tests would also have to be conducted.

## Determine Whether the Question Can Be Answered

When marketing researchers promise more than they can deliver, they hurt the credibility of marketing research. It is extremely important for researchers to avoid being impelled—either by overeagerness to please or by managerial machismo—into an effort that they know has a limited probability of success. In most cases, you can discern in advance the likelihood of success by identifying the following:

- Instances in which you know for certain that information of the type required exists or can be readily obtained
- Situations in which you are fairly sure, based on similar prior experiences, that the information can be gathered
- Cases in which you know that you are trying something quite new and there is a real risk of drawing a complete blank

## State the Research Objectives

The culmination of the problem definition process is a statement of the research objectives. These objectives are stated in terms of the precise information necessary to address the marketing research problem/opportunity. Well-formulated objectives serve as a road map in pursuing the research project. They also serve as a standard that later will enable managers to evaluate the quality and value of the work by asking, "Were the objectives met?" and, "Do the recommendations flow logically from the objectives and the research findings?"

# Research Objectives As Hypotheses

**hypothesis**
An assumption or theory (guess) that a researcher or manager makes about some characteristic of the population being investigated.

A **hypothesis** is an assumption or theory guess that a researcher or manager makes about some characteristic of the population being investigated. A hypothesis must be susceptible to data through actual testing. So a statement that claims, "There are 1000 angels on the head of a pin," is not a hypothesis. It cannot be confronted with real-world data.

A hypothesis tends to be predictive in nature. For example, a car dealership might hypothesize that all purchasers of a new Honda car who receive a letter assuring them that they have just purchased the finest car on the market will be more content with their purchase than those who do not receive the letter.

Hypotheses are often stated in a null format. That is, "There is no difference between ___ and ___". So, "There is no difference in contentment between Honda purchasers who received the image reinforcement letter and those who did not." The final conclusion of the researcher will be to retain the null hypothesis or reject the null hypothesis based upon data.

Academic research is almost always cloaked in hypotheses. In practice, marketing research studies, outside of academia, rarely formally state hypotheses. However, they are inferred through statistical testing. We will delve into this topic in more detail in Chapter 16.

# Marketing Research Process

We have just discussed the first step in the marketing research process: identifying the problem/opportunity and stating the marketing research objectives. The other steps in the process are creating the research design, choosing the method of research, selecting the sampling procedure, collecting the data, analyzing the data, writing and presenting the report, and following up on any recommendations that were made as a result of the report (see Exhibit 3.2). The overview of the process in this section forms the foundation for the remainder of the text. The following chapters examine specific aspects of the marketing research process.

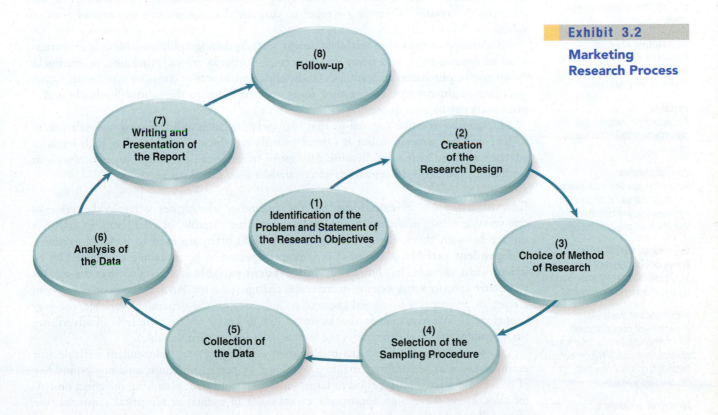

**Exhibit 3.2**

**Marketing Research Process**

Matt Meadows/Photolibrary / Getty Images

Scanning bar code information is a means of observation research that is widely used today.

**research design**
The plan to be followed to answer the marketing research objectives.

**descriptive studies**
Research studies that answer the questions who, what, when, where, and how.

**variable**
A symbol or concept that can assume any one of a set of values.

**causal studies**
Research studies that examine whether the value of one variable causes or determines the value of another variable.

**dependent variable**
A symbol or concept expected to be explained or influenced by the independent variable.

**independent variable**
A symbol or concept over which the researcher has some control and that is hypothesized to cause or influence the dependent variable.

**temporal sequence**
An appropriate causal order of events.

## Creating the Research Design

The **research design** is a plan for addressing the research objectives or hypotheses. In essence, the researcher develops a structure or framework to answer a specific research problem/opportunity. There is no single best research design. Instead, different designs offer an array of choices, each with certain advantages and disadvantages. Ultimately, trade-offs are typically involved. A common trade-off is between research costs and the quality of the decision-making information provided. Generally speaking, the more precise and error-free the information obtained, the higher the cost. Another common trade-off is between time constraints and the type of research design selected. Overall, the researcher must attempt to provide management with the best information possible, subject to the various constraints under which he or she must operate. The researcher's first task is to decide whether the research will be descriptive or causal.

**Descriptive Studies**  **Descriptive studies** are conducted to answer who, what, when, where, and how questions. Implicit in descriptive research is the fact that management already knows or understands the underlying relationships among the variables in the problem. A **variable** is simply a symbol or concept that can assume any one of a set of values.

A descriptive study for Starbucks might include demographic and lifestyle characteristics of typical, light, and heavy patronizers of Starbucks stores, purchasers of Starbucks baked goods, purchasers of Starbucks sandwiches, and buyers of coffee to take home. Other questions might determine drive time from work or home to the nearest Starbucks and if purchasers pay by cash or credit.

Descriptive research can tell us that two variables, such as advertising and sales, seem to be somehow associated, but it cannot provide convincing evidence that high levels of advertising cause high sales. Because descriptive research can shed light on associations or relationships, it helps the researcher select variables for a causal study.

**Causal Studies**  In **causal studies**, the researcher investigates whether the value of one variable causes or determines the value of another variable, in an attempt to establish linkage between them. Experiments (see Chapter 8) often are used to measure causality. A **dependent variable** is a symbol or concept expected to be explained or affected by an independent variable. In contrast, an **independent variable** is a variable that the market researcher can, to some extent, manipulate, change, or alter. An independent variable in a research project is a presumed cause of or influence on the dependent variable, the presumed effect. For example, Starbucks would like to know whether the level of advertising (independent variable) determines the level of sales (dependent variable).

A causal study for Starbucks might involve changing one independent variable (for example, the number of direct mailings offering a 10 percent discount on a one-pound bag of coffee over a six-month period to target customers) and then observing the effect on coffee sales. Here, there is an appropriate causal order of events, or **temporal sequence**; the effect follows closely the hypothesized cause. Temporal sequence is one criterion that must be met for causality.

A second criterion for causality is **concomitant variation**—the degree to which a presumed cause (direct-mail promotion) and a presumed effect (coffee sales) occur together or vary together. If direct-mail promotions are a cause of increased coffee sales, then when the number of direct-mail promotions is increased, coffee sales should go up, and when the number of promotions is decreased, sales should fall. If, however, an increase in direct-mail promotions does not result in an increase in coffee sales, the researcher must conclude that the hypothesis about the relationship between direct-mail promotions and coffee sales is not supported.

An ideal situation would be one in which sales of coffee increased markedly every time Starbucks increased its e-mail promotions (up to a saturation level). But, alas, we live in a world where such perfection is rarely achieved. One additional saturation e-mail might bring a small increase in sales and the next e-mail a larger increment, or vice versa. And during the next six-month period, an increase in e-mail promotions might produce no increase or even a decline in sales.

Remember, even perfect concomitant variation would not prove that A causes B. All the researcher could say is that the association makes the hypothesis more likely.

An important issue in studying causality is recognizing the possibility of **spurious association**, in which other variables are actually causing changes in the dependent variable. In an ideal situation, the researcher would demonstrate a total absence of other causal factors. However, in the real world of marketing research, it is very difficult to identify and control all other potential causal factors. Think for a moment of all the variables that could cause sales of one-pound bags of coffee to increase or decrease—for example, blogs, prices, newspaper and television advertising, coupons, mobile advertising, discounts, and weather. The researcher may be able to lower spurious associations by trying to hold constant these other factors. Alternatively, the researcher may look at changes in sales in similar socioeconomic areas.

**concomitant variation**
The degree to which a presumed cause and a presumed effect occur or vary together.

**spurious association**
A relationship between a presumed cause and a presumed effect that occurs as a result of an unexamined variable or set of variables.

## Choosing a Basic Method of Research

A research design, either descriptive or causal, is chosen based on a project's objectives. The next step is to select a means of gathering data. There are three basic research methods: (1) survey, (2) observation, and (3) experiment. Survey research is often descriptive in nature but can be causal. Observation research is typically descriptive, and experiment research is almost always causal.

**Surveys** **Survey research** involves an interviewer (except in mail and Internet and mobile surveys) who interacts with respondents to obtain facts, opinions, and attitudes. A questionnaire is used to ensure an orderly and structured approach to data gathering. Face-to-face interviews may take place in the respondent's home, a shopping mall, a place of business, or virtually any other venue.

**survey research**
Research in which an interviewer (except in mail and Internet surveys) interacts with respondents to obtain facts, opinions, and attitudes.

**Observations** **Observation research** is examining patterns of behavior as opposed to asking consumers why they do what they do. This may involve people watching consumers or the use of a variety of machines. Kimberly-Clark (K-C), the maker of Huggies, Kleenex, and other household staples, outfits consumers with mini video cameras mounted to visors and linked to a recording device. Paid participants wear the somewhat-strange-looking eye gear, known internally as the Consumer Vision System (CVS), while doing chores or shopping.

Under the system, K-C discovered that mothers who used Huggies Baby Wash, a bathing lotion, had trouble holding the bottle and needed two hands to open and dispense its contents. "[Moms] almost always have to have one hand on the baby at one time," said Becky Walter, K-C director of innovation, design, and testing.[4]

K-C redesigned the product with a grippable bottle and a large lid that could easily be lifted with a thumb. The result was a significant increase in market share. Observation research is discussed in detail in Chapter 7.

**observation research**
Typically, descriptive research that monitors respondents' actions without direct interaction.

**experiments**
Research to measure causality, in which the researcher changes one or more independent variables and observes the effect of the changes on the dependent variable.

**Experiments** **Experiments** are the third method researchers use to gather data. Experiment research is distinguished by the researcher's changing one or more independent variables—price, package, design, shelf space, advertising theme, or advertising expenditures—and observing the effects of those changes on a dependent variable (usually sales). The objective of experiments is to measure causality. The best experiments are those in which all factors other than the ones being manipulated are held constant. This enables the researcher to infer with confidence that changes in sales, for example, are caused by changes in the amount of money spent on advertising.

Holding all other factors constant in the external environment is a monumental and costly, if not impossible, task. Factors such as competitors' actions, weather, and economic conditions in various markets are beyond the control of the researcher. One way researchers attempt to control factors that might influence the dependent variable is to use a laboratory experiment—that is, an experiment conducted in a test facility rather than in the natural environment. Researchers sometimes create simulated supermarket environments, give consumers scrip (play money), and then ask them to shop as they normally would for groceries. By varying package design or color over several time periods, for example, the researcher can determine which package is most likely to stimulate sales. Although laboratory techniques can provide valuable information, it is important to recognize that the consumer is not in a natural environment; how people act in a test facility may differ from how they act in an actual shopping situation. Experiments are discussed in detail in Chapter 9.

## Selecting the Sampling Procedure

A sample is a subset from a larger population. Although the basic nature of the sample is specified in the research design, selecting the sampling procedure is a separate step in the research process. Several questions must be answered before a sampling procedure is selected. First, the population or universe of interest must be defined. This is the group from which the sample will be drawn. It should include all the people whose opinions, behaviors, preferences, attitudes, and so on will yield information needed to answer the research problem—for example, all persons who eat Mexican food at least once every 60 days.

**probability sample**
A subset of a population where every element in the population has a known nonzero chance of being selected.

**nonprobability sample**
A subset of a population in which the chances of selection for the various elements in the population are unknown.

After the population has been defined, the next question is whether to use a probability sample or a nonprobability sample. A **probability sample** is a sample for which every element in the population has a known nonzero probability of being selected. Such samples allow the researcher to estimate how much sampling error is present in a given study. All samples that cannot be considered probability samples are nonprobability samples. **Nonprobability samples** are those in which the chances of selection for the various elements in the population are unknown. Researchers cannot statistically calculate the reliability of a nonprobability sample; that is, they cannot determine the degree of sampling error that can be expected. Sampling is the topic of Chapter 13.

## Collecting the Data

Most survey-based data are now collected on the Internet or on mobile devices. Interviewer-based data collection is usually done by marketing research field services. Field service firms, found throughout the country, specialize in collecting data through personal and telephone interviewing on a subcontract basis. A typical interviewer-based research study involves data collection in several cities and requires working with a comparable number of field service firms. To ensure that all subcontractors do everything exactly the same way, detailed field instructions should be developed for every job. Nothing should be left to chance; in particular, no interpretations of procedures should be left to the subcontractors.

In addition to doing interviewing, field service firms often provide group research facilities, mall intercept locations, test product storage, and kitchen facilities for preparing test food products. They may also conduct retail audits (counting the amount of product sold from retail shelves).

## Analyzing the Data

After the data have been collected, the next step in the research process is data analysis. The purpose of this analysis is to interpret and draw conclusions from the mass of collected data. The marketing researcher may use a variety of techniques, beginning with simple frequency analysis and culminating in complex multivariate techniques. Data analysis will be discussed later in the text.

## Writing and Presenting the Report

After data analysis is completed, the researcher must prepare the report and communicate the conclusions and recommendations to management. This is a key step in the process because a marketing researcher who wants project conclusions acted on must convince the manager that the results are credible and justified by the data collected.

The researcher usually will be required to present both written and oral reports on a project. The nature of the audience must be kept in mind when these reports are being prepared and presented. The oral report should begin with a clear statement of the research objectives, followed by an outline of the methodology. A summary of major findings should come next. The report should end with a presentation of conclusions and recommendations for management. In today's fast-paced world of marketing research, long, elaborately written reports are virtually a thing of the past. Decision makers today typically want only a copy of the PowerPoint presentation or an executive summary.

**Judging the Quality of a Report** Because most people who enter marketing become research users rather than research suppliers, it is important to know what to look for in a research report. The ability to evaluate a research report is crucial. As with many other items we purchase, the quality of a research report is not always readily apparent. Nor does paying a high price for a project necessarily guarantee superior quality. The basis for measuring a report's quality lies in the research proposal. Does the report meet the objectives established in the proposal? Has the methodology outlined in the proposal been followed? Are the conclusions based on logical deductions from the data analysis? Do the recommendations seem prudent, given the conclusions?

**Using the Internet to Disseminate Reports** It is becoming increasingly commonplace for research suppliers and clients to publish reports directly to the Web. Most companies, such as Texas Instruments, locate this material not in public areas on the Web but on corporate intranets or in password-protected locations on websites. Publishing reports on the Web has a number of advantages:

1. The reports become immediately accessible to managers and other authorized and interested parties worldwide.

2. The reports can incorporate full multimedia presentation, including text, graphs, various types of animation, audio comments, and video clips.

3. The reports are fully searchable. Suppose a manager is interested in any material relating to advertising. Instead of manually scanning a long and detailed report for such mentions, he or she can search the report for comments relating to advertising.

## Following Up

After a company has spent a considerable amount of effort and money on marketing research and the preparation of a report, it is important that the findings be used. Management should determine whether the recommendations were followed and, if not, why not. As you will learn in the next section, one way to increase the likelihood that research conducted by a corporate marketing department will be used is to minimize conflict between that department and other departments within the company.

# Managing the Research Process

## The Research Request

**research request**
An internal document used by large organizations that describes a potential research project, its benefits to the organization, and estimated costs; it must be formally approved before a research project can begin.

Before conducting a research project, a company such as Microsoft® might require approval of a formal research request. Moderate- and large-size retailers, manufacturers, and nonprofit organizations often use the **research request** as a basis for determining which projects will be funded. Typically, in larger organizations there are far more requests by managers for marketing research information than monies available to conduct such research. Requiring a research request is a formalized approach to allocating scarce research dollars.

It is very important for the brand manager, new product specialist, or whoever is in need of research information to clearly state in the formal research request why the desired information is critical to the organization. Otherwise, the person with approval authority may fail to see why the expenditure is necessary.

In smaller organizations, the communication link between brand managers and marketing researchers is much closer. Their day-to-day contact often removes the need for a formal research request. Instead, decisions to fund research are made on an ad hoc basis by the marketing manager or the director of marketing research.

Completion and approval of the request represent a disciplined approach to identifying research problems and obtaining funding to solve them. The degree of effort expended at this step in the research process will be reflected in the quality of the information provided to the decision maker because a well-conceived research request will guide the design, data-gathering, analysis, and reporting processes toward a highly focused objective. The sections of a formal research request are as follows:

1. *Action.* The decision maker should describe the action to be taken on the basis of the research. This will help the decision maker focus on what information should be obtained and guide the researcher in creating the research design and in analyzing the results.

2. *Origin.* The decision maker should state the events that led to a need for a decision. This will help the researcher understand more deeply the nature of the management decision problem.

3. *Information.* The decision maker should list the questions that she or he needs to have answered to take action. Carefully considering the questions will improve the efficiency of the research.

4. *Use.* This section should explain how each piece of information will be used to help make the actual decision. By giving logical reasons for each part of the research, it will ensure that the questions make sense in light of the action to be taken.

5. *Target groups and subgroups.* By describing those from whom information must be gathered to address the research problem, this section will help the researcher design the sample procedure for the research project.

6. *Logistics.* Time and budget constraints always affect the research technique chosen for a project. For this reason, approximations of the amount of money available and the amount of time left before results are needed must be included as a part of the research request.

7. *Comments.* Any other comments relevant to the research project must be stated so that, once again, the researcher can fully understand the nature of the problem.

## Request for Proposal

The research request is an internal document used by management to determine which projects to fund. A **request for proposal (RFP)** is a solicitation sent to marketing research suppliers inviting them to submit a formal proposal to conduct research, including a bid. The RFP is the lifeblood of a research supplier. Receiving it is the initial step in getting new business and, therefore, revenue.

A typical RFP provides background data on why a study is to be conducted, outlines the research objectives, describes a methodology, and suggests a time frame. In some RFPs, the supplier is asked to recommend a methodology or even help develop the research objectives. Most RFPs also ask for (1) a detailed cost breakdown, (2) the supplier's experience in relevant areas, and (3) references. Usually, a due date for the proposal will be specified.

Suppliers must exercise care in preparing their proposals in response to the RFP. More than one client has said, "We find the quality of the proposals indicative of the quality of work produced by the firm." Thus, a research supplier that doesn't have the necessary time to adequately prepare a proposal should simply not submit a bid.

**request for proposal (RFP)**
A solicitation sent to marketing research suppliers inviting them to submit a formal proposal, including a bid.

# The Marketing Research Proposal

When marketing research suppliers receive an RFP, they respond to the potential client with a research proposal. The **research proposal** is a document that presents the research objectives, research design, timeline, and cost of a project. We have included an actual proposal (disguised) prepared by two project managers at Decision Analyst (a large international marketing research firm) in Appendix 3A. Most research proposals today are short (three to five pages) and are transmitted back to the potential client as an e-mail attachment. A proposal for the federal government can run 50 pages or longer. The federal proposal will include a number of standard forms mandated by the government.

Most proposals contain the following elements:

**research proposal**
A document developed, usually in response to an RFP, that presents the research objectives, research design, timeline, and cost of a project.

I.  Title Page

    This includes the title of the project from the RFP, the names of the preparers of the proposal, and contact information; who the proposal is being prepared for; and the date.

II. Statement of the Research Objectives

    The objectives are often stated in the RFP. If not, they must be determined as described earlier in the chapter.

III. Study Design

    This presents a statement of how the data will be gathered and who will be sampled and the sample size.

IV. Areas of Questioning

    This is not found in all proposals, but in our experience we have found it to be very helpful. It is a tentative list of survey topics based on the research objectives.

**V.** Data Analysis

This states which techniques will be used to analyze the data.

**VI.** Personnel Involved

This provides a complete list of all supervisory and analytical personnel who will be involved in the project and a short vita of each. Each person's responsibility is also outlined. This element is typically not included when the client and supplier have an ongoing relationship. It is mandatory in most government work.

**VII.** Specifications and Assumptions

Most RFPs are relatively short and don't spell out every detail. In order to make certain that the supplier and potential client are on the same page, it is a good idea to list the specifications and assumptions that were made when creating the proposal (see Appendix 3-A).

Exhibit 3.3 details the benefits of a good proposal to both the client and the supplier.

**VIII.** Services

This spells out exactly what the research supplier will do (see Appendix 3-A). For example, who is designing the questionnaire? Is it the client, the supplier, or is it a joint effort? Again, the purpose is to make sure that the client and the research supplier operate from the same set of expectations.

**IX.** Cost

This specifies the cost and payment schedule.

**X.** Timing

This states when various phases of the project will be completed and provides a final completion date.

Preparing proposals may be the most important function a research supplier performs, inasmuch as proposals, and their acceptance or rejection, determine the revenue of the firm. If a research firm's proposals are not accepted, the company will have no funds and will

| EXHIBIT 3.3 | Benefits of a Good Proposal |
|---|---|
| **Client** | **Supplier** |
| Serves as a road map for the project | Serves as a road map for the project |
| • Specifies research methodology<br>• Specifies timeline<br>• Specifies deliverables<br>• Specifies projected costs<br>• Allows for planning-team member involvement and resource allocation | • Identifies specific responsibilities of the vendor<br>• Identifies the role the client has in fielding the research<br>• Allows for planning-team member involvement and resource allocation |
| Ensures that competing vendors carefully consider: | Serves as a valuable tool for managing client expectations, especially when the client: |
| • Project specifications<br>• Research design/methodology<br>• Project cost | • Contributes to delays or revises project timeline<br>• Mandates changes to project scope<br>• Requests additional or alternative deliverables<br>• Cancels the project |
| Ensures that the selected vendor has an explicit understanding of business decisions the research will affect | |
| Prompts the client to consider unique capabilities that individual firms offer, which might contribute to project success | Provides an objective method for clients to examine vendor qualifications |

*Source:* Matthew Singer, "Writer's Lock," *Marketing Research* (Fall 2006), p. 38.

ultimately go out of business! Moreover, if the price that is quoted is too low, the researcher may get the job but lose money. If the price is too high, the proposal may be outstanding, but the researcher will lose the work to a competitor.

## What to Look for in a Marketing Research Supplier

Market Directions, a Kansas City marketing research firm, asked marketing research clients around the United States to rate the importance of several statements about research companies and research departments. Replies were received from a wide range of industries, resulting in the following top 10 list. A desirable marketing researcher:

1. Maintains client confidentiality.
2. Is honest.
3. Is punctual.
4. Is flexible.
5. Delivers against project specifications.
6. Provides high-quality output.
7. Is responsive to the client's needs.
8. Has high-quality control standards.
9. Is customer-oriented in interactions with client.
10. Keeps the client informed throughout a project.[5]

The two most important qualities, confidentiality and honesty, are ethical issues; the remaining factors relate to managing the research function and maintaining good communications.

Good communications are a necessity. Four of the qualities on the top 10 list—flexibility, responsiveness to clients' needs, customer orientation, and keeping the client informed—are about good communications. A successful marketing research organization requires good communications both within the research company and with clients.

How important is communication? Consider this: Managers spend at least 80 percent of every working day in direct communication with others. In other words, 48 minutes of every hour are spent in meetings, on the telephone, or talking informally. The other 20 percent of a typical manager's time is spent doing desk work, most of which is communication in the form of reading and writing.[6] Communications permeate every aspect of managing the marketing research function.

# What Motivates Decision Makers to Use Research Information?

When research managers communicate effectively, generate quality data, control costs, and deliver information on time, they increase the probability that decision makers will use the research information they provide. Yet academic research shows that political factors and preconceptions can also influence whether research information is used. Specifically, the determinants of whether or not a manager uses research data are (1) conformity to prior expectations, (2) clarity of presentation, (3) research quality, (4) political acceptability within the firm, and (5) lack of challenge to the status quo.[7] Managers and researchers both agree that technical quality is the most important determinant of research use. However, managers are less likely to use research that does not conform to preconceived notions or is not politically acceptable. This does not mean, of course, that researchers should alter their findings to meet management's preconceived notions.

Marketing managers in industrial firms tend to use research findings more than do their counterparts in consumer goods organizations.[8] This tendency among industrial managers is attributed to a greater exploratory objective in information collection, a greater degree of formalization of organizational structure, and a lesser degree of surprise in the information collected.

David Santee, president of True North Marketing Insights, discusses why marketing research must become more strategic in the Practicing Marketing Research box.

# PRACTICING MARKETING RESEARCH

## Marketing Research Needs to be More Strategic

David Santee addresses marketing researchers and makes a plea for the research industry to become more strategic.

Although it may not always be apparent, senior executives want our information and our insights. In fact, they want us to be strategic partners. A thought-provoking study by the Market Research Executive Board found that 65 percent of senior leaders want market research to be a strategic partner. But here's the kicker—only 25 percent view us that way. In other words, they want it, but we are not delivering.

Market research is changing: from being tactical to becoming strategic; from delivering data to delivering solution; from being technical to becoming consultative; from being an order-taking staff function to becoming a proactive partner. Our market has changed, too. Just like those companies that vanished because they did not recognize a change in the market, we are seeing a change in our market. Will we recognize it?

Most of us are not positioning ourselves as marketplace experts or strategists. We are not called on to help define a strategy—or to be the strategic partner that senior management wants us to be. The reason we're not considered for this role is because we're truly not there yet. Our industry isn't there yet. Our skill sets are not there yet. Before we can fix the problem, we have to recognize that the problem exists.

At issue are not tactical everyday decision—whether a product should be green or blue, which ad breaks through the best, which option tastes the best, or even measuring our customer satisfaction. The real issue is with the more important strategic decisions that can significantly influence a company's success—the ones that can set the course for the next several years. Those typically made by the operating committee who makes the really big decisions. The only relevant learning in a company is the learning done by those with a power to act.[9]

### Questions

1. Explain what is meant by the last sentence in the story above.

2. Why is "becoming strategic" so important to marketing researchers?

# SUMMARY

The process for correctly defining the research problem consists of a series of steps: (1) recognize the problem or opportunity, (2) find out why the information is being sought, (3) understand the decision-making environment, (4) use the symptoms to help clarify the problem, (5) translate the management problem into a marketing research problem, (6) determine whether the information already exists, (7) determine whether the question can be answered, and (8) state the research objectives. If the problem is not defined correctly, the remainder of the research project will be a waste of time and money.

The steps in the market research process are as follows:

1. Identification of the problem/opportunity and statement of the marketing research objectives

2. Creation of the research design

3. Choice of the method of research

4. Selection of the sampling procedure
5. Collection of data
6. Analysis of data
7. Preparation and presentation of the research report
8. Follow-up

In specifying a research design, the researcher must determine whether the research will be descriptive or causal. Descriptive studies are conducted to answer who, what, when, where, and how questions. Causal studies are those in which the researcher investigates whether one variable (independent) causes or influences another variable (dependent). The next step in creating a research design is to select a research method: survey, observation, or experiment. Survey research involves an interviewer (except in mail and Internet and mobile surveys) interacting with a respondent to obtain facts, opinions, and attitudes. Observation research, in contrast, monitors respondents' actions and does not rely on direct interaction with people. An experiment is distinguished by the fact that the researcher changes one or more variables and observes the effects of those changes on another variable (usually sales). The objective of most experiments is to measure causality.

A sample is a subset of a larger population. A probability sample is one for which every element in the population has a known nonzero probability of being selected. All samples that cannot be considered probability samples are nonprobability samples. Any sample in which the chances of selection for the various elements in the population are unknown can be considered a nonprobability sample.

In larger organizations, it is common to have a research request prepared after the statement of research objectives. The research request generally describes the action to be taken on the basis of the research, the reason for the need for the information, the questions management wants to have answered, how the information will be used, the target groups from whom information must be gathered, the amount of time and money available to complete the project, and any other information pertinent to the request. The request for proposal (RFP) is the document used by clients to solicit proposals from marketing research suppliers.

Marketing research proposals are developed in response to an RFP. In some cases, the proposals are created based on an informal request such as in a telephone conversation between a client and research supplier. The research proposal gives the research objectives, research design, timeline, and cost. Research proposals are the tool that generates revenue for the research firm.

Good communications are the foundation of research management and the basis for getting decision makers to use research information. The information communicated to a decision maker depends on the type of research being conducted.

# KEY TERMS

opportunity identification 47
situation analysis 48
exploratory research 48
pilot studies 48
experience surveys 49
case analysis 49
marketing research objective 51
marketing research problem 51
management decision problem 51

hypothesis 52
research design 54
descriptive studies 54
variable 54
causal studies 54
dependent variable 54
independent variable 54
temporal sequence 54
concomitant variation 55

spurious association 55
survey research 55
observation research 55
experiments 56
probability sample 56
nonprobability sample 56
research request 58
request for proposal (RFP) 59
research proposal 59

# QUESTIONS FOR REVIEW & CRITICAL THINKING

1. The definition of the research problem is one of the critical steps in the research process. Why? Who should be involved in this process?

2. What role does exploratory research play in the marketing research process? How does exploratory research differ from other forms of marketing research?

3. Give some examples of symptoms of problems and then suggest some underlying real problems.

4. Give several examples of situations in which it would be better to take a census of the population than a sample.

5. Critique the following methodologies and suggest more appropriate alternatives:

   a. A supermarket is interested in determining its image. Cashiers drop a short questionnaire into the grocery bag of each customer prior to bagging the groceries.

   b. To assess the extent of its trade area, a shopping mall stations interviewers in the parking lot every Monday and Friday evening. After people park their cars, interviewers walk up to them and ask them for their zip codes.

   c. To assess the potential for new horror movies starring alien robots, a major studio invites people to call a 900 number and vote yes if they would like to see such movies or no if they would not. Each caller is billed a $2 charge.

6. You have been charged with determining how to attract more business majors to your school. Outline the steps you would take, including sampling procedures, to accomplish this task.

7. What can researchers do to increase the chances that decision makers will use the marketing research information they generate?

8. Explain the critical role of the research proposal.

9. Divide the class into teams of four or five. Half of the teams should prepare short RFPs on the following topics:

   a. Food on campus
   b. Role of fraternities and sororities on campus
   c. Entertainment in your city
   d. Your university website
   e. Role of student internships in education
   f. Online purchasing of school supplies
   g. Purchasing music on the Internet

   The RFPs should state clearly and precisely the research objectives and other pertinent information. The remaining teams should create proposals in response to the RFPs.

## WORKING THE NET

1. Go to the Internet and search on "mobile marketing research." Report your findings to the class.

2. Describe how putting research reports on the Web can benefit managers.

3. Go to a search engine and type "writing RFPs." Explain what kind of help is available to prepare RFPs.

## REAL-LIFE RESEARCH • 3.1

### Let's Go Out to Eat!

In retail environments, creating positive customer experiences can make any customer more valuable to the business, sometimes increasing the average transaction amount up to 50 percent. However, in a restaurant environment, because customers are rarely in a position to order and eat twice as much as they planned, there is less opportunity to increase the transaction amount by providing a great experience. Still, creating a positive experience for the customer and executing service standards has been shown to effect at least some increase in average ticket amounts.

Although the results are not as dramatic as those for retail, customers who have a highly satisfying experience in a restaurant spend slightly more money than those who were just satisfied (Figure 1). Part of this increase can be attributed to up-sell effects when a server mentions a particular appetizer or menu item (Figure 2). However, higher average ticket amounts are not merely the result of suggestive selling; restaurant staff can increase average check amounts by creating a great dining experience that customers want to enhance and make longer by sampling additional menu items. The immediate effect on sales from providing a great customer experience may be small, but it makes a big impact on the business when multiplied over thousands of transactions for an individual restaurant or restaurant chain.

### Pretty Intuitive

Customers who have a highly satisfying experience tell us time and again that they are going to return to that restaurant more often than those who don't have a highly satisfying

▶ Drive-thru guests show the largest difference in average ticket amount

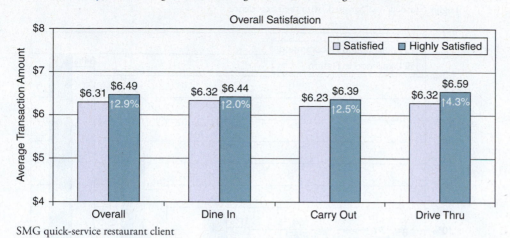

SMG quick-service restaurant client

**Figure 1**

**"Highly Satisfied" Guests Spend Slightly More than "Satisfied" Guests**

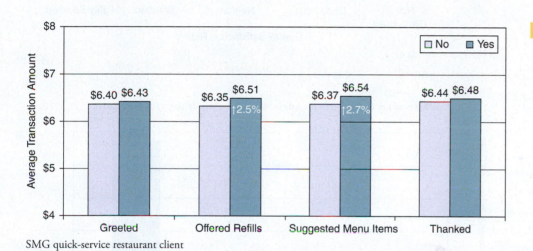

SMG quick-service restaurant client

**Figure 2**

**"Offered Refills" and "Suggested Menu Items" Show Largest Difference in Average Spend**

experience. That's pretty intuitive, right? What might not be as intuitive is the difference between a good experience and a great experience. When the restaurant is working well—the server is friendly and knowledgeable, the food tastes great, and the atmosphere is humming—that's when you create a loyal guest. On average, results show that when comparing those who say they had an exceptional experience to those who were merely satisfied, twice as many who had the exceptional experience are likely to return and three times as many are likely to recommend that restaurant to their friends and family (Figure 3). This pattern is true for restaurants at all ends of the service spectrum, from quick-service to white-tablecloth. Simply put, creating a great customer experience creates loyal customers.

Just because people say they are going to do something, however, does not mean they will necessarily follow through. When someone says he is loyal to a restaurant, is he really loyal? Maybe someone else says she will come back more often, but will she really do it? This can be measured by tying customer satisfaction results to credit-card or loyalty-club data. For one casual-dining concept, customers who said they were highly likely to come back in the next 30 days did so at almost twice the rate of customers who said they were likely to return in the next 30 days (Figure 4). Imagine the impact on traffic and revenue if restaurants could provide the kind of experience that would convert just 5 or 10 percent of their guests from having good experiences to having the kind of experience that would engender this kind of loyalty.

**Guests Who Rate Their Overall Experience a "5" Are More Likely to Return and Recommend**

▶ Guests are three times as likely to recommend to others and twice as likely to return if they were "Highly Satisfied" vs. "Satisfied" with their experience

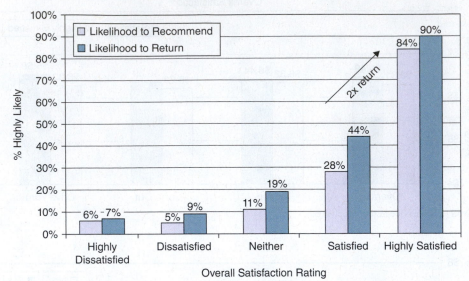

SMG fast-food client

**Intent to Return Mirrors Actual Return in Next 30 Days**

▶ Customers who say they are "Highly Likely to Return" actually return at twice the rate

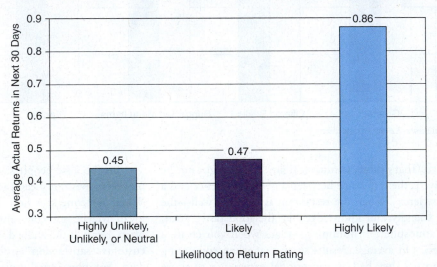

SMG casual-dining client

## Spend More Money

One interesting finding is that when customers visit a restaurant because of a recommendation or a previous positive experience, they actually spend more money. This is in sharp contrast to the people who visited primarily because of a promotion or advertisement. Those people actually spent less than people who visited for any other reason. In one quick-service restaurant (QSR) example, it was found that customers who visited because of a positive recommendation from a trusted friend or family member spent approximately 14 percent more than those who visited because of a promotion or advertisement.

## Servers Are the Key

How do restaurants build those positive experiences that customers want to repeat and recommend to others? It starts at the front line. Servers are the key to converting a customer from merely satisfied to loyal. Executing a simple set of service standards can have a big impact on driving guest satisfaction with their experience. Figure 5 illustrates that by simply greeting guests, checking back with them regularly, thanking them for their business, and ensuring that a manager is visible in the dining room, restaurants can nearly quadruple guest satisfaction compared to a guest who receives zero or just one of those behaviors. So although retaining the best servers is the most effective way to drive satisfaction and loyalty, ensuring that simple service behaviors are consistently executed may be the most attainable way to improve the guests' experiences.

One way managers and executives can create buy-in from servers is to go back to the data and show them the kind of impact their actions can have on their own income. By again tying guest feedback to transaction information, it can be shown that for guests who experienced all of the prescribed service behaviors, not only are they more loyal to the restaurant but also they really do tip their servers better. In fact, for one casual dining concept there was a marked increase in tip value when guests experienced all of the service behaviors instead of just one (Figure 6). Everybody in the restaurant wins when service becomes the focus.[10]

## Questions

1. Would you say that this was an exploratory study? If not, what are the research questions?

2. Is this research causal or descriptive? Why?

3. Explain how the Olive Garden might use this information; McDonald's.

4. What might be included in an RFP to do further research?

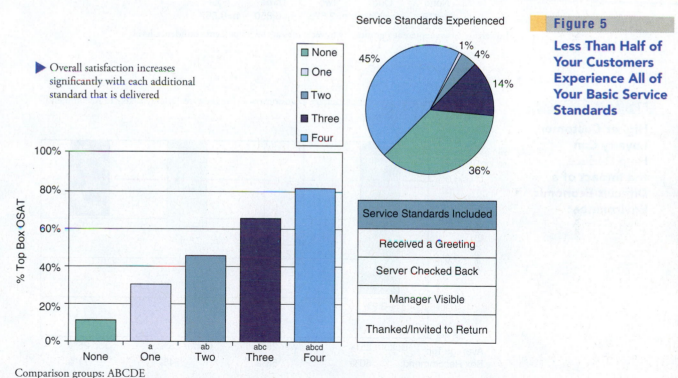

▶ Overall satisfaction increases significantly with each additional standard that is delivered

Service Standards Experienced

None — 45%
One — 1%
Two — 4%
Three — 14%
Four — 36%

**Figure 5**

**Less Than Half of Your Customers Experience All of Your Basic Service Standards**

| Service Standards Included |
| --- |
| Received a Greeting |
| Server Checked Back |
| Manager Visible |
| Thanked/Invited to Return |

Comparison groups: ABCDE
Lowercase letters represent significantly lower scores at the 95% confidence level

**Figure 6**

**Tip Percentage Increases Significantly When More Than Three Service Standards Are Delivered**

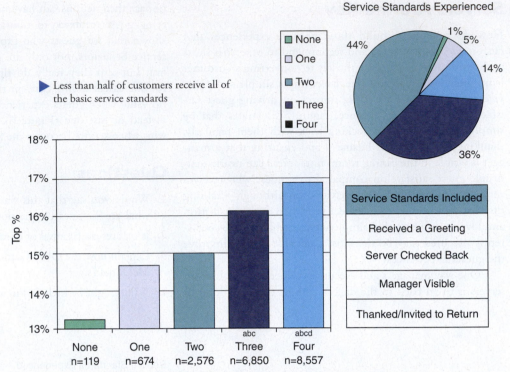

▶ Less than half of customers receive all of the basic service standards

Lowercase letters represent significantly lower scores at the 95 percent confidence level

**Figure 7**

**Higher Customer Loyalty Can Help Reduce the Impact of a Difficult Economic Environment**

▶ Restaurants with a greater percentage of customers saying they are "Highly Likely to Recommend" have better comp sales

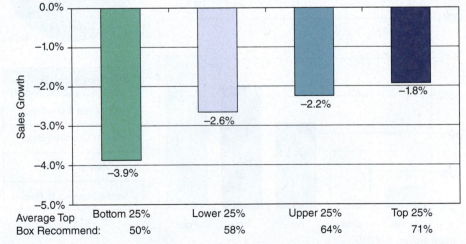

*Note:* SMG refers to Service Management Group, a Kansas City, Missouri, marketing research firm.

# APPENDIX 3A
# A MARKETING RESEARCH PROPOSAL

## Decision Analyst, Inc. Proposal to Conduct a Brand Equity Study

**CONFIDENTIAL**

**Prepared For:**
**Fun City Gaming, Inc.**

**Prepared by:**
**Kathi McKenzie & Sally DanforthJanuary 2013**

# Background

Fun City Gaming, Inc. currently operates a multilevel dockside riverboat casino and a land-based pavilion with three restaurants and a hotel, all located on the Arlen River. The casino offers 1,500 slot machines and 70 table games, and is the "flagship" of the Fun City franchise. The Fun City Casino has four primary competitors currently operating in the area, all within a roughly 30-mile radius of the Fun City. The Fun City Casino ranks second in revenue but first in profit among these competitors. In addition to these competitors, additional competition will be provided by the planned "River Wild" casino, which will likely begin construction in about a year. This casino will be located in Saint George, minutes from the Fun City Casino.

Fun City is currently undergoing a large redevelopment, involving construction of a completely new gaming vessel, significant upgrades to the pavilion, addition of new restaurants, and a new parking garage. The gaming vessel will feature 2,500 slot machines, 84 table games, high-limit gaming areas, and upgraded décor. The new Fun City will offer superior features to the current product as well as to primary competitors.

In order to be financially feasible, this project must increase business from current customers as well as attract customers from competitive casinos, some of whom may have to travel past competitive casinos to arrive at Fun City. In addition, the new offering should be especially attractive to premium casino players.

# Objectives

The overall objective of this study would be to help management position the new Fun City offering. Key questions to be addressed include:

■   What should be the positioning of the new casino?
■   Should the Fun City name be used, or should it be rebranded?
■   If rebranded, what name should be used?

# Study Design

This study would be conducted using a targeted telephone survey among 800 gamblers within a 100-mile radius of the Fun City Casino location. Specifically, we will survey 400 within the Arlen Valley portion of this area and 400 in the area eastward, where the majority of current/future competition lies. Respondents will be screened based on past 12-month casino usage.

# Areas of Questioning

Decision Analyst would work closely with Fun City Gaming in developing the questionnaire. Assuming that we have three to four potential positionings to test, tentative survey topics would include:

■   Current casino usage and gambling behavior.
■   Awareness and overall rating for the Fun City name, as well as names of key competitors and other names owned by Fun City Gaming that might be used for the new casino.
■   Rating of the Fun City and key competitors on several (8 to 10) image attributes.

- Exposure to brief description of the "new" (redeveloped) casino. Each respondent would be exposed to the description with *one* of the potential positionings. This will result in a readable sample size for each positioning.
- Overall rating and rating on key image attributes for the "new" casino.
- Rating of the Fun City name and other potential names on overall appeal and fit with this description.
- Projected use of new casino; effect on gambling habits and share of casino visits.

Data will be analyzed both by area of residence and by gambling value (high/medium/low value gamblers).

# Data Analysis

Factor analysis will be conducted, and the factors that are most related to the overall rating of the casino will be identified. On the basis of these factors, a perceptual map will be created to show visually the relationship between the current Fun City and competitive brands, based on brand image. The image projected by the new casino description will also be shown on this map, and a gap analysis conducted to highlight possible differences in image projected by each of the three to four positionings.

# Personnel Involved

This project will be supervised by Kathi McKenzie and Sally DanGorth. Kathi will be the overall supervisor and Sally will be responsible for the data analysis and presentation. (*Note:* A short bio of each person would normally be attached.)

# Specifications/Assumptions

The cost estimate is based on the following assumptions:

- Number of completed interviews = 800
- Average interview length = 20 minutes
- Average completion rate = 0.62
- Complete per hour Assumed incidence = 25%
- No open-ended questions
- Type of sample: targeted random digit
- Up to two banners of statistical tables in Word format
- Factor analysis, two perceptual maps (total sample and high-value gambler), and gap analysis
- Report Personal presentation, if desired

# Services

Decision Analyst, Inc. would:

- Develop the questionnaire, in conjunction with Fun City Gaming management.
- Generate sample within the target area.

- Program the survey.
- Manage and administer the project.
- Monitor and oversee all telephone interviewing.
- Process data, specify cross-tabulations, and compile statistical tables.
- Analyze the data and prepare presentation-style report, if desired.

# Cost

The cost to conduct this study, as described, would be $61,900, plus or minimum a 10 percent contingency fee, which would only be spent with specific prior approval of Fun City Gaming. This cost estimate does not include the cost of any travel outside of the Dallas–Fort Worth area. Any overnight deliveries or travel expenses would be billed at cost at the end of the study.

Decision Analyst would closely monitor data collection. If the actual data collection experience differed from the stated specifications and assumptions, we would notify you immediately to discuss the options available.

# Timing

After approval of the final questionnaire, the project would require approximately five to six weeks, as outlined below:

| | |
|---|---|
| Survey programming and quality control | 3–4 days |
| Data collection | 3 weeks |
| Final data tabulations | 3 days |
| Final report | 1–2 weeks |

# Secondary Data and Big Data Analytics

## LEARNING OBJECTIVES

1. Understand the advantages and disadvantages of secondary data.

2. Comprehend data mining and behavioral targeting.

3. Learn the advantages of big data analytics, how to make it actionable, and the importance of data visualization.

What are secondary data? What are their advantages and disadvantages? How is data mining used by managers to extract insights from databases? Most importantly, how do managers manage the huge flow of information they have available? You will learn the answers to these questions in chapter four.

## Nature of Secondary Data

**Secondary data** consist of information that has already been gathered and might be relevant to the problem at hand. **Primary data**, in contrast, are survey, observation, and experiment data collected to solve a particular problem. It is highly unlikely that any marketing research problem is entirely unique or has never occurred before. It also is probable that someone else has investigated the problem or one similar to it in the past. Therefore, secondary data can be a cost-effective and efficient means of obtaining information for marketing research. There are two basic sources of secondary data: the company itself (internal databases) and other organizations, such as Acxion, (external databases).

Secondary information originating within the company includes annual reports, reports to stockholders, sales data, customer profiles, purchase patterns, product testing results (perhaps made available to the news media), Internet and mobile tracking of customers,

**secondary data**
Data that have been previously gathered.

**primary data**
New data gathered to help solve the problem under investigation.

company website tracking, and house periodicals composed by company personnel for communication to employees, customers, or others. Often, all this information is incorporated into a company's internal database.

Outside sources of secondary information include innumerable government (federal, state, and local) departments and agencies that compile and publish summaries of business data, as well as trade and industry associations, business periodicals, and other news media that regularly publish studies and articles on the economy, specific industries, and even individual companies. Acxiom uses more than 23,000 computer servers to collect, collate, and analyze consumer data. The firm has created the world's largest consumer database. The servers process more than 50 trillion data "transactions" a year. The database contains information on over 500 million consumers worldwide, with about 1,500 data points per person. Acxiom customers include firms like E*Trade, Ford, Wells Fargo, Macy's and just about all major firms seeking consumer insights. Acxiom integrates online, mobile, and offline data to create in-depth consumer behavior portraits. The firm's proprietary software, called PersonicX, assigns consumers to one of 70 detailed socioeconomic clusters. For example, the "savvy single" cluster means that this group's mobile, upper-middle-class who do their banking online, attend pro sports events, are sensitive to price—and respond to free-shipping offers.[3]

## Advantages of Secondary Data

Marketing researchers use secondary information because it can often be obtained at a fraction of the cost, time, and inconvenience associated with primary data collection. Additional advantages of using secondary information include the following:

- *Secondary data may help to clarify or redefine the problem during the exploratory research process* (see Chapter 3).   Consider the experience of a local YMCA. Concerned about a stagnant level of membership and a lack of participation in traditional YMCA programs, it decided to survey members and nonmembers. Secondary data revealed that there had been a tremendous influx of young single persons into the target market, while the number of "traditional families" had remained constant. The problem was redefined to examine how the YMCA could attract a significant share of the young single adult market while maintaining its traditional family base.

- *Secondary data may actually provide a solution to the problem.* It is highly unlikely that the problem is unique; there is always the possibility that someone else has addressed the identical problem or a very similar one. Thus, the precise information desired may have been collected, but not for the same purpose.

  Many states publish a directory of manufacturers (typically available online) that contains information on companies: location, markets, product lines, number of plants, names of key personnel, number of employees, and sales levels. When a consulting company specializing in long-range strategic planning for members of the semiconductor industry needed a regional profile of its potential clients, it used individual state directories to compile the profile; no primary data collection was necessary.

- *Secondary data may provide primary data research method alternatives.* Each primary data research endeavor is custom-designed for the situation at hand; consequently, the marketing researcher should always be open to sources that suggest research alternatives. For example, when we started work on a research project for a large southwestern city's convention and visitor's bureau, we obtained a research report prepared by *Meeting and Convention Planners* magazine. In designing our questionnaire, we used a series of scales from the magazine's questionnaire. Not only were the scales well designed, but results from our study could be compared with the magazine's data.

- *Secondary data may alert the marketing researcher to potential problems and/or difficulties.* In addition to alternatives, secondary information may divulge potential dangers. Unpopular collection methods, sample selection difficulties, or respondent hostility may be uncovered. For example, examination of a study of anesthesiologists by a researcher planning to conduct a study of their satisfaction with certain drugs discovered a high refusal rate in a telephone survey. The researcher had planned to use a telephone study but instead switched to a mail questionnaire with a response incentive.

- *Secondary data may provide necessary background information and build credibility for the research report.* Secondary information often yields a wealth of background data for planning a research project. It may offer a profile of potential buyers versus non-buyers, industry data, desirable new product features, language used by purchasers to describe the industry, and the advantages and disadvantages of existing products. Language used by target consumers can aid in phrasing questions that will be meaningful to respondents. Sometimes background data can satisfy some of the research objectives, eliminating the need to ask certain questions; shorter questionnaires typically have higher completion rates. And secondary data can enrich research findings by providing additional insights into what the data mean or by corroborating current findings. Finally, secondary data can serve as a reference base for subsequent research projects.

- *Secondary data may provide the sample frame.* If a company, such as UPS, wants to track its levels of customer satisfaction each quarter, the names of customers must come from its database. Thus, the customer list is the sample frame, and the sample frame is the list or device from which a sample is drawn.

## Limitations of Secondary Data

Despite the many advantages of secondary data, they also pose some dangers. The main disadvantages of secondary information are lack of availability, lack of relevance, inaccuracy, and insufficiency.

**Lack of Availability**  For some research questions, there are simply no available data. Suppose Kraft General Foods wants to evaluate the taste, texture, and color of three new gourmet brownie mixes. No secondary data exist that can answer these questions; consumers must try each mix and then evaluate it. If McDonald's wants to evaluate its image in Phoenix, Arizona, it must gather primary data. If BMW wants to know the reaction of college students to a new two-seater sports car design, it must show prototypes to the students and evaluate their opinions. Of course, secondary data may have played a major role in the engineer's design plan for the car.

**Lack of Relevance**  It is not uncommon for secondary data to be expressed in units or measures that cannot be used by the researcher. For example, Joan Dermott, a retailer of oriental rugs, determined that the primary customers for her rugs were families with a total household income of $80,000 to $120,000. Higher-income consumers tended to purchase pricier rugs than those Dermott carried. When she was trying to decide whether to open a store in another Florida city, she could not find useful income data. One source offered class breakdowns of $40,000 to $90,000, $90,000 to $110,000, $110,000 to $150,000, and so forth. Another secondary source broke down incomes into less than $50,000, $50,000 to $70,000, and more than $70,000. Even if the given income brackets had met Joan's needs, she would have faced another problem: outdated information. One study had been conducted in 2001 and the other in 2007. In

Florida's dynamic markets, the percentages probably were no longer relevant. This is often the case with U.S. Census data, which are nearly a year old before they become available.

**Inaccuracy** Users of secondary data should always assess the accuracy of the data. There are a number of potential sources of error when a researcher gathers, codes, analyzes, and presents data. Any report that does not mention possible sources and ranges of error should be suspect.

Using secondary data does not relieve the researcher from attempting to assess their accuracy. A few guidelines for determining the accuracy of secondary data are as follows:

1. *Who gathered the data?* The source of the secondary data is a key to their accuracy. Federal agencies, most state agencies, and large commercial marketing research firms generally can be counted on to have conducted their research as professionally as possible. Marketing researchers should always be on guard when examining data in which a hidden agenda might be reflected. A chamber of commerce, for instance, is always going to put its best foot forward. Similarly, trade associations often advocate one position over another.

2. *What was the purpose of the study?* Data are always collected for some reason. Understanding the motivation for the research can provide clues to the quality of the data. A chamber of commerce study conducted to provide data that could be used to attract new industry to the area should be scrutinized with a great deal of caution. There have been situations in which advertising agencies have been hired by clients to assess the impact of their own advertising programs. In other words, they have been asked to evaluate the quality of the job they were doing for their clients!

3. *What information was collected?* A researcher should always identify exactly what information was gathered and from whom. For example, in a dog food study, were purchasers of canned, dry, and semimoist food interviewed, or were just one or two types of dog food purchasers surveyed? In a voters' survey, were only Democrats or only Republicans interviewed? Were the respondents registered voters? Was any attempt made to ascertain a respondent's likelihood of voting in the next election? Were self-reported data used to infer actual behavior?

4. *When was the information collected?* A shopping mall study that surveyed shoppers only on weekends would not reflect the opinions of "typical" mall patrons. A telephone survey conducted from 9:00 A.M. to 5:00 P.M. would vastly underrepresent working persons. A survey of Florida visitors conducted during the summer probably would reveal motivations and interests different from those of winter visitors.

5. *How was the information collected?* Were the data collected by mail, telephone, mobile device, Internet, or personal interview? Each of these techniques offers advantages and disadvantages. What was the refusal rate? Were decision makers or their representatives interviewed? In short, the researcher must attempt to discern the amount of bias injected into the data by the information-gathering process. A mail survey with a 1 percent response rate (that is, only 1 percent of those who received the survey mailed it back) probably contains a lot of self-selection bias.

6. *Is the information consistent with other information?* A lack of consistency between secondary data sets should dictate caution. The researcher should delve into possible causes of the discrepancy. Differences in the sample, time frame, sampling methodology, questionnaire structure, and other factors can lead to variations in studies. If possible, the researcher should assess the validity of the different studies as a basis for determining which, if any, study should be used for decision making.

**Insufficiency** A researcher may determine that available data are relevant and accurate but still not sufficient to make a decision or bring closure to a problem. For example, a manager for Walmart may have sufficient secondary data on incomes, family sizes, number of competitors, and growth potential to determine in which of five Iowa towns Walmart wishes to locate its next store. But if no traffic counts exist for the selected town, primary data will have to be gathered to select a specific site for the store.

# Internal Databases

For many companies, a computerized database containing information about customers and prospects has become an essential marketing tool. An internal database is simply a collection of related information developed from data within the organization.

## Creating an Internal Database

A firm's sales activities can be an excellent source of information for creating an **internal database.** A traditional starting point has been the firm's sales or inquiry processing and tracking system. Typically, such a system is built on salespersons' *call reports.* A call report provides a blueprint of a salesperson's daily activities. It details the number of calls made, characteristics of each firm visited, sales activity resulting from the call, and any information picked up from the client regarding competitors, such as price changes, new products or services, credit term modifications, and new product or service features. An internal marketing database built on sales results, customer preferences, Internet, mobile, and social data can be a powerful marketing tool.

**internal database**
A collection of related information developed from data within the organization.

## Data Mining

American Express uses a neural network to examine the hundreds of millions of entries in its database that tell how and where individual cardholders transact business. A **neural network** is a computer program that mimics the processes of the human brain and thus is capable of learning from examples to find patterns in data. The result is a set of *purchase propensity scores* for each cardholder. Based on these scores, AmEx matches offers from affiliated merchants to the purchase histories of individual cardholders and encloses these offers with their monthly statements. The benefits are reduced expenses for AmEx and information of higher value for its cardholders; American Express is engaged in data mining.

**neural network**
A computer program that mimics the processes of the human brain and thus is capable of learning from examples to find patterns in data.

**Data mining** is the use of statistical and other advanced software to discover nonobvious patterns hidden in big data. The objective is to identify patterns that marketers can use in creating new strategies and tactics to increase a firm's profitability. Camelot Music Holdings used data mining to identify a group of high-spending, 65-plus customers (members of its frequent shopper club) who were buying lots of classical and jazz music and movies. Further data mining revealed that a large percentage also bought rap and alternative music; these were grandparents buying for the grandkids. Now, Camelot tells the senior citizens what's hot in rap and alternative music, as well as in traditional music.

**data mining**
The use of statistical and other advanced software to discover nonobvious patterns hidden in a database.

Data mining involves searching for interesting patterns and following the data trail wherever it leads. The discovery process often requires sifting through massive quantities of data; electronic point-of-sale transactions, inventory records, and online customer orders matched with demographics can easily use up several terabytes of data storage space. Probability sampling, descriptive statistics, and multivariate statistics are all tools of data mining that make the task manageable. (Probability sampling was discussed in Chapter 3; descriptive statistics programs and multivariate statistics will be covered in Chapters 14 through 18.) Other, more advanced data mining tools, such as genetic algorithms and case-based reasoning systems, must be left for an advanced text.

## Behavioral Targeting

**behavioral targeting**
The use of online and offline data to understand a consumer's habits, demographics, and social networks in order to increase the effectiveness of online advertising.

**Behavioral targeting** is the use of online and offline data to understand a consumer's habits, demographics, and social networks in order to increase the effectiveness of online advertising. Acxiom's PersonicX, for example, is used for behavioral targeting. As the Internet has matured, nontargeted advertising has decreased in efficiency. One study found that only 4 percent of Internet users account for 67 percent of all display ad clicks. Another recent study by DoubleClick reported an average click-through rate of just 0.1 percent. Translated, that means that only one out of a thousand people actually click through the average display ad. Behavioral targeting attempts to change the odds in favor of the advertiser. In fact, recent research confirms that targeted ad click-throughs and conversion rates are significantly higher than nontargeted ads.[4]

EXelate Media, a research firm that collects and sells Web data, announced an alliance with Nielsen Holdings, America's largest marketing research firm. The deal tied eXelate's data on more than 150 million Internet users to Nielsen's database on 115 million American households to provide more detailed profiles of consumers.

EXelate gathers online consumer data through deals with hundreds of websites. The firm determines a consumer's age, sex, ethnicity, marital status, and profession by scouring website registration data. It pinpoints, for example, which consumers in the market to buy a car are fitness buffs, based on their Internet searches and the sites they frequent. It gathers and stores the information using tracking cookies, or small strings of data that are placed on the hard drive of a consumer's computer when that consumer visits a participating site. A more detailed discussion of the tracking process can be found in Chapter 8.

An auto maker, for instance, could use EXelate and Nielsen's databases to target ads promoting a sports car to people who visit auto blogs, search online for sports cars, and fit into a group Nielsen calls the "young digerati." This group includes tech-savvy, affluent consumers who live in trendy apartments or condos, are 25 to 44 years old, make about $88,000 a year, and typically read *The Economist.*[5]

The addition of social networking data has been a huge boost to behavioral targeting. Users of Facebook and other social sites reveal interests, connections, and tastes like never before. In the past, online advertisers have found it very effective to promote to persons who have bought from them, visited their site, or interacted with an ad. The problem comes in with generating demand among people who may not even know the product. This is where social data comes into play. Companies like Media 68 takes an advertiser's customer data and links it to social user information it licenses from social networking sites. The technology matches a prospect with his or her closest friends. So a remessaging campaign can target the original customer plus his or her friends. Instead of reaching one prospect, the campaign may reach 8 or 10 million prospects. It is the idea that "birds of a feather flock together."[6]

Lotame and 33across are among the other companies aiming to mine social networking data for advertisers. Lotame attempts to use social data to get at influencers. It trolls social networks, blogs, and message boards for users who have created content about specific topics. Then it expands the circle by adding in people who consumed that user-generated content. Finally, it adds people who look like those content creators and consumers.[7]

Both eBay and Spring have used 33across to improve their online advertising effectiveness.

# Big Data Analytics

Recall that big data is the accumulation and analysis of massive quantities of information. One research and consulting firm says that an organization with five total terabytes of active business data is one with big data.[8] A terabyte is a billion bytes, so a firm would be considered as working with big data if it had active business data of 5 billion bytes or more. Big data offers a firm:

- Deeper insights—Rather than looking at market segments, classifications, groups or other summary-level information, big data researchers have insights into all the individual, all the products, all the parts, all the events, and all the transactions.

- Broader insights—Big data analytics takes into account all the data, structured and unstructured, to understand the complex, evolving, and interrelated conditions to produce more accurate insights.[9]

An example of deeper and broader insights would be where a Cable TV supplier showed that 95 percent of all appointments made were met on time. This sounds impressive until you know that there were 3,000 appointments in a day, so 150 customers waited at home in vain each day. If you can then tie the missed appointments to call data, survey data, and repurchase data along with tweets and Facebook comments, a manager could begin calculating how much revenue and word-of-mouth damage occurred, in addition to the extra cost of rescheduling and expediting visits.[10]

## Defining Relationships

For scientists and marketing researchers, big data analytics represents a paradigm shift. The traditional scientific method involves getting information about a problem, creating a hypothesis, and then testing data to accept or reject the null hypothesis. Hypothesis-driven research is based on well-defined parameters created by the researcher. It limits exploration to what the mind can imagine. Data-driven science allows us to collect data and then see what it tells us. This is a sharp reversal from traditional science.

Big data is more about "what" than "why." There are many contexts where "why" is a luxury and "what" is good enough. When Amazon uses big data analytics on sales data to find books that are often bought together, the recommendation doesn't need to know why many customers who bought *War and Peace,* for instance, also bought *The Idiot.* Amazon may not care why the two books were linked. But it can pitch *War and Peace* to *Idiot* buyers and vice versa.

Sometimes after the "what" is revealed, then traditional research may be needed to answer "why." For example, if big data tells healthcare researchers that people who walk are less obese, then, logically, the next important question is, "Why do so few people walk?" And what will happen if we give overweight people an app for their smartphone to help them track physical activity? These questions are the job of traditional marketing research.

## The Big Data Breakthrough

Not long ago, the notion of big data analytics was just a dream. Traditional databases, usually written in a language called SQL (pronounced sequel), store data in tables, columns, and rows but are limited when it comes to storing strings of words such as those found in an e-mail or text message. They are also unable to handle pictures or video.

New types of databases that began emerging in late 2009, such as MongoDB, Cassandra, and Simple DB, don't have these limitations, and allow analysts to create queries against all these types of data.

Such databases, known collectively as NoSQL (for "not only SQL"), can make a huge difference to companies analyzing very large data sets, even if they are fairly conventional. For example, analysts at risk consultant Verisk Analytics run various models and analytics against billions of customer records in order to help identify fraudulent insurance claims.[11]

Perry Rotella, vice president and chief information officer at Cerisk, said using a traditional DB2 database from International Business Machines "would be a six-hour job" that had to run overnight. Analysts would pore over the results and generate new queries that would have to run again. He said it took weeks every time analysts needed to create a new statistical model. The company recently changed to a NoSQL database that allows analysts to run the same type of queries in 30 seconds.[12]

Recently developed programs known as natural language processing and machine learning rely on the computer programs themselves to find patterns and even elucidate the meaning of ambiguous words based on context. With natural language processing, the program can figure out whether a term like "bomb" is being used to describe a Broadway play versus something a terrorist would use.

Until recently, complex computer programs needed to run on expensive hardware, such as enormous mainframe computers. Today, an open-source software framework called Hadoop—developed at Yahoo with contributions from technology developed by Google, and named after a child's toy elephant—allows queries to be split up by the program.

Different analytic tasks are distributed among many inexpensive servers, each of which solves a part of the puzzle, before reassembling the queries when the work is completed. The ability to distribute complex queries to a large number of inexpensive computers helps people get very quick responses to complicated questions with a large number of variables.

Online automotive market Edmunds.com can help auto dealers predict how long a given car will remain on their lots by comparing car makes, models and other features against the number of days inventory cars at that price point averaged on a lot in a given dealer's regions. The predictions help minimize the number of days a car remains unsold —"one of the most important sales metrics for dealers," said Philip Potloff, Edmunds.com's chief information officer.[13]

Becky Wu, senior vice president of Research for Luth Research, discusses why the promise of big data analytics is very real in the Practicing Marketing Research box.

# PRACTICING MARKETING RESEARCH

## Big Data Unmasks a Wealth of Knowledge

One increasingly critical area of big data is consumer behaviors tracked across computer and mobile devices by using metering technologies like that of Luth Research's ZQ Intelligence platform. This type of data matters a lot because consumers' life is deeply intertwined with digital technologies and media. In every minute:

- 2 million search queries take place via Google.
- 571 new websites are launched.
- People download 47,000 mobile apps from Apple App Store.
- Consumers spend $272,000 with online retailers.

These mind-boggling numbers aside, what is noteworthy is all of these activities are trackable and are in fact being tracked. These data, existing outside of traditional research methods, create unique value to market research in a few notable ways:

- Behavior-centric data free marketing researchers from having to do the job of recording what consumers do. Instead, survey and other research methods can focus on their true mission—getting to the why behind behaviors.
- It comes with precise big data, including time stamp and geo-location (in the case of mobile tracking). This distinct benefit provides contextual understanding of when and where behaviors and decisions take place, which has been long missing from traditional market research.
- Passive tracking generates a vast among of continuous data. The resulting data surpasses what surveys can provide without overburdening respondents.[14]

## Questions

1. How can real-time tracking help marketing decision makers?
2. Do tracking and traditional marketing research benefit each other? If so, how?

## Making Big Data Actionable

Output that is too complex can be overwhelming or even mistrusted. What is needed are intuitive tools that can aid everyday decision making. In the traditional world of marketing research, a product manager or other marketing manager would go to the marketing research department (or send out an RFP) describing a problem. Researchers would then conduct the research by interviewing people, which then leads to analysis of the data. Next, would be a PowerPoint presentation. Finally, managers might or might not take action. In the new world of big data analytics, customer insights are delivered to people who run various business functions on a regular basis. For example, store managers, product managers, and call-center supervisors receive an ongoing set of insights that are tailored to their specific roles.

Automated decision making also plays an important role in big data analytics. For example, an online shopper may receive product recommendations on a real-time basis, such as while the consumer is in the purchase process. Big data analytics could prompt credit card offers to customers while in a branch bank or in contact with a call center. Automation of big data requires that an experience be created for the individual consumer that is tailored enough to his or her needs that it will generate an incremental response.[15]

## Data Visualization

Of course, not all big data output results in automated decision making. Yet the output must be organized and rationalized. Most people cannot recall a string of numbers any longer than a phone number. So how could anyone make sense out of a billion numbers or more? The answer is pictures, or data visualization. **Data visualization** is the use of picture visualization techniques to illustrate the relationship within data. Recall the wind currents across the U.S. example in Chapter 2. Data visualization companies, such as Gooddata, Ayasdi, Tidemark, and Platfora, turn large data sets into pictures that lead companies intuitively to the information that is more important to them.

Exhibit 4.1 shows an example of credit card transactions; the red dots indicate fraud. By clicking on the red dots, managers can get more information on how the frauds were carried out. This can help the company develop new ways to prevent further incidents, such as by adding new rules to their transaction system.

**data visualization**
The use of picture visualization techniques to illustrate the relationship within data.

## Battle over Privacy

There is a downside to big data: consumer privacy. The researchers say that their data contains no personally identifiable information. In one survey, only 32 percent said that they

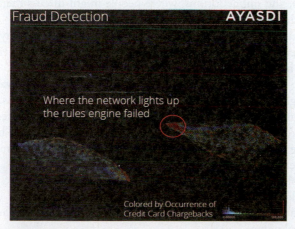

*Source:* Ayasdi, Inc.

were comfortable with advertisers using their browsing history to deliver more relevant ads. How much tracking actually goes on? *The Wall Street Journal* picked 50 websites that account for about 40 percent of all U.S. page views. The 50 sites installed a total of 3,180 tracking cookies on a test computer used to conduct the study. Only one site, Wikipedia.org, installed none. Twelve sites, including Comcast.net and MSN.com, installed more than 100 tracking tools apiece. Dictionary.com installed 168 tracking tools that didn't let users decline to be tracked and 121 tools that, according to privacy statements, didn't rule out collecting financial or health data.[17]

Congress is considering laws to limit tracking. The Federal Trade Commission is developing privacy guidelines for the industry. If "you were in the Gap, and the sales associate said to you, 'OK, from now on, since you shopped here today, we are going to follow you around the mall and view your consumer transactions,' no person would ever agree to that," Senator George LeMieux of Florida said in a Senate hearing on Internet privacy.[18]

The computer consultant Tom Owad has published the results of an experiment that provided a lesson in just how easy it is to extract sensitive personal data from the Net. Mr. Owad wrote a simple piece of software that allowed him to download public wish lists that Amazon.com customers post to catalog products that they plan to purchase or would like to receive as gifts. These lists usually include the name of the list's owner and his or her city and state.

Using a couple of standard-issue PCs, Mr. Owad was able to download over 250,000 wish lists over the course of a day. He then searched the data for controversial or politically sensitive books and authors, from Kurt Vonnegut's *Slaughterhouse-Five* to the Koran. He then used Yahoo People Search to identify addresses and phone numbers for many of the list owners.

Mr. Owad ended up with maps of the United States showing the locations of people interested in particular books and ideas, including George Orwell's *1984*. He could just as easily have published a map showing the residences of people interested in books about treating depression or adopting a child. "It used to be," Mr. Owad concluded, "you had to get a warrant to monitor a person or a group of people. Today, it is increasingly easy to monitor ideas. And then track them back to people."

What Mr. Owad did by hand can increasingly be performed automatically, with data mining software that draws from many sites and databases. One of the essential characteristics of the Net is the interconnection of diverse stores of information. The *openness* of databases is what gives the system much of its power and usefulness. But it also makes it easy to discover hidden relationships among far-flung bits of data.[19]

An emerging technique that is upsetting many privacy advocates is called *scraping*. Firms offer to harvest online conversations and collect personal details from social networking sites, resumé sites, and online forums, where people might discuss their lives. (Scraping is discussed in more detail in Chapter 8.)

Recently, the website PatientsLikeMe.com noticed suspicious activity on its "Mood" discussion board. There, people exchange highly personal stories about their emotional disorders, ranging from bipolar disease to a desire to cut themselves.[20]

It was a break-in. A new member of the site, using sophisticated software, was scraping, or copying, every single message off PatientsLikeMe's private online forums.

PatientsLikeMe managed to block and identify the intruder: Nielsen Holdings, the privately held New York media research firm. Nielsen monitors online "buzz" for clients, including major drug makers, which, Nielsen says, buy data gleaned from the Web to get insight from consumers about their products.

"I felt totally violated," says Bilal Ahmed, a 33-year-old resident of Sydney, Australia, who used PatientsLikeMe to connect with other people suffering from depression.[21] He used a pseudonym on the message boards, but his PatientsLikeMe profile linked to his blog, which contains his real name.

After PatientsLikeMe told users about the break-in, Mr. Ahmed deleted all his posts, plus a list of drugs he uses. "It was very disturbing to know that your information is being sold," he says. Nielsen says it no longer scrapes data from private message boards.[22]

Behavioral tracking has become the foundation of the online advertising industry. Online advertising is why a company like Google can spend millions and millions of dollars on free services like its search engine, Gmail, mapping tools, Google Groups, and more.

And it's not just Google. Facebook, Yahoo, MSN, and thousands of blogs, news sites, and comment boards use advertising to support what they do. And personalized advertising is more valuable than advertising aimed at just anyone. Marketers will pay more to reach you if you are likely to use their products or services.

The Internet is in an arms race over control of personal data. Facebook's 60 billion plus value is testimony to value of tracking over a billion people. The "like" and "share" buttons enable Facebook to track people online. New firms, like Disconnect, enable users to block tracking. Many companies are realizing the value of blocking Internet tracking. Snapchat, for example, offers a photo-deleting app. Ipredator blocks your identify on the Web. And Silent Circle encrypts calls, texts, and emails.

Mike Zaneis, general counsel for the Interactive Advertising Bureau, a group that represents online marketers, is worried about the effect of privacy tools on the digital ad market, which had revenue of $36.6 billion in 2012. "It's an economic trade-off: You go to a website, you see ads. If you block those ads, you're starving the content creators," says Zaneis. "It would put tens of thousands of small publishers out of business if you had widespread, mass adoption of these tools.[23]

Exhibit 4.2 details several ways that you can limit prying eyes.

**Identity Theft**  People have a right to be concerned. Identity theft cost $54 billion annually.[24] One company that has come under fire is ChoicePoint. Since spinning off from the credit bureau Equifax in 1997, it has been buying up databases and data mining operations. Businesses, individuals, even the FBI, now rely on its storehouse. Other customers: Nigerian scammers who apparently used the data to steal people's identities.

The problem was unreliable safeguards. To ensure that only certain businesses had access to its data, ChoicePoint set up certain requirements that potential customers must meet. A man named Olatunji Oluwatosin—and possibly others—used fake names and a Hollywood copy shop fax machine to create fictitious small businesses requesting ChoicePoint service. Before Oluwatosin was caught—after someone at ChoicePoint grew suspicious about one of his applications—he accessed at least 145,000 names. (Oluwatosin pleaded no contest to felony identity theft in California in February 2005; he served a 16-month sentence.)[25] ChoicePoint no longer sells consumer data that includes driver license numbers and Social Security numbers.[26]

In many cases, finding Social Security and credit card numbers or medical records on the Internet doesn't require much computer expertise. Instead, such information is accessible to anyone who knows where to look.

Eric Johnson, a professor at Dartmouth College's Tuck School of Business, has found files containing names, Social Security, and health insurance numbers belonging to thousands of individuals exposed by so-called peer-to-peer software.

The software, such as LimeWire, which allows computers to connect directly to one another, is most often used to trade music and video files, but is capable of transmitting any data, including workplace documents and spreadsheets.

By entering basic search terms like hospital names into the software, Mr. Johnson said he turned up a 1,718-page document containing insurance details and diagnoses leaked by a medical-testing lab. He said he also found spreadsheets from a hospital system that contained contact information and Social Security numbers for more than 20,000 patients.

"There's no hacking or anything like that going on," he said. "We were just searching."[27]

| **EXHIBIT 4.2** | How to Cover Your Tracks Online |
|---|---|

**Simple Steps**

Major browsers including Microsoft Corp.'s Internet Explorer, Mozilla Foundation's Firefox, Google Inc.'s Chrome, and Apple Inc.'s Safari have privacy features. To have the highest privacy option, upgrade to the latest version of the browser you use.

**Check and Delete Cookies:** All popular browsers let users view and delete cookies installed on their computer. Methods vary by browser.

For instance, on Internet Explorer 8 (the most widely used browser), go to the "Tools" menu, pull down to "Internet Options," and under the "General" tab there are options for deleting some or all cookies.

**Adjust Browser Settings:** Once you've deleted cookies, you can limit the installation of new ones. Major browsers let you accept some cookies and block others. To maintain logins and settings for sites you visit regularly, but limit tracking, block "third-party" cookies. Safari automatically does this; other browsers may be set manually.

No major browsers let you track or block beacons (a beacon is a file that keeps track of your navigation through a website or a series of websites), without installing extra software known as "plug-ins."

**Turn on "Private" Browsing:** All major browsers offer a "private browsing" mode to limit cookies. Chrome calls it "Incognito," Internet Explorer calls it "InPrivate Browsing." But this option is available only in the latest version, IE8.

Private browsing doesn't block cookies. It deletes cookies each time you close the browser or turn off private browsing, effectively hiding your history.

**Monitor "Flash Cookies":** Another kind of cookie uses Adobe Systems Inc.'s popular Flash program to save information on your computer. Flash is the most common way to show video online. As with regular cookies, Flash cookies can be useful for remembering preferences, such as volume settings for videos. But marketers also can use Flash cookies to track what you do online.

To identify the Flash cookies on your computer and adjust your settings, you need to go to an Adobe website: *www.macromedia. com/support/documentation/en/flashplayer/help/settings_manager.html.* You can delete Flash cookies stored on your computer and specify whether you want to accept future third-party Flash cookies.

**Advanced Steps**

**Install Privacy "Plug-ins":** Small programs called "add-ons" or "plug-ins" can help maintain privacy. Some let you monitor trackers that can't be seen through the browser; others allow you to delete cookies on a regular schedule.

Not all browsers can use all plug-ins. And some plug-ins can be tricky to set up. With those caveats, some plug-ins may be worth a look:

**Better Privacy:** This plug-in offers control over Flash cookies. It doesn't block them, but lets you set rules for deleting them—a distinction that can be helpful if you frequent sites that require you to use third-party Flash cookies to see their content. Better Privacy (available only for Firefox) is at https://addons.mozilla.org/en-US/firefox/addon/betterprivacy/.

**Ghostery:** Available at ghostery.com, it helps control beacons. It alerts you when there's a beacon on a page you're viewing, tells you who placed it, and details the company's privacy policy. With Internet Explorer or Firefox, you can then block the beacon from capturing information on your computer.

*Source:* Jennifer Valentino DeVries, "How to Avoid the Prying Eyes," *The Wall Street Journal* (July 31–August 1, 2010), p. W3.

Mr. Johnson said he contacts the organizations, but even if they remove the peer-to-peer software from employee computers, copies of the shared files may still be available online.

In many cases, known cyber criminals download files containing sensitive personal information, said Rick Wallace, a researcher at Tiversa Inc., a security company that looks for leaked files on behalf of corporate clients. Tiversa found more than 13 million leaked files that contained information about its customers in one 12-month period.

Cyber criminals often sell the credit card numbers and other personal information they find in hacker chat rooms that aren't secret but can only be found by people in the know—although anyone who types "fullz" and "cvv2" into Google's search engine can see a sampling.

Often, data come from breaches where hackers have bypassed weak security systems, said Steven Peisner, president of Sellitsafe Inc., which helps merchants avoid processing fraudulent purchases. He estimates he sees about 15,000 or so stolen accounts being published each month in these dark corners of the Internet.[28]

**Governmental Actions** Three key laws (one a state law) have been passed to protect consumers from identity theft. These are:

### Federal Laws

**Gramm-Leach-Bliley Act (Financial Services Modernization Act):** aimed at financial companies. Requires those corporations to tell their customers how they use their personal information and to have policies that prevent fraudulent access to it. Partial compliance has been required since 2001.

**Health Insurance Portability and Accountability Act:** aimed at the healthcare industry. Limits disclosure of individuals' medical information and imposes penalties on organizations that violate privacy rules. Compliance has been required for large companies since 2003.

**The Fair Credit Reporting Act (FCRA):** enforced by the Federal Trade Commission, promotes accuracy in consumer reports, and is meant to ensure the privacy of the information in them.

**The Children's Online Privacy Protection Act (COPPA):** aims to give parents control over what information is collected from their children online and how such information may be used.

*The rule applies to:*

- Operators of commercial websites and online services directed to children under 13 that collect personal information from them.
- Operators of general audience sites that knowingly collect personal information from children under 13.
- Operators of general audience sites that have a separate children's area and that collect personal information from children under 13.

*The rule requires operators to:*

- Post a privacy policy on the homepage of the website and link to the privacy policy on every page where personal information is collected.
- Provide notice about the site's information collection practices to parents and obtain verifiable parental consent before collecting personal information from children.
- Give parents a choice as to whether their child's personal information will be disclosed to third parties.
- Provide parents access to their child's personal information and the opportunity to delete the child's personal information and opt out of future collection or use of the information.
- Not condition a child's participation in a game, contest, or other activity on the child's disclosing more personal information than is reasonably necessary to participate in that activity.
- Maintain the confidentiality, security and, integrity of personal information collected from children.

### State Laws

**California's Notice of Security Breach Law:** if any company or agency that has collected the personal information of a California resident discovers that nonencrypted information has been taken by an unauthorized person, the company or agency must tell the resident. Compliance has been required since 2003. (Some 30 other states are considering similar laws.)

Meineke uses geographic information systems to map its stores and competitors in relation to its customer base. Go to http://www.meineke.com to find out how it positions its website based on customer information.

# Geographic Information Systems

**geographic information system (GIS)**

Computer-based system that uses secondary and/or primary data to generate maps that visually display various types of data geographically.

**A geographic information system (GIS)** provides both a means of maintaining geographic databases and a tool capable of complex spatial analysis to provide information for a big data database.. Spatial analysis is the analysis of phenomena distributed in space and having physical dimensions (the location of, proximity to, or orientation of objects, such as stores, with respect to one another). A geographic database can store and provide access to corporate data, such as customer locations, facilities, logistic routes, and competitors. As a spatial analysis tool, this corporate data can be immersed with secondary demographic data and digitized maps to analyze and maximize the effects of locations. Utilities, oil companies, large retailers, and government agencies have long used these systems. Today, the technology accounts for several billion dollars a year in hardware, software, and consulting sales. There are three reasons for this boom. The cost of a GIS has fallen dramatically, the ease of use for business-related analysis has improved, and GIS data can now be transmitted over the Internet fairly easily. GIS is now one of the hottest business information tools. Companies as diverse as Chase Manhattan, Domino's Pizza, Ace Hardware, Gold's Gym, and Subaru America have embraced mapping as an easier and more powerful way to manage geographic data than mind-numbing printouts, spreadsheets, and charts. GIS offers researchers, managers, and clients an intuitive way to organize data and to see relationships and patterns.[29]

GIS analysts and geographers talk about lines, points, and polygons (areas), while marketing researchers talk about roads, stores, and sales territories. But lines, points, and polygons are how business data are represented within a geographic database. Applications using lines include finding the quickest truck routes for long-haul freight companies and the shortest routes for local delivery trucks. UPS calculates daily delivery routes, based on "estimated travel times, in-home time, truck capacity, optimal stop sequence."GPS (global positioning system) receivers in the vehicles can communicate with a GIS to receive real-time weather and road conditions to the drivers. Applications involving points focus on finding the best potential sites for retail bank branches and devising the best strategy for a network of miniwarehouses. Applications involving areas range from finding the best markets for hardware sales to identifying the best location for a new Taco Bell. A GIS can also answer detailed marketing questions. If a marketing researcher for Target wants to know how many of the company's high-performance stores have trading areas that overlap by at least 50 percent with trading areas for Walmart, a GIS analyst can run a spatial query on a geographic database to address the question.

Aftermarket auto repair is a highly competitive $90 billion-a-year business in which dealerships have improved their services and market share. To stay ahead of the competition, Meineke Discount Muffler Corporation has turned to GIS. Meineke's 900 franchisees continuously send detailed customer and service records to Meineke headquarters in Charlotte, North Carolina. Records include customer's name and home address; vehicle make, model, and year; work performed; and payment method. They also explain how the customer learned about Meineke. These data are integrated with demographics, average commute times, market area incomes, and the like, within a geographic database. Meineke can then map its stores, competitors, and other retail outlets in relation to its customer base. GIS analysis is used to compute site selection, market share analysis, and inventory management.

Using TargetPro GIS software from MapInfo Corporation, Meineke analysts have developed GIS models (geographic formulas), allowing them to specify an actual or proposed retail location and then create an easy to understand report. Meineke can customize trade areas as it sees fit. If marketing research shows that some customers will not cross a river or a state boundary to get to the nearest outlet but will drive two miles farther to another Meineke franchise in a different zip code, the company can use TargetPro to create a map that reflects those shopping patterns. Meineke uses GIS to determine optimal inventory levels by analyzing demographics, commute times, and historical sales figures, which can point to short- and long-term potential business.

"We can place a store on the map, draw a radius around it, then ask the system how many vehicles are in the area," said Paul Baratta, director of real estate and international development for Meineke. "There might be 75,000 cars in a given neighborhood, but another layer of data might show that 65,000 of those are Lexus brands. How many people are going to put mufflers on a car that they're trading in every two years? [GIS] looks at the information in a different way."[30]

MapInfo is now combining GIS and predictive data analysis software to predict not only which markets offer the best potential for expansion—down to specific intersections—but also how each new store will affect revenue across the chain, generating color-coded maps of the best locales. For example, in the fast-food business, clustering with similar merchants is often beneficial because diners typically will drive only five minutes for quick food and tend to go where they have myriad options. But as Arby's learned, specific products can affect behavior. MapInfo discovered that diners drove as much as 20 percent farther for an Arby's roast beef sandwich than for the chain's chicken offering. The reason? Shoppers could get chicken elsewhere but considered roast beef a "destination" product.[31]

# Decision Support Systems

A **decision support system (DSS)** is designed to support the needs and styles of individual decision makers. In theory, a DSS represents something close to the ultimate in data management. We say "in theory" because, for the most part, the ideal has not been realized in practice. However, there have been some notable exceptions with firms using big data analytics. Characteristics of a true DSS are as follows:

- *Interactive.* The manager gives simple instructions and sees results generated on the spot. The process is under the manager's direct control; no computer programmer is needed, and there is no need to wait for scheduled reports.

**decision support system (DSS)**
An interactive, personalized information management system, designed to be initiated and controlled by individual decision makers.

- *Flexible.* It can sort, regroup, total, average, and manipulate data in a variety of ways. It will shift gears as the user changes topics, matching information to the problem at hand. For example, the chief executive can see highly aggregated figures, while the marketing analyst can view detailed breakouts.

- *Discovery-oriented.* It helps managers probe for trends, isolate problems, and ask new questions.

- *Easy to learn and use.* Managers need not be particularly knowledgeable about computers. Novice users can elect a standard, or default, method of using the system, bypassing optional features to work with the basic system immediately. The opportunity to gradually learn about the system's possibilities minimizes the frustration that frequently accompanies use of new computer software.

Managers use a DSS to conduct sales analyses, forecast sales, evaluate advertising, analyze product lines, and keep tabs on market trends and competitors' actions. A DSS not only allows managers to ask "what if" questions but also enables them to view any given slice of the data.

Here's a hypothetical example of using a DSS provided by a manager of new products:

*To evaluate sales of a recently introduced new product, we can "call up" sales by the week, then by the month, breaking them out at [the vice president's] option by, say, customer segments. As he works at his terminal, his inquiries could go in several directions, depending on the decision at hand. If his train of thought raises questions about monthly sales last quarter compared to forecasts, he wants his decision support system to follow along and give him answers immediately.*

*He might see that his new product's sales were significantly below forecast. Forecasts too optimistic? He compares other products' sales to his forecasts and finds that the targets were very accurate. Something wrong with the product? Maybe his sales department is getting insufficient leads, or is not putting leads to good use. Thinking a minute about how to examine that question, he checks ratios of leads converted to sales, product by product. The results disturb him. Only 5 percent of the new product's leads generate orders compared to the company's 12 percent all-product average. Why? He guesses that the sales force is not supporting the new product vigorously enough. Quantitative information from the DSS perhaps could provide more evidence to back that suspicion. But already having enough quantitative knowledge to satisfy himself, the VP acts on his intuition and experience and decides to have a chat with his sales manager.*

# SUMMARY

Secondary data are previously gathered information that might be relevant to the problem at hand. They can come from sources internal to the organization or external to it. Primary data are survey, observation, or experiment data collected to solve the particular problem under investigation.

Using secondary data has several advantages. Secondary data may (1) help to clarify or redefine the problem during the exploratory research process, (2) actually provide a solution to the problem, (3) provide primary data research method alternatives, (4) alert the marketing researcher to potential problems and difficulties, and (5) provide necessary background data, and build credibility for the research report. The disadvantages of using secondary data include lack of availability, lack of relevance, inaccuracy, and insufficient data.

A database is a collection of related data. A traditional type of internal marketing database is founded on customer information. For example, a customer database may have demographic and perhaps psychographic information about existing customers and purchase data such as when the goods and services were bought, the types of merchandise procured, the dollar amount of sales, and any promotional information associated with sales. A database can be created from recorded conversations, social media posts, YouTube videos, GPS tracking data, in-store tracking cameras, credit card transactions, and the list goes on. An internal database also may contain competitive intelligence, such as new products offered by competitors and changes in competitors' service policies and prices.

Data mining has dramatically increased users' ability to get insightful information out of databases. It can be used to acquire new customers, retain existing customers, abandon accounts that are not cost-effective, and engage in market-based analyses.

Big data analytics enables managers to achieve broader and deeper insights into their customers, markets, the competitive environment, and business trends. Big data can find patterns in data that would otherwise go unnoticed. Big data analytics tells managers what is out there. The big breakthrough in understanding big data came when data scientists developed algorithms to analyze unstructured data, such as a YouTube video. A key element in understanding big data output is data visualization.

The proliferation of databases on and off the Internet and behavioral targeting have raised consumer and government concerns over privacy. Several laws have been passed to protect our privacy. These include the Gramm-Leach-Bliley Act, the Health Insurance Portability and Accountability Act, the Fair Credit Reporting Act, the Children's Online Privacy Act, and California's Notice of Security Breach Law.

Geographic information systems, which consist of a demographic database, digitized maps, and software, enable users to add primary data from a current study (or secondary corporate data) to the mix. The result is computer-generated maps that can reveal a variety of strategic findings to marketing managers; for example, a map may indicate an optimal location for a new retail store.

Decision support systems are designed from the individual decision maker's perspective. DSS systems are interactive, flexible, discovery-oriented, and easy to learn; they can offer many benefits to small and large firms alike.

## KEY TERMS & DEFINITIONS

secondary data **73**
primary data **73**
internal database **77**

neural network **77**
data mining **77**
behavioral targeting **78**

Data visualization **81**
geographic information system (GIS) **86**
decision support system (DSS) **87**

## QUESTIONS FOR REVIEW & CRITICAL THINKING

1. Why should companies consider creating a big data database? Name some types of information that might be found in this database and the sources of this information.

2. Why has big data analytics become so popular with firms such as United Airlines, American Express, and Ford Motor Company?

3. It has been said that big data analytics turns the scientific method on its head. What does this mean?

4. Why are secondary data often preferred to primary data?

5. What pitfalls might a researcher encounter in using secondary data?

6. Why has behavioral targeting become so popular with marketers? Why is it controversial?

7. In the absence of company problems, is there any need to conduct marketing research or develop a decision support system?

8. What is data visualization? Why is it important?

9. Divide the class into groups of four or five. Each team should go to the Internet and look up big data analytics. Each team should then report to the class on how a specific company is effectively using big data to improve their marketing efficiency.

*(Team Exercise)*

## WORKING THE NET

1. Go to *http://acxiom.com* and describe to the class what products it offers.

2. Go to www.Ayasdi.com and explain what it does. Why are its services valuable to many firms?

3. Go to the National Opinion Research Center at *www.norc .org* and describe what new reports are available for researchers.

4. You are interested in home-building trends in the United States, as your company, Whirlpool, is a major supplier of kitchen appliances. Go to *http://www.nahb.com* and describe what types of information at this site might be of interest to Whirlpool.

5. Go to *http://www.claritas.com.* Describe types of secondary data available at this site.

6. Go to *www.marketresearch.com* and explain what types of reports are available.

7. Go to *www.comscore.com* and explain what it offers to its customers.

8. Go to *www.Nielsen.com* and read about BuzzMetrics. Explain how it works and why it is a valuable tool to some marketers.

# REAL-LIFE RESEARCH • 4.1

## The Interesting and Curious World of Nate Silver

The question on the table is whether big data—that is, the accumulation and analysis of massive quantities of information—will change our world, or whether it's just another overhyped technology with a too-good-to-be-true story line. Silver is arguably peerless at interpreting data in the domains of sports and politics. Early in his career, he created an analytical model for baseball stats known as PECOTA, which did an exceedingly good job of identifying the minor-league prospects most likely to perform well in the majors. More recently, his FiveThirtyEight.com blog famously analyzed polling and economic data to predict the results of the 2008 presidential election (calling 49 or 50 states correctly) and the 2012 election (going 50 for 50). He has since dabbled in predictions of Oscar winners, NCAA basketball champions, and the geographic distribution of support for gay marriage. For at least the past five years, his methods and models have been questioned, doubted, and ridiculed. But in response he has shown every doubter, with almost unerring consistency, that a super nerd with a big data set and a killer algorithm can be a winner.

So is big data going to change the world or not? "The revolutions we recognize in retrospect," Silver says, "aren't usually the ones we recognize in advance." He's right, as usual, but he's not precisely addressing the question. We live in a complex world that barely makes sense. Often, we expect too much of computers and not enough of ourselves. "People blame the data," he notes, "when they should be asking better questions."

Silver is quick to point out that the most familiar, and arguably most successful, applications of big data involve National Weather Service predictions and hurricane warnings, which rely on huge data sets and wizardly models and have become increasingly accurate and precise. But other familiar examples abound, too. The quants on Wall Street have been helping hedge funds interpret complex trading data for years. Watson, the IBM computer that won at *Jeopardy!* and is now being applied to medical treatment and financial planning, is a success with a certain kind of big data—"unstructured data" as IBM likes to call it, which describes information formatted as natural language rather than numerical figures. Palantir, a wilfully obscure company that crunches big data in the name of national security, is another. Above all are Amazon, Facebook, Google, and Twitter, which stand as the foremost practitioners at making informed conclusions from customer data.

It isn't lost on Silver that he arrives at his moment of fame just as his field is debating whether the newest statistical tools are truly transformative or whether the expectations for big data, already quite high, might always outpace the reality. The fact that large data sets have existed in one form or another for decades, if not centuries, doesn't mean that nothing new and significant has happened in the past year or two. If you ask a half dozen of the country's leading data scientists, including Silver, you can arrive at a rough consensus that things are indeed changing. Buy why? As Silver sees it, "We've gotten a lot better in a few things, and a little better in a lot of things."

For starters, far more data are available to us today, thanks in large part to the information, records, and measurements generated by call phones, sensors, and web traffic. We have more computer-processing power, and at a lower cost. The interplay between different kinds of databases is more robust, helping to reveal patterns—about consumers, politics, sports, disease, markets, media—that were harder to discern before. And the ability to get specific data in real time and course-correct quite quickly is growing, too.

Big data is not just about business and profits. Apart from its efforts to track infectious diseases such as the flu, Google has used its vast trove of data to create a state-of-the-art language-translation program. IBM has applied its data-crunching abilities to identify previously undetectable health risks in premature babies. General Electric is creating new jet engines with sensors that can collect and transmit mind-boggling amounts of information about performance and thereby help flag potential problems. In the meantime, a host of companies with less familiar names are mining similar ore. Osito, a Silicon Valley startup, has an app that gathers data about the location and daily patterns of its users to provide them with helpful information throughout the day. (If the roads are clogged, Osito might tell you to leave early for your next appointment.) Or there's Kaggle, a company that identifies "data challenges" from corporations and not-for-profits and puts tens of thousands of data scientists into competition with one another to solve them. Recently, in response to a challenge posed by Cornell University and an oceanographic big data company called Marineexplore, Kaggle asked its users to come up with an algorithm for improving buoy systems to prevent ships from colliding with endangered whale species. (The prize was $10,000.) Another competition asked users to

create an algorithm that analyzes patient health records to predict how many days they will spend in the hospital in the next year. (The prize was $3 million.)[32]

## Questions

1. Will big data analytics put marketing researchers out of business? Why?
2. Go to Nate Silver's blog, www.fivethirtyeight.com and tell the class what topics he is currently discussing.
3. The case discusses several current nonbusiness uses of big data. Can you think of other nonbusiness problems that big data analytics might solve?
4. What factors have led to the big data era?

## CHAPTER 5

# Qualitative Research

### LEARNING OBJECTIVES

1. Define qualitative research and understand its popularity.

2. Learn about focus groups, how to conduct them, and their advantages and disadvantages.

3. Compare other forms of qualitative research with focus groups.

4. Appreciate the future of qualitative research.

What is qualitative research, and what are the advantages and disadvantages? Why are focus groups so popular, and what are the trends in focus group research? What other qualitative tools are available to marketing researchers? These are the areas that will be covered in Chapter 5.

## Nature of Qualitative Research

**qualitative research**
Research whose findings are not subject to quantification or quantitative analysis.

**quantitative research**
Research that uses mathematical analysis.

**Qualitative research** is a term used loosely to refer to research whose findings are not subject to quantification or quantitative analysis. A quantitative study may determine that a heavy user of a particular brand of tequila is 21 to 35 years of age and has an annual income of $40,000 to $60,000. While **quantitative research** might be used to find statistically significant differences between heavy and light users, qualitative research could be used to examine the attitudes, feelings, and motivations of the heavy user. Advertising agencies planning a campaign for tequila might employ qualitative techniques to learn how heavy users express themselves and what language they use—essentially, how to communicate with them.

The qualitative approach was derived from the work of the mid-eighteenth-century historian Giambattista Vico. Vico wrote that only people can understand people, and that they do so through a faculty called *intuitive understanding*. In sociology and other social sciences, the concept of *Verstehen*, or the intuitive experiment, and the use of empathy have been associated with major discoveries (and disputes).

# Qualitative Research versus Quantitative Research

Exhibit 5.1 compares qualitative and quantitative research on several levels. Perhaps most significant to managers is the fact that qualitative research typically is characterized by small samples—a trait that has been a focal point for criticism of all qualitative techniques. In essence, many managers are reluctant to base important strategy decisions on small-sample research because it relies so greatly on the subjectivity and interpretation of the researcher. They strongly prefer a large sample, with results analyzed on a computer and summarized into tables. These managers feel comfortable with marketing research based on large samples and high levels of statistical significance because the data are generated in a rigorous and scientific manner.

# Popularity of Qualitative Research

Companies are now spending over $5 billion annually on qualitative research.[1] Why does the popularity of qualitative research continue to grow? First, qualitative research is usually much cheaper than quantitative research. Second, there is no better way to understand the in-depth motivations and feelings of consumers. When, in a popular form of qualitative research, product managers unobtrusively observe from behind a one-way mirror, they obtain firsthand experiences with flesh-and-blood consumers. Instead of plodding through a computer printout or consultant's report that requires them to digest reams of numbers, the product manager and other marketing personnel observe consumers' reactions to concepts and hear consumers discuss their own and their competitors' products at length, in their own language. Sitting behind a one-way mirror can be a humbling experience for a new product-development manager when the consumer begins to tear apart product concepts that were months in development in the sterile laboratory environment.

A third reason for the popularity of qualitative research is that it can improve the efficiency of quantitative research. Reckitt Benckiser PLC, the maker of Woolite and Lysol, knew women were not happy with how glasses were cleaned in a dishwasher. Focus groups learned that, over time, glasses washed in a dishwasher tended to become cloudy and stained. The company decided to embark on a major quantitative study to determine the extent of the perceived "staining" problem among households with dishwashers. The quantitative

| EXHIBIT 5.1 | Qualitative versus Quantitative Research | |
|---|---|---|
| | **Qualitative Research** | **Quantitative Research** |
| Types of questions | Probing | Limited probing |
| Sample size | Small | Large |
| Amount of information from each respondent | Substantial | Varies |
| Requirements for administration | Interviewer with special skills | Interviewer with fewer special skills or no interviewer |
| Type of analysis | Subjective, interpretive | Statistical, summation |
| Hardware | Sound recorders, projection devices, video recorders, pictures, discussion guides | Questionnaires, computers, printouts, mobile devices |
| Degree of replicability | Low | High |
| Researcher training | Psychology, sociology, social psychology, consumer behavior, marketing, marketing research | Statistical, decision models, decision support systems, computer programming, marketing, marketing research |
| Type of research | Exploratory | Descriptive or causal |

study verified that consumers were indeed unhappy with how their glasses looked after numerous rounds in the dishwasher. They also were willing to pay a reasonable price to find a solution. Reckitt Benckiser introduced Finish Glass Protector, a dishwasher detergent that protects glassware from mineral corrosion. Thus qualitative research led to a well-conceived quantitative study that verified demand for the new product.

It is becoming more common for marketing researchers to combine qualitative and quantitative research into a single study or a series of studies. The Finish glass example showed how qualitative research can be used prior to quantitative research; in other research designs, the two types of research are conducted in the reverse order. For instance, the patterns displayed in quantitative research can be enriched with the addition of qualitative information on the reasons and motivations of consumers. One major insurance company conducted a quantitative study in which respondents were asked to rank the importance of 50 service characteristics. Later, focus groups were conducted in which participants were asked to define and expound on the top 10 characteristics. Most of these characteristics dealt with client–insurance agent interactions. From these focus groups the researchers found that "agent responds quickly" may mean either a virtually instantaneous response or a response within a reasonable time; that is, it means "as soon as is humanly possible for emergencies" and "about 24 hours for routine matters." The researchers noted that had they not conducted focus groups after the quantitative study, they could only have theorized about what "responds quickly" means to customers.

In the final analysis, all marketing research is undertaken to increase the effectiveness of decision making. Qualitative research blends with quantitative measures to provide a more thorough understanding of consumer demand. Qualitative techniques involve open-ended questioning and probing. The resulting data are rich, human, subtle, and often very revealing.

## Limitations of Qualitative Research

Qualitative research can and does produce helpful and useful information—yet it is held in disdain by some researchers. One drawback relates to the fact that marketing successes and failures many times are based on small differences in attitudes or opinions about a marketing mix, and qualitative research does not distinguish those small differences as well as large-scale quantitative research does. However, qualitative research is sometimes able to detect problems that escape notice in a quantitative study. For example, a major manufacturer of household cleaners conducted a large quantitative study in an effort to learn why its bathroom cleanser had lackluster sales when, in fact, its chemical compound was more effective than those used by leading competitors. The quantitative study provided no clear-cut answer. The frustrated product manager then turned to qualitative research, which quickly found that the muted pastel colors on the package did not connote "cleansing strength" to the shopper. In light of this finding and the finding that a number of people were using old toothbrushes to clean between their bathroom tiles, the package was redesigned with brighter, bolder colors and with a brush built into the top.

A second limitation of qualitative studies is that they are not necessarily representative of the population of interest to the researcher. One would be hard-pressed to say that a group of 10 college students was representative of all college students, of college students at a particular university, of business majors at that university, or even of marketing majors! Small sample size and free-flowing discussion can lead qualitative research projects down many paths. Because the subjects of qualitative research are free to talk about what interests them, a dominant individual in a group discussion can lead the group into areas of only tangential interest to the researcher. It takes a highly skilled researcher to get the discussion back on track without stifling the group's interest, enthusiasm, and willingness to speak out.

# Focus Groups

Focus groups had their beginnings in group therapy used by psychiatrists. Today, a **focus group** consists of 8 to 12 participants who are led by a moderator in an in-depth discussion on one particular topic or concept. The goal of focus group research is to learn and understand what people have to say and why. The emphasis is on getting people to talk at length and in detail about the subject at hand. The intent is to find out how they feel about a product, concept, idea, or organization; how it fits into their lives; and their emotional involvement with it.

Focus groups are much more than merely question-and-answer interviews. A distinction is made between *group dynamics* and *group interviewing*. The interaction associated with **group dynamics** is essential to the success of focus group research; this interaction is the reason for conducting research with a group rather than with individuals. One idea behind focus groups is that a response from one person will become a stimulus for another person, thereby generating an interplay of responses that will yield more information than if the same number of people had contributed independently.

The idea for group dynamics research in marketing came from the field of social psychology, where studies indicated that, unknown to themselves, people of all walks of life and in all occupations would talk more about a topic and do so in greater depth if they were encouraged to act spontaneously instead of reacting to questions. Normally, in group dynamics, direct questions are avoided. In their place are indirect inquiries that stimulate free and spontaneous discussions. The result is a much richer base of information, of a kind impossible to obtain by direct questioning.

**focus group**
Group of 8 to 12 participants who are led by a moderator in an in-depth discussion on one particular topic or concept.

**group dynamics**
Interaction among people in a group.

## Popularity of Focus Groups

How popular are focus groups? Most marketing research firms, advertising agencies, and consumer goods manufacturers use them. Today, most marketing research expenditures for qualitative research are spent on focus groups. The majority of focus research projects in the United States take place in over 750 focus facilities and are directed by over 1,000 moderators. The most common formats of qualitative research are focus groups and individual depth interviews (IDIs). Today, both forms of qualitatives are being conducted online and on mobile devices, as we will discuss in Chapter 7.

Focus group research is a globally accepted form of marketing research. It is estimated that over 650,000 focus groups are conducted worldwide each year. Approximately 250,000 focus group sessions take place in the United States annually.[2]

Focus groups tend to be used more extensively by consumer goods companies than by industrial goods organizations, as forming industrial groups poses a host of problems not found in consumer research. For example, it is usually quite easy to assemble a group of 12 homemakers; however, putting together a group of 10 engineers, sales managers, or financial analysts is far more costly and time-consuming.

Lewis Stone, former manager of Colgate-Palmolive's Research and Development Division, says the following about focus groups:

*If it weren't for focus groups, Colgate-Palmolive Co. might never know that some women squeeze their bottles of dishwashing soap, others squeeeeeze them, and still others squeeeeeeeeeze out the desired amount. Then there are the ones who use the soap "neat." That is, they put the product directly on a sponge or washcloth and wash the dishes under running water until the suds run out. Then they apply more detergent.*

*Stone was explaining how body language, exhibited during focus groups, provides insights into a product that are not apparent from reading questionnaires on habits and practices.*

*Focus groups represent a most efficient way of learning how one's products are actually used in the home. By drawing out the panelists to describe in detail how they do certain tasks . . . you can learn a great deal about possible need-gaps that could be filled by new or improved products, and also how a new product might be received.*[3]

Thus, an "experiencing" approach represents an opportunity to learn from a flesh-and-blood consumer. Reality in the kitchen or supermarket differs drastically from that in most corporate offices. Focus groups allow the researcher to experience the emotional framework in which the product is being used. In a sense, the researcher can go into a person's life and relive with him or her all the satisfactions, dissatisfactions, rewards, and frustrations experienced when the product is taken home.

Robert L. Wehling, senior vice president of global marketing and consumer knowledge at the Procter & Gamble Company, issued the following mandate to researchers: "Know the individual consumer's heart and you will own the future! Get to know this changing consumer personally. Not as an average but as a person."[4]

## Conducting Focus Groups

On the following pages, we will consider the process of conducting focus groups, illustrated in Exhibit 5.2. We devote considerable space to this topic because there is much potential for researcher error in conducting focus groups.

**focus group facility**
Research facility consisting of a conference room or living room setting and a separate observation room with a one-way mirror or live audiovisual feed.

**Setting** Focus groups are usually held in a **focus group facility**. The setting is often a conference room, with a large, one-way mirror built into one wall. Microphones are placed in an unobtrusive location (usually the ceiling) to record the discussion. Behind the mirror is the viewing room, which holds chairs and note-taking benches or tables for the clients. The viewing room also houses the recording or videotaping equipment. The photo in Exhibit 5.3 illustrates a focus group in progress.

Some research firms offer a living-room setting as an alternative to the conference room. It is presumed that the informality of a living room (a typical homelike setting) will make the participants more at ease. Another variation is to televise the proceedings to a remote viewing room rather than use a one-way mirror. This approach offers clients the advantage of being able to move around and speak in a normal tone of voice without being heard through the wall.

**Exhibit 5.2**

**Steps in Conducting a Focus Group**

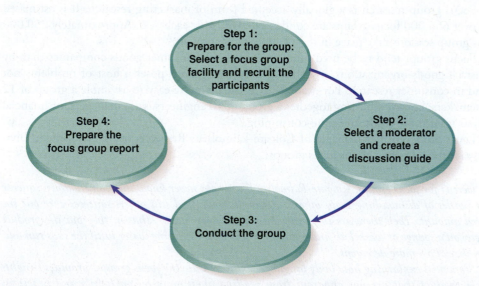

Step 1:
Prepare for the group:
Select a focus group facility and recruit the participants

Step 2:
Select a moderator and create a discussion guide

Step 3:
Conduct the group

Step 4:
Prepare the focus group report

Exhibit 5.3

**A Focus Group in Progress**

*Decision Analyst; Jerry W. Thomas, moderator*

**Participants** Participants for focus groups are recruited from a variety of sources. Two traditional procedures are mall-intercept interviewing and random telephone screening. (Both methods are described in detail in Chapter 6.) Researchers normally establish criteria for the group participants. For example, if Quaker Oats is researching a new cereal, it might request as participants mothers who have children between 7 and 12 years old and who have served cold cereal, perhaps of a specific brand, in the past three weeks.

Other focus group recruiters go to where the target market is to find qualified respondents. This type of recruiting means going to nursery schools to find moms with kids, health clubs to find people with active lifestyles, the home improvement center to find do-it-yourselfers, supermarkets to find primary food shoppers, and community centers to find senior citizens.

Usually, researchers strive to avoid repeat, or "professional," respondents in focus groups. Professional respondents are viewed by many researchers as actors or, at the very least, less than candid participants. Questions also may be raised regarding the motives of the person who would continually come to group sessions. Is she or he lonely? Does she or he really need the respondent fee that badly? It is highly unlikely that professional respondents are representative of many, if any, target markets. Unfortunately, field services find it much easier to use repeat respondents than to recruit a new group of individuals each time. Most field services keep a database of individuals, along with their demographics and purchase patterns, who are willing to participate in focus groups. Sample screening questions to identify repeat respondents are shown in Exhibit 5.4.

Although there is no ideal number of participants, a typical group will contain 8 participants. If the group contains more than 8 people, group members will have little time to express their opinions. Rarely will a group last more than two hours; an hour and a half is more common. The first 10 minutes is spent on introductions and an explanation of procedures. This leaves about 80 useful minutes in the session, and up to 25 percent of that time may be taken by the moderator. With 10 people in the group, an average of only six minutes per individual is left for actual discussion. If the topic is quite interesting or of a technical nature, fewer than 8 respondents may be needed. The type of group will also affect the number recruited.

Why do people agree to participate in focus groups? Research shows that the number one reason is money.[5] Other motivations, in rank order, are (2) the topic was interesting,

Sometimes it is important to talk with people who have participated in previous research because they have experience talking about certain topics. At other times, it is important to talk with people who have never participated in an opinion study. Often we are looking for a mix of different experiences. What type of opinion studies, if any, have you ever participated in? (DO NOT READ LIST.)

|  | ALL MENTIONS |
|---|---|
| One-on-one in-person depth interview | 1 |
| Group interview with two or more participants | 2 |
| Mock jury or trial | 3 |
| Product placement test with a follow-up interview | 4 |
| Mail interview | 5 |
| Internet survey | 6 |
| Phone survey | 7 |
| Other (SPECIFY) | 8 |
| None | 9 |

**1A.** When was the last time you participated in a

_____ Group interview with two or more participants

_____ (LIST A NOTHER TYPE OF RESEARCH YOU MIGHT CONSIDER INAPPROPRIATE.)

**IF WITHIN THE LAST SIX MONTHS, THANK AND TERMINATE.**

**1B.** What were the topics of all of the group interviews in which you have participated?

_____

_____

**IF ONE OF THE TOPICS LISTED BELOW IS MENTIONED, THANK AND TERMINATE.**

(   ) MP3 Players

(   )

**1C.** Are you currently scheduled to participate in any type of market research study?

CIRCLE

Yes   1 → (THANK AND TERMINATE)

No    2    → (CONTINUE)

*Source:* Merril Shugoll and Nancy Kolkebeck, "You Get What You Ask For," *Quirk's Marketing Research Review* (December 1999), pp. 61–65. Reprinted by permission.

(3) it was a convenient time, (4) focus groups are fun, (5) respondent knew a lot about the product, (6) curiosity, and (7) focus groups offer an opportunity to express opinions. The study also found that participants who came only for the money were less committed to research and tended to fulfill their roles in a more perfunctory way.

**Moderator** Having qualified respondents and a good focus group moderator are the keys to a successful focus group. A **focus group moderator** needs two sets of skills. First, the moderator must be able to conduct a group properly. Second, he or she must have good business skills in order to effectively interact with the client. Key guidelines for conducting a focus group include the following:

■ Show respect for respondents.
■ Own the room—clear demonstration of invisible leadership.
■ Speak clearly and loudly.
■ Set expectations and gives all the industry disclosures.
■ Ask short questions and actively listens.

**focus group moderator**
Person hired by the client to lead the focus group; this person should have a background in psychology or sociology or, at least, marketing.

- Move things along without rushing, curtailing tangents.
- Avoid "serial interviewing" (interviewing the first person, then the second, third and so forth).
- Show creativity and adaptability in the moment.
- Change activities about every 20 minutes.
- Move around—do not stay glued to the chair.
- Maintain an open body position.
- Move from general to specific questions within a topic area.
- Create a safe opportunity for diverse opinions.
- Work along a logical path showing planning of questions.
- Handle both thought leaders and shy respondents with ease.
- Miss no opportunity to probe for additional information.[6]

This list is all about creating rapport. *Rapport* means to be in a close or sympathetic relationship. A moderator develops a free and easy sense of discourse about anything with respondents. These strangers meet and are helped to a common ground through the ease of rapport. In a comfortable, nonthreatening, lively place, they can talk about anything at all—about sausage, insurance, tires, baked goods, magazines. In research the moderator is the bridge builder, and rapport is the bridge between people's everyday lives and the client's business interest.

**Discussion Guide** Regardless of how well trained and personable the moderator is, a successful focus group requires a well-planned discussion guide. A **discussion guide** is a written outline of the topics to be covered during the session. Usually the moderator generates the guide based on research objectives and client information needs. It serves as a checklist to ensure that all salient topics are covered and in the proper sequence. For example, an outline might begin with attitudes and feelings toward eating out, then move to fast foods, and conclude with a discussion of the food and decor of a particular chain. It is important to get the research director and other client observers, such as a brand manager, to agree that the topics listed in the discussion guide are the most important ones to be covered. It is not uncommon for a team approach to be used in generating a discussion guide.

The guide tends to lead the discussion through three stages. In the first stage, rapport is established, the rules of group interactions are explained, and objectives are given. In the second stage, the moderator attempts to provoke intensive discussion. The final stage is used for summarizing significant conclusions and testing the limits of belief and commitment.

Exhibit 5.5 shows an actual discussion guide for diet breads by a Decision Analyst moderator. The groups were held in several cities around the country.

**Focus Group Length** Many managers today prefer shorter (around an hour) focus groups. Yet the average group today is still about 90 minutes. Although shorter groups may be the trend, there is much to be said for longer focus groups. By a longer group, we mean two hours or longer. A long group helps managers get more things done in a single session, and it also allows the respondents to get more involved, participate in more time-consuming tasks, and interact more extensively.

The issue of group length is not an isolated one; rather, it is intertwined with a second key factor: the number of questions in the discussion guide. One of the biggest problems with focus groups today, in our opinion, is the tendency to prepare discussion guides that pose far too many questions, which virtually precludes any depth of coverage or any significant group interactions. Managers want to get their money's worth, so it makes sense for them to ask every possible question. The "focus group" turns into a group interrogation or survey but without the controls and statistical power of scientific surveys.

**discussion guide**
Written outline of topics to be covered during a focus group discussion.

**I. Introduction**
A. Recording/observers
B. Casual, relaxed, informal
C. No right or wrong answers
D. Be honest. Tell the truth
E. Discussion rules
- Talk one at a time.
- Don't dominate the discussion.
- Talk in any order.
- Listen to others.

**II. General Attitudes toward Bread**
A. Eating more or less bread now, compared to two years ago? Explore reasons.
B. Advantages of bread, compared to other foods?
C. Disadvantages of bread, compared to other foods?
D. Words/mental images associated with great tasting bread?
E. Foods bread goes with best? Why?

**III. Usage/Purchase of Bread**
A. When and where is bread consumed most often?
B. How does bread usage vary by household member? Why?
C. Types of bread used most frequently?
D. Likes/dislikes of each type of bread?
E. Brands preferred? Why these brands? Vary by family member?

**IV. Bread Consumption When Dieting**
A. Changes in bread consumption related to dieting? Why?
B. Types of bread eaten when dieting, if any reasons?
C. Role of bread in dieting?

**V. Attitudes toward Diet Breads**
A. Awareness of diet breads/brands?
B. Experiences with diet breads/brands?
C. Satisfaction with each brand? Why like or not like? Brand perceptions?
D. Important factors/product attributes associated with preferred brands?

**VI. The Perfect Diet Bread**
A. Product characteristics?
- Taste
- Texture
- Color
- Crust
B. Nutritional benefits?
C. Packaging preferences?

**VII. Show and Discuss Advertising Concepts**
A. Overall reactions to each concept?
B. Likes/dislikes for each concept?
C. Main idea for each concept?
D. Believability?

**VIII. Reactions to Diet Bread Samples**
A. Overall reactions to each bread?
B. Reactions to taste?
C. Reactions to texture and mouth feel?
D. Reaction to slice shape and thickness?
E. Reaction to loaf shape and size?
F. Reaction to color?
G. Reaction to feel in hand?

*www.decisionanalyst.com*

| EXHIBIT 5.6 | Response Time per Question per Respondent | | |
|---|---|---|---|
| | Focus Group Length | | |
| Number of Questions | 75 min. | 90 min. | 120 min. |
| 15 | :30 | :36 | :48 |
| 20 | :23 | :27 | :36 |
| 25 | :18 | :22 | :29 |
| 30 | :15 | :18 | :24 |
| 35 | :13 | :15 | :21 |
| 40 | :11 | :14 | :18 |

**Note:** The analysis assumes a group comprising 10 respondents.

In order to think more explicitly and logically about the number of questions to ask, managers should examine the interactions between the length of the focus group and the size of the discussion guide. As illustrated in Exhibit 5.6, more questions and less time combine to create a research environment that elicits responses that are mere survey-like sound bites. Also, moderators who have to plow through 40 questions in 90 minutes are likely to feel rushed, unable to probe interesting responses, and inclined to be abrupt with long-winded or slow individuals. As we move up and to the right in the table, these pressures and constraints diminish. With fewer questions and more time, respondents can elaborate their answers, moderators can probe more effectively, and the pace becomes more relaxed, natural, and humanistic.

**The Client's Role** The client, of course, selects the supplier and sometimes the moderator as well. The client typically selects the markets where the groups will be held and specifies the characteristics of the group respondents. Sometimes the client will hand a finished discussion guide to the moderator, and, in other circumstances, the moderator and the client work together to create a final guide.

The client should go over not only the discussion guide with the moderator but the product or service being discussed as well. For example, a moderator was doing a group on new earpieces, and the client had not shown the moderator how they worked. The moderator was not told that, if you wore glasses, the frames would interfere with putting on the earpieces. When the moderator attempted to demonstrate the earpieces, they would not fit in his ears. Obviously, this created a negative impression among group participants.

**Focus Group Report** Typically, after the final group in a series is completed, there will be a moderator debriefing, sometimes called **instant analysis**. This tradition has both pros and cons. Arguments for instant analysis include the idea that it serves as a forum for combining the knowledge of the marketing specialists who viewed the group with that of the moderator. It gives the client an opportunity to hear and react to the moderator's initial perceptions, and it harnesses the heightened awareness and excitement of the moment to generate new ideas and implications in a brainstorming environment.

The shortcomings include the possibility of biasing future analysis on the part of the moderator with this "hip-shooting commentary," conducted without the benefit of time to reflect on what transpired. Instant analysis will be influenced by recency, selective recall, and other factors associated with limited memory capabilities; it does not allow the moderator to hear all that was said in a less than highly involved and anxious state. There is nothing wrong with a moderator debriefing, as long as the moderator explicitly reserves the right to change her or his opinion after reviewing the tapes.

**instant analysis**
Moderator debriefing, offering a forum for brainstorming by the moderator and client observers.

Today, a formal focus group report is typically a PowerPoint presentation. The written report is nothing more than a copy of the PowerPoint slides.

## Focus Group Trends

**Online and Mobile Groups**  A very popular trend in focus group research is conducting the groups online and over mobile devices. This topic is discussed in detail in Chapter 7. Even when focus groups are conducted in traditional focus group facilities, there is a growing tendency for clients to watch the sessions online. The advantage to the clients is that they can avoid the time and expense of traveling to a distant city. Over 40 percent of all focus groups conducted in traditional facilities involve video transmissions.

**Focus Group Panels**  Typically, a screening question for participating in a focus group is: "Have you participated in a focus group within the last six months?" If the answer is yes, they are disqualified. The notion is that clients don't want professional respondents but want "fresh participants." A different model now being used by some firms is a focus group panel. The idea is to establish a group of about 8 to 12 qualified respondents who agree to participate in a series of interviews on a given product, service, or topic. Once recruited, the same group of respondents would then agree to meet once a month for approximately a six-month period.

One advantage of the panel is that a variety of topics can be addressed and then revisited if necessary. For example, assume that a consumer packaged-goods company is seeking to launch a new line of salad dressings. Its qualitative panel starts out first with the seeds of new ideas for a line of salad dressings. The next session refines those ideas to the point where packaging, graphics, and flavor concepts are developed. And before the subsequent session, advertising stimuli boards can be created with positioning statements and potential names generated. This, ultimately, can save clients time and money.

The key advantages of focus group panels are as follows:

- *Consumer panels can be significantly less expensive versus recruiting the same number of separate groups over the same time period.* Because the same people are used each month, there are no additional recruiting costs—only simple reminder calls are required. This more streamlined design can result in a 25 to 30 percent reduction in cost to clients.

- *A summary is sufficient.* Because quick feedback is critical, and the entire process is so fluid, the company doesn't require a full report. A topline summary works well and can be delivered just a few days after the panel convenes.

- *Companies appreciate the discipline that consumer panels can impose in the process.* They know that each month they need to meet with marketing, packaging, and R&D to determine what issues still exist. Meanwhile, the various internal departments welcome the concept of having a voice in the panel content each month.[7]

**Using the Rotated Opposed View (ROV)**  The ROV methodology uses a two-hour session to reveal and diagnose differing viewpoints and find the criteria on which to build a bridge between them. Candidates form two groups: high- and low-intensity users of the product with the same socioeconomic profile. Both the usage frequency and perception of the product are intentionally polarized to ensure that the participants have opposing viewpoints.

The session begins with the low-intensity users outlining their reasons for not using the product, why they do not identify with the brand, and highlighting any competitor products that are preferred.

Meanwhile, the high-intensity users watch and listen from behind mirrored glass in the viewing room, along with their own moderator. With some targeted probing from the moderator, the session "viewers" are then invited to express their opposing opinions on paper, ready for the next session.

After 45 minutes, the roles are reversed and the high-intensity users become the "viewed" and the session repeats as before. In this second session, however, the high-intensity users discuss their affinity for the brand, their reasons for purchase, and why they select this particular product over the other available. They also openly discuss areas where they agree and disagree with the low-intensity users.

At the end of the split-sessions, the two user groups are brought together and the differences between their usage of the product and attitudes are explored to find commonalities. In a "pitch and object" session, the high-intensity users pitch the product to the low-intensity users, who then explain their objections before the group collectively identifies common ground. This process continues until some consensus is found.

The outcome is the generation of unique insights into the mind, attitudes, and reasoning of the consumers, and it also proves a valuable experience for the participants. Both the separate and collective components of the session can deliver invaluable information for the development of marketing strategies.[8]

The ROV technique creates quality, free-flowing participant engagement. It is also a good methodology for developing new insights. It helps product managers understand the views of those who don't like the product or service.

**Adding Marketing Professionals as Respondents** When the product or service concept warrants it, marketing professionals (e.g., advertising executives, new product development managers, and marketing officers) are mixed in with typical consumers. These professionals are referred to as *prosumers*. British Airways was looking to challenge American Airlines and Virgin Atlantic for dominance of business-class related travel on the airlines' transatlantic routes. The qualitative research being conducted with consumers was not getting the research team the kind of insights it was seeking. The team decided it would need to shake things up if it was going to achieve any breakthroughs that would help British Airways differentiate its business-class travel experience.

The research team took an unusual step. It set up focus groups that involved the usual target—regular business travelers. But the team added product-development and marketing professionals who frequently traveled from New York to London—precisely the kind of professional who would typically be intentionally screened out.

After a joint focus group that included both consumers and these "prosumers," the prosumers group joined British Airways' leadership team for a gloves-off creative session that incorporated what was learned in the focus group, but also took into account the prosumers' understanding of the types of informed, innovative thinking the research team was seeking.

One of those prosumers, a research and development director at Unilever, shared the confidence that when she travels, she likes a seat that fully reclines but does not like to be sleeping in full-recline mode next to strangers or business associates. And she presumed that many women travelers would probably agree with her. From that observation, an idea was born. Now, seats that cradle passengers and pullout privacy panels are designed into almost all international business-travel sections.

"Her professional experience—understanding demographics, knowing that we were looking for breakthrough ideas—and her ability to express her ideas in a useful way to the research team made her a key part of the process," says Christopher Miller, founder of Lancaster, Pennsylvania-based Innovation Focus, Inc. "That creative tension, where respondents speak both personally and as a professional, has become the foundation of this process.[9]

The marketing team at WD-40 Company got precisely that—breakthroughs—when it used the process to help with its product development efforts. The team's project involved WD-40 Company professionals, two prosumers and a small group of consumers. In the creative session following the focus groups, it was a prosumer who wondered whether the lubricant could be put in a handheld pen format. That outside-the-box idea is now known as the No-Mess Pen. And another prosumer who needed to cover a very large piece of equipment with WD-40 tossed out the question of whether the product could be put into a bug spray-style fogger. The answer was yes. That business-to-business product is now called the Big Blast Can.[10]

## Benefits and Drawbacks of Focus Groups

The benefits and drawbacks of qualitative research in general also apply to focus groups. But focus groups have some unique pros and cons that deserve mention.

**Advantages of Focus Groups** The interactions among respondents can stimulate new ideas and thoughts that might not arise during one-on-one interviews. And group pressure can help challenge respondents to keep their thinking realistic. Energetic interactions among respondents also make it likely that observation of a group will provide firsthand consumer information to client observers in a shorter amount of time and in a more interesting way than will individual interviews.

Another advantage focus groups offer is the opportunity to observe customers or prospects from behind a one-way mirror, video feed, or online. In fact, there is growing use of focus groups to expose a broader range of employees to customer comments and views. "We have found that the only way to get people to really understand what customers want is to let them see customers, but there are few people who actually come in contact with customers," says Bonnie Keith, corporate market research manager at Hewlett-Packard. "Right now, we are getting people from our manufacturing and engineering operations to attend and observe focus groups."

Another advantage of focus groups is that they can be executed more quickly than many other research techniques. In addition, findings from groups tend to be easier to understand and to have a compelling immediacy and excitement. "I can get up and show a client all the charts and graphs in the world, but it has nowhere near the impact of showing 8 or 10 customers sitting around a table and saying that the company's service isn't good," says Jean-Anne Mutter, director of marketing research at Ketchum Advertising.

**Disadvantages of Focus Groups** Unfortunately, some of the strengths of focus groups also can become disadvantages. For example, the immediacy and apparent understandability of focus group findings can cause managers to be misled instead of informed. Mutter says, "Even though you're only getting a very small slice, a focus group gives you a sense that you really understand the situation." She adds that focus groups can strongly appeal to "people's desire for quick, simple answers to problems, and I see a decreasing willingness to go with complexity and to put forth the effort needed to really think through the complex data that will be yielded by a quantitative study."

Gary Willets, director of marketing research for NCR Corporation, echoes this sentiment. He notes, "What can happen is that you will do the focus group, and you will find out all of these details, and someone will say, 'OK, we've found out all that we need to know.' The problem is that what is said in a focus group may not be all that typical. What you really want to do is do a qualitative study on the front end and follow it up with a quantitative study." Focus groups, like qualitative research in general, are essentially inductive in approach. The research is data-driven, with findings and conclusions being drawn directly from the information provided. In contrast, quantitative studies generally follow a deductive approach, in which formulated ideas and hypotheses are tested with data collected specifically for that purpose.

Other disadvantages relate to the focus group process. For example, focus group recruiting may be a problem if the type of person recruited responds differently to the

# PRACTICING MARKETING RESEARCH

## Recruiting Must Be Done Right

Bad, inept recruiting is my pet peeve, probably because it's more difficult to work around than mediocre moderating or reporting. As a client, we go to great lengths to identify the types and mix of folks we want in our group, whether recruited from a list we provide or not. And we try to do our homework on our end to understand the implications of every criterion we request. We always ask for quotes based on several more recruits than we need with the understanding that we want our minimum of good respondents to show—we don't mind paying for extras to be sure we have the minimum. And we always allow three-plus weeks for recruiting—so if there is a problem, we should know with still enough time to make adjustments and adheres to our schedule.

We challenge our vendors to tell us up front if they think the honorarium is too low for what we want. We beg them to let us know immediately of any recruiting problems so we have time to assess and redirect most appropriately.

Despite paying the recruiting subcontractor and the vendors to check the quotas, we always recheck the quotas since we've learned not to depend entirely on the vendor or recruiters to do so properly. Sloppy or inadequate recruiting isn't just about ignoring instructions; it can have a significant impact on the usefulness of the groups. For instance, if we ask for the person who takes the child to the doctor, that's who we need in the groups. The reactions of a father of young children to new pediatric office visit requirements might be very different than a mom's reaction, and if mom takes the children to the doctor, what she thinks is more important than what dad thinks.[11]

## Questions

1. Why is recruiting so important for focus groups and other forms of qualitative research?
2. Do you think that paying respondents will bias their responses? Why or why not?

issues being discussed than do other target segments. White middle-class individuals, for example, participate in qualitative research in numbers disproportionate to their presence in the marketplace.

Getting the right respondents is critical to having a good focus group. Linda Lynch, marketing research director at Blue Cross Blue Shield, discusses her frustration with poor respondent recruiting in the Practicing Marketing Research box.

The greatest potential for distortion is during the group interview itself. As a participant in the social interaction, the moderator must take care not to behave in ways that prejudice responses. The moderator's style may contribute to bias. For example, an aggressive, confronting style may lead respondents to say whatever they think the moderator wants them to say, to avoid attack. Or "playing dumb" may create the perception that the moderator is insincere or phony and cause respondents to withdraw.

Respondents also can be a problem. Some individuals are simply introverted and do not like to speak out in group settings. Other people may attempt to dominate the discussion. These are people who know it all—or think they do—and answer every question first, without giving others a chance to speak. A dominating participant may succeed in swaying other group members. If a moderator is abrupt with a respondent, it can send the wrong message to other group members—"You'd better be cautious, or I will do the same thing to you." Fortunately, a good moderator can stifle a dominant group member and not the rest of the group. Simple techniques used by moderators include avoiding eye contact with a dominant person; reminding the group that "we want to give everyone a chance to talk"; saying "Let's have someone else go first"; or, if someone else is speaking and the dominant person interrupts, looking at the initial speaker and saying, "Sorry, I cannot hear you."

# Other Qualitative Methodologies

Most of this chapter has been devoted to focus groups because of their pervasive use in marketing research. However, several other qualitative techniques are also used, albeit on a much more limited basis.

## Individual Depth Interviews

**individual depth interviews**
One-on-one interviews that probe and elicit detailed answers to questions, often using nondirective techniques to uncover hidden motivations.

**Individual depth interviews (IDI)** are relatively unstructured one-on-one interviews. The interviewer is thoroughly trained in the skill of probing and eliciting detailed answers to each question. Sometimes psychologists are used as depth interviewers: They may employ nondirective clinical techniques to uncover hidden motivations. IDIs are the second most popular form of qualitative research.

The direction of a depth interview is guided by the responses of the interviewee. As the interview unfolds, the interviewer thoroughly probes each answer and uses the replies as a basis for further questioning. For example, a depth interview might begin with a discussion of snack foods. The interviewer might follow each answer with "Can you tell me more?" "Would you elaborate on that?" or "Is that all?" The interviewer might then move into the pros and cons of various ingredients, such as corn, wheat, and potatoes. The next phase could delve into the sociability of the snack food. Are Fritos, for example, more commonly eaten alone or in a crowd? Are Wheat Thins usually reserved for parties? When should you serve Ritz crackers?

The advantages of depth interviews over focus groups are as follows:

1. Group pressure is eliminated, so the respondent reveals more honest feelings, not necessarily those considered most acceptable among peers.

2. The personal one-on-one situation gives the respondent the feeling of being the focus of attention—that his or her thoughts and feelings are important and truly wanted.

3. The respondent attains a heightened state of awareness because he or she has constant interaction with the interviewer and there are no group members to hide behind.

4. The longer time devoted to individual respondents encourages the revelation of new information.

5. Respondents can be probed at length to reveal the feelings and motivations that underlie statements.

6. Without the restrictions of cultivating a group process, new directions of questioning can be improvised more easily. Individual interviews allow greater flexibility to explore casual remarks and tangential issues, which may provide critical insights into the main issue.

7. The closeness of the one-on-one relationship allows the interviewer to become more sensitive to nonverbal feedback.

8. A singular viewpoint can be obtained from a respondent without influence from others.

9. The interview can be conducted anywhere, in places other than a focus group facility.

10. Depth interviews may be the only viable technique for situations in which a group approach would require that competitors be placed in the same room. For example, it might be very difficult to do a focus group on systems for preventing bad checks with managers from competing department stores or restaurants.

11. When the research objective is to understand individual decision processes or individual responses to marketing stimuli (e.g., Web sites), IDIs are typically the choice. IDIs allow detailed exploration of a single respondent's reactions without contamination.

They are particularly valuable when researchers want individual reactions placed in the context of the individual's experiences.

12. If the topic is highly sensitive (e.g., serious illnesses), use of IDIs is indicated. Subjects that are highly personal (e.g., bankruptcy) or very detailed (e.g., divorce decrees) are best probed deeply with IDIs.

13. A great deal of what we communicate is nonverbal, such as facial and body expressions, and voice tone and inflection. Even a simple phrase like, "That's Great," can have multiple meanings. Is the speaker being sincere or using sarcasm?

The disadvantages of depth interviews relative to focus groups are as follows:

1. The total cost of depth interviews can be more expensive than focus groups, but not on a cost per respondent minute (see the next section).

2. Depth interviews do not generally get the same degree of client involvement as focus groups. It is difficult to convince most client personnel to sit through multiple hours of depth interviews so as to benefit firsthand from the information.

3. Because depth interviews are physically exhausting for the moderator, they do not cover as much ground in one day as do focus groups. Most moderators will not do more than four or five depth interviews in a day, whereas they can involve 20 people in a day in two focus groups.

4. Focus groups are called for when consensus or debate is required to explore disparate views. Groups generate opportunities for point-counterpoint discussion and resolutions.

5. Focus groups give the moderator an ability to leverage the dynamics of the group to obtain reactions that might not be generated in a one-on-one session.[12]

Rheingold USA, a San Francisco research firm, analyzed several Super Bowl commercials using IDIs. Its objective was to access the underlying messages of the ads. Questions to elicit these insights include: What went through your mind at every step of the commercial? Which questions do the scenes and their elements trigger? How does the commercial answer these questions? Which questions remain unanswered, and how do you, the viewer, feel about that? What are your internal answers to these questions to make sense out of the commercial? How does this connect to the advertised product? How does it make you feel about the product? Which elements are crucial to attract you or repel you from the product?

The first ad was for the VW Passat. You can watch it at:

*www.youtube.com/watch?v=0rDU8K63hbo.*

*Plot: A little kid, dressed up as Darth Vader, plays in a nice upper-middle-class family home and tries to work Darth Vader magic on the washing machine, the dog, and his sister's doll. But his willpower does not make anything move. When his father gets home with the VW Passat, the kid tries to work his magic on the car as well. And, surprisingly, the car starts and the lights turn on. As a viewer, we see the parents behind the kitchen window, while it becomes obvious that the father started the car remotely with his key.*

Respondents feel touched by the atmosphere conveyed in the ad and talk about the sweetness of this family's life: "He recognizes the struggles of his boy and wants to help him." "This is a close family, they give their child independence and are supportive of his creativity." "Isn't that great? His kid means the world to him." "This is monumental to the kid. He is in heaven and will talk about this his whole life!"

On the surface, respondents see an ideal for their own life achievements and accordingly view the Passat to be the perfect car for the happy, average family. However, when digging deeper into respondents' minds, the often-unconscious darker or more Darth Vader-y side behind the scenes reveals itself: "Darth Vader is so powerful and stands above everything." "It is kind of scary to see that little kid running around like that." Some even drew the connection to a dark side of VW: "This company was started by Adolf Hitler ..."

Respondents first state that the fun of this commercial lies within the sweetness of the little boy and the beauty of the family life. However, what we seem to truly enjoy is the powerful, almost almighty position we get into. The viewer becomes a confidant of the father, secretly enjoying playing a trick on the little boy: "It is almost as if I had pushed the button. I can totally see myself doing this to our son."

According to the researcher, what we often do not want to admit is that driving is strongly connected to the feeling of being almighty: We try to show off, escape from what we want to leave behind, explore something new, and use the car as a tool to provide us with extended powers we would not have by ourselves.

The researchers claim that the Passat had a secret message: "I am not only the average, middle-of-the-road, unedgy, maybe even sometimes boring car; I can also help you feel almighty and powerful. I literally provide the key to it!"

The researchers believe that the IDIs showed with this commercial that Volkswagen was able to touch the viewers' secret ambitions of almightiness and power when driving a car without threatening them, and that it offered them a "sweet and safe middle-class cover" that would not overtly confront them.[13]

Good depth interviewers, whether psychologists or not, are hard to find and expensive. A second factor that determines the success of depth research is proper interpretation. The unstructured nature of the interview and the clinical nature of the analysis increase the complexity of the task. Small sample sizes, the difficulty of making comparisons, the subjective nature of the researcher's interpretations, and high costs have all contributed to the lack of popularity of depth interviewing. Classic applications of depth interviews include the following:

- Communication checks (e.g., review of print, radio, or TV advertisements or other written materials)
- Sensory evaluations (e.g., reactions to varied formulations for deodorants or hand lotions, sniff tests for new perfumes, or taste tests for a new frosting)
- Exploratory research (e.g., defining baseline understanding or a product, service, or idea)
- New product development, prototype stage
- Packaging or usage research (e.g., when clients want to "mirror" personal experience and obtain key language descriptors)

A variation of the depth interview is called customer care research (CCR). The basic idea is to use depth interviewing to understand the dynamics of the purchase process. The following seven questions are the basis for CCR:

1. What started you on the road to making this purchase?
2. Why did you make this purchase now?
3. What was the hardest part of this process? Was there any point where you got stuck?
4. When and how did you decide the price was acceptable?
5. Is there someone else with whom I should talk to get more of the story behind this purchase?
6. If you've purchased this product before, how does the story of your last purchase differ from this one?
7. At what point did you decide you trusted this organization and this person to work with in your best interests?[20]

**Cost of Focus Groups versus IDI** In a standard, eight-person, 90-minute focus group, there are nine people (eight participants plus moderator) sharing the floor. On average, therefore, each respondent is allotted 10 minutes of talk time across those 90 minutes (90 minutes divided by nine people).

The cost of a focus group of this type is about $13,000. That number includes everything: recruiter, moderator, participant stipend, food, facility, report write-up, and the cost of getting a few observers to the event. Divide 80 minutes of participant talk time (the moderator doesn't count) into the $13,000 expense, and your cost per respondent minute in this case is $162.50 ($13,000/80).

If, however, a typical in-depth interview runs 30 minutes and costs between $600 and $800 (including recruiting, interviewing, participant stipend, and reporting), the cost per respondent minute is in the range of $20 to $27. The big difference results from the amount of time the respondent spends talking, which is typically about 20 to 25 of those 30 minutes in an in-depth phone interview.

Thus, when considering the cost per respondent minute, in-depth interviews can provide much greater value. Of course, the quality of both the focus groups and the IDI determines the real value of the research.

**Using Hermeneutics** Some IDI researchers use a technique called hermeneutic research to achieve their goals. **Hermeneutic research** focuses on interpretation as a basis of understanding the consumer. Interpretation comes about through "conversations" between the researcher and the participant. In hermeneutic research, the researcher answers the participant's questions and, as in the traditional method, the researcher only questions the respondent. There are no predetermined questions, but questions arise spontaneously as the conversation unfolds.

For example, a researcher and consumer in conversation about why that individual purchased a high-end home theater system may discuss the reasons for making the purchase, such as holding movie parties, enjoying a stay-at-home luxury, or immersing oneself in sporting events. The researcher may interpret "holding movie parties" as a reason for purchase to mean that without the system, the consumer would not hold the parties at all, and so the researcher will return to the consumer for additional information. Upon reviewing the data and talking more, the researcher and consumer determine that why the item was purchased and why it is used (which may or may not be the same) are not as telling as how the product makes its owner feel. In this case, the owner may feel confident as an entertainer, more social, powerful, wealthy, relaxed, or rejuvenated. Talking and probing more about the use of the home theater, the researcher uncovers both new data and new issues to address or consider moving forward.

Writing an IDI report, whether or not hermeneutics are used, is quite different from writing a quantitative report.

**hermeneutic research**
Research that focuses on interpretation through conversations.

**Using the Delphi Method** The **Delphi Method** is often used in new product development when firms are looking for creative new ideas to incorporate in products or services. The term *Delphi* has its roots in Greek history. The city of Delphi was a hub of activity, combining culture, religion, and perspective into one highly populated area of information. Delphi was also home to the Oracle of Pythia, a woman believed to offer great insight into the future. The Oracle was a great influence to visitors, who believed this knowledge of the future would help them succeed in life.

Typically, the Delphi Method relies on people who are experts in some area. It may be product development researchers, marketing managers, professional people (MDs, engineers, etc.), magazine editors, executives, priests, and so forth. Obviously, the type of experts used depends on the objectives of the Delphi session. If one is looking for more efficient ways to handle materials management in a warehouse, the experts may simply be the workers in the warehouse.

**Delphi Method**
Rounds of individual data collection from knowledgeable people. Results are summarized and returned to the "participants for further refinement.

The Delphi Method involves a number of rounds of data collection. In the classical Delphi procedure, the first round is unstructured, in order to allow individual experts relative freedom to identify and elaborate the pertinent issues from their point of view. These issues are then consolidated by the researcher(s) into a structured questionnaire.

This questionnaire is subsequently used to elicit the opinions and judgments of the panel of experts in a quantitative form. The responses are analyzed and statistically summarized and presented back to the panelists for further consideration. Respondents are then given the opportunity to alter prior opinions on the basis of feedback. The number of rounds varies from 2 to 10, but seldom goes beyond one or two iterations.

The key characteristics of Delphi are anonymity, iteration, feedback, and aggregation of group responses. The objective is to obtain the most reliable consensus of opinion via a series of intensive questionnaires, interspersed with opinion feedback.

The purpose of anonymity in a Delphi study is to exclude group interaction, which can cause a number of problems, such as group conflict and individual dominance. Delphi relies on a structured, indirect approach to group decision making; that is, participants don't meet, relying instead on statistical aggregation of individual predictions and ideas.

Controlled feedback, developed from the results of a round, is presented back to the panel of experts at the start of the next round. The form of the feedback varies depending on the topic. It may simply be an aggregation of ideas, or, if the group is estimating sales of a proposed new product, then quantitative estimates, for example, medians, may be given. Sometimes the Delphi Method creates scenarios—for example, how can we create a better customer relationship management (CRM) software that will enable us to take market share from the two market leaders? Scenarios can be used to answer two types of questions: (1) Precisely how might some hypothetical situation come about, step by step? And (2) what alternatives exist, for each actor, at each step, for preventing, diverting, or facilitating the process?

The iteration, controlled feedback, and aggregation of group responses aim to produce as many high-quality responses and opinions as possible on a given issue(s) from a panel of experts to enhance decision making. By feeding back responses from the panel to each member in the group, through a series of iterations, experts are able to adjust their estimates on the basis of others' comments.

## Projective Tests

**projective test**
Technique for tapping respondents' deepest feelings by having them project those feelings into an unstructured situation.

Projective techniques are sometimes incorporated into depth interviews. The origins of projective techniques lie in the field of clinical psychology. In essence, the objective of any **projective test** is to delve below surface responses to obtain true feelings, meanings, and motivations. The rationale behind projective tests comes from the knowledge that people are often reluctant or unable to reveal their deepest feelings. In some instances, they are unaware of those feelings because of psychological defense mechanisms.

Projective tests are techniques for penetrating a person's defense mechanisms to allow true feelings and attitudes to emerge. Generally, a respondent is presented with an unstructured and nebulous situation and asked to respond. Because the situation is ill-defined and has no true meaning, the respondent must impose her or his own frame of reference. In theory, the respondent "projects" personal feelings into the unstructured situation, bypassing defense mechanisms because the respondent is not referring directly to herself or himself. As the individual talks about something or someone else, her or his inner feelings are revealed.

Why is projection important? Consumers (or doctors, voters, managers, or whomever we are studying) may not tell us everything that influences them. Three obstacles stand in the way:

1. Respondents may be unconscious or unaware of a particular influence.
2. They may be aware of an influence, but feel it is too personal or socially undesirable to admit (e.g., prestige image or racial bias).

**3.** They may be aware that they perceive a product a particular way, but they may not bother to mention this because, in their view, it is not a logical, rational reason for buying or not buying the product. Some doctors, for example, are adamant that what they prescribe has nothing to do with the sound of a drug's name or the attractiveness of the manufacturer's logo, and is based solely on decision-making factors such as research findings, clinical experience, and patient compliance.[14]

Most projective tests are easy to administer and are tabulated like other open-ended questions. They are often used in conjunction with nonprojective open- and closed-ended questions. A projective test may gather "richer," and perhaps more revealing, data than do standard questioning techniques. Projective techniques are used often in image questionnaires and concept tests, and occasionally in advertising pretests. It is also common to apply several projective techniques during a depth interview.

The most common forms of projective techniques used in marketing research are word association tests, sentence and story completion tests, cartoon tests, photo sorts, consumer drawings, storytelling, and third-person techniques. Other techniques, such as psychodrama tests and the Thematic Apperception Test (TAT), have been popular in treating psychological disorders but of less help in marketing research.

**Word Association Tests**  Word association tests are among the most practical and effective projective tools for marketing researchers. An interviewer reads a word to a respondent and asks him or her to mention the first thing that comes to mind. Usually, the individual will respond with a synonym or an antonym. The words are read in quick succession to avoid allowing time for defense mechanisms to come into play. If the respondent fails to answer within three seconds, some emotional involvement with the word is assumed.

Word association tests are used to select brand names, advertising campaign themes, and slogans. For example, a cosmetic manufacturer might ask consumers to respond to the following words as potential names for a new perfume: infinity, encounter, flame, desire, precious, erotic. One of these words or a synonym suggested by respondents might then be selected as the brand name.

**word association test**
Projective test in which the interviewer says a word and the respondent must mention the first thing that comes to mind.

**Analogies**  Slightly different from word associations, analogies draw a comparison between two items in terms of their similarities. For example, a researcher investigating consumers' perceptions of Ford automobiles may ask: "I'm going to read you a list of stores, and then I'd like you to tell me which of these is most similar to Ford cars. If possible, try to give the first answer that comes to mind. The stores are: Neiman Marcus, Walmart, Macy's, JC Penney, Kmart, Nordstrom, Target, and Lord & Taylor." As a follow-up, the researcher would then ask: "What is it about [Store X] that is most similar to Ford cars? How are the qualities of Ford cars similar to this store?" This line of questioning induces the respondent to talk (indirectly) about his or her perceptions of Ford cars.

The use of analogies in this instance is not to determine which store(s) people associate with Ford cars but, rather, to get people to talk about their perceptions of Ford cars in ways they might otherwise be unable to do. Because perceptions of stores vary, some respondents may choose Store A, and some may choose Store B. The researcher should be less concerned with identifying the store(s) that respondents tend to select and more concerned with determining the reasons respondents give for the choices they make. Person A may select a different store from Person B, but this is of little significance if these two individuals share similar perceptions of the stores they chose, and hence of the Ford brand.[15]

**analogy**
Drawing a comparison between two items in terms of their similarities.

**Personification**  A technique similar to analogies, personification involves drawing a comparison between a product and a person. To continue with the example from above, the researcher might say, "Think about the Ford brand, and imagine it were a person. Who would this brand be? How would you describe this person? What personality characteristics would this person have? In what ways do you associate this person with the brand?"

**personification**
Drawing a comparison between a product and a person.

During this type of exercise, the researcher should encourage the participant to discuss such things as the person's values, beliefs, goals, lifestyle, appearance, age, occupation, socioeconomic status, hobbies, and interests. All of these can speak volumes about the respondent's attitudes toward the brand and can go significantly beyond the output of standard lines of questioning.

**sentence and story completion test**
Projective test in which respondents complete sentences or stories in their own words.

### Sentence and Story Completion Tests

**Sentence and story completion tests** can be used in conjunction with word association tests. The respondent is furnished with an incomplete story or group of sentences and asked to complete it. A few examples of incomplete sentences follow:

1. Best Buy is . . .
2. The people who shop at Best Buy are . . .
3. Best Buy should really . . .
4. I don't understand why Best Buy doesn't . . .

Here's an example of a story completion test:

*Sally Jones just moved to Chicago from Los Angeles, where she had been a salesperson for IBM. She is now a district manager for the Chicago area. Her neighbor Rhonda Smith has just come over to Sally's apartment to welcome her to Chicago. A discussion of where to shop ensues. Sally notes, "You know, I've heard some things about Best Buy. . . ." What is Rhonda's reply?*

As you can see, story completion tests provide a more structured and detailed scenario for the respondent. Again, the objective is for the interviewees to put themselves in the role of the imaginary person mentioned in the scenario.

Some researchers consider sentence and story completion tests to be the most useful and reliable of all the projective tests. Decision Analyst is now offering both online sentence completion and online word association research to its clients.

**cartoon test**
Projective test in which the respondent fills in the dialogue of one of two characters in a cartoon.

### Cartoon Tests

The typical **cartoon test** consists of two characters with balloons, similar to those seen in comic books; one balloon is filled with dialogue, and the other balloon is blank (see Exhibit 5.7). The respondent is asked to fill in the blank balloon.

### Exhibit 5.7

### Cartoon Test

Note that the cartoon figures in Exhibit 5.7 are left vague and without expression so that the respondent is not given clues regarding a suggested type of response. The ambiguity is designed to make it easier for the respondent to project his or her feelings into the cartoon situation.

Cartoon tests are extremely versatile and highly projective. They can be used to obtain differential attitudes toward two types of establishments and the congruity or lack of congruity between these establishments and a particular product. They can also be used to measure the strength of an attitude toward a particular product or brand, or to ascertain what function is being performed by a given attitude.

**Photo Sorts** With **photo sorts**, consumers express their feelings about brands by manipulating a specially developed photo deck depicting different types of people, from business executives to college students. Respondents connect the individuals in the photos with the brands they think they would use.

BBDO Worldwide, one of the country's largest advertising agencies, has developed a trademarked technique called Photosort. A Photosort conducted for General Electric found that consumers thought the brand attracted conservative, older, business types. To change that image, GE adopted the "Bring Good Things to Life" campaign. A Photosort for Visa found the credit card to have a wholesome, female, middle-of-the-road image in customers' minds. The "Everywhere You Want to Be" campaign was devised to interest more high-income men.

Another Photosort technique, entitled Pictured Aspirations Technique (PAT), was created by Grey Advertising, a large New York advertising agency. The technique attempts to uncover how a product fits into a consumer's aspirations. Consumers sort a deck of photos according to how well the pictures describe their aspirations. In research done for Playtex's 18-hour bra, this technique revealed that the product was out of sync with the aspirations of potential customers. The respondents chose a set of pictures that depicted "the me they wanted to be" as very energetic, slim, youthful, and vigorous. But the pictures they used to express their sense of the product were a little more old-fashioned, a little stouter, and less vital and energetic looking. Out went the "Good News for Full-Figured Gals" campaign, with Jane Russell as spokesperson, and in came the sexier, more fashionable concept of "Great Curves Deserve 18 Hours."

**Consumer Drawings** Researchers sometimes ask consumers to draw what they are feeling or how they perceive an object. **Consumer drawings** can unlock motivations or express perceptions. For example, the McCann-Erickson advertising agency wanted to find out why Raid roach spray outsold Combat insecticide disks in certain markets. In interviews, most users agreed that Combat is a better product because it kills roaches without any effort on the user's part. So the agency asked the heaviest users of roach spray—low-income women from the southern United States—to draw pictures of their prey (see Exhibit 5.8). The goal was to get at their underlying feelings about this dirty job.

All of the 100 women who participated in the agency's interviews portrayed roaches as men. "A lot of their feelings about the roach were very similar to the feelings that they had about the men in their lives," said Paula Drillman, executive vice president at McCann-Erickson. Many of the women were in common-law relationships. They said that the roach, like the man in their life, "only comes around when he wants food." The act of spraying roaches and seeing them die was satisfying to this frustrated, powerless group. Setting out Combat disks may have been less trouble, but it just didn't give them the same feeling. "These women wanted control," Drillman said. "They used the spray because it allowed them to participate in the kill."

**Storytelling** As the name implies, **storytelling** requires consumers to tell stories about their experiences. It is a search for subtle insights into consumer behavior.

**photo sort**
Projective technique in which a respondent sorts photos of different types of people, identifying those people who she or he feels would use the specified product or service.

**consumer drawings**
Projective technique in which respondents draw what they are feeling or how they perceive an object.

**storytelling**
Projective technique in which respondents are required to tell stories about their experiences, with a company or product, for example; also known as the *metaphor technique*.

"One night I just couldn't take the horror of these bugs sneaking around in the dark. They are always crawling when you can't see them. I had to do something. I thought wouldn't it be wonderful if when I switch on the light the roaches would shrink up and die like vampires to sunlight. So I did, but they just all scattered. But I was ready with my spray so it wasn't a total loss. I got quite a few . . . continued tomorrow night when nighttime falls."

"A man likes a free meal you cook for him; as long as there is food he will stay."

"I tiptoed quietly into the kitchen, perhaps he wasn't around. I stretched my arm up to turn on the light. I hoped I'd be alone when the light went on. Perhaps he is sitting on the table I thought. You think that's impossible? Nothing is impossible with that guy. He might not even be alone. He'll run when the light goes on I thought. But what's worse is for him to slip out of sight. No, it would be better to confront him before he takes control and 'invites a companion'."

**Exhibit 5.8**

**Consumer Drawings That Helped Identify Respondents' Need for Control**
*Source:* Courtesy of McCann- Erickson, New York.

Gerald Zaltman, a Harvard Business School professor, has created a metaphor laboratory to facilitate the storytelling process. (A *metaphor* is a description of one thing in terms that are usually used to describe another; it can be used to represent thoughts that are tacit, implicit, and unspoken.) Zaltman elicits metaphors from consumers by asking them to spend time over several weeks thinking about how they would visually represent their experiences with a company. To help them with the process, he asks them to cut out magazine pictures that somehow convey those experiences. Then, consumers come to his lab and spend several hours telling stories about all of the images they chose and the connections between the images and their experiences with the firm.

One metaphor study was conducted on pantyhose. "Women in focus groups have always said that they wear them because they have to, and they hate it," says Glenda Green, a marketing research manager at DuPont, which supplies the raw material for many pantyhose manufacturers. "We didn't think we had a completely accurate picture of their feelings, but we hadn't come up with a good way to test them."[16] DuPont turned to storytelling for better insights. Someone brought a picture of a spilled ice cream sundae, capturing the rage she feels when she spots a run in her hose. Another arrived with a picture of a beautiful woman with baskets of fruit. Other photos depicted a Mercedes and Queen Elizabeth. "As we kept probing into the emotions behind the choice of these photos, the women finally began admitting that hose made them feel sensual, sexy, and more attractive to men," says Green. "There's no way anyone would admit that in a focus group." Several stocking manufacturers used this information to alter their advertising and package design.

Another example of what storytelling can uncover is told in the following story:

*A fine-jewelry retail chain sought to overcome an industry downturn through innovation. First, it held eight focus groups in two markets, inviting women of prime jewelry-buying ages to discuss topics that included: preferences for different gems, material and styles; comparisons between the chain and its competitors; and reactions to store designs and salespeople. Disappointed by the lack of "Eureka!" moments in the 16 hours of groups, the chain then collected 100 purchase stories in two stores over two weekends.*

*The first surprise to management was that 70 percent of the stories were told by men, a demographic ignored when planning the focus groups. When they were asked, "What was going on in your life that led you to come here today?" one key element kept surfacing in their stories: the need to not only buy a jewelry gift but to present it as a romantic surprise. The romantic surprise was as important a part of what they needed as the jewelry itself, but jewelry stores were doing little to meet this need.*

*The men described their struggles to find a container for the purchase that would help accomplish their goal. They also battled to find the right setting for making the presentation. And they sweated profusely to find the right words to accompany it. In other words, the stores provided only one component of the four-piece product that was needed.*

*While men had never thought to directly ask jewelers for the other components, the struggles in their stores shouted out an innovation opportunity: Changing the company's product definition from "fine jewelry" to "surprise, romantic presentations of the right jewelry in the right package, in the right setting and with the right words" and repositioning store associates as resources to help men assemble all four components of the complete product.*

*Men weren't asking jewelry stores for this kind of help—not because they didn't need it, but because stores never signaled an ability to provide it. But two weekends of customer story-collecting not only uncovered the need but also fathered jewelry presentation ideas that the chain later used to deliver the full package.*[17]

**Third-Person Technique**   Perhaps the easiest projective technique to apply, other than word association, is the **third-person technique**. Rather than directly asking respondents what they think, researchers couch the question in terms of "your neighbor," "most people," or some other third party. Rather than asking a mother why she typically does not fix a nutritionally balanced breakfast for her children, a researcher might ask, "Why don't many people provide their families nutritionally balanced breakfasts?" The third-person technique is often used to avoid questions that might be embarrassing or evoke hostility if posed directly to a respondent.

**third-person technique**
Projective technique in which the interviewer learns about respondents' feelings by asking them to answer for a third party, such as "your neighbor" or "most people."

# Future of Qualitative Research

The rationale behind qualitative research tests is as follows:

1. The criteria employed and the evaluations made in most buying and usage decisions have emotional and subconscious content, which is an important determinant of buying and usage decisions.

2. Such content is adequately and accurately verbalized by the respondent only through *indirect* communicative techniques.

To the extent that these tenets remain true or even partially correct, the demand for qualitative applications in marketing research will continue to exist. But the problems of small sample sizes and subjective interpretation will continue to plague some forms of qualitative research. Inability to validate and replicate qualitative research will further deter its use.

On the positive side, the use of focus groups will grow. Focus group research can provide data and insights not available through any other techniques. Low cost and ease of application will lend even greater impetus to use online and mobile focus groups. Finally, the qualitative–quantitative split will begin to close as adaptations and innovations allow researchers to enjoy the advantages of both approaches simultaneously.

## SUMMARY

Qualitative research refers to research whose findings are not subject to quantification or quantitative analysis. It is often used to examine consumer attitudes, feelings, and motivations. Qualitative research, particularly the use of focus groups, continues to grow in popularity for three reasons. First, qualitative research is usually cheaper than quantitative studies. Second, it is an excellent means of understanding the in-depth motivations and feelings of consumers. Third, it can improve the efficiency of quantitative research.

Qualitative research is not without its disadvantages. Sometimes, qualitative research does not distinguish small differences in attitudes or opinions about a marketing mix as well as large-scale quantitative studies do. Also, respondents in qualitative studies are not necessarily representative of the population of interest to the researcher. And the quality of the research may be questionable, given the number of individuals who profess to be experts in the field, yet lack formal training.

Focus groups are the most popular type of qualitative research. A focus group typically consists of 8 to 12 paid participants who are led by a moderator in an in-depth discussion on a particular topic or concept. The goal of the focus group is to learn and understand what people have to say and why. The emphasis is on getting people to talk at length and in detail about the subject at hand. The interaction associated with group dynamics is essential to the success of focus group research. The idea is that a response from one person will become a stimulus for another person, thereby generating an interplay of responses that will yield more information than if the same number of people had contributed independently.

Most focus groups are held in a group facility, which is typically set up in a conference room, with a large one-way mirror built into one wall. Microphones are placed in unobtrusive locations to record the discussion. Behind the mirror is a viewing room. The moderator plays a critical role in the success or failure of the group and is aided in his or her efforts by a well-planned discussion guide.

A number of other qualitative research methodologies are used but on a much more infrequent basis. One such technique is depth interviews. Individual depth interviews are unstructured one-on-one interviews. The interviewer is thoroughly trained in the skill of probing and eliciting detailed answers to each question. He or she often uses nondirective clinical techniques to uncover hidden motivations. Other qualitative techniques are hermeneutics and the Delphi Method. The use of projective techniques represents another form of qualitative research. The objective of any projective test is to delve below the surface responses to obtain true feelings, meanings, or motivations. Some common forms of projective techniques are word association tests, analogies, personification sentence and story completion tests, cartoon tests, photo sorts, consumer drawings, storytelling, and third-person techniques.

## KEY TERMS

qualitative research 92

quantitative research 92

focus group 95

group dynamics 95

focus group facility 96

focus group moderator 98

discussion guide 99

instant analysis 101

individual depth interviews 106

hermeneutic research 109

Delphi Method 109

projective test 110

word association test 111

analogy 111

personification 111

sentence and story completion test 112

cartoon test 112

photo sort 113

consumer drawings 113

storytelling 113

third-person technique 115

# QUESTIONS FOR REVIEW & CRITICAL THINKING

1. What are the major differences between quantitative and qualitative research?

2. What are some of the possible disadvantages of using focus groups?

3. Create a story completion test for downloading music from the Internet.

4. What can the client do to get more out of focus groups?

5. What is the purpose of a projective test? What major factors should be considered in using a projective technique?

6. Divide the class into groups of four and eight. The groups of four will select a topic below (or one suggested by your instructor) and create a discussion guide. One of the four will then serve as the group moderator. One of the groups of eight will serve as participants in the focus group.

The groups should last at least 20 minutes and be observed by the remainder of the class. Suggested topics:

a. New video games

b. Buying a hybrid gasoline/electric car

c. Student experiences at the student union

d. The quality of existing frozen dinners and snacks and new items that would be desired by students

e. How students spend their entertainment dollars and what additional entertainment opportunities they would like to see offered

7. Take a consumer drawing test—draw a typical Pepsi drinker and a typical Coke drinker. What do the images suggest about your perceptions of Coke and Pepsi drinkers?

8. Use the metaphor technique to tell a story about going to the supermarket.

9. Create five sentence completion and story tests about your university.

# WORKING THE NET

Go to *http://www.insideheads.com*. Watch the video about online focus groups. Report your findings to the class.

Go to *http://www.grca.org*. Explain the goals and functions of the organization. What resources do they offer marketing researchers and qualitative research practitioners? What are the benefits of joining the organization?

# REAL-LIFE RESEARCH • 5.1

## McDonald's Listening Tour

According to the Centers for Disease Control and Prevention, more than one-third of U.S. adults and approximately 17 percent—or 12.5 million—children and adolescents are obese. It goes without saying that marketers are regularly the targets for consumer advocacy groups looking to take action against the obesity epidemic, and fast-food restaurants and other purveyors of fatty and sugary foods are often at the center of the obesity debate.

McDonald's formulated a corporate response by announcing a long-term plan geared toward offering improved nutrition choices, including adding produce and low-fat dairy options to Happy Meals, reducing sodium and added sugars across its menu, and increasing customers' access to nutrition information. The plan also includes a long-term qualitative research project, a nationwide "listening tour" featuring McDonald's leadership and key decision makers, including senior director of Nutrition Cindy Goody, McDonald's USA president Jan Fields, and CMO Neil Golden.

The listening tour was designed to gather input from local audiences on the company's nutritional messaging, sustainability, and overall brand promotion. McDonald's menu has changed over the years, and the goal of the tour was to take feedback from various audiences. This would help with menu adjustments and help to determine how the company can be more sustainable. The entire premise was based on a two-way dialogue.

McDonald's approached the sessions with guidelines that varied, depending on the audience. It was not simply a wide-open discussion on any topic that came to mind. Several tour stops were to speak with minority consumers; other stops included the BlogHer conference, a social networking conference for female bloggers. Other groups visited included the American Dietetic Association's Food & Nutrition Conference, a group of PTA members and educators in Washington, DC, and a group of students at Duke University.

McDonald's found out that most people felt the firm was on the right track. In other cases, the company found that it needed to do a better job telling McDonald's story. It was not getting credit for things that it was doing. For example, McDonald's has an iPhone app with nutritional information, but very few knew about it. Others didn't realize that McDonald's menu is completely customizable. If you don't want

pickles, then you don't have to have pickles. And if you want lettuce and tomato, all you have to do is ask.[18]

## Questions

1. Is the listening tour really qualitative research? Why or why not?

2. After the findings are presented to management, should quantitative research be done?

3. Couldn't McDonald's just have done focus groups instead?

4. Other than focus groups, what qualitative techniques might McDonald's have used?

© Alex/iStockphoto

## CHAPTER 6

# Traditional Survey Research

## LEARNING OBJECTIVES

1. Understand the reasons for the popularity of survey research.

2. Learn about the types of errors in survey research.

3. Distinguish the types of surveys.

4. Gain insight into the factors that determine the choice of particular survey methods.

Survey research is the use of a questionnaire to gather facts, opinions, and attitudes; it is the most popular way to gather primary data. What are the various types of survey research? As noted previously, not everyone is willing to participate in a survey. What kind of errors does that create? What are the other types of errors encountered in survey research? Why have Internet and mobile survey research become so popular, and what are their drawbacks? These questions are answered in this chapter.

# Popularity of Survey Research

Some 126 million Americans have been interviewed at some point in their lives. Each year, about 70 million people are interviewed in the United States, which is the equivalent of over 15 minutes per adult per year. Surveys have a high rate of usage in marketing research compared to other means of collecting primary data, for some very good reasons:

- *The need to know why.* In marketing research, there is a critical need to have some idea about why people do or do not do something. For example, why did they buy or not buy a particular brand? What did they like or dislike about it? Who or what influenced them? We do not mean to imply that surveys can prove causation, only that they can be used to develop some idea of the causal forces at work.

- *The need to know how.* At the same time, the marketing researcher often finds it necessary to understand the process consumers go through before taking some action. How did they make the decision? What time period passed? What did they examine or consider? When and where was the decision made? What do they plan to do next?

■ *The need to know who.* The marketing researcher also needs to know who the person is and who played an influencing role in the decision making process, from a demographic or lifestyle perspective.

# Types of Errors in Survey Research

When assessing the quality of information obtained from survey research, the manager must determine the accuracy of those results. This requires careful consideration of the research methodology employed in relation to the various types of errors that might result (see Exhibit 6.1).

**random error, or random sampling error**
Error that results from chance variation.

## Sampling Error

Two major types of errors may be encountered in connection with the sampling process. They are random error and systematic error, sometimes referred to as bias.

Surveys often attempt to obtain information from a representative cross section of a target population. The goal is to make inferences about the total population based on the responses given by respondents sampled. Even when all aspects of the sample are investigated properly, the results are still subject to a certain amount of **random error** (or **random**

**Exhibit 6.1**

**Types of Survey Error**

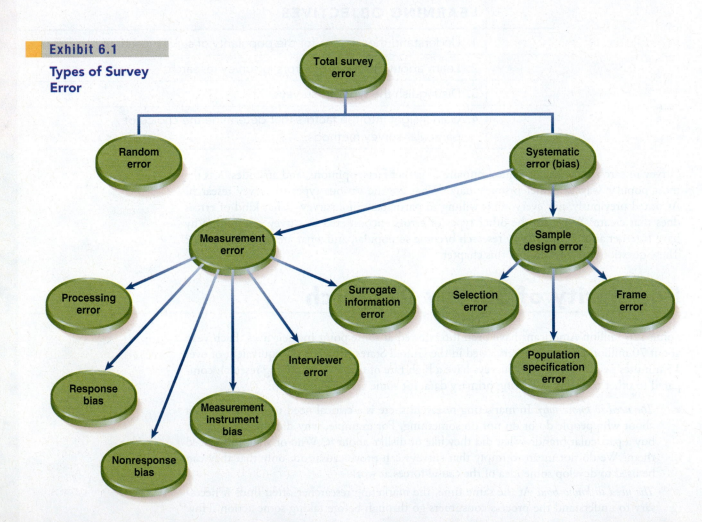

sampling error) because of chance variation. **Chance variation** is the difference between the sample value and the true value of the population mean. This error cannot be eliminated, but it can be reduced by increasing the sample size. It is possible to estimate the range of random error at a particular level of confidence. Random error and the procedures for estimating it are discussed in detail in Chapters 13 and 14.

## Systematic Error

**Systematic error**, or **bias**, results from mistakes or problems in the research design or from flaws in the execution of the sample design. Systematic error exists in the results of a sample if those results show a consistent tendency to vary in one direction (consistently higher or consistently lower) from the true value of the population parameter. Systematic error includes all sources of error except those introduced by the random sampling process. Therefore, systematic errors are sometimes called *nonsampling errors*. The nonsampling errors that can systematically influence survey answers can be categorized as *sample design error* and *measurement error*.

**Sample Design Error** **Sample design error** is a systematic error that results from a problem in the sample design or sampling procedures. Types of sample design errors include frame errors, population specification errors, and selection errors.

**Frame Error** The **sampling frame** is the list of population elements or members from which units to be sampled are selected. **Frame error** results from using an incomplete or inaccurate sampling frame. The problem is that a sample drawn from a list that is subject to frame error may not be a true cross section of the target population. A common source of frame error in marketing research is the use of a published telephone directory as a sampling frame for a telephone survey. Many households are not listed in a current telephone book because they do not want to be listed or are not listed accurately because they have recently moved or changed their telephone number. Research has shown that those people who are listed in telephone directories are systematically different from those who are not listed in certain important ways, such as socioeconomic levels. This means that if a study purporting to represent the opinions of all households in a particular area is based on listings in the current telephone directory, it will be subject to frame error.

**Population Specification Error** **Population specification error** results from an incorrect definition of the population or universe from which the sample is to be selected. For example, suppose a researcher defined the population or universe for a study as people over the age of 35. Later, it was determined that younger individuals should have been included and that the population should have been defined as people 20 years of age or older. If those younger people who were excluded are significantly different in regard to the variables of interest, then the sample results will be biased.

**Selection Error** Selection error can occur even when the analyst has a proper sampling frame and has defined the population correctly. **Selection error** occurs when sampling procedures are incomplete or improper or when appropriate selection procedures are not properly followed. For example, door-to-door interviewers might decide to avoid houses that do not look neat and tidy because they think the inhabitants will not be agreeable to doing a survey. If people who live in messy houses are systematically different from those who live in tidy houses, then selection error will be introduced into the results of the survey. Selection error is a serious problem in nonprobability samples, a subject discussed in Chapter 13.

**Measurement Error** Measurement error is often a much more serious threat to survey accuracy than is random error. When the results of public opinion polls are given in the media and in professional marketing research reports, an error figure is frequently reported (say, plus or minus 5 percent). The television viewer or the user of a marketing research

**chance variation**
The difference between the sample value and the true value of the population mean.

**systematic error, or bias**
Error that results from problems or flaws in the execution of the research design; sometimes called *nonsampling error*.

**sample design error**
Systematic error that results from an error in the sample design or sampling procedures.

**sampling frame**
The list of population elements or members from which units to be sampled are selected.

**frame error**
Error resulting from an inaccurate or incomplete sampling frame.

**population specification error**
Error that results from incorrectly defining the population or universe from which a sample is chosen.

**selection error**
Error that results from incomplete or improper sample selection procedures or not following appropriate procedures.

**measurement error**
Systematic error that results from a variation between the information being sought and what is actually obtained by the measurement process.

A population must be defined before research can begin. Errors can occur if a population is not defined correctly or if selection procedures are not followed properly.

Grant Faint /Getty Images

study is left with the impression that this figure refers to total survey error. Unfortunately, this is not the case. This figure refers only to random sampling error. It does not include sample design error and speaks in no way to the measurement error that may exist in the research results. **Measurement error** occurs when there is variation between the information being sought (true value) and the information actually obtained by the measurement process. Our main concern in this text is with systematic measurement error. Various types of error may be caused by numerous deficiencies in the measurement process. These errors include surrogate information error, interviewer error, measurement instrument bias, processing error, nonresponse bias, and response bias.

### Surrogate Information Error

**surrogate information error**
Error that results from a discrepancy between the information needed to solve a problem and that sought by the researcher.

**Surrogate information error** occurs when there is a discrepancy between the information actually required to solve a problem and the information being sought by the researcher. It relates to general problems in the research design, particularly failure to properly define the problem. A few years ago, Kellogg spent millions developing a line of 17 breakfast cereals that featured ingredients that would help consumers cut down on their cholesterol. The product line was called Ensemble. It failed miserably in the marketplace. Yes, people want to lower their cholesterol, but the real question was whether they would purchase a line of breakfast cereals to accomplish this task. This question was never asked in the research. Also, the name "Ensemble" usually refers to either an orchestra or something you wear. Consumers didn't understand either the product line or the need to consume it.

### Interviewer Error

**interviewer error, or interviewer bias**
Error that results from the interviewer's influencing—consciously or unconsciously—the answers of the respondent.

**Interviewer error, or interviewer bias**, results from the interviewer's influencing a respondent—consciously or unconsciously—to give untrue or inaccurate answers. The dress, age, gender, facial expressions, body language, or tone of voice of the interviewer may influence the answers given by some or all respondents. This type of error is caused by problems in the selection and training of interviewers or by the failure of interviewers to follow instructions. Interviewers must be properly trained and supervised to appear neutral at all times. Another type of interviewer error occurs when deliberate cheating takes place. This can be a particular problem in door-to-door interviewing, where interviewers may be tempted to falsify interviews and get paid for work they did not actually do. The procedures developed by the researcher must include safeguards to ensure that this problem will be detected (see Chapter 15).

**Measurement Instrument Bias**  Measurement instrument bias (sometimes called *questionnaire bias*) results from problems with the measurement instrument or questionnaire (see Chapter 12). Examples of such problems include leading questions or elements of the questionnaire design that make recording responses difficult and prone to recording errors. Problems of this type can be avoided by paying careful attention to detail in the questionnaire design phase and by using questionnaire pretests before field interviewing begins.

**measurement instrument bias**
Error that results from the design of the questionnaire or measurement instrument; also known as *questionnaire bias*.

**Input Error**  Input errors may be due to mistakes that occur when information from survey documents is entered into the computer. For example, a document may be scanned incorrectly. Individuals filling out surveys on a smartphone or laptop may hit the wrong keys.

**input error**
Error that results from the incorrect input of information into a computer file or database.

**Nonresponse Bias**  Ideally, if a sample of 400 people is selected from a particular population, all 400 of those individuals should be interviewed. As a practical matter, this will never happen. Response rates of 5 percent or less are common in mail surveys. The question is, "Are those who did respond to the survey systematically differ in some important way from those who did not respond?" Such differences lead to **nonresponse bias**. We recently examined the results of a study conducted among customers of a large savings and loan association. The response rate to the questionnaire, included in customer monthly statements, was slightly under 1 percent. Analysis of the occupations of those who responded revealed that the percentage of retired people among respondents was 20 times higher than in the local metropolitan area. This overrepresentation of retired individuals raised serious doubts about the accuracy of the results.

**nonresponse bias**
Error that results from a systematic difference between those who do and those who do not respond to a measurement instrument.

Obviously, the higher the response rate, the less the possible impact of nonresponse because nonrespondents then represent a smaller subset of the overall picture. If the decrease in bias associated with improved response rates is trivial, then allocating resources to obtain higher response rates might be wasteful in studies in which resources could be used for better purposes.

Nonresponse error occurs when the following happens:

- A person cannot be reached at a particular time.
- A potential respondent is reached but cannot or will not participate at that time (for example, the telephone request to participate in a survey comes just as the family is sitting down to dinner).
- A person is reached but refuses to participate in the survey. This is the most serious problem because it may be possible to achieve future participation in the first two circumstances.

The **refusal rate** is the percentage of persons contacted who refused to participate in a survey. Although response rates for mobile and Internet surveys hover around 60 percent with panel surveys even higher, telephone and mail response rates are very low. Pew Research has found that the response rate for a typical telephone survey was 36 percent in 1997 and only 8 percent in 2012.[1] The movement from landlines to smartphones has been a contributing factor. Comparing 1997 to 2012, we find that:

**refusal rate**
Percentage of persons contacted who refused to participate in a survey.

|  | 1997 | 2012 |
|---|---|---|
| **Telephone Contact Rate** Percentage of households in which an adult was reached | 90% | 62% |
| **Telephone Cooperation Rate** Percentage of households contacted that yielded an interview | 43% | 14% |
| **Telephone Response Rate** Percentage of household sampled that yielded an interview | 36% | 9% |

*Source:* "Accessing the Representativeness of Public Opinion Surveys," Pew Research Center for the People and the Press, May 15, 2013.

**response bias**
Error that results from the tendency of people to answer a question incorrectly through either deliberate falsification or unconscious misrepresentation.

**Response Bias** If there is a tendency for people to answer a particular question in a certain way, then there is **response bias**. Response bias can result from deliberate falsification or unconscious misrepresentation.

*Deliberate falsification* occurs when people purposefully give untrue answers to questions. There are many reasons why people might knowingly misrepresent information in a survey. They may wish to appear intelligent, they may not reveal information that they feel is embarrassing, or they may want to conceal information that they consider to be personal.

For example, in a survey about fast-food buying behavior, the respondents may have a fairly good idea of how many times they visited a fast-food restaurant in the past month. However, they may not remember which fast-food restaurants they visited or how many times they visited each restaurant. Rather than answering "Don't know" in response to a question regarding which restaurants they visited, the respondents may simply guess.

*Unconscious misrepresentation* occurs when a respondent is legitimately trying to be truthful and accurate but gives an inaccurate response. This type of bias may occur because of question format, question content, or various other reasons.

Strategies for minimizing survey errors are summarized in Exhibit 6.2.

| EXHIBIT 6.2 | Types of Errors and Strategies for Minimizing Errors |
|---|---|
| **I. Random error** | This error can be reduced only by increasing sample size. |
| **II. Systematic error** | This error can be reduced by minimizing sample design and measurement errors. |
|    **A. Sample design error** | |
|      Frame error | This error can be minimized by getting the best sampling frame possible and doing preliminary quality control checks to evaluate the accuracy and completeness of the frame. |
|      Population specification error | This error results from incorrect definition of the population of interest. It can be reduced or minimized only by more careful consideration and definition of the population of interest. |
|      Selection error | This error results from using incomplete or improper sampling procedures or not following appropriate selection procedures. It can occur even with a good sampling frame and an appropriate specification of the population. It is minimized by developing selection procedures that will ensure randomness and by developing quality control checks to make sure that these procedures are followed in the field. |
|    **B. Measurement error** | |
|      Surrogate information error | This error results from seeking and basing decisions on the wrong information. It results from poor design and can be minimized only by paying more careful attention to specification of the types of information required to fulfill the objectives of the research. |
|      Interviewer error | This error occurs because of interactions between the interviewer and the respondent that affect the responses given. It is minimized by careful interviewer selection and training. In addition, quality control checks should involve unobtrusive monitoring of interviewers to ascertain whether they are following prescribed guidelines. |
|      Measurement instrument bias | Also referred to as *questionnaire bias*, this error is minimized only by careful questionnaire design and pretesting. |
|      **Input** error | This error can occur in the process of transferring data from questionnaires to the computer. It is the result of incorrect keystrokes from a respondent. Use software checks to find illogical response patterns or improperly scanned machine-scored questionnaires. |
|      Nonresponse bias | This error results from the fact that those people chosen for the sample who actually respond are systematically different from those who are chosen and do not respond. It is particularly serious in connection with mail surveys. It is minimized by doing everything possible (e.g., shortening the questionnaire, making the questionnaire more respondent friendly, doing callbacks, providing incentives, contacting people when they are most likely to be at home) to encourage those chosen for the sample to respond. |
|      Response bias | This error occurs when something about a question leads people to answer it in a particular way. It can be minimized by paying special attention to questionnaire design. In particular, questions that are hard to answer, might make the respondent look uninformed, or deal with sensitive issues should be modified (see Chapter 12). |

# Types of Surveys

Asking people questions is the essence of the survey approach. But what type of survey is best for a given situation? The non-Internet survey alternatives discussed in this chapter are door-to-door interviews, executive interviews, mall-intercept interviews, telephone interviews, self-administered questionnaires, and mail surveys.

## Door-to-Door Interviews

**Door-to-door interviews**, in which consumers are interviewed in person in their homes, were at one time thought to be the best survey method. This conclusion was based on a number of factors. First, the door-to-door interview is a personal, face-to-face interaction with all the attendant advantages—immediate feedback from the respondent, the ability to explain complicated tasks, the ability to use special questionnaire techniques that require visual contact to speed up the interview or improve data quality, and the ability to show the respondent product concepts and other stimuli for evaluation. Second, the participant is at ease in a familiar, comfortable, secure environment.

Door-to-door interviews began a steep decline in the early 1970s and have now virtually disappeared altogether from the U.S. marketing research scene. The primary reason is the cost of paying an interviewer's travel time, mileage, and survey time, as well as ever-rising refusal rates. The method is still used in some government research. For example, some of the most recent U.S. Census was done door-to-door. Door-to-door interviewing is also the most popular form of interviewing in many developing countries..

**door-to-door interviews**
Interviews conducted face to face with consumers in their homes.

## Executive Interviews

Marketing researchers use **executive interviews** as the industrial equivalent of door-to-door interviews. This type of survey involves interviewing businesspeople at their offices concerning industrial products or services. For example, if Hewlett-Packard wants information about user preferences for features that might be offered in a new line of office printers, it needs to interview prospective user-purchasers of the printers. It would thus be appropriate to locate and interview these people at their offices.

This type of interviewing is expensive. First, individuals involved in the purchasing decision for the product in question must be identified and located. Sometimes lists can be obtained from various sources, but more frequently screening must be conducted over the telephone. A particular company may indeed have individuals of the type being sought, but locating them within a large organization can be expensive and time-consuming. Once a qualified person is located, the next step is to get that person to agree to be interviewed and to set a time for the interview. This is not usually as hard as it might seem because most professionals seem to enjoy talking about topics related to their work.

Finally, an interviewer must go to the particular place at the appointed time. Long waits are frequent; cancellations are common. This type of survey requires highly skilled interviewers because they are frequently interviewing on topics they know little about. Executive interviews have essentially the same advantages and disadvantages as door-to-door interviews. More and more executive interviews are moving online.

**executive interviews**
Industrial equivalent of door-to-door interviewing.

## Mall-Intercept Interviews

**Mall-intercept interviews** are still a common method for conducting personal interviews. This survey approach is relatively simple. Shoppers are intercepted in public areas of shopping malls and either interviewed on the spot or asked to come to a permanent interviewing facility in the mall. Approximately 350 malls throughout the country have permanent survey facilities operated by marketing research firms. An equal or greater number of malls permit marketing

**mall-intercept interviews**
Interviews conducted by intercepting mall shoppers (or shoppers in other high-traffic locations) and interviewing them face to face.

researchers to interview on a daily basis. Many malls do not permit marketing research interviewing, however, because they view it as an unnecessary nuisance to shoppers.

Mall surveys are less expensive than door-to-door interviews because respondents come to the interviewer rather than the other way around. Interviewers spend more of their time actually interviewing and less of their time hunting for someone to interview. Also, mall interviewers do not have the substantial travel time and mileage expenses associated with door-to-door interviewing. In addition to low cost, mall-intercept interviews have many of the advantages associated with door-to-door interviews in that respondents can try test products on the spot.

However, a number of serious disadvantages are associated with mall-intercept interviewing. First, it is virtually impossible to get a sample representative of a large metropolitan area from shoppers at a particular mall. Even though malls may be large, most of them draw shoppers from a relatively small local area. In addition, malls tend to attract certain types of people, based on the stores they contain. Studies also show that some people shop more frequently than others and therefore have a greater chance of being selected. Finally, many people refuse mall interviews. In summary, mall-intercept interviewing cannot produce a good or representative sample except in the rare case in which the population of interest is coincident with or is a subset of the population that shops at a particular mall.

Second, the mall environment is not always viewed as a comfortable place to conduct an interview. Respondents may be ill at ease, in a hurry, or preoccupied by various distractions outside the researcher's control. These factors may adversely affect the quality of the data obtained. Even with all its problems, the popularity of mall-intercept interviews has declined only slightly in recent years.

## Telephone Interviews

Until 1990, telephone interviewing was the most popular form of survey research. The advantages of telephone interviewing are compelling. First, telephoning is a relatively inexpensive way to collect survey data. Second, the telephone interview has traditionally produced a high-quality sample. Ninety-five percent of all Americans have some type of phone. *Random-digit sampling*, or *random-digit dialing*, is a frequently used sampling approach (see Chapter 13). The basic idea is simple: Instead of drawing a sample from the phone book or other directory, researchers use telephone numbers generated via a random-number procedure. This approach ensures that people with unlisted numbers and those who have moved or otherwise changed their telephone numbers since the last published phone book are included in the sample in the correct proportion. The huge disadvantage, as already noted, is the extremely low completion rate.

**Predictive Dialing** Today, random digit dialing has been merged with software to create predictive dialing. Predictive dialing gives interviewers more time for the actual interviews, since they are not dialing phone numbers; thus, it increases the efficiency of the interviewing process. The dialer automatically calls a number, screens the unnecessary calls such as answering machines and busy signals, then connects a waiting interviewer with a potential respondent. The software will prioritize recalls to meet a preset appointment time and deliver real-time reporting of numbers dialed and attempted, along with completed interviews.

**call center telephone interviews**
Interviews conducted by calling respondents from a centrally located marketing research facility.

**Call Center Telephone Interviews** **Call center telephone interviews** are conducted from a facility set up for that purpose. The reason for the popularity of call center phone interviews is fairly straightforward—in a single word, control. First, the interviewing process can be monitored; most call center telephone interviewing facilities have unobtrusive monitoring equipment that permits supervisors to listen in on interviews as they are being conducted. Interviewers who are not doing the interview properly can be corrected, and those who are incapable of conducting a proper interview can be terminated. One supervisor can monitor from 10 to 20 interviewers. Ordinarily, each interviewer is monitored at least once per shift. Second, completed interviews are edited on the spot as a further quality control check. Interviewers can be immediately informed of any deficiencies in their work. Finally, interviewers' working hours are controlled.

Virtually all research firms have computerized the call center telephone interviewing process. In **computer-assisted telephone interviews (CATI)**, each interviewer is seated in front of a personal computer. When a qualified respondent gets on the line, the interviewer starts the interview by pressing a key or series of keys on the keyboard. The questions and multiple-choice answers appear on the screen one at a time. The interviewer reads the question and enters the response, and the computer skips ahead to the appropriate next question. For example, the interviewer might ask whether the respondent has a dog. If the answer is yes, there might be a series of questions regarding what type of dog food the person buys. If the answer is no, those questions would be inappropriate. The computer takes into account the answer to the dog ownership question and skips ahead to the next appropriate question.

In addition, the computer can help customize questionnaires. For example, in the early part of a long interview, a respondent is asked the years, makes, and models of all the cars he or she owns. Later in the interview, questions might be asked about each specific car owned. The question might come up on the interviewer's screen as follows: "You said you own a 2014 GMC truck. Which family member drives this vehicle most often?" Other questions about this vehicle and others owned would appear in similar fashion.

Another advantage of CATI is that computer tabulations can be run at any point in the study. Based on preliminary tabulations, certain questions might be dropped, saving time and money in subsequent interviewing. If, for example, 98.3 percent of those interviewed answer a particular question in the same manner, there is probably no need to continue asking the question. Tabulations may also suggest the need to add questions to the survey. If an unexpected pattern of product use is uncovered in the early stages of interviewing, questions can be added that delve further into this behavior. Finally, management may find the early reporting of survey results useful in preliminary planning and strategy development.

Gaining respondent cooperation is the key to a successful telephone interview. Bonnie Eisenfeld, a Philadelphia-based marketing research consultant, talks about the importance of respecting the respondent in the Practicing Marketing Research box.

**computer-assisted telephone interviews (CATI)**
Call center telephone interviews in which interviewers enter respondents' answers directly into a computer.

# PRACTICING MARKETING RESEARCH

## *Respondent Respect Improves Marketing Research for All*

The most common complaints that I hear about surveys are: the questions were confusing, the multiple choices available did not include the answer the respondent wanted to give, and the interview seemed interminable and boring. People do not like receiving a telephone call at home in the middle of dinner, and they most particularly do not like it when an interview takes longer than promised. If the caller said the questionnaire would take 5 minutes and it took 20 minutes, the respondent gets irritated and will probably refuse the next request to participate. Research faux pas such as these indicate a lack of respect for the respondent.

To ensure that respondents continue to participate in the market research process, market researchers need to understand the process from the respondents' point of view and we need to show respect and appreciation.

### Respondents are motivated by a combination of factors.

Respondents who agree to participate in surveys are motivated by a combination of factors. They may participate because of interest in the topic, realization that their opinions are important, the opportunity to talk about themselves and their opinions, a desire to be helpful, the chance to voice their satisfaction or dissatisfaction, and a chance to influence a product or service in some way.

They may be curious about the topic or curious to know what their peers have to say. From a more self-serving perspective, respondents may believe that ultimately the findings will benefit them. Time availability is a big issue, but busy respondents will often make time if they are offered an incentive they value in return for their participation.

### Design a questionnaire to allow respondents to express themselves.

Respondents want to express their thoughts and opinions, they really do. If a questionnaire containing tightly constructed multiple-choice or scaled responses does not capture respondents' real thoughts, they feel frustrated. So even if your questionnaire is mostly closed-ended, you should allow for open-ended responses, also.

Try to avoid questions that have long lists of multiple choices, as respondents will get bored and may terminate early. At best, their responses will be perfunctory and without thought.

Pre-test the questionnaire for logic and clarity and revise it until you have eliminated any confusing questions. Also, test for how long the questionnaire takes to complete. It may look short on paper, but if you want thoughtful answers, you need to allow time for each respondent to think. Keep the questionnaire as short as possible to meet your research objectives.

### Recruit respondents with their needs in mind.

Time is a valuable commodity to most people. Researchers should allow enough project time so that willing respondents can do the interview or complete a questionnaire when it's best for them. It is particularly important if you have a small sample to build in the time for multiple callbacks and referrals. The people you are targeting have jobs, families, obligations, meetings, hobbies, vacations, and other parts of their lives that are more important to them than your research project. You are lucky if they take the time to respond to your questions.

To recruit respondents, create a pre-call communication message that includes a detailed explanation of the project, the purpose of the research, the importance of the selected respondents' participation and the type of organization sponsoring the study. It is customary to promise anonymity and confidentiality to respondents.[2]

## Questions

1. Do you always or very frequently refuse to participate in marketing research surveys? Why?

2. Have you ever participated in a survey and then felt frustrated afterwards? What happened?

3. What can researchers do to get more people to participate in marketing research surveys?

# Self-Administered Questionnaires

**self-administered questionnaires**

Questionnaires filled out by respondents with no interviewer present.

The self-administered and mail survey methods explained in this section have one thing in common. They differ from the other survey methods discussed in that no interviewer is involved. The major disadvantage of **self-administered questionnaires** is that no one is present to explain things to the respondent and clarify responses to open-ended questions. For example, if someone were asked via an open-ended question why he or she does not buy a particular brand of soft drink, a typical answer might be "because I don't like it." From a managerial perspective, this answer is useless. It provides no information that can be used to alter the marketing mix and thereby make the product more attractive. An interviewer conducting the survey, however, would "probe" for a response—after receiving and recording the useless response, the interviewer would ask the respondent what it was that he or she did not like about the product. The interviewee might then indicate a dislike for the taste. Next, the interviewer would ask what it was about the taste that the person did not like. Here the interviewer might finally get something useful, with the respondent indicating that the product in question was, for example, "too sweet." If many people give a similar response, management might elect to reduce the sweetness of the drink. The point is that, without probing, management would have only the useless first response.

Some have argued that the absence of an interviewer is an advantage in that it eliminates one source of bias. There is no interviewer whose appearance, dress, manner of speaking, or failure to follow instructions may influence respondents' answers to questions.

Self-administered interviews are often used in malls or other central locations where the researcher has access to a captive audience. Airlines, for example, often have programs in which questionnaires are administered during the flight. Passengers are asked to rate various aspects of the airline's services, and the results are used to track passenger perceptions of service over time. Many hotels, restaurants, and other service businesses provide brief questionnaires to patrons to find out how they feel about the quality of service provided (see Exhibit 6.3).

A recent development in the area of direct computer interviewing is kiosk-based computer interviewing. Kiosks are developed with multimedia, touch-screen computers contained in freestanding cabinets. These computers can be programmed to administer complex surveys, show full-color scanned images (products, store layouts), and play sound and video clips. Kiosks have been used successfully at trade shows and conventions and are now being used in retail environments, where they have many applications. From a research standpoint, kiosk-based interviewing can be used in place of exit interviews to capture data on recent experiences. Kiosks have other definite advantages: This form of interviewing tends to be less expensive, and internal control is higher because the survey is preprogrammed.

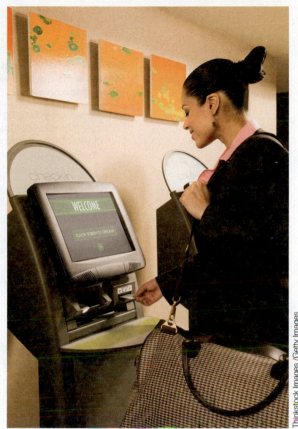

Thinkstock Images /Getty Images

Kiosk-based computer interviewing is a relatively new and successful way of capturing data on consumers' recent experiences. Go to *www .intouchsurvey.com* to find out more about the kiosk-based offerings of In-Touch Survey Systems, Inc.

## Mail Surveys

Two general types of mail surveys are used in marketing research: ad hoc mail surveys and mail panels. In **ad hoc mail surveys** (sometimes called *one-shot mail surveys*), the researcher selects a sample of names and addresses from an appropriate source and mails questionnaires to the people selected. Ordinarily, there is no prior contact, and the sample is used only for a single project. However, the same questionnaire may be sent to nonrespondents several times to increase the overall response rate. In contrast, **mail panels** operate in the following manner:

1. A sample group is precontacted by letter. In this initial contact, the purpose of the panel is explained, and people are usually offered a gratuity.

2. As part of the initial contact, consumers are asked to fill out a background questionnaire on the number of family members, their ages, education level, income, types of pets, types of vehicles and ages, types of appliances, and so forth.

3. After the initial contact, panel participants are sent questionnaires from time to time. The background data collected on initial contact enable researchers to send questionnaires only to appropriate households. For example, a survey about dog food usage and preferences would be sent only to dog owners.

A mail panel is a type of longitudinal study. **A longitudinal study** is one that questions the same respondents at different points in time. Several companies, including Synovate, NPD Research, and The Gallop Panel, operate large (more than 100,000 households) consumer mail panels.

**ad hoc mail surveys**
Questionnaires sent to selected names and addresses without prior contact by the researcher; sometimes called *one-shot mail surveys*.

**mail panels**
Precontacted and prescreened participants who are periodically sent questionnaires.

**longitudinal study**
Study in which the same respondents are resampled over time.

**Exhibit 6.3**

**Customer Survey**

*Source:* Courtesy of Accent Marketing & Research, Ltd., London.

# GATWICK EXPRESS
Customer Survey

+ ⌈0 1 2 3 4 5 6 7 8 9 R⌉

**Self-Administered Questionnaire: Airport Travel**
**Please fill out the following questionnaire. Check the appropriate boxes and write your answers in the space provided.**

1. Where are you flying from? Where are you going? Please list the departure and arrival times of your flights as well as the airline you are flying with.
   - Departure Location: _____
     - Departure Time: _____
     - Airline/Flight Number: _____
   - Arrival Locations _____
     - Arrival Time: _____
     - Airline/Flight Number: _____

2. Which class are you sitting in?
   - First Class ○
   - Coach ○

3. Are your flights direct? If not, where is your layover? How long is your layover?
   _____

4. Where do you live?
   _____

5. What is your age, gender, and yearly household income?
   - Age _____
   - Gender _____
   - Income _____

6. How many adults are in your party? How many children?
   - Adults _____
   - Children _____

7. Why are you flying today? Check all that apply.
   - Business ○
   - Vacation ○
   - Visiting friends or relatives ○
   - Other ○

8. How many times have you flown in the last 12 months?
   _____

9. How did you book your flight?
   - Online ○
   - Through a travel agency ○
   - Over the phone ○

10. How did you first hear about the airline you are flying with today?
    _____

11. Did you consider alternative modes of transportation? If so, which ones? And why did you ultimately choose to fly with the airline you chose?
    _____

12. Please comment on your travel experience today with your particular airline.
    Comments:
    _____

**Thank you for completing today's airline travel questionnaire. Enjoy your flight!**

On first consideration, mail appears to be an attractive way to collect survey data. There are no interviewers to recruit, train, monitor, and pay. The entire study can be sent out and administered from a single location. Hard-to-reach respondents can be readily surveyed. Mail surveys appear to be convenient, efficient, and inexpensive. The promise of anonymity is another benefit. While personal and telephone interviews may indicate that all information collected will be kept confidential, blind mail surveys absolutely guarantee it. This is particularly important to someone who may be asked to provide information of a confidential or personal nature.

| EXHIBIT 6.4 | Tactics Employed to Increase Mail Survey Response Rates |

- Advance postcard or telephone call alerting respondent to survey
- Follow-up postcard or phone call
- Monetary incentives (half-dollar, dollar)
- Premiums (pencil, pen, keychain, etc.)
- Postage stamps rather than metered envelopes
- Self-addressed, stamped return envelope
- Personalized address and well-written cover letter
- Promise of contribution to favorite charity
- Entry into drawings for prizes
- Emotional appeals
- Affiliation with universities or research institutions
- Personally signed cover letter
- Multiple mailings of the questionnaire
- Reminder that respondent participated in previous studies (for mail panel participants)

Like self-administered questionnaires, mail surveys of both types encounter the problems associated with not having an interviewer present. In particular, no one is there to probe responses to open-ended questions, a real constraint on the types of information that can be sought. The number of questions—and, consequently, the quantity of obtainable information—is usually more limited in mail surveys than in surveys involving interviewers.

Ad hoc mail surveys suffer from a high rate of nonresponse and attendant systematic error. Nonresponse in mail surveys is not a problem as long as everyone has an equal probability of not responding. However, numerous studies have shown that certain types of people—such as those with more education, those with high-level occupations, women, those less interested in the topic, and students—have a greater probability of not responding than other types. Response rates in ad hoc mail surveys may run anywhere from less than 5 percent to more than 50 percent, depending on the length of the questionnaire, its content, the group surveyed, the incentives employed, and other factors. Those who operate mail panels claim response rates in the vicinity of 70 percent.

Many strategies designed to enhance response rates have been developed. Some of the more common ones are summarized in Exhibit 6.4. The question must always be, "Is the cost of the particular strategy worth the increased response rate generated?" Unfortunately, there is no clear answer to this question that can be applied to all procedures in all situations.

Mail surveying is declining in popularity in commercial marketing research. Today, many research projects that, in the past, would have been conducted by mail are now being moved to the Internet and mobile devices.

Non-Internet survey alternatives discussed in this section are summarized in Exhibit 6.5.

# Determination of the Survey Method

A number of factors may affect the choice of a survey method in a given situation. The researcher should choose the survey method that will provide data of the desired types, quality, and quantity at the lowest cost. The major considerations in the selection of a survey method are summarized in Exhibit 6.6.

## Sampling Precision

The required level of sampling precision is an important factor in determining which survey method is appropriate in a given situation. Some projects, by their very nature, require a high level of sampling accuracy, whereas this may not be a critical consideration in other projects. If sampling accuracy were the only criterion, the appropriate data-collection

| EXHIBIT 6.5 | Non-Internet Forms of Survey Research |
|---|---|
| **Type of Interview** | **Description** |
| Door-to-door interviews | Interviews are conducted in respondents' homes (rarely used today in the United States). |
| Executive interviews | Interviews of industrial product users (e.g., engineers, architects, doctors, executives) or decision makers are conducted at their place of business. |
| Mall-intercept interviews | Interviews with consumers are conducted in a shopping mall or other high-traffic location. Interviews may be done in a public area of the mall, or respondents may be taken to a private test area. |
| Call center telephone interviews | Interviews are conducted from a telephone facility set up for that purpose. These facilities typically have equipment that permits supervisors to unobtrusively monitor the interviewing while it is taking place. Many of these facilities do national sampling from a single location. An increasing number have computer-assisted interviewing capabilities. At these locations, the interviewer sits in front of a computer terminal with a personal computer. The questionnaire is programmed into the computer, and the interviewer uses the keyboard to directly enter responses. |
| Self-administered questionnaires | Self-administered questionnaires are most frequently employed at high-traffic locations such as shopping malls or in captive audience situations such as classrooms and airplanes. Respondents are given general information on how to fill out the questionnaire and are expected to fill it out on their own. Kiosk-based point-of-service touch screens provide a way to capture information from individuals in stores, health clinics, and other shopping or service environments. |
| Ad hoc (one-shot) mail surveys | Questionnaires are mailed to a sample of consumers or industrial users, without prior contact by the researcher. Instructions are included; respondents are asked to fill out the questionnaire and return it via mail. Sometimes a gift or monetary incentive is provided. |
| Mail panels | Questionnaires are mailed to a sample of individuals who have been precontacted. The panel concept has been explained to them, and they have agreed to participate for some period of time, in exchange for gratuities. Mail panels typically generate much higher response rates than do ad hoc mail surveys. |

| EXHIBIT 6.6 | Factors That Determine the Selection of a Particular Survey Method |
|---|---|
| **Factor** | **Comment** |
| Sampling precision | If the need for accuracy in the study results is not great, less rigorous and less expensive sampling procedures may be appropriate. |
| Budget | It is important to determine how much money is available for the survey portion of the study. |
| Need to expose respondent to various stimuli and have respondent perform specialized tasks | Taste tests and prototype usage tests usually require face-to-face contact. Card sorts, certain visual scaling methods, and the like require either face-to-face contact or the Internet. |
| Quality of data required | It is important to determine how accurate the results of the study need to be. |
| Length of questionnaire | Long questionnaires are difficult to do by mail, over the phone, or in a mall. |
| Incidence rate | Are you looking for people who make up 1 percent of the total population or 50 percent of the population? If you are looking for a needle in a haystack, you need an inexpensive way to find it. The Internet is probably the best source. |
| Degree of structure of questionnaire | Highly unstructured questionnaires, such as IDI, may require data collection by personal interview. |
| Time available to complete survey | There might not be time to wait for responses via snail-mail. The Internet is the fastest way to go. |

technique would probably be call center telephone interviewing, an online survey of a sample drawn from a huge Internet panel, or some other form of polling of a sample drawn from customer lists. The appropriate survey method for a project not requiring a high level of sampling accuracy might be the mail approach or some type of mall survey.

The trade-off between the call center telephone survey, Internet panel, and the mail survey methods in regard to sampling precision is one of accuracy versus cost. A call center telephone survey employing a random-digit dialing sampling procedure that includes cell phone and smart phones might produce a better sample than the mail survey method. However, the mail survey will most likely cost less. Often, Internet samples will provide both lower cost and greater accuracy.

## Budget

The commercial marketing researcher frequently encounters situations in which the budget available for a study has a strong influence on the survey method used. For example, assume that for a particular study the budgetary constraint for interviewing is $10,000 and the sample size required for the necessary accuracy is 1,000. If the cost of administering the questionnaire using the mall-intercept method is $34.50 per interview and the cost of administering it via Internet survey is $1.50 per interview, the choice is fairly clear—assuming that nothing about the survey absolutely requires face-to-face contact.

## Requirements for Respondent Reactions

In some studies, the marketing researcher needs to get respondent reactions to various marketing stimuli—perhaps product prototype usage (a new style of smartphone keyboard) or a taste test. In these cases, the need to get respondent reactions to stimuli normally requires personal contact between interviewer and respondent.

© webphotographeer/iStockphoto

Taste tests typically require food preparation. This preparation must be done under controlled conditions so that the researcher can be certain that each person interviewed is responding to the same stimulus. The only viable survey alternative for tests of this type is the mall-intercept approach or some variant. One variant, for example, is recruiting people to come to properly equipped central locations, such as community centers, to sample products and be interviewed.

Some surveys require face-to-face interaction because of the need to use special measurement techniques or eye tracking devices, or to obtain specialized forms of information. The tasks are so complex that the interviewer must be available to explain the tasks and ascertain whether the respondents understand what is required of them.

Taste tests are most often conducted in a controlled environment because of their unique requirements. Can you imagine conducting this type of research through a mail survey?

## Quality of Data

The quality of data required is an important determinant of the survey method. Data quality is measured in terms of validity and reliability. (These two concepts are discussed in detail in Chapter 10.) *Validity* refers to the degree to which a measure reflects the characteristic of interest. In other words, a valid measure provides an accurate reading of whatever the researcher is trying to measure. *Reliability* refers to the consistency with which a measure produces the same results with the same or comparable populations.

Many factors beyond the interviewing method affect data quality. Sampling methods, questionnaire design, specific scaling methods, and interviewer training are a few of them. However, each of the various interviewing methods has certain inherent strengths and weaknesses in terms of data quality. These strengths and weaknesses are summarized in Exhibit 6.7.

The important point here is that the issue of data quality may override other considerations such as cost. For example, although the least expensive way to get responses to a long questionnaire with many open-ended questions might be via a mall-intercept interview, the data obtained by this method might be so biased—because of respondent fatigue, distraction, and carelessness—that the results would be worthless at best and misleading at worst.

| EXHIBIT 6.7 | Strengths and Weaknesses of Selected Non-Internet Data-Collection Methods in Terms of Quality of Data Produced | |
|---|---|---|
| **Method** | **Strengths** | **Weaknesses** |
| Mall-intercept interview | Interviewer can show, explain, and probe. | Many distractions are inherent in the mall environment; respondent may be in a hurry, not in proper frame of mind to answer survey questions; there is more chance for interviewer bias; nonprobability sampling problems arise. |
| Call center telephone interview | Supervisor can monitor the interviewing process easily; excellent samples can be obtained; interviewer can explain and probe. | Respondent may be distracted by things going on at their location; problems arise in long interviews and interviews with many open-ended questions. Many refuse to participate. |
| Self-administered questionnaire | Interviewer and associated biases are eliminated; respondent can complete the questionnaire when convenient; respondent can look up information and work at own pace. | There is no interviewer to show, explain, or probe; sample may be poor because of nonresponse; who actually completes the questionnaire cannot be controlled. |
| Mail survey | Same strengths as for self-administered method. | Same weaknesses as for self-administered questionnaire; sample quality is better with mail panel. |

## Length of the Questionnaire

The length of the questionnaire—the amount of time it takes the average respondent to complete the survey—is an important determinant of the appropriate survey method to use. If the questionnaire for a particular study takes an hour to complete, the choices of survey method are extremely limited. Telephone, mall-intercept, and most other types of surveys, with the exception of personal interviews, will not work. People shopping at a mall ordinarily do not have an hour to spend being interviewed. Terminations increase and tempers flare when interviewers must try to keep respondents on the phone for an hour. Response rates plummet when people receive through the mail questionnaires that take an hour or more to complete. The trick is to match the survey technique to the length of the questionnaire.

While there is no hard-and-fast rule, the following maximum lengths have been recommended:

- Face-to-face (in-home, office)      25 minutes
- Telephone                           20 minutes
- Mall intercept                      15 minutes
- Online                              20 minutes
- Individual depth interview          40 minutes

## Incidence Rate

Recall that the incidence rate refers to the percentage of people, households, or businesses in the general population that would qualify as interviewees in a particular study. Search costs, which correlate with the time spent trying to locate qualified respondents, sometimes exceed the costs of interviewing. In situations where the researcher expects incidence rates to be low and search costs high, it is important to select the method or combination of methods that will provide the desired survey results at a reasonable cost.

Doing a low-incidence rate study in a mall would be very expensive. This approach should be taken only if there is some compelling reason for doing so—a long in-depth interview, for example. The lowest-cost survey alternative for the low-incidence study is probably the Internet panel, assuming that this approach meets the other data-collection requirements of the study. One advantage of the Internet panel is that it can be prescreened; people can be asked a number of questions, usually including some on product usage. For example, if panel members were asked during prescreening whether anyone in their household participated in downhill or alpine skiing, the Internet panel operator could—at very low cost—pull out only those households with one or more skiers for a survey of Alpine skiers.

## Structure of the Questionnaire

In addition to the length of the questionnaire, the degree of structure required in the questionnaire may be a factor in determining which survey method is most appropriate for a given study. *Structure* refers to the extent to which the questionnaire follows a set sequence or order, has a predetermined wording of questions, and relies on closed-ended (multiple-choice) questions. A questionnaire that does all these things would be structured; one that deviates from these set patterns would be considered unstructured. A questionnaire with little structure, such as an individual depth interview, requires a face-to-face interview. Very brief, highly structured questionnaires do not require face-to-face contact between interviewer and respondent. Mail, telephone, self-administered, and online surveys are viable options for studies of this type.

## Time Available to Complete the Survey

If the client needs to have survey results quickly, the Internet is the best choice. Generally, call center telephone and mall-intercept interviews can also be completed in a timely manner.

## SUMMARY

Surveys are popular for several reasons. First, managers need to know why people do or do not do something. Second, managers need to know how decisions are made. Third, managers need to know what kind of person, from a demographic or lifestyle perspective, is making the decision to buy or not to buy a product.

There are two major categories of errors in survey research: random error and systematic error, or bias. Systematic error can be further broken down into measurement error and sample design error. Types of sample design error include selection, population specification, and frame errors. Frame error results from the use of an incomplete or inaccurate sampling frame. Population specification error results from an incorrect definition of the universe or population from which the sample is to be selected. Selection error results from adopting incomplete or improper sampling procedures or not properly following appropriate selection procedures.

The second major category of systematic error is measurement error. Measurement error occurs when there is a discrepancy between the information being sought (true value) and the information actually obtained by the measurement process. Measurement error can be created by a number of factors, including surrogate information error, interviewer error, measurement instrument bias, processing error, nonresponse bias, and response bias. Surrogate information error results from a discrepancy between the information actually required to solve a problem and the information sought by the researcher. Interviewer error occurs when an interviewer influences a respondent to give untrue or inaccurate answers. Measurement instrument bias is caused by problems within the questionnaire itself. Processing error results from mistakes in the transfer of information from survey documents to the computer. Nonresponse bias occurs when a particular individual in a sample cannot be reached or refuses to participate in the survey. Response bias arises when interviewees tend to answer questions in a particular way, whether out of deliberate falsification or unconscious misrepresentation.

There are several types of traditional surveys. Mall-intercept interviews are conducted with shoppers in public areas of shopping malls, either by interviewing them in the mall or by asking them to come to a permanent interviewing facility within the mall. Executive interviews are the industrial equivalent of door-to-door interviews; they involve interviewing professional people at their offices, typically concerning industrial products or services. Call center telephone interviews are conducted from a facility set up for the specific purpose of doing telephone survey research. Computer-assisted telephone interviewing (CATI) is a form of call center interviewing. Each interviewer is seated in front of a computer terminal or personal computer. The computer guides the interviewer and the interviewing process by exhibiting appropriate questions on the computer screen. The data are entered into the computer as the interview takes place. A self-administered questionnaire is filled out by the respondent. The big disadvantage of this approach is that probes cannot be used to clarify responses. Mail surveys can be divided into ad hoc, or one-shot, surveys and mail panels. In ad hoc mail surveys, questionnaires are mailed to potential respondents without prior contact. The sample is used for only a single survey project. In a mail panel, consumers are precontacted by letter and are offered an incentive for participating in the panel for a period of time. If they agree, they fill out a background questionnaire. Then, periodically, panel participants are sent questionnaires.

The factors that determine which survey method to use include the degree of sampling precision required, budget size, whether respondents need to react to various stimuli or to perform specialized tasks, the quality of data required, the length of the questionnaire, the degree of structure of the questionnaire, and the time available to complete the survey.

## KEY TERMS

random error, or random sampling error **120**

chance variation **121**

systematic error, or bias **121**

sample design error **121**

sampling frame **121**

frame error **121**

population specification error **121**

selection error **121**

measurement error **121**

surrogate information error **122**

interviewer error, or interviewer bias **122**

measurement instrument bias **123**

input error **123**

nonresponse bias **123**

refusal rate **123**

response bias **124**

door-to-door interviews **125**

executive interviews **125**

mall-intercept interviews **125**

call center telephone interviews **126**

computer-assisted telephone interviews (CATI) **127**

self-administered questionnaires **128**

ad hoc mail surveys **129**

mail panels **129**

longitudinal study **129**

## QUESTIONS FOR REVIEW & CRITICAL THINKING

1. The owner of a hardware store in Eureka, California, is interested in determining the demographic characteristics of people who shop at his store versus those of people who shop at competing stores. He also wants to know what his image is relative to the competition. He would like to have the information within three weeks and is working on a limited budget. Which survey method would you recommend? Why?

2. Discuss this statement: "A mall-intercept interview is representative only of people who shop in that particular mall. Therefore, only surveys that relate to shopping patterns of consumers within that mall should be conducted in a mall-intercept interview."

3. A colleague is arguing that the best way to conduct a study of attitudes toward city government in your community is through a mail survey because it is the cheapest method. How would you respond to your colleague? If time were not a critical factor in your decision, would your response change? Why?

4. Discuss the various types of sample design errors and give examples of each.

5. Why is it important to consider measurement error in survey research? Why is this typically not discussed in professional marketing research reports?

6. What types of error might be associated with the following situations?
   a. Conducting a survey about attitudes toward city government, using the telephone directory as a sample frame.
   b. Interviewing respondents only between 8:00 A.M. and 5:00 P.M. on features they would like to see in a new condominium development.
   c. Asking people if they have visited the public library in the past two months.
   d. Asking people how many tubes of toothpaste they used in the past year.
   e. Telling interviewers they can probe using any particular example they wish to make up.

# REAL-LIFE RESEARCH • 6.1

## Pitney Bowes Places a Premium on Satisfaction

Pitney Bowes is a mail and document servicing company with over $5 billion in sales. From a Pitney Bowes perspective, every single customer is vital to the organization's success. The company has in-depth conversations with multiple people in an organization to dig deep and understand their needs and concerns. For example, monthly in-depth telephone surveys with multiple contacts at each customer company explore sales support, machine performance, response time, satisfaction with service reps, ease of doing business, and overall satisfaction.

If customers report that they are merely satisfied, service managers have three days to resolve problems and develop an action plan to make customers happy.

Managers review satisfaction results each week and analytic teams looks for trends by region, sales rep, models, etc., to drive strategies and new programs. Reports track satisfaction but, more importantly, help uncover what drives satisfaction.

The goal is to talk about specifics but also to explore whether they would recommend Pitney Bowes and how it ranks among their most trusted providers. If Pitney Bowes is not the absolute best, it wants to find out what it needs to do to excel in their eyes.

### Dramatic increase

Since reengineering its measurement program several years ago, Pitney Bowes has seen a dramatic increase in customer satisfaction and business performance. Today, 86 percent of customers report that they are very satisfied, and 96 percent of customers would recommend Pitney Bowes.

Other divisions within Pitney Bowes provide desktop applications to millions of customers who conduct millions of transactions every day. "Many of our customers purchase technology online and never actually meet with a Pitney Bowes representative, so we needed to build a robust mechanism that made it easy for us to capture, hear, and analyze customer concerns," says Gael Lundeen, vice president of customer experience for Pitney Bowes.

Highlights of this measurement program include:

- Monthly e-mail surveys that focus on 20 critical customer-facing processes. Over the past 16 months, more than 180,000 customer satisfaction surveys have been completed.
- If any customers report that they are dissatisfied, the appropriate business units are alerted. They respond and are required to report results.
- As part of the survey process, customers are also asked to contribute ideas and suggestions. To date, 25 percent of customers have responded, which has led to 44,000 new ideas.

### Constantly search

Vendors like Pitney Bowes constantly search for new ways to exceed expectations and act on the insights they collect. They understand that there are limited pools of potential customers and that satisfaction, loyalty, and purchase behavior are closely aligned.

### When it comes to customer satisfaction, what does the vendor actual measure?

When a company says, "90 percent of our customers are satisfied," what exactly does that mean? Actually, leading technology vendors do not measure whether a customer is satisfied. They only care about whether a customer is *very* satisfied.

While surveys and feedback mechanisms vary from company to company, most employ a sliding scale that runs from very satisfied, satisfied and somewhat satisfied down to neutral, somewhat dissatisfied, dissatisfied and very dissatisfied. Buyers should be wary of providers who cite anything other than top-box statistics.

In many countries, including the United States, "satisfaction" is akin to cultural politeness. When customers claim they are satisfied or somewhat satisfied, that often means there are underlying issues with the vendor that have yet to be addressed.

"Very satisfied" is the gold standard. While few companies will be able to cite numbers in the 90+ percent range when using this scale, it says a lot when vendors set this as the goal. Companies that measure themselves against this top-box standard are more likely to find ways to delight their customers over time.

### How often does a vendor measure customer satisfaction?

To be successful, a customer satisfaction measurement program needs to be ongoing, a best practice that is often misperceived. Requesting feedback from customers once a year is not enough for anyone looking to improve business processes.

Given the critical nature of technology, software and systems need to demonstrate success in the eyes of a customer

every day. Business needs and market conditions may change quickly, which is why many vendors conduct satisfaction surveys on a monthly basis.[4]

## Questions

1. What are the various types of surveys that could be used to measure satisfaction? What are some of the advantages and disadvantages of each?

2. Should customer satisfaction be measured daily? If yes, isn't this very expensive? Why measure every day?

3. Assume that you have 2,000 customers, and 95 percent of your customers are very satisfied. Isn't that good enough?

4. Is it important to know why a customer is satisfied? Why?

business news
business news
business news **articles**
business news **network**
business news **daily**
business news **americas**
newspapers

**CHAPTER**

**7**

# Online Marketing Research—The Growth of Mobile and Social Media Research

## LEARNING OBJECTIVES

1. Examine the online world as it applies to marketing research.

2. Use the Internet to gather secondary data for marketing research.

3. Understand the nature of online focus groups, online individual depth interviews, and marketing research online communities.

4. Appreciate online survey research and ways to conduct it.

5. Learn the importance of online panel management in maintaining data quality.

6. Appraise the growing use of surveys on smart devices and the importance of social media marketing research.

Chapter 7 explores the ever-increasing role of the Internet in secondary data searches, qualitative research, and survey research, all fostered by digital devices and social media. Online observation research, another form of research growing at a sizzling pace, is covered in Chapter 8.

# The Online World

The world's Internet population will total almost 3 billion users by the time you read this paragraph. In the United States and Canada, over 80 percent of the population is online, spanning every ethnic, socioeconomic, and educational divide. Around the globe, a little over a third of the world's population now has Internet access. The United States has the highest Internet penetration, followed by Oceania/Australia (68%); Europe (61%); Latin America/Caribbean (40%); Middle East (36%), Asia (26%), and Africa (14%).[1]

The popularity of online research continues to grow, with the vast majority of America's marketing research companies conducting some form of online research. Today, online survey research has replaced computer-assisted telephone interviewing (CATI) as the most popular mode of data collection. Internet data collection is also rated as having the greatest potential for further growth.

# Using the Internet for Secondary Data

Recall from Chapter 4 that secondary data can play a key role early in the marketing research process. It can clarify the problem, perhaps suggest a methodology for approaching the problem, and, if you are really lucky, provide a solution so that the time and cost of primary research are avoided.

## Sites of Interest to Marketing Researchers

Exhibit 7.1 details a number of different sites where researchers can go to obtain secondary information, including competitive intelligence. You will note that a rich variety of data are available on many different topics. Although a lot of information is free, some, such as that offered by Nielsen Site Reports, must be purchased. To learn about the demographics and psychographics of your zip code, go to http://www.claritas.com/MyBestSegments/Default.jsp#. Then select "zip code look-up" and type in your zip code.

Several excellent periodical, newspaper, and book databases are also available to researchers. We have also posted these on our website at *www.wiley.com/college/McDaniel*. Some can be directly accessed via the Internet and others through your local library's website.

## Newsgroups

A primary means of communicating with other professionals and special-interest groups on the Internet is through newsgroups. Newsgroups function much like bulletin boards for a particular topic or interest. Topics cover just about anything. They range from companies, sports, products, services, investing, brands, to animals. Users post messages to a news server, which then sends them to participating servers. Then, other users can access the newsgroup and read the postings. The groups can be moderated, where a person decides which postings will be part of the discussion, or unmoderated, where everything is posted. To participate, a person must subscribe to the group, which is usually free. Nearly all newsgroups are found on Usenet, which is a collection of servers around the world.

| EXHIBIT 7.1 | Secondary Data Available Online for Marketing Researchers | |
|---|---|---|
| **Organization** | **URL** | **Description** |
| American Marketing Association | www.marketingpower.com | Enables users to search all of the AMA's publications by using keywords. |
| American Fact Finder | www.factfinder.census.gov | Provides ongoing data collected by the Census Bureau. |
| BLS Consumer Expenditure Surveys | www.bls.gov/cex | Provides information on the buying habits of consumers, including data on their expenditures, income, and credit ratings. |
| Bureau of Economic Analysis | www.bea.gov | Offers a wide range of economic statistics. |
| Bureau of Transportation Statistics | www.bts.gov | Serves as a comprehensive source for a wide range of statistics on transportation. |
| American City Business Journals | www.bizjournals.com | Offers a wealth of articles, reports, news, and data on everything from ratings of America's best small cities to statistics on men's and women's salaries. Current articles and reports, as well as an extensive archive dating back to 1994, provide insight and analysis of key business and economic trends. |
| Center for International Earth Science Network | www.ciesin.org | Serves as an excellent source of demographic information concerning the United States. |
| Centers for Disease Control/National Center for Health Statistics | www.cdc.gov/nchs | Maintains data on vital events, health status, lifestyle, exposure to unhealthy influences, onset and diagnosis of illness and disability, and use of health–care, through the National Center for Health Statistics. The NCHS, a subdivision of the Centers for Disease Control and Prevention, is the federal government's principal agency for vital and health statistics. |
| Clickz.com | www.clickz.com | Provides statistics on Internet research: weekly usage statistics, online populations, browser statistics and more. |
| The Dismal Scientist | www.dismal.com | Provides timely economic information, with comprehensive data and analyses at the metro, state, and national levels. This authoritative site also has data and analyses of global issues, including situations facing Asia, South America, and Europe. Visitors can rank states and metro areas on more than 100 economic, socioeconomic, and demographic categories. |
| Easy Analytic Software, Inc./The Right Site | www.easidemographics.com | Offers demographic site reports, or three-ring studies, including current estimates for population and households. Each three-ring study has census estimates for race, ethnicity, age distribution, and income distribution, as well as weather data. |
| EconData.net | www.econdata.net | Enables users to access a tremendous number of links to government, private, and academic data sources. Check out the list of top 10 data sources at this premier site for researchers interested in economics and demographics. |
| FreeDemographics | www.freedemographics.com | Offers free demographic market analysis reports. |
| Harris InfoSource | www.harrisinfo.com | Provides business-to-business data on American manufacturers and key decision makers. |
| Hoovers | www.hoovers.com | Gives company descriptions and industry information. |
| Internet Public Library | www.ipl.org/div/aon | Offers a collection of over 1,100 Internet sites providing information about a wide variety of professional and trade associations. |
| Marketing Research Association | www.mra-net.org | Offers causes and solutions of "declining respondent cooperation" and links to research suppliers. |
| Mediamark Research/ Top-Line Reports | www.mediamark.com/mri/ docs/toplinereports.html | Allows marketers and researchers to access demographic data on magazines, cable TV, and 53 different product or service categories. Top-Line Reports breaks down cable TV networks' viewers according to age, sex, and income. Magazines are listed by total audience, circulation, readers per copy, median age, and income. |

(continued)

| EXHIBIT 7.1 | (Continued) | |
|---|---|---|
| **Organization** | **URL** | **Description** |
| Opinion Research (ORC International) | www.opinionresearch.com | Offers consulting and research services. Its website claims expertise in a broad range of industries, including information technology and telecommunications, healthcare, financial services, public services, energy and utilities market research, and more. |
| Population Reference Bureau | www.prb.org | Source of demographic information on population issues. |
| *Quirks* | www.quirks.com | Magazine for market researchers. |
| Service Intelligence | www.serviceintelligence.com | Has an area devoted to customer stories of unpleasant experiences with airlines, banks, restaurants, and other service businesses. However, "hero" stories are also included. |
| Social Security Administration | www.socialsecurity.gov/policy | Provides a range of government statistics about social security beneficiaries. |
| U.S. Census Bureau | www.census.gov | Serves as the source for all federal census data. |
| U.S. Department of Agriculture/Economic Research Service | www.ers.usda.gov | Offers a wide range of agricultural statistics. |
| USAData | www.usadata.com | Provides access to consumer lifestyle data on a local, regional, and national basis. |
| U.S. Government | www.fedstats.gov | Serves as a source for statistics and reports for more than 100 government agencies. Also links to other sources of relevant information. Highly recommended site, but you might have to dig a little. |
| Valuation Resources | www.valuationresources.com | Offers a directory of resources that address subjects such as industry overview, issues, trends, and outlook, industry financial information and financial ratios, and compensation and salary surveys for a wide variety of industries. |
| Wikipedia | www.wikipedia.org | Functions as the free encyclopedia that anyone can edit. |
| World Fact Book | www.cia.gov/library/publications/the-world-factbook | Provides detailed information about countries of the world, including political and economic aspects. |
| WorldOpinion | www.worldopinion.com | Offers thousands of marketing research reports. This is perhaps the premier site for the marketing research industry. |

With over 200,000 newsgroups currently in existence and more being added every day, there is a newsgroup for nearly every hobby, profession, and lifestyle. Most browsers come with newsgroup readers. If you do not already have a newsgroup reader, you can go to one of the search engines and search for a freeware or shareware newsgroup reader. These newsgroup readers function much like e-mail programs. To find a particular newsgroup, follow these steps:

1. Connect to the Internet in your usual way.

2. Open your newsreader program.

3. Search for the topic of interest. Most newsreaders allow you to search the names of the newsgroups for key words or topics. Some newsreaders, like Microsoft Internet Explorer, also allow you to search the brief descriptions that accompany most newsgroups.

4. Select the newsgroup of interest.

5. Begin scanning messages. The title of each message generally indicates its subject matter.

Newsgroup messages look like e-mail messages. They contain a subject title, author, and message body. Unlike normal e-mail messages, however, newsgroup messages are threaded discussions. This means that any reply to a previous message will appear linked to that message. Therefore, you can follow a discussion between two or more people by starting at the original message and following the links (or threads) to each successive reply. Images, sound files, and video clips can be attached to messages for anyone to download and examine.

## Blogs

The traditional definition of a blog, or weblog, was a frequent, chronological publication of personal thoughts and web links. Now companies are also using blogs to communicate directly with customers and other businesses. More recently, market researchers have used blogs to monitor brands, track trends, profile customers, and identify unmet needs. Blogs are growing to be an important tool in the exploratory research stage of many formal survey projects.[7]

Companies also use blogs to talk to customers and to other businesses. Blogging gained popularity with the introduction of automated published systems, most notably at *blogger-atblogger.com*. Marketing researchers are finding blogs to be an important source of information on just about any topic imaginable. Researchers have used them to recruit respondents for surveys. Although blogs can be found on most search engines, several engines such as blogsearchengine.com are dedicated to blog searches.

Blogs can also be used as a form of individual depth interviews (IDI). For a study of women's handbags, 150 women from 17 cities around the globe such as Rome, Istanbul, Shanghai and San Francisco were recruited to talk about what was in their bags, their relationships to their bags, and the different roles that bags played in their lives. All participants were "handbag enthusiasts," but none had prior blogging experience.

Researchers posted topics for women to cover in three parts, giving respondents two days to reply to each part. It was reasoned that this would give women time to think over each series of questions, allowing them to reply in more depth and detail than they might in a more traditional interview process. Importantly, it also gave them the opportunity to take and post photos to illustrate their bags and their contents.[2]

These blogs opened up a rich and insightful world. What struck the researchers most was the confessional nature of the blogs, the ease and pleasure women took in revealing the detailed contents of their bags, the stories behind certain objects and the rich, often complicated relationships they had with individual bags. A few sample comments were:

**Remembering that first bag**
"My very first really incredible special important purse I ever had was my red leather Betsey Johnson purse. My boyfriend gave it to me as a gift for my nineteenth birthday. It reminded me of my grandma's Louis Vuitton purses. As a little girl, of course I had no idea what a Louis was, but I knew somehow that they were very important. Excuse my French, but I thought they were a bit ugly. I knew they were important because when it rained, my grandma would hide them so daintily under her coat or umbrella and make the maddest dash to a car I had ever seen."

**On my relationships to my bags**
"Wow, I never really thought about our relationship. Hmmm. Well, I guess you could say the Balenciaga is 'my Sherpa bitch.' She (yes, she is a girl) is always holding my 'shit' for me."

"This bag knows me to the fullest extent. We have been caught up in many different pickles together and have made it out just fine! This bag would have many great things to say about me, if another bag asked. It would describe us as a team and tell that other purse how much I have taught it and shown it off."

"I suppose I would think of this bag as being an escort and definitely a he. I feel it is support under my arm and feel confident with it going about my day-to-day business, whatever that entails. Whereas the embroidered one and the little creamy grosgrain one are like girlfriends that go out with me in the evenings and make me feel feminine and girly."[3]

# Online Qualitative Research

A popular form of online qualitative research is focus groups. Traditional online groups are what the name implies. The goal is to get 8 to 10 participants online at the same time, for a moderator to send questions to the participants, and the participants to provide their comments. These online bulletin board focus groups had a number of disadvantages. Since the moderator is typing a question and the focus group participants are typing replies, all non-verbal communication was lost. Both inflection in voice tone and body language are keys to fully understanding what a person means. Also, it is invariable that some respondents type faster than others, creating a suboptimal interview flow. As one moderator notes, "Often-times I was in the middle of the second sections of my guide when some people were just answering questions from the first section."[4]

Unlike in traditional qualitative groups, online participants don't wait for others to respond before offering their answers to a question; everyone responds at (or around) the same time. As such, moderators are challenged to read a burst of responses and respond with meaningful probes to each individual participant. This actually limits the ability to probe, thereby eliminating one key characteristic of qualitative research.[5]

## Webcam Online Focus Groups

The many disadvantages of bulletin board focus groups have been eliminated by the use of webcams and webcam focus group software. Webcams connect participants and a moderator. Voice data often goes over a phone line to reduce demands on bandwidth, making the videoconference experience much more fluid.

The video-based online focus group marries the benefits of traditional qualitative research and the promised benefits of online focus groups:

- Moderators can see and hear participants, meaning that there is greater context to a participant's responses and probing is not compromised.
- Participants can log in from any part of the country (or the world, for that matter), thus eliminating the need for the moderator or clients to travel to a limited number of markets.
- Built-in collaboration tools enable the moderator to show multiple forms of stimuli (concepts, advertisements, storyboards) to the group.[6]

Webcam groups require more screening than a traditional offline focus group. Additional questions include: one to evaluate a recruit's comfort level participating in a webcam-based interview (strong comfort required); a question about broadband access on the computer they will use for the interview (broadband access required); a question about personal comfort using a computer and the Internet; and a question about webcam ownership.[7] Some research companies will send webcams to hard-to-find qualified respondents.[8]

Many companies offer webcam-based software and hosting such as QualMeeting by 20/20 Research.

## Improving Virtual Focus Groups with Telepresence

Telepresence was invented by Cisco to simplify virtual business meetings. Cisco and Tata Communications set up a network of public telepresence rooms located in 30 cities around the world. Each telepresence location features three HD video screens in a semi-circle (to create an identical room on the "other side"); reflective lighting for a more three-dimensional feel; full-duplex audio; directional, voice-activated video and audio; simultaneous sharing of laptop screen; and the ability to conference multiple locations at once. See Exhibit 7.2.

"Compared to traditional videostreaming, the big difference is that this isn't a remote viewing technology. This is a remote participating technology. You can moderate from another city. It's not videostreaming over the web to your desktop. It's everyone sitting around what appears to them to be the same table, engaged in dialogue as if we were physically in the same room," notes Jonathan Hilland, CEO of Mindwave Research.[9]

Participants arrive at the telepresence facility in their city. The moderator is often in a telepresence room with other participants. The participants in each location sit around a semicircle table facing three television screens. The screens display a live feed from rooms in one city or in several other cities that are set up to look identical; the screens appear to "complete" the room. Up to two participants can be seen on each screen for a total of six persons seen on the screen at one time. Above each television screen is a camera, aimed at the two-person section of the semicircle directly across from it. In front of each two-person section of the semicircle is a microphone. The audio is designed to be directional, so the voice of the person speaking feeds only from behind the screen on which the respondent appears.[10] Although participants may be in six cities around the world, each has the virtual sense of being at the same conference table with the others.

## Using Channel M2 to Conduct Online Focus Groups

Channel M2 provides market researchers with user-friendly virtual interview rooms, recruiting, and technical support for conducting virtual qualitative research efficiently and effectively. By using Channel M2, the moderator and client can see and hear every respondent. You can see a demo at *www.channelM2.com*.

Focus group recruiting at M2 uses a blend of e-mail recruitment (from a global panel with access to over 15 million online consumers) and telephone verification and confirmation. Specifically, e-mails elicit involvement and direct participants to an online qualification questionnaire to ensure that each meets screening criteria. Telephone follow-up confirms that respondents qualify. Prior to the interview, respondents know they must show photo ID on camera so as to verify identity. Specifically, respondents are directed to show their driver's license to their webcam.

Channel M2 focus groups begin by the participants logging onto a web page where everyone sees and hears each other, and communicates in a group setting. Participants are recruited using traditional methods and are then sent a web camera so that both verbal and nonverbal reactions can be recorded. Installation of the webcam is simple, aided by Channel M2 tech support one to two days prior to the interview.

Participants are then provided instructions via e-mail, including a link to the Channel M2 interviewing room and a toll-free teleconference number to call. Upon clicking on the link, participants sign on and see the Channel M2 interview room, complete with live video of the other participants, text chat, screen or slide sharing, and whiteboard.

Once the focus group is underway, questions and answers occur in "real time" in a lively setting. Participants comment spontaneously, both verbally or via text messaging, yet the moderator can provide direction exactly as they would in a traditional setting.

Recently, Channel M2 has introduced real-time voice analysis. The program details the respondent's: emotional mindset (excitement, stress, fear, embarrassment); cognitive processes (rejection, confusion, uncertainty); and veracity (truth, deceit, conflict). When one of these flags pop up, the moderator can probe more deeply to clarify the situation. Voice analysis can be used later in the focus group analysis to remove the comments of any participant who was determined by the software to be untruthful.[11]

## Using the Web to Find Focus Group Participants

The Internet is proving to be an excellent tool to locate group participants that fit a very specific set of requirements. Researchers are tapping online bulletin boards such as Craigslist, which attracts 60 million visitors each month to its classified advertisements. The site is most useful "when you're trying to find niche users to a small population of users that is hard to find," says Tim Plowman, an anthropologist who works at Cheskin, a marketing consulting firm.

Point Forward, Inc., a Redwood City, California, marketing research firm, has used Craigslist to find people who fit very specific categories, such as people who travel frequently between the United States and Mexico, says Vice President Michael Barry.

A Craigslist posting by a different marketing research firm offered $350 to $900 to New York residents willing to give researchers a tour of their liquor cabinets, take them on a liquor-shopping trip, or make a video-based documentary of a social event they were planning.

Screening questions included: "When you are out for drinks or purchasing alcohol in a store, do people tend to ask for your advice on which brands of liquor to buy? If yes, how often does that happen?"[12]

## Online Individual Depth Interviews (IDI)

Individual online depth interviews are typically conducted like a webcam focus group interview except the IDI is longer and with only one person at a time. Bulletin board IDIs aren't efficient because the extensive typing required and there is no nonverbal feedback. Prior to webcam research, some marketing researchers combined an IDI telephone interview and the Internet to show stimuli.[13] This approach still lacks the ability to view nonverbal cues. Individual depth interviews conducted either on or offline offer richer content and deeper insights than most focus groups. Online IDIs may be the only way to reach people such as physicians or busy executives.

# Marketing Research Online Communities (MROC)

A **marketing research online community (MROC)** is a carefully selected group of consumers who agree to participate in an ongoing dialogue. The information value emerges from the richer, more complex understanding that researchers get from a MROC. All community interaction takes place on a custom-designed website. Membership is by invitation only.[14] During the life of the community—which may last anywhere from a few days to a continuous process—community members respond to questions on a regular basis. These discussions, which typically take the form of qualitative "dialogues," are augmented by the ability of community members to talk to one another about topics that are of interest to them as well.

The popularity and power of web communities initially came from several key benefits. Web communities

- Engage customers in a space where they are most comfortable, allowing clients to interact with them on a deeper level.
- Uncover "exciters" and "eureka moments," resulting in customer-derived innovations.
- Establish brand advocates who are emotionally invested in a company's success.
- Offer real-time results, enabling clients to explore ideas that normal time constraints prohibit.
- Create a forum in which natural dialogue allows customers to initiate topics important to them.[15]

In addition, web communities help companies create a customer-centered organization by putting employees into direct contact with consumers from the comfort of their own desks.

Since communities provide advantages in speed, flexibility, and 24/7 access to consumers, they let the organization be agile in its research decision making and prudent in its spending.

By adding a research focus to the web community environment, this holistic perspective deepens as the community becomes a way to

- Map the psyche of consumer segments.
- Brainstorm new ideas.
- Co-create and test new products.
- Observe natural consumer behavior.
- Rally the company around a customer-centered perspective.[16]

Beyond that, communities provide even greater value when the insights gained can be quickly shifted from the community space to the traditional market research space. This tight integration with more mainstream research approaches ensures that the community is both feeding new research initiatives and being fueled by insights gained from traditional research projects.

This type of cross-pollination takes another step toward a new research paradigm, one that integrates web communities and traditional research. This new paradigm offers the potential to

- Increase the efficiency of research by quickly finding the most appropriate forum for exploration of new insights.
- Reduce costs by using the community to follow up on questions left unanswered from ad hoc research studies.
- Improve the way consumer insights and implications are shared across organizational departments.

**marketing research online community (MROC)**
Carefully selected group of consumers who agree to participate in an ongoing dialogue with a corporation.

Unlike Internet surveys, participants in a research community talk to each other as well as to researchers and marketers. Consumers exchange ideas in their own language and raise questions and answers that researchers sometimes did not even think to ask. In other words, the social context and interaction are important and help provide a holistic understanding. This can only be achieved by creating engagement at different levels, however. First, there is a need for natural engagement; consumers have to identify with the topic or the brand under investigation. A second form of engagement is method engagement. Researchers should propose questions in a fun and challenging way to increase participation and the quality of input. Using gamification (point scoring, competition with others, rules of play) can spice up the research questioning. Including entertaining video clips or having celebrities ask questions can also increase respondent participation.[18]

Many marketers focus on the absolute number of people in MROC. Although this is important, what is more valuable is the number of interactions per discussion thread, which can only be created through engagement with consumers. Larger communities (over 100 members) require more participation in building efforts by the moderator. **Lurking**—which occurs when community members remain in the community but don't actively participate—can increase when there are too many members or an overwhelming number of posts. A paradox? Not really. When participants see too much information, they disconnect because they are convinced that their opinion has already been voiced and adds little or no value to the discussion.[19]

Researchers from InSites Consulting, based in the Netherlands and New York, discuss giving participants in MROCs more active roles in the communities in the Practicing Marketing Research Box.

# PRACTICING
# MARKETING RESEARCH

## Making Participants Researchers

In MROC, we are the researchers, they are the participants. What would happen if we were to bring down these walls and turn participants into researchers? Our recent case studies demonstrate that community participants are not only perfectly capable of taking on the role as co-researchers, it's also a way to close cultural, generational and knowledge gaps. By placing participants in the role of co-researcher, we can analyze a research question from multiple perspectives.

Without introducing the official role of a "co-moderator" we already see some members start behaving as moderators by asking questions or raising general issues. Of the 15 more recent communities we have set up, this moderator behavior is visible in the "off-topic rooms" of 12 of them. (Off-topic rooms are areas on the community where members can start their own discussion and talk about anything they want. This moderator behavior is observed when members start new topics with question(s) about the brand/topic of the research, to trigger a new discussion and

ultimately to contribute to the end goal of the research community. These are questions that are new to the research and that clients and researchers have not asked. For example, in a recent community about coffee, one member started a discussion on reasons why we drink coffee:

*We have been talking about drinking coffee for a few weeks now and I think it's not only just because it's tasty, comforting, energizing, etc. For me, I think it's a peace of mind. I used to work on a farm. Around 10 a.m., everyone came to the kitchen for a break and we drank coffee together. There was then some talking, and when the coffee was finished, everyone went back to work. Sitting down and having a break was only done if there was coffee! So, coffee is about having a break and relaxing. Do you agree? What are your reasons for drinking coffee?*

This natural moderator behavior already shows there's potential for empowering participants to be part of the research team and become actual co-moderators. There are various ways to introduce co-moderators into the community. We have identified two types of co-moderator: by role and by mission.

## Role

The co-moderator task "by role" is endorsed as another moderator in the MROC of a specific room (i.e., the social corner). The co-moderator is encouraged to start discussions, moderate, summarize, and report back to the moderator. In the community "Come Dine With Me" that we ran for Campbell's, 23 percent of the participants indicated upfront they were interested in being a co-moderator. Ultimately, the selected co-moderator took his role very seriously and started completely new topics in a dedicated room. By qualitative coding of the discussion, we concluded that the efforts of the co-moderator-by-role resulted in two times more interaction in the discussion compared to threads started by a regular (non–co-moderator) member.

## Multiple Perspectives

Next to moderating, participants can also add value when they are involved during the analysis phase, also referred to as *crowd-interpretation*. The rationale behind crowd-interpretation is that analysis of data is biased by a researcher's gaze. To get all potential interpretations and insights hidden in the data, we need to include multiple perspectives.

Recently, we conducted an insight community in cooperation with Air France and LKM where we wanted to detect new needs of transfer passengers. After an observational stage where transfer passengers reported their journey, we invited the community members to interpret each other's contributions.

From previous research, we know that consumers who are knowledgeable about the topic are most suitable for interpreting research results.

The crowd-interpretation was done in a game. During the first round, members had to give their interpretation on the input of their peers. In the second round, the original contributor could rate the analysis. Upon each correct analysis, a member could receive points. Consumers who were best in the analysis (highest amount of points) won the game and got a special incentive. Comparing the results of the researcher group with those of the participants, we concluded that involving co-researchers led to up to 21 percent more new insights.[20]

## Questions

1. Is it a good idea to let members of a MROC play the role of marketing researchers? Why or why not?

2. Are MROCs a substitute for online focus groups and/or IDIs? Why or why not?

3. Should all companies be using MROCs? If no, which types should not?

# Online Survey Research

The Internet has forever changed the way we conduct survey research. As noted earlier, a vast majority of all U.S. research firms are now conducting online research. In the United States, the online population is now closely tracking the U.S. population in most key demographic areas. Moreover, the number of Internet users around the world continues to explode. As the number of users grows worldwide, characteristics of a country's population and Internet user characteristics tend to meld. The reason for the phenomenal growth of online research is straightforward. The advantages far outweigh the disadvantages.

## Advantages of Online Surveys

Most companies today face shorter product life cycles, increased competition, and a rapidly changing business environment. Management decision makers are having to make complex, rapid-fire decisions, and Internet research can help by providing timely information. The specific advantages of online surveys include the following:[21]

- **Rapid deployment, real-time reporting** Online surveys can be broadcast to thousands of potential respondents simultaneously. Respondents complete surveys and the results are tabulated and posted for corporate clients to view as the returns arrive. Thus, Internet survey results can be in the decision maker's hands in significantly less time than traditional survey results.

■ *Reduced costs* The use of electronic survey methods can cut costs by 25 to 40 percent and provide results in half the time it takes to do traditional telephone surveys. Data-collection costs account for a large proportion of any traditional marketing research budget. Telephone surveys are labor-intensive efforts incurring training, telecommunications, and management costs. Online surveys eliminate these costs almost completely. Although the costs of traditional survey techniques rise in proportion to the number of interviews desired, electronic solicitations can grow in volume with less increase in project costs.

■ *Ready personalization* Internet surveys can be highly personalized for greater relevance to each respondent's own situation, thus speeding up the response process. Respondents appreciate being asked only pertinent questions, being able to pause and then resume the survey as needed, and having the ability to see previous responses and correct inconsistencies.

■ *High response rates* Busy respondents may be growing increasingly intolerant of "snail mail" or telephone-based surveys. Online surveys take less time to complete than phone interviews do, can be accomplished at the respondent's convenience (after work hours), and are much more stimulating and engaging. Graphics, interactivity, links to incentive sites, and real-time summary reports make the interview more enjoyable. The result: much higher response rates.

■ *Ability to contact the hard-to-reach* Certain groups are among the most difficult to reach (doctors, high-income professionals, CIOs in Global 2000 firms). Most of these groups are well represented online. Internet surveys provide convenient anytime/anywhere access that makes it easy for busy professionals to participate.

■ *Simplified and enhanced panel management* Internet panels are electronic databases, linked via the Internet, that are committed to providing feedback and counsel to research firms and their clients. They may be large or small, syndicated or proprietary, and they may consist of customers, potential customers, partners, or employees. Internet panels can be built and maintained at less cost and time required for traditional panels. Once a panel is created and a questionnaire is finalized, surveys can be deployed, data are collected, and top-level results are reported within days.

A sophisticated database tracks panelist profile data and survey responses, facilitating longitudinal studies and data mining to yield insights into attitudes and behaviors over time and across segments. Response rates are high, typically 20 to 60 percent, because respondents have agreed in advance to participate in the survey. These participants tend to provide more detailed and thoughtful answers than do those in traditional surveys, because they don't have to give demographic and lifestyle information (it's already been captured) and because they become engaged in the panel over time.

■ *External Internet panels simplify life for research suppliers* The availability of huge Internet panels maintained by firms such as Harris Interactive, SSI, Greenfield Online, Research Now, and Decision Analyst makes the sampling process much easier for research companies that utilize these panels. We will discuss these panels in detail later in the chapter. Moreover, the cost to use the panels has dropped as the number of panel suppliers has increased.[22]

## Disadvantages of Online Surveys

The most common complaint about the use of online surveys traditionally was that Internet users are not representative of the population as a whole. As mentioned earlier, this comment has largely disappeared in the United States. Harris Interactive and DSS Research have conducted over 300 surveys using parallel modes (telephone and Internet) and found that the research produced similar results. In all of the studies, it was rare to find a statistically significant difference between the sampling modes.[23] DSS concluded that the Internet panel methodology offered the best alternative for market share measurement and competitive benchmarking objectives based on cost (half the cost of telephone), speed (can be completed in less than half the time of telephone), and accuracy of measurement.

Lee Smith, COO of Insight Express, conducted a side-by-side comparison of online research and mail surveys. He found that online research delivered data of the same quality as using mail surveys in one-eighth the time and at one-eighth the cost.[24] Other research has shown that in most countries where the Internet penetration rate exceeds 20 percent, online surveys tend to yield results similar to those found in traditional methods such as telephone or paper-and-pencil survey research.[25]

A second problem exists when an **unrestricted Internet sample** is set up on the Internet. This means anyone who wishes to complete the questionnaire can do so. It is fully self-selecting and probably representative of no one except web surfers. The problem gets worse if the same Internet user can access the questionnaire over and over. For example, the first time *InfoWorld*, a computer user magazine, conducted its Readers' Choice survey on the Internet, the results were so skewed by repeat voting for one product that the entire survey was publicly abandoned and the editor had to ask for readers' help to avoid the problem again. All responsible organizations conducting surveys over the Internet easily guard against this problem by providing unique passwords to those individuals they invite to participate. These passwords permit one-time access to the survey.

A third problem is that the sample frame needed may not be available on the Internet. Assume that Guido's, a popular Italian restaurant in Dayton, Ohio, wanted to know how its customers perceived the food quality and service compared with that of the big chains, such as Olive Garden. A large Internet panel, such as Greenfield Online, is probably not going to have enough members in Dayton, Ohio, that patronize Guido's to give a representative sample. If Guido's doesn't have customer e-mail addresses, then an Internet sample isn't feasible.

Other problems include a lack of *callback* procedures to clarify open-end responses, potential for questionnaire programming errors, and a lack of bandwidth (some potential respondents can't complete the survey or download photos and video quickly). Many companies and researchers have become concerned with the quality of online samples. Procter & Gamble states that a high-quality online sample must include only respondents who are real people whose identify and location can be authenticated; are qualified to answer the survey based on screening and behavioral criteria we determine; only take each survey once; and answer questions thoughtfully.[26]

As a result, all research suppliers for Procter & Gamble must do the following:

- Use objective quality criteria that are predetermined, replicable and standardized.
- Rely on automated processes to meet quality requirements.
- Ensure that potentially fraudulent respondents cannot easily identify or circumvent the quality measures in place.
- Uniformly apply quality requirements to all projects when requested, regardless of sample source, survey technology, and geography.
- Deliver reports demonstrating the impact of applying the quality requirements.
- Protect and secure all personally identifiable and confidential information collected from respondents, suppliers and/or clients.[27]

**unrestricted Internet sample**
Self-selected sample group consisting of anyone who wishes to complete an Internet survey.

# Methods of Conducting Online Surveys

There are several basic methods for conducting online surveys: web survey software, survey design websites, and web hosting.

**Web Survey Software** Web survey software includes software systems specifically designed for web questionnaire construction and delivery. In a typical use, the questionnaire is constructed with an easy-to-use edit feature, using a visual interface, and then automatically transmitted to a web server system. The web server distributes the questionnaire and files responses in a database. The user can query the server at any time for completion statistics, descriptive statistics on responses, and graphical displays of data. Several popular online survey research software packages are IBM SPSS Quanquest, Sawtooth CiW, Infopoll, and SurveyGold.

**Gaining Survey Completions** Do-it-yourself software, such as IBM SPSS Quanquest, requires that you offer the respondent a good experience if you expect the person to complete the survey. The more engaged respondents are, the better quality insights they will provide. The following tips can help create a better experience for the interviewee:

- As with any questionnaire, use language that is less "research-ese" and more conversational.
- Be honest and upfront about the time required to complete a study.
- Provide more opportunities for participants to provide open-ended answers and truly express themselves.
- Ensure that all possible answer choices are given; avoid overuse of "other."
- Keep survey to less than 20 minutes in length and provide participants with progress information as they advance through the survey.
- Consider using graphics when possible or appropriate to make the experience more visually engaging.
- Explore new ways to facilitate interaction between respondents and a researcher.
- Make studies more informative—participants are particularly motivated by acquiring new knowledge and information about a product or topic.
- Offer participants the opportunity to be contacted again to receive updates on projects of products being tested.[28]

How important are incentives in online research? And does the cosmetic appearance of the questionnaire have an impact on completion rates? Decipher Inc. conducted an online study to address these questions.[29] It conducted a survey using a domestic customer list provided by eBay Inc. Over 1,900 eBay members participated in a 7-minute online survey. The recruits were sent an e-mail invitation containing a link that directed them to the survey. The study employed four parallel cells:

| | Survey Design | Incentive |
|---|---|---|
| Cell 1 | Plain | None |
| Cell 2 | Fancy | None |
| Cell 3 | Fancy | 1 in 500 chance to win $1,000 |
| Cell 4 | Fancy | Guaranteed $2 cash to first 500 qualified completes |

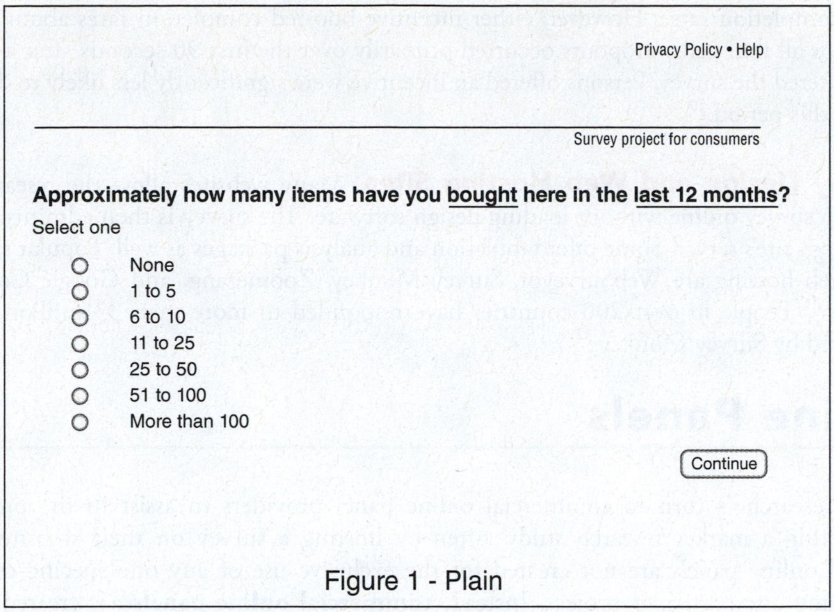

Privacy Policy • Help

Survey project for consumers

**Approximately how many items have you <u>bought</u> here in the <u>last 12 months?</u>**

Select one

○  None
○  1 to 5
○  6 to 10
○  11 to 25
○  25 to 50
○  51 to 100
○  More than 100

Continue

Figure 1 - Plain

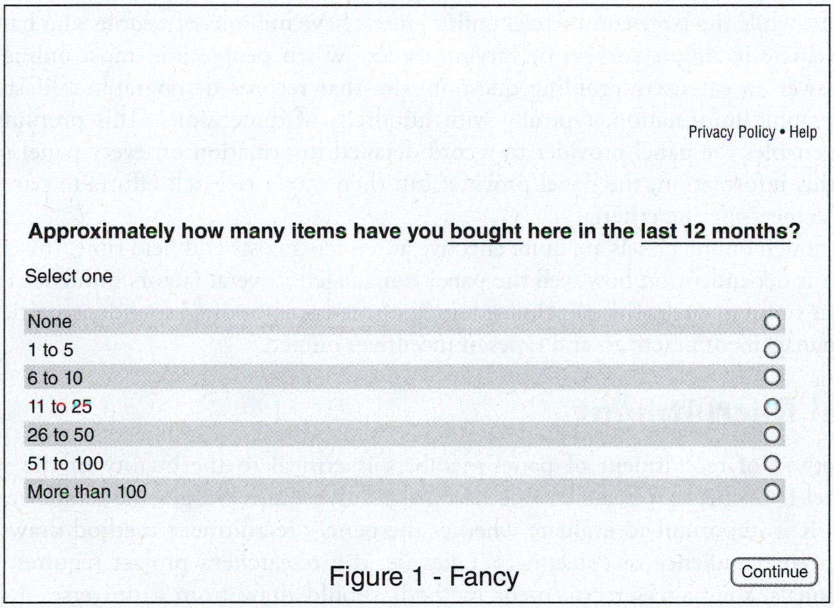

**Exhibit 7.3**

**Does a Fancy Survey Design Matter?**

*Source:* Jamin Brazil, Aaron Jue, Chandra Mullins, and Jamye Plunkett, "Capture Their Interest," *Quirk's Marketing Research Review* (July/August 2006), p. 48.

Privacy Policy • Help

**Approximately how many items have you <u>bought</u> here in the <u>last 12 months?</u>**

Select one

None                              ○
1 to 5                            ○
6 to 10                           ○
11 to 25                          ○
26 to 50                          ○
51 to 100                         ○
More than 100                     ○

Figure 1 - Fancy

Continue

As can be seen from the setup, a comparison between Cell 1 and Cell 2 measured the effect of a plain versus fancy survey design. Color, the use of tables, and the right-aligned buttons distinguished the fancy from the plain survey design (see Exhibit 7.2).

A comparison between Cells 2 and 3 or Cells 2 and 4 measured incentive effects. Finally, a comparison between Cells 3 and 4 measured the effects of the different types of incentive: a cash prize drawing or a smaller, guaranteed cash incentive.

The appearance of the survey had no measurable impact on the completion rate (in both instances, about 77 percent completed the survey). Nor did the type of incentive affect completion rates. However, either incentive boosted completion rates about 10 percent. For all four cells, dropouts occurred primarily over the first 90 seconds after a respondent entered the survey. Persons offered an incentive were significantly less likely to drop out during this period.[30]

**Survey Design and Web Hosting Sites** Many websites allow the researcher to design a survey online without loading design software. The survey is then administered on the design site's server. Some offer tabulation and analysis packages as well. Popular sites that offer web hosting are WebSurveyor, Survey Monkey, Zoomerang, and Google Consumer Surveys.[31] People in over 200 countries have responded to more than 33 million surveys produced by Survey Monkey.[32]

# Commercial Online Panels

**commercial online panels**
Group of individuals who have agreed to receive invitations to do online surveys from a particular panel company such as eRewards or SSI. The panel company charges organizations doing surveys for access to the panel. Charges are usually so much per survey depending on survey length and the type of people being sought for the survey. The panel company controls all access to the members of its panel.

Many researchers turn to commercial online panel providers to assist in the process of completing a market research study, often by hosting a survey on their website. Commercial online panels are not created for the exclusive use of any one specific company or for any one particular project. Instead, **commercial online panels** are created for the use of multiple projects by many different companies. The companies providing access to the online panels have invested in the pre-recruitment of people who opt to participate in online market research surveys. Some online panels are for use by a specific industry, such as construction, medical, or technology industries, and may have a few thousand panel members, while the large commercial online panels have millions of people who have opted to participate in online surveys of varying topics. When people join most online panels, they answer an extensive profiling questionnaire that records demographic, lifestyle, and psychographic information, typically with hundreds of dimensions. This profiling information enables the panel provider to record detailed information on every panel member. Using this information, the panel provider can then target research efforts to panel members who meet specific criteria.

Although online panels are quite effective at reducing costs and field time, the quality of the data is dependent on how well the panel is managed. Several factors influence the quality of an online panel. These include the recruitment methods, respondent participation, panel management practices, and types of incentives offered.

## Panel Recruitment

The method of recruitment of panel members is critical to the quality of the panel. If the panel is to meet a researcher's needs for a study requiring a general audience of consumers, it is important to evaluate whether the panel's recruitment method draws from a representative audience of consumers. Likewise, if a researcher's project requires business professionals, the panel's recruitment methods should draw from a universe of business professionals. Ideally, a panel should represent a diverse sampling of the population under study. Panel member recruitment methodology is a key distinction among online panels. There are essentially two methods for recruiting for an online panel: open source and by invitation only.

**open online panel recruitment**
Any person with Internet access can self-select to be in a research panel.

Intercepting people as they surf the Internet through ads is known as open recruitment. **Open online panel recruitment** allows any person who has access to the Internet to "self-select" and enroll in a market research panel. This provides the benefit of building a panel quickly with people who are Internet-savvy and responsive to online advertising.

A key drawback is the lack of control over who is recruited. A panel with open recruitment may sign up millions of web surfers who share similar characteristics, but may include only people who are responsive to web ads and/or "seek out" an opportunity to join an online panel by using search engines. This leaves out a large percentage of the general population.

In many cases, open recruitment leads to an overabundance of panel members who participate in many different panels and complete an inordinate amount of surveys. These are known in the industry as "professional survey takers"—people who sign up to take hundreds of surveys in order to enter into sweepstakes drawings or other types of incentives. The primary concerns associated with professional survey takers are that (1) they can give false or misleading information in an attempt to get through a survey quickly without regard to providing well-considered responses; (2) they tend to go through surveys in a perfunctory manner, which shows up in the time they take to complete the survey; and (3) they can make up a disproportionate amount of survey responders, leading to biased and unrepresentative research data. To the detriment of Internet marketing research, some websites have been developed to recruit people to sign up for several panels at one time. However, it is important to consider that not all online panels are made up of professional survey takers. This is why it is so important to understand the recruitment methods used by an online panel before employing them in the research process.

A research study may focus on people who meet a specific criterion such as golfing once a week.

The other method used for recruiting respondents to an online panel, the by-invitation-only method, was first used by Research Now, one of America's largest commercial online panel providers. **Closed online panel recruitment**, or by invitation only, invites only prevalidated individuals, or individuals who share known characteristics, to enroll in a market research panel. Most often, this is accomplished by inviting customers from large, highly trusted leading brands who collectively have a large, diverse base of customers in a given population (i.e., general consumers or business professionals). In recruiting for its consumer panel, for example, Research Now has partnered with large, well-known companies that have large, diverse customer bases. Similarly, in recruiting for its panel of business professionals, they have partnered with major airlines, hotels, and car rental companies. There is some natural overlap in the recruiting since business professionals who travel are also consumers, but Research Now pays close attention to panelist enrollment to ensure there isn't panelist duplication.

**closed online panel recruitment**
Inviting only prevalidated individuals or those with shared known characteristics to enroll in a research panel.

The "by-invitation-only" method enables a panel researcher to recruit people with specific demographics into the panel in order to meet a client's needs for a representative sample of the understudy population, or to meet specific needs. For example, in order to recruit affluent panel members, the panel provider may recruit customers from upscale retailers to join the panel. To recruit teenagers, a panel provider may recruit customers of specific clothing retailers that specialize in the teen market. To recruit business decision makers, a panel provider may recruit customers from companies that cater to businesspeople, such as airlines, hotels, car rental companies, and subscribers to business publications.

Using a "by-invitation-only" recruitment method gives a panel provider greater control over who is invited to the panel and greatly reduces the likelihood of professional survey takers. One particular area that requires attention with this approach is that the panel composition is dependent on the people who are invited to join the panel and may be biased by customers of a specific recruitment source. Thus, it is important that a "by-invitation-only" panel have a large number of diverse recruitment sources by working with companies in many different areas to ensure balanced representation in the panel.

## Respondent Participation

Respondent participation is critical to the success of the research process in order to minimize nonresponse bias. Therefore, it is important to understand the panel management practices and incentives employed by an online panel. Response rates for online surveys can vary dramatically, with some populations having average response rates less than 5 percent, others with response rates closer to 30 percent, and sometimes well over 60 percent for pre-screened individuals, who have been alerted to expect to receive a survey at a specific time or date. The diminishing response rates observed with telephone interviewing have played a key role in the increased usage of online panels.

Ensuring participation is a function of several factors, including to what extent panel members are engaged in the research process, their experience with surveys and the panel in general, and the topic of the research. Of course, one of the primary drivers of participation is the incentive program.

Generally, online panels use two incentive models: the sweepstakes model and the pay-all model. The sweepstakes model offers survey participants a chance to be entered into a drawing for a prize, often hundreds or thousands of dollars, albeit with extremely low odds of winning. Pay-all incentive models pay each respondent a small incentive for their time and participation each time they take part in a survey.

The choice of incentive model is not trivial. A sound incentive model influences not only survey response rates but also retention rates for panel members—which becomes very important when there is a need to use profiling information for targeting a specific type of respondent. Panel members who do not feel adequately compensated for their time and effort are much less likely to participate in research studies.

## Panel Management

In addition to effective panel recruitment and respondent cooperation programs, online panel providers must have effective ongoing management of their panel to ensure a high level of quality. Panels must continually see that that their participants have positive experiences with every research project. Among other components, good panel management includes frequency controls to see that panel members are not surveyed too little or too much. Panel members should be given enough survey opportunities to stay effectively engaged in the research process, but not surveyed too much as to be burdened with survey invitations. Other keys to guaranteeing a positive panel member's experience is providing respondent privacy, safeguarding personal information, and protecting members from bogus research that attempts to use online surveys as a sales channel (this is the practice of *sugging*—selling under the guise of research).

Panel providers are continually recruiting new members to keep up with the growth in demand for online samples, as well as replace any panel members who may drop out. Even with exceptional panel member retention, some panel members will become less active in responding to surveys. In addition, panels will often recruit new members to assist in growing certain hard-to-reach segments and/or balancing the panel to have maximum representation of the overall population. Ensuring a growing supply of engaged, active panel members is a constant goal of every panel provider.

Finally, panel management includes ensuring panel freshness. As panel members change, their profiles must be updated. A single, 25-year-old college student with an annual income of $12,000 from last year may now be a married 26-year-old accountant with a new baby and a household income of $45,000. Updating profiles ensures that panel providers are able to consistently target qualified people for surveys.

# Mobile Internet Research— The Future Is Now

By the end of 2013, the number of smartphone, cell phones, and tablets on the planet exceeded the world's human population. Smartphone traffic grew by 81 percent in 2012 alone. Fifty-six percent of American adults now own a smartphone, and 57 percent of adults use their phone to go online (the number jumps to 79 percent of adults in households with incomes over $75,000). Thirty-four percent of adults own a tablet.[33]

People carry their lives on their mobile devices, using them to take and store pictures, read news, keep in touch with friends and colleagues, and engage with apps that make their lives easier and more fun. The mobile experience is far more intimate than the desktop experience, and mobile users want to feel that the content that they are consuming on their devices is equally personal. Mobile has the unparalleled capability to reach a customer anywhere, but it also means that an infinite number of distractions compete for his or her attention.

## Advantages of Mobile

Today, one quarter of survey respondents prefer to participate in survey research via their mobile devices.[34] This number will continue to rise. The only question is, how fast? With traditional survey research, researchers ask consumers to recall their experiences. Smartphones enable researchers to not only observe consumers' whereabouts through geolocation, geofencing, and mobile analytics but to ask them for real-time feedback via mobile surveys. Geofencing is the creation of a virtual fence around a location.[35]

When a person with a smartphone crosses a geofence, a location-specific survey can be triggered. For example, a person might leave a Macy's store and be pinged to answer a few questions about the shopping experience. Other questions may focus on each of locating a product, in-store promotional effectiveness, and shopper intent-to-purchase versus just browsing.

Mobile research offers several advantages in addition to intercepting respondents at specific locations:

- *Increased response rates.* Respondents respond at higher rates (and more quickly) on mobile devices vs. current methods.
- *Increased convenience.* Respondents have better experiences when they can provide feedback when and where they want to.
- *Broader reach.* The ability to reach respondents in developing and remote countries creates a huge opportunity to capture insights in those regions.
- *Richer content.* Respondents can easily share media (e.g., photos, videos, voice recordings, etc.) via mobile devices.[36]

- *Broader demographic reach.* Respondent cooperation from all demographic groups is higher.
- *Immediate feedback.* Mobile surveys provide immediate feedback on research questions concerning marketing campaigns, ad testing, and more.
- *Cost savings.* Researchers receive faster reply to surveys, shorter project completion time.
- *Additional options.* Use as a mobile recruiting tool to direct respondents to online surveys, or connect with hard-to-reach groups. It is another way of reaching people on the go.[37]

## A Few Bumps at the Beginning

Anxious to be a trendsetter, some research firms moved to mobile surveys without a well-thought-out game plan. Simply taking a survey designed for a Mac or PC and converting it to a text-messaging (SMS) format was a recipe for disaster. Responding to a complex, 40-minute, slow-loading survey by typing out the responses led to high incompletion rates. So while mobile research is still quite new, surveys conducted via text-messaging are already scarce. The industry focus has shifted to surveys conducted via WAP or via a survey application designed for a specific phone operating system like an iPhone or Android device.[38]

Both WAP (or web-based mobile surveys) and app-based surveys have their own benefits and challenges. WAP surveys allow for cross-platform text and multimedia surveys (meaning they're compatible with mobile browsers on multiple operating systems). Device compatibility is over 70 percent. The downside is that mobile browser speed can vary considerably based on the wireless connection. App-based surveys are device-specific (meaning an iPhone app won't work on an Android phone; thus, multiple versions of the app are necessary to allow for cross-platform research) but generally bring faster delivery and upload times. This may ultimately work to increase respondent satisfaction with the survey-taking process. In addition, survey apps can be developed on and integrated into preexisting apps, which may present marketers with opportunities to add in survey functionality to apps that have served other functions to date.[39]

Gone are the days when surveys had to be programmed and loaded on an actual PC. Today, tablets can easily access surveys and instantly feed data into online reporting toolsets via a basic wireless connection. Researchers are even using tablet PCs to evolve qualitative research into hybrid quant/qual techniques. For example, respondents are given a short quant survey to quantify individual preferences, after which survey results can be instantly aggregated and summarized via real-time online reporting tools. Afterward, a focus group discussion of preference or other drivers can take place, incorporating the initial quantitative survey data into the qualitative group discussion.[40]

## Designing a Mobile Survey

Survey designers must be proactive in the design of both the questionnaire and user—interface in order to give mobile respondents an excellent survey experience. First and foremost, mobile surveys need to be short. Ten questions or fewer is a good rule. This is because it takes longer to navigate on mobile devices due to limitations of the user interfaces and data transfer speeds. Second, a good mobile survey will minimize the number of pages. Each time the page refreshes, the respondent has to wait. It is important not to put too many questions on a page, as mobile devices also have less memory to work with, so a page with too many elements may cause the device to become slow or nonresponsive.

Third, the type of questions should be kept simple. Single-dimension radio, checkbox, or "select" questions are better than multidimensional grid questions, which could be difficult to complete due to mobile devices' small screens. Also, limit the use of open-ended questions, as they require typing. Finally, all nonessential content should be minimized. It takes extra load time and visual space for every element that appears on the screen. Even a progress bar increases the load time and the need for vertical scrolling.[41]

The immediacy of mobile surveys, along with geolocation and geofencing, enables a new range of survey incentives. Many companies are offering real-time incentives such as a virtual coupon for the store that you are approaching.

The advantages of mobile surveys are illustrated by Toluna, an Internet and mobile marketing research company. A Toluna client wanted to conduct a survey during the Super Bowl regarding the ads that ran during the game. The client wanted to get a read on real-time reactions—but most people who watch the Super Bowl aren't simultaneously sitting in front of their desktop computers. They are, however, multitasking, using their mobile phones (63 percent of those 18- to 24-year-old smartphone owners in the United States text, use apps, check e-mail, surf the Internet, or participate in social networking discussion while watching TV at least once a week). Only a mobile survey could gather the immediate data that the agency craved. Respondents were recruited in advance of game day and then, during the Super Bowl, surveys were pushed out in real time to ask about commercials as their aired.[42]

# Social Media Marketing Research

Social media, such as Facebook, Twitter, Pinterest, and LinkedIn, give opportunities to marketing researchers to understand their customers and potential customers like never before. Companies can ask themselves, "Who are our fans? What can they teach us about our brand?" Answers to these questions first require building dialogue and customer communities about a company or brand.

Much social media marketing research is different from traditional survey research. Rather than a product manager asking a research team to determine X, Y, and Z, and then having the researchers conduct the survey and provide the requested feedback, social media research is more interactive, via a few questions and observations over time. By analyzing social media exchanges about a product or service, researchers can learn what factors customers use to determine value, as well as the way they speak about the product, service, or brand. Much social media research is based on forms of observation, and these will be discussed in more detail in Chapter 8.

Dr. Pepper spent years building its 8.5-million-strong fan base on Facebook. Now, careful tracking and testing with those Facebook users who say they "like" the soft drink helps the brand figure out how to hone its marketing messages. It sends out two messages daily on its Facebook fan page, and then listens to the fan's reactions. Using tools from Facebook, Dr. Pepper can measure how many times a message is viewed, how many times it is shared with other Facebook users, and what fan responses say.

"We mine the data to understand what is appreciated, and what is not," says Robert Stone, director of interactive media services for Dr. Pepper Snapple Group.[43]

For example, the company learned that diehard Dr. Pepper fans like edgy one-liners. One of the best performing messages: "If liking you is wrong, we don't want to be right." And they dislike messages that focus on prices and special offers. "It just isn't relevant to their passion about the brand," Mr. Stone says.[44]

## Conduction a Facebook Focus Group

The National Cattlemen's Beef Association (NCBA) was interested in understanding beef consumption habits of millennials (those between the ages of 13 and 30). A group of respondents were recruited who not only met the age criteria to be considered a millennial but also met certain demographic and psychographic screening criteria specific to this study: eat beef at least twice a month; have some level of involvement in meal planning and/or prep; use Facebook regularly (at least twice a week) and have at least 25 friends on Facebook; can answer a series of attitudinal questions about current and future life plans; and are part of a representative mix of gender, age, and marital status.[45]

Participants were recruited the same was they would for any other online focus group or IDI—with one exception. After qualifying and agreeing to take part in the study, participants were asked to visit a Facebook page the researchers set up for the group, become its friend, and then return to the survey and answer some additional questions to verify that they had indeed visited the site. The latter measure was added to ensure that they were comfortable navigating on Facebook.

One of the concerns with using Facebook as the platform was a general lack of security associated with using an open social networking site. To remedy this, once the group was fully recruited, the researchers simply changed the settings of the page to the highest level of privacy (by invite only).

Participants would need to be engaged in this discussion for six weeks. The researchers knew that a study of that length could lead to participant burnout, so they initiated processes to minimize the impact:

- A new topic was posted about two to three times per week. This reduced the need for the participants to come to the group every day and avoided inundating them with daily messages.

- The moderator of the discussion was a millennial himself who understood the principles of moderating and knew how to engage the group in a fun and unintimidating way. He was talking to his peers on Facebook, something he does regularly anyway.

- The moderator validated the opinions of the participants. He added his commentary to their responses and occasionally would try out a new idea that was developed based on their answers. These millennials knew they were being listened to because the discussion was built around what they had said previously.

- Random prize drawings were held throughout the six weeks of the discussion. In addition to the honorarium they received for taking part in the discussion, participants would occasionally be offered a chance to win a gift card for giving the best idea, sharing recipes and cooking ideas, or just being selected at random among those who participated that day.[46]

The aim was to have 60 millennials fully participate in the discussion. Some drop-off was expected, particularly given the length of time and the season in which this session was conducted (it began mid-November and ran right up to the week of Christmas). A total of 227 millennials qualified and agreed to take part in the group. Of this, 119 *friended* the group (52 percent) and, of those, 66 were actively engaged (55 percent). These were 27 topics posted, with 1,545 total responses by the participants. This equates to about 57 responses per topic and about 22 responses per participant.[47]

The National Cattlemen's Beef Association obtained valuable insights on how to improve packaging, distribution, in-store promotions, and social media marketing. The focus group allowed for a rich, colorful, and dynamic dialogue between participants and the moderator.

# Conducting Surveys

For researchers wanting to conduct traditional survey research, social media can be used as a respondent recruiting tool. Persons who "like" a product or service or members of web communities, can be sent an email with a link to an external site where the person can take the web survey.

There are many apps available for administering social media surveys. Survey Monkey's app enables the researcher to embed a survey on Facebook. A survey can be created by using a Survey Monkey template, or one can choose from the Survey Monkey Question Bank. Survey Monkey's advice is to make the survey short, offer incentives, and make it fun. That is, be friendly and show some personality.

Facebook also offers tools for conducting surveys at http://apps.facebook.com/opinionpolls. For example, to ask a question or questions to a group, you click ASK QUESTION at the top of a group. Next, you enter a question and add poll options if you wish. Then click POST to share it with the group.

TwitPolls lets Twitter users ask questions of their followers and receive tallied results at the cost of the user-determined survey time frame. The app allows brands and companies to gather real-time feedback from their followers without forcing followers to leave the Twitter environment.

All social media have apps for survey research. The researcher must decide which social media will provide the survey population of interest and which app offers the tools needed to best extract the type of decision-making information needed.

# SUMMARY

Over 3 billion people worldwide are online. In the United States and Canada, the figure is over 80 percent. Over 90 percent of U.S. research firms are conducting online research. Secondary data can play a key role in the marketing research process. It can clarify a problem, suggest a particular research methodology, or sometimes actually provide a solution to the problem. Exhibit 7.1 offers an extensive list of online sources of secondary data. The Internet has, in many ways, revolutionized the gathering of secondary data. Now, rather than wait for replies from government agencies or other sources, users can find millions of pieces of information on the Internet. Trips to the library may become a thing of the past for many researchers. Search engines and directories contain links to millions of documents throughout the world. Special-interest discussion groups and blogs on the Internet can also be valuable sources of secondary data.

More and more focus groups are being conducted online. Traditional online focus groups were in a bulletin board format. Moderators typed questions and respondents typed replies. All nonverbal communication was lost. People have different levels of typing ability, which also created problems. Webcam focus groups with voice connections and software create a more traditional offline-like focus group. Also, respondents can be in various cities around the world. Telepresence creates a virtual traditional focus group environment that simulates all participants being in the same room.

Channel M2 provides virtual focus group interview rooms where respondents participate via a webcam. Questions and answers occur in real time, thus simulating a traditional focus group. Asynchronous focus groups are time-extended focus groups conducted much like an online chat group. Web community research is where a group of consumers agree to participate in an ongoing dialogue with a company. The discussion may last a year or more, and participants respond to questions that are regularly posted to the community. Insights from the community can be used as a basis for traditional marketing research. Recently, Channel M2 introduced real-time voice analysis. The program details the respondent's emotional mindset, cognitive processes, and veracity.

Firms are now conducting individual depth interviews (IDI) online. IDIs are conducted like a webcam online focus group, except just with one person at a time.

Marketing research online communities (MROC) are increasing in popularity. MROCs are by invitation only and may last from a few days to a continuous process. MROCs have many advantages listed in the chapter and provide researchers with a richer and more complex understanding of concepts, brands, strategies, and consumer behavior.

Internet surveys offer rapid deployment and real-time reporting, dramatically reduced costs, ready personalization, high response rates, ability to reach low-incidence respondents, simplified and enhanced panel management, and profitability for survey research firms. The disadvantages are the potential nonrepresentativeness of Internet users, lack of callback procedures to clarify open-end responses, bandwidth problems, and the fact that the sample frame needed may not be available on the Internet.

A number of tips are given for improving completion rates for online surveys. One study found that appearance had no impact, but financial incentives did improve completions. When formatting a survey, radio buttons should be used with a predetermined set of options. Drop-down boxes are appropriate when respondents are familiar with the categories, such as the state where you live. Fill-in boxes require clear, concise directions. They should be used sparingly because they have a high skip rate.

Commercial online panels are used for multiple projects by many different companies. While panels reduce cost and field time, the quality of the data requires good panel management. Panel recruitment can be by open source or "by invitation only." The by-invitation-only method is highly preferred

for quality purposes. Good panel management requires the blocking of professional survey takers. Typically, Internet panels use either a "pay-all" or a sweepstakes strategy to gain respondent cooperation. Pay-all tends to be much more effective.

Well over half of all Americans own a smartphone, and more than a third own a tablet. Thus, more marketing research is being conducted on these devices. Mobile surveys offer real-time feedback, such as when a consumer is shopping, plus geolocation software denotes the respondent's exact location and the survey is automatically time-stamped. Mobile surveys offer advantages detailed in the chapter. Researchers quickly found that SMS surveys didn't work very well compared to WAP and app-based surveys. Yet, the latter two methods also have their challenges. Mobile surveys need to be short, minimize the number of page views, ask simple questions, and minimize nonessential content.

Social media research enables marketing researchers to understand consumers like never before. Firms can build communities about the firm or brands and then carry on a continuous dialogue about the brand. These is much more interaction between the researchers and the community members than in traditional research. Also, there is more observation of what is said about the brand and who says it. Focus groups, individual depth interviews, and survey research can all be conducted via social media.

## KEY TERMS

Marketing research online community (MROC) **147**

unrestricted Internet sample **151**
commercial online panel **154**

open online panel recruitment **154**
closed online panel recruitment **155**

## QUESTIONS FOR REVIEW & CRITICAL THINKING

1. Do you think that eventually all marketing research will be done with mobile devices? Why or why not?
2. Explain the relationship between blogs, MROCs, and marketing research.
3. Discuss the advantages and disadvantages of online focus groups.
4. Do you think that a company such as Caterpillar could benefit from web community research? Ford? United Airlines?
5. Discuss the popularity of online survey research. Why is it so popular?
6. Describe some ways to recruit for online panels.

7. How does one avoid professional survey takers with online panels?

8. Is panel management a critical task for a quality online panel?

9. What are the keys to a good mobile survey?

10. What is geofencing, and how can it be used in survey research?

11. Explain the difference between a traditional marketing research survey and a social media community research project.

12. How can one conduct a focus group using Facebook?

## WORKING THE NET

1. Go to Exhibit 7.1 and, using it as a resource, determine the 10 highest-income counties in the United States; where the highest ratio of pickup trucks per capita is found; the oldest median age zip code in America; a list of key decision makers in the U.S. steel industry; a reader profile on *Fast Company* magazine; where most avocados are grown; and this week's smartphone usage in the United States.

2. Compare and contrast the offerings of *www.surveysampling. com*; *www.zommerang.com; www.researchnow.com*; and *www.surveymonkey.com.*

3. Conduct a one- or two-question survey using the Survey Monkey Facebook app or TwitPolls on Twitter.

4. Can surveys be conducted on YouTube, LinkedIn, Google, or Pinterest? If so, explain how.

5. Go to www.gutcheckit.com and explain its Instant Research Communities.

## REAL-LIFE RESEARCH • 7.1

### Procter & Gamble Uses Its Online Community to Help Develop Scents for a New Product Line

When Procter & Gamble was developing scents for a new product line, it asked members of its online community to simply record the scents that they encountered over the course of a day that made them feel good. By week's end, they had images, videos and simple text messages about cut grass, fresh paint, play dough, and other aromas that revealed volumes about how scent triggers not just nostalgia but feeling of competence, adventurousness, comfort, and other powerful emotions.

This scents project illustrates how mobile enables discovery around a specific sensation. But P&G also embarked on an ambitious attempt to get a more holistic understanding of its consumer—who she is, where she goes, what she sees. So, using a research application, community members were asked to share beauty moments—the sensory experiences and encounters with beauty products and brands that they have during the week, both at home and out in the world. A great deal was learned about how they feel at different times of day, in different contexts, about what triggers them to use an existing product or try a new one.

Beauty is a highly subjective attribute and feeling beautiful is a highly dynamic state. So P&G enlisted its community members to help it go deeper, not just through more personal, one-to-one sharing via these mobile apps buy through collective collaboration. After all, while emerging new tools and apps make people more accurate reports, they still have to be willing to do it. That's why it's so important to be able to establish intimacy, trust and relationship in one venue, like an online community or series of advisory group meetings or online chats that you can then apply to mobile projects, and vice versa.

In this example, P&G was trying to discover the parallels and discrepancies between how other see them. So community members simply used their phones to take pictures of themselves in the moment—at home or at work—and post them, along with their own critique. Then other community members privately and anonymously commented on the images.

"This is me after work. I am still wearing work clothes, tired, but feeling good," wrote one brave volunteer beneath her uploaded picture. "I see my smile, yet again, I also see that my face needs powdering and my eyes are tired."

But is that what other women saw when they looked at her? Some glances were pretty sharply appraising. "She seems to have a bit of acne," one unsentimental member wrote. "Her nose ring doesn't go with the rest of her," wrote another. "Bright, happy eyes!" observed one admirer. "Absolutely great smile. White teeth," wrote another. Overall, the "critics" were kinder than the subject.

Is it surprising to learn that young women are harder on themselves than others tend to be? Probably not. But the deeper lesson in this experience is about the positive potential of collaboration—between technologies (mobile vs. online), between consumers and between consumers and brands.

## Questions

1. Do you think P & G used the right research method to answer the research question? What about mall interviews or IDIs?

2. How does a company recruit the "right" respondents for its online and social media communities?

3. Researchers talk about getting "richer understanding" from online communities. What does this really mean?

4. How might a firm like Estee Lauder use this information? Should they also create an online community? Have they done so already?

© Denis Zbukarev/iStockphoto

# Primary Data Collection: Observation

## LEARNING OBJECTIVES

1. Develop a basic understanding of observation research.

2. Learn the approaches to observation research.

3. Understand the types of machine observation.

4. Appreciate how online tracking is changing and its growing use in social media.

5. Learn how virtual shopping environments are created and used in marketing research.

What is observation research, and how is it used in marketing research? What is ethnography, and why is it so popular? Observation research has exploded on the Internet and social media. Why? Why is online observation research so controversial? What are the machines that can be used in observation research, and what kind of data do they produce? We will answer these questions in Chapter 8.

# Nature of Observation Research

Instead of asking people questions, as a survey does, observation research depends on watching what people do. Specifically, **observation research** can be defined as the systematic process of recording patterns of occurrences or behaviors without normally questioning or communicating with the people involved. (Mystery shopping is an exception.) A marketing researcher using the observation technique witnesses and records events as they occur or

**observation research**
Systematic process of recording patterns of occurrences or behaviors without normally communicating with the people involved.

| EXHIBIT 8.1 | Observation Situations |
|---|---|
| **Situations** | **Example** |
| **People watching people** | Observers stationed in supermarkets watch consumers select frozen Mexican dinners, with the purpose of seeing how much comparison shopping people do at the point of purchase. |
| **People watching phenomena** | Observers stationed at an intersection count vehicles moving in various directions to establish the need for a traffic light. |
| **Machines watching people** | Movie or video cameras record consumers selecting frozen Mexican dinners. |
| **Machines watching phenomena** | Advanced software programs record people navigating the Internet. |

compiles evidence from records of past events. The observation may involve watching people or watching phenomena, and it may be conducted by human observers or by machines. Exhibit 8.1 gives examples of some common observation situations.

## Conditions for Using Observation

Three conditions must be met before most types of observation can be successfully used as a data-collection tool for marketing research:

1. The needed information must be either observable or inferable from behavior that is observable. For example, if a researcher wants to know why an individual purchased a new Toyota Sequoia rather than a Ford Expedition, observation research will not provide the answer.

2. The behavior of interest must be repetitive, frequent, or in some manner predictable. Otherwise, the cost of most forms of observation makes the approach prohibitively expensive.

3. The behavior of interest for many types of observation must be of relatively short duration. Observation of the entire decision-making process for purchasing a new home, which might take several weeks or months, is not feasible.

## Approaches to Observation Research

Researchers can choose from a variety of observation approaches. They are faced with the task of choosing the most effective approach for a particular research problem, from the standpoint of cost and data quality. The dimensions along which observation approaches vary are (1) natural versus contrived situations, (2) open versus disguised observation, (3) human versus machine observers, and (4) direct versus indirect observation.

**Natural versus Contrived Situations** Counting how many people enter a Macy's store during certain hours is a good example of a completely natural situation. The observer plays no role in the behavior of interest. Those being observed should have no idea that they are under observation. At the other extreme is recruiting people to do their shopping in a simulated supermarket (rows of stocked shelves set up in a field service's mall facility) so that their behavior can be carefully observed. In this case, the recruited people must be given at least some idea that they are participating in a study. The participants might be given grocery carts and told to browse the shelves and pick out items that they might normally use. The researchers might use alternative point-of-purchase displays for several products under study. To test the effectiveness of the various displays, the observers would note how long the shopper paused in front of the test displays and how often the product was actually selected. Today, many firms, such as Frito-Lay and Procter & Gamble, use online simulated environments.

A contrived environment enables the researcher to better control extraneous variables that might have an impact on a person's behavior or the interpretation of that behavior. Use of such an environment also tends to speed up the data-gathering process. The researcher does not have to wait for natural events to occur but instead instructs the participants to perform certain actions. Because more observations can be collected in the same length of time, the result will be either a larger sample or faster collection of the targeted amount of data. The latter should lower the costs of the project.

The primary disadvantage of a contrived setting is that it is artificial, and thus the observed behavior may be different from what would occur in a real-world situation. The more natural the setting, the more likely it is that the behavior will be normal for the individual being observed.

### Open versus Disguised Observation
Does the person being observed know that he or she is being observed? It is well known that the presence of an observer may have an influence on the phenomena being observed. Two general mechanisms work to bias the data. First, if people know they are being observed (as in **open observation**), they may behave differently. Second, the appearance and behavior of the observer offer potential for bias similar to that associated with the presence of an interviewer in survey research.

**Disguised observation** is the process of monitoring people who do not know they are being watched. A common form of disguised observation is observing behavior from behind a one-way mirror. For example, a product manager may observe respondent reactions to alternative package designs from behind a one-way mirror during a focus group discussion.

**open observation**
Process of monitoring people who know they are being watched.

**disguised observation**
Process of monitoring people who do not know they are being watched.

### Human versus Machine Observers
In some situations, it is possible and even desirable to replace human observers with machines—when machines can do the job less expensively, more accurately, or more readily. Traffic-counting devices are probably more accurate, definitely cheaper, and certainly more willing than human observers. It would not be feasible, for example, for Nielsen Holdings to have human observers in people's homes to record television viewing habits. Movie cameras, audiovisual equipment, and software record behavior much more objectively and in greater detail than human observers ever could. The electronic scanners found in most retail stores provide more accurate and timely data on product movement than human observers ever could.

### Direct versus Indirect Observation
Some of the observation carried out for marketing research is direct observation of current behavior or artifacts. For example, the contents of 100 women's purses in Portland, Oregon and Plano, Texas were examined as part of an observational study. Nearly every participant (99 percent) had something of a financial nature such as a credit or debit card, checkbook or wallet. Women who were married, college educated, and with high incomes carried the most cards. Ninety-eight percent of the women carried reward and membership cards. Office supplies, like paper and pens, were found in 93 percent of the purses. Other items discovered, in rank order, were: beauty and hair care, identification, receipts, cell phones and accessories, insurance cards, food and candy, health-care products, coupons, glasses, photos, trash, nail care products, feminine care products, tissues, hand sanitizers, food/drink supplies such as napkins and toothpicks, oral care products, religious items, weapons, keepsakes, and cameras. Only 8 percent carried a camera.[1]

In some cases, past behavior must be observed. To do this, the researcher must turn to some record of the behavior. Archaeologists dig up sites of old settlements and attempt to determine the nature of life in early societies from the physical evidence they find. **Garbologists** sort through people's garbage to analyze household consumption patterns. Marketing research usually is much more mundane. In a product prototype test, it may be important to learn how much of the test product the consumer used. The most accurate way to find this out is to have the respondent return the unused product so that the researcher

**garbologists**
Researchers who sort through people's garbage to analyze household consumption patterns.

can see how much is left. If a study involved the in-home use of a laundry soil and stain remover, it would be important to know how much of the remover each respondent actually used. All of the respondents' answers to questions would be considered from this usage perspective.

Pictures can also be used to see what people have done in certain situations. For example, a global study conducted by New York-based GfK NOP created a massive visual database with the goal of better understanding global consumers. Part of that research was photographing people's kitchens, which in many cultures is the "heart of the home." Examples of the kind of understanding the researchers gleaned from the photos are shown in Exhibit 8.2.

## Advantages of Observation Research

Watching what people actually do rather than depending on their reports of what they did has one very significant and obvious advantage: Firsthand information is not subject to many of the biasing factors associated with the survey approach. Specifically, the researcher avoids problems associated with the willingness and ability of respondents to answer questions. Also, some forms of data are gathered more quickly and accurately by observation. Letting a scanner record the items in a grocery bag is much more efficient than asking the shopper to enumerate them. Similarly, rather than asking young children which toys they like, major toy manufacturers prefer to invite target groups of children into a large playroom and observe via a one-way mirror which toys are chosen and how long each holds the child's attention.

## Disadvantages of Observation Research

The primary disadvantage of many types of observation research is that only behavior and physical personal characteristics usually can be examined. The researcher does not learn about motives, attitudes, intentions, or feelings. Also, with the exception of online observation, only public behavior is observed; private behavior—such as dressing for work or committee decision making within a company—is beyond the scope of observation

**Exhibit 8.2**

**Pictures Can Help Understand Global Consumers**

© wonry / iStockphoto

research. A second problem is that present observed behavior may not be projectable into the future. The fact that a consumer purchases a certain brand of milk after examining several alternatives does not mean that he or she will continue to do so in the future.

Observation research can be time-consuming and costly if the observed behavior occurs rather infrequently. For example, if observers in a supermarket are waiting to watch the purchase behavior of persons selecting Lava soap, they may have a long wait. And if the choice of consumers to be observed is biased (e.g., shoppers who go grocery shopping after 5:00 p.m.), distorted data may be obtained.

# Human Observation

As noted in Exhibit 8.1, people can be employed to watch other people or certain phenomena. For example, people can act as mystery shoppers, observers behind one-way mirrors, or recorders of shopper traffic and behavior patterns.

## Ethnographic Research

Ethnographic research comes to marketing from the field of anthropology. The popularity of the technique in commercial marketing research is increasing. **Ethnographic research**, or the study of human behavior in its natural context, involves observation of behavior and physical settings. Ethnographers directly observe the population they are studying. As "participant observers," ethnographers can use their intimacy with the people they are studying to gain richer, deeper insights into culture and behavior—in short, what makes people do what they do. Over $450 million annually is spent on ethnographic research.[2] Today, corporations, such as Procter & Gamble and Microsoft, have their own in-house ethnographers. Procter & Gamble conducted ethnographic research in Mexico City among lower-middle-class families. The research led to Downy Single Rinse, a fabric softener that removed a step from the less mechanized laundry process there. Ethnographic studies can cost anywhere from $5,000 to as much as $800,000, depending on how deeply a company wants to delve into its customers' lives.

One of the first uses of ethnographic research in an informal manner goes back to the Spanish Civil War in the 1930s. Forrest Mars Sr., when he wasn't dodging bullets, was observing soldiers coating their chocolate with sugar. The result of this ethnographic research was the creation of M&M's candy (named for Mars and business associate Bruce Murrie).[3]

**ethnographic research**
Study of human behavior in its natural context, involving observation of behavior and physical setting.

© Niels Poulsen std /Alamy

**Advantages of Ethnographic Research** Both focus groups and individual depth interviews rely on retrospection. That is, they ask respondents to recall their behavior and the behavior of others. Human memory, of course, can sometimes be faulty.

In addition, respondents sometimes reply in a socially desirable manner. A man may be reading adult magazines but claims to be reading *Fortune* and *BusinessWeek*.

Ethnographic research offers a number of advantages. These include the following:

- Ethnography is reality-based. It can show exactly how consumers live with a product, not just what they say about it or how they remember using it.
- It can reveal unexpressed needs and wants.
- It can discover unexploited consumer benefits.
- It can reveal product problems.
- It can show how, when, why, and where people shop for brands—and how they perceive it compared to competitive products.
- It can show who in the family actually uses a product and perhaps uncover a whole new potential demographic target.

- It takes advantage of consumers' experience with the category and their hands-on creativity as they demonstrate their ideas for new products and product improvements.
- It can test new products in a real context.
- It can reveal advertising execution ideas that derive directly from consumer experience.
- It can help form a better relationship with your consumers, based on an intimate knowledge of their lifestyles.[4]

Because individuals generally acclimate to an observer's presence over time (often quickly), their behavior becomes relatively unbiased by the observer—resulting in a more accurate characterization of behavior.

Although the ethnographic researcher's principal activity is observing behavior, active interviews or discussion with respondents is a key component. Getting respondents' perspectives on actions, through dialogue, is informative. Furthermore, the ethnographic data can be utilized in mixed method studies, for comparing and contrasting it with data from other sources. For example, a research manager could leverage observational data of the sales reps interacting with customers and prospects, and compare it with information from in-depth district and regional sales manager interviews—identifying any disconnects between what's being done and what's expected.

**Conducting Ethnographic Research** The first step is to find participants. Afterward, the observation process can begin. A highly skilled ethnographer is typically trained in anthropology. The research begins with systematic observation and inquiry. The ethnographer is trained to examine human culture: symbols, codes, myths, rituals, beliefs, values, rules for social interaction, and conceptual categories and perceptions. Many so-called ethnographists' interviews occur over a 90-minute period, too brief for close environmental observation and questioning. (Three to four hours per ethnographic observation and interview is far more productive.)

In a study on how consumers think about and use home printers, a highly trained ethnographer would ask:

- What are the meanings and processes of printing in their most elemental senses, as if the ethnographer had never seen a printer?
- Can we understand the symbolism of printing by exploring how respondents classify nonprinted versus printed matter?
- Anthropologists use a construct called binary opposition:

| Binary Opposition | |
|---|---|
| **Nonprinted Matter** | **Printed Matter** |
| Intangible | Tangible |
| Fleeting | Lasting |
| Public | Private |

- What are the consumer myths, stories, and beliefs about printing versus not printing and about different brands of printers?
- How do printing rituals serve as rites of passage that transform consumers from one state of being into another?
- Are people who print and save hard copies different in a "tribal" way from people who see printing as antiquated and wasteful?
- Are there social or business situations that demand or deny printing choices, and, if so, why?

These questions and observations would undoubtedly enrich new-product development and marketing communications, helping shape product design, brand positioning, and advertising content.[5] In contrast to the above, ethnography-lite would consist of limited observations (under an hour) and a few individual depth interviews. This form of research is often conducted by people who do not have advanced training in anthropology or sociology. Unfortunately, a number of studies are conducted in this manner, which often yield very few insights.

The next step is to analyze and interpret all of the data collected to find themes and patterns of meaning. This is no simple task. Hours and hours of audio and video must be transcribed and restudied. Even for the well-trained and experienced ethnographer, the amount of data can at times be overwhelming. But through careful and thorough analysis of the data, themes and categories emerge and applicable findings become clear. It often helps to bring in a second ethnographer who was not present during the field work to give his or her own objective appraisal.[6] Ethnographers usually create frameworks to help companies think about their consumers and understand what it all means.

Triangulation—the process of checking findings against what other people say and against similar research already conducted—is a way to verify the accuracy of collected data. While traditional ethnography stops with the description of the group studies, this is not sufficient for businesses. They need actionable guidelines, recommendations, and an outline of strategy. The findings must be presented in a fashion that will enable companies to create innovative and successful solutions.

For managers at Cambridge SoundWorks, it was a perplexing problem: In retail outlets across the country, men stood wide-eyed when sales reps showed off the company's hi-fi, "blow-your-hair-back" stereo speakers. So why didn't such unabashed enthusiasm for the product translate into larger—and bigger ticket—sales?

To find out, the Andover, Massachusetts, manufacturer and retailer of stereo equipment hired research firm Design Continuum, in West Newton, Massachusetts, to follow a dozen prospective customers over the course of two weeks. The researchers' conclusion: The high-end speaker market suffered from something referred to as "the spouse acceptance factor." While men adored the big black boxes, women hated their unsightly appearance. Concerned about the way the speakers would "look" in the living room, women would talk their husbands out of buying a cool but hideous and expensive piece of stereo equipment. Even those who had purchased the product had trouble showing it off: Men would attempt to display the loudspeakers as trophies in living rooms, while women would hide them behind plants, vases, and chairs. "Women would come into the store, look at the speakers and say, 'that thing is ugly,'" says Ellen Di Resta, principal at Design Continuum. "The men would lose the argument and leave the store without a stereo. The solution was to give the target market what men and women *both* wanted: a great sound system that looks like furniture so you don't have to hide it."

Armed with this knowledge, Cambridge SoundWorks unveiled a new line. The furniture-like Newton Series of speakers and home theater systems comes in an array of colors and finishes. The result: The Newton Series is the fastest-growing and best-selling product line in the firm's 14-year history.

Marriott hired IDEO, Inc., to rethink the hotel experience for an increasingly important customer: the young, tech-savvy road warrior. "This is all about looking freshly at business travel and how people behave and what they need," explains Michael E. Jannini, Marriott's executive vice president for brand management.[7]

To better understand Marriott's customers, IDEO dispatched a team of seven consultants, including a designer, anthropologist, writer, and architect, on a six-week trip. Covering 12 cities, the group hung out in hotel lobbies, cafés, and bars, and asked guests to graph what they were doing hour by hour.

This is what they learned: Hotels are generally good at serving large parties but not small groups of business travelers. Researchers noted that hotel lobbies tend to be dark and better suited to killing time than conducting casual business. Marriott lacked places where guests could comfortably combine work with pleasure outside their rooms. IDEO consultant and Marriott project manager Dana Cho recalls watching a female business traveler drink wine in the lobby while trying not to spill it on papers spread out on a desk. "There are very few hotel services that address [such] problems," says Cho.[8]

Having studied IDEO's findings, in January Marriott announced plans to reinvent the lobbies of its Marriott and Renaissance Hotels, creating for each a social zone, with small tables, brighter lights, and wireless web access, that is better suited to meetings. Another area will allow solo travelers to work or unwind in larger, quiet, semiprivate spaces where they won't have to worry about spilling coffee on their laptops or papers.

Jim Stengel, Procter & Gamble's chief marketing officer, notes, "I'm a big observational guy." So he has urged the P&G marketers to spend lots of time with consumers in their homes, watching the ways they wash their clothes, clean their floors, and diaper their babies, and asking them about their habits and frustrations. Back in 2000, the typical brand marketer spent less than 4 hours a month with consumers. Says Stengel: "It's at least triple that now."[9]

Brian Green, a senior researcher for Herman Miller, Inc., a manufacturer of office furnishings and accessories, described a recent ethnographic project that was global in scope. His report is given in the Practicing Marketing Research box.

# PRACTICING MARKETING RESEARCH

## As the World Works

My ethnography-based research touched four continents and involved interactions with more than 10,000 people over the course of three-and-a-half months on the road. After over 730 hours of field research, more than 3,000 pictures, and almost 30 hours of participant-generated video footage, the study yielded a plethora of rich data.

### The Ways People Interact

The primary purpose of this internationally inclusive study was to bring focus to physical and virtual work behaviors. Our team wanted to identify the ways people interact and how employers are supporting and fostering that behavior. What we learned would inform Herman Miller's new product development and create knowledge that could be shared with customers.

### Observation

This was the cornerstone of the methodologies. We worked with the customer contacts to determine which departments in their buildings were best to observe. With this there is definitely some sample bias but it is quite intentional. We were looking for study participants who spend more time interacting with others as a function of their jobs.

The observation tended to happen across a floor or two of an office building. This helped assure that one subset didn't cloud the research findings.

We were often given a desk to sit at as a home base. From there, we spent our time watching employees' interactions. While there was a risk that having us on-site might alter the employees' behavior, this didn't appear to get in the way. The employees' interactions were between themselves; we weren't really part of the office dynamic. In fact, most employees didn't pay any attention to us.

### Participant Documentation

We asked employees to use an interaction log, which is a one-page form with check boxes, to chart the characteristics of interaction. We wanted an easy way to paint a picture of each interaction. It captured things like the number of people participating in the interaction, duration, space where it occurred, technology and tools that were used, and the levels of privacy they had, both visual and acoustical.

A subsample of the participants, typically 10 to 15 over two days, was asked to complete the log. We didn't want this to become a burden, so each of these participants completed the log for only one of the two research days. The volume of completed logs intrigued us. In most cases, people were surprised how many logs and how many interactions they had in the course of a day.

## Online Survey

The online survey was administered to all workers at the customer sites. Our survey gathered information similar to the interaction log. Employees were asked to think about one of their most recent interactions. They were then presented with six different types of space and asked which typified where the interaction happened. The spaces were depicted with photography from their own spaces and a written description. Once they selected a space type they were asked about the characteristics of the interaction. The survey was customized for each research site with the company's logo information and images from their company environment.

## Focus Groups

We gathered 8-to-10 employees for focus groups at each site to help us better understand what we were seeing. We explored their most-favorite and least-favorite spaces. They talked about where they go to get heads-down, focused work done and where they go to interact. We asked where participants bump into others and have unplanned by meaningful conversation. We also discussed what tools and technologies were utilized in these spaces.

## Video Diaries

Day-in-the-life video diaries captured employee interactions. Employees were asked to find situations that might be insightful and in which they could tell us why they were doing things the way they did. We asked that they capture the environment around them when they were interacting. The videos provided a wealth of information from the participants' perspectives.

## Pictures

We took many pictures at each site to document the types of areas and the interactions that took place within them. Photos were later categorized and tagged with descriptors.

## Utilization Study

At the beginning of each site visit, we asked the company to provide floor plans of their spaces. These were used to chart interactions. Because we toured the space every half-hour, documenting where the interactions occurred, we were able to create a heat map of the space. This showed where interactions were happening and where they weren't. We captured characteristics of the interactions, such as how many people were interacting, with what technology, which work tools were used, and postures of the participants.

## Results Were Rich

As one might expect, the building, its interior layout and its furnishings play a huge role in how people interact in the work environment.

The utilization study yielded one of the more interesting statistical nuggets. We observed and charted that 70 percent of the interactions took place around the individual offices. On the one hand, this makes sense—it is, after all, where the people work. On the other hand, this reinforces the notion that people don't need formal conference rooms to interact with their colleagues.

Through the focus groups, we found that people go through an almost-unconscious checklist to determine if they should find a meeting space or stay in their individual space. When someone walks up to an individual's desk, that individual considers the following:

- How long is this going to take?
- Do we need to have anyone else join us for the discussion?
- Are there any tools (e.g., whiteboard, tack board, projector, teleconference phone, etc.) that we need for a successful outcome?
- Is the topic we are discussing appropriate for those around us?

When people are driven to a meeting space, they avoid areas that don't meet their needs. People know what works for them and what doesn't. The primary drivers that determine where people go when an interaction needs to become more formal are:

- Proximity—People typically won't bypass areas that work in favor of a "cooler" space further away.
- Availability—Is the place available for collaboration?
- Technology—Does it have the right technology tools for the task at hand?
- Lighting—Does the place have access to natural light? Is there adequate lighting?
- Tools (e.g., whiteboard, tack board, etc.)—Does the collaboration space have the tools that will make the meeting productive?

The long-held view that the corporate environment is going away is in stark contrast to the value placed on the office by the participants. These people used words like *increased efficiency*, *clarity of communication*, and *better personal connection* to describe what they value about the office. Even in the age of technology and telecommuting, face-to-face interactions are still held in high regard.[10]

## Questions

1. How might Herman Miller use these research findings?
2. Are there other research techniques that could have been used to obtain the same information? If so, what are they?
3. Are there advantages to combining ethnographic research with other types of research? If yes, describe those advantages.

**Ethnography and Focus Groups** Of course, both ethnography and focus groups are forms of qualitative research. Yet most research clients see the two techniques playing different roles in the overall research process. Sometimes both methodologies are used on the same project:

■ Ethnography for strategic understanding, exploratory research at the beginning of the creative/innovation process.

■ Focus groups/IDIs for tactical issues—reactions to stimuli (ads, visuals, concepts, etc.), often ones that have been developed in the first phase. In a sense, these methods have been repositioned in some clients' minds.

I think of focus groups to get narrow things. If I have eight concepts, [I want to know] what's working better than another, what language is working better, etc. When I'm trying to get something deeper and something I didn't know how to ask, I would use one-on-ones. If I have the choice and the time—there's time and money associated with ethnography—I'd opt for ethnography hands-down every time. *(pharmaceutical client)*

Focus groups still have their place for consensus building and culling down ideas. For innovation, I do think ethnography has an advantage. *(consultant)*

It's rare that we do a study that doesn't have both ethnography and focus groups. They both have their purposes. We try [ideas] out in the focus groups based on earlier insights and ideas drawn from the ethnography. Focus groups yield time and efficiency that can lead to tighter and more effective surveys." *(financial services client)*[11]

## Mystery Shoppers

**mystery shoppers**
People who pose as consumers and shop at a company's own stores or those of its competitors to collect data about customer–employee interactions and to gather observational data; they may also compare prices, displays, and the like.

**Mystery shoppers** are used to gather observational data about a store (e.g., are the shelves neatly stocked?) and to collect data about customer–employee interactions. In the latter case, of course, there is communication between the mystery shopper and the employee. The mystery shopper may ask, "How much is this item?" "Do you have this in blue?" or "Can you deliver this by Friday?" The interaction is not an interview, and communication occurs only so that the mystery shopper can observe the actions and comments of the employee. Mystery shopping is, therefore, classified as an observational marketing research method, even though communication is often involved. It is estimated that 70 percent of America's national retailers use the technique: Walmart, McDonald's, Starbucks, Blockbuster, Jiffy Lube, Rite Aid, PF Chang's restaurants, and Whole Foods Markets are some of the big-name clients that rely on mystery shoppers.

"The No. 1 thing we're trying to do is reinforce a company's training," explains David Rich, president of ICC/Decision Services, which deploys mystery shoppers for such clients as Levi's and Godiva.[12] Mystery shopping gives managers nearly instant feedback on whether their workers are smiling when they ought to, making customers feel at ease, or inviting them to get fries with that. Many companies tie bonuses to performance on mystery inspections, giving employees an incentive to be nice.

The mystery-shopping concept has four basic levels, which differ in the depth and type of information collected:

■ *Level 1*—The mystery shopper conducts a mystery telephone call. Here, the mystery shopper calls the client location and evaluates the level of service received over the phone, following a scripted conversation.

■ *Level 2*—The mystery shopper visits an establishment and makes a quick purchase; little or no customer–employee interaction is required. For example, in a Level 2 mystery shop, a mystery shopper purchases an item (e.g., gas, a hamburger, or a lottery ticket) and evaluates the transaction and image of the facility.

- *Level 3*—The mystery shopper visits an establishment and, using a script or scenario, initiates a conversation with a service and/or sales representative. Level 3 mystery shopping usually does not involve an actual purchase. Examples include discussing different smartphone packages with a sales representative, reviewing services provided during an oil change, and so forth.

- *Level 4*—The mystery shopper performs a visit that requires excellent communication skills and knowledge of the product. Discussing a home loan, the process for purchasing a new car, or visiting apartment complexes serve as examples.

Mystery shopping can have one or several objectives. As mentioned earlier, a common objective is measuring employee training. Other objectives are:

- Enabling an organization to monitor compliance with product/service delivery standards and specifications.

- Enabling marketers to examine the gap between promises made through advertising/sales promotion and actual service delivery.

- Helping monitor the impact of training and performance improvement initiatives on compliance with or conformance to product/service delivery specifications.

- Identifying differences in the customer experience across different times of day, locations, product/service types, and other potential sources of variation in product/service quality.[13]

One mystery-shopping firm that specializes in chain, mid-priced restaurants, gathers the following types of data:

- Telephone skills/hostess services
- Guest experience
- Food quality and temperature
- Facility conditions
- Cleanliness of restroom facilities
- Parking lot condition
- Dress code compliance
- Visibility and interaction of management staff
- Compliance with franchise agreement[14]

Understanding a restaurant's service and environment is critical to the success of Fridays, Olive Garden, and Chili's. For example, one survey of 4,000 diners in midpriced chains found that when food delivery was less than 10 minutes, 57 percent stated that they "definitely would return." That percentage dropped to 17 percent when delivery was longer than 15 minutes.[15]

Today, mystery-shopping companies use smartphones for providing real-time insights using web-based reporting systems. In the past, summary reports often took a minimum of a week to 10 days after the shoppers left the field. Today, technology allows for same-day client reports.[16]

## One-Way Mirror Observations

The discussion of focus groups in Chapter 5 noted that focus group facilities almost always provide **one-way mirror observation**, which allows clients to observe the group discussion as it unfolds. New product development managers, for example, can note

**one-way mirror observation**
Practice of watching behaviors or activities from behind a one-way mirror.

consumers' reactions to various package prototypes as the moderator demonstrates them. (One researcher spent 200 hours watching mothers change diapers to gather information for the redesign of disposable diapers.) In addition, the clients can observe the degree of emotion exhibited by the consumer as he or she speaks. One-way mirrors are also sometimes used by child psychologists and by toy designers to observe children at play. At the Fisher-Price Play Lab, some 3,500 children per year pass through. It is set up like a preschool classroom. On the other side of the glass is a narrow carpeted room with about 10 chairs and two video cameras. Nearly all Fisher-Price toys have been taken for a spin in the Play Lab at some point in their development.

The lighting level in the observation room must be very dim relative to that in the focus group room. Otherwise, the focus group participants can see into the observation room. Several years ago, we (the authors) were conducting a focus group of orthopedic surgeons in St. Louis, Missouri. One physician arrived approximately 20 minutes early and was ushered into the group room. A young assistant product manager for the pharmaceutical manufacturer was already seated in the observation room. The physician, being alone in the group room, decided to take advantage of the large framed mirror on the wall for some last-minute grooming. He walked over to the mirror and began combing his hair. At the same time, the assistant product manager, sitting about a foot away on the other side of the mirror, decided to light a cigarette. As the doctor combed his hair, there was suddenly a bright flash of light, and another face appeared through the mirror. What happened next goes beyond the scope of this text. In recent years, the trend has been to inform participants of the one-way mirror and to explain who is in the other room watching and why. Another trend is to use a hidden video camera and broadcast the live feed to one or more remote locations.

# Machine Observation

The observation methods discussed so far have involved people observing things or consumers. Now we turn our attention to observation by machines. We begin with popular and controversial topics of neuromarketing.

**Neuromarketing**
The process of researching the brain patterns and certain physiological measures of consumers to marketing stimuli.

**electroencephalograph (EEG)**
Machine that measures electrical pulses on the scalp and generates a record of electrical activity in the brain.

## Neuromarketing

**Neuromarketing** is the process of researching the brain patterns and certain physiological measures of consumers to marketing stimuli. Brain patterns are typically measured by an **electroencephalograph (EEG)** that records the brain's electrical activity. Functional magnetic resonance imaging (fMRI) measures the changes in the flow of blood related to neural activity in the brain. Physiological measures include blood pressure, heart rate, and sweating.

Neuromarketing is a so-called hot area in marketing research. It has both strong proponents and detractors. The largest firm in the field is NeuroFocus, a Nielsen Holdings company. The firm has invented a portable, wireless EEG that sends data directly to a remote laptop of iPad. Consumers are paid to wear the device while watching TV, viewing ad or product prototypes, watching movies, or possibly shopping in a store or mall. An EEG measures electrical activity in virtually real-time. In contrast, an MRI records changes in blood flow in the brain that results in about a five second delay in the reading. MRIs provide clear, high-resolution pictures but cannot match an EEG for speed. For example, imagine that you are asked to generate an action verb in response to the word *ball*. Within 200 milliseconds, your brain has absorbed the request. Impulses move to the motor cortex and drive your articulators to respond, and you might say "throw." This process happens far too fast for an MRI to record. But an EEG can capture virtually every neurological impulse that results from that single word: *ball*. According to proponents, this is where neuromarketing exists—at the very creation of an unconscious idea, in the wisp of time between the instant your brain receives a stimulus and subconsciously reacts. There, data are unfiltered, uncorrupted by your conscious mind, which hasn't yet had the chance to formulate and deliver a response in words or gestures.[17]

NeuroFocus tests just two dozen subjects for its corporate clients. It is claimed that this is possible because people's brains are remarkably alike, even though there are some differences between male and female brains, and between those of children and senior citizens. And NeuroFocus collects a massive amount of input, recording and analyzing billions of data points during a typical neurological testing project.[18]

Intel hired NeuroFocus to better understand how people felt about Intel the brand. Previous research found that most people know Intel and like the brand. But when asked to name tech leaders, Intel came out lower on the list. Thus, Intel managers wanted a deeper understanding of consumer's feeling about the brand.

NeuroFocus structured its test for Intel using the Evoked Response Potential test, a staple of neuroscience. Test subjects were paid to come to a NeuroFocus lab and put on a cap with 64 sensors that would measure electrical activity across the brain. Because the United States and China are two very important markets for Intel, NeuroFocus tested groups of 24 consumers (half men, half women) in Berkeley, California, and in a midsize city in China's Sichuan Province.

In a quiet room, each test subject was shown the words *achieve, possibilities, explore, opportunity, potentiality, identify, discover, resolves,* and *solves problems.* Each went by on a TV screen at half-second intervals. The subject was instructed to press a button whenever she saw a word with a letter underscored by a red dot. After several minutes of this subconscious-priming word test, she was shown a few Intel ads. Following this, the words were again presented on the screen, this time without the dots.[19]

The exercise served two functions: First, the red dots focused the subject's attention; second, they gave NeuroFocus a baseline measure of the brain's response, since each time a test subject saw the red dot, her brain created the "click" reaction. A so-called "a-ha" moment.

When NeuroFocus later analyzed the EEG readings, it looked for those same "a-ha" moments from the period during which the subject had viewed the Intel ads. The words that provoked the most such responses were *achieve* and *opportunity.* Women in the United States and in China had virtually the same response post-advertisements, as did American men and Chinese men. The differences were in the genders; in both countries, men and women had strikingly different reactions. *Achieve* prompted the most intense reactions among women, while men gravitated toward *opportunity.* The results ultimately led Intel to change its promotional strategy.[20]

Despite the success of NeuroFocus, Graham Page, executive vice president of Consumer Neuroscience, Millward Brown, one of America's largest marketing research firms, urges caution. Page says:

- There are still significant practical hurdles. The technologies are not available everywhere, and the logistics of brainwave measurement or brain scanning are not trivial. Testing robust numbers of participants is often expensive—or worse, not done.
- The extreme claims of some of the early practitioners in the field have inspired some skepticism.
- Many of our clients believe their work in this area has the potential to generate significant competitive advantage and so are understandably coy about sharing too much publicly.
- Most marketers quickly realize that neuroscience methods in isolation can be hard to interpret and don't stand alone.[21]

Graham Page continues, "This last point is crucial. Over the last six years we have examined all the main techniques in the area and compared them to the existing qualitative and quantitative work we do to ensure a realistic perspective on what the science can and can't say. We've seen that there is clear and significant value in certain neuroscience methods, but only when used alongside existing methods rather than as a replacement and only if interpreted with care by people with experience in the field. Neuroscience-based methods do not reveal the inner truth; rather, they provide additional perspective on consumers' responses to brands and marketing, which needs interpretation in the light of other information. A holistic approach reveals greater insight than conventional or neuroscience methods along.[22]

We now turn our attention to two older technologies that also fall under the neuromarketing umbrella—galvanic skin response GSR) and eye tracking.

**galvanic skin response (GSR)**
Change in the electric resistance of the skin associated with activation responses; also called *electrodermal response*.

### Galvanic Skin Response
**Galvanic skin response (GSR)**, also known as *electrodermal response*, is a change in the electric resistance of the skin associated with activation responses. A small electric current of constant intensity is sent into the skin through electrodes attached to the palmar side of the fingers. The changes in voltage observed between the electrodes (caused by the moisture of sweating) indicate the level of stimulation. Because the equipment is portable and not expensive, measuring GSR is a simple way to assess emotional reaction to a stimulus. GSR is used primarily to measure stimulus response to advertisements but is sometimes used in packaging research.

### Eye Tracking
There has been a surge in the use of eye-tracking research as the equipment has gotten more sophisticated. Tobii Technology has introduced glasses that look and feel like modern eyewear and allows subjects to walk around freely in a real-world environment. They can browse in stores, use a computer, try out a new product, or read an advertisement.[23] Unilever, Kimberly-Clark, Con Agra, Heinz, and Kellogg all use eye-tracking research. Tobii creates virtual store shelves for Procter & Gamble to test the pulling power of new package designs.

Eye tracking is used to precisely measure what someone is looking at. An infrared light is directed into the eye. The light enters the retina and is reflected back to a camera. The vector between the center of the pupil and the corneal reflection is measured and point-of-regard is found. Using trigonometry, the system calculates eye movements.[24]

Eye tracking can document:

1. *Visibility.* Do people even see and notice a package on a cluttered shelf, a display in an enormous store or a link on a cluttered web screen?

2. *Engagement.* Do these marketing efforts hold their attention, or are they quickly bypassed?

3. *Viewing patterns/communication hierarchy.* Which specific elements or messages draw attention and are consistently seen/read—and which are frequently overlooked?

These three dimensions provide important direction in terms of when eye tracking is most likely to be valuable. Because eye tracking measures visibility and engagement, it is typically most relevant in situations in which the marketer is buying "space" (such as a direct-mail envelope, an ad in a magazine, or a package on a shelf) and attempting to capture a viewer's time and attention.[25]

Marketing Metrics conducted an eye-tracking study involving 45 different direct mail pieces across 33 different companies. The goal was to determine how long mail recipients view and interact with a direct mail piece before they make the critical decision of keeping it (to share with someone else in the household or for later reference or usage) or throw it away. Additional behavioral insights on how recipients view and interact with advertisements

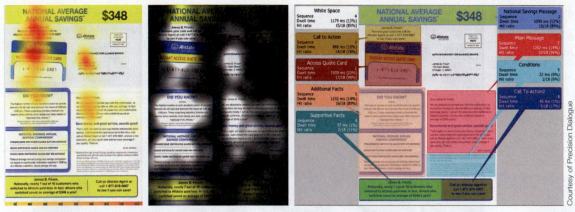

*Source:* Cathleen Zapata, "What Caught Their Eye?" *Quirk's Marketing Research Review*, May 2012, 35.

Courtesy of Precision Dialogue

**Exhibit 8.3**

**A Heat Map, Focus Map and Key Performance Indicators for an Allstate Direct Mail Piece**

received in the mail were also obtained. A mix of 18 participants was tested at MetricsLab in Cleveland. Participants included nine male and nine female direct mail recipients, median age 35, with a variety of interests, needs, and experiences.[26]

Keep rates for the direct mail pieces ranged from 0 for the Bradford Exchange and several others to 83 percent for Dick's Sporting Goods. Respondents said that they would keep it for later or share with someone in the household.

Several types of output from eye tracking are heat maps, focus maps, and key performance indicators (see Exhibit 8.3). Heat maps highlight areas that users see most often. Areas viewed more often are darker in color (shown in red) than areas viewed less often (yellow). Areas without color were not directly viewed. Focus maps are similar to heat maps but show areas viewed less often in black. Areas that are clear were directly viewed more often.

The chart of key performance indicators displays statistics for identified areas of interest. The sequence of one area of interest is the order that area was viewed, taking into account all identified areas. Areas that are not designated as an area of interest are described as white space. The dwell time is the number of microseconds that users looked at the specific area of interest. The percentage next to the dwell time tells what percentage of the overall viewing time was spent on this item. The hit ratio describes the number of users who focused on that area of interest, out of the total number of users included in the analysis[27].

We now turn our attention to other forms of machine observation.

## Facial Action Coding Services (FACS)

Researchers at the University of California at San Francisco identified the 43 muscle movements responsible for all human facial expression (see Exhibit 8.4). They spent seven years categorizing roughly 3,000 combinations of such movements and the emotions they convey—the "eyelid tightener" expresses anger, for instance, and the "nasolabial fold deepener" manifests sadness. The system has proved to be highly accurate; the FBI and CIA reportedly use the FACS method to determine the emotions of suspects during interrogations.[28]

Sensory Logic, a Saint Paul, Minnesota, research firm, uses FACS to get to the "truth." The firm's clients include Target, Nextel, General Motors, and Eli Lilly, according to Don Hill, the firm's president (see *www.sensorylogic.com*). To measure initial gut reactions to a commercial or ad, Hill first attaches electrodes to the side of a subject's mouth (monitoring the zygomatic muscle, for smiles), above the eyebrow (corrugator muscle, for frowns), and on two fingers (for sweat). He says the facial muscle movements reflect appeal, whereas perspiration translates into what he calls "impact"—emotional power. After Hill takes initial readings, he removes the electrodes and he videotapes an interview with each subject. Later,

© Cameron Whitman/iStockphoto

**Exhibit 8.4**

**Which One Is Blowing Smoke?**

Dan Hill, president of Sensory Logic, says that some of the consumers who tell you they like what you're selling don't really mean it. Here he shows us how to tell who's being genuine and who's just making nice.

his FACS-trained team reviews the video, second by second, cataloguing emotions. In a study of automobile Super Bowl commercials, Hill found that consumers' facial expressions were a strong predictor of future sales.[29]

Even some of Hill's happy customers say that face reading has limitations. For one thing, not everyone believes that pitches have to aim for the heart. "A lot of the advertising we do is a more rational sell," a General Motors researcher says, "so emotional research doesn't apply."[30]

## Gender and Age Recognition Systems

NEC Electronics of Japan has developed technology to recognize gender and approximate age of consumers. It has married this system with digital signs that can be placed in malls, airports, and other heavily trafficked public areas. Mall retailers, for example, can tailor their message to a person as they walk by. The system can also count the number of persons who walked past the flat-panel digital signs during any specific time period. The program uses an algorithm that draws on a database on thousands of faces as a reference. It looks at distinguishing points of the face, from the shape of the ears and eyes to hair color, to determine the age. The database expands as more people walk past the camera, allowing the program to make better judgment calls with time.

NEC also has installed the recognition system in vending machines in Japan. When a person stands in front of a vending machine, the system reads a consumer's profile. It then recommends snacks and drinks that fit the person's profile.

Consumers, meanwhile, may object to getting their faces scanned, without their knowledge. Likewise, retailers may not want to involve themselves in what some may perceive as a violation of privacy. To date, the systems have not been installed in the United States.[31]

## In-Store Tracking

In-store security cameras are now being used to track shopper behavior. RetailNext takes video feeds from the security cameras and runs them through proprietary software to track shoppers. Cameras can be combined with motion sensors to determine, for example, how often a brand is picked up but not placed in the shopping cart. Companies such as T-Mobile, Family Dollar Stores, and American Apparel are using the system.

RetailNext's data sometimes refute conventional wisdom. For instance, many food manufacturers pay a premium for their products to be displayed at the end of an aisle. But customers pay greater attention to products placed in the center of an aisle, according to RetailNext's analysis.[32] *Why* they do that might be material for another study.

Luxury retailer Montblanc began testing RetailNext's video analytics at a store in Miami. Employees have used it to generate maps showing which parts of the store are best-trafficked and to decide where to place in-store decorations, salespeople, and merchandise. The technology has boosted sales 20 percent, and Montblanc plans to expand it to other stores.[33]

A variation of in-store tracking is an iPhone app being tested by Neiman Marcus. Shoppers download the app from iTunes and opt in to the service. Sensors are installed at key entry points of the store, so when a shopper with the app passes within range, she's alerted to which of her preferred sales associates is in the store right now—plus new-product arrivals, sales, fashion trends and upcoming store events. Shoppers can use the app to make appointments or leave messages for associates; mark favorite products, which are automatically shared with their favorite sales associates; and scan QR codes on store signage for trend and product information. Neiman's can synch past purchase data, too, enabling sales associates to provide relevant, tailored recommendations.[34]

Location-based tools like Foursquare are trickling down from restaurants and specialty retail to packaged goods. A number of grocers and some drugstores are testing check-ins, providing tailored, real-time offers. Walgreens is the first retailer to adopt a new service from LocalResponse to monitor GPS services, such as Foursquare and Yelp, for "check-in" notifications. When a shopper "checks-in" at a Walgreens store, the service tweets an ad to the shopper based on his location. For example, Walgreens tweeted over 5,000 ads for Halls cough drops: "Check out Halls new cough drops in the cold aisle."[35]

## Television Audience Measurement and Tracking

For the past decade or so, watching television in America has been defined by the families recruited by Nielsen Media Research who have agreed to have an electronic meter attached to their televisions or to record in a diary what shows they watch. Traditional "people meters" are electronic TV-set-top boxes that continually record which channel is tuned in. Today, the trend is away from traditional people meters to direct measurement from "set-top boxes" (STB). These are the boxes installed by the likes of Direct TV, Dish Network, and the cable companies to enable you to watch television programs. As the technology develops, researchers will be able to tap second-by-second viewing habits of millions of households. In contrast, Nielsen's national people meter panel consists of only 18,000 people.

In the past, TV programs were typically viewed in the home, or perhaps a sports bar, on TV sets. Today, that has changed. More and more people are viewing TV programs on laptops, iPads, and other tablets and portable devices. A recent survey found 18 percent of the respondents watch full-length TV shows on tablets.[26] Nielsen has created new technology that now lets it measure mobile viewing as well as viewing on traditional TV sets. This is very important to the television networks because TV ratings (viewers per program) dropped in 2013. This meant that TV broadcast networks had to charge less for each of their advertising slots. Although some audiences may have declined, it is possible that viewers simply switched to viewing on mobile devices, which wasn't previously measured.

## TiVo Targeting

TiVo has created Power\\Watch, a panel of 48,000 TiVo households who have opted-in to having their personally identifiable viewing information collected and responding to monthly online surveys. Those who opt in have a chance to win a $1,000 Amazon shopping spree and other prizes. Advertisers will now be able to look at the TV-tuning behaviors of households based on attitudes and other behavioral characteristics such as intent to purchase a new vehicle, types of favorite movies, political affiliation, and travel plans.[37]

TiVo says it also licenses anonymous viewing data to TV-targeting firm TRA, which matches second-by-second data from 1.7 million set-top boxes from TiVo and a major cable operator with other types of data— including some 57 million frequent-shopping cards. The matching is done through Experian, a big data company that knows which set-top box and which frequent-shopping card belongs to a particular street address. (It doesn't share the address with TRA.)

The method can turn up surprising associations: TRA found that watchers of *Jersey Shore* were also regular buyers of yogurt.[38]

## Cablevision Targeting

Cablevision can beam different ads to different set-top boxes, even when they're tuned to the same channel.

This technology figures out which subscribers should see which ad by anonymously matching the names and addresses of Cablevision's subscribers with information provided by big data firms. Cablevision says it doesn't share subscriber data with advertisers, or use or share viewership information. Cablevision now offers advertisers targeted ads across its entire viewing market.

## Symphony IRI Consumer Network

The Symphony IRI Consumer Network is a continuous household purchase panel that receives purchasing data from the National Consumer Panel (NCP), a joint venture between Symphony IRI and the Nielsen Holdings. Households are recruited to the NCP and given incentives to record all of their UPC-based purchases, with a handheld in-home scanning device.

The data available from the panel includes the following:

- Average amount of product purchased by each household during a specific period.
- Total projected category or product volume sold in the specific period.
- Projected number of households that purchased the category or product within the specific period.
- The average number of shopping trips when the product was purchased.
- The average volume sold for the product per purchase occasion.[31]

Symphony IRI also offers its Marketplace Insights On Demand, which provides online and offline survey data from the Consumer Network panel. When a client wants more information about what is happening in the marketplace, it can turn to Insights surveys. The types of information that can be obtained from the surveys include:

- *Retailer competitive landscape insights:* What percent of a retailer's shopper base also shops elsewhere? How do shoppers' dollars per trip in one retailer compare to another?

- *Category competitive landscape insights:* How much spending is the retailer missing when the shoppers shop elsewhere? For shoppers who do not buy the category at the retailer, where are they buying the category?
- *Consumer purchasing dynamics insights:* Understand the drivers behind category dynamics and describe purchasing behavior for key customer segments.[39]

# Tracking

Online tracking is fundamentally another form of observation research. The objective is to deliver the right message to the right audience at the right time. Orbitz found that Mac users spend around 30 percent more on hotel rooms than their PC counterparts. Also, Mac users are 40 percent more likely to book a four- or five-star hotel. Therefore, when Mac users want to book a hotel, they are shown more expensive options than PC users looking for a room in the same city.[40]

Whereas survey research lets researchers find out the "why" and "how," tracking (also called behavioral tracking), answers the "where," "how much," and "how often" questions. Tracking helps close the gap between what consumers tell you they think and what they intend to do and what they actually do.

Traditional Internet tracking is via cookies. A cookie is a piece of text stored by a user's web browser. It can be used for authentication, storing site preferences, shopping cart contents, and other useful functions. Cookies can also be used for tracking the Internet user's web browsing habits. A *flash cookie* is a cookie placed on a computer via Adobe System's popular Flash program. Using Flash is the most common way to show video online.

Lotame Solutions, Inc., a New York company, uses sophisticated software called a "beacon" to capture what people are typing on a website — their comments on monies, say, or their interest in parenting and pregnancy. Lotame packages that data into profiles about individuals, without determining a person's name, and sells the profiles to companies seeking customers.

Perhaps the most controversial monitoring comes from "third-party cookies." They work like this: The first time a site is visited, it installs a tracking file, which assigns the computer a unique ID number. Later, when the user visits another site affiliated with the same tracking company, it can take note of where that user was before and where he is now. This way, over time the company can build a robust profile.

Until recently, trackers have had a problem on how to track and target the same consumer across multiple devices—desktops and laptops, smartphones, and tablets. Cookies work well when a person is using one device like a laptop or desktop. The trail is more difficult to follow when a user switches to a mobile device. When users frequently switch between, say, a desktop and mobile device, they are referred to as *digitally agnostic*. A recent study found that digitally agnostic users can switch screens up to 27 times an hour.[41] Several new companies, such as Tapad and Drawbridge, have attacked this problem. Tapad analytics examines 150 billion data points—from cookies, cellphone IDs (which link individual phones to app downloads and web browsing), Wi-Fi connections, website registrations, browsing history, and other inputs. Tapad looks for commonalities that link one device with another.

If a tablet and a laptop share the same Wi-Fi network, for example, that's a positive sign. So are browsing patterns—say, two devices share a history of visiting sports websites. Each correlation nudges higher the likelihood that the same person owns both devices. Based on those probabilities, Tapad clients serve potential customers ads across platforms. A target might see one ad on a work computer, another on the mobile web on the commute home, and a third while sitting with a tablet on the couch. Companies such as American Airlines, Audi, and TurboTax are using Tapad.[42]

## Your E-Reader Is Reading You

There are some 40 million e-readers and 65 million tablets in use in the United States.[43] Amazon, Apple, and Google can easily track how far readers are getting in books, how long they spend reading them, and which search terms they use to find books. Amazon knows, for example, that 18,000 readers underlined the passage, "Because sometimes things happen to people and they're not equipped to deal with them." This is from *Catching Fire,* the second book in the *Hunger Games* trilogy.[44]

The digital reading platform Copia, which has 50,000 subscribers, collects detailed demographic and reading data—including the age, gender, and school affiliation of people who bought particular titles, as well as how many times the books were downloaded, opened, and read—and shares its findings with publishers. Copia aggregates the data so that individual users aren't identifiable, and shares that information with publishers who request it.[45]

## Social Media Tracking

One of the greatest advantages of social media research lies within tracking research that monitors brand sentiment over discrete units of time. Because social media data are tagged with times and dates, and because information is stored publicly online until such time as the creator deletes it, historical data can be instantly available. Understanding how consumers talk about a product, brand, or service, or what they expect, delivers invaluable direction on how to create a successful marketing mix. One company wanted to enter a product category that was new to it, yet a logical extension of its brand. By using social media tracking, the firm could see what people were saying about existing companies in the product category. The researchers determined what was liked and disliked, which helped play a role in designing the new line extension.

Facebook is the largest social media site, with over 1.2 billion users. Google is gaining steam with 345 million users. Pinterest continues to grow as it sheds its "women only" image, and others like Slideshare, Tumblr, Path, and Mobi also will take more social media market share. Twitter shows no signs of decline, but it will be interesting to see how it innovates to keep up with Google+. Twitter recently added a micro video app "Vine" as a move toward real-time video sharing. Vine allows a maximum of 6 seconds.[46] Let's take a closer look at tracking on three social media sites: Facebook, Twitter, and Pinterest.

**Facebook** When you decide to sign up for a new account, Facebook inserts two tracking cookies into your browser: a session cookie and a browser cookie. If you choose not to become a member, you get only the browser cookie. From then on, every time you visit a webpage that has a Facebook Like button, or any other Facebook plug-in, the social networking website is informed of the date, time, and web address of the webpage you have clicked. Other information (e.g., IP addresses, operating system, and browser version) is also recorded. If you are logged into Facebook and surfing the web, the session cookie logs your activity. It also records your name, e-mail, friends, and all profile-related data. If you are not logged on, or if you are a nonmember, the browser cookie conducts the logging and reports a unique identifier but no other personal information.[47]

For advertisers, Facebook offers conversion tracking. A **conversion** is an action that a person takes based on an advertiser's website such as checking out, registering, adding an item to the shopping cart, or viewing a particular page. Virtually any page on a website can represent a conversion, and the advertiser can create and add the conversion tracking code on any page of its website.[48] Conversion tracking helps businesses measure the return on investment of their Facebook ads by reporting on the actions people take after viewing those ads. Advertisers can create pixels that track conversion, add them to the pages of their website where the conversions will happen, and then track these conversions back to ads they're running on Facebook.

**Cost per impression** is the cost to offer potential customers one opportunity to see an advertisement. It is often expressed in a cost-per-thousand basis (CPM). Facebook's analytics optimize the process for advertisers so that persons most likely to make a conversion are the ones exposed to the ads. Conversion tracking helps businesses leverage *optimized cost per impression* (oCPM) to show ads to people who are more likely to convert off Facebook.[49]

If an advertiser wants to track the conversions that happen of its website as a result of ads that they are running on Facebook, the firm can create a conversion tracking pixel to put on its website. Using the conversion-tracking pixel tool, the advertiser can create a JavaScript code snippet to place on the conversion pages. For example, if the company wants to track checkouts, it would put the conversion-tracking pixel on the checkout confirmation page that people see after completing a checkout. Whenever a person loads that page in his or her browser, the code tells Facebook that the conversion event has occurred. Facebook then matches that conversion event against the set of people who have viewed and/or clicked on an ad so that Facebook can provide the advertiser with information that helps understand the return on investment for the ad spending.[50]

Facebook is testing technology that would greatly expand the scope of data that it collects about its users. The social network might start collecting data on minute user interactions with its content, such as how long a user's cursor hovers over a certain part of its website, or whether a user's newsfeed is visible at a given moment on the screen of his or her mobile phone.

Facebook collects two kinds of data, demographic and behavioral. The *demographic* data—such as where a user lives or went to school—document a user's life beyond the network. The *behavioral data*—such as one's circle of Facebook friends, or "likes"—are captured in real time on the network itself. The ongoing tests would greatly expand the behavioral data that are collected.[51]

**Pinterest** Pinterest is a pinboard-style photo-sharing site, which allows users to create and manage theme-based image collections, such as hobbies, interest, and events. You can browse other pinboards for images, repin images to your own pinboard, and like photos. In 2014, Pinterest announced the availability of *Promoted Pins* to advertisers. These pins, paid for by advertisers, are shown at the top of search results and category feeds. Ads are contextual, so a search on "Halloween" might produce an ad for an online costume shop. Pinterest is different from other social media in that it focuses on things rather than messaging or relationships. A Georgia Tech study found that the most common verbs used on the site were *use, look, want,* and *need*.[51] These all relate to shopping. Part of Pinterest tracking is when a person goes on sites that have a "Pin It" button and then pins something from that website.

**conversion**
An action that a person takes based on an advertiser's website, such as checking out, registering, adding an item to the shopping cart, or viewing a specific page.

**cost per impression**
The cost to offer potential customers one opportunity to see an advertisement. Often expressed in terms of cost per thousand (CPM).

In addition to buying Promoted Pins, which are optimized through analytics, an advertiser might have its own site on Pinterest. Pinterest Analytics are available to anyone who has a Verified Business Account. Information available to a businessperson, by customized dates, includes:

- **Pins**: Images pinned from your site
- **Pinners**: How many people are pinning images from your website
- **Repins**: Which pins originating from your site are being repinned
- **Repinners**: The number of visitors repinning your pins
- **Impressions**: How often your pins are shown on Pinterest
- **Reach**: How many unique visitors saw your pins
- **Clicks**: How many times users click on your website
- **Visitors**: How many visitors clicked through to your website from Pinterest
- **Popularity:** Most recent pins, most repinned, and most clicked

Some questions that can be answered by analyzing the data from Pinterest Analytics:

1. What content are your visitors repinning?
2. How many different people are pinning images from your site?
3. What pins are bringing the most traffic from Pinterest to your site?

Using this information, a person can determine what other images should be pinned on Pinterest, what images/products to feature and highlight on their site or social media campaigns, as well as how to adjust placement of products on the site. From the Most Repinned section, one can glean insight into Pinterest's followers. If you click on an individual pin, the number of repins is shown, and then you can click on the number to see *who* pinned this image. You can then visit their profiles to see what else they like to pin, follow them if they share interesting content, and work on maturing the relationship from social signal to engagement to relationship to action.[54]

Several third-party analytics can also help a business optimize its Pinterest site. Curalate (http://www.curalate.com) enables a person to track and measure the sharing of visual content. Octopin (http://www.octopin) enables a researcher to identify the sites' top influencers and engaged audience. It allows for trading your site's reputation and brand image. Pinleague (http://www.pinleague.com) allows a firm to track the growth of its site over time, measure ROI, and track competitors.[55]

**Twitter** Twitter analyzes tweets, retweets, location, and people you follow to determine which *Promoted Tweets* (ads) to inject into your timeline. The "tweet" buttons embedded in websites all over the web can also function as tracking devices. Twitter announced in 2012 that it would use tracking data to offer more relevant Promoted Tweets. Twitter recently acquired MoPub, which places ads within mobile apps.[56]

Recently, Twitter announced a new targeted advertising initiative. It used a local florist shop as an example that wants to advertise a Valentine's Day special on Twitter...

They'd prefer to show their ad to flower enthusiasts who frequent their website or subscribe to their newsletter. To get the special offer to those people who are also on Twitter, the shop may share with us a scrambled, unreadable email address (a hash) or browser information (a browser cookie ID). We can then match that information to accounts in order to show them a Promoted Tweet with the Valentine's Day deal.[57]

Like other social media, a member of Twitter can access his or her own tracking data. Twitter Counter lets a firm, or person, obtain statistics on followers, following, and daily tweets. Tweet stats provide graphs on a user's account, such as tweets per hour, per month, tweet timeline, and reply statistics. Twitalyzer enables users to examine a number of measures of success in social media, including influence and popularity. Tweeps answers questions such as: What do they tweet about? How much do they tweet? How social are they? Do they use hashtags? Do they share URLs? These statistics are updated several times each day to help a user keep up with the fast moving world of Twitter.[58]

# Observation Research and Virtual Shopping

Advances in computer technology have enabled researchers to simulate an actual retail store environment on a computer screen. Depending on the type of simulation, a shopper can "pick up" a package by touching its image on the monitor and rotate it to examine all sides. Like buying on most online retailers, the shopper touches the shopping cart to add an item to the basket. During the shopping process, the computer unobtrusively records the amount of time the consumer spends shopping in each product category, the time the consumer spends examining each side of a package, the quantity of product the consumer purchases, and the order in which items are purchased.

Computer-simulated environments like this one offer a number of advantages over older research methods. First, unlike focus groups, concept tests, and other laboratory approaches, the virtual store duplicates the distracting clutter of an actual market. Consumers can shop in an environment with a realistic level of complexity and variety. Second, researchers can set up and alter the tests very quickly. Once images of the product are scanned into the computer, the researcher can make changes in the assortment of brands, product packaging, pricing, promotions, and shelf space within minutes. Data collection is also fast and error-free because the information generated by the purchase is automatically tabulated and stored by the computer. Third, production costs are low because displays are created electronically. Once the hardware and software are in place, the cost of a test is largely a function of the number of respondents, who generally are given a small incentive to participate. Fourth, the simulation has a high degree of flexibility. It can be used to test entirely new marketing concepts or to fine-tune existing programs. The simulation also makes it possible to eliminate much of the noise that exists in field experiments.[59]

Kimberly-Clark has refined the virtual shopping experience even more. Located in Appleton, Wisconsin, the firm's virtual testing lab has a woman standing in a room surrounded by three screens showing a store aisle, a retina-tracking device recording her every glance.

Asked by a Kimberly-Clark researcher to find a "big box" of Huggies Natural Fit diapers in size three, the woman pushed forward on a handle like that of a shopping cart, and the video simulated her progress down the aisle. Spotting Huggies' red packages, she turned the handle to the right to face a dizzying array of diapers. After pushing a button to get a kneeling view of the shelves, she reached forward and tapped the screen to put the box she wanted in her virtual cart.

Kimberly-Clark hopes these virtual shopping aisles will provide better understanding of consumer behavior and make the testing of new products faster, more convenient, and more precise.[60]

Kimberly-Clark's lab also features a U-shaped floor-to-ceiling screen that re-creates in vivid detail interiors of the big retailers that sell the company's products—a tool that the company will use in presentations to executives in bids to win shelf space. A separate area is reserved for real replicas of store interiors, which can be customized to match the flooring, light fixtures, and shelves of retailers such as Target Corp. and Wal-Mart Stores, Inc.

Kimberly-Clark says its studio allows researchers and designers to get a fast read on new product designs and displays without having to stage real-life tests in the early stages of development. Doing the research in a windowless basement, rather than an actual test market, also avoids tipping off competitors early in the development process.

"We're trying to test ideas faster, cheaper, and better," says Ramin Eivaz, a vice president at Kimberly-Clark focusing on strategy. Formerly, new product testing typically took eight months to two years. Now, that time is cut in half, he says. Projects that test well with the virtual-reality tools will be fast-tracked to real-store trials, Mr. Eivaz says.[61]

Virtual-shopping research is growing rapidly as companies such as Frito-Lay, Goodyear, Procter & Gamble, General Mills, and Coca-Cola realize the benefits from this type of observation research. About 40,000 new consumer package goods are introduced in the United States each year. All are vying for very limited retail shelf space. Manufacturers always welcome any process, such as virtual shopping, that can speed product development time and lower costs.

To sell retailers on new products, manufacturers are revealing more about their product pipelines to drum up interest early on. Kimberly-Clark has brought in executives from major retail chains to see the Appleton facility. Kimberly-Clark uses the data from its virtual-reality tests with consumers to tout the performance of products in development.

"It no longer works to show up on a retailer's doorstop with your new product and say, 'Isn't this pretty?'" Mr. Eivaz says. "We need to be an indispensable partner to our retailers and show we can do more for them."[62]

## SUMMARY

Observation research is the systematic process of recording patterns of occurrences or behaviors without questioning or normally communicating with the people involved. For many types of observation to be used successfully, the needed information must be observable and the behavior of interest must be repetitive, frequent, or in some manner predictable. The behavior of interest also should be of a relatively short duration. There are four dimensions along which observation approaches vary: (1) natural versus contrived situations, (2) open versus disguised observation, (3) human versus machine observers, and (4) direct versus indirect observation.

The biggest advantage of observation research is that researchers can see what people actually do rather than having to rely on what they say they did, thereby avoiding many biasing factors. Also, some forms of data are more quickly and accurately gathered by observation. The primary disadvantage of many forms of research is that the researcher learns nothing about motives, attitudes, intentions, or feelings.

People watching people or objects can take the form of ethnographic research, mystery shopping, one-way mirror observations (e.g., child psychologists might watch children play with toys), and shopper pattern and behavior studies.

Machine observation may involve neuromarketing, using measures such as functional magnetic resonance imaging, electroencephalography, galvanic skin response, and eye tracking. Other forms of machine observation include fraud action coding service, gender and age recognition systems, in-store tracking, and television audience measurement and tracking. Symphony IRI employs handheld scanners with its National Consumer Panel to scan all household purchases with UPC codes. These data are then used to measure consumer shopping patterns and sales by product category and brand.

Online tracking is used to deliver the right message, to the right audience, at the right time. Tracking, also called behavioral tracking, can answer "where," "how much," and "how often" questions. Traditional tracking was done with cookies, which works well with laptops and desktops. Now, new technology lets firms track consumers across mobile devices as well. Social media tracking helps marketers understand how consumers talk about a brand or a product or what they expect from a brand. Social media like Google+, Facebook, Pinterest, and Twitter offer sophisticated forms of tracking to help advertisers deliver messages to those most likely to be potential purchasers.

Virtual shopping using advanced computer technology to create a simulated shopping environment is a rapidly growing form of observation research. It reduces the cost and time it takes to bring new products to the market.

## KEY TERMS

observation research **165**

open observation **167**

disguised observation **167**

garbologists **167**

ethnographic research **169**

mystery shoppers **174**

one-way mirror observation **175**

Neuromarketing **176**

electroencephalograph (EEG) **176**

galvanic skin response (GSR) **178**

conversion **185**

cost per impression **185**

## QUESTIONS FOR REVIEW & CRITICAL THINKING

1. You are charged with the responsibility of determining whether men are brand conscious when shopping for racquetball equipment. Outline an observation research procedure for making that determination.

2. Fisher-Price has asked you to develop a research procedure for determining which of its prototype toys is most appealing to 4- and 5-year-olds. Suggest a methodology for making this determination.

3. What are the biggest drawbacks of observation research?

4. Compare the advantages and disadvantages of observation research with those of survey research.

5. It has been said that "people buy things not for what they will do, but for what they mean." Discuss this statement in relation to observation research.

6. How might a mystery shopper be valuable to the following organizations?
   a. JetBlue Airlines
   b. Macy's Department Store
   c. H&R Block

7. Use ethnographic research to evaluate the dining experience at your student center. What did you learn?

8. Describe how tracking research can benefit an online retailer.

9. Do you think that virtual shopping will replace other forms of marketing research? Why or why not?

10. Do you think that in-store tracking is too intrusive? Why or why not?

11. Were you aware of all the types of information that social media gathers about you? Are you comfortable with this?

Do you like the fact that only ads of potential interest to you will be shown?

12. Divide the class into teams of five. Each team should select a different retailer (services are okay for mystery shopping). Two members of the team should prepare a list of 10 to 15 questions to be answered. A sample of questions for an Eye Care Clinic is shown below. The remaining three members of the team should become mystery shoppers with the goal of answering the questions created by the team. After the shopping is complete, the team should combine their findings and make a report to the class. *(Team Exercise)*

*Sample Mystery Shopping Questions for an Eye Care Clinic*

1. Was the phone answered within three rings?

2. How long did you have to wait for an appointment?

3. Were you given clear directions to the office?

4. Did you receive a new patient packet in the mail?

5. Were signs directing you to the office clear and visible?

6. Did the receptionist greet you when you entered the office?

7. How long did you wait before being taken into a room for the pre-exam?

8. Did all staff members have a name tag on?

9. Was the facility clean?

10. Were your eyes dilated before you saw the doctor?

11. Were exam procedures explained clearly?

12. Were you given an opportunity to ask the doctor questions?

13. Were your questions answered promptly and respectfully?

14. Were you directed to the optical shop after your exam?

15. Were your glasses/contacts ready when promised?

## WORKING THE NET

1. Go to *www. iriworldwide.com* **and** *www.nielsen.com* and report what types of observation research are being conducted by the two research firms.

2. Go to *www.doubleclick.com* and read its latest research findings. Make an oral presentation to your class.

3. Go to *www.mysteryshop.org* to learn more about mystery shopping.

4. Go to www.facebook.com and report what it says about optimized cost per impressions.

5. Go to www.google.com/analytics and explain what services it offers.

## REAL-LIFE RESEARCH • 8.1

### Eating Well and Doing Good

The emergence of socially responsible business models has changed the way some consumers think about businesses, but it has also changed the way businesses think about consumers. Buy-one-give-one (B1G1)[B1G1?] companies, for example, give one product or an equal value in cash to charitable causes for each one purchased, requiring the businesses to understand two different categories of consumers: those who would normally consume their products and those who may consume them due to the firms' humanitarian model.

This was one of the primary marketing challenges for 1-For-1 Foods, an Indiana-based B1G1 nutrition-bar start-up that retails in the greater Chicagoland area and gives one bar to homeless shelters in the area in which each bar is purchased. 1-For-1 Foods realized that its actual target market extended far beyond health and fitness buffs to socially conscious consumers who might not normally buy premium nutrition bars.

To better understand these different audiences and learn how they relate to intersect, 1-For-1 Foods turned to Culture Concepts, a Milwaukee research company, for some pro bono research help. As a young company, 1-For-1 Foods didn't have a very formidable marketing budget. So, to help reduce logistical and incentive costs while ensuring credible and useful results, Culture Concepts proposed conducting a set of ethnographic studies on larger groups of people and augmenting the results with online ethnographic research.

Using this approach, three separate studies were conducted. The first observed a group of avid nutrition-bar consumers on a hiking trip and documented their conversations, habits, and interactions with health-food products. The second study observed owners of shoes sold by TOMS—a fast-growing Los Angeles-based company that gives one pair of shoes to underprivileged children for every pair purchased—socializing in public and in private, paying particular attention to the value they placed on their shoes and TOMS' buy one-give-one model. The third study used a digital ethnographic approach that observed what different peer groups of nutrition-bar consumers and TOMS shoes consumers were saying about these products via social media. Highly detailed profiles of the most active consumers of each product were constructed using publicly available online information in order to capture the other priorities of each set of consumers.

### An Ideal Setting

For the first ethnographic study, the researchers worked with independent coffee shops in the Chicago area to locate health-bar consumers. Because of the social focus of the study, rather than choose a number of individual participants, Culture Concepts selected a group of friends consisting of 10 male and female health-food consumers from multiple generations that could be observed collectively. After talking with the group about the requirements of the study, it was suggested that a hiking trip that the group was planning would be an ideal setting for an ethnographic study.

Using a preplanned hiking trip as the setting for the study guaranteed that all the participants would be immersed in an environment that felt natural and meaningful to them, ensuring that their behavior would be authentic and insightful. The three-day study resulted in extensive documentation of the personalities, social and individual behaviors and value expressions of the hikers. It is worth noting that most of the data was documented in writing due to the lack of electricity on the trip. However, solar chargers were used to replenish their smartphone batteries so some video could be recorded.

Particular attention was paid to how the hikers interacted with nutrition bars and other health-food products that they had brought with them. A number of powerful insights emerged as a result of these observations. One important finding was that health bars appeared to add value to the hikers' experience both physically and psychologically. On a basic and quite obvious level, health bars provided a portable and convenient form of nutritional sustenance. On a higher level, however, health bars seemed to serve as tangible symbols of a healthy lifestyle that unified the experience of natural food with the natural environment, acting as a visible expression of the hikers' worldview. As one participant said, "[Nutrition bars] stand for who I am and what I believe to be important."

The deeper meaning of health bars was further evidenced by the social value that they added to the group dynamic. The hikers consistently consumed health bars together and often shared and exchanged different bar brands. Most of the hikers demonstrated genuine interest in discovering new brands and hearing peer reviews of popular ones. Additionally, lending further credence to the idea that health bars have a social value proposition, half of the hikers reported that they consumer health bars in a similarly social way at their gyms or after working out.

## Shadowed the Group

Working with several different shoe retailers, we identified a number of TOMS shoes owners to participate in the second ethnographic study. Like the previous study on nutrition-bar consumers, a group of six friends—men and women in their twenties and thirties—who all owned at least one pair of TOMS shoes was chosen for observation. We shadowed the group for a day, accompanying them on a shopping excursion and to dinner at a downtown Chicago restaurant. Particularly salient topics of discussion included health care, corporate corruption, global warming, iPhone rumors, and new movies.

These touchpoints gave us useful information about the values of a core audience, and also served as a reference for participant responses during one-on-one exit interviews that were conducted after the observation period. During these interviews, participants were asked what types of ideas they associate with TOMS and with socially responsible business models in general. A significant portion of their responses to these questions corresponded with the conversation topics from earlier in the day. For example, some ideas that the participants associated with TOMS included the health and wellbeing of others; the value of ethical corporations; authenticity, and trendiness. Additionally, almost all of the participants associated the idea of socially responsible business with environmental friendliness.

The insights gathered from these live ethnographic studies were then used to inform an online ethnography that analyzed conversations about nutrition bars and B1G1 products on social media networks and profiled a number of consumers who were ardent evangelists of these products. The study of online conversations validated a number of hypotheses that emerged from the live ethnographies and using publicly available information to profile key audience members was a quick, affordable, and comprehensive way to get a detailed view of consumers' value and lifestyle.

Culture Concepts learned that health bars are not always consumed in isolation, and that many times they are paired with other healthy activities, such as hiking or working out. Health bars can sometimes even become a topic of conversation, the facilitators of social interaction. The fact that they can facilitate social experiences suggests that they can be symbolic, not merely symptomatic, of a healthy lifestyle.

Health bars are more than a source of nutrition. To some, they're a symbol of a lifestyle, a culture, and a particular set of values that are shared among health-conscious consumers. In order to tap into those sentiments, marketing and advertising cannot just focus on the nutritional value of the product but should also feature healthy activities and healthy people in ways that glorify and reinforce the values of that particular consumer culture.

From TOMS shoes consumers, the researchers learned that their personal sociopolitical beliefs are very much linked to their loyalty to TOMS. The B1G1 model is at the heart of why they value TOMS and a socially conscious focus is important to them when they select both products and peers. This culture of socially conscious consumers prizes integrity and authenticity in their politics and their purchases. They place a higher value on things that are raw, real and worn, that are not pretentious and nonconformist. Thus, messages directed at this audience should be honest and simple, and packaging should look natural and organic.

Ensuring that the entire product experience resonates with socially conscious consumers is pivotal to getting them to remain loyal to B1G1 brands. It is not enough to have a socially conscious business model. If the brand experience doesn't meet their expectations and conform to their values, then even the best B1G1 brand will be seen as a poseur and pretender. Simply put, the ethos of socially conscious brands needs to correspond to the ethos of socially conscious consumers.

## At the Intersection

The 1-For-1 Foods consumer sits at the intersection of two consumer cultures, espousing the values of both health-conscious consumers and socially conscious consumers. Of all the live ethnography participants from both groups, over half consumed both nutrition bars and owned TOMS shoes, demonstrating that there is tangible overlap between these two core constituencies. Beyond the overlapping of consumer product preferences, there is also a salient overlapping of values. Both segments demonstrate deep consideration for human health, whether their own or that of others, and an underlying concern for the environment. These values of vitality and sustainability inform the perceptions and behaviors of these groups, transforming what they believe and what they buy.[63]

## Questions

1. Do you think that 1-For-1 Foods has enough information to create a successful marketing strategy? If not, what other questions need to be answered and what research methodology should be used?

2. What other types of research could have been used to gather the insights uncovered in the studies?

3. Could this research have been done using tracking data and Google Analytics? Why or why not?

4. Is a hiking trip a proper venue for ethnographic research? What about dinner at a restaurant?

5. Now that qualitative research has been done, should 1-For-1 Foods do quantitative research? Why or why not?

© prodakszyn/iStockphoto

# Primary Data Collection: Experimentation and Test Markets

## LEARNING OBJECTIVES

1. Understand the nature of experiments.

2. Gain insight into requirements for proving causation.

3. Learn about the experimental setting.

4. Examine experimental validity.

5. Compare types of experimental designs.

6. Understand extraneous variables

7. Analyze experimental design, treatment, and effects.

8. Examine the limitations of experimental research.

9. Evaluate selected experimental designs.

10. Gain insight into test marketing.

In this chapter, we cover issues related to the use of experiments for data collection in marketing research. Field experiments, laboratory experiments and test markets are the major experimental approaches covered. We also present the evidence you have to provide to prove that one thing likely caused another (not easy), different types of experimental designs and sources of error in experiments.

# What Is an Experiment?

Experimentation is often presented as a third type of data collection to go along with survey and observation. Strictly speaking, experimentation is not a form of data collection at all, but rather, a research strategy. It is appropriate whenever we are attempting to determine the effect or impact of one thing on another. Common examples would be the effect of advertising on sales or the effect of price on sales. Research based solely on surveys or observations without any type of experimental design is strictly descriptive in nature. By contrast, surveys or observations are used to take the necessary measurements for research that employs experimental designs.

Research based on experimentation is fundamentally different from research based on surveys or observation.[1] In the case of both survey and observation research, the researcher is, in essence, a passive assembler of data. The researcher asks people questions or observes what they do. In experimental research, the situation is very different: The researcher becomes an active participant in the process.

**experiment**

Research approach in which one variable is manipulated and the effect on another variable is observed.

In concept, an **experiment** is straightforward. The researcher changes or manipulates one thing (called an *experimental, treatment, independent,* or *explanatory variable*) to observe the effect on something else (referred to as a *dependent variable*). In marketing experiments, the dependent variable is frequently some measure of sales, such as total sales or market share; experimental variables are typically marketing mix elements, such as price, amount or type of advertising, and changes in product features.

# Demonstrating Causation

**causal research**

Research designed to determine whether a change in one variable likely caused an observed change in another.

Experimental research is often referred to as **causal** (not casual) **research** because it is the only type of research that has the potential to demonstrate that a change in one variable *causes* some predictable change in another. To demonstrate causation (that *A* likely caused *B*), one must be able to show three things:

1. Correlation or concomitant variation
2. Appropriate time order of occurrence
3. Elimination of other possible causal factors

Please note that we are using the terms *causation* and *causality* in the scientific sense.[2] The scientific view of causation is quite different from the popular view, which often implies that there is a single cause of an event. For example, when someone says in everyday conversation that *X* is the cause of some observed change in *Y*, he or she generally means that *X* is the only cause of the observed change in *Y*. But the scientific view holds that *X* is almost always only one of a number of possible determining conditions that caused the observed change in *Y*.

In addition, the everyday view of causality implies a completely deterministic relationship, while the scientific view implies a probabilistic relationship. The popular view is that if *X* is the cause of *Y*, then *X* must always lead to *Y*. The scientific view holds that *X* can be a cause of *Y* if the presence of *X* makes the occurrence of *Y* more probable or likely.

Finally, the scientific view holds that one can never definitively prove that *X* is a cause of *Y* but only infer that a relationship exists. In other words, causal relationships are always inferred and never demonstrated conclusively beyond a shadow of a doubt. Three types of evidence—correlation, appropriate time order of occurrence, and elimination of other possible causal factors—are used to infer causal relationships.

## Concomitant Variation

To provide evidence that a change in *A* caused a particular change in *B*, one must first show that there is correlation between *A* and *B*; in other words, *A* and *B* must vary together in some predictable fashion. This might be a *positive* or an *inverse* relationship. Two variables that we usually expect to be related in a positive manner are advertising and sales. They would be positively related if sales increased by some predictable amount when advertising increased by a certain amount. Two variables that might be related in an inverse manner are price and sales. They would be inversely (negatively) related if sales increased when price decreased and decreased when price increased. The researcher can test for the existence and direction of statistical relationships by means of a number of statistical procedures, including chi-square analysis, correlation analysis, regression analysis, and analysis of variance to mention a few. All of these statistical procedures are discussed later in the text (chi-square, correlation analysis, and regression analysis in Chapter 16 and analysis of variance in Chapter 17).

However, correlation alone does not prove causation. Simply because two variables happen to vary together in some predictable fashion does not prove that one causes the other. For example, suppose you found a high degree of correlation between sales of a product in the United States and the GDP (gross domestic product) of Germany. This might be true simply because both variables happened to be increasing at a similar rate. Further examination and consideration might show that there is no true link between the two variables. To infer causation, you must be able to show correlation—but correlation alone is not proof of causation.

## Appropriate Time Order of Occurrence

The second requirement for demonstrating that a causal relationship likely exists between two variables involves showing that there is an appropriate time order of occurrence. To demonstrate that $A$ caused $B$, one must be able to show that $A$ occurred before $B$ occurred. For example, to demonstrate that a price change had an effect on sales, you must be able to show that the price change occurred before the change in sales was observed. However, showing that $A$ and $B$ are correlated and that $A$ occurred before $B$ still does not provide evidence strong enough to let us conclude that $A$ is the likely cause of an observed change in $B$.

## Elimination of Other Possible Causal Factors

The most difficult thing to demonstrate in marketing experiments is that the change in $B$ was not caused by some factor other than $A$. For example, suppose a company increased its advertising expenditures and observed an increase in sales. Correlation and appropriate time order of occurrence are present. But has a likely causal relationship been demonstrated? The answer is no. It is possible that the observed change in sales is due to some factor or factors other than the increase in advertising. For example, at the same time advertising expenditures were increased, a major competitor might have decreased advertising expenditures, or increased price, or pulled out of the market. Even if the competitive environment did not change, one or a combination of other factors may have influenced sales. For example, the economy in the area might have received a major boost for some reason that has nothing to do with the experiment. For any of these reasons, or many others, the observed increase in sales might have been caused by many other things other than or in addition to the increase in advertising expenditures. Much of the discussion in this chapter is related to designing experiments so as to eliminate or adjust for the effects of other possible causal factors.

# Experimental Setting

Experiments can be conducted in a laboratory or a field setting.[3] Most experiments in the physical sciences are conducted in a laboratory setting; while many marketing experiments are field experiments.

## Laboratory Experiments

**Laboratory experiments** provide a number of important advantages.[4] The major advantage of conducting experiments in a laboratory is the ability to control extraneous causal

**laboratory experiments**
Experiments conducted in a controlled setting.

factors—temperature, light, humidity, and so on—and focus on the effect of a change in *A* on *B*. In the lab, the researcher can effectively deal with the third element of proving causation (elimination of other possible causal factors) and focus on the first two elements (correlation variation and appropriate time order of occurrence). This additional control strengthens our ability to infer that an observed change in the dependent variable was caused by a change in the experimental, or treatment, variable. Because of this, laboratory experiments are having greater internal validity (discussed in greater detail in the next section). But, they suffer from the fact that the controlled and possibly sterile environment of the laboratory is not a good analog of the marketplace. For this reason, the findings of laboratory experiments sometimes do not hold up when transferred to the marketplace. Because of this, laboratory experiments are seen as having greater problems with external validity (see the next section). However, laboratory experiments are probably being used to a greater extent in marketing research today than in the past because of their many advantages.

## Field Experiments

**field experiments**
Tests conducted outside the laboratory in an actual environment, such as a marketplace.

**Field experiments** are conducted in an actual market environment. Test markets, discussed later in this chapter, are a frequently used type of field experiment. Field experiments solve the problem of the realism of the environment but open up a whole new set of problems. The major problem is that in the field the researcher cannot control all the other factors that might influence the dependent variable, such as the actions of competitors, the weather, the economy, societal trends, and the political climate.

# Experimental Validity

*Validity* is defined as the degree to which an experiment actually measures what the researcher was trying to measure (see Chapter 10). The validity of a measure depends on the extent to which the measure is free from both systematic and random error. Two specific kinds of validity are relevant to experimentation: internal validity and external validity.

**internal validity**
Extent to which competing explanations for the experimental results observed can be ruled out.

**Internal validity** refers to the extent to which competing explanations for the experimental results observed can be ruled out. If the researcher can show that the experimental, or treatment, variable actually produced the differences observed in the dependent variable, then the experiment can be said to be internally valid. This kind of validity requires evidence demonstrating that variation in the dependent variable was caused by exposure to the treatment variable and not other possible causal factors.

**external validity**
Extent to which causal relationships measured in an experiment can be generalized to outside persons, settings, and times.

**External validity** refers to the extent to which the causal relationships measured in an experiment can be generalized to outside persons, settings, and times.[5] The issue here is how representative the subjects and the setting used in the experiment are of other populations and settings to which the researcher would like to apply the results. Field experiments offer a higher degree of external validity and a lower degree of internal validity than do laboratory experiments.

# Experimental Notation

In the discussion of experiments, we will use a standard system of notation, as follows:

- *X* is used to indicate the exposure of an individual or a group to an experimental treatment. The experimental treatment is the factor whose effects we want to measure and compare. Experimental treatments may be factors such as different prices, package designs, point-of-purchase displays, advertising approaches, or product forms.

■ $O$ (for observation) is used to refer to the process of taking measurements on the test units. *Test units* are individuals, groups of individuals, or entities whose response to the experimental treatments is being tested. Test units might include individual consumers, groups of consumers, retail stores, total markets, or other entities that might be the targets of a firm's marketing program. Observations may be made using observation techniques discussed in Chapter 8 or survey methods discussed in Chapter 6.

■ Different time periods are represented by the horizontal arrangement of the $X$s and $O$s. For example,

$$O_1 \; X \; O_2$$

■ would describe an experiment in which a preliminary measurement $O_1$ was taken of one or more test units, then one or more test units were exposed to the experimental variable $X$, and then a measurement $O_2$ of the test units was taken. The $X$s and $O$s can be arranged vertically to show simultaneous exposure and measurement of different test units. For example, the following design involves two different groups of test units:

$$X_1 \; O_1$$
$$X_2 \; O_2$$

The two groups of test units received different experimental treatments at the same time ($X_1$ and $X_2$), and then the two groups were measured simultaneously ($O_1$ and $O_2$).[6]

# Extraneous Variables

In interpreting experimental results, the researcher would like to be able to conclude that the observed response is due to the effect of the experimental variable. However, many factors stand in the way of the ability to reach this conclusion. In anticipation of these possible problems, the researcher needs to design the experiment so as to eliminate as many extraneous factors as possible as causes of the observed effect.

## Examples of Extraneous Variables

Examples of extraneous factors or variables that pose a threat to experimental validity are history, maturation, instrument variation, selection bias, mortality, testing effects, and regression to the mean.[7]

### History
**History** refers to the intervention, between the beginning and end of the experiment, of any variable or event—other than those manipulated by the researcher (experimental variables)—that might affect the value of the dependent variable. Early tests of Prego spaghetti sauce by the Campbell Soup Company provide an example of a possible problem with extraneous variables. Campbell executives claim that Ragu, a competing brand, greatly increased its advertising levels and use of cents-off deals during the Prego tests. They believe that this increased marketing activity was designed to get shoppers to stock up on Ragu and make it impossible for Campbell to get an accurate reading of potential sales for its Prego product.

**history**
Intervention, between the beginning and end of an experiment, of outside variables or events that might change the dependent variable.

### Maturation
**Maturation** refers to changes in subjects during the course of the experiment that are a function of time; it includes getting older, hungrier, more tired, and the like. Throughout the course of an experiment, the responses of people to a treatment variable may change because of these maturation factors and not because of the treatment variable. The likelihood that maturation will be a serious problem in a particular experiment, depends on the length of the experiment. The longer the experiment runs, the more likely it is that maturation will present problems for interpreting the results.

**maturation**
Changes in subjects occurring during the experiment that are not related to the experiment but that may affect subjects' response to the treatment factor.

**instrument variation**
Changes in measurement instruments (e.g., interviewers or observers) that might affect measurements.

## Instrument Variation
**Instrument variation** refers to any changes in measurement instruments that might explain differences in the measurements taken. It is a serious problem in marketing experiments where people are used as interviewers or observers to measure the dependent variable. If measurements on the same subject are taken by different interviewers or observers at different points in time, differences between measurements may reflect variations in the way the interviewing or observation was done by different interviewers or observers. On the other hand, if the same interviewer or observer is used to take measurements on the same subject over time, differences may reflect the fact that the particular observer or interviewer has become less interested and is doing a sloppier job.

**selection bias**
Systematic differences between the test group and the control group due to a biased selection process.

## Selection Bias
The threat to validity posed by **selection bias** is encountered in situations where the experimental or test group is systematically different from the population to which the researcher would like to project the experimental results or from the control group (if the design includes one). In projecting the results to a population that is systematically different from the test group, the researcher may get results very different from those obtained in the test because of differences in the makeup of the two groups. Similarly, an observed difference between a test group and an untreated control group (not exposed to the experimental variable) may be due to differences between the two groups and not to the effect of the experimental variable. Researchers can ensure equality of groups through either randomization or matching. *Randomization* involves assigning subjects to test groups and control groups at random. *Matching* involves what the name suggests—making sure that there is a one-to-one match between people or other units in the test and control groups in regard to key characteristics (e.g., age, income, education, etc.). Specific matching procedures are discussed later in this chapter.

**mortality**
Loss of test units or subjects during the course of an experiment, which may result in a nonrepresentativeness.

## Mortality
**Mortality** refers to the loss of test units during the course of an experiment. It is a problem because there is no easy way to know if the lost units would have responded to the treatment variable in the same way as those units that remained throughout the entire experiment. An experimental group that was representative of the population or that matched a control group may become nonrepresentative because of the systematic loss of subjects with certain characteristics. For example, in a study of music preferences of the population, if nearly all the subjects under the age of 25 were lost during the course of the experiment, then the researcher would likely get a biased picture of music preferences at the end of the experiment. As a result, the findings would lack external validity.

**testing effect**
Effect that is a by-product of the research process itself.

## Testing Effects
**Testing effects** result from the fact that the process of experimentation can produce its own effect on the responses observed. For example, measuring attitude toward a product before exposing subjects to an ad may act as a treatment variable, influencing perception of the ad. Testing effects come in two forms:

- *Main testing effects* are the possible effects of earlier observations on later observations. For example, students taking the GMAT for the second time tend to do better than those taking the test for the first time, even though the students have no information about the items they actually missed on the first test. This effect also can be reactive in the sense that responses to the first administration of an attitude test have some effect on attitudes that is reflected in subsequent applications of the same test.

- *Interactive testing effect* is the effect of a prior measurement on a subject's response to a later measurement. For example, if subjects are asked about their awareness of advertising for various products (pre-exposure measurement) and then exposed to advertising for one or more of these products (treatment variable), post measurements would likely reflect the joint effect of the pre-exposure and the treatment condition.

**Regression to the Mean**  **Regression to the mean** refers to the observed tendency of subjects with extreme behavior to move toward the average for that behavior during the course of an experiment. Test units may exhibit extreme behavior because of chance, or they may have been specifically chosen because of their extreme behavior. The researcher might, for example, have chosen people for an experimental group because they were extremely heavy users of a particular product or service. In such situations, their tendency to move toward the average behavior may be interpreted as having been caused by the treatment variable when in fact it has nothing to do with the treatment variable.

**regression to the mean**
Tendency of subjects with extreme behavior to move toward the average for that behavior during the course of an experiment.

## Controlling Extraneous Variables

Causal factors that threaten validity must be controlled in some manner to establish a clear picture of the effect of the manipulated variable on the dependent variable. Extraneous causal factors are ordinarily referred to as *confounding variables* because they confound the treatment condition, making it impossible to determine whether changes in the dependent variable are due solely to the treatment conditions.

Four basic approaches are used to control extraneous factors: randomization, physical control, design control, and statistical control.

**Randomization** is carried out by randomly assigning subjects to treatment conditions so that extraneous causal factors related to subject characteristics can reasonably be assumed to be represented equally in each treatment condition, thus canceling out extraneous effects.

**Physical control** of extraneous causal factors involves somehow holding constant the value or level of the extraneous variable throughout the experiment. Another approach to physical control is matching respondents in regard to important personal characteristics (e.g., age, income, lifestyle) before assigning them to different treatment conditions. The goal is to make sure there are no important differences between characteristics of respondents in the test and control groups.

**Design control** is the control of extraneous factors by means of specific types of experimental designs developed for this purpose. These designs are discussed later in this chapter.

Finally, **statistical control** can be used to account for extraneous causal factors if these factors can be identified and measured throughout the course of the experiment. Procedures such as analysis of covariance can adjust for the effects of a confounded variable on the dependent variable by statistically adjusting the value of the dependent variable for each treatment condition.

**randomization**
Random assignment of subjects to treatment conditions to ensure equal representation of subject characteristics.

**physical control**
Holding constant the value or level of extraneous variables throughout the course of an experiment.

**design control**
Use of the experimental design to control extraneous causal factors.

**statistical control**
Adjusting for the effects of confounded variables by statistically adjusting the value of the dependent variable for each treatment condition.

# PRACTICING MARKETING RESEARCH

## Data Use: The Insidious Top-box and Its Effects on Measuring Line Share[8]

Consumers have limited budgets and consumption capacities, so when companies want to make changes to a product line, managers want to know how those changes would affect the choices people make within the category. To find out, marketers often use the "top-box" measurement tool of purchase intent. A survey using top-box presents a given product that respondents will rate on a scale typically ranging from "definitely will buy" to "definitely will not buy."

A clear response would seem to provide the information a manager would need.

Even though the response from the survey participant is clear, the answer for the company is not. One potential line extension may rate higher in a top-box scenario, but the top-box comparison offers no indication of whether the higher-rated option will steal share from competitors or pull from other products in the line. Top-box is also known for producing inflated results. Again, this is because it measures desire, not actual choice. It often fails to make distinctions within a broad spectrum of desire, and, as shown in Figure 1, is less able to produce results that clearly demonstrate perceived differences among various product concepts.

Marketers would benefit from using alternative methods, such as conjoint analyses and discrete choice, that measure choice, not simply model it. Researchers should create equivalent test groups from the sample, establishing a control group using a full set of relevant competing products, including those they currently offer, and systematically introduce the test product altering a single different variable for each other test group. This is essentially an application of the scientific method. This approach allows experimenters to manipulate any variable within the test sample or element within the marketing mix. Experimenters can even compare different strategies, such as a product adaptation versus a line extension.

For the marketer who is concerned with growing business and acquiring relevant information on product interaction and line share, rethinking the tools used to gather this data is a worthwhile exercise.

## Questions

1. Do you think top-box measurement would be more accurate if only one option were presented rather than multiple options? Why or why not?

2. Do you think any marketing research method can accurately predict action rather than simply assess desire?

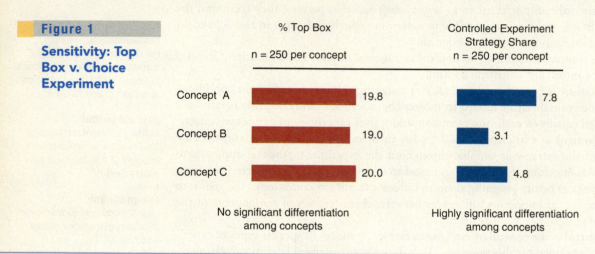

**Figure 1**

**Sensitivity: Top Box v. Choice Experiment**

# Experimental Design, Treatment, and Effects

**experimental design**
Test in which the researcher has control over and manipulates one or more independent variables.

In an **experimental design**, the researcher has control over and manipulates one or more independent variables. In the experiments we discuss, typically only one independent variable is manipulated. Nonexperimental designs, which involve no manipulation, are often referred to as ex post facto (after the fact) research—an effect is observed, and then some attempt is made to attribute this effect to some causal factor.

An experimental design includes four elements:

1. The *treatment*, or experimental, *variable* (independent variable) that is manipulated
2. The *subjects* who participate in the experiment
3. A *dependent variable* that is measured
4. Some *plan or procedure* for dealing with extraneous causal factors

**treatment variable**
Independent variable that is manipulated in an experiment.

The **treatment variable** is the independent variable that is manipulated or changed. *Manipulation* refers to a process in which the researcher sets the levels of the independent variable to test a particular causal relationship. To test the relationship between price (independent variable) and sales (dependent variable), a researcher might expose subjects to three different levels of price and record the level of purchases at each price level. As the variable that is manipulated, price is the single treatment variable, with three treatment conditions or levels.

An experiment may include a test, or treatment, group, and a control group. A *control group* is a group in which the independent variable is not changed during the course of the experiment. A *test group* is a group that is exposed to manipulation (change) of the independent variable.

The term **experimental effect** refers to the effect of the treatment variable on the dependent variable. The goal is to determine the effect of each treatment condition (level of treatment variable) on the dependent variable. For example, suppose that three different markets are selected to test three different prices, or treatment conditions. Each price is tested in each market for three months. In Market 1, a price 2 percent lower than existing prices for the product is tested; in Market 2, a price 4 percent lower is tested; and in Market 3, a price 6 percent lower is tested. At the end of the three-month test, sales in Market 1 are observed to have increased by less than 1 percent over sales for the preceding 3-month period. In Market 2, sales increased by 3 percent; and in Market 3, sales increased by 5 percent. The change in sales observed in each market is the experimental effect.

**experimental effect**
Effect of the treatment variable on the dependent variable.

# Limitations of Experimental Research

As the preceding discussion shows, experiments are an extremely powerful form of research—the only type of research that can truly explore the existence and nature of causal relationships between variables of interest. Given these obvious advantages over other research designs for primary data collection, you might ask why experimental research is not used more often in marketing. There are many reasons, including the cost of experiments, the issue of security, and problems associated with implementing experiments.

## High Cost of Experiments

To some degree, when making comparisons of the costs of experiments with the costs of surveys or observation-based research, we are comparing apples to oranges. Experiments can be very costly in both money and time. In many cases, managers may anticipate that the costs of doing an experiment would exceed the value of the information gained. Consider, for example, the costs of testing three alternative advertising campaigns in three different geographic areas. Three different campaigns must be produced; airtime must be purchased in all three markets; the timing in all three markets must be carefully coordinated; some system must be put into place to measure sales before, during, and after the test campaigns have run; measurements of other extraneous variables must be made; extensive analysis of the results must be performed; and a variety of other tasks must be completed in order to execute the experiment. All of this will cost a bare minimum of $1 million for a low-profile product and as much as tens of millions for a high-profile brand. When we add the amount of time required to do all this to the cost, you can see why this is a strong impediment to greater use of experimental designs in marketing.

## Security Issues

Conducting a field experiment in a test market involves exposing a marketing plan or some key element of a marketing plan in the actual marketplace. Undoubtedly, competitors will find out what is being considered well in advance of full-scale market introduction. This advance notice gives competitors an opportunity to decide whether and how to respond. In any case, the element of surprise is lost. In some instances, competitors have actually "stolen" concepts that were being tested in the marketplace and gone into national distribution before the company testing the product or strategy element completed the test marketing.

## Implementation Problems

Problems that may hamper the implementation of an experiment include difficulty gaining cooperation within the organization, contamination problems, differences between test markets and the total population, and the lack of an appropriate group of people or geographic area for a control group.

It can be extremely difficult to obtain cooperation within the organization to execute certain types of experiments. For example, a regional marketing manager might be very reluctant to permit her market area to be used as a test market for a reduced level of advertising or a higher price. Quite naturally, her concern would be that the experiment might lower sales for the area.

**Contamination** occurs when buyers from outside the test area come into the area to purchase the product being tested, thereby distorting the results of the experiment. Outside buyers might live on the fringes of the test market area and receive TV advertisements—intended only for those in the test area—that offer a lower price, a special rebate, or some other incentive to buy a product. Their purchases will indicate that the particular sales-stimulating factor being tested is more effective than is actually the case.

In some instances, test markets may be so different, and the behavior of consumers in those markets so different, that a relatively small experimental effect is difficult to detect. This problem can be dealt with by careful matching of test markets and other similar strategies designed to ensure a high degree of equivalency of test units.

Finally, in some situations, no appropriate geographic area or group of people may be available to serve as a control group. This may be the case in a test of industrial products, whose very small number of purchasers are concentrated geographically. An attempt to test a new product among a subset of such purchasers would almost certainly be doomed to failure.

**contamination**
Inclusion in a test of a group of respondents who are not normally there; for example, buyers from outside the test market who see an advertisement intended only for those in the test area and enter the area to purchase the product being tested.

# Selected Experimental Designs

This section presents examples of pre-experimental, true experimental, and quasi-experimental designs.[9] In outlining these designs, we use the system of notation introduced earlier.

## Pre-Experimental Designs

Pre-experimental designs are research designs that do not include basic elements required in true experimental designs. Because of their simplicity, they may make sense in certain situations, but they produce results that are difficult to interpret. Studies using **pre-experimental designs** are often difficult to interpret because they offer little or no control over the influence of extraneous factors. As a result, these studies often are not much better than descriptive studies when it comes to making causal inferences. With these designs, the researcher has little control over aspects of exposure to the treatment variable (such as to whom and when) and measurements. However, these designs frequently are used in commercial test marketing because they are simple and inexpensive.

**pre-experimental designs**
Designs that offer little or no control over extraneous factors.

**One-Shot Case Study Design** The **one-shot case study design** involves exposing test units (people, test markets, etc.) to the treatment variable for some period of time and then taking a measurement of the dependent variable. Using standard notation, the design is shown as follows:

**one-shot case study design**
Pre-experimental design with no pretest observations, no control group, and an after measurement only.

$$X\ O_1$$

There are two basic weaknesses in this design. No pretest observations are made of the test units that will receive the treatment, and no control group of test units that did not receive the treatment is observed. As a result, the design does not deal with the effects of any of the extraneous variables discussed previously. Therefore, the design lacks internal validity and, most likely, external validity as well. This design is useful for suggesting causal hypotheses but does not provide a strong test of such hypotheses. Many test markets for new products (not previously on the market) are based on this design because it is simpler and less costly.

**One-Group Pretest–Posttest Design**   The **one-group pretest–posttest design** is the design employed most frequently for testing changes in established products or marketing strategies. The fact that the product was on the market before the change provides the basis for the pretest measurement ($O_1$). The design is shown symbolically as follows:

$$O_1 \quad X \quad O_2$$

Pretest observations are made of a single group of subjects or a single test unit ($O_1$) that then receives the treatment. Finally, a posttest observation is made ($O_2$). The treatment effect is estimated by $O_2 - O_1$.

History is a threat to the internal validity of this design because an observed change in the dependent variable might be caused by an event that took place outside the experiment between the pretest and posttest measurements. In laboratory experiments, this threat can be controlled by insulating respondents from outside influences. Unfortunately, this type of control is impossible in field experiments.

Maturation is another threat to this type of design. An observed effect might be caused by the fact that subjects have grown older, smarter, more experienced, or the like between the pretest and the posttest.

This design has only one pretest observation. As a result, the researcher knows nothing of the pretest trend in the dependent variable. The posttest score may be higher because of an increasing trend of the dependent variable in a situation where this effect is not the treatment of interest.

Bias can creep into any design as discussed next in the Practicing Marketing Research box.

**one-group pretest–posttest design**
Pre-experimental design with pre- and postmeasurements but no control group.

# PRACTICING MARKETING RESEARCH

## What Happens When Your Selection Bias Is the Interviewer's Gender?[10]

In creating an experimental design to test variables in a market research strategy, selection bias usually means a threat to validity because the test group is too different from the desired target population the researcher wants to probe. But what if the selection bias starts with the market researcher's gender? What impact might that have on the experimental validity? Recently, German researchers found that surveys sent by women or with women's names get better responses than men's.

Stefan Althoff is a marketing researcher manager for Lufthansa Technik in Hamburg, Germany. In 2004, his department started an online customer survey. They received a very low response. A week later they sent out reminders, but the writer signing the letter was named Julia. The response rate jumped to 30 percent. For many of the subsequent online surveys, Lufthansa Technik had women sign their e-mail surveys and reminders, and anecdotally the researchers had the impression respondents read and completed the surveys faster than before when men had signed them. They called this the Anita Effect—the impact of a sender's gender on response.

In January 2006, Althoff and colleagues ran an in-house employee survey at Lufthansa Technik regarding intranet usage. Their sample was two groups of 105 men each in which one group got a mailed invitation to participate from a female, one from men. The response rate for the 210 men was 80 percent, but for the men receiving invitations from the female sender, it was 83.9 percent and from men, it was only 74.3 percent.

In March 2006, Althoff and his associates tested the Anita Effect again, this time with a survey of registered users of UNIpark and associated with the academic market. Althoff split 460 users into four groups and asked them to evaluate UNIpark's Web site homepage and the utility of Globalpark's online survey software. Althoff and crew (which included a woman researcher) varied the gender of the e-mail invitations, but the results were significant: "The response rate was higher from the group that received an invitation mailed from a female sender," Althoff commented.

## Questions

1. What types of possible (even if subtle) bias might result from male respondents answering an e-mail survey sent or signed by a female?

2. Althoff pzlanned to test the impact of different women's names on response rate. Consider which three female names might be the most attractive and least attractive to male respondents.

## True Experimental Designs

**true experimental design**
Research using an experimental group and a control group, to which test units are randomly assigned.

In a **true experimental design**, the experimenter randomly assigns treatments to randomly selected test units. In our notation system, the random assignment of test units to treatments is denoted by (R). Randomization is an important mechanism that makes the results of true experimental designs more valid than the results of pre-experimental designs. True experimental designs are superior because randomization takes care of many extraneous variables. The principal reason for choosing randomized experiments over other types of research designs is that they clarify causal inference.[11] Two examples of true experimental designs are discussed in this section: before and after with control group design and after-only with control group design.

| EXHIBIT 9.1 | Examples of True Experimental Designs |
|---|---|

**Situation:** California Tan wants to measure the sales effect of a point-of-purchase display. The firm is considering two true experimental designs.

| After-Only with Control Group Design | Before and After with Control Group Design |
|---|---|

**After-Only with Control Group Design**

Basic design:

| | | |
|---|---|---|
| Experimental Group: | (R) × | $O_1$ |
| Control Group: | (R) | $O_2$ |

Sample: Random sample of stores that sell their products. Stores are randomly assigned to test and control groups. Groups can be considered equivalent.
Treatment ($X$): Placing the point-of-purchase display in stores in the experimental group for 1 month.
Measurements ($O_1$, $O_2$): Actual sales of company's brand during the period that the point-of-purchase displays are in test stores.
Comments:

Because of random assignment of stores to groups, the test group and control group can be considered equivalent. Measure of the treatment effect of $X$ is $O_1 - O_2$. If $O_1 = 125,000$ units and $O_2 = 113,000$ units, then treatment effect = 12,000 units.

**Before and After with Control Group Design**

Basic design:

| | | | |
|---|---|---|---|
| Experimental Group: | (R) | $O_1$ | X | $O_2$ |
| Control Group: | (R) | $O_3$ | | $O_4$ |

Sample: Same as after-only design.
Treatment ($X$): Same as after-only design.
Measurements ($O_1$ to $O_4$):

$O_1$ and $O_2$ are pre- and postmeasurements for the experimental group;
$O_3$ and $O_4$ are the same for the control group.

Results:

$O_1 = 113,000$ units
$O_2 = 125,000$ units
$O_3 = 111,000$ units
$O_4 = 118,000$ units

Comments:

Random assignment to groups means that the groups can be considered equivalent.

Because groups are equivalent, it is reasonable to assume that they will be equally affected by the same extraneous factors.

The difference between pre- and postmeasurements for the control group ($O_4 - O_3$) provides a good estimate of the effects of all extraneous factors on both groups. Based on these results, $O_4 - O_3 = 7,000$ units. The estimated treatment effect is $(O_2 - O_1) - (O_4 - O_3) = (125,000 - 113,000) - (118,000 \ 2 \ 111,000) = 5,000$ units.

## Before and After with Control Group Design

**Before and After with Control Group Design** The **before and after with control group design** can be presented symbolically as follows:

Experimental Group:     $(R)$    $O_1$     $X$      $O_2$

Control Group:          $(R)$    $O_3$           $O_4$

Because the test units in this design are randomly assigned to the experimental and control groups, the two groups can be considered equivalent. Therefore, they are likely to be subject to the same extraneous causal factors, except for the treatment of interest in the experimental group. For this reason, the difference between the pre- and postmeasurements of the control group $(O_4 - O_3)$ should provide a good estimate of the effect of all the extraneous influences experienced by each group. The true impact of the treatment variable $X$ can be known only when the extraneous influences are removed from the difference between the pre- and postmeasurements of the experimental group. Thus, the true impact of $X$ is estimated by $(O_2 - O_1) - (O_4 - O_3)$. This design generally controls for all but two major threats to validity: mortality and history.

Mortality is a problem if units drop out during the study and these units differ systematically from the ones that remain. This results in a selection bias because the experimental and control groups are composed of different subjects at the posttest than at the pretest. History will be a problem in those situations where factors other than the treatment variable affect the experimental group but not the control group, or vice versa. Examples of this design and the after-only with control group design are provided in Exhibit 9.1.

## After-Only with Control Group Design

**After-Only with Control Group Design** The **after-only with control group design** ensures that test and control groups can be considered equivalent; it can be shown symbolically as follows:

Experimental Group:     $(R)$    $X$    $O_1$

Control Group:          $(R)$      $O_2$

Notice that the test units are randomly $(R)$ assigned to experimental and control groups. This random assignment should produce experimental and control groups that are approximately equal in regard to the dependent variable before presentation of the treatment to the experimental group. It can reasonably be assumed that test unit mortality (one of the threats to internal validity) will affect each group in the same way.

Considering this design in the context of the sun tan lotion example described in Exhibit 9.1, we can see a number of problems. Events other than the treatment variable may have occurred during the experimental period in one or a few stores in the experimental group. If a particular store in the experimental group ran a sale on certain other products and, as a result, had a larger than average number of customers in the store, suntan lotion sales might have increased because of the heavier traffic. Events such as these, which are store-specific (history), may distort the overall treatment effect. Also, there is a possibility that a few stores might drop out during the experiment (mortality threat), resulting in selection bias because the stores in the experimental group will be different at the posttest.

## Quasi-Experiments

When designing a true experiment, the researcher often must create artificial environments to control independent and extraneous variables. Because of this artificiality, questions are raised about the external validity of the experimental findings. Quasi-experimental designs have been developed to deal with this problem. They generally are more feasible in field settings than are true experiments.

**before and after with control group design**
True experimental design that involves random assignment of subjects or test units to experimental and control groups and pre- and postmeasurements of both groups.

**after-only with control group design**
True experimental design that involves random assignment of subjects or test units to experimental and control groups, but no premeasurement of the dependent variable.

**quasi-experiments**
Studies in which the researcher lacks complete control over the scheduling of treatments or must assign respondents to treatments in a nonrandom manner.

In **quasi-experiments**, the researcher lacks complete control over the scheduling of treatments or must assign respondents to treatments in a *nonrandom* fashion. These designs frequently are used in marketing research studies because cost and field constraints often do not permit the researcher to exert direct control over the scheduling of treatments and the randomization of respondents. Examples of quasi-experiments are interrupted time-series designs and multiple time-series designs.

**interrupted time-series design**
Research in which repeated measurement of an effect "interrupts" previous data patterns.

**Interrupted Time-Series Designs** Interrupted time-series designs involve repeated measurement of an effect both before and after a treatment is introduced that "interrupts" previous data patterns. Interrupted time-series experimental designs can be shown symbolically as follows:

$$O_1 \quad O_2 \quad O_3 \quad O_4 \quad X \quad O_5 \quad O_6 \quad O_7 \quad O_8$$

A common example of this type of design in marketing research involves the use of consumer purchase panels. A researcher might use a panel to make periodic measurements of consumer purchase activity (the $O$s), introducing a new promotional campaign (the $X$) and examining the panel data for an effect. The researcher has control over the timing of the promotional campaign but cannot be sure when the panel members were exposed to the campaign or whether they were exposed at all.

This design is very similar to the one-group pretest–posttest design

$$O_1 \quad X \quad O_2$$

However, time-series experimental designs have greater interpretability than the one-group pretest–posttest design because the many measurements allow more understanding of the effects of extraneous variables. If, for example, sales of a product were on the rise and a new promotional campaign was introduced, the true effect of this campaign could not be estimated if a pretest–posttest design were used. However, the rising trend in sales would be obvious if a number of pretest and posttest observations had been made. Time-series designs help determine the underlying trend of the dependent variable and provide better interpretability in regard to the treatment effect.

The interrupted time-series design has two fundamental weaknesses. The primary weakness is our inability to control history. Although maintaining a careful log of all possibly relevant external happenings can reduce this problem, we have no way of determining the appropriate number and timing of pretest and posttest observations.

The other weakness of this design comes from the possibility of interactive effects of testing and evaluation apprehension resulting from the repeated measurements taken on test units. For example, panel members may become "expert" shoppers or simply become unnaturally conscious of their shopping habits. Under these circumstances, it may be inappropriate to make generalizations to other populations.

**multiple time-series design**
Interrupted time-series design with a control group.

**Multiple Time-Series Designs** If a control group is added to an interrupted time-series design, then researchers can be more certain in their interpretation of the treatment effect. This design, called the **multiple time-series design**, can be shown symbolically as follows:

Experimental Group: $\quad O_1 \quad O_2 \quad O_3 \quad O_4 \quad O_5 \quad O_6$

Control Group: $\quad O_1 \quad O_2 \quad O_3 \quad O_4 \quad O_5 \quad O_6$

The researcher must take care in selecting the control group. For example, if an advertiser were testing a new advertising campaign in a test city, that city would constitute the experimental group and another city that was not exposed to the new campaign would be chosen as the control group. It is important that the test and control cities be roughly equivalent in regard to characteristics related to the sale of the product (e.g., competitive brands available).

# Test Markets

The development of products and services goes through a sequence of steps, beginning with idea generation, screening of ideas, concept testing, business analysis, prototype development, test marketing, and commercialization. Marketers may or may not test market a product or service depending on its expected rate of diffusion, the degree to which it is different from existing competitive offerings, and a host of other factors.

Test marketing is a common form of experimentation used by marketing researchers. The term **test market** is used rather loosely to refer to any research that involves testing a new product or change in an existing marketing strategy (e.g., product, price, place promotion) in a single market, group of markets, or region of the country through the use of experimental or quasi-experimental designs.[12]

New product introductions play a key role in a firm's financial success or failure. The conventional wisdom in the corporate world is that new products will have to be more profitable in the future than they were in the past because of higher levels of competition and a faster pace of change. Estimates of new-product failure rates vary all over the place and range to more than 90 percent. Testing at McDonald's is discussed in the Practicing Marketing Research box.

**test market**
Real-world testing of a new product or some element of the marketing mix using an experimental or quasi-experimental design.

# PRACTICING MARKETING RESEARCH

## Testing at McDonald's[13]

Big companies such as McDonald's, with locations all over the globe, can perform test marketing in their own stores. Take the McLobster, for instance. I'm sure it began during an idea-generation session. Someone might have said, "Hey, what is missing in our Canadian/New England market?" Or maybe they just liked the idea of going into the lobster sandwich business and asked themselves, "Who would eat this?" Or maybe it wasn't an internal idea source, maybe it was external, coming from consumers or a supplier. The McLobster passed the idea-screening stage, "Which helps spot good ideas and drop poor ones as soon as possible."

Next, came the product concept, "a detailed version of the idea stated in meaningful consumer terms." This would go something like, "The McLobster: real Atlantic lobster spread over the length of a bun and smothered in creamy, white McLobster sauce … mmm, I'm lovin' it!" Then they turned it into a product image, where it became more than just a description—either as a drawing or a physical representation of the McLobster.

Eventually, after the marketing strategy development stage where McDonald's described its target market, the company could explore the planned value proposition, and the sales, market share, and profit goals. Finally, McDonald's would have performed a business analysis on the McLobster, reviewing sales, costs, and profit projections to see if they fit with the objectives of the company.

Then would have come the fun parts, such as product development, where McDonald's would actually create the McLobster. Perhaps seafood specialists would be consulted. McDonald's wouldn't then just commercialize the product to every McDonald's that serves to its target market, though. It would first have to do test marketing, by introducing the product and marketing program into real-market conditions at certain locations within its target market.

Test marketing is easy for a company like McDonald's, which can experiment with its products within its own restaurants, simply by doing small, local promotions and offering it on the menu with a big "NEW" next to it. The McLobster must not have been profitable enough to mass commercialize, but to my understanding, it was reintroduced over the years as a seasonal product in limited markets.

### Questions

1. What are the characteristics of a good test market?
2. Why is test marketing easier for companies like McDonald's?

As you probably recognize, test-market studies have the goal of helping marketing managers make better decisions about new products and additions or changes to existing products or marketing strategies. A test-market study does this by providing a real-world test for evaluating products and marketing programs. Marketing managers use test markets to evaluate proposed national programs with many separate elements on a smaller, less costly scale. The basic idea is to determine whether the estimated profits from rolling the product out on a national basis justify the potential risks. Test-market studies are designed to provide information in regard to the following issues:

- Estimates of market share and volume.
- The effects that the new product will have on sales of similar products (if any) already marketed by the company. This is referred to as the *cannibalization rate*.
- Characteristics of consumers who buy the product. Demographic data will almost surely be collected, and lifestyle, psychographic, and other types of classification data are often collected. This information is useful in refining the marketing strategy for the product. For example, knowing the demographic characteristics of likely purchasers will help in developing a media plan that will effectively and efficiently reach target customers. Knowing the psychographic and lifestyle characteristics of target customers will provide valuable insights into how to position the product and the types of promotional messages that will appeal to them.
- The behavior of competitors during the test. This may provide some indication of what competitors will do if the product is introduced nationally.

Other types of research may precede or follow experiments or test markets as suggested in the Practicing Marketing Research box that follows.

# PRACTICING MARKETING RESEARCH

## *Unlocking the Potential*[14]

Innovation is a disruptive force that fuels progress. But innovation doesn't happen in a vacuum. New products and services must be tested and often retested to measure viability.

An example of innovation is the CardLock service from PSCU Financial Services, a St. Petersburg, Florida, financial services and payment processing company serving more than 600 credit unions and 14 million cardholders across the country. Introduced in late summer 2009, CardLock aims to strengthen fraud prevention by enabling cardholders to lock or unlock their credit or debit cards, effectively turning them off or on. Cardholders can call a toll-free number or visit a special website to lock or unlock their account in seconds using a simple four-digit key code.

Before going to market, PSCU Financial Services conducted research to test the viability of the CardLock concept, a process detailed here.

CardLock was not created in a vacuum. A vision was developed and the idea was championed internally to gain acceptance and endorsement by key corporate stakeholders. A cross-department task force convened to discuss the idea. The team hammered out a product concept, discussed technical requirements, analyzed secondary data on the concept, and provided anecdotal feedback about the market and the potential benefit to credit unions and their members.

### Distinct Differentiator

It was determined that no other product like CardLock existed in the marketplace, giving PSCU a distinct differentiator. But before any product development took place, a research plan was needed to fully test the concept.

Stakeholders provided input and ultimately endorsed and supported a research plan. Stakeholders needed answers to the following questions: Does it fit a need? Does it have market potential? And, what features and functionality are needed to make it successful? At this point, the company contacted SRA Research Group to consult on the potential ways to approach a variety of issues around this research.

The research plan was divided into three distinct phases: a quantitative segmentation study; a series of focus groups; and, if the concept made it far enough, credit union in-market testing. The process was atypical. Many research projects start with qualitative and then move to quantitative. Based on its experience, SRA indicated that one of the typical pitfalls in product development is qualitative research being used to push an idea to market. And, PSCU needed confidence that a market existed before it could explore features and functionality—a more costly endeavor. Hence, the quantitative survey was done first.

## Phase 1: Consumer Segmentation Study

The company needed a reliable pulse of consumer demand. To that end, PSCU conducted an online survey using a nationally representative panel. Qualifications to participate in the survey were primarily limited to owning either a debit or credit card. A total of 1,080 responded to the survey.

A detailed concept statement for CardLock was introduced. The survey included questions on level of interest (with and without a fee); reasons for or against enrolling; likelihood of use; number of credit and debit cards owned; and experience with card fraud. Survey results were compared across age, income, education, presence of children, number of cards owned, home-ownership status, and financial institution affiliation.

Overall, about 4 in 10 expressed interest in the CardLock concept. Level of interest was sustained even after introducing a $1 monthly fee to the concept.

Two key drivers of interest included the need to be protected from fraud—an obvious driver—and peace of mind. Those not interested generally felt they didn't need it or were concerned about convenience (i.e., forgetting to unlock or forgetting their password). The big takeaway was that, to drive maximum adoption, product developers had to ensure CardLock was easy to use.

Research confirmed distinct marketable segments. Those with the most interest included online shoppers, frequent travelers, younger consumers, renters and those who were victims of card fraud.

With evidence from the research that a market existed for the product, with pockets of great interest among certain segments, internal stakeholders had confidence to move forward with the next phase of the research.

## Phase 2: Consumer Focus Groups

PSCU was confident it had a product with market potential. Before rushing it to market, the company needed some direction on what features and functionality to offer in order to drive greater adoption and usage. The company needed to know how consumers would use the product, what concerns they have, and what roadblocks they might experience. Focus groups were ultimately selected as the method of choice, as they allow for rich discussion that can bring new insights to light and make products even more effective. SRA Research Group was commissioned to conduct this phase of the research.

Researchers elected to conduct four focus groups in two markets. These markets were chosen out of convenience and, to some extent, out of a need for a more neutral consumer group. Survey research from phase one indicated that younger consumers were more interested in the concept than older consumers. Therefore, each of the four sessions was devoted to one of four specific age groups: 18-to-24, 25-to-34, 35-to-44, and 45-to-54. Those 55 and older were not considered a strong market based on the quantitative research.

After a careful review of the quantitative research, it was decided that invitees had to own at least one debit or credit card, have some interest in the concept and exhibit some of the segment characteristics identified in phase one (i.e., routine traveler, online shopper, etc.). SRA carefully monitored the mix of respondents to ensure all of the potential interest groups were represented in the sessions.

The discussion guide was developed and categorized into four key sections. The first section covered panelists' card usage patterns and behaviors. The second section covered panelists' perception of the ideal card. If they could build a card from scratch, what would it look like?

A clear product concept statement was supplied to each group. The moderator then solicited feedback. What was their reaction? Would they register their card for the service? Why or why not? How would they prefer to register? How would they like to be notified in the event someone tried to use a locked card? How often would they use it? What's missing from the product?

Convenience was a major consideration mentioned in the groups. The system needed to be quick to lock and unlock, otherwise respondents would not use it.

The groups also included a short discussion on card fraud. This was a bit tricky in that we wanted to avoid the lengthy war stories but still understand the depth of concern that consumers have about this issue.

Much to our collective surprise, many participants only had a limited understanding of their liability under existing cardholder agreements. Despite this, panelists generally understood the value of the service and expressed interest. Having control gave some of them much-needed peace of mind. In addition to the additional control, the inconvenience of dealing with card fraud was a major motivating factor driving interest.

In all, the consumer focus groups gave product development managers great insight on how to build features and functionality to drive adoption and usage. They also provided an in-depth view into how consumers could be motivated to sign up for this type of service. Now, product development managers needed to test the water.

## Phase 3: Credit Union Testing

At this stage, CardLock development was near complete. But, PSCU realized that credit unions needed to become comfortable with it before they would champion the benefits to their own membership—a key to the product's success. Pilot-testing the new solution to a handful of credit unions would also serve to provide valuable in-market data.

A decision was made to pilot the new solution to three credit unions. Employees of these credit unions were given full access to CardLock. Their use was monitored. How often did they turn their cards on and off? How long did they leave their cards locked? Were there any technical glitches? PSCU conducted weekly check-in calls with pilot coordinators and conducted an on-site feedback session at the end of the pilot period. The in-market test ran for 10 weeks and was considered a success.

### Added Sense of Control

After much due diligence, CardLock moved through the product development pipeline and became an official product. A press release was sent to major credit union trade publications announcing the new service. Since its debut, many credit unions have enrolled.

Market research paved the way for CardLock. The time and investment in both consumer research and in-market testing proved extremely beneficial. It helped to transform a concept into a truly viable and innovative product. In the end, a need was identified, a market was cornered, and peace of mind was achieved.

### Questions

1. What contributions did each of the research components—quantitative focus groups and in-market test—make in the process of getting a successful product to market?
2. How did PSCU leverage the learning from each phase of the research?

Lifestyle data are often collected to find out about the characteristics of possible consumers. This information helps a firm refine the marketing strategy for its product. What might lifestyle data reveal about consumers who would purchase this iPhone?

© sgm/Shutterstock

## Types of Test Markets

Most test markets can be categorized into four types—traditional, scanner or electronic, controlled, and simulated.[15] The *traditional or standard test market* involves testing the product and other elements of the marketing mix through regular channels of distribution. Traditional test markets take a relatively long time (6 months or more is not uncommon), are costly, and immediately tell the competition what you are planning. Some believe the traditional test market provides the best read on how a product and any associated marketing mix elements will actually do if introduced because it is the most like the real marketplace. However, other options, discussed in this section, can provide good estimates at a fraction of the cost, more quickly and without giving the competition advance warning regarding what we are planning to do.

*Scanner or electronic test markets* are markets where research firms have panels of consumers who carry scannable cards for use in buying particular products, especially those sold through grocery stores. These panels permit us to analyze the characteristics of those consumers who buy and those who don't buy the test products. Purchase/nonpurchase by individual panel participants can be related to their detailed demographic data, past purchase history, and, in some cases, media viewing habits. Firms offering scanner panels include ACNielsen and Information Resources. This approach offers speed, lower cost, and some security regarding the marketing strategy or changes in strategy we are considering. The major criticism of this approach is what some argue is its unrepresentative sampling: Those who agree to participate in these panels may not be representative of the broader populations of consumers in these and other markets.

*Controlled test markets* are managed by research suppliers who ensure that the product is distributed through the agreed upon types and numbers of outlets. Research suppliers who offer controlled test markets, such as ACNielsen, pay distributors to provide the required amount of shelf space for test products. Research suppliers carefully monitor sales of the product in these controlled test markets. They enable clients to get their products into test markets more quickly, often supply more realistic levels of distribution, and provide better monitoring of product movement. Some test markets are more popular than others, as discussed in the following Practicing Marketing Research box.

# PRACTICING MARKETING RESEARCH

## Why Columbus, Ohio?[16]

In the high-security test kitchen at Wendy's International, they're working on what they hope will be the next big thing: the Black Label Burger. But don't start drooling just yet. Before it goes to your town, it first has to make the grade here: Columbus, Ohio. White-coated food technicians do the cooking and send the samples to volunteer tasters, who grade it on things like onion flavor and messiness.

It's the last step before it goes out to the test market, and Senior VP Lori Estrada has high hopes: "We're still waiting on our consumer scores, but I'm anticipating based on what we know going into this that they're going to be great."

The test burger then goes to a real Wendy's. Even when it's on the menu here, spokesman Denny Lynch says, they're still find-tuning.

The consumer "guinea pigs" come in all demographics here. With the Ohio State University and dozens of other colleges, the student population here is massive, and there's a strong international presence. It all adds up to a near-perfect cross-section of the country's consumers. It's Middle America—but that doesn't mean its average. There is an interesting blend of a funky culture—creativity, diversity—and a corporate culture that really mixes it up, making it a unique test bed, as opposed to just being average. So the thinking is, if an idea can make it here, it can make it anywhere.

## Questions

1. Why is Columbus, Ohio, seen as a good test market by many marketers? Do you see it as a good test market? Why or why not?

2. Is there such a thing as an "average" market? Justify your answer regardless of whether you agree or don't agree.

*STMs (simulated test markets)* are just what the name implies—simulations of the types of test markets noted above. They can be conducted more quickly than the other approaches, at a lower cost, and can produce results that are highly predictive of what will actually happen. In these simulated test markets, a more limited amount of information is used in conjunction with mathematical models that include estimates of the effects of different marketing variables that can be adjusted to fit the situation. A number of different companies, including ACNielsen (Bases), Harris Interactive (Litmus), and Synovate (MarkeTest), offer these services and each one has special features. However, they all share the following elements:

- A sample of consumers is selected based on the expected or known characteristics of the target consumer for the test product.

- Consumers sampled are recruited to come to a central location testing facility to view commercials for the test product and competitive products.

- Consumers are then given the opportunity to purchase the test product in the actual marketplace or in a simulated store environment.

- Purchasers are contacted after they have had time to use the product. They are asked how likely they are to repurchase and for their evaluations of the product.

- The above information is used with the proprietary model of the STM company to generate estimates of sales volume, market share, and other key market metrics.[17]

## Costs of Test Marketing

Test marketing is expensive. A simple two-market test can cost a bare minimum of $1 million and probably much more. A long-running, more complex test can cost in the tens of millions of dollars. These estimates refer only to direct costs, which may include the following:

- Production of commercials
- Payments to an advertising agency for services
- Media time, charged at a higher rate because of low volume
- Syndicated research information
- Customized research information and associated data analysis
- Point-of-purchase materials
- Coupons and sampling
- Higher trade allowances to obtain distribution[18]

Many *indirect costs* are also associated with test marketing, including the following:

- Cost of management time spent on the test market
- Diversion of sales activity from existing products
- Possible negative impact of a test market failure on other products with the same family brand
- Possible negative trade reactions to products if the firm develops a reputation for not doing well
- Cost of letting competitors know what the firm is doing, thereby allowing them to develop a better strategy or beat the firm to the national market[19]

Test markets are expensive, and, as a result, they should be used only as the last step in a research process that has shown the new product or strategy has potential. In some situations, it might be cheaper to go ahead and launch the product, even if it fails.

## Decision to Conduct Test Marketing

From the preceding discussion, you can see that test markets offer at least two important benefits to the firm conducting the test.[20]

- First and foremost, the test market provides a vehicle by which the firm can obtain a good estimate of a product's sales potential under realistic market conditions. A researcher can develop estimates of the product's national market share on the basis of these test results and use this figure to develop estimates of future financial performance for the product.
- Second, the test should identify weaknesses of the product and the proposed marketing strategy for the product and give management an opportunity to correct those weaknesses. It is much easier and less expensive to correct these problems at the test market stage than after the product has gone into national distribution.

These benefits must be weighed against costs and a number of other negatives associated with test markets.[21] The financial costs of test markets are not insignificant. And test markets give competitors an early indication of what the firm is planning to do. They thus share the opportunity to make adjustments in their marketing strategy; or, if the idea is simple and not legally protected, they may be able to copy it and move into national distribution faster than the original firm can.

Four major factors should be taken into account in determining whether to conduct a test market:

1. *Weigh the cost and risk of failure against the probability of success and associated profits.* If estimated costs are high and you are uncertain about the likelihood of success, then you should lean toward doing a test market. On the other hand, if both expected costs and the risk of product failure are low, then an immediate national rollout without a test market may be the appropriate strategy.

2. *Consider the likelihood and speed with which competitors can copy your product and introduce it on a national basis.* If the product can be easily copied, then it may be appropriate to introduce the product without a test market.

3. *Consider the investment required to produce the product for the test market versus the investment required to produce the product in the quantities necessary for a national rollout.* In cases where the difference in investment required is very small, it may make sense to introduce the product nationally without a test market. However, in cases where a very large difference exists between the investment required to produce the product for test market and that required for a national rollout, conducting a test market before making a decision to introduce the product nationally makes good sense.

4. *Consider how much damage an unsuccessful new product launch would inflict on the firm's reputation.* Failure may hurt the firm's reputation with members of the channel of distribution (retailers) and impede the firm's ability to gain their cooperation in future product launches.

## Steps in a Test Market Study

Once the decision has been made to conduct test marketing, a number of steps must be carried out if we are to achieve a satisfactory result.

### Step One: Define the Objective
As always with these kinds of lists, the first step is to define the objectives of the test. Typical test market objectives include the following:

- Develop share and volume estimates.
- Determine the characteristics of people who are purchasing the product.
- Determine the frequency and purpose of purchase.
- Determine where (retail outlets) purchases are made.
- Measure the effect of sales of the new product on sales of similar existing products in the line.

### Step Two: Select a Basic Approach
After specifying the objectives of the test market exercise, the next step is to decide on the appropriate type of test market, given the stated objectives.

Earlier in the chapter, we discussed the characteristics, advantages, and disadvantages of four types of test markets:

- Traditional or standard test market
- Scanner or electronic test market
- Controlled test market
- Simulated test market (STM) (See Practicing Marketing Research on page 216 for more discussion of STMs.)

Selecting markets for a test is an important decision. Significant regional differences should be considered in choosing cities as test markets. To find some readily apparent regional differences between Seattle and Miami, visit *www.ci.seattle.wa.us* and *www.miami.com*.

General Mills used the "rolling rollout" when it introduced MultiGrain Cheerios to the public. Visit *www.generalmills.com* to find out what new products the company may be introducing.

The decision regarding which type of test market to use in a given situation depends on how much time you have, how much budget you have, and how important it is to keep the competition in the dark about what you are planning to do.

### Step Three: Develop Detailed Test Procedures

After the objectives and a basic approach for the test have been developed, the researcher must develop a detailed plan for conducting the test. Manufacturing and distribution decisions must ensure that adequate product is available and that it is available in most stores of the type that sell that particular product class. In addition, the detailed marketing plan for the test must be specified, including the basic positioning approach, the actual commercials to be used, pricing strategy, media plan, and various promotional elements.

### Step Four: Select Test Markets

The selection of markets for the test is an important decision. A number of factors must be taken into account in making this decision.

First, there are the overall standards:[22]

- There should be a minimum of two test markets, in addition to a control market, for an existing national brand or a minimum of three markets for testing a new brand.

- The markets selected should be geographically dispersed; if the brand is a regional brand, the markets should cover several dispersed markets within that region.

- Markets should be demographically representative of the United States, unless, for instance, a pronounced ethnic skew is desirable for a specific brand.

- Depending on the product purchase cycle, the test should be run for at least 6 months, up to 12 months, before the results can be considered projectable. If the product is purchased infrequently, it is advisable to run the test for even longer than a year.

- The market must have a variety of media outlets, including at least four television stations, cable penetration no more than 10 percent above or below the U.S. average, at least four radio stations, a dominant local newspaper with daily and Sunday editions, a Sunday supplement with a syndicated edition, or a local supplement of similar quality.

# PRACTICING MARKETING RESEARCH

## Quick Scans of Product-Specific Test Markets

Some locations just seem to specialize in favorable conditions for selected test market trials, such as for high-end beer, premium vodkas, or Brazilian steakhouses.

Miller Brewing Company of Milwaukee, Wisconsin, decided to test market three kinds of low-calorie, craft-style light beers in only four cities starting in 2008: Minneapolis, Minnesota; Charlotte, North Carolina; San Diego, California; and Baltimore, Maryland. Their goal was to establish a new category for light craft-style beers and to capitalize on three noticeable trends in the beer industry: the shift toward lighter beers (fewer calories and carbohydrates), more variety, and the, so-called premiumization–high-end, quality-perceived offerings. It's a solid idea because craft beer sales for 2006 were up 17.8 percent and those four cities have the right combination of demographics to warrant the test market.[23]

Fuller's, a London brewery founded in 1711, selected Denver, Colorado, as the premium United States locale to test market its high-end London Pride beer. Why Denver? The area is home to a hefty quantity of beer drinkers who prefer the high-end brews and presumably won't mind spending $8 for a London Pride six-pack. People there, research has found, are "friendly" to premium or craft-style beers. Even better, craft beer commands a 10 percent market share in Colorado, putting it third in the nation. Fuller's marketing approach included radio ads that trolled for the golf and outdoors-focused types who are more the "microbrew set," the company said.[24] Anheuser-Busch is test-running its Purus vodka, distilled in Italy and fetching $35 a bottle retail, in Boston, New York, Washington, and Annapolis. Why there? The company wants to attract the "modern luxury connoisseur" to their organic wheat-based Purus, and they want to test-position it in those cities' most exclusive lounges and restaurants as well as in a handful of specialty groceries and liquor stores. Again, there's evidence of sober thinking behind the approach: U.S. sales of upper-end or ultra-premium vodkas more than doubled between 2003 and 2006. Typical consumers? Young drinkers, aged 21 to 30, who care more about image than price.[25]

What U.S. city did International Restaurant Concepts of Lakewood, Colorado, select to test market its Tucanos Brazilian Grill steakhouse? Provo, Utah. At first glance, Provo's demographics would seem against it: of its 100,000 residents, 87 percent are white and only 10 percent Hispanic, so where's the market for Tucanos's churrascaria? It turns out that because Provo is the home of Brigham Young University and runs a missionary training center for the Church of the Latter-Day Saints, many of the thousands of Mormon students sent out in the field have been posted to Brazil. In addition, the university population comprises many international students—all of which generates an ethnically diverse and language-rich community and good test market.[26]

## Questions

1. What characteristics do the cities of Minneapolis, Charlotte, San Diego, and Baltimore possess that make them good markets for introducing premium-level beers?

2. How would you tailor a test market experimentation for Brazilian cuisine in a Mormon-saturated region whose members, nonetheless, are well-traveled and versed in Brazilian foods?

# PRACTICING MARKETING RESEARCH

## Simulated test marketing research enables you to experiment and hone in on the best marketing plan.[27]

Although it's true that some marketers use simulated test marketing technology to test a few alternative plans and pick the winner in terms of projected volume or sales, there's really no reason to put a cap on the number to try out. And here's why.

Now, more than ever, marketers need plans that enhance new product/service performance as much as possible. Marketers everywhere—even the ones with great products and services ready to go—need to ask themselves: "Do I have the right combination of strategy and tactics that will generate the most return in terms of share, revenue, and/or profit from my investment?"

When we asked a leading consumer packaged goods manufacturer recently about the reasons behind the company's 90 to 95 percent failure rate, the company explained that "a faulty marketing plan and/or the failure to implement the plan" more often than not upended performance.

Beyond its uses as a forecasting tool, simulated test marketing research enables you to experiment with different inputs—from strategic elements such as the target and positioning to tactical elements such as GRPs and budget allocation across different traditional and digital media—and narrow in on the marketing plan most likely to support performance objectives in the real world.

We've never seen a plan recommended based on simulated test marketing recommended that didn't beat the ones submitted by marketing management. Sometimes the margin is modest; sometimes the difference is overwhelming.

Simulated test marketing applications go beyond prelaunch planning and forecasting. Marketers can also use one cleverly done to improve the marketing plan postlaunch. Marketers can see the current trajectory of a new product/service or program based on as little as 30 days of actual, real-world results. If they see a big difference between the prelaunch and postlaunch forecasts of awareness, sales, and profits, they have the time—and the simulated test marketing technology—to do some reformulating of the plan and get innovation ROI on track.

Though more and more marketers regularly use technology to test different and numerous configurations of new products and services, we're hard pressed to find too many that use it to formulate the marketing plan. Turning to technology tools such as simulated test marketing will go a long way to improving the performance of innovation efforts.

### Questions

1. What is a simulated test market, or STM? How does it differ from a traditional test market?
2. Can simulated test markets be used only to estimate projected volume or sales? What other uses do they have?

**Step Five: Execute the Plan** Once the plan is in place, the researcher can begin execution. At this point, a key decision has to be made: how long should the test run? The average test runs for 6 to 12 months. However, shorter and longer tests are not uncommon. The test must run long enough for an adequate number of repeat purchase cycles to be observed in order to provide a measure of the "staying power" of a new product or marketing program. The shorter the average period, the shorter the test needs to be. Cigarettes, soft drinks, and packaged goods are purchased every few days, whereas such products as shaving cream and toothpaste are purchased only every few months. The latter would require a longer test. Whatever the product type, the test must be continued until the repeat purchase rate stabilizes. The percentage of people making repeat purchases tends to drop for some period of time before reaching a relatively constant level. Repeat purchase rate is critical to the process of estimating ultimate sales of the product. If the test ends too soon then sales will be overestimated.

Two other considerations in determining the length of the test relate to the expected speed of competitor reaction and the costs of running the test. If there is reason to expect that competitors will react quickly to the test marketing (introduce their own versions of the new product), then the test should be as short as possible. Minimizing the length of the test reduces the amount of time competitors have to react. Finally, the value of additional information to be gained from the test must be balanced against the cost of continuing to run the test. At some point, the value of additional information will be outweighed by its cost.

### Step Six: Analyze the Test Results

Results should be evaluated throughout the test period. However, after completion of the experiment, a more careful and thorough evaluation of the data must be performed. This analysis will focus on four areas:

- *Purchase data.* The purchase data are most important in most experiments or test markets. The levels of initial purchase (trial) throughout the course of the experiment provide an indication of how well the advertising and promotion program worked. The repeat rate (percentage of initial triers who made second and subsequent purchases) provides an indication of how well the product met the expectations created through advertising and promotion. Of course, the trial and repeat purchase results provide the basis for estimating sales and market share in the broader market.
- *Awareness data.* How effective were the media expenditures and media plan in creating awareness of the product? Do consumers know how much the product costs? Do they know its key features?
- *Competitive response.* Ideally, the responses of competitors should be monitored during the period of the test market. For example, competitors may try to distort test results by offering special promotions, price deals, and quantity discounts. Their actions may provide some indication of what they will do if the product moves into national distribution and some basis for estimating the effect of these actions.
- *Source of sales.* If the product is a new entry in an existing product category, it is important to determine where sales are coming from. In other words, which brands did the people who purchased the test product previously purchase? This information provides a true indication of real competitors. If the firm has an existing brand in the market, it also indicates to what extent the new product will take business from existing brands and from the competition.

Based on the evaluation, a decision will be made to improve the marketing program or the product, drop the product, or move the product into national or regional distribution.

## Other Types of Product Tests

In addition to the four types of test markets, there are other means by which companies can gauge potential for a new product. One alternative is a *rolling rollout*, which usually follows a pretest. A product is launched in a certain region rather than in one or two cities. Within a matter of days, scanner data provides information on how the product is doing. The product can then be launched in additional regions; ads and promotions can be adjusted along the way to a national introduction. General Mills has used this approach for products such as MultiGrain Cheerios.

Another alternative is to try a product out in a foreign market before rolling it out globally. Specifically, one or a few countries can serve as test markets for a continent or even the world. This *lead country strategy* has been used by Colgate-Palmolive, Procter & Gamble, and many others.

## SUMMARY

Experimental research is used to test whether a change in an independent variable causes some predictable change in a dependent variable. To show that a change in *A* likely caused an observed change in *B*, one must show three things: correlation, appropriate time order of occurrence, and the elimination of other possible causal factors. Experiments can be conducted in a laboratory or a field setting. The major advantage of conducting experiments in a laboratory is that the researcher can more readily control extraneous factors. However, in marketing research, laboratory settings typically do not appropriately replicate the marketplace. Experiments conducted in the actual marketplace are called field experiments. The major difficulty with field experiments is that the researcher cannot control all the other factors that might influence the dependent variable.

In experimentation, we are concerned with internal and external validity. Internal validity refers to the extent to which competing explanations (other possible factors) of the experimental results observed can be ruled out. External validity refers to the extent to which causal relationships measured in an experiment can be generalized to other settings. Extraneous variables are other independent variables that may affect the dependent variable and thus stand in the way of our ability to conclude that an observed change in the dependent variable was due to the effect of the experimental, or treatment, variable. Extraneous factors include history, maturation, instrument variation, selection bias, mortality, testing effects, and regression to the mean. Four basic approaches are used to control extraneous factors: randomization, physical control, design control, and statistical control.

In an experimental design, the researcher has control over and manipulates one or more independent variables. Nonexperimental designs, which involve no manipulation, are referred to as ex post facto research. An experimental design includes four elements: the treatment, subjects, a dependent variable that is measured, and a plan or procedure for dealing with extraneous causal factors. An experimental effect is the effect of the treatment variable on the dependent variable.

Experiments have an obvious advantage in that they are the only type of research that can demonstrate the existence and nature of causal relationships between variables of interest. Yet the amount of actual experimentation done in marketing research is limited because of the high cost of experiments, security issues, and implementation problems. There is evidence to suggest that the use of experiments in marketing research is growing.

Pre-experimental designs offer little or no control over the influence of extraneous factors and are thus generally difficult to interpret. Examples include the one-shot case study design and the one-group pretest–posttest design. In a true experimental design, the researcher is able to eliminate all extraneous variables as competitive hypotheses to the treatment. Examples of true experimental designs are the before and after with control group design and the after-only with control group design.

In quasi-experiments, the researcher has control over data-collection procedures but lacks complete control over the scheduling of treatments. The treatment groups in a quasi-experiment normally are formed by assigning respondents to treatments in a nonrandom fashion. Examples of quasi-experimental designs are the interrupted time-series design and the multiple time-series design.

Test marketing involves testing a new product or some element of the marketing mix by using experimental or quasi-experimental designs. Test markets are field experiments and they are extremely expensive to conduct. The steps in conducting a test market study include defining the objectives for the study, selecting the basic approach to be used, developing detailed procedures for the test, selecting markets for the test, executing the plan, and analyzing the test results.

## KEY TERMS

experiment **194**

causal research **194**

laboratory experiments **195**

field experiments **196**

internal validity **196**

external validity **196**

history **197**

maturation **197**

instrument variation **198**

selection bias **198**

mortality **198**

testing effect **198**

regression to the mean **199**

randomization **199**

physical control **199**

design control **199**

statistical control **199**

experimental design **200**

treatment variable **200**

experimental effect **201**

contamination **202**

pre-experimental designs **202**

one-shot case study design **201**

one-group pretest–posttest design **203**

true experimental design **204**

before and after with control group design **205**

after-only with control group design **205**

quasi-experiments **206**

interrupted time-series design **206**

multiple time-series design **206**

test market **207**

# QUESTIONS FOR REVIEW & CRITICAL THINKING

1. Divide the class into as many as six groups, as appropriate. Each group will have the task of recommending a test market design and addressing the associated questions for one of the following scenarios:

*(Team Exercise)*

- Design a test of a new pricing strategy for orange juice concentrate. The brand is an established brand, and we are only interested in testing the effect of a 5 percent price increase and a 5 percent decrease. All other elements of the marketing mix will remain the same.
- A soft-drink company has determined in taste tests that consumers prefer the taste of their diet product when sweetened with Splenda® in comparison to Equal®. Now they are interested in determining how the new sweetener will play in the marketplace. Design a test market that will achieve this goal.
- A national pizza chain wants to test the effect on sales of four different discount coupons. Design a test that will do this in a way that gives a clear read. Your focus should be on the effect on sales volume. Financial analysis after the test results are in will address the revenue and profit impact.
- A national value-priced hotel chain needs to understand the business impact of including a free buffet-style breakfast to guests. Design and justify a test that will do this.
- A credit card company needs to test its strategy for attracting college students to its card. It is going to continue using booths in student unions and other high-traffic campus locations. It has been offering free CDs from a list to those who sign up for its card, but since other card companies are using this approach, the company wants to try some alternatives. It is considering free MP3 downloads from iTunes and t-shirts featuring popular music groups. Design a test that will tell the company which option to choose if its goal is to increase signups by the largest amount.

2. Tico Taco, a national chain of Mexican fast-food restaurants, has developed the "Super Sonic Taco," which is the largest taco in the market and sells for $1.19. Tico Taco has identified its target customers for this new product as men under 30 who are not concerned about health issues, such as fat content or calories. It wants to test the product in at least four regional markets before making a decision to introduce it nationally. What criteria would you use to select test cities for this new product? Which cities would you recommend using? Why would you recommend those cities?

3. Of the primary data-collection techniques available to the researcher (survey, observation, experiment), why is the experiment the only one that can provide conclusive evidence of causal relationships? Of the various types of experiments, which type or types provide the best evidence of causation or noncausation?

4. What are some important independent variables that must be dealt with in an experiment to test consumer reactions to a pilot for a new TV series? Explain why those variables are important.

5. Managers of the student center at your university or college are considering three alternative brands of frozen pizza to be offered on the menu. They want to offer only one of the three and want to find out which brand students prefer. Design an experiment to determine which brand of pizza the students prefer.

6. Night students at the university or college are much older than day students. Introduce an explicit control for day versus night students in the preceding experiment.

7. Why are quasi-experiments much more popular in marketing research than true experiments?

8. How does history differ from maturation? What specific actions might you take to deal with each in an experiment?

9. A manufacturer of microwave ovens has designed an improved model that will reduce energy costs and cook food evenly throughout. However, this new model will increase the product's price by 30 percent because of extra components and engineering design changes. It decides to test market the new oven in a market area with an extremely high household income level. In addition, the producer offers a discount coupon to facilitate product sales. The company wants to determine what effect the new model will have on sales of its microwave ovens. Do you see any potential problems with a sales forecast based on the results of the test market sales? What would you do differently?

10. Discuss various methods by which extraneous causal factors can be controlled.

11. Discuss the alternatives to traditional test marketing. Explain their advantages and disadvantages.

## WORKING THE NET

1. Visit *www.questionpro.com/akira/showLibrary.do? categoryID516&mode51* to take a psychographics profile with 269 focused questions distributed into 15 categories. What kind of consumer are you? How would you design a test market to attract a customer like yourself?

2. Consult www.city-data.com Research city demographics for Cedar Rapids, Iowa; Eau Claire, Wisconsin; and Grand Junction, Colorado, to evaluate why *Advertising Age* (2005) ranked them among the top seven most popular test market sites in the United States for matching the average American demographic profile.

## REAL-LIFE RESEARCH • 9.1

### Texas Red Soft Drinks

Texas Red is the oldest soft-drink company in Texas. During the 1980s, the company went through bankruptcy because of its inability to compete with the big national soft drink brands. In 2003, a group of investors purchased the brand name from the bankruptcy court and reincarnated it with distribution primarily through specialty grocery stores and selected theme restaurants. The company is currently available in 267 grocery stores and 123 restaurants across Texas.

The "new" Texas Red has experienced solid growth and financial performance over its almost 8-year history. However, the competitive environment remains tough with the big national brands at one end of the spectrum and other specialty soft-drink producers at the other end. It is critical that Texas Red spend its limited marketing budget in the most efficient manner to drive business to its retail and restaurant locations.

In recent months, the management team at Texas Red has been divided in regard to the best marketing strategy for the company. One contingent wants to pursue a strategy based on a low price relative to other specialty soft drinks. The other group wants to focus on enhancing awareness and image of the brand with a focus on its long history in the state

of Texas and the unique aspects and high quality of its products. The difference of opinion between the two factions has become heated and somewhat divisive. Furthermore, time is running out to get their marketing strategy in place for the coming year.

Toby Newbern, director of marketing, knows that it is important to make the right decision and to break the deadlock quickly so that the company can move on with its plans and business development activities. He wants to design a test that will settle the issue once and for all in a scientific manner. Texas Star has always focused on an upscale demographic target. Toby's research plan calls for testing the price-oriented campaign in one market and the image-oriented campaign in another. The impact on sales in the respective markets will indicate the effectiveness of the two approaches. He faces a number of decisions. First, he needs to choose the markets for the test. Second, there is the question of how long to run the test. Finally, it is necessary to sort out what happens in the two test markets from the general trend for Texas Red.

### Questions

1. Is the test market approach the best way to tackle this problem, all things considered? Are there other viable options and, if so, what are the options?

2. Which of the experimental designs discussed in the chapter would be most feasible for this project? Why that design?

3. How many markets should be used for the test? What should be the characteristics of these markets?

4. What sort of evidence, from the test, would definitively break the deadlock between the two groups with different visions as the company?

# REAL-LIFE RESEARCH • 9.2

## Alcon

Alcon Laboratories has just completed a series of product tests for a new over-the-counter eyedrop product. This product proved very effective in clearing up bloodshot eyes in clinical trials and has been perceived to be effective by consumers in market tests.

At this point, the effectiveness of the product, both clinically and in terms of consumer perceptions, has been demonstrated. There is now a debate between two different factions on the product and marketing teams regarding pricing. One group feels strongly that the product should be priced only slightly, in the range of 5 percent, higher than the competition. Members of this group are of the opinion that demand for these types of nonprescription eye drop products is relatively elastic. Further, they think that their proven clinical and perceptual advantages are not enough to overcome a price differential of 10 percent, and possibly not enough to overcome a differential of even 5 percent. They think that higher differentials will lead consumers to choose a competitive product.

The other group believes that the advantages of the new product and the associated claims that they can make based on the clinical trials will justify a price differential of 20 to 25 percent. Their thinking in this matter is partially supported by focus group results and some similar experiences with related products. These differences have been the subject of several meetings, some of them quite heated, with neither group willing to change its position. The issue has become highly dysfunctional and is starting to hurt the company in terms of delays in the introduction of what many see as an innovative new product. Senior managers who have to approve the launch and the pricing see some logic in the arguments advanced by each side and do not think that they have the information necessary to make an informed decision. They do not want to make the decision on an arbitrary basis or to be seen as favoring one group over the other for no apparent reason. They have decided that the best course is to conduct a market test and to make the final decision based on the results of that test.

## Questions

1. The company used an interrupted time series design for a similar problem involving a particular product feature. Describe a test that would utilize an interrupted time series design to address the pricing question. Would this type of test provide a definitive answer to their question? Why or why not?

2. What other type of experimental design might the company utilize to answer the question it is trying to deal with? Describe how that design would work in this case. Would that approach be superior to the interrupted time series design? Why or why not?

3. Regardless of the approach used, when comparing the effectiveness of the two prices, would you be more interested in total unit sales or total revenue when comparing results? Justify your response.

# CHAPTER 10

# The Concept of Measurement

## LEARNING OBJECTIVES

1. Analyze the concept of measurement.

2. Define what is a concept.

3. Learn the nature of a construct.

4. Write a concept constitutively.

5. Define a concept operationally.

6. Create a measurement scale.

7. Evaluate the reliability and validity of a measurement.

What is the nature of measurement? Describe the steps that are involved. Explain the three levels of measurement and their differences. What are the notions of validity and reliability? Why are they so critically important to the concept of measurement? These are the topics of Chapter 10.

## Measurement Process

**measurement**
Process of assigning numbers or labels to persons, objects, or events in accordance with specific rules for representing quantities or qualities of attributes.

**rule**
Guide, method, or command that tells a researcher what to do.

**Measurement** is the process of assigning numbers or labels to persons, objects, or events in accordance with specific rules for representing quantities or qualities of attributes. Measurement, then, is a procedure used to assign numbers that reflect the amount of an attribute possessed by a person, object, or event. Note that it is not the person, object, or event that is being measured, but, rather, its attributes. A researcher, for example, does not measure a consumer per se but instead, measures that consumer's attitudes, income, brand loyalty, age, and other relevant factors.

The concept of rules is key to measurement. A **rule** is a guide, a method, or a command that tells a researcher what to do. For example, a rule of measurement might state, "Assign

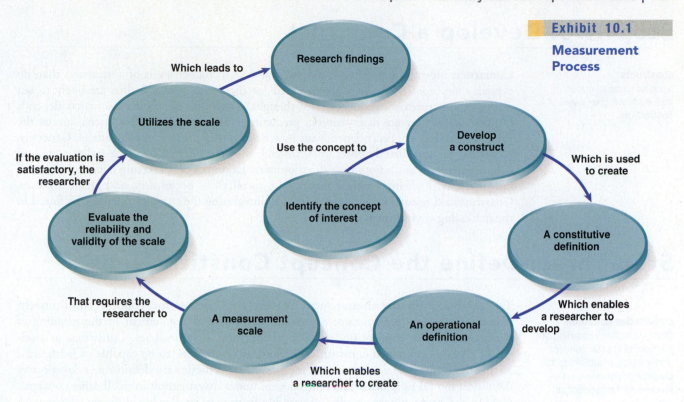

**Exhibit 10.1**

**Measurement Process**

the numbers 1 through 5 to people according to their disposition to do household chores. If they are extremely willing to do any and all household chores, assign them a 1. If they are not willing to do any household chores, assign them a 5." The numbers 2, 3, and 4 would be assigned based on the *degree* of their willingness to do chores, as it relates to the absolute end points of 1 and 5.

A problem often encountered with rules is a lack of clarity or specificity. Some things are easy to measure because rules are easy to create and follow. The measurement of gender, for example, is quite simple, as the researcher has concrete criteria to apply in assigning a 1 for a male and a 2 for a female. Unfortunately, many characteristics of interest to a marketing researcher—such as brand loyalty, purchase intent, and total family income—are much harder to measure because of the difficulty of devising rules to assess the true value of these consumer attributes. The steps a researcher should take to measure a phenomenon appear in Exhibit 10.1.

# Step One: Identify the Concept of Interest

The measurement process begins with identification of the concept of interest. A *concept* is an abstract idea generalized from particular facts. It is a category of thought used to group sense data together "as if they were all the same." All perceptions regarding a stoplight at the intersection of South and Main streets form a category of thought, though a relatively narrow one. Perceptions of all stoplights, regardless of location, would be a broader concept, or category of thought.

# Step Two: Develop a Construct

**constructs**
Specific types of concepts that exist at higher levels of abstraction.

**Constructs** are specific types of concepts that exist at higher levels of abstraction than do everyday concepts. Constructs are invented for theoretical use and thus are likely to cut across various preexisting categories of thought. The value of specific constructs depends on how useful they are in explaining, predicting, and controlling phenomena, just as the value of everyday concepts depends on how helpful they are in everyday affairs. Generally, constructs are not directly observable. Instead, they are inferred by some indirect method from results such as findings on a questionnaire. Examples of marketing constructs include brand loyalty, high-involvement purchasing, social class, personality, and channel power. Constructs aid researchers by simplifying and integrating the complex phenomena found in the marketing environment.

# Step Three: Define the Concept Constitutively

**constitutive definition**
Statement of the meaning of the central idea or concept under study, establishing its boundaries; also known as *theoretical*, or *conceptual*, *definition*.

The third step in the measurement process is to define the concept constitutively. A **constitutive** (or *theoretical*, or *conceptual*) **definition** is a statement of the meaning of the central idea or concept under study, establishing its boundaries. Constructs of a scientific theory are defined constitutively. Thus, all constructs, to be capable of being used in theories, must possess constitutive meaning. Like a dictionary definition, a constitutive definition should fully distinguish the concept under investigation from all other concepts, making the study concept readily discernible from very similar but different concepts. A vague constitutive definition can cause an incorrect research question to be addressed. For instance, to say that researchers are interested in studying marital roles would be so general as to be meaningless. To say that they want to examine the marital roles of newlyweds (married less than 12 months) from 24 to 28 years of age with 4 years of college may not even suffice. While one researcher may be interested in communication patterns as partners assume certain roles, a second researcher may be interested in parenting roles.

# Step Four: Define the Concept Operationally

**operational definition**
Statement of precisely which observable characteristics will be measured and the process for assigning a value to the concept.

A precise constitutive definition makes the operational definition task much easier. An **operational definition** specifies which observable characteristics will be measured and the process for assigning a value to the concept. In other words, it assigns meaning to a construct in terms of the operations necessary to measure it in any concrete situation.

Because it is overly restrictive in marketing to insist that all variables be operationally defined in directly measurable terms, many variables are stated in more abstract terms and measured indirectly, based on theoretical assumptions about their nature. For example, it is impossible to measure an attitude directly, because an attitude is an abstract concept that refers to things inside a person's mind. It is possible, nonetheless, to give a clear theoretical definition of an attitude as an enduring organization of motivational, emotional, perceptual, and cognitive processes with respect to some aspect of the environment. On the basis of this definition, instruments have been developed for measuring attitudes indirectly, by asking questions about how a person feels, what the person believes, and how the person intends to behave.

In summary, an operational definition serves as a bridge between a theoretical concept and real-world events or factors. Constructs such as "attitude" and "high-involvement purchasing" are abstractions that cannot be observed. Operational definitions transform such constructs into observable events. In other words, they define or give meaning to a construct by spelling out what the researcher must do to measure it. There are many different potential operational definitions for any single concept, regardless of how exact the constitutive definition may be. The researcher must choose the operational definition that fits most appropriately with the objectives of the research.

An example of a constitutive definition, a corresponding operational definition, and a resultant measurement scale are shown in Exhibit 10.2. The operational definition of role ambiguity was developed by two marketing professors for use with salespeople and customer service personnel. The theoretical notion is that role ambiguity leads to job stress and impedes a worker's ability to improve performance and obtain job-based rewards, leading to job dissatisfaction.

*Construct equivalence* deals with how people see, understand, and develop measurements of a particular phenomenon. The problem confronting the global marketing researcher is that, because of sociocultural, economic, and political differences, construct perspectives may be neither identical nor equivalent.

In England, Germany, and Scandinavia, beer is generally perceived as an alcoholic beverage. In Mediterranean lands, however, beer is considered akin to soft drinks. Therefore, a study of the competitive status of beer in northern Europe would have to build in questions on wine and liquor. In Italy, Spain, or Greece, the comparison would have to be with soft drinks.

In Italy, it's common for children to have a bar of chocolate between two slices of bread as a snack. In France, bar chocolate is often used in cooking. But a German housewife would be revolted by either practice. In France, fragrance is measured on a hot–cold continuum. In the United States and the United Kingdom, hot and cold are not attributes assigned to fragrances.

The examples provided in the Global Research feature on page XXX highlight the construct equivalence problem faced by global marketing researchers.

| EXHIBIT 10.2 | Constitutive and Operational Definitions of Role Ambiguity |
|---|---|
| **Constitutive Definition** | Role ambiguity is a direct function of the discrepancy between the information available to the person and that which is required for adequate performance of a role. It is the difference between a person's actual state of knowledge and the knowledge that provides adequate satisfaction of that person's personal needs and values. |
| **Operational Definition** | Role ambiguity is the amount of uncertainty (ranging from very uncertain to very certain on a 5-point scale) an individual feels regarding job-role responsibilities and expectations from other employees and customers. |
| **Measurement Scale** | The measurement scale consists of 45 items, with each item assessed by a 5-point scale with category labels 1 = very certain, 2 = certain, 3 = neutral, 4 = uncertain, 5 = very uncertain. Samples of the 45 items follow:<br>• How much freedom of action I am expected to have<br>• How I am expected to handle nonroutine activities on the job<br>• The sheer amount of work I am expected to do<br>• To what extent my boss is open to hearing my point of view<br>• How satisfied my boss is with me<br>• How managers in other departments expect me to interact with them<br>• What managers in other departments think about the job I perform<br>• How I am expected to interact with my customers<br>• How I should behave (with customers) while on the job<br>• If I am expected to lie a little to win customer confidence<br>• If I am expected to hide my company's foul-ups from my customers<br>• About how much time my family feels I should spend on the job<br>• To what extent my family expects me to share my job-related problems<br>• How my co-workers expect me to behave while on the job<br>• How much information my co-workers expect me to convey to my boss |

*Source:* Adapted from Jagdip Singh and Gary K. Rhoads, "Boundary Role Ambiguity in Marketing-Oriented Positions: A Multidimensional, Multifaceted Operationalization," *Journal of Marketing Research* 28 (August 1991), pp. 328–338. Reprinted by permission of the American Marketing Association.

# Step Five: Develop a Measurement Scale

**scale**
Set of symbols or numbers so constructed that the symbols or numbers can be assigned by a rule to the individuals (or their behaviors or attitudes) to whom the scale is applied.

Exhibit 10.2 includes a scale that ranges from "very certain" to "very uncertain." A **scale** is a set of symbols or numbers so constructed that the symbols or numbers can be assigned by a rule to the individuals (or their behaviors or attitudes) to whom the scale is applied. The assignment on the scale is indicated by the individual's possession of whatever the scale is supposed to measure. Thus, a salesperson who feels he knows exactly how he is supposed to interact with customers would mark *very certain* for that item on the scale in Exhibit 10.2.

Creating a measurement scale begins with determining the level of measurement that is desirable or possible. Exhibit 10.3 describes the four basic levels of measurement: nominal, ordinal, interval, and ratio.

## Nominal Level of Measurement

**nominal scales**
Scales that partition data into mutually exclusive and collectively exhaustive categories.

**Nominal scales** are among those most commonly used in marketing research. A nominal scale partitions data into categories that are mutually exclusive and collectively exhaustive, implying that every bit of data will fit into one and only one category and that all data will fit somewhere on the scale. The term *nominal* means "name-like," indicating that the numbers assigned to objects or phenomena are naming or classifying them but have no true number value; that is, the numbers cannot be ordered, added, or divided. The numbers are simply labels or identification numbers and nothing else. Examples of two nominal scales follow:

| EXHIBIT 10.3 | The Four Basic Levels of Measurement | | | |
|---|---|---|---|---|
| **Level** | **Basic Empirical Description*** | **Operations** | **Typical Descriptive Typical Usage** | **Statistics** |
| Nominal | Uses numerals to identify objects, individuals, events, or groups | Determination of equality/ inequality | Classification (male/ female; buyer/nonbuyer) | Frequency counts, percentages/modes |
| Ordinal | In addition to identification, provides information about the relative amount of some characteristic possessed by an event, object, etc. | Determination of greater or lesser | Rankings/ratings (preferences for hotels, banks, etc.; social class; ratings of foods based on fat content, cholesterol) | Median (mean and variance metric) |
| Interval | Possesses all the properties of nominal and ordinal scales plus equal intervals between consecutive points | Determination of equality of intervals | Preferred measure of complex concepts/ constructs (temperature scale, air pressure scale, level of knowledge about brands) | Mean/variance |
| Ratio | Incorporates all the properties of nominal, ordinal, and interval scales plus an absolute zero point | Determination of equality of ratios | Preferred measure when precision instruments are available (sales, number of on-time arrivals, age) | Geometric mean/ harmonic mean |

*Because higher levels of measurement contain all the properties of lower levels, higher level scales can be converted into lower level ones (i.e., ratio to interval or ordinal or nominal, or interval to ordinal or nominal, or ordinal to nominal).
*Source:* Adapted from S. S. Stevens, "On the Theory of Scales of Measurement," *Science* 103 (June 7, 1946), pp. 677–680.

| Gender: | (1) Male | (2) Female | |
|---------|----------|------------|---|
| Geographic area: | (1) Urban | (2) Rural | (3) Suburban |

The only quantifications in numerical scales are the number and percentage of objects in each category—for example, 50 males (48.5 percent) and 53 females (51.5 percent). Computing a mean of 2.4 for geographic area would be meaningless; only the mode, the value that appears most often, would be appropriate.

## Ordinal Level of Measurement

**Ordinal scales** have the labeling characteristics of nominal scales plus an ability to order data. Ordinal measurement is possible when the transitivity postulate can be applied. (A *postulate* is an assumption that is an essential prerequisite to carrying out an operation or line of thinking.) The *transitivity postulate* is described by the notion that "if *a* is greater than *b*, and *b* is greater than *c*, then *a* is greater than *c*." Other terms that can be substituted for *is greater than* are *is preferred to*, *is stronger than*, and *precedes*. An example of an ordinal scale follows:

> Please rank the following online dating services from 1 to 5, with 1 being the most preferred and 5 the least preferred.
>
> *www.spark.com* _____
> *www.eharmony.com* _____
> *www.match.com* _____
> *www.zoosk.com* _____
> *www.friendfinder.com* _____

Ordinal numbers are used strictly to indicate rank order. The numbers do not indicate absolute quantities, nor do they imply that the intervals between the numbers are equal. For example, a person ranking fax machines might like HP only slightly more than Canon and view Sharp as totally unacceptable. Such information would not be obtained from an ordinal scale.

Because ranking is the objective of an ordinal scale, any rule prescribing a series of numbers that preserves the ordered relationship is satisfactory. In other words, Spark could have been assigned a value of 30; eharmony, 40; Match, 27; Zoosk, 32; and FriendFinder, 42. Or any other series of numbers could have been used, as long as the basic ordering was preserved. In the case just cited, FriendFinder is 1; eHarmony 2; Zoosk 3; Spark 4; and Match 5. Common arithmetical operations such as addition and multiplication cannot be used with ordinal scales. The appropriate measure of central tendency is the mode or the median. A percentile or quartile measure is used for measuring dispersion.

A controversial (yet rather common) use of ordinal scales is to rate various characteristics. In this case, the researcher assigns numbers to reflect the relative ratings of a series of statements, then uses these numbers to interpret relative distance. Recall that the marketing researchers examining role ambiguity used a scale ranging from *very certain* to *very uncertain*. The following values were assigned:

| (1) | (2) | (3) | (4) | (5) |
|-----|-----|-----|-----|-----|
| **Very Certain** | **Certain** | **Neutral** | **Uncertain** | **Very Uncertain** |

If a researcher can justify the assumption that the intervals are equal within the scale, then the more powerful parametric statistical tests can be applied. (Parametric statistical tests will be discussed in Chapters 16 and 17.) Indeed, some measurement scholars argue that equal intervals should be normally assumed.

**ordinal scales**
Scales that maintain the labeling characteristics of nominal scales and have the ability to order data.

*The best procedure would seem to be to treat ordinal measurements as though they were interval measurements but to be constantly alert to the possibility of gross inequality of intervals. As much as possible about the characteristics of the measuring tools should be learned. Much useful information has been obtained by this approach, with resulting scientific advances in psychology, sociology, and education. In short, it is unlikely that researchers will be led seriously astray by heeding this advice, if they are careful in applying it.*[1]

## Interval Level of Measurement

**interval scales**
Scales that have the characteristics of ordinal scales, plus equal intervals between points to show relative amounts; they may include an arbitrary zero point.

**Interval scales** contain all the features of ordinal scales with the added dimension that the intervals between the points on the scale are equal. The concept of temperature is based on equal intervals. Marketing researchers often prefer interval scales over ordinal scales because they can measure how much of a trait one consumer has (or does not have) over another. An interval scale enables a researcher to discuss differences separating two objects. The scale possesses properties of order and difference but with an arbitrary zero point. Examples are the Fahrenheit and Celsius scales; the freezing point of water is zero on one scale and 32 degrees on the other.

The arbitrary zero point of interval scales restricts the statements that a researcher can make about the scale points. One can say that 80°F is hotter than 32°F or that 64°F is 16° cooler than 80°F. However, one cannot say that 64°F is twice as warm as 32°F. Why? Because the zero point on the Fahrenheit scale is arbitrary. To understand this point, consider the transformation of the two Fahrenheit temperatures to Celsius using the formula Celsius 3 $(F - 32)(5/9)$; 32°F equals 0°C, and 64°F equals 17.8°C. The statement we made about the Fahrenheit temperatures (64° is twice as warm as 32°) does not hold for Celsius. The same would be true of rankings of online dating services on an interval scale. If Match had received a 20 and Zoosk a 10, we cannot say that Match is liked twice as much as Zoosk, because a point defining the absence of liking has not been identified and assigned a value of zero on the scale.

Interval scales are amenable to computation of an arithmetic mean, standard deviation, and correlation coefficients. The more powerful parametric statistical tests such as *t* tests and *F* tests can be applied. In addition, researchers can take a more conservative approach and use nonparametric tests if they have concern about the equal intervals assumption.

## Ratio Level of Measurement

**ratio scales**
Scales that have the characteristics of interval scales, plus a meaningful zero point so that magnitudes can be compared arithmetically.

**Ratio scales** have all the characteristics of those scales previously discussed as well as a meaningful absolute zero or origin. Because there is universal agreement as to the location of the zero point, comparisons among the magnitudes of ratio-scaled values are acceptable. Thus, a ratio scale reflects the actual amount of a variable. Physical characteristics of a respondent such as age, weight, and height are examples of ratio-scaled variables. Other ratio scales are based on area, distance, money values, return rates, population counts, and lapsed periods of time.

Because some objects have none of the property being measured, a ratio scale originates at a zero point with absolute empirical meaning. For example, an investment (albeit a poor one) can have no rate of return, or a census tract in New Mexico could be devoid of any persons. An absolute zero implies that all arithmetic operations are possible, including multiplication and division. Numbers on the scale indicate the actual amounts of the property being measured. A large bag of McDonald's french fries weighs 8 ounces, and a regular bag at Burger King weighs 4 ounces; thus, a large McDonald's bag of fries weighs twice as much as a regular Burger King bag of fries.

# Step Six: Evaluate the Reliability and Validity of the Measurement

An ideal marketing research study would provide information that is accurate, precise, lucid, and timely. Accurate data imply accurate measurement, or $M = A$, where $M$ refers to measurement and $A$ stands for complete accuracy. In marketing research, this ideal is rarely, if ever, achieved. Instead,

$$M = A + E$$
$$\text{where } E = \text{errors}$$

Errors can be either random or systematic, as noted in Chapter 6. Systematic error results in a constant bias in the measurements caused by faults in the measurement instrument or process. For example, if a faulty ruler (on which one inch is actually one and a half inches) is used in Pillsbury's test kitchens to measure the height of chocolate cakes baked with alternative recipes, all cakes will be recorded at less than their actual height. *Random error* also influences the measurements but not systematically. Thus, random error is transient in nature. A person may not answer a question truthfully because he is in a bad mood that day.

Two scores on a measurement scale can differ for a number of reasons.[2] Only the first of the following eight reasons does not involve error. A researcher must determine whether any of the remaining seven sources of measurement differences are producing random or systematic error:

1. *A true difference in the characteristic being measured.* A perfect measurement difference is solely the result of actual differences. For example, John rates McDonald's service as 1 (excellent) and Sandy rates its service as 4 (average), and the variation is due only to actual attitude differences.

2. *Differences due to stable characteristics of individual respondents*, such as personality, values, and intelligence. Sandy has an aggressive, rather critical personality, and she gives no one and nothing the benefit of the doubt. She actually was quite pleased with the service she received at McDonald's, but she expects such service and so gave it an average rating.

3. *Differences due to short-term personal factors*, such as temporary mood swings, health problems, time constraints, or fatigue. Earlier on the day of the study, John had won $400 in a "Name That Tune" contest on a local radio station. He stopped by McDonald's for a burger after he picked up his winning check. His reply on the service quality questionnaire might have been quite different if he had been interviewed the previous day.

4. *Differences caused by situational factors*, such as distractions or others present in the interview situation. Sandy was giving her replies while trying to watch her 4-year-old nephew, who was running amok on the McDonald's playground; John had his new fiancée along when he was interviewed. Replies of both people might have been different if they had been interviewed at home while no other friend or relative was present.

5. *Differences resulting from variations in administering the survey.* Interviewers can ask questions with different voice inflections, causing response variation. And because of such factors as rapport with the interviewee, manner of dress, sex, or race, different

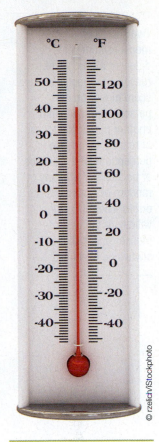

© rzelich/iStockphoto

Commonly used temperature scales are based on equal intervals and an arbitrary zero point. Marketing researchers often prefer interval scales because they can measure how much more of a trait one consumer has than another.

Two scores on a measurement scale can differ for a number of reasons. McDonald's may score higher on one person's survey than on another person's because of real differences in perceptions of the service or because of a variety of random or systematic errors. The reliability and validity of the type of measurement should always be checked.

Andre Jenny Stock Connection Worldwide/NewsCom

interviewers can cause responses to vary. Interviewer bias can be as subtle as a nodding of the head. One interviewer who tended to nod unconsciously was found to bias some respondents. They thought that the interviewer was agreeing with them when he was, in fact, saying, "Okay, I'm recording what you say—tell me more." A survey administered on a mobile device may vary from the same survey done by telephone.

6. *Differences due to the sampling of items included in the questionnaire.* When researchers attempt to measure the quality of service at McDonald's, the scales and other questions used represent only a portion of the items that could have been used. The scales created by the researchers reflect their interpretation of the construct (service quality) and the way it is measured. If the researchers had used different words or if items had been added or removed, the scale values reported by John and Sandy might have been different.

7. *Differences due to a lack of clarity in the measurement instrument.* A question may be ambiguous, complex, or incorrectly interpreted. A survey that asked, "How far do you live from McDonald's?" and then gave choices "(1) less than 5 minutes, (2) 5 to 10 minutes," and so forth, would be ambiguous; someone walking would undoubtedly take longer to get to the restaurant than a person driving a car or riding a bike. This topic is covered in much greater detail in Chapter 11.

8. *Differences due to mechanical or instrument factors.* Blurred questionnaires, lack of space to fully record answers, missing pages in a questionnaire, incorrect computer keystrokes, or a thumb hitting the wrong button on a mobile device can result in differences in responses.

Linda Naiditch, with Matthew Greenwald & Associates—a Washington, DC, research firm—discusses a technique for minimizing errors in questionnaire design in the Practicing Marketing Research box below.

# PRACTICING MARKETING RESEARCH

## Designing a Better Questionnaire

You don't know what you don't know. This truism often lurks in my mind as I am designing a questionnaire. I feel it is my job to ask just the right questions so that my clients can obtain the information they need. But I can't be sure if I have hit the mark if I do not know how respondents will understand and interpret my questions. Perhaps the best way to illustrate my concern about the unknown is to ask you to imagine what would happen if:

■ Respondents don't see an answer that reflects their thinking in a list of response options to particular question.

■ A listing of attributes does not include all the factors that would be relevant to the client's objectives.

■ Respondents think a term means something different than what you intended.

■ Respondents completely misunderstand the thrust of the question.

■ You just didn't think of something and leave out what would be an important component to the study.

Well, the simple answer is that the results you deliver to clients would either be incomplete or based on suboptimal data that you thought was just fine.

Researchers currently use a variety of methods to try to avoid these problems, including having research colleagues review the draft questionnaire; conducting qualitative research before moving on to the quantitative research; and conducting and monitoring pretest interviews. Each of those methods can help. But even when we use all three methods, our questions can still be off-target, incomplete, or worded in a way that is not effective because there is still something that we don't know.

Research colleagues who help us with their expert review can often see gaps and help fill them in. But we and our colleagues often have very different life experiences from the subjects who will be completing the survey, so we cannot think like them or imagine every situation that might apply to them.

To overcome these problems, our firm has turned to *cognitive interviewing*. Cognitive interviewing is a specialized type of pretest that focuses on respondents' thinking process as they hear or read questions in a survey. It actively delves into how they interpret the meaning of questions and possible responses, what they think about when they are considering how to answer, how they decide on their answers, and what their answers mean. Our methods are primarily drawn from Gordon B. Willis's *Cognitive Interviewing: A Tool For Improving Questionnaire Design:*

■ Ask respondents to rephrase the question, or the response options, in their own words.

■ Ask respondents to tell the interviewer what they are thinking as they consider the question, consider their answer, and decide on their actual response.

■ Ask respondents what specific words or phrases in selected questions mean to them.

■ Ask how easy or difficult a question is to answer and, if it is not easy, to probe for the causes of difficulty.

■ Look for any cues that might indicate an issue, including hesitation or information provided in one question that seems to conflict with the information provided in another.

In addition, we sometimes ask respondents how they would answer a precoded question before they have seen the response options, to ensure that we have presented all relevant categories. We may also repeat a question with slightly different wording later in the questionnaire to see if it elicits a different response. If we hear responses that seem inconsistent, we probe for the reason why. We observe and listen for nonverbal cues that a respondent is having difficulty or is confused.

A few examples of cognitive interviews that we conducted on a recent publicly released survey about nutrition illustrates their value. In a survey about nutrition, one trend question asked respondents to rate how much impact factors such as taste, price, healthfulness, and sustainability have on their food selection. With our understanding that "sustainability" can connote ecological, economic and social aspects of food production and sales, and knowing that a surprisingly high proportion of the population reported in a past study that it significantly impacted their food purchase decision, we decided to explore the concept in our cognitive interviews.

A young woman named Angie explained that, to her, sustainability meant how long food would remain fresh if she put it in the freezer. Similarly, a middle-aged man thought it related to a food's shelf life. With such different meanings to different people, the term would not be useful.

Later, in a cognitive interview with a middle-aged man name David, we posed the question shown in Figure 1 from the same draft questionnaire.

| | Not at all Important | Not too Important | Somewhat Important | Very Important | Not Sure |
|---|---|---|---|---|---|
| a. Trans fat content | 1 | 2 | 3 | 4 | 5 |
| b. Total fat content | 1 | 2 | 3 | 4 | 5 |
| c. Mono- and poly-saturated fat content | 1 | 2 | 3 | 4 | 5 |
| d. Saturated fat content | 1 | 2 | 3 | 4 | 5 |
| e. Omega-3 content | 1 | 2 | 3 | 4 | 5 |
| f. Omega-6 content | 1 | 2 | 3 | 4 | 5 |

**Figure 1**

When you are deciding whether to buy a particular food, how important, if at all, is each of the following:

In explaining his answers to this question, David noted that some of the food components listed are good to include in one's diet, such as omega-3s, while others such as trans fats and saturated fats are bad. When we initially drafted the question, we expected it would measure how much weight, if any, respondents placed on these ingredients, regardless of whether they are good or bad for one's health. David, however, chose the "very important" option when he wanted to indicate that a food component was a good one that he sought to include in his diet and "not at all important" to convey the component was something bad to be avoided.

David's thinking prompted us to revisit this question in depth with the client, and we ultimately separated the question into two parts. The first asked yes/no whether the respondent considered whether the food they purchased contained these types of fats, then a follow-up question was posed to learn whether the respondent was seeking to consumer or avoid each one.

Finally, one more example from David's interview.

*To the best of your knowledge, is your blood pressure…*

*1. High or higher than normal*

*2. Normal (or in the normal range)*

*3. Low or lower than normal*

*4. Not sure*

David responded to this question with a question to us: "How should I answer if my underlying blood pressure is high but it is normal because of medication I take?" That was a forehead-slapping moment where we knew we needed two versions of the "normal" response option—one "without medication" and one "with medication." The revised question turned out to be very useful in analysis of differences between subgroups of respondents.[3]

## Questions

1. Can cognitive interviewing help reduce error? If so, what type, random or systematic?

2. What are some of the benefits of cognitive interviewing?

3. One scholar recommends three rounds of cognitive interviews, each with 10 interviews. What are the advantages and disadvantages of this process? Isn't one round enough?

## Reliability

A measurement scale that provides consistent results over time is reliable. If a ruler consistently measures a chocolate cake as 9 inches high, then the ruler is said to be reliable. Reliable scales, gauges, and other measurement devices can be used with confidence and with the knowledge that transient and situational factors are not interfering with the measurement process. Reliable instruments provide stable measures at different times under different conditions. A key question regarding reliability is "If we measure some phenomenon over and over again with the same measurement device, will we get the same or highly similar results?" An affirmative answer means that the device is reliable.

Thus, **reliability** is the degree to which measures are free from random error and, therefore, provide consistent data. The less error there is, the more reliable the observation is, so a measurement that is free of error is a correct measure. A reliable measurement, then, does not change when the concept being measured remains constant in value. However, if the concept being measured does change in value, the reliable measure will indicate that change. How can a measuring instrument be unreliable? If your weight stays constant at 150 pounds

**reliability**
Degree to which measures are free from random error and, therefore, provide consistent data.

but repeated measurements on your bathroom scale show your weight to fluctuate, the scale's lack of reliability may be due to a weak spring.

There are three ways to assess reliability: test–retest, the use of equivalent forms, and internal consistency.

### Test–Retest Reliability

**Test–retest reliability** is obtained by repeating the measurement with the same instrument, approximating the original conditions as closely as possible. The theory behind test–retest is that if random variations are present, they will be revealed by differences in the scores between the two tests. **Stability** means that very few differences in scores are found between the first and second administrations of the test; the measuring instrument is said to be stable. For example, assume that a 30-item department store image measurement scale was administered to the same group of shoppers at two different times. If the correlation between the two measurements was high, the reliability would be assumed to be high.

There are several problems with test–retest reliability. First, it may be very difficult to locate and gain the cooperation of respondents for a second testing. Second, the first measurement may alter a person's response on the second measurement. Third, environmental or personal factors may change, causing the second measurement to change.

**test–retest reliability**
Ability of the same instrument to produce consistent results when used a second time under conditions as similar as possible to the original conditions.

**stability**
Lack of change in results from test to retest

### Equivalent Form Reliability

The difficulties encountered with the test–retest approach can be avoided by creating equivalent forms of a measurement instrument. For example, assume that the researcher is interested in identifying inner-directed versus outer-directed lifestyles. Two questionnaires can be created containing measures of inner-directed behavior (see Exhibit 10.4) and measures of outer-directed behavior. These measures should receive about the same emphasis on each questionnaire. Thus, although the questions used to ascertain the lifestyles are different on the two questionnaires, the number of questions used to measure each lifestyle should be approximately equal. The recommended interval for administering the second equivalent form is two weeks, although in some cases the two forms are given one after the other or simultaneously. **Equivalent form reliability** is determined by measuring the correlation of the scores on the two instruments.

**equivalent form reliability**
Ability of two very similar forms of an instrument to produce closely correlated results.

| EXHIBIT 10.4 | Statements Used to Measure Inner-Directed Lifestyles |
| --- | --- |

I often don't get the credit I deserve for things I do well.
I try to get my own way regardless of others.
My greatest achievements are ahead of me.
I have a number of ideas that someday I would like to put into a book.
I am quick to accept new ideas.
I often think about how I look and what impression I am making on others.
I am a competitive person.
I feel upset when I hear that people are criticizing or blaming me.
I'd like to be a celebrity.
I get a real thrill out of doing dangerous things.
I feel that almost nothing in life can substitute for great achievement.
It's important for me to be noticed.
I keep in close touch with my friends.
I spend a good deal of time trying to decide how I feel about things.
I often think I can feel my way into the innermost being of another person.
I feel that ideals are powerful motivating forces in people.
I think someone can be a good person without believing in God.
The Eastern religions are more appealing to me than Christianity.
I feel satisfied with my life.
I enjoy getting involved in new and unusual situations.
Overall, I'd say I'm happy.
I feel I understand where my life is going.
I like to think I'm different from other people.
I adopt a commonsense attitude toward life.

There are two problems with equivalent forms that should be noted. First, it is very difficult, and perhaps impossible, to create two totally equivalent forms. Second, if equivalence can be achieved, it may not be worth the time, trouble, and expense involved. The theory behind the equivalent forms approach to reliability assessment is the same as that of the test–retest. The primary difference between the test–retest and the equivalent forms methods is the testing instrument itself. Test–retest uses the same instrument, whereas the equivalent forms approach uses a different, but highly similar, measuring instrument.

**internal consistency reliability**
Ability of an instrument to produce similar results when used on different samples during the same time period to measure a phenomenon.

**Internal Consistency Reliability** **Internal consistency reliability** assesses the ability to produce similar results when different samples are used to measure a phenomenon during the same time period. The theory of internal consistency rests on the concept of equivalence. *Equivalence* is concerned with how much error may be introduced by using different samples of items to measure a phenomenon; it focuses on variations at one point in time among samples of items. A researcher can test for item equivalence by assessing the homogeneity of a set of items. The total set of items used to measure a phenomenon, such as inner-directed lifestyles, is divided into two halves; the total scores of the two halves are then correlated. Use of the **split-half technique** typically calls for scale items to be randomly assigned to one half or the other. The problem with this method is that the estimate of the coefficient of reliability is totally dependent on how the items were split. Different splits result in different correlations when, ideally, they should not.

**split-half technique**
Method of assessing the reliability of a scale by dividing the total set of measurement items in half and correlating the results.

To overcome this problem, many researchers now use the *Cronbach alpha technique*, which involves computing mean reliability coefficient estimates for all possible ways of splitting a set of items in half. A lack of correlation of an item with other items in the scale is evidence that the item does not belong in the scale and should be omitted. One limitation of the Cronbach alpha is that the scale items require equal intervals. If this criterion cannot be met, another test called the KR-20 can be used. The *KR-20 technique* is applicable for all dichotomous or nominally scaled items.

## Validity

**validity**
The degree to which what the researcher was trying to measure was actually measured.

Recall that the second characteristic of a good measurement device is validity. **Validity** addresses the issue of whether what the researcher was trying to measure was actually measured. When Pontiac brought out the Aztek, research said that the car would sell between 50,000 and 70,000 units annually, despite the controversial styling. After selling only 27,000 cars per year, the model was discontinued. Unfortunately, the research measuring instrument was not valid. The validity of a measure refers to the extent to which the measurement instrument and procedure are free from both systematic and random error. Thus, a measuring device is valid only if differences in scores reflect true differences on the characteristic being measured rather than systematic or random error. You should recognize that a necessary precondition for validity is that the measuring instrument be reliable. An instrument that is not reliable will not yield consistent results when measuring the same phenomenon over time.

A scale or other measuring device is basically worthless to a researcher if it lacks validity because it is not measuring what it is supposed to. On the surface, this seems like a rather simple notion, yet validity often is based on subtle distinctions. Assume that your teacher gives an exam that he has constructed to measure marketing research knowledge, and the test consists strictly of applying a number of formulas to simple case problems. A friend receives a low score on the test and protests to the teacher that she "really understands marketing research." Her position, in essence, is that the test was not valid. She maintains that, rather than measuring knowledge of marketing research, the test measured memorization of formulas and the ability to use simple math to find solutions. The teacher could repeat the exam only to find that student scores still fell in the same order. Does this mean that the

| EXHIBIT 10.5 | Assessing the Validity of a Measurement Instrument |
|---|---|
| Face validity | The degree to which a measurement instrument seems to measure what it is supposed to, as judged by researchers. |
| Content validity | The degree to which measurement items represent the universe of the concept under study. |
| Criterion-related validity | The degree to which a measurement instrument can predict a variable that is designated a criterion. |
| | a. Predictive validity: The extent to which a future level of a criterion variable can be predicted by a current measurement on a scale. |
| | b. Concurrent validity: The extent to which a criterion variable measured at the same point in time as the variable of interest can be predicted by the measurement instrument. |
| Construct validity | The degree to which a measurement instrument confirms a hypothesis created from a theory based on the concepts under study. |
| | a. Convergent validity: The degree of association among different measurement instruments that purport to measure the same concept. |
| | b. Discriminant validity: A measure of the lack of association among constructs that are supposed to be different. |

protesting student was incorrect? Not necessarily; the teacher may be systematically measuring the ability to memorize rather than a true understanding of marketing research.

Unlike the teacher attempting to measure marketing research knowledge, a brand manager is interested in successful prediction. The manager, for example, wants to know if a purchase intent scale successfully predicts trial purchase of a new product. Thus, validity can be examined from a number of different perspectives, including face, content, criterion-related, and construct validity (see Exhibit 10.5).

**Face Validity**  **Face validity** is the weakest form of validity. It is concerned with the degree to which a measurement seems to measure what it is supposed to measure. It is a judgment call by the researcher, made as the questions are designed. Thus, as each question is scrutinized, there is an implicit assessment of its face validity. Revisions enhance the face validity of the question until it passes the researcher's subjective evaluation. Alternatively, *face validity* can refer to the subjective agreement of researchers, experts, or people familiar with the market, product, or industry that a scale logically appears to be accurately reflecting what it is supposed to measure. A straightforward question such as "What is your age?" followed by a series of age categories generally is agreed to have face validity. Most scales used in marketing research attempt to measure attitudes or behavioral intentions, which are much more elusive.

**face validity**
Degree to which a measurement seems to measure what it is supposed to measure.

**Content Validity**  **Content validity** is the representativeness, or sampling adequacy, of the content of the measurement instrument. In other words, does the scale provide adequate coverage of the topic under study? Say that McDonald's has hired you to measure its image among adults 18 to 30 years of age who eat fast-food hamburgers at least once a month. You devise the following scale:

**content validity**
Representativeness, or sampling adequacy, of the content of the measurement instrument.

| Modern building | 1 | 2 | 3 | 4 | 5 | Old-fashioned building |
| Beautiful landscaping | 1 | 2 | 3 | 4 | 5 | Poor landscaping |
| Clean parking lots | 1 | 2 | 3 | 4 | 5 | Dirty parking lots |
| Attractive signs | 1 | 2 | 3 | 4 | 5 | Unattractive signs |

A McDonald's executive would quickly take issue with this scale, claiming that a person could evaluate McDonald's on this scale and never have eaten a McDonald's hamburger. In fact, the evaluation could be made simply by driving past a McDonald's. The executive could further argue that the scale lacks content validity because many important components of image—such as the quality of the food, cleanliness of the eating area and restrooms, and promptness and courtesy of service—were omitted.

The determination of content validity is not always a simple matter. It is very difficult, and perhaps impossible, to identify all the facets of McDonald's image. Content validity ultimately becomes a judgmental matter. One could approach content validity by first carefully defining precisely what is to be measured. Second, an exhaustive literature search and focus groups could be conducted to identify all possible items for inclusion on the scale. Third, a panel of experts could be asked their opinions on whether an item should be included. Finally, the scale could be pretested and an open-ended question asked that might identify other items to be included. For example, after a more refined image scale for McDonald's has been administered, a follow-up question could be "Do you have any other thoughts about McDonald's that you would like to express?" Answers to this pretest question might provide clues for other image dimensions not previously considered.

## Criterion-Related Validity

**criterion-related validity**
Degree to which a measurement instrument can predict a variable that is designated a criterion.

**Criterion-related validity** examines the ability of a measuring instrument to predict a variable that is designated a criterion. Suppose that we wish to devise a test to identify marketing researchers who are exceptional at moderating focus groups. We begin by having impartial marketing research experts identify from a directory of researchers those they judge to be best at moderating focus groups. We then construct 300 items to which all the group moderators are asked to reply yes or no, such as "I believe it is important to compel shy group participants to speak out" and "I like to interact with small groups of people." We then go through the responses and select the items that the "best" focus group moderators answered one way and the rest of the moderators answered the other way. Assume that this process produces 84 items, which we put together to form what we shall call the Test of Effectiveness in Focus Group Moderating (TEFGM). We feel that this test will identify good focus group moderators. The criterion of interest here is the ability to conduct a good focus group. We might explore further the criterion-related validity of TEFGM by administering it to another group of moderators, each of whom has been designated as either "best" or "not as good." Then we could determine how well the test identifies the section to which each marketing researcher is assigned. Thus, criterion-related validity is concerned with detecting the presence or absence of one or more criteria considered to represent constructs of interest.

A politician is interested in what issues those likely to vote perceive as important. The predictive validity of the politician's measures may determine whether he or she is elected.

Mark Cowan/UPI/Landov

Two subcategories of criterion-related validity are predictive validity and concurrent validity. **Predictive validity** is the extent to which a future level of a criterion variable can be predicted by a current measurement on a scale. A voter-motivation scale, for example, is used to predict the likelihood that a person will vote in the next election. A savvy politician is not interested in what the community as a whole perceives as important problems but only in what persons who are likely to vote perceive as important problems. These are the issues that the politician would address in speeches and advertising. Another example of predictive validity is the extent to which a purchase-intent scale for a new Pepperidge Farm pastry predicts actual trial of the product.

**Concurrent validity** is concerned with the relationship between the predictor variable and the criterion variable, both of which are assessed at the same point in time—for example, the ability of a home pregnancy test to accurately determine whether a woman is pregnant right now. Such a test with low concurrent validity could cause a lot of undue stress.

**Construct Validity** Construct validity, though not often consciously addressed by many marketing researchers on a day-to-day basis, is extremely important to marketing scientists. Assessing construct validity involves understanding the theoretical foundations underlying the obtained measurements. A measure has **construct validity** if it behaves according to the theory behind the prediction. Purchase behavior can be observed directly; someone either buys product A or does not. Yet scientists have developed constructs on lifestyle, involvement, attitude, and personality that help explain *why* someone does or does not purchase something. These constructs are largely unobservable. Researchers can observe behavior related to the constructs—that is, the purchase of a product. However, they cannot observe the constructs themselves—such as an attitude. Constructs help scientists communicate and build theories to explain phenomena.

You might think of construct validity as a *labeling* issue. When you measure a notion (construct) called "high involvement," is that what you are really measuring? Viewed in a slightly different manner, when a researcher claims construct validity, he or she essentially has a theory of how phenomena, people, and measures relate to each other (and other theoretical terms). In other words, the researcher offers us a theoretical pattern. When the researcher claims construct validity, he or she is claiming that the observed pattern in a research project corresponds to the theoretical pattern. In this instance, how the researcher thought the world works is how it works.

Although construct validity is presented here with various other types of validity, it really stands above all others. Why? Because construct validity relates back to the very essence of what you are trying to measure. If your research lacks construct validity, little else matters.[4]

Two statistical measures of construct validity are convergent and discriminant validity. **Convergent validity** reflects the degree of correlation among different measures that purport to measure the same construct. **Discriminant validity** reveals the lack of—or low—correlation among constructs that are supposed to be different. Assume that we develop a multi-item scale that measures the propensity to shop at discount stores. Our theory suggests that this propensity is caused by four personality variables: high level of self-confidence, low need for status, low need for distinctiveness, and high level of adaptability. Furthermore, our theory suggests that propensity to shop at discount stores is not related to brand loyalty or high-level aggressiveness.

Evidence of construct validity exists if our scale does the following:

- Correlates highly with other measures of propensity to shop at discount stores, such as reported stores patronized and social class (convergent validity).
- Has a low correlation with the unrelated constructs of brand loyalty and a high level of aggressiveness (discriminant validity)

**predictive validity**
Degree to which a future level of a criterion variable can be forecast by a current measurement scale.

**concurrent validity**
Degree to which another variable, measured at the same point in time as the variable of interest, can be predicted by the measurement instrument.

**construct validity**
Degree to which a measurement instrument represents and logically connects, via the underlying theory, the observed phenomenon to the construct.

**convergent validity**
Degree of correlation among different measurement instruments that purport to measure the same construct.

**discriminant validity**
Measure of the lack of association among constructs that are supposed to be different.

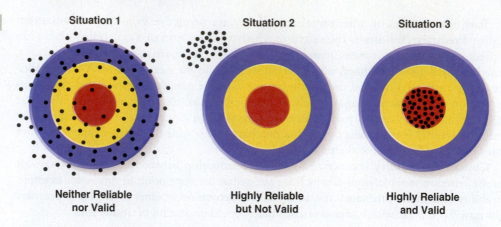

Situation 1 — Neither Reliable nor Valid

Situation 2 — Highly Reliable but Not Valid

Situation 3 — Highly Reliable and Valid

All the types of validity discussed here are somewhat interrelated in both theory and practice. Predictive validity is obviously very important on a scale to predict whether a person will shop at a discount store. A researcher developing a discount store patronage scale probably would first attempt to understand the constructs that provide the basis for prediction. The researcher would put forth a theory about discount store patronage—that, of course, is the foundation of construct validity. Next, the researcher would be concerned with which specific items to include on the discount store patronage scale, and whether these items relate to the full range of the construct. Thus, the researcher would ascertain the degree of content validity. The issue of criterion-related validity could be addressed in a pretest by measuring scores on the discount store patronage scale and actual store patronage.

## Reliability and Validity—A Concluding Comment

The concepts of reliability and validity are illustrated in Exhibit 10.6. Situation 1 shows holes all over the target, which could be caused by the use of an old rifle, being a poor shot, or many other factors. This complete lack of consistency means there is no reliability. Because the instrument lacks reliability, thus creating huge errors, it cannot be valid. Measurement reliability is a necessary condition for validity.

Situation 2 denotes a very tight pattern (consistency), but the pattern is far removed from the bull's-eye. This illustrates that an instrument can have a high level of reliability (little variance) but lack validity. The instrument is consistent, but it does not measure what it is supposed to measure. The shooter has a steady eye, but the sights are not adjusted properly. Situation 3 shows the reliability and validity that researchers strive to achieve in a measurement instrument; it is on target with what the researcher is attempting to measure.

## SUMMARY

Measurement consists of using rules to assign numbers or labels to objects in such a way as to represent quantities or qualities of attributes. A measurement rule is a guide, a method, or a command that tells a researcher what to do. Accurate measurement requires rules that are both clear and specific.

The measurement process comprises the following steps: (1) identify the concept of interest, (2) develop a construct, (3) define the concept constitutively, (4) define the concept operationally, (5) develop a measurement scale, and (6) evaluate the reliability and validity of the scale. A constitutive definition is a statement of the meaning of the central concept under study, establishing its boundaries. An operational definition specifies which observable characteristics will be measured and the process for assigning a value to the concept.

There are four basic levels of measurement: nominal, ordinal, interval, and ratio. A nominal scale partitions data into categories that are mutually exclusive and collectively exhaustive. The numbers assigned to objects or phenomena have no true numerical meaning; they are simply labels. Ordinal scales have the labeling characteristics of nominal scales plus an ability to order data. Interval scales contain all the features of ordinal scales, with the added dimension that the intervals between the points on the scale are equal. Interval scales enable the researcher to discuss differences separating two objects. They are amenable to computation of an arithmetic mean, standard deviation, and correlation coefficients. Ratio scales have all the characteristics of previously discussed scales, as well as a meaningful absolute zero or origin, thus permitting comparison of the absolute magnitude of the numbers and reflecting the actual amount of the variable.

Measurement data consist of accurate information and errors. Systematic error results in a constant bias in the measurements. Random error also influences the measurements but is not systematic; it is transient in nature. Reliability is the degree to which measures are free from random error and therefore provide consistent data. There are three ways to assess reliability: test–retest, internal consistency, and use of equivalent forms. Validity addresses whether the attempt at measurement was successful. The validity of a measure refers to the extent to which the measurement device or process is free from both systematic and random error. Types of validity include face, content, criterion-related, and construct validity.

## KEY TERMS

measurement 222
rule 222
constructs 224
constitutive definition 224
operational definition 224
scale 226
nominal scales 226
ordinal scales 227
interval scales 228

ratio scales 228
reliability 232
test–retest reliability 233
stability 233
equivalent form reliability 233
internal consistency reliability 234
split-half technique 234
validity 234
face validity 235

content validity 235
criterion-related validity 236
predictive validity 237
concurrent validity 237
construct validity 237
convergent validity 237
discriminant validity 237

## QUESTIONS FOR REVIEW & CRITICAL THINKING

*(Team Activity)*

1. What is measurement?
2. Differentiate among the four types of measurement scales, and discuss the types of information obtained from each.
3. How does reliability differ from validity? Give examples of each.
4. Give an example of a scale that would be reliable but not valid. Also give an example of a scale that would be valid but not reliable.
5. What are three methods of assessing reliability?
6. What are three methods of assessing validity?
7. Divide the class into teams of four or five. Each team should go to the Internet and find the results of a survey with data. Each team should then determine the face validity and content validity of the research. Also, each team should suggest a method for assessing reliability of the survey.

## WORKING THE NET

Go to a web search engine and look up "validity and reliability." Describe to the class the new insights you gain into these important concepts.

Go to *http://www.nielsen.com/us/en/nielsen-solutions/nielsen-measurement.html* and determine exactly what Nielsen measures. Next, report to the class how these constructs are measured.

## REAL-LIFE RESEARCH 10.1

### Profiles on Women Shoppers

When you consider that women control more than $7 trillion in domestic spending and more than 85 percent of purchase decisions across most major categories, it's no wonder that marketers are anxious to crack the code—and persuade women to crack open their wallets.

To better understand how to motivate women and to provide insight into the unconscious drivers of female behaviors and purchase decisions, Wilmette, Illinois, research company Insights in Marketing LLC developed five Female Behavioral Insight (FBI) profiles that aim to create a complete and clearer picture of what matters to American women.

Here's a snapshot of the FBI profiles:

**Profile 1** (26 percent of women): She is driven and focused on being successful in whatever she does. These are the women who want to have it all. Whether she is a leader of a Fortune 500 company or the CEO of her family, she is determined to accomplish her goals. She's often torn between her work life and home life. But, with a laser-sharp focus, she never loses sight of her goals, knowing that with enough tenacity, she'll win.

**Profile 2** (21 percent of women): She is a happy traditionalist who is conservative and risk-avoidant. You're most likely to find her at home with friends and family. She is the quintessential nurturer who takes care of herself by caring for others, whether it's emotionally or physically. She prefers to be behind the scenes rather than center stage and is guided by a strong belief system, structure, and routines.

**Profile 3** (20 percent of women): She is deliberate and highly curious about why people do what they do. Routine is the backbone to her life and she gets comfort from knowing what's going to happen next. She is happiest when things are going according to plan but life and the unpredictable world around her make her feel off balance. She can handle a few curveballs but struggles when too many come her way. If there are rules, she will follow them, because rules define guidelines and expectations.

**Profile 4** (17 percent of women): Self-reliant and struggling to maintain control over things around her, she feels that she is the only one who can solve her problems. She's keenly aware of the setbacks and of disappointments that have befallen her, driving her to surround herself with an emotional fortress. Despite her seeming independence, she needs reinforcement and positive feedback from others.

**Profile 5** (16 percent of women): Driven by an unquenchable curiosity, she is a bubbly, social butterfly who is open to anything. She doesn't climb a mountain or try the newest restaurant just for bragging rights; rather, she does it just to satisfy her own curiosity. Fearless and unreserved, she is resistant to anything boring or repetitive. She believes that people should seek out and pursue what makes them happy. She wants everyone to fully experience all that life has to offer so she goes out of her way to be inviting, inclusive, and generous.[5]

### Questions

1. What is the construct in the research? Give a constitutive definition.
2. What level(s) of measurement could the researchers have used? Give examples.
3. What could the researchers have used to measure reliability?
4. How might the researchers approach the measurement of validity?
5. What can the researchers do to demonstrate construct validity?
6. Do you see this scale as having value to marketing researchers? Why or why not?

© Mira/Alamy

# Using Measurement Scales to Build Marketing Effectiveness

## LEARNING OBJECTIVES

1. Explain the linkage among attitudes, behavior, and marketing effectiveness.

2. Understand the concept of scaling.

3. Compare the various types of attitude scales.

4. Examine some basic considerations in selecting a type of scale.

5. Realize the importance of attitude measurement scales in management decision making.

What are the various ways to measure attitudes? Why is it useful to measure attitudes? What factors should be considered in creating an attitude scale? These questions will be addressed in this chapter.

# Attitudes, Behavior, and Marketing Effectiveness

An attitude is a psychological construct, a way of conceptualizing an intangible. Attitudes cannot be observed or measured directly; their existence is inferred from their consequences. An **attitude** is an enduring organization of motivational, emotional, perceptual, and cognitive processes with respect to some aspect of a person's environment. In marketing research, it is a learned predisposition to respond in a consistently favorable or unfavorable manner toward an object or concept. Attitudes tend to be long lasting and consist of clusters of interrelated beliefs. They encompass a person's value system, which represents her or his standards of good and bad, right and wrong, and so forth. Thus, an individual may have a

**attitude**
Enduring organization of motivational, emotional, perceptual, and cognitive processes with respect to some aspect of a person's environment.

specific attitude toward Disney World, based on beliefs about a need for entertainment, cartoon characters, fantasy, crowds of people, waiting in lines, and many other things. Disney World also may be highly valued as good, clean, wholesome fun.

## Link between Attitudes and Behavior

The link between attitudes and behavior is complex. Predictions of future behavior for a group of consumers tend to be more accurate than those for a single consumer. Specifically, researchers have identified the following links:

1. The more favorable the attitude of consumers, the higher the incidence of product usage; the less favorable the attitude, the lower the incidence of product usage.

2. The less favorable people's attitudes toward a product, the more likely they are to stop using it.

3. The attitudes of people who have never tried a product tend to be distributed around the mean in the shape of a normal distribution.[1]

4. When attitudes are based on actually trying and experiencing a product, attitudes predict behavior quite well. Conversely, when attitudes are based on advertising, attitude–behavior consistency is significantly reduced.[2]

Some marketing researchers have become rather pessimistic about the ability of attitude research to predict behavior.[3] The present view of most researchers, however, is that one must learn to recognize the factors that influence the extent to which measured attitudes accurately predict behavior. Six factors should be considered in assessing whether attitude research findings will predict behavior:[4]

1. *Involvement of the consumer.* Attitudes are likely to predict purchase behavior only under conditions of high involvement.

2. *Attitude measurement.* The measure of attitude has to be reliable, valid, and at the same level of abstraction as the measure of behavior. For example, if the behavior involves contributing to a specific charity, such as the American Cancer Society, the attitude measure cannot ask less specific (i.e., more abstract) questions about consumers' attitudes

Attitude measurement must be reliable, valid, and specific to the particular behavior. If the behavior is that of contributing to the American Cancer Society, the questions asked should refer to that charity. Go to *www.cancer.org* to find out what information is available to help in framing such questions.

© AtnoYdur/iStockphoto

toward charities in general. A similar consistency must be applied to the variable of time. If the behavior involves buying a new Porsche within the next six months, the measure should include a time parameter. The longer the time between attitude measurement and the behavior, the weaker the relationship is.

3. *Effects of other people.* The feelings of other people toward the purchase and the consumer's motivation to comply with these feelings influence the extent to which attitudes predict behavior.

4. *Situational factors.* If situational factors, such as holidays, time pressures, or sickness intervene, measured attitudes may fail to predict behavior well.

5. *Effects of other brands.* Even though a consumer's attitude toward a brand may be quite favorable, if that consumer's attitude toward another brand is even more favorable, the other brand will probably be purchased. One reason the "attitude toward the object" model is often unable to accurately predict behavior is that it fails to include measures of attitudes toward other objects.

6. *Attitude strength.* For an attitude to influence behavior, it must be held with sufficient strength and conviction to be activated in memory.[5] The degree of association between an attitude and an object varies across a continuum. At one end of the continuum is the nonattitude: The consumer has neither positive nor negative feelings about a particular brand. At the other end of the continuum is the extreme attitude: The consumer feels very strongly about the brand.

## Enhancing Marketing Effectiveness

Attitudes are truly the essence of the "human change agent" that all marketers strive to influence. Marketing managers realize that there is not a perfect correlation between attitudes and behavior. Yet, in designing or modifying a marketing mix, managers know that attitude measures are often the best tool available for finding an effective mix. When Toyota is trying to decide which of three potential new designs will sell the most hybrid cars, it relies on attitude research. The implicit assumption is the design most preferred in attitude research testing will sell the most hybrids, all other things being equal. Thus, marketing managers measure attitudes in an attempt to predict behavior; correct predictions will enable managers to bring the "right" new product to the marketplace. This new product will be accompanied by the "right" marketing mix, again usually based to some extent on attitude research. Demographic data and past purchase patterns also are important data sources in deciding on a new marketing mix.

# Scaling Defined

The term **scaling** refers to procedures for attempting to determine quantitative measures of subjective and sometimes abstract concepts. It is defined as a procedure for assigning numbers (or other symbols) to properties of an object in order to impart some numerical characteristics to the properties in question. Actually, numbers are assigned to *indicants* of the properties of objects. The rise and fall of mercury in a glass tube (a thermometer) is an indicant of temperature variations.

A scale is a measurement tool. Scales are either unidimensional or multidimensional. **Unidimensional scales** are designed to measure only one attribute of a concept, respondent, or object. Thus, a unidimensional scale measuring consumers' price sensitivity might include several items to measure price sensitivity, but combined into a single measure; all interviewees' attitudes are then placed along a linear continuum, called *degree of price sensitivity*. **Multidimensional scales** are based on the premise that a concept, respondent, or object might be better described using several dimensions. For example, target customers for Jaguar automobiles may be defined in three dimensions: level of wealth, degree of price sensitivity, and appreciation of fine motor cars.

**scaling**
Procedures for assigning numbers (or other symbols) to properties of an object in order to impart some numerical characteristics to the properties in question.

**unidimensional scales**
Scales designed to measure only one attribute of a concept, respondent, or object.

**multidimensional scales**
Scales designed to measure several dimensions of a concept, respondent, or object.

# Attitude Measurement Scales

Measurement of attitudes relies on less precise scales than those found in the physical sciences and hence is much more difficult. Because an attitude is a construct that exists in the mind of the consumer, it is not directly observable—unlike, for example, weight in the physical sciences. In many cases, attitudes are measured at the nominal or ordinal level. Some more sophisticated scales enable the marketing researcher to measure at the interval level. One must be careful not to attribute the more powerful properties of an interval scale to the lower-level nominal or ordinal scales.

## Graphic Rating Scales

**graphic rating scales**
Measurement scales that include a graphic continuum, anchored by two extremes.

**Graphic rating scales** offer respondents a graphic continuum, typically anchored by two extremes. Exhibit 11.1 depicts three types of graphic rating scales that might be used to evaluate La-Z-Boy recliners. Scale A represents the simplest form of a graphic scale. Respondents are instructed to mark their response on the continuum. After respondents have done so, scores are ascertained by dividing the line into as many categories as desired and assigning a score based on the category into which the mark has been placed. For example, if the line were 6 inches long, every inch might represent a category. Scale B offers the respondent slightly more structure by assigning numbers along the scale.

Responses to graphic rating scales are not limited to simply placing a mark on a continuum, as scale C illustrates. Scale C has been used successfully by many researchers to speed up interviews. Respondents are asked to touch the thermometer on the screen or mobile device that best depicts their feelings.

Graphic ratings scales are also sometimes called "sliders" when used in online and mobile surveys. The respondent simply uses his or her finger to slide the scale along a

**Exhibit 11.1**

**Four Types of Graphic Rating Scales**

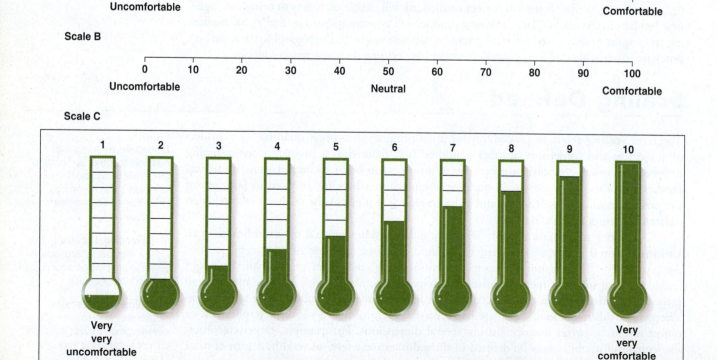

Scale A

Uncomfortable ——————————————————————— Comfortable

Scale B

0    10    20    30    40    50    60    70    80    90    100
Uncomfortable                    Neutral                   Comfortable

Scale C

1    2    3    4    5    6    7    8    9    10

Very very uncomfortable                                    Very very comfortable continuum. On some slides, a number will pop-up above the slider as it is moved along the scale (see Scale D in Exhibit 11.1).

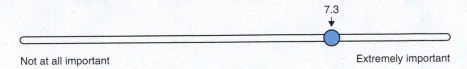

Graphic rating scales can be constructed easily and are simple to use. They enable a researcher to discern fine distinctions, assuming that the rater has adequate discriminatory abilities. Numerical data obtained from the scales are typically treated as interval data.

One disadvantage of graphic rating scales is that overly extreme anchors tend to force respondents toward the middle of the scale. Also, some research has suggested that such scales are not as reliable as itemized rating scales.

## Itemized Rating Scales

**Itemized rating scales** are similar to graphic rating scales, except that respondents must select from a limited number of ordered categories rather than placing a mark on a continuous scale. (Purists would argue that scale C in Exhibit 11.1 is an itemized rating scale.) Exhibit 11.2 shows some examples of itemized rating scales taken from nationwide marketing research surveys. Starting items are rotated on each questionnaire to eliminate the order bias that might arise from starting with the same item each time. Another example in the form of slider scales is discussed in the Practicing Marketing Research feature below.

**itemized rating scales**
Measurement scales in which the respondent selects an answer from a limited number of ordered categories.

# PRACTICING MARKETING RESEARCH

## Comparing the Traditional Likert Scale and Alternative Slider Scales[6]

Survey Sampling International ran a series of surveys designed to examine the differences between the performances of a "standard" 5-point Likert scale and a Flash-based slider scale. The two scales were assessed based on data collected, engagement, and respondent satisfaction with the instrument.

The experiment focused on two key ratings issues: equivalency of ratings and the spaces between ratings. In setting up the experiment, respondents were given a traditional Likert scale containing four statements and were asked at the end to rate how well they felt the instrument allowed them to express their true opinions. Respondents were then given a second scale on which they were allowed to rescore previous items on a scale up to 5 points in the direction of any adjacent ranks. While respondents generally expressed satisfaction with the accuracy of the traditional scale, a substantial portion chose to rerate, especially those posting ratings of agree/disagree slightly (as much as 75 percent). On the whole, the results indicated conclusively that the instrument did not offer a fine enough range

of responses to precisely reflect respondents' opinions. In addition, items ranked the same could not be assumed to indicate equivalency of respondent opinions.

In the next stage of the experiment, respondents were asked to rate the statements again using a series of slider scales. Each of the four sliders was text anchored at the end and did not include any visual illustrative elements. The first slider offered the traditional labels; the second kept the hash marks but removed the text; the third removed the marks; and the fourth added a numerical score between 1 and 5 to indicate the position of the slider. The following table offers an example of responses for all six ranking instruments. Responses were for this statement: The highest standards of morals and ethics is [sic] the most important thing in life.

Data distributions varied noticeably across the different designs, indicating that design did matter with regard to how respondents answered. In applying averages and mean scores, however, the data generally seemed to align across the scale designs. The clear takeaway was that the slider scales generally offered greater granularity in terms of response options. That granularity was reflected in respondent attitudes as, overall, respondents using slider scales reported higher satisfaction levels regardless of the slider design.

| | Disagree Strongly | Disagree Slightly | Neither/ Nor | Agree Slightly | Agree Strongly |
|---|---|---|---|---|---|
| Traditional | 12 | 40 | 105 | 231 | 201 |
| Rescored Traditional | 6 | 12 | 61 | 57 | 154 |
| Labeled Slider | 4 | 25 | 77 | 125 | 129 |
| Mark Slider | 1 | 17 | 92 | 88 | 114 |
| Blank Slider | 1 | 8 | 27 | 21 | 97 |
| Slider with Score | 4 | 10 | 51 | 47 | 124 |

## Questions

1. Using the following scale, assess the following statement: The assessment of the Likert scale in comparison to the slider scale is accurate.

2. Now given the opportunity, would you place your answer somewhere in between its current position and a position adjacent to it? Why or why not?

3. In answering the previous questions, do you think you have been able to accurately express your opinions regarding the given statement? Explain.

Scale A was used by a dot-com company in determining what features and services it should add to its website. Scale B was used in measuring satisfaction with an online travel site. Scale C was used by an e-commerce music retailer to better understand how people select a music website. Scale D was also an Internet survey, conducted by a producer of customer relationship management software. Examples of other itemized rating scales are shown in Exhibit 11.3.

Although itemized rating scales do not allow for the fine distinctions that can be achieved in a graphic rating scale, they are easy to construct and administer. And the definitive categories found in itemized rating scales usually produce more reliable ratings.

| **Exhibit 11.2** | If offered, how likely would you be to use the following areas on this site? |
|---|---|

**Itemized Rating Scales Used in Internet and Mall Surveys**

**Scale A**

**a.** Auctions
Not at all likely to use   01   02   03   04   05   06   07   **Extremely likely to use**

**b.** Fee-based education tools
Not at all likely to use   01   02   03   04   05   06   07   **Extremely likely to use**

**c.** Event registration
Not at all likely to use   01   02   03   04   05   06   07   **Extremely likely to use**

**d.** Online shopping markets
Not at all likely to use   01   02   03   04   05   06   07   **Extremely likely to use**

**e.** Recruiting
Not at all likely to use   01   02   03   04   05   06   07   **Extremely likely to use**

**f.** Research subscription
Not at all likely to use   01   02   03   04   05   06   07   **Extremely likely to use**

**g.** Trading community
Not at all likely to use   01   02   03   04   05   06   07   **Extremely likely to use**

**h.** Training/seminars
Not at all likely to use   01   02   03   04   05   06   07   **Extremely likely to use**

## Scale B

Submitting a Request for a Hotel Reservation

We'd like to get your feedback regarding your experience in submitting a request for a hotel reservation at our website today. Please rate your satisfaction with each of the following aspects of *fasthotels.com* based on **your experience this visit**.

|  | Very Satisfied | | | | Very Dissatisfied |
|---|---|---|---|---|---|
|  | 1 | 2 | 3 | 4 | 5 |
| Ability to access the offer page | o | o | o | o | o |
| Ability to locate hotel information | o | o | o | o | o |
| Ability to locate city information | o | o | o | o | o |
| Clarity of how the bonus program works | o | o | o | o | o |
| Clarity of the purchase agreement | o | o | o | o | o |

Please rate the extent to which you are satisfied that *Fasthotels.com* **has communicated** each of the following to you during this visit:

|  | Very Satisfied | | | | Very Dissatisfied |
|---|---|---|---|---|---|
|  | 1 | 2 | 3 | 4 | 5 |
| Your hotel reservation is/will be nonchangeable | o | o | o | o | o |
| Your hotel reservation is/will be nonrefundable | o | o | o | o | o |

How **satisfied** would you say you were with **this visit** to *Fasthotels.com*?

o Very satisfied

o Satisfied

o Somewhat satisfied

o Neither satisfied nor dissatisfied

o Somewhat dissatisfied

o Dissatisfied

o Very dissatisfied

## Scale C

What factors influence your choice of music websites? (Rate the importance of each item.)

|  | Not at All Important | | | | Very Important |
|---|---|---|---|---|---|
| Customer benefits or rewards for shopping | o | o | o | o | o |
| Customer service or delivery options | o | o | o | o | o |
| Ease of use of website | o | o | o | o | o |
| Low prices | o | o | o | o | o |
| Real-time audio sampling of CDs | o | o | o | o | o |
| Reviews and artist information | o | o | o | o | o |

## Scale D

How interested would you be in obtaining additional information about this customer relationship management solution for your business?

o Extremely interested        o interested        o interested

o interested        o Not interested

How likely is it that your business will invest in this type of customer relationship management solution within the next 12 months?

o Extremely likely        o likely        o likely

o likely        o Not likely

| EXHIBIT 11.3 | Selected Itemized Rating Scales | | | |
|---|---|---|---|---|
| **Characteristic of Interest** | | | **Rating Choices** | |
| **Purchase-Intent** | Definitely will buy | Probably will buy | Probably will not buy | Definitely will not buy | |
| **Level of Agreement** | Strongly agree | Somewhat agree | Neither agree nor disagree | Somewhat disagree | Strongly disagree |
| **Quality** | Very good | Good | Neither good nor bad | Fair | Poor |
| **Dependability** | Completely dependable | Somewhat dependable | Not very dependable | Not dependable at all | |
| **Style** | Very stylish | Somewhat stylish | Not very stylish | Completely unstylish | |
| **Satisfaction** | Completely satisfied | Somewhat satisfied | Neither satisfied nor dissatisfied | Somewhat dissatisfied | Completely dissatisfied |
| **Cost** | Extremely expensive | Expensive | Neither expensive nor inexpensive | Slightly inexpensive | Very inexpensive |
| **Ease of Use** | Very easy to use | Somewhat easy to use | Not very easy to use | Difficult to use | |
| **Color Brightness** | Extremely bright | Very bright | Somewhat bright | Slightly bright | Not bright at all |
| **Modernity** | Very modern | Somewhat modern | Neither modern nor old-fashioned | Somewhat old-fashioned | Very old-fashioned |

When researchers, for some reason, are interested in the most extreme-position views, they might elect to use a two-stage format. Research has shown that a two-stage format can provide better data quality in detecting extreme views than a single-stage itemized rating scale. Following is an example of the two-stage approach.[7]

## Traditional One-Stage Format

"How effective do you believe Senator Foghorn is in having your money stay in the community?"

| Very effective | Somewhat effective | Somewhat ineffective | Very ineffective | Don't know |
|---|---|---|---|---|
| 4 | 3 | 2 | 1 | 0 |

## Two-Stage Format

"How effective do you believe Senator Foghorn is in having your money stay in the community?"

**How effective?**
☐ Effective
☐ Ineffective
☐ No opinion

**Would that be very or somewhat?**
☐ Very
☐ Somewhat

**noncomparative scales**
Measurement scales in which judgment is made without reference to another object, concept, or person.

## Rank-Order Scales

Itemized and graphic scales are considered to be **noncomparative scales** because the respondent makes a judgment without reference to another object, concept, or person.

**Rank-order scales**, by contrast, are **comparative scales** because the respondent is asked to compare two or more items and rank each item. Rank-order scales are widely used in marketing research, for several reasons. They are easy to use and give ordinal measurements of the items evaluated. Instructions are easy to understand, and the process typically moves at a steady pace. Some researchers claim that rank-order scales force respondents to evaluate concepts in a realistic manner. Exhibit 11.4(A) illustrates a series of rank-order scales taken from a study on eye shadows. Exhibit 11.4(B) shows an online scale on automobile resale value percentage.

Rank-order scales possess several disadvantages. If all of the alternatives in a respondent's choice set are not included, the results could be misleading. For example, a respondent's first choice on all dimensions in the eye shadow study might have been Mineral Fusion, which was not included. A second problem is that the concept being ranked may be completely outside a person's choice set, thus producing meaningless data. Perhaps a respondent doesn't use eye shadow and feels that the product isn't appropriate for any woman. Another limitation is that the scale gives the researcher only ordinal data. Nothing is learned about how far apart the items stand or how intensely the respondent feels about the ranking of an item. Finally, the researcher does not know why the respondent ranked the items as he or she did.

**rank-order scales**
Measurement scales in which the respondent compares two or more items and ranks them.

**comparative scales**
Measurement scales in which one object, concept, or person is compared with another on a scale.

---

**Exhibit 11.4**

**Series of Rank-Order Scales Used to Evaluate Eye Shadows and Car Resale Values**

### Eye Shadow Scales

Please rank the following eye shadows, with 1 being the brand that best meets the characteristic being evaluated and 6 the worst brand on the characteristic being evaluated. The six brands are listed on card C. (HAND RESPONDENT CARD C.) Let's begin with the idea of having high-quality compacts or containers. Which brand would rank as having the highest quality compacts or containers? Which is second? (RECORD BELOW.)

| | Q.48. Having High-Quality Container | Q.49. Having High-Quality Applicator | Q.50. Having High-Quality Eye Shadow |
|---|---|---|---|
| Avon | _____ | _____ | _____ |
| Cover Girl | _____ | _____ | _____ |
| Estee Lauder | _____ | _____ | _____ |
| L'Oreal | _____ | _____ | _____ |
| Sephora | _____ | _____ | _____ |
| Revlon | _____ | _____ | _____ |

| Card C | | |
|---|---|---|
| Avon | Cover Girl | Estee Lauder |
| L'Oreal | Natural Wonder | Revlon |

### Car Resale Value Scale

Based on your personal experience or what you have seen, heard or read, please rank the following car brands according to the resale value percentage—that is, the brand that enables you to recover the largest dollar amount (percentage) of your original purchase price of the vehicle.

Place a "1" next to the brand that has the highest resale value percentage, a "2" next to the brand that has the next highest resale value percentage, and so forth. Remember, no two cars can have the same ranking.

_____ Chevrolet

_____ Toyota

_____ BMW

_____ Ford

Here are some characteristics used to describe sun-care products in general. Please tell me which characteristic in each pair is more important to you when selecting a sun-care product.

| | |
|---|---|
| a. Tans evenly | b. Tans without burning |
| a. Prevents burning | b. Protects against burning and tanning |
| a. Good value for the money | b. Goes on evenly |
| a. Not greasy | b. Does not stain clothing |
| a. Tans without burning | b. Prevents burning |
| a. Protects against burning and tanning | b. Good value for the money |
| a. Goes on evenly | b. Tans evenly |
| a. Prevents burning | b. Not greasy |

## Paired Comparisons

**paired comparison scales**
Measurement scales that ask the respondent to pick one of two objects in a set, based on some stated criteria.

**Paired comparison scales** ask a respondent to pick one of two objects from a set, based on some stated criteria. The respondent, therefore, makes a series of paired judgments between objects. Exhibit 11.5 shows a paired comparison scale used in a national study for sun care products. Only part of the scale is shown; the data-collection procedure typically requires the respondent to compare all possible pairs of objects.

Paired comparisons overcome several problems of traditional rank-order scales. First, it is easier for people to select one item from a set of two than to rank a large set of data. Second, the problem of order bias is overcome; there is no pattern in the ordering of items or questions to create a source of bias. On the negative side, because all possible pairs are evaluated, the number of paired comparisons increases geometrically as the number of objects to be evaluated increases arithmetically. Thus, the number of objects to be evaluated should remain fairly small to prevent interviewee fatigue.

## Constant Sum Scales

**constant sum scales**
Measurement scales that ask the respondent to divide a given number of points, typically 100, among two or more attributes, based on their importance to him or her.

To avoid long lists of paired items, marketing researchers use **constant sum scales** more often than paired comparisons. Constant sum scales require the respondent to divide a given number of points, typically 100, among two or more attributes based on their importance to him or her. Respondents must value each item relative to all other items. The number of points allocated to each alternative indicates the ranking assigned to it by the respondent, as well as the relative magnitude of each alternative as perceived by the respondent. A constant sum scale used in a national study of tennis sportswear is shown in Exhibit 11.6. Another advantage of the constant sum scale over a rank-order or paired comparison scale is that if the respondent perceives two characteristics to have equal value, he or she can so indicate.

A major disadvantage of this scale is that the respondent may have difficulty allocating the points to total 100 if there are a lot of characteristics or items. Most researchers feel that 10 items is the upper limit on a constant sum scale.

## Semantic Differential Scales

**semantic differential scales**
Measurement scales that examine the strengths and weaknesses of a concept by having the respondent rank it between dichotomous pairs of words or phrases that could be used to describe it; the means of the responses are then plotted as a profile or image.

The semantic differential was developed by Charles Osgood, George Suci, and Percy Tannenbaum.[8] The focus of their original research was on the measurement of meaning of an object to a person. The object might be a savings and loan association and the meaning its image among a certain group of people.

The construction of a **semantic differential scale** begins with determination of a concept to be rated, such as the image of a company, brand, or store. The researcher selects dichotomous (opposite) pairs of words or phrases that could be used to describe the concept.

Below are seven characteristics of women's tennis sportswear. Please allocate 100 points among the characteristics such that the allocation represents the importance of each characteristic to you. The more points that you assign to a characteristic, the more important it is. If the characteristic is totally unimportant, you should not allocate any points to it. When you've finished, please double-check to make sure that your total adds to 100.

| Characteristics of Tennis Sportswear | Number of Points |
|---|---|
| Is comfortable to wear | _____ |
| Is durable | _____ |
| Is made by well-known brand or sports manufacturers | _____ |
| Is made in the United States | _____ |
| Has up-to-date styling | _____ |
| Gives freedom of movement | _____ |
| Is a good value for the money | _____ |
| | 100 points |

**Exhibit 11.6**

**Constant Sum Scale Used in Tennis Sportswear Study**

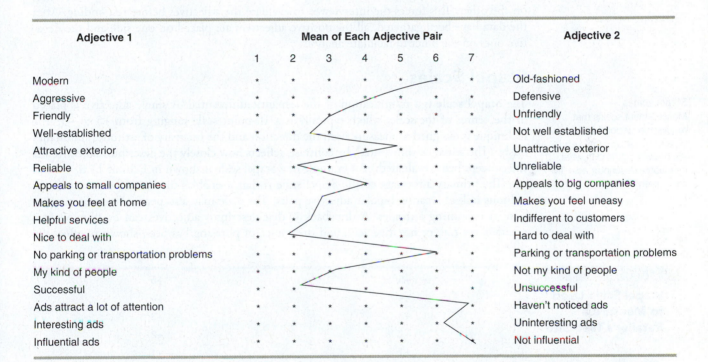

**Exhibit 11.7**

**Semantic Differential Profile of an Arizona Savings and Loan Association**

Respondents then rate the concept on a scale (usually 1 to 7). The mean of the responses for each pair of adjectives is computed, and the means are plotted as a profile or image.

Exhibit 11.7 is an actual profile of an Arizona savings and loan association as perceived by noncustomers with family incomes of $80,000 and above. A quick glance shows that the firm is viewed as somewhat old-fashioned, with rather plain facilities. It is viewed as well-established, reliable, successful, and probably very nice to deal with. The institution has parking problems and perhaps entry and egress difficulties. Its advertising is viewed as dismal.

The semantic differential is a quick and efficient means of examining the strengths and weaknesses of a product or company image, versus those of the competition. More importantly, however, the semantic differential has been shown to be sufficiently reliable and valid for decision making and prediction in marketing and the behavioral sciences.[9] Also, the semantic differential has proved to be statistically robust (generalizable from one group of subjects to another) when applied to corporate image research.[10] This makes possible the measurement and comparison of images held by interviewees with diverse backgrounds.

Although these advantages have led many researchers to use the semantic differential as an image measurement tool, it is not without disadvantages. First, the semantic differential suffers from a lack of standardization. It is a highly generalized technique that must be adapted for each research problem. There is no single set of standard scales; hence, the development of customized scales becomes an integral part of the research.

The number of divisions on the semantic differential scale also presents a problem. If too few divisions are used, the scale is crude and lacks meaning; if too many are used, the scale goes beyond the ability of most people to discriminate. Researchers have found the seven-point scale to be the most satisfactory.

Another disadvantage of the semantic differential is the *halo effect*. The rating of a specific image component may be dominated by the interviewee's overall impression of the concept being rated. Bias may be significant if the image is hazy in the respondent's mind. To partially counteract the halo effect, the researcher should randomly reverse scale adjectives so that all the "good" ones are not placed on one side of the scale and the "bad" ones on the other. This forces the interviewee to evaluate the adjectives before responding. After the data have been gathered, all the positive adjectives are placed on one side and the negative ones on the other to facilitate analysis.

## Stapel Scales

**Stapel scales**
Measurement scales that require the respondent to rate, on a scale ranging from +5 to –5, how closely and in what direction a descriptor adjective fits a given concept.

The **Stapel scale** is a modification of the semantic differential. A single adjective is placed in the center of the scale, which typically is a 10-point scale ranging from +5 to –5. The technique is designed to measure both the direction and the intensity of attitudes simultaneously. (The semantic differential, by contrast, reflects how closely the descriptor adjective fits the concept being evaluated.) An example of a Stapel scale is shown in Exhibit 11.8.

The primary advantage of the Stapel scale is that it enables the researcher to avoid the arduous task of creating bipolar adjective pairs. The scale may also permit finer discrimination in measuring attitudes. A drawback is that descriptor adjectives can be phrased in a positive, neutral, or negative vein, and the choice of phrasing has been shown to affect the

**Exhibit 11.8**

**Stapel Scale Used to Measure a Retailer's Web Site**

| | |
|---|---|
| +5 | +5 |
| +4 | +4 |
| +3 | +3 |
| +2 | +2 |
| +1 | +1 |
| Cheap Prices | Easy to Navigate |
| –1 | –1 |
| –2 | –2 |
| –3 | –3 |
| –4 | –4 |
| –5 | –5 |

Select a "plus" number for words you think describe the Web site accurately. The more accurately you think the word describes the website, the larger the "plus" number you should choose. Select a "minus" number for words you think do not describe the website accurately. The less accurately you think the word describes the Web site, the larger the "minus" number you should choose. Therefore, you can select any number from 15 for words you think are very accurate all the way to –5 for words you think are very inaccurate.

scale results and the person's ability to respond.[11] The Stapel scale has never had much popularity in commercial research and is used less frequently than the semantic differential.

## Likert Scales

The **Likert scale** is another scale that avoids the problem of developing pairs of dichotomous adjectives. The scale consists of a series of statements expressing either a favorable or an unfavorable attitude toward the concept under study. The respondent is asked to indicate the level of her or his agreement or disagreement with each statement by assigning it a numerical score. The scores are then totaled to measure the respondent's attitude.

Exhibit 11.9 shows two Likert scales for an Internet game site targeted toward teenagers. Scale A measures attitudes toward the registration process; scale B evaluates users' attitudes toward advertising on the website.

With the Likert scale, the respondent is required to consider only one statement at a time, with the scale running from one extreme to the other. A series of statements (attitudes) can be examined, yet there is only a single set of uniform replies for the respondent to choose from.

Rensis Likert created this scale to measure a person's attitude toward concepts (e.g., unions), activities (e.g., swimming), and so forth. He recommended the following steps in building the scale:

1. The researcher identifies the concept or activity to be scaled.
2. The researcher assembles a large number of statements (75 to 100) concerning the public's sentiments toward the concept or activity.
3. Each test item is classified by the researcher as generally "favorable" or "unfavorable" with regard to the attitude under study. No attempt is made to scale the items; however, a pretest is conducted that involves the full set of statements and a limited sample of respondents.
4. In the pretest, the respondent indicates agreement (or not) with *every* item, checking one of the following direction-intensity descriptors:
   a. Strongly agree
   b. Agree
   c. Undecided
   d. Disagree
   e. Strongly disagree
5. Each response is given a numerical weight (e.g., 5, 4, 3, 2, 1).
6. The individual's *total attitude score* is represented by the algebraic summation of weights associated with the items checked. In the scoring process, weights are assigned so that the direction of attitude—favorable to unfavorable—is consistent over items. For example, if 5 were assigned to "strongly agree" for favorable items, 5 should be assigned to "strongly disagree" for unfavorable items.
7. After seeing the results of the pretest, the researcher selects only those items that appear to discriminate well between high and low *total* scorers. This may be done by first finding the highest and lowest quartiles of subjects on the basis of *total* score and then comparing the mean differences on each *specific* item for these high and low groups (excluding the middle 50 percent of subjects).
8. The 20 to 25 items finally selected are those that have discriminated "best" (i.e., exhibited the greatest differences in mean values) between high and low total scorers in the pretest.
9. Steps 3 through 5 are then repeated in the main study.

**Likert scales**
Measurement scales in which the respondent specifies a level of agreement or disagreement with statements expressing either a favorable or an unfavorable attitude toward the concept under study.

People's attitudes toward activities like snowboarding can be measured using Likert scales.

Likert created the scale so that a researcher could look at a summed score and tell whether a person's attitude toward a concept was positive or negative. For example, the maximum favorable score on a 20-item scale would be 100; therefore, a person scoring 92 would be presumed to have a favorable attitude. Of course, two people could both score 92 and yet have rated various statements differently. Thus, specific components of their overall attitude could differ markedly. For example, if respondent A strongly agreed (5) that a particular bank had good parking and strongly disagreed (1) that its loan programs were the best in town and respondent B had the exact opposite attitude, both would have summed scores of 6.

In the world of marketing research, Likert-like scales are very popular. They are quick and easy to construct and can be administered by telephone or via the Internet. Commercial researchers rarely follow the textbook-like process just outlined. Instead, the scale usually is developed jointly by a client project manager and a researcher. Many times, the scale is created following a focus group.

## Purchase-Intent Scales

**purchase-intent scales**
Scales used to measure a respondent's intention to buy or not buy a product.

Perhaps the single scale used most often in marketing research is the **purchase-intent scale**. The ultimate issue for marketing managers is, will they buy the product or not? If so, what percentage of the market can I expect to obtain? The purchase-intent question normally is asked for all new products and services and product and service modifications by manufacturers, retailers, and even nonprofit organizations.[12]

During new-product development, the purchase-intent question is first asked during concept testing to get a rough idea of demand. The manager wants to quickly eliminate potential turkeys, take a careful look at those products for which purchase-intent is moderate, and push forward the products that seem to have star potential. At this stage, investment is minimal and product modification or concept repositioning is an easy task.

As the product moves through development, the product itself, promotion strategy, price levels, and distribution channels become more concrete and focused. Purchase-intent is evaluated at each stage of development and demand estimates are refined. The crucial go–no go decision for national or regional rollout typically comes after test marketing.

Immediately before test marketing, commercial researchers have another critical stage of evaluation. Here, the final or near-final version of the product is placed in consumers' homes in test cities around the country. After a period of in-home use (usually two to six weeks), a follow-up survey is conducted among participants to find out their likes and dislikes, how the product compares with what they use now, and what they would pay for it. The critical question near the end of the questionnaire is purchase-intent.

Question 21 in Exhibit 11.10 is a purchase-intent question taken from a follow-up study on in-home placement of a flytrap. The trap consisted of two 3-inch disks held about one-quarter inch apart by three plastic pillars; it looked somewhat like a large, thin yo-yo. The trap contained a pheromone to attract the flies and a glue that would remain sticky for six months. Supposedly, the flies flew in but never out. Centered on the back side of one of

Exhibit 11.9

Likert Scales Used by an Internet Game Site

## Scale A

How did you feel about the registration process when you became a new user?

| | Strongly disagree | Somewhat disagree | Neutral | Somewhat agree | Strongly agree |
|---|---|---|---|---|---|
| The registration was simple. | o | o | o | o | o |
| The registration questions were "nonthreatening." | o | o | o | o | o |
| Registration here will protect my privacy. | o | o | o | o | o |
| The registration did not take a long time to complete. | o | o | o | o | o |
| The registration informed me about the site. | o | o | o | o | o |

## Scale B

How do you feel about the following statements?

| | Strongly disagree | Somewhat disagree | Neutral | Somewhat agree | Strongly agree |
|---|---|---|---|---|---|
| Allowing companies to advertise on the Internet allows me to access free services. | o | o | o | o | o |
| I do not support advertising on this site even though it provides me with free entertainment. | o | o | o | o | o |
| There is extremely too much advertising on the Internet. | o | o | o | o | o |
| There is extremely too much advertising on this site. | o | o | o | o | o |
| It's easy for me to ignore the advertising on this site and just play the game. | o | o | o | o | o |

the disks was an adhesive tab so that the disk could be attached to a kitchen window. The concept was to eliminate flies in the kitchen area without resorting to a pesticide. Question 22 was designed to aid in positioning the product, and question 23 (akin to the net promoter scale discussed below) traditionally was used by the manufacturer as a double-check on purchase-intent. If 60 percent of the respondents claimed that they definitely would buy the product and 90 percent said they definitely would not recommend the product to their friends, the researcher would question the validity of the purchase-intent.

The purchase-intent scale has been found to be a good predictor of consumer choice of frequently purchased and durable consumer products.[13] The scale is very easy to construct, and consumers are simply asked to make a subjective judgment of their likelihood of buying a new product. From past experience in the product category, a marketing manager can translate consumer responses on the scale to estimates of purchase probability. Obviously, everyone who "definitely will buy" the product will not do so; in fact, a few who state that they definitely will not buy actually will buy the product. The manufacturer of the flytrap is a major producer of both pesticide and nonpesticide pest-control products. Assume that, based on historical follow-up studies, the manufacturer has learned the following about purchase-intent of nonpesticide home-use pest-control products:

21. If a set of three traps sold for approximately $5.00 and was available in the stores where you normally shop, would you:

(51)

| | |
|---|---|
| definitely buy the set of traps | 1 |
| probably buy | 2 |
| probably not buy | 3 |
| definitely not buy | 4 |

22. Would you use the traps (a) instead of or (b) in addition to existing products?

(52)

| | |
|---|---|
| instead of | 1 |
| in addition to | 2 |

23. Would you recommend this product to your friends?

(53)

| | |
|---|---|
| definitely | 1 |
| probably | 2 |
| probably not | 3 |
| definitely not | 4 |

- 63 percent of the "definitely will buy" actually purchase within 12 months.
- 28 percent of the "probably will buy" actually purchase within 12 months.
- 12 percent of the "probably will not buy" actually purchase within 12 months.
- 3 percent of the "definitely will not buy" actually purchase within 12 months.

Suppose that the flytrap study resulted in the following:

- 40 percent—definitely will buy
- 20 percent—probably will buy
- 30 percent—probably will not buy
- 10 percent—definitely will not buy

Assuming that the sample is representative of the target market,

$$(0.4)(63\%) + (0.2)(28\%) + (0.3)(12\%) + (0.1)(3\%)$$
$$= 35.7\% \text{ market share}$$

Most marketing managers would be deliriously happy about such a high market share prediction for a new product. Unfortunately, because of consumer confusion, the product was killed after the in-home placement despite the high prediction.

It is not uncommon for marketing research firms to conduct studies containing a purchase-intent scale in cases where the client does not have historical data to use as a basis for weighing the results. A reasonable but conservative estimate would be 70 percent of the "definitely will buy," 35 percent of the "probably will buy," 10 percent of the "probably will not buy," and zero of the "definitely will not buy."[14] Higher weights are common in the industrial market.

Some companies use the purchase-intent scale to make go–no go decisions in product development without reference to market share. Typically, managers simply add the "definitely will buy" and "probably will buy" percentages and compare that total to a predetermined go–no go threshold. Combining "definitely" and "probably" is referred to as a top two box score. One consumer goods manufacturer, for example, requires a box score of 80 percent or higher at the concept testing stage and 65 percent for a product to move from in-home placement tests to test marketing.

## Scale Conversions[15]

A considerable amount of voice-of-the-customer (VOC) data, also called customer satisfaction studies, is collected using tracking studies. Tracking studies simply follow changes in consumers' attitudes and purchase behavior over time. For example, VOC research may be conducted every quarter or every six months. Sometimes situations arise in firms, such as policy changes, that require changes in the VOC research methodology. One such change is moving from one scale (say, 5-point) to another scale (say, 10-point). There could be many reasons for that kind of change, but it raises the obvious question: How can data collected using the two scales be compared?

The objective is to aid the researcher in comparing data that are measured in different ways and make informed decisions. The underlying assumption here is that the scale wording is sufficiently comparable that scale conversions can be attempted. Although several techniques can be used for scale conversion, we will examine a simple, straightforward method here.

In the scale equivalence approach, no attempt is made to modify the data in any way. Instead, the focus is on identifying the appropriate way of reporting that would enable scores to become comparable. This wouldn't be applicable in all situations and is useful primarily in situations where "boxed" scores (top-two box, top-three box, etc.) are reported.

Consider four scales (in terms of scale points) that are commonly used in marketing research: 5-point, 7-point, 10-point, and 11-point scales. Often, the results of a study using these kinds of scales are reported using boxed scores. Questions then relate to how a study using a 5-point scale and reporting on "top-two box" scores can be translated when the new scale has, say, 7 points. In the approach of scale equivalence, we look at the proportion of a scale each scale point covers.

For example, each scale point on a 5-point scale covers 20 percent of the scale. That is, if we were generating completely random data to respond to this scale, we would expect approximately 20 percent of the responses to be 1, 20 percent to be 2, and so on. Therefore, a top-two box score would cover 40 percent of the scale points on a 5-point scale. Similarly, for a 7-point scale, each scale point accounts for approximately 14 percent of the scale, and top-two box scores would account for about 28 percent of the scale points. Exhibit 11.11 shows the box score distributions for the four scales.

The boxed numbers show, for example, that a top-two box score on a 5-point scale accounts for approximately the same proportion of the scale as a top-three box score on a 7-point scale, or a top-four box score on a 10-point scale (approximately 40 percent).

| EXHIBIT 11.11 | Box Score Distributions for Four Scales | | | | |
| --- | --- | --- | --- | --- | --- |
| Scale | Top 1 | Top 2 | Top 3 | Top 4 | Top 5 |
| 5-point | 20% | 40% | | | |
| 7-point | 14% | 28% | 42% | | |
| 10-point | 10% | 20% | 30% | 40% | |
| 11-point | 9% | 18% | 27% | 36% | 45% |

| EXHIBIT 11.12 | Approximate Conversions for Boxed Scores among Four Scales | | |
|---|---|---|---|
| **11-Point Scale** | **10-Point Scale** | **7-Point Scale** | **5-Point Scale** |
| ? | Top-4 Box | Top-3 Box | Top-2 Box |
| Top-3 Box | Top-3 Box | Top-2 Box | ? |
| Top-2 Box | Top-2 Box | ? | Top Box |

Hence, when data using these scales are to be compared, the relevant number of top boxes could be used. More generally, Exhibit 11.12 provides (approximate) conversions for boxed scores among the four scales. A question mark (?) indicates that a simple conversion is not available.

## Net Promoter Score (NPS)

One way to avoid the confusion of using scales with differing numbers of scale points is to use the net promoter score (NPS) as the measure of satisfaction. The concept of NPS first appeared in the *Harvard Business Review* in 2003.[16] Its appeal is its simplicity involving one question, "Would you recommend this company (or brand) to a friend?" The scale ranges from 0 to 10. The **net promoter score** is the percent of promoters (those rating 7 or 10) minus the percent of detractors (those rating 0 – 6). Those rating a 7 or 8 are considered passive or benign. Acceptance of NPS was swift by companies large and small. It meant no more surveys with lots of questions or mystifying models to understand. The key strategy is to maximize high scores and to eliminate or minimize low scores. Jeff Immelt, CEO of General Electric, said, "This is the best customer relationship metric that I have ever seen."[17]

Research from the Temkin Group, Waban, Massachusetts, found that 81 percent of promoters are very likely to repurchase from the company in the future and 64 percent are very likely to forgive the company if it makes a mistake. For detractors, those numbers are 16 percent and 24 percent, respectively.[18]

Not everyone is a strong supporter of NPS. For example, Exhibit 11.13 shows three different scenarios with an NPS of 20 percent (promoters minus detractors). With Company

**net promoter score**
A measure of satisfaction; the percentage of promoters minus the percentage of detractors when answering the question, "Would you recommend this to a friend?"

**Exhibit 11.13**

*Source:* Randy Hanson, "Life after NPS," *Marketing Research* (Summer 2011), 10.

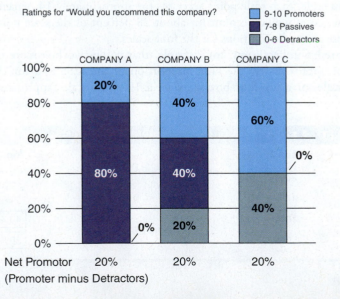

**NPS RESULTS FOR THREE COMPANIES**

Ratings for "Would you recommend this company?"

- 9-10 Promoters
- 7-8 Passives
- 0-6 Detractors

A, there are no detractors, but 80 percent are passive. Company B has an equal amount of promoters and passives with 20 percent detractors. Company C has no passives, but a large number (40 percent) of detractors. Thus, even though the NPS is the same for all three firms, each requires a different marketing and customer relationship strategy.

Also, an increasing NPS over time can mean more promoters, less detractors, or both. Again, depending on why the NPS has gone up, different strategies may be necessary.

Another issue is those labeled *passives*. Some argue that passives are, in fact, not passive. As stated earlier, passives are those who assign a 7 or 8 on the "Would you recommend...." question. TARP Worldwide, of Arlington, Virginia, found that passives were significantly less loyal and very likely to spread negative word-of-mouth.[19] John Goodman, vice-chairman of TARP, says, "Think about how you would react if someone came to you and said, "I just went to this restaurant and I'd definitely give it a 7." What you hear is them saying, "It was barely adequate," or, "They didn't do a bad job." Would you rush right out to that restaurant? We think not."[20] TARP has also found passives to be much more price-sensitive.

# Considerations in Selecting a Scale

Many questions arise in selecting a scale. Considerations include the nature of the construct being measured, type of scale, balanced versus nonbalanced scale, number of scale categories, and forced versus nonforced choice.

## The Nature of the Construct Being Measured

A basic check of the appropriateness of a scale is confirmation that it is drawn directly from the overall objective of the research study. The scope of the research objectives has a fundamental effect on the manner in which scales are used for survey measurement.

## Type of Scale

Most commercial researchers lean toward scales that can be administered via the Internet or on a mobile device to save interviewing expense. Ease of administration and development also are important considerations. For example, a rank-order scale can be quickly created, whereas developing a semantic differential (rating) scale is often a long and tedious process. The client's decision-making needs are always of paramount importance. Can the decision be made using ordinal data, or must the researcher provide interval information? Researchers also must consider the respondents, who usually prefer nominal and ordinal scales because of their simplicity. Ultimately, the choice of which type of scale to use will depend on the problem at hand and the questions that must be answered. It is not uncommon to find several types of scales in one research study. For example, an image study for a grocery chain might have a ranking scale of competing chains, a semantic differential to examine components of the chain's image, and a NPS scale.

Marketing researchers sometimes borrow scales directly from other studies or Internet sites. Many online survey sites have libraries of scales available. (See surveymonkey.com; researchrockstar.com; marketingscales.com; and questionpro.com.) There are also several scale handbooks that facilitate the appropriate measures and encourage researchers to standardize on previously developed and validated measures.[21] This makes the research stream more cumulative. Marketing researchers often find that these borrowed scales work just fine. Sometimes, however, they don't work very well.

A marketing researcher should fully understand the nature of the construct that was measured, the scope of the measurement, and the content and phrasing of the scale items for relevance to a new population before borrowing a scale. In sum, the caveat is, "Borrow with caution."[22]

## Balanced versus Nonbalanced Scale

**balanced scales**
Measurement scales that have the same number of positive and negative categories.

**nonbalanced scales**
Measurement scales that are weighted toward one end or the other of the scale.

A **balanced scale** has the same number of positive and negative categories; a **nonbalanced scale** is weighted toward one end or the other. If the researcher expects a wide range of opinions, then a balanced scale probably is in order. If past research or a preliminary study has determined that most opinions are positive, then using a scale with more positive gradients than negative ones will enable the researcher to ascertain the degree of positiveness toward the concept being researched. We have conducted a series of studies for the YMCA and know that its overall image is positive. Thus, we used the following categories to track the YMCA's image: (1) outstanding, (2) very good, (3) good, (4) fair, (5) poor.

## Number of Scale Categories

The number of categories to be included in a scale is another issue that must be resolved by the marketing researcher. If the number of categories is too small—for example, good, fair, poor—the scale is crude and lacks richness. A 3-category scale does not reveal the intensity of feeling that, say, a 10-category scale offers. Yet, a 10-category scale may go beyond a person's ability to accurately discriminate among categories. Research has shown that rating scales with either 5 or 7 points are the most reliable.[23]

With an even number of scale categories, there is no neutral point. Without a neutral point, respondents are forced to indicate some degree of positive or negative feelings on an issue. Persons who are truly neutral are not allowed to express their neutrality. On the other hand, some marketing researchers say that putting a neutral point on a scale gives the respondent an easy way out, allowing the person with no really strong opinion to avoid concentrating on his or her actual feelings. Of course, it is rather unusual for any individual to be highly emotional about a new flavor of salad dressing, a package design, or a test commercial for a pickup truck!

## Forced versus Nonforced Choice

As mentioned in the discussion of semantic differential scales, if a neutral category is included it typically will attract those who are neutral and those who lack adequate knowledge to answer the question. Some researchers have resolved this issue by adding a "Don't know" response as an additional category. For example, a semantic differential might be set up as follows:

| | | | | | | | | | |
|---|---|---|---|---|---|---|---|---|---|
| **Friendly** | 1 | 2 | 3 | 4 | 5 | 6 | 7 | **Unfriendly** | Don't Know |
| **Unexciting** | 1 | 2 | 3 | 4 | 5 | 6 | 7 | **Exciting** | Don't Know |

A "Don't know" option, however, can be an easy out for the lazy respondent.

If it has a neutral point, a scale without a "Don't know" option does not force a respondent to give a positive or negative opinion. A scale without a neutral point or a "Don't know" option forces even those persons with no information about an object to state an opinion. The argument for forced choice is that the respondent has to concentrate on his or her feelings. The arguments against forced choice are that inaccurate data are recorded and that some respondents may refuse to answer the question. A questionnaire that continues to require respondents to provide an opinion when, in fact, they lack the necessary information to do so can create ill will and result in early termination of the interview.

# Attitude Measures and Management Decision Making

So far in this chapter we have discussed the nature of attitudes, various types of measurement scales, and some considerations in creating a scale. We now turn our attention to making attitude research more valuable for management decision making.

In the wide spectrum of features of a product or brand, there are some that predispose consumers to action (that is, to preference for the product, to actual purchase, to making recommendations to friends, and so on) and others that do not. Attitudes that are most closely related to preference or to actual purchase decisions are said to be **determinant attitudes**. Other attitudes—no matter how favorable—are not determinant. Obviously, marketers need to know which features lead to attitudes that "determine" buying behavior, for these are the features around which marketing strategy must be built.[24]

With reference to determinant attitudes, Nelson Foote, manager of the consumer and public relations research program for General Electric, commented: "In the electrical appliance business, we have been impressed over and over by the way in which certain characteristics of products come to be taken for granted by consumers, especially those concerned with basic functional performance or with values like safety."

"If these values are missing in a product, the user is extremely offended," he said. "But if they are present, the maker or seller gets no special credit or preference because, quite logically, every other maker and seller is assumed to be offering equivalent values. In other words, the values that are salient in decision making are the values that are problematic— that are important, to be sure, but also those which differentiate one offering from another."

In proprietary studies evaluating such automobile attributes as power, comfort, economy, appearance, and safety, for example, consumers often rank safety as first in importance. However, these same consumers do not see various makes of cars as differing widely with respect to safety; therefore, safety is not a determinant feature in the actual purchase decision. This fact should rightly lead the company to concentrate on raising its performance in features other than safety. However, if safety is totally ignored, the brand may soon be perceived as being so unsafe that it loses some of its share of the market. At this point, safety would achieve determinance, a quality it would hold until concentration on safety by the "unsafe" company brought its product back into line with those of other companies.

To identify determinant attitudes and discern their relative degree of determinance, researchers must go beyond the scaling of respondents' attitudes. The study design must include a methodology for measuring determinance, for it will not naturally develop in the course of scaling. There are three major approaches to identifying determinant attitudes: (1) direct questioning, (2) indirect questioning, and (3) observation.

**determinant attitudes**
Those consumer attitudes most closely related to preferences or to actual purchase decisions.

## Direct Questioning

The most obvious way to approach determinant attitudes is to ask consumers directly what factors they consider important in a purchasing decision. Through direct questioning, respondents may be asked to explain their reasons for preferring one product or brand over another. Or they may be asked to rate their "ideal brand" for a given product in terms of several product attributes so that a model profile can be constructed (see the discussion of semantic differential scales).

This approach has the appeal of seeming to get directly to the issue of "Why do you buy?" Unfortunately, it rests on two very questionable assumptions: (1) respondents know why they buy or prefer one product over another, and (2) they will willingly explain what these reasons are.

Another direct questioning approach is "dual questioning," which involves asking two questions concerning each product attribute that might be determinant. Consumers are first asked what factors they consider important in a purchasing decision and then asked how they perceive these factors as differing among the various products or brands.

Exhibits 11.14 and 11.15 illustrate this approach through ratings of attitudes toward savings and loan associations, given during a survey of the general public in the Los Angeles area. (The various benefits or claims are ranked in descending order in each exhibit so that comparisons between the exhibits can be made more easily.) Notice that some items are high in rated importance but are not thought to differ much among the various savings and loan associations (for example, safety of money, interest rate earned). Thus, while safety of money is ranked first in importance, about half of all respondents feel there is no difference among savings and loan associations in terms of safety; therefore, safety of funds is probably not a determinant feature. Conversely, some items show big differences among the various associations but are considered to be of relatively little importance in determining the choice of a savings and loan (e.g., years in business, parking convenience).

On the other hand, "interest rate earned" has a very high importance ranking, and far fewer respondents feel there is no difference among the various associations relative to interest rate. Financial strength is rated somewhat lower in importance but is second highest in terms of the difference between associations. Therefore, financial strength appears to be relatively determinant of attitudes. Similarly, the researcher can proceed through the rest of the ratings to identify those attitudes that seem to influence the choice among various savings and loans most strongly and thus, presumably, are determinant attitudes.

## Indirect Questioning

Another approach to identifying determinant attitudes is indirect questioning, of which there are many forms. Recall from Chapter 5 that indirect questioning is any interviewing approach that does not directly ask respondents to indicate the reasons why they bought a product or service or which features or attributes are most important in determining choice.

## Observation

A third technique for identifying buying motives is observation research (see Chapter 8). For example, in one study, supermarket shoppers were observed, and detailed reports were recorded of their movements and statements while interacting with certain products on display in several different stores. The authors drew conclusions concerning who does the shopping, the influence of children and adult males on purchasing decisions, the effect of pricing, where brand choices seem to be made, and how much package study is involved. One of the findings of this study was that shoppers seemed to reject certain candy packaging in favor of other packaging. This finding suggests that package design might be a determinant feature, though by no means the only one.[25] (The disadvantages of observation research were discussed in Chapter 8.)

## Choosing a Method for Identifying Determinant Attitudes

Direct questioning, indirect questioning, and observation each have some limitations in identifying determinant attitudes. Therefore, the marketing researcher should use two or more of the techniques. Convergent findings will offer greater assurance that the attitudes identified are indeed determinant attitudes. Several statistical tools can aid the researcher in this process; they will be discussed in Chapters 15 to 18.

| EXHIBIT 11.14 | Importance Ratings of Savings and Loan Characteristics | | | |
|---|---|---|---|---|
| Benefit or Claim | Big Difference | Small Difference | No Difference | Don't Know |
| Years in business | 53% | 31% | 10% | 6% |
| Financial strength | 40 | 32 | 22 | 6 |
| Parking convenience | 37 | 35 | 22 | 6 |
| Safety of money | 36 | 15 | 47 | 2 |
| Management ability | 35 | 26 | 27 | 12 |
| Government insurance | 35 | 11 | 51 | 3 |
| Branch location convenience | 34 | 36 | 28 | 2 |
| Attitude of personnel | 34 | 28 | 33 | 5 |
| Interest rate earned | 33 | 30 | 35 | 2 |
| Speed/efficiency of service | 32 | 28 | 35 | 5 |
| Ease of withdrawing money | 29 | 18 | 48 | 5 |
| Compounding frequency | 28 | 36 | 31 | 5 |
| Time required to earn interest | 26 | 34 | 33 | 7 |
| Building/office attractiveness | 24 | 44 | 30 | 2 |
| Other services offered | 21 | 34 | 29 | 16 |
| Premiums offered | 15 | 36 | 38 | 11 |

*Source:* James Myers and Mark Alpert, "Determinant Buying Attitudes: Meaning and Measurement," *Marketing Management* (Summer 1997), p. 53. Reprinted by permission of the American Marketing Association.

| EXHIBIT 11.15 | Difference Ratings of Savings and Loan Characteristics |
|---|---|
| Benefit or Claim | Average Ratings* |
| Safety of money | 1.4 |
| Interest rate earned | 1.6 |
| Government insurance | 1.6 |
| Financial strength | 2.0 |
| Ease of withdrawing money | 2.0 |
| Management ability | 2.0 |
| Attitude of personnel | 2.1 |
| Speed/efficiency of service | 2.2 |
| Compounding frequency | 2.2 |
| Branch location convenience | 2.3 |
| Time required to earn interest | 2.3 |
| Parking convenience | 2.4 |
| Years in business | 2.5 |
| Other services offered | 3.1 |
| Building/office attractiveness | 3.4 |
| Premiums offered | 4.0 |

*1—extremely important; 2—very important; 3—fairly important; 4—slightly important, etc.

*Source:* James Myers and Mark Alpert, "Determinant Buying Attitudes: Meaning and Measurement," *Marketing Management* (Summer 1997), p. 52. Reprinted by permission of the American Marketing Association.

# SUMMARY

An attitude is an enduring organization of motivational, emotional, perceptual, and cognitive processes with respect to some aspect of a person's environment. In marketing research, it is a learned predisposition to respond in a consistently favorable or unfavorable manner toward an object or concept.

The term *scaling* refers to procedures for attempting to determine quantitative measures of subjective and sometimes abstract concepts. It is defined as a procedure for assigning numbers or other symbols to properties of an object in order to impart some numerical characteristics to the properties in question. Scales are either unidimensional or multidimensional. A unidimensional scale is designed to measure only one attribute of a concept, respondent, or object. Multidimensional scaling is based on the premise that a concept, respondent, or object might be better described using several dimensions.

One type of scale is called a graphic rating scale. Respondents are presented with a graphic continuum, typically anchored by two extremes. Itemized rating scales are similar to graphic rating scales except that respondents must select from a limited number of categories rather than placing a mark on a continuous scale. A rank-order scale is a comparative scale because respondents are asked to compare two or more items with each other. Paired comparison scales ask the respondent to pick one of two objects from a set, based on some stated criteria. Constant sum scales require the respondent to divide a given number of points, typically 100, among two or more attributes, based on their importance to him or her. Respondents must value each item relative to all other items. The number of points allocated to each alternative indicates the ranking assigned to it by the respondent.

The semantic differential was developed to measure the meaning of an object to a person. The construction of a semantic differential scale begins with determination of a concept to be rated, such as a brand image; then the researcher selects dichotomous pairs of words or phrases that could be used to describe the concept. Respondents next rate the concept on a scale, usually 1 to 7. The mean of the responses is computed for each pair of adjectives, and the means are plotted as a profile or image. In the Stapel scale, a single adjective is placed in the center of the scale. Typically, a Stapel scale is designed to simultaneously measure both the direction and the intensity of attitudes. The Likert scale is another scale that avoids the problem of developing pairs of dichotomous adjectives. The scale consists of a series of statements expressing either a favorable or an unfavorable attitude toward the concept under study. The respondent is asked to indicate the level of his or her agreement or disagreement with each statement by assigning it a numerical score. Scores are then totaled to measure the respondent's attitude.

The scale that is very important to marketing researchers is the purchase-intent scale. This scale is used to measure a respondent's intention to buy or not buy a product. The purchase-intent question usually asks a person to state whether he would definitely buy, probably buy, probably not buy, or definitely not buy the product under study. The purchase-intent scale has been found to be a good predictor of consumer choice of frequently purchased consumer durable goods.

Another very popular, yet controversial scale is called the net promoter score. It asks, "Would you recommend this company to a friend?" on a 0–10 scale. The score is the percent of promoters minus the percent of detractors. Researchers have found that promoters are likely to repurchase from the firm and to forgive them if they make a mistake. Disadvantages are that the score is too general and that passives are too often ignored but are likely to create negative word-of-mouth advertising.

Sometimes, it is necessary to do scale conversions in tracking studies when, over time, the number of points on a scale changes. Scale equivalence can be created when box scores are used as evaluation measures.

Several factors should be considered in selecting a particular scale for a study. The first is the type of scale to use: rating, ranking, sorting, or purchase-intent. Next, consideration must be given to the use of a balanced scale versus a nonbalanced scale. The number of categories also must be determined. A related factor is whether to use an odd or even number of categories. Finally, the researcher must consider whether to use forced or nonforced choice sets.

Attitudes that predispose consumers to action are called determinant attitudes. Marketing researchers need to identify which attitudes, of all those measured, are determinant. This can be accomplished by direct questioning, indirect questioning, and observation research.

# KEY TERMS

attitude **241**

scaling **243**

unidimensional scales **243**

multidimensional scales **243**

graphic rating scales **244**

itemized rating scales **245**

noncomparative scales  248

rank-order scales  249

comparative scales  249

paired comparison scales  250

constant sum scales  250

semantic differential scales  250

Stapel scales  252

Likert scales  253

purchase-intent scales  254

net promoter score  258

balanced scales  260

nonbalanced scales  260

determinant attitudes  261

## QUESTIONS FOR REVIEW & CRITICAL THINKING

1. Discuss some of the considerations in selecting a rating, ranking, or purchase-intent scale.

2. What are some of the arguments for and against having a neutral point on a scale?

3. Compare and contrast the semantic differential scale, Stapel scale, and Likert scale. Under what conditions would a researcher use each one?

4. The local department store in your hometown has been besieged by competition from the large national chains. What are some ways that target customers' attitudes toward the store could be changed?

5. Develop a Likert scale to evaluate the parks and recreation department in your city.

6. Develop a purchase-intent scale for students eating at the university's cafeteria. How might the reliability and validity of this scale be measured? Why do you think purchase-intent scales are so popular in commercial marketing research?

7. When might a researcher use a graphic rating scale rather than an itemized rating scale?

8. What is the difference between a rating and a ranking? Which is best for attitude measurement? Why?

9. Develop a rank-order scale for soda preferences of college students. What are the advantages and disadvantages of this type of scale?

10. What are determinant attitudes and why are they important?

11. Explain the concept of scale equivalence.

12. Why is the net promoter score popular yet controversial?

13. Discuss the relationship between customer satisfaction and profits.

14. Divide the class into teams. Each team should create five adjective pairs of phrases that could be used in a semantic differential to measure the image of your college or university. The instructor will then aggregate the suggestions into a single semantic differential. Each team member should then conduct five interviews with students not in the class. The data can then be analyzed later in the term when statistical analysis is covered.

*(Team Exercise)*

## WORKING THE NET

SBI (Strategic Business Insights) is a spinoff of the Stanford Research Institute. One of its most popular products is called VALS (Values and Life Style Survey). SBI uses VALS to segment the marketplace on the basis of personality traits that drive consumer behavior. VALS is used in all phases of the marketing mix. The survey categorizes consumers into one of eight personality types. GEOVALS applies the power of VALS to local marketing efforts by identifying the concentration of the VALS consumer group residing within a specific block group or zip code.

Go to *www.strategicbusinessinsights.com*, click on "Take the VALS survey."

1. Explain the theory behind the creation of VALS.

2. Do you agree with your VALS classification? Learn more by going to "The VALS Types" link.

3. What kind of scale was used in the survey? Could other types of scales have been used?

4. Explain how a marketer could use GEOVALS.

## REAL-LIFE RESEARCH • 11.1

# Improving the Long-Term Prognosis of Pharmaceutical Brands

Over the past several years, pharmaceutical companies have begun leveraging customer loyalty and engagement research to strengthen competitive positionings, improve customer experiences, and deliver more engaging marketing. For pharmaceutical companies, winning the loyalty game means achieving a greater share of physicians who will give their company and product the benefit of the doubt; while creating fewer disloyal physicians—those who will avoid their product whenever possible.

As Figure 1 shows, there is a wide range of manufacture recognition. (Each row represents the products made by one company.) The firms at the top have successfully promoted their overall brands and most physicians know which companies make their products. The bottom row shows, however, that there are still medications whose manufacturers are known by fewer physicians.

## Two-Pronged Effort

As Figure 2 shows, building deeper relationships with physicians requires a two-pronged effort: converting ambivalent physicians to loyal ones and fixing the problems that are making some physicians disloyal. Further analysis of other data reveals an important discovery: The two lists of priorities are not the same. The implication is that different strategies are required to build loyalty and to eliminate disloyalty.

Figure 3 shows the strongest four attributes in terms of their impact on loyalty—with typical results from this kind of analysis. We learn that physicians are more likely to be loyal if they believe that the company: (1) treats physicians fairly in their interaction; (2) provides a consistently high level of service; (3) delivers valuable services; and (4) understands the physician's practice.

The bar chart represents the percent of physicians who are delighted with each of three companies. Imagine for a minute that you are Company A. You are faced with Company B, which has convinced over half of physicians that it has achieved excellence in three of the four areas. Your company is fairly close in two of those areas. To create a brand position—a structure of brand pillars that can generate a

---

**Figure 1**

**Awareness of the Pharmaceutical Company That Markets Each Brand**

Promote company as well as brand: 57% aware

Do not promote company: 43% aware

◆ Company 1
■ Company 2
● Company 3
◆ Company 4
Company 5
● Company 6

30%          50%          70%
Know Which Company Makes The Product

---

**Figure 2**

**Building Loyalty— Converting Ambivalent to Loyal Prescribers and Converting Disloyal to Ambivalent**

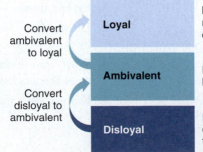

Convert ambivalent to loyal

Convert disloyal to ambivalent

**Loyal** — Loyal prescribers prescribe and recommend more because of key enhancers

**Ambivalent** — Prescribers who are not loyal because key enhancers are not being provided

**Disloyal** — Prescribers avoid prescribing or recommending when possible due to key dissatisfiers

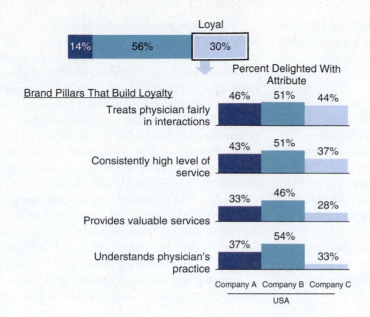

Figure 3

Understanding the
Causes of Loyalty

leadership position in the minds of your customers—you need to find at least one area that you can own. In this case, it will be "providing valuable services." To complete the bundle, close the gap on those areas where it is feasible, given the size of the gap and the resources that would be required.

## Strong Impact

Figure 4 shows the four strongest drivers of disloyalty. While one of the factors (understanding the physician's practice) operates in both directions—loyalty and disloyalty—the other three have a strong impact on disloyalty without having much of an impact on loyalty.

We learn that the strongest driver of physician disloyalty is the belief that a company does not look out for patients' interests. Another key factor is the perception that the company, its marketing channels and sales force are not focused on physicians' needs. And a third cause of disloyalty is simply not seeing value in the company's services.

Company B still dominates, with lower levels of dissatisfaction than competitors on most items. But here, Company A has an area of strength—few physicians believe that it does a poor job of looking out for patients' interests. So Company A's first job is to consciously maintain this advantage. Its other job is to eliminate weaknesses (e.g., learning why some physicians

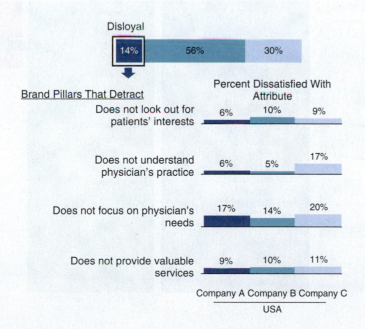

Figure 4

Understanding
the Causes of
Disloyalty

believe it does not focus on physicians' needs) and then take advantage of disloyalty to competitors by demonstrating that it will fulfill this basic need when competitors do not.

## Measuring and managing

In today's pharmaceutical industry, where it is no longer the rep and samples alone that build loyalty, the multichannel experience is what creates perceptions of value, strengthening brand pillars and, in turn, developing loyalty (Figure 5). Pharma companies now face the challenge of measuring and managing the entire multichannel experience. Interestingly, in different therapeutic areas, very different channels have assumed the mantle of supporting actors that supplement the leading role of the rep.

Drill-down analysis identifies channels that have the strongest impact on perceptions of a company—those channels that lead physicians to see the firm as delivering any or all of the key loyalty (and disloyalty) drivers.

Figure 6 shows a channel drill-down analysis for one critical brand pillar: "provides valuable services." It will not surprise anyone in pharma that the sales rep is the strongest pillar. Samples are also critical in those therapeutic areas where samples are a way that physicians can provide valuable support to patients. But many other factors now play a role, from video details to medical liaisons to patient assistance and the entire spectrum of resources that has created the multichannel customer experience. This shows how a multifaceted and intricate brand-building process can be simplified by prioritizing high-impact channels that strengthen a brand pillar and lead to loyalty.

To build the perception that the company provides exceptionally valuable services, marketers need to pay attention to the op-box ratings of each channel that leads to the perception of excellence in those brand pillars that support loyalty. Our results show that Company A will need to focus its attention on sampling and video details (similar to a sales rep visit but conducted on an audiovisual platform). This company's reps

Figure 5

**Which Channels and Resources Build Brand Pillars**

- **For each brand pillar, determine which channels and resources convince customers that your company and brand delivers on the brand promise**

- **Then deliver excellent performance on these channels and resources**

In-Person

Web

Email

Call Center

Direct Mail

V-Detail

2008 2009 2010 2011

**Brand Pillars That Drive Loyalty**

Treat physicians fairly

Providing valuable services

*Each company must determine the brand pillars that motivate loyalty among its customers and prospects*

**Loyalty & Engagement**

- Satisfaction, loyalty to client

- Emotional & rational attachment

**ROI**
- NRx
- TRx

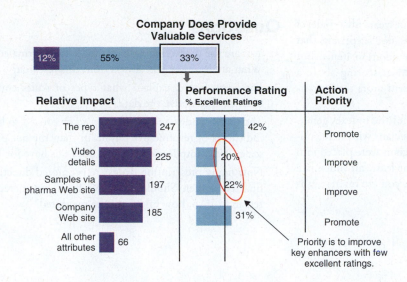

and website are providing an outstanding experience for many physicians. But the percent of physicians giving the highest ratings on video details and samples is sub-par.

## Metrics Vary Widely

As in other industries, the metrics used to measure loyalty in health care vary widely. Net promoter is the most famous metric. The critical question is how much benefit accrues from the additional complexity of an index, compared to the simplicity of a single question. The pharmaceutical industry is rich with data on actual customer behavior, including scripts written or revenue resulting from an individual physician's prescribing behavior. Figure 7 shows the results of an analysis in which physician opinion data are merged with actual prescription revenue per physician. Each pair of bars compares loyal physicians —however measured—with physicians who are not loyal.

In each instance, the loyal physicians (represented by the orange bars) are responsible for more revenue per physician than the ones who are not loyal (the gray bars). The key question is: How much more revenue? Comparing promoters to detractors achieves a 25 percent differential, which is to say that promoters prescribe 25 percent more than detractors. (Promoters selected 9 or 10 on the recommendation sale, whereas detractors selected 0 to 6). When we apply the same scale and calculations to a satisfaction question, it discriminates somewhat better, with extremely satisfied physicians (scores of 9 or 10) prescribing 35 percent more than not-very-satisfied ones (those who chose 0 to 6).

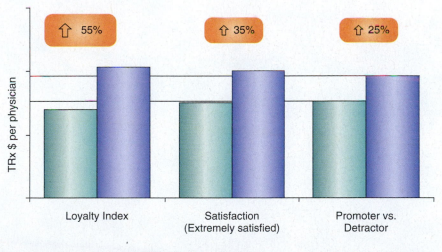

Results compare prescribing behavior among loyal vs. disloyal, as defined by each metric
Satisfaction (extremely satisfied vs. not satisfied) and Promoter vs. Detractor are based on the same calculation: 9-10 considered loyal and 0-6 considered disloyal on a 10 point scale. For the loyalty index, loyal customers score above a threshold and disloyal are below a threshold.

Opinion researchers have known for years that indexes outperform individual questions, so it is not surprising that the loyalty index outperforms the single-question items. But by how much? Loyal physicians (defined as scoring above a threshold on the index) prescribe 55 percent more than physicians who are not loyal.

It is important to note that all three of the indexes generated roughly the same percentage of physicians who were considered loyal. They differ on which physicians were placed into the loyal category. In pharmaceuticals, at least, an index is a more accurate measure of loyalty, if what you are interest in is more prescriptions and more revenue.[26]

## Questions

1. You are the marketing manager for a big pharma company. What are four key take aways from this research?

2. For every figure, explain what types of scales could have been used to derive the data.

3. The loyalty index and satisfaction score proved to be better indicators of revenue per physician than the net promoter scale. What implications, if any, does this have for NPS?

4. Now many prescription drugs are promoted directly to the final consumer. Should this have been considered in the research? If so, how might this be measured?

# Questionnaire Design

## LEARNING OBJECTIVES

1. Understand the role of the questionnaire in the data-collection process.

2. Become familiar with the criteria for a good questionnaire.

3. Learn the process for questionnaire design.

4. Understand how software, the Internet, and mobile devices are influencing questionnaire design.

5. Understand the impact of the questionnaire on data-collection costs.

At a high level, questionnaire or survey instrument design is both art and science. When dealing with questionnaire specifics, such as how to ask certain types of questions, there is plenty of science in the form of methodological research that has been conducted by academics and marketing research professionals. In this chapter, we will provide both overall guidance on questionnaire design and best practices for handling specific issues based on the findings of methodological research studies.

## Role of a Questionnaire

Survey research, by definition, relies on the use of a questionnaire. A **questionnaire** is a set of questions designed to generate the data necessary to accomplish the objectives of the research project; it is a formalized schedule for collecting information from respondents. You have most likely seen or even filled out a questionnaire recently. Creating a good questionnaire requires both hard work and imagination.

A questionnaire standardizes the wording and sequencing of questions and imposes uniformity on the data-gathering process. Every respondent sees or hears the same words;

**questionnaire**
Set of questions designed to generate the data necessary to accomplish the objectives of the research project; also called an *interview schedule* or *survey instrument*.

**Exhibit 12.1**

**Questionnaire's Pivotal Role in the Research Process**

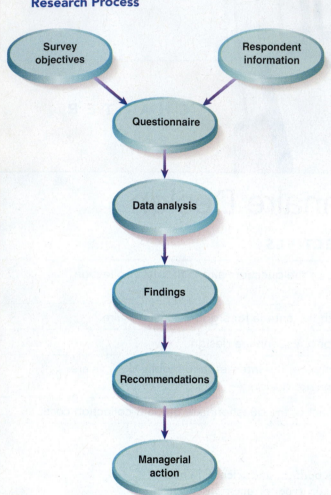

every interviewer asks identical questions. Without such standardization, interviewers could ask whatever they wanted, and researchers would be left wondering whether respondents' answers were a consequence of interviewer influence or interpretation; a valid basis for comparing respondents' answers would not exist. The jumbled mass of data would be unmanageable from a tabulation standpoint. In a very real sense, then, the questionnaire is a control device.

The questionnaire (sometimes referred to as an *interview schedule* or *survey instrument*) plays a critical role in the data-collection process. An elaborate sampling plan, well-trained interviewers, proper statistical analysis techniques, and good editing and coding are all for naught if the questionnaire is poorly designed. Improper design can lead to incomplete information, inaccurate data, and, of course, higher costs. The questionnaire is the tool that creates the basic product (respondent information).

Exhibit 12.1 illustrates the pivotal role of the questionnaire. It is positioned between survey objectives (drawn from the manager's problem) and respondent information. In this position, it must translate the objectives into specific questions to solicit the required information from respondents.

The questionnaire must translate the survey objectives into a form understandable to respondents and "pull" the requisite information from them. At the same time, it must recover their responses in a form that can be easily summarized and translated into findings and recommendations that will satisfy a manager's information requirements. Questionnaires also play a key role in determining survey costs, discussed in detail later in the chapter.

# Criteria for a Good Questionnaire

To design a good questionnaire, researchers must consider a number of issues: Does it provide the necessary decision-making information for management? Does it consider the respondent? Does it solicit responses in an unbiased manner? Does it meet editing, coding, and data analysis requirements?

## Does It Provide the Necessary Decision-Making Information?

A primary role of any questionnaire is to provide the information required for management decision making. Any questionnaire that fails to provide important insights for management or decision-making information should be discarded or revised. Therefore, the managers who will be using the data should always approve the questionnaire. By signing off on the questionnaire, the manager is saying, "Yes, this instrument will supply the data I need to reach a decision." If the manager does not sign off, then the marketing researcher must continue to revise the questionnaire.

## Does It Consider the Respondent?

The number of surveys taken annually has mushroomed as companies have an ever-increasing need for information about the marketplace. Poorly designed, confusing, and overly lengthy surveys have literally turned off thousands of potential respondents.

The researcher designing a questionnaire must consider not only the topic and the type of respondent, but the interviewing environment and questionnaire length as well. Respondents will answer somewhat longer questionnaires when they are interested in the topic and when they perceive that they will have little difficulty in responding to the questions. The design of surveys for mobile devices has created new challenges for questionnaire design as more people want to complete surveys by that means.[1] A promising new approach to engaging respondents in questionnaires is gamification, where we create some type of game out of the experience.[2]

A questionnaire should be designed explicitly for the intended respondents. For example, although a parent typically is the purchaser of cold cereals, the child, either directly or indirectly, often makes the decision as to which brand. Thus, a taste test questionnaire about cold cereals should be formulated in children's language. On the other hand, a survey about *purchasing* cold cereals should be worded in language suitable for adults. One of the most important tasks of questionnaire design is to fit the questions to prospective respondents. The questionnaire designer must strip away any marketing jargon and business terminology that could be misunderstood by the respondent. In fact, it is best to use simple, everyday language, as long as the result is not insulting or demeaning to the respondent.

## Does It Meet Editing and Coding Requirements?

Once the information has been gathered, it will have to be coded for data analysis. A questionnaire should be designed with these later processes in mind.

A questionnaire should always fit the respondent. Although parents typically purchase cereal, children often make the decision about what kind to buy. A taste test questionnaire for children should be worded in language they can understand.

**editing**

Going through each questionnaire to ensure that skip patterns were followed and the required questions filled out.

**skip pattern**

Sequence in which questions are asked, based on a respondent's answer.

**Editing** refers to going through each questionnaire to make certain that skip patterns were followed and required questions were filled out. In current-day marketing research, editing only applies to mail and other paper copy surveys. Issues around questionnaire logic are dealt with in the programming for all computer- and mobile device-administered surveys.

The **skip pattern** is the sequence in which questions are asked, based on a respondent's answer. Exhibit 12.2 shows a clearly defined skip pattern from question 4a to question 5a for persons who answer no to question 4a.

Most marketing research data analysis software automatically catches coding errors. Computer-aided telephone interviewing (CATI) and Internet software programs take care of skip patterns automatically. Flexibility is programmed into a questionnaire in two ways:

- Skip patterns (branching) take the respondent to different sets of questions based on the answers given to prior questions. This could be a "simple skip," in which questions are skipped because they would not be relevant to the respondent, or could be "dynamic branching," in which one of many possible sets of questions is presented to the participant depending on the way that he or she responded to a question.

- Piping integrates responses from a question into later questions. A participant could be asked to type an answer to an open-ended question (e.g., year, make, and model of the car they drive most often), and the text of that answer could be incorporated into the wording of the next question (e.g., "how would you rate your 2010 Toyota Corolla overall?").

The issue of coding responses to open-ended questions applies to all types of surveys and is addressed in detail in Chapter 15.

In summary, a questionnaire serves many masters. First, it must accommodate all the research objectives in sufficient depth and breadth to satisfy the information requirements of the manager. Next, it must "speak" to the respondent in understandable language and at the appropriate intellectual level. Furthermore, it must be convenient for the interviewer to administer or the respondent to complete, and it must allow the interviewer to quickly record respondent answers or the respondent to record their answers. At the same time, the questionnaire must be easy to edit and check for completeness. It also should facilitate coding.

Tips for designing questionnaires to improve response rates are covered in the following Practicing Market Research feature.

**Exhibit 12.2**

**Example of a Questionnaire Skip Pattern**

**4a.** Do you usually use a hair conditioner on your child's hair?

    (1) (  ) No (SKIP to 5a)        (2) (  ) Yes (ASK Q. 4b)

**4b.** Is that a conditioner that you pour on or a conditioner that you spray on?

    (1) (  ) Cream rinse that you pour on

    (2) (  ) Cream rinse that you spray on

**4c.** About how often do you use a hair conditioner on your child's hair? Would you say less than once a week, once a week, or more than once a week?

    (1) (  ) Less than once a week

    (2) (  ) Once a week

    (3) (  ) More than once a week

**5a.** Thinking of the texture of your child's hair, is it. . . . (READ LIST)

    (1) (  ) Fine      (2) (  ) Coarse      (3) (  ) Regular

**5b.** What is the length of your child's hair? (READ LIST)

    (1) (  ) Long      (2) (  ) Medium      (3) (  ) Short

# Does It Solicit Information In An Unbiased Manner: Questionnaire Design Process

Designing a questionnaire involves a series of logical steps, as shown in Exhibit 12.3. The steps may vary slightly when performed by different researchers, but all researchers tend to follow the same general sequence. Committees and lines of authority can complicate the process, so it is wise to clear each step with the individual who has the ultimate authority for the project. This is particularly true for the first step: determining survey objectives, resources, and constraints. Many work hours have been wasted because a researcher developed a questionnaire to answer one type of question and the "real" decision maker wanted something entirely different. It also should be noted that the design process itself—specifically, question wording and format—can raise additional issues or unanswered questions. This, in turn, can send the researcher back to step one for a clearer description of the information sought.

## Step One: Determine Survey Objectives, Resources, and Constraints

The research process often begins when a manager needs decision-making information that is not available internally or from secondary sources. At this point, the manager most likely approaches the research department with her need. How this process works is covered in the discussion of uses of marketing research in Chapter 2.

**Exhibit 12.3**

**Questionnaire Design Process**

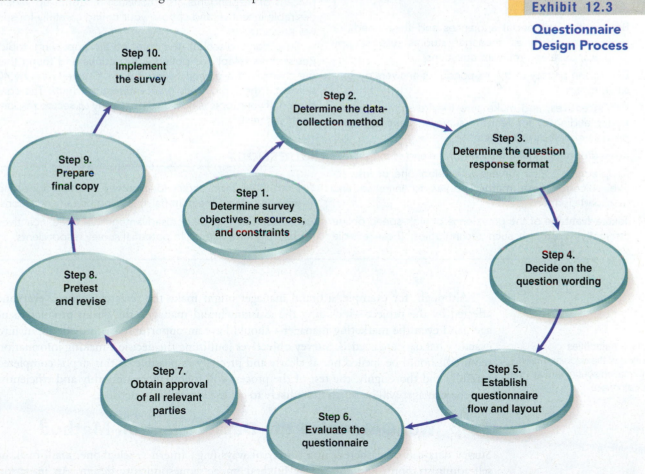

# PRACTICING MARKETING RESEARCH

## Tips for Maximizing User Response in Online Surveys

No other methodology now rivals the Internet for market research. You can target almost any kind of respondent group, and they can answer thoughtfully and thoroughly at their leisure. Here are 10 valuable tips for online survey development:

1. Make sure you would enjoy taking the survey. Put your screening and data management questions first. Use drop-down lists sparingly. Keep your directions clear. Go light on the number of product attributes, no more than 20. Give them an out, such as a "don't know" or "I prefer to not answer" option.

2. Don't forget the respondents are doing you a favor; find ways to make the experience enjoyable for them.

3. Make the attribute ratings easy on the viewer's eyes.

4. Keep the surveys as short as possible; long spells boredom or fatigue.

5. Be sensitive to special audiences and their needs or preferences, such as teenager studies (use snappy graphics; pose age-relevant questions).

6. Ensure the privacy of the respondent's answers on sensitive topics.

7. Use incentives, and make sure they're suitable to the target audience; for lengthy surveys, make sure you provide generous incentives.

8. Keep dropout trigger questions for the end of the survey.

9. Supplement e-mail surveys with telephone or interactive voice-response methodologies to increase and hold participation.

10. Take advantage of the prevalence of high-speed online interactivity through such technologies; these enable market researchers to sample consumer response to commercials or simulated shopping environments.[3]

What factors influence a person's decision to answer an online survey in the first place? According to Janet Westergaard, president of Esearch.com in Rolling Hills, California, here they are in order: (1) incentive offered, 66 percent; (2) available time when survey is presented, 56 percent; (3) survey topic, 37 percent; and (4) survey length, 30 percent.

Westergaard noted gender differences, too. Males are more attracted to incentives, whereas women value their available time higher; the time factor is most critical for respondents aged 18 to 30 (72 percent said so) compared to people 311 years old (50 percent said so). Men respond more strongly to the topic and survey length (46 percent) compared to women (31 percent). Overall, both men and women (47 percent) said incentive was the biggest factor, followed by whether they had the time to spare (27 percent). The actual topic was a determining factor to only 12.6 percent of respondents. The conclusion: Come up with a desirable incentive and choose your timing carefully for survey presentation.[4]

Still, don't discount the lure of an appealing topic. Researchers telephone-polled 2,300 adults and found that the chances of a person taking part in a survey rises by 40 percent if the topic holds great interest for them. The conclusion: If your topic is hot, divulge it early to secure respondents' interest.[5]

## Questions

1. Draft three "hot" topics for a survey and find appealing ways to present the material in leading or early questions.

2. Consider the merits, or disadvantages, of three incentives that might be offered to potential survey respondents.

---

Although, for example, a brand manager might make the research request, everyone affected by the project—including the assistant brand manager, the group product manager, and even the marketing manager—should have an opportunity to provide input into exactly what data are needed. **Survey objectives** (outlining the decision-making information required) should be spelled out as clearly and precisely as possible. If this step is completed carefully and thoroughly, the rest of the process will follow more smoothly and efficiently, and the manager will be much more likely to get the information needed.

**survey objectives**
Outline of the decision-making information sought through the questionnaire.

## Step Two: Determine the Data-Collection Method

Survey data can be gathered, in a variety of ways (e.g., Internet, telephone, mail, mall, or self-administration), and the survey method impacts questionnaire design. An in-person interview in a mall will have constraints (such as a time limitation) not encountered with an Internet questionnaire. A self-administered questionnaire, in a doctor's office for example, must be explicit and is usually rather short with few skip patterns; because no interviewer will be present to guide the respondent through the survey. A telephone interview may require a rich and extensive verbal description of a concept to make certain the respondent understands the idea being discussed. Obviously, a taste test cannot be conducted by telephone or Internet, at least not easily. In an Internet survey, respondents can be shown pictures or videos to demonstrate a concept. The kind of information you need to obtain to fulfill the research objectives dictates the options you have to collect the data.

The forms of data collection we rely on have always evolved as society and technology have changed over time. Up until the 1950s, door-to-door interviewing was the primary mode of survey data collection, with the respondents interviewed in their home. This was followed by heavy reliance on telephone interviewing, and the emergence of mall-intercept interviewing for those surveys requiring face-to-face contact, getting people to taste products, evaluate advertising, etc. Mail surveys have always been used and continue play a significant role to this day as indicated in the Practicing Marketing Research box below.

In the 1990s, online interviewing emerged, with the respondent using a desktop or laptop computer. Later, we had to contend with the fact that a growing number of households had only a wireless phone or phones—almost 40 percent in 2012. To be representative, telephone samples should include a mix of wireless numbers given that the wireless-only households are demographically and psychographically different from households that have wireless phones. In addition, mobile devices have begun to play a major and growing role in survey data collection with an estimates 25 to 30 percent of online surveys completed using these devices.[7] The impact of these devices on questionnaire design is discussed later in this chapter. The Practicing Marketing Research box on page 279 highlights the growing importance of online surveys and how they need to be designed differently.

# PRACTICING MARKETING RESEARCH

## An Iowa City Finds Mail Survey Fits Its Needs[6]

A course in statistical methods was part of my statistics major program at Iowa State College. Mail surveys were covered in the course—for about six seconds. "We won't bother with that since you can't get a decent return percentage," the professor said. Imagine my surprise when I went to work for Meredith Publishing a few years later only to learn how wrong the professor was.

We did mail surveys with subscribers of *Better Homes & Gardens* and *Successful Farming* and achieved response rates of 80 to 85 percent. The last one I did for *Successful Farming* several years later got 75 percent. These days, employing all the tricks, I can still get 50 percent. One approach is the use of an incentive—typically a dollar bill—with the survey letter. The dollar adds little weight to the postage but carries a lot of weight toward the success of the survey. It's too small for people to consider it payment but it gets their attention so they will read the cover letter—and that's paramount because the magic is in the letter.

Recently, I was hired to do some research by the city of North Liberty, Iowa, and my first recommendation was to do a mail survey. North Liberty is just north of Iowa City and is one of the fastest-growing municipalities in the state. The city had some specific needs regarding demand for public transit and had tried to do its own surveying previously, without success.

Dean Wheatley, city planner for North Liberty, explains the purpose of the project: "We needed a good unbiased understanding of how residents feel about specific existing and potential city services. In these times of lean budgets and ever-increasing demands, it is important to focus attention where it is most needed and not to try to be the provider of everything every person or group is interested in. For this survey, we were expecting to provide assistance to a transit committee and to a parks and recreation committee by helping to narrow and define public interests. We also asked questions to help staff and the city council understand the level of satisfaction with existing and potential services and projects."

## On a volunteer basis

An earlier North Liberty survey covered only public transit, and people were invited to complete it on a volunteer basis through various avenues—the city's website; by picking them up at city hall; and by copying it out of the local paper. As you might expect, only people with an interest in public transit bothered to take the survey—104 out of a population of about 10,000.

I knew that a mail survey could certainly do better than that, but doing mail surveys for municipalities precludes the use of the dollar bill. Taxpayers don't look favorably upon their elected representatives and city officials wasting tax dollars on that kind of foolishness. It kind of starts the survey cooperation process off on the wrong foot. So in order to increase response rates, my advice was to field a survey covering a range of subject matter, so there would be something of interest to everyone.

What response can you expect from citizens when their leaders want their opinion? My experience has been that 35 to 40 percent is the best you can achieve, assuming ideal conditions—good questions people are glad you asked; citizen respect (or strong disrespect) for leaders; willingness by the leaders to pay for the mail survey tricks. Make no mistake, cheaper is not the reason to recommend mail surveys. Proper mail techniques are more costly than people expect, and doing things the right way can put mail survey expenditures on par with those of telephone surveys.

But mail bests telephone in its ability to cover lists of items to be rated. While telephone interviews can turn into drudgery having to read lists and reread rating scales, everything is clearly laid out in front of the respondent in a mail questionnaire. Another plus for mail surveys is that everyone has an address. This gives me confidence that I'm dealing with random sampling. I'm not as confident as time goes by with telephone interviewing. Not everyone has a landline anymore, and private numbers have always been a problem, although less so in my part of the country. A large and increasing percentage of households, especially younger people, only have a cell phone.

To obtain a random sample, it is necessary to employ hybrid methods that combine landline and cell phone samples. Although no marketing research call is heartily welcomed these days, this kind of call coming to a cell phone is actively resented, according to anecdotal evidence. This certainly calls into question the quality of what you can manage to obtain in the interview. Web-based surveys, although quick and inexpensive, are definitely out for a citizen survey such as this one. Too many people have no access to the Internet, and it precludes random sampling.

I like web surveys a lot when I have a list that properly represents a universe, such as an employee roster, but that's definitely not the case for municipal citizen surveys. Trying to develop a hybrid method for these kinds of surveys is definitely overkill, adding unnecessary complication and cost to what can be a very straightforward solution.

## Built-in biases

Every method has built-in biases. Web and cell phone surveys skew toward younger people. Mail survey response is more likely to be from older people, the more thoughtful, and those who tend to be more patient. Interestingly, these characteristics tend to describe those with a higher likelihood of voting. It follows, then, that mail surveys will tend to do a better job of measuring the attitudes and predicting likely behaviors of voters. Like it or not, it's important to know what voters think. People with a problem and those who are otherwise negative will always be much more vocal than those who are happy. It's pretty easy to get knocked off balance by all the noise from these folks and wonder whether their views are valid and merit some sort of action. On the other hand, inaction on an issue a lot of folks are worked up on has its risks as well. Make no mistake; we're talking about getting reelected here.

I'm not in love with mail surveys, in spite of how it may seem. As a consultant who only charges for his time, I really don't care what method I recommend, only that it is best for the job at hand. Mail surveys have some downsides and are not good for every situation. They are unsuitable for measuring awareness, for example, since there's no way to prevent people from looking things up so they can appear to be "smart" on the survey. The recipient of the survey is also able to inspect the entire questionnaire before deciding to answer it or not. They also take longer to execute than telephone or web surveys.

## Existing alternatives

In the best interest of the client, I usually look for existing alternatives that might meet the client's needs, and I did so in this case. There are at least two firms that I am aware of that specialize in these kinds of surveys for municipalities. I've seen their work, and they do an exceptional job. They pretty much pull out all the stops from a technical standpoint. Their reports are clearly written and well-presented, with many excellent and useful features. They definitely cover the waterfront of concerns for any municipality, and they each have a long list of clients. Their questions are largely standardized, so they are able to show trends through time for yearly or every-other-year waves of interviewing and can show a municipality's scores versus all other cities or versus cities of their size. This is a highly useful feature. I would not hesitate to recommend either to a client whose need fit their services.

However, their one drawback is affordability. Large municipalities obviously feel they can afford the services, based on the firms' client lists. While a few smaller cities and towns are customers, most would find it too expensive. North Liberty certainly fell in that category, so I designed a streamlined approach very similar to what the other firms do, as it turns out, but much more affordable. I charged North Liberty $2,600 for planning, several meetings, material development, advice on methodology, data entry, tabulation, a written report, and a presentation. The town took care of printing, assembly, and postage, and paid for those themselves. Take away the need for meetings and travel and handle everything by e-mail, and my charge drops to $2,000.

The specialty firms employ mail surveys, too, but I did a simple random sample of households, while they use stratified random samples. They make fairly extensive efforts to do follow-ups; I only did the original mailing with no follow-ups. I can't disagree with what they do, but the results bear out my streamlining of the process. In the North Liberty project, we mailed out to a net of 1,005 after undeliverables. We received responses from 334 households at the cutoff, a 33.2 percent return, with no incentives used.

### Worked well

For North Liberty, the mail survey worked well, Wheatley says. "Using the survey results documentation we are able to honestly and factually report and act on the priorities among the survey questions posed. It helps us respond to anecdotal accounts and claims by enabling us to cite statistically valid resident interests."

As he points out, when municipalities endeavor to learn their citizens' opinions, it is critical that this learning is achieved through scientific, projectable surveying. The survey must settle the issues and not leave room for continued argument. I love it when people say, "Well, it wasn't a scientific survey." Then why did you bother? Nothing you could count on was learned. The object is not to use the latest trendy method; it is to learn truth you can trust.

Further, working with a professional researcher gets a third party involved, so that it's not city officials who get attacked by those who don't like the results. A professional researcher can provide a cogent and understandable defense of the findings.

## Questions

1. What were the advantages of mail surveys in the applications discussed in the Practicing Marketing Research feature? Would you always have these advantages in any mail survey application?

2. What are the biases in mail surveys discussed in this application?

3. Are mail surveys always the best option? Why/why not?

# PRACTICING MARKETING RESEARCH

## Tips for Effective Mobile Surveying[8]

The proliferation of smart, web-ready mobile devices continues unabated, and for many consumers these machines are replacing their desktop and laptop computers, which, until recently, were the primary means to collect online survey data. In 2011 the percentage of surveys being taken on mobile devices was less than 2 percent. However, the United States and other nations have experienced a major shift to a more mobile-centric culture since then.

With this prolific adoption of mobile devices, CatalystMR is now seeing 25 to 30 percent of its online surveys being completed on mobile devices versus desktop and laptop computers. Coupled with the accelerated use of mobile devices to access e-mail, with 36 percent of all e-mails in the United States being opened on mobile devices (Knotice, Sept. 2012)[9], a mobile data collection strategy must be at the forefront of consideration when conducting online research.

For data collection within the United States, consideration for feature phones (or nonsmart web-enabled devices) is not crucial because of dropping market share and consumer behavior differences. In the United States, those with nonsmart Internet-accessible phones don't tend to surf the web or make purchases on their feature phones as compared to modern smartphones.

Because international smartphone adoption over feature phones has not been as rapid in many parts of the world due to cultural (Internet-accessible feature phones are popular) and economic differences, surveys being conducted abroad require special consideration and programming to allow feature phones to take online mobile surveys.

In other words, it's more important to make the survey accessible to a feature phone in other parts of the world compared to North America and Europe. While there is a continued trend toward smartphone adoption internationally, in regions of the world such as Asia-Pacific and Latin America for example, the ownership and usage including Internet surfing and online purchasing of feature phones exceed that of smartphones and tablets. In these regions and most parts of the world with the exception of Europe and North America, consumers surf the Internet on full-featured phones.

Mobile devices are continuing to evolve rapidly, as is the technology available for conducting surveys on these devices and the behavior of those using them. As a result, any overview of best practices is a constantly moving target. Nevertheless, assembling a list of best practices is still a worthwhile endeavor.

## Number of questions and survey length

A couple of years ago, CatalystMR was advising its clients that five to seven minutes was a pretty firm ceiling for mobile survey length and should not be exceeded. However, tolerance of longer surveys is increasing as devices continue to improve and respondents use these devices more frequently. In fact, for many people, mobile is a preferred platform to communicate rather than a desktop. Additionally, respondents recognize and accept that mobile devices have less screen space to work with than desktop and laptop computers. Our current recommendation for top-end survey length on mobile devices is roughly the same as our recommendation for desktop-only surveys: 20 minutes or less, with an ideal of 10 to 15 minutes or less for mobile devices, especially smartphones.

With survey lengths exceeding 20 minutes, we see a drop-off of respondents completing the survey, regardless of device type. With that said, always remember: The shorter the better. You need to take into consideration the respondent's relationship with the brand, the customer's expectations, the marketing effect of the survey, the incentive amount, panel versus non panel, and other factors that might lead you to conduct a very brief survey, perhaps only 5 to 15 simple questions.

Respondents using tablets are more tolerant of longer surveys than those taking surveys on smartphones, primarily due to the need to scroll more on a smaller screen and general fatigue. Those taking a survey on a feature phone are less tolerant than smartphone users for similar reasons. For the purposes of feature-phone users, these respondents should be given a scaled-down version of the survey to lessen respondent fatigue and to mitigate the dropout rate.

With all this in mind, it should still be expected that a mobile survey will experience a higher dropout or abandonment rate than that of a desktop survey. However, survey results trend the same whether online or via mobile. With few exceptions, such as surveys that require a large viewing screen (i.e., conjoint studies, large or complex grid presentations, etc.), we have found that survey results are not affected by the platform used to take the survey.

## When to scale down the questions asked in mobile vs. desktop

If your survey exceeds 15 minutes, consider limiting the number of questions asked on mobile devices. To avoid respondent fatigue and higher-than-necessary dropout rates on these devices, think about asking up to 10 minutes of questions as the core of your research. For example, if you have a battery of questions asking respondents to rate their satisfaction on 15 items, consider asking smartphone users about the most important 10 items. Or perhaps rotate blocks of attributes so that all attributes are rated by a subset of respondents.

## Survey design: question types, setup, and logic

*Scale questions* should be limited to five points, or seven points at most. Ten-point scale questions take up too much screen real estate and therefore require scrolling left/right or pinching a mobile screen's viewable area so small that the screen presentation causes the question to be difficult to manage.

Try to limit the amount of text on each attribute. Overly wordy attribute text takes up more valuable screen real estate and increases the need for scrolling.

*Ranking questions* are fully functional on smartphones and tablet devices. Once again, just keep in mind that overly wordy text or too many items to rank can make the page too complex visually for smaller screen sizes. On smartphones, always consider that longer questions will require vertical scrolling, which makes those questions more difficult to navigate.

*Other question types* including numeric, radio (single-response), checkbox (multiple response), text, and pull-down work perfectly on smartphones and tablets.

To minimize scrolling, the best practice is to program *one question per screen*.

*Survey logic:* Any survey logic available in an online survey is similarly available in a mobile survey.

*One survey engine—platform-agnostic:* The same survey that runs on a desktop runs on a mobile web-enabled mobile device because the survey engine is the same. In our firm's case, because the survey engine is the same and CatalystMR tracks user agent data such as device type, user agent data can drive survey logic. This means that you have the ability to customize survey logic based on the device accessing the survey.

## Device information

Our survey system, for example, captures many data points automatically from the user's device. We can report this data back in an easily understood format.

## Survey introduction (including pop-up invitations)

Special consideration needs to be paid to the introduction and invitation text for your survey. Consider the following to improve the traffic to your survey:

- Make the invitation engaging.
- Use graphically rich e-mail invitations because they produce better results and are not automatically screened out by most spam filters today.
- Keep the invitation text short, clear, and compelling. The invitation will only have the viewer's attention for a few seconds, so make the words you use count.
- If the survey invitations are only being sent to a specified group, let the respondent know this. This can convey the idea that the respondent has a special opportunity to give feedback.

## Questions

1. What are the major constraints associated with the use of mobile devices to complete surveys?

2. What are the major considerations regarding number of questions in survey length when designing surveys for mobile devices?

3. When considering administration of surveys on mobile devices, what are the considerations regarding question types, set up and logic?

## Step Three: Determine the Question Response Format

Once the data-collection method has been determined, decisions must be made regarding the types of questions to be used in the survey. Three major types of questions are used in marketing research: open-ended, closed-ended, and scaled-response questions.

**Open-Ended Questions**    **Open-ended questions** are those to which the respondent replies in her or his own words. In other words, the researcher does not limit the response choices.

Open-ended questions offer several advantages to the researcher. They enable respondents to give their general reactions to questions like the following:

1. What advantages, if any, do you think ordering from an e-retailer company offers compared with buying from local retail outlets? (*Probe:* What else?)

2. Why do you have one or more of your rugs or carpets professionally cleaned rather than cleaning them yourself or having someone else in the household clean them?

3. What do you think is most in need of improvement here at the airport?

4. What is there about the color of _____ [product] that makes you like it the best? (*Probe:* What color is that?)

5. Why do you say that brand [the one you use most often] is better?

Each of the preceding questions was taken from a different nationwide survey covering five products and services. Note that open-ended questions 2 and 4 are part of a skip pattern. Before being asked question 2, the respondent has already indicated that he or she uses a professional carpet cleaning service and does not depend on members of the household.

Similarly, open-ended questions may suggest additional alternatives not listed in a closed-ended response format. For example, a previously unrecognized advantage of using an e-retail company might be uncovered in responses to question 1. A closed-ended question on the same subject would not have this advantage.

One manufacturer for which the authors consult always ends product placement questionnaires with the following: "Is there anything else that you would like to tell us about the product that you have tried during the past three weeks?" This probe seeks any final tidbit of information that might provide additional insight for the researcher.

Alexa Smith, president of Research Department in New York City, suggests several open-ended questions that can be asked for greater insights in the Practicing Marketing Research box on page 283.

**open-ended questions**
Questions to which the respondent replies in her or his own words.

Open-ended questions are not without their problems. Editing and coding can consume great amounts of time and money if done manually. Editing open-ended responses requires collapsing the many response alternatives into some reasonable number. If too many categories are used, data patterns and response frequencies may be difficult to interpret. Even if a proper number of categories is used, editors may still have to interpret what the interviewer has recorded and force the data into a category. If the categories are too broad, the data may be too general and important meaning may be lost.

**Probing** Often, open-ended questions require probing. Probing means that an interviewer encourages the respondent to elaborate or continue the discussion.[10] Powerful probes will advance a discussion quickly away from top-of-mind responses and seat-of-the-pants answers—and access deeper information, allowing insight into the baseline thinking that drives behavior.

Probes fall into three distinct areas: proactive, reactive, and spontaneous. The last one is also called a "natural probe," since it just pops up instantly in the mind of a researcher who knows that deeper insights need to be expressed. For example, a respondent says: "I get upset when the line is too long at checkout." A natural probe has to be: "What upsets you?"

By contrast, a proactive probe is one that can be planned ahead of time, and it might look like the following:

The original question might be: "What were some key factors of importance to you when buying your last car?" And the proactive probe might be: "In reviewing those key factors in your mind, which one stands out as critical to buying decisions?" A proactive probing series can be planned ahead of time to lead the discussion to fertile areas for discussion, aimed at reaching the study purpose. And from time to time, a family of proactive probes might have a visitor from the "natural" probe family as well.

Reactive probes are almost like "natural probes," except that they are more "knee jerk" in character. The most common ones are: "What makes you say that?" Or: "What is the basis for that belief on your part?" Those kinds of probes question the baseline thinking of a respondent, rather than relying on a report of behavior. A few examples of probes are as follows.

If a food study on tacos asked, "What, if anything besides meat, do you normally add to a taco you have prepared at home?", coding categories would need to be determined to categorize answers to this open-ended question.

Thomas Firak Photography /Getty Images

**Request for elaboration:** "Tell me more about that." Give me an example of . . . ."

**Request for word association:** "What do you mean by . . . .? "What does the term _____ mean to you?"

**Request for clarification:** "How does that differ from. . . .?" "In what circumstances do you. . . .?"

**Request for comparison:** "How is _____ similar to _____?" "Which costs more, X or Y?"

**Request for classification:** "Where does _____ fit?" "What else is in the category of _____?" [11]

# PRACTICING MARKETING RESEARCH

## Useful Open-Ended Questions [12]

Here are some open-ended questions, often overlooked, that lead to greater insight:

- **What would it take to get you to use or buy a product or service?** Such a question is useful at the end of a focus group or in-depth interview. At minimum, it can provide a handy summation of the findings that have gone before. It can also serve as a forum for problems and issues that have not yet surfaced. In a study about children's magazines developed in Europe, for example, the respondents said the text would need to be simplified and the illustrations improved for the magazines to be acceptable for children in the United States.

- **What is the best thing about the product, service, or promotion?** This question yields far more than the typical "What do you like about it?" question and can be useful as an addition to the traditional "likes" question. A food company had developed a frozen breakfast item that did not seem to be winning any awards for quality and taste. But asking what respondents liked about the food item yielded little because respondents were dissatisfied with the product. By asking what the *best* thing about it was, however, the company found it was "the idea." Many of the participants in the study were working mothers and longed for a quick and convenient hot breakfast item they could provide for their families. Based on answers to a question on simple likes, the whole idea might have been thrown out, but based on "the best thing," the client knew the company was on to something and that the product just needed taste and quality improvements.

- **What is the worst thing about the product, service, or promotion?** The corollary to "the best thing," this question also often yields surprising answers. Respondents

who talked about going to the dentist responded rationally to what they disliked, including pain, expense, and insecurity about their personal experience. When asked, "What is the worst thing that can happen when you go to the dentist?" many said, "You could die!" Dying in the dentist's chair is a rare occurrence, but the response taught the study's sponsor something about the level of fear people were dealing with.

- **Main idea registration.** At the least, the researcher needs to know if respondents have the correct understanding of an idea. Asking for main idea registration is often a good shortcut to identifying communications problems with a concept that would otherwise impede acceptance of an idea. Sometimes the executional elements of a concept can provide a sticking point that can be distracting. A quick fix may be either to verbally correct the misunderstanding or to rewrite the concepts in between focus groups or interviews. If respondents do not understand the intended message, they often find it difficult to answer a question about whether anything is confusing or hard to understand.

- **How would friends and close associates relate to this idea?** Sometimes an idea or a concept can be so blatant that it causes a consumer backlash. This can happen when a company tries to create an upscale, status-conscious image for its product or service. In this case, consumers will indicate something to the effect that they would never be so snobbish as to relate to the idea. When this happens, the merit of the strategy can become apparent if the question is moved into the third person, such as "Do you know friends and associates who would relate to this idea?" If respondents say yes, then the researcher can determine what friends and associates would like about the idea. In telling how their friends and associates would relate to the idea, consumers are really talking about themselves in a more socially sanctioned way. A surprising number of clients are not aware of this and tend to pass the moderator admonishing notes about just wanting to know what respondents themselves think.

■ **What do you do just before you use a product or service?** Elderly women were asked this question in the context of reading their favorite magazine and how

special the experience was when they explained that they take their shoes off, put on their favorite slippers, change into comfortable clothes, and go off by themselves to read the magazine. Reading the magazine was something they did entirely for themselves, and the publisher learned that the magazine was truly a valued companion to these women.

Precoding open-ended questions can partially overcome these problems. Assume that this question was to be asked in a food study: "What, if anything, do you normally add to a taco that you have prepared at home, besides meat?" Coding categories for this open-ended question might be as follows:

| Response | Code |
| --- | --- |
| Avocado | 1 |
| Cheese (Monterey Jack, cheddar) | 2 |
| Guacamole | 3 |
| Lettuce | 4 |
| Mexican hot sauce | 5 |
| Olives (black or green) | 6 |
| Onions (red or white) | 7 |
| Peppers (red or green) | 8 |
| Pimento | 9 |
| Sour cream | 0 |
| Other | X |

These answers would be listed on the questionnaire, and a space would be provided to write in any nonconforming reply in the "Other" category. In a telephone interview, the question would still qualify as open-ended because the respondents would not see the categories and the interviewer would be instructed not to divulge them. Precoding necessitates that the researcher have sufficient familiarity with previous studies of a similar nature to anticipate respondents' answers. Otherwise, a pretest with a fairly large sample is needed.

A basic problem with open-ended questions lies in the interpretation-processing area. A two-phase judgment must be made. First, the researcher must decide on an appropriate set of categories, and then each response must be evaluated to determine into which category it falls.

A final difficulty with open-ended questions is their inappropriateness on some self-administered questionnaires. With no interviewer there to probe, respondents may give a shallow, incomplete, or unclear answer. On a self-administered questionnaire without precoded choices, answers to the taco question might read "I use a little bit of everything" or "I use the same things they use in restaurants." These answers would have virtually no value to a researcher.

**closed-ended questions**
Questions that require the respondent to choose from a list of answers.

**Closed-Ended Questions** A **closed-ended question** requires the respondent to make a selection from a list of responses. The primary advantage of closed-ended questions is simply the avoidance of many of the problems associated with open-ended questions. Reading response alternatives may jog a person's memory and generate a more realistic response.

Interviewer bias is minimized because the interviewer is simply clicking a box, circling a category, recording a number, or punching a key. Because the option of expounding on a topic is not given to a respondent, there is no bias toward the articulate. Finally, coding can be done automatically with questionnaire software programs.

It is important to realize the difference between a precoded open-ended question and a multiple-choice question. A precoded, open-ended question allows the respondent to answer in a freewheeling format; the interviewer simply checks coded answers as they are given. Probing is used, but a list is never read. If the answer given is not one of the precoded ones, it is written verbatim in the "Other" column. In contrast, a closed-ended question requires that a list of alternatives be read by the respondent or interviewer, depending on the survey method—with or without an interviewer.

Traditionally, marketing researchers have separated closed-ended questions into two types: **dichotomous questions**, with a two-item response option, and **multiple-choice** (or multichotomous) **questions**, with a multi-item response option.

**dichotomous questions**
Closed-ended questions that ask the respondents to choose between two answers.

**multiple-choice questions**
Closed-ended questions that ask the respondent to choose among several answers; also called *multichotomous questions*.

**Dichotomous Questions**  In a dichotomous question, the two response categories are sometimes implicit. For instance, the implicit response options to the question "Did you buy gasoline for your automobile in the last week?" are "Yes" and "No." Even if the respondent says, "I rented a car last week, and they filled it up for me. Does that count?" the question would still be classified as dichotomous. A few examples of dichotomous questions follow:

1. Did you heat the Danish roll before serving it?
   Yes        1
   No         2

2. The federal government doesn't care what people like me think.
   Agree      1
   Disagree   2

3. Do you think that inflation will be greater or less than it was last year?
   Greater than    1
   Less than       2

Because the respondent is limited to two fixed alternatives, dichotomous questions are easy to administer and usually evoke a rapid response. Many times, a neutral response option is added to dichotomous questions, "Don't know" or "No response."

**Multiple-Choice Questions**  With multiple-choice questions, replies do not have to be coded as they do with open-ended questions, but the amount of information provided is more limited. The respondent is asked to give one alternative that correctly expresses his or her opinion or, in some instances, to indicate all alternatives that apply. Some examples of multiple-choice questions follow:

1. I'd like you to think back to the last footwear of any kind that you bought. I'll read you a list of descriptions and would like for you to tell me into which category it falls.

   | | | | |
   |---|---|---|---|
   | Dress and/or formal | 1 | Specialized athletic shoes | 4 |
   | Casual | 2 | Boots | 5 |
   | Canvas-trainer-gym shoes | 3 | | |

2. Please check the age group to which you belong.

   | | | | |
   |---|---|---|---|
   | A. Under 17 | 1 | D. 35–49 years | 4 |
   | B. 17–24 years | 2 | E. 50–64 years | 5 |
   | C. 25–34 years | 3 | F. 65 and over | 6 |

**3.** In the last 3 months, have you used Noxzema Skin Cream . . . (CHECK ALL THAT APPLY)

| | |
|---|---|
| as a facial wash? | 1 |
| for moisturizing the skin? | 2 |
| for treating blemishes? | 3 |
| for cleansing the skin? | 4 |
| for treating dry skin? | 5 |
| for softening skin? | 6 |
| for sunburn? | 7 |
| for making the facial skin smooth? | 8 |

Question 1, from a mall intercept interview, may not cover all possible alternatives and, thus, may not capture a true response. Where, for example, would an interviewer record work shoes? The same thing can be said for question 3. Not only are all possible alternatives not included, but also respondents cannot elaborate or qualify their answers. The problem could be easily overcome by adding an "Any other use?" alternative to the question and asking the respondent to specify the type of shoe. If certain types, such as work shoes, come up frequently, then it may be possible to add that type of shoe to the list.

The multiple-choice question has two additional disadvantages. First, the researcher might have to spend time generating the list of possible responses. This phase may require brainstorming or intensive analysis of focus group tapes or secondary data. This may not be a problem if the particular questions have been asked in previous studies and the options are well known. Second, the researcher must settle on a range of possible answers. If the list is too long, respondents may become confused or lose interest. A related problem with any list is *position bias*. Respondents typically will choose either the first or the last alternative, all other things being equal. When Internet questionnaire software and CATI systems are used, however, position bias is eliminated by automatically the items on the list.

**scaled-response questions**
Closed-ended questions in which the response choices are designed to capture the intensity of the respondent's feeling.

**Scaled-Response Questions** The last response format to be considered is **scaled-response questions**, which are closed-ended questions where the response choices are designed to capture intensity of feeling. Consider the following questions:

**1.** Now that you have used the product, would you say that you would buy it or not?
(CHECK ONE)
Yes, would buy it
No, would not buy it

**2.** Now that you have used the product, would you say that you . . .
(CHECK ONE)
definitely would buy it?
probably would buy it?
might or might not buy it?
probably would not buy it?
definitely would not buy it?

The first question fails to capture intensity. It determines the direction (yes or no) but it cannot compare with the second question in completeness or sensitivity of response. The latter also has the advantage of being metric in nature. Technically, the question generates ordinal data, but it is typically treated as metric. See Chapter 10 for discussion of different types of data scales,

A primary advantage of using scaled-response questions is that scaling permits measurement of the intensity of respondents' answers. Also, many scaled-response forms incorporate numbers that can be used directly as codes. Finally, the marketing researcher can use much more powerful statistical tools with some scaled-response questions (see Chapter 17).

# Step Four: Decide on the Question Wording

Once the marketing researcher has decided on the specific types of questions and the response formats, the next task is the actual writing of the questions. Wording specific questions can require a significant investment of the researcher's time unless questionnaire software or a survey website like Perseus or Zoomerang is used. This may not be a big issue for research firms in that many questions will be usable on many types of surveys as well as whole sections of questionnaires and general questioning approaches.

Four general guidelines about the wording of questions are useful to bear in mind: (1) the wording must be clear, (2) the wording must not bias the respondent, (3) the respondent must be able to answer the questions, and (4) the respondent must be willing to answer the questions.

**Make Sure the Wording Is Clear** Once the researcher has decided that a question is absolutely necessary, the question must be stated so that it means the same thing to all respondents. Ambiguous terminology—for example, "Do you live within 5 minutes of here?" or "Where do you usually shop for clothes?"—should be avoided. The respondent's answer to the first question will depend on such factors as mode of transportation (maybe the respondent walks), driving speed, and perceptions of elapsed time. (The interviewer would do better to display a map with certain areas delineated and ask whether the respondent lives within the area outlined.) The second question depends on the type of clothing being purchased and the meaning of the word "Where."

**Clarity** also calls for the use of reasonable terminology. A questionnaire is not a vocabulary test. Jargon should be avoided, and verbiage should be geared to the target audience. The question "What is the level of efficacy of your preponderant dishwashing liquid?" probably would be greeted by a lot of blank stares. It would be much simpler to ask "Are you (1) very satisfied, (2) somewhat satisfied, or (3) not satisfied with your current brand of dishwashing liquid?" Words with precise meanings, universal usage, and minimal connotative confusion should be selected. When respondents are uncertain about what a question means, the incidence of "No response" or "Don't know" answers increases.

A further complication in wording questions is the need to tailor the language to the target respondent group, are you surveying lawyers or construction laborers. This advice may seem painfully obvious, but there are instances in which failure to relate to respondents' frames of reference has been disastrous. A case in point is the use of the word *bottles* (or *cans*) in this question: "How many bottles of beer do you drink in a normal week?" Because in some southern states beer is sold in 32-, 12-, 8-, 7-, 6-, and even 4-ounce bottles, a "heavy" drinker (defined as someone who consumes eight bottles of beer per week) may drink as little as 32 ounces while a "light" drinker (defined as someone who consumes up to three bottles) may actually drink as much as 96 ounces.

Clarity can be improved by stating the general purpose of the survey at the beginning of the interview. To put the questions in the proper perspective, the respondent needs to understand the general topic of survey and what is expected of him or her in a very generic sense. This does not include identifying the sponsor of the survey, which might bias the respondent.

Sometimes questions are asked with categories that are not mutually exclusive. For example:

What is your total yearly household income before taxes?

1. Under $40,000
2. $40,000–$60,000
3. $60,000–$80,000
4. Over $80,000

**clarity**
Achieved by avoiding ambiguous terminology, using reasonable, vernacular language adjusted to the target group, and asking only one question at a time.

So if a respondent's family income is $60,000, does he or she pick answer 2 or 3?

Here is a question with conflicting meaning:

Please indicate the product you use most often. Check all that apply.[12]

1. Cell phone
2. Toaster
3. Microwave
4. Vacuum cleaner

In this question, "use most often" and "check all that apply" are conflicting instructions.

Researchers must also be careful in determining when to allow multiple responses. The following question on an Internet survey allowed only one answer but should have been "check all that apply."

What time of the day do you like to check your e-mail?

- Morning
- Midday
- Evening
- Night
- Check e-mail once per week or less
- Do not use e-mail[13]

Researchers must allow all valid responses. The example below is quite obvious but, in some cases, response categories are much more subtle.

What is your favorite color?

- Red
- Green
- Blue

To achieve clarity in wording, the researcher should avoid asking two questions in one, sometimes called a *double-barreled question*. For example, "How did you like the taste and texture of the coffee cake?" should be broken into two questions, one concerning taste and the other texture. Each question should address only one aspect of evaluation.

**Avoid Biasing the Respondent** Questions such as "Do you often shop at lower-class stores like Super Shop?" and "Have you purchased any high-quality Black & Decker tools in the past 6 months?" show an obvious bias. Leading questions, such as "Weren't you pleased with the good service you received last night at the Holiday Inn?" is also quite obviously biased. However, bias may be much more subtle than that illustrated in these examples.

Sponsor identification early in the interviewing process can distort answers. An opening statement such as "We are conducting a study on the quality of banking for Northeast National Bank and would like to ask you a few questions" should be avoided. Similarly, it will not take long, for example, for a person to recognize that the survey is being conducted for Miller beer if, after the third question, every question is related to this product. This issue can be avoided by mixing in questions about other brands.

**Consider the Respondent's Ability to Answer the Questions** In some cases, a respondent may never have acquired the information needed to answer the question. For example, a husband may not know which brand of sewing thread is preferred by his wife, and respondents will know nothing about a brand or store that they have never encountered. A question worded so as to imply that the respondent should be able to answer it will often elicit a reply that is nothing more than a wild guess. This creates measurement error, since uninformed opinions are being recorded.

Another problem is forgetfulness. For example, you probably cannot remember the answers to all these questions: What was the name of the last movie you saw in a theater? Who were the stars? Did you have popcorn? How many ounces were in the container? What price did you pay for the popcorn? Did you purchase any other snack items? Why or why not? The same is true for the typical respondent. Yet a brand manager for Mars, Incorporated wants to know what brand of candy you purchased last, what alternative brands you considered, and what factors led you to the brand selected. Because brand managers want answers to these questions, market researchers ask them. This, in turn, creates measurement error. Often, respondents will give the name of a well-known brand, like Milky Way or Hershey. In other cases, respondents will mention a brand that they often purchase, but it might not be the last brand purchased.

To avoid the problem of a respondent's inability to recall, the researcher should keep the referenced time periods relatively short. For example, if the respondent says yes to the question "Did you purchase a candy bar within the past 7 days?" then brand and purchase motivation questions can be asked. A poor question for Dish Network customers might be, "How many movies have you rented in the past year to view at home on Dish Network?" It could be replaced with the following:

a. How many movies have you rented in the past month to view on Dish Network?
b. Would you say that, in the last month, you rented more movies, fewer movies, or about the average number of movies you rent per month? (IF "MORE" or "LESS," ASK THE FOLLOWING QUESTION)
c. What would you say is the typical number of movies you rent per month?

Here are two questions from actual marketing research studies. The first is from a mail survey and the second from a telephone survey. Question one: In the past three months, how much have you spent on movies you saw advertised in the newspaper? Most people haven't a clue as to how much they have spent on movies in the last three months unless it is "nothing." And they certainly don't recall which of the movies were advertised where. Also, what if the respondent bought tickets for the whole family? Question two: Of your last 10 drinks of scotch, how many were at home? At a friend's? At a restaurant? At a bar or tavern? A light scotch drinker might have consumed 10 drinks over a period of not less than two years! Maybe he carries around a scotch intake logbook, but it's doubtful.

The above questions are bad, but the following questions, from a real mail panel survey, were written by either a careless questionnaire designer or one who lives quite differently from most of us:

■ *Question*: How many times in an average day do you apply your usual underarm product? One to two times per day? Three to four times per day? Five to six times per day? More than six times per day?

■ *Question*: How many times in an average day do you shower/bathe? One time per day? Two times per day? Three times per day? Four times per day? Five or more times per day?

Good grooming is important, but these questions are over the line.

## Consider the Respondent's Willingness to Answer the Question
A respondent may have a very good memory, yet not be willing to give a truthful reply. If an event is perceived as embarrassing, sensitive in nature, threatening, or divergent from the respondent's self-image, it is likely either not to be reported at all or to be distorted in a socially desirable direction.

Embarrassing questions that deal with topics such as borrowing money, personal hygiene, sexual activities, and criminal records must be phrased carefully to minimize measurement error. One technique is to ask the question in the third person—for example, "Do you think that most people charge more on their credit cards than they should? If yes, follow up with "Why do they do that?" By generalizing to "most people," the researcher may be able to learn more about individual respondents' attitudes toward credit and debt.

Another method for soliciting embarrassing information is for the interviewer to state, prior to asking the question, that the behavior or attitude is not unusual—for example, "Millions of Americans suffer from hemorrhoids; do you or any member of your family suffer from this problem?" This technique, called *using counterbiasing statements*, makes embarrassing topics less intimidating for respondents to discuss.

## Step Five: Establish Questionnaire Flow and Layout

After the questions have been properly formulated, the next step is to sequence them and develop a layout for the questionnaire. Questionnaires are not constructed haphazardly; there should be a logic to the positioning of each section (see Exhibit 12.4). Experienced marketing researchers know that good questionnaire development is a key to obtaining a completed interview. A well-organized questionnaire usually elicits answers that are more carefully thought out and detailed. Researcher wisdom has led to the following general guidelines concerning questionnaire flow.

### Use Screening Questions to Identify Qualified Respondents
These questions are based on the population of interest. Only qualified respondents are interviewed, and specific minimum numbers (quotas) of various types of qualified respondents may be sought. For example, a food products study generally has quotas of users of specific brands, a magazine study screens for readers, and a cosmetic study screens for brand awareness.

**screeners**
Questions used to identify appropriate respondents.

**Screeners** (screening questions) may appear on the questionnaire, or a screening questionnaire may be filled out for everyone who is interviewed. Any demographics obtained provide a basis against which to compare persons who qualify for the full study. A long screening questionnaire can significantly increase the cost of the study, as more information must be obtained from every contact with a respondent. But it provides important data on the nature of nonusers, nontriers, and persons unaware of the product or service being researched. Short screening questionnaires, such as the one presented in Exhibit 12.5, quickly eliminate unqualified persons and enable the interviewer to move immediately to the next potential respondent.

| EXHIBIT 12.4 | How a Questionnaire Should Be Organized | | |
|---|---|---|---|
| **Location** | **Type** | **Examples** | **Rationale** |
| Screeners | Qualifying questions | "Have you been snow skiing in the past 12 months?" "Do you own a pair of skis?" | The goal is to identify target respondents. |
| First few questions | Warm-ups | "What brand of skis do you own?" "How many years have you owned them?" | Easy-to-answer questions show the respondent that the survey is simple. |
| First third of questions | Transitions | "What features do you like best about the skis?" | Questions related to research objectives require slightly more effort. |
| Second third | Difficult and complicated questions | "Following are 10 characteristics of snow skis. Please rate your skis on each characteristic, using the scale below." | The respondent has committed to completing the questionnaire. |
| Last third | Classifying and demographic questions | "What is the highest level of education you have attained?" | The respondent may leave some "personal" questions blank, but they are at the end of the survey. |

Most importantly, screeners provide a basis for estimating the costs of a survey. A survey in which all persons are qualified to be interviewed is much cheaper to conduct than one with a 5 percent incidence rate (percentage of people screened who are expected to qualify). Many surveys are placed with field services at a flat rate per completed questionnaire. The rate is based on a stated average interview time and incidence rate. Screeners are used to determine whether, in fact, the incidence rate holds true in a particular city. If it does not, the flat rate is adjusted accordingly.

**Begin with a Question That Gets the Respondent's Interest** After introductory comments and screens to find a qualified respondent, the initial questions should be simple, interesting, and nonthreatening. To open a questionnaire with an income or age question is likely to be disastrous. These are often considered threatening and tend to immediately put the respondent on the defensive. The initial question should be easy to answer without much forethought.

**Ask General Questions First** Once the interview progresses beyond the opening warm-up questions, the questionnaire should proceed in a logical fashion. First, general questions are asked to get the person thinking about a concept, company, or type of product; then the questionnaire moves to the specifics. For example, a questionnaire on shampoo might begin with, "Have you purchased a hair spray, hair conditioner, or hair shampoo within the past six weeks?" Then it would ask about the frequency of shampooing, brands purchased in the past three months, satisfaction and dissatisfaction with brands purchased, repurchase intent, characteristics of an "ideal" shampoo, respondent's hair characteristics, and finally demographics.

**Ask Questions That Require "Work" in the Middle** Initially, the respondent will be only vaguely interested in and understanding of the nature of the survey. As the interest-building questions appear, momentum and commitment to the interview will build. When the interview shifts to questions with scaled-response formats, the respondent must be motivated to understand the response categories and options. Alternatively, questions might necessitate some recall or opinion formation on the part of the respondent. Established interest and commitment must sustain the respondent in this part of the interview.

---

| | |
|---|---|
| Hello. I'm from Data Facts Research. We are conducting a survey among men, and I'd like to ask you a few questions. | **Exhibit 12.5**<br><br>**Screening Questionnaire That Seeks Men 15 Years of Age and Older Who Shave at Least Three Times a Week with a Blade Razor** |

1. Do you or does any member of your family work for an advertising agency, a marketing research firm, or a company that manufactures or sells shaving products?

   (TERMINATE)                                                     Yes ( )

   (CONTINUE WITH Q. 2)                                    No ( )

2. How old are you? Are you . . . (READ LIST)

   (TERMINATE)                               Under 15 yrs. old? ( )

   (CHECK QUOTA CONTROL FORM—IF QUOTA GROUP FOR WHICH THE RESPONDENT QUALIFIES IS NOT FILLED, 15 to 34 yrs. old? ( ) CONTINUE, IF QUOTA GROUP IS FILLED, THEN TERMINATE.)                Over 34 yrs. old? ( )

3. The last time you shaved, did you use an electric razor or a razor that uses blades?

   (TERMINATE)                                 Electric Razor ( )

   (CONTINUE WITH Q. 4)                               Blade Razor ( )

4. How many times have you shaved in the past 7 days?

   (IF LESS THAN THREE TIMES, TERMINATE. IF THREE OR MORE TIMES, CONTINUE WITH THE MAIN QUESTIONNAIRE.)

**Position Sensitive, Threatening, and Demographic Questions at the End** As mentioned earlier, the objectives of a study sometimes necessitate questions on topics about which respondents may feel uneasy. These topics should be covered near the end of the questionnaire to ensure that most of the questions are answered before the respondent becomes defensive or breaks off the interview. Another argument for placing sensitive questions toward the end is that by the time these questions are asked, interviewees have been conditioned to respond. In other words, the respondent has settled into a pattern of seeing or hearing a question and giving an answer.

**Put Instructions in Capital Letters** To avoid confusion and to clarify what is a question and what is an instruction, all instructions for self-administered questionnaires should be in capital letters—for example, "IF 'YES' TO QUESTION 13, SKIP TO QUESTION 17." Capitalizing helps bring the instructions to the interviewer's or respondent's attention. Of course, this is done automatically on computer-based surveys.

**Use a Proper Introduction and Closing** Every questionnaire must have an introduction and closing. The Council for Marketing and Opinion Research (CMOR) has developed a model survey introduction and closing based on research findings from a number of different studies. CMOR recommends the following:[14]

## Model Introduction/Opening

- In order to gain the trust of the respondent, the interviewer should provide his or her first name or agreed on contact name.
- Provide the name of the company that the interviewer represents and the name of the client/sponsor of the research, if appropriate, and if there is good reason to believe this will not bias responses based on the goals of the research. It would not, for example, be a good idea to identify the sponsor if we are conducting an image survey.
- Explain the nature of the study topic/subject matter in general terms.
- State, as early in the interview as possible, that no selling will be involved as a result of the survey.
- The respondent should be told the approximate length of the survey.
- It is recommended as standard practice to obtain two-party consent to monitoring/recording; that is, both the respondent and the interviewer should be informed that the call might be monitored/recorded for quality control purposes.
- Reinforce the fact that the respondent's time is appreciated/valued.
- Invite the respondent to participate in the survey, determine if the interview time is convenient, and, if not, offer an alternative callback time and date to complete the survey.

*Hello, my name is _____, and I'm calling from (company). Today/Tonight we are calling to gather opinions regarding (general subject), and are not selling anything. This study will take approximately (length) and may be monitored (and recorded) for quality purposes. We would appreciate your time. May I include your opinions?*

## Model Closing

- At the conclusion of the survey, thank the respondent for his or her time.
- Express the desired intention that the respondent had a positive survey experience.
- Remind the respondent that his or her opinions do count.

*Thank you for your time and cooperation. I hope this experience was a pleasant one. Please remember that your opinion counts! Have a good day/evening.*

# Step Six: Evaluate the Questionnaire

Once a rough draft of the questionnaire has been designed, the marketing researcher should take a step back and critically evaluate it. This phase may seem redundant, given the careful thought that went into each question. But recall the crucial role played by the questionnaire. At this point in the questionnaire development, the following issues should be considered: (1) For each question, is the question necessary? (2) Is the questionnaire too long? (3) Will the questions provide the information needed to accomplish the research objectives?

**Is the Question Necessary?** Perhaps the most important criterion for this phase of questionnaire development is the necessity for a given question. Sometimes researchers and brand managers want to ask questions because "they were on the last survey we did like this" or because "it would be nice to know." Excessive numbers of demographic questions are very common. Asking for education data, numbers of children in multiple age categories, and extensive demographics on the spouse simply is not warranted by the nature of many studies.

Each question must serve a purpose. Unless it is a screener, an interest generator, or a required transition, it must be directly and explicitly related to the stated objectives of the survey. Any question that fails to satisfy at least one of these criteria should be omitted.

**Is the Questionnaire Too Long?** At this point, the researcher should role-play the survey, with volunteers acting as respondents. Although there is no magic number of interactions, the length of time it takes to complete the questionnaire should be averaged over a minimum of five trials. Any questionnaire to be administered in a mall or over the telephone should be a candidate for cutting if it averages longer than 20 minutes. Sometimes mall-intercept interviews can run slightly longer if an incentive is provided to the respondent. Internet and telephone surveys should take less than 15 minutes to complete.

Gift cards (prepaid Visa cards, for example) are probably the most commonly used incentive today.. The use of incentives can actually lower survey costs because response rates increase and terminations during the interview decrease.

A technique that can reduce the length of questionnaires is called a split-questionnaire design. It can be used when the questionnaire is long and the sample size is large. The questionnaire is split into one core component (such as demographics, usage patterns, and psychographics) and a number of subcomponents. Respondents complete the core component plus a randomly assigned subcomponent.

**Will the Questions Provide the Information Needed to Accomplish the Research Objectives?** The researcher must make certain that the questionnaire contains sufficient numbers and types of questions to meet the decision-making needs of management. A suggested procedure is to carefully review the written objectives for the research project and then write each question number next to the objective that the particular question will address. For example, question 1 applies to objective 3, question 2 to objective 2, and so forth. If a question cannot be tied to an objective, the researcher should determine whether the list of objectives is complete. If the list is complete, the question should be omitted. If the researcher finds an objective with no questions listed beside it, appropriate questions should be added. Tips for writing a good questionnaire are provided in the Practicing Marketing Research feature on page 294.

# Step Seven: Obtain Approval of All Relevant Parties

After the first draft of the questionnaire has been completed, copies should be distributed to all parties who have direct authority over the project. Practically speaking, managers may step in at any time in the design process with new information, requests, or concerns. When this happens, revisions are often necessary. It is still important to get final approval of the first draft, even if managers have already intervened in the development process.

Managerial approval commits management to obtaining a body of information via a specific instrument (questionnaire). If the question is not asked, the data will not be gathered. Thus, questionnaire approval tacitly reaffirms what decision-making information is needed and how it will be obtained. For example, assume that a new product questionnaire asks about shape, material, end use, and packaging. By approving the form, the new-product development manager is implying, "I know what color the product will be," or, "It is not important to determine color at this time."

## Step Eight: Pretest and Revise

**pretest**
Trial run of a questionnaire.

When final managerial approval has been obtained, the questionnaire must be pretested. No survey should be conducted without a pretest. Moreover, a pretest does not mean that one researcher is administering the questionnaire to another researcher. Ideally, a pretest is administered to target respondents for the study. In a **pretest**, researchers look for misinterpretations or confusion on the part of respondents, lack of continuity, poor skip patterns, additional alternatives for precoded and closed-ended questions, and general respondent reaction to the interview. The pretest should be conducted in the same mode as the final interview—that is, if the study is to be an Internet survey, then the pretest should be too.

## Step Nine: Prepare Final Questionnaire Copy

Even the final copy phase does not allow the researcher to relax. Precise instructions must be created when an interviewer is involved—for example, where to interview, target respondents, and when to show respondents test items such as alternative product designs. In a mail survey, compliance and subsequent response rates may be affected positively by a professional-looking questionnaire. For telephone interviews, the survey is typically read from a computer screen. Survey software for online interviews often lets the designer choose backgrounds, formats, and so forth.

# PRACTICING MARKETING RESEARCH

## Tips for Writing a Good Questionnaire[15]

If you have ever sent what you thought was a "final" questionnaire to a marketing research supplier, only to have it returned to you full of wording changes, deletions, and other editorial comments, you're not alone. Writing a questionnaire does not, at first glance, appear to be a very difficult task: just figure out what you want to know, and write questions to obtain that information. But although writing questions is easy, writing good questions is not. Here are some dos and don'ts when writing questions.

1. *Avoid abbreviations, slang, or uncommon words that your audience might not understand.* For example: What is your opinion of PPOs? It is quite possible that not

everyone knows that PPO stands for preferred provider organization. If the question targets the general public, the researcher might run into problems. However, if the question is for physicians or hospital administrators, then the acronym PPO is probably acceptable.

2. *Be specific.* The problem with vague questions is that they generate vague answers. For example: What is your household income? As respondents come up with numerous interpretations to this question, they will give all kinds of answers—income before taxes, income after taxes, and so on. Another example: How often did you attend sporting events during the past year? (1) Never, (2) Rarely, (3) Occasionally, (4) Regularly. Again, this question is open for interpretation. People will interpret "sporting event" and the answer list differently—does "regularly" mean weekly, monthly, or what?

3. *On the other hand, don't overdo it.* When questions are too precise, people cannot answer them. They will either refuse or guess. For example: How many books did you read [last year]? You need to give them some ranges: (1) None, (2) 1–10, (3) 11–25, (4) 26–50, (5) More than 50.

4. *Make sure your questions are easy to answer.* Questions that are too demanding will also lead to refusals or guesses. For example: Please rank the following 20 items in order of importance to you when you are shopping for a new car. You're asking respondents to do a fair amount of calculating. Don't ask people to rank 20 items; have them pick the top 5.

5. *Don't assume too much.* This is a fairly common error, in which the question writer infers something about people's knowledge, attitudes, or behavior. For example: Do you tend to agree or disagree with the president's position on gun control? This question assumes that the respondent is aware that the president has a position on gun control and knows what that position is. To avoid this error, the writer must be prepared to do some educating. For example: "The president has recently stated his position on gun control. Are you aware that he has taken a stand on this issue?" If the answer is yes, then continue with: "Please describe in your own words what you understand his position on gun control to be." And, finally, "Do you tend to agree or disagree with his stand?"

6. *Watch out for double questions and questions with double negatives.* Combining questions or using a double negative leads to ambiguous questions and answers. For example: "Do you favor the legalization of marijuana for use in private homes but not in public places?" If this question precisely describes the respondent's position, then a "yes" answer is easily interpreted. But a "no" could mean the respondent favors use in public places but not in private homes, or opposes both, or favors both. Similarly, here is an example of a question with a double negative: "Should the police chief not be directly responsible to the mayor?" The question is ambiguous; almost any answer will be even more so.

7. *Check for bias.* A biased question can influence people to respond in a manner that does not accurately reflect their positions. There are several ways in which questions can be prejudiced. One is to imply that respondents should have engaged in a certain behavior. For example: "The movie, *XYZ*, was seen by more people than any other movie this year. Have you seen this movie?" So as not to appear "different," respondents may say yes even though they haven't seen the movie. The question should be: "Have you seen the movie, *XYZ*?" Another way to bias a question is to have unbalanced answer choices. For example: "Currently our country spends XX billion dollars a year on foreign aid. Do you feel this amount should be (1) increased, (2) stay the same, (3) decreased a little, (4) decreased somewhat, (5) decreased a great deal?" This set of responses encourages respondents to select a "decrease" option, since there are three of these and only one increase option.

## Pretesting: The Survey before the Survey

All the rewriting and editing in the world won't guarantee success. However, pretesting is the least expensive way to make sure your questionnaire research project is a success. The primary purpose of a pretest is to make certain that the questionnaire gives the respondent clear, understandable questions that will evoke clear, understandable answers.

After completion of the pretest, any necessary changes should be made. Managerial approval should then be reobtained before going forward. If the original pretest results in extensive design and question alterations, a second pretest is in order.

# Step Ten: Implement the Survey

Completion of the questionnaire establishes the basis for obtaining the desired decision-making information from the marketplace. As discussed in Chapter 2, most mall and telephone research interviewing is conducted by field service firms. It is their job to complete the interviews and deliver the raw results back to the researcher. In essence, field services are the in-person interviewers, the production line of the marketing research industry. A series of forms and procedures must be issued with the questionnaire to make certain that the field service firm gathers the data correctly, efficiently, and at a reasonable cost. Depending on the data-collection method, these may include supervisor's instructions, interviewer's instructions, screeners, call record sheets, and visual aids.

**Supervisor's Instructions** **Supervisor's instructions** inform the field services firm of the nature of the study, start and completion dates, quotas, reporting times, equipment and facility requirements, sampling instructions, number of interviewers required, and

**supervisor's instructions**
Written directions to the field service firm on how to conduct the survey.

validation procedures. In addition, detailed instructions are required for any taste test that involves food preparation. Quantities typically are measured and cooked using rigorous measurement techniques and devices.

A vital part of any study handled by a field service, supervisor's instructions establish the parameters for conducting the research. Without clear instructions, the interview may be conducted 10 different ways in 10 different cities. A sample page from a set of supervisor's instructions is shown in Exhibit 12.6.

**field management companies**
Firms that provide such support services as questionnaire formatting, screener writing, and coordination of data collection.

## Field Management Companies

**Field management companies**, such as QFact, On-Line Communications, and Direct Resource, can provide all or a combination of the following services: questionnaire formatting, screener writing, development of instructional and peripheral materials, shipping

**Exhibit 12.6**

**Sample Page of Supervisor's Instructions for a Diet Soft Drink Taste Test**

| | |
|---|---|
| **Purpose** | To determine from diet soft-drink users their ability to discriminate among three samples of Diet Dr Pepper and give opinions and preferences between two of the samples |
| **Staff** | 3–4 experienced interviewers per shift |
| **Location** | One busy shopping center in a middle to upper-middle socioeconomic area. The center's busiest hours are to be worked by a double shift of interviewers. |
| | In the center, 3–4 private interviewing stations are to be set up, and a refrigerator and good counterspace made available for product storage and preparation. |
| **Quota** | 192 completed interviews broken down as follows: |
| | A minimum of 70 Diet Dr Pepper users |
| | A maximum of 122 other diet brand users |
| **Project materials** | For this study, you are supplied the following: |
| | 250 Screening Questionnaires |
| | 192 Study Questionnaires |
| | 4 Card A's |
| **Product/preparation** | For this study, our client shipped to your refrigerated facility 26 cases of soft-drink product. Each case contains 24 10-oz. bottles—312 coded with an *F* on the cap, 312 with an *S*. |
| | Each day, you are to obtain from the refrigerated facility approximately 2–4 cases of product—1–2 of each code. Product must be transported in coolers and kept refrigerated at the location. It should remain at approximately 42°F. |
| | In the center, you are to take one-half of the product coded *F* and place the #23 stickers on the bottles. The other half of the *F* product should receive #46 stickers. |
| | The same should be done for product *S*—one-half should be coded #34, the other half #68. A supervisor should do this task before interviewing begins. Interviewers will select product by *code number*. Code number stickers are enclosed for this effort. |
| | Each respondent will be initially testing three product samples as designated on the questionnaire. Interviewers will come to the kitchen, select the three designated bottles, open and pour 4 oz. of each product into its corresponding coded cup. The interviewer should cap and *refrigerate* leftover product when finished pouring and take only the 3 *cups* of product on a tray to respondent. |

services, field auditing, and all coordination of data collection, coding, and tab services required for the project. Generally lean on staff, these companies provide the services clients need without attempting to compete with the design and analytical capabilities of full-service companies and ad agency research staffs.

A number of full-service companies and qualitative professionals have discovered that using field management companies can be cost-effective; it can increase productivity by allowing them to take on more projects while using fewer of their internal resources. Several qualitative researchers have developed ongoing relationships with field management companies, whose personnel function as extensions of the consultant's staff, setting up projects and freeing up the researcher to conduct groups, write reports, and consult with clients.

Of course, like any other segment of the research industry, field management has its limitations. By definition, field management companies generally do not have design and analytical capabilities. This means that their clients may, on occasion, need to seek other providers to meet their full-service needs. In addition, because this is a relatively new segment of the industry; experience, services, and standards vary tremendously from firm to firm. It's advisable to carefully screen prospective companies and check references. These limitations notwithstanding, field management companies provide a way for researchers to increase their productivity in a cost-effective manner, while maintaining the quality of the information on which their company's decisions and commitments are based.

# Impact of the Internet on Questionnaire Development

As with most other aspects of marketing research, the Internet has affected questionnaire development and use in several ways. For example, a marketing research company can now create a questionnaire and send it as an e-mail attachment to management for comments and approval or actually let them go through it online just as a respondent or interviewer would; once approved, a programmed version can be placed on the research firm's or client's server to be administered an Internet survey. Or researchers can simply use an Internet company like Vovici, Inquisite, Web Surveyor, SSI Web, or many others to create a survey on the Internet.

Survey Monkey, for example, is a leading Internet self-service questionnaire-building site. It allows marketing researchers to create online surveys quickly and then view real-time results anytime and anywhere, using remote access. The advantage is that the marketing research client has no questionnaire software to install, and no programming or administration is required. All operations are automated and performed through its website, surveymonkey.com. This includes survey design, respondent invitation, data collection, analysis, and results reporting. An extensive list of DIY (do it yourself) survey platforms with review information can be found at: http://www.survey-reviews.net/index.php/reviews/. Most recently, Google has introduced Google Consumer Surveys. With this service, Google provides a complete suite of tools to create surveys, get respondents, and summarize results. A description of these services can be found at: http://www.google.com/insights/consumersurveys/how.

Internet survey tools have become increasingly sophisticated, making do-it-yourself or DIY surveys more feasible. DIY research is discussed in greater detail in the Practicing Marketing Research box on page 298.

# PRACTICING MARKETING RESEARCH

## A Beginner's Guide to DIY Research[16]

The idea of do-it-yourself (DIY) survey research is not new. For years, researchers have been using various tools to conduct customer-facing surveys, providing companies with insight to help improve their client relationships. Fast-forward to 2012 and social media and similar technologies are creating exponentially more opportunities in client-based research, giving companies more tools and more information than they could ever utilize.

With these new opportunities come new challenges and, too often, researchers simply aren't equipped with the knowledge and tools required to derive real value from client research.

Don't ask yourself whether you should perform client-based research (you absolutely should). Ask yourself, instead, how you can do the best possible DIY research for your company, which includes knowing the dangers of the DIY approach and when it's time to call in the pros.

### Benefits of DIY research

DIY research is often seen as a viable short-term alternative to full-fledged market research projects, especially when budget is constrained.

1. **Convenience.** For many companies, the primary benefit of DIY research is convenience. If you're simply looking for quick feedback on a few straightforward topics that do not require much analysis, you can use a basic online tool such as SurveyMonkey.

2. **Perspective.** If you're the person in charge of conducting survey methodology and analysis, you will gain a firsthand, in-depth understanding of your clients' needs and how to best meet them. This benefit can also have a notable downside in that your clients may be unwilling to truly open up to their day-to-day contact at the company—you.

3. **Cost.** Cost-savings is often touted as another benefit of the DIY survey approach. Depending on how in-depth the survey is and the number of questions asked, you could be looking at no additional cost aside from time spent creating it. Step it up a notch with more questions and customizable features and you're still not looking at budget-breaking numbers. If you're a small business or don't need serious data, a DIY survey is the ticket.

### Dangers of a DIY approach

A carefully crafted DIY research project can deliver important insights. However, a DIY approach has some potential downsides. These challenges threaten data quality and ultimately, your target objectives.

1. **Wasted data.** DIY surveys run the risk of failing to connect survey questions to organizational objectives. Ideally, every aspect of the survey should deliver data for making specific business decisions and accomplishing clearly articulated organizational goals. Many DIY surveys are populated with random questions that the organization wants answered or thinks should be asked, even though those questions aren't linked to business objectives.

2. **Flawed results.** DIY surveys can contain fundamental flaws that reverberate throughout data analysis and decision-making. If your research fails to deliver the necessary insights, or worse yet, delivers inaccurate results, important decisions could be made based on faulty information. When creating DIY surveys, people often forget to keep the end in mind.

   Account managers taking a DIY approach should be aware of the effect their personal connection to the client could have on survey responses. A client who has a long-standing relationship with the account manager will likely be hesitant to disclose negative elements of his or her interaction with the company. Consider opting for an independent third party—or even another individual within the organization—to ensure meaningful responses.

3. **Poorly crafted questions.** When it comes to survey mechanics, question phrasing can be another stumbling block for DIY researchers. Even when the meaning of specific questions may seem obvious, survey participants will struggle to respond to questions that are vague, unclear or imprecise. It's important to accurately match the type of question (e.g. open-ended vs. Likert scale [strongly disagree through strongly agree]) to the information you're attempting to uncover and the nature of the survey. Shortcomings in question phrasing and structure will inevitably translate into muddled client responses.

4. **Alienated clients.** One of the more serious pitfalls of DIY research is the possibility that your research tools or methodology might alienate clients. If the survey is highly repetitive, fails to value the participants' time, or reinforces negative stereotypes, DIY surveys can inflict serious damage on client relationships and, ultimately, your bottom line. Although you might see the survey as going above and beyond, your client might think otherwise.

## Call in the pros

Researchers need to understand that DIY research is not a panacea. Although technology has extended the ability to capture meaningful client insights, there are still many scenarios that call for professional research expertise. In fact, knowing when it's time to call in the pros can be the determining factor in the quality and effectiveness of your entire research agenda.

Ask yourself: What am I trying to accomplish with this survey? What data do I need to collect, and why? Those questions should be among the first you ask yourself when starting the survey process. If you're serious about gaining additional insight into problem areas and identifying unknown issues, call in the pros. They'll have databases of tried-and-true questions that produce the responses and data you need.

Likewise, if you want to dig deep and are unsure if your clients will answer your survey truthfully, calling in a third party will eliminate any uneasiness your client may feel. In turn, you may find the results are more honest.

As the stakes go up, the limits of DIY research become more apparent. When companies want to find solutions to long-term problems or require very specific, actionable insights, it becomes important to outsource research to a professional. In addition to providing end-to-end management of the research process, the pros offer expertise in data analysis and other critical aspects of client surveys.

An important part of the research process involves the transformation of data into targeted actions. In addition to optimizing data collection, qualified research organizations can help you translate findings into actions and business outcomes that will benefit both you and your clients.

## Best practices in DIY research

If you choose to adopt a DIY approach, you'll assume responsibility for the integrity of survey methodology, including the integration of several best practices into the DIY research process.

1. **Survey purpose.** The first step in successful research is to consider how you will use the survey results. Be prepared to address any issues or weaknesses that are raised in the survey because clients will expect you to make corrective improvements based on the results.

2. **Strategic segmentation.** One of the most dangerous mistakes in DIY research is to try to accomplish too much in a single survey. It isn't necessary to survey your entire client base or cover every possible research angle in a single survey vehicle. Instead, break surveys up into manageable segments that will make it easier for the team to translate results into actions.

3. **Participation rates.** Participation rates can make or break the success of DIY surveys. If possible, it's helpful to introduce surveys to clients in person rather than using an e-mail blast. Another strategy to boost participation is to conduct the survey via phone or in face-to-face meetings, recognizing that the price of higher participation will be an additional time investment. If you send a survey out via e-mail, include a status bar. Having an end in sight will boost participation.

4. **Types of questions.** Most DIY surveys should include a combination of Likert scale and open-ended questions. While Likert scale questions reveal participants' attitudes or feelings about specific issues, open-ended questions provide qualitative data that can be invaluable to you. When possible, avoid using "neutral" as a response option. Make your client pick a side. Additionally, provide a comment section at the end so they can address anything they weren't able to during the survey.

5. **Analysis and averages.** Keeping in mind that the goal of DIY research should always be actionable insights, the most effective research mechanisms are often one-to-one surveys. Research that delivers results in the form of averages has limited value because it may not deliver actionable results. For example, a survey showing that a third of your clients find your ordering process cumbersome isn't nearly as useful as one revealing that your largest client is struggling to adapt to your new Web-based ordering solution. A good rule of thumb is that even though averages can be helpful, surveys that deliver granular, one-to-one results can make it easier to attach targeted actions to your research.

## Best served by a combination

In the end, most researchers discover that their agenda is best served by a combination of DIY and outsourced, professional research opportunities. The quick feedback that can be achieved through DIY surveys can be a great lead-in to the deep insights and solutions to long-term problems that can be accomplished with a professional client management provider.

## Questions

1. What are some of the benefits of DIY research? Which one of these really stands out to you? Why do you say that?

2. What are the major pitfalls of DIY research? Which one of these represents the greatest threat to the quality of the research?

3. At what point should you call in the pros? Explain your answer.

# Adapting to Mobile Device Questionnaires

When we deploy a survey for web administration, targeted respondents are in control regarding the device used to complete the survey. They can use any web-enabled device. We previously noted that recent estimates indicate that 25 to 30 percent of the web surveys are completed using a smartphone or tablet. Not only are respondents in control as to device used, they are also in control as to when and where they complete the survey or whether they complete it at all. They may be riding on a train or in a car pool, waiting at an airport or other location, or just sitting on a park bench.

Many have access to desktops, laptops, tablets, and smartphones and may use one or the other, depending on the day and time. In order to encourage as many people as possible to complete the survey, we must make it easy to complete, regardless of the hardware platform they are using at a particular time. Mobile devices, particularly smartphones, suffer from limitations in the amount of screen real estate available. Therefore, when deploying web surveys, we must keep these limitations in mind.

It is possible for our servers to detect the operating systems being used by respondents and deploy slightly different versions of the survey depending on the operating system—Mac, Windows, IOS, Android, etc.—being used by the respondent and deploy a version optimized for that platform. In general, we are interested in discriminating between desktop/laptops and tablets/smartphones. Although tablets generally have more screen size to work with than smartphones, they can be treated similarly in terms of questionnaire design.

Some general rules for creating web surveys for mobile devices in order to minimize the need to scroll, pinch, and so on include:

- Present grids/batteries as individual questions.
- Keep the number of scale points on rating items in the 5 to 7, at a maximum, range.
- Generally work to minimize question wording.
- Keep answer lists to maximum of 10 to 12 items.
- Shoot for a 10-minute survey.
- Redesign programmed questions that seek comparisons between two different graphics (ads) in creative ways.

Tips for designing mobile friendly questionnaires are provided in the Practicing Marketing Research box below.

# PRACTICING MARKETING RESEARCH

## Top 10 Tips for Designing a Mobile-Friendly Questionnaire[17]

1. **Remember the reality of the real estate**. Mobile phone screens are a small fraction of the size of PC screens and, though larger, tablet screens are still only half or less the size of PC screens.

2. **Design for both portrait (vertical) and landscape (horizontal) view**. Your respondents will choose their preferred view, so the questionnaire must work in both orientations:

   a. Item lists should be short enough for the full list to be visible in landscape view.

   b. Scales should be narrow enough to be fully visible in portrait view.

   c. To be safe, mention the size of the scale in the question text (i.e., using the 5-point scale below) in case they can only see part of it. Also, consider using the top of the scale on the left, since it will not make sense for a scale to end at 3—but if you start at 1, they might not realize a scale goes all the way to 10, because they can only see 7 or 8 without sliding the screen to the right.

3. **Reduce the number of words in the questions**. People communicate with fewer words on mobile. We may need to replace longer questions with shorter ones that

retain the same meaning and remain well defined. This could be a real challenge!

4. **Redesign Flash elements**. Flash is not supported on mobile devices.

5. **Start with the mobile design and size up**. A design that works well for a mobile will work well on a PC. So size up instead of starting with a PC-design and trying to scale down.

6. **Design the functional elements first**. Anything that people have to touch, like "next" buttons, radio buttons or check boxes, should be as large as possible and have as much space around them as possible. Traditionally, questionnaire designers focused on the text then fitted the functional elements around it. In a mobile world, we need to reverse the process.

7. **Test on multiple devices**. Also test thoroughly in both portrait and landscape view.

8. **Avoid scrolling designs**. Instead of asking people to scroll or pinch to expand, reduce the number of items in a list or grid. Scrolling is much faster on the mobile phone (so users may see just the beginning and end of the list and miss the items in the middle). The transition to mobile can be an ideal time to rethink the design of grid questions.

9. **Make text boxes as large as you can**. Research shows that the larger the box, the more words are typed in open-ended responses.

10. **Resist the temptation to use the full functionality of the phone**. Features like the spinning "wheels" seen in mobile calendars are attractive from the design point of view, but could be awkward for users and cause incompatible or unexpected results.

## Questions

1. Why should you design mobile-friendly questionnaires in both portrait and landscape views?

2. Why should you test your mobile friendly questionnaire on multiple mobile devices?

**Facebook as a Survey Research Platform** In late 2010, Facebook launched Facebook Questions. It allows users to post surveys and questions about subjects of their choice, soliciting their friends—or the entire Facebook population—for information and opinions. As this text went to print, the service had gone through beta testing and will be further developed with the test group's feedback in mind.

YOSHIKATSU TSUNO/AFP/Getty Images

In the global market of today, a product may be tested in many countries at the same time. The need for questionnaires in several different languages has grown considerably in the last decade.

Whether Facebook Questions will serve as a casual form of research or a more recreational "What song is it that goes X?" or "Which shoes look better with this belt?" remains to be seen, but company and brand Facebook pages will also have the ability to gauge how consumers feel about new products or potential launches and also establish a forum where users and brand fans can be heard right from the comfort of their own Facebook profiles.

Facebook Questions will appear on the user's profile and will also appear in the user's friends' News Feed, so answers are anticipated to be personalized and especially relevant to the poster. Photos can also be added if the user is trying to identify something, such as a type of flower in their garden.

The "social" aspect of Facebook Questions comes in the form of question suggestions and the helpful/unhelpful checkbox. Whenever polls or questions have been answered, users can post them to their own or their friends' profiles, and if a user sees a question for which a friend might have an answer, the user can "suggest" that question for a friend. Facebook Questions will also have a feature similar to ones seen on Digg, Amazon.com, and Yahoo! Answers, where the users' viewing or responding to the question can (anonymously) mark whether they found a respondent's answer helpful or unhelpful. The most helpful answers will rise to the top. Users are also able to "follow" questions, so that a notification will be sent when another user responds to the question.[18]

# Costs, Profitability, and Questionnaires

A discussion of questionnaires is not complete without mentioning their impact on job costs and profitability. Marketing research suppliers often bid against one another for a project. A supplier who overestimates costs may lose the job to a lower-cost competitor. In all survey research, the questionnaire and incidence rate (see Chapter 6) are the core determinants of a project's estimated data-collection costs. When one of America's largest research suppliers examined costs and bids for all of its projects conducted by central-location telephone interviewing, it found that it had overestimated project costs 44 percent of the time during a recent 18-month period. The resulting overbidding had translated into millions of dollars of lost sales opportunities.

To avoid overbidding, managers must have a better understanding of data collection costs. In one central-location telephone study with a 50 percent incidence rate and calls lasting an average of 15 minutes, MARC, a large international marketing research firm, found that only 30 percent of the data-collection costs involved asking the questions. Seventy percent of the data-collection costs were incurred trying to reach a qualified respondent.[19]

Exhibit 12.7 depicts the numerous roadblocks an interviewer can encounter trying to get a completed interview. Each roadblock adds to the costs. MARC, for example, has found that simply adding a security screener to a questionnaire can increase the cost of interviewing by as much as 7 percent.

Another major source of extra cost in survey research is premature termination of interviews. Respondents terminate interviews for four major reasons: the subject matter, redundant or difficult-to-understand questions, questionnaire length, and changing the subject during an interview. People like to talk about some subjects and not others. For example, the subject of gum is no problem, but bringing up mouthwash results in many terminations. Exhibit 12.8 reveals that a 20-minute interview on gum results in few terminations (actual data). However, many people terminate a mouthwash interview within 3 minutes, or in the 19- to 22-minute range. Terminations of a leisure travel interview don't become a serious problem until the interview reaches 20 minutes in length. Terminations usually mean that the interview must be redone and all the time spent interviewing the respondent was wasted. However, preliminary research has found that callbacks on terminated interviews can sometimes result in a completed interview.[20] (The same research on callbacks to persons who originally refused to be surveyed was not productive.)

Once managers understand the actual costs of data collection, they should be in a better position to bid on jobs with a high degree of cost accuracy. Better information should result in less overbidding and therefore more contracts.

| EXHIBIT 12.7 | Difficulties in Finding a Qualified Respondent in a Central-Location Telephone Interview |
| --- | --- |

**1. Failed Attempts**
- Busy
- No answer
- Answering machine
- Business number
- Phone/language problem
- Discontinued line

**2. Cooperation Problems**
- Respondent not at home
- Respondent refused to be interviewed

**3. Screener Determines Respondent Not Eligible**
- Failed security test (works for marketing research firm, advertising agency, or the client)
- Doesn't use the product
- Demographic disqualification (wrong gender, age, etc.)
- Quota filled (For example, survey has a quota of 500 users of Tide and 500 users of other clothes washing powders. Interviewer already has 500 Tide users; the current respondent uses Tide.)

**4. Respondent Terminated during Interview**

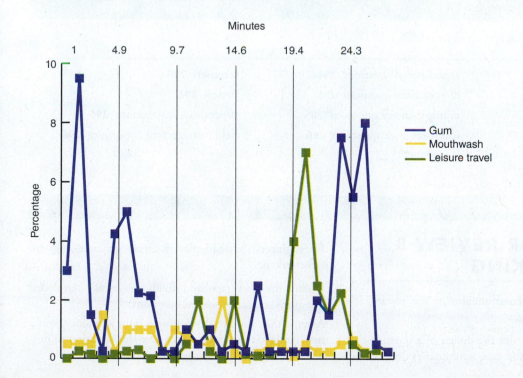

| Exhibit 12.8 |
| --- |

**Actual Respondent Termination Patterns for Interviews in Three Different Product Categories**

## SUMMARY

The questionnaire plays a critical role in the data-collection process. The criteria for a good questionnaire may be categorized as follows: (1) providing the necessary decision-making information, (2) fitting the respondent, and (3) meeting editing, coding, and data processing requirements.

The process of developing a questionnaire is a sequential one:

Step One. Determine survey objectives, resources, and constraints.
Step Two. Determine the data-collection method.
Step Three. Determine the question response format.
Step Four. Decide on the question wording.
Step Five. Establish questionnaire flow and layout.
Step Six. Evaluate the questionnaire.
Step Seven. Obtain approval of all relevant parties.
Step Eight. Pretest and revise.
Step Nine. Prepare final questionnaire copy.
Step Ten. Implement the survey.

The three different types of questions—open-ended, closed-ended, and scaled-response questions—each have advantages and disadvantages. In establishing the wording and positioning of questions within the questionnaire, the researcher must try to ensure that the wording is clear and does not bias the respondent and that the respondent will be able and willing to answer the questions.

During the implementation of survey research, procedures must be followed to ensure that the data are gathered correctly, efficiently, and at a reasonable cost. These include preparing supervisor's instructions, interviewer's instructions, screeners, call record sheets, and visual aids. Many research organizations are now turning to field management companies to actually conduct the interviews.

Questionnaire software and the Internet are having a major impact on survey design. Vovici Web surveyor, SSI Web, and others enable researchers to go to the website and create online surveys.

The role of the questionnaire in survey research costs can be a decisive one. If a research firm overestimates data-collection costs, chances are that it will lose the project to another supplier. Most data-collection costs are associated not with conducting the actual interview, but with finding a qualified respondent. A respondent's propensity to terminate an interview, which can be costly, is often based on the nature of the topic discussed.

## KEY TERMS

questionnaire **271**
editing **274**
skip pattern **274**
survey objectives **276**
open-ended questions **281**

closed-ended questions **284**
dichotomous questions **285**
multiple-choice questions **285**
scaled-response questions **286**
clarity **287**

screeners **290**
pretest **294**
supervisor's instructions **295**
field management companies **296**

## QUESTIONS FOR REVIEW & CRITICAL THINKING

1. Explain the role of the questionnaire in the research process.

2. How do respondents influence the design of a questionnaire? Give some examples (e.g., questionnaires designed for engineers, baseball players, army generals, migrant farmworkers).

3. Discuss the advantages and disadvantages of open-ended questions and closed-ended questions.

4. Assume that you are developing a questionnaire about a new sandwich for McDonald's. Use this situation to outline the procedure for designing a questionnaire.

5. Give examples of poor questionnaire wording, and explain what is wrong with each question.

6. Once a questionnaire has been developed, what other factors need to be considered before the questionnaire is put into the hands of interviewers?

7. Why is pretesting a questionnaire important? Are there some situations in which pretesting is not necessary?

8. Design three open-ended and three closed-ended questions to measure consumers' attitudes toward BMW automobiles.

9. What's wrong with the following questions?
   a. How do you like the flavor of this high-quality Maxwell House coffee?
   b. What do you think of the taste and texture of this Sara Lee coffee cake?
   c. We are conducting a study for Bulova watches. What do you think of the quality of Bulova watches?

10. What do you see as the major advantages of using a field management company? What are the drawbacks?

11. Discuss the advantages and disadvantages of web-based questionnaires.

12. Divide the class into groups of four or five. Next, match the groups evenly into supplier and client teams. The instructor will then pair a client team with a supplier team. Each client team should pick some aspect of the university such as student housing, student transportation, sports, sororities, fraternities, food on campus, or some other aspect of student life. Next, the client team should create four management objectives for their topic and construct a questionnaire to meet the management objectives. In addition, the questionnaire should include the following demographics: age, gender, major, and others determined by your instructor. Once the client team approves the questionnaire, both the client and supplier team members should complete 10 interviews each. The results should then be presented to the class. *Note:* This data can be formatted into SPSS for more detailed analysis later in the text.

*(Team Activity)*

## WORKING THE NET

1. Visit https://contribute.surveymonkey.com/?ut_source=header, create a free account, and take a series of free online surveys and evaluate the programs, questions, approach, assumptions, and results.

2. Log on to *www.surveymonkey.com* and *www.inquisite.com* and consider how suitable, or not, their online polling software would be for conducting market research for new customers for iPhone.

3. See what it's like to be at the receiving end of an online survey; take one or two surveys at *www.greenfield.com* and click on "Take a Survey."

## *REAL-LIFE RESEARCH • 12.1*

### Understanding Buyer Behavior

Yes, what you see below is an actual questionnaire (with very minimal modifications). It was a student-designed questionnaire (not from a business school) intended to understand shopping behavior in a Midwestern city. It violates numerous principles of questionnaire design. See how many you can find as you read through the instrument.

### Survey Instrument

1. How old are you? _____
2. How old is your husband/wife? _____
3. How long have you been married? _____
4. What is the highest level of education you or your husband/wife have achieved?
   a. No formal education
   b. Primary education
   c. Secondary education
   d. College
   e. Two-year college
   f. Four-year college
   g. Graduate college
5. What is the highest level of education your partner has achieved?
   a. No formal education
   b. Primary education
   c. Secondary education

**d.** College

**e.** Two-year college

**f.** Four-year college

**g.** Graduate college

6. Are you currently employed or engaged in an income-generating business?

**a.** Yes

**b.** No

7. (IF ANSWER IS YES, PROCEED WITH QUESTION #8. OTHERWISE, SKIP TO QUESTION #9.) How much do you make per month from your employment and/or business?

**a.** _____ Enter amount in dollars.

8. Is your husband/wife currently employed or engaged in an income-generating business?

**a.** Yes

**b.** No

9. (IF ANSWER IS YES, PROCEED WITH QUESTION #10. OTHERWISE, SKIP TO QUESTION #11.) How much does your husband/wife make per month from his employment and/or business?

**a.** _____ Enter amount in dollars.

10. Do you and your husband have any children?

**a.** Yes

**b.** No

11. (IF ANSWER IS YES, PROCEED WITH QUESTION #12. OTHERWISE, SKIP TO QUESTION #14.) How many children do you have?

**a.** _____ Enter exact number.

12. What are the ages of your children? _____

13. Do they go to school? Where? _____

14. Between you and your husband, who is the dominant decision maker concerning general family issues such as where to live, when to go on vacations, what furniture to buy, etc.? a. I am b. My husband c. Neither or both

15. Are there any other adult family members living with you and your husband?

**a.** Yes

**b.** No

**c.** Sometimes. Who? _____

16. Where do you shop? _____

17. Why there and not at another place? _____
_____
_____
_____

18. How would you describe what they sell?

**a.** Very good

**b.** Quite good

**c.** Not very good

**d.** Poor

19. How did you learn about this store?

**a.** On TV

**b.** On the Internet

**c.** Through friends

**d.** Advertisement

**e.** Newspaper

**f.** I just happened to be passing by

20. I think my friends would enjoy shopping at this store.

**a.** Very strongly agree

**b.** Somewhat agree

**c.** Agree

**d.** Don't really agree

**e.** Strongly disagree

21. What do you like best? _____
_____
_____
_____

22. What could be improved? _____
_____
_____
_____

## Questions

1. Critique each question and explain how it could be improved.

2. Suggest some questions that could be used to understand shopping behavior, for both goods and services, in a Midwestern city.

3. How should the revised questionnaire be reordered?

# REAL-LIFE RESEARCH • 12.2

## Sonic Goes Mobile

Sonic Drive-Ins has recently reviewed information for a number of surveys involving various types of product evaluations. All the surveys were completed online with customers recruited from their proprietary panel. In addition to the actual survey data and other information, the online interviewing system captures the browser that the respondent used to complete the survey. Analyzing the "browser used" data, Sonic has observed a slow but steady increase in the number of individuals completing the survey on mobile browsers, including tablets and smartphones. The most recent results show a big jump in this percentage from a year ago, with an average of nearly 30 percent of the more recent surveys completed on mobile browsers.

Several managers have attempted completing some of these surveys using their own tablets and smartphones. They like the idea that using these platforms increase the options for the consumer and that these devices permit consumers to take the surveys at times and in places when and where they previously could not. However, their experiences in testing the surveys on their mobile devices have suggested that they may need to change the way they design questionnaires to accommodate smartphones and tablets.

## Questions

1. What are the impediments and difficulties associated with completing surveys on mobile devices?

2. What changes does Sonic need to make in its survey designs to take advantage of these new survey platforms?

3. What about mixing survey results taken on laptop computers and those taken on mobile devices? What cautions, if any, would you have?

4. Might the inclusion of mobile devices, along with laptops and desktops, improve the quality of the sample? Why do you say that?

# Basic Sampling Issues

## LEARNING OBJECTIVES

1. Understand the concept of sampling.

2. Learn the steps in developing a sampling plan.

3. Understand the concepts of sampling error and nonsampling error.

4. Understand the differences between probability samples and nonprobability samples.

5. Understand sampling implications of surveying over the Internet.

# Concept of Sampling

**sampling**
Process of obtaining information from a subset of a larger group.

**Sampling**, as the term is used in marketing research, is the process of obtaining information from a subset (a sample) of a larger group (the universe or population). We then take the results from the sample and project them to the larger group. The motivation for sampling is to be able to make these estimates more quickly and at a much lower cost than would be possible by any other means. It has been shown time and again that sampling a small percentage of a population can produce very accurate estimates about the population. An example that you are probably familiar with is polling in connection with political elections. Most major polls for national elections use samples of 1,000 to 1,500 people to make predictions regarding the voting behavior of tens of millions of people and their predictions have proven to be remarkably accurate.

The key to making accurate predictions about the characteristics or behavior of a large population on the basis of a relatively small sample lies in the way in which individuals are selected for the sample. It is critical that they be selected in a scientific manner, which ensures that the sample is representative—that it is a true miniature of the population. All of the major types of people who make up the population of interest should be represented in the sample in the same proportions in which they are found in the larger population. This same requirement remains as we move into the range of new online- and social-media-based data acquisition approaches. Sample size is no substitute for selection methods that ensure representativeness. This sounds simple, and as a concept, it is simple. However, achieving this goal in sampling from a human population is not easy.

## Population

In discussions of sampling, the terms *population* and *universe* are often used interchangeably.[1] In this textbook, we will use the term **population**, or *population of interest*, to refer to the entire group of people about whom we need to obtain information. Defining the population of interest is usually the first step in the sampling process and often involves defining the target market for the product or service in question.

Consider a product concept test for a new nonprescription cold symptom-relief product, such as Contac. You might take the position that the population of interest includes everyone, because everyone gets colds from time to time. Although this is true, not everyone buys a nonprescription cold symptom-relief product when he or she gets a cold. In this case, the first task in the screening process would be to determine whether people have purchased or used one or more of a number of competing brands during some time period. Only those who had purchased or used one of these brands would be included in the population of interest. The logic here is that unless the new product is really innovative in some sense, sales will have to come from current buyers in the product category.

Defining the population of interest is a key step in the sampling process. There are no specific rules to follow. The researcher must apply logic and judgment in addressing the basic issue: Whose opinions are needed in order to satisfy the objectives of the research? Often, the definition of the population is based on the characteristics of current or target customers.

**population**
Entire group of people about whom information is needed; also called *universe* or *population of interest*.

## Sample versus Census

In a **census**, data are obtained from or about every member of the population of interest. Censuses are seldom employed in marketing research, as populations of interest to marketers normally include thousands or millions of individuals. The cost and time required to collect data from a population of this magnitude are so great that censuses are out of the question. It has been demonstrated repeatedly that a relatively small but carefully chosen sample can very accurately reflect the characteristics of the population from which it is drawn. A **sample** is a subset of the population. Information is obtained from or about a sample and used to make estimates about various characteristics of the total population. Ideally, the sample from or about which information is obtained is a representative cross section of the total population.

Note that the popular belief that a census provides more accurate results than a sample is not necessarily true. In a census of a human population, there are many impediments to actually obtaining information from every member of the population. The researcher may not be able to obtain a complete and accurate list of the entire population, or certain members of the population may refuse to provide information or be difficult to find. Because of these barriers, the ideal census is seldom attainable, even with very small populations. You may have read or heard about these types of problems in connection with the 2000 and 2010 U.S. Census.[2]

**census**
Collection of data obtained from or about every member of the population of interest.

**sample**
Subset of all the members of a population of interest.

# Developing a Sampling Plan

The process of developing an operational sampling plan is summarized in the seven steps shown in Exhibit 13.1. These steps are defining the population, choosing a data-collection method, identifying a sampling frame, selecting a sampling method, determining sample size, developing operational procedures, and executing the sampling plan.

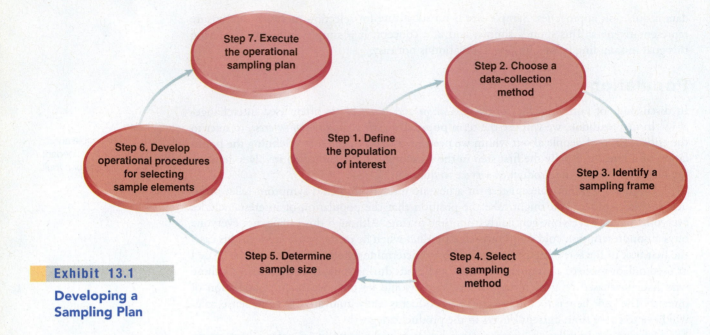

**Exhibit 13.1**

**Developing a Sampling Plan**

## Step One: Define the Population of Interest

The first issue in developing a sampling plan is to specify the characteristics of those individuals or things (for example, customers, companies, stores) from whom or about whom information is needed to meet the research objectives. The population of interest is often specified in terms of geographic area, demographic characteristics, product or service usage characteristics, brand awareness measures, or other factors (see Exhibit 13.2). In surveys, the question of whether a particular individual does or does not belong to the population of interest is often dealt with by means of screening questions discussed in Chapter 12. Even with a list of the population and a sample from that list, we still need screening questions to qualify potential respondents. Exhibit 13.3 provides a sample sequence of screening questions.

# PRACTICING MARKETING RESEARCH

## Driver's Licenses and Voter Registration Lists as Sampling Frames[3]

Medical researchers at the University of North Carolina at Chapel Hill wanted to provide the most representative sampling frame for a population-based study of the spread of HIV among heterosexual African Americans living in eight rural North Carolina counties. They found that the list of driver's licenses for men and women aged 18 to 59 gave them the "best coverage" and a "more nearly complete sampling frame" for this population, one that permitted "efficient sampling," followed by voter registration lists. It far exceeded all census lists and at least four other available population lists.

Telephone directories, for example, are inadequate because they do not publish unlisted numbers, thereby eliminating those people from the study. Medicare lists only tally the elderly, disabled, or those with diagnosed diseases. Motor vehicle registries only cover people who own cars, and random-digit dialing does not tell a researcher whether the person called belongs to the targeted demographic subset. Census lists are not good enough, either, the researchers found, because driver's license files often exceeded in number the projected population based on the census, highlighting its inaccuracy. Furthermore, the list of registered drivers was superior to voter registration lists in identifying men in the desired population, inasmuch as fewer men were registered to vote than women.

In 1992, other medical researchers had employed driver's license lists as a sampling frame for their studies of bladder and breast cancer among adult blacks. But in 1994, a congressional act restricted the release of driver's license lists to applications for statistical analysis but not direct contact of license holders. Unfortunately for market researchers, subsequent congressional, judicial review, and legislation at the state level in selected states have kept this sampling frame methodology in a state of uncertainty and flux.

## Questions

1. What kinds of usable data could a statistical analysis of driver's license lists generate, and how would you go about the study?
2. Identify two other market research categories in which driver's license lists would excel in providing accurate data.

In addition to defining who will be included in the population of interest, researchers should define the characteristics of individuals who should be excluded. For example, most commercial marketing research surveys exclude some individuals for so-called security reasons. Very frequently, one of the first questions on a survey asks whether the respondent or anyone in the respondent's immediate family works in marketing research, advertising, or the product or service area at issue in the survey (see, for example, question 5 in Exhibit 13.3). If the individual answers yes to this question, the interview is terminated. This type of question is called a *security question* because those who work in the industries in question are viewed as security risks. They may be competitors or work for competitors, and managers do not want to give them any indication of what their company may be planning to do.

There may be other reasons to exclude individuals. For example, Dr Pepper/Seven Up, Inc. might wish to do a survey among individuals who drink five or more cans, bottles, or glasses of soft drink in a typical week but do not drink Dr Pepper, because the company is interested in developing a better understanding of heavy soft-drink users who do not drink its product. Therefore, researchers would exclude those who drank one or more cans, bottles, or glasses of Dr Pepper in the past week.

| EXHIBIT 13.2 | Some Bases for Defining the Population of Interest |
| --- | --- |
| Geographic Area | What geographic area is to be sampled? This is usually a question of the client's scope of operation. The area could be a city, a county, a metropolitan area, a state, a group of states, the entire United States, or a number of countries. |
| Demographics | Given the objectives of the research and the target market for the product, whose opinions, reactions, and so on are relevant? For example, does the sampling plan require information from women over 18, women 18–34, or women 18–34 with household incomes over $35,000 per year who work and who have preschool children? |
| Usage | In addition to geographic area and/or demographics, the population of interest frequently is defined in terms of some product or service use requirement. This is usually stated in terms of use versus nonuse or use of some quantity of the product or service over a specified period of time. The following examples of use screening questions illustrate the point:<br><br>• Do you drink five or more cans, bottles, or glasses of diet soft drinks in a typical week?<br>• Have you traveled to Europe for vacation or business purposes in the past two years?<br>• Have you or has anyone in your immediate family been in a hospital for an overnight or extended stay in the past two years? |
| Awareness | The researcher may be interested in surveying those individuals who are aware of the company's advertising, to explore what the advertising communicated about the characteristics of the product or service. |

Hello. I'm _____ with _____ Research. We're conducting a survey about products used in the home. May I ask you a few questions?

1. Have you been interviewed about any products or advertising in the past 3 months?

   Yes                                          (TERMINATE AND TALLY)

   No                                           (CONTINUE)

2. Which of the following hair care products, if any, have you used in the past month? (HAND PRODUCT CARD TO RESPONDENT; CIRCLE ALL MENTIONS)

   1 Regular shampoo

   2 Dandruff shampoo

   3 Conditioner

3. You said that you have used a conditioner in the past month. Have you used a conditioner in the past week?

   Yes (used in the past week)                  (CONTINUE FOR "INSTANT" QUOTA)

   No (not used in past week)                   (TERMINATE AND TALLY)

4. Into which of the following groups does your age fall? (READ LIST, CIRCLE AGE)

   X            Under 18            (CHECK AGE QUOTAS)

   1            18–24

   2            25–34

   3            35–44

   X            45 or over

5. Previous surveys have shown that people who work in certain jobs may have different reactions to certain products. Now, do you or does any member of your immediate family work for an advertising agency, a marketing research firm, a public relations firm, or a company that manufactures or sells personal care products?

   Yes                                          (TERMINATE AND TALLY)

   No                                           (CONTINUE)

   (IF RESPONDENT QUALIFIES, INVITE HIM OR HER TO PARTICIPATE AND COMPLETE NAME GRID BELOW)

## Step Two: Choose a Data-Collection Method

The selection of a data-collection method has implications for the sampling process that we need to consider:

- Mail surveys suffer from biases associated with low response rates (which are discussed in greater detail later in this chapter).

- Telephone surveys have a less significant but growing problem with nonresponse, and suffer from call screening technologies used by potential respondents and the fact that an increasing percentage of people have mobile phones only. Currently, the best estimates put the percentage of wireless-only-households at 38.2 percent.[4]

- Internet surveys have problems with professional respondents (discussed in Chapter 7) and the fact that the panel or e-mail lists used often do not provide appropriate representation of the population of interest. Similar issues apply when using Facebook, Twitter, or other social media platforms as sample sources.

- The bigness of big data can be seductive and lead us not to question its representativeness in cases where it may not be representative of the population because it may come from limited sources. "Big" does not ensure representativeness.

Increasingly researchers are turning to methodologies that involve blending sample based on interviews collected by different means such as mail-telephone-Internet panel, Internet panel-SMS (text), Internet panel-social media, etc. As respondents become more difficult to reach by the old standbys, we have to offer new means of responding that are engaging and convenient. In the process, we need to make sure samples are still representative and results are still accurate.[5] The issue is discussed in the Practicing Marketing Research feature below.

# PRACTICING MARKETING RESEARCH

## Blending Social Media into Online Panels[6]

Social media participants represent a large potential opportunity to source respondents for market research purposes. They represent a different population of respondents from those typically found in online panels. By virtue of their difference and abundance, we must find ways to include them in our online research.

However, their difference is both a resource and a potential problem. The existing panels have been providing valuable data for years, and a sudden inclusion of new respondents has the potential to create data inconsistencies that should be cautiously avoided. We have proposed a conservative and measured way of including these new sources in a granular fashion. Their inherent difference within each demographic cell dictates the maximum blending percentage we feel can comfortably be added to a host population of online panel respondents.

At this time, it is better to err on the conservative side when merging these respondents into existing panels. Thus, we have incorporated worst-case scenarios involving sample size, income, and the amount of statistically measured difference that we allow into our sampling population.

The management of online samples is shifting from quota fulfillment to a concern for total sample frame. This type of approach is sensitive to the overriding philosophy that those who use these samples must be confident that the change that they see in their data is real and not an artifact generated by shifts in the constituent elements of the sample source being employed. Sample providers have a responsibility to be transparent about their sample frame. It is only through clarity that research practitioners can understand how to interpret their data, and it is only through that clarity that end users will know what reliance to place on it.

Once methods are employed to assure quality they cannot be "one time" credentials that pale with time. They are neither static nor do they transcend geographies. In the best of worlds, they are sensitive to changing social, political, and economic conditions. As in all other quality metrics, we do not consider the blending ratios to be static; therefore, comparative analysis must be an ongoing endeavor.

## Step Three: Identify a Sampling Frame

The third step in the process is to identify the **sampling frame**, which is a list of the members or elements of the population from which units to be sampled are to be selected. Identifying the sampling frame may simply mean specifying a procedure for generating such a list. In the ideal situation, the list of population members is complete and accurate. Unfortunately, there usually is no such list. For example, the population for a study may be defined as those individuals who have spent two or more hours on the Internet in the past week; there is no complete listing of these individuals. In such instances, the sampling frame specifies a procedure that will produce a representative sample with the desired characteristics.

For example, a telephone book might be used as the sample frame for a telephone survey sample in which the population of interest is all households in a particular city. However, the telephone book does not include households that do not have telephones and those

**sampling frame**
List of population elements from which units to be sampled can be selected or a specified procedure for generating such a list.

with unlisted numbers. It is well established that those with listed telephone numbers are significantly different from those with unlisted numbers in regard to a number of important characteristics. Subscribers who voluntarily unlist their phone numbers are more likely to be renters, live in the central city, have recently moved, have larger families, have younger children, and have lower incomes than their counterparts with listed numbers.[7] There are also significant differences between the two groups in terms of purchase, ownership, and use of certain products. Sample frame issues are discussed in the Practicing Marketing Research feature on page 317.

Unlisted numbers are more prevalent in the western United States, in metropolitan areas, among nonwhites, and among those in the 18- to 34-year age group. These findings have been confirmed in a number of studies.[8] The implications are clear: if representative samples are to be obtained in telephone surveys, researchers should use procedures that will produce samples including appropriate proportions of households with unlisted numbers. Address-based sampling discussed in the Practicing Marketing Research feature on page 315 offers a new approach to the problems of getting a proper sample frame.

**random-digit dialing**
Method of generating lists of telephone numbers at random.

One possibility is **random-digit dialing**, which generates lists of telephone numbers at random. This procedure can become fairly complex. Fortunately, companies such as Survey Sampling offer random-digit samples at a very attractive price. Details on the way such companies draw their samples can be found at *www.surveysampling.com/products_samples .php*. Developing an appropriate sampling frame is often one of the most challenging problems facing the researcher.[9]

As noted earlier, there is a growing challenge associated with the fact that an increasing number of households do not have a traditional landline and rely on mobile phones only. Currently, almost 40 percent of households use mobile phones only.[10] Fortunately, we can purchase mobile phone sample from suppliers such as SSI.

## Step Four: Select a Sampling Method

The fourth step in developing a sampling plan is selection of a sampling method, which will depend on the objectives of the study, the financial resources available, time limitations, and the nature of the problem under investigation. The major alternatives in sampling methods can be grouped under two headings: probability and nonprobability sampling methods (see Exhibit 13.4).

**Exhibit 13.4**

**Classification of Sampling Methods**

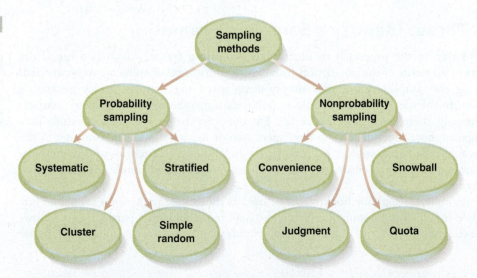

**Exhibit 13.5**

**Example of Operational Sampling Plan**

In the instructions that follow, reference is made to follow your route around a block. In cities, this will be a city block. In rural areas, a block is a segment of land surrounded by roads.

1. If you come to a dead end along your route, proceed down the opposite side of the street, road, or alley, traveling in the other direction. Continue making right turns, where possible, calling at every third occupied dwelling.

2. If you go all the way around a block and return to the starting address without completing four interviews in listed telephone homes, attempt an interview at the starting address. (This should seldom be necessary.)

3. If you work an entire block and do not complete the required interviews, proceed to the dwelling on the opposite side of the street (or rural route) that is nearest the starting address. Treat it as the next address on your Area Location Sheet and interview that house only if the address appears next to an "X" on your sheet. If it does not, continue your interviewing to the left of that address. Always follow the right turn rule.

4. If there are no dwellings on the street or road opposite the starting address for an area, circle the block opposite the starting address, following the right turn rule. (This means that you will circle the block following a clockwise direction.) Attempt interviews at every third dwelling along this route.

5. If, after circling the adjacent block opposite the starting address, you do not complete the necessary interviews, take the next block found, *following a clockwise direction*.

6. If the third block does not yield the dwellings necessary to complete your assignment, proceed to as many blocks as necessary to find the required dwellings; follow a clockwise path around the primary block.

*Source:* From "Belden Associates Interviewer Guide," reprinted by permission. The complete guide is over 30 pages long and contains maps and other aids for the interviewer.

# PRACTICING MARKETING RESEARCH

## How to Achieve Near Full Coverage for Your Sample Using Address-Based Sampling[11]

Address-Based Sampling (ABS) offers potential benefits in comparison to a strictly telephone-based method of contact. Landlines offer access to only about 75 percent of U.S. households, and contacting people via wireless devices can be a complicated process. Market research firm Survey Sampling International (SSI), however, has found that using an ABS approach can almost completely fill that access gap.

SSI combines a telephone database with a mailing list—entries with a telephone number are contacted normally, while entries possessing only the address are sent a survey in the mail. Using the U.S. Postal Service's (USPS) Delivery Sequence File (DSF) combined with other commercial databases offering more complete information on individual households, SSI has been able to achieve coverage of 95 percent of postal households and 85 percent of those addresses matched to a name. Between 55 and 65 percent are matched to a telephone number, and demographic data can be accessed as well when creating a sample.

The trend toward mobile is making telephone surveys more difficult. Twenty percent of U.S. households have no landline. This is especially true of people in their 20s. ABS, however, still offers access to households that use a cell phone as the primary or only mode of communication, but it also provides greater geodemographic information and selection options than would an approach based strictly on a wireless database.

While ABS does face certain challenges—mail surveys are generally more expensive and multimode designs can lead to variable response rates—there are methods that can be used to compensate. Selection criteria can be modified to maximize the delivery efficiency of mailers. Appended telephone numbers can be screened as well to improve accuracy and response rates. On the whole, ABS helps research achieve a more complete sample with greater response rates and also allows respondents an option of exercising their preferred response channel.

### Questions

1. Can you think of any demographic segments that might still be difficult to reach via ABS?

2. What are some ways researchers could use to mitigate the increased costs of mail surveys?

**probability samples**
Samples in which every element of the population has a known, nonzero likelihood of selection.

**nonprobability samples**
Samples in which specific elements from the population have been selected in a nonrandom manner.

© uschools/iStockphoto

The population for a study must be defined. For example, a population for a study may be defined as those individuals who have spent two or more hours on the Internet in the past week.

**sample size**
The identified and selected population subset for the survey, chosen because it represents the entire group.

**Probability samples** are selected in such a way that every element of the population has a known, nonzero likelihood of selection.[12] Simple random sampling is the best-known and most widely used probability sampling method. With probability sampling, the researcher must closely adhere to precise selection procedures that avoid arbitrary or biased selection of sample elements. When these procedures are followed strictly, the laws of probability hold, allowing calculation of the extent to which a sample value can be expected to differ from a population value. This difference is referred to as *sampling error*. The debate continues regarding whether online panels produce probability samples. These issues are discussed in the feature on page 317.

**Nonprobability samples** are those in which specific elements from the population have been selected in a nonrandom manner. *Nonrandomness* results when population elements are selected on the basis of convenience—because they are easy or inexpensive to reach. *Purposeful nonrandomness* occurs when a sampling plan systematically excludes or overrepresents certain subsets of the population. For example, if a sample designed to solicit the opinions of all women over the age of 18 were based on a telephone survey conducted during the day on weekdays, it would systematically exclude working women.

Probability samples offer several advantages over nonprobability samples, including the following:

- The researcher can be sure of obtaining information from a representative cross section of the population of interest.

- Sampling error can be computed.

- The survey results can be projected to the total population. For example, if 5 percent of the individuals in a probability sample give a particular response, the researcher can project this percentage, plus or minus the sampling error, to the total population.

Probability samples also have a number of disadvantages, the most important of which is that they are usually more expensive to implement than nonprobability samples of the same size. The rules for selection increase interviewing costs and professional time spent in designing and executing the sample design.[13]

## Step Five: Determine Sample Size

Once a sampling method has been chosen, the next step is to determine the appropriate **sample size**. (The issue of sample size determination is covered in detail in Chapter 14.) In the case of nonprobability samples, researchers tend to rely on such factors as available budget, rules of thumb, and number of subgroups to be analyzed in their determination of sample size. However, with probability samples, researchers use formulas to calculate the sample size required, given target levels of *acceptable error* (the acceptable difference between sample result and population value) and *levels of confidence* (the likelihood that the confidence interval—sample result plus or minus the acceptable error—will take in the true population value). As noted earlier, the ability to make statistical inferences about population values based on sample results is the major advantage of probability samples.

## Step Six: Develop Operational Procedures for Selecting Sample Elements

The operational procedures to be used in selecting sample elements in the data-collection phase of a project should be developed and specified, whether a probability or a nonprobability sample is being used.[14] However, the procedures are much more critical to the successful execution of a probability sample, in which case they should be detailed, clear, and unambiguous and should eliminate any interviewer discretion regarding the selection of specific sample elements. Failure to develop a proper operational plan for selecting sample elements can jeopardize the entire sampling process. Exhibit 13.5 provides an example of an operational sampling plan.

# PRACTICING MARKETING RESEARCH

## Can a Single Online Respondent Pool Offer a Truly Representative Sample?[15]

Online research programs can often benefit by building samples from multiple respondent pools. Achieving a truly representative sample is a difficult process for many reasons. When drawing from a single source, even if researchers were to use various verification methods, demographic quotas, and other strategies to create a presumably representative sample, the selection methods themselves create qualitative differences—or allow them to develop over time. The same is true of the parameters under which the online community or respondent pool was formed (subject matter mix, activities, interaction opportunities, etc.). Each online community content site is unique, and members and visitors choose to participate because of the individual experience their preferred site provides. As such, the differences between each site start to solidify as site members share more and more similar experiences and differences within the site's community decrease. (Think, birds of a feather flock together.)

As such, researchers cannot safely assume that any given online respondent pool offers an accurate probability sample of the adult U.S. or Internet population. Consequently, both intrinsic (personality traits, values, locus of control, etc.) and extrinsic (panel tenure, survey participation rates, etc.) differences will contribute variations to response-measure distribution across respondent pools. To control distribution of intrinsic characteristics in the sample while randomizing extrinsic characteristics as much as possible, researchers might need to use random selection from multiple respondent pools.

The GfK Research Center for Excellence in New York performed a study to see how the distribution of intrinsic and extrinsic individual differences varied between respondent pools. Respondents were drawn from five different online resource pools, each using a different method to obtain survey respondents. A latent class regression method separated the respondents into five underlying consumer classes according to their Internet-usage driver profiles.

Researchers then tested which of the intrinsic characteristics tended to appear within the different classes. No variable appeared in more than three classes. Furthermore, the concentration of each class varied considerably across the five respondent pools from which samples were drawn.

Within the classes themselves, variations appeared in their demographic distributions. One of the five experienced a significant skew based on gender, and two other classes exhibited variable age concentrations, with one skewed toward younger respondents and the other toward older ones.

Overall, GfK's study revealed numerous variations across different respondent resource pools. As their research continues, current findings suggest that researchers must be aware of these trends, especially in choosing their member acquisition and retention strategies and in determining which and how many respondent pools to draw from.

### Questions

1. If one respondent pool is not sufficient, how many do you think you would have to draw from to get a truly representative sample? Why do you think that?

2. When creating a sample, how would you propose accounting for the types of extrinsic characteristics mentioned?

## Step Seven: Execute the Operational Sampling Plan

The final step in the sampling process is execution of the operational sampling plan. This step requires adequate checking to ensure that specified procedures are followed.

# Sampling and Nonsampling Errors

**population parameter**
A value that accurately portrays or typifies a factor of a complete population, such as average age or income.

Consider a situation in which the goal is to determine the average number of minutes per day spent using smart phones for the population of smart phone owners. If the researcher could obtain accurate information about all members of the population, he or she could simply compute the population parameter average gross income. A **population parameter** is a value that defines a true characteristic of a total population. Assume that $\mu$ (the population parameter, average minutes per day spent using smart phones) is 65.4. As already noted, it is almost always impossible to measure an entire population (take a census). Instead, the researcher selects a sample and makes inferences about population parameters from sample results. In this case, the researcher might take a sample of 400 from a population of many millions. An estimate of the average minutes per day spent using smart phones of the members of the population ($\varepsilon$) would be calculated from the sample values. Assume that the average for the sample members is 64.7 minutes per day. A second random sample of 400 might be drawn from the same population, and the average again computed. In the second case, the average might be 66.1 minutes per day. Additional samples might be chosen, and a mean calculated for each sample. The researcher would find that the means computed for the various samples would be fairly close but not identical to the true population value in most cases.

The accuracy of sample results is affected by two general types of error: sampling error and nonsampling (measurement) error. The following formula represents the effects of these two types of error on estimating a population mean:

$$\bar{X} = \mu \pm \varepsilon_s \pm \varepsilon_{ns}$$

where $\bar{X} =$ Sample mean

$\mu =$ true population mean

$\varepsilon_s =$ sampling error

$\varepsilon_{ns} =$ nonsampling, or measurement, error

**sampling error**
Error that occurs because the sample selected is not perfectly representative of the population.

**Sampling error** results when the sample selected is not perfectly representative of the population. There are two types of sampling error: administrative and random. *Administrative error* relates to the problems in the execution of the sample plan—that is, flaws in the design or execution of the sample that cause it to be nonrepresentative of the population. These types of error can be avoided or minimized by careful attention to the design and execution of the sample. *Random sampling error* is due to chance and cannot be avoided. This type of error can be reduced, but never totally eliminated, by increasing the sample size. **Nonsampling**, or measurement **error**, includes all factors other than sampling error that may cause inaccuracy and bias in the survey results.

**nonsampling error**
All errors other than sampling error; also called *measurement error*.

# Probability Sampling Methods

As discussed earlier, every element of the population should have a known and equal likelihood of being selected for a probability sample. There are four types of probability sampling methods: simple random sampling, systematic sampling, stratified sampling, and cluster sampling.

# PRACTICING MARKETING RESEARCH

## Sampling and Data Collection with Internet Panels

*Michelle Dodd, Director, Strategic Customer Insights & Research, AT&T*

Going once, going twice....sold to the lowest bidder!

Is it really that simple to select an Internet panel partner? The short answer is no. Selecting which Internet panel(s) to work with on a given project has many factors that must be taken into consideration.

First you start with getting bids. As usual, you need the bid "ASAP," since it is then incorporated into your proposal. You need to know the feasibility and cost since they ultimately impact your recommendation on data collection methodology. Some Internet panels are very responsive and quick to turn around their bids while others seem to need two to three days. The basic facts you must provide to the panels are the geography of interest, the estimated survey length and the qualifying incidence they can expect. If you must collect the data in a very short time frame (less than one week), that will be factored in as well.

The next item to consider is your previous experience with these panels. Do their bids tend to be pretty accurate? Are they consistently able to meet (or even exceed) their estimated feasibility? Do they overpromise, leaving you in a lurch to finish collecting data in another way? Do you tend to find more speeders, duplicate respondents or fraudulent respondents in their population? Does the project manager respond to your questions in a timely manner and keep you updated as often as you like during the project?

So now you have bids from several different panels. How do you select one? One of the first criteria to consider is whether or not any one panel can fulfill all of your quota requirements on its own. It is preferable to field a study using just one panel than having to use two or more panels. This is primarily due to managing quotas and the reduced possibility of having duplicate respondents in your sample. If you are dealing with a limited geography and/or low incidence, it is likely that you will need to use multiple panels in order to meet your target quotas.

If you are fortunate enough to have more than one panel that can meet your quota requirements on its own, then cost and customer service come to the forefront of consideration. If you feel confident that each panel can successfully fill your quota requirements, you will likely select the one with the lower cost per interview (CPI). But customer service should not be overlooked. Most panels have good project managers that will work with you to get your study tested, launched and completed within the needed time frame. But if you are sweating bullets the whole time your project is in the field, wondering if you will meet quotas and meet your timeline, then a lower cost may not be worth it in the long run.

At the completion of the data collection phase, you may need to get data from a third party (such as Acxiom or Knowledge Based Marketing) appended to supplement or enhance your analysis. Not all Internet panels can or will help with this task. Some Internet panels do not capture name and physical address information on their panelists. Others may have this information but are not willing to share it. So if this is a possible requirement on your project, it is important to flesh it out up front to make sure that your panel partner(s) can and will provide this information for panelists who complete a survey on your project.

## Simple Random Sampling

Simple random sampling is the purest form of probability sampling. For a simple random sample, the known and equal probability is computed as follows:

$$\text{Probability of selection} = \frac{\text{Sample size}}{\text{Population size}}$$

For example, if the population size is 10,000 and the sample size is 400, the probability of selection is 4 percent:

$$.04 = \frac{400}{10,000}$$

**simple random sample**
Probability sample selected by assigning a number to every element of the population and then using a table of random numbers to select specific elements for inclusion in the sample.

If a sampling frame (listing of all the elements of the population) is available, the researcher can select a **simple random sample** as follows:

1. Assign a number to each element of the population. A population of 10,000 elements would be numbered from 1 to 10,000.

2. Using a table of random numbers (such as Exhibit 1 in Appendix Three, "Statistical Tables"), begin at some arbitrary point and move up, down, or across until 400 (sample size) five-digit numbers between 1 and 10,000 have been chosen. The numbers selected from the table identify specific population elements to be included in the sample.

Simple random sampling is appealing because it seems easy and meets all the necessary requirements of a probability sample. It guarantees that every member of the population has a known and equal chance of being selected for the sample. Simple random sampling begins with a current and complete listing of the population. Such listings, however, are extremely difficult, if not impossible, to obtain. Simple random samples can be obtained in telephone surveys through the use of random digit dialing. They can also be generated from computer files such as customer lists; software programs are available or can be readily written to select random samples that meet all necessary requirements.

## Systematic Sampling

**systematic sampling**
Probability sampling in which the entire population is numbered and elements are selected using a skip interval.

Because of its simplicity, **systematic sampling** is often used as a substitute for simple random sampling. It produces samples that are almost identical to those generated via simple random sampling. It is a compromise for expediency, does not meet the strict rules and has a very small risk of producing a nonrepresentative sample.

To produce a systematic sample, the researcher first numbers the entire population, as in simple random sampling. Then determines a *skip interval* and selects names based on this interval. The skip interval can be computed very simply through use of the following formula:

$$\text{Skip interval} = \frac{\text{Population size}}{\text{Sample size}}$$

For example, if you were using a local telephone directory and had computed a skip interval of 100, every 100th name would be selected for the sample. The use of this formula would ensure that the entire list was covered.

A random starting point should be used in systematic sampling. For example, if you were using a telephone directory, you would need to draw a random number to determine the page on which to start—say, page 53. You would draw another random number to determine the column to use on that page—for example, the third column. You would draw a final random number to determine the actual starting element in that column—say, the 17th name. From that beginning point, you would employ the skip interval until the desired sample size had been reached.

The main advantage of systematic sampling over simple random sampling is economy. Systematic sampling is often simpler, less time-consuming, and less expensive to execute than simple random sampling. The greatest danger lies in the possibility that hidden patterns within the population list may inadvertently be pulled into the sample. However, this danger is remote.

## Stratified Sampling

**Stratified samples** are probability samples that are distinguished by the following procedural steps:

1. The original, or parent, population is divided into two or more mutually exclusive and exhaustive subsets (e.g., male and female).

2. Simple random samples of elements from the two or more subsets are chosen independently of each other.

Although the requirements for a stratified sample do not specify the basis on which the original or parent population should be separated into subsets, common sense dictates that the population be divided on the basis of factors related to the characteristic of interest in the population. For example, if you are conducting a political poll to predict the outcome of an election and can show that there is a significant difference in the way men and women are likely to vote, then gender is an appropriate basis for stratification. If you do not do stratified sampling in this manner, then you do not get the benefits of stratification, and you have expended additional time, effort, and resources for no benefit. With gender as the basis for stratification, one stratum, then, would be made up of men and one of women. These strata are mutually exclusive and exhaustive in that every population element can be assigned to one and only one (male or female) and no population elements are unassignable. The second stage in the selection of a stratified sample involves drawing simple random samples independently from each stratum.

Researchers prefer stratified samples to simple random samples because of their potential for greater statistical efficiency.[16] That is, if two samples are drawn from the same population—one a properly stratified sample and the other a simple random sample—the stratified sample will have a smaller sampling error. Also, reduction of sampling error to a certain target level can be achieved with a smaller stratified sample. Stratified samples are statistically more efficient because one source of variation has been eliminated.

If stratified samples are statistically more efficient, why are they not used all the time? There are two reasons. First, the information necessary to properly stratify the sample frequently may not be available. For example, little may be known about the demographic characteristics of consumers of a particular product. To properly stratify the sample and to get the benefits of stratification, the researcher must choose bases for stratification that yield significant differences between the strata in regard to the measurement of interest. When such differences are not identifiable, the sample cannot be properly stratified. Second, even if the necessary information is available, the potential value of the information may not warrant the time and costs associated with stratification.

In the case of a simple random sample, the researcher depends entirely on the laws of probability to generate a representative sample of the population. With stratified sampling, the researcher, to some degree, forces the sample to be representative by making sure that important dimensions of the population are represented in the sample in their true population proportions. For example, the researcher may know that although men and women are equally likely to be users of a particular product, women are much more likely to be heavy users. In a study designed to analyze consumption patterns of the product, failure to properly represent women in the sample would result in a biased view of consumption patterns. Assume that women make up 60 percent of the population of interest and men account for 40 percent. Because of sampling fluctuations, a properly executed simple random sampling

**stratified sample**
Probability sample that is forced to be more representative through simple random sampling of mutually exclusive and exhaustive subsets.

procedure might produce a sample made up of 55 percent women and 45 percent men. This is the same kind of error you would obtain if you flipped a coin 10 times. The ideal result of 10 coin tosses would be five heads and five tails, but more than half the time you would get a different result. In similar fashion, a properly drawn and executed simple random sample from a population made up of 60 percent women and 40 percent men is not likely to consist of exactly 60 percent women and 40 percent men. However, the researcher can force a stratified sample to have 60 percent women and 40 percent men.

Three steps are involved in implementing a properly stratified sample:

1. *Identify salient (important) demographic or classification factors*—Factors that are correlated with the behavior of interest. For example, there may be reason to believe that men and women have different average consumption rates of a particular product. To use gender as a basis for meaningful stratification, the researcher must be able to show with actual data that there are significant differences in the consumption levels of men and women. In this manner, various salient factors are identified. Research indicates that, as a general rule, after the six most important factors have been identified, the identification of additional salient factors adds little in the way of increased sampling efficiency.[17]

2. *Determine what proportions of the population fall into the various subgroups under each stratum* (for example, if gender has been determined to be a salient factor, determine what proportion of the population is male and what proportion is female). Using these proportions, the researcher can determine how many respondents are required from each subgroup. However, before a final determination is made, a decision must be made as to whether to use proportional allocation or disproportional, or optimal, allocation.

**proportional allocation**
Sampling in which the number of elements selected from a stratum is directly proportional to the size of the stratum relative to the size of the population.

Under **proportional allocation**, the number of elements selected from a stratum is directly proportional to the size of the stratum in relation to the size of the population. With proportional allocation, the proportion of elements to be taken from each stratum is given by the formula $n/N$, where $n$ = the size of the stratum and $N$ = the size of the population.

**disproportional, or optimal, allocation**
Sampling in which the number of elements taken from a given stratum is proportional to the relative size of the stratum and the standard deviation of the characteristic under consideration.

**Disproportional**, or **optimal**, **allocation** produces the most efficient samples and provides the most precise or reliable estimates for a given sample size. This approach requires a double weighting scheme. Under this scheme, the number of sample elements to be taken from a given stratum is proportional to the relative size of the stratum and the standard deviation of the distribution of the characteristic under consideration for all elements in the stratum. This scheme is used for two reasons. First, the size of a stratum is important because those strata with greater numbers of elements are more important in determining the population mean. Therefore, such strata should have more weight in deriving estimates of population parameters. Second, it makes sense that relatively more elements should be drawn from those strata having larger standard deviations (more variation) and relatively fewer elements should be drawn from those strata having smaller standard deviations. Allocating relatively more of the sample to those strata where the potential for sampling error is greatest (largest standard deviation) is cost-effective and improves the overall accuracy of the estimates. There is no difference between proportional allocation and disproportional allocation if the distributions of the characteristic under consideration have the same standard deviation from stratum to stratum.[18]

3. *Select separate simple random samples from each stratum.* This process is implemented somewhat differently than traditional simple random sampling. Assume that the stratified sampling plan requires that 240 women and 160 men be interviewed. The researcher will sample from the total population and keep track of the number of men and women interviewed. At some point in the process, when, for example, 240 women and 127 men have been interviewed, the researcher will interview only men until the target of 160 men is reached. In this manner, the process generates a sample in which the proportion of men and women conforms to the allocation scheme derived in step 2.

Stratified samples are not used as often as one might expect in marketing research. The reason is that the information necessary to properly stratify the sample is often not available in advance. Stratification cannot be based on guesses or hunches but must be based on hard data regarding the characteristics of the population and the relationship between these characteristics and the behavior under investigation. Stratified samples are frequently used in political polling and media audience research. In those areas, the researcher is more likely to have the information necessary to implement the stratification process.

## Cluster Sampling

The types of samples discussed so far have all been single unit samples, in which each sampling unit is selected separately. In the case of **cluster samples**, the sampling units are selected in groups.[19] There are two basic steps in cluster sampling:

1. The population of interest is divided into mutually exclusive and exhaustive subsets such as geographic areas.
2. A random sample of the subsets (e.g., geographic areas) is selected.

If the sample consists of all the elements in the selected subsets, it is called a *one-stage cluster sample.* However, if the sample of elements is chosen in some probabilistic manner from the selected subsets, the sample is a *two-stage cluster sample.*

Both stratified and cluster sampling involve dividing the population into mutually exclusive and exhaustive subgroups. However, in stratified samples the researcher selects a sample of elements from each subgroup, while in cluster samples, the researcher selects a sample of subgroups and then collects data either from all the elements in the subgroup (one-stage cluster sample) or from a sample of the elements (two-stage cluster sample).

All the probability sampling methods discussed to this point require sampling frames that list or provide some organized breakdown of all the elements in the target population. Under cluster sampling, the researcher develops sampling frames that specify groups or clusters of elements of the population without actually listing individual elements. Sampling is then executed by taking a sample of the clusters in the frame and generating lists or other breakdowns for only those clusters that have been selected for the sample. Finally, a sample is chosen from the elements of the selected clusters.

The most popular type of cluster sample is the area sample in which the clusters are units of geography (for example, city blocks). Cluster sampling is considered to be a probability sampling technique because of the random selection of clusters and the random selection of elements within the selected clusters.

Cluster sampling assumes that the elements in a cluster are as heterogeneous as those in the total population. If the characteristics of the elements in a cluster are very similar, then that assumption is violated and the researcher has a problem. In the city-block sampling just

Harry Lynch/Getty Images

A stratified sample may be appropriate in certain cases. For example, if a political poll is being conducted to predict who will win an election, a difference in the way men and women are likely to vote would make gender an appropriate basis for stratification.

**cluster sample**
Probability sample in which the sampling units are selected from a number of small geographic areas to reduce data collection costs.

324 | CHAPTER 13 | BASIC SAMPLING ISSUES

**multistage area sampling**
Geographic areas selected for national or regional surveys in progressively smaller population units, such as counties, then residential blocks, then homes.

described, there may be little heterogeneity within clusters because the residents of a cluster are very similar to each other and different from those of other clusters. Typically, this potential problem is dealt with in the sample design by selecting a large number of clusters and sampling a relatively small number of elements from each cluster.

Another possibility is **multistage area sampling**, or **multistage area probability sampling**, which involves three or more steps. Samples of this type are used for national surveys or surveys that cover large regional areas. Here, the researcher randomly selects geographic areas in progressively smaller units.

From the standpoint of statistical efficiency, cluster samples are generally less efficient than other types of probability samples. In other words, a cluster sample of a certain size will have a larger sampling error than a simple random sample or a stratified sample of the same size. To understand the greater cost efficiency and lower statistical efficiency of a cluster sample, consider the following example. A researcher needs to select a sample of 200 households in a particular city for in-home interviews. If she selects these 200 households via simple random sampling, they will be scattered across the city. Cluster sampling might be implemented in this situation by selecting 20 residential blocks in the city and randomly choosing 10 households on each block to interview.

It is easy to see that interviewing costs will be dramatically reduced under the cluster sampling approach. Interviewers do not have to spend as much time traveling, and their mileage is dramatically reduced. In regard to sampling error, however, you can see that simple random sampling has the advantage. Interviewing 200 households scattered across the city increases the chance of getting a representative cross section of respondents. If all interviewing is conducted in 20 randomly selected blocks within the city, certain ethnic, social, or economic groups might be missed or over- or underrepresented.

As noted previously, cluster samples are, in nearly all cases, statistically less efficient than simple random samples. It is possible to view a simple random sample as a special type of cluster sample, in which the number of clusters is equal to the total sample size, with one sample element selected per cluster. At this point, the statistical efficiency of the cluster sample and that of the simple random sample are equal. From this point on, as the researcher decreases the number of clusters and increases the number of sample elements per cluster, the statistical efficiency of the cluster sample declines. At the other extreme, the researcher

The most popular type of cluster sample is the area sample, in which the clusters are units of geography (for example, city blocks). A researcher, conducting a door-to-door survey in a particular metropolitan area, might randomly choose a sample of city blocks from the metropolitan area, select a sample of clusters, and then interview a sample of consumers from each cluster. All interviews would be conducted in the clusters selected, dramatically reducing interviewers' travel time and expenses. Cluster sampling is considered to be a probability sampling technique because of the random selection of clusters and the random selection of elements within the selected clusters.

© LHB Photo/Alamy

might choose a single cluster and select all the sample elements from that cluster. For example, he or she might select one relatively small geographic area in the city where you live and interview 200 people from that area. How comfortable would you be that a sample selected in this manner would be representative of the entire metropolitan area where you live?

Given the minimal use of face-to-face interviewing today, the incentives for the use of cluster sampling, which center on cost efficiencies, are also minimal.

# Nonprobability Sampling Methods

In a general sense, any sample that does not meet the requirements of a probability sample is, by definition, a nonprobability sample. We have already noted that a major disadvantage of nonprobability samples is the inability to calculate sampling error for them. This suggests the even greater difficulty of evaluating the overall quality of nonprobability samples. How far do they deviate from the standard required of probability samples? The user of data from a nonprobability sample must make this assessment, which should be based on a careful evaluation of the methodology used to generate the nonprobability sample. Is it likely that the methodology employed will generate a reasonable cross section of individuals from the target population? Or is the sample hopelessly biased in some particular direction? These are the questions that must be answered. Four types of nonprobability samples are frequently used: convenience, judgment, quota, and snowball samples.

## Convenience Samples

**Convenience samples** are primarily used, as their name implies, for reasons of convenience. Companies such as Frito-Lay often use their own employees for preliminary tests of new product formulations developed by their R&D departments. At first, this may seem to be a highly biased approach. However, these companies are not asking employees to evaluate existing products or to compare their products with a competitor's products. They are asking employees only to provide gross sensory evaluations of new product formulations (for example, saltiness, crispness, greasiness). In such situations, convenience sampling is an efficient and effective means of obtaining the required information. This is particularly true in an exploratory situation, where there is a pressing need to get an inexpensive approximation of true value.

Some believe that the use of convenience sampling is growing at a faster rate than the growth in the use of probability sampling.[20] The reason, as suggested is the growing availability of databases of consumers in low-incidence and hard-to-find categories. For example, suppose a company has developed a new athlete's foot remedy and needs to conduct a survey among those who suffer from the malady. Because these individuals make up only 4 percent of the population, researchers conducting a telephone survey would have to talk with 25 people to find 1 individual who suffered from the problem. Purchasing a list of individuals known to suffer from the problem can dramatically reduce the cost of the survey and the time necessary to complete it. Although such a list might be made up of individuals who used coupons when purchasing the product or sent in for manufacturers' rebates, companies are increasingly willing to make the trade-off of lower cost and faster turnaround for a lower-quality sample.

**convenience samples**
Nonprobability samples based on using people who are easily accessible.

## Judgment Samples

The term **judgment sample** is applied to any sample in which the selection criteria are based on the researcher's judgment about what constitutes a representative sample. Most test markets and many product tests conducted in shopping malls are essentially

**judgment samples**
Nonprobability samples in which the selection criteria are based on the researcher's judgment about representativeness of the population under study.

judgment sampling. In the case of test markets, one or a few markets are selected based on the judgment that they are representative of the population as a whole. Malls are selected for product taste tests based on the researcher's judgment that the particular malls attract a reasonable cross section of consumers who fall into the target group for the product being tested.

## Quota Samples

**quota samples**
Nonprobability samples in which quotas, based on demographic or classification factors selected by the researcher, are established for population subgroups.

**Quota samples** are typically selected in such a way that demographic characteristics of interest to the researcher are represented in the sample in target proportions. Thus, many people confuse quota samples and stratified samples. There are, however, two key differences between a quota sample and a stratified sample. First, respondents for a quota sample are not selected randomly, as they must be for a stratified sample. Second, the classification factors used for a stratified sample are selected based on the existence of a correlation between the factor and the behavior of interest. There is no such requirement in the case of a quota sample. The demographic or classification factors of interest in a quota sample are selected on the basis of researcher judgment.

## Snowball Samples

**snowball samples**
Nonprobability samples in which additional respondents are selected based on referrals from initial respondents.

In **snowball samples**, sampling procedures are used to select additional respondents on the basis of referrals from initial respondents. This procedure is used to sample from low-incidence or rare populations—that is, populations that make up a very small percentage of the total population.[21] The costs of finding members of these rare populations may be so great that the researcher is forced to use a technique such as snowball sampling. For example, suppose an insurance company needed to obtain a national sample of individuals who have switched from the indemnity form of healthcare coverage to a health maintenance organization (HMO) in the past six months. It would be necessary to sample a very large number of consumers to identify 1,000 that fall into this population. It would be far more economical to obtain an initial sample of 200 people from the population of interest and have each of them provide the names of an average of four other people to complete the sample of 1,000.

The main advantage of snowball sampling is a dramatic reduction in search costs. However, this advantage comes at the expense of sample quality. The total sample is likely to be biased because the individuals whose names were obtained from those sampled in the initial phase are likely to be very similar to those initially sampled. As a result, the sample may not be a good cross section of the total population. There is general agreement that some limits should be placed on the number of respondents obtained through referrals, although there are no specific rules regarding what these limits should be. This approach may also be hampered by the fact that respondents may be reluctant to give referrals.

# Internet Sampling

The advantages of Internet interviewing are compelling, as discussed in Chapter 6:

- *Target respondents can complete the survey when it is convenient for them*. It can be completed late at night, over the weekend, and at any other time they choose.
- *Data collection is relatively inexpensive*. Once basic overhead and other fixed costs are covered, interviewing is essentially volume-insensitive. Thousands of interviews can be

conducted at an actual data-collection cost of just a few dollars per survey. Cost for a telephone survey may be three to five times higher depending on the study.

- *The interview can be administered under software control.* This allows the survey to follow skip patterns and do other "smart" things.
- *The survey can be completed quickly.* Hundreds or thousands of surveys can be completed in a day or less.[22]

A growing body of research shows that surveys conducted by Internet, using panels owned by firms such as SSI and Research Now, produce results comparable to those produced by telephone surveys.[23] Increasingly, researchers are blending data from online panels with data generated from telephone, mail, and other data-collection techniques to deal with the limitations of each method used alone. Issues in this type of sample blending are covered in the Practicing Marketing Research feature below.

# PRACTICING MARKETING RESEARCH

## How Building a Blended Sample Can Help Improve Research Results[24]

Most researchers prefer building a sample from a single source. In many cases, however, getting a truly representative sample from a single source is becoming more difficult. Survey Sampling International (SSI) has used a blended sample approach of panels, web traffic, and aligned interest groups, and has found the resulting quality of the data is higher than with a single source sample.

Using a blended sample source creates two benefits: (1) It helps capture the opinions of people who would not otherwise join panels; and (2) it increases heterogeneity. As the breadth of sources increases, however, it is important to identify the unique biases of each of those sources and control for it in order to ensure high sample quality. The only way to achieve this balance is to understand where the bias is coming from. By using a panel exclusively, for example, you might eliminate individuals with valuable opinions who just aren't willing to commit to joining the panel.

Researchers should also make sure their samples are consistent and predictable. Studies indicate that controlling just for demographics and other traditional balancing factors does not always account for the variations created by the distinct characteristics of different sample sources. Demographic quotas may work, but only if the selected stratification relates directly to the questionnaire topic. Comparing sources to external benchmarks can improve consistency as well, but often those benchmarks are not readily available.

SSI's research on variance between data sources indicates that psychographic and neurographic variables have a greater capacity to influence variance between diverse sources than traditional demographic variables have. Even still, these variables do not account for all the possible variance, so researchers must continue testing in order to ensure consistency within the blended sampling method.

SSI offers the following suggestions for creating a blended sample:

- Consider including calibration questions—Look for existing external benchmarks for your survey topic.
- Understand the sample blending techniques used to create your sample—Tell your sample provider what kind of source smoothing and quality control methods are being used.
- Know your sources—Ask your sample provider how source quality is being maintained.
- Plan ahead—Incorporate blending into the sample plan from the start.
- Ensure that respondents are satisfied with the research experience—Be aware that significantly high nonresponse and noncompletion rates can introduce bias as well.

## Questions

1. Beyond the variables discussed, can you think of any others that might be relevant when creating a blended sample?
2. Do you think a blended sample would be useful, and if so, would you be inclined to try it? Are there any situations in which you would think a single-source sample would be more effective? Why?

# SUMMARY

The population, or universe, is the total group of people in whose opinions the researcher is interested. A census involves collecting the needed information from every member of the population of interest. A sample is simply a subset of a population. The steps in developing a sampling plan are: define the population of interest, choose the data-collection method, identify the sampling frame, select the sampling method, determine sample size, develop and specify an operational plan for selecting sampling elements, and execute the operational sampling plan. The sampling frame is a list of the elements of the population from which the sample will be drawn or a specified procedure for representing the list.

In probability sampling methods, samples are selected in such a way that every element of the population has a known, nonzero likelihood of selection. Nonprobability sampling methods select specific elements from the population in a nonrandom manner. Probability samples have several advantages over nonprobability samples, including reasonable certainty that information will be obtained from a representative cross section of the population, a sampling error that can be computed, and survey results that can be projected to the total population. However, probability samples are more expensive than nonprobability samples and usually take more time to design and execute.

The accuracy of sample results is determined by both sampling and nonsampling error. Sampling error occurs because the sample selected is not perfectly representative of the population. There are two types of sampling error: random sampling error and administrative error. Random sampling error is due to chance and cannot be avoided; it can only be reduced by increasing sample size.

Probability samples include simple random samples, systematic samples, stratified samples, and cluster samples. Nonprobability samples include convenience samples, judgment samples, quota samples, and snowball samples. At the present time, Internet samples tend to be convenience samples. That may change in the future as better e-mail sampling frames become available.

# KEY TERMS

sampling **308**

population **309**

census **309**

sample **309**

sampling frame **313**

random-digit dialing **314**

probability samples **316**

nonprobability samples **316**

sample size **316**

population parameter **318**

sampling error **318**

nonsampling error **318**

simple random sample **320**

systematic sampling **321**

stratified sample **321**

proportional allocation **322**

disproportional, or optimal, allocation **322**

cluster sample **323**

multistage area sampling **324**

convenience samples **325**

judgment samples **325**

quota samples **326**

snowball samples **326**

# QUESTIONS FOR REVIEW & CRITICAL THINKING

1. What are some situations in which a census would be better than a sample? Why are samples usually employed rather than censuses?

2. Develop a sampling plan for examining undergraduate business students' attitudes toward Internet advertising.

3. Give an example of a perfect sampling frame. Why is a telephone directory usually not an acceptable sampling frame?

4. Distinguish between probability and nonprobability samples. What are the advantages and disadvantages of each? Why are nonprobability samples so popular in marketing research?

5. Distinguish among a systematic sample, a cluster sample, and a stratified sample. Give examples of each.

6. What is the difference between a stratified sample and a quota sample?

7. American National Bank has 1,000 customers. The manager wishes to draw a sample of 100 customers. How could this be done using systematic sampling? What would be the impact on the technique, if any, if the list were ordered by average size of deposit?

8. Do you see any problem with drawing a systematic sample from a telephone book, assuming that the telephone book is an acceptable sample frame for the study in question?

9. Describe snowball sampling. Give an example of a situation in which you might use this type of sample. What are the dangers associated with this type of sample?

10. Name some possible sampling frames for the following:

   a. Patrons of sushi bars
   b. Smokers of high-priced cigars
   c. Snowboarders

   d. Owners of DVD players
   e. People who have visited one or more countries in Europe in the last year
   f. People who immigrated to the United States within the last two years
   g. People with allergies

11. Identify the following sample designs:

   a. The names of 200 patrons of a casino are drawn from a list of visitors for the last month, and a questionnaire is administered to them.
   b. A radio talk show host invites listeners to call in and vote yes or no on whether handguns should be banned.
   c. A dog-food manufacturer wants to test a new dog food. It decides to select 100 dog owners who feed their dogs canned food, 100 who feed their dogs dry food, and 100 who feed their dogs semimoist food.
   d. A poll surveys men who play golf to predict the outcome of a presidential election.

## WORKING THE NET

1. Toluna offers *QuickSurveys*, a self-service tool that enables you to conduct market research quickly, easily and cost effectively. You can:

   - Create a survey of up to five questions.
   - Select up to 2,000 nationally representative respondents.
   - Pay online using a credit card or PayPal.
   - Immediately follow the results live online and complete within 24 hours (speed of completion may vary by country.

With this system, once your survey has been created it will automatically appear live on targeted specific areas of Toluna.com—a global community site that provides a forum where over 4 million members interact and poll each other on a broad range of topics. Visit *www.toluna-group.com* to view a *QuickSurveys* flash demo.

2. Throughout 2008, Knowledge Networks worked in conjunction with the Associated Press and Yahoo! to repeatedly poll 2,230 people (from random telephone sampling) about likely election results and political preferences. Visit *www.knowledgenetworks.com* and evaluate their methodology and ultimate accuracy (or inaccuracy) on this topic.

## REAL-LIFE RESEARCH • 13.1

### The Research Group

The Research Group has been hired by the National Internet Service Providers Association to determine the following:

- What specific factors motivate people to choose a particular Internet service provider (ISP)?
- How do these factors differ between choosing an ISP for home use and choosing an ISP for business use?

- Why do people choose one ISP over the others? How many have switched ISPs in the past year? Why did they switch ISPs?
- How satisfied are they with their current ISP?
- Do consumers know or care whether an ISP is a member of the National Internet Service Providers Association?
- What value-added services do consumers want from ISPs (e.g., telephone support for questions and problems)?

The Research Group underbid three other research companies to get the contract. In fact, its bid was more than

25 percent lower than the next lowest bid. The primary way in which The Research Group was able to provide the lowest bid related to its sampling methodology. In its proposal, The Research Group specified that college students would be used to gather the survey data. Its plan called for randomly selecting 20 colleges from across the country, contacting the chairperson of the marketing department, and asking her or him to submit a list of 10 students who would be interested in earning extra money. Finally, The Research Group would contact the students individually with the goal of identifying five students at each school who would ultimately be asked to get 10 completed interviews. Students would be paid $10 for each completed survey. The only requirement imposed in regard to selecting potential respondents was that they had to be ISP subscribers at the time of the survey. The Research Group proposal suggested that the easiest way to do this would be for the student interviewers to go to the student union or student center during the lunch hour and ask those at each table whether they might be interested in participating in the survey.

## Questions

1. How would you describe this sampling methodology?
2. What problems do you see arising from this technique?
3. Suggest an alternative sampling method that might give the National Internet Service Providers Association a better picture of the information it desired.

## REAL-LIFE RESEARCH • 13.2

### Community Bank

Joe Stewart of Community Bank has been tasked by the board of directors of the bank with conducting a survey in the community they serve. Community has been a rapidly growing bank serving a single large metropolitan area with five branch banks. It appeals primarily to mid-size commercial customers and has the advantage of being able to cater to the unique needs of the market it serves. Community Bank has been very effective in working around the more homogenized strategies used by the large national banks and has been more agile in this than even some of its other local competitors.

However, its growth is slowing and the board and senior management believe it is time to conduct a market survey among consumers to identify possible opportunities that they have overlooked in their focus on the commercial market. Initially, the thought was to conduct a random sample of consumers in the market. This thought came from several board members and some senior managers who had taken statistics and a few marketing research courses in their college curricula.

Joe has been doing some work using Excel and has determined, for example, that if they do a random sample, then only about 3.8 percent of the people that they survey would be expected to fall within the $200,000 or higher annual household income category. This figure parallels the percentage of households that fall into this category from the most recent U.S. population census. Given that it has already been determined that Community Bank's budget would support a maximum sample size of 1,000, this would produce only about 38 people in the sample that fall into this category. Similar comparisons have been made for other key subgroups, and Joe has consistently been finding that the expected sample size numbers in many of these targeted subgroups are too small to inspire much confidence in the conclusions they draw about these subgroups.

## Questions

1. Is there another type of probability sample that would better suit the needs of Community Bank? What is that sample type, and how would it better meet its needs?
2. Assuming that Joe thinks this (your answer to question 1) would be a better alternative, how would he justify his recommendations to the board and senior management?
3. What sample size should the bank be seeking in important sub groups? What is the basis for your response?

© Aerial Archives/Alamy

## CHAPTER 14

# Sample Size Determination

## LEARNING OBJECTIVES

1. Gain an appreciation of a normal distribution.

2. Understand population, sample, and sampling distributions.

3. Understand how to compute the sampling distribution of the mean.

4. Learn how to determine sample size.

5. Understand how to determine statistical power.

# Determining Sample Size for Probability Samples

The process of determining sample size for probability samples involves financial, statistical, and managerial issues. As a general rule, the larger the sample, the smaller the sampling error. However, larger samples cost more money, and the resources available for a project are always limited. Although the cost of increasing sample size tends to rise on a linear basis (double the sample size, almost double the cost) with data collection costs, sampling error decreases at a rate equal to the square root of the relative increase in sample size. If sample size is quadrupled, data collection cost is almost quadrupled, but the level of sampling error is reduced by only 50 percent.

Managerial issues and research objectives must be reflected in sample size calculations. How accurate do estimates need to be, and how confident do managers need to be that true population values are included in the chosen confidence interval? Some cases require high levels of precision (small sampling error) and confidence that population values fall in the small range of sampling error (the confidence interval). Other cases may not require the same level of precision or confidence.

Online interviewing and Internet panels, along with social-media–driven sampling, have had an impact of feasible sample sizes. The Practicing Marketing Research box below provides an example of what can be achieved in the way of sample size quickly and at reasonable cost. With 4,300 consumers interviewed every weekday, we can get very precise measures of key metrics in a very timely manner.

# PRACTICING MARKETING RESEARCH

## The Super Bowl's Real Results: The Brands that Lifted Purchase Consideration Most[1]

You loved Budweiser Super Bowl ads like "Puppy Bowl," but you aren't thinking about buying Bud more than before, new research from YouGov BrandIndex suggests. M&M's, on the other hand, has significantly increased its odds on your next shopping trip.

"There can definitely be a difference between someone seeing an ad that they liked creatively that made them laugh or cry or smile, and wanting to go out and buy that product," said Ted Marzilli, CEO at YouGov BrandIndex.

YouGov BrandIndex, which says it interviews 4,300 people each weekday from an online panel that's designed to be representative of the U.S. population, crunched the numbers on Super Bowl advertisers before and after the game. It found that Budweiser, GoDaddy, Doritos, and Microsoft got people talking or increased the positive buzz about them more than other Super Bowl advertisers. But of those four, only Doritos made the top 10 for a lift in purchase consideration.

Even the good news for M&M's, Doritos, and other brands such as Jeep only goes so far at this point, Mr. Marzilli said. "What this doesn't show you, because we're looking at this only two days after the Super Bowl, is how long that purchase consideration lasts," he said.

Other brands may have been trying to increase good buzz more than anything else. RadioShack, among others, seemed to do itself a favor with its 1980s-themed Super Bowl ad, according to YouGov BrandIndex. And as far as Budweiser goes, the Super Bowl is less of an investment in the grand scheme of its annual marketing than it is for smaller marketers, Mr. Marzilli noted.

**YouGov BrandIndex**

### Super Bowl: Purchase Consideration

| Brand | Baseline Period (Jan 1-20) | Pre Super Bowl Period (Jan 21-26) | 2 Day Post Game (Feb 3-4) | Change 2-Day Post Game vs Pre SB Period | Change 2-Day Post Game vs Baseline |
|---|---|---|---|---|---|
| M&M's | 41.8 | 41.7 | 48.4 | 6.7 | 6.6 |
| Jeep | 11.5 | 11.2 | 14.1 | 2.9 | 2.7 |
| Audi | 7.1 | 6.9 | 9.7 | 2.8 | 2.6 |
| Hyundai | 13.1 | 13.2 | 15.2 | 2.0 | 2.1 |
| Doritos | 38.1 | 41.2 | 40.1 | −1.0 | 2.0 |
| Kia | 11.1 | 11.7 | 13.1 | 1.4 | 2.0 |
| RadioShack | 25.6 | 24.0 | 27.1 | 3.1 | 1.5 |
| AXE | 12.8 | 15.7 | 17.7 | −2.0 | 0.9 |
| Budweiser | 11.2 | 12.1 | 11.2 | −0.8 | 0.1 |
| Microsoft | 32.7 | 32.5 | 32.1 | −0.3 | −0.5 |

## YouGov BrandIndex

### Super Bowl: Word of Mouth

| Brand | Baseline Period (Jan 1-20) | Pre Super Bowl Period (Jan 21-26) | 2 Day Post Game (Feb 3-4) | Change 2-Day Post Game vs Pre SB Period | Change 2-Day Post Game vs Baseline |
|---|---|---|---|---|---|
| Doritos | 14.6 | 18.8 | 26.1 | 7.3 | 11.5 |
| Microsoft | 10.7 | 14.0 | 17.8 | 3.8 | 7.1 |
| Budweiser | 7.5 | 9.2 | 12.9 | 3.7 | 5.3 |
| Cheerios | 14.3 | 17.4 | 19.0 | 1.6 | 4.8 |
| Pepsi | 13.8 | 13.6 | 17.4 | 3.8 | 3.6 |
| M&M's | 14.3 | 13.2 | 17.5 | 4.3 | 3.3 |
| Coca Cola | 18.7 | 19.1 | 21.8 | 2.7 | 3.1 |
| Kia | 6.8 | 6.4 | 9.j0 | 2.7 | 2.3 |
| Audi | 4.6 | 3.6 | 6.9 | 3.3 | 2.3 |
| Jeep | 9.2 | 8.6 | 10.8 | 2.2 | 1.6 |

## YouGov BrandIndex

### Super Bowl: Buzz

| Brand | Baseline Period (Jan 1-20) | Pre Super Bowl Period (Jan 21-26) | 2 Day Post Game (Feb 3-4) | Change 2-Day Post Game vs Pre SB Period | Change 2-Day Post Game vs Baseline |
|---|---|---|---|---|---|
| Go Daddy.com | −0.1 | 1.6 | 17.2 | 15.6 | 17.2 |
| Budweiser | 9.7 | 11.1 | 17.8 | 6.7 | 8.1 |
| M&M's | 21.9 | 25.2 | 29.3 | 4.0 | 7.4 |
| Doritos | 17.9 | 23.2 | 25.0j | 1.8 | 7.1 |
| RadioShack | 4.1 | 3.7 | 10.0 | 6.3 | 5.9 |
| Audi | 11.5 | 9.3 | 16.2 | 6.9 | 4.8 |
| Jeep | 12.9 | 9.4 | 17.3 | 7.9 | 4.4 |
| Microsoft | 11.5 | 15.2 | 15.9 | 0.6 | 4.4 |
| Cheerios | 25.2 | 28.0 | 29.4 | 1.4 | 4.2 |
| AXE | 6.5 | 9.0 | 9.1 | 0.1 | 2.6 |

The score for buzz on the chart here ranges from +100 to −100 and is compiled by subtracting negative feedback from positive on the question, "If you've heard anything about the brand in the last two weeks, through advertising, news, or word of mouth, was it positive or negative?" A zero score would mean equal positive and negative feedback.

Scores for word of mouth and purchase consideration range from 0 percent to 100 percent. Word of mouth reflects the brands that respondents said they had talked about with friends and family online or in person during the past two weeks. Purchase consideration reflects the brands respondents said they would consider when they were next in the market.

## Budget Available

The sample size for a project is often determined, at least indirectly, by the budget available. Thus, it may be the last project factor determined. A brand manager may have $50,000 available in the budget for a new product test. After deduction of other project costs (e.g., research design, questionnaire development, data processing, analysis and reporting), the amount remaining determines the size of the sample. Of course, if the dollars available will not produce an adequate sample size, then management must make a decision: either additional funds must be found, or the project should be canceled.

Although this approach may seem highly unscientific and arbitrary, it is a fact of life in a corporate environment. Financial constraints challenge the researcher to develop research designs that will generate data of adequate quality for decision-making purposes at low cost. For example, it may be possible to collect the data in a less expensive way—via Internet rather than by telephone, for example. This "budget available" approach forces the researcher to explore alternative data-collection approaches and to carefully consider the value of information in relation to its cost.

## Rule of Thumb

Potential clients may specify in their RFP (request for proposal) that they want a sample of 200, 400, 500, or some other size. Sometimes, this number is based on desired sampling error. In other cases, it is based on nothing more than past experience. The justification for the specified sample size may boil down to a "gut feeling" that a particular sample size is necessary or appropriate.

If the researcher determines that the sample size requested is not adequate to support the objectives of the proposed research, then she or he has a professional responsibility to present arguments for a larger sample size and let the client make the final decision. If the client rejects arguments for a larger sample size, then the researcher may decline to submit a proposal based on the belief that an inadequate sample size will produce results with so much error that they may be misleading.[2]

## Number of Subgroups Analyzed

In any sample size determination problem, consideration must be given to the number and anticipated size of various subgroups of the total sample that must be analyzed and about which statistical inferences must be made. For example, a researcher might decide that a sample of 400 is quite adequate overall. However, if male and female respondents must be analyzed separately and the sample is expected to be 50 percent male and 50 percent female, then the expected sample size for each subgroup is only 200. Is this number adequate for making the desired statistical inferences about the characteristics and behavior of the two groups? If the results are to be analyzed by both sex and age, then the problem gets even more complicated.

Assume that it is important to analyze four subgroups of the total sample: men under 35, men 35 and over, women under 35, and women 35 and over. If each group is expected to make up about 25 percent of the total sample, a sample of 400 will include only 100 respondents in each subgroup. The problem is that as sample size gets smaller, sampling error gets larger, and it becomes more difficult to tell whether an observed difference between groups is a real difference or simply a reflection of sampling error.

Other things being equal, the larger the number of subgroups to be analyzed, the larger the required sample size. It has been suggested that a sample should provide, at a minimum, 100 or more respondents in each major subgroup and 20 to 50 respondents in each of the less important subgroups.[3]

## Traditional Statistical Methods

You probably have been exposed in other classes to traditional approaches for determining sample size for simple random samples. These approaches are reviewed in this chapter. Three pieces of information are required to make the necessary calculations for a sample result:

- An estimate of the population standard deviation
- The acceptable level of sampling error
- The desired level of confidence that the sample result will fall within a certain range (result ± sampling error) of true population values

With these three pieces of information, the researcher can calculate the size of the simple random sample required.[4] The following section covers the logic behind our ability to make these calculations, starting with the normal distribution.

# Normal Distribution

## General Properties

The properties of the normal distribution are crucial to classical statistical inference. There are several reasons for its importance. First, many variables encountered by marketers have probability distributions that are close to the normal distribution. Examples include the number of cans, bottles, or glasses of soft drink consumed by soft drink users, the number of times that people who eat at fast-food restaurants go to such restaurants in an average month, and the average hours per week spent viewing television. Second, the normal distribution is useful for a number of theoretical reasons; one of the more important of these relates to the central limit theorem. According to the **central limit theorem**, for any population, regardless of its distribution, the distribution of sample means or sample proportions approaches a normal distribution as sample size increases. The importance of this tendency will become clear later in the chapter. Third, the normal distribution is a useful approximation of many other discrete probability distributions. If, for example, a researcher measured the heights of a large sample of men in the United States and plotted those values on a graph, a distribution similar to the one shown in Exhibit 14.1 would result. This

**central limit theorem**
Idea that a distribution of a large number of sample means or sample proportions will approximate a normal distribution, regardless of the distribution of the population from which they were drawn.

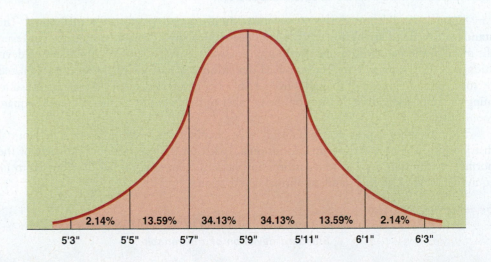

**Exhibit 14.1**

**Normal Distribution for Heights of Men**

| EXHIBIT 14.2 | Area under Standard Normal Curve for $Z$ Values (Standard Deviations) of 1, 2, and 3 |
|---|---|
| **$Z$ Values (Standard Deviation)** | **Area under Standard Normal Curve(%)** |
| 1 | 68.26 |
| 2 | 95.44 |
| 3 | 99.74 |

**normal distribution**
Continuous distribution that is bell-shaped and symmetric about the mean; the mean, median, and mode are equal.

distribution is a **normal distribution**, and it has a number of important characteristics, including the following:

1. The normal distribution is bell-shaped and has only one mode. The mode is a measure of central tendency and is the particular value that occurs most frequently. (A bimodal, or two-mode, distribution would have two peaks or humps.)

2. The normal distribution is symmetric about its mean. This is another way of saying that it is not skewed and that the three measures of central tendency (mean, median, and mode) are all equal.

3. A particular normal distribution is uniquely defined by its mean and standard deviation.

4. The total area under a normal curve is equal to one, meaning that it takes in all observations.

5. The area of a region under the normal distribution curve between any two values of a variable equals the probability of observing a value in that range when an observation is randomly selected from the distribution. For example, on a single draw, there is a 34.13 percent chance of selecting from the distribution shown in Exhibit 14.1 a man between 5'7" and 5'9" in height.

**proportional property of the normal distribution**
Feature that the number of observations falling between the mean and a given number of standard deviations from the mean is the same for all normal distributions.

6. The area between the mean and a given number of standard deviations from the mean is the same for all normal distributions. The area between the mean and plus or minus one standard deviation takes in 68.26 percent of the area under the curve, or 68.26 percent of the observations. This **proportional property of the normal distribution** provides the basis for the statistical inferences we will discuss in this chapter.

## Standard Normal Distribution

**standard normal distribution**
Normal distribution with a mean of zero and a standard deviation of one.

**standard deviation**
Measure of dispersion calculated by subtracting the mean of the series from each value in a series, squaring each result, summing the results, dividing the sum by the number of items minus 1, and taking the square root of this value.

Any normal distribution can be transformed into a standard normal distribution. The **standard normal distribution** has the same features as any normal distribution. However, the mean of the standard normal distribution is always equal to zero, and the standard deviation is always equal to one. The **standard deviation** is a measure of dispersion calculated by subtracting the mean of the series from each value in a series, squaring each result, summing the results, dividing the sum by the number of items minus 1, and taking the square root of this value.

The probabilities provided in Table 2 in Appendix 2 are based on a standard normal distribution. A simple transformation formula, based on the proportional property of the normal distribution, is used to transform any value $X$ from any normal distribution to its equivalent value $Z$ from a standard normal distribution:

$$Z = \frac{Value\ of\ the\ variable - Mean\ of\ the\ variable}{Standard\ deviation\ of\ the\ variable}$$

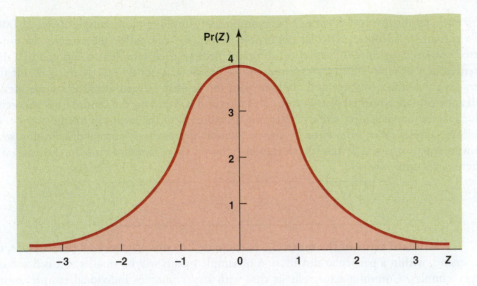

Symbolically, the formula can be stated as follows:

$$Z = \frac{X - \mu}{\sigma}$$

*where*
$X$ = value of the variable
$\mu$ = mean of the variable
$\sigma$ = standard deviation of the variable

The areas under a standard normal distribution (reflecting the percent of all observations) for various $Z$ values (*standard deviations*) are shown in Exhibit 14.2. The standard normal distribution is shown in Exhibit 14.3.

# Population and Sample Distributions

The purpose of conducting a survey using a sample is to make inferences about the population, not to describe the sample. The population, as defined earlier, includes all possible individuals or objects from whom or about which information is needed to meet the objectives of the research. A sample is a subset of the total population.[5]

A **population distribution** is a frequency distribution of all the elements of the population. It has a mean, usually represented by the Greek letter $\mu$; and a standard deviation, usually represented by the Greek letter $\sigma$.

A **sample distribution** is a frequency distribution of all the elements of an individual (single) sample. In a sample distribution, the mean or average is usually represented by $\bar{X}$ and the standard deviation is usually represented by $S$.

**population distribution**
Frequency distribution of all the elements of a population.

**sample distribution**
Frequency distribution of all the elements of an individual sample.

# Sampling Distribution of the Mean

At this point, it is necessary to introduce a third distribution, the sampling distribution of the sample mean. Understanding this distribution is crucial to understanding the basis for our ability to compute sampling error for simple random samples. The **sampling distribution of the mean** is a probability distribution of the means of all possible samples of a given size drawn from a given population. Although this distribution is seldom calculated, its known properties have tremendous practical significance. Actually, deriving a distribution

**sampling distribution of the mean**
Theoretical frequency distribution of the means of all possible samples of a given size drawn from a particular population; it is normally distributed.

of sample means involves drawing a large number of simple random samples (e.g., 25,000) of a certain size from a particular population. Then, the means for the samples are computed and arranged in a frequency distribution. Because each sample is composed of a different subset of sample elements, all the sample means will not be exactly the same. If the samples are sufficiently large and random, then the resulting distribution of sample means will approximate a normal distribution. This assertion is based on the central limit theorem, which states that as sample size increases, the distribution of the means of a large number of random samples taken from virtually any population approaches a normal distribution with a mean equal to $\mu$ and a standard deviation (referred to as *standard error* in this case) $S_{\bar{x}}$, where $n =$ sample size and

$$S_{\bar{x}} = \frac{\sigma}{\sqrt{n}}$$

**standard error of the mean**
Standard deviation of a distribution of sample means.

The **standard error of the mean** ($S_{\bar{x}}$) is computed in this way because the variance, or dispersion, within a particular distribution of sample means will be smaller if it is based on larger samples. Common sense tells us that with larger samples individual sample means will, on the average, be more "accurate" or closer to the population mean.

It is important to note that the central limit theorem holds regardless of the shape of the population distribution from which the samples are selected. This means that, regardless of the population distribution, the sample means selected from the population distribution will tend to be normally distributed.

The notation ordinarily used to refer to the means and standard deviations of population and sample distributions and sampling distribution of the mean is summarized in Exhibit 14.4. The relationships among the population distribution, sample distribution, and sampling distribution of the mean are shown graphically in Exhibit 14.5.

## Basic Concepts

Consider a case in which a researcher takes 1,000 simple random samples of size 200 from the population of all consumers who have eaten at a fast-food restaurant at least once in the past 30 days. The purpose is to estimate the average number of times these individuals eat at a fast-food restaurant in an average month.

If the researcher computes the mean number of visits for each of the 1,000 samples and sorts them into intervals based on their relative values, the frequency distribution shown in Exhibit 14.6 might result. Exhibit 14.7 graphically illustrates these frequencies in a histogram, on which a normal curve has been superimposed. As you can see, the histogram closely approximates the shape of a normal curve. If the researcher draws a large enough number of samples of size 200, computes the mean of each sample, and plots these means, the resulting distribution is a normal distribution. The normal curve shown in Exhibit 14.7 is the sampling distribution of the mean for this particular problem. The sampling distribution of the mean for simple random samples that have 30 or more observations has the following characteristics:

| EXHIBIT 14.4 | Notation for Means and Standard Deviations of Various Distributions | |
|---|---|---|
| **Distribution** | **Mean** | **Standard Deviation** |
| Population | $\mu$ | $\sigma$ |
| Sample | $\bar{X}$ | $S$ |
| Sampling | $\mu_{\bar{x}} = \mu$ | $S_{\bar{x}}$ |

- The distribution is a normal distribution.
- The distribution has a mean equal to the population mean.
- The distribution has a standard deviation, the standard error of the mean.

$$\sigma_{\bar{X}} = \frac{\sigma}{\sqrt{n}}$$

© marko turk/Age Fotostock

This statistic is referred to as the standard error of the mean (instead of the standard deviation) to indicate that it applies to a distribution of sample means rather than to the standard deviation of a single sample or a population. Keep in mind that this calculation applies *only* to a simple random sample. Other types of probability samples (for example, stratified samples and cluster samples) require more complex formulas for computing standard error. Note that this formula does not account for any type of bias, including nonresponse bias discussed in the feature on page 340.

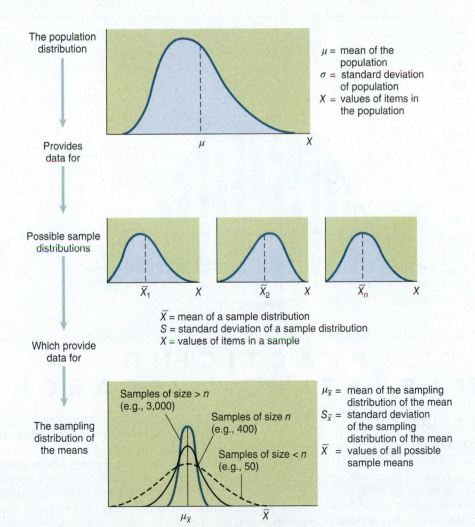

The population distribution

$\mu$ = mean of the population
$\sigma$ = standard deviation of population
$X$ = values of items in the population

Provides data for

Possible sample distributions

$\bar{X}$ = mean of a sample distribution
$S$ = standard deviation of a sample distribution
$X$ = values of items in a sample

Which provide data for

The sampling distribution of the means

Samples of size $> n$ (e.g., 3,000)
Samples of size $n$ (e.g., 400)
Samples of size $< n$ (e.g., 50)

$\mu_{\bar{x}}$ = mean of the sampling distribution of the mean
$S_{\bar{x}}$ = standard deviation of the sampling distribution of the mean
$\bar{X}$ = values of all possible sample means

**Exhibit 14.5**

**Relationships of the Three Basic Types of Distribution**

*Source:* Adapted from D. H. Sanders et al., *Statistics, A Fresh Approach,* 4th ed. (New York: McGraw-Hill, 1990). Reprinted with permission of the McGraw-Hill Companies.

| EXHIBIT 14.6 | Frequency Distribution of 1,000 Sample Means: Average Number of Times Respondent Ate at a Fast-Food Restaurant in the Past 30 Days | |
|---|---|---|
| **Number of Times** | | **Frequency of Occurrence** |
| 2.6–3.5 | | 8 |
| 3.6–4.5 | | 15 |
| 4.6–5.5 | | 29 |
| 5.6–6.5 | | 44 |
| 6.6–7.5 | | 64 |
| 7.6–8.5 | | 79 |
| 8.6–9.5 | | 89 |
| 9.6–10.5 | | 108 |
| 10.6–11.5 | | 115 |
| 11.6–12.5 | | 110 |
| 12.6–13.5 | | 90 |
| 13.6–14.5 | | 81 |
| 14.6–15.5 | | 66 |
| 15.6–16.5 | | 45 |
| 16.6–17.5 | | 32 |
| 17.6–18.5 | | 16 |
| 18.6–19.5 | | 9 |
| Total | | 1,000 |

### Exhibit 14.7

**Actual Sampling Distribution of Means for Number of Times Respondent Ate at Fast-Food Restaurant in Past 30 Days**

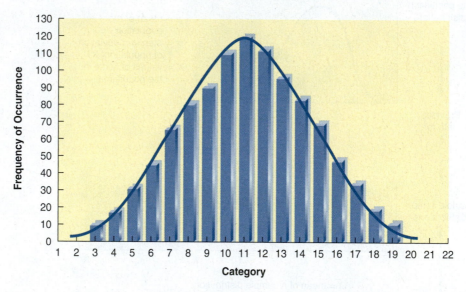

# PRACTICING MARKETING RESEARCH

## Nonresponse Bias in a Dutch Alcohol Consumption Study[6]

The fact that some people fail to respond to a poll or respond only selectively to certain questions, ignoring others, can distort the accuracy of a survey. Market researchers call this nonresponse bias, and researchers at the Addiction Research Institute in Rotterdam, The Netherlands, concluded that it can be a serious problem. In fact, response rates to surveys in The Netherlands had dropped from 80 percent in the 1980s to 60 percent at the end of the 1990s, and were still continuing to decline, all leading to a smaller sample size and accuracy loss in population estimates. People who don't respond to polls may have relevant characteristics different from responders.

In 2002, the researchers reviewed the results of a study done in 1999 on alcohol usage. Their research assumption was that abstainers probably didn't respond because they lacked interest in the subject and excessive drinkers did not respond because they were embarrassed by their usage. This hypothesis was borne out in the subsequent study. In designing their study, they knew that nonresponse bias cannot be corrected simply by weighting data based on demographic variables. They needed to poll the nonrespondents and evaluate if their answers differed from responders.

Originally, a random sample of 1,000 people, aged 16 to 69 years, was taken from the city registry of Rotterdam. Everyone received a mailed questionnaire about his or her alcohol consumption. After two reminders were sent, the response rate was 44 percent. For the follow-up study, the researchers chose 25 postal areas in Rotterdam and a secondary sample of 310 people. Of these, 133 had already responded to the first survey, and 177 did not, so these two groups were called primary respondents and primary nonrespondents, respectively. Members of the latter group were approached in person by the researchers in a series of five in-person attempts to conduct the interview at their homes. In the end, 48 primary nonrespondents could not be reached, leaving a final sample size for primary nonrespondents of 129.

Both groups were asked the same two questions: (1) Do you ever drink alcohol?; and (2) Do you ever drink six or more alcoholic beverages in the same day? The net response rate from the nonrespondents to both questions was 52 percent—in other words, even more nonresponse (48 percent) was encountered in the follow-up study.

More importantly, the Dutch researchers discovered, first, that alcohol abstainers were underrepresented, but not frequent, excessive drinkers; second, that the underrepresentation of abstainers was greater among women than men, greater for those older than 35, and greater for those who were Dutch versus other nationalities; and third, that a thorough nonresponse follow-up study is called for (as mentioned, weighting data to accommodate this is insufficient) to evaluate nonresponse biases in any future studies. The potential answers of those who don't answer are valuable and statistically necessary for any study.

## Questions

1. The nonresponse bias came in with the extremes (abstainers and heavy drinkers) regarding alcohol use. Is there any weighting approach that might compensate for these two important groups of nonresponders so that a follow-up study would not be needed?

2. For the 48 percent who failed to respond to the second study, would a mailed questionnaire, ensuring privacy, be worth the expense in terms of the improvement in statistical accuracy it might generate?

## Making Inferences on the Basis of a Single Sample

In practice, there is no need for taking all possible random samples from a particular population and generating a frequency distribution and histogram like those shown in Exhibits 14.6 and 14.7. Instead, the researcher wants to take one simple random sample and make statistical inferences about the population from which it was drawn. The question is, what is the probability that any one simple random sample of a particular size will produce an estimate of the population mean that is within one standard error (plus or minus) of the true population mean? The answer, based on the information provided in Exhibit 14.2, is that there is a 68.26 percent probability that any one sample from a particular population will produce an estimate of the population mean that is within plus or minus one standard error of the true value, because 68.26 percent of all sample means fall in this range. There is a 95.44 percent probability that any one simple random sample of a particular size from a given population will produce a value that is within plus or minus two standard errors of the true population mean, and a 99.74 percent probability that such a sample will produce an estimate of the mean that is within plus or minus three standard errors of the population mean.

## Point and Interval Estimates

The results of a sample can be used to generate two kinds of estimates of a population mean: point and interval estimates. The sample mean is the best **point estimate** of the population mean. Inspection of the sampling distribution of the mean shown in Exhibit 14.7 suggests that a particular sample result is likely to produce a mean that is relatively close to the population mean. However, the mean of a particular sample could be any one of the sample means shown in the distribution. A small percentage of these sample means are a

**point estimate**
Particular estimate of a population value.

The sampling distribution of the proportion is used to estimate the percentage of the population that watches a particular television program.

OJO Images/Robert Daly /Getty Images

**interval estimate**
Interval or range of values within which the true population value is estimated to fall.

**confidence level**
Probability that a particular interval will include true population value; also called *confidence coefficient.*

**confidence interval**
Interval that, at the specified confidence level, includes the true population value.

considerable distance from the true population mean. The distance between the sample mean and the true population mean is the sampling error.

Given that point estimates based on sample results are exactly correct in only a small percentage of all possible cases, interval estimates generally are preferred. An **interval estimate** is a particular interval or range of values within which the true population value is estimated to fall. In addition to stating the size of the interval, the researcher usually states the probability that the interval will include the true value of the population mean. This probability is referred to as the **confidence level**, and the interval is called the **confidence interval**.

Interval estimates of the mean are derived by first drawing a random sample of a given size from the population of interest and calculating the mean of that sample. This sample mean is known to lie somewhere within the sampling distribution of all possible sample means, but exactly where this particular mean falls in that distribution is not known. There is a 68.26 percent probability that this particular sample mean lies within one standard error (plus or minus) of the true population mean. Based on this information, the researcher states that he or she is 68.26 percent confident that the true population value is equal to the sample value, plus or minus one standard error. This statement can be shown symbolically, as follows:

$$\overline{X} - 1\sigma_{\overline{X}} \leq \mu \leq \overline{X} + 1\sigma_{\overline{X}}$$

By the same logic, the researcher can be 95.44 percent confident that the true population value is equal to the sample estimate 62 (technically 1.96) standard errors, and 99.74 percent confident that the true population value falls within the interval defined by the sample value 63 standard errors.

These statements assume that the standard deviation of the population is known. However, in most situations, this is not the case. If the standard deviation of the population were known, by definition the mean of the population would also be known, and there would be no need to take a sample in the first place. Because information on the standard deviation of the population is lacking, its value is estimated based on the standard deviation of the sample.

## Sampling Distribution of the Proportion

Marketing researchers frequently are interested in estimating proportions or percentages rather than or in addition to estimating means. Common examples include estimating the following:

- The percentage of the population that is aware of a particular ad.
- The percentage of the population that accesses the Internet one or more times in an average week.
- The percentage of the population that has visited a fast-food restaurant four or more times in the past 30 days.
- The percentage of the population that watches a particular television program.

In situations in which a population proportion or percentage is of interest, the sampling distribution of the proportion is used.

The **sampling distribution of the proportion** is a relative frequency distribution of the sample proportions of a large number of random samples of a given size drawn from a particular population. The sampling distribution of a proportion has the following characteristics:

- It approximates a normal distribution.
- The mean proportion for all possible samples is equal to the population proportion.
- The standard error of a sampling distribution of the proportion can be computed with the following formula:

**sampling distribution of the proportion**
Relative frequency distribution of the sample proportions of many random samples of a given size drawn from a particular population; it is normally distributed.

$$S_P = \sqrt{\frac{P(1-P)}{n}}$$

where  $S_P$ = standard error of sampling distribution of proportion
$P$ = estimate of population proportion
$n$ = sample size

Consider the problem of estimating the percentage of all adults who have accessed Twitter in the past 90 days. As in generating a sampling distribution of the mean, the researcher might select 1,000 random samples of size 200 from the population of all adults and compute the proportion of all adults who have accessed Twitter in the past 90 days for all 1,000 samples. These values could then be plotted in a frequency distribution and this frequency distribution would approximate a normal distribution. The estimated standard error of the proportion for this distribution can be computed using the formula provided earlier.

For reasons that will be clear to you after you read the next section, marketing researchers have a tendency to prefer dealing with sample size issues as problems of estimating proportions rather than means.

# Determining Sample Size

## Problems Involving Means

Consider once again the task of estimating how many times the average fast-food restaurant user visits a fast-food restaurant in an average month. Management needs an estimate of the average number of visits to make a decision regarding a new promotional campaign that is being developed. To make this estimate, the marketing research manager for the organization intends to survey a simple random sample of all fast-food users. The question is, what information is necessary to determine the appropriate sample size for the project? The formula for calculating the required sample size for problems that involve the estimation of a mean is as follows:[7]

$$n = \frac{Z^2 \sigma^2}{E^2}$$

where  $Z$ = level of confidence expressed in standard errors

$\sigma$ = population standard deviation

$E$ = acceptable amount of sampling error

Three pieces of information are needed to compute the sample size required:

1. The acceptable or allowable level of sampling error $E$.

2. The acceptable level of confidence $Z$. In other words, how confident does the researcher want to be that the specified confidence interval includes the population mean?

3. An estimate of the population standard deviation $\sigma$.

**allowable sampling error**
Amount of sampling error the researcher is willing to accept.

The level of confidence $Z$ and **allowable sampling error** $E$ for this calculation must be set by the researcher in consultation with his or her client. As noted earlier, the level of confidence and the amount of error are based not only on statistical criteria but also on financial and managerial criteria. In an ideal world, the level of confidence would always be very high and the amount of error very low. However, because this is a business decision, cost must be considered. An acceptable trade-off among accuracy, level of confidence, and cost must be developed. High levels of precision and confidence may be less important in some situations than in others. For example, in an exploratory study, you may be interested in developing a basic sense of whether attitudes toward your product are generally positive or negative. Precision may not be critical. However, in a product concept test, you would need a much more precise estimate of sales for a new product before making the potentially costly and risky decision to introduce that product in the marketplace.

**population standard deviation**
Standard deviation of a variable for the entire population.

Making an estimate of the **population standard deviation** presents a more serious problem. As noted earlier, if the population standard deviation were known, the population mean also would be known (the population mean is needed to compute the population standard deviation), and there would be no need to draw a sample. How can the researcher estimate the population standard deviation before selecting the sample? One or some combination of the following four methods might be used to deal with this problem:

1. *Use results from a prior survey.* The firm may have conducted a prior survey dealing with the same or a similar issue. In this situation, a possible solution to the problem is to use the results of the prior survey as an estimate of the population standard deviation.

2. *Conduct a pilot survey.* If this is to be a large-scale project, it may be possible to devote some time and resources to a small-scale pilot survey of the population. The results of this pilot survey can be used to develop an estimate of the population standard deviation that can be used in the sample size determination formula.

3. *Use secondary data.* In some cases, secondary data can be used to develop an estimate of the population standard deviation.

4. *Use judgment.* If all else fails, an estimate of the population standard deviation can be developed based solely on judgment. Judgments might be sought from a variety of managers in a position to make educated guesses about the required population parameters.

It should be noted that after the survey has been conducted and the sample mean and sample standard deviation have been calculated, the researcher can reassess the accuracy of the estimate of the population standard deviation used to calculate the required sample size. At this time, if appropriate, adjustments can be made in the initial estimates of sampling error.[8]

Let's return to the problem of estimating the average number of fast-food visits made in an average month by users of fast-food restaurants:

- After consultation with managers in the company, the marketing research manager determines that an estimate is needed of the average number of times that fast-food consumers visit fast-food restaurants. She further determines that managers believe that a high degree of accuracy is needed, which she takes to mean that the estimate should be within .10 (one-tenth) of a visit of the true population value. This value (.10) should be substituted into the formula for the value of $E$.

- In addition, the marketing research manager decides that, all things considered, she needs to be 95.44 percent confident that the true population mean falls in the interval defined by the sample mean plus or minus $E$ (as just defined). Two (technically, 1.96) standard errors are required to take in 95.44 percent of the area under a normal curve. Therefore, a value of 2 should be substituted into the equation for $Z$.

- Finally, there is the question of what value to insert into the formula for $\sigma$. Fortunately, the company conducted a similar study one year ago. The standard deviation in that study for the variable—the average number of times a fast-food restaurant was visited in the past 30 days—was 1.39. This is the best estimate of $\sigma$ available. Therefore, a value of 1.39 should be substituted into the formula for the value of $\sigma$. The calculation follows:

$$
\begin{aligned}
n &= \frac{Z^2 \sigma^2}{E^2} \\
&= \frac{2^2 (1.39)^2}{(.10)^2} \\
&= \frac{4(1.93)}{.01} \\
&= \frac{7.72}{.01} \\
&= 772
\end{aligned}
$$

Based on this calculation, a simple random sample of 772 is necessary to meet the requirements outlined.

## Problems Involving Proportions

Now let's consider the problem of estimating the proportion or percentage of all adults who have accessed Twitter in the past 90 days. The goal is to take a simple random sample from the population of all adults to estimate this proportion.[9]

- As in the problem involving fast-food users, the first task in estimating the population mean on the basis of sample results is to decide on an acceptable value for $E$. If, for example, an error level of 34 percent is acceptable, a value of .04 should be substituted into the formula for $E$.

- Next, assume that the researcher has determined a need to be 95.44 percent confident that the sample estimate is within 34 percent of the true population proportion. As in the previous example, a value of 2 should be substituted into the equation for $Z$.

■ Finally, in a study of the same issue conducted one year ago, 5 percent of all respondents indicated they had purchased something over the Internet in the past 90 days. Thus, a value of .05 should be substituted into the equation for $P$.

The resulting calculations are as follows:

Given the requirements, a random sample of 119 respondents is required. It should be noted that, in one respect, the process of determining the sample size necessary to estimate a proportion is easier than the process of determining the sample size necessary to estimate a mean: If there is no basis for estimating $P$, the researcher can make what is sometimes referred to as the most-pessimistic, or worst-case, assumption regarding the value of $P$. Given the values of $Z$ and $E$, what value of $P$ will require the largest possible sample? A value of .50 will make the value of the expression $P(1 - P)$ larger than any possible value of $P$. There is no corresponding most-pessimistic assumption that the researcher can make regarding the value of $\sigma$ in problems that involve determining the sample size necessary to estimate a mean with given levels of $Z$ and $E$.

## Determining Sample Size for Stratified and Cluster Samples

The formulas for sample size determination presented in this chapter apply only to simple random samples. There also are formulas for determining required sample size and sampling error for other types of probability samples such as stratified and cluster samples. Although many of the general concepts presented in this chapter apply to these other types of probability samples, the specific formulas are much more complicated.[10] In addition, these formulas require information that frequently is not available or is difficult to obtain. For these reasons, sample size determination for other types of probability samples is beyond the scope of this introductory text.

## Sample Size for Qualitative Research

The issue of sample size for qualitative research often comes up when making decisions about the number of traditional focus groups, individual depth interviews or online bulletin board focus groups to conduct. Given the relatively small sample sizes we intentionally use in qualitative research, the types of sample size calculation discussed in this chapter are never going to help us answer this question. Experts have discussed rules based on experience, with some analysis suggesting that after we have talked to 20–30 people in a qualitative setting, the general pattern of responses begins to stabilize. This issue is discussed in greater detail in the Practicing Marketing Research feature on page 347.

## Population Size and Sample Size

You may have noticed that none of the formulas for determining sample size takes into account the size of the population in any way. Students (and managers) frequently find this troubling. It seems to make sense that one should take a larger sample from a larger population. But this is not the case. Normally, there is no direct relationship between the size of the population and the size of the sample required to estimate a particular population parameter with a particular level of error and a particular level of confidence. In fact, the size of the population may have an effect only in those situations where the size of the sample is large in relation to the size of the population. One rule of thumb is that an adjustment should be made in the sample size if the sample size is more than 5 percent of the size of the total population. The normal presumption is that sample elements are drawn independently of one another (**independence assumption**). This assumption is justified when the sample is small relative to the population. However, it is not appropriate when the sample is a relatively large (5 percent or more) proportion of the population. As a result, the researcher must adjust the results obtained with the standard formulas. For example, the formula for the standard error of the mean, presented earlier, is as follows:

**independence assumption**
Assumption that sample elements are drawn independently.

$$\sigma_{\bar{x}} = \frac{\sigma}{\sqrt{n}}$$

For a sample that is 5 percent or more of the population, the independence assumption is dropped, producing the following formula:

$$\sigma_{\bar{x}} = \frac{\sigma}{\sqrt{n}} \sqrt{\frac{N-n}{N-1}}$$

# PRACTICING MARKETING RESEARCH

## Sample Size for Qualitative Research[11]

In a qualitative research project, how large should the sample be? How many focus groups, individual depth interviews (IDIs), or online bulletin board focus groups are needed? One suggested rule is to make sure you do more than one group on a topic because any one group may be idiosyncratic. Another guideline is to continue doing groups or IDIs until we have reached a saturation point and are no longer hearing anything new. These rules are intuitive and reasonable, but they are not solidly grounded and do not really give us an optimal qualitative sample size. The approach proposed here gives some specific answers.

First, the importance of sample size in qualitative research must be understood.

### Size Does Matter, Even for a Qualitative Sample

In qualitative work, we are trying to discover something. We may be seeking to uncover the reasons why consumers are or are not satisfied with a product; the product attributes that are important to users; possible consumer perceptions of celebrity spokespersons; the various problems that consumers experience with our brand; or other kinds of insights. It is up to a subsequent quantitative study to estimate, with statistical precision, the importance or prevalence of each perception.

The key point is this: Our qualitative sample must be big enough to ensure that we are likely to hear most or all of the perceptions that might be important.

### Discovery Failure Can Be Serious

What might go wrong if a qualitative project fails to uncover an actionable perception (or attribute, opinion, need, experience, etc.)? Here are some possibilities:

A source of dissatisfaction is not discovered—and not corrected. In highly competitive industries, even a small incidence of dissatisfaction could dent the bottom line.

In the qualitative testing of an advertisement, a copy point that offends a small but vocal subgroup of the market is not discovered until a public relations fiasco erupts.

When qualitative procedures are used to pretest a quantitative questionnaire, an undiscovered ambiguity in the wording of a question may mean that some of the subsequent quantitative respondents give invalid responses. Thus, qualitative discovery failure eventually can result in quantitative estimation error due to respondent miscomprehension.

Therefore, size does matter in a qualitative sample, though for a different reason than in a quantitative sample. The following example shows how the risk of discovery failure may be easy to overlook even when it is formidable.

## Basing the Decision on Calculated Probabilities

So, how can we figure the sample size needed to reduce the risk as much as we want? I am proposing two ways. One would be based on calculated probabilities similar to what we do for quantitative sample size estimation, but different.

The other way of figuring an appropriate sample size would be to consider the findings of some actual studies. Based on various studies, a sample size of 30 seems to be the point at which we will find out all the unique things that occur with any frequency.

Until someone comes up with a more definitive answer, an *N* of 30 respondents is a reasonable starting point for deciding the qualitative sample size that can reveal the full range (or nearly the full range) of potentially important customer perceptions. An *N* of 30 reduces the probability of missing a perception with a 10 percent incidence to less than 5 percent (assuming random sampling) and is at the upper end of the range found in the studies. If focus groups are desired, and we want to count each respondent separately toward the *N* we choose (e.g., getting an *N* of 30 from three groups with 10 respondents in each), then it is important for every respondent to have sufficient airtime on the key issues. Also, it is critical for the moderator to control dominators and bring out the shy people, lest the distinctive perceptions of less-talkative customers are missed.

## Questions

1. Is sample size important in qualitative research? Why do you say that?

2. What is a reasonable target sample size for qualitative studies? What is that sample size based on?

---

**finite population correction factor (FPC)**
An adjustment to the required sample size that is made in cases where the sample is expected to be equal to 5 percent or more of the total population.

The factor $(N - n)/(N - 1)$ is referred to as the **finite population correction factor (FPC)**.

$$\sigma_{\bar{x}} = \frac{\sigma}{\sqrt{n}} \sqrt{\frac{N-n}{N-1}}$$

In those situations in which the sample is 5 percent or more of the population, the researcher can appropriately reduce the required sample size using the FPC. This calculation is made using the following formula:

$$n' = \frac{nN}{N + n - 1}$$

where $\quad n' =$ reviced sample size
$n =$ original sample size
$N =$ population size

If the population has 2,000 elements and the original sample size is 400, then

$$n' = \frac{400(2000)}{2000 + 40 - 1} = \frac{800,000}{2399}$$
$$= 333$$

# PRACTICING MARKETING RESEARCH

## Estimating with Precision How Many Phone Numbers Are Needed

Calculating how many phone numbers are needed for a project may seem like a difficult task, but following a few basic rules can make it simple. The formula used by Survey Sampling, Inc. (SSI) to calculate sample size involves four factors: (1) the number of completed interviews needed, (2) the working phone (or "reachable") rate, (3) the incidence rate, and (4) the contact/completion rate.

### Completed Interviews

The number of completed interviews is based on the sample size calculation formula for simple random samples. It is the final sample size you want to achieve.

### Working Phone Rate

The working phone rate varies with the sampling methodology used. An SSI RDD sample yields a 60 percent working phone rate. That is a good number to use in the formula for estimation purposes.

### Incidence Rate

The incidence rate is the percentage of contacts that will qualify for the interview. Or put another way, what percentage of people who answer the phone (or reply to your mail questionnaire) will pass your screening questions? Accurate incidence data are critical to determining proper sample size. An incidence figure that is too high will leave you short of sample once your study is in the field.

### Contact/Completion Rate

The last factor is the contact/completion rate. SSI defines this rate as the percentage of people who, once they qualify for your study, will agree to cooperate by completing the interview. There are several important elements you should consider when trying to reasonably estimate the completion rate:

- Contact rate
- Length of interview
- Sensitivity of topic
- Time of year
- Number of attempts/callbacks
- Length of time in the field

Provided that the interview is short (less than 10 minutes) and nonsensitive in nature, sufficient callbacks are scheduled, and the study will be in the field for an adequate period of time, SSI estimates a 30 percent completion rate. The completion rate should be adjusted according to the specifications of each study. If the subject matter is sensitive or the interview is long, the completion rate should be reduced. If the length of time in the field is less than one week, SSI recommends increasing the sample size by at least 20 percent.

### An Example

Suppose you wish to complete 300 interviews in the United Kingdom. Using a random-digit sample, you can expect a working phone rate of 60 percent. Start by dividing the number of completed interviews you need (300) by the working phone rate (.60), to yield 500. You need to reach heavy soft drink users (17 percent of adults), and you estimate that 30 percent of the people contacted will complete the interview. Divide 500 by the incidence rate for the group under study (.17) and then by the completion rate (.30). This calculation shows you need 9,804 phone numbers to complete this survey.[12]

---

With the FPC adjustment, a sample of only 333 is needed, rather than the original 400.

The key is not the size of the sample in relation to the size of the population, but whether the sample selected is truly representative of the population. Empirical evidence shows that relatively small but carefully chosen samples can quite accurately reflect characteristics of the population. Many well-known national surveys and opinion polls, such as the Gallup Poll and the Harris Poll, are based on samples of fewer than 2,000. These polls have shown that the behavior of tens of millions of people can be predicted quite accurately using samples that are minuscule in relation to the size of the population.

If you wish to complete 300 interviews in the United Kingdom, you need to determine the contact/completion rate in order to figure out how many calls will actually have to be made to complete the survey.

Lou Jones/ZUMA Press/NewsCom

## Determining How Many Sample Units Are Needed

Regardless of how the target sample size is determined, the researcher is confronted with the practical problem of figuring out how many sampling units (telephone numbers, addresses, and so on) will be required to complete the assignment. For example, if the target final sample size is 400, then obviously more than 400 telephone numbers will be needed to complete a telephone survey.

Some of the numbers on the list will be disconnected, some people will not qualify for the survey because they do not meet the requirements for inclusion in the population, and some will refuse to complete the survey. These factors affect the final estimate of the number of phone numbers, which may be used to place an order with a sample provider, such as Survey Sampling, Inc., or to ask the client for customer names and phone numbers for a satisfaction survey. This estimate must be reasonably accurate because the researcher wants to avoid paying for more numbers than are needed; on the other hand, the researcher doesn't want to run out of numbers during the survey and have to wait for more.

Estimating the number of sample units needed for a telephone sample is covered in the feature on page 349.

# Statistical Power

**statistical power**
Probability of not making a type II error.

Although it is standard practice in marketing research to use the formulas presented in this chapter to calculate sample size, these formulas all focus on *type I error*, or the error of concluding that there is a difference when there is not a difference. They do not explicitly deal with *type II error*, or the error of saying that there is no difference when there is a difference. The probability of not making a type II error is called **statistical power**.[13] The standard formulas for calculating sample size implicitly assume a power of 50 percent. For example, suppose a researcher is trying to determine which of two product concepts has stronger appeal to target customers and wants to be able to detect a 5 percent difference in the percentages of target customers who say that they are very likely to buy the products. The standard sample size formulas indicate that a sample size of approximately 400 is needed for each

| EXHIBIT 14.8 | Sample Size Required to Detect Differences between Proportions from Independent Samples at Different Levels of Power and an Alpha of 0.25 | | | | | |
|---|---|---|---|---|---|---|
| **Difference to Detect** | **Power** | | | | | |
| | **50%** | **60%** | **70%** | **75%** | **80%** | **90%** |
| 0.01 | 19,205 | 24,491 | 30,857 | 34,697 | 39,239 | 52,530 |
| 0.05 | 766 | 977 | 1,231 | 1,384 | 1,568 | 2,094 |
| 0.10 | 190 | 242 | 305 | 343 | 389 | 518 |
| 0.15 | 83 | 106 | 133 | 150 | 169 | 226 |

product test. By using this calculation, the researcher implicitly accepts the fact that there is a 50 percent chance of incorrectly concluding that the two products have equal appeal.

Exhibit 14.8 shows the sample sizes required, at an alpha (probability of incorrectly rejecting the null hypothesis) of 0.25, for specific levels of power and specific levels of differences between two independent proportions. Formulas are available to permit power calculations for any level of confidence; however, they are somewhat complex and will not help you understand the basic concept of power. Programs available on the Internet can be used to make these calculations. To reproduce the numbers in Exhibit 14.8, go to *https://www.dssresearch.com/KnowledgeCenter/toolkitcalculators/statisticalpowercalculators.aspx* and do the following:

- Click on the Percentage, Two Sample option under Sample Size.
- Enter the Sample 1 Percentage and the Sample 2 Percentage in the boxes so that the figures entered reflect the differences you want to be able to detect and the values are in the expected range. These figures are set at the 50 percent level (value of $p$ in the standard sample size formula).
- Below those boxes, enter the Alpha and Beta Error Levels. Alpha is the value you would use for $E$ in the standard sample size formula, and beta is the probability of incorrectly failing to reject the null hypothesis of no difference when a real difference exists. Power is equal to 1 – beta.
- Click on the Calculate Sample Size button at the bottom of the screen for the answer.

# SUMMARY

Determining sample size for probability samples involves financial, statistical, and managerial considerations. Other things equal, the larger the sample, the smaller the sampling error. In turn, the cost of the research grows with the size of the sample.

There are several methods for determining sample size. One is to base the decision on the funds available. In essence, sample size is determined by the budget. Although seemingly unscientific, this approach is often a realistic one in the world of corporate marketing research. A second approach is the so-called rule of thumb method, which involves determining the sample size based on a gut feeling or common practice. The client often requests samples of 300, 400, or 500 in a request for proposal (RFP). A third technique for determining sample

size is based on the number of subgroups to be analyzed. Generally speaking, the more subgroups that need to be analyzed, the larger the required total sample size.

In addition to these methods, there are a number of statistical formulas for determining sample size. Three pieces of data are required to make sample size calculations: an estimate of the population standard deviation, the level of sampling error that the researcher or client is willing to accept, and the desired level of confidence that the sample result will fall within a certain range of the true population value.

The normal distribution is crucial to statistical sampling theory. The normal distribution is bell-shaped and is symmetric about its mean. The standard normal distribution has the features of a normal distribution; however, the mean of the standard normal distribution is always equal to zero, and the standard deviation is always equal to one. A transformation formula is used to transform any value $X$ from any normal distribution to its equivalent value $Z$ from a standard normal distribution. The central limit theorem states that the distribution of the means of a large number of random samples taken from virtually any population approaches a normal distribution with a mean equal to $\mu$ and a standard deviation equal to $S_{\bar{x}}$, where

$$S_{\bar{x}} = \frac{\sigma}{\sqrt{n}}$$

The standard deviation of a distribution of sample means is called the standard error of the mean.

When the results of a sample are used to estimate a population mean, two kinds of estimates can be generated: point and interval estimates. The sample mean is the best point estimate of the population mean. An interval estimate is a certain interval or range of values within which the true population value is estimated to fall. Along with the magnitude of the interval, the researcher usually states the probability that the interval will include the true value of the population mean—that is, the confidence level. The interval is called the confidence interval.

The researcher interested in estimating proportions or percentages rather than or in addition to means uses the sampling distribution of the proportion. The sampling distribution of the proportion is a relative frequency distribution of the sample proportions of a large number of random samples of a given size drawn from a particular population. The standard error of a sampling distribution of proportion is computed as follows:

$$S_p = \sqrt{\frac{P(1-P)}{n}}$$

The following are required to calculate sample size: the acceptable level of sampling error $E$, the acceptable level of confidence $Z$, and an estimate of the population standard deviation 3. The formula for calculating the required sample size for situations that involve the estimation of a mean is as follows:

$$n = \frac{Z^2\sigma^2}{E^2}$$

The following formula is used to calculate the required sample size for problems involving proportions:

$$n = \frac{Z^2[P(1-P)]}{E^2}$$

Finally, statistical power is the probability of not making a type II error. A type II error is the mistake of saying that there is not a difference when there is a difference. The standard sample size formula implicitly assumes a power of 50 percent. It may be important to use different levels of power depending on the nature of the decision in question.

# KEY TERMS

central limit theorem  **335**

normal distribution  **336**

proportional property of the normal distribution  **336**

standard normal distribution  **336**

standard deviation  **336**

population distribution  **337**

sample distribution  **337**

sampling distribution of the mean  **337**

standard error of the mean  **338**

point estimate  **341**

interval estimate  **342**

confidence level  **342**

confidence interval  **342**

sampling distribution of the proportion  **343**

allowable sampling error  **344**

population standard deviation  **344**

independence assumption  **347**

finite population correction factor (FPC)  **348**

statistical power  **350**

# QUESTIONS FOR REVIEW & CRITICAL THINKING

1. Explain how the determination of sample size is a financial, statistical, and managerial issue.

2. Discuss and give examples of three methods that are used in marketing research for determining sample size.

3. A marketing researcher analyzing the fast-food industry noticed the following: The average amount spent at a fast-food restaurant in California was $3.30, with a standard

deviation of $0.40. Yet in Georgia, the average amount spent at a fast-food restaurant was $3.25, with a standard deviation of $0.10. What do these statistics tell you about fast-food consumption patterns in these two states?

4. Distinguish among population, sample, and sampling distributions. Why is it important to distinguish among these concepts?

5. What is the finite population correction factor? Why is it used? When should it be used?

6. Assume that previous fast-food research has shown that 80 percent of the consumers like curly french fries. The researcher wishes to have a standard error of 6 percent or less and be 95 percent confident of an estimate to be made about curly french fry consumption from a survey. What sample size should be used for a simple random sample?

7. You are in charge of planning a chili cook-off. You must make sure that there are plenty of samples for the patrons of the cook-off. The following standards have been set: a confidence level of 99 percent and an error of less than 4

ounces per cooking team. Last year's cook-off had a standard deviation in amount of chili cooked of 3 ounces. What is the necessary sample size?

8. Based on a client's requirements of a confidence interval of 99.74 percent and acceptable sampling error of 2 percent, a sample size of 500 is calculated. The cost is estimated at $20,000. The client replies that the budget for this project is $17,000. What are the alternatives?

9. A marketing researcher must determine how many telephone numbers she needs to order from a sample provider to complete a survey of ATM users. The goal is to complete 400 interviews with ATM users. From past experience, she estimates that 60 percent of the phone numbers provided will be working phone numbers. The estimated incidence rate (percentage of people contacted who are ATM users) is 43 percent. Finally, she estimates from previous surveys that 35 percent of the people contacted will agree to complete the survey. How many telephone numbers should she order?

# WORKING THE NET

1. Log on to *http://research-advisors.com/documents/SampleSize-web.xls* to get a download of an Excel spreadsheet for a sample size table. The spreadsheet enables users to change the margin of error, confidence level, and population size. Experiment with different combinations.

2. For an online statistical power calculator, go to: *https://www.dssresearch.com/KnowledgeCenter/toolkitcalculators/samplesizecalculators.aspx* Estimate the statistical

power (type II error or beta error) for existing survey projects.

3. Use the sample size calculator online at *https://www.dssresearch.com/KnowledgeCenter/toolkitcalculators/samplesizecalculators.aspx* to work out these problems. What size samples are needed for a statistical power of 70 percent in detecting a difference of 5 percent between the estimated percentages of recent CD buyers in two independent samples? Assume an expected percentage in the range of 50 percent and an alpha error of 5 percent.

# REAL-LIFE RESEARCH • 14.1

## Concomm

Concomm Telecom is a major provider of comprehensive communications services for residential users. It offers a package including local and long-distance telephone, digital cable, Internet, and monitored home security service. Concomm is in the process of building awareness of its brand in selected areas of the southwestern United States. The company plans to

spend $22 million to promote awareness and brand image of its comprehensive package of services in the target area. Brand image and awareness are important to Concomm because it is competing with a number of much larger and better financed competitors, including AT&T, Verizon, and Comcast.

In the first year of the brand image campaign, Concomm spent $12 million pursuing the same goals of increasing awareness and brand image. In order to see if the campaign was successful, the company conducted tracking research by telephone. It conducted a pretest before the campaign began and a posttest at the end of the year. The surveys were designed to measure awareness and image of Concomm. Changes in either measure from the pretest to the posttest were to be attributed to the effects of the ad campaign. No other elements of the marketing strategy were changed during the course of the campaign.

Unaided, or top-of-mind, awareness ("What companies come to mind when you think of companies that provide residential communication services?") increased from 21 percent in the pretest to 25 percent in the posttest. In the pretest, 42 percent reported having a positive image of Concomm. This figure increased to 44 percent in the posttest. Though both key measures increased, the same sizes for the two tests were relatively small. Random samples of 100 consumers were used for both tests. Sampling error for the measure of awareness at 95.44 percent confidence is ± 8.7 percent. The comparable figure for the image measure is ± 9.9 percent. The value used for $P$ in the formula is the posttest result. With these relatively large sampling errors and the relatively small changes in awareness and image, Concomm could only say with 95.44 percent confidence that awareness in the posttest was 25 percent ± 8.7 percent, or in the range of 16.3 percent to 33.7 percent. In regard to the image measure, it could only say with 95.44 percent confidence that the percentage of consumers with a positive image of Concomm in the posttest was 44 percent ± 9.9 percent, or in the range of 34.1 percent to 53.9 percent. Based on the relatively small changes in awareness

and image and the relatively large errors associated with these measures, Concomm could not conclude with any confidence that either measure had actually changed.

The CEO of Concomm is concerned about the amount of money being spent on advertising and wants to know whether the advertising is actually achieving what it is supposed to achieve. She wants a more sensitive test so that a definitive conclusion can be reached regarding the effect of the advertising.

## Questions

1. Show how the sampling errors for the posttest measures were calculated.

2. If the CEO wants to have 95.44 percent confidence that the estimates of awareness and positive image are within ± 2 percent of the true value, what is the required sample size?

3. What is the required sample size if the CEO wants to be 99.74 percent confident?

4. If the current budget for conducting telephone interviews is $20,000 and the cost per interview is $19, can Concomm reach the goal specified in question 3? With the $20,000 budget, what error levels can it reach for both measures? What is the budget required to reach the goal set in question 3?

## REAL-LIFE RESEARCH • 14.2

### Building a Village

Village Home Builders is a major builder of upscale spec homes in six major markets in the Southwest. In 2013 the company built over 200 homes in the $500,000 plus price range. Management has a gut feel that the market and tastes of their target customers are changing in subtle ways. It has tasked Greg Morse of their marketing staff with the project task of conducting a market segmentation project among target customers to get an in depth understanding of what they are looking for in today's market.

Greg Morse of Village is faced with some challenges regarding the sample size for this important project. He is working with both a local marketing research firm and a management-consulting firm, given the strategic importance of the project. Management committed $75,000 to the project at a time when budgets are fairly tight at Village. The charges of the management-consulting firm come out of a separate budget and are not covered by the $75,000, which is solely committed to the marketing research.

Given the various markets and subgroups that Village, the marketing research firm, and the management consulting firm have identified and agreed that need to be properly represented in the sample, they have come up with a preliminary estimate of a required sample size of at least 2,000 consumers. Joe has just received the proposal from the marketing research firm and he feels that the methodology, deliverables and other elements of the proposal are right on target. However, a quick review of the cost section of the proposal and shows that they have a problem. Note that the marketing research firm was not told that there is a budget of $75,000 available for the project. It is typical not to inform the researchers of how much you have available to avoid their designing the research to fit the budget, making sure that they spend every dime, as well as other related problems. The estimates from the research firm are shown in the following table. As you can see, the total of $83,700 is well beyond the budget for the project. Joe has two basic choices: Go back to senior management and justify a larger budget for the project or go back to the research firm with change specifications, requesting that they reprice the research based on the new specifications.

**Village Home Builders**
**Market Segmentation Research**
**Cost Estimates**

| Item | Quantity | Units | Rate | Amount |
|---|---|---|---|---|
| **Development** | | | | |
| Finalizing details of project design | 8 | hours | $125 | $1,000 |
| Database work | 5 | hours | $100 | $500 |
| Survey instrument design | 30 | hours | $125 | $3,750 |
| **Data Collection** | 2000 | surveys | $15 | $30,000 |
| **Data Processing** | | | | |
| Coding | 2500 | lines | $0.50 | $1,250 |
| Tabulation | 20 | hours | $100 | $2,000 |
| **Analysis** | | | | |
| Analytical | 50 | hours | $175 | $8,750 |
| Analysis | 65 | hours | $150 | $9,750 |
| Report preparation | 40 | hours | $125 | $5,000 |
| **General and administrative** | | | | $21,700 |
| **Total** | | | | **$83,700** |

## Questions

1. Which approach do you think Joe should take? Try to get more money for the project or try to reduce the cost of the project? Some of both? Justify your answer.

2. If, for example, Joe chose to get more money for the project from senior management, then outline his arguments for an increase in funds.

3. If Joe decided to respecify the research and get the research firm to adjust its price, where would you suggest cost reductions could or should be made? What about reductions in sample size? Reducing sample size to around 1,600 would get the project costs down to available budget levels? Note that other costs won't change much, if at all, with a lower sample size. What are the pros and cons of reducing sample size?

 • **SPSS JUMP START FOR CHI-SQUARE TEST**

# Exercise 1: Sample Size Determination Using the Sample Means Method SPSS-H1

1. Go to the Wiley website at *www.wiley.com/college/mcdaniel* and download the *Segmenting the College Student Market for Movie Attendance* database to SPSS windows. Using the *Segmenting the College Student Market for Movie Attendance* database, assume that the most important items in the survey are in question 5, which has nine movie items in which respondents rate their relative importance (download a copy of the *Segmenting the College Student Market for Movie Attendance* questionnaire). Notice the computer coding for each of the variables, which is the same as that in the *variable view* option on the SPSS Data Editor.

2. The Sample Means method of sample size determination consists of:
   i. required confidence level ($z$)
   ii. level of tolerable error ($e$)
   iii. estimated population variance ($\sigma$)
   iv. estimated sample size ($n$)
   v. *Formula:* $n = (z^2 * \sigma^2)/e^2$

3. Of the various methods of deriving sample size, estimated population standard deviation can be estimated based on prior studies, expert judgment, or by conducting a pilot sample. For this problem, we are going to estimate population standard deviation using a **pilot sample**. To do this you will use only the first 200 cases in the *Segmenting the College Student Market for Movie Attendance* database. Invoke the *data/select cases* sequence to select the first 200 cases in the database. We are assuming that these are responses to a pilot sample, and we will use them to estimate the needed sample size.

4. Use the *analyze/descriptive statistics/descriptive* sequence to compute the standard deviation for variables Q5a–Q5i. We are assuming that each of the nine variables is equally important with respect to the research objective.

5. From your knowledge of sample size determination, you should know that the variable to select for sample size determination is the one with the largest standard deviation. Select that variable.

   Answer the following questions:

1. Which of the nine movie theater items had the largest standard deviation?

   _____

2. Invoke the sample means method of sample size determination to make the necessary computations for each of the following:
   **a.** Compute sample size, given the following:
      i. Required confidence level ($Z$) is 95.44%.
      ii. Tolerable error ($e$) is .1 or 1/10 of a response point.
      iii. Standard deviation ($\sigma$) = _____
      iv. Sample size ($n$) = _____

   **b.** Compute sample size, given the following:
      i. Required confidence level ($Z$) is 99.72%.
      ii. Tolerable level ($e$) is .1 or 1/10 of a response point.
      iii. Standard deviation ($\sigma$) = _____
      iv. Sample size ($n$) = _____

3. How do your computed sample sizes in the problems above compare to the total number of cases in the *Segmenting the College Student Market for Movie Attendance* database?

   _____

4. We are going to assume that the objective of our research concerning students' attendance at movies can be expressed as a dichotomy (greater or lesser, etc.); for example, it doesn't matter how much one group attends movies over another group, but just *who* attends the most. To accomplish this we can use the much less complicated *sample proportions* formula. We are going to assume that we have no prior studies, hence, in the sample proportions formula $P = .5$ and $(1 − P) = .5$. **You will not need SPSS to assist you with this computation.**

surveysolutions XP

**a.** Compute sample size given the following:
   **i.** Required confidence level ($Z$) is 95.44 percent.
   **ii.** Tolerable error ($e$) is .05 or accuracy within 5 percent of the true population mean.
   **iii.** Standard deviation $P = .5$ and $(1 - P) = .5$
   **iv.** Sample size ($n$) = _____

**c.** Compute sample size, given the following:
   **i.** Required confidence level ($Z$) is 99.72 percent.
   **ii.** Tolerable error ($e$) is .03 or accuracy within 3 percent of the true population mean.
   **iii.** Standard deviation $P = .5$ and $(1 - P) = .5$
   **iv.** Sample size ($n$) = _____

# Exercise 2: Determining the Reliability/Confidence of Sample Results

1. In the subsequent exercise, the objective will not be to determine the needed sample size, but to evaluate the confidence level of results derived from the entire *Segmenting the College Student Market for Movie Attendance* database. To evaluate this type of confidence, using the sample means formula, solve for $Z$ instead of $n$. Hence, use the formula $Z^2 = n * e^2/\sigma^2$. Then take the square root of $Z^2$. Go to the normal distribution table in the appendix of your text to determine the confidence level associated with the database. For the sample proportions formula, solve for $Z$ using the formula $Z^2 = (n * e^2)/[P(1 - P)]$, then take the square root of $Z^2$.

2. For this problem again assume that question #5 has the most important questions in the questionnaire, with respect to the research objectives. Using the *analyze/descriptive statistics/descriptives* sequence, compute the standard deviation for variables Q5a–Q5i. We are assuming that each of the nine variables are equally important with respect to the research objective. **Again, choose the variable with the largest standard deviation** to input into the analysis.

3. Given the preceding, compute the confidence level associated with the *Segmenting the College Student Market for Movie Attendance* database, given the following:
   **1. a.** Tolerable error is .1 or 1/10 of a response point
      **b.** Sample size = 500
      **c.** Standard deviation _____
   **2.** Confidence Level = _____ %
   **3.** How do the results in 2, above, compare to the results in 2 of the sample size determination problem?

   _____

   **4.** Sample Proportions Formula: Given the following information, compute the confidence level associated with the *Segmenting the College Student Marketing for Movie Attendance* database. *You will not need SPSS to make this computation.*
      **a.** Tolerable error is .05 or 5%.
      **b.** Sample size = 500
      **c.** Standard deviation $P = .5$ and $(1 - P) = .5$
      Confidence Level = _____ %
      How do the results in this problem compare to the confidence level in #2 of (3)?

Monty Rakusen/Getty Images

# 15

# Data Processing and Fundamental Data Analysis

## LEARNING OBJECTIVES

1. Get an overview of the data analysis procedure.

2. Understand validation and editing.

3. Learn how to code questions in surveys.

4. Understand the process of data entry so that information can be read by a computer.

5. Understand the importance of cleaning questionnaires so that they are free of errors.

6. Be familiar with tabulation and statistical analysis.

7. Gain insight into the graphic representations of data.

8. Comprehend descriptive statistics.

Okay, now we have reached the point where the survey is in the field (data collection is under way). At this point, we need to begin a number of processes that will, upon their completion, prepare the data for the analysis phase. Although some of the elements are clerical in nature, these processes are critical in making sure that the data have integrity and are free of errors related to the process of capturing respondent answers to our questions and moving those answers to tabular, graphical and statistical displays. The steps in this process are covered in this chapter.

## Overview of the Data Analysis Procedure

Once data collection has been completed and questionnaires have been returned, the researcher may be facing anywhere from a few hundred to several thousand interviews.

DSS Research recently completed a mail study involving 1,300 questionnaires of 10 pages each. The 13,000 pages amounted to a stack of paper more than 3 feet high. How should a researcher transform all the information contained on 13,000 pages of completed questionnaires into a format that will permit the summarization necessary for detailed analysis? At one extreme, the researcher could read all the interviews, make notes while reading them, and draw some conclusions from this review of the questionnaires. The limitations of this approach are fairly obvious. Instead of this haphazard and inefficient approach, professional researchers follow a five-step procedure for data analysis:

| | |
|---|---|
| Step One. | Validation and editing (quality control) |
| Step Two. | Coding |
| Step Three. | Data entry |
| Step Four. | Logical cleaning of data |
| Step Five. | Tabulation and statistical analysis |

If responses are captured electronically, the process is considerably less daunting, but still needs to be followed as appropriate.

# Step One: Validation and Editing

The purpose of the first step is twofold. The researcher wants to make sure that all the interviews actually were conducted as specified (validation) and that the questionnaires have been filled out properly and completely (editing).

## Validation

First, the researcher must determine, to the extent possible, that each of the questionnaires to be processed represents a valid interview. Here, we are using the term *valid* in a different sense than in Chapter 10. In Chapter 10, validity was defined as the extent to which the item being measured was actually measured. In this chapter, **validation** is defined as the process of ascertaining that interviews were conducted as specified. In this context, no assessment is made regarding the validity of the measurement. The goal of validation is solely to detect interviewer fraud or failure to follow key instructions. You may have noticed that questionnaires presented throughout the text almost always have a place to record the respondent's name, address, and telephone number. This information is seldom used in any way in the analysis of the data; it is collected only to provide a basis for validation.

**validation**
Process of ascertaining that interviews actually were conducted as specified.

Professional researchers know that interviewer cheating does happen. Various studies have documented the existence and prevalence of interviewer falsification of several types. For this reason, validation is an integral and necessary step in the data processing stage of a marketing research project.

After all the interviews have been completed, the research firm recontacts a certain percentage of the respondents surveyed by each interviewer. Typically, this percentage ranges from 10 to 20 percent. If a particular interviewer surveyed 50 people and the research firm normally validates at a 10 percent rate, 5 respondents surveyed by that interviewer would be recontacted to determine:

1. Was the person actually interviewed?
2. Did the person who was interviewed qualify to be interviewed according to the screening questions on the survey? For example, the interview may have required that the person

being interviewed come from a family with an annual household income of $25,000 or more. On validation, the respondent would again be asked whether the annual household income for his or her family was $25,000 or more per year.

3. Was the interview conducted in the required manner? For example, a mall survey should have been conducted in the designated mall. Was this particular respondent interviewed in the mall or was she or he interviewed at some other place, such as a restaurant or someone's home?

4. Did the interviewer cover the entire survey? Sometimes interviewers recognize that a potential respondent is in a hurry and may not have time to complete the entire survey. If respondents for that particular survey are difficult to find, the interviewer may be motivated to ask the respondent a few questions at the beginning and a few questions at the end and then fill out the rest of the survey without the respondent's input. Validation for this particular problem would involve asking respondents whether they were asked various questions from different points in the interview.

Validation may involve checking for other problems. For example: Was the interviewer courteous? Did the interviewer speculate about the client's identity or the purpose of the survey? Does the respondent have any other comments about the interviewer or the interview experience?

The purpose of the validation process, as noted earlier, is to ensure that interviews were administered properly and completely. Researchers must be sure that the research results on which they are basing their recommendations reflect the legitimate responses of target individuals.

In the case of online interviews from Internet panels a substantial amount of checking that represents a form of validation must be done. Details of procedures used by DSS Research are provided in the Practicing Marketing Research feature below.

Robert Shafer /Getty Images

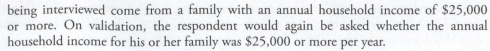

# PRACTICING MARKETING RESEARCH

## DSS Research Online Data Collection Quality Assurance Procedures[1]

### Respondent Selection

The following guidelines will be used when identifying and selecting potential respondents to include in our Internet surveys:

■ **Use reputable Internet panels.** The recruitment, maintenance, and quality control procedures of panel companies are critical to insuring the best possible respondent sample. Only panels that use a double opt-in registration process and validate their panel membership through physical address verification are eligible for usage. Panel companies must also limit the number of surveys in which panelists can participate in a given period of time

and have procedures in place to minimize the chances of panelists having multiple accounts with the same organization. The primary characteristics to consider when evaluating a panel company are:

i. *Method of recruitment.* Ensure that panelists are recruited from reputable sources and voluntarily agree to participate. Aggregators (automatically pulling e-mail addresses and phone numbers from websites, blogs, forums, etc.) should not be accepted. Panels should be built and managed exclusively for market research purposes.

ii. *Frequency of replenishment.* Indicate the frequency in which inactive panelists are removed and new ones added. Panelist retention rates and overall rate of growth are indicators of panelist involvement and level of activity/inactivity.

iii. *Maximum number of surveys completed per month.* Make sure limits are in place to keep panelists from becoming professional respondents.

iv. *Verification of identity.* Determine what steps panel companies use to verify the identities of those individuals who become members of their panel. These steps should include the identification and removal of individuals with multiple accounts and multiple individuals in the same household should also be removed.

v. *Profile information collected.* Determine the type of demographic and behavioral information collected from panelists for use in profiling members and pre-screening for certain target populations. There should be a plan in place to update this information on a regular basis and identify panelists with significant variations (i.e., gender change or dramatic age difference in subsequent wave) for possible removal from the panel.

vi. Incentives used. Determine what types of incentives are offered by the panel and the frequency with which those incentives are dispersed. Infrequent drawings and low odds of winning can discourage reliable participation.

vii. *Disciplinary procedures.* Examine the steps taken by each panel to address individuals suspected of speeding or cheating during a survey.

viii. *Typical response rates.* The typical response rate for a panel will indicate how engaged those individuals are with the panel, whether the panel's incentive program is equitable and whether panelists are being oversurveyed or allowed to remain inactive for long periods of time.

ix. *Privacy policies in place.* Panel companies should have clearly defined policies and data storage protection procedures to ensure the privacy of their members and to protect access to their member databases.

x. *Customer service.* Having responsive representatives that can quickly provide quotes, estimate number of completes and get surveys fielded is imperative. Quick turnaround is often needed on proposals and data collection. Client objectives and project scope can change quickly, so panel companies must be responsive and flexible.

■ **Continually monitor Internet panel performance.** The response rate, respondent quality, and customer service of Internet panels are continually monitored. Response rates and respondent quality issues (speeders, duplicates, inattentive, etc.) are always reported back to the panel company.

## Online Data Collection Quality Assurance— Respondent Cooperation and Attention Issues

These steps are taken to maximize respondent cooperation and to eliminate respondents who did not give sufficient attention to the questions being asked or intentionally tried to "cheat" the system to be included in a survey in which they did not qualify:

■ **Check for multiple responses and out-of-area respondents.** DSS uses a software tool to identify individuals who are attempting to complete multiple surveys either by having multiple accounts with a single panel or by having accounts with multiple panel companies. The system creates a unique fingerprint of each computer to identify multiple surveys from the same computer, regardless of which panel or username is used. It also examines IP addresses and information regarding the panelists' ISP to identify panelists who are attempting to access a survey that falls outside the targeted region or country. When panelists are identified as attempting to access the same survey multiple times or access a survey outside their geography, they are blocked from further access to the survey and reported to the panel company for further action.

■ **Exclude speeders.** Anyone who speeds through a survey at such a rate that they could not possibly have given reasonable consideration to the survey questions will be excluded from the sample and not compensated for their time.

■ **Setting a minimum survey length.** The minimum allowed speed is set prior to survey launch as an initial guideline to flag potential speeders among the first respondents. The initial limit is estimated at 40 to 50 percent of the expected survey length. The first respondents are not immediately terminated based on falling below this limit, but are set aside for later review. Once more, surveys are collected; an absolute survey minimum is set. Any early surveys that fell below the newly established survey limit are removed from the final sample. The absolute survey minimum is determined once a sufficient number of responses have been received by computing the median survey length and then setting a limit of roughly 50 or 60 percent of the median length. Survey traits (complexity, variety of skip patterns, variation in characteristics of target population, etc.) and experience are used to set the final limit. Once the final limit is set, any respondents that finish the survey below the minimum time limit are terminated and their panel ID is sent to the panel company as a suspected speeder. The proportion of speeders identified is monitored throughout the survey, and the minimum time limit is adjusted upward or downward if it is determined that the initial limit was inappropriate.

■ **Examining individual questions.** The length of time spent on each question is also collected for analyses. Prior to finalizing the sample for data processing, the distribution of time spent on each question is examined. Any extreme anomalies are examined further, looking for respondents who sped quickly through multiple questions before stopping or slowed considerably on one or two questions to avoid looking like a speeder.

- **Exclude straight liners/flat liners and those who provide contradictory responses.** Another area of concern in any survey is inattentiveness. Respondents who appear to be clicking answers without reading the questions or always picking the same point of a scale are flagged as suspects for further evaluation. Straight lining (providing the same response to a long series of questions) on a long battery of items is certainly suspicious, but doing so on an attitude battery that includes both positively and negatively worded statements results in discarding of that respondent's survey due to their clear lack of attention. Asking the same or a similar question at two different points in the survey is another way of detecting inattention. Small deviations in responses between similar or identical questions are normal, but those who provide contradictory responses (e.g., someone who indicates they are "very satisfied" at the beginning of the survey and "somewhat dissatisfied" at a later point in the survey) are rejected from the final sample. Inconsistencies such as a person who reports being a senior executive, but later reports a very low household income, are flagged and excluded unless a reasonable explanation is identified to account for these responses.

- **Monitor key demographic and behavioral characteristics to be sure the sample is representative of the target market.** Gender, age, and education level are typically monitored during the screening process to ensure that the Internet sample is not biased toward younger, better-educated individuals than would be found in that population using all survey modes. If a key market variable is already well known (e.g., market share, market penetration, etc.), survey responses can be compared directly to the known parameter. Panels that have trouble maintaining representative samples should be reevaluated.

- **Do not allow responses to key questions or screening questions to be changed.** Respondents are prevented from going back and changing their responses to any screening questions once they have been terminated from the survey. If they are not prevented from going back to change a response, they could try a different answer that does not screen them out of the survey, continuing as if the acceptable answer had been given from the beginning. Likewise, if there is a critical question in the main body of the survey that you want to be sure captures the respondents' initial impressions (e.g., unaided awareness of competing brands), respondents will be prevented from going back and changing those initial responses.

- **Remove respondents before fielding has ended.** As much as possible, analyses of speeders, straight liners or flat liners (same answer to all questions in a rating battery), and inattentive responders should be done throughout the data collection process in order to keep project quotas on target. In some cases, oversampling may be done to allow a few respondents to be removed during data processing without adversely affecting the final sample size.

- **Extend survey fielding.** Extending data collection over several days helps any survey methodology to garner a more representative sample. Whenever possible, allow surveys to remain in the field for at least three to five days. At least a week is preferred, even though data collection might easily be completed overnight.

## Editing

**editing**
Process of ascertaining that questionnaires were filled out properly and completely.

Whereas validation involves checking for interviewer cheating and failure to follow instructions, **editing** involves checking for interviewer and respondent mistakes. Paper questionnaires usually are edited at least twice before being submitted for data entry. First, they may be edited by the field service firm that conducted the interviews, and then they are edited by the marketing research firm that hired the field service firm to do the interviewing. CATI, Internet, and other software-driven surveys have built-in logical checking. The editing process for paper surveys involves manual checking for a number of problems, including the following:

1. *Whether the interviewer failed to ask certain questions or record answers for certain questions.* In the questionnaire shown in Exhibit 15.1, no answer was recorded for question 19. According to the structure of the questionnaire, this question should have been asked of all respondents. Also, the respondent's name does not give a clear indication of gender. The purpose of the first edit—the field edit—is to identify these types of problems when there is still time to recontact the respondent and determine the appropriate answer to questions that were not asked. This may also be done at the second edit (by the marketing research firm), but in many instances there is not time to recontact the respondent and the interview has to be discarded.

| **EXHIBIT 15.1** | **Sample Questionnaire** |
| --- | --- |

**Consumer Survey**
**Mobile Telephone Survey Questionnaire**

Long Branch—Asbury, N.J.
(01-03) <u>001</u>

Date <u>1-05-01</u>

Respondent Telephone Number <u>201-555-2322</u>

Hello. My name is Sally with POST Research. May I please speak with the male or female head of the household?

(IF INDIVIDUAL NOT AVAILABLE, RECORD NAME AND CALLBACK INFORMATION ON SAMPLING FORM.)

(WHEN MALE/FEMALE HEAD OF HOUSEHOLD COMES TO PHONE): Hello, my name is _____,
with POST Research. Your number was randomly selected, and I am not trying to sell you anything. I simply want to ask you a few questions about a new type of telephone service.

1. First, how many telephone calls do you make during a typical day?

|  | (04) |
| --- | --- |
| 0–2 | 1 |
| 3–5 | 2 |
| 6–10 | ③ |
| 11–15 | 4 |
| 16–20 | 5 |
| More than 20 | 6 |
| Don't know | 7 |

Now, let me tell you about a new service called cellular mobile telephone service, which is completely wireless. You can get either a portable model that may be carried in your coat pocket or a model mounted in any vehicle. You will be able to receive calls and make calls, no matter where you are. Although cellular phones are wireless, the voice quality is similar to your present phone service. This is expected to be a time-saving convenience for household use.

This new cellular mobile phone service may soon be widely available in your area.

2. Now, let me explain to you the cost of this wireless service. Calls will cost 26 cents a minute plus normal toll charges. In addition, the monthly minimum charge for using the service will be $7.50 and rental of a cellular phone will be about $40. Of course, you can buy the equipment instead of leasing it. At this price, do you think you would be very likely, somewhat likely, somewhat unlikely, or very unlikely to subscribe to the new phone service?

|  |  | (05) |
| --- | --- | --- |
| Very likely | | 1 |
| Somewhat likely | | ② |
| Somewhat unlikely | | 3 |
| Very unlikely | (GO TO QUESTION 16) | 4 |
| Don't know | (GO TO QUESTION 16) | 5 |

INTERVIEWER—IF "VERY UNLIKELY" OR "DON'T KNOW," GO TO QUESTION 16.

3. Do you think it is likely that your employer would furnish you with one of these phones for your job?

|  |  | (06) |
| --- | --- | --- |
| No | (GO TO QUESTION 5) | 1 |
| Don't know | (GO TO QUESTION 5) | 2 |
| Yes | (CONTINUE) | ③ |

INTERVIEWER—IF "NO" OR "DON'T KNOW," GO TO QUESTION 5; OTHERWISE CONTINUE.

4. If your employer did furnish you with a wireless phone, would you also purchase one for household use?

|  |  | (07) |
| --- | --- | --- |
| Yes | (CONTINUE) | ① |
| No | (GO TO QUESTION 16) | 2 |
| Don't know | (GO TO QUESTION 16) | 3 |

5. Please give me your best estimate of the number of mobile phones your household would use (write in "DK" for "Don't know").

Number of Units _____<u>01</u>_____ (08–09)

6. Given that cellular calls made or received will cost 26 cents a minute plus normal toll charges during weekdays, how many calls on the average would you expect to make in a typical weekday?

RECORD NUMBER _____<u>06</u>_____ (10–11)

*(continued)*

**EXHIBIT 15.1** (Continued)

7.    About how many minutes would your average cellular call last during the week?

RECORD NUMBER _____05_____ (12–13)

8.    Weekend cellular calls made or received will cost 8 cents per minute plus normal toll charges. Given this, about how many cellular calls on the average would you expect to make in a typical Saturday or Sunday?

RECORD NUMBER _____00_____ (14–15)

9.    About how many minutes would your average cellular call last on Saturday or Sunday?

RECORD NUMBER _____ (16–17)

10.   You may recall from my previous description that two types of cellular phone units will be available. The vehicle phone may be installed in any vehicle. The portable phone will be totally portable—it can be carried in a briefcase, purse, or coat pocket. The totally portable phones may cost about 25 percent more and may have a more limited transmitting range in some areas than the vehicle phone. Do you think you would prefer portable or vehicle phones if you were able to subscribe to this service?

                                                                              (18)
Portable .................................................................... 1
Vehicle...................................................................... ②
Both ......................................................................... 3
Don't know................................................................ 4

11.   Would you please tell me whether you, on the average, would use a mobile phone about once a week, less than once a week, or more than once a week from the following geographic locations.

| | Less Than Once a Week | Once a Week | More Than Once a Week | Never | |
|---|---|---|---|---|---|
| Monmouth County | 1 | 2 | ③ | 4 | (19) |
| (IF "NEVER," SKIP TO QUESTION 16) | | | | | |
| Sandy Hook | 1 | 2 | 3 | ④ | (20) |
| Keansburg | 1 | 2 | 3 | ④ | (21) |
| Atlantic Highlands | 1 | 2 | ③ | 4 | (22) |
| Matawan-Middletown | ① | 2 | 3 | 4 | (23) |
| Red Bank | ① | 2 | 3 | 4 | (24) |
| Holmdel | 1 | 2 | ③ | 4 | (25) |
| Eatontown | 1 | ② | 3 | 4 | (26) |
| Long Branch | 1 | 2 | 3 | ④ | (27) |
| Freehold | 1 | 2 | 3 | ④ | (28) |
| Manalapan | 1 | 2 | 3 | ④ | (29) |
| Cream Ridge | 1 | 2 | 3 | ④ | (30) |
| Belmar | 1 | 2 | 3 | ④ | (31) |
| Point Pleasant | 1 | 2 | ③ | 4 | (32) |

I'm going to describe to you a list of possible extra features of the proposed cellular service. Each option I'm going to describe will cost not more than $3.00 a month per phone. Would you please tell me if you would be very interested, interested, or uninterested in each feature:

| | Very Interested | Interested | Uninterested |
|---|---|---|---|
| 12.  Call forwarding (the ability to transfer any call coming in to your mobile phone to any other phone). | ① | 2 | 3  (33) |
| 13.  No answer transfer (service that redirects calls to another number if your phone is unanswered). | 1 | 2 | ③  (34) |

**EXHIBIT 15.1**   *(Continued)*

|  | Very Interested | Interested | Uninterested |
|---|---|---|---|
| 14. Call waiting (a signal that another person is trying to call you while you are using your phone). | 1 | ② | 3  (35) |
| 15. Voice mailbox (a recording machine that will take the caller's message and relay it to you at a later time. This service will be provided at $5.00 per month). | 1 | 2 | ③  (36) |

16. What is your age group? (READ BELOW)

(37)

Under 25 ...........................................................1
25–44 ...............................................................2
45–64 ...............................................................3
65 and over ......................................................4
Refused, no answer, or don't know .........................5

17. What is your occupation?

(38)

Manager, official, or proprietor.....................1
Professional (doctors, lawyers, etc.) .........................2
Technical (engineers, computer
programmers, draftsmen, etc.) .....................3
Office worker/clerical .....................................4
Sales .............................................................5
Skilled worker or foreman ..............................6
Unskilled worker ............................................7
Teacher..........................................................8
Homemaker, student, retired .........................9
Not now employed..........................................X
Refused..........................................................Y

18. Into which category did your total family income fall in 2002? (READ BELOW)

(39)

Under $15,000 ...............................................1
$15,000–$24,999 ..........................................2
$25,000–$49,999 ..........................................3
$50,000–$74,999 ..........................................4
$75,000 and over ...........................................5
Refused, no answer, don't know.........................6

19. (INTERVIEWER—RECORD SEX OF RESPONDENT):

(40)

Male ...............................................................1
Female ...........................................................2

20. May I have your name? My office calls about 10 percent of the people I talk with to verify that I have conducted the interview.
Gave name.........................................................1
Refused.............................................................2

_____*Jordan Beasley*_____
Name

Thank you for your time. Have a good day.

2. *Whether skip patterns were followed.* According to the **skip pattern** in question 2 in Exhibit 15.1, if the answer to this question is "Very unlikely" or "Don't know," the interviewer should skip to question 16. The editor needs to make sure that the interviewer followed instructions. Sometimes, particularly during the first few interviews in a particular study, interviewers get mixed up and skip when they should not or fail to skip when they should. In electronic surveys, this issue is dealt with in survey programming and is not going to happen.

**skip pattern**
Sequence in which later questions are asked, based on a respondent's answer to an earlier question or questions.

**Exhibit 15.2**

**Recording of Open-Ended Questions**

**Exhibit 15.2**

**Recording of Open-Ended Questions**

**A.** Example of Improper Interviewer Recording of Response to an Open-Ended Question

Question: Why do you go to Burger King most often among fast food/quick service restaurants? (PROBE)

*Response recorded:*

The consumer seemed to think Burger King had better tasting food and better quality ingredients.

**B.** Example of Interviewer Failure to Probe a Response

Question: Same as Part A.

*Only response recorded:*

*Because I like it.*

**C.** Example of Proper Recording and Probing

Question: Same as Part A.

*Response recorded:*

*Because I like it. (P)\* I like it, and I go there most often because it is the closest place to where I work. (AE)\*\* No.*

\*(P) is an interviewer mark indicating he or she has probed a response.

\*\*(AE) is interviewer shorthand for "Anything else?" This gives the respondent an opportunity to expand on the original answer.

**3.** ***Whether the interviewer paraphrased respondents' answers to open-ended questions.*** Marketing researchers and their clients usually are very interested in the responses to open-ended questions. The quality of the responses, or at least what was recorded, is an excellent indicator of the competence of the interviewer who recorded them. Interviewers are trained to record responses verbatim and not to paraphrase or insert their own language. They also are instructed to probe the initial response. The first part of Exhibit 15.2 shows an example of an interviewer's paraphrasing and interpretation of a response to an open-ended question. The second part of Exhibit 15.2 shows the result of interviewer failure to probe a response. The response is useless from a decision-making perspective. It comes as no surprise that the respondent goes to Burger King most often because he likes it. The third part of Exhibit 15.2 shows how an initial meaningless response can be expanded to a useful response by means of proper probing. A proper probe to the answer "Because I like it" would be "Why do you like it?" or "What do you like about it?" The respondent then indicates that he goes there most often because it is the fast-food restaurant most convenient to his place of work.

The person doing the editing must make judgment calls in regard to substandard responses to open-ended questions. She or he must decide at what point particular answers are so limited as to be useless, and whether respondents should be recontacted.

The editing process is extremely tedious and time-consuming. However, it is a very important step in the processing of survey responses.

# Step Two: Coding

**Coding**
Process of grouping and assigning numeric codes to the various responses to a question.

As discussed in Chapter 12, **coding** refers to the process of grouping and assigning numeric codes to the responses to a particular question. Most questions on surveys are closed-ended and precoded, meaning that numeric codes have already been assigned to the various responses on the questionnaire. All answers to closed-ended questions should be precoded, as they are in question 1 on the questionnaire in Exhibit 15.1. Note that each answer has a numeric code to its right; the answer "0–2" has the code 1, the answer "3–5" has the code 2, and so on. The interviewer can record the response by circling the numeric code next to the answer given by the respondent. In this case, the respondent's answer was seven calls per day. The code 3 next to the category "6–10" (calls per day) is circled.

Open-ended questions create a coding dilemma. They were phrased in an open-ended manner because the researcher either had no idea what answers to expect or wanted a richer response than is possible with a closed-ended question. As with editing, the process of coding responses to open-ended questions can be tedious and time-consuming. In addition, the procedure is to some degree subjective.[2] For these reasons, researchers tend to avoid open-ended questions unless they are absolutely necessary.

## Coding Process

The process of coding responses to open-ended questions includes the following steps:

1. *List responses.* Coders at the research firm prepare lists of the actual responses given to each open-ended question on a particular survey. In studies of a few hundred respondents, all responses may be listed. With larger samples, responses given by a sample of respondents are listed.

2. *Consolidate responses.* A sample list of responses to an open-ended question is provided in Exhibit 15.3. Examination of this list indicates that a number of the responses can be interpreted to mean essentially the same thing; therefore, they can be appropriately consolidated into a single category. This process of consolidation might yield the list shown in Exhibit 15.4. Consolidating requires a number of subjective decisions—for example, does response number 4 in Exhibit 15.3 belong in category 1, or should it have its own category? These decisions typically are made by a qualified research analyst and may involve client input.

---

| **EXHIBIT 15.3** | **Sample of Responses to Open-Ended Question** |
|---|---|

**Question: Why do you drink that brand of beer? (BRAND MENTIONED IN ANSWER TO PREVIOUS QUESTION)**

**Sample responses:**

1. Because it tastes better.
2. It has the best taste.
3. I like the way it tastes.
4. I don't like the heavy taste of other beers.
5. It is the cheapest.
6. I buy whatever beer is on sale. It is on sale most of the time.
7. It doesn't upset my stomach the way other brands do.
8. Other brands give me headaches. This one doesn't.
9. It has always been my brand.
10. I have been drinking it for over 20 years.
11. It is the brand that most of the guys at work drink.
12. All my friends drink it.
13. It is the brand my wife buys at the grocery store.
14. It is my wife's/husband's favorite brand.
15. I have no idea.
16. Don't know.
17. No particular reason.

| EXHIBIT 15.4 | Consolidated Response Categories and Codes for Open-Ended Responses from Beer Study | |
|---|---|---|
| **Response Category Descriptor** | **Response Items from Exhibit 14.1 Included** | **Assigned Numeric Code** |
| Tastes better/like taste/tastes better than others | 1, 2, 3, 4 | 1 |
| Low/lower price | 5, 6 | 2 |
| Does not cause headache, stomach problems | 7, 8 | 3 |
| Long-term use, habit | 9, 10 | 4 |
| Friends drink it/influence of friends | 11, 12 | 5 |
| Wife/husband drinks/buys it | 13, 14 | 6 |

| EXHIBIT 15.5 | Example Questionnaire Setup for Open-Ended Questions |
|---|---|

**37.** Why do you drink that brand of beer? (BRAND MENTIONED IN PREVIOUS QUESTION)?

(48) _____ 2

*Because it's cheaper. (P) Nothing. (AE) Nothing.*

3. *Set codes.* A numeric code is assigned to each of the categories on the final consolidated list of responses. Code assignments for the sample beer study question are shown in Exhibit 15.4.

4. *Enter codes.* After responses have been listed and consolidated and codes set, the last step is the actual entry of codes. This involves several substeps:
   **a.** Review responses to individual open-ended questions on questionnaires.
   **b.** Match individual responses with the consolidated list of response categories and determine the appropriate numeric code for each response.
   **c.** Write the numeric code in the appropriate place on the questionnaire for the response to the particular question (see Exhibit 15.5) or enter the appropriate code in the database electronically.[3]

Here's an example of the process, using the listing of responses shown in Exhibit 15.3 and the consolidation and setting of codes shown in Exhibit 15.4.

■ You turn to the first questionnaire and read this response to the question "Why do you drink that brand of beer?": "Because it's cheaper."

■ You compare this response with the consolidated response categories and decide that it best fits into the "Low/lower price" category. The numeric code associated with this category is 2 (see Exhibit 15.4).

■ You enter the code in the appropriate place on the questionnaire (see Exhibit 15.5).

## Automated Coding Systems and Text Processing

With CATI, Internet, and SMS text surveys, data entry is completely eliminated for closed-ended questions. However, even when the text of open-ended questions is electronically captured, some type of coding process is still required. A number of developments are replacing the tedious coding process for open-ended questions.

The TextSmart module of SPSS is one example of the new breed of automated coding systems. Algorithms based on semiotics[4] are at the heart of these systems and show great

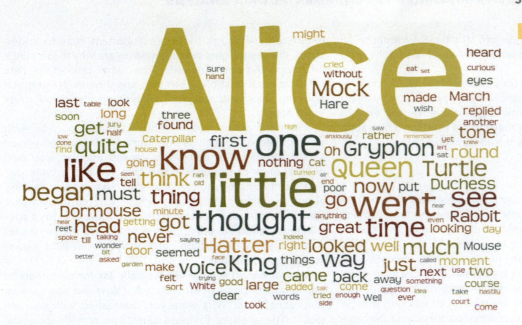

**Exhibit 15.6**

**Word Cloud Created from Text of Alice in Wonderland**

*Source:* Textisbeautiful.net

promise for speeding up the coding process, reducing its cost, and increasing its objectivity. Basically, these algorithms use the power of computers to search for patterns in open-ended responses and in group responses, based on certain keywords and phrases.

Semantria provides a number of different text processing tools and options to process results from open-ended questions and achieve degrees of summarization not previously possible and, it does it all, very quickly. Take a look at the website at semantria.com. The Practicing Marketing Research feature on page 372 provides an example of how one organization used their services.

Word clouds are but another way to summarize responses to open- ended questions or any kind of free text response. Examples can be found at wordle.net and textisbeautiful.net. Both sites provide tools to generate word clouds from text that you enter (copy and paste). Some clients find these useful; others do not. The clouds give greater prominence to words that appear more frequently in the source text. Most of the tools permit you to adjust clouds with different fonts, layouts, and color schemes. An example is provided in Exhibit 15.6.

# PRACTICING MARKETING RESEARCH

## Trying to Make Some Sense of It All[5]

The advent of data warehouses gave businesses the power to collect, store, and analyze information from multiple corporate systems in a single, high-performance environment. However, business managers were limited to analyzing only structured data. Structured data consist of tidy or fixed answers and numerals arranged in rows and columns. These data are easily stored, categorized, queried, reported, and rolled up by a database. Text analytics opens the floodgates to new insights by allowing companies to analyze unstructured, free-form data in the same way structured data has been analyzed in enterprise data warehouses.

Systems that interact with customers are inherently filled with a large amount of unstructured, free-form text. For example, notes entered from a call center, open-ended responses on a customer survey, and comments posted on the Internet all are defined as unstructured text. Text analytics, also known as text mining, is a technology that turns that unstructured information into structured information so that it can be properly analyzed by business intelligence systems.

There are many approaches and techniques used to turn text into structured information. Each approach has varying levels of accuracy and utility. In this article, we will explore those techniques and how they can be used in combination to uncover hidden insights stored within the text.

## Missing or ignoring

Currently, there is an explosion of free-form text information being generated by consumers. Studies show that as much as 80 percent of the information that is created in a corporation is free-form or text in nature. At the same time, computer technology can not accurately process and understand language in its traditional form because computers are made to simply match patterns, compare, and sort. Therefore, companies are missing or ignoring a large percentage of the valuable information that could be helpful to their business.

Companies have numerous internal systems such as call centers, e-mail, and automated feedback systems to gather and manage customer information. However, public Internet comments are posted for all to see, providing low-cost access to relevant customer thoughts and feelings about a company and its competitors. Businesses and their competitors can use this information to do competitive research, understand general market trends, and pinpoint emerging problems early on in the product development life cycle. However, due to the free-form nature and sheer volume of this information, it is an expensive and cumbersome process to gather and understand unstructured data.

Transaction or feedback surveys typically contain one or more verbatim questions such as, "How can we improve?" or "Please describe the problem you had." Responses to these are typically very helpful individually. But what if you had a few thousand? How would you summarize them?

For these reasons, businesses are turning to text analytics systems and technologies to automatically process and analyze text in all its forms and transform it to be utilized in identifying trends, early warning signs, product issues, suggestions for improvement, and cries for help from customers.

## Answering the "why"

Traditional business intelligence systems that analyze structured data are very good for statistically reporting the current state of customers and markets—sales are up or sales are down; customers are satisfied or customers are unsatisfied; this region seems to be performing better than that region, etc. Although these are important facts to understand, the key insights that are missing are why those things are happening now. Answering the "why" behind the data is typically not possible, even with investments in interpolation, modeling and statistical analysis on traditional structured data.

However, when you combine structured data with unstructured data, such as free-form replies to open-ended survey questions or comments on the Internet, you add another layer of depth that can give you a complete picture. For example, you can see what customers are saying about a poorly performing product, why customers in a specific region for a specific type of product and for a specific time period are unhappy and what were the key issues that drove low satisfaction. Text analytics can help understand these questions.

Well-designed surveys will typically ask for customers to rate products or services, then ask, "Why did you give us that rating?" or "Why were you dissatisfied with our service?" The answers to those questions provide powerful insights. However, until recently this has been difficult to analyze. Businesses have traditionally relied on verbatim coding systems where vendors or analysts manually review a random sample of a few hundred responses and then create codes to categorize them into common issues.

Although manually reviewing a sample of responses provides some level of accuracy, there are some inherent flaws in that process. First and foremost is that you are not looking at all of the data. If you have thousands or hundreds of thousands of responses, you are only able to cost-effectively analyze a small fraction of the available information. The second flaw is human bias. Whenever humans are making decisions about the data, there is always a tendency for people to respond and categorize based on the way they are feeling that day. Eye strain and fatigue also play a role in delivering inconsistent results. One day, an analyst might categorize a particular issue as a customer service problem, the next day or week they might think it is more of a product problem.

In addition, customers may have complex issues that are not easily categorized with traditional coding schemes. In this case, you may need multiple interdependent codes, but that can make it even more difficult for human analysts to be consistent. All of these challenges to analyzing free-form, open-ended comments in surveys are prevalent today. Text analytics delivers the capability to automatically process and analyze large volumes of free-form text with consistency and accuracy.

## Variety of methods

A variety of methods have been developed for performing text analytics. These include:

**Keyword or statistical analysis:** The most traditional method is keyword analysis, which uses a type of pattern recognition. A Google search is a good example of this.

**Natural language processing:** To overcome the inherent flaws of keyword searching and analysis, providers of text analytics have developed more sophisticated natural language processing (NLP)-based technologies. These systems have been around for some time but have had varying levels of success. Natural language processing requires training the computer to think like a human. In other words, training a computer to understand language the way humans understand language. This requires understanding basic grammar rules and word forms such as verbs, nouns, adjectives, prepositional phrases, etc. Once the system understands the basic structure of language, it can use that new information to derive the true meaning of words and phrases.

**Named entity recognition (NER):** NER is the process of identifying and extracting classes of entities—persons, places, and things such as companies, products, people, organizations, locations, dates, and so on, stored in free-form text. This technique requires that the analyst know in advance the specific entities to be extracted and then assign them to predetermined groups or classes. The resulting extractions can then be stored in a database and used to understand the frequency of mentions or broad topics discussed in the targeted source. This type of analysis is superior to keyword approaches since it is capable of using NLP to distinguish between nouns and verbs and only extract the appropriate mentions of the targeted terms.

**Targeted event extraction:** Event extraction is a technical term that defines a process of creating complex rules to locate and classify data based on targeted terms that are often referred to as triggers. After locating a trigger word, the rules define common attributes that occur in relation to that term. Using the suit example above, an analyst would create rules such as looking for the trigger term "sue" and then identify the plaintiff, defendant, jurisdiction and date for all lawsuits mentioned in the targeted documents.

**Exhaustive fact extraction:** This new method of text analytics patented by Attensity uses linguistic heuristics and patterns to discern the key facts and concepts contained in the source text. These patterns can then be universally applied to the entire corpus of text data, allowing the system to generate and exhaustive database of all available facts in one structured database. The analyst is then able to utilize traditional database queries to report on the most frequently occurring topics expressed in the text. The advantage to this approach is that the analyst is not forced to determine the problems, issues or topics to be analyzed prior to executing the fact extraction process. This means that emerging issues and new insights can be discovered in a timely and efficient manner.

Regardless of the technologies used to understand text, the analyst will need to consider many additional factors based on how the comments are generated and stored. Consider the different ways text is generated on a social media site. One is Twitter, where users are constrained to 140 characters, and hence use lots of acronyms, codes, hashtags, and cryptic language. Another is a customer product review, in which customers write a narrative description of their experience with a specific product. Still another is a customer survey with a directed question asking for a directed response.

These conditions present great challenges for text analytics. Although NLP technology will be required to provide accurate results, the best text analytics systems will utilize a variety of approaches adapted to the type and purpose of the source information.

## Actionable insights

One of the most common things that can be learned using text analytics is when a customer expresses some sort of positive or negative emotion in conjunction with a company or brand interaction. Considering all of the things that could be expressed by customers in a free-form comment, general sentiment is relatively easy to discern since the way that people describe being upset or unhappy is universal.

However, the most valuable insights gained from customer comments are those that are called actionable insights. Actionable insights actually point to a specific condition or state within a customer's experience that the company could have an immediate impact on, such as a specific product problem. Another example is an issue with an operational procedure or policy that causes some frustration in customers or perhaps a poor interaction with a customer service agent regarding a refund. Unlike expressions of general sentiment, these are specific types of insights that can point to specific actions a company can take to keep customers from leaving or to directly increase loyalty and satisfaction.

## Questions

1. Why has text analytics become almost a necessity today?
2. Please describe the different approaches to text analytics or processing?

# PRACTICING MARKETING RESEARCH

## How One Company Used Semantria Text Analytics to Improve Insights[6]

Schwan's Home Service, Inc., a business unit of the Schwan Food Company, markets and distributes approximately 400 frozen foods under the Schwan's® brand through home-delivery and mail order services. Featured product lines include the company's signature ice cream, pizza, choice meats, seafood, ethnic specialties, breakfast items, and desserts.

Schwan's sends out weekly national surveys to their customer base for feedback on products, service, quality of goods, and other criteria. However, with thousands of survey responses coming in per month, there isn't enough manpower to process them all in the old school way. Until recently, Schwan's had no efficient way to monitor the qualitative data coming in. This was a big shortcoming because the most valuable survey information was in the comments section. They did not have a way to get reliable, real-time insights into direct customer feedback. Initially, Schwan's team read each comment one by one, manually coded them, and tried to determine trending themes. Most of the information they extracted seemed to fall under broad categories, such as "this product is great!" or "I'm very pleased with the service." Nice compliments, but terrible in terms of actionable data. As such, the insights remained uncovered, and still they had no way of hearing the voice of the customer. To remedy this, Schwan's turned to Semantria's Excel Add-In for a solution. Currently, the Schwan's team exports their open-ended survey data from their survey systems, and then opens it in Microsoft Excel with the Semantria Add-In installed. With a few clicks, the Add-In processes Schwan's data, categorizes all of the comments according to a custom taxonomy (set of categories), singles out the main themes and ideas therein, and detects the sentiment signals around trending customer issues. Semantria turns its unstructured, open-ended responses into actionable data in a matter of seconds.

Schwan's originally used Semantria to analyze their content that had low scores, with the intention of extracting the most common customer complaints, tracking these complaints to their source, and then remedying the issue at the point of origin. With the assistance of Semantria's Data Analysis team, Schwan's built a set of categories customized for their needs in a matter of hours. Using this taxonomy, all of Schwan's open-ended responses are now quickly categorized and grouped. Furthermore, using Excel's basic VLOOKUP function in conjunction with Semantria's Queries, Schwan's is able to pull in sentiment scores, important keywords, and other text analytics data, group it by problem type, and associate it back to the original customer and delivery ID within minutes.

In less than a month of working with Semantria, the Schwan's team received insights and sentiment scores from customers regarding their products and service, giving them concrete data to act on, as opposed to bare scores. They are currently working on a communication plan with senior managers to pass information along through their warehouse locations, assisted by the results of Semantria queries around keywords such as "delivery." Nathan M. Schwan's Market Research Analyst, explains: "We have statistical software that pulls customer data every week for client demographics; location, delivery driver, and customer number. We utilize Semantria, in combination with survey results from our clients rating our products and services, to better understand what our customers think about our business. We take that knowledge, connect it to client verbatims, tie them back to customers, and find out where the problems exist."

Schwan's expects Semantria to allow it to improve on its customer service, and respond quicker to "general" customer concerns. The Schwan's team is also using the program to identify positive and problematic areas of other parts of the business. They expect their use of Semantria to drive productive growth.

## Questions

1. Why was Schwan not using results to open-ended questions?

2. How did Semantria help them deal with this limitation?

3. What are they getting out of open-ended questions now that they didn't get before? How hard is it?

# Step Three: Data Entry

**data entry**
Process of converting information to an electronic format.

Once the questionnaires have been validated, edited, and coded, it's time for the next step in the process—data entry. Of course, this step only applies to situations where data have been captured on paper surveys such as mail and self-administered surveys. We use the term **data entry** here to refer to the process of converting information to a form that can be read by a computer. This process requires a data entry device, such as a personal computer, and a storage medium, such as computer disk or hard drive.

## Intelligent Entry Systems

Most data entry is done by means of intelligent entry systems. With **intelligent data entry**, the information entered is checked for internal logic. Intelligent entry systems can be programmed to avoid certain types of errors at the point of data entry, such as invalid or wild codes and violation of skip patterns.

Consider question 2 on the questionnaire in Exhibit 15.1. The five valid answers have the associated numeric codes 1 through 5. An intelligent data entry system programmed for valid codes would permit the data entry operator to enter only one of these codes in the field reserved for the response to this question. If the operator attempts to enter a code other than those defined as valid, the device will inform the data entry operator in some manner that there is a problem. The data entry device, for example, might beep and display a message on the screen that the entered code is invalid. It will not advance to the next appropriate field until the code has been corrected. Of course, it is still possible to incorrectly enter a 3 rather than the correct answer 2. Referring again to question 2, note that if the answer to the question is "Very unlikely" or "Don't know," then the data entry operator should skip to question 16. An intelligent data entry device will make this skip automatically.

## The Data Entry Process

The validated, edited, and coded questionnaires have been given to a data entry operator seated in front of a personal computer. The data entry software system has been programmed for intelligent entry. The actual data entry process is ready to begin. Usually, the data are entered directly from the questionnaires, because experience has shown that a large number of errors are introduced when questionnaire data are transposed manually to coding sheets. Going directly from the questionnaire to the data entry device and associated storage medium is much more accurate and efficient. To better understand the mechanics of the process, look again at Exhibit 15.1.

- In the upper right-hand corner of the questionnaire, the number 001 is written. This number uniquely identifies the particular questionnaire, which should be the first questionnaire in the stack that the data entry operator is preparing to enter. This number is an important point of reference because it permits the data entry staff to refer back to the original document if any errors are identified in connection with the data input.

- To the left of the handwritten number 001 is (01–03). This tells the data entry operator that 001 should be entered into fields 01–03 of the data record. Throughout the questionnaire, the numbers in parentheses indicate the proper location on the data record for the circled code for the answer to each question. Question 1 has (04) associated with the codes for the answers to the question. Thus, the answer to this question would be entered in field 04 of the data record. Now, take a look at the open-ended question in Exhibit 15.5. As with closed-ended questions, the number in parentheses refers to the field on the data record where the code or codes for the response to this question should be entered. Note the number 2 written in to the right of (48); a 2 should be entered in field 48 of the data record associated with this questionnaire.

Exhibit 15.1 clearly illustrates the relationship between the layout of the questionnaire, in terms of codes (numbers associated with different answers to questions) and fields (places on the data record where the code is entered) and the layout of the data record.

**intelligent data entry**
Form of data entry in which the information being entered into the data entry device is checked for internal logic.

## Scanning

As all students know, the scanning of documents (test scoring sheets) has been around for decades. It has been widely used in schools and universities as an efficient way to capture and score responses to multiple-choice questions. However, until more recently, its use in marketing research has been limited. This limited use can be attributed to two factors: setup costs and the need to record all responses with a No. 2 pencil. Setup costs include the cost of special paper, special ink in the printing process, and very precise placement of the bubbles for recording responses. The break-even point, at which the savings in data entry costs exceeded the setup costs for scanning is in the 5,000 to 10,000 survey range. Therefore, for most surveys, scanning was not feasible.

However, changes in **scanning technology** and the advent of personal computers have changed this equation. Today, questionnaires prepared with any one of a number of Windows word-processing software packages and printed on a laser printer or by a standard printing process can be readily scanned, using the appropriate software and a scanner attached to a personal computer or network. In addition, the latest technology permits respondents to fill out the survey using almost any type of writing implement (any type of pencil, ballpoint pen, or ink pen). This eliminates the need to provide respondents with a No. 2 pencil and greatly simplifies the process of mailing surveys. Finally, the latest technology does not require respondents to carefully shade the entire circle or square next to their response choices; they can put shading, a check mark, an X, or any other type of mark in the circle or square provided for the response choice.[7]

As a result of these developments, the use of scannable surveys is growing dramatically. An analyst who expects more than 400 to 500 surveys to be completed will find scannable surveys to be cost-effective.

Though no reliable volume figures are available, it is an accepted fact that the amount of survey data being captured electronically is increasing. For example, electronic data capture is used in computer-assisted telephone interviewing, Internet surveys, and TouchScreen kiosk surveys.

**scanning technology**
Form of data entry in which responses on questionnaires are read in automatically by the data entry device.

# Step Four: Logical Cleaning of Data

At this point, the data from all questionnaires have been entered and stored on a network or individual computer hard drive. It is time to do final error checking before proceeding to the tabulation and statistical analysis of the survey results. Many colleges have one or more statistical software packages available for the tabulation and statistical analysis of data, including SAS (Statistical Analysis System) and SPSS (Statistical Package for the Social Sciences), which have proven to be the most popular statistical packages. Most colleges have personal computer versions of SPSS and SAS, in addition to other computer statistical packages. The number of packages for desktops and other personal devices is large and growing.

Regardless of which computer package is used, it is important to do a final computerized error check of the data, or what is sometimes referred to as **logical or machine cleaning of data.** This may be done through error checking routines and/or one-way frequency tabulations.

Some computer packages permit the user to write **error-checking routines.** These routines include a number of statements to check for various conditions. For example, if a particular field on the data records for a study should be coded with only a 1 or a 2, a logical statement can be written to check for the presence of any other code in that field. Some of the more sophisticated packages generate reports indicating how many times a particular condition was violated and the data records on which it was violated. With this list, the user can refer to the original questionnaires and determine the appropriate values.

The purpose of this step is to make sure that the data are logically consistent. If they are not, then some of the resulting tabular analyses will not add up. In most cases, the

**logical or machine cleaning of data**
Final computerized error check of data.

**error-checking routines**
Computer programs that accept instructions from the user to check for logical errors in the data.

discrepancies will be small, but any discrepancies make clients uneasy and may lead them to question the integrity of the entire survey.

# Step Five: Tabulation and Statistical Analysis

The survey results are now on a hard drive and free of logical, data entry and interviewer recording errors. The next step is to tabulate the survey results.

## One-Way Frequency Tables

The most basic tabulation is the **one-way frequency table**, which shows the number of respondents who gave each possible answer to each question. An example of this type of table appears in Exhibit 15.7. This table shows that 144 consumers (48 percent) said they would choose a hospital in Saint Paul, 146 (48.7 percent) said they would choose a hospital in Minneapolis, and 10 (3.3 percent) said they didn't know which location they would choose. A printout is generated with a one-way frequency table for every question on the survey. In most instances, a one-way frequency table is the first summary of survey results seen by the research analyst. In addition to frequencies, these tables typically indicate the percentage of those responding who gave each possible response to a question.

**one-way frequency table**
Table showing the number of respondents choosing each answer to a survey question.

An issue that must be dealt with when one-way frequency tables are generated is what base to use for the percentages for each table. There are three options for a base:

1. **Total respondents.** If 300 people are interviewed in a particular study and the decision is to use total respondents as the base for calculating percentages, then the percentages in each one-way frequency table will be based on 300 respondents.

2. **Number of people asked the particular question.** Because most questionnaires have skip patterns, not all respondents are asked all questions. For example, suppose question 4 on a particular survey asked whether the person owned any dogs and 200 respondents indicated they were dog owners. Since questions 5 and 6 on the same survey were to be asked only of those individuals who owned a dog, questions 5 and 6 should have been asked of only 200 respondents. In most instances, it would be appropriate to use 200 as the base for percentages associated with the one-way frequency tables for questions 5 and 6.

3. **Number of people answering the question.** Another alternative base for computing percentages in one-way frequency tables is the number of people who actually answered a particular question. Under this approach, if 300 people were asked a particular question but 28 indicated "Don't know" or gave no response, then the base for the percentages would be 272.

| EXHIBIT 15.7 | One-Way Frequency Table |
|---|---|
| **Q.30 If you or a member of your family were to require hospitalization in the future, and the procedure could be performed in Minneapolis or Saint Paul, where would you choose to go?** | |

| | Total |
|---|---|
| Total | 300 |
| | 100% |
| To a hospital in Saint Paul | 144 |
| | 48.0% |
| To a hospital in Minneapolis | 146 |
| | 48.7% |
| Don't know/no response | 10 |
| | 3.3% |

Ordinarily, the number of people who were asked a particular question is used as the base for all percentages throughout the tabulations, but there may be special cases in which other bases are judged appropriate. Exhibit 15.8 is a one-way frequency table in which three different bases are used for calculating percentages.

Some questions, by their nature, solicit more than one response from respondents. For example, consumers might be asked to name all brands of vacuum cleaners that come to mind. Most people will be able to name more than one brand. Therefore, when these answers are tabulated, there will be more responses than respondents. If 200 consumers are surveyed and the average consumer names three brands, then there will be 200 respondents and 600 answers. The question is, should percentages in frequency tables showing the results for these questions

| **EXHIBIT 15.8** | **One-Way Frequency Table Using Three Different Bases for Calculating Percentages** | | |
|---|---|---|---|
| **Q.35 Why would you not consider going to Saint Paul for hospitalization?** | | | |
| | **Total\* Respondents** | **Total Asked** | **Total Answering** |
| Total | 300 | 64 | 56 |
| | 100% | 100 % | 100% |
| They aren't good/service poor | | | |
| | 18 | 18 | 18 |
| Saint Paul doesn't have the services/equipment that Minneapolis does | 6% | 28 % | 32% |
| | 17 | 17 | 17 |
| Saint Paul is too small | 6% | 27 % | 30% |
| | 6 | 6 | 6 |
| Bad publicity | 2% | 9 % | 11% |
| | 4 | 4 | 4 |
| Other | 1% | 6 % | 7% |
| | 11 | 11 | 11 |
| Don't know/no response | 4% | 17 % | 20% |
| | 8 | 8 | |
| | 3% | 13 % | |

\*A total of 300 respondents were surveyed. Only 64 were asked this question because in the previous question those respondents said they would not consider going to Saint Paul for hospitalization. Only 56 respondents gave an answer other than "Don't know."

The base for each percentage must be determined before one-way frequency tables are run. If a survey question asks whether the person has a dog and 200 respondents indicate that they do, further questions designated for dog owners should have only 200 respondents.

© Kai Chiang/iStockphoto

be based on the number of respondents or the number of responses? Exhibit 15.9 shows percentages calculated using both bases. Most commonly, marketing researchers compute percentages for multiple-response questions on the basis of the number of respondents, reasoning that the client is primarily interested in the proportion of people who gave a particular answer.

## Cross Tabulations

**Cross tabulations** are likely to be the next step in analysis. They represent a simple-to-understand, yet powerful, analytical tool. Many marketing research studies go no further than cross tabulations in terms of analysis. The idea is to look at the responses to one question in relation to the responses to one or more other questions. Exhibit 15.10 shows a simple cross tabulation that examines the relationship between cities consumers are willing to consider for hospitalization and the age of the consumers. This cross tabulation includes frequencies and percentages, with the percentages based on column totals. This table shows an interesting relationship between age and likelihood of choosing Minneapolis or Saint Paul for hospitalization. Consumers in successively older age groups are increasingly likely

**cross tabulation**
Examination of the responses to one question relative to the responses to one or more other questions.

| EXHIBIT 15.9 | Percentages for a Multiple-Response Question Calculated on the Bases of Total Respondents and Total Responses |
|---|---|

**Q.34 To which of the following towns and cities would you consider going for hospitalization?**

| | Total Respondents | Total Responses |
|---|---|---|
| Total | 300 | 818 |
| | 100% | 100% |
| Minneapolis | 265 | 265 |
| | 88.3% | 32.4% |
| Saint Paul | 240 | 240 |
| | 80.0% | 29.3% |
| Bloomington | 112 | 112 |
| | 37.3% | 13.7% |
| Rochester | 92 | 92 |
| | 30.7% | 11.2% |
| Minnetonka | 63 | 63 |
| | 21.0% | 7.7% |
| Eagan | 46 | 46 |
| | 15.3% | 5.6% |

| EXHIBIT 15.10 | Sample Cross Tabulation |
|---|---|

**Q.30 If you or a member of your family were to require hospitalization in the future, and the procedure could be performed in Minneapolis or Saint Paul, where would you choose to go?**

| | | | Age | | |
|---|---|---|---|---|---|
| | Total | 18–34 | 35–54 | 55–64 | 65 or Over |
| Total | 300 | 65 | 83 | 51 | 100 |
| | 100% | 100% | 100% | 100% | 100% |
| To a hospital in Saint Paul | 144 | 21 | 40 | 25 | 57 |
| | 48.0 | 32.3% | 48.2% | 49.0% | 57.0% |
| To a hospital in Minneapolis | 146 | 43 | 40 | 23 | 40 |
| | 48.7% | 66.2% | 48.2% | 45.1% | 40.0% |
| Don't know/no response | 10 | 1 | 3 | 3 | 3 |
| | 3.3% | 1.5% | 3.6% | 5.9% | 3.0% |

| EXHIBIT 15.11 | Cross-tabulation Table with Column, Row, and Total Percentages* | | |
|---|---|---|---|
| **Q.34 To which of the following towns and cities would you consider going for hospitalization?** | | | |
| | **Total** | **Male** | **Female** |
| Total | 300 | 67 | 233 |
| | 100.0% | 100.0% | 100.0% |
| | 100.0% | 22.3% | 77.7% |
| | 100.0% | 22.3% | 77.7% |
| Saint Paul | 265 | 63 | 202 |
| | 88.3% | 94.0% | 86.7% |
| | 100.0% | 23.6% | 76.2% |
| | 88.3% | 21.0% | 67.3% |
| Minneapolis | 240 | 53 | 187 |
| | 80.0% | 79.1% | 80.3% |
| | 100.0% | 22.1% | 77.9% |
| | 80.0% | 17.7% | 62.3% |
| Bloomington | 112 | 22 | 90 |
| | 37.3% | 32.8% | 38.6% |
| | 100.0% | 19.6% | 80.4% |
| | 37.3% | 7.3% | 30.0% |

*Percentages listed are column, row, and total percentages, respectively.

to choose Saint Paul and increasingly less likely to choose Minneapolis. Following are a number of considerations regarding the setup of cross-tabulation tables and the determination of percentages within them:

- The previous discussion regarding the selection of the appropriate base for percentages applies to cross-tabulation tables as well.

- Three different percentages may be calculated for each cell in a cross-tabulation table: column, row, and total percentages. Column percentages are based on the column total, row percentages are based on the row total, and total percentages are based on the table total. Exhibit 15.11 shows a cross-tabulation table in which the frequency and all three of the percentages are shown for each cell in the table.

- A common way of setting up cross-tabulation tables is to use columns to represent factors such as demographics and lifestyle characteristics, which are expected to be predictors of the state of mind, behavior, or intentions data, shown as rows of the table. In such tables, percentages usually are calculated on the basis of column totals. This approach permits easy comparisons of the relationship between, say, lifestyle characteristics and expected predictors such as sex or age. For example, in Exhibit 15.10, this approach facilitates examination of how people in different age groups differ in regard to the particular factor under examination. Exhibit 15.12 shows a cross-tabulation with the results to multiple questions shown as columns.

### Death of Crosstabs?

There are some indications that the historical high interest in cross tabulations on the part of marketing researchers and their clients is beginning to wane. Some of the issues around this change are discussed in greater detail in Chapter 19. However, the new generation of managers is much less interested in sorting through reams of printed output to find gems than were their predecessors. Increasingly, they are simply looking for "the answer." As a result, we may see more reliance on tools such as the Q software, discussed in the Practicing Marketing Research feature on page 379. These tools can be used to extract those survey results that are directly responsive to the research objectives.

# PRACTICING MARKETING RESEARCH

## Q Data Analysis Software a Very Functional Choice[8]

The Australian software design firm Numbers International recently released a new data analysis program called Q. Q offers researchers a wide range of advanced statistical testing and modeling tools, packaged in a way that allows even those not specializing in statistical analysis to get meaningful results when studying survey data of almost any question format.

Although some of its features may require some familiarization to fully grasp, Q is supported by numerous tools to help researchers get started. A 60-page quick-start guide provides an overview of tables, functions, and modeling tools, and an instant-start guide summarizes them into a one-page reference sheet. The software also comes with help functions, tutorials, and online training tools.

Unlike many analytical software packages, Q provides researchers with easy and direct access to the basic data, and it keeps them engaged with the data throughout the analytical process. Erik Heller, general manager of the Sydney office for market research firm Sweeney Research, has adopted Q with great success. He comments, "Where Q differentiates itself from other tools like SPSS is the extent to which it is intuitive and easy for people to immerse themselves in the data."

Most analytical functions are accessible through drop-down menus and toolbars and allow users to manipulate the data from the main view. Q's tools also allow for significant analytical depth. For those who just need basic reports of the data, Q offers straight crosstabs but also provides advance multivariate analysis to help identify deeper, more complex trends. When venturing into these more involved multivariate methods, however, Q always starts the researcher at the same level of the basic data and builds the analytical process up from there. The research stays grounded in progressively verifiable results. As the researcher proceeds, Q helps organize tables and data sets and can package them for delivery once the analysis is done. As Heller adds, "It is very easy for someone who is not that involved in the data analysis to go into the data and run some additional crosstabs." Q offers free Reader software, which allows recipients to easily view and access these reports even if its analytical functions are limited.

One slight weakness in the software is its limited range of output functions. With no support for Excel or Power-Point and limited chart and graph options, the final reports that Q is able to produce may be less dynamic than those of some other data analysis programs. The current version of Q is also not the ideal choice for time-series analysis and multiwave research projects. Ultimately, its biggest weaknesses may be attributed to merely an overemphasis of function over style.

## Questions

1. How is using the Q software different from using the traditional crosstab approach?
2. Do you think using Q would increase the amount of thinking required of the analyst? Explain your answer.

# Graphic Representations of Data

You have heard the saying, "One picture is worth a thousand words." Graphic representations of data use pictures rather than tables to present research results. Results—particularly key results—can be presented most powerfully and efficiently through graphs.

Marketing researchers have always known that important findings identified by cross tabulation and statistical analysis could be best presented graphically. However, in the early years of marketing research, the preparation of graphs was tedious, difficult, and time-consuming. The advent of personal computers, coupled with graphics software and laser printers, has changed all of this. Spreadsheet programs such as Excel have extensive graphics capabilities. In addition, programs designed for creating presentations, such as PowerPoint, permit the user to generate a wide variety of high-quality graphics with ease. With these programs, it is possible to do the following:

- Quickly produce graphs.
- Display those graphs on the computer screen.

■ Make desired changes and redisplay.

■ Print final copies on a laser or inkjet printer.

All of the graphs shown in the next several pages were produced using a personal computer, a laser printer, and a graphics software package.

## Line Charts

Line charts are one of the simplest forms of graphs. They are particularly useful for presenting measurements over time. The results reveal similar sales patterns for 2001 and 2002, with peaks in June and generally low sales in January through March and September through December. Just Add Water is evaluating the sales data to identify product lines that it might add to improve sales during those periods.

| EXHIBIT 15.12 | A Stub and Banner Table |
|---|---|

**North Community College—Anywhere, U.S.A. Q.1c. Are you single, married, or formerly married?**

| | | Zones | | | Gender | | Age | | |
|---|---|---|---|---|---|---|---|---|---|
| | Total | 1 | 2 | 3 | M | F | 18–34 | 35–54 | 55 and over |
| Total | 300 | 142 | 103 | 55 | 169 | 131 | 48 | 122 | 130 |
| | 100% | 100% | 100% | 100% | 100% | 100% | 100% | 100% | 100% |
| Married | 228 | 105 | 87 | 36 | 131 | 97 | 36 | 97 | 95 |
| | 76% | 74% | 84% | 65% | 78% | 74% | 75% | 80% | 73% |
| Single | 5 | 1 | 2 | 2 | 4 | 1 | 2 | 1 | 2 |
| | 2% | 1% | 2% | 4% | 2% | 1% | 4% | 1% | 2% |
| Formerly | 24 | 11 | 10 | 3 | 12 | 12 | 3 | 9 | 12 |
| married | 8% | 8% | 10% | 5% | 7% | 9% | 6% | 7% | 9% |
| Refused | 43 | 25 | 4 | 14 | 22 | 21 | 7 | 15 | 21 |
| to answer | 14% | 18% | 4% | 25% | 13% | 16% | 15% | 12% | 16% |

| EXHIBIT 15.13 | |
|---|---|

| Race | | | Family Profile | | Vote History | | Registered Voter | |
|---|---|---|---|---|---|---|---|---|
| | | | Child | Child | 2–3 | 4 Times or | | |
| White | Black | Other | < 18 Years | > 18 Years | Times | More | Yes | No |
| 268 | 28 | 4 | 101 | 53 | 104 | 196 | 72 | 228 |
| 100% | 100% | 100% | 100% | 100% | 100% | 100% | 100% | 100% |
| 207 | 18 | 3 | 82 | 39 | 80 | 148 | 58 | 170 |
| 77% | 64% | 75% | 81% | 74% | 77% | 76% | 81% | 75% |
| 5 | — | — | — | — | 2 | 3 | 1 | 4 |
| 2% | — | — | — | — | 2% | 2% | 1% | 2% |
| 18 | 6 | — | 5 | 6 | 10 | 14 | 3 | 21 |
| 7% | 21% | — | 5% | 11% | 10% | 7% | 4% | 9% |
| 38 | 4 | 1 | 14 | 8 | 12 | 31 | 10 | 33 |
| 14% | 14% | 25% | 14% | 15% | 12% | 16% | 14% | 14% |

## Pie Charts

Pie charts are another type of graph that is frequently used. They are appropriate for displaying marketing research results in a wide range of situations. Exhibit 15.14 shows radio music preferences gleaned from a survey of residents of several Gulf Coast metropolitan areas in Louisiana, Mississippi, and Alabama. Note the three-dimensional effect produced by the software for this example.

## Bar Charts

Bar charts may be the most flexible of the three types of graphs discussed in this section. Anything that can be shown in a line graph or a pie chart can also be shown in a bar chart. In addition, many things that cannot be shown—or effectively shown—in other types of graphs can be readily illustrated in bar charts. Four types of bar charts are discussed here.

1. **Plain bar chart.** As the name suggests, plain bar charts are the simplest form of bar chart. The same information displayed in the pie chart in Exhibit 15.14 is shown in the bar chart in Exhibit 15.15. Draw your own conclusions regarding whether the pie chart or the bar chart is the more effective way to present this information. Exhibit 15.15 is a traditional two-dimensional chart. Most of the software packages available today can take the same information and present it with a three-dimensional effect, as shown

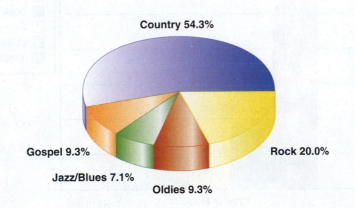

**Exhibit 15.14**

**Three-Dimensional Pie Chart for Types of Music Listened to Most Often**

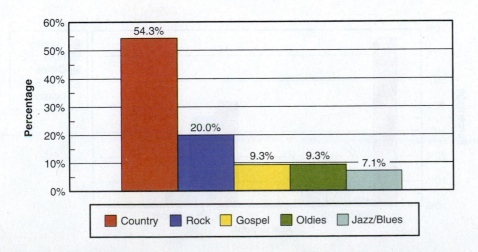

**Exhibit 15.15**

**Simple Two Dimensional Bar Chart for Types of Music Listened to Most Often**

in Exhibit 15.16. Again, decide for yourself which approach is visually more appealing and interesting.

2. **Clustered bar chart.** The clustered bar chart is one of three types of bar charts useful for showing the results of cross tabulations. The radio music preference results are cross tabulated by age in Exhibit 15.17. The graph shows that country music is mentioned most often as the preferred format by those over 35 and those 35 or under. The graph also shows that rock music is a close second for those 35 or under and is least frequently mentioned by those over 35. The results suggest that if the target audience is those in the 35 or under age group, then a mix of country and rock music is appropriate. A focus on country music probably would be the most efficient approach for those over 35.

3. **Stacked bar chart.** Like clustered bar charts, stacked bar charts are helpful in graphically representing cross-tabulation results. The same music preference data shown in Exhibit 15.16 are presented as a stacked bar chart in Exhibit 15.18.

4. **Multiple-row, three-dimensional bar chart.** This type of bar chart provides what we believe to be the most visually appealing way of presenting cross-tabulation information. The same music preference data displayed in Exhibits 15.17 and 15.18 are presented in a multiple-row, three-dimensional bar chart in Exhibit 15.19.

**Exhibit 15.16**

**Simple Three-Dimensional Bar Chart for Types of Music Listened to Most Often**

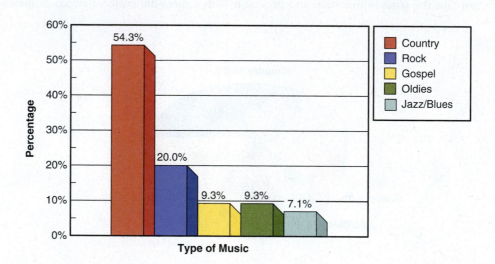

**Exhibit 15.17**

**70% Clustered Bar Chart for Types of Music Listened to Most Often by Age**

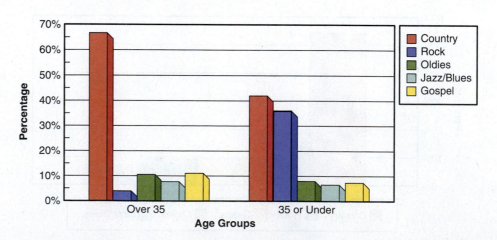

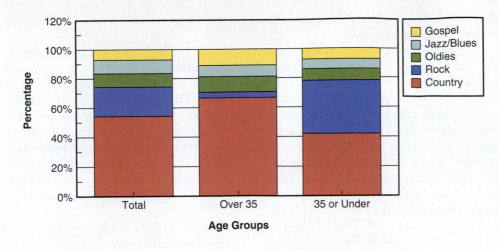

**Exhibit 15.18**

**Stacked Bar Chart for Types of Music Listened to Most Often by Age**

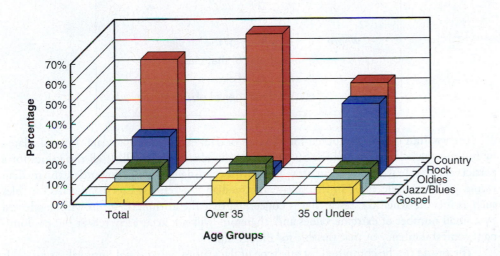

**Exhibit 15.19**

**Multiple-Row, Three- Dimensional Bar Chart for Types of Music Listened to *Most* Often by Age**

PowerPoint and other presentation packages offer an array of other specialized graph types, and you are encouraged to explore those options. The key is to use the right type of graph to clearly and effectively display key findings.

# Descriptive Statistics

Descriptive statistics are an efficient means of summarizing the basic characteristics of large sets of data. In a statistical analysis, the analyst calculates one number or a few numbers that reveal something about the characteristics of large sets of data.

## Measures of Central Tendency

Before beginning this section, you should review the types of data scales presented in Chapter 10. Recall that there are four basic types of measurement scales: nominal, ordinal, interval, and ratio. Nominal and ordinal scales are sometimes referred to as nonmetric scales, whereas interval and ratio scales are called metric scales. Many of the statistical procedures discussed in this section and in following sections require metric scales, whereas others are designed for nonmetric scales.

The three measures of central tendency are the arithmetic mean, median, and mode. The **mean** is properly computed only from interval or ratio (metric) data. It is computed by adding the values for all observations for a particular variable, such as age, and dividing the resulting sum by the number of observations. With survey data, the exact value of the variable may not be known; it may be known only that a particular case falls in a particular category. For example, an age category on a survey might be 18 to 34 years of age. If a person falls into this category, the person's exact age is known to be somewhere between 18 and 34. With grouped data, the midpoint of each category is multiplied by the number of observations in that category, the resulting totals are summed, and the total is then divided by the total number of observations. This process is summarized in the following formula:

**mean**
Sum of the values for all observations of a variable divided by the number of observations.

$$\overline{X} = \frac{\sum_{i=1}^{h} f_i X_i}{n}$$

where  $f_i$ = frequency of the $i$th class
$X_i$ = midpoint of that class
$h$ = number of classes
$n$ = total number of observations

The **median** can be computed for all types of data except nominal data. It is calculated by finding the value below which 50 percent of the observations fall. If all the values for a particular variable were put in an array in either ascending or descending order, the median would be the middle value in that array. The median is often used to summarize variables such as income when the researcher is concerned that the arithmetic mean will be affected by a small number of extreme values and, therefore, will not accurately reflect the predominant central tendency of that variable for that group.

**median**
Value below which 50 percent of the observations fall.

The **mode** can be computed for any type of data (nominal, ordinal, interval, or ratio). It is determined by finding the value that occurs most frequently. In a frequency distribution, the mode is the value that has the highest frequency. One problem with using the mode is that a particular data set may have more than one mode. If three different values occur with the same level of frequency and that frequency is higher than the frequency for any other value, then the data set has three modes. The mean, median, and mode for sample data on beer consumption are shown in Exhibit 15.20.

**mode**
Value that occurs most frequently.

## Measures of Dispersion

Frequently used measures of dispersion include standard deviation, variance, and range. Whereas measures of central tendency indicate typical values for a particular variable, measures of dispersion indicate how spread out the data are. The dangers associated with relying only on measures of central tendency are suggested by the example shown in Exhibit 15.21. Note that average beer consumption is the same in both markets—three cans/bottles/glasses. However, the standard deviation is greater in market two, indicating more dispersion in the data. Whereas the mean suggests that the two markets are the same, the added information provided by the standard deviation indicates that they are different.

The formula for computing the standard deviation for a sample of observations is as follows:

**EXHIBIT 15.20**  Mean, Median, and Mode for Beer Consumption Data

A total of 10 beer drinkers (drink one or more cans, bottles, or glasses of beer per day on the average) were interviewed in a mall-intercept study. They were asked how many cans, bottles, or glasses of beer they drink in an average day.

| Respondent | Number of Cans/ Bottles/Glasses Per Respondent Day |
|---|---|
| 1 | 2 |
| 2 | 2 |
| 3 | 3 |
| 4 | 2 |
| 5 | 5 |
| 6 | 1 |
| 7 | 2 |
| 8 | 2 |
| 9 | 10 |
| 10 | 1 |

Mode = 2 cans/bottles/glasses

Median = 2 cans/bottles/glasses

Mean = 3 cans/bottles/glasses

**EXHIBIT 15.21**  Measures of Dispersion and Measures of Central Tendency

Consider the beer consumption data presented below for two markets.

| Respondent | Number of Cans/ Bottles/Glasses Market One | Number of Cans/ Bottles/Glasses Market Two |
|---|---|---|
| 1 | 2 | 1 |
| 2 | 2 | 1 |
| 3 | 3 | 1 |
| 4 | 2 | 1 |
| 5 | 5 | 1 |
| 6 | 1 | 1 |
| 7 | 2 | 1 |
| 8 | 2 | 3 |
| 9 | 10 | 10 |
| 10 | 1 | 10 |
| Mean | 3 | 3 |
| Standard deviation | 2.7 | 3.7 |

Though mean consumption is the same in both markets the standard deviation shows there is much more dispersion in consumption in Market Two.

Occupation is an example of a categorical variable. The only results that can be reported for a variable of this type are the frequency and the relative percentage with which each category was encountered.

$$S = \sqrt{\frac{\sum\limits_{i=1}^{n}(X_i - \overline{X})^2}{n-1}}$$

where  $S$ = sample standard deviation

$X_i$ = value of the *i*th observation

$\overline{X}$ = sample mean

$n$ = sample size

The variance is calculated by using the formula for standard deviation with the square root sign removed. That is, the sum of the squared deviations from the mean is divided by the number of observations minus 1. Finally, the range is equal to the maximum value for a particular variable minus the minimum value for that variable.

## Percentages and Statistical Tests

© tom carter/Alamy

When performing basic data analysis, the research analyst is faced with the decision of whether to use measures of central tendency (mean, median, mode) or percentages (one-way frequency tables, cross tabulations). Responses to questions either are categorical or take the form of continuous variables. Categorical variables such as "Occupation" (coded 1 for professional/managerial, 2 for clerical, etc.) limit the analyst to reporting the frequency and relative percentage with which each category was encountered. Variables such as age can be continuous or categorical, depending on how the information was obtained. For example, an interviewer can ask people their actual age or ask them which category (under 35, 35 or older, etc.) includes their age. If actual ages are available, mean age can be readily computed. If categories are used, one-way frequency tables and cross tabulations are the most obvious choices for analysis. However, continuous data can be put into categories, and means can be estimated for categorical data by using the formula for computing a mean for grouped data (presented earlier).

Finally, statistical tests are available that can indicate whether two means—for example, average expenditures by men and average expenditures by women at fast-food restaurants—or two percentages differ to a greater extent than would be expected by chance (sampling error) or whether there is a significant relationship between two variables in a cross-tabulation table. These tests are discussed in Chapter 16.

## SUMMARY

Once the questionnaires have been returned from the field, a five-step process takes place. These steps are (1) validation and editing, which are quality control checks, (2) coding, (3) data entry, (4) logical cleaning of data, and (5) tabulation and statistical analysis. The first step in the process, making sure that the data have integrity, is critical. Otherwise, the age-old adage is true: "Garbage in, garbage out." Validation involves determining with as much certainty as possible that each questionnaire is, in fact, a valid interview. A valid interview in this sense is one that was conducted in an appropriate manner. The objective of validation is to detect interviewer fraud or failure to follow key instructions. Validation is accomplished by recontacting a certain percentage of the respondents surveyed by each interviewer. Any surveys found to be fraudulent are eliminated from the database. After the validation process is completed, editing begins. Editing involves checking for interviewer and respondent mistakes—making certain that all required questions were answered, that skip patterns were followed properly, and that responses to open-ended questions were accurately recorded. The process of "validating" online surveys is quite different.

Upon completion of the editing, the next step is to code the data. Most questions on surveys are closed-ended and pre-coded, which means that numeric codes already have been assigned to the various responses on the questionnaire. With open-ended questions, the researcher has no idea in advance what the responses will be. Therefore, the coder must establish numeric codes for response categories by listing actual responses to open-ended questions and then consolidating those responses and assigning numeric codes to the consolidated categories. Once a coding sheet has been created, all questionnaires are coded using the coding sheet categories.

The next step is data entry. Today, most data entry is done by means of intelligent entry systems that check the internal logic of the data. The data typically are entered directly from the questionnaires. New developments in scanning technology have made a more automated approach to data entry cost-effective for smaller projects. Of course, data entry is not required for online surveys.

Machine cleaning of data is a final, computerized error check of the data, performed through the use of error checking routines and/or marginal reports. Error checking routines indicate whether or not certain conditions have been met. A marginal report is a type of frequency table that helps the user determine whether inappropriate codes were entered and whether skip patterns were properly followed.

The final step in the traditional data analysis process is tabulation of the data. The most basic tabulation involves a one-way frequency table, which indicates the number of respondents who gave each possible answer to each question. Generating one-way frequency tables requires the analyst to determine a basis for percentages. For example, are the percentages to be calculated based on total respondents, number of people asked a particular question, or number answering a particular question? Tabulation of data is often followed by cross tabulation—examination of the responses to one question in relation to the responses to one or more other questions. Cross tabulation is a powerful and easily understood approach to the analysis of survey research results. New ways to track what we need from the data are supplanting the traditional crosstabs.

Statistical measures provide an even more powerful way to analyze data sets. The most commonly used statistical measures are those of central tendency: the arithmetic mean, median, and mode. The arithmetic mean is computed only from interval or ratio data by adding the values for all observations of a particular variable and dividing the resulting sum by the number of observations. The median can be computed for all types of data except nominal data by finding the value below which 50 percent of the observations fall. The mode can be computed for any type of data by simply finding the value that occurs most frequently. The arithmetic mean is, by far, the most commonly used measure of central tendency.

In addition to central tendency, researchers often want to have an indication of the dispersion of the data. Measures of dispersion include standard deviation, variance, and range.

## KEY TERMS

validation 359

editing 362

skip pattern 365

coding 366

data entry 372

intelligent data entry 373

scanning technology 374

logical or machine cleaning of data 374

error-checking routines 374

one-way frequency table 375

cross tabulation 377

mean 384

median 384

mode 384

## QUESTIONS FOR REVIEW & CRITICAL THINKING

1. What is the difference between measurement validity and interview validation?

2. Assume that Sally Smith, an interviewer, completed 50 questionnaires. Ten of the questionnaires were validated by calling the respondents and asking them one opinion question and two demographic questions over again. One respondent claimed that his age category was 30–40, when the age category marked on the questionnaire was 20–30. On another questionnaire, in response to the question, "What is the most important problem facing our city government?" the interviewer had written, "The city council is too eager to raise taxes." When the interview was validated, the respondent

said, "The city tax rate is too high." As a validator, would you assume that these were honest mistakes and accept the entire lot of 50 interviews as valid? If not, what would you do?

3. What is meant by the editing process? Should editors be allowed to fill in what they think a respondent meant in response to open-ended questions if the information seems incomplete? Why or why not?

4. Give an example of a skip pattern on a questionnaire. Why is it important to always follow the skip patterns correctly?

5. It has been said that, to some degree, coding of open-ended questions is an art. Would you agree or disagree? Why? Suppose that, after coding a large number of questionnaires, the researcher notices that many responses have ended up in the "Other" category. What might this imply? What could be done to correct this problem?

6. Describe an intelligent data entry system. Why are data typically entered directly from the questionnaire into the data entry device?

7. What is the purpose of machine cleaning data? Give some examples of how data can be machine cleaned. Do you think that machine cleaning is an expensive and unnecessary step in the data tabulation process? Why or why not?

8. It has been said that a cross tabulation of two variables offers the researcher more insightful information than does a one-way frequency table. Why might this be true? Give an example.

9. Illustrate the various alternatives for using percentages in one-way frequency tables. Explain the logic of choosing one alternative method over another.

10. Explain the differences among the mean, median, and mode. Give an example in which the researcher might be interested in each of these measures of central tendency.

11. Calculate the mean, median, mode, and standard deviation for the following data set:

| Respondent | Times Visited Whitehall Mall in Past 6 Months | Times Visited Northpark Mall | Times Visited Sampson Mall in Past 6 Months |
|---|---|---|---|
| A | 4 | 7 | 2 |
| B | 5 | 11 | 16 |
| C | 13 | 21 | 3 |
| D | 6 | 0 | 1 |
| E | 9 | 18 | 14 |
| F | 3 | 6 | 8 |
| G | 2 | 0 | 1 |
| H | 21 | 3 | 7 |
| I | 4 | 11 | 9 |
| J | 14 | 13 | 5 |
| K | 7 | 7 | 12 |
| L | 8 | 3 | 25 |
| M | 8 | 3 | 9 |

12. Enter the following data into an Excel spreadsheet. Include the column headings (Q1, Q2, and Q3), as well as the numeric values. The definitions of the numeric values are provided at the bottom of the table. Use the Pivot Table feature in Excel (found under the Data option) to cross tabulate the likelihood of purchase (row) by gender (column) and income level (column). What conclusions can you draw about the relationship between gender and likelihood of purchase and that between income and likelihood of purchase?

| Respondent | Likelihood of Purchase | Gender | Income |
|---|---|---|---|
| A | 5 | 2 | 3 |
| B | 4 | 2 | 3 |
| C | 4 | 2 | 2 |

| Respondent | Likelihood of Purchase | Gender | Income |
|---|---|---|---|
| D | 3 | 1 | 2 |
| E | 1 | 1 | 2 |
| F | 5 | 2 | 3 |
| G | 5 | 2 | 3 |
| H | 4 | 2 | 3 |
| I | 1 | 1 | 2 |
| J | 1 | 1 | 2 |
| K | 2 | 1 | 1 |
| L | 5 | 2 | 3 |
| M | 5 | 2 | 3 |
| N | 4 | 1 | 3 |
| O | 3 | 1 | 2 |
| P | 3 | 1 | 2 |
| Q | 4 | 2 | 3 |
| R | 5 | 2 | 3 |
| S | 2 | 1 | 1 |
| T | 2 | 1 | 1 |

Likelihood of purchase: very likely 5 5, likely 5 4, undecided 5 3, unlikely 5 2, very unlikely 5 1 Gender: male 5 1, female 5 2
Income: under $30,000 5 1, $30,000 to $75,000 5 2, over $75,000 5 3

13. Using data from a newspaper or magazine article, create the following types of graphs:

   a. Line graph
   b. Pie chart
   c. Bar chart

## WORKING THE NET

1. Microsoft Office Online offers data graphics software called Microsoft Office Visio 2007 enabling users to construct their own data graphics, adjust color shapes to fit the data, and customize data format; try out the downloadable demonstration offered at: *http://office. microsoft.com/en-us/visio-help/demo-let-data-tell-its-story-with-data-graphics-HA010182979.aspx*.

2. To stay updated on the newest software and algorithms for statistical uses, visit the website of the *Journal of Statistical Software* at: *www.jstatsoft.org*.

## REAL-LIFE RESEARCH • 15.1

### Waffle World

Waffle World is a chain of 175 restaurants that serve nothing but different forms of waffles. Or, at least, every item they serve includes waffles. It has recently completed a taste test of a new Belgium waffle breakfast sandwich. In the test, people are asked to indicate which of the following best described the overall taste of a new waffle breakfast sandwich. Immediately following that question, a follow-up question asked respondents to indicate why they gave the particular response. This was a completely open-ended question; their responses can be found in a file named waffletastetest.xlsx on the website for this test.

## Questions

1. Code the results using the traditional approach to coding discussed in the text. What conclusions can you draw based on these results?

2. Go to the Semantria.net site and sign up for a free account. Run the results through the Semantria program and see what you get. What conclusions would you draw from these results?

3. Go to the textisbeautiful.net site and run the responses through their programming to get a word cloud based on the responses. What conclusions would you draw based on this word cloud?

4. Which approach do you find to be the most insightful and useful for managers? Why do you say that?

## REAL-LIFE RESEARCH • 15.2

### Tico Taco

Tico Taco has recently opened its seventeenth store in Wyoming. Currently, the chain offers tacos, fajitas, and burritos. Management is considering offering a super taco that would be two times as large as their regular taco and would contain 6 ounces of ground beef. The basic taco has spiced ground beef, lettuce, and cheese. Management feels that the super taco should offer more options.

A marketing research study was undertaken to determine what those other options should be. A key question on the survey was, "What, if anything, do you normally add to a taco that you have prepared at home besides meat?" The question is open-ended, and the coding categories that have been established for the question are shown in the table.

| Responses | Code |
|---|---|
| Avocado | 1 |
| Cheese (Monterey Jack/cheddar) | 2 |
| Guacamole | 3 |
| Lettuce | 4 |
| Mexican hot sauce | 5 |
| Olive (black/green) | 6 |
| Onion (red/white) | 7 |
| Peppers (red/green) | 8 |
| Pimiento | 9 |
| Sour cream | 0 |
| Other | X |

## Questions

1. How would you code the following responses?

   a. I usually add a green, avocado-tasting hot sauce.

   b. I cut up a mixture of lettuce and spinach.

   c. I'm a vegetarian; I don't use meat at all. My taco is filled only with guacamole.

   d. Every now and then I use a little lettuce, but normally I like cilantro.

2. Is there anything wrong with having a great number of responses in the "Other" category? What problem does this present for the researcher?

## SPSS EXERCISES FOR CHAPTER 15

# Exercise 1: Machine Cleaning Data

1. Go to the Wiley website at **www.wiley.com/college/mcdaniel** and download the Segmenting the College Student Market for Movie Attendance database to SPSS Windows. This database will have several errors for you to correct. In the SPSS Data Editor, go the variable view option and notice the **computer coding** for each variable.

2. Also from the Wiley website, download a copy of the Segmenting the College Student Market for Movie Attendance questionnaire. Notice the computer coding for each of the variables, which is the same as that in the variable view option on the SPSS Data Editor. This information will be important in finding errors in the database.

3. In the SPSS Data Editor, invoke the analyze/descriptive statistics/frequencies sequence to obtain frequencies for all of the variables in the database.

4. From the SPSS Viewer output screen, determine which variables have input errors. Summarize the errors using the followings template as a guide.

| Questionnaire Number | Variable Containing error | Incorrect Value | Correct Value |
| --- | --- | --- | --- |
| | | | |

Go back to the data view screen of the SPSS Data Editor.

5. Another possible source of errors is in question 8. Notice that in this question, the sum of the answers should be 100 percent. Create a summated variable for question 8 (Q8a 3 Q8b 3 Q8c 3 Q8d) to check for errors by invoking the transform/compute sequence. Now, compute a frequency distribution for Q8sum. The values that are not "100" indicate an input error. (Such an error could be the result of the respondent not totaling percentages to 100, but for this machine-cleaning exercise, the assumption is that it is an input error.) Summarize the errors using the template above.

6. Once you have completed summarizing the variables containing errors, go back to the data view screen of the SPSS Data Editor. Position the cursor on each of the variables containing errors. Use the Ctrl-f function to find the questionnaire numbers where the errors occurred. At this point, you will need the corrected database, or the database with no errors. Your professor has access to this database with no errors. After getting the corrected database, finish filling in the table in part (4) above with the correct values. Then make the changes in your database, so that you have a database with no errors. Be sure to resave your database after correcting it for errors.

7. After machine cleaning your data, rerun the analyze/descriptive statistics/frequencies sequence to obtain frequencies for your corrected database.

8. You will use the results of this exercise to answer the questions in Exercises 2 and 4.

# Exercise 2: Analysis of Data with Frequency Distributions

If you did not complete Exercise 1, you will need the corrected database from your professor. After getting the corrected database, use the analyze/descriptive statistics/frequencies sequence to obtain frequency distributions for all of the variables in your database except the questionnaire number (Q No).

If you completed Exercise 1, you will have a corrected database, which consists of frequency distributions for each of the variables in the database.

Answer the following questions.

1. What percentage of all respondents attended at least 1 movie in the past year? _____%

2. What percentage of all respondents never buy food items at a movie? _____%

3. Produce a table indicating the percentage of all respondents who consider each of the movie theater items in question 5 of the questionnaire very important. List the top five movie items in descending order (start with the movie items that have the highest percentage of very important responses).

## For example:

| Movie Item | Percentage of Respondents |
| --- | --- |
| Movie item with the highest percentage | 75.0% |
| Movie item with the 2nd highest percentage, etc. | 39.2% |

4. What percentage of respondents consider the "newspaper" a very important source of information about movies playing at movie theaters? _____%

5. What percentage of respondents consider the "Internet" a very unimportant source of information about movies playing at movie theaters? _____%

6. By observing the distribution of responses for Q8a, Q8b, Q8c, and Q8d, which is the most popular purchase option for movie theater tickets? _____

7. Produce a table listing in descending order the percentage of respondents that consider each of the movie theater information sources (Q7) very important.

## For example:

| Movie Theater Information Sources | Percentage of Respondents Indicating Very Important |
| --- | --- |
| Internet | 55% |
| Newspaper | 31% |

# Exercise 3: Analysis of Data with Descriptive Statistics

If you did not complete Exercise 1 or 2, you will need the corrected database from your professor. The objective of this exercise is to analyze data using measures of central tendency and measures of dispersion. To analyze means and standard deviations, use the analyze/ descriptive statistics/descriptives sequences. To analyze medians and modes, use the analyze/ descriptive statistics/frequencies sequence, and select statistics. You will see the box with all three measures of central tendency (mean, median, and mode).

On the questionnaire, question 5 utilizes a 4-point Itemized Rating scale (illustrated below). This scale is balanced and can be assumed to yield interval scale/metric data. Given the preceding, invoke SPSS to calculate the mean and standard deviation for all of the variables in question 5 (Q5a–Q5i).

| Very unimportant | Somewhat unimportant | Somewhat important | Very important |
|---|---|---|---|
| 1 | 2 | 3 | 4 |

Answer the following questions.

1. Using only the **mean** for each of the variables, which of the movie theater items was considered "most important"? _____

2. Using only the **standard deviation** for each of the variables, for which question was there the greatest amount of agreement? _____ *Hint:* Least amount of dispersion regarding the response to the movie item

3. Questions 4 and 6 utilize multiple-choice questions that yield nonmetric data, but that are ordinal scale. The appropriate measures of central tendency for nonmetric data are the median and the mode.

   a. What is the median response for question 4, concerning the amount a person spends on food/drink items at a movie? _____

| Never buy food items at movies | Up to $7.49 | $7.50 to $14.99 | $15.00 or more |
|---|---|---|---|
| (0) | (1) | (2) | (3) |

   b. Concerning question 6, the distance a person would drive to see a movie on a "big screen," what is the mode of that distribution of responses?

| Zero | 1 to 9 miles | 11 to 24 miles | 25 to 49 miles | 503 miles |
|---|---|---|---|---|
| (0) | (1) | (2) | (3) | (4) |

4. In this question the objective will be to compare the results of median and mean responses for Q3.

   a. Mean response: _____

   b. Median response: _____

   c. Standard deviation: _____

   d. Minimum response: _____

   e. Maximum response: _____

5. When the responses to a question contain extreme values, the mean response can lie in the upper or lower quartile of the response distribution. In such a case, the median value would be a better indicator of an average response than the mean value. Given the

information you obtained from answering question 4 above, is the mean or median a better representative of the "average" response to Q3?

_____

_____

_____

## Exercise 4: Analysis of Demographic Characteristics Using Charts

If you completed Exercise 1 and/or Exercise 2, you will have the information to complete this exercise.

If you did not complete either Exercise 1 or 2, you will need to get a corrected soft-drink database from your professor. After getting the database, use the **analyze–descriptive statistics/frequencies** sequence to obtain frequency distributions for the demographic questions (questions 11–14).

Complete the following.

1. Display the demographic data for each of the four demographic variables in tables.

2. For each demographic variable, illustrate the table results using some type of graphic representation of the data (pie charts, line charts, or bar charts).

*Note:* Some students who are proficient in Excel may want to paste their databases into an Excel spreadsheet for the geographical depiction of the demographic variables.

Monty Rakusen /Getty Images

# Statistical Testing of Differences and Relationships

## LEARNING OBJECTIVES

1. Learn how to evaluate differences and changes.

2. Understand the concept of hypothesis development and how to test hypotheses.

3. Be familiar with several of the more common statistical tests of goodness of fit, hypotheses about one mean, hypotheses about two means, and hypotheses about proportions.

4. Learn the hypotheses about one mean.

5. Learn the hypotheses about two means.

6. Learn the hypotheses about proportions.

7. Learn about analysis of variance.

8. Understand the *P* values and significance testing.

This chapter addresses statistical techniques that can be used to determine whether observed differences are likely to be real differences or whether they are likely attributable to sampling error.

# Evaluating Differences and Changes

The issue of whether certain measurements are different from one another is central to many questions of critical interest to marketing managers. Some specific examples of managers' questions follow:

■ Our posttest measure of top-of-mind awareness (first brand mentioned unaided) is slightly higher than the level recorded in the pretest. Did top-of-mind awareness really increase or is there some other explanation for the increase? Should we fire or commend our agency?

■ Our overall customer satisfaction score increased from 92 percent 3 months ago to 93.5 percent today. Did customer satisfaction really increase? Should we celebrate?

■ Satisfaction with the customer service provided by our cable TV system in Dallas is, on average, 1.2 points higher on a 10-point scale than is satisfaction with the customer service provided by our cable TV system in Cincinnati. Are customers in Dallas really more satisfied? Should the customer service manager in Cincinnati be replaced? Should the Dallas manager be rewarded?

■ In a recent product concept test, 19.8 percent of those surveyed said they were very likely to buy the new product they evaluated. Is this good? Is it better than the results we got last year for a similar product? What do these results suggest in terms of whether to introduce the new product?

■ A segmentation study shows that those with incomes of more than $30,000 per year frequent fast-food restaurants 6.2 times per month on average. Those with incomes of $30,000 or less go an average of 6.7 times. Is this difference real—is it meaningful?

■ In an awareness test, 28.3 percent of those surveyed have heard of our product on an unaided basis. Is this a good result?

These are the common questions in marketing and marketing research. Although considered boring by some, statistical hypothesis testing is important because it helps researchers get closer to the answers to these questions. We say "closer" because certainty is never achieved in answering these questions in marketing research.

# Statistical Significance

The basic motive for making statistical inferences is to generalize from sample results to population characteristics. A fundamental tenet of statistical inference is that it is possible for numbers to be different in a mathematical sense but not significantly different in a statistical sense. For example, suppose cola drinkers are asked to try two cola drinks in a blind taste test and indicate which they prefer; the results show that 51 percent prefer one test product and 49 percent prefer the other. There is a mathematical difference in the results but the difference would appear to be minor and unimportant. The difference probably is well within the range of accuracy of researchers' ability to measure taste preference and thus probably is not significant in a statistical sense. Three different concepts can be applied to the notion of differences when we are talking about results from samples:

■ *Mathematical differences.* By definition, if numbers are not exactly the same, they are different. This does not, however, mean that the difference is either important or statistically significant.

■ *Statistical significance.* If a particular difference is large enough to be unlikely to have occurred because of chance or sampling error, then the difference is **statistically significant.**

■ *Managerially important differences.* One can argue that a difference is important from a managerial perspective only if results or numbers are sufficiently different. For example, the difference in consumer responses to two different packages in a test market might be statistically significant but yet so small as to have little practical or managerial significance.[1]

This chapter covers different approaches to testing whether results are statistically significant. The Practicing Marketing Research feature on page 397 covers issues related to statistical significance testing.

**statistical significance**
A difference that is large enough that it is not likely to have occurred because of chance or sampling error.

As you review the material in this chapter, keep three things in mind:

1. **Random samples are assumed.** All of the tests we will discuss in this chapter assume the data come from random samples. Some have additional assumptions, but all assume random samples. If the data you are working with do not come from random samples, then the significance tests are not appropriate.

2. **Big data does not mean "good" data.** Big data presents some special challenges. First of all, don't be totally swayed by the sheer amount of data you have, no matter how much data, it must come from random samples. With really big data—thousands, tens of thousands or hundreds of thousands of observations—if the obervations come from random samples, then very small differences will be statistically significant because sample size always figures into the calculation of significance.

3. **Don't overrely on significance testing.** Placing total reliance on significance testing is not a good idea. If, on the one hand, we are testing many measures from a particular study conducted at different points in time to access the changes that have taken place, then some percentage will give false positives (indicate significant differences incorrectly). On the other hand, routinely dismissing differences that are not significant can lead us to miss important findings.

# PRACTICING MARKETING RESEARCH

## Let's Test Everything[2]

The logic of statistical (stat) testing is not complex, but it can be difficult to understand, because it is the reverse of everyday logic and what normal people expect. Basically, to determine if two numbers differ significantly, it is assumed that they are the same. The test then determines whether this notion can be rejected, and we can say that the numbers are "statistically significantly different at the (some pre-determined) confidence level."

While it is not complex, the logic can be subtle. One subtlety leads to a common error, aided and abetted by automatic computer stat testing—overtesting. Suppose there is a group of 200 men and one of 205 women, and they respond to a new product concept on a purchase intent scale. The data might look like that shown in Table A.

Statistical logic assumes that the two percentages to be tested are from the same population—they do not differ. Therefore, it is assumed that men have the same purchase interest as women. The rules also assume that the numbers are unrelated, in the sense that the percentages being tested are free to be whatever they might be, from 0 percent to 100 percent. Restricting them in any way changes the probabilities, and the dynamics of the statistical test.

**Table A**
**Purchase Intent Among Men and Women**

| Base: total per group | Men (200) % | | Women (205) % |
|---|---|---|---|
| Definitely would buy | 3 | | 21 |
| Probably would buy | 10 | | 19 |
| Def./Prob. would buy | 13 | S | 40 |
| Might or might not buy | 40 | | 35 |
| Probably would not buy | 30 | | 20 |
| Definitely would not buy | 17 | | 5 |
| Total | 100 | | 100 |

*S = the percentages differ significantly at the 95% confidence level.*

The right way to test for a difference in purchase intent is to pick a key measure to summarize the responses, and test that measure. In Table A, the Top Two Box score was tested—the combined percentages from the top two points on the scale ("definitely would buy" plus "probably would buy"). Within the group of men, this number could have turned out to be anything. It just happened to be 13 percent. Within the group of women, it could have been anything, and, as it turns out, was 40 percent. Within each group, the number was free to be anything from 0 percent to 100 percent, so picking this percentage to test follows the statistical rule. The stat test indicates that the idea that these percentages are from the same place (or are the same) can be rejected, so we can say they are "statistically significantly different at the 95 percent confidence level."

Something different often happens in practice, though. Because the computer programs that generate survey data do not "know" what summary measure will be important, these programs test everything. When looking at computer-generated data tables, the statistical results will look something like those shown in Table B.

If the Top Two Box score is selected ahead of time, and that is all that is examined (as in Table A), then this automatic testing is very helpful. It does the work, and shows that 13 percent differs from 40 percent. The other stat test results are ignored. However, if the data are reported as shown in Table B, there is a problem.

The percentages for the men add to 100 percent. If one percentage is picked for testing, it is "taken out" of the scale, in a sense. The other percentages are no longer free to be whatever they might be. They must add to 100 percent minus the set, fixed percent that was selected for testing. Percentages for the men can vary from 0 percent to 87 percent, but they can't be higher, because 13 percent is "used up." Similarly, percentages for the women can vary from 0 percent to 60 percent, but 40 percent is used already. When you look at testing in the other rows, or row by row, you are no longer using the confidence level you think you are using—it becomes something else.

Statistically, if one said of Table B that the percentages that "definitely would buy" and the percentages that "definitely/probably would buy" both differ at the 95 percent confidence level, it would be wrong. One of them does, but the other difference is at some unknown level of significance, probably much less than 95 percent, given one related significant difference.

| Table B — Purchase Intent Among Men and Women | | | |
|---|---|---|---|
| Base: total per group | Men (200) % | | Women (205) % |
| Definitely would buy | 3 | S | 21 |
| Probably would buy | 10 | | 19 |
| Def./Prob. would buy | 13 | S | 40 |
| Might or might not buy | 40 | | 35 |
| Probably would not buy | 30 | | 20 |
| Definitely would not buy | 17 | D | 5 |
| Total | 100 | | 100 |

*S = the percentages differ significantly at the 95% confidence level.*
*D = the percentages differ directionally at the 90% confidence level.*

Stat tests are very useful. Each one answers a specific question about a numerical relationship. The one most commonly asked about scale responses is whether two numbers differ significantly. If they are the right two numbers, and the proper test is used, the question is easily answered. If they are the wrong two numbers, or the wrong test has been used, the decision maker can be misled.

## Questions

1. How is it that statistical testing is the reverse of everyday logic? Explain.

2. What is the most common question we address with statistical tests about scale responses?

# Hypothesis Testing

**hypothesis**
Assumption or theory that a researcher or manager makes about some characteristic of the population under study.

A **hypothesis** is an assumption or theory guess that a researcher or manager makes about some characteristic of the population being investigated. The marketing researcher is often faced with the question of whether research results are different enough from the norm that some element of the firm's marketing strategy should be changed. Consider the following situations.

- The results of a tracking survey show that awareness of a product is lower than it was in a similar survey conducted six months ago. Are the results significantly lower? Are the results sufficiently lower to call for a change in advertising strategy?

- A product manager believes that the average purchaser of his product is 35 years of age. A survey is conducted to test this hypothesis and the survey shows that the average purchaser of the product is 38.5 years of age. Is the survey result different enough from the product manager's belief to cause him to conclude that his belief is incorrect?

■ The marketing director of a fast-food chain believes that 60 percent of her customers are female and 40 percent are male. She does a survey to test this hypothesis and finds that, according to the survey, 55 percent are female and 45 percent are male. Is this result different enough from her original theory to permit her to conclude that her original theory was incorrect?

All of these questions can be evaluated with some kind of statistical test. In hypothesis testing, the researcher determines whether a hypothesis concerning some characteristic of the population is likely to be true, given the evidence. A statistical hypothesis test allows us to calculate the probability of observing a particular result if the stated hypothesis is actually true.[3]

There are two basic explanations for an observed difference between a hypothesized value and a particular research result. Either the hypothesis is true and the observed difference is likely due to sampling error or the hypothesis is false and the true value is some other value.

## Steps in Hypothesis Testing

Five steps are involved in testing a hypothesis. First, the hypothesis is specified. Second, an appropriate statistical technique is selected to test the hypothesis. Third, a decision rule is specified as the basis for determining whether to reject or fail to reject (FTR) the null hypothesis $H_0$. Please note that we did not say "reject $H_0$ or accept $H_0$." Although a seemingly small distinction, it is an important one. The distinction will be discussed in greater detail later on. Fourth, the value of the test statistic is calculated and the test is performed. Fifth, the conclusion is stated from the perspective of the original research problem or question.

**Step One: Stating the Hypothesis**  Hypotheses are stated using two basic forms: the null hypothesis $H_0$ and the alternative hypothesis $H_a$. The **null hypothesis** $H_0$ (sometimes called the *hypothesis of the status quo*) is the hypothesis that is tested against its complement, the alternative hypothesis $H_a$ (sometimes called the *research hypothesis of interest*). Suppose the manager of Burger City believes that his operational procedures will guarantee that the average customer will wait 2 minutes in the drive-in window line. He conducts research, based on the observation of 1,000 customers at randomly selected stores at randomly selected times. The average customer observed in this study spends 2.4 minutes in the drive-in window line. The null hypothesis and the alternative hypothesis might be stated as follows:

**null hypothesis**
The hypothesis of status quo, no difference, no effect.

■ Null hypothesis $H_0$: Mean waiting time = 2 minutes.
■ Alternative hypothesis $H_a$: Mean waiting time $\neq$ 2 minutes.

It should be noted that the null hypothesis and the alternative hypothesis must be stated in such a way that both cannot be true. The idea is to use the available evidence to ascertain which hypothesis is more likely to be true.

**Step Two: Choosing the Appropriate Statistical Test**  As you will see in the following sections of this chapter, the analyst must choose the appropriate statistical test, given the characteristics of the situation under investigation. A number of different statistical tests, along with the situations where they are appropriate, are discussed in this chapter. Exhibit 16.1 provides a guide to selecting the appropriate test for various situations. All the tests in this table are covered in detail later in this chapter. The following Practicing Marketing Research feature further addresses this issue.

**EXHIBIT 16.1** Statistical Tests and Their Uses

| Area of Application | Subgroups or Samples | Level Scaling | Test | Special Requirements | Example |
|---|---|---|---|---|---|
| Hypotheses about frequency distribution | One | Nominal | $\chi^2$ | Random sample | Are observed differences in the number of people responding to three different promotions likely/not likely due to chance? |
| | Two or more | Nominal | $\chi^2$ | Random sample, independent samples | Are differences in the number of men and women responding to a promotion likely/not likely due to chance? |
| Hypotheses about means | One (large sample) | Metric (interval or ratio) | $Z$ test for one mean | Random sample, $n \geq 30$ | Is the observed difference between a sample estimate of the mean and some set standard or expected value of the mean likely/not likely due to chance? |
| | One (small sample) Two (large sample) | Metric (interval or ratio) Metric (interval or ratio) | $t$ test for one mean $Z$ test for one mean | Random sample, $n < 30$ Random sample, $n \geq 30$ | Same as for small sample above Is the observed difference between the means for two subgroups (mean income for men and women) likely/not likely due to chance? |
| | Three or more | Metric (interval or ratio) | One-way ANOVA | Random sample | Is the observed variation between means for three or more subgroups (mean expenditures on entertainment for high-, moderate-, and low-income people) likely/not likely due to chance? |
| Hypotheses about proportions | One (large sample) | Metric (interval or ratio) | $Z$ test for one proportion | Random sample, $n \geq 30$ | Is the observed difference between a sample estimate of proportion (percentage who say they will buy) and some set standard or expected value likely/not likely due to chance? |
| | Two (large sample) | Metric (interval or ratio) | $Z$ test for two proportions | Random sample, $n \geq 30$ | Is the observed difference between estimated percentages for two subgroups (percentage of men and women who have college degrees) likely/not likely due to chance? |

# PRACTICING MARKETING RESEARCH

## Choosing the Right Test for the Right Situation[4]

How's a researcher to know which kind of statistical testing procedure software to use to generate marketing research data tables? Three basic rules can help marketers determine which testing procedure should be employed in a given situation:

- There is a difference between "two groups" and "three or more groups."
- There is a difference between percentages and means.
- There is a difference between matched samples and independent samples.

When testing percentages with dependent groups, chi-squares should be used for three or more groups, and Z tests should be used for two groups. When testing means, ANOVAs (Analysis of Variance) are used in the case of three or more group, and t tests are used for the two-group case. (See the accompanying table.)

| Which Test Should I Use? | | |
|---|---|---|
| When measuring... | 2 Groups | 3+ Groups |
| Percentages | Z test | chi-square |
| Means | t test | ANOVA |

Although analytic software can be very useful for quickly processing survey data, researchers must be careful how they use it. Default settings in many analytic software packages will run the same test automatically, frequently violating the first rule above when testing three or more groups. Thus, in the case of percentages, many software tools will often apply multiple $Z$ tests instead of a chi-square and, in the case of means, multiple $t$ tests instead of an ANOVA.

Statistically, using the wrong test in these instances will result in a confidence level below what you think you are using. For example, when comparing the percentages in three different groups, the chi-square method will determine whether they vary statistically by running a single test comparing percentages for all three groups simultaneously. In contrast, the $Z$ test will run three separate tests, comparing group A to group B, B to C, and C to A individually. Ultimately, it is possible that the tests could produce different outcomes, where one test would suggest a statistically significant difference exists across the three groups while others would suggest no statistically significant differences or only find differences between one or two groups.

Essentially, the chi-square test is taking all the information into account at once, whereas the $Z$ test is running multiple tests on selected portions of the data. In most cases, the results of using the wrong test will probably not lead marketing managers to any critical mistakes based on the research; however, using the wrong testing method can seriously undermine credibility. As a matter of quality control, this error can be easily avoided if researchers are careful to use the right tests and settings when performing their analysis.

## Questions

1. Aside from the automatic settings in analytic software mentioned above, can you think of any other procedural factors that might cause a researcher to misapply certain tests?

2. If you have access to analytic software, run a $Z$ test and a chi-square test on the same set of data (you might try pulling one from earlier in the chapter) and compare the results. Were they significantly different? If they did not produce the same results, can you see why?

**Step Three: Developing a Decision Rule** Based on our previous discussions of distributions of sample means, you may recognize that one is very unlikely to get a sample result that is exactly equal to the value of the population parameter. The problem is determining whether the difference, or deviation, between the actual value of the sample mean and its expected value based on the hypothesis could have occurred by chance (e.g., 5 times out of 100) if the statistical hypothesis is true. A **decision rule**, or standard, is needed to determine whether to reject or fail to reject the null hypothesis. Statisticians state such decision rules in terms of significance levels.

**decision rule**
Rule or standard used to determine whether to reject or fail to reject the null hypothesis.

The significance level ($\alpha$) is critical in the process of choosing between the null and alternative hypotheses. The level of significance—.10, .05, or .01, for example—is the probability that is considered too low to justify acceptance of the null hypothesis.

Consider a situation in which the researcher has decided that she wants to test a hypothesis at the .05 level of significance. This means that she will reject the null hypothesis if the test indicates that the probability of occurrence of the observed result (e.g., the difference between the sample mean and its expected value) because of chance or sampling error is less than 5 percent. Rejection of the null hypothesis is equivalent to supporting the alternative hypothesis, but statistically, we can only state that the null hypothesis is not true.

**Step Four: Calculating the Value of the Test Statistic** In this step, the researcher does the following:

- Uses the appropriate formula to calculate the value of the statistic for the test chosen.
- Compares the value just calculated to the critical value of the statistic (from the appropriate table), based on the decision rule chosen.
- Based on the comparison, determines to either reject or fail to reject the null hypothesis $H_0$.

**Step Five: Stating the Conclusion** The conclusion summarizes the results of the test. It should be stated from the perspective of the original research question.

## Types of Errors in Hypothesis Testing

Hypothesis tests are subject to two general types of errors, typically referred to as type I error and type II error. A **type I error** involves rejecting the null hypothesis when it is, in fact, true. The researcher may reach this incorrect conclusion because the observed difference between the sample and population values is due to sampling error. The researcher must decide how willing she or he is to commit a type I error. The probability of committing a type I error is referred to as the *alpha* ($\alpha$) *level*. Conversely, $1 - \alpha$ is the probability of making a correct decision by not rejecting the null hypothesis when, in fact, it is true.

A **type II error** involves failing to reject the null hypothesis when it actually is false. A type II error is referred to as a *beta* ($\beta$) *error*. The value $1 - \beta$ reflects the probability of making a correct decision in rejecting the null hypothesis when, in fact, it is false. The four possibilities are summarized in Exhibit 16.2.

As we consider the various types of hypothesis tests, keep in mind that when a researcher rejects or fails to reject the null hypothesis, this decision is never made with 100 percent certainty. There is a probability that the decision is correct, and there is a probability that the decision is not correct. The level of $\alpha$ is set by the researcher, after consulting with his or her client, considering the resources available for the project, and considering the implications of making type I and type II errors. However, the estimation of $\beta$ is more complicated and is beyond the scope of our discussion. Note that type I and type II errors are not complementary; that is, $\alpha + \beta \neq 1$.

It would be ideal to have control over $n$ (the sample size), $\alpha$ (the probability of a type I error), and $\beta$ (the probability of a type II error) for any hypothesis test. Unfortunately, only two of the three can be controlled. For a given problem with a fixed sample size, $n$ is fixed, or controlled. Therefore, only one of $\alpha$ and $\beta$ can be controlled.

Assume that for a given problem you have decided to set $\alpha = .05$. As a result, the procedure you use to test $H_0$ versus $H_a$ will reject $H_0$ when it is true (type I error) 5 percent of the time. You could set $\alpha = 0$ so that you would never have a type I error. The idea of never rejecting a correct $H_0$ sounds good. However, the downside is that $\beta$ (the probability of a type II error) is equal to 1 in this situation. As a result, you will always fail to reject $H_0$ when it is false. For example, if $\alpha = 0$ in the fast-food service time example, where $H_0$ is mean waiting time = 2 minutes, then the resulting test of $H_0$ versus $H_a$ will automatically fail to reject $H_0$ (mean waiting time = 2 minutes) whenever the estimated waiting time is any value other than 2 minutes. If, for example, we did a survey and determined that the mean waiting time for the people surveyed was 8.5 minutes, we would still fail to reject (FTR) $H_0$. As you can see, this is not a good compromise. We need a value of $\alpha$ that offers a more reasonable compromise between the probabilities of the two types of errors. Note that in the situation in which $\alpha = 0$ and $\beta = 1$, $\alpha + \beta = 1$. As you will see later on, this is not true as a general rule.

The value of $\alpha$ selected should be a function of the relative importance of the two types of errors. Suppose you have just had a diagnostic test. The purpose of the test is to determine

**type I error ($\alpha$ error)**
Rejection of the null hypothesis when, in fact, it is true.

**type II error ($\beta$ error)**
Failure to reject the null hypothesis when, in fact, it is false.

| EXHIBIT 16.2 | Type I and Type II Errors | |
|---|---|---|
| **Actual State of the Null Hypothesis** | **Fail to Reject $H_0$** | **Reject $H_0$** |
| $H_0$ is true | Correct ($1 - \alpha$) | Type I error ($\alpha$) |
| $H_0$ is false | Type II error ($\beta$) | Correct ($1 - \beta$) |

whether you have a particular medical condition that is fatal in most cases. If you have the disease, a treatment that is painless, inexpensive, and totally without risk will cure the condition 100 percent of the time. Here are the hypotheses to be tested:

$H_0$: Test indicates that you do not have the disease.

$H_a$: Test indicates that you do have the disease.

Thus,

$\alpha = P$ (rejecting $H_0$ when it is true)
= (test indicates that you have the disease when you do not have it)

$\beta = P$ (FTR $H_0$ when in fact it is false)
= $P$ (test indicates that you do not have the disease when you do have it)

Clearly, a type I error (measured by $\alpha$) is not nearly as serious as a type II error (measured by $\beta$). A type I error is not serious because the test will not harm you if you are well. However, a type II error means that you will not receive the treatment you need, even though you are ill.

The value of $\beta$ is never set in advance. When $\alpha$ is made smaller, $\beta$ becomes larger for a given sample size. If you want to minimize type II error, then you choose a larger value for $\alpha$ in order to make $\beta$ smaller. In most situations, the range of acceptable values for $\alpha$ is .01 to .1. You may also increase the sample size in order to reduce $\beta$ for a given level of $\alpha$.

In the case of the diagnostic test situation, you might choose a value of $\alpha$ at or near .1 because of the seriousness of a type II error. Conversely, if you are more concerned about type I errors in a given situation, then a small value of $\alpha$ is appropriate. For example, suppose you are testing commercials that were very expensive to produce, and you are concerned about the possibility of rejecting a commercial that is really effective. If there is no real difference between the effects of type I and type II errors, as is often the case, an $\alpha$ value of .05 is commonly used.

## Accepting $H_0$ versus Failing to Reject (FTR) $H_0$

Researchers often fail to make a distinction between accepting $H_0$ and failing to reject $H_0$. However, as noted earlier, there is an important distinction between these two decisions. When a hypothesis is tested, $H_0$ is presumed to be true until it is demonstrated as likely to be false. In any hypothesis testing situation, the only other hypothesis that can be accepted is the alternative hypothesis $H_a$. Either there is sufficient evidence to support $H_a$ (reject $H_0$) or there is not (fail to reject $H_0$). The real question is whether there is enough evidence in the data to conclude that $H_a$ is correct. If we fail to reject $H_0$, we are saying that the data do not provide sufficient support of the claim made in $H_a$—not that we accept the statement made in $H_0$.

## One-Tailed versus Two-Tailed Test

Tests are either one-tailed or two-tailed. The decision as to which to use depends on the nature of the situation and what the researcher is trying to demonstrate. For example, when the quality control department of a fast-food organization receives a shipment of chicken breasts from one of its vendors and needs to determine whether the product meets specifications in regard to fat content, a one-tailed test is appropriate. The shipment will be rejected if it does not meet minimum specifications. On the other hand, the managers of the meat company that supplies the product should run two-tailed tests to determine two factors. First, they must make sure that the product meets the minimum specifications of their customer before they ship it. Second, they want to determine whether the product exceeds specifications because this can be costly to them. If they are consistently providing a product that exceeds the level of quality they have contracted to provide, their costs may be unnecessarily high.

The classic example of a situation requiring a two-tailed test is the testing of electric fuses. On the one hand, a fuse must trip, or break contact, when it reaches a preset temperature, or a fire may result. On the other hand, you do not want the fuse to break contact before it reaches the specified temperature or it will shut off the electricity unnecessarily. The test used in the quality control process for testing fuses must, therefore, be two-tailed.

## Example of Performing a Statistical Test

Income is an important determinant of the sales of luxury cars. Lexus North America (LNA) is in the process of developing sales estimates for the Southern California market, one of its key markets. According to the U.S. Census, the average annual family income in the market is $55,347. LNA has just completed a survey of 250 randomly selected households in the market to obtain other measures needed for its sales forecasting model. The recently completed survey indicates that the average annual family income in the market is $54,323. The actual value of the population mean ($\mu$) is unknown. This gives us two estimates of m: the census result and the survey result. The difference between these two estimates could make a substantial difference in the estimates of Lexus sales produced by LNA's forecasting model. In the calculations, the U.S. Census Bureau estimate is treated as the best estimate of $\mu$.

# P R A C T I C I N G
# M A R K E T I N G   R E S E A R C H

## More Tips on Significance Testing

*Paul Schmiege, Analytical Science, DSS Research*

© Roger Gates

On the quantitative side of the marketing research industry, you spend a great deal of time measuring and comparing. But unlike grabbing a yardstick and measuring a physical quantity, your measurements have sampling error. (*Sampling error* is a technical term and does not connote a mistake.) Then, when you compare two measurements, both of which have sampling error, you cannot be 100 percent confident that a difference even exists. That's where statistics comes in and says, "Though you can't be 100 percent confident, you can test to see if we are 95 percent or 90 percent confident that a difference exists."

The point of making comparisons is to help lead you as interpreters of data to evaluations. "Is this difference important, is it something that we should act on, should we continue with the same advertising strategy to increase unaided awareness?" Unfortunately, statistics cannot answer those questions for you.

The distinction between testing a difference with a statistical test and evaluating the meaning or relevance of said difference is important to remember. The singlemost common test in marketing research is the two-sample *t* test. You use it to answer questions like this: "Last year, the percentage of respondents aware of our brand on an unaided basis was 43.2 percent. This year, the corresponding percentage is 47.5 percent. Is this difference significant?" This type of question is so common you might not ever see any other test in your entire career. Because the two-sample *t* test is so important, it is good to keep at least two points in mind about it:

■ The two-sample *t* test is a two-tail test. It asks, "Does a significant difference exist?" It does not ask, "Is the first significantly greater than the second?" or "Is the first significantly less than the second?" Consequently, if a significant difference exists you should say, "A statistically significant difference exists, and that observed difference is higher (or lower)."

■ The two-sample *t* test is run with the assumption of equal variances. The true standard deviation for the combined populations is unknown, so you "pool" the two sample standard deviations together to calculate something similar to a weighted average. In academic research, you would first test whether to assume equal or unequal variance, but you will probably never have to do that in the business world.

For any given observed difference, there are sample sizes large enough that the difference will be significant in a two-sample *t* test (sample sizes go in the denominator of the equation). Or, to think of it from another perspective, when you start testing with larger and larger sample sizes, smaller and smaller differences become statistically significant, but practical significance remains the same. Is a 0.5 percent increase worth telling management about, even if it should happen to be statistically significant? Probably not.

In the end, always remember that the technical term *statistical significance* is not the same as the more intuitive terms like *practical significance* or *importance*. At the heart of its technical meaning, significance in the field of statistics means the difference is likely greater than we would expect due to sampling error. Don't mistake a statistical test, a useful tool in the evaluation, for the evaluation itself.

LNA decides to statistically compare the census and survey estimates. The statistics for the sample are

$$\bar{X} = \$54,323$$
$$S = \$4,323$$
$$n = 250$$

The following hypotheses are produced:

$$H_0 : \mu = \$55,347$$
$$H_a : \mu \neq \$55,347$$

The decision makers at LNA are willing to use a test that will reject $H_0$ when it is correct only 5 percent of the time ($\alpha = .05$). This is the significance level of the test. LNA will

© Jack Puccio/iStockphoto

The quality control department of a fast-food organization would probably do a one-tailed test to determine whether a shipment of chicken breasts met product specifications. However, the managers of the meat company that supplied the chicken breasts would probably do a two-tailed test.

reject H$_0$ if the difference between the sample mean and the Census estimate is larger than can be explained by sampling error at $\alpha = .05$

Standardizing the data so that the result can be directly related to $Z$ values in Exhibit 2 in Appendix 3, we have the following criterion:

Reject H$_0$ if is larger than can be explained by sampling error at $\alpha = .05$. This expression can be rewritten as

$$\left| \frac{\overline{X} - \$55,347}{S / \sqrt{n}} \right| > k$$

What is the value of $k$? If H$_0$ is true and the sample size is large ($\geq 30$), then (based on the central limit theorem) $X$ approximates a normal random variable with a mean equal to 0 and a standard deviation equal to 1.

That is, if H$_0$ is true, $(\overline{X} - \$55,347 / SI\sqrt{n})$ approximates a standard normal variable $Z$ for samples of 30 or larger with a mean equal to 0 and a standard deviation equal to 1.

$$\text{Mean} = \mu = \$55,347$$
$$\text{Standard deviation} = \frac{S}{\sqrt{n}}$$

We will reject H$_0$ if $|Z| > k$. When $|Z| > k$, either $Z > k$ or $Z < -k$, as shown in Exhibit 16.3. Given that

$$P(|Z| > k) = .05$$

the total shaded area is .05, with .025 in each tail (two-tailed test). The area between 0 and $k$ is .475. Referring to Exhibit 2 in Appendix 3, we find that $k = 1.96$. Therefore, the test is

$$\text{Reject H}_0 \text{ if } \left| \frac{\overline{X} - \$55,347}{S / \sqrt{n}} \right| > 1.96$$

and FTR H$_0$ otherwise. In other words,

**Exhibit 16.3**

**Shaded Area Is Significance Level $\alpha$**

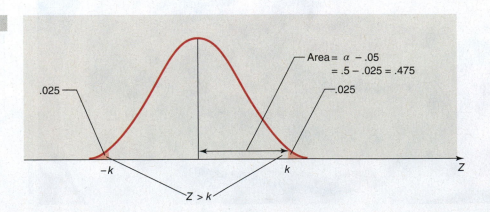

$$\text{Reject } H_0 \text{ if } \left|\frac{\overline{X} - \$55{,}347}{S/\sqrt{n}}\right| > 1.96 \text{ or if } \left|\frac{\overline{X} - \$55{,}347}{S/\sqrt{n}}\right| < 1.96$$

The question is whether $54,323 is far enough away from $55,347 for LNA to reject $H_0$? The results show that

$$Z = \frac{\overline{X} - \$55{,}347}{S/\sqrt{n}}$$

$$= \frac{\$54{,}323 - \$55{,}347}{\$4{,}322/\sqrt{250}} = -3.75$$

Because $-3.75 < -1.96$, we reject $H_0$. On the basis of the sample results and $\alpha = .05$, the conclusion is that the average household income in the market is not equal to $55,347. If $H_0$ is true ($\mu = \$55{,}347$), then the value of $X$ obtained from the sample ($54,323) is 3.75 standard deviations to the left of the mean on the normal curve for $X$. A value of $X$ this far away from the mean is very unlikely (probability is less than .05). As a result, we conclude that $H_0$ is not likely to be true, and we reject it.

Having said all this, we caution against an overreliance on statistical tests and significance/nonsignificance. The Practicing Marketing Research feature below covers this point in greater detail.

# PRACTICING MARKETING RESEARCH

## Does Statistical Precision Validate Results?[5]

The presence of statistical significance in marketing research analysis can be deceptive. *Statistical* significance does not necessarily mean that the difference has any *practical* significance. In addition to large sample sizes, there are many potential sources of error that can create problems for researchers when identifying statistically significant differences.

Generally, two kinds of error affect the validity of statistical measurements. *Random error* introduces error variance, but as it occurs randomly across respondents, it does not add statistical bias to the data. *Systematic error* is consistent across respondents, creating a bias within the data that may or may not be known. Typically, the causes for these kinds of error fall into two categories: sampling error, arising in the process of building a respondent pool; and measurement error, arising from the way the questionnaire is constructed.

### Sampling Error

Three major sources of sampling error include under coverage, nonresponse, and self-selection.

1. *Under coverage*—Under coverage occurs when a certain segment of the population is not adequately represented.
2. *Nonresponse*—Nonresponse error is a result of portions of the population being unwilling to participate in research projects.
3. *Self-selection*—Self-selection can result from respondents having control over survey completion. For instance, participants in an online survey panel might get bored and opt out before the survey is over.

### Measurement Error

The following six types of measurement error can result in random or systematic error.

1. *Question interpretation*—Respondents may interpret vague or ambiguously worded questions differently.
2. *Respondent assumptions*—Regardless of the way a question is worded, respondents still bring personal assumptions to the table, including any number of varying external factors influencing their understanding of the question.
3. *Question order*—Respondents might answer a question differently depending on where it falls in the survey, as

their opinions might be influenced by their thoughts on surrounding questions.

4. *Method variance*—Researchers must be aware of potential errors introduced by the method used to deliver the survey.

5. *Attribute wording*—The way in which survey attributes are described may elicit different answers from respondents.

6. *Omitting important questions*—Systematic error most commonly results from inadequate coverage of critical variables within the question battery. Absent variables can significantly affect the results of data analysis.

## Managerial Significance

Researchers must be careful to differentiate between resultant random and systematic errors. Furthermore, they must also realize that statistical precision does not necessarily indicate that the difference is actionable or meaningful.

Rather than focusing on statistical significance in and of itself, researchers need to identify results that have managerial significance—results that are relevant to the decision-making process. Given a large enough sample, any null hypothesis can be discounted, and any two unequal means can be shown to be statistically different. An absence of statistical significance between two supposedly "different" populations may be just as relevant as any demonstrated statistical significance. As such, statistical testing should be used as a tool to discover practical insights, not to define them.

## Questions

1. Of the potential causes for error described above, which do you think would be easiest to identify? Hardest? Explain your reasoning.

2. Can you think of any ways that could help researchers determine whether occurrences of statistical significance in their results have managerial significance?

# Commonly Used Statistical Hypothesis Tests

A number of commonly used statistical hypothesis tests of differences are presented in the following sections. Many other statistical tests have been developed, but a full discussion of all of them is beyond the scope of this text.

The distributions used in the following sections for comparing the computed and tabular values of the statistics are the $Z$ distribution, the $t$ distribution, the $F$ distribution, and the chi-square ($\chi^2$) distribution. The tabular values for these distributions appear in Exhibits 2, 3, 4, and 5 of Appendix 3.

## Independent versus Related Samples

In some cases, one needs to test the hypothesis that the value of a variable in one population is equal to the value of that same variable in another population. Selection of the appropriate test statistic requires the researcher to consider whether the samples are independent or related. **Independent samples** are those in which measurement of the variable of interest in one sample has no effect on measurement of the variable in the other sample. It is not necessary that there be two different surveys, only that the measurement of the variable in one population has no effect on the measurement of the variable in the other population. In the case of **related samples**, measurement of the variable of interest in one sample may influence measurement of the variable in another sample.

If, for example, men and women were interviewed in a particular survey regarding their frequency of eating out, there is no way that a man's response could affect or change the way a woman would respond to a question in the survey. Thus, this would be an example of independent samples. By contrast, consider a situation in which the researcher needed to determine the effect of a new advertising campaign on consumer awareness of a particular brand. To do this, the researcher might survey a random sample of consumers

**independent samples**
Samples in which measurement of a variable in one population has no effect on measurement of the variable in the other.

**related samples**
Samples in which measurement of a variable in one population may influence measurement of the variable in the other.

before introducing the new campaign and then survey the same sample of consumers 90 days after the new campaign was introduced. These samples are not independent. The measurement of awareness 90 days after the start of the campaign may be affected by the first measurement.

## Degrees of Freedom

Many of the statistical tests discussed in this chapter require the researcher to specify degrees of freedom in order to find the critical value of the test statistic from the table for that statistic. The number of **degrees of freedom** is the number of observations in a statistical problem that are not restricted or are free to vary.

The number of degrees of freedom (d.f.) is equal to the number of observations minus the number of assumptions or constraints necessary to calculate a statistic. Consider the problem of adding five numbers when the mean of the five numbers is known to be 20. In this situation, only four of the five numbers are free to vary. Once four of the numbers are known, the last value is also known (can be calculated) because the mean value must be 20. If four of the five numbers were 14, 23, 24, and 18, then the fifth number would have to be 21 to produce a mean of 20. We would say that the sample has $n - 1$ or 4 degrees of freedom. It is as if the sample had one less observation—the inclusion of degrees of freedom in the calculation adjusts for this fact.

**degrees of freedom**
Number of observations in a statistical problem that are free to vary.

# Goodness of Fit

## Chi-Square Test

As noted earlier in the text, data collected in surveys are often analyzed by means of one-way frequency counts and cross tabulations.[6] The purpose of a cross tabulation is to study relationships among variables. The question is, do the numbers of responses that fall into the various categories differ from what one would expect? For example, a study might involve partitioning users into groups by gender (male, female), age (under 18, 18 to 35, over 35), or income level (low, middle, high) and cross tabulating on the basis of answers to questions about preferred brand or level of use. The **chi-square** $(\chi^2)$ **test** enables the research analyst to determine whether an observed pattern of frequencies corresponds to, or fits, an "expected" pattern.[7] It tests the "goodness of fit" of the observed distribution to an expected distribution. We will look at the application of this technique to test distributions of cross-tabulated categorical data for a single sample and for two independent samples. A case where chi-square is used is provided in the Practicing Marketing Research feature below.

**chi-square test**
Test of the goodness of fit between the observed distribution and the expected distribution of a variable.

# PRACTICING MARKETING RESEARCH

## Study Results Using Chi-Square Guide Improvements-Myrtle Beach Golf Passport Program[8]

Since the opening of America's first golf course in Charleston in 1786, golf has played a big role in the economy of South Carolina. Economic activity from visiting golfers on

and off golf courses in South Carolina created a $2.72 billion economic impact in 2007.

The unique importance of golf and tourism to the area created an opportunity to study how a local affinity marketing program, Myrtle Beach Golf Passport, affects the large number of visitors to the area, as well as those golfers who live in Myrtle Beach.

Myrtle Beach Golf Passport was created in 1993, enabling eligible residents, as well as those who own second homes in the area, the opportunity to enjoy reduced golf fees all year round. This program has been favorably received by over 10,000 members and has enjoyed a 75 percent annual renewal.

## Build on that success

Looking to build on that success, a marketing research study was undertaken to determine if Passport should be expanded from simply reducing greens fees to include other areas of golf vacation activities such as attractions, restaurants and retail locations.

The Passport group agreed to cooperate in the marketing research effort and helped to generate lists of attractions, restaurants, and retail shopping locations that might become part of the Passport affinity marketing program, as detailed below.

**Attractions.** Ten participating attractions cover events for adults and children and represent the main attractions in the Myrtle Beach area.

**Restaurant types.** Participating restaurants represent a cross-section of restaurants available in the Myrtle Beach area.

**Retail shopping locations.** The 10 retail shopping locations represent both golf specialty retail outlets and general-merchandise retail locations.

The survey questionnaire was distributed e-mail using several different lists. In addition to a variety of demographic items, the survey participants were asked if they were an occasional visitor, seasonal visitor, part-time resident, or full-time resident in the area. They were then grouped into visitor and resident segments. For each of the attractions, restaurant types and retail shopping locations, the participants indicated whether they never, rarely, sometimes or always visited each of the attractions, restaurant types, and retail shopping locations.

The survey yielded responses from 529 residents and 199 visitors, for a total sample size of 728. These data were then analyzed for differences between the visitor and resident segments.

**Low level of willingness.** Overall, the attractions showed fewer participants willing to always visit them, ranging from 1.2 percent for Myrtle Waves to 8.5 percent for Carolina Opry. In contrast, the restaurants showed a low of 2.3 percent for theme restaurants and a high of 33.7 percent for steakhouses. Retailer scores ranged from a low of 1 percent for Old Golf Shop and a high of 57.2 percent for Martin's PGA Superstore.

**Attractions.** Significant chi squares were found for the six attractions listed below along with their p values: Alabama Theater ($p < .0001$), Carolina Opry ($p < .0001$), Dixie Stampede ($p < .002$), Legends in Concert ($p < .0001$), Medieval Times ($p < .0001$), and Ripley's Aquarium ($p < .003$).

In all cases, residents were significantly more willing to visit these attractions compared to visitors. However, the percentages of Passport members who always or sometimes visit any of the attractions were low, averaging only 19.8 percent and ranging from a low of 10.7 percent to 39.0 percent. The unwillingness of the majority of visitor Passport members to visit attractions sometimes or always makes attractions a low priority for inclusion in a discount program for Passport members who are visitors. The results for residents weren't much better, showing an average of 26.1 percent and ranging from a low of 9.9 percent to 43.9 percent of residents who are sometimes or always visiting attractions.

**Restaurant types.** Significant chi squares were found for two restaurant types (listed along with their p values): Italian restaurants ($p < .002$) and seafood restaurants ($p < .008$).

A majority of visitors who are Passport members either sometimes or always visit restaurants in high percen-tages for the following: steakhouses (79.2), seafood (77.8 percent), Italian (68.0 percent), and sports bars (51.1 percent).

Although residents and visitors showed no significant difference for steakhouses, the combined percentage for all Passport members who say they either sometimes or always visit steakhouse restaurants was 83.6 percent, the highest for restaurants as a group.

**Retail shopping locations.** Significant chi squares were found for the five retail shopping locations, listed here along with their p values: Coastal Grand Mall ($p < .0001$), Colonial Mall ($p < .04$), Golf Dimensions Superstore ($p < .044$), Inlet Square Mall ($p < .0001$), and MacFrugal's Golf (Murrells Inlet) ($p < .034$).

A majority of visitors who are Passport members either sometimes or always visit retail shopping locations in high percentages.

The most frequently visited retail shopping locations are either golf specialty stores or diversified retail centers.

## Recommendations

The study results were presented by the research team to the Myrtle Beach Area Golf Course Owners Association at a golf owners' conference. The following recommendations were made:

- The opportunities for offering discounts in the Passport program are, in descending order of potential value: shopping, restaurants, and attractions.

- Since a majority of Passport owners who were either residents or visitors did not indicate they either sometimes or always go to any of the attractions, this category was not recommended by the research team for discount offers. The lack of a broad appeal indicates no interest.

■ Discounts for steakhouses and seafood restaurants were highly recommended by the research team for both visitor and resident Passport members. This recommendation was based on high percentages of both segments saying they would either sometimes or always visit a steakhouse or seafood restaurant.

Discounts at retail shopping outlets were also recommended by the research team, but were confined to golf shops. Merchandise discounts were made available through Passport for members and guests at most pro shops (10 percent), Golf Dimensions (10 percent), and Callaway Performance Center (10 percent).

## Utilization has been high

All of these special discounts have been made available and marketed on the enhanced owners' website, myrtlebeachgolfpassport.com. Utilization has been high on the 81 courses represented on the website, and the program may be expanded to include more restaurants and golf retail outlets if partners can be found.

## Questions

1. What did the chi-square statistic tell the researchers in this case?

2. What did they find regarding the potential value of shopping, restaurants, and attractions?

**Chi-Square Test of a Single Sample** Suppose the marketing manager of a retail electronics chain needs to test the effectiveness of three special deals (deal 1, deal 2, and deal 3). Each deal will be offered for a month. The manager wants to measure the effect of each deal on the number of customers visiting a test store during the time the deal is on. The number of customers visiting the store under each deal is as follows:

| Deal | Month | Customers per Month |
|------|-------|---------------------|
| 1 | April | 11,700 |
| 2 | May | 12,100 |
| 3 | June | 11,780 |
| Total | | 35,580 |

The marketing manager needs to know whether there is a significant difference between the numbers of customers visiting the store during the time periods covered by the three deals. The chi-square $(\chi^2)$ one-sample test is the appropriate test to use to answer this question. This test is applied as follows:

1. Specify the null and alternative hypotheses.
   - Null hypothesis $H_0$: The numbers of customers visiting the store under the various deals are equal.
   - Alternative hypothesis $H_a$: There is a significant difference in the numbers of customers visiting the store under the various deals.

2. Determine the number of visitors who would be expected in each category if the null hypothesis were correct $(E_i)$. In this example, the null hypothesis is that there is no difference in the numbers of customers attracted by the different deals. Therefore, an equal number of customers would be expected under each deal. Of course, this assumes that no other factors influenced the number of visits to the store. Under the null (no difference) hypothesis, the expected number of customers visiting the store in each deal period would be computed as follows:

$$E_i = \frac{TV}{N}$$

where $TV$ = total number of visits

$N$ = total number of visits

Thus,

$$\chi^2 = \frac{35,580}{3} = 11,860$$

The researcher should always check for cells in which small expected frequencies occur because they can distort $\chi^2$ results. No more than 20 percent of the categories should have an expected frequency of less than 5, and none should have an expected frequency of less than 1. This is not a problem in this case.

**3.** Calculate the $\chi^2$ value, using the formula

$$\chi^2 = \sum_{i=1}^{k} \frac{(O_i - E_i)^2}{E_i}$$

For this example,

$O_i$ = observed number in $i$th category

where $E_i$ = expected number in $i$th category

$k$ = number of categories

For this example,

$$\chi^2 = \frac{(11,700 - 11,860)^2}{11,860} + \frac{(12,100 - 11,860)^2}{11,860} + \frac{(11,780 - 11,860)^2}{11,860}$$

$$= 7.6$$

**4.** Select the level of significance $\alpha$. If the .05 level of significance ($\alpha$) is selected, the tabular $\chi^2$ value with 2 degrees of freedom ($k - 1$) is 5.99. (See Exhibit 4 in Appendix 3 for $k - 1 = 2$ d.f., $\alpha = .05$.)

**5.** State the result. Because the calculated $\chi^2$ value (7.6) is higher than the table value (5.99), we *reject the null hypothesis*. Therefore, we conclude with 95 percent confidence that customer response to the deals was significantly different. Unfortunately, this test tells us only that the overall variation among the cell frequencies is greater than would be expected by chance. It does not tell us whether any individual cell is significantly different from the others.

**Chi-Square Test of Two Independent Samples** Marketing researchers often need to determine whether there is any association between two or more variables. Before formulation of a marketing strategy, questions such as the following may need to be answered: Are men and women equally divided into heavy-, medium-, and light-user categories? Are purchasers and nonpurchasers equally divided into low-, middle-, and high-income groups? The chi-square ($\chi^2$) test for two independent samples is the appropriate test in such situations.

| EXHIBIT 16.4 | Data for 32 Test of Two Independent Samples |
|---|---|

| Visits to Convenience Store by Males | | | | Visits to Convenience Stores by Females | | | |
|---|---|---|---|---|---|---|---|
| Number $X_m$ | Frequency $f_m$ | Percent | Cumulative Percent | Number $X_f$ | Frequency $f_f$ | Percent | Cumulative Percent |
| 2 | 2 | 4.4 | 4.4 | 2 | 5 | 7.0 | 7.0 |
| 3 | 5 | 11.1 | 15.6 | 3 | 4 | 5.6 | 12.7 |
| 5 | 7 | 15.6 | 31.1 | 4 | 7 | 9.9 | 22.5 |
| 6 | 2 | 4.4 | 35.6 | 5 | 10 | 14.1 | 36.6 |
| 7 | 1 | 2.2 | 37.8 | 6 | 6 | 8.5 | 45.1 |
| 8 | 2 | 4.4 | 42.2 | 7 | 3 | 4.2 | 49.3 |
| 9 | 1 | 2.2 | 44.4 | 8 | 6 | 8.5 | 57.7 |
| 10 | 7 | 15.6 | 60.0 | 9 | 2 | 2.8 | 60.6 |
| 12 | 3 | 6.7 | 66.7 | 10 | 13 | 18.3 | 78.9 |
| 15 | 5 | 11.1 | 77.8 | 12 | 4 | 5.6 | 84.5 |
| 20 | 6 | 13.3 | 91.1 | 15 | 3 | 4.2 | 88.7 |
| 23 | 1 | 2.2 | 93.3 | 16 | 2 | 2.8 | 91.5 |
| 25 | 1 | 2.2 | 95.6 | 20 | 4 | 5.6 | 97.2 |
| 30 | 1 | 2.2 | 97.8 | 21 | 1 | 1.4 | 98.6 |
| 40 | 1 | 2.2 | 100.0 | 25 | 1 | 1.4 | 100.0 |

$$n_m = 45 \qquad\qquad n_f = 71$$

Mean number of visits by males, $\overline{X}_m = \dfrac{\sum X_m f_m}{45} = 11.5$ 　　　 Mean number of visits by females, $\overline{X}_f = \dfrac{\sum X_f f_f}{71} = 8.5$

The technique will be illustrated using the data from Exhibit 16.4. A convenience store chain wants to determine the nature of the relationship, if any, between gender of customer and frequency of visits to stores in the chain. Frequency of visits has been divided into three categories: 1 to 5 visits per month (light user), 6 to 14 visits per month (medium user), and 16 and above visits per month (heavy user). The steps in conducting this test follow.

1. State the null and alternative hypotheses.
   - Null hypothesis $H_0$: There is no relationship between gender and frequency of visits.
   - Alternative hypothesis $H_a$: There is a significant relationship between gender and frequency of visits.

2. Place the observed (sample) frequencies in a $k \times r$ table (cross tabulation or contingency table), using the $k$ columns for the sample groups and the $r$ rows for the conditions or treatments. Calculate the sum of each row and each column. Record those totals at the margins of the table (they are called *marginal totals*). Also, calculate the total for the entire table ($N$).

| | Male | Female | Totals |
|---|---|---|---|
| 1–5 visits | 14 | 26 | 40 |
| 6–14 visits | 16 | 34 | 50 |
| 15 and above visits | 15 | 11 | 26 |
| Totals | 45 | 71 | 116 |

## SPSS JUMP START FOR CHI-SQUARE TEST

Steps that you need to go through to do the chi-square test problem shown in the book are provided below along with the output produced. Use the data set **Chisqex**, which you can download from the website for the text.

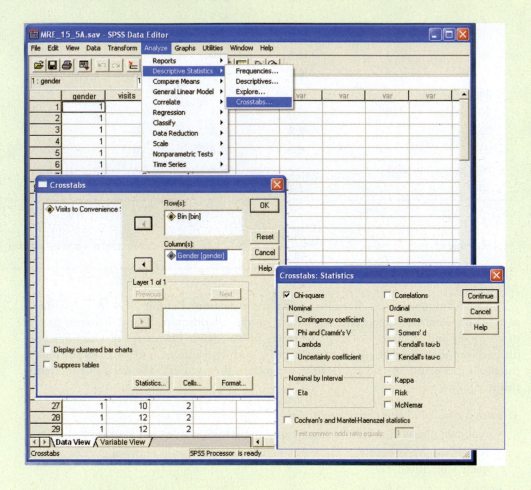

## Steps in SPSS

1. Select Analyze → Descriptive Statistics → Crosstabs.
2. Move **bin** to Rows.
3. Move **gender** to Columns.
4. Click Statistics.
5. Check box for Chi-square.
6. Click Continue.
7. Click OK.

# SPSS Output for Chi-Square Test

## Crosstabs

### Case Processing Summary

| | Cases | | | | | |
|---|---|---|---|---|---|---|
| | Valid | | Missing | | Total | |
| | N | Percent | N | Percent | N | Percent |
| Bin * Gender | 116 | 100.0% | 0 | .0% | 116 | 100.0% |

### Bin * Gender Crosstabulation

Count

| | | Gender | | Total |
|---|---|---|---|---|
| | | Male | Female | |
| Bin | 1-5 visits | 14 | 26 | 40 |
| | 6-14 visits | 16 | 34 | 50 |
| | 15 and above visits | 15 | 11 | 26 |
| Total | | 45 | 71 | 116 |

### Chi-Square Tests

| | Value | df | Asymp. Sig. (2-sided) |
|---|---|---|---|
| Pearson Chi-Square | 5.125[a] | 2 | .077 |
| Likelihood Ratio | 5.024 | 2 | .081 |
| Linear-by-Linear Association | 2.685 | 1 | .101 |
| N of Valid Cases | 116 | | |

a. 0 cells (.0%) have expected count less than 5. The minimum expected count is 10.09.

3. Determine the expected frequency for each cell in the contingency table by calculating the product of the two marginal totals common to that cell and dividing that value by $N$.

| | Male | Female |
|---|---|---|
| 1-5 visits | $\frac{45 \times 40}{116} = 15.5$ | $\frac{71 \times 40}{116} = 24.$ |
| 6-14 visits | $\frac{45 \times 50}{116} = 19.4$ | $\frac{71 \times 50}{116} = 30.$ |
| 15 and above visits | $\frac{45 \times 26}{116} = 10.1$ | $\frac{71 \times 26}{116} = 15.$ |

The $\chi^2$ value will be distorted if more than 20 percent of the cells have an expected frequency of less than 5 or if any cell has an expected frequency of less than 1. The test should not be used under these conditions.

4. Calculate the value of $\chi^2$ using

$$\chi^2 = \sum_{i=1}^{r} \sum_{j=1}^{k} \frac{(O_{ij} - E_{ij})^2}{E_{ij}}$$

where  $O_{ij}$ 5 observed number in the $i$th row of the $j$th column

$E_{ij}$ 5 expected number in the $i$th row of the $j$th column

For this example,

$$\chi^2 = \frac{(14-15.52)^2}{15.52} + \frac{(26-24.48)^2}{24.28} + \frac{(16-19.4)^2}{19.4}$$
$$+ \frac{(34-30.6)^2}{30.6} + \frac{(15-10.09)^2}{10.09} + \frac{(11-15.91)^2}{15.91}$$
$$= 5.1$$

5. State the result. The tabular $\chi^2$ value at a .05 level of significance and $(r-1) \times (k-1) = 2$ degrees of freedom is 5.99 (see Exhibit 4 of Appendix 3). Because the calculated $\chi^2 = 5.1$ is less than the tabular value, we *fail to reject (FTR) the null hypothesis* and conclude that there is no significant difference between males and females in terms of frequency of visits.

# Hypotheses about One Mean

### Z Test

One of the most common goals of marketing research studies is to make some inference about the population mean. If the sample size is large enough ($n \geq 30$), the appropriate test statistic for testing a hypothesis about a single mean is the **Z test**. For small samples ($n \geq 30$) the *t* test with $n - 1$ degrees of freedom (where $n$ = sample size) should be used.

Mobile Connection, a Dallas mobile phone and accessories chain, recently completed a survey of 200 consumers in its market area. One of the questions was "Compared to other mobile phone stores in the area, would you say Mobile Connection is much better than average, somewhat better than average, average, somewhat worse than average, or much worse than average?" Responses were coded as follows:

**Z test**
Hypothesis test used for a single mean if the sample is large enough and drawn at random.

| Response | Code |
|---|---|
| Much better | 5 |
| Somewhat better | 4 |
| Average | 3 |
| Somewhat worse | 2 |
| Much worse | 1 |

The mean rating of Mobile Connection is 3.4. The sample standard deviation is 1.9. How can the management of Mobile Connection be confident that its stores' mean rating is significantly higher than 3 (average in the rating scale)? The $Z$ test for hypotheses about one mean is the appropriate test in this situation. The steps in the procedure follow.

1. Specify the null and alternative hypotheses.
   - Null hypothesis $H_0 : M \leq 3$ ($M$ = response on rating scale) $\leq 3$
   - Alternative hypothesis $H_a : M \leq 3$

2. Specify the level of sampling error ($\alpha$) allowed. For $\alpha = .05$ the table value of $Z(\text{critical}) = 1.64$. (See Exhibit 3 in Appendix 2 for d.f. $= \infty$, .05 significance, one-tail. The table for $t$ is used because $t = Z$ for samples greater than 30.) Management's need to be very confident that the mean rating is significantly higher than 3 is interpreted

to mean that the chance of being wrong because of sampling error should be no more than .05 (an $\alpha = .05$).

3. Determine the sample standard deviation ($S$), which is given as $S = 1.90$.

$$S_{\bar{x}} = \frac{S}{\sqrt{n}}$$

where $S_{\bar{x}}$ = estimated standard error of the mean

4. Calculate the estimated standard error of the mean, using the formula

$$S_{\bar{x}} = \frac{S}{\sqrt{n}}$$

where $S_{\bar{x}}$ = estimated standard error of the mean

In this case,

$$S_{\bar{x}} = \frac{1.9}{\sqrt{200}} = 0.13$$

5. Calculate the test statistic:

$$Z = \frac{(\text{Sample mean}) - \left( \begin{array}{c} \text{Population mean specified} \\ \text{under the null hypothesis} \end{array} \right)}{\text{Estimated standard error of the mean}}$$

$$= \frac{3.4 - 3}{0.13} = 3.07$$

6. State the result. *The null hypothesis can be rejected* because the calculated $Z$ value (3.07) is larger than the critical $Z$ value (1.64). Management of Video Connection can infer with 95 percent confidence that its video stores' mean rating is significantly higher than 3.

## t Test

As noted earlier, for small samples $(n < 30)$, the **t test** with $n - 1$ degrees of freedom is the appropriate test for making statistical inferences. The $t$ distribution also is theoretically correct for large samples $(n \geq 30)$. However, it approaches and becomes indistinguishable from the normal distribution for samples of 30 or more observations. Although the $Z$ test is generally used for large samples, nearly all statistical packages use the $t$ test for all sample sizes.

To see the application of the $t$ test, consider a soft-drink manufacturer that test markets a new soft drink in Denver. Twelve supermarkets in that city are selected at random and the new soft drink is offered for sale in these stores for a limited period. The company estimates that it must sell more than 1,000 cases per week in each store for the brand to be profitable enough to warrant large-scale introduction. Actual average sales per store per week for the test are shown in the accompanying table.

Here is the procedure for testing whether sales per store per week are more than 1,000 cases:

*t* test
Hypothesis test used for a single mean if the sample is too small to use the Z test.

1. Specify the null and alternative hypotheses.
   - Null hypothesis $H_a: \bar{X} \geq 1{,}000$ cases per store per week
   - ($\bar{x}$ = average sales per store per week).
   - Alternative hypothesis $H_a: \bar{X} \geq 1{,}000$ cases per store per week.

| Store | Average Sales per Week ($X_i$) |
|-------|-------------------------------|
| 1 | 870 |
| 2 | 910 |
| 3 | 1,050 |
| 4 | 1,200 |
| 5 | 860 |
| 6 | 1,400 |
| 7 | 1,305 |
| 8 | 890 |
| 9 | 1,250 |
| 10 | 1,100 |
| 11 | 950 |
| 12 | 1,260 |

$$\text{Mean sales per week, } \bar{X} = \frac{\sum_{i=1}^{n} X_i}{n} = 1087.1$$

2. Specify the level of sampling error ($\alpha$) allowed. For $\alpha = .05$, the table value of $t$(critical) = 1.796. (See Exhibit 3 in Appendix 3 for $12 - 1 = 11$ d.f., $\alpha = .05$, one-tail test. A one-tailed $t$ test is appropriate because the new soft drink will be introduced on a large scale only if sales per week are more than 1,000 cases.)

3. Determine the sample standard deviation ($S$) as follows:

$$S = \sqrt{\frac{\sum_{i=1}^{n}(X_i - \bar{X})^2}{n-1}}$$

where
- $X_i$ = observed sales per week in $i$th store
- $\bar{X}$ = average sales per week
- $n$ = number of stores

For the sample data,

$$S = \sqrt{\frac{403{,}822.9}{(12-1)}} = 191.6$$

Further discussion of the $t$ test is provided in the SPSS feature on page 419.

**4.** Calculate the estimated standard error of the mean $\left(S\overline{X}\right)$, using the following formula:

$$S_{\overline{X}} = \frac{S}{\sqrt{n}}$$

$$= \frac{191.6}{\sqrt{12}} = 55.3$$

●
# SPSS JUMP START FOR t TEST

Steps that you need to go through to do the *t*-test problem shown in the book are provided below along with the output produced. Use the data set **TTestex**, which you can download from the website for the text.

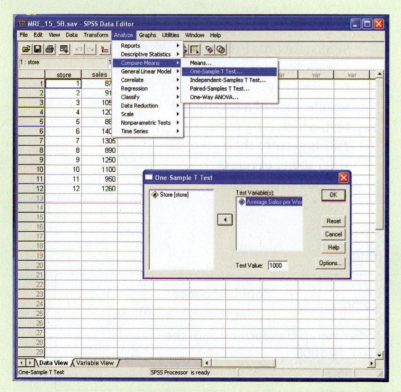

**1.** Select Analyze → Compare Means → One-Sample T Test.

**2.** Move **sales** to Test Variable(s).

**3.** Input 1000 after Test Value.

**4.** Click OK.

## SPSS Output for T Test

**T-Test**

**One-Sample Statistics**

| | N | Mean | Std. Deviation | Std. Error Mean |
|---|---|---|---|---|
| Average Sales per Week | 12 | 1087.08 | 191.602 | 55.311 |

**One-Sample Test**

| | Test Value = 1000 | | | | | |
|---|---|---|---|---|---|---|
| | | | | | 95% Confidence Interval of the Difference | |
| | t | df | Sig. (2-tailed) | Mean Difference | Lower | Upper |
| Average Sales per Week | 1.574 | 11 | .144 | 87.083 | -34.65 | 208.82 |

## Note:

SPSS here only lists the significance for a two-tailed test. We need the significance of a one-tailed test, which is half this. .072 is greater than = .05 so fail to reject the null hypothesis.

**5.** Calculate the *t*-test statistic:

$$Z = \frac{(\text{Sample mean}) - \left(\begin{array}{c}\text{Population mean}\\ \text{under the null hypothesis}\end{array}\right)}{\text{Estimated standard error of the mean}}$$
$$= \frac{1{,}087.1 - 1000}{55.3} = 1.6$$

**6.** State the result. *The null hypothesis cannot be rejected* because the calculated value of *t* is less than the critical value of *t*. Although mean sales per store per week ($\bar{X} = 1087.1$) are higher than 1,000 units, the difference is not statistically significant, based on the 12 stores sampled. On the basis of this test and the decision criterion specified, the large-scale introduction of the new soft drink is not warranted.

# Hypotheses about Two Means

Marketers are frequently interested in testing differences between groups. In the following example of testing the differences between two means, the samples are independent.

The management of a convenience store chain is interested in differences between the store visit rates of men and women. Believing that men visit convenience stores more often than women, management collected data on convenience store visits from 1,000 randomly selected consumers. Testing this hypothesis involves the following steps:

1. Specify the null and alternative hypotheses.
   - Null hypothesis $H_0: M_m - M_f \leq 0$; the mean visit rate of men ($M_m$) is the same as or less than the mean visit rate of women ($M_f$).
   - Alternative hypothesis $H_a: M_m - M_f > 0$; the mean visit rate of men ($M_m$) is higher than the mean visit rate of women ($M_f$).
   
   The observed difference in the two means (Exhibit 16.4) is $11.49 - 8.51 = 2.98$.

2. Set the level of sampling error ($\alpha$). The managers decided that the acceptable level of sampling error for this test is $\alpha = .05$. For $\alpha = .05$ the table value of $Z$(critical) $= 1.64$. (See Exhibit 3 in Appendix 3 for d.f. $= \infty$, .05 significance, one-tail. The table for $t$ is used because $t = Z$ for samples greater than 30.)

3. Calculate the estimated standard error of the differences between the two means as follows:

$$S_{X_{m-f}} = \sqrt{\frac{S_m^2}{n_m} + \frac{S_f^2}{n_f}}$$

where

$S_m$ = estimated standard deviation of population $m$ (men)
$S_f$ = estimated standard deviation of population $f$ (women)
$n_m$ = sample size for sample $m$
$n_f$ = sample size for sample $f$

Therefore,

$$S_{X_{m-f}} = \sqrt{\frac{(8.16)^2}{45} + \frac{(5.23)^2}{71}} = 1.37$$

Note that this formula is for those cases in which the two samples have unequal variances. A separate formula is used when the two samples have equal variances. When this test is run in SAS and many other statistical packages, two $t$ values are provided—one for each variance assumption.

4. Calculate the test statistic $Z$ as follows:

$$Z = \frac{\left(\begin{array}{c}\text{Difference between means} \\ \text{of first and second sample}\end{array}\right) - \left(\begin{array}{c}\text{Difference between means} \\ \text{under the null hypothesis}\end{array}\right)}{\text{Standard error of the differences between the two means}}$$

$$= \frac{(11.49 - 8.51) - 0}{1.37} = 2.18$$

Before launching new services designed for families with an annual income of more than $50,000, the bank needs to be certain about the percentage of its customers who meet or exceed this threshold income.

Comstock Images /Getty Images

**5.** State the result. The calculated value of $Z$ (2.18) is larger than the critical value (1.64), so *the null hypothesis is rejected*. Management can conclude with 95 percent confidence $(1 - \alpha = .95)$ that, on average, men visit convenience stores more often than do women.

# Hypotheses about Proportions

In many situations, researchers are concerned with phenomena that are expressed in terms of percentages.[9] For example, marketers might be interested in testing for the proportion of respondents who prefer brand A versus those who prefer brand B, or those who are brand loyal versus those who are not.

## Proportion in One Sample

**hypothesis test of proportions**

Test to determine whether the difference between proportions is greater than would be expected because of sampling error.

A survey of 500 customers conducted by a major bank indicated that slightly more than 74 percent had family incomes of more than $70,000 per year. If this is true, the bank will develop a special package of services for this group. Before developing and introducing the new package of services, management wants to determine whether the true percentage is greater than 60 percent. The survey results show that 74.3 percent of the bank's customers surveyed reported family incomes of $70,000 or more per year. The procedure for the **hypothesis test of proportions** follows:

1. Specify the null and alternative hypotheses.
   - Null hypothesis $H_0$: $P \leq .60$.
   - Alternative hypothesis $H_a$: $P > .60$ ($P$ = proportion of customers with family incomes of $70,000 or more per year).

2. Specify the level of sampling error ($\alpha$) allowed. For $\alpha = .05$, the table value of $Z$(critical) $= 1.64$. (See Exhibit 3 in Appendix 3 for d.f. $= \infty$, .05 significance, one-tail. The table for $t$ is used because $t = Z$ for samples greater than 30.)

3. Calculate the estimated standard error, using the value of $P$ specified in the null hypothesis:

$$S_P = \sqrt{\frac{P(1-P)}{n-1}}$$

where $P$ = proportion specified in the null hypothesis
$n$ = sample size

Therefore,

$$S_P = \sqrt{\frac{.6(1-.6)}{35-1}} = .022$$

4. Calculate the test statistic as follows:

$$Z = \frac{(\text{Observed proportion} - \text{Proportion under null hypothesis})}{\text{Estimated standard error } (S_P)}$$

$$= \frac{0.743 - 0.60}{.022} = 6.5$$

The *null hypothesis is rejected* because the calculated $Z$ value is larger than the critical $Z$ value. The bank can conclude with 95 percent confidence ($1 - \alpha = .95$) that more than 60 percent of its customers have family incomes of $70,000 or more. Management can introduce the new package of services targeted at this group.

## Two Proportions in Independent Samples

In many instances, management is interested in the difference between the proportions of people in two different groups who engage in a certain activity or have a certain characteristic. For example, management of a convenience store chain had reason to believe, on the basis of a research study, that the percentage of men who visit convenience stores nine or more times per month (heavy users) is larger than the percentage of women who do so. The specifications required and the procedure for testing this hypothesis are as follows.

1. Specify the null and alternative hypotheses:
   - Null hypothesis $H_0$: $P_m - P_f \leq 0$; the proportion of men ($P_m$) reporting nine or more visits per month is the same as or less than the proportion of women ($P_f$) reporting nine or more visits per month.
   - Alternative hypothesis $H_a$: $P_m - P_f > 0$; the proportion of men ($P_m$) reporting nine or more visits per month is greater than the proportion of women ($P_f$) reporting nine or more visits per month.

The sample proportions and the difference can be calculated from Exhibit 16.4 as follows:

$$P_m = \frac{26}{45} = .58$$

$$P_f = \frac{30}{71} = .42$$

$$P_m - P_f = .58 - .42 = .16$$

2. Set the level of sampling error $\alpha$ at .10 (management decision). For $\alpha = .10$, the table value of $Z$(critical) $= 1.28$. (See Exhibit 3 in Appendix 3 for d.f. $= \infty$, .10 significance, one-tail. The table for $t$ is used because $t = Z$ for samples greater than 30.)

3. Calculate the estimated standard error of the differences between the two proportions as follows:

$$S_{P_{m-f}} = \sqrt{P(1-P)\left(\frac{1}{n_m} + \frac{1}{n_f}\right)}$$

where $P = \dfrac{n_m P_m + n_f P_f}{n_m + n_f}$

$P_m$ = proportion in sample $m$ (men)

$P_f$ = proportion in sample $f$ (women)

$n_m$ = size of sample $m$

$n_f$ = size of sample $f$

Therefore,

$$P = \frac{45(.58) + 71(.41)}{45 + 71} = .42$$

$$\text{and } S_{P_{m-f}} = \sqrt{.48(1-.48)\left(\frac{1}{45} + \frac{1}{71}\right)} = .1$$

4. Calculate the test statistic.

$$Z = \frac{\left(\begin{array}{c}\text{Difference between} \\ \text{observed proportions}\end{array}\right) - \left(\begin{array}{c}\text{Difference between proportions} \\ \text{under the null hypothesis}\end{array}\right)}{\text{Estimated standard error of the differences between the two means}}$$

$$= \frac{(.58 - .42) - 0}{.10} = 1.60$$

5. State the result. *The null hypothesis is rejected* because the calculated $Z$ value (1.60) is larger than the critical $Z$ value (1.28 for $\alpha = .10$). Management can conclude with 90 percent confidence $(1 - \alpha = .90)$ that the proportion of men who visit convenience stores nine or more times per month is larger than the proportion of women who do so.

It should be noted that if the level of sampling error $\alpha$ had been set at .05, the critical $Z$ value would equal 1.64. In this case, we would fail to reject (FTR) the null hypothesis because $Z$(calculated) would be smaller than $Z$(critical).

# Analysis of Variance (ANOVA)

When the goal is to test the differences among the means of two or more independent samples, **analysis of variance (ANOVA)** is an appropriate statistical tool. Although it can be used to test differences between two means, ANOVA is more commonly used for hypothesis tests regarding the differences among the means of several ($C$) independent groups (where $C > 3$). It is a statistical technique that permits the researcher to determine whether the variability among or across the $C$ sample means is greater than expected because of sampling error.

The $Z$ and $t$ tests described earlier normally are used to test the null hypothesis when only two sample means are involved. However, in situations in which there are three or more samples, it would be inefficient to test differences between the means two at a time. With five samples and associated means, 10 $t$ tests would be required to test all pairs of means. More important, the use of $Z$ or $t$ tests in situations involving three or more means increases the probability of a type I error. Because these tests must be performed for all possible pairs of means, the more pairs, the more tests that must be performed. And the more tests performed, the more likely it is that one or more tests will show significant differences that are really due to sampling error. At an $\alpha$ of .05, this could be expected to occur in 1 of 20 tests on average.

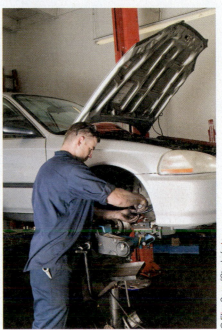

One-way ANOVA is often used to analyze experimental results. Suppose the marketing manager for a chain of brake shops was considering three different services for a possible in-store promotion: wheel alignment, oil change, and tune-up. She was interested in knowing whether there were significant differences in potential sales of the three services.

Sixty similar stores (20 in each of three cities) were selected at random from among those operated by the chain. One of the services was introduced in each of three cities. Other variables under the firm's direct control, such as price and advertising, were kept at the same level during the course of the experiment. The experiment was conducted for a 30-day period, and sales of the new services were recorded for the period.

Average sales for each shop are shown as follows. The question is, are the differences among the means larger than would be expected due to chance?

A brake shop might use analysis of variance to analyze experimental results with respect to several new services before deciding on a particular new service to offer.

| Chicago (Wheel Alignment) | | Cleveland (Oil Change) | | Detroit (Tune-Up) | |
|---|---|---|---|---|---|
| 310 | 318 | 314 | 321 | 337 | 310 |
| 315 | 322 | 315 | 340 | 325 | 312 |
| 305 | 333 | 350 | 318 | 330 | 340 |
| 310 | 315 | 305 | 315 | 345 | 318 |
| 315 | 385 | 299 | 322 | 320 | 322 |
| 345 | 310 | 309 | 295 | 325 | 335 |
| 340 | 312 | 299 | 302 | 328 | 341 |
| 330 | 308 | 312 | 316 | 330 | 340 |
| 320 | 312 | 331 | 294 | 342 | 320 |
| 315 | 340 | 335 | 308 | 330 | 310 |
| $\bar{X} = 323$ | | $\bar{X} = 315$ | | $\bar{X} = 328$ | |

1. Specify the null and alternative hypotheses.
   - Null hypothesis $H_0$: $M_1 = M_2 = M_3$; mean sales of the three items are equal.
   - Alternative hypothesis $H_a$: The variability in group means is greater than would be expected because of sampling error.

2. Sum the squared differences between each subsample mean and the overall sample mean weighted by sample size ($n_j$). This is called the *sum of squares among groups* or *among group variation* (SSA). SSA is calculated as follows:

$$SSA = \sum_{j=1}^{C} n_j (\overline{X}_j - \overline{X}_t)^2$$

In this example, the overall sample mean is

$$\overline{X}_t = \frac{20(323) + 20(315) + 20(328)}{60} = 322$$

Thus,

$$SSA = 20(323 - 322)^2 + 20(315 - 322)^2 + 20(328 - 322)^2$$
$$= 1720$$

The greater the differences among the sample means, the larger the SSA will be.

3. Calculate the variation among group means as measured by the *mean sum of squares among groups* (MSA). The MSA is calculated as follows:

$$MSA = \frac{\text{Sum of squares among groups (SSA)}}{\text{Degrees of freedom (d.f.)}}$$
$$\text{where} \quad \text{Degrees of freedom} = \text{number of groups } (C) - 1$$

In this example,

$$d.f. = 3 - 1 = 2$$

Thus,

$$MSA = \frac{1720}{2} = 860$$

4. Sum the squared differences between each observation ($Xij$) and its associated sample mean $\overline{x}_j$ accumulated over all $C$ levels (groups). Also called the *sum of squares within groups* or *within group variation*, it is generally referred to as the *sum of squared error* (SSE). For this example, the SSE is calculated as follows:

$$SSE = \sum_{j=1}^{C} \sum_{i=1}^{n_j} (X_{ij} - \overline{X}_j)^2$$
$$= (6644) + (4318) + (2270) = 13{,}232$$

5. Calculate the variation within the sample groups as measured by the mean sum of squares within groups. Referred to as *mean square error* (MSE), it represents an estimate of the random error in the data. The MSE is calculated as follows:

$$\text{MSE} = \frac{\text{Sum of squares within groups (SSE)}}{\text{Degrees of freedom (d.f.)}}$$

The number of degrees of freedom is equal to the sum of the sample sizes for all groups minus the number of groups ($C$):

$$\text{d.f.} = \left(\sum_{j=1}^{K} n_j\right) - C$$
$$= (20 + 20 + 20) - 3 = 57$$

Thus,

$$\text{MSE} = \frac{13,232}{57} = 232.14$$

As with the $Z$ distribution and $t$ distribution, a sampling distribution known as the *F distribution* permits the researcher to determine the probability that a particular calculated value of $F$ could have occurred by chance rather than as a result of the treatment effect. The $F$ distribution, like the $t$ distribution, is really a set of distributions whose shape changes slightly depending on the number and size of the samples involved. To use the **F test**, it is necessary to calculate the degrees of freedom for the numerator and the denominator.

**F test**
Test of the probability that a particular calculated value could have been due to chance.

6. Calculate the $F$ statistic as follows:

$$F = \frac{\text{MSA}}{\text{MSE}}$$
$$= \frac{860}{232.14} = 3.70$$

The numerator is the MSA, and the number of degrees of freedom associated with it is 2 (step 3). The denominator is the MSE, and the number of degrees of freedom associated with it is 57 (step 5).

7. State the results. For an alpha of .05, the table value of $F$ (critical) with 2 (numerator) and 57 (denominator) degrees of freedom is approximately 3.15. (See Table 5 in Appendix 3 for d.f. for denominator = 57, d.f. for numerator = 2, .05 significance.) The calculated $F$ value (3.70) is greater than the table value (3.15), and so *the null hypothesis is rejected*. By rejecting the null hypothesis, we conclude that the variability observed in the three means is greater than expected due to chance.

The results of an ANOVA generally are displayed as follows:

| Source of Variation | Sum of Squares | Degrees of Freedom | Mean Square | F Statistic |
|---|---|---|---|---|
| Treatments | 1,720 (SSA) | 2 (C − 1) | 860 (MSA) | 3.70 calculated |
| Error | 13,232 (SSE) | 57 (n − C) | 232.14 (MSE) | |
| Total | 14,592 (SST) | 59 (n − 1) | | |

An example of an ANOVA application is provided in the Practicing Marketing Research feature below.

# PRACTICING MARKETING RESEARCH

## 12 Coins, 3 Shops, 2 Microbiologists, and 1 Test—ANOVA[10]

ANOVA, or the analysis of variance, is a statistical test devised in the 1920s by the English statistician, Ronald A. Fisher. British microbiologists Richard Armstrong and Anthony Hilton, both at Aston University in Birmingham, England, have found it to be the "most appropriate method" for statistical analysis of complex data sets—in this case coins collected from a butcher's shop, news agent's office, and a sandwich shop.

The researchers took four coins randomly from each premise and analyzed them for bacterial populations. Armstrong and Hilton described their procedure as a one-way ANOVA with four replications performed in a randomized test design. The procedure took into account the variation between the various observations and partitioned these variations into portions correlated with the differences they found between the three shops and even the variation among the four coins collected in each shop. Even so, this was a single-factor ANOVA experiment, the only variable being the shop.

They next performed a factorial experiment, studying several factors at once, namely, the influence of the type of dishcloth (cloth or sponge) and the prior rinsing of the material on the quantity of bacteria transferred to a food preparation surface as well as interactions between the two

variables. Then they performed an even more factorially complex ANOVA study to determine how well two strains of bacteria survived on inoculated pound notes measured at 10 time intervals. The ANOVA method enabled them to discern a subtle pattern of three-factor interactions among the variables (such as the slight interaction between surface type and bacterial strain), the decline of bacterial numbers over time in variance with the type of surface, and the decline of one bacterial strain in numbers faster than the other in the same circumstance.

Each of these investigations yielded a data-rich ANOVA table, information that health inspectors surely would find practical and immediately useful. The researchers had high praise for the ANOVA technique, calling it a "powerful method of investigation" for applied microbiology because it could highlight the effect of single factors as well as their interaction. Even better, combining different factors in one study is efficient and often reduces the number of replications needed.

### Questions

1. Can you devise a four-factor ANOVA test for the microbiologists?

2. The microbiologists applied their different ANOVA tests to food-service-related shops. How might it be applied to a dentist's office?

# P Values and Significance Testing

For the various tests discussed in this chapter, a standard—a level of significance and associated critical value of the statistics—is established, and then the value of the statistic is calculated to see whether it beats that standard. If the calculated value of the statistic exceeds the critical value, then the result being tested is said to be statistically significant at that level.

EXHIBIT 16.5    Sample *t*-Test Output

```
Stat.   Grouping: GENDER (pcs. sta)
Basic   Group 1: G_1:1
Stats   Group 2: G_2:0

        Mean     Mean                                    Valid N   Valid N
Variable  G_1:1    G_2:0   t value   df      P           G_1:1     G_2:0

ADDED PAY 16.82292 20.04717  -1.32878  200  .185434       96        106
```

However, this approach does not give the exact probability of getting a computed test statistic that is largely due to chance. The calculations to compute this probability, commonly referred to as the *p* value, are tedious to perform by hand. Fortunately, they are easy for computers. The **p value** is the most demanding level of statistical (not managerial) significance that can be met, based on the calculated value of the statistic. Computer statistical packages usually use one of the following labels to identify the probability that the distance between the hypothesized population parameter and the observed test statistic could have occurred due to chance:

- *p* value
- ≤ PROB
- PROB =

The smaller the *p* value, the smaller the probability that the observed result occurred by chance (sampling error).

An example of computer output showing a *p* value calculation appears in Exhibit 16.5. This analysis shows the results of a *t* test of the differences between means for two independent samples. In this case, the null hypothesis $H_0$ is that there is no difference between what men and women would be willing to pay for a new communications service. (The variable name is GENDER, with the numeric codes of 0 for males and 1 for females. Subjects were asked how much they would be willing to pay per month for a new wireless communications service that was described to them via a videotape. Variable ADDEDPAY is their response to the question.) The results show that women are willing to pay an average of $16.82 for the new service and men are willing to pay $20.04. Is this a significant difference?

The calculated value for *t* of −1.328 indicates, via the associated *p* value of .185, that there is an 18.5 percent chance that the difference is due to sampling error. If, for example, the standard for the test were set at .10 (willing to accept a 10 percent chance of incorrectly rejecting $H_0$), then the analyst would *fail to reject* $H_0$ in this case.

**P value**

Exact probability of getting a computed test statistic that is due to chance. The smaller the *p* value, the smaller the probability that the observed result occurred by chance.

# SUMMARY

The purpose of making statistical inferences is to generalize from sample results to population characteristics. Three important concepts applied to the notion of differences are mathematical differences, managerially important differences, and statistical significance.

A hypothesis is an assumption or theory that a researcher or manager makes about some characteristic of the population being investigated. By testing, the researcher determines whether a hypothesis concerning some characteristic of the population is valid. A statistical hypothesis test permits the researcher to calculate the probability of observing the particular result if the stated hypothesis actually were true. In hypothesis testing, the first step is to specify the hypothesis. Next, an appropriate statistical technique should be selected to test the hypothesis. Then, a decision rule must be specified as the basis for determining whether to reject or fail to reject the hypothesis. Hypothesis tests are subject to two types of errors called type I ($\alpha$ error) and type II ($\beta$ error). A type I error involves rejecting the null hypothesis when it is, in fact, true. A type II error involves failing to reject the null hypothesis when the alternative hypothesis actually is true. Finally, the value of the test statistic is calculated, and a conclusion is stated that summarizes the results of the test.

Marketing researchers often develop cross tabulations, whose purpose usually is to uncover interrelationships among the variables. Usually the researcher needs to determine whether the numbers of subjects, objects, or responses that fall into some set of categories differ from those expected by chance. Thus, a test of goodness of fit of the observed distribution in relation to an expected distribution is appropriate. One common test of goodness of fit is chi square.

Often, marketing researchers need to make inferences about a population mean. If the sample size is equal to or greater than 30 and the sample comes from a normal population, the appropriate test statistic for testing hypotheses about means is the $Z$ test. For small samples, researchers use the $t$ test with $n - 1$ degrees of freedom when making inferences ($n$ is the size of the sample).

When researchers are interested in testing differences between responses to the same variable, such as advertising, by groups with different characteristics, they test for differences between two means. A $Z$ value is calculated and compared to the critical value of $Z$. Based on the result of the comparison, they either reject or fail to reject the null hypothesis. The $Z$ test also can be used to examine hypotheses about proportions from one sample or independent samples.

When researchers need to test for differences among the means of three or more independent samples, analysis of variance is an appropriate statistical tool. It is often used for hypothesis tests regarding the differences among the means of several independent groups. It permits the researcher to test the null hypothesis that there are no significant differences among the population group means.

## KEY TERMS

| | | |
|---|---|---|
| statistical significance **396** | independent samples **408** | hypothesis test of proportions **422** |
| hypothesis **398** | related samples **408** | analysis of variance (ANOVA) **425** |
| null hypothesis **399** | degrees of freedom **409** | $F$ test **427** |
| decision rule **401** | chi-square test **409** | $p$ value **429** |
| type I error ($\alpha$ error) **402** | $Z$ test **416** | |
| type II error ($\beta$ error) **402** | $t$ test **417** | |

## QUESTIONS FOR REVIEW & CRITICAL THINKING

1. Explain the notions of mathematical differences, managerially important differences, and statistical significance. Can results be statistically significant and yet lack managerial importance? Explain your answer.

2. Describe the steps in the procedure for testing hypotheses. Discuss the difference between a null hypothesis and an alternative hypothesis.

3. Distinguish between a type I error and a type II error. What is the relationship between the two?

4. What is meant by the terms *independent samples* and *related samples*? Why is it important for a researcher to determine whether a sample is independent?

5. Your university library is concerned about student desires for library hours on Sunday morning (9:00 A.M.–12:00 P.M.). It has undertaken to survey a random sample of 1,600 undergraduate students (one-half men, one-half women) in each of four status levels (i.e., 400 freshmen, 400 sophomores, 400 juniors, 400 seniors). If the percentages of students preferring Sunday morning hours are those shown below, what conclusions can the library reach?

| | Seniors | Juniors | Sophomores | Freshmen |
|---|---|---|---|---|
| Women | 70 | 53 | 39 | 26 |
| Men | 30 | 48 | 31 | 27 |

6. A local car dealer was attempting to determine which premium would draw the most visitors to its showroom.

An individual who visits the showroom and takes a test drive is given a premium with no obligation. The dealer chose four premiums and offered each for one week. The results are as follows.

| Week | Premium | Total Given Out |
|------|---------|-----------------|
| 1 | Four-foot metal stepladder | 425 |
| 2 | $50 savings bond | 610 |
| 3 | Dinner for four at a local steakhouse | 510 |
| 4 | Six pink flamingos plus an outdoor thermometer | 705 |

Using a chi-square test, what conclusions can you draw regarding the premiums?

7. A market researcher has completed a study of pain relievers. The following table depicts the brands purchased most often, broken down by men versus women. Perform a chi-square test on the data and determine what can be said regarding the cross tabulation.

| Pain Relievers | Men | Women |
|----------------|-----|-------|
| Anacin | 40 | 55 |
| Bayer | 60 | 28 |
| Bufferin | 70 | 97 |
| Cope | 14 | 21 |
| Empirin | 82 | 107 |
| Excedrin | 72 | 84 |
| Excedrin PM | 15 | 11 |
| Vanquish | 20 | 26 |

8. A child psychologist observed 8-year-old children behind a one-way mirror to determine how long they would play with a toy medical kit. The company that designed the toy was attempting to determine whether to give the kit a masculine or a feminine orientation. The lengths of time (in minutes) the children played with the kits are shown below. Calculate the value of $t$ and recommend to management whether the kit should have a male or a female orientation.

| Boys | Girls | Boys | Girls |
|------|-------|------|-------|
| 31 | 26 | 67 | 9 |
| 12 | 38 | 67 | 9 |
| 41 | 20 | 25 | 16 |
| 34 | 32 | 73 | 26 |
| 63 | 16 | 36 | 81 |
| 7 | 45 | 41 | 20 |
| | | 15 | 5 |

9. American Airlines is trying to determine which baggage handling system to put in its new hub terminal in San Juan, Puerto Rico. One system is made by Jano Systems, and the second is manufactured by Dynamic Enterprises. American has installed a small Jano system and a small Dynamic Enterprises system in two of its low-volume terminals. Both terminals handle approximately the same quantity of baggage each month. American has decided to select the system that provides the minimum number of instances in which passengers disembarking must wait 20 minutes or longer for baggage. Analyze the data that follow and determine whether there is a significant difference at the .95 level of confidence between the two systems. If there is a difference, which system should American select?

| Minutes of Waiting | Jano Systems (Frequency) | Dynamic Enterprises (Frequency) |
|--------------------|--------------------------|---------------------------------|
| 10–11 | 4 | 10 |
| 12–13 | 10 | 8 |
| 14–15 | 14 | 14 |
| 16–17 | 4 | 20 |
| 18–19 | 2 | 12 |
| 20–21 | 4 | 6 |
| 22–23 | 2 | 12 |
| 24–25 | 14 | 4 |
| 26–27 | 6 | 13 |
| 28–29 | 10 | 8 |
| 30–31 | 12 | 6 |
| 32–33 | 2 | 8 |
| 34–35 | 2 | 8 |
| 36 or more | 2 | 2 |

10. Menu space is always limited in fast-food restaurants. However, McDonald's has decided that it needs to add one more salad dressing to its menu for its garden salad and chef salad. It has decided to test market four flavors: Caesar, Ranch-Style, Green Goddess, and Russian. Fifty restaurants were selected in the North-Central region to sell each new dressing. Thus, a total of 200 stores were used in the research project. The study was conducted for two weeks; the units of each dressing sold are shown in the following table. As a researcher, you want to know if the differences among the average daily sales of the dressings are larger than can be reasonably expected by chance. If so, which dressing would you recommend be added to the inventory throughout the United States?

| Day | Caesar | Ranch-Style | Green Goddess | Russian |
|---|---|---|---|---|
| 1 | 155 | 143 | 149 | 135 |
| 2 | 157 | 146 | 152 | 136 |
| 3 | 151 | 141 | 146 | 131 |
| 4 | 146 | 136 | 141 | 126 |
| 5 | 181 | 180 | 173 | 115 |
| 6 | 160 | 152 | 170 | 150 |
| 7 | 168 | 157 | 174 | 147 |
| 8 | 157 | 167 | 141 | 130 |
| 9 | 139 | 159 | 129 | 119 |
| 10 | 144 | 154 | 167 | 134 |
| 11 | 158 | 169 | 145 | 144 |
| 12 | 172 | 183 | 190 | 161 |
| 13 | 184 | 195 | 178 | 177 |
| 14 | 161 | 177 | 201 | 151 |

## WORKING THE NET

1. Calculating the *p* value and performing a *Z* or *t* test are much easier when done by computers. For a *p* value calculator, usable without fee, visit: *www.graphpad.com/quickcalcs/PValue1.cfm.*
   For a *Z* test calculator, also free to use, visit: *www.changbioscience.com/stat/ztest.html*

For a *t* test online calculator, available also with no charge, visit: *www.graphpad.com/quickcalcs/ttest1.cfm.*

2. Educators at Tufts University offer a helpful tutorial on reading the output from a one-way analysis of variance, an ANOVA table. Study this at: *http://www. JerryDallal. com/LHSP/aov1out.htm.*

## REAL-LIFE RESEARCH • 16.1

### Analyzing Global Bazaar Segmentation Results

Nala Chan is an advertising executive with Stewart Bakin Advertising. She is responsible for the Global Bazaar account and has just finished reviewing the results of a recent customer study in the top 40 U.S. markets. The study was conducted by Internet panel in 2011 and included people who shopped at

Global Bazaar in the 30 days prior to the date of the survey. The accompanying table shows selected survey results broken down by market segments (columns) identified in research previously conducted by Global. The first two rows are based on actual sales data; the rest of the table shows results from the most recent survey with statistical testing of differences. The first six rows show key metrics used by Global to guide its marketing strategy. Some of the key metrics come from actual sales data, whereas others come from the recent survey. All results, except those for the first two rows, are for the segments or based on segment column totals.

| | Market Segments | | | | |
|---|---|---|---|---|---|
| Variable | Single 18–25 | Single 26–40 | Married 18–25 | Married 26–40 | Married over 40 |
| Percent of current customer base[a] | 15% | 20% | 27% | 29% | 9% |
| Percent of sales[a] | 10% | 13% | 29% | 34% | 14% |

| | Market Segments | | | | |
|---|---|---|---|---|---|
| **Variable** | **Single 18–25** | **Single 26–40** | **Married 18–25** | **Married 26–40** | **Married over 40** |
| Top of mind awareness of Global Bazaar[a] | 34%* | 29%* | 45% | 51%** | 53%** |
| Image index (100-point scale)[b] | 69%* | 70%* | 85% | 92%** | 93%** |
| Likely to shop at Global Bazaar in next 30 days | 21%* | 19%* | 33% | 39%** | 42%** |
| Likely to shop at a competitive store in next 30 days | 38%** | 40%** | 28% | 23%* | 25%* |
| Number of children under 23 years | | | | | |
| Average number | 2.38 | 2.10 | 0 | 0 | 0.29 |
| Income | | | | | |
| Median income | $28,000* | $39,500 | $44,430 | $56.580** | $69,170** |
| % HH income over $75,000 | 29% | 28% | 15.3%* | 28% | 36% |
| Education | | | | | |
| % College degree or more | 9%* | 29%** | 26%** | 21% | 21% |
| Ethnic makeup | | | | | |
| % white | 94% | 92% | 91% | 95% | 95% |
| % black | 3% | 4% | 6% | 2% | 4% |
| % Hispanic | 2% | 2% | 2% | 2% | 1% |
| % Other | 4% | 4% | 3% | 4% | 2% |

[a]Based on actual customer data. Significance testing not appropriate.

[b]Index developed by Global Bazaar based on multiple measures from survey—higher is better.

*Significantly lower than average for all customers surveyed.

**Significantly higher than average for all customers surveyed.

## Questions

1. Which segment provides the largest percentage of sales?

2. In which segment does Global have the highest top of mind awareness?

3. Which two segments account for over 60 percent of sales?

4. In what segment does Global perform most poorly? Explain all the dimensions of their poor performance in this segment.

5. Based on these results, what advice would you give to Global?

# REAL-LIFE RESEARCH • 16.2

## AT&T Wireless

Marc Mulwray is the new marketing research director for AT&T Wireless. Marc was hired to help AT&T address new challenges from Verizon, Sprint, and T-Mobile in the highly competitive environment for wireless customers. New deals and pricing plans, new claims about network speed and new device offerings seem to emerge daily.

One of the crucial challenges for AT&T is that of current customer retention, as other players try to pull customers away with deals, including paying their cost to break their contracts with AT&T. Current customer retention is especially important as growth in the total number of wireless customers has waned given that nearly everyone has a wireless phone or tablet.

Marc has been charged with determining how many current AT&T customers will switch to another wireless provider over the next six months given the current deals offered by competitors. To address this question, Marc and his team designed and fielded a national survey among its current customers. The survey covered a number of areas, including customer demographics, psychographics, wireless usage, and so on; but the key questions relate to their likelihood to switch to various other carriers in response to the deals, pricing and phones they are offering. Surveys were administered online based on e-mail invitations with links to the survey. The survey was completed by 1,200 customers who gave complete answers to all questions.

Initial results indicate that 14 percent of customers are likely to switch. The margin of error is 2.8 percent, which means that (at the 95 percent confidence level) the actual percentage of customers switching could be as low as 11.2 percent or as high as 16.8 percent. Given that AT&T has more than 100 million customers, this is a difference in customers lost of 16.8 million minus 11.2 million or 5.6 million. AT&T senior management is concerned about this error range of ±2.8 percent, which means that error spans a total of 5.6 percentage points. Further customer retention efforts must be budgeted now, and AT&T senior managers want firmer numbers on which to base strategies and budgets.

## Questions

1. How could the error range be reduced without collecting more data? Would you recommend taking this approach? Why or why not?

2. Do you think AT&T senior management would find this approach to reducing the error range satisfactory?

3. If 1,000 more respondents were surveyed and 20 percent of them indicated that they would switch, what would the error range become?

## SPSS EXERCISES FOR CHAPTER 16

## Exercise 1: Analyzing Data Using Cross-Tabulation Analysis

*Note:* Go to the Wiley website at ***www.wiley.com/college/mcdaniel*** and download the Segmenting the College Student Market for Movie Attendance database to SPSS windows. Use the analyze/descriptive statistics/crosstab sequence to obtain cross-tabulated results. In addition, click on the "cell" icon and make sure the observed, expected, total, row, and column boxes are checked. Then, click on the "statistics" icon and check the chi-square box. Once you run the analysis, on the output for the chi-square analysis, you will only need the Pearson chi-square statistic to assess whether or not the results of the crosstab are statistically significant.

In this exercise, we are assessing whether persons who attend movies at movie theaters are demographically different from those who do not. Invoke the crosstab analysis for the following pairs of variables:

a. Q1 & Q11

b. Q1 & Q12

c. Q1 & Q13

d. Q1 & Q14

Answer questions 1–6 using only the sample data. Do not consider the results of the *chi-square test.*

1. What % of males do not attend movies at movie theaters? _____%

2. What % of all respondents are African American and do not attend movies at movie theaters? _____%

3. What % of respondents not attending movies at movie theaters are in the 19–20 age category? _____%

4. Which classification group is most likely to attend movies at movie theaters? _____

5. Which age category is least likely to attend movies at a movie theater? _____

6. Are Caucasians less likely to attend movie theaters than African Americans? _____

For question 7, the objective is to determine statistically whether, in the population from which the sample data was drawn, there were demographic differences in persons who attend and do not attend movies at movie theaters. We do this by using the results of the *chi-square test for independent samples*.

7. Evaluate the chi-square statistic in each of your crosstab tables. Construct a table to summarize the results. For example:

| Variables | Pearson Chi-Square | Degrees of Freedom | Asymp sig. | Explanation |
|---|---|---|---|---|
| Q1(attend or not attend movies at movie theaters & Q12 (gender) | 2.71 | 1 | .10 | We can be 90% confident that based on our sample results, males differ significantly from females in their tendency to attend or not attend movies at movie theaters. |

## Exercise 2: *t/Z* Test for Independent Samples

Use the *analyze/compare means/independent samples t-test* sequence to complete this exercise. This exercise compares males and females regarding the information sources they utilize to search for information about movies at movie theaters. SPSS calls the variable in which the means are being computed the *test variable,* and the variable in which we are grouping responses the *grouping variable.*

*Note:* In statistics, if a sample has fewer than 30 observations or cases, then we invoke a *t* test. If there are 30 or more cases, we invoke a *Z* test, as *the t test values and Z test values are virtually the same; hence SPSS refers only to a t test.*

## Answer the following questions.

The result of the *t* test generates a table of **group statistics**, which is based only on the **sample** data. The other output table generated by the *t* test has statistical data from which we can determine whether or not the sample results can be generalized to the population from which the sample data was drawn. If the *t* test is significant, then we can use the group statistics to determine the specifics of the computed results. For example, a significant *t* test may tell us that males differ from females regarding the importance they place on the newspaper as an information source, but the group statistics tell us "who" considers it most important.

From our *sample data*, can we generalize our results to the population by saying that males differ from females regarding the importance they place on various information sources to get information about movies at movie theaters by:

1. the newspaper (Q7a)?
2. the Internet (Q7b)?
3. phoning in to the movie theater for information (Q7c)?
4. the television (Q7d)?
5. friends or family (Q7e)?

You may want to use the template below to summarize your *t* test results. For example:

| Variables | Variance Prob of Sig Diff | Means Prob of Sig Diff | Interpretation of Results |
|---|---|---|---|
| Q12 (gender) & Q7a (newspaper) | .000 | .035 | 96.5% confident that based on our sample results, males differ significantly from females concerning the importance they place on the newspaper as an information source about movies at movie theaters **(means test).** 100% confident that males and females were significantly different regarding the variance of response within each gender **(variance test).** |

# Exercise 3: ANOVA Test for Independent Samples

Invoke the *analyze/compare means/One-Way ANOVA* sequence to invoke the ANOVA test to complete this exercise. This exercise compares the responses of freshmen, sophomores, juniors, seniors, and graduate students to test for significant differences in the importance placed on several movie theater items. For the ANOVA test, SPSS calls the variable in which means are being computed the *independent variable* and the variable in which we are grouping responses the *factor variable*. Be sure to click the *options* icon and check *descriptives* so that the output will produce the mean responses by student classification for the sample data. As with the *t* test, the ANOVA test produces a table of *descriptives* based on sample data. If our ANOVA test is significant, the *descriptives* can be used to determine, for example, which student classification places the most importance on comfortable seats.

Answer the following questions:

From our sample data, can we generalize our results to the population by saying that there are significant differences across the classification of students by the importance they place on the following movie theater items?

1. Video arcade at the movie theater (Q5a)?
2. Soft drinks and food items (Q5b)
3. Plentiful restrooms (Q5c)
4. Comfortable chairs (Q5d)

5. Auditorium-type seating (Q5e)

6. Size of the movie theater screens (Q5f)

7. Quality of the sound system (Q5g)

8. Number of screens at a movie theater (Q5h)

9. Clean restroom (Q5i)

10. Using only the *descriptive statistics,* which classification group (Q13) places the least amount of importance on clean restrooms (Q5i)? _____

11. Using only the *descriptive statistics,* which classification group (Q13) places the greatest amount of importance on quality of sound system (Q5i)? _____

Summarize the results of your ANOVA analysis using a table similar to the one below.

| Variables | Degrees of Freedom | F-Value | Probability of Insignificance | Interpretation of Results |
|---|---|---|---|---|
| Q5a (importance of a video arcade) & Q13 (student classification) | 4,461 | 12.43 | .001 | 99.9% confident that based on the sample results, students differ significantly by classification concerning the importance placed on there being a video arcade at the movie theater. |

# CHAPTER 17

# Bivariate Correlation and Regression

## LEARNING OBJECTIVES

1. Learn the bivariate analysis of association.

2. Understand bivariate regression analysis.

3. Define the correlation analysis.

In this chapter, we will cover techniques that will permit you to evaluate the relationships between two variables.

# Bivariate Analysis of Association

**bivariate techniques**
Statistical methods of analyzing the relationship between two variables.

**independent variable**
Variable believed to affect the value of the dependent variable.

**dependent variable**
Variable expected to be explained or caused by the independent variable.

In many marketing research studies, the interests of the researcher and manager go beyond issues that can be addressed by the statistical testing of differences discussed in Chapter 16. They may be interested in the degree of association between two variables. Statistical techniques appropriate for this type of analysis are referred to as **bivariate techniques**. When more than two variables are involved, the techniques employed are known as *multivariate techniques*. Multivariate techniques are discussed in Chapter 18.

When the degree of association between two variables is analyzed, the variables are classified as the **independent** (predictor) **variable** and the **dependent** (criterion) **variable**. Independent variables are those that are believed to affect the value of the dependent variable. Independent variables such as price, advertising expenditures, or number of retail outlets may, for example, be used to predict and explain sales or market share of a brand—the dependent variable. Bivariate analysis can help provide answers to questions such as the following: How does the price of our product affect its sales? What is the relationship between household income and expenditures on entertainment?

It must be noted that none of the techniques presented in this chapter can be used to prove that one variable caused an observed change in another variable. They can only be used to describe the nature of statistical relationships between variables.

The analyst has a large number of bivariate techniques from which to choose. This chapter discusses two procedures that are appropriate for metric (ratio or internal) data—bivariate regression and Pearson's product–moment correlation—and one that is appropriate for ordinal (ranking) data—Spearman rank-order correlation. Other statistical procedures that can be used for analyzing the statistical relationship between two variables include the two-group *t* test, chi-square analysis of crosstabs or contingency tables, and ANOVA (analysis of variance) for two groups. All of these procedures were introduced and discussed in Chapter 16.

# Bivariate Regression

**Bivariate regression analysis** is a statistical procedure appropriate for analyzing the relationship between two variables when one is considered the dependent variable and the other the independent variable. For example, a researcher might be interested in analyzing the relationship between sales (dependent variable) and advertising (independent variable). If the relationship between advertising expenditures and sales can be accurately captured by regression analysis, the researcher can use the resulting model to predict sales for different levels of advertising. When the problem involves using two or more independent variables (e.g., advertising and price) to predict the dependent variable of interest, multiple regression analysis (discussed in Chapter 18) is appropriate.

**bivariate regression analysis** Analysis of the strength of the linear relationship between two variables when one is considered the independent variable and the other the dependent variable.

## Nature of the Relationship

One way to study the nature of the relationship between the dependent and the independent variable is to plot the data in a **scatter diagram**. The dependent variable $Y$ is plotted on the vertical axis, whereas the independent variable $X$ is plotted on the horizontal axis. By examining the scatter diagram, one can determine whether the relationship between the two variables, if any, is linear or curvilinear. If the relationship appears to be linear or close to linear, linear regression is appropriate. If a nonlinear relationship is shown in the scatter diagram, curve-fitting nonlinear regression techniques are appropriate. These techniques are beyond the scope of this discussion.

**scatter diagram** Graphic plot of the data with dependent variable on the $Y$ (vertical) axis and the independent variable on the $X$ (horizontal) axis. Shows the nature of the relationship between the two variables, linear or nonlinear.

Exhibit 17.1 depicts several kinds of underlying relationships between the $X$ (independent) and $Y$ (dependent) variables. Scatter diagrams (a) and (b) suggest a positive linear relationship between $X$ and $Y$. However, the linear relationship shown in (b) is not as strong as that portrayed in (a); there is more scatter in the data shown in (b). Diagram (c) shows a perfect negative, or inverse, relationship between variables $X$ and $Y$. An example might be the relationship between price and sales. As price goes up, sales go down. As price goes down, sales go up. Diagrams (d) and (e) show nonlinear relationships between the variables; appropriate curve-fitting techniques should be used to mathematically describe these relationships. The scatter diagram in (f) shows no relationship between $X$ and $Y$. The Practicing Marketing Research box on page 440 provides a creative application of regression.

**Exhibit 17.1**

**Types of Relationships Found in Scatter Diagrams**

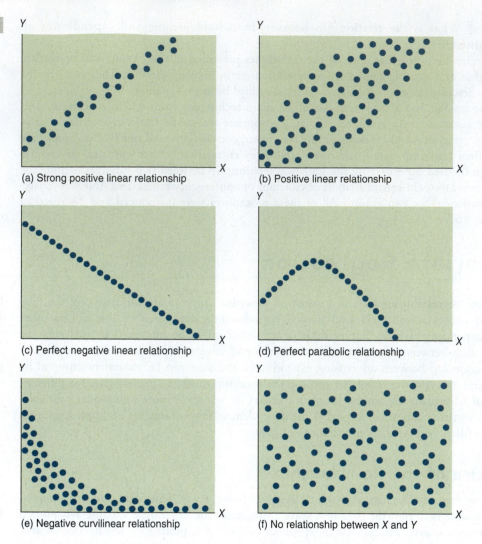

(a) Strong positive linear relationship

(b) Positive linear relationship

(c) Perfect negative linear relationship

(d) Perfect parabolic relationship

(e) Negative curvilinear relationship

(f) No relationship between X and Y

# PRACTICING MARKETING RESEARCH[1]

MTV's *Teen Mom* has been very controversial. But it has become a tool of public health. A study released by the National Bureau of Economic Research declares that MTV's "*Teen Mom* franchise—which also includes the original *Teen Mom* and *16 and Pregnant*—had a measurable effect on reducing teen pregnancy rates.

The study shows that a program on MTV can drive teen behavior in positive ways. The study does explain a baffling statistic, said Phillip Levine, a Wellesley College economist, who co-wrote the report with University of Maryland economist Melissa Kearney. Since 1991, teen pregnancy rates nationwide had been declining by about 2.5 percent per year. But around 2009, the drop suddenly grew more dramatic: about 7.5 percent per year.

"You just don't see numbers like that," said Levine, who has long researched the economics of reproductive health.

The usual-suspect explanations—new types of contraception, new forms of sex ed—didn't seem to fit. A poor economy was a likely factor. But he and Kearney also stumbled across a press release from the National Campaign to Prevent Teen Pregnancy, crediting *16 and Pregnant*.

So they ran the numbers, analyzing Nielsen ratings and related tweets and searches. They cross-referenced teen birth data and did some regression-analysis jujitsu. And they concluded that—while the economy played a role—the show itself caused a 5.7 percent reduction in teen pregnancy rates.

Some have questioned, with good reason, whether correlation really is causation. Still, it's hard to underestimate the power of the *Teen Mom* reach. Tuesday's premiere was the number one show on all of television for viewers between 12 and 34. Which makes it worth asking: What makes the show stick?

It could be that breathless tabloid coverage of booty shorts. But it also could be the trappings of reality TV itself. Levine, who hadn't watched *Teen Mom* before he started the study, said he expected heart-to-hearts between girls and their boyfriends, philosophical discussions about contraception. Instead, he said, "A lot of the show is about conflict"—between a girl and her boyfriend, a girl and her ex, a girl and her parents, and a girl and herself.

Data show that girls have better outcomes when they can talk about sex with trusted, nonjudgmental adults, said

Boston City Councilor Ayanna Pressley, who has worked to develop comprehensive sex ed for Boston schools. If *Teen Mom* turned out to be a supplemental text, would that be so bad? The answer isn't to shut it out, but to watch it very closely. And discuss.

## Questions

1. What did regression analysis show about the impact of *Teen Mom* on teen pregnancy?

2. What, if anything, did regression tell us about the reasons for the decline in teen pregnancies?

## Example of Bivariate Regression

Stop 'N Go conducted a research effort designed to measure the effect of vehicular traffic past a particular store location on annual sales at that location. To control for other factors, researchers identified 20 stores that were virtually identical on all other variables known to have a significant effect on store sales (e.g., square footage, amount of parking, demographics of the surrounding neighborhood). This particular analysis is part of an overall effort by Stop 'N Go to identify and quantify the effects of various factors that affect store sales. The ultimate goal is to develop a model that can be used to screen potential sites for store locations and select, for actual purchase and store construction, the ones that will produce the highest level of sales.

After identifying the 20 sites, Stop 'N Go took a daily traffic count for each site over a 30-day period. In addition, from internal records, the company obtained total sales data for each of the 20 test stores for the preceding 12 months (see Exhibit 17.2).

| EXHIBIT 17.2 | Annual Sales and Average Daily Vehicular Traffic | |
|---|---|---|
| Store Number($i$) | Average Daily Vehicular Count in Thousands ($X_i$) | Annual Sales in Thousands of Dollars ($Y_i$) |
| 1 | 62 | 1121 |
| 2 | 35 | 766 |
| 3 | 36 | 701 |
| 4 | 72 | 1304 |
| 5 | 41 | 832 |
| 6 | 39 | 782 |
| 7 | 49 | 977 |
| 8 | 25 | 503 |
| 9 | 41 | 773 |
| 10 | 39 | 839 |
| 11 | 35 | 893 |
| 12 | 27 | 588 |
| 13 | 55 | 957 |

(continued)

| EXHIBIT 17.2 | (Continued) | |
|:---:|:---:|:---:|
| Store Number(*i*) | Average Daily Vehicular Count in Thousands ($X_i$) | Annual Sales in Thousands of Dollars ($Y_i$) |
| 14 | 38 | 703 |
| 15 | 24 | 497 |
| 16 | 28 | 657 |
| 17 | 53 | 1209 |
| 18 | 55 | 997 |
| 19 | 33 | 844 |
| 20 | 29 | 883 |

A scatterplot of the resulting data is shown in Exhibit 17.3. Visual inspection of the scatterplot suggests that total sales increase as average daily vehicular traffic increases. The question now is how to characterize this relationship in a more explicit, quantitative manner.

**Least-Squares Estimation Procedure** The least-squares procedure is a fairly simple mathematical technique that can be used to fit data for $X$ and $Y$ to a line that best represents the relationship between the two variables. No straight line will perfectly represent every observation in the scatterplot. This is reflected in discrepancies between the actual values (dots on the scatter diagram) and predicted values (values indicated by the line). Any straight line fitted to the data in a scatterplot is subject to error. A number of lines could be drawn that would seem to fit the observations in Exhibit 17.3.

The least-squares procedure results in a straight line that fits the actual observations (dots) better than any other line that could be fitted to the observations. Put another way, the sum of the squared deviations from the line (squared differences between dots and the line) will be lower for this line than for any other line that can be fitted to the observations.

The general equation for the line is $Y = a + bX$. The estimating equation for regression analysis is

$$Y = \hat{a} + \hat{b}X + e$$

where   $Y =$ dependent variable, annual sales in
thousands of dollars

$\hat{a} =$ estimated $Y$ intercept for regression line

$\hat{b} =$ estimated slope of regression line,
regression coefficient

$X =$ independent variable, average daily vehicular
traffic in thousands of vehicles

$e =$ error, difference between actual value and value
predicted by regression line

**Exhibit 17.3**

**Scatterplot of Annual Sales by Traffic**

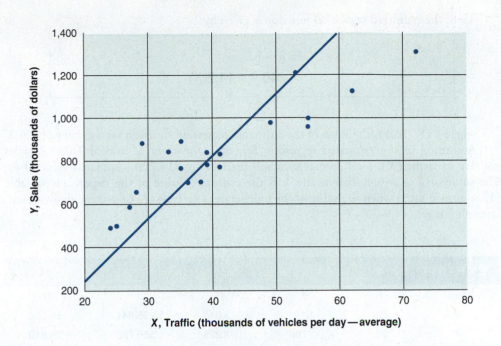

Values for $\hat{a}$ and $\hat{b}$ can be calculated from the following equations:

$$\hat{b} = \frac{\sum X_i Y_i - n\overline{X}\,\overline{Y}}{\sum X_i^2 - n(\overline{X})^2}$$

$$\hat{a} = \overline{Y} - \hat{b}\overline{X}$$

where  $\overline{X}$ = mean value of $X$

  $\overline{Y}$ = mean value of $Y$

  $n$ = sample size (number of units in the sample)

With the data from Exhibit 17.4, $\hat{b}$ is calculated as follows:

$$\hat{b} = \frac{734,083 - 20(40.8)(841.3)}{36,526 - 20(40.8)^2} = 14.7$$

The value of $\hat{a}$ is calculated as follows:

$$\hat{a} = \overline{Y} - \hat{b}\overline{X}$$

$$= 841.3 - 14.72(40.8) = 240.9$$

Thus, the estimated regression function is given by

$$\hat{Y} = \hat{a} + \hat{b}X$$
$$= 240.9 + 14.7(X)$$

where $\hat{Y}$ ($Y$ - hat) is the value of the estimated regression function for a given value of $X$.

According to the estimated regression function, for every additional 1,000 vehicles per day in traffic ($X$), total annual sales will increase by \$14,720 (estimated value of $b$). The value of $\hat{a}$ is 240.9. Technically, $\hat{a}$ is the estimated value of the dependent variable ($Y$, or annual sales) when the value of the independent variable ($X$, or average daily vehicular traffic) is zero.

| EXHIBIT 17.4 | | Least-Squares Computation | | | |
|---|---|---|---|---|---|
| Store | X | Y | X² | Y² | XY |
| 1 | 62 | 1,121 | 3,844 | 1,256,641 | 69,502 |
| 2 | 35 | 766 | 1,225 | 586,756 | 26,810 |
| 3 | 36 | 701 | 1,296 | 491,401 | 25,236 |
| 4 | 72 | 1,304 | 5,184 | 1,700,416 | 93,888 |
| 5 | 41 | 832 | 1,681 | 692,224 | 34,112 |
| 6 | 39 | 782 | 1,521 | 611,524 | 30,498 |
| 7 | 49 | 977 | 2,401 | 954,529 | 47,873 |
| 8 | 25 | 503 | 625 | 253,009 | 12,575 |
| 9 | 41 | 773 | 1,681 | 597,529 | 31,693 |
| 10 | 39 | 839 | 1,521 | 703,921 | 32,721 |
| 11 | 35 | 893 | 1,225 | 797,449 | 31,255 |
| 12 | 27 | 588 | 729 | 345,744 | 15,876 |
| 13 | 55 | 957 | 3,025 | 915,849 | 52,635 |
| 14 | 38 | 703 | 1,444 | 494,209 | 26,714 |
| 15 | 24 | 497 | 576 | 247,009 | 11,928 |
| 16 | 28 | 657 | 784 | 431,649 | 18,396 |
| 17 | 53 | 1,209 | 2,809 | 1,461,681 | 64,077 |
| 18 | 55 | 997 | 3,025 | 994,009 | 54,835 |
| 19 | 33 | 844 | 1,089 | 712,336 | 27,852 |
| 20 | 29 | 883 | 841 | 779,689 | 25,607 |
| Sum | 816 | 16,826 | 36,526 | 15,027,574 | 734,083 |
| Mean | 40.8 | 841.3 | | | |

 • 

## SPSS JUMP START FOR REGRESSION

Steps that you need to go through to do the bivariate regression problem shown in the book follow, along with the output produced. Use the data set **Bivregex**, which you can download from the website for the text.

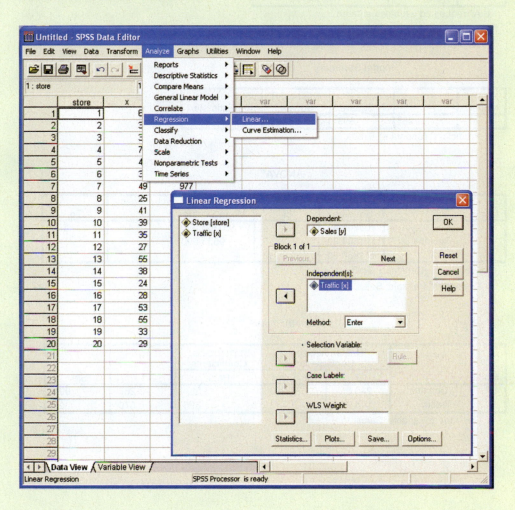

## Steps in SPSS

1. Select Analyze → Regression → Linear.
2. Move **y** to Dependent.
3. Move **x** to Independent(s).
4. Click OK.

# SPSS Output for Regression

## Regression

### Variables Entered/Removed[b]

| Model | Variables Entered | Variables Removed | Method |
|---|---|---|---|
| 1 | Traffic[a] | . | Enter |

a. All requested variables entered.

b. Dependent Variable: Sales

### Model Summary

| Model | R | R Square | Adjusted R Square | Std. Error of the Estimate |
|---|---|---|---|---|
| 1 | .896[a] | .803 | .792 | 97.640 |

a. Predictors: (Constant). Traffic

### ANOVA[b]

| Model | | Sum of Squares | df | Mean Square | F | Sig. |
|---|---|---|---|---|---|---|
| 1 | Regression | 700255.40 | 1 | 700255.399 | 73.451 | .000[a] |
| | Residual | 171604.80 | 18 | 9533.600 | | |
| | Total | 871860.20 | 19 | | | |

a. Predictors: (Constant). Traffic

b. Dependent Variable: Sales

### Coefficients[a]

| Model | | Unstandardized Coefficients | | Standardized Coefficients | t | Sig. |
|---|---|---|---|---|---|---|
| | | B | Std. Error | Beta | | |
| 1 | (Constant) | 240.857 | 73.383 | | 3.282 | .004 |
| | Traffic | 14.717 | 1.717 | .896 | 8.570 | .000 |

a. Dependent Variable: Sales

**Regression Line** Predicted values for $Y$, based on calculated values for $\hat{a}$ and $\hat{b}$ are shown in Exhibit 17.5. In addition, errors for each observation $(Y - \hat{Y})$ are shown. The regression line resulting from the values is plotted in Exhibit 17.6.

**Strength of Association: $R^2$** The estimated regression function describes the nature of the relationship between $X$ and $Y$. Another important factor is the strength of the relationship between the variables. How widely do the actual values of $Y$ differ from the values predicted by the model?

| EXHIBIT 17.5 | | Predicted Values and Errors for Each Observation | | | | |
|---|---|---|---|---|---|---|
| **Store** | **X** | **Y** | **$\hat{Y}$** | **$Y - \hat{Y}$** | **$(Y - \hat{Y})^2$** | **$(Y - \bar{Y})^2$** |
| 1 | 62 | 1,121 | 1,153.3 | –32.2951 | 1,043 | 78,232 |
| 2 | 35 | 766 | 755.9 | 10.05716 | 101 | 5,670 |
| 3 | 36 | 701 | 770.7 | –69.6596 | 4,852 | 19,684 |
| 4 | 72 | 1,304 | 1,300.5 | 3.537362 | 13 | 214,091 |
| 5 | 41 | 832 | 844.2 | –12.2434 | 150 | 86 |
| 6 | 39 | 782 | 814.8 | –32.8098 | 1,076 | 3,516 |
| 7 | 49 | 977 | 962.0 | 15.02264 | 226 | 18,414 |
| 8 | 25 | 503 | 608.8 | –105.775 | 11,188 | 114,447 |
| 9 | 41 | 773 | 844.2 | –71.2434 | 5,076 | 4,665 |
| 10 | 39 | 839 | 814.8 | 24.19015 | 585 | 5 |
| 11 | 35 | 893 | 755.9 | 137.0572 | 18,785 | 2,673 |
| 12 | 27 | 588 | 638.2 | –50.2088 | 2,521 | 64,161 |
| 13 | 55 | 957 | 1,050.3 | –93.2779 | 8,701 | 13,386 |
| 14 | 38 | 703 | 800.1 | –97.0931 | 9,427 | 19,127 |
| 15 | 24 | 497 | 594.1 | –97.0586 | 9,420 | 118,542 |
| 16 | 28 | 657 | 652.9 | 4.074415 | 17 | 33,966 |
| 17 | 53 | 1,209 | 1,020.8 | 188.1556 | 35,403 | 135,203 |
| 18 | 55 | 997 | 1,050.3 | –53.2779 | 2,839 | 24,242 |
| 19 | 33 | 844 | 726.5 | 117.4907 | 13,804 | 7 |
| 20 | 29 | 883 | 667.6 | 215.3577 | 46,379 | 1,739 |
| Sum | 816 | 16,826 | 16,826 | | 171,605 | 871,860 |
| Mean | 40.8 | 841 | | | | |

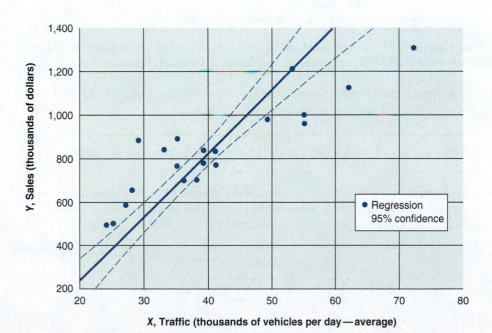

**Exhibit 17.6**

**Least-Squares Regression Line Fitted to Sample Data**

**coefficient of determination**
Percentage of the total variation in the dependent variable explained by the independent variable.

The **coefficient of determination**, denoted by $R^2$, is the measure of the strength of the linear relationship between $X$ and $Y$. The coefficient of determination measures the percentage of the total variation in $Y$ that is "explained" by the variation in $X$. The $R^2$ statistic ranges from 0 to 1. If there is a perfect linear relationship between $X$ and $Y$ (all the variation in $Y$ is explained by the variation in $X$), then $R^2$ equals 1. At the other extreme, if there is no relationship between $X$ and $Y$, then none of the variation in $Y$ is explained by the variation in $X$, and $R^2$ equals 0.

$$R^2 = \frac{\text{Explained variation}}{\text{Total variation}}$$

where

$$\text{Explained variation} = \text{Total variation} - \text{Unexplained variation}$$

The coefficient of determination for the Stop 'N Go data example is computed as follows. [See Exhibit 17.5 for calculation of $(Y - \hat{Y})^2$ and $(Y - \bar{Y})^2$.]

$$
\begin{aligned}
R^2 &= \frac{\text{Total variation} - \text{Unexplained variation}}{\text{Total variation}} \\
&= 1 - \frac{\text{Unexplained variation}}{\text{Total variation}} \\
&= 1 - \frac{\sum_{i=1}^{n}(Y_i - Y_i)^2}{\sum_{i=1}^{n}(Y_i - \bar{Y})^2} \\
&= 1 - \frac{171,605}{871,860} = .803
\end{aligned}
$$

Of the variation in $Y$ (annual sales), 80 percent is explained by the variation in $X$ (average daily vehicular traffic). There is a very strong linear relationship between $X$ and $Y$.

**Statistical Significance of Regression Results**  In computing $R^2$, the total variation in $Y$ was partitioned into two component sums of squares:

$$\text{Total variation} = \text{Explained variation} + \text{Unexplained variation}$$

The total variation is a measure of variation of the observed $Y$ values around their mean $\bar{Y}$. It measures the variation of the $Y$ values without any consideration of the $X$ values.

Total variation, known as the *total sum of squares* (SST), is given by

$$\text{SST} = \sum_{i-1}^{n}(Y_i - \bar{Y})^2 = \sum_{i=1}^{n}Y_i^2 - \left(\frac{\sum_{i=1}^{n}Y_i^2}{n}\right)$$

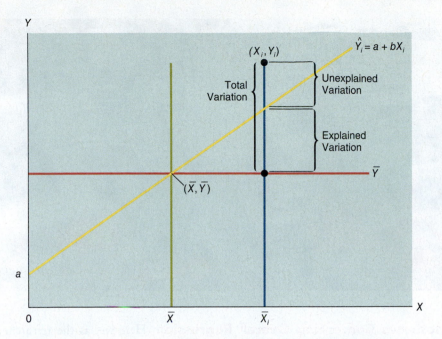

**Exhibit 17.7**

**Measures of Variation in a Regression**

The explained variation, or the **sum of squares due to regression** (SSR), is given by

**sum of squares due to regression**
Variation explained by the regression.

$$SSR = \sum_{i=1}^{n}(\hat{Y}_i - \overline{Y})^2 = a\sum_{i=1}^{n}Y_i + b\sum_{i=1}^{n}X_iY_i - \left(\frac{\sum_{i=1}^{n}Y_i}{n}\right)^2$$

Exhibit 17.7 depicts the various measures of variation (i.e., sum of squares) in a regression. SSR represents the differences between $Y_i$ (the values of $\overline{Y}$ predicted by the estimated regression equation) and $\overline{Y}$ (the average value of $Y$). In a well-fitting regression equation, the variation explained by regression (SSR) will represent a large portion of the total variation (SST). If $Y_i = \hat{Y}_i$ at each value of $X$, then a perfect fit has been achieved. All the observed values of $Y$ are then on the computed regression line. Of course, in that case, $SSR \neq SST$.

The unexplained variation, or **error sum of squares** (SSE), is obtained from

**error sum of squares**
Variation not explained by the regression.

$$SSE = \sum_{i=1}^{n}(Y_i - \hat{Y})^2 = \sum_{i=1}^{n}Y_i^2 - a\sum_{i=1}^{n}Y_i - b\sum_{i=1}^{n}X_iY_i$$

In Exhibit 17.7, note that SSE represents the residual differences (error) between the observed and predicted $Y$ values. Therefore, the unexplained variation is a measure of scatter around the regression line. If the fit were perfect, there would be no scatter around the regression line and SSE would be zero.

In studying the relationship between vehicular traffic and sales, the coefficient of determination may be used to measure the percent of the total variation.

© TIM MCCAIG/iStockphoto

**Hypotheses Concerning Overall Regression** Here we, as the researchers, are interested in hypotheses regarding the computed $R^2$ value for the problem. Is the amount of variance explained in the result (by our model) significantly greater than we would expect due to chance? Or, as with the various statistical tests discussed in Chapter 16, to what extent can we rule out sampling error as an explanation of the results? Analysis of variance (an $F$ test) is used to test the significance of the results.

An analysis of variance table is set up as shown in Exhibit 17.8. The computer output for our example appears in Exhibit 17.9. The breakdowns of the total sum of squares and associated degrees of freedom are displayed in the form of an analysis of variance (ANOVA) table. We use the information in this table to test the significance of the linear relationship between $Y$ and $X$. As noted previously, an $F$ test will be used for this purpose. Our hypotheses are as follows:

- Null hypothesis $H_0$: There is no linear relationship between $X$ (average daily vehicular traffic) and $Y$ (annual sales).
- Alternative hypothesis $H_a$: There is a linear relationship between $X$ and $Y$.

As in other statistical tests, we must choose $\alpha$. This is the likelihood that the observed result occurred by chance, or the probability of incorrectly rejecting the null hypothesis. In this case, we decide on a standard level of significance: $\alpha = .05$. In other words, if the calculated value of $F$ exceeds the tabular value, we are willing to accept a 5 percent chance of incorrectly rejecting the null hypothesis. The value of $F$, or the $F$ ratio, is computed as follows (see Exhibit 17.9):

$$F = \frac{MSR}{MSE}$$
$$= \frac{700,255}{9,534} = 73.5$$

We will reject the null hypothesis if the calculated $F$ statistic is greater than or equal to the table, or critical, $F$ value. The numerator and denominator degrees of freedom for this $F$ ratio are 1 and 18, respectively. As noted earlier, it was decided that an alpha level of .05 ($\alpha = .05$) should be used.

| EXHIBIT 17.8 | Analysis of Variance | | | |
|---|---|---|---|---|
| Source of Variation | Degrees of Freedom | Sum of Squares | Mean Square | F Statistic |
| Regression (explained) | 1 | SSR | | |
| Residual (unexplained) | $n-2$ | SSE | | |
| Total | $n-1$ | SST | | |

| EXHIBIT 17.9 | Regression Analysis Output | | | | | |
|---|---|---|---|---|---|---|
| STAT. MULTIPLE REGRESS. | Regression Summary for Dependent Variable: R = .89619973 $R^2$ = .80317395 Adjusted $R^2$ = .79223917 F(1,18) = 73.451 p, .00000 Std. Error of estimate: 97.640 | | | | | |
| N = 20 | BETA | St. Err. of BETA | B | St. Err. of B | t(18) | p-level |
| Intercpt X | .896200 | .104570 | 240.8566 14.7168 | 73.38347 1.71717 | 3.282164 8.570374 | .004141 .000000 |

The table, or critical, value of $F$ with 1 (numerator) and 18 (denominator) degrees of freedom at $\alpha = .05$ is 4.49 (see Exhibit 5 in Appendix 2). Because the calculated value of $F$ is greater than the critical value, we reject the null hypothesis and conclude that there is a significant linear relationship between the average daily vehicular traffic ($X$) and annual sales ($Y$). This result is consistent with the high coefficient of determination $R^2$ discussed earlier.

**Hypotheses about the Regression Coefficient ß** Finally, we may be interested in making hypotheses about $\beta$, the regression coefficient. As you may recall, $\beta$ is the estimate of the effect of a one-unit change in $X$ on $Y$. The hypotheses are as follows:

- Null hypothesis $H_0$ : $\beta = 0$.
- Alternative hypothesis $H_a$ : $\beta \neq 0$.

The appropriate test is a $t$ test, and, as you can see from the last line of Exhibit 17.9, the computer program calculates the $t$ value (8.57) and the $p$ value (probability of incorrectly rejecting the null hypothesis of .0000). See Chapter 16 for a more detailed discussion of $P$ values. Given the $\alpha$ criterion of .05, we would reject the null hypothesis in this case.

The Practicing Marketing Research feature below shows how regression can be used to guide customer satisfaction improvement.

# PRACTICING MARKETING RESEARCH[2]

## Using Regression Analysis for Key Driver Analysis

Key driver analysis is a broad term used to cover a variety of analytical techniques. It always involves at least one dependent or criterion variable and one or (typically) multiple independent or predictor variables whose effect on the dependent variable needs to be understood. The dependent variable is usually a measure on which the manager is trying to improve the organization's performance. Examples include overall satisfaction, loyalty, value, and likelihood to recommend.

When conducting a key driver analysis, there is a very important question that needs to be considered: Is the objective of the analysis explanation or prediction?

Answering this question before starting the analysis is very useful because it helps in choosing not only the analytical method to be used but also, to some extent, the choice of variables. When the objective of the analysis is explanation, we try to identify a group of independent variables that can explain variations in the dependent variable and that are actionable. For example, overall satisfaction with a firm can be explained by attribute satisfaction scores. By improving the performance on those attributes identified as key drivers, overall satisfaction can be improved. If the predictors used are not actionable, then the purpose of the analysis is defeated.

In the case of prediction, we try to identify variables that can best predict an outcome. This is different from explanation because the independent variables here do not have to be actionable, since we are not trying to change the dependent variable. As long as the independent variables can be measured, predictions can be made. For example, in the financial services industry, it is important to be able to predict (rather than change) the creditworthiness of a prospective customer from the customer's profile.

Beyond the issue of explanation versus prediction, there are two other questions that help in the choice of analytical technique to be used:

1. Is there one, or more than one, dependent variable?

2. Is the relationship being modeled linear or nonlinear?

In the remainder of this article we will discuss analytical methods that would be appropriate if one or both of these questions is answered in the affirmative.

### Single dependent variable

Key driver analyses often use a single dependent variable, and the most commonly used method is multiple regression analysis. A single scaled dependent variable is explained using multiple independent variables. Typically, the scale for the dependent variable ranges from 5 points to 10 points and is usually an overall measure, such as satisfaction or likelihood to recommend.

The independent variables are some measures of attribute satisfaction, usually measured on the same scale as the dependent variable, but not necessarily. There are two main

parts to the output that are of interest to the manager: the overall fit of the model and the relative importance.

The overall fit of the model is often expressed as $R^2$, or the total variance in the dependent variable that can be explained by the independent variables in the model. $R^2$ values range from 0 to 1, with higher values indicating better fit. For attitudinal research, values in the range of 0.4 to 0.6 are often considered to be good. Relative importance of the independent variables is expressed in the form of coefficients or beta weights. A weight of 0.4 associated with a variable means that a unit change in that variable can lead to a 0.4 unit change in the dependent variable. Thus, beta weights are used to identify the variables that have the most impact on the dependent variable.

While regression models are quite robust and have been used for many years, they do have some drawbacks. The biggest (and perhaps most common) is the problem of multicollinearity. This is a condition where the independent variables have very high correlations among them, and hence, their impact on the dependent variable is distorted. Different approaches can be taken to address this problem.

A data reduction technique such as factor analysis can be used to create factors out of the variables that are highly correlated. Then the factor scores (which are uncorrelated with each other) can be used as independent variables in the regression analysis. Of course, this would make interpretation of the coefficients harder than when individual variables are used. Another method of combating multicollinearity is to identify and eliminate redundant variables before running the regression. But this can be an arbitrary solution that may lead to the elimination of important variables.

## Questions

1. What is key driver analysis? What role does regression analysis play in this type of analysis?

2. How can you use the results from key driver to improve, say, customer satisfaction? Explain.

# Correlation for Metric Data: Pearson's Product–Moment Correlation

**correlation analysis**
Analysis of the degree to which changes in one variable are associated with changes in another.

**Pearson's product–moment correlation**
Correlation analysis technique for use with metric data.

Correlation is the degree to which changes in one variable (the dependent variable) are associated with changes in another. When the relationship is between two variables, the analysis is called simple, or bivariate, **correlation analysis**. With metric data, **Pearson's product–moment correlation** may be used. Additional discussion of issues around this type of analysis is provided in the Practicing Market Research features on page 453 and page 456.

In our example of bivariate regression, we used the coefficient of determination $R^2$ as a measure of the strength of the linear relationship between $X$ and $Y$. Another descriptive measure, called the *coefficient of correlation R*, describes the degree of association between

$X$ and $Y$. It is the square root of the coefficient of determination with the appropriate sign ($+$ or $-$):

$$R = \pm\sqrt{R^2}$$

The value of $R$ can range from $-1$ (perfect negative correlation) to $+1$ (perfect positive correlation). The closer $R$ is to $\pm 1$, the stronger the degree of association between $X$ and $Y$. If $R$ is equal to zero, then there is no association between $X$ and $Y$.

If we had not been interested in estimating the regression function, we could have computed $R$ directly from the data for the convenience store example, using this formula:

$$R = \frac{n\sum XY - (\sum X)(\sum Y)}{\sqrt{[n\sum X^2 - (\sum X)^2][n\sum Y^2 - (\sum Y)^2]}}$$

$$= \frac{20(734,083) - (816)(16,826)}{\sqrt{[20(36,526) - (816)^2][20(15,027,574) - (16,826)^2]}}$$

$$= .896$$

# PRACTICING MARKETING RESEARCH

## Rethinking the Applicability of Pearson's Product–Moment Correlation[3]

Is Pearson's product–moment correlation the best way to test reliability between a test and its retest scores? Maybe not, say Miaofen Yen, PhD, RN, and Li-Hua Lo, PhD, RN, both professors at National Cheng Jung University in Tainan, Taiwan. In statistics, the authors explain, the reliability of a measure means "the proportion of the observed score variance due to the true scores, that is, the ratio of true score variance to total score variance." Typically, statisticians use the Pearson correlation to calculate the reliability of results from test to retest, especially in nursing research, which is the domain of the authors. But research shows that this method has three limitations.

First, Pearson's calculation is designed to show the relationship between two variables, but it is inappropriate to apply this correlation to two data sets on the same variable. Second, when multiple tests are employed, it's hard to discern variations from test to test; when one concept is measured three times, generating three scores, one cannot create correlation coefficients for all three scores at the same time. Third, Pearson's is unable to detect systematic errors (e.g., a miscalibrated measurement device that consistently reads 10 pounds heavier) even though test and retest scores may be "perfectly correlated," as Miaofen and Li-Hua say.

An alternative approach called intraclass correlation, or ICC, and also known as generalizing coefficient, addresses these three limitations. Three issues need to be borne in mind when using ICC: First, the study design should focus on reliability, not correlation; second, the correct statistical model must be selected—either a one-way or a two-way random model depending on study conditions; and third, the number of measures in the study must be carefully considered.

Miaofen Yen and Li-Hua Lo demonstrated the strength of ICC on a study of competence for breast self-examination. The study looked at perceived competence and perceived barriers to the self-exam. The doctors engaged 10 nurses to complete the research study twice over a two-week period, polling them on 20 questions, each with a 5-point scale. Then they used ICC to run the test–retest reliability gauge. The calculations produced two ICC coefficients: The first was a single measure ICC (0.640), and the second was an average measure ICC (0.781). But it was the first result that the researchers found most applicable because in practical terms they would only give the test once.

The ICC value of 0.640 was close to the Pearson's value of 0.643, but ICC showed its merit in the area of discerning systematic error. When a systematic error of 12 points was introduced, the two resulting coefficients were found to be different. Pearson's was 0.643 and ICC was 0.554, demonstrating ICC's greater sensitivity to systematic error and its suitability for test–retest reliability.

## Questions

and evaluate whether ICC would have given better results.

1. Find several published examples of test–retest reliability studies done with Pearson's product–moment correlation

2. Why is Pearson's correlation unable to accurately reflect systematic errors, and how does ICC better accommodate this function?

In this case, the value of $R$ indicates a positive correlation between the average daily vehicular traffic and annual sales. In other words, successively higher levels of sales are associated with successively higher levels of traffic. Issues related to using both bivariate and multivariate correlation to get a more complete picture are discussed in the Practicing Marketing Research feature on page 457.

Another way to summarize and present correlation results is provided in the Practicing Marketing Research feature on page 455.

•

# SPSS JUMP START FOR CORRELATION

Steps that you need to go through to do the correlation problem shown in the book are provided below along with the output produced. Use the data set **Correx**, which you can download from the website for the text.

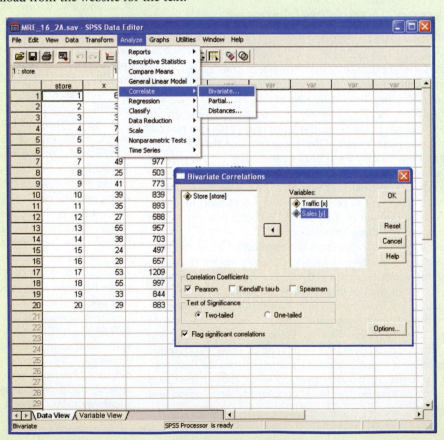

## Steps in SPSS

1. Select *Analyze → Correlate → Bivariate.*
2. Move **x** to Variables.
3. Move **y** to Variables.
4. Click OK.

# SPSS Output for Correlation

## Correlations

**Correlations**

| | | Traffic | Sales |
|---|---|---|---|
| Traffic | Pearson Correlation | 1 | .896** |
| | Sig. (2-tailed) | . | .000 |
| | N | 20 | 20 |
| Sales | Pearson Correlation | .896** | 1 |
| | Sig. (2-tailed) | .000 | . |
| | N | 20 | 20 |

**. Correlation is significant at the 0.01 level

surveysolutions XP

# PRACTICING MARKETING RESEARCH

## Do Your "BESD" When Explaining Correlation Results[4]

A correlation coefficient ranges from −1 to 1, with higher numbers (in either the positive or negative direction), indicating a stronger association between variables.

Two frequently used methods of explaining correlation often fall short of providing clients with a clear understanding of what the results mean.

One way is by computing the "percent of variance accounted for," which is done by squaring the correlation coefficient. Thus, if the correlation between two variables, say education and income, is .5, we can say that 25 percent of the variance in income is accounted for by variation in education.

The second way has sometimes been called the "soft-drink description." This is the process of dividing correlations into the categories of small, medium, and large. Many researchers consider correlations below .3 small, those from .3 to .5 medium, and those greater than .5 large. This way

of explaining the importance of correlations is easily grasped and provides some direction for clients.

A third technique developed by social scientists in the 1980s—the binomial effect size display (BESD)—helps to bring to life the importance (or unimportance) of your results. For example, say your goal was to predict repeat purchase behavior among a group of customers—half of whom have made a repeat purchase, half of whom have not—using a customer attitudes index and the correlation is .50 and that "25 percent of the variance in repeat purchase behavior is explained by variation in scores on the index." Your client might think the result is not very important ("Only 25 percent?!"). He or she would be wrong, and the BESD can show why.

We begin by constructing a 2×2 matrix as shown in Table 1, with two levels for the customer attitudes index (scorers in the top half and scorers in the bottom half) and two levels for purchase behavior (repeat purchase/no repeat purchase). Computing the cell entries begins with the assumption that there is no correlation between the measures. If this were the case, we would expect that 50 percent of the customers who scored in the top half of the index made repeat purchases and 50 percent who scored in the bottom half of the index made repeat purchases. This would give us 50 percent in each cell, since all rows and columns must add to 100 percent.

| TABLE 1 | Example of binomial effect size display for a correlation of Q | | |
|---------|-------------------------------------------------------------|-----|-----|
| | | **REPEAT PURCHASE?** | |
| CUSTOMER ATTITUDES INDEX SCORE | | Yes | No |
| | Top Half | 50% | 50% |
| | Bottom Half | 50% | 50% |

To represent the correlation in the matrix, remove the decimal point from the correlation, divide this number by two, and add the result (25) to the top left cell. Now adjust all cells so that all rows and columns add to 100 (see Table 2).

The BESD tells us that 75 percent of those who scored in the top half on the customer attitudes index made a repeat purchase, and only 25 percent of those scoring in the bottom half did so. The meaning of this result is easily grasped, and the implications are fairly clear. Moving from bottom to top on the customer attitudes index increases

the probability of a repeat purchase by three times—an important result.

| TABLE 2 | Example of binomial effect size display for a correlation of .5 | | |
|---------|-------------------------------------------------------------|-----|-----|
| | | **REPEAT PURCHASE?** | |
| CUSTOMER ATTITUDES INDEX SCORE | | Yes | No |
| | Top Half | 75% | 25% |
| | Bottom Half | 25% | 75% |

The BESD is a flexible technique because it can be used with any kind of data that can be meaningfully dichotomized. So, the next time you want to communicate the importance of your correlation results in a way that is meaningful to your client (and in a way that will keep him or her awake during your presentation), remember to do your BESD.

## Questions

1. What are two traditional ways to explain correlation results to a client? Describe each.

2. What is the BESD approach? Does it make results easier to digest by clients? Why/why not?

# PRACTICING MARKETING RESEARCH

## Pearson's Product–Moment Correlation Fine-Tunes Medical Statistics[5]

Pearson's product–moment correlation is an appropriate statistical tool for cases involving a comparison between two variables, $X$ and $Y$, with metric data. It produces a coefficient, called $r$, which results from dividing the covariance of two variables by the product of their standard deviations. It measures the degree of a linear relationship between two variables, indicating this as a range of $+1$ to $-1$.

Statisticians may thank an English professor named Karl Pearson (1857–1936) for this calculation. In 1911, Pearson founded the Department of Applied Statistics at University College in London, England, the first academic statistics department in the world. Since then, researchers in many fields, especially medicine, have relied on Pearson's to fine-tune their data, as the following medical example vividly shows.

### Chronic Fatigue Syndrome Studies

Researchers at the Human Performance Laboratory and Department of Internal Medicine at Vrije Universiteit Brussel in Brussels, Belgium, assembled a test group of 427 women with clinically diagnosed chronic fatigue syndrome (CFS) and a control group of 204 age-matched women with sedentary lifestyles to participate in an exercise program to test heart rate. The women used a stationary ergometric bicycle and pedaled for 8 to 12 minutes as their oxygen levels, heart rate, and other physical parameters were monitored.

The researchers used the Pearson's calculation to study variations in the associations between variables within each group (test and control). They also employed Pearson's to discern any differences in the exercise parameters between the two groups. The purpose was to yield a better understanding of how exercise capacity varied between both groups. As the data show, Pearson's provided clear-cut correlations.

The calculation showed, for example, the correlation differences in terms of workload at anaerobic threshold

(WAT, reduced oxygen intake) for maximum heart rate was 0.37 for CFS women compared to 0.70 for control-group sedentary women. It also showed that the maximum respiratory quotient for CFS women was positively associated with WAT ($r = 0.26$; $P < .001$ [$P =$ difference]) and negatively associated with HRAT (heart rate at anaerobic threshold: $r = 0.15$; $P < .01$). Among women in the control group, the maximum respiratory quotient was positively correlated with the resting heart rate ($r = 0.17$; $P < .02$), and negatively correlated with WAT ($r = 0.24$; $P < .002$).

Overall, Pearson's showed that "variation in heart rate was strongly related to changes in exercise capacity in patients with CFS." The researchers state that theirs was the first large-scale study to assess exercise capacity in a large population of CFS sufferers; the report, aided by Pearson's correlation, validated the belief that people with CFS have significantly reduced exercise capacity, sometimes up to 50 percent.

## Questions

1. Explain the statistical operating principle that accounts for Pearson's ability to clearly show differences between the two groups as reflected in the $r$ values.

2. Is there an $r$ value, possibly on the high side, that would seem suspect if reported for this study?

# PRACTICING MARKETING RESEARCH

## When Bivariate and Multivariate Correlation Combined Give the Best Picture

Social researchers Douglas Kirby, Karin Coyle, and Jeffrey B. Gould wanted to assess the relationships between conditions of poverty and birthrates among young teenagers in California. They collected data from 1,811 zip codes in which any teenage births had been recorded over a six-year period. They excluded all zip code areas that did not have at least 200 young women aged 15–17 (which they called "young-teenage birthrates") to get a sample of 1,192 zip codes.

Their dependent variable was the mean of the yearly birthrates for women in this group. Their independent variables included 19 demographic features, which they culled from a list of 177 social indicators. Of these 19 independent measures, 3 dealt with ethnicity and 16 represented other factors such as education, employment, marital status, income level, and housing status.

Using these data, the researchers calculated the simple bivariate correlation and regression coefficients between young teenage birthrate and the 19 social measures, one at a time. Their bivariate analysis results showed that the number of families living in conditions of poverty in a given zip code was "highly related" to the birthrate among teenagers 15–17. The bivariate correlations, they concluded, "show that a single variable, the proportion of households living below the poverty line, is highly related to the young-teen-age birthrate." Bivariate analysis also demonstrated that median household income and the number of homes receiving public assistance are also highly related and that three of the four poverty measures have the largest regression coefficients.

But the researchers wanted to look at a bigger picture of relationships and control for the "correlates" of family poverty level. So they shifted to multivariate correlation to make connections among multiple manifestations of poverty, low educational levels and employment status, and high levels of employment. They found that these factors also have a "large impact" on teenage birthrates. Multivariate correlation showed that the number of families living at or below poverty levels "remained by far the most important predictor" of teenage birthrate.[6]

Similarly, researcher and author Clayton E. Cramer found that the sequential application of bivariate and then multivariate correlation produced the best results in his study of the effectiveness of the Brady Handgun Violence Prevention Act of 1993. Bivariate analysis is easy to perform, Cramer says, and works well for certain types of research problems, such as comparing brands of gun ammunition or suggesting that factor A did not cause factor B or that factor A affected factor B.

But when you tackle "hard social problems" such as those associated with crime and gun control, using only two variables is insufficient for figuring out true causality. "Unlike bivariate correlation analysis, multivariate correlation analysis can help identify some truly subtle relationships—where a 3 percent increase in A may cause a 1 percent increase in B." Multivariate analysis is "a devilishly complex technique," and scientists using it can make legitimate mistakes which are hard to detect except by other scientists, Cramer says, but application of it produced strong data that the Brady Law had no effect on homicide rates.[7]

## SUMMARY

The techniques used to analyze the relationship between variables taken two at a time are called bivariate analyses. Bivariate regression analysis allows a single dependent variable to be predicted from knowledge about a single independent variable. One way to examine the underlying relationship between a dependent and an independent variable is to plot them on a scatter diagram. If the relationship appears to be linear, then linear regression analysis may be used. If it is curvilinear, then curve-fitting techniques should be applied. The general equation for a straight line fitted to two variables is given by

$$Y = a + bX$$

where   $Y$ = dependent variable

$X$ = independent variable

$a$ = Y intercept

$b$ = amount Y increases with each unit increase in X

Both $a$ and $b$ are unknown and must be estimated. This process is known as simple linear regression analysis. Bivariate least-squares regression analysis is a mathematical technique for fitting a line to measurements of the two variables $X$ and $Y$. The line is fitted so that the algebraic sum of deviations of the actual observations from the line is zero and the sum of the squared deviations is less than it would be for any other line that might be fitted to the data.

The estimated regression function describes the nature of the relationship between $X$ and $Y$. In addition, researchers want to know the strength of the relationship between the variables. This is measured by the coefficient of determination, denoted by $R^2$. The coefficient of determination measures the percent of the total variation in $Y$ that is "explained" by the variation in $X$. The $R^2$ statistic ranges from 0 to 1. An analysis of variance (ANOVA) approach also can be used for regression analysis. The total variation is known as the total sum of squares (SST). The explained variation, or the sum of squares due to regression (SSR), represents the variability explained by the regression. The unexplained variation is called the error sum of squares (SSE).

Correlation analysis is the measurement of the degree to which changes in one variable are associated with changes in another. Correlation analysis will tell the researcher whether the variables are positively correlated, negatively correlated, or independent.

## KEY TERMS

bivariate techniques **438**

independent variable **438**

dependent variable **438**

scatter diagram **439**

bivariate regression analysis **439**

coefficient of determination **448**

sum of squares due to regression **449**

error sum of squares **449**

correlation analysis **452**

Pearson's product–moment correlation **452**

## QUESTIONS FOR REVIEW & CRITICAL THINKING

1. Give examples of three marketing problems for which correlation analysis would be appropriate.

2. A sales manager of a life insurance firm administered a standard multiple-item job satisfaction scale to all the members of the firm's salesforce. The manager then correlated (Pearson's product–moment correlation) job satisfaction score with years of school completed for each salesperson. The resulting correlation was .11. On the basis of this analysis, the sales manager concluded: "A salesperson's level of education has little to do with his or her job satisfaction." Would you agree or disagree with this conclusion? Explain the basis for your position.

**3.** What purpose does a scatter diagram serve?

**4.** Explain the meaning of the coefficient of determination. What does this coefficient tell the researcher about the nature of the relationship between the dependent and independent variables?

**5.** It has been observed in the past that when an AFC team wins the Super Bowl, the stock market rises in the first quarter of the year in almost every case. When an NFC team wins the Super Bowl, the stock market falls in the first quarter in most cases. Does this mean that the direction of movement of the stock market is caused by which conference wins the Super Bowl? What does this example illustrate?

**6.** The following table gives data collected by a convenience store chain for 20 of its stores.
Column 1: ID number for each store
Column 2: Annual sales for the store for the previous year in thousands of dollars
Column 3: Average number of vehicles that pass the store each day, based on actual traffic counts for one month
Column 4: Total population that lives within a two-mile radius of the store, based on 1990 census data
Column 5: Median family income for households within a two-mile radius of the store, based on 2000 census data

| Store ID No. | Annual Sales (thousands of dollars) | Average Daily Traffic | Population in 2-Mile Radius | Average Income in Area |
|---|---|---|---|---|
| 1 | $1,121 | 61,655 | 17,880 | $28,991 |
| 2 | $ 766 | 35,236 | 13,742 | $14,731 |
| 3 | $ 595 | 35,403 | 19,741 | $ 8,114 |
| 4 | $ 899 | 52,832 | 23,246 | $15,324 |
| 5 | $ 915 | 40,809 | 24,485 | $11,438 |
| 6 | $ 782 | 40,820 | 20,410 | $11,730 |
| 7 | $ 833 | 49,147 | 28,997 | $10,589 |
| 8 | $ 571 | 24,953 | 9,981 | $10,706 |
| 9 | $ 692 | 40,828 | 8,982 | $23,591 |
| 10 | $1,005 | 39,195 | 18,814 | $15,703 |
| 11 | $ 589 | 34,574 | 16,941 | $ 9,015 |
| 12 | $ 671 | 26,639 | 13,319 | $10,065 |
| 13 | $ 903 | 55,083 | 21,482 | $17,365 |
| 14 | $ 703 | 37,892 | 26,524 | $ 7,532 |
| 15 | $ 556 | 24,019 | 14,412 | $ 6,950 |
| 16 | $ 657 | 27,791 | 13,896 | $ 9,855 |
| 17 | $1,209 | 53,438 | 22,444 | $21,589 |
| 18 | $ 997 | 54,835 | 18,096 | $22,659 |
| 19 | $ 844 | 32,916 | 16,458 | $12,660 |
| 20 | $ 883 | 29,139 | 16,609 | $11,618 |

Answer the following:

**a.** Which of the other three variables is the best predictor of sales? Compute correlation coefficients to answer the question.

**b.** Do the following regressions:

**(1)** Sales as a function of average daily traffic

**(2)** Sales as a function of population in a two-mile radius

**c.** Interpret the results of the two regressions.

**7.** Interpret the following:

**a.** $Y = .11 + .009X$, where $Y$ is the likelihood of sending children to college and $X$ is family income in thousands of dollars. Remember: It is family income in *thousands*.

(1) According to our model, how likely is a family with an income of $100,000 to send their children to college?

(2) What is the likelihood for a family with an income of $50,000?

(3) What is the likelihood for a family with an income of $17,500?

(4) Is there some logic to the estimates? Explain.

b. $Y = .25 - .0039X$, where $Y$ is the likelihood of going to a skateboard park and $X$ is age.

(1) According to our model, how likely is a 10-year-old to go to a skateboard park?

(2) What is the likelihood for a 60-year-old?

(3) What is the likelihood for a 40-year-old?

(4) Is there some logic to the estimates? Explain.

8. The following ANOVA summary data are the result of a regression with sales per year (dependent variable) as a function of promotion expenditures per year (independent variable) for a toy company.

$$F = \frac{MSR}{MSE} = \frac{34,276}{4,721}$$

The degrees of freedom are 1 for the numerator and 19 for the denominator. Is the relationship statistically significant at a $= .05$? Comment.

## WORKING THE NET

1. For an informative and practical tutorial with examples and graphs on different regression models with count data (including Poisson, negative binomial, zero-inflated count models, and others), visit: *www.ats.ucla.edu/stat/stata /seminars/count_presentation/count.htm*.

2. For a free online statistical calculator to work with the Pearson's product–moment correlation, see: *www.wessa .net*.

3. Take a look at the video on correlation at *http://www .youtube.com/watch?v=Fd-V9W7dK04*.

## REAL-LIFE RESEARCH • 17.1

### Axcis Athletic Shoes

Fred Luttrell is the new product development manager for Axcis Athletic Shoe Company. He recently completed consumer testing of 12 new shoe concepts. As part of this test, a panel of consumers was asked to rate the 12 shoe concepts on two attributes, overall quality and style. A 10-point scale was used, with anchors at $10 =$ best possible and $1 =$ worst possible.

The panel of 20 consumers met as a group and came up with the ratings as a group. Fred believes that there is a relationship between the style ratings and the overall quality ratings. He believes that shoes receiving higher ratings on style also will tend to receive higher ratings on overall quality. The ratings results for the 12 shoe concepts are as follows.

| Shoe Model | Style Rating | Quality Rating | Shoe Model | Style Rating | Quality Rating |
|---|---|---|---|---|---|
| 1 | 9 | 8 | 7 | 9 | 7 |
| 2 | 7 | 7 | 8 | 7 | 9 |
| 3 | 6 | 8 | 9 | 8 | 6 |
| 4 | 9 | 9 | 10 | 10 | 9 |
| 5 | 8 | 7 | 11 | 6 | 5 |
| 6 | 5 | 5 | 12 | 9 | 10 |

### Questions

1. Which of the statistical procedures covered in this chapter is appropriate for addressing Fred's theory? Why would you choose that technique over the other?

2. Use the technique that you chose to determine whether Fred's theory is supported by the statistical evidence. State the appropriate null and alternative hypotheses. Is Fred's theory supported by the statistical evidence? Why or why not?

# REAL-LIFE RESEARCH • 17.2

## Lambda Social Hotspot

Lambda Networks has had great success selling mobile hotspots with a social twist. With Lambda, you pay for data as you go and take it with you on your 4G mobile hotspot You can post to Facebook, check the news, video chat with your friends, check sports scores, and anything else you do online. Lambda works in 100 major U.S. cities covering approximately 200 million people across the country.

The Lambda personal hotspot has an open Wi-Fi signal, so anyone near you can connect to it  If they do, you'll both receive 100MB of free data  The system lets you own data, instead of it owning you, and your data never expirs. The company has been growing rapidly, but a careful look at the data shows that it is losing 1.3 customers for every two they gain.

Jon Kelly and Jayme Meriah of Lambda have been having a heated debate regarding additional budget that Jayme is seeking to improve customer service and other aspects of the customer experience, including improvements in the company website and development of a mobile version of the website. Recent results from their customer tracking research point to a decided downward trend in customer ratings of their service.

Kelly has taken the position that customer satisfaction is really not that important and that the company should not be spending additional funds for customer service–related activities. He points to the fact that sales are increasing briskly as proof of his position. He would like to spend the additional budget on advertising and promotion activities, believing that this will go farther in improving the growth in sales. Jayme has pointed out that she believes that improving the customer experience and customer satisfaction is important in building customer loyalty and improving customer retention, taking the position that it is less expensive to retain a customer than to get a new customer.

Jon has challenged Jayme, asking for some evidence that there is a relationship between customer satisfaction and customer loyalty. Jayme has been analyzing data from their customer satisfaction tracking survey and, in particular, has used regression analysis to look at the relationship between customer satisfaction and customer loyalty.

The data from 25 randomly selected respondents are provided below. Satisfaction is measured on a 10-point scale with 1 = completely unsatisfied and 10 = completely satisfied. Loyalty is also measured on a 10-point scale, with 1 = "I plan to drop my service in the near future" and 10 = "I plan to continue my service indefinitely."

| Respondent | Satifaction Rating | Loyality Score |
|---|---|---|
| 1 | 9 | 9 |
| 2 | 8 | 8 |
| 3 | 7 | 6 |
| 4 | 8 | 9 |
| 5 | 7 | 8 |
| 6 | 8 | 7 |
| 7 | 9 | 9 |
| 8 | 7 | 7 |
| 9 | 7 | 8 |
| 10 | 8 | 8 |
| 11 | 6 | 6 |
| 12 | 7 | 7 |
| 13 | 8 | 8 |
| 14 | 9 | 9 |
| 15 | 8 | 8 |
| 16 | 7 | 8 |
| 17 | 7 | 6 |
| 18 | 8 | 7 |
| 19 | 8 | 9 |
| 20 | 9 | 8 |
| 21 | 5 | 4 |
| 22 | 9 | 7 |
| 23 | 7 | 8 |
| 24 | 8 | 9 |
| 25 | 8 | 9 |

## Questions

1. Based on the argument, which variable should be the dependent variable? Why do you say that?

2. Run a bivariate regression with your dependent variable. What is the correlation between the two variables? What is the $R^2$ statistic? What does it tell us? What is the regression coefficient? What does it tell us?

3. Does this analysis tend to support Jon's position or Jayme's? Why do you say that?

## SPSS EXERCISES FOR CHAPTER 17

### Exercise 1: Bivariate Regression

Use the *analyze/regression/linear* sequence to invoke bivariate regression analysis. This exercise attempts to explain the variation in the *number of movies the respondent attends in an average month* (*Q3*). Hence, **Q3** is the **dependent variable**. Invoke the bivariate regression procedure for the following pairs of variables:

1. Q3 and Q5d (movie theater item—importance of comfortable chairs)
2. Q3 and Q5e (movie theater item—auditorium type seating)
3. Q3 and Q7a (movie theater information source—newspaper)
4. Q3 and Q7b (movie theater information source—Internet)
5. Q3 and Q7c (movie theater information source—phone in for information)
6. Q3 and Q9 (self-perception of how physically active)
7. and Q10 (self-perception of how socially active)

Summarize the results of the bivariate regression analysis by filling in tables similar to the following ones.

| Model | Regression coefficient | t | Sig. |
|---|---|---|---|
| Constant | | | |
| Q5d | | | |
| Q5e, etc. | | | |

| Variables | Model $R^2$ | Model *F*-value | Sig. |
|---|---|---|---|
| Q5d | | | |
| Q5e, etc. | | | |

1. At the 95 percent level of confidence, which of the regression models (list the pairs of variables) are significant (list the dependent variables)?

   _____

   _____

2. *Interpretation of the regression coefficients:* Use the following table to summarize the regression coefficient, $\beta$, in each of the seven regression models.

| Model | Regression Coefficient $\beta$ | t | Sig. of $\beta$ | Interpretation of the Regression Coefficient $\beta$ |
|---|---|---|---|---|
| Example Q3 & Q5b | .244 | 4.147 | .000 | A one-unit increase in Q5b is associated with a .244 increase in monthly movie attendance |

3. Using the regression results, compute Y(Q3) if Q5d = 4. _____

4. Using the regression results, compute Y(Q3) if Q7c = 2. _____

5. Using the regression results, compute Y(Q3) if Q9 = 3. _____

6. Which of the seven models in the bivariate regression analysis _____ explained the most variation in Q3 (*Hint:* $R^2$)?

7. In which of the seven models does the independent variable's _____ regression coefficient cause the largest change in Q3 for a one-unit change in the independent variable?

## Exercise 2: Pearson's Product–Moment Correlation

Use the *analyze/correlate/bivariate* sequence to invoke bivariate correlation analysis. This exercise utilizes the metric correlation technique (Pearson's), which requires that both variables in the bivariate analysis be of at least interval measurement scale. The objective of this exercise is to examine the association between various pairs of variables.

Invoke the bivariate correlation procedure utilizing the Pearson coefficient to evaluate the association between the following pairs of variables:

a. Q3 and Q8a (purchase option for movie tickets—Internet)

b. Q9 (self-perception of how physically active) and Q10 (self-perception of how socially active)

c. Q8a (purchase option for movie tickets—Internet) and Q7b (importance of the Internet as a source of information about movies at movie theaters)

d. Q5b (movie theater item—importance of soft drinks and food items) and Q9 (self-perception of how physically active)

e. Q5h (movie theater item—number of screens at a movie theater) and Q10 (self-perception of how socially active)

With the results of the bivariate correlation using the Pearson coefficient, fill in a table similar to the following.

| Variables | Pearson Coefficient (include 3) | Probability of an Insignificant Correlation in the Population (based on the Sample Results) | Interpretation of the Results |
| --- | --- | --- | --- |
| | | | |
| | | | |

Questions to Answer: (Assume a significant relationship requires at least a **95 percent** level of confidence.)

1. Of the five correlations computed, which pair of variables had the strongest association? _____

2. Of the three correlations computed, which pair of variables had the weakest association? _____

3. Do people who perceive themselves as more physically active have a greater or lesser need for food and drink at a movie theater? _____

4. Are people who use the Internet to purchase movie tickets more or less likely to use the Internet to get information about movies at movie theaters? _____

surveysolutions XP

Yellow Dog Productions/Getty Images

# Multivariate Data Analysis

## LEARNING OBJECTIVES

1. Define multivariate data analysis.

2. Gain insights into multivariate software.

3. Describe Multiple Discriminant Analysis.

4. Understand cluster analysis.

5. Understand factor analysis.

# Multivariate Analysis Procedures

Advances in computer hardware and software have provided the basis for remarkable developments in the use of powerful statistical procedures for the analysis of marketing research data. These developments have made it possible to analyze large amounts of complex data with relative ease. In particular, multivariate analysis procedures have been extremely significant in this data analysis revolution. The hot job market for people with skills in this area is discussed in the accompanying Practicing Marketing Research feature.

**multivariate analysis**
A general term for statistical procedures that simultaneously analyze multiple measurements on each individual or object under study.

The term **multivariate analysis** refers to the simultaneous analysis of multiple measurements on each individual or object being studied.[1] Some experts consider any simultaneous statistical analysis of more than two variables to be multivariate analysis. Multivariate analysis procedures are extensions of the univariate and bivariate statistical procedures discussed in Chapters 16 and 17.

A number of techniques fall under the heading of multivariate analysis procedures. In this chapter, we will consider five of these techniques:

- Multiple regression analysis
- Multiple discriminant analysis
- Cluster analysis
- Factor analysis
- Conjoint analysis

# PRACTICING MARKETING RESEARCH

## Data Scientist: The Sexiest Job of the Twenty-First Century[2]

Statisticians have been in high demand for many years due to the rapid increase in corporate databases throughout the world. However, the rise of social media and mobile applications has created a flood of information content that overwhelms traditional data storage and analyses. In May 2013, independent research organization SINTEF stated that "a full 90 percent of all the data in the world has been generated over the last two years. The Internet companies are awash with data that can be grouped and utilized."[3] Companies like Yahoo, Google, Facebook, and eBay have had to invent new ways of capturing and processing the massive amount of information they receive on a daily basis. Much of this information lacks the form and structure of traditional databases, requiring new types of analysts and new methods of analysis. These analysts are referred to as data scientists because they work with a variety of different data elements in an exploratory fashion, much like an engineer or scientist. What once was megabytes and gigabytes of facts and figures is now terabytes, petabytes, and exabytes of data that include images, text, video, tweets, blogs, online and offline behaviors, global positioning coordinates, and so on.

One of the key tasks of a data scientist is to make sense of these disparate sources that cannot easily be linked together. All the raw data in the world, in and of itself, is not very useful until patterns and relationships can be identified. Data scientists must use cutting-edge tools, open-source programs, and custom programming to manipulate available information. Beyond these technical skills, they also must understand their company's underlying business model in order to separate meaningful relationships from random patterns and coincidental correlations. Furthermore, data scientists need to be able to prepare clear and concise visuals that connect all these pieces into a coherent story that senior management can comprehend and act upon. Universities have not yet caught up to the requirements of this new role, so corporations are often training employees from within and drawing from other disciplines such as computer science, math, economics, biology, and other sciences. Introverts with limited social skills may be excellent database administrators or statisticians, but they may lack the communication skills required to interact with customers and various departments throughout an organization on their way to uncovering meaningful opportunities and solutions.

Google, for example, employs data scientists to continuously find new ways to deliver the right ads to the most receptive people to maximize advertising effectiveness and ad revenue. LinkedIn studies existing relationships and connections to recommend the best groups for members to join and to identify individuals they should add to their networks. Amazon is constantly revising its algorithms for product recommendations, ad placement and special offers to provide maximum value to its customers. All these companies and thousands others seek data scientists to address these questions and to find opportunities to address needs that are not yet served and often unrecognized at the time of their discovery.

As many data scientists point out, however, the use of statistics is not without its challenges. If not carefully analyzed, the massive amount of data available can overwhelm statistical models, and even strong statistical correlations in the data do not necessarily indicate a causal relationship. Still, as the explosion of available data continues, the ability to identify mathematically abnormal relationships in the data creates a wealth of opportunities. Organizations need to be able to properly explain these abnormalities though, and that's why they need the best analysts and communicators. These skill sets are quickly becoming the kind you can take to the bank!

### Questions

1. Where have you recently seen the use of statistics and data analysis where you might not have expected it? How was it being used?

2. Top companies are finding that many talented analysts and statisticians actually have backgrounds in other disciplines such as economics, mathematics, and computer sciences. How do you think these disciplines relate to and inform the approach to data analysis?

---

You may have been exposed to multiple regression analysis in introductory statistics courses. The remaining procedures are less widely studied. Summary descriptions of the techniques are provided in Exhibit 18.1.

Although awareness of multivariate techniques is far from universal, they have been around for decades and have been widely used for a variety of commercial purposes. Fair Isaac & Co. has built a $740 million business around the commercial use of multivariate techniques.[4]

| EXHIBIT 18.1 | Brief Descriptions of Multivariate Analysis Procedures |
|---|---|
| Multiple regression analysis | Enables the researcher to predict the level of magnitude of a dependent variable based on the levels of more than one independent variable. |
| Multiple discriminant analysis | Enables the researcher to predict group membership on the basis of two or more independent variables. |
| Cluster analysis | Is a procedure for identifying subgroups of individuals or items that are homogeneous within subgroups and different from other subgroups. |
| Factor analysis | Permits the analyst to reduce a set of variables to a smaller set of factors or composite variables by identifying underlying dimensions in the data. |
| Conjoint analysis | Provides a basis for estimating the utility that consumers associate with different product features or attributes. |

The firm and its clients have found that they can predict with surprising accuracy who will pay their bills on time, who will pay late, and who will not pay at all. The federal government uses secret formulas, based on the firm's analyses, to identify tax evaders. Fair Isaac has also shown that results from its multivariate analyses help in identifying the best sales prospects. A range of multivariate procedures are covered in the Practicing Marketing Research feature below.

# Multivariate Software

The computational requirements for the various multivariate procedures discussed in this chapter are substantial. As a practical matter, running the various types of analyses presented requires a computer and appropriate software. Until the late 1980s, most types of multivariate analyses discussed in this chapter were done on mainframe or minicomputers because personal computers were limited in power, memory, storage capacity, and range of software available. Those limitations are in the past. Personal computers have the power to handle just about any problem that a marketing researcher might encounter. Most problems can be solved in a matter of seconds, and a wide variety of outstanding software is available for multivariate analysis. SPSS is the most widely used by professional marketing researchers.

# PRACTICING MARKETING RESEARCH

## Eleven Techniques for Analyzing Data[5]

The astute marketing researcher knows that different marketing questions often require different types of analytical tools. With the wide array of tools at their disposal, researchers need to understand the strengths and weaknesses of each. Here are 11 techniques that researchers may consider—and when.

1. **Multiple Regression Analysis**—analyzes one metric dependent variable in relation to multiple metric independent variables. Normality, linearity, and equal variance assumptions must be carefully observed. Often used in forecasting.

2. **Logistic Regression Analysis**—consists of a variation of multiple regression designed to create a probabilistic assessment of a binary choice, comparing predicted and observed events. Estimates the likelihood of belonging

to each group and predicts consumer behavior in the presence of alternate choices.

3. **Discriminant Analysis**—organizes people and observations into homogeneous groups. Requires metric independent variables with high normality. Used for classifying people according to specific characteristic, for instance, buyer and nonbuyer. Comparable to logistic regression when there are only two categories in the dependent variable, but logistic regression has fewer assumptions to be met.

4. **Multivariate Analysis of Variance (MANOVA)**—compares categorical independent variables with multiple metric dependent variables, determining dependence relationships across various groups. Used in experiment design. If sample sizes are too large, the model becomes impractical.

5. **Factor Analysis**—reduces a wide range of related variables into a smaller set of uncorrelated factors. No dependent variables. Major analysis methods include common factor analysis and principal component analysis.

6. **Cluster Analysis**—creates subgroups out of similar individuals or objects within a large data set. Not all individuals or objects may fit within the defined subgroups. Major clustering methods include hierarchical, nonhierarchical, and a combination of the two.

7. **Multidimensional Scaling (MDS)**—uses perceptual mapping to convert consumer judgments into multidimensional distances. An exploratory technique, useful when dealing with unknown comparison bases. Typically requires four times as many objects as dimensions.

8. **Correspondence Analysis**—creates a perceptual map of object attribute ratings through dimensional reduction. Useful when assessing a wide range of attributes since it does not require that all individuals evaluate every attribute. A combination of independent and dependent variables can result in difficulties in interpretation.

9. **Conjoint Analysis**—also known as *tradeoff analysis*, measures the relative value of the features that comprise a product or service. Results can be used to predict product preferences and forecast demand under a wide variety of scenarios.

10. **Canonical Correlation**—correlates independent and dependent variables simultaneously, using metric independent variables or nonmetric categorical variables. Has fewest restrictions of any multivariate technique, but also fewest assumptions.

11. **Structural Equation Modeling (SEM)**—employs a variety of techniques (e.g., LISREL, latent variable analysis, confirmatory factor analysis) to simultaneously examine numerous relationships between variable sets. SEM is used to develop or validate theoretical models regarding causal relationships between independent variables and one or more dependent variables.

## Questions

1. What questions do you think you should be asking when choosing a multivariate analysis technique?

2. Have you ever done a project in which the analytical technique chosen was not the best fit? What difficulties did you encounter as a result?

SPSS includes a full range of software modules for integrated database creation and management, data transformation and manipulation, graphing, descriptive statistics, and multivariate procedures. It has an easy-to-use, graphical interface. Additional information on the SPSS product line can be found at *http://www.spss.com/software/statistics* and *http://www.spss.com/software/modeler*. A number of other useful resources are available at the SPSS site:

- Technical support, product information, FAQs (frequently asked questions), various downloads, and product reviews
- Examples of successful applications of multivariate analysis to solve real business problems
- Discussions of data mining and data warehousing applications

As we move into discussing analytical techniques, don't forget that we've got to capture the data first to feed our models. This is often the bigger challenge, as discussed in the Practicing Marketing Research feature from the banking industry on page 468. This is particularly true when we move into the realm of big data. We employ many of the same analytical techniques discussed in this chapter, but first we've got to capture the data and get the information in a form we can use. More on this issue later in the chapter.

# PRACTICING MARKETING RESEARCH

## Mastering Data Management[6]

Certain banks are farther along than others in being able to drive customer acquisition through data and analytics, and those institutions have started to master their own data management, says Chandan Sharma, global managing director of financial services marketing for Verizon Enterprise Solutions.

"They've elevated data management to a high-level... they also recognize the importance of creating these functions around data management in the right place within their organization," he observes. "It's then easy to have a cross-enterprise view of the customer."

Sioux Falls, South Dakota–based Great Western Bank ($9 billion in assets) is one example of an institution that has done extensive work around data management, and is now using that work as a stage to launch new customer acquisition and marketing initiatives.

"Our biggest challenge in using data and analytics for marketing and customer acquisition has been data quality, making sure that the codes are there for different documents and records," says Ron Van Zanten, the bank's vice president of data quality.

To address this issue, the bank created a data committee with members from different teams across the organization, Van Zanten shares. The committee, which reports up into Great Western's business intelligence operations council, created standard definitions that teams across the organization now use for different tiers, pricing, and terms on accounts. Those definitions are now standardized across Great Western's various systems, Van Zanten reports.

That data quality work has served to gain buy-in from employees across the organization by building trust in the bank's data, Van Zanten adds. "If you have people in your organization who look at a report, and they say, 'My loan numbers don't match up,' and that's true, then it brings

about doubt across the organization in what you're doing," he explains. "We can now validate our data, and the work that we're doing with it."

Gaining that buy-in across the organization isn't always easy. Van Zanten's team has been working to centralize Great Western's data in its data warehouse. Sometimes parts of an organization can be reluctant to give up their data, he notes.

"We've taken the 'source of truth' from different silos and put it in our warehouse... some people have to give up the keys to their kingdoms. But this is now freeing up our staff to do new things, instead of producing the same old reports," he remarks.

With this clean, well-defined data in hand, Great Western has started to cast a net for more profitable customers to help grow the bank. Great Western used to give away free checking to new customers in its branches, but now with the knowledge gained through its data management, the bank is working to entice customers who will have a more sticky relationship with the bank and buy value-add services, Van Zanten says.

Recently, Great Western started purchasing demographic data from Experian to add to its own data and started to build profiles of what profitable customers look like and how to market to them, Van Zanten reports.

"We've built a new system so when a new customer opens an account, we can see what similar customers like. If they open a debit card, we can offer things like direct deposit and push e-statements... and entice them to a more sticky relationship," he adds.

The bank has also worked to better price its products for profitability by factoring in the cost of expenses on products into their price. "We can bake in the cost of funds transfers and operational costs, and take direct income and expenses on accounts, and then post those against savings and loans," Van Zanten explains.

Great Western can now assign a numeric digit for onboarding a particular account, such as a consumer checking or a small business account, and fully understand the cost of servicing that account.

# Multiple Regression Analysis

Researchers use multiple regression analysis when their goal is to examine the relationship between two or more metric predictor (independent) variables and one metric dependent (criterion) variable.[7] Under certain circumstances, described later in this section, nominal predictor variables can be used if they are recoded as binary variables.

Multiple regression analysis is an extension of bivariate regression, discussed in Chapter 17. Instead of fitting a straight line to observations in a two-dimensional space, multiple regression analysis fits a plane to observations in a multidimensional space. The output obtained and the interpretation are essentially the same as for bivariate regression. The general equation for multiple regression is as follows:

**multiple regression analysis**
Procedure for predicting the level or magnitude of a (metric) dependent variable based on the levels of multiple independent variables.

$$Y = a + b_1 X_1 + b_2 X_2 + b_3 X_3 + \cdots + b_n X_n$$

where
- $Y$ = dependent or criterion variable
- $a$ = estimated constant
- $b_1 - b_n$ = coefficients associat ed with the predictor variables so that a change of one unit $X$ will cause a change of $b_1$ units in $Y$; values for the coefficients are estimated from the regression analysis
- $X_1 - X_n$ = predictor (independent) variables that influence influence the dependent variable

For example, consider the following regression equation (in which values for $a$, $b_1$, and $b_2$ have been estimated by means of regression analysis):

$$\hat{Y} = 200 + 17X_1 + 22X_2$$

where
- $\hat{Y}$ = estimated sales in units
- $X_1$ = advertising expenditures
- $X_2$ = number of salespersons

This equation indicates that sales increase by 17 units for every \$1 increase in advertising and 22 units for every one-unit increase in number of salespersons.

## Applications of Multiple Regression Analysis

There are many possible applications of multiple regression analysis in marketing research:

- Estimating the effects of various marketing mix variables on sales or market share
- Estimating the relationship between various demographic or psychographic factors and the frequency with which certain service businesses are visited
- Determining the relative influence of individual satisfaction elements on overall satisfaction
- Quantifying the relationship between various classification variables, such as age and income, and overall attitude toward a product or service
- Determining which variables are predictive of sales of a particular product or service

Multiple regression analysis can serve one or a combination of two basic purposes: (1) predicting the level of the dependent variable, based on given levels of the independent variables, and (2) understanding the relationship between the independent variables and the dependent variable.

## Multiple Regression Analysis Measures

**coefficient of determination**
Measure of the percentage of the variation in the dependent variable explained by variations in the independent variables.

In the discussion of bivariate regression in Chapter 17, a statistic referred to as the **coefficient of determination**, or $R^2$, was identified as one of the outputs of regression analysis. This statistic can assume values from 0 to 1 and provides a measure of the percentage of the variation in the dependent variable that is explained by variation in the independent variables. For example, if $R^2$ in a given regression analysis is calculated to be .75, this means that 75 percent of the variation in the dependent variable is explained by variation in the independent variables. The analyst would always like to have a calculated $R^2$ close to 1. Frequently, variables are added to a regression model to see what effect they have on the $R^2$ value.

As models get larger, more independent or predictor variables, it is wise to look at a variation of the $R^2$ statistic called **adjusted $R^2$**, as the measure of fit for a regression model. The standard $R^2$ value tends to increase with every predictor variable that is added to the model, regardless of whether that variable truly adds to the explanatory power of the model. The adjusted $R^2$ corrects the coefficient of determination based on the relationship between the number of predictor variables and the overall sample size, producing a more rational estimate of model fit when several independent variables are included. The adjusted $R^2$ will always be less than or equal to $R^2$, being similar to the standard measure when the amount of sample per independent variable is large and producing a negative result when the sample size is very small and there are many predictors included in the model.

**regression coefficients**
Estimates of the effect of individual independent variables on the dependent variable.

The $b$ values, or **regression coefficients**, are estimates of the effect of individual independent variables on the dependent variable. It is appropriate to determine the likelihood that each individual $b$ value is the result of chance. This calculation is part of the output provided by virtually all statistical software packages. Typically, these packages compute the probability of incorrectly rejecting the null hypothesis of $b_n = 0$.

## Dummy Variables

In some situations, the analyst needs to include nominally scaled independent variables such as gender, marital status, occupation, and race in a multiple regression analysis.

Multiple regression analysis can be used to estimate the relationship between various demographic or psychographic factors and the frequency with which a service business is hired.

© Brian McEntire/iStockphoto

**Dummy variables** can be created for this purpose. Dichotomous, nominally scaled independent variables can be transformed into dummy variables by coding one value (e.g., female) as 0 and the other (for example, male) as 1. For nominally scaled independent variables that can assume more than two values, a slightly different approach is required. If there are $K$ categories, $K - 1$ dummy variables are needed to uniquely identify every category. (Including $K$ categories would over identify the model since the last category is represented by "0s" on the previous $K - 1$ variables.) Consider a question regarding racial group with three possible answers: African American, Hispanic, or Caucasian. Binary or dummy variable coding of responses requires the use of two dummy variables, $X_1$ and $X_2$, which might be coded as follows:

**dummy variables**
In regression analysis, a way of representing two-group or dichotomous, nominally scaled independent variables by coding one group as 0 and the other as 1.

|  | $X_1$ | $X_2$ |
|---|---|---|
| If person is African American | 1 | 0 |
| If person is Hispanic | 0 | 1 |
| If person is Caucasian | 0 | 0 |

## Potential Use and Interpretation Problems

The analyst must be sensitive to certain problems that may be encountered in the use and interpretation of multiple regression analysis results. These problems are summarized in the following sections.

**Collinearity** One of the key assumptions of multiple regression analysis is that the independent variables are not correlated (collinear) with each other.[8] If they are correlated, the predicted $Y$ value is unbiased, and the estimated $B$ values (regression coefficients) will have inflated standard errors and will be inaccurate and unstable. Larger than expected coefficients for some $b$ values are compensated for by smaller than expected coefficients for others. This is why you still produce reliable estimates of $Y$ and why you can get sign reversals and wide variations in $b$ values with **collinearity**, but still produce reliable estimates of $Y$.

**collinearity**
Correlation of independent variables with each other, which can bias estimates of regression coefficients.

The simplest way to check for collinearity is to examine the matrix showing the correlations between each variable in the analysis. One rule of thumb is to look for correlations between independent variables of .30 or greater. If correlations of this magnitude exist, then the analyst should check for distortions of the $b$ values. One way to do this is to run regressions with the two or more collinear variables included and then run regressions again with the individual variables. The $b$ values in the regression with all variables in the equation should be similar to the $b$ values computed for the variables run separately.

A number of strategies can be used to deal with collinearity. Two of the most commonly used strategies are (1) to drop one of the variables from the analysis if two variables are heavily correlated with each other and (2) to combine the correlated variables in some fashion (e.g., create an index or use factor analysis to combined related variables) to form a new composite independent variable, which can be used in subsequent regression analyses.

**Causation** Although regression analysis can show that variables are associated or correlated with each other, it cannot prove **causation**. Causal relationships can be confirmed only by other means (see Chapter 9). A strong logical or theoretical basis must be developed to support the idea that a causal relationship exists between the independent variables and the dependent variable. However, even a strong logical base and supporting statistical results demonstrating correlation are only *indicators* of causation.

**causation**
Inference that a change in one variable is responsible for (caused) an observed change in another variable.

**Standardizing Regression Coefficients** The magnitudes of the regression coefficients associated with the various independent variables can be compared directly only if

**scaling of coefficients**
A method of directly comparing the magnitudes of the regression coefficients of independent variables by scaling them in the same units or by standardizing the data.

they are scaled in the same units or if the data have been standardized. Consider the following example:

$$\hat{Y} = 50 + 20X_1 + 20X_2$$

where $\hat{Y}$ = estimated sales volume

$X_1$ = advertising expenditures in thousands of dollars

$X_2$ = number of salespersons

At first glance, it appears that an additional dollar spent on advertising and another salesperson added to the salesforce have equal effects on sales. However, this is not true because $X_1$ and $X_2$ are measured in different kinds of units. Direct comparison of regression coefficients requires that all independent variables be measured in the same units (e.g., dollars or thousands of dollars) or that the data be standardized. *Standardization* is achieved by taking each number in a series, subtracting the mean of the series from the number, and dividing the result by the standard deviation of the series. This process converts any set of numbers to a new set with a mean of 0 and a standard deviation of 1. The formula for the standardization process is as follows:

$$\frac{X_i - \bar{X}}{\sigma}$$

where $X_i$ = individual number from a series of numbers

$\bar{X}$ = mean of the series

$\sigma$ = standard deviation of the series

**classification matrix**
A matrix or table that shows the percentages of people or things correctly and incorrectly classified by the discriminant model.

**Sample Size** The value of $R^2$ is influenced by the number of predictor variables relative to sample size.[9] Several different rules of thumb have been proposed; they suggest that the number of observations should be equal to at least 10 to 15 times the number of predictor variables. For the preceding example (sales volume as a function of advertising expenditures and number of salespersons) with two predictor variables, a minimum of 20 to 30 observations would be required.

# Multiple Discriminant Analysis

**multiple discriminant analysis**
Procedure for predicting group membership for a (nominal or categorical) dependent variable on the basis of two or more independent variables.

**metric scale**
A type of quantitative that provides the most precise measurement.

**nominal or categorical**
A type of nonmetric qualitative data scale that only uses numbers to indicate membership in a group (e.g., 1 = male, 2 = female). Most mathematical and statistical procedures cannot be applied to nominal data.

Although **multiple discriminant analysis** is similar to multiple regression analysis,[10] there are important differences. In the case of multiple regression analysis, the dependent variable must be **metric**; in multiple discriminant analysis, the dependent variable is **nominal or categorical** in nature. For example, the dependent variable might be usage status for a particular product or service. A particular respondent who uses the product or service might be assigned a code of 1 for the dependent variable, and a respondent who does not use it might be assigned a code of 2. Independent variables might include various metric measures, such as age, income, and number of years of education. The goals of multiple discriminant analysis are as follows:

- Determine if there are statistically significant differences between the average discriminant score profiles of two (or more) groups (in this case, users and nonusers).
- Establish a model for classifying individuals or objects into groups on the basis of their values on the independent variables.
- Determine how much of the difference in the average score profiles of the groups is accounted for by each independent variable.

The general discriminant analysis equation follows:

$$Z = b_1X_1 + b_2X_2 + \cdots + b_nX_n$$

$$\text{where} \quad Z = \text{discriminant score}$$
$$b_1 - b_n = \text{discriminant weights}$$
$$X_1 - X_n = \text{independent variables}$$

The **discriminant score**, usually referred to as the *Z score*, is the score derived for each individual or object by means of the equation. This score is the basis for predicting the group to which the particular object or individual belongs. *Discriminant weights*, often referred to as **discriminant coefficients**, are computed by means of the discriminant analysis program. The size of the discriminant weight (or coefficient) associated with a particular independent variable is determined by the variance structure of the variables in the equation. Independent variables with large discriminatory power (large differences between groups) have large weights and those with little discriminatory power have small weights.

The goal of discriminant analysis is the prediction of a categorical variable. The analyst must decide which variables would be expected to be associated with the probability of a person or object falling into one of two or more groups or categories. In a statistical sense, the problem of analyzing the nature of group differences involves finding a linear combination of independent variables (the discriminant function) that shows large differences in group means. Multiple discriminant analysis outperforms multiple regression analysis in some applications where they are both appropriate.

> **discriminant score**
> Score that is the basis for predicting to which group a particular object or individual belongs; also called *Z score*.

> **discriminant coefficient**
> Estimate of the discriminatory power of a particular independent variable; also called *discriminant weight*.

## Applications of Multiple Discriminant Analysis

Discriminant analysis can be used to answer many questions in marketing research:

- How are consumers who purchase various brands different from those who do not purchase those brands?
- How do we target likely buyers for a new product from our database of existing customers in order to conduct the most effective prelaunch marketing campaign?
- How do consumers who frequent one fast-food restaurant differ in demographic and lifestyle characteristics from those who frequent another fast-food restaurant?
- How do consumers who have chosen either indemnity insurance, HMO coverage, or PPO coverage differ from one another in regard to healthcare use, perceptions, and attitudes?

# Cluster Analysis

The term **cluster analysis** generally refers to statistical procedures used to identify objects or people that are similar in regard to certain variables or measurements. The purpose of cluster analysis is to classify objects or people into some number of mutually exclusive and exhaustive groups so that those within a group are as similar as possible to one another (this is true in general, but techniques such as fuzzy clustering compute probabilities of membership rather than assigning records uniquely to a single group).[11] In other words, clusters should be homogeneous internally (within cluster) and heterogeneous externally (between clusters).

> **cluster analysis**
> General term for statistical procedures that classify objects or people into some number of mutually exclusive and exhaustive groups on the basis of two or more classification variables.

## Procedures for Clustering

A number of different procedures (based on somewhat different mathematical and computer routines) are available for clustering people or objects. Some examples of clustering techniques include *K*-means, two-stage, nearest neighbor, decision trees, ensemble analysis, random forest, BIRCH, and self-organizing neural networks. However, the general approach underlying all of these procedures involves measuring the similarities among people or objects in regard to their values on the variables used for clustering.[12] Similarities among the people or objects being clustered are normally determined on the basis of some type of distance measure. This approach is best illustrated graphically. Suppose an analyst wants to group, or cluster, consumers on the basis of two variables: monthly frequency of eating out and monthly frequency of eating at fast-food restaurants. Observations on the two variables are plotted in a two-dimensional graph in Exhibit 18.2. Each dot indicates the position of one consumer in regard to the two variables. The distance between any pair of points is positively related to how similar the corresponding individuals are when the two variables are considered together (the closer the dots, the more similar the individuals). In Exhibit 18.2, consumer *X* is more like consumer *Y* than like either *Z* or *W*.

Inspection of Exhibit 18.2 suggests that three distinct clusters emerge on the basis of simultaneously considering frequency of eating out and frequency of eating at fast-food restaurants:

- Cluster 1 includes those people who do not frequently eat out or frequently eat at fast-food restaurants.
- Cluster 2 includes consumers who frequently eat out but seldom eat at fast-food restaurants.
- Cluster 3 includes people who frequently eat out and also frequently eat at fast-food restaurants.

The fast-food company can see that its best targets are to be found among those who, in general, eat out frequently and eat at fast food restaurants specifically. To provide more insight for the client, the analyst should develop demographic, psychographic, and behavioral profiles of consumers in cluster 3.

As shown in Exhibit 18.2, clusters can be developed from scatterplots. However, this time-consuming, trial-and-error procedure becomes more tedious as the number of variables used to develop the clusters or the number of objects or persons being clustered increases. You can readily visualize a problem with two variables and fewer than 100 objects. Once the number of variables increases to three and the number of observations increases to 500 or

**Exhibit 18.2**

**Cluster Analysis Based on Two Variables**

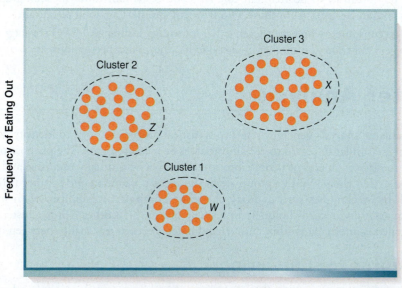

Clustering people according to how frequently and where they eat out is a way of identifying a particular consumer base. An upscale restaurant can see that its customers fall into cluster 2 and possibly cluster 3 in Exhibit 18.2.

more, visualization becomes impossible. Fortunately, computer algorithms are available to perform this more complex type of cluster analysis. The mechanics of these algorithms are complicated and beyond the scope of this discussion. The basic idea behind most of them is to start with some arbitrary cluster boundaries and modify the boundaries until a point is reached where the average interpoint distances within clusters are as small as possible relative to average distances between clusters.

Additional discussion of using cluster analysis for market segmentation in provided in the accompanying Practicing Marketing Research feature.

**K-means cluster analysis**
Multivariate procedure that groups people or objects into clusters based on their closeness to each other on a number of variables.

# PRACTICING MARKETING RESEARCH

## How to Segment a Market Using Cluster Analysis

*Mike Foytik, Chief Technical Officer, DSS Research*

Although many alternative statistical techniques have come and gone over the years, traditional *K*-means cluster analysis has proven to be a reliable and efficient way of segmenting any market. Cluster analysis is the one approach that is readily available in all statistical packages and provides satisfactory results in all but the most extreme circumstances.

Before running cluster analysis, or any other form of segmentation, you must first determine what "basis" variables should be chosen to define the segments. Your segmentation solution can only be as good as the variables you choose to build that solution. In order to select the right basis variables, review the overall objectives of the segmentation. Whatever insights you hope to uncover in the marketplace or characteristics you are trying to reveal must be present in your basis variables. If the objective is to identify the best customers for a new product you are offering, product preference must be included as a basis variable along with attitudes or demographic characteristics that might be correlated with their product preference.

Research objectives, past experience, knowledge of the market, qualitative research and analysis of the available data may all be used to identify the best basis variable candidates. Unless you have a very specific, narrowly defined objective for segmenting your market, it is generally better to start with a wide array of basis variables and narrow the selection through analyses and testing.

Once your basis variables are selected, various data manipulation and transformations are needed to prepare your dataset for cluster analysis. If using basis variables with different rating scales, standardization is in order to prevent a larger scale from dominating the clusters. Dummy variables, log and nonlinear transformations, and composite variables may need to be created to accentuate patterns in the data or to rescale items with large magnitude. You should look at the response distribution of potential basis variables to ensure there is enough variation on each item to effectively differentiate respondents.

The more items included as basis variables related to a common theme, the more the resulting solution will be focused on that theme. To avoid including too many related items as basis variables, factor analysis or correlation analysis can be used to select a representative subset from a large array of potential basis variables. We have found it more beneficial to select a subset of raw variables from a factor solution rather than using the factor scores themselves as basis variables.

Once your basis variables are determined, running a cluster analysis is very easy. Just input the basis variables, select the number of clusters you wish to identify in your data and you are on your way. However, evaluating the results and identifying the best solution is a skill that can only be developed through trial and error. The better you understand what you are looking for, the more likely you are to arrive at a solution that meets your needs. There are different metrics that can help you determine how many clusters/segments should be in your final solution, but there is no single criterion that gives the absolute best results every time.

You can narrow your set of potential solutions by using heuristics such as requiring a minimum segment size that is at least 10 percent of your overall sample and opting for the solution with the fewest segments when there does not appear to be a clear cut advantage between two or more options. If an extremely small segment (usually less than 1 percent of your sample) keeps appearing in your output, consider treating that segment as outliers and removing them from the analysis. To modify an existing solution that does not quite meet your objectives, try swapping some basis variables with other correlated measures, simply remove some items that do not appear to be contributing to the overall results, add related items to strengthen the impact of a particular characteristic you believe is underrepresented in the solution or search for new basis variables to realign the segments along a dimension not showing up in the current solutions.

Analysis of variance (ANOVA) is an excellent tool for evaluating the results of any segmentation solution being considered. First, use ANOVA to ensure you have sufficient variation amongst all your basis variables. Then apply ANOVA to all relevant survey questions and external data points to determine how well the solution differentiates respondents on all items of interest. By highlighting the highest and lowest items on each survey question that product significant variation across segments (high $F$-value on ANOVA test), you can quickly focus your attention on the items that best differentiate and define each segment. Once you can attach a meaningful name or persona to each segment and those segments address your overall objectives, you have a solution worth considering.

Don't give up too quickly if a meaningful solution is not immediately identified. Try lots of data runs, rethink your basis variables and look for ways to pull parts of one solution you like together with segments from another solution that has positive traits.

# Factor Analysis

**factor analysis**
Procedure for simplifying data by reducing a large set of variables to a smaller set of factors or composite variables by identifying underlying dimensions of the data.

The purpose of **factor analysis** is data simplification.[13] The objective is to summarize the information contained in a large number of metric measures (e.g., rating scales) with a smaller number of summary measures, called *factors*. As with cluster analysis, there is no dependent variable.

Many phenomena of interest to marketing researchers are actually composites, or combinations, of a number of measures. These concepts are often measured by means of rating questions. For instance, in assessing consumer response to a new automobile, a general concept such as "luxury" might be measured by asking respondents to rate different cars on attributes such as "quiet ride," "smooth ride," or "plush carpeting." The product designer wants to produce an automobile that is perceived as luxurious but knows that a variety of features probably contribute to this general perception. Each attribute rated should measure a slightly different facet of luxury. The set of measures should provide a better representation of the concept than a single global rating of "luxury."

Several measures of a concept can be added together to develop a composite score or to compute an average score on the concept. Exhibit 18.3 shows data on six consumers who

| EXHIBIT 18.3 | Importance Ratings of Luxury Automobile Features | | | |
|---|---|---|---|---|
| **Respondent** | **Smooth Ride** | **Quiet Ride** | **Acceleration** | **Handling** |
| Bob | 5 | 4 | 2 | 1 |
| Roy | 4 | 3 | 2 | 1 |
| Hank | 4 | 3 | 3 | 2 |
| Janet | 5 | 5 | 2 | 2 |
| Jane | 4 | 3 | 2 | 1 |
| Ann | 5 | 5 | 3 | 2 |
| Average | 4.50 | 3.83 | 2.33 | 1.50 |

each rated an automobile on four characteristics. You can see that those respondents who gave higher ratings on "smooth ride" also tended to give higher ratings on "quiet ride." A similar pattern is evident in the ratings of "acceleration" and "handling." These four measures can be combined into two summary measures by averaging the pairs of ratings. The resulting summary measures might be called "luxury" and "performance" (see Exhibit 18.4).

## Factor Scores

Factor analysis produces one or more factors, or composite variables, when applied to a number of variables. A **factor**, technically defined, is a linear combination of variables. It is a weighted summary score of a set of related variables, similar to the composite derived by averaging the measures. However, in factor analysis, each measure is first weighted according to how much it contributes to the variation of each factor.

**factor**
A linear combination of variables that are correlated with each other.

In factor analysis, a factor score is calculated on each factor for each subject in the data set. For example, in a factor analysis with two factors, the following equations might be used to determine factor scores:

$$F_1 = .40A_1 + .30A_2 + .02A_3 + .05A_4$$
$$F_2 = .01A_1 + .04A_2 + .45A_3 + .37A_4$$
$$\text{where} \quad F_1 - F_n = \text{factor scores}$$
$$A_1 - A_n = \text{attribute ratings}$$

With these formulas, two factor scores can be calculated for each respondent by substituting the ratings she or he gave on variables $A_1$ through $A_4$ into each equation. The coefficients in the equations are the factor scoring coefficients to be applied to each respondent's ratings. For example, Bob's factor scores (see Exhibit 18.4) are computed as follows:

$$F_1 = .40(5) + .30(4) + .02(2) + .05(1) = 3.29$$
$$F_2 = .01(5) + .04(4) + .45(2) + .37(1) = 2.38$$

In the first equation, the factor scoring coefficients, or weights, for $A_1$ and $A_2$ (.40 and .30) are large, whereas the weights for $A_3$ and $A_4$ are small. The small weights on $A_3$ and $A_4$ indicate that these variables contribute little to score variations on factor 1 ($F_1$). Regardless of the ratings a respondent gives to $A_3$ and $A_4$, they have little effect on his or her score on $F_1$. However, variables $A_3$ and $A_4$ make a large contribution to the second factor score ($F_2$),

| EXHIBIT 18.4 | Average Ratings of Two Factors | |
|---|---|---|
| **Respondent** | **Luxury** | **Performance** |
| Bob | 4.5 | 1.5 |
| Roy | 3.5 | 1.5 |
| Hank | 3.5 | 2.5 |
| Janet | 5.0 | 2.0 |
| Jane | 3.5 | 1.5 |
| Ann | 5.0 | 2.5 |
| Average | 4.25 | 1.92 |

whereas $A_1$ and $A_2$ have little effect. These two equations show that variables $A_1$ and $A_2$ are relatively independent of $A_3$ and $A_4$ because each variable takes on large values in only one scoring equation.

The relative sizes of the scoring coefficients are also of interest. Variable $A_1$ (with a weight of .40) is a more important contributor to factor 1 variation than is $A_2$ (with a smaller weight of .30). This finding may be very important to the product designer when evaluating the implications of various design changes. For example, the product manager might want to improve the perceived luxury of the car through product redesign or advertising. The product manager may know, based on other research, that a certain expenditure on redesign will result in an improvement of the average rating on "smooth ride" from 4.3 to 4.8. This research may also show that the same expenditure will produce a half-point improvement in ratings on "quiet ride." The factor analysis shows that perceived luxury will be enhanced to a greater extent by increasing ratings on "smooth ride" than by increasing ratings on "quiet ride" by the same amount.

## Factor Loadings

**factor loading**
Correlation between factor scores and the original variables.

The nature of the factors derived can be determined by examining the **factor loadings**. Using the scoring equations presented earlier, a pair of factor scores ($F_1$ and $F_2$) are calculated for each respondent. Factor loadings are determined by calculating the correlation (from $-1$ to $+1$) between each factor ($F_1$ and $F_2$) score and each of the original ratings variables. Each correlation coefficient represents the loading of the associated variable on the particular factor. If $A_1$ is closely associated with factor 1, the loading or correlation will be high, as shown for the sample problem in Exhibit 18.5. Because the loadings are correlation coefficients, values near $-1$ or $+1$ indicate a close positive or negative association. Variables $A_1$ and $A_2$ are closely associated (highly correlated) with scores on factor 1, and variables $A_3$ and $A_4$ are closely associated with scores on factor 2.

Stated another way, variables $A_1$ and $A_2$ have high loadings on factor 1 and serve to define the factor; variables $A_3$ and $A_4$ have high loadings on and define factor 2.

| EXHIBIT 18.5 | Factor Loadings for Two Factors | |
|---|---|---|
| | **Correlation with** | |
| **Variable** | **Factor 1** | **Factor 2** |
| $A_1$ | .85 | .10 |
| $A_2$ | .76 | .06 |
| $A_3$ | .06 | .89 |
| $A_4$ | .04 | .79 |

## Naming Factors

Once each factor's defining variables have been identified, the next step is to name the factors. This is a somewhat subjective step, combining intuition and knowledge of the variables with an inspection of the variables that have high loadings on each factor. Usually, a certain consistency exists among the variables that load highly on a given factor. For instance, it is not surprising to see that the ratings on "smooth ride" and "quiet ride" both load on the same factor. Although we have chosen to name this factor "luxury," another analyst, looking at the same result, might decide to name the factor "prestige."

## Number of Factors to Retain

In factor analysis, the analyst is confronted with a decision regarding how many factors to retain. The final result can include from one factor to as many factors as there are variables. The decision is often made by looking at the percentage of the variation in the original data that is explained by each factor.

There are many different decision rules for choosing the number of factors to retain. Probably the most appropriate decision rule is to stop factoring when additional factors no longer make sense. The first factors extracted are likely to exhibit logical consistency; later factors are usually harder to interpret, for they are more likely to contain a large amount of random variation.

# Conjoint Analysis

**Conjoint analysis** is a popular multivariate procedure used by marketers to help determine what features a new product or service should include and how it should be priced. It can be argued that conjoint analysis has become popular because it is a more powerful, more flexible, and often less expensive way to address these important issues than is the traditional concept testing approach.[14]

Conjoint analysis is not a completely standardized procedure.[15] A typical conjoint analysis application involves presenting various product or service combinations in a carefully controlled exercise, then estimating the relative value of each feature tested. The type of conjoint approach (e.g., ratings-based, discrete choice, graded pairs, dual choice, full profile, partial profile, adaptive choice, etc.) affects how the exercise is presented and what statistical procedures are most appropriate for analyzing the results. Fortunately, conjoint analysis is not difficult to understand conceptually, as we demonstrate in the following example concerning the attributes of golf balls.

**conjoint analysis**
Multivariate procedure used to quantify the value that consumers associate with different levels of product/service attributes or features.

## Example of Conjoint Analysis

Put yourself in the position of a product manager for Titleist, a major manufacturer of golf balls. From focus groups recently conducted, past research studies of various types, and your own personal experience as a golfer, you know that golfers tend to evaluate golf balls in terms of three important features or attributes: average driving distance, average ball life, and price.

You also recognize a range of feasible possibilities for each of these features or attributes, as follows:

1. Average driving distance
   - 10 yards more than the golfer's average
   - Same as the golfer's average
   - 10 yards less than the golfer's average

2. Average ball life
   - 54 holes
   - 36 holes
   - 18 holes
3. Price per ball
   - $2.00
   - $2.50
   - $3.00

From the perspective of potential purchasers, these attributes have a natural order (i.e., longer distance and longer ball life are always preferred over shorter options), so we can easily identify the ideal configuration. This is not always the case when dealing with attributes such as brand, physical appearance, or color. For this example, the consumer's ideal golf ball would have the following characteristics:

- Average driving distance—10 yards above average
- Average ball life—54 holes
- Price—$2.00

From the manufacturer's perspective, which is based on manufacturing cost, the ideal golf ball would probably have these characteristics:

- Average driving distance—10 yards below average
- Average ball life—18 holes
- Price—$3.00

This golf ball profile is based on the fact that it costs less to produce a ball that travels a shorter distance and has a shorter life. The company confronts the eternal marketing dilemma: the company would sell a lot of golf balls, but would go broke if it produced and sold the ideal ball from the golfer's perspective. However, the company would sell very few balls if it produced and sold the ideal ball from the manufacturer's perspective. As always, the "best" golf ball from a business perspective lies somewhere between the two extremes.

A traditional approach to this problem might produce information of the type displayed in Exhibit 18.6. As you can see, this information does not provide new insights regarding which ball should be produced. The preferred driving distance is 10 yards above average and the preferred average ball life is 54 holes. These results are obvious without any additional research.

## Considering Features Conjointly

In conjoint analysis, rather than having respondents evaluate features individually, the analyst asks them to evaluate features conjointly or in combination so that advantages for one attribute can only be chosen at the expense of another attribute. The results of asking two different golfers to rank different combinations of "average driving distance" and "average ball life" conjointly are shown in Exhibits 18.7 and 18.8.

As expected, both golfers agree on the most and least preferred balls. However, analysis of their second through eighth rankings makes it clear that the first golfer is willing to trade off ball life for distance

Conjoint analysis could be used by a manufacturer of golf balls to determine the relative importance of these three features of a golf ball and to see which ball meets the most needs of both consumer and manufacturer.

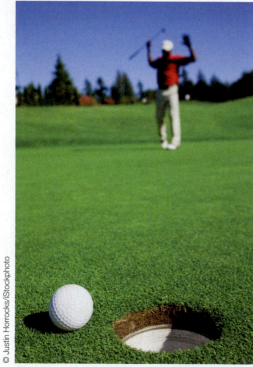

© Justin Horrocks/iStockphoto

| EXHIBIT 18.6 | Traditional Nonconjoint Rankings of Distance and Ball Life Attributes |
| --- | --- |

| Average Driving Distance | | Average Ball Life | |
| --- | --- | --- | --- |
| Rank | Level | Rank | Level |
| 1 | 275 yards | 1 | 54 holes |
| 2 | 250 yards | 2 | 36 holes |
| 3 | 225 yards | 3 | 18 holes |

| EXHIBIT 18.7 | Conjoint Rankings of Combinations of Distance and Ball Life for Golfer 1 |
| --- | --- |

| | Ball Life | | |
| --- | --- | --- | --- |
| Distance | 54 holes | 36 holes | 18 holes |
| 275 yards | 1 | 2 | 4 |
| 250 yards | 3 | 5 | 7 |
| 225 yards | 6 | 8 | 9 |

| EXHIBIT 18.8 | Conjoint Rankings of Combinations of Distance and Ball Life for Golfer 2 |
| --- | --- |

| | Ball Life | | |
| --- | --- | --- | --- |
| Distance | 54 holes | 36 holes | 18 holes |
| 275 yards | 1 | 3 | 6 |
| 250 yards | 2 | 5 | 8 |
| 225 yards | 4 | 7 | 9 |

(accept a shorter ball life for longer distance), while the second golfer is willing to trade off distance for longer ball life (accept shorter distance for a longer ball life).

This type of information is the essence of the special insight offered by conjoint analysis. The technique permits marketers to see which product attribute or feature potential customers are willing to trade off (accept less of) to obtain more of another attribute or feature. People make these kinds of purchasing decisions every day (for example, they may choose to pay a higher price for a product at a local market for the convenience of shopping there).

## Estimating Utilities

The next step is to calculate a set of values, or **utilities**, for the three levels of price, the three levels of driving distance, and the three levels of ball life in such a way that, when they are combined in a particular mix of price, ball life, and driving distance, they predict each golfer's rank order for that combination. Estimated utilities for golfer 1 are shown in Exhibit 18.9. As you can readily see, this set of numbers perfectly predicts the original rankings. The relationship among these numbers or utilities is fixed, though there is some arbitrariness in their magnitude or scale. In other words, the utilities shown in Exhibit 18.9 can be multiplied or divided by any constant and the same relative results will be obtained. Utilities for this simple example can be computed using ordinary least squares regression, but the exact procedures for estimating utilities of more complex exercises are beyond the scope of this discussion.

**utilities**
The relative value of attribute levels determined through conjoint analysis.

| EXHIBIT 18.9 | Ranks (in parentheses) and Combined Metric Utilities for Golfer 1—Distance and Ball Life | | |
|---|---|---|---|
| | **Ball Life** | | |
| **Distance** | **54 holes** | **36 holes** | **18 holes** |
| 275 yards | (1) 150 | (2) 125 | (4) 100 |
| 250 yards | (3) 110 | (5) 85 | (7) 60 |
| 225 yards | (6) 50 | (8) 25 | (9) 0 |

They are normally calculated by using procedures related to regression, analysis of variance, linear programming, logic, or hierarchical Bayes analysis.

The trade-offs that golfer 1 is willing to make between "ball life" and "price" are shown in Exhibit 18.10. This information can be used to estimate a set of utilities for "price" that can be added to those for "ball life" to predict the rankings for golfer 1, as shown in Exhibit 18.11.

This step produces a complete set of utilities for all levels of the three features or attributes that successfully capture golfer 1's trade-offs. These utilities are shown in Exhibit 18.12.

## Simulating Buyer Choice

For various reasons, the firm might be in a position to produce only 2 of the 27 golf balls that are possible with each of the three levels of the three attributes. The possibilities are shown in Exhibit 18.13. If the calculated utilities for golfer 1 are applied to the two golf balls the firm is able to make, then the results are the total utilities shown in Exhibit 18.14. These results indicate that golfer 1 will prefer the ball with the longer life over the one with

| EXHIBIT 18.10 | Conjoint Rankings of Combinations of Price and Ball Life for Golfer 1 | | |
|---|---|---|---|
| | **Ball Life** | | |
| **Price** | **54 holes** | **36 holes** | **18 holes** |
| $2.00 | 1 | 2 | 4 |
| $2.50 | 3 | 5 | 7 |
| $3.00 | 6 | 8 | 9 |

| EXHIBIT 18.11 | Ranks (in parentheses) and Combined Metric Utilities for Golfer 1—Price and Ball Life | | |
|---|---|---|---|
| | **Ball Life** | | |
| **Price** | **54 holes** | **36 holes** | **18 holes** |
| $2.00 | (1) 70 | (2) 45 | (4) 20 |
| $2.50 | (3) 55 | (5) 30 | (7) 5 |
| $3.00 | (6) 50 | (8) 25 | (9) 0 |

| EXHIBIT 18.12 | Complete Set of Estimated Utilities for Golfer 1 | | | | |

| Distance | | Ball Life | | Price | |
|---|---|---|---|---|---|
| Level | Utility | Level | Utility | Level | Utility |
| $275 yards | 100 | 54 holes | 50 | $2.00 | 20 |
| 250 yards | 60 | 36 holes | 25 | $2.50 | 5 |
| 225 yards | 0 | 18 holes | 0 | $3.00 | 0 |

| EXHIBIT 18.13 | Ball Profiles for Simulation | |

| Attribute | Distance Ball | Long-Life Ball |
|---|---|---|
| Distance | 275 | 250 |
| Life | 18 | 54 |
| Price | $2.50 | $3.00 |

| EXHIBIT 18.14 | Estimated Total Utilities for the Two Sample Profiles | | | |

| | Distance Ball | | Long-Life Ball | |
|---|---|---|---|---|
| Attribute | Level | Utility | Level | Utility |
| Distance | 275 | 100 | 250 | 60 |
| Life | 18 | 0 | 54 | 50 |
| Price | $2.50 | 5 | $3.00 | 0 |
| Total utility | | 105 | | 110 |

the greater distance because it has a higher total utility. The analyst need only repeat this process for a representative sample of golfers to estimate potential market shares for the two balls. In addition, the analysis can be extended to cover other golf ball combinations.

The three steps discussed here—collecting trade-off data, using the data to estimate buyer preference structures, and predicting choice—are the basis of any conjoint analysis application. Although the trade-off matrix approach is simple, useful for explaining conjoint analysis, and effective for problems with small numbers of attributes, it is seldom used in the real world.

One of the most common approaches to conducting conjoint analysis is the use of a discrete choice or choice-based conjoint exercise. Two or more products are shown side-by-side with details provided on each key attribute being tested. Respondents are asked to select a single product from amongst the options shown. The exercise is repeated multiple times in order to present a wide variety of product designs, but no individual sees more than a fraction of the sometimes thousands or even millions of possible product combinations.

Computer-driven exercises might further adapt the exercise to each respondent, based on prior answers and personal demographics, to spend more time on the factors that seem to be driving product choice. Menu-based conjoint analysis can replicate the choices consumers make when choosing between "value meals" and a la carte items from a restaurant menu. Other computer-driven exercises allow respondents to design their own product with appropriate design constraints and pricing factored in to each option chosen, much the way consumers configure their own Dell computer online or select upgrades for a new car. These and many other approaches can be used to capture the information needed for estimating respondent utilities when designed, executed, and analyzed properly.

As suggested earlier, there is much more to conjoint analysis than has been discussed in this section. However, if you understand this simple example, then you understand the basic concepts that underlie conjoint analysis.

### Limitations of Conjoint Analysis

Like many research techniques, conjoint analysis suffers from a certain degree of artificiality. Respondents may be more deliberate in their choice processes in this context than in a real situation. The survey may provide more product information than respondents would get in a real market situation. If key attributes or popular options within key attributes are excluded from the study, demand estimates could be severely impacted. Testing too many attributes or features will diminish the amount of attention that can be given to each individual's most desired features, reducing measurement precision. The presentation of information (e.g., the order in which attributes are listed; whether pictures are used for some attributes, but not others; how price is displayed; etc.) can greatly impact what features respondents focus on and, ultimately, how they make their decisions. It is important to either be as neutral as possible in the presentation of a conjoint exercise or else try to replicate how the product or service is actually evaluated and compared in the marketplace in order to avoid biasing results.

Finally, it is important to remember that the advertising and promotion of any new product or service can lead to consumer perceptions that are very different from those created via factual descriptions used in a survey. Also keep in mind that consumers can't purchase something they don't know exists, so conjoint analysis operates under the assumptions of full awareness, unrestricted access, and complete knowledge of all product features.

# Big Data and Hadoop

*Big data* is the term used to describe large and complex data sets. Companies have been collecting transaction-based information since the beginning of the computer age. However, the sheer volume of information has grown exponentially over the last few years and the types of information now being generated does not easily fit into traditional hierarchical database structures. Big data describes the new data capture and management approaches that are designed to handle the higher volume, faster acquisition rates, and broader array of data types. Most of the tools for big data are still evolving, and individuals with the skills to capitalize on them are in short supply.

Hadoop is an open-source platform distributed by Apache for managing large amounts of information across hundreds or thousands of networked computers. Each computer works independently on a small portion of the total dataset so that a task such as clustering several billion records can be handled in a fraction of the time taken for more conventional database structures. There are numerous backup copies of each data chunk, so that any failure can be immediately picked up by another computer with access to the same information. Google and Yahoo have had a hand in developing the platform and underlying technology for Hadoop as they sought ways to store and access the vast array of search information they were collecting.

Today, many companies that deal with big data—such as Amazon, eBay, Facebook, Google, IBM, LinkedIn, Spotify, Twitter, and Yahoo—use Hadoop to manage their information.

# Predictive Analytics[16]

Predictive analytics describes a wide array of tools and techniques that are used to extract and analyze information from data sets. Statistics, machine learning, database management, and computer programming all play a part in identifying patterns and transforming data into insights. It is an increasingly important set of tools for businesses to transform the exponentially growing quantities of digital data into business intelligence as firms seek informational advantages to improve efficiency and effectiveness. Predictive analytics can apply to big data or traditional databases, observational data like loyalty card usage, Internet sources like social media text, and web tracking data or primary survey research results. Fraud detection, trend analyses, targeted direct marketing, predicting heavy users, and identifying likely buyers are just some of the applications for predictive analytics.

## Using Predictive Analytics

**Acquiring a Data Set**  Before applying predictive analytics, an organization must assemble a target data set relevant to the problem of interest. Predictive analytics can only uncover patterns and relationships that exist in the available data. Typically, the data set must be large enough to include all the patterns and combinations that are likely to be found in the real world.

In the past, assembling such large data sets was very costly and time consuming. Today, most companies capture terabytes of information on their customers as a normal course of business, and many social media companies provide access to massive amounts of data in real time for anyone to tap into. In addition, third-party vendors provide a wide variety of data elements that can be purchased for just about any household or company in the United States.

**Pre-processing**  Once assembled, the data set must be cleaned in a process where observations that contain excessive noise, errors and missing data are edited or excluded. Data transformations may be used to smooth out irregular distributions and minimize extreme values. Imputing missing values from comparable records and building predictive models to fill-in missing information is often used. Linking multiple data sets is also part of pre-processing available data.

**Modeling**  A variety of techniques may be employed as part of the modeling process:

- **Clustering.** This is a task of discovering groups and structures in the data that are similar on certain, selected sets of variables. These are groupings that are not obvious and are not based on a single set of variables or small number of items. Clustering normally requires evaluating numerous solutions before finding the best option. Cluster analysis, one of the techniques discussed earlier in this chapter, is commonly used to reveal hidden groupings or identify unexpected associations.

- **Classification.** Readily available information such as demographics and geography might be used to classify individuals on key behaviors such as purchase frequency or product preference. Proprietary information such as online ads viewed or previous products purchased can be very effective at predictive future behaviors whenever such information is available. Customer segments identified through clustering might also be modeled in order to predict which segment new customers and prospects belong. Successful models can be applied to new customers and records that could not be processed directly due to missing data.

- **Estimation.** Calculations such as risk scores, fraud detection, retention rates, lifetime value, and likelihood to purchase rates may be calculated for individuals or groups. These calculations can be used to predict future outcomes based on limited present-day data. They can also be used to monitor individuals or groups in order to detect changes in behavior that allow the organization to react before customers or revenues are lost.

**Validating Results**  A final step of knowledge discovery from the target data and modeling is to attempt to verify the patterns produced by the predictive modeling algorithms in a wider data set. Not every pattern and relationship identified in previous steps turns out to be valid in the real world. In the evaluation process, the patterns or models identified in the wider data set are applied to a test data set that was not used to develop the predictive modeling algorithm. The resulting output is compared to the desired output.

For example, an algorithm developed to predict those most likely to respond to a mail offer would be developed or trained on certain past mail offers. Once developed or trained, the algorithm developed from the test mailings would be applied to other mailings not used in the development of the algorithm or to actual results from a mailing recently completed. If the predictive model does not meet the desired accuracy standards, then it is necessary to go through the previous steps again in order to develop an algorithm or model with the desired level of accuracy.

**Applying the Results** Once the models and calculations are in place and have been validated, they are applied to existing and future customer records to improve the efficiency and effectiveness of marketing efforts. For example, specific information captured from a new sales inquiry can be used to classify an individual into the correct market segment. Based on their market segment, the most appropriate product offering can be prepared and the marketing messages can be adjusted to most resonate with that individual. Purchasing prospect lists with specific information appended to each record allows an organization to avoid wasting marketing dollars on unlikely purchasers (based on applied predictive models) and focus resources on the most likely buyers and those with the greatest potential lifetime value.

The Practicing Marketing Research feature below provides on example of how predictive modeling is used by a major retailer and also touches on the privacy issues discussed in the next section.

# PRACTICING MARKETING RESEARCH

## How Target Figured out a Teen Girl Was Pregnant Before Her Father Did[17]

Every time you go shopping, you share intimate details about your consumption patterns with retailers. And many of those retailers are studying those details to figure out what you like, what you need, and which coupons are most likely to make you happy. Target, for example, has figured out how to data-mine its way into your womb, to figure out whether you have a baby on the way long before you need to start buying diapers.

Charles Duhigg outlines in the *New York Times* how Target tries to hook parents-to-be at that crucial moment before they turn into rampant—and loyal—buyers of all things pastel, plastic, and miniature. He talked to Target statistician Andrew Pole—before Target freaked out and cut off all communications—about the clues to a customer's impending bundle of joy. Target assigns all customers a Guest ID number, tied to their credit card, name, or e-mail address, that becomes a bucket that stores a history of everything they've bought and any demographic information Target has collected from them or bought from other sources. Using that, Pole looked at historical buying data for all the ladies who had signed up for Target baby registries in the past.

Move up http://i.forbesimg.com t Move down

He ran different analyses, analyzing the data, and some useful patterns emerged. Lots of people buy lotion, but one of Pole's colleagues noticed that women on the baby registry were buying larger quantities of unscented lotion around the beginning of their second trimester. Another analyst noted that sometime in the first 20 weeks, pregnant women loaded up on supplements like calcium, magnesium, and zinc. Many shoppers purchase soap and cotton balls, but when someone suddenly starts buying lots of scent-free soap and extra-big bags of cotton balls, in addition to hand sanitizers and washcloths, it signals they could be getting close to their delivery date.

As Pole's computers crawled through the data, he was able to identify about 25 products that, when analyzed together, allowed him to assign each shopper a "pregnancy prediction" score. More important, he could also estimate her due date to within a small window, so Target could send coupons timed to very specific stages of her pregnancy.

Take a fictional Target shopper named Jenny Ward, who is 23, lives in Atlanta and in March bought cocoa-butter lotion, a purse large enough to double as a diaper bag, zinc and magnesium supplements, and a bright blue rug. There's, say, an 87 percent chance that she's pregnant, and that her delivery date is sometime in late August.

And perhaps that it's a boy, based on the color of that rug?

So Target started sending coupons for baby items to customers according to their pregnancy scores. An angry man went into a Target outside of Minneapolis, demanding to talk to a manager. "My daughter got this in the mail!" he said. "She's still in high school, and you're sending her coupons for baby clothes and cribs? Are you trying to encourage her to get pregnant?"

The manager didn't have any idea what the man was talking about. He looked at the mailer. Sure enough, it was addressed to the man's daughter and contained advertisements for maternity clothing, nursery furniture, and pictures of smiling infants. The manager apologized, and then called a few days later to apologize again. On the phone, though, the father was somewhat abashed. "I had a talk with my daughter," he said. "It turns out there's been some activities in my house I haven't been completely aware of. She's due in August. I owe you an apology."

What Target discovered fairly quickly is that it creeped people out that the company knew about their pregnancies in advance.

"If we send someone a catalog and say, 'Congratulations on your first child!' and they've never told us they're pregnant, that's going to make some people uncomfortable," Pole told me. "We are very conservative about compliance with all privacy laws. But even if you're following the law, you can do things where people get queasy."

So Target got sneakier about sending the coupons. The company can create personalized booklets; instead of sending people with high pregnancy scores books of coupons solely for diapers, rattles, strollers, and the *Go the F*** to Sleep* book, they more subtly spread them about:

"Then we started mixing in all these ads for things we knew pregnant women would never buy, so the baby ads looked random. We'd put an ad for a lawn mower next to diapers. We'd put a coupon for wineglasses next to infant clothes. That way, it looked like all the products were chosen by chance.

"And we found out that as long as a pregnant woman thinks she hasn't been spied on, she'll use the coupons. She just assumes that everyone else on her block got the same mailer for diapers and cribs. As long as we don't spook her, it works."

So the Target philosophy toward expecting parents might be similar to the first-date philosophy: Even if you've fully stalked the person on Facebook and Google beforehand, pretend like you know less than you do so as not to creep the person out.

Duhigg suggests that Target's gangbusters revenue growth in the 2000s—$44 billion in 2002, when Pole was hired, to $67 billion in 2010—is attributable to Pole's helping the retail giant corner the baby-on-board market, citing company president Gregg Steinhafel boasting to investors about the company's "heightened focus on items and categories that appeal to specific guest segments such as mom and baby."

## Privacy Concerns and Ethics

Most believe that predictive modeling is ethically neutral. However, the ways in which data are collected for predictive modeling and the types of data acquired can raise questions regarding privacy, legality, and ethics. For example, monitoring telephone calls and Internet usage for national security or law enforcement purposes has raised privacy concerns.

## Commercial Predictive Modeling Software and Applications

Database providers like Oracle and Microsoft provide tools optimized for their platform. Popular big data platform, Hadoop, has a variety of open-source and commercial tools available. There are an increasing number of highly integrated packages for predictive modeling, including:

- Angoss KnowledgeSTUDIO
- Clarabridge
- RapidMiner
- SAS Enterprise Miner
- SPSS Modeler
- *STATISTICA* Data Miner

# SUMMARY

Multivariate analysis refers to the simultaneous analysis of multiple measurements on each individual or object being studied. Some of the more popular multivariate techniques include multiple regression analysis, multiple discriminant analysis, cluster analysis, factor analysis, and conjoint analysis.

Multiple regression analysis enables the researcher to predict the magnitude of a dependent variable based on the levels of more than one independent variable. Multiple regression fits a plane to observations in a multidimensional space. One statistic that results from multiple regression analysis is called the coefficient of determination, or $R^2$. The value of this statistic ranges from 0 to 1. It provides a measure of the percentage of the variation in the dependent variable that is explained by variation in the independent variables. The *b* values, or regression coefficients, indicate the effect of the individual independent variables on the dependent variable.

Whereas multiple regression analysis requires that the dependent variable be metric, multiple discriminant analysis uses a dependent variable that is nominal or categorical in nature. Discriminant analysis can be used to determine if statistically significant differences exist between the average discriminant score profiles of two (or more) groups. The technique can also be used to establish a model for classifying individuals or objects into groups on the basis of their scores on the independent variables. Finally, discriminant analysis can be used to determine how much of the difference in the average score profiles of the groups is accounted for by each independent variable. The discriminant score, called a *Z* score, is derived for each individual or object by means of the discriminant equation.

Cluster analysis enables a researcher to identify subgroups of individuals or objects that are homogeneous within the subgroup, yet different from other subgroups. Cluster analysis requires that all independent variables be metric, but there is no specification of a dependent variable. Cluster analysis is an excellent means for operationalizing the concept of market segmentation.

The purpose of factor analysis is to simplify massive amounts of data. The objective is to summarize the information contained in a large number of metric measures such as rating scales with a smaller number of summary measures called factors. As in cluster analysis, there is no dependent variable in factor analysis. Factor analysis produces factors, each of which is a weighted composite of a set of related variables. Each measure is weighted according to how much it contributes to the variation of each factor. Factor loadings are determined by calculating the correlation coefficient between factor scores and the original input variables. By examining which variables load heavily on a given factor, the researcher can subjectively name that factor.

Perceptual maps can be produced by means of factor analysis, multidimensional scaling, discriminant analysis, or correspondence analysis. The maps provide a visual representation of how brands, products, companies, and other objects are perceived relative to each other on key features such as quality and value. All the approaches require, as input, consumer evaluations or ratings of the objects in question on some set of key characteristics.

Conjoint analysis is a technique that can be used to measure the trade-offs potential buyers make on the basis of the features of each product or service available to them. The technique permits the researcher to determine the relative value of each level of each feature. These estimated values are called utilities and can be used as a basis for simulating consumer choice.

Predictive modeling draws on statistics, machine learning, artificial intelligence, and computer programming to identify patterns in market data sets. It is becoming increasingly important as the available data grow exponentially.

# KEY TERMS

multivariate analysis **464**

multiple regression analysis **469**

coefficient of determination **470**

regression coefficients **470**

dummy variables **471**

collinearity **471**

causation **471**

scaling of coefficients **471**

classification matrix **472**

multiple discriminant analysis **472**

metric scale **472**

nominal or categorical **472**

discriminant score **473**

discriminant coefficient **473**

cluster analysis **473**

K-means cluster analysis **475**

factor analysis **476**

factor **477**

factor loading **478**

conjoint analysis **479**

utilities **481**

# QUESTIONS FOR REVIEW & CRITICAL THINKING

1. Distinguish between multiple discriminant analysis and cluster analysis. Give several examples of situations in which each might be used.

2. What purpose does multiple regression analysis serve? Give an example of how it might be used in marketing research. How is the strength of multiple regression measures of association determined?

3. What is a dummy variable? Give an example using a dummy variable.

4. Describe the potential problem of collinearity in multiple regression. How might a researcher test for collinearity? If collinearity is a problem, what should the researcher do?

5. A sales manager examined age data, education level, a personality factor that indicated level of introvertedness/extrovertedness, and level of sales attained by the company's 120-person salesforce. The technique used was multiple regression analysis. After analyzing the data, the sales manager said, "It is apparent to me that the higher the level of education and the greater the degree of extrovertedness a salesperson has, the higher will be an individual's level of sales. In other words, a good education and being extroverted cause a person to sell more." Would you agree or disagree with the sales manager's conclusions? Why?

6. The factors produced and the results of the factor loadings from factor analysis are mathematical constructs. It is the task of the researcher to make sense out of these factors. The following table lists four factors produced from a study of cable TV viewers. What label would you put on each of these four factors? Why?

| | | Factor Loading |
|---|---|---|
| Factor 1 | I don't like the way cable TV movie channels repeat the movies over and over. | .79 |
| | The movie channels on cable need to spread their movies out (longer times between repeats). | .75 |
| | I think the cable movie channels just run the same things over and over and over. | .73 |
| | After a while, you've seen all the pay movies, so why keep cable service. | .53 |
| Factor 2 | I love to watch love stories. | .76 |
| | I like a TV show that is sensitive and emotional. | .73 |
| | Sometimes I cry when I watch movies on TV. | .65 |
| | I like to watch "made for TV" movies. | .54 |
| Factor 3 | I like the religious programs on TV (negative correlation). | −.76 |
| | I don't think TV evangelism is good. | .75 |
| | I do not like religious programs. | .61 |
| Factor 4 | I would rather watch movies at home than go to the movies. | .63 |
| | I like cable because you don't have to go out to see the movies. | .55 |
| | I prefer cable TV movies because movie theaters are too expensive. | .46 |

7. The following table is a discriminant analysis that examines responses to various attitudinal questions from cable TV users, former cable TV users, and people who have never used cable TV. Looking at the various discriminant weights, what can you say about each of the three groups?

| | | Discriminant Weights | | |
|---|---|---|---|---|
| | | **Users** | **Formers** | **Nevers** |
| **Users** | | | | |
| A19 | Easygoing on repairs | −.40 | | |
| A18 | No repair service | −.34 | | |
| A7 | Breakdown complainers | +.30 | | |

| | | Discriminant Weights | | |
| --- | --- | --- | --- | --- |
| | | **Users** | **Formers** | **Nevers** |
| A5 | Too many choices | −.27 | | |
| A13 | Antisports | −.24 | | |
| A10 | Antireligious | +.17 | | |
| **Formers** | | | | |
| A4 | Burned out on repeats | | +.22 | |
| A18 | No repair service | | +.19 | |
| H12 | Card/board game player | | +.18 | |
| H1 | High-brow | | −.18 | |
| H3 | Party hog | | +.15 | |
| A9 | DVD preference | | +.16 | |
| **Nevers** | | | | |
| A7 | Breakdown complainer | | | −.29 |
| A19 | Easygoing on repairs | | | +.26 |
| A5 | Too many choices | | | +.23 |
| A13 | Antisports | | | +.21 |
| A10 | Antireligious | | | −.19 |

8. The following table shows regression coefficients for two dependent variables. The first dependent variable is willingness to spend money for cable TV. The independent variables are responses to attitudinal statements. The second dependent variable is stated desire never to allow cable TV in their homes. By examining the regression coefficients, what can you say about persons willing to spend money for cable TV and those who will not allow cable TV in their homes?

9. Explain what predictive analytics encompasses. Provide examples of some marketing problems to which you might apply predictive analytics.

10. Describe the steps in the predictive analytics process.

11. What is Hadoop? How does it relate to big data?

| | Regression Coefficients |
| --- | --- |
| **Willing to Spend Money for Cable TV** | |
| Easygoing on cable repairs | −3.04 |
| Cable movie watcher | 2.81 |
| Comedy watcher | 2.73 |
| Early to bed | −2.62 |
| Breakdown complainer | 2.25 |
| Lovelorn | 2.18 |
| Burned out on repeats | −2.06 |
| **Never Allow Cable TV in Home** | |
| Antisports | 0.37 |
| Object to sex | 0.47 |
| Too many choices | 0.88 |

# WORKING THE NET

1. A good discussion of cluster analysis can be found at *http://faculty.darden.virginia.edu/GBUS8630/doc/M-0748.pdf.*

2. For some easy to digest and comprehensive information on multivariate analysis, including how to run these analyses in SPSS, visit *http://core.ecu.edu/psyc/wuenschk/spss/SPSS-MV.htm*

# REAL-LIFE RESEARCH • 18.1

## Satisfaction Research for Pizza Quik

*The Problem* Pizza Quik is a regional chain of pizza restaurants operating in seven states in the Midwest. Pizza Quik has adopted a total quality management (or TQM) orientation.[18] As part of this orientation, the firm is committed to the idea of market-driven quality. That is, it intends to conduct a research project to address the issue of how its customers define quality and to learn from the customers themselves what they expect in regard to quality.

*Research Objectives* The objectives of the proposed research are:

- To identify the key determinants of customer satisfaction
- To measure current customer satisfaction levels on those key satisfaction determinants
- To determine the relative importance of each key satisfaction determinant in deriving overall satisfaction
- To provide recommendations to management regarding where to direct the company's efforts

*Methodology* The first objective was met by means of qualitative research. A series of focus groups were conducted with customers to determine which attributes of Pizza Quik's product and service are most important to them. Based on this analysis, the following attributes were identified:

- Overall quality of food
- Variety of menu items
- Friendliness of Pizza Quik's employees
- Provision of good value for the money
- Speed of service

In the second stage of the research, central-location telephone interviews were conducted with 1,200 randomly selected individuals who had purchased or eaten at a Pizza Quik restaurant (in the restaurant or take-out) in the past 30 days. Key information garnered in the survey included:

- Overall rating of satisfaction with Pizza Quik on a 10-point scale (1 = poor and 10 = excellent)
- Rating of Pizza Quik on the five key satisfaction attributes identified in the qualitative research, using the same 10-point scale as for overall satisfaction
- Demographic characteristics

*Results and Analysis* Extensive cross tabulations and other traditional statistical analyses were conducted. A key part of the analysis was to estimate a regression model with overall satisfaction as the dependent variable and satisfaction with key product and service attributes as the predictors. The results of this analysis were:

$$S = .48X_1 + .13X_2 + .27X_3 + .42X_4 + .57X_5$$

where

$$S = \text{overall satisfaction rating}$$
$$X_1 = \text{rating of food quality}$$
$$X_2 = \text{rating of variety of menu}$$
$$X_3 = \text{rating of friendliness of employees}$$
$$X_4 = \text{rating of value}$$
$$X_5 = \text{rating of speed of service}$$

Average ratings on the 10-point scale for overall satisfaction and the five key attributes were:

$$S = 7.3$$
$$X_1 = 6.8$$
$$X_2 = 7.7$$
$$X_3 = 8.4$$
$$X_4 = 6.9$$
$$X_5 = 8.2$$

The regression coefficients provide estimates of the relative importance of the different attributes in determining overall satisfaction. The results show that $X_5$ (rating of speed of service) is the most important driver of overall satisfaction. The results also indicate that a one-unit increase in average rating on speed of service will produce an increase of .57 in average satisfaction rating. For example, the current average rating on speed of service is 8.2. If, by providing faster service, Pizza Quik could increase this rating to 9.2, then it would expect the average satisfaction rating to increase to 7.87. $X_1$ (rating of food quality) and $X_4$ (rating of value) are not far behind speed of service in their effect on overall satisfaction according to the regression estimates. At the other extreme, $X_2$ (rating of variety of menu) is least important in determining overall satisfaction, and $X_3$ (rating of friendliness of employees) is in between in importance.

The performance ratings provide a different picture. According to the average ratings, customers believe Pizza

Quik is doing the best job on $X_3$ (friendliness of employees) and the worst job on $X_1$ (food quality).

## Questions

1. Plot the importance and performance scores in a matrix. One axis would be importance from low to high and the other would be performance from low to high.

2. Which quadrant should you pay the most attention to? Why?

3. Which quadrant or quadrants should you pay the least attention to? Why?

4. Based on your analysis, where would you advise the company to focus its effort? What is the rationale behind this advice?

## REAL-LIFE RESEARCH • 18.2

### Gibson's Uses Predictive Analytics

Gibson's Family Discount Centers runs medium-size discount stores in almost 100 locations in smaller markets in Texas and Oklahoma. Gibson's Family Discount, as its name suggests, has always appealed to shoppers looking for bargains and discounts. It covers a wide range of merchandise comparable in scope to what you might find at a Walmart. However, it does not sell groceries beyond a very limited selection of things similar to what you might find in a 7-Eleven store. Gibson's has been steadily expanding in its market area over the last five years. It is particularly concerned with lagging sales of all clothing items.

Based on advice from its advertising agency, Gibson's has recently purchased a list of over one million households in its target area. The list includes names of all household members, addresses, and extensive data about the household from Acxiom. The information on each household also includes responses to a number of survey questions. Surveys were conducted in malls and shopping centers, by mail, from Internet panel members, and via survey invitations sent to e-mail lists.

Gibson's still relies heavily on mail circulars sent weekly to households in its target area. There are just under 2 million

households in that area, so the list it purchased covers about half of the households. Gibson's is hopeful that it can get the same kind of information about the other 1 million households over time. However, it wants to use the current list to improve the efficiency of its marketing efforts. In particular, it is interested in increasing sales of clothing items. As noted above, sales of clothing, in general, have lagged sales in relation to sales of the other items they carry.

Gibson's management is aware of the trend of increasing the use of predictive analytics and believes that Gibson's can improve marketing efficiency in general and clothing sales in particular by using these tools. To this end, Gibson's recently hired a young man, David Resendez, who previously worked as a predictive analyst for Target stores. Prior to joining Target, David graduated with a master's degree in predictive analytics from Northwestern University.

As his first assignment for Gibson's, David conducted a market segmentation study by Internet panel of just over 3,218 randomly selected households in the target geography and identified six segments based on a number of demographic, behavioral, attitudinal, and other variables. Cluster analysis was used to find the segments. Names for the segments were generated by looking at detailed characteristics of each segment and attempting to come up with a name or descriptor for each segment that best characterized it. A few summary items for the six segments are provided in the table below:

| Item | Online Buyers | Specialty Store Shoppers | Shop-aholics | Upscale Brand Loyalists | Classic Savers | Bargain Hunters |
|---|---|---|---|---|---|---|
| Number in study (total n=3,218) | 349 | 599 | 253 | 445 | 742 | 830 |
| Size of segment (% total) | 11% | 19% | 8% | 14% | 23% | 26% |
| % of clothing spending* | 7% | 19% | 11% | 11% | 19% | 18% |
| Average age | 32.3 | 39.7 | 36.7 | 42.3 | 41.5 | 41.9 |
| Average income | $113K | $125K | $103K | $128K | $103K | $77K |
| Average clothing spend | $1,220 | $1,613 | $1,842 | $1,323 | $1,270 | $1,118 |
| Overall opinion of Gibson's brand (% 6 - Extremely positive or 5) | 22% | 13% | 18% | 9% | 39% | 44% |

Looking at the six segments, David has recommended that the Classic Savers and Bargain Hunters segments are the best targets. He presented the results to management. After some heated discussion about the segments, management accepted the results.

In the pre-acceptance debate, one faction of management took the position that every household is a potential customer, while the other faction took the position that they need to focus on those households that are the most likely customers for the things they sell in their stores. Based on acceptance of the segments, management has tasked David with analyzing the 1 million household list and predicting which group or segment each household falls into. The two groups are Classic Savers plus Bargain Hunters (Group 1) or any of the other four segments (Group 2).

The potential financial impact is huge. For example, in our survey data from the segmentation it was estimated that just 42 percent of those in the market fall into the target segments. If we follow the analytics, then only about 420,000 households from our list would be targeted and 580,000 would not. Based on mailing of circulars only, eliminating the 580,000 saves $22,620,000 per year (52 weeks × 580,000 eliminated × $.75 cost per circular, printing, postage and processing).

The overall research design took into account that Gibson's would do the segmentation study and then apply the results to the 1 million households list. The process is:

- Conduct the market segmentation study and identify segments as described above.

- Append the same data we have for the 1 million households to the respondents from the market segmentation study respondents using the Acxiom data. This is done based on respondent address.

- Predict segment membership using segments from the market segmentation as the dependent variable and the appended Acxiom variables as predictors. The reason is that we will not have the responses to the segmentation survey questions when we go to the 1 million households list. We will only have the Acxiom data.

- The task is to predict whether people fall into one of the two groups: Classic Savers plus Bargain Hunters (Group 1) or any of the other four segments (Group 2). David chose multiple discriminant analysis for this task. Results are provided below:

**Standardized Discriminant Function Coefficients**

| Variable | Function 1 |
|---|---|
| Function1Less than 10 purchases high end brands | .934 |
| Spending on leisure travel last year | −.063 |
| Importance of price on 1–10 scale | .086 |
| Stay at home, homemaker | .070 |
| $ spent at lower end stores | .163 |

- Evaluate the predictive power of the multiple discriminant analysis model. Results are shown in the following table. At an overall rate of almost 79 percent correct predictions, it was deemed that segment membership was highly predictable based on using the Acxiom data.

- Apply the model to the one million households database, predicting segment membership and focusing marketing efforts on the group that includes Classic Savers plus Bargain Hunters.

**Classification Results[a,c]**

| | Segments | | Predicted Group | | Total |
|---|---|---|---|---|---|
| | | | 1.00 | 2.00 | |
| Original | Count | 1.00 | 1063 | 284 | 1347 |
| | | 2.00 | 405 | 1466 | 1871 |
| | % | 1.00 | 78.9 | 21.1 | 100.0 |
| | | 2.00 | 21.6 | 78.4 | 100.0 |

a. 78.6% of original grouped cases correctly classified.
b. Cross validation is done only for those cases in the analysis. In cross validation, each case is
c. 78.6% of cross-validated grouped cases correctly classified.

# Questions

1. What role did the Acxiom data play in the whole process? Would this application have been possible without the Acxiom data? Why or why not?

2. If you wanted to reach all Classic Savers plus Bargain Hunters, to how many of the one million households from the list would you need to mail to be sure?

3. What are the limitations of the approach illustrated in the case? What are the pros and cons?

# APPENDIX

## Role of Marketing Research in the Organization and Ethical Issues

## Marketing Research across the Organization

1. The question of data interpretation is not fully resolved in business today. Someone must still look at the data and decide what they really mean. Often this is done by the people in marketing research. Defend the proposition that persons in engineering, finance, and production should interpret all marketing research data when the survey results affect their operations. What are the arguments against this position?

2. Marketing research data analysis for a large electric utility found that confidence in the abilities of the repairperson is the customers' primary determinant of their satisfaction or dissatisfaction with the electric utility. Armed with these findings, the utility embarked on a major advertising campaign extolling the heroic characteristics of the electric utility repairperson. The repair people hated the campaign. They knew that they couldn't live up to the customer expectations created by the advertising. What should have been done differently?

3. When marketing research is used in strategic planning, it often plays a role in determining long-term opportunities and threats in the external environment. Threats, for example, may come from competitors' perceived future actions, new competitors, governmental policies, changing consumer tastes, or a variety of other sources. Management's strategic decisions will determine the long-term profitability, and perhaps even the survival, of the firm. Most top managers are not marketing researchers or statisticians; therefore, they need to know how much confidence they can put into the data. Stated differently, when marketing researchers present statistical results, conclusions, and recommendations, they must understand top management's tolerance for ambiguity and imprecision. Why? How might this understanding affect what marketing researchers present to management? Under what circumstances might the level of top management's tolerance for ambiguity and imprecision shift?

## Ethical Dilemma: Branding the Black Box in Marketing Research

Marketing research discovered branding in the mid-1980s and it experienced phenomenal growth in the 1990s, which continues today. Go to virtually any large marketing research firm's website, and you'll see a vast array of branded research products for everything from market segmentation to customer value analysis—all topped off with a diminutive $^{SM, TM}$, or $^®$. Here's just a sample: MARC's Designor$^{SM}$, Market Facts' Brand Vision$^®$, Maritz Research's 80/203$^®$ Relationship Manager, and Total Research's TRBC$^{TM}$, a scale bias correction algorithm.

A common denominator across some of these products is that they are proprietary, which means the firms won't disclose exactly how they work. That's why they're also known pejoratively as black boxes. A black box method is proprietary—a company is able to protect its product development investment. And if customers perceive added value in the approach, suppliers can charge a premium price to boot. (Black boxes and brand names are not synonymous. Almost all proprietary methods have a clever brand name, but there are also brand names attached to research methods that are not proprietary.)

At least two factors have given rise to this branding frenzy. First, competitive pressures force organizations to seek new ways to differentiate their product offerings from those of their competitors. Second, many large research companies are publicly held, and publicly held companies are under constant pressure to increase sales and profits each quarter. One way to do this is to charge a premium price for services. If a company has a proprietary method for doing a marketing segmentation study, presumably it can charge more for this approach than another firm using publicly available software such as SPSS or SAS. Ironically, it is possible that some black boxes are perfectly standard software such as SPSS and SAS; but if their proponents won't say how they work, or which techniques are used, these methods are still black boxes.

## Questions

1. Is the use of branded black box models unethical?

2. Should marketing research suppliers be forced to explain to clients how their proprietary models work?

3. Should firms be required by law to conduct validity and reliability tests on their models to demonstrate that they are better than nonproprietary models?

**Source:** Terry Grapentine, "You Can't Take Human Nature Out of Black Boxes," *Marketing Research* (Winter 2001), p. 21.

## SPSS EXERCISES FOR CHAPTER 18

## Exercise 1: Multivariate Regression

This exercise uses multivariate regression to explain and predict how many movies a respondent attends in a month.

1. Go to the website for the text and download the Movie database.

2. Open the database in SPSS and view the variables under Variable View. We will be using the independent variables Q2 Q4 Q6 Q8a Q8b Q8c Q8d Q9 Q10 Q12 and Q13 to predict the dependent variable Q3.

   We are including the variables Q4 and Q6 as is. Strictly speaking, is this proper? What might you want to do instead and why? Why might you decide to leave a variable in bins instead? Would it ever be proper to use a variable like Q11 as is?

3. Go to Analyze → Descriptive Statistics → Descriptives and move Q3 Q2 Q4 Q6 Q8a Q8b Q8c Q8d Q9 Q10 Q12 and Q13 to the Variable(s) box and click OK. Multivariate techniques require that every variable have a legitimate value. If a respondent did not answer every question, then the analyst must either ignore the observation entirely or impute estimates for the missing values. The default for statistical software is to ignore those observations automatically. We will not do imputation for this exercise.

   a. What will the sample size be for later multivariate techniques?

   b. Is this sample size large enough for multivariate regression?

   c. What would some possible problems be if the sample size were not large enough?

   d. Are the minimum and maximum values for each variable within the proper range? A value that is out of range would indicate either a data input error or a user-defined missing value like "Refused" or "Don't Know." Data input errors should be corrected or deleted. User-defined missing values should be declared in SPSS.

   e. Are all the variables within the proper range?

4. Go to Analyze → Regression → Linear.

   Move Q3 to Dependent.

   Move Q2 Q4 Q6 Q8a Q8b Q8c Q8d Q9 Q10 Q12 Q13 to Independent(s).

   Change Method to Stepwise.

   Click OK.

   a. Which independent variables did the stepwise regression select? Why not the rest?

   b. Is each variable chosen significant?

   c. Are the variables that have not been chosen necessarily insignificant?

   d. Is the model significant?

   e. Does this method guarantee that you get the "best" model?

5. Go to Analyze → Descriptive Statistics → Descriptives and remove Q6 Q8a Q8b Q8c Q8d Q9 Q10 and Q12 from the Variable(s) box, so that only Q3 Q2 Q4 and Q13 remain in the box and then click OK.

   What is the sample size now?

6. Go to Analyze → Regression → Linear.

   Move Q3 to Dependent.

   Remove Q6 Q8a Q8b Q8c Q8d Q9 Q10 and Q12 from Independent(s) so that only Q2 Q4 and Q13 remain.

   Change Method to Enter.

   Click OK.

   a. How and why does this model differ from the model based on stepwise regression?

   b. Which model is better?

## Interpretation

1. How does stated importance affect the number of times one attends movies?

2. How does spending money on snacks affect the number of times one attends movies?

3. How does student classification affect the number of times one attends movies?

4. If a sophomore thought that going to the movies was somewhat important and typically spent $12 on snacks, how many times per month would he or she attend movies, based on this model?

5. Do any of the variables, according to the results, appear to have an effect on the number of times one attends movies, or does it seem that other factors not covered in this survey are driving movie attendance?

## Exercise 2: Factor Analysis

This exercise uses factor analysis to explore how survey respondents consider various aspects of a theater visit.

1. Go to the website for the text and download the Movie database.

2. Open the database in SPSS and view the variables under Variable View. Notice that question 5 has 9 importance rating items.

3. Go to Analyze → Descriptive Statistics → Descriptives and move Q5a through Q5i to the Variable(s) box and click OK.

   a. Which item is the most important?

   b. Which item is the least important?

Multivariate techniques require that every variable have a legitimate value. If a respondent did not answer every question, then the analyst must either ignore the observation entirely or impute estimates for the missing values. The default for statistical software is to ignore those observations automatically. We will not get involved with imputation for this exercise.

a. What will the sample size be for later multivariate techniques?

b. Is this sample size large enough for factor analysis?

c. What would some possible problems be if the sample size were not large enough?

d. It is a good idea to check that the minimum and maximum values for each variable are within the proper range. A value that is out of range indicates either a data input error or a user-defined missing value such as "Refused" or "Don't Know." Data input errors should be corrected or deleted. User-defined missing values should be declared in SPSS.

e. Are all the variables within the proper range?

4. Go to Analyze → Descriptive Statistics → Descriptives and move Q5a through Q5i to the Variables box and click OK.

  Examine the resulting correlations matrix.

  a. Other than the 1's down the main diagonal of the matrix, what is the highest correlation in absolute value?

  b. Does any variable "just not fit" with the others?

  c. Does multicollinearity appear to exist among some of the items?

5. Go to Analyze → Data Reduction → Factor.

  Move Q5a through Q5i to the Variables box.

  Click the Rotation button, place a check in front of "Varimax," and click Continue.

  Click the Options button.

  Place a check in front of "Sorted by size."

  Place a check in front of "Suppress absolute values less than" and set the value after it to .25.

  Click Continue.

  Click OK.

  SPSS produces a lot of output Factor Analysis. It is possible to create much more output than we have generated here by setting various subcommands and options.

  a. How many factors did SPSS create?

  b. Why did it stop at that number?

  c. How could you change the defaults to create a different number of factors?

  d. Go to the output entitled Total Variance Explained. How much variance was explained in this Factor Analysis?

  e. Go to the output entitled Rotated Component Matrix. Why are some elements in this matrix blank?

  f. Do the components or factors make sense?

  g. Can you identify a common theme for each component or factor?

## Interpretation

1. Is this a good factor solution? Why do you say that?

2. How might you create a better factor solution?

3. What understanding has this analysis helped you gain about how moviegoers perceive their movie-going experience?

4. What recommendations would you give a manager of a movie house based on this analysis?

Jon Feingersh /Getty Images

# Communicating the Research Results

## LEARNING OBJECTIVES

1. Become aware of the primary purposes of a research report.

2. Learn how to organize and prepare a research report.

3. Gain insight into how to interpret and present marketing research results.

4. Learn how to make a personal presentation.

The research report is the culmination of all of our efforts. It is critical that it clearly conveys key findings and their implications. This chapter addresses this important issue.

# The Research Report

The research objectives, the decisions to be made based on the research, and a vision of the analysis and the report to be written should have guided the researcher through the design and execution of the research. For a survey-based project, the development of the questionnaire, in particular, should have been based on continuous reference to the research objectives. Now, we have the data, it has been cross tabulated, statistical testing has been performed, extensive statistical analysis has been conducted, and the researcher and her team have spent time sifting through all of this information and relating it back to the original objectives and the decisions associated with those objectives. This process could go on and on, but deadlines in the schedule push the process to a conclusion, often faster than we would like.

The researcher has a tremendous amount of information—piles of crosstabs, reams of statistical analyses, tons of notes, and an assortment of other pieces of information. The challenge is: How to package all of this in a coherent report that efficiently and effectively communicates the key findings and the decision implications of those findings? We like to think of this process as one of trying to figure out how to tell a story. Before you can tell a story, you have to have a pretty good idea of where the story is going to end up. All the analysis brings one to that conclusion. Once you know or have ascertained the key points that you want to make, it becomes much easier to map out what you need to get across to your readers to bring them to that same conclusion.

It is important that a research firm have a consistent style for reporting. This puts all analysts on the same page so that even a glance at a report will tell clients it was produced by a certain research firm. Having said all this, we must admit that when a client has a different internal standard for reporting, it is sometimes necessary to follow a different approach than the one recommended above. In some cases, the client may even dictate that the research supplier produce the report on the client's PowerPoint template according to the client's style rules. The Practicing Marketing Research feature below provides tips on preparing a great report.

# PRACTICING MARKETING RESEARCH

## How to Write a Research Report[1]

It happens all too often. As a market researcher, you slave away for countless hours in pursuit of insightful data but, to your shock, your research report flops and your data are dead in the water.

What went wrong? Chances are, it is how you presented the findings. The data-driven writing may either be so dry that it bored the reader to tears, or the real takeaways are buried underneath so many figures that your readers can't follow along.

Before you next open Microsoft Word, learn what you can do to hook readers from the first word to the last.

### Think Before You Write

Before you begin, while you're writing, and during your final review, keep these three items top of mind: Know your reader, your data, and the context for your research.

Orly Maravankin, executive vice president of GfK Custom Research North American in New York, says it helps for researchers to speak to business leaders or clients up front to get a clear understanding of their business objectives. Doing this helps you understand what you should accomplish with your reports. Beyond that, read your company's (or client's) annual business report, get a sense of the cultural and social trends surrounding your study, and determine the insight the data supports, she says.

"First and foremost, you have to figure out what you're really trying to say. What are the primary things you want your audience to walk away with?" says Fred John, senior business leader of intelligence and planning for MasterCard Inc. Typically, readers aren't looking for numbers but for insights into what business actions they should take. "The key thing is not to simply report what you found," he adds.

### Tell a Story

As you get ready to write, storyboard, or visually outline, your research so you can find ways to organize and tighten your thoughts, says Ed Stalling, chief storyteller at Maritz Research Inc. in Fenton, Missouri, who splits his time between reviewing company research reports and promoting writing tips and concepts to employees. From that outline, the context for the research should seem more apparent, he says, and you can better appreciate which aspects of the data matter most. Remember when you're writing that you're trying to tell a story with a distinct beginning, middle, and end. "You have to go beyond the nuts and bolts if you want to connect with clients."

That doesn't mean you should save all the good stuff for the very end of the report "when everyone's checked out mentally," John says. One approach is to write your research report like a newspaper story, where the headline calls out the "news" behind your research and the opening sentences of each section summarize the most important arguments, says Larry Gibson, a Minneapolis-based consultant and senior associate at research consultancy Eric Marder Associates Inc. and presenter of the tutorial Writing Research Reports and Creating Presentation Structures that Work at the AMA's Applied Research Methods conference. "The most important place in any given document is where you have the first words in the first paragraph," he says. "They either grab you or they don't."

To keep people engaged throughout, make sure you write in concise, conversational language: Use active voice, avoid long sentences, and eliminate jargon. "It would probably help if it read more like people talking as opposed to something put together by a bunch of robots," John says.

Since the "what does it mean" aspect is so important, make sure your conclusions are clearly expressed so that a reader casually skimming the report understands what you're saying, Gibson says. Use the tone of your writing to make the data come alive with an engaging point of view. For help on establishing tone, turn to some of your favorite business columnists, dissect their writing styles and ask why you're drawn to their words, John says.

After you finish writing, take some time away from the report so you can revise it with fresh eyes. Share your work with a colleague who doesn't know much about what you're writing and with someone who knows it well to see if they understand your points and stay interested throughout.

## Questions

1. Should you save all your good stuff for the end of your report? Why do you say that?

2. How do you keep people engaged throughout a report of presentation? Why is that important?

3. Are report readers looking for numbers or for insights into what business actions they should take? Why do you say that?

4. According to the author, what is the first thing you need to do before you begin a report or presentation? Why is that important? Is it easy?

# Organizing the Report

The traditional research report follows an outline like the following one:

1. **Title Page.** The title page should be dominated by the name of the project. Other elements that should be included are the name of the client organization, name of the research firm, and date of the report.

2. **Table of Contents.** This should not exceed one page and should list the major sections of the report along with the page numbers on which they start. It is a convenience for the reader and, often, the researcher in that it permits quick reference for finding specific information in the report.

3. **Executive Summary.** This is perhaps the most difficult part of the report to write, because it must succinctly cover the key findings and any recommendations that flow from those findings. Not all reports include recommendations. Whether they include recommendations depends on the nature of the research, what is expected from the research firm, and what the research found. However, all research reports should include key findings. What makes it tough to do the executive summary is that it should be short (two to four pages at a maximum), and many researchers find it very difficult to summarize the massive amount of information available to them in just two to four pages. It is easy to be long-winded, but it is difficult to be compact in your summarization. The executive summary should not summarize every single finding but should focus on those findings that are important and relevant to the goals of the research.

4. **Background.** The background sets the context for the research and addresses such things as the overall goal of the research, the decisions that need to be made, the company's strength and weaknesses regarding the issue in question, and other similar information.

It should not be more than one or two pages. Again, it is often difficult to compress a lot of information down to its essentials.

5. **Methodology.** Here we should discuss how the research was done and why it was done that way. Issues that need to be addressed include who was interviewed, why we chose to interview those people, how they were interviewed (for example, telephone survey, mail survey, Internet survey, or some hybrid of these methods), why they were interviewed in that manner, how they were selected, what type of sampling methodology did we use, whether the sample is a representative sample, how many people we interviewed, how we processed the completed surveys, what special statistical procedures were used and why we used those procedures, and other related questions. It is not necessary that this section be long—one to two pages is appropriate. If it is necessary to address some technical elements of the methodology in a more extensive manner, then more detailed information on, for example, statistical procedures used should be provided in an appendix.

6. **Findings.** This is typically the longest section of the report and should summarize results for almost every question on the survey.

7. **Appendices.** This final section of the report provides a number of supporting items such as a copy of the questionnaire, a set of cross tabulations for every question on the survey (client can look up specific issues not addressed in the findings), and other supporting material such as detailed technical information on special research procedures and techniques.

# Interpreting the Findings

**executive summary**
Portion of a research report that explains why the research was done, what was found, what those findings mean, and what action, if any, management should undertake.

The most difficult task for individuals writing research reports for the first time is interpreting the findings to arrive at conclusions and then using these conclusions to formulate recommendations. The **executive summary** is that portion of the report that explains what the research found, what the results mean, and what action, if any, should be taken, based on the research findings. The difficulties of this process are completely understandable, given that the marketing researcher is often inundated with piles of computer printouts, stacks of questionnaires, hundreds of pages of cross tabulations, the results of hundreds of statistical tests, pages and pages of statistical analysis printouts, and a scratchpad full of notes on the project. There is, however, a systematic method that the researcher can follow to draw conclusions.

The research objectives (there they are again) and background stated early in the marketing research process should serve as the primary guide for interpreting findings and drawing conclusions.

**conclusions**
Generalizations that answer the questions raised by the research objectives or otherwise satisfy the objectives.

**Conclusions** are generalizations that answer the questions raised by the research objectives or otherwise satisfy the objectives. These conclusions are derived through the process of *induction,* or generalizing from small pieces of information. The researcher must distill and merge the information and then develop a few descriptive statements that generalize the results. In short, the conclusion of a research report should be a statement or series of statements that communicate the results to the reader but do not necessarily include any of the data derived from the statistical analysis. The real process of developing the report requires the art of the storyteller, as described in the Practicing Marketing Research feature on page 503.

# PRACTICING MARKETING RESEARCH

## More Insights, Less Data—Why Your Research Should Tell a Story[2]

Researchers are caring by nature. We worry about many things during a project. We make sure every last detail of the survey is perfect. We write—and rewrite—questions, thinking about that one person who might not understand what we mean. We continually test the survey and monitor it all very closely as the "completes" start coming in. Are we going over quota? What is the drop-off? Is the survey too long?

Over the course of writing the report, we develop a keen insight into all the subtleties and details of the data we are examining. Because of this, we want to make sure clients (internal or external) know about every last interesting difference we find. This typically results in a 50-plus-page report with hundreds, if not thousands, of data points and a variety of graphs, charts, and tables. We, of course, sum it up in a concise executive summary, hoping that it will interest a senior executive just enough to dive into the rest of the immensely interesting minutiae of data.

And that is our problem: We are hoping that someone is going read it.

### No matter how compelling

In my almost 20 years in the field, my experience has been that no matter how compelling we make the deck, no marketing manager or senior executive wants to read half of a report to find out why his new product idea sucks and how to fix it. They don't even want to read half of a report if it's good news. In fact, the typical experience is that they are going to take the three or four key ideas talked about in the presentation and make them their talking points. They rarely go back to the deck.

So what does that mean for us?

We need to become strategic storytellers. While this is not a new idea and you may be saying, "I am already doing this," the new economic reality of shrinking budgets, tighter deadlines and fewer in-house research resources has made it more important than ever that we change how we tell our stories and who we tell them to, as our clients are more frequently not researchers themselves anymore.

### Inspire our clients

Stories are engaging, they take us places, they inspire us— and that is what we, as insight professionals, need to do: inspire our clients to take action. More and more clients just want to know the three things they can do right now to fundamentally change their business, especially senior executives whose time is already spread thin. They want it in a

quick, easy-access format that is engaging (and, dare I say, fun) to read.

Yes, the clients have paid for answers to all the questions they asked, but we need to become a lot smarter about how we tell these stories. We should not be afraid to leave results on the cutting-room floor if they start to dilute the main thread of the story. Only focus on a handful of questions that truly tell the story of the data, rather than worrying about making sure there's a chart or graph for every question in the main deck. Clients will actually be more satisfied because it is easy to understand the story and make decisions based on the results.

### More about insights, less about data

Trust me. It can be done, no matter how long the questionnaire or how many different inputs there are. It takes a different perspective on how to put together a report.

My company has done it with segmentation studies, brand health studies, and especially with many of our tracking studies. A great, and maybe somewhat extreme, example of this is a recent brand health study we conducted for one of our automotive clients. The survey itself was almost 20 minutes long. Each of three banner (crosstabs) books was more than 700 pages. In the end, we were able to distill the data down to 20 key slides that strategically told the story. Our work was well received—and socialized—by the client.

### Starting at the finish line

The single most important aspect of doing this is what we call starting at the finish line, or business objectives of the study. What problems are they trying to solve? How will this data be used in the decision-making process? Who is the ultimate audience?

If the client can't answer these initial questions, we push them to go and find the answers within their organization. If they still can't come up with answers, we ask them to think about the end presentation. What 5 or 10 things would they like to stand up and say, based on this study? Once these are established, we have a great sense of the true goals of the project and can start working toward developing the story based on this foundation. We often are also adding secondary data and competitive assessments that go beyond the study itself and help support the story.

### Even more reflective

Don't get me wrong. It is not easy. I am not implying that we only selectively analyze the results. What I am suggesting doesn't actually make report development easier or shorter. It, in fact, makes it much harder. Very tough decisions need to be made on what stays in the deck and what goes in the appendix —or is even jettisoned—but the end product will be even more reflective of our caring nature.

## Questions

1. What does the author mean by "starting at the finish line"? Does that approach make sense to you? Why or why not?

2. What is the difference between data and insights? What are today's decision makers looking for?

3. Do decision makers want to go through a detailed 50-page Power Point deck to arrive at the conclusions? Why do you say that?

4. Should your research report and presentation tell a story? Why do you say that?

5. Do you want to inspire clients with your report and presentation? What are the advantages, if any, of doing that?

## Format of the Report

The format and preparation of marketing research reports have changed dramatically over the last 15 years. The pressure to find more efficient and effective ways to communicate research results has pushed researchers toward brevity and a heavy reliance on presentation software to tell their stories. Microsoft's PowerPoint continues to dominate the presentation software market today.

It is expected, today, that a marketing research report should tell its story with pictures, videos, and graphics. This is what clients expect and what the researcher is expected to deliver. It is not unusual for clients to specify that they want graphics-based reports in their RFPs (requests for proposals). Research reports that might have included 50 or more pages of text and a handful of graphs in the past are now presented in a limited amount of text, perhaps just a few pages if it were all strung together, and 20 or 30 pages of graphs and tables. This approach enables time-pressed executives to quickly grasp the story and the key findings and move ahead to conclusions and recommendations. Most clients today just want a copy of the PowerPoint presentation instead of a long, detailed old-school report.

Graphics, text boxes, bulleted lists, and the like are used to interpret the meaning of various graphs. Examples of pages from a report prepared using presentation software are provided in Exhibits 19.1 through 19.9.

## Formulating Recommendations

**recommendations**
Conclusions applied to marketing strategies or tactics that focus on a client's achievement of differential advantage.

**Recommendations** are gained from the process of deduction. The marketing researcher applies the conclusions to the research objectives to provide direction for marketing strategies or tactics. A recommendation usually focuses on how the client can gain a differential advantage. A *differential advantage* is a true benefit offered by a potential marketing mix that the target market cannot obtain anywhere else (for example, American Airlines having exclusive U.S. carrier landing rights at a foreign airport).

In some cases, a marketing researcher may not be able to make specific recommendations and can only make more general ones. For example, the marketing researcher might not have sufficient information about the resources and experience base of the company or the decision maker for whom the report is being prepared. Or the researcher may have been told that the recommendations will be determined by the decision maker. Under these circumstances, the researcher offers conclusions and stops at that.

The final report is the culmination of the research effort. The quality of the report and its recommendations often determine whether a client will return to a research supplier.

Within a corporation, an internal report prepared by a research department may have less impact, but a history of preparing excellent reports may lead to merit salary increases and, ultimately, promotion for a research staff member.

## The Presentation

Clients may expect a presentation of the research results. A presentation serves many purposes. It requires that the interested parties assemble and become reacquainted with the research objectives and methodology. It also provides an opportunity for all interested parties to hear any unexpected events or findings, and the rationale behind them, and showcases the research conclusions and recommendations. In fact, for some decision makers in the company, the presentation will be their *only* exposure to the findings; they will never read the report. Other managers may only skim the report, using it as a memory-recall trigger for points made in the presentation. In short, effective communication in the presentation is absolutely critical. The Practicing Marketing Research feature below provides good guidelines for constructing presentations.

# PRACTICING MARKETING RESEARCH

## Guidelines for Effective Presentation[3]

Good researchers deliver accurate information. Great researchers deliver business insights. The challenge for many research managers is how to be perceived as insightful thinkers who are actively involved in corporate strategy sessions, rather than as pure "data heads" who have little more to offer than the basic information their studies kick out.

Let's suppose you're a market researcher with at least several years of experience and a track record of delivering pretty good presentations. Chances are, you may be reaching that point in your career where you want to be more than just a trusted conduit for research data—you want to have a larger, more strategic role. In short, you want an invitation to sit at the table where the business implications of your team's research are discussed.

So what's the best way to get an invitation to the party? Or to revitalize your career and really get noticed? The first place to start is with your presentations themselves—and realize that "pretty good" just isn't good enough. In my opinion, as someone who has both sat through hundreds of presentations (including many, many painfully boring ones) and given hundreds of presentations to audiences ranging from middle managers to corporate boards, the best way to get a seat at the decision-making table is to deliver presentations that (1) are engaging and (2) actually provide meaningful, relevant insights to decision makers. In other words, if you want to play at the senior level, you have to give senior-level presentations.

Follow these guidelines to give more effective research presentations.

### Change perceptions

So how do you craft a senior-level presentation—and get a more favorable response from top management? How do you change organizational perceptions so you're viewed as something other than a faithful number cruncher?

First, it's important to understand that data is one thing, but its significance—or what it actually means for the business—is quite another. Many research presentations are simply too long, too academic and/or too conceptual. They are data-intensive when they really need to be insight-intensive.

The purpose of a presentation is not to showcase all your hard work or to tell the audience everything you know about a particular topic. Rather, the purpose is to communicate insights that can help make critical business decisions easier. Top management wants to know "What do we do differently next Tuesday as a result of your work?" And that's all they want to know.

If you have a tendency—as we all do—to be enamored of all the wonderful data you brought into this world, the first step toward delivering a presentation that has an impact is to take a machete to your jungle of data. Eliminate everything that isn't perfectly relevant to your core story. By imposing some rigorous self-detachment, you can begin to learn how to separate the hard-won raw data from the more significant or larger business story it supports.

### Follow the fab five

In 25+ years of observing and guiding others in crafting presentations, I've seen great presentations and really bad presentations. There are many aspects that contribute to a compelling, effective presentation. If one adheres to the following "fab five" principles I've devised, you're generally ensured an engaged audience who will embrace your message—and, more importantly, act on it.

1. *Keep it tight.*
Many research presentations appear to be sold by weight—they can run 75 to 80 pages or more. In today's business climate, no one has time to sit through 40 pages, let alone 80. Keep your findings brief and focused on insights. And don't waste time on the nitty-gritty details of methodology or the analytical techniques employed—no one cares. Management trusts you to do good work and just wants to know what you learned.

2. *Keep it simple.*
The work we do is often very complex, but our success depends on our ability to make it appear simple—so the audience can easily follow what we're saying. Sometimes, in attempting to keep a presentation brief, we seem to compete to see who can get the most information on one slide. Data are not your offspring—it's OK to leave them behind. Remember to tell the audience just what's important—and resist the urge to tell them every little thing you learned along the way.

3. *Focus on the audience's needs—not yours.*
In all cases, the idea is to engage the audience—it's all about them. The purpose of a business presentation is not to showcase how incredibly hard you worked or how remarkable your research models are, nor is it to demonstrate your formidable command of presentation software. You just need to explain what the findings mean for the business.

4. *Be engaged—and engaging.*
You don't have the right to be boring! A researcher I know once said, "How excited can we get about this? It's only research." Yikes! If we want others to take us seriously and become engaged in the value we can bring to strategic discussions, we need to be engaged ourselves. Excitement and enthusiasm are contagious. Our presentations need to tell a great story, not read like a dictionary.

5. *Take a risk.*
In our efforts to be consummate professionals, many of us are almost fanatic about presenting absolutely accurate information. Consequently, we sometimes resist drawing conclusions on anything outside the specific scope of our study findings. The fact is that executives make calculated guesses based on imperfect information all day, every day. If we can't join them in embracing uncertainty and taking an informed risk, we won't be invited to the table when the big strategic decisions are made. Run with the big dogs—take a risk, answer the questions, and explain what the findings mean for the business.

## Identify what they will rarely tell you

If your presentations are characterized by careful tables of data, really densely packed slides, ripe with all kinds of great information and impressive discussions of methodology, chances are, your audience is bored to tears—but they'll rarely tell you. With presentations, as with life in general, most people tend to keep their toughest responses bottled up inside because they don't want to hurt anyone's feelings—especially if they see you as a sincere, well-intentioned data geek.

**"The Five Things Top Management Wants To Tell Research—But Just Can't."**

1. "You're boring us to tears."

2. "Enough with all the numbers already—what do we do?!"

3. "I don't have all day to listen to you—how about 10 pages next time instead of 50?"

4. "I don't care what fancy methodology you used—what's the bottom line?"

5. "Take a position, will you?"

Want to look at engaged, interested faces instead of the unfocused stares of people about to slip into unconsciousness? Then, once again, present clear, concise, simple insights instead of data findings.

## Strive to be viewed in a different light

Insights don't require dense charts and tables with eight-point type—they do require clear, concise, simple information for people who don't care about research details but do care very much about the business implications of your work. Want a seat at the table where the decision-making happens? Give your organization's decision makers the business implications of your research and why it should matter to them—in 15 pages or less—and before you know it, you'll be viewed in a different light. You'll be a regular at the strategy table.

## Questions

1. What does the author mean by "taking a risk"? What is the risk? What is the potential reward?

2. What do insights require? What don't they require?

3. If you deliver a presentation with careful tables of data, really densely packed slides, ripe with all kinds of great information and impressive discussions of methodology, what effect will it likely have on your audience?

4. How can the presenter engage his or her audience?

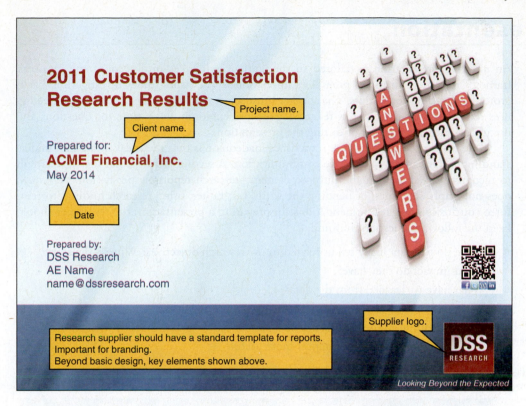

**Exhibit 19.1**

**Sample Title Slide**

## 2011 Customer Satisfaction Research Results

Project name.

Client name.

Prepared for:
**ACME Financial, Inc.**
May 2014

Date

Prepared by:
DSS Research
AE Name
name@dssresearch.com

Supplier logo.

**DSS** RESEARCH

*Looking Beyond the Expected*

Research supplier should have a standard template for reports.
Important for branding.
Beyond basic design, key elements shown above.

---

**Exhibit 19.2**

**Sample Table of Contents**

## Table of contents

Not more than a page. Helps user refer to specific areas of interest. List major sections.

| | |
|---|---|
| **Background and Objectives** | 2 |
| **Executive Summary** | 3 |
| **Methodology** | 5 |
| **Research Findings** | 6 |
|     Overall Satisfaction | 7 |
|     Plan Loyalty | 8 |
|     Network, Policies, and Other Plan Items | 10 |
|     Quality and Compensation Issues | 14 |
|     ACME Staff | 21 |
|     ACME Processes | 26 |
|     Communications | 32 |
|     Demographics | 34 |
| **Appendices** | |
|     Appendix A: Key Driver Statistical Model | 38 |
|     Appendix B: Questionnaire | 48 |
|     Appendix C: Crosstabulations | 49 |

# Making a Presentation

An effective presentation is tailored to the audience. It takes into account the receivers' frame of reference, attitudes, prejudices in relation to the issues under investigation, backgrounds, and time constraints. The speaker must select words, concepts, and illustrative figures to which the audience can relate. A good presentation allows time for questions and discussion, either at the end or during the presentation.

One reason presentations are sometimes inadequate is that the speaker lacks an understanding of the barriers to effective communication. A second factor is that the speaker fails to recognize or admit that the purpose of many research reports is persuasion. *Persuasion* does not imply stretching or bending the truth, but rather, using research findings to reinforce conclusions and recommendations. In preparing a presentation, the researcher should keep the following questions in mind:

- What do the data really tell us related to the research objectives? What is the story?
- What impact do they have?
- What have we learned from the data?
- What do we need to do, given the information we now have?
- How can future studies of this nature be enhanced?
- What could make this information more useful?

Bernhard Lang /Getty Images

## Background and Objectives

Keep it concise. Put key objectives in bulleted list.

**Background.** ACME, like other progressive organizations, wants to develop a program to assess customer satisfaction with the services they receive from the organization. This information will be used in ACME's quality improvement efforts. The goal is to provide rational direction for those efforts.

**Objectives.** This type of research is designed to achieve the following objectives:

- Measure overall satisfaction with ACME compared to the competition.
- Measure customer satisfaction with ACME's new website where all transactions with ACM can be handled.
- Measure satisfaction with specific elements of all other programs and services provided to customers by ACME.
- Identify major reasons for satisfaction/dissatisfaction.
- Evaluate and classify program and service elements on the basis of their importance to customers and the ACME's perceived performance of ACME (i.e., identify areas of strength and opportunities for improvement).

**Exhibit 19.3**

**Sample Background and Objectives**

---

## Executive summary

Focus on key findings, not just reiteration of detailed results.

**The majority are loyal, but satisfaction declined.**

- Four out of five customers see their relationship with ACME continuing on a long-term basis. Over half are categorized as secure or favorable and can be considered loyal to ACME.
- Two-thirds report they are satisfied with ACME in 2014. However, this is a significant decline from 80.1% in 2010.
- ACME overall satisfaction and loyalty measures are significantly lower than the National Average.

**Heavy Users are highly satisfied; Light Users less so.**

- Heavy users report significantly higher satisfaction than light users and are more likely to see their relationship with ACME continuing on a long-term basis.
- Although only a small percentage of customers is categorized as alienated, Light Users make up a higher proportion of this group.

**ACME processes are primary areas of strength.**

- Both the customer service and application processes are identified through key driver analysis as areas of strength for ACME.
- Satisfaction with the billing process continues an upward trend. Ratings are on par with the National Average and significantly higher than in 2013.

**Staff ratings remain strong, with knowledge a key asset.**

- The majority of customers are satisfied with all aspects related to ACME staff. About four out of five are satisfied with staff knowledge, the area of highest satisfaction across all staff levels.
- Although still high, relatively lower staff ratings are associated with accessibility related measures. Key driver analysis identifies ease of reaching staff as an opportunity for improvement.

Continued on next page

**Exhibit 19.4(a)**

**Sample First Page of Executive Summary**

**Exhibit 19.4(b)**

**Sample First Page of Executive Summary**

## Executive summary

> Provide direction.

**Key opportunities relate to compensation issues, policies and procedures.**

- In 2011, significantly fewer customers are satisfied with reimbursement levels and agree that ACME compensates fairly, both opportunities for improvement identified through key driver analysis.

- Other opportunities for improvement include a number of ACME policies and procedures:
  - Is committed to improving quality of patient care
  - Has utilization guidelines that are clinically appropriate
  - Has administrative policies and procedures that encourage quality care
  - Controls cost without sacrificing quality of care

- In addition, those considered alienated or at risk report high levels of dissatisfaction with their ability to provide input on policies and procedures affecting care and strong disagreement that ACME controls cost without sacrificing quality of care.

- Continue to focus improvement efforts on these measures for the greatest impact on physician satisfaction.

---

**Exhibit 19.5**

**Sample Methodology Slide**

## Methodology

> Explain what was done in a simple, straightforward manner.

**Questionnaire.** DSS was responsible for developing the survey instrument. ACME approved the final draft of the questionnaire. A copy of the mail survey instrument used is provided in Appendix B.

**Methodology employed.** Eligible respondents included a list of customers provided by ACME. The sample design is as follows:

| | 2014 | | | 2013 | | | 2012 | | |
|---|---|---|---|---|---|---|---|---|---|
| | Heavy Users | Light Users | Overall | Heavy Users | Light Users | Overall | Heavy Users | Light Users | Overall |
| Completed surveys | 52 | 60 | **112** | 101 | 71 | **172** | 87 | 71 | **158** |
| Mailed Surveys | 200 | 200 | **400** | 200 | 200 | **400** | 200 | 200 | **400** |
| Returned undeliverable surveys | NA | NA | **4** | NA | NA | **8** | NA | NA | **14** |
| Response rate | 26.0% | 30.0% | **28.0%** | 50.5% | 35.5% | **43.0%** | 43.5% | 35.5% | **39.5%** |
| Adjusted response rate** | NA | NA | **28.3%** | NA | NA | **43.9%** | NA | NA | **40.9%** |
| Sample error* | NA | NA | **±7.9%** | NA | NA | **±5.6%** | NA | NA | **±6.1%** |
| Initial survey mailed | February 28, 2014 | | | March 7, 2013 | | | February 28, 2012 | | |
| Second survey mailed | March 21, 2014 | | | March 28, 2013 | | | March 21, 2012 | | |
| Last day to accept surveys | April 27, 2014 | | | May 2, 2013 | | | April 25, 2012 | | |

**Data collection.** All data were collected by DSS Research.

**Data processing and analysis.** DSS processed all completed surveys and analyzed the results. A complete set of survey tabulations is provided in Appendix C of this report.

* At 95% confidence, using the most pessimistic assumption regarding variance (p=0.5).
** Excludes undeliverables.

**Exhibit 19.6**

**Graphics Make Communication More Effective**

## Loyalty

Over half of customers are categorized as secure or favorable and can be considered loyal to ACME. One in four are at risk, though not necessarily dissatisfied. Only a small percentage are categorized as alienated. The Specialists Segment makes up a greater proportion of this group.

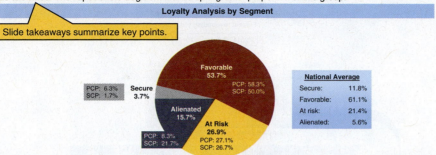

**Loyalty Analysis by Segment**

Slide takeaways summarize key points.

Favorable 53.7% — PCP: 58.3% SCP: 50.0%

Secure 3.7% — PCP: 6.3% SCP: 1.7%

Alienated 15.7%

At Risk 26.9% — PCP: 27.1% SCP: 26.7% / PCP: 8.3% SCP: 21.7%

| National Average | |
|---|---|
| Secure: | 11.8% |
| Favorable: | 61.1% |
| At risk: | 21.4% |
| Alienated: | 5.6% |

**Questions used to determine "loyalty":**

- Q13 - Overall, how satisfied are you with ACME? *Very satisfied, satisfied, dissatisfied, very dissatisfied*
- Q15 - Would you recommend ACME to your patients who asked your advice about which managed care plan to join? *Definitely yes, probably yes, probably not, definitely not*
- Q16 - Would you recommend ACME to a physician who was interested in contracting with a managed care plan? *Definitely yes, probably yes, probably not, definitely not*
- Q17 - I see my relationship with ACME continuing on a long-term basis. *Strongly agree, agree, disagree, strongly disagree*

**Definitions of groups:**

- **Secure** – Top box answer on all four questions. Very satisfied and loyal to ACME.
- **Favorable** – Top-two-box answer on all four questions (but not top box on all four). Satisfied and fairly loyal to ACME.
- **At Risk** – Bottom-two-box answer on one, two or three (but not all) of the four questions. Not necessarily satisfied and has questionable loyalty to ACME.
- **Alienated** – Bottom-two-box answer on all four questions. Dissatisfied and likely to leave ACME.

**Exhibit 19.7**

**Multiple Graphics Provide Summary on a Topic**

## Quality and compensation issues – ACME

The majority of customers are positive toward ACME policies and procedures, although at significantly lower levels than the National Average.

**Q2. How much do you agree or disagree that ACME...?**

Percent responding *strongly agree* or *agree*...

2011 ■ 2010 ■ 2009

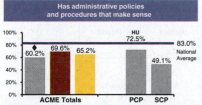

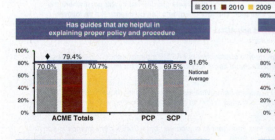

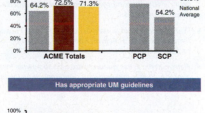

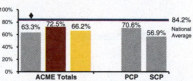

**Has guides that are helpful in explaining proper policy and procedure**

ACME Totals: 70.0%, 79.4%, 70.7% — PCP 70.6% — SCP 69.5% — 81.6% National Average

**Is committed to improving customer service**

ACME Totals: 64.2%, 72.5%, 71.3% — PCP HU 76.0% — SCP 54.2% — 85.5% National Average

**Has administrative policies and procedures that make sense**

ACME Totals: 60.2%, 69.6%, 65.2% — PCP HU 72.5% — SCP 49.1% — 83.0% National Average

**Has appropriate UM guidelines**

ACME Totals: 63.3%, 72.5%, 66.2% — PCP 70.6% — SCP 56.9% — 84.2% National Average

♦ Indicates 2011 ACME Total results are significantly higher or lower than the National Average at the 0.05 level.
**HU** Indicates PCP results are significantly higher than the specialist results at the 0.05 level.

## Exhibit 19.8

**Graphics and Tables Work Together**

### Physician communications - Internet access and usage

Internet access continues to increase among customers. Broadband is the most common connection type, used by more than half.

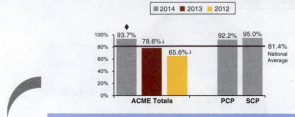

**Q10. Do you and your staff currently have access to the Internet?**

Percent responding *yes…*

- 2014
- 2013
- 2012

| | ACME Totals | PCP | SCP |
|---|---|---|---|
| | 93.7% ♦ | 92.2% | 95.0% |
| | 78.6% ↓ | | |
| | 65.6% ↓ | | |

81.4% National Average

If yes..

**Q11. If yes, which of the following do you use?^\*\***

| | ACME Total 2014 | Usage level | |
|---|---|---|---|
| | | Heavy | Light |
| Base: | (n=101) | (n=46) | (n=55) |
| Broadband | 55% | 52% | 58% |
| Dial-up | 23.8% | 19.6% | 0 |
| Other | 20.8% | 28.3% | 14.5% |

^ New question in 2011.
\*\* Note: National Average data not available.
↓↑ Indicates that year's result is significantly higher or lower than the 2011 ACME result at the 0.05 level.
♦ Indicates 2011 ACME Total results are significantly higher or lower than the National Average at the 0.05 level.

## Exhibit 19.9

**Graphics and Text Tell How to Interpret Statistical Results**

### Key Driver Statistical Model - POWeR™ Chart

**Classification matrix.** The importance and performance results for each item in the model are plotted in a matrix like the one shown to the right. This matrix provides a quick summary of what is most important to customers and how ACME is doing on those items. The matrix is divided into four quadrants. The quadrants are defined by the point where the medians of the importance and performance scales intersect. The four quadrants can be interpreted as follows:

- *Power. These items are very important to customers and ACME's performance levels on these items are high. Promote and leverage your strengths in this quadrant.*

- *Opportunity. Items in this quadrant are very important to customers, but ACME's performance is below average. Focus your resources on improving processes that underlie these items and look for significant improvements in your satisfaction scores.*

- *Wait. Though still important to customers, these items are somewhat less important than those that fall on the right hand of the chart. Relatively speaking, ACME's performance is low on these items. Dealing with these items can wait until more important items have been dealt with.*

- *Retain. Items in this quadrant are also somewhat less important to customers, but ACME's performance is above average. Simply maintain your performance on these items.*

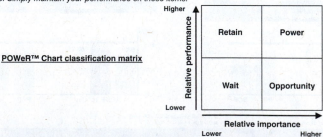

POWeR™ Chart classification matrix

# PRACTICING MARKETING RESEARCH

## The Market Researchers' Wish List[4]

It's not uncommon for market researchers to also participate in the technology development at their firm. Confirmit, a market research firm, polls those researchers in its Market Research Software Survey, to get feedback on emerging industry trends and the role technology is playing in companies across the industry. A recent survey identified some changes in reporting methods and how researchers were using software in these areas.

In a single year, Confirmit found significant shifts in the distribution methods being used for research reports. PowerPoint presentations remained the most popular over that period, but fell from being used in 56 percent of all projects to 48 percent. Microsoft Word documents, printed tabs, and Acrobat PDFs all declined as well. Online results delivery remained static, and interactive analysis—the only distribution method to increase in usage—rose slightly, from 8 to 10 percent. And while it appears that many researchers are using multiformat delivery, even that modality appears to be on the decline. Even though 52 percent of companies considered crosstab report production capabilities as essential, only 14 percent of companies actually used them.

Concerning researchers' wishes for analysis and reporting tools, two main points seemed to emerge. First, 74 percent rated PowerPoint issues as one of their top three priorities, asking software developers to create some solution that would automate the process of having to manually manipulate imported data and charts into presentation-quality material. Second, three-fifths of respondents assessed the state of online analysis tools to be unsatisfactory, and they were actively looking for alternate solutions to what was available. A smaller proportion, 38 percent, expressed a desire for better desktop analytical tools as a top-three priority as well.

## Questions

1. Which distribution methods do you think would be most useful for research reports? Are some better suited for particular situations? Would you use multiformat delivery?

2. Have you used any software for generating research reports? How well did it work? What would be at the top of your wish list, based on your experience?

## Presentations by Internet

With PowerPoint, publishing presentations to the web is easier than ever. Publication to the web enables individuals to access the presentation, regardless of where they are or when they need to access it. In addition, researchers can present results at multiple locations on the Internet. The steps are very simple:

1. Open your presentation in PowerPoint. To see what your slides will look like on the web, choose "Web Page Preview" from the "File" menu. After you have made any edits, choose "Save as Web Page" from the same menu.

2. The "Save As" dialog box allows you to change the title of your presentation to whatever you want displayed in the title bar of your visitor's browser.

3. The "Publish" button takes you to the "Publish as Web Page" dialog box, where you can customize your presentation.

4. The "Web Options" dialog box lets you specify the way your published file will be stored on the Web server and whether to update internal links to these files automatically.

See the Practicing Marketing Research Feature above for information on trends in report delivery.

## SUMMARY

The six primary sections of a contemporary marketing research report are, in order: the table of contents, background and objectives, executive summary, methodology, findings, and appendixes with supporting information.

The primary objectives of the marketing research report are to state the specific research objectives, explain why and how the research was done, present the findings of the research, and provide conclusions and recommendations. Most of these elements are contained in the executive summary. The conclusions do not necessarily contain statistical numbers derived from the research but rather generalize the results in relation to the stated objectives. Nor do conclusions suggest a course of action. This is left to the recommendations, which direct the conclusions to specific marketing strategies or tactics that would place the client in the most positive position in the market.

The marketing research report of today makes heavy use of graphics to present key findings. For most researchers, PowerPoint is the software of choice for creating research reports. In terms of mechanics, reports minimize the use of words, feed information to clients in "minibites," and make extensive use of bulleted charts and graphics. In addition to the written report, which is often nothing more than a copy of the PowerPoint presentation, a presentation of research results is often required. It is common for research reports to be published on the Internet by the client or by the researcher at the client's request. This has the advantage of making the results available to individuals worldwide in the client's organization. The Internet can also be used to support simultaneous presentation of the research results in multiple locations.

## KEY TERMS

executive summary 502

conclusions 502

recommendations 504

## QUESTIONS FOR REVIEW & CRITICAL THINKING

1. What are the roles of the research report? Give examples.

2. Distinguish among findings, conclusions, and recommendations in a research report.

3. Why should research reports contain executive summaries? What should be contained in an executive summary?

## WORKING THE NET

1. Go to *http://www.gallup.com* and examine some of the special reports on American opinions, such as those found under "Economy." Do these reports meet the criteria discussed in the text for good marketing research reports? Why or why not?

2. Go to *http://www.slideshare.net/*. Click on Today's Top Slideshares, Review several of the presentations you find to be particularly interesting. Think about what you like and don't like about each one.

# REAL-LIFE RESEARCH • 19.1

## The United Way

The United Way was concerned about the attitudes of non-donors toward the organization with the theory that their reasons for not donating are tied to their perceptions of United Way. It is also interested in getting a sense of what factors might convert nondonors to donors. The executive summary from the research report is provided below. Each heading and the text that follows were provided on PowerPoint slides in the report, and the presentation was provided by the research firm that conducted the study of these issues.

## Executive Summary Objectives and Methodology

- The general purposes of this study were to determine the attitudes of nondonors toward the United Way, to assess the reasons for not donating, and to ascertain factors that may influence nondonors to contribute in the future.
- The study relied on primary data gathered through online surveys.
- The study employed a probability sample.
- Responses were obtained from 726 respondents.

## Findings

- The percentage with positive perceptions of the United Way was greater than the percentage having negative perceptions. However, the majority had no opinions about United Way.
- Only 5.2 percent rated United Way fair or poor in providing benefits to those in need.
- United Way actually spends 9 to 10 percent of contributions on administrative costs, although 80.6 percent believed that the United Way used more than 10 percent of its contributions on administrative costs.
- Primary reasons for not contributing were contribution to other charities or religious organizations, personal financial circumstances, lack of knowledge of how donated funds are used, personal beliefs, absence of favorite charities, pressure to contribute, and preference to donate time rather than money.

- Of those who were asked to contribute, pressure seemed somewhat important in influencing their decision not to contribute.
- Of those who indicated that personal financial reasons influenced their decision not to give, 35.6 percent indicated they would give to United Way if asked.
- Other charities and religious denominations are clearly in competition with United Way for donations.
- Many respondents indicated that they would contribute if they could specify the charity to receive their contributions, had more knowledge about the United Way and the charities it supports, were asked to give, had less pressure to give, could use payroll deduction, and had the option of spreading contributions over time.
- Of those whose place of employment participated in the United Way campaign, 49.6 percent had been asked to give but did not.
- Workplace campaigns reach a large number of executives and professional and administrative personnel in the higher-income brackets but do not reach a significant number of service personnel or lower-income households.

## Conclusions

- Negative perceptions do not appear to be a major factor affecting reasons for not contributing. However, a positive perception does not necessarily translate into a contribution.
- Noncontributors lack sufficient information regarding the United Way to form an accurate perception of the organization.
- There is a lack of knowledge concerning the United Way and the organizations to which it allocates contributions.
- Respondents believe that the United Way uses more for administrative costs than it actually does.
- The United Way is in competition for a limited number of charity dollars.

## Recommendations

- Conduct additional research to determine noncontributor's level of knowledge of the United Way and the purpose that the United Way serves.

- Increase education for potential contributors regarding the United Way's purpose, the organizations it supports, and the United Way's reasonable administrative costs.

- Expand the frequency of campaigns in the workplace and develop ways to increase awareness of the methods of contributing.

- Develop appropriate competitive marketing strategy to address the United Way's competitors.

## Questions

1. Do you think that the executive summary provides guidance for decision-making information?

2. Are all of the elements present that should be included in an executive summary as discussed in this chapter?

3. Do the findings, conclusions, and recommendations logically follow from the objectives? Why or why not?

## REAL-LIFE RESEARCH • 19.2

## TouchWell Storefront Concept and Naming Research

TouchWell is a large health insurance plan serving major markets in Texas, including Dallas / Fort Worth (DFW), Houston, Austin, and San Antonio. TouchWell is attempting to adapt to a changing health insurance environment transitioning from a situation where:

- 60% of consumers receive coverage through their employer or their spouse's employer.

- 8% purchased health insurance on their own directly from a carrier.

- 16% received coverage through some type of government program, including Medicare and Medicaid.

- 16% are uninsured.

Passage of the Affordable Care Act in 2010 promises to change the landscape for TouchWell and other health insurers:

- Fewer consumers will receive their coverage through employers as employers, particularly small ones, begin to drop employee coverage.

- More of those who had employer-sponsored coverage previously will buy on their own directly from carriers through federal- or state-sponsored health insurance marketplaces, which began in the fall of 2013.

- The uninsured will be able to purchase through the health insurance market places, noted above, with a level of government subsidy, up to 100%.

The main issue that TouchWell wants to address in the research project for which results are shown is the fact that more consumers will be buying directly from carriers. This means that, as with other consumer goods, their brands will become increasingly important and they need to have closer contact with consumers. To address these changes, TouchWell executives have made the decision to open "stores" in selected areas throughout the markets they serve. They believe that consumers are going to need convenient channels through which they can communicate and interact with health insurance organizations. They have observed that a few other health insurers in other parts of the country have opened retail stores and believe that they need to do the same to remain competitive. They are interested in understanding the overall appeal of their storefront location concept in different markets and across different demographic groups, want to test various name options they have come up, and need to quantify the relative importance of different store features.

The methodology used in TouchWell's recently project and selected research results are provided on the following pages.

## Questions

1. Comment on the general effectiveness of the presentation. Are the slides easy to understand? Do they effectively convey key information? What suggestions would you make for improving the presentation?

2. Comment on the "overall concept appeal" results. What does this slide convey? Does it provide a clear picture? What changes, if any, would you make in the presentation of this information?

3. Comment on the "naming comparison" results slide. A strong contingent of managers favors the TouchWell Care Café name. What would you say to them? What would be your first choice among the names tested based on the research findings? Second choice? Third choice?

4. How would your recommendations for services to offer differ based on appeal of service? Likelihood to use service? Which one do you think is more important?

5. What would your recommendations be regarding key characteristics of the centers?

# Health Insurance Storefront Naming Research

Prepared for:
**TouchWell**
April 2014

Prepared by:
Acme Research

## Methodology

**Questionnaire.** Acme worked with TouchWell to develop the survey instrument for Internet administration.

**Data collection.** All data were collected by Acme Research via an online survey.

**Sample design.**

- **Qualified respondents.** Member and non-member consumers ages 18-80 who live within one of the TouchWell markets.

- **Sample source.** Sample was provided by an online panel company with supplemental sample provided by Touch Well.

- **Sample type.** Stratified probability sample.

- **Sample size.** 800 surveys were completed (400 members and 400 non-members).

- **Sampling error.** A sample of 800 consumers yields a sampling error of ±3.5%, at 95% confidence using the most pessimistic assumption regarding variance (p = 0.5).

**Data processing and tabulation.** Acme processed all completed surveys and analyzed the results. All data were weighted by ethnicity, gender, income, education and age to accurately reflect true population proportions.

Percentages lower than 5.0% are not labeled in charts or graphs where space does not permit.

Unless otherwise noted, all charts represent the top three box scores on a 10-point scale.

## Concept description

We would like to get your opinion on a new idea about creating a place dedicated to promoting health and well-being for you and your family.

A health insurance company is planning to open **storefront locations throughout Texas** where you, your neighbors, and others in your community can interact face-to-face with a health concierge.

What will make the storefront unique is that you will be able to:

- Obtain personalized answers to health insurance questions and get help in navigating the complexities of the health care system at a one-stop-shop location.
- Get advice from friendly and caring staff about how to stay healthy, get better, or live effectively with a health condition.
- Learn about resources and tools available to manage your health, including benefits of your heath insurance coverage, and help from government programs, and community organizations.
- Make arrangements for using healthcare such as selecting doctors, obtaining referrals if needed, and making appointments.
- Resolve customer service problems such as those related to ID cards, and claims and billing issues.

Not only will the storefront will be open to everyone in the community, but members of the health insurance company will find it an especially convenient place to manage their health care needs and general well-being.

## Overall concept appeal

Nearly half find the storefront concept appealing, with more than four in 10 indicating that the association of the concept with TouchWell made it more appealing and nearly as many indicating that the concept made them feel more positive about TouchWell. Additionally, more than four in 10 indicated that they would be likely to visit the storefront.

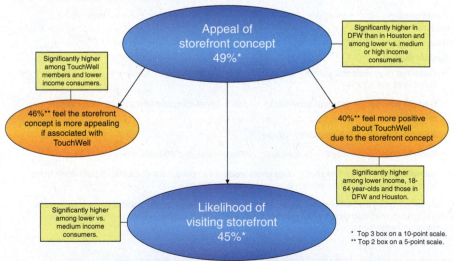

Q3. Based on the description above, how appealing is the storefront idea you just read about? Q4. How likely would you be to visit the storefront if it was offered in your neighborhood? Q5. If the storefront located in your neighborhood was brought to you by TouchWell, would that change your opinion about the storefront idea? Q6. If the storefront located in your neighborhood was brought to you by TouchWell, would that change your opinion about TouchWell?

## Naming comparison

With or without the presentation of visuals, the clear top two choices among all groups are TouchWell Care Center and TouchWell Customer Care Center.

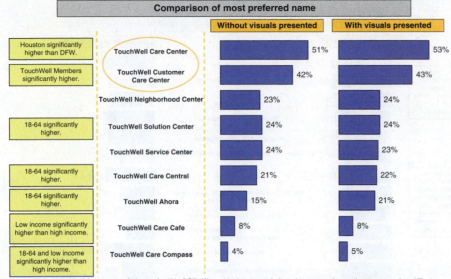

| | Comparison of most preferred name | | |
| --- | --- | --- | --- |
| | | Without visuals presented | With visuals presented |
| Houston significantly higher than DFW. | TouchWell Care Center | 51% | 53% |
| TouchWell Members significantly higher. | TouchWell Customer Care Center | 42% | 43% |
| | TouchWell Neighborhood Center | 23% | 24% |
| 18-64 significantly higher. | TouchWell Solution Center | 24% | 24% |
| | TouchWell Service Center | 24% | 23% |
| 18-64 significantly higher. | TouchWell Care Central | 21% | 22% |
| 18-64 significantly higher. | TouchWell Ahora | 15% | 21% |
| Low income significantly higher than high income. | TouchWell Care Cafe | 8% | 8% |
| 18-64 and low income significantly higher than high income. | TouchWell Care Compass | 4% | 5% |

Q7a. How well does each of the following names fit the storefront idea? Q7b. We want to show you again the various name options as they may appear in real life at a storefront. For each option, tell us how well the name fits the storefront idea.

## Naming comparison

TouchWell Care Center is the top choice.

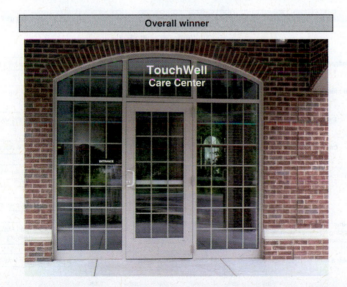

**Overall winner**

### Appeal and likelihood to use services

The most appealing services of the 29 tested are related to clinical navigation/care coordination, sales, education and health screens. Likelihood to use does not consistently follow appeal. For example, fitness/exercise classes are 11th in appeal but are the most likely to be used.

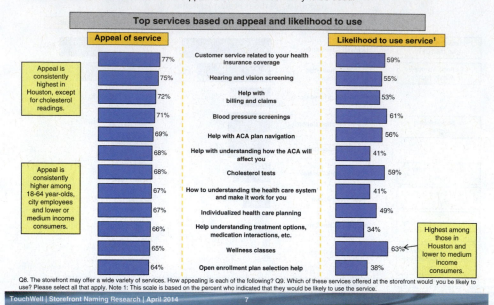

**Top services based on appeal and likelihood to use**

| Appeal of service | | Likelihood to use service[1] |
|---|---|---|

Appeal is consistently highest in Houston, except for cholesterol readings.

Appeal is consistently higher among 18-64 year-olds, city employees and lower or medium income consumers.

| Service | Appeal | Likelihood |
|---|---|---|
| Customer service related to your health insurance coverage | 77% | 59% |
| Hearing and vision screening | 75% | 55% |
| Help with billing and claims | 72% | 53% |
| Blood pressure screenings | 71% | 61% |
| Help with ACA plan navigation | 69% | 56% |
| Help with understanding how the ACA will affect you | 68% | 41% |
| Cholesterol tests | 68% | 59% |
| How to understanding the health care system and make it work for you | 67% | 41% |
| Individualized health care planning | 67% | 49% |
| Help understanding treatment options, medication interactions, etc. | 66% | 34% |
| Wellness classes | 65% | 63% |
| Open enrollment plan selection help | 64% | 38% |

Highest among those in Houston and lower to medium income consumers.

Q8. The storefront may offer a wide variety of services. How appealing is each of the following? Q9. Which of these services offered at the storefront would you be likely to use? Please select all that apply. Note 1: This scale is based on the percent who indicated that they would be likely to use the service.

### Importance of storefront characteristics

Knowledgeable and friendly staff members, personalized service and convenient locations are the most important store characteristics in driving likelihood to visit.

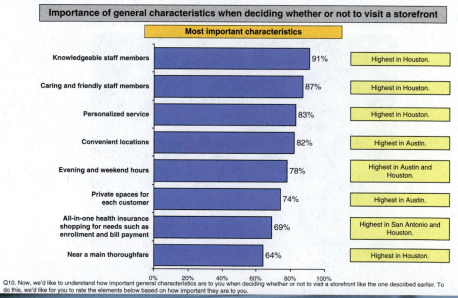

**Importance of general characteristics when deciding whether or not to visit a storefront**

**Most important characteristics**

| Characteristic | % | Note |
|---|---|---|
| Knowledgeable staff members | 91% | Highest in Houston. |
| Caring and friendly staff members | 87% | Highest in Houston. |
| Personalized service | 83% | Highest in Houston. |
| Convenient locations | 82% | Highest in Austin. |
| Evening and weekend hours | 78% | Highest in Austin and Houston. |
| Private spaces for each customer | 74% | Highest in Austin. |
| All-in-one health insurance shopping for needs such as enrollment and bill payment | 69% | Highest in San Antonio and Houston. |
| Near a main thoroughfare | 64% | Highest in Houston. |

Q10. Now, we'd like to understand how important general characteristics are to you when deciding whether or not to visit a storefront like the one described earlier. To do this, we'd like for you to rate the elements below based on how important they are to you.

## Sources of information

Nearly three-quarters rely on their doctor or pharmacist for health information. Family and friends had traditionally been number two, but has been supplanted by the Internet.

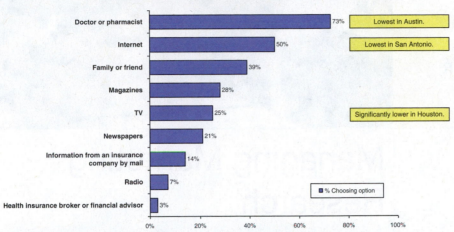

**Sources of information about improving and/or maintaining health**

| Source | % |
|---|---|
| Doctor or pharmacist | 73% — *Lowest in Austin.* |
| Internet | 50% — *Lowest in San Antonio.* |
| Family or friend | 39% |
| Magazines | 28% |
| TV | 25% — *Significantly lower in Houston.* |
| Newspapers | 21% |
| Information from an insurance company by mail | 14% |
| Radio | 7% |
| Health insurance broker or financial advisor | 3% |

■ % Choosing option

Q2. Which of the following, if any, do you rely on for information about improving and/or maintaining your health?

## Respondent profile

The majority indicated that they are in excellent, very good or good health, and half are a college graduate or have post-graduate education. Significantly more in San Antonio are married, and those in Houston have the lowest income and fewer are male.

| | Total | Location | | | | Age | | Member/Non-member | |
|---|---|---|---|---|---|---|---|---|---|
| | | DFW (B) | Austin (C) | San Antonio (D) | Houston (E) | 18-64 (F) | 65-80 (G) | Member (H) | Non-Member (I) |
| **Health status** | | | | | | | | | |
| Excellent, very good or good | 87% | 86% | 85% | 83% | 90% | 89% G | 78% | 84% | 87% |
| **Level of education** | | | | | | | | | |
| College graduate or more | 50% | 53% | 52% | 44% | 51% | 55% G | 37% | 49% | 52% |
| **Marital status** | | | | | | | | | |
| Married | 44% | 46% E | 38% | 50% CE | 31% | 41% | 52% F | 46% | 42% |
| **Income** | | | | | | | | | |
| Low (Just under $50,000 or less per year) | 49% | 48% | 39% | 45% | 67% BCD | 39% | 57% F | 48% | 49% |
| Medium ($50,000 to just under $100,000 per year) | 29% | 31% | 35% | 33% | 25% | 32% | 28% | 32% | 30% |
| High ($100,000 or more per year) | 22% | 21% E | 26% E | 22% E | 8% | 29% G | 15% | 20% | 21% |
| **Gender** | | | | | | | | | |
| Male | 48% | 51% E | 55% E | 42% | 38% | 46% | 54% F | 47% | 49% |

A capital letter (ABC) indicates a significantly higher figure than the corresponding column.

Gerard Launet /Getty Images

# 20

# Managing Marketing Research

## LEARNING OBJECTIVES

1. Understand what clients want from a marketing research supplier or department.

2. Learn about managing a marketing research supplier organization.

3. Learn about communication.

4. Gain insights into the unique management issues of managing a corporate marketing research department.

5. Learn about client profitability management.

6. Gain insights into staff management and development.

7. Learn how to manage a marketing research department.

The marketing research industry is going through interesting times. Large, multinational research firms are growing by acquisition and organic growth, marketers are challenging their research partners to provide more value, the Internet and digital innovations continue to transform the marketplace, and new research technologies are being developed and commercialized. A study of 249 marketing research professionals found respondents claiming that these are exciting times but also challenging times.[1] They predict that the future of the marketing research profession will be driven more by a combination of creativity and technical capability. This means that the industry must attract managers with unique skill sets to survive and grow in this environment.

A second survey of 512 research professionals conducted by Rockhopper Research of Summit, New Jersey, identified a number of problems faced by the industry today:

- 73 percent felt that research is becoming commoditized and clients are less willing to pay for quality.
- 70 percent said clients are demanding shorter time lines for projects and faster delivery of findings.
- 63 percent agreed that nonresearcher management are conducting their own surveys on the web.
- 45 percent foresaw less demand for primary research, thanks to managers who think they can learn anything they need by going online.[2]

We will examine how research managers on both the supplier side and in the corporate research departments are meeting the challenges and opportunities in today's business environment.

# Marketing Research Supplier Management

## What Do Clients Want?

Managing a marketing research supplier organization involves understanding what clients want and expect, maintaining good communications with the client, effectively managing the research process, good time management, cost management, and client profitability management. If a marketing research department in a large organization is conducting its own research, then it will also face these same managerial issues. If it farms out its research, then good management requires selecting the right vendor. A research department must also try to become less of an "order-taker" and play a greater role in the marketing decision-making process within the organization.

Market Directions, a marketing research firm in Kansas City, Missouri, asked marketing research clients across the United States to rate the importance of several statements about research companies and research departments. Replies from a wide range of industries are summarized in the following top-10 list:

1. Maintains client confidentiality.

2. Is honest.

3. Is punctual.

4. Is flexible.

5. Delivers against project specifications.

6. Provides high-quality output.

7. Is responsive to the client's needs.

8. Has high quality-control standards.

9. Is customer-oriented in interactions with client.

10. Keeps the client informed throughout a project.[3]

The two most important factors, confidentiality and honesty, are ethical issues, which were covered earlier in the text. The remaining issues relate to managing the research function and maintaining good communication.

# PRACTICING MARKETING RESEARCH

## The 10 commandments of MR client management[4]

It is essential to have a philosophy that allows you to think about clients beyond the project if you want to establish lasting working relationships—in business and beyond. Built over many years of successes and failures, here are my 10 commandments of client management.

1. **A mistake or two along the way is forgiven when you have a relationship with a client.** We'll start off with a bang and address the most important of the 10 commandments, since all others feed off of it. This is why someone can do 20 projects with a client and continually be on the thinnest of ice and someone else can do only a few projects with a client but be positioned much better for long-term survival.

2. **When you open your mouth and speak to a client, if the best you can do is break even, think hard about what you are going to say.** Whenever we speak, there are three possible outcomes: score points, lose points, or break even. When talking with clients, you may have a decent idea when your comment is going to score points. Likewise, you probably know what *won't* bring a smile to your client's face. It's that huge expanse in the middle that is so open to interpretation. The more thought you give to comments that occupy this space, the better off you'll be. The goal is to minimize this neutral territory, moving thoughts to one side or the other.

3. **Stay two or three steps ahead of the client at all times.** Anticipating what may happen before it happens adds a layer of quality to what you're doing. This is ever-so-important for research projects, which are a mix of both art and science. Staying ahead of the game allows for the art to come into play—adding quality and new ideas. At the end of the day, the client will have greater confidence in you as the caretaker of their project, providing you with greater opportunities for additional projects down the road.

4. **As a project director, you are an extension of the revenue generator. But you should always take ownership of the project you are working on.** Project directors are usually second in command and may even be the research supplier's primary voice, but they are not responsible for generating revenue. As such, it would be very easy for project directors to perform according to their secondary role on a project. Project directors need to know that their behavior with clients is every bit as important as the behavior exhibited by revenue generators themselves. As a project director, if you truly believe the outcome of the research engagement rests on your shoulders, the client will have the greatest opportunity to experience a successful research effort. The bottom line is that both the revenue generator and the project director need to own the project.

5. **Never wait for a client to do anything!** Let's say a client has signed off on a project schedule that indicates you will send the first draft of the survey on Monday and will get comments back no later than 5 p.m. on Wednesday. As Wednesday afternoon approaches with no communication from the client, you can either assume the comments will arrive by 5 p.m. or you can reach out to the client and ask if any clarification is needed. Of course, the real purpose of the communication is to remind the client of the deadline. When almost all project mistakes rest on your shoulders, never wait for a client to do anything.

6. **Never rely on verbal conversations with clients for important issues—get it in writing.** This has ramifications far beyond the MR world. How many times have you had conversations about important topics that later became a back-and-forth with major differences of opinion? You're either insisting you didn't use the exact words the other person is attributing to you or you're insisting you really meant something different than what the other person interpreted. Things can get very messy when it's all about the words that came out of your mouth.

   If you have to enter into a conversation with a client about an important topic and that conversation serves as the sole transcript, you could be in trouble down the road. Why? Because when it's your word against the client's word, you lose, even when you're right.

7. **At times, making your ideas the client's ideas helps cement a partnership.** This may be the most controversial of the commandments and probably the most difficult to achieve. At first, it seems to fly in the face of conventional wisdom concerning the management of clients. After all, your responsibility as a revenue generator is to occasionally suggest innovative ideas as you build trust with a client and become viewed as a valuable resource. While that may be true, it is human nature to want to be seen as more than simply a yes-man. A partnership works best when there's give and take between a revenue generator and client. Sometimes, having both parties own an idea is preferred.

8. **Know when (not) to call or e-mail a client.** Of course, there are active forms of communication (e.g., face-to-face discussions and live phone calls), but there are also passive forms of communication (e.g., e-mails and voicemails).

Understanding appropriate usage is the difference between a harmless communication and a disaster.

Let's say you were awarded a global study from a client involving 10 countries. The schedule indicates data collection should be finished by Friday in all countries, but two countries are lagging behind. You have determined that a new approach is needed to get the remaining completed interviews, which will add one week to the schedule unless you can make up time in other phases of the project. Sending an e-mail to the client or leaving a voicemail message about the bad news is asking for trouble. However, sending an e-mail or leaving a voicemail message asking the client to call you about a matter that needs to be discussed is perfectly fine. Typically, anything that is negative—or even neutral—should only be addressed during a live conversation. Generally speaking, if you're unsure whether e-mail or voicemail is appropriate, don't use it.

9. **Strive for face time with the client.** Sometimes, when you take a situation to the extreme, the solution becomes crystal clear. If you never actually saw your client in the flesh, are the odds great that you would develop a relationship strong enough to overcome mistakes? Of course, the answer is absolutely not. While regular face time with a client can be difficult due to distance, strive for face time whenever possible.

10. **Do what is best for the project. If it is also best for you, that's great. If it isn't, put yourself second and do what is best for the study.** This is a mouthful but crucial to successful client management. A marketing research project can easily take on a life of its own. A study that appeared to be smooth and simple with a straightforward timeline can go awry very quickly. At the end of the day, it's not about you, it's about the project. It's harsh, but if the project is cramping your lifestyle, so be it. It's only temporary.

## Questions

1. Is it important to get face time with the client? Can't you just rely on telephone calls, texts, e-mails and other forms of non–face-to-face communications? Why do you say that?

2. Can you rely totally on verbal communications with clients on key project issues? Why or why not?

3. Can you sit back and wait for clients to do things they are supposed to do? Justify your response.

A survey of client firms found a generally high level of satisfaction with research suppliers (4.08 on a 5-point scale)[5] Clients were most satisfied with data quality and on-time delivery. Relative cost had the lowest average score. Three suppliers consistently score well in this annual survey. They are the Cincinnati-based firm, Directions Research and Burke, Inc., as well as Syracuse, New Yor-–based KS&R.

## Consolidating the Number of Acceptable Suppliers

Beginning in 2010, and continuing today, research clients are reducing their supplier lists, constantly reviewing contracts to see which ones can be eliminated, amended, or terminated. The key to staying on the acceptable vendor lists, according to research buyers, is in the contribution a supplier makes to the company. This means understanding the clients' industry, tracking industry trends, and customizing their offerings to meet the clients' unique needs.[6]

# Communication

The key to good supplier–client relations is excellent communication. Every project should have a liaison who serves as a communication link between the supplier and the client. In large firms, this individual may be an account executive or a project manager, while in small firms, he or she may be an owner or a partner. But whatever the job title, the liaison must communicate accurately, honestly, and frequently with the client.

Before a project begins, the communication liaison should go over the project objectives, methodology, and timing with the client to make certain that there are no misunderstandings. The client should then sign off on the questionnaire, thereby agreeing that the questionnaire is sufficient to gather the raw data needed to accomplish the research objectives.

John Colias, vice president of MARC Research, says the following about communication between a research supplier and its client:

*When a company hires a market research firm to design a study, the supplier must operate as part of the team of researchers and marketers. To be an effective member of the team, the supplier must also intimately understand the marketing questions. This understanding results from interactive dialogue among the researcher, marketer, and the supplier about the marketing questions and business decisions. Such a dialogue crystallizes the research objectives into concrete deliverables that directly influence business decisions.[7]*

The liaison must ascertain how often the client wants progress reports. At a minimum, these reports should be issued weekly. The report should cover the status of the project, unusual problems encountered, and, if it is a cost-plus project, expenses incurred to date. *Cost-plus* refers to actual costs plus an additional markup to cover overhead. Cost-plus projects are typically found in situations where a research department of a large corporation, such as Ford Motors, conducts a project for another department.

# The Key Role of the Project Manager

Because a majority of all research projects are conducted by relatively large research supplier firms, most research clients interact with a project manager and not a company owner. Thus, to the research client, the project manager is the supplier. The best project director helps the client define the research objectives and research design, executes the project flawlessly, monitors the project closely, delivers beyond expectations, and provides insights about the findings.

The project directors that a client wants to use over and over again are those whom the client doesn't have to worry about. This type of project director understands all aspects of the research process, is familiar with the project's objectives, and ensures that the outcome will be above expectations. The client may find out about problems that arise during the project but knows the project director will fix them. The project director provides a safety net; the client is assured that at the end of the project there will be excellence, not disaster. Project directors of this caliber raise the bar for other market research suppliers[8]

On the other hand, a poor project director can result in a supplier being dropped from the acceptable vendor list. Actions that can destroy a supplier–client relationship are as follows:

- The project director is never around to take calls; he or she delegates everything to a junior person who can't answer questions or solve problems.
- The project director does not report problems that occur during the project, and the client is surprised when they finally erupt at the end.
- Projects consistently come in late or over budget with no advance notice[9]

# Managing the Research Process

**Research management** has seven important goals beyond excellent communication: building an effective organization, assurance of data quality, adherence to time schedules, cost control, client profitability management, and staff management and development. The project manager is key to this process. Some tips for project managers are provided in the Practicing Marketing Research feature on page 528.

## Organizing the Supplier Firm

Traditionally, most marketing research firms were organized around functions. Large suppliers, for example, may have separate departments for sampling, questionnaire programming, field, coding, tabulation, statistics, and sales. Even the client service staff may be separate from those who manage projects and write questionnaires and reports. Each of these departments has a head who is expert in the functions of that department and manages work assignments within the department. Projects flow from department to department.

A functional form of organization allows technical people to perform backroom tasks such as programming and data analysis and the "people people" to handle project management and client contact. It provides for knowledgeable supervision, so that, for example, beginners in sample design are working under the direction of veteran experts. It permits the development of good work processes and quality standards, so that tasks are performed consistently. It lets the difficulty of a given project be matched with the skill of the person doing it, so that routine work is given to junior staff and the most complex tasks are reserved for the expert. This matching of work and skill levels leads to happier staff and lower project costs.

Yet functional organizations are not without their problems. Department staff can become focused on the execution of their task, to the detriment of the whole process and the client. Departmental standards and scheduling policies may take on lives of their own, optimizing the efficiency and quality of a department's work but making timely completion of the whole project difficult. By becoming removed from client contact, departments can become inwardly oriented, viewing clients as problems rather than the source of their livelihood. Interdepartmental communication and scheduling can become time-consuming and flawed, as project managers or operations schedulers negotiate each project's schedule with a series of independent department heads. Each department may feel that it is performing perfectly, yet the whole process viewed from the outside can seem rigid, bureaucratic, and ineffective.

In response to problems like these, some companies are organizing by teams. They are breaking up functional departments and organizing their staff into units based around client groups or research types. These teams include people with all or most of the skills necessary to complete a study from beginning to end. A typical team might include several client service/project management people, a field director, a questionnaire programmer, and a tab specwriter. Staff members are frequently cross-trained in multiple functions. The team is almost always headed by a senior staff member with a client service or project management background.

There are many variations on this theme. Within the teams, work may remain specialized (the specwriter does the tables), or there can be extensive cross-training (everyone does tables). Highly specialized functions (such as statistical analysis) that are carried out by one or two experts may remain as functional departments, available to all. A hybrid approach is also possible, where some functions are moved within the teams, while others (such as field management) remain as separate departments.

Because each client group controls its own resources, scheduling and communication are easier. With no department heads or central scheduling to go through, the group head directly prioritizes the work of everyone working on his or her projects.

# PRACTICING MARKETING RESEARCH

## Managing Projects with Ease[10]

Managing a project can seem daunting because projects can differ in size from small and simple to large and complex. Whether you are planning a project, a charity event, your dream house by the ocean, or a website, you need good project management skills to succeed.

Project management is defined as the discipline of planning, organizing, securing, and managing resources to bring about the successful completion of specific project goals and objectives.

The project manager (PM) is responsible for everything that is required to make the project a succes—whether directly or indirectly. The PM is at the center of everything related to the project. Controlling the contributions of seniors and peers is just as important as managing the work team.

Do you have what it takes to be a PM? Here are a few questions to ask yourself to determine if you have what it takes:

- Are you organized and detailed?
- Will you be at ease communicating with a wide range of people, including employees?
- Can you follow up with people without fear of "bothering" them?
- Is efficient record keeping easy for you?
- Would people describe you as a natural leader and motivator?
- Can you work independently with little need for supervision or praise?
- Do you manage your personal time and money effectively?

If you answered yes to most of these questions, be assured that you have the basic project management skills needed. In addition, you will enjoy project management and your job.

Here are a few tips to help with your next big project:

First, you need to *define the project* that includes the scope and overall objectives. Asking all of the people involved in the project what the objectives are and having them defined and prioritized is crucial to your success. Be careful to promise only what you think the budget, resources and time allowed will permit. Overall, the project definition should include the following:

- Project description
- Goal(s) that are measurable and achievable in the given time frame

- A small list of objectives
- Success criteria
- Alternate plan if you need to change direction

Second, you need to *create a plan*. This is the most important part of this process because without a plan, your project will be impossible to control. Often, planning is ignored in an attempt to get right into the project. However, if done correctly the plan will save time, money, confusion, and problems.

Not only should this plan include the people and resources that will be required to complete the project, but it should also estimate the time and effort required for each activity. Determine a realistic schedule with milestones that indicate critical dates to complete each activity and most importantly, involve the project team in these estimates. Utilizing a software package (there are many including Microsoft products) is helpful to create a project schedule, deliverables, tasks, durations, and the resources to complete each task.

Be sure to *identify the risks*.

You need to understand and recognize upfront possible problems, changes and challenges. Getting your team to help with the solutions will create a better work environment, while not identifying these risks effectively is a common reason why projects fail or don't meet expectations.

The third key to a PM's success is *communication*. Ironically, while everyone recognizes the contribution of good communications to success, it remains a problem area on many projects and in many companies. Perhaps it is because we all communicate differently and receive information differently. The PM must know the team and know what method(s) works best such as: meetings, e-mail, video-conferencing, phone calls, cand so on.

Fourth, the PM needs to *create a calm balance*. No matter what happens during a project, grace under pressure is an absolute must. The PM has the unique ability to bridge differences, find common threads and move the group to a common understanding and acceptance of the project's goals, objectives, and perhaps most importantly, what their individual roles will be or will not be.

Fifth, *learning from the past* can help PMs avoid costly mistakes that occurred on similar projects in the past. In addition, it helps companies take advantage of previous successes.

Learning from the past involves evaluating past mistakes, as well as the mistakes of others. This can be difficult because sometimes we are too close to the project to see all of the potential weaknesses. Although learning from others can also be difficult, it is less so because there may be documentation or individuals available to provide further insights.

Last, and perhaps an important step commonly overlooked, is to *celebrate* the project's completion. Your team has worked hard, and its efforts need to be recognized and rewarded. The celebration can be as elaborate as a party away from the company's premises, or as simple as gift certificates to movies/restaurants,cand so on. This sort of team building is important and it will boost employee morale and productivity.

## Questions

1. What things is the marketing research project manager responsible for? Does this include controlling the contributions of seniors and peers?

2. Why is communication so important in the project management process? How would you characterize good communication from a project manager?

3. Why is it so important for project managers to learn from the past?

Technical and operations personnel become closer to clients and more aligned with their needs. By reducing the organizational distance between the client and these staff members, it is easier for them to appreciate the client's situation and focus on serving his or her needs.

Staff may develop more flexibility and broader skills. Cross-training and cross-assignment of work are easier when all the people involved report to the same person[11]

## Data Quality Management

Perhaps the most important objective of research management is to ensure the quality or integrity of the data produced by the research process. You have probably heard announcers on television say, "The poll had a margin of error of 3 percent." Some problems and implicit assumptions are associated with this statement. First, you learned in the discussion of sampling error in Chapter 13 that this statement is missing an associated level of confidence. In other words, how confident are the pollsters that the poll has a margin of error of 3 percent? Are they 68.26 percent confident, 95.44 percent confident, 99.74 percent confident, or confident at some other level? Second, this statement does not make clear that the margin of error applies only to *random sampling error*. The implicit, or unstated, assumption is that there are no other sources of error, that all other sources of error have been effectively dealt with by the research design and procedures, or that all other sources of error have been effectively randomized by taking summary measures across the entire sample. By definition, error is random when there are just as many errors in one direction as in the other direction, leaving overall measures, such as averages, unaffected. Marketing research managers can help assure high-quality data by having policies and procedures in place to minimize sources of error (see Chapter 6).

A recent Harris poll found that there are a lot of misperceptions about error out there. After surveying 1,052 U.S. adults, Harris reported the following:

- Fifty-two percent of all adults believe, wrongly, that statements about "the margin of error being plus or minus 3 percent" mean that "all of the results of the survey are accurate to within a maximum of 3 percent given all types of error."

- A 66 percent majority of adults believe, wrongly, that the phrase "margin of error" includes calculation of errors caused by "how the questions are worded."

Effective time management is becoming increasingly important in all aspects of professional life. One requirement of research management is to keep a project on the schedule specified by the client.

- Large minorities believe, wrongly, that the calculation of the margin of error includes errors in developing a representative base or weighting errors (45 percent), mistakes made by interviewers (45 percent), and errors because of where the questions are placed in the survey (40 percent).

- Only 12 percent of the public agrees that the words "margin of error" should only address one specific source of error, sampling error—as they almost always do.

A 56 percent majority believes that statements about margin of error do not make it clear that this calculation excludes all sources of error except for sampling error for a pure random sample[12]

Marketing researchers must not only attempt to minimize error, but also do a better job of explaining the term *margin of error*. Simply saying "a survey statistic has a margin of error of plus or minus 3 percent" gives the typical audience a false impression of accuracy. Readers should be informed of other possible sources of error, such as interviewer bias or question wording, even if it is not feasible or practical to calculate these errors.

Also, managers must have in place procedures to ensure the careful proofing of all text, charts, and graphs in written reports and other communications provided to the client. Mistakes may mislead a client into making the wrong decision. Suppose the data suggest purchase intent at 18 percent, but the report shows 81 percent; this typographical mistake could easily lead to an incorrect decision. If the client finds even small mistakes, the credibility of the researcher and all of the research findings may be brought into serious question. The rule of thumb is to never provide information to the client that has not been very carefully checked.

## Time Management

A second goal of research management is to keep the project on schedule. Time management is important in marketing research because clients often have a specified time schedule that they must meet. For example, it may be absolutely imperative that the research results be available on March 1 so that they can be presented at the quarterly meeting of the new product committee. The findings will affect whether the test product will receive additional funding for development.

Two problems that can play havoc with time schedules are inaccuracies in estimates of the incidence rate and the interview length. A lower-than-expected incidence rate will require more interviewing resources than originally planned to get the job done on time. If the research manager does not have idle resources to devote to the project, then it will take longer to complete. The same is true for a longer-than-anticipated interview.

Recall that the *incidence rate* is the percentage of persons or households out of the general population that fit the qualifications to be interviewed in a particular study. Often, estimates of incidence rate are based not on hard-and-fast data but on data that are incomplete, relatively inaccurate, or dated. Incidence rate problems can not only increase the amount of time required to complete the sample for the project but also negatively affect the costs of the data-collection phase of the research.

The project manager must have early information regarding whether or not a project can be completed on time. If a problem exists, the manager must first determine whether anything can be done to speed up the process. Perhaps training additional interviewers would help expedite completion of the survey. A second option might be to increase the incentive to complete an online survey. The researcher must inform the client that the project is going to take longer than expected. The researcher can then explore with the client whether a time extension is possible or what changes the client might be willing to make to get the project completed on the original time schedule. For example, the client might be willing to reduce the total sample size or shorten the length of the interview by eliminating questions that are judged to be less critical. Thus, it is very important that the system be structured so that both the researcher and the client are alerted to potential problems within the first few days of the project.

Time management, like cost control, requires that systems be put in place to inform management as to whether the project is on schedule. Policies and procedures must be established to efficiently and quickly solve schedule problems and promptly notify the client about the problem and potential solutions.

## Cost Management

In comparison to data quality and time management, cost management is straightforward. All it requires is adherence to good business practices, such as procedures for cost tracking and control. In particular, good procedures for cost control include the following elements:

- Systems that accurately capture data collection and other costs associated with the project on a daily basis.
- Daily reporting of costs to the communication liaison. Ideally, reports should show actual costs in relation to budget.
- Policies and practices in the research organization that require the liaison to communicate the budget picture to clients and to senior managers at the research company.
- Policies and practices that quickly identify overbudget situations and then find causes and seek solutions.

If the project is overbudget because the client provided information that proved to be erroneous (for example, incidence rate, interview length), then it is imperative that the client be offered options early in the process: a higher cost, smaller sample size, shorter interview, or some combination of these. If the firm waits until the project is complete to communicate this problem to the client, the client is likely to say, "You should have told me sooner—there is nothing I can do now." In this situation, the firm will probably have to swallow the cost overrun.

**Outsourcing** From the early 2000s until 2009, the hot trend was outsourcing. By 2010, the tide had turned toward insourcing. The term **outsourcing** as used in this text is having personnel in another country perform some, or all, of the functions involved in a marketing research project. When a research firm sets up a wholl-owned foreign subsidiary, it is called **captive outsourcing**. Simple outsourcing is where a domestic research company enters into a relationship with a foreign company that provides a variety of marketing research functions. For example, Cross-Tab Services of Mumbai, India, offers online survey programming, data processing, data analysis, and other services. Other services that may be outsourced are data management and panel management. A number of issues need to be considered when one is outsourcing, as shown in Exhibit 20.1.

**outsourcing**
Having personnel in another country perform some, or all, of the functions involved in a marketing research project.

**captive outsourcing**
When a research firm creates a wholly owned foreign facility for outsourcing.

**Insourcing** Some firms (mostly on the client side), have moved to insourcing as a way to cut costs. Rather than use suppliers, they are conducting online surveys themselves. It is a means of generating more research insights with a smaller budget. This is a boon for firms likesConfirmIT, which offer a software platform that enables suppliers, and research clients to create and deliver surveys, collect data, and prepare and share detailed analysis. Market-Sight and Vovici offer much the same thing with slightly different twists. As insourcing accelerates, online research tool vendors should experience annual growth rates of 15 to 20 percent.[13] Insourcing began with routine studies of customers and some qualitative research. It is now shifting to online marketing research communities and enterprise customer satisfaction and loyalty feedback management.

| EXHIBIT 20.1 | Outsourcing Issues |
|---|---|
| **Issues** | **Management Strategies** |
| Confidentiality | Proper confidentiality and data security agreements need to be signed with third-party providers and senior personnel of captive centers. Frequent audits are also recommended to ensure compliance. |
| Infrastructure | It is important that the destination country and the city selected within the country have access to required infrastructure such as power, bandwidth, good connectivity through airports, hotel facilities for visits by customer's team, and, of course, talented workers. |
| Quality of deliverables | Careful documentation is important for processes executed in any location, but they are doubly important in the case of offshore outsourcing. Also, proper systems and protocols must be laid down for communication between teams in the client country and in the vendor country. |
| Domain knowledge | It is important to ensure that the senior members of the team in the offshore location have a strong domain understanding of market research and do not have just an IT or data processing background. |
| Cultural issues | It is necessary to understand the culture of the offshore location and the sensitivities of the people. Cultural misunderstandings can cause misgivings and can affect the quality of work. |
| Job losses in the client country and associated negative publicity for the agency | Good people can be retained and be provided jobs in other roles in the same agency in order to fuel the growth that will result from the cost savings realized. It is important to have a proper PR initiative to explain the benefits of offshoring to the economy of the client country. (Economic studies have shown that in the long term, offshoring leads to greater benefits for the economy of the client country and actually creates more jobs.) |
| Employee liability | This risk is not an issue if one outsources to third-party providers. If one is going the captive route, then it is important to carefully study the employment laws of the destination country to ensure no legal conflicts. |

*Source:* Ashwin Mittal and Kedar Sohoni, "A Brief Guide to Oursourcing," *Quirk's Marketing Research Review* (November 2005), p. 70.

## Client Profitability Management

While marketing research departments in large companies may be able to focus on doing "on-demand" projects for internal clients, marketing research suppliers have to think about profitability. The old adage that 20 percent of the clients generate 80 percent of the profits is often true.

Custom Research Incorporated (CRI), of Minneapolis, realized that it had too many clients—or too few good ones.[14] The company divided its clients into four categories based on the client's perceived value to CRI's bottom line (see Exhibit 20.2). Only 10 of CRI's 157 customers fell into the most desirable category (generating a high dollar volume and a high profit margin). Another 101 customers contributed very little to the top or bottom line. In short, CRI was spending too much time and too many valuable employee resources on too many unprofitable customers.

In assessing which customers to keep, CRI calculated the profit for each one by subtracting all direct costs and selling expenses from the total revenues brought into CRI by that customer for the year. That is, CRI asked, "What costs would we not incur if this customer went away?" The cutoff points for high and low scores were purely subjective; they corresponded to CRI's goals for profit volume and profit margin. CRI management decided that it had to systematically drop a large number of old customers and carefully screen potential new customers. CRI's screening questions for new customers are shown in Exhibit 20.3.

Using the customer's analysis, CRI went from 157 customers and $11 million in revenue to 78 customers and $30 million in revenue. Most importantly, profits more than doubled. Managers had calculated they'd need to reap about 20 to 30 percent more business from some two dozen companies to help make up for the roughly 100 customers they planned to "let go" within 2 years. This was accomplished by building a close personal relationship with the clients that remained. The process involved CRI's researching the industry, the client company, and its research personnel to fully understand the client's needs. For each client, CRI created a Surprise and Delight plan to deliver a "value-added" bonus to the client. For example, Dow Brands received some complimentary software that CRI knew the company needed. This one-on-one relationship marketing has been the key to CRI's success.

Exhibit 20.2

**CRI's Client Profitability Analysis**

**HIGH/LOW**
About half of these customers were new ones that CRI figured would become more profitable over time. The other half were right on the line—on the verge of high/high.

**HIGH/HIGH**
At the top: These customers had pared down their suppliers and clearly valued an ongoing relationship with CRI. They accounted for 29% of sales.

| HIGH VOLUME LOW MARGIN **11** CUSTOMERS | HIGH VOLUME HIGH MARGIN **10** CUSTOMERS |
| --- | --- |
| LOW VOLUME LOW MARGIN **101** CUSTOMERS | LOW VOLUME HIGH MARGIN **35** CUSTOMERS |

**LOW/LOW**
CRI once believed it could make many of these customers more loyal, but time revealed that this group wanted to work with various suppliers.

**LOW/HIGH**
These were small customers who were very profitable. Was there more potential for sales in this group?

| EXHIBIT 20.3 | Screening Questions Used by CRI and the Rationale for Each Question |
| --- | --- |
| **Question** | **Rationale** |
| How did you hear about us? | A bad answer: "I found you in the Yellow Pages." Unlike many companies, CRI doesn't ask this question so that it can decide how to divvy up the marketing dollars. "If someone finds us in the Yellow Pages, they have no reason to use us over anyone else," CRI cofounder Judy Corson explains. A good answer: "A colleague of mine worked with you at another company." |
| What kind of work is it (in terms of industry or scope)? | More than anything, the answer reveals whether the caller is trying to price a quick, one-time project or one that's totally outside CRI's realm. If so, the caller is referred to an indirect competitor. |
| What's your budget? | That's akin to asking someone how much money he or she makes, but the prospect's response to a ballpark guess on the cost of the project helps CRI ascertain what the client has in mind. |
| What are your decision criteria? | CRI knows that it doesn't fare well in blind bidding or in drawn-out, committee-style decisions, so it's interested in dealing with callers who have some level of decision-making power—and assiduously avoids getting involved in anything that smells like a bidding war. |
| Whom are we competing against for your business? | CRI likes to hear the names of its chief rivals, a half-dozen large companies, including the M/A/R/C Group, Market Facts, and Burke Marketing Research. |
| Why are you thinking of switching? | "There's a two-edged sword here," explains cofounder Jeff Pope. "Clients that are hard to break into are better because they don't switch too easily. But you need a way to get in—so a legitimate need for a new supplier is OK." Each month only 2 or 3 of 20 to 30 callers answer enough questions correctly to warrant more attention. So why spend time with the rest? "Do unto others. . . . You never know where people will go." |

*Source:* Susan Greco, "Choose or Lose," *INC.* (December 1998), pp. 57–59, 62–66.

# Staff Management and Development

The primary asset of any marketing research firm is its people. Proprietary techniques and models can help differentiate a marketing research company, but eventually its success depends on the professional nature of its staff and their determination to deliver a quality product. Consequently, recruiting and retaining a competent, enthusiastic staff are crucial and constant management challenges.

Kathleen Knight is president and CEO of BAIGlobal, Incorporated, a Tarrytown, New York, marketing research firm. She offers several suggestions for staff development in a research firm:

1. *Create an environment that encourages risk taking, experimentation, and responsibility.* The benefits to the research firm, such as new service development, new techniques, and business growth, outweigh any potential risks. However, employees need to feel that they will be supported in taking risks. New ideas and different business approaches need to be treated with respect and given room to develop.

2. *Foster recognition and accountability.* Recognize good effort and reward it. One of the best forms of reward is visibility within the company. Make sure that everyone knows when an outstanding job was done and that excellence matters.

3. *Provide job autonomy within a certain structure.* Marketing research is a technical science, and the numbers have to add up. But it also is a business, and projects have to generate money to pay the bills. Within these boundaries, there are many different ways to get the job done. Let employees put their personal stamp on a project and they will feel like true partners in their work.

4. *Attract and support people with entrepreneurial attitudes.* Set business goals and management parameters; then let the staff determine the path to take to get the job done. This allows each person to leverage his or her own abilities and achieve the highest level of success.

5. *Connect rewards to a business result.* Providing open financial data to researchers seems to create a business consciousness that is exciting for all. Often, very talented researchers know little about the financial dynamics of the industry. They welcome the chance to learn and thus become more accountable for bottom-line results.

# PRACTICING MARKETING RESEARCH

## 10 Tips for a Winning Proposal

Emily Waters and Sarah Dellomo both Account Executives DSS Research

© Roger Gates

© Roger Gates

A well-crafted proposal will help you generate more business and win new clients. Keep these tips in mind when responding to requests for proposal (RFPs):

1. **Follow all instructions provided in the RFP.** This includes information requests, page length guidelines, formatting instructions and labeling. Closely following instructions demonstrates your attention to detail, while failure to comply with instructions can result in disqualification of your proposal.

2. **Fully answer all of the questions asked, but don't go overboard providing extraneous information.** Your responses should be clear and concise.

3. **Remember to "sell" your company.** Be sure to stress the key reasons why potential clients should choose you. What differentiates your company from the rest? Clients want to avoid making risky decisions, so take the opportunity to highlight why you're the right choice.

4. **Avoid submitting a "stock" proposal.** There will often be opportunities to borrow from your past proposals, but customize your content enough to avoid delivering a generic, "cookie cutter" proposal.

5. **Know your audience.** Proposals prepared for new clients are often more detailed than those for existing clients who are already familiar with your company. If you are given the evaluation criteria that will be most important to your audience, tailor your proposal toward those areas.

6. **Know how much contact is appropriate and allowed.** In some cases, you will be required to work through a

designated contact and communication with others will be prohibited. However, if the RFP process is less structured, you may be allowed to have direct contact with decision makers. In this case, you have a valuable opportunity to influence the decision in your favor.

7. **Plan ahead!** Turnaround times for proposals are often short. Review the RFP early and compile a list of questions for your potential client. Most RFPs provide a deadline for submitting your questions, so you'll only get one shot at having them answered. If you will also require information from subcontractors or colleagues to complete the response, request that information as early as possible to avoid a last minute rush.

8. **Clearly outline your assumptions about project specifications and pricing.** You will rarely be given every piece of information you need to price a project, so you'll need to make some assumptions. Use your experience and available data from similar projects to make reasonable assumptions. Don't be afraid to ask your colleagues for their opinions if you lack significant experience with the type of project on which you're bidding. Be sure to clearly state all assumptions in your proposal.

9. **Only propose an alternative solution when you are asked for one.** If you are asked to provide alternative solutions or suggestions, by all means, provide them. But if you're not specifically asked to change the RFP specifications, stick to what you're asked for.

10. **Submit your response on time!** Late proposals are generally not considered. Be sure to submit your response on time or all of your hard work will be wasted! If you are required to submit hard copies, plan ahead to be sure they arrive at their destination on time.

6. *Open your financial books.* Research firms can provide senior employees with full financial information to let them know how well they are doing across the months and years. The bottom line is the best aggregate measure of performance—individually, as a group, and as a firm. Opening the books establishes a common mission and goal across the organization.

7. *Offer diversity within your organization.* It's fun and exciting to learn new products, serve new clients, and work with a new research team. A chance at a new position is often the spark someone needs to really do well within a firm. And the possibility of this kind of job change seems to add to the satisfaction that employees feel. If you pay attention to individuals and create a career path across disciplines within your organization, it's more likely that talented researchers will stay.

8. *Provide clear promotional paths.* Employees like to know how they can advance and want to feel some control over their careers. Clear criteria and expectations go a long way toward helping researchers feel comfortable. In the marketing research business, the best training is as an apprentice, working with senior researchers doing interesting work. Talented people will grow and prosper where the expectations are that senior managers will be mentors, that junior staff will learn, and that excellent work produced together will lead to everyone's career advancement.[15]

# Managing a Marketing Research Department

A manager of a marketing research department within a corporation faces a different set of issues from a research supplier. Among these issues are effective spending of the research budget, prioritizing projects for the corporation, retaining skilled staff, selecting the right research suppliers, moving the marketing research function to a more strategic role in the firm, and measuring return on investment for marketing research.

## Allocating the Research Department Budget[16]

No matter who controls the research project budget, it's important to spend money and (most importantly) research staff time wisely. That is especially important when the clients (new-product development managers or brand managers) fund each project and cannot understand why the marketing research department doesn't have the staff time to do whatever they want. In that case, many research heads are learning how to prioritize projects. There are several effective ways to accomplish that.

A research study found that only about 20 percent of research projects are focused on strategically important issues. The other 80 percent of projects are focused on tactical issues, such as setting prices, advertising, distributing products, or adding new features to existing products. Researchers and clients agree that they would prefer to spend more time on the strategic issues, such as identifying promising new markets or developing new products and services.[17]

For example, one research group took it upon itself to improve its firm's new-product development process by bringing together experts from marketing research, marketing, research and development, manufacturing, and sales to design a new process.

Another research group head learned to facilitate strategic planning (an ad hoc effort in her firm), so that she could help her executive team plan when cross-functional action was needed.

Several research heads said that they try to meet with their clients annually before budgeting season begins to talk about what research issues will be most important to clients in the coming year. Both parties then agree on the vital projects for the coming year and on how much time or money to allocate to them. While everyone admits that unforeseen circumstances almost always force the plans to be altered, having an annual plan enables a manager to adapt quickly and be flexible.

Many department heads say that they believe it's important for the research group to have a discretionary budget for important projects. That is considered especially important if research projects are usually funded by the clients. One new director of research used the discretionary budget to study why demand for his organization's main product appeared to be dropping in the face of a changing industry. Another researcher paid for a project on store designs because he felt that the designs were probably holding back sales—and he was right. Still another group paid to learn scenario planning and used it to help clients pick options for new-product testing.

## Prioritizing Projects

Estimating the financial return from a research project is a great way to rationalize spending across projects because it provides a quantitative methodology that helps clients identify "must-have" versus "nice-to-have" projects. It is not only an effective way of turning away less important work; it also helps strengthen relations with clients because it shows that researchers are thinking about their bottom line, too. We will present a way to measure return on investment (ROI) for marketing research, created by research consultants Diane Schmalensee and A. Dawn Lesh, later in the chapter.

Estimating the ROI for a given project has several advantages. First, estimating the expected returns on research before beginning work may help: Focus the research on important research objectives and clarify client needs; differentiate projects that are likely to be implemented (and thus have a higher ROI) from those that may not lead to action; clarify how much money and time it is worth spending on a project given its expected financial payoff.

Second, measuring the payoff of research does not end during the planning stages. Ideally, researchers check back with their clients after the work is completed to validate the actual payoff. This permits researchers and clients to learn how accurate the original ROI estimate was as well as how to improve future estimates.

Finally, having ROI discussions with clients both before and after projects is a great way to show that the research function is a partner with its clients—sharing client objectives and spending research monies effectively. This process has the added benefit of allowing overworked research staff to shrink or delay less important research.

## Retaining Skilled Staff

When researchers are feeling overworked and finding it difficult to meet client needs without sacrificing their personal time needs, they begin to burn out and think about working elsewhere. Losing a skilled staff member can damage a research group. It means more work for the remaining staff members, and it can leave a hole in valuable client relationships. It is especially important to recognize and reward hard-working staff members. How can this be done? Research shows that staff members of marketing research departments value doing interesting and fulfilling work, getting recognition for a job well done, and earning adequate pay.[18] What is adequate pay? A 2013 client-side salary survey shows average compensation by job title in Exhibit 20.4.

A few techniques for retaining key research staff are as follows:

1. *Conduct regular performance reviews that give continuing feedback on a job well done*—or offer ways to improve. Many staff members think their bosses play favorites during performance reviews. So department heads try to use clear performance criteria for each position and offer objective appraisals for everyone.

2. *Offer public recognition for great work.* Some groups mention great work during staff meetings; post client comments on a "wall of fame" in the department; have bosses send personal letters to staff members at home, praising their work; hold pizza parties for teams that have performed "above and beyond"; or simply have the head of the department stop by a staff member's office to offer congratulations and thanks.

3. *Give differential pay raises that recognize superior performance.* Although across-the-board, uniform pay increases are often used (because they are the easiest to administer), they do not recognize the high performers—and they allow the lower performers to believe they are doing adequate work.

4. *Vary the work.* In order to keep everyone interested, some research groups identify one-off projects and then allow staff members to volunteer for them. Examples of special

| EXHIBIT 20.4 | Client-Side Researchers' Compensation | | |
|---|---|---|---|
| **Job Title** | **Base** | **Bonus/Other** | **Total** |
| Senior Vice President or Vice President | $167,732 | $84,922 | $252,654 |
| Market Research Director/Senior Direction | $133,035 | $54,319 | $187,354 |
| Market Research Manager | $97,355 | $28,442 | $125,797 |
| Account Executive/Manager | $36,750 | $9,000 | $45,750 |
| Customer Insights Manager | $98,453 | $36,797 | $135,250 |
| Director of Marketing | $123,950 | $62,776 | $186,726 |
| Brand Manager or Product Manager | $79,222 | $7,000 | $86,222 |
| Project Manager | $84,694 | $21,769 | $106,463 |
| Senior Research Analyst | $76,404 | $14,169 | $90,573 |
| Research Analyst | $58,591 | $20,482 | $79,073 |
| Statistician | $86,889 | $22,667 | $109,556 |
| Research Assistant | $35,417 | $8,300 | $43,717 |
| Sales/Account Representative | $23,000 | $16,000 | $39,000 |

*Source:* Emily Goon, "A Report On The 2013 Quirk's Salary Review of Corporate Researchers, *Quirk's Marketing Research Review,* June 2013, p 66.

projects could include a project that will feed into the firm's strategic plans, formation of a high-visibility cross-functional team, or a project that uses a new technique or addresses an unusually interesting topic.[19]

Bonnie Eisenfeld, an independent marketing research consultant, talks about some nonquantitative skill aspects of an ideal marketing research job seeker in the following Practicing Marketing Research box.

## Selecting the Right Marketing Research Suppliers

Once the nature, scope, and objectives of the project have been determined, the next step is to assess the capabilities of alternative suppliers. Some research vendors have a particular area of specialization, offering special expertise and experience and greater insights in their specialty areas than generalist firms. Some firms specialize in advertising or customer satisfaction research, while others are devoted to a particular technique (e.g., conjoint analysis or market segmentation) or data-collection method (e.g., mall intercepts, mail surveys, or Internet panels). Still other research firms specialize in particular products (e.g., fast food) or industries (e.g., health care).

Marketing research firms, at least those doing custom work, get business by means of requests from clients. Marketing efforts of research firms have the goal of getting or being included in these requests from client organizations. To be included, you need to make prospective clients aware of your organization and convince them that you have the capability to do a great job on the type of project in question. Prospective clients develop a stable of research firms they know or believe can deliver what they want in terms of high-quality, actionable results at a reasonable cost.

The request from a prospective client can take a very informal or a very formal form. At the informal end of the spectrum, the request may come in the form of a telephone call or email that provides key information about what the client wants to do (research objectives, characteristics of people they want to interview, their thoughts on the form of data collection, sample size and other sampling details, any specialized analytical techniques they view as appropriate, the time schedule they need, and other pertinent details). The expected response from the research firm may be nothing more than a brief e-mail outlining methodology, costs, and time schedule. The request from the client may be sent to only a single, trusted firm or to a handful of firms with whom the client has experience.

At the other end of the spectrum, the client may send a formal RFP (request for proposal) that runs to 20-plus pages and provides extremely detailed information about the project and asks for information covering:

- The research firm and its experience in the product / service area and with the particular type of research in question
- Recommended methodology
- Background information on project lead and other key project team members
- Quality control procedures
- Financial condition of the research firm
- Detailed proposed schedule for completion of the work
- Detailed costs to do the research
- References who can comment on work provided by the research firm

Regardless of the degree of detail and formality of the RFP from the client and the response from the research firm, the next step for the prospective client is to review the proposals, ask any questions, select the firm the client thinks will do the best job, consider costs, make the final selection, and inform the firms who submitted proposals that they have won or not won the project.

# PRACTICING MARKETING RESEARCH

## Soft Skills of an Ideal Marketing Researcher

Ideal marketing researchers need good quantitative skills. More importantly, in today's competitive and dynamic markets, new researchers need other skills and characteristics.

### Lifelong Learners

The best researchers are avid readers, travelers, online searchers, or news junkies—in short, lifelong learners. Their accumulated knowledge and skills are often applied in surprising ways. For example, analogies from evolutionary biology can help explain the competitive situation in a market.

Researchers are curious people. They want to know about human behavior, attitudes and opinions, and their underlying reasons and motivations. A curious person asks question, listens carefully to the answers, and probes for more information from respondents.

One test for curiosity in the hiring process is to observe how many questions the candidate asks in the interview, particularly questions on subjects other than compensation. However, watching a candidate conduct a research interview or focus group is the better test.

### Easy Adapters

In addition to a solid academic background, successful hires must be able to adapt easily and understand that brevity is prized in the business world. New researchers have to get used to corporate deadlines and move faster, sometimes sacrificing methodological precision and sometimes arriving at conclusions with less-than-perfect data.

In addition to a broad educational background, I advise new entrants to get experience as an interviewer. There is no substitute for the learning you acquire from actually conducting an interview. It enhances your ability to write a real-life questionnaire that respondents will be willing to answer.

### Partners

The in-house researcher is not just a messenger between corporate management and an outside vendor. Ideally, a researcher should act as a partner with the strategist or decision maker. He or she must understand the context and information needs of the business and, based on management's research objectives, help create questions and then collect data to answer the questions. Thus, every researcher should take advantage of opportunities for education and training offered by their organization to obtain the business knowledge necessary for context.[20]

## Questions

1. What skills do you think are required to be a great marketing researcher?
2. Where would you rank communication skills on your list?

---

A research department manager should beware of firms committed to a particular technique and/or data-collection method because they may be more likely to "force" the department's research project into their particular model, rather than tailor the research to fit the specific needs of the research department's project.

Research department managers must consider the size of the firms in their decision. The size of the vendor is an extremely important decision criterion. It is important not to overwhelm a small firm with an enormous project, and, conversely, a small project may not get the proper attention at a large firm.

The general rule is to favor the smallest firm consistent with the scope of the project. However, any project that accounts for 30 percent or more of a marketing research supplier's annual revenues may be too large for that firm to handle effectively.

The research department manager should establish, upfront, the individual who will be managing the project. It should be determined in advance who would be responsible for the day-to-day management of the project. That is, will it be the person who "sold" the project or a project director hundreds of miles away? If the contact becomes unavailable, will competent support staff be available?

The research department manager needs to become acquainted with the backgrounds of the potential vendors. There are some general questions that every potential vendor should be asked to determine the stability of the company and its qualifications to complete the project in a satisfactory manner. These questions would include:

- How long has the vendor been in business?
- For what other companies has the vendor conducted research projects? Remember it is imperative to request references and check them for each firm.
- What are the academic backgrounds and experience of those persons who will be working on the project, that is, the project director, field director, data processing manager, and so forth? Does the composition of the project team strike the right balance between top-level management and technical researchers and analysts?
- Does the success of the project depend on the capabilities of a subcontractor? If the marketing research supplier will be subcontracting any elements of the project, it is important that the subcontractor and his or her qualifications be identified.

Also, the research manager should review the quality control standards of each potential vendor. The validity of the results of any research project is dependent on the quality control measures practiced by the vendor. For example, on telephone studies, what are the procedures with respect to callbacks, monitoring, and validation? It is prudent to avoid firms that do not follow generally accepted practices in their operations.

The reputations of the firms must be considered in the decision. Reputation is important, but a department should not pay a larger premium for it. However, some situations may require the services of a prestigious research firm because a company plans to publicize the results, or use them in advertisements, so having the best reputation available may actually be a good investment. For example, Dell touts its standings in J. D. Power Customer Satisfaction surveys.

Finally, a manager should avoid letting price be the sole determining factor in the selection. When reviewing proposals, price should be the last item to be considered.[21]

Today, many client companies are looking beyond traditional selection criteria and are seeking a partner as opposed to a research provider. "Suppliers should try to be better business consultants," partnering with buyers to get to know buyers' companies and industries thoroughly, says Beth Shriver, staff research manager at Akron, Ohio–based diversified energy company FirstEnergy Corporation. Through partnerships—rather than just supplier/buyer relationships—research vendors can help buyers make better use of the copious amounts of data that most companies already have in-house, Shriver says.[22]

Gala Amoroso, Marketing Research Director at McCormick & Company, the huge consumer packaged goods firm, claims she also wants closer relationships with her research suppliers. "A partner, to me, would be the difference between a company we call when we have a project . . . versus a company we talk to whether we have a project or not," she says. A partner-like supplier would move beyond filling McCormick's research needs to anticipate its needs, finding ways to mine insights from the company's existing data, and working with the company to unearth better and better insights, she says.[23]

Selecting the right supplier in the United States can be a difficult task. The problem expands exponentially in developing countries.

# Moving Marketing Research into a Decision-Making Role

A more strategic managerial question regarding the marketing research department is the role and importance of marketing research in the managerial decision-making process. The researchers' challenge is to shed their long-held traditional role as a support function—one that reacts to requests from project and new-product development managers and then focuses on producing the numbers but not on their meaning to the business. Changes in the way marketing research is integrated with decision-making at Newell Rubbermaid, discussed in the following Practicing Marketing Research feature, provide a good example.

# PRACTICING MARKETING RESEARCH

## Newell Rubbermaid Shakes Up CMO Model by Putting Research in Charge[24]

Since Richard Davies became Newell's chief marketing officer, he's instituted big changes for the company that markets such brands as Paper Mate pens, Graco baby products, Rubbermaid storage products, Calphalon cookware, and much more. He's consolidated marketing staff and agencies and given unprecedented authority to an expanded and independent research group.

Despite reducing staff, the company opened a 130-person marketing floor at its corporate headquarters in Atlanta, along with growing outposts in Shanghai and Sao Paulo and a center for writing instruments in London. And Newell has roughly doubled its market research staff to more than 20 and seen a similar rise in its overall spending on research. It's also preparing to ramp up spending on media.

Now comes the hard part: proving it all works, especially since the approach is, in many ways, at odds with standard practice at big multibrand behemoths like Procter & Gamble Co. and Unilever.

When Mr. Davies was lured to Newell by CEO Mike Polk in late 2012, he quickly saw the need for change. The CMO was in charge of developing capabilities, processes, and training, but the marketing organization had no central authority. Instead, it was divided up among business units that controlled their own marketing budgets and decisions.

One consequence, Mr. Davies said, was "a lack of investment in consumer understanding," with some brands relying on consumer-habit studies that were 10 years old. Marketing people and spending also weren't aligned with company priorities such as growing in Asia and Latin America, and expanding writing instruments. By consolidating into a single marketing department, Mr. Davies said he could increase "consumer insights" spending while reducing spending overall.

The consolidation also made it possible to trim agencies and attract the likes of BBH and PHD, which never would have considered a $250 million account divided among so many category and country fiefdoms as the old Newell had, Mr. Davies said.

To find those agencies, named in October following reviews, Mr. Davies rejected the conventional pitch process he finds "a complete waste of time and agency resources." Instead, he talked with agency leaders about such things as "what makes great advertising and what work they've done it the past they're proud of, and what could be improved."

Part of that is based on Mr. Davies's theory that "any big agency can hire great talent. It then comes down to the quality of the leadership. How do they want to work with us? How do they find us as a client?"

Making that process easier was that Mr. Davies was the decision maker. "My predecessor was responsible for marketing as a capability, developing skills and training," Mr. Davies said. "I look after that, but I also look after the day job of marketing. I'm responsible for the advertising and mix development. And that's really helpful, because as we develop new approaches, processes, and techniques, I don't need to persuade people to do it, that it's a good idea. I can tell them to do it."

"Certainly for a company our size, we don't have the time to go around trying to influence people that this is how they should do things," he said. "Maybe some of the bigger companies don't have the time, either. I don't know."

Perhaps an even bigger departure for Newell's marketing department under Mr. Davies is the unprecedented authority for market research, which also reports to him. While Mr. Davies wants product concepts and ad ideas tested with consumers, he's also given researchers authority to tell marketers an idea isn't even worth testing yet.

Mr. Davies believes such power should be the rule rather than the exception, because researchers are the voice of the consumer. "You lose count of the number of companies who claim the consumer is boss," he said. "But the question is, do they really make the consumer the boss or not?"

Of course, the market ultimately will judge. Mr. Davies pointed to market-share gains after Newell research showed the importance of a free-flowing pen to consumers. That translated into Paper Mate InkJoy pens, backed by heavy sampling combined with TV ads focused on how easily the pen flows.

Newell parlayed another insight—that Brazilian construction workers were spending too much of their hard-earned cash on saw blades—into a two-sided replacement blade from its Irwin tool division, which was also backed by heavy sampling.

## Questions

1. How did Newell Rubbermaid change the way marketing research fit into its organization and into its decision-making process?

2. What are the early indicators of how well or poorly these changes have worked?

Experts agree that, to earn the ear of senior management, researchers must move beyond the task of simply crunching numbers and churning out results; they need to understand the underlying business issues at stake and adjust the information they gather and how they analyze it. They also must reach out to other departments, building relationships and a better understanding of the issues companywide. "We need to evolve just from doing research to doing insights," says Peter Daboll, chief of insights for Sunnyvale, California–based Yahoo! Inc. "If you want to be at the table you have to be senior. [To be senior means to] go from collecting, collating and presenting to anticipating, reconciling and recommending. . . . [Executives] want the freaking answer, not the tool to give them the answer."[25]

"I strongly emphasize that while [the research managers and associates] may be in my official marketing research department—it's my insistence that they view themselves as members of the business team" first and foremost, says Daryl Papp, Lilly's director of U.S. market research. He adds that about half of his department comprises professionals who come from areas of marketing other than research for a several-year "broadening assignment" to learn about the company's businesses. Papp believes that having marketing researchers sit side by side with other colleagues who aspire to high-level management helps contribute to the business-oriented mentality in his department.[26]

The Market Research Executive Board (MREB) reports that 69 percent of senior executives want research to be a strategic partner, but only 29 percent of them currently view research as such. Furthermore, execs who view research as a strategic partner are much more likely to have changed decisions based on research than those who view research as an analytic resource (57 percent vs. 33 percent).[27]

Marketing research departments can take several specific actions to increase their internal standing and achieve strategic, consultative relevance. These are: Be driven by impact; bring leadership to strategic priorities; develop rich consumer and market insights; use creativity to innovate; and communicate for impact.[28]

**Driven by Impact** In some research departments, success is defined by a project that is well executed—a questionnaire that the client is happy with, fieldwork that's done on time and on budget, a report or presentation that often summarizes "all the news that's fit to print," Then the researcher moves on to his or her next project. Performance reviews focus on quality of project management skills.

Contrast this with what the company's senior management wants from research. The company is investing substantial dollars in research, so it wants to see marketplace impact as a result of its investment. And senior managers' time is increasingly precious, so they just want to know the key insights and how the company should act on the insights. If there is little or no marketplace impact as a result of the research investment, why should they keep investing?

Marketplace impact doesn't happen automatically from identifying insights. Insights must be integrated with business economics and organizational strengths and weaknesses, then communicated and subsequently acted on by the appropriate internal function.

Research departments need to provide an environment in which marketplace impact is integral to the department's vision and mission, an environment that makes provoking impact part of the research culture and that rewards impact.

**Bring Leadership to Strategic Priorities** Researchers often complain that they spend too much time and money researching tactical issues while major strategic issues struggle to get budget. When this happens, it speaks "opportunity" and is a clear indication that research programs and budgets are not reviewed at a high enough level in the organization. It may be that the research budget is controlled by a brand-level marketing person and that the rolled-up departmental research budget is never reviewed with senior management. Or it may be that senior management doesn't believe (or isn't aware) that research can help with the major strategic issues.

Research department managers must understand the major strategic issues facing the company. Then, they must determine what information is required to address these issues. Finally, a research strategic plan must be created and presented to senior management.

### Develop Rich Consumer and Market Insights
An **insight** includes discovery together with marketplace impact: "Insight is new knowledge that has the potential to create significant marketplace impact."

A recent *Forbes* article provides a vision of the marketing research department of the future (see Practicing Marketing Research feature below).

**insight**
Newer knowledge that has the potential to create significant marketing impact.

# PRACTICING MARKETING RESEARCH

## Here's What the Marketing Organization of the Future Should Look Like[29]

2020 isn't the future; the future is now. Every day, the look and feel and function of marketing is transforming radically—and so the means to keep up must be transforming, too. Marketing organizations that aren't restructuring to meet the demands of 2020—of today, for that matter—will be left by the wayside.

But what must that restructured organization look like? To answer that question, the Association of National Advertisers, together with the World Federation of Advertisers and EffectiveBrands, a global marketing strategy consulting firm, has been conducting an ongoing global study—including a quantitative and qualitative survey—of senior marketing leaders over the past several months

that's unprecedented in size and scope. Marc deSwaan Arons, executive chairman of EffectiveBrands, will, with a panel of CMOs, present some of the initial findings from the research project to attendees at the annual ANA Masters of Marketing conference this weekend in Phoenix. Forbes is a partner in the project, in addition to the ANA and the WFA, along with Spencer Stuart, Adobe and MetrixLab.

And according to the project, called Marketing2020, the winning companies will have highly integrated organizations—that is, hub-and-spokes structures whereby the CMO is in the middle, with roles akin to product manager, marketing strategies manager, advertising director, PR manager, market-research director and promotion director creating the spokes and rim of the wheel. Silos are finally nonexistent; the integration and interconnectedness of this new model enables full coordination of all constituents.

So where the organizational structure had looked like this:

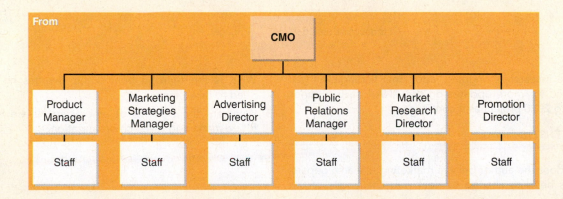

It will now look like this:

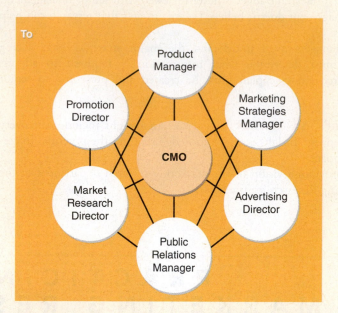

Nonnegotiable characteristics of the 2020 marketing organization: a goal of business growth; a clear purpose; complete internal alignment of functional areas; clearly defined roles and responsibilities of each individual; research centers and data-informed efforts; an amalgam of agency partners as well as an in-house agency-like team; cross-platform social-media engagement; a strong CMO-CEO connection.

The research also concludes that a chief experience officer will be necessary at all successful organizations. This can be the CMO, or the CEO, or another individual charged with overseeing marketing staff grouped as "Think" (analytics marketers), "Feel" (engagement marketers), and "Do" (production/content marketers).

The most successful CMOs, meanwhile, will take on additional responsibilities, like IT or HR.

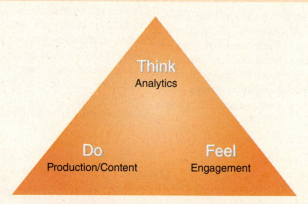

As the research is ongoing, additional findings will gel. Stay tuned for more updates on the ANA/EffectiveBrands Marketing 2020 project as it continues.

## Questions

1. How does the author believe marketing research departments need to change to deal with challenges of the future?

2. What is the thinking behind the changes he believes need to take place?

3. What are the benefits of embracing his views on the future marketing research organization?

The toolkit for identifying insights has expanded in recent years. Online research capabilities have made segmentation and other quantitative techniques much more affordable, and enabled virtual-shopping capabilities. Ethnographic research has become mainstream. Neuroscience, eye-tracking and facial-coding methodologies are evolving. Hosted online panel communities provide an opportunity for dialogue with consumers, and among consumers, over time. Listening to social media has become extremely important.

The challenge today is in unearthing insights that lead to competitive advantage, that can be leveraged to trigger an emotional consumer response and that ultimately provides the opportunity for significant marketplace impact.

**Use Creativity to Innovate** Senior management loves innovation because it can lead to higher current and future earnings. **Innovation** is the successful implementation of creative ideas within an organization. **Creativity** is the ability to generate and recognize potentially useful ideas. Creativity then, is a necessary prerequisite for innovation. Marketing researchers can build innovation into presentations and research recommendations by following the creative problem-solving process (see Exhibit 20.5).

**Communicate for Impact** The richest insight in the world doesn't add value unless some action is taken. Research needs to take responsibility for making change happen as a result of insight development. Communicating for impact is critical. The job of the presentation is to create impact—period. Anything else is superfluous.

The following pointers will help create impact:

- Tell a story with your presentation, and tell it succinctly.
- Leverage visual storytelling, incorporating video where possible.

**innovation**
The successful implementation of creative ideas within an organization.

**creativity**
The ability to generate and recognize potentially useful ideas.

---

**Exhibit 20.5**

**The Creative Problem-Solving Process**

Creative problem solving begins with an assessment of the situation. The process then follows three phases with two of the phases consisting of multiple steps. Each step has a convergence part and a divergence part. Divergence is when issues, wishes, ideas, or actions are elicited. Convergence is when they are winnowed down to one or a few for further exploration.

Phase one is problem exploration and consists of these three steps:

1. **Identify the challenge:** Here a vision is imagined in divergent mode, then identified in convergent mode.

2. **Facts and feelings exploration:** This is the classic research step. A divergent list of facts, feelings, and relevant data is made. In convergence mode, salient data points are identified.

3. **Problem framing and reframing:** The original vision is reexamined in light of the salient data, and alternate problem frames are generated in divergent mode. One challenge statement is selected in convergence—and transformed into a question that inspires answers to solve the problem.

Phase two of the process is idea generation. It has one step:

4. **Idea generation:** As many ideas as possible are generated to answer the question converged upon in problem framing. The goal is a breakthrough option or idea. In convergence, the ideas are clustered and combined, and ultimately one or a small subset is selected.

The last phase, phase three, is getting into action. It has two steps:

5. **Solution development:** The idea(s) selected in step 4 is (are) examined and improved using criteria developed/diverged upon for the challenge. Ideas are enhanced by building them up to better match key criteria using additional ideation.

6. **Action planning:** In this final step, a process for implementing the idea is developed and mapped out. Divergent thinking takes place around assistors, resistors, and ways to make the plan exciting, and convergence creates a standard action/work plan.

Source: Greg Fraley, "Create or Perish," February 2009, p. 56.

- Know your audience and their ingoing beliefs. Address potential problems before delivering the presentation.

- Your audience wants to know what they should do, not what you did.

- Your job doesn't end when the presentation is given. Take responsibility for making action happen.[30]

## Measuring Marketing Research's Return on Investment (ROI)

The old view of marketing as an art form disappeared long ago. In its place is the notion of strict accountability. Marketing expenditures become investments, with performance measures coming from the world of finance. So it has become increasingly fashionable in large corporations to demand that marketing research prove its worth. The approach that is gaining in popularity is return on investment (ROI). Recall that ROI is a ratio calculated by dividing the after-tax income from an investment by the dollar amount of the investment. Five arguments can be made against using ROI to measure the value of marketing research to an organization:

1. *ROI is theoretically flawed because it divides the profit return by the expenditure instead of subtracting it.* All reputable bottom-line metrics, such as profit, cash flow, payback, and shareholder value, subtract expenditure from income. Dividing one into the other distorts the result.

2. *ROI was invented to compare alternative uses of capital, based on projected percentage return on that capital.* Market research (MR), however, is usually a stream of costs that continue for the purposes of comparison in each and every year. Market research is rarely an investment in the true sense of the word.

3. *Improving ROI tends to suboptimize expenditure.* Most investments have diminishing profit returns. The early profits give the greatest ROI, but maximizing productivity (i.e., total profit return) requires more expenditure beyond that. Would you rather, at the same low level of risk, have a 100 percent return on $2 or an 80 percent return on $1,000? This objection arises directly from the division rather than subtraction anomaly.

4. *ROI usually focuses on the short term.* It does not consider the effects on the marketing asset (brand equity) or the dynamic development of marketing over longer time periods.

5. *ROI is useful only for comparing alternative expenditures.* Research should inform marketing mix decisions, not control them. Such a comparison does not contrast like with like. Internal information, such as the management accounts or budgets, is a closer comparison, as it fights with marketing metrics for space on the dashboard used by top management to help drive the business. And yet, when did anyone call for the ROI on the internal accounting function?[31]

Despite the negatives, ROI deserves further examination into how it can be operationalized. Two approaches are ROI Lite and ROI Complete created by Dawn Lesh, president of New York-based A. Dawn Lesh International, and Diane Schmalensee, president of Schmalensee Partners in Chestnut Hill, Massachusetts.[32]

**ROI Lite**  To measure ROI Lite, MR asks the client for two estimates during pre-project planning:

1. The anticipated dollar value of the decision that will be based on the research.

2. The anticipated increase in confidence of making the "right" decision. For example, instead of saying a decision is worth $10 million, a client might say it's worth $8 million to $12 million. Or a client could say he or she expects his or her confidence to rise 40 to 60 percent.

With the answers to these questions, MR can calculate the expected ROI Lite using the following formula:

$$\text{ROI Lite} = \frac{\$\text{Value} \times \text{Increased confidence}}{\text{Cost of research}}$$

For example, assume a firm has to decide which of five creative approaches to use in a $2 million advertising campaign.

- Since it is uncertain how the advertising will affect sales, the firm decides to use the $2 million campaign cost as the value estimate. No one knows which of the five approaches is best, so the confidence of randomly picking the best one is only 20 percent.
- The firm believes that after the research it will be 80 percent confident of making the best decision (an increase of 60 percent).
- The cost of the copy testing is $250,000.

$$\text{ROI Lite} = \frac{\$2 \text{ million} \times 60\%}{\$250,000} = \frac{\$1.2 \text{ million}}{\$250,000} = 480\%$$

This ROI Lite discussion can help determine how much to invest in the research. If the dollar value of a decision is small or the expected decrease in uncertainty is low, then the budget should be kept small. After the research is completed, MR meets again with the client to revise the ROI Lite estimate in light of what was learned.

**ROI Complete**  ROI Complete is similar to ROI Lite except that it adds the concept of the likelihood of taking action. MR and the client discuss the estimated likelihood of taking action with and without the research. If the firm usually acts without research, then MR may not be able to raise the likelihood of acting, and the firm should not spend much money on the research. However, if the firm seldom acts without research, then the research is more valuable:

$$\text{ROI Complete} = \frac{\$\text{Value} \times \text{Increased confidence} \times \text{Increased likelihood of acting}}{\text{Cost of research}}$$

The following equation is used:
For example, suppose the decision is whether or not to enter a new market.

- Costs (including research, manufacturing, and marketing) are estimated to be $20 million, and potential revenue is estimated at $50 million in the first year. The client and MR agree to use the first year's net income of $30 million as the expected dollar value. (Note that a few sophisticated MR departments calculate the net present value of the continuing revenue stream, but we have kept the example simple.)
- The executives know that entering a new market is risky. They are only 10 percent confident of making the right decision without research. With the research, they estimate that they will be 70 percent confident—an increase of 60 percent.
- The executives often act without research. The estimated likelihood of acting without research (based on past history) is 50 percent. They expect this would rise to 80 percent after the research—an increase of 30 percent.
- The cost of the research is $1 million. The firm decides to go forward with the research because there will be an anticipated positive 540 percent ROI by the end of the first year:

$$\text{ROI Complete} = \frac{\$30 \text{ million} \times 60\% \times 30\%}{\$1 \text{ million}} = \frac{\$5.4 \text{ million}}{\$1 \text{ million}} = 540\%$$

$$\text{ROI Complete} = \frac{\$30 \text{ million} \times 60\% \times 30\%}{\$1 \text{ million}} = \frac{5.4}{1} = 540\%$$

After the research is completed, MR and the client recalculate ROI.

What if the research says the firm should not enter the market? In that case, the research still has a positive ROI since it saves the firm from investing in a losing venture. Using the previous example, suppose that the research made the firm 80 percent certain it would lose its $20 million investment. Before the research, the firm was 50 percent likely to act and make a losing decision, which means the return on the research is 800 percent:

$$\text{Actual ROI} = \frac{\$20 \text{ million} \times 80\% \times 50\%}{\$1 \text{ million}} = \frac{8}{1} = 800\%$$

What if the research convinces the firm to avoid the market it originally preferred (as shown above) but to invest in an alternative market that would generate a new profit of $30 million in the first year? Assume the firm is 70 percent confident that the alternative is the best one (an increase of 60 percent since it had only 10 percent confidence in it before the research). Also assume that the research increases the likelihood of actually entering a new market by 30 percent. Then the ROI is even higher:

$$\text{Actual ROI} = \frac{(\$20 \text{ million} \times 80\% \times 50\%) + (\$30 \text{ million} \times 60\% \times 30\%)}{\$1 \text{ million}}$$
$$= \frac{\$8 \text{ million} + \$5.4 \text{ million}}{\$1 \text{ million}} = 1,340\%$$

What if the client decides not to act even though the research projects a positive outcome? This often happens when there are changes in leadership or other uses for the capital. In that case, ROI is 0 percent, but the post-research discussion makes clear that this is the client's choice and not MR's fault.

It's not always easy to ask clients how likely they are to take action. Sometimes firms commission research simply to bless a decision that has already been made. Or firms may expect the research to increase their knowledge without necessarily leading to action. Examples of this would be new segmentation research or customer satisfaction tracking. In these cases, the likelihood of acting and the dollar value would depend entirely on what was learned. One MR director said, "Just like estimating the return on IT investments, there are so many assumptions necessary that you can never be sure your estimate will be close. For some kinds of exploratory research, you won't know until you're done whether it will produce anything of financial value." Because these discussions are difficult, some MR groups prefer to use ROI Lite rather than ROI Complete.[33]

The benefits of quantifying the economic value of research include:

- Increased credibility with senior management and other functional areas
- Increased focus on the factors in the processes that drive the most economic value
- A greater probability that research will be viewed as an investment rather than an expense

- More ammunition in defending the research budget
- Better prioritization and allocation of research resources
- More incentive for the research department to stay involved through execution.[34]

# SUMMARY

Supplier research marketing management has six important goals beyond excellent communication: creation of an effective organization, assurance of data quality, adherence to time schedules, cost control, client profitability management, and staff management and development. Many research firms are transitioning to a team-based organization from the traditional functional organizational structure. Marketing research managers can help ensure high-quality data by attempting to minimize sources of error. Researchers should also strive for better client and audience understanding of the margin of error concept. Time management requires a system to notify management of potential problems and policies to solve behind-schedule situations both efficiently and quickly. Cost management demands good cost-tracking and cost control processes. Client profitability management requires that the marketing research supplier determine how much each client contributes to the researcher's overall profitability. Unprofitable clients should be dropped; marginally profitable clients should be developed into high-profit clients or dropped. The supplier should use relationship marketing to build a solid, increasingly profitable long-term relationship with clients identified as high-profit contributors. Finally, staff management and development requires that employees be encouraged to take risks and assume responsibility, be recognized for a job well done, and be offered job autonomy, financial rewards tied to business results, new challenges, and a clear career path.

While outsourcing has been popular for some time, many client-side firms have begun to insource as well. Outsourcing can often save time and money. Outsource firms offer programming, data processing, data analysis, data management, and panel management. Some important issues when considering outsourcing are confidentiality, infrastructure, quality of deliverables, domain, knowledge, culture considerations,

potential negative publicity from job losses, and employee liability. Insourcing can also conserve resources and save time. The availability of sophisticated online research tools has resulted in many firms doing Internet surveys themselves. Insourcing has spread from basic online survey to research online communities, and enterprise customer satisfaction and loyalty feedback management.

A manager of a marketing research department within a corporation faces a different set of issues than from a research supplier. Among these are effective spending of the research budget, prioritizing projects for the corporation, retaining skilled staff, selecting the right research suppliers, moving the marketing research function to a more strategic role in the firm, and measuring return on investment for marketing research.

One technique for prioritizing projects is to focus first on strategic projects and then on the tactical. This is also true for allocating the corporate research budget. Also, projects should be funded that have the highest potential ROI. Ways to retain key staff are to offer interesting and fulfilling work, recognizing someone for a job well done, and offering competitive pay.

A manager of a corporate research department must develop methodologies and skills for selecting the right research suppliers. This includes assessing competing supplier capabilities and reviewing the quality controls of each supplier. Today, many client-side companies are moving beyond traditional selection criteria and are asking for a partner as opposed to simply a research supplier.

The objective of many research departments is to move from being simply data collectors to partners in the strategic decision process. The chapter makes a number of suggestions on how to make this a reality. Finally, a number of corporations are now measuring the ROI on marketing research. This tool, when applied to marketing research can lead to increased credibility with senior management and other advantages.

# KEY TERMS

research management **527**

outsourcing **531**

captive outsourcing **531**

insight **543**

innovation **545**

creativity **545**

## QUESTIONS FOR REVIEW & CRITICAL THINKING

1. Should a survey presentation say, "The margin of error is plus or minus 3 percent"? If not, what problem does it present?

2. Describe four different ways a manager can help ensure high data quality.

3. What policies need to be put in place to ensure that research projects are handled in a timely manner? What steps should be taken if a project falls behind schedule?

4. How can a research supplier develop its employees?

5. Should every firm conduct a client profitability study? Why or why not?

6. Is outsourcing beneficial to the marketing research industry? Why or why not? What about insourcing?

7. Explain the relationship between insights, creativity, and innovation.

8. How should one allocate a corporate marketing research budget? Is this the only way?

9. What is an acceptable method of prioritizing research projects in a research department?

10. What should marketing research do in order to play a more strategic role in the organization?

11. Assume that a company is trying to determine whether to enter a new market. The estimated first year's revenue is $2.2 million. Because management knows a little about this market, it is 20 percent confident that it can make the right decision without research. With research, management will be 80 percent confident. The estimated likelihood of moving into the market without research is 40 percent. This figure would rise to 80 percent after the research. The cost of the research is $400,000. What is the ROI after the first year?

12. What steps and actions should a research supplier take to try to become a strategic partner with a research client?

## WORKING THE NET

1. Go to *www.warc.com* and find an article on managing marketing research firms or projects. Summarize this article for the class.

2. Go to Google or another search engine and look up "marketing research proposals." Find some specific examples of proposals. Choose one that you find interesting Critique that proposal from the standpoint of a research buyer who has received it, looking for things you like and don't like about it, comment on items you find clear or unclear and think about what is missing and what doesn't need to be there. Present your findings to the class.

## REAL-LIFE RESEARCH • 20.1

### Walther Research Deals with Managing Project Managers

Larry Walther started his research company in 1992 in Phoenix, Arizona. He began with a few local clients and two employees. Interviewers were hired as subcontractors and were paid only when his clients paid Larry. In order to make ends meet, he opened several mall locations and set up a focus group facility. By taking in work as a field service as well as a full-service research company, he began to grow. In 1997, his sales reached $1 million, and he had 20 employees. Today the firm has 300 employees.

Larry's growth slowly led to the creation of a functional organization structure. This seemed to happen as much by chance as by design. For example, to get control over the 15 client service/salespeople, they were put into a separate department. The same thing happened with questionnaire design and programming, advanced analytics, database management, and so forth.

Larry's company has grown beyond his wildest dreams, yet all is not well in the organization. Recently, he lost a number of key people, and morale seems to be low throughout the company. Some clients have complained about late projects and unsatisfactory reports. In fact, he recently lost one of his oldest and best clients. Much of the problem, but certainly not all, seems to be his project managers and a lack of project control. An informal survey by Larry of his best clients found:

- The field service recruited unqualified respondents.
- Underqualified interviewers were used for executive interviews.
- The moderator could not keep up with changes that were made in the discussion guide.
- The report lacked depth, interpretation, or insight.
- The presentation or report was disorganized and confusing.

Larry also heard this story from one of his better clients: The client's project report was due to the client on a Friday. The project director was leaving for vacation that day and arranged for someone else in Larry's firm to send the report to the client. However, the project director neglected to tell the client that she was going on vacation and did not give the client the name and phone number of the alternate contact person. The day the report was due, the client called the project director and got a message that she was on vacation. Naturally, the client panicked and called one of Larry's senior assistants asking, "Where's my report?" The client got the report that day as expected, but the relationship with Walther Research has suffered severe damage.

## Questions

1. Larry is considering reorganizing. What should he do?
2. What are the advantages of keeping a functional organizational structure? What are the disadvantages?
3. What might he gain from a team structure? Are there any risks in moving to this form of organization?
4. What should Larry do about directing and controlling his project managers?

# REAL-LIFE RESEARCH • 20.2

## Johnny Jets Drive-Ins

Johnny Jets Drive-Ins is a quick-service restaurant (QSR) organization with more than 4,500 locations in 27 states. Johnny Jets offers customers the option to eat at the restaurant location (in car, inside, patio) or to take out. Regardless of which option customers choose, they order from their smart phones, tablets, or computers on location or remotely, or from a touch screen menu board at the restaurant.

Johnny Jets has enjoyed a high degree of growth and very positive financial returns since starting 17 years ago. Growth has slowed over the last two years as the increase in the number of new locations has stalled.

**Need for market segmentation** Management feels Johnny Jets has reached a level of maturity where growth will need to come more from increasing sales at existing locations and that they need to be more efficient and effective in their marketing efforts. A major factor behind this thinking is that it has secured most of the best locations based on its store location modeling system and that its opportunities for growth from new sites will be much more limited in the future.

It has hired a very large, well-known management-consulting firm to help assess the challenges and strategic options. This firm has been analyzing the data for the last three months and its initial recommendations are that Johnny Jets:

- Needs to find the natural segments that exist in the QSR or fast-food market based on consumer attitudes, behaviors, demographics, and other factors.

- Identify, within the overall QSR segmentation schema, the segment or segments that find their restaurants most appealing.
- Evaluate the opportunities to appeal to additional segments in the QSR space, or, essentially, extend its reach.
- Focus more efficiently and effectively on the targeted segments by making appropriate changes in restaurant location strategy, modifying marketing appeals or positioning, changing product offerings, and making appropriate changes in other elements of the marketing mix.

**Selecting a research firm** Johnny Jets has not previously conducted strategy research and has concluded, with the help of the consulting firm, that the research firms they have used for taste tests and tracking research do not have the capabilities and expertise to conduct the market segmentation work needed. Through industry contacts and input from the management-consulting firm, Johnny Jets narrowed the list of research firms to four that have experience in the QSR industry and in market segmentation. RFPs were sent to those four firms outlining the objectives, specifying the timeline for the research, requesting detailed information about each firm—history, resources, experience, background on key project team members, quality control procedures, financial condition—and describing recommended methodology, detailed time schedule for the project, and cost.

**Evaluating proposals** Management received proposals from three of the four firms. One declined to submit a proposal based on the fact that it had a major conflict of interest in that is was engaged in similar work for the major competitor of Johnny Jets. A team at Johnny Jets evaluated the proposals and has determined:

- All three of the responding firms are qualified.
- The proposed methodologies from the three firms exhibit a high degree of similarity.
- All can meet the timeline required.
- Prices proposed by the three differ by approximately 10 percent from the lowest to highest.

Management is leaning toward the proposal from DSS Research, which is about 7 percent higher than the lowest-cost bid. Reasons for favoring DSS include:

- The DSS methodology shows somewhat more creativity and appears to offer a solution that is more actionable.
- The DSS price is roughly in the middle of the three estimates received.
- The references provided by DSS were more enthusiastic about the company than the references provided by the others.
- Finally, managers like the DSS response to the proposal section that asked, "Why should Johnny Jets choose you as a research partner?"

The DSS response to that section is provided below:

- **Flawless execution of your project** based on experience, dedicated account management teams, and technology.
- **Experienced staff.** Our 400 + knowledgeable and experienced employees enable us to get the job done and respond quickly and effectively to your needs.
- **Focused knowledge and experience in the QSR market.** We stay up to date on developments in the industry and have a deep understanding of the industry and the constituencies it serves.
- **Everything done in-house to control quality, timing, and cost.**
- **Commitment to clients.** It's in our DNA; always go the extra mile for every client.
- **Proactive, responsive project management.** Our project managers, processes and survey management system (SMS) keep you fully informed and engaged in the research process.
- **Dedication to quality.** Based on his academic background, including his published research and his industry-leading textbooks, Mike Nixon of DSS understands the importance of quality research and stresses it throughout the organization.
- **Highest response rates** based on best practices in data collection produce lower nonresponse bias and more accurate results.
- **Strong analytics.** Mr. Nixon has taught and extensively written about a wide range of powerful analytic techniques for researchers. He created our Marketing Science group as a platform to deliver the best possible analytics to clients to and to give them the power of decision-making information.
- **Clear and insightful reporting.** Our reporting package gives you all the information you need to meet your objectives.
- **Unparalleled value.** Our internal systems enable us to carefully track costs and identify areas where inefficiencies exist. This internal infrastructure, combined with our extensive QSR experience, allows us to offer competitive pricing, resulting in one of the best research values around.

## Questions

1. Comment on the process that Johnny Jets used to select a research firm. What, if anything, would you do differently?

2. Was it appropriate for the one firm to decline to submit a proposal based on conflicts? Why do you say that?

3. What do you think of the DSS response to the, "Why should Johnny Jets choose RESEARCH FIRM NAME?" question in the RFP?

4. Based on the information provided, would you choose DSS to do the research?

# APPENDIX ONE

## Statistical Tables

**1**
**Random Digits**

**2**
**Standard Normal Distribution: Z-values**

**3**
**t-Distribution**

**4**
**Chi-Square Distribution**

**5**
**F-Distribution**

| EXHIBIT 1 | Random Digits | | | | | | | | |
|---|---|---|---|---|---|---|---|---|---|
| 63271 | 59986 | 71744 | 51102 | 15141 | 80714 | 58683 | 93108 | 13554 | 79945 |
| 88547 | 09896 | 95436 | 79115 | 08303 | 01041 | 20030 | 63754 | 08459 | 28364 |
| 55957 | 57243 | 83865 | 09911 | 19761 | 66535 | 40102 | 26646 | 60147 | 15702 |
| 46276 | 87453 | 44790 | 64122 | 45573 | 84358 | 21625 | 16999 | 13385 | 22782 |
| 55363 | 07449 | 34835 | 15290 | 76616 | 67191 | 12777 | 21861 | 68689 | 03263 |
| | | | | | | | | | |
| 69393 | 92785 | 49902 | 58447 | 42048 | 30378 | 87618 | 26933 | 40640 | 16281 |
| 13186 | 29431 | 88190 | 04588 | 38733 | 81290 | 89541 | 70290 | 40113 | 08243 |
| 17726 | 28652 | 56836 | 78351 | 47327 | 18518 | 92222 | 55201 | 27340 | 10493 |
| 36520 | 64465 | 05550 | 30157 | 82242 | 29520 | 69753 | 72602 | 23756 | 54935 |
| 81628 | 36100 | 39254 | 56835 | 37636 | 02421 | 98063 | 89641 | 64953 | 99337 |
| | | | | | | | | | |
| 84649 | 48968 | 75215 | 75498 | 49539 | 74240 | 03466 | 49292 | 36401 | 45525 |
| 63291 | 11618 | 12613 | 75055 | 43915 | 26488 | 41116 | 64531 | 56827 | 30825 |
| 70502 | 53225 | 03655 | 05915 | 37140 | 57051 | 48393 | 91322 | 25653 | 06543 |
| 06426 | 24771 | 59935 | 49801 | 11082 | 66762 | 94477 | 02494 | 88215 | 27191 |
| 20711 | 55609 | 29430 | 70165 | 45406 | 78484 | 31639 | 52009 | 18873 | 96927 |
| | | | | | | | | | |
| 41990 | 70538 | 77191 | 25860 | 55204 | 73417 | 83920 | 69468 | 74972 | 38712 |
| 72452 | 36618 | 76298 | 26678 | 89334 | 33938 | 95567 | 29380 | 75906 | 91807 |
| 37042 | 40318 | 57099 | 10528 | 09925 | 89773 | 41335 | 96244 | 29002 | 46453 |
| 53766 | 52875 | 15987 | 46962 | 67342 | 77592 | 57651 | 95508 | 80033 | 69828 |
| 90585 | 58955 | 53122 | 16025 | 84299 | 53310 | 67380 | 84249 | 25348 | 04332 |
| | | | | | | | | | |
| 32001 | 96293 | 37203 | 64516 | 51530 | 37069 | 40261 | 61374 | 05815 | 06714 |
| 62606 | 64324 | 46354 | 72157 | 67248 | 20135 | 49804 | 09226 | 64419 | 29457 |
| 10078 | 28073 | 85389 | 50324 | 14500 | 15562 | 64165 | 06125 | 71353 | 77669 |
| 91561 | 46145 | 24177 | 15294 | 10061 | 98124 | 75732 | 00815 | 83452 | 97355 |
| 13091 | 98112 | 53959 | 79607 | 52244 | 63303 | 10413 | 63839 | 74762 | 50289 |
| | | | | | | | | | |
| 73864 | 83014 | 72457 | 22682 | 03033 | 61714 | 88173 | 90835 | 00634 | 85169 |
| 66668 | 25467 | 48894 | 51043 | 02365 | 91726 | 09365 | 63167 | 95264 | 45643 |
| 84745 | 41042 | 29493 | 01836 | 09044 | 51926 | 43630 | 63470 | 76508 | 14194 |
| 48068 | 26805 | 94595 | 47907 | 13357 | 38412 | 33318 | 26098 | 82782 | 42851 |
| 54310 | 96175 | 97594 | 88616 | 42035 | 38093 | 36745 | 56702 | 40644 | 83514 |
| | | | | | | | | | |
| 14877 | 33095 | 10924 | 58013 | 61439 | 21882 | 42059 | 24177 | 58739 | 60170 |
| 78295 | 23179 | 02771 | 43464 | 59061 | 71411 | 05697 | 67194 | 30495 | 21157 |
| 67524 | 02865 | 39593 | 54278 | 04237 | 92441 | 26602 | 63835 | 38032 | 94770 |
| 58268 | 57219 | 68124 | 73455 | 83236 | 08710 | 04284 | 55005 | 84171 | 42596 |
| 97158 | 28672 | 50685 | 01181 | 24262 | 19427 | 52106 | 34308 | 73685 | 74246 |
| | | | | | | | | | |
| 04230 | 16831 | 69085 | 30802 | 65559 | 09205 | 71829 | 06489 | 85650 | 38707 |
| 94879 | 56606 | 30401 | 02602 | 57658 | 70091 | 54986 | 41394 | 60437 | 03195 |
| 71446 | 15232 | 66715 | 26385 | 91518 | 70566 | 02888 | 79941 | 39684 | 54315 |
| 32886 | 05644 | 79316 | 09819 | 00813 | 88407 | 17461 | 73925 | 53037 | 91904 |
| 62048 | 33711 | 25290 | 21526 | 02223 | 75947 | 66466 | 06332 | 10913 | 75336 |
| | | | | | | | | | |
| 84534 | 42351 | 21628 | 53669 | 81352 | 95152 | 08107 | 98814 | 72743 | 12849 |
| 84707 | 15885 | 84710 | 35866 | 06446 | 86311 | 32648 | 88141 | 73902 | 69981 |
| 19409 | 40868 | 64220 | 80861 | 13860 | 68493 | 52908 | 26374 | 63297 | 45052 |
| 57978 | 48015 | 25973 | 66777 | 45924 | 56144 | 24742 | 96702 | 88200 | 66162 |
| 57295 | 98298 | 11199 | 96510 | 75228 | 41600 | 47192 | 43267 | 35973 | 23152 |
| | | | | | | | | | |
| 94044 | 83785 | 93388 | 07833 | 38216 | 31413 | 70555 | 03023 | 54147 | 06647 |
| 30014 | 25879 | 71763 | 96679 | 90603 | 99396 | 74557 | 74224 | 18211 | 91637 |
| 07265 | 69563 | 64268 | 88802 | 72264 | 66540 | 01782 | 08396 | 19251 | 83613 |
| 84404 | 88642 | 30263 | 80310 | 11522 | 57810 | 27627 | 78376 | 36240 | 48952 |
| 21778 | 02085 | 27762 | 46097 | 43324 | 34354 | 09369 | 14966 | 10158 | 76089 |

## EXHIBIT 2 | Standard Normal Distribution: Z-values

Entries in the table give the area under the curve between the mean and Z standard deviations above the mean. For example, for $Z = 1.25$, the area under the curve between the mean and Z is .3944.

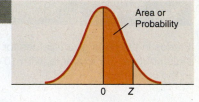

Area or Probability

| Z | .00 | .01 | .02 | .03 | .04 | .05 | .06 | .07 | .08 | .09 |
|---|---|---|---|---|---|---|---|---|---|---|
| .0 | .0000 | .0040 | .0080 | .0120 | .0160 | .0199 | .0239 | .0279 | .0319 | .0359 |
| .1 | .0398 | .0438 | .0478 | .0517 | .0557 | .0596 | .0636 | .0675 | .0714 | .0753 |
| .2 | .0793 | .0832 | .0871 | .0910 | .0948 | .0987 | .1026 | .1064 | .1103 | .1141 |
| .3 | .1179 | .1217 | .1255 | .1293 | .1331 | .1368 | .1406 | .1443 | .1480 | .1517 |
| .4 | .1554 | .1591 | .1628 | .1664 | .1700 | .1736 | .1772 | .1808 | .1844 | .1879 |
| .5 | .1915 | .1950 | .1985 | .2019 | .2054 | .2088 | .2123 | .2157 | .2190 | .2224 |
| .6 | .2257 | .2291 | .2324 | .2357 | .2389 | .2422 | .2454 | .2486 | .2518 | .2549 |
| .7 | .2580 | .2612 | .2642 | .2673 | .2704 | .2734 | .2764 | .2794 | .2823 | .2852 |
| .8 | .2881 | .2910 | .2939 | .2967 | .2995 | .3023 | .3051 | .3078 | .3106 | .3133 |
| .9 | .3159 | .3186 | .3212 | .3238 | .3264 | .3289 | .3315 | .3340 | .3365 | .3389 |
| 1.0 | .3413 | .3438 | .3461 | .3485 | .3508 | .3531 | .3554 | .3577 | .3599 | .3621 |
| 1.1 | .3643 | .3665 | .3686 | .3708 | .3729 | .3749 | .3770 | .3790 | .3810 | .3830 |
| 1.2 | .3849 | .3869 | .3888 | .3907 | .3925 | .3944 | .3962 | .3980 | .3997 | .4015 |
| 1.3 | .4032 | .4049 | .4066 | .4082 | .4099 | .4115 | .4131 | .4147 | .4162 | .4177 |
| 1.4 | .4192 | .4207 | .4222 | .4236 | .4251 | .4265 | .4279 | .4292 | .4306 | .4319 |
| 1.5 | .4332 | .4345 | .4357 | .4370 | .4382 | .4394 | .4406 | .4418 | .4429 | .4441 |
| 1.6 | .4452 | .4463 | .4474 | .4484 | .4495 | .4505 | .4515 | .4525 | .4535 | .4545 |
| 1.7 | .4554 | .4564 | .4573 | .4582 | .4591 | .4599 | .4608 | .4616 | .4625 | .4633 |
| 1.8 | .4641 | .4649 | .4656 | .4664 | .4671 | .4678 | .4686 | .4693 | .4699 | .4706 |
| 1.9 | .4713 | .4719 | .4726 | .4732 | .4738 | .4744 | .4750 | .4756 | .4761 | .4767 |
| 2.0 | .4772 | .4778 | .4783 | .4788 | .4793 | .4798 | .4803 | .4808 | .4812 | .4817 |
| 2.1 | .4821 | .4826 | .4830 | .4834 | .4838 | .4842 | .4846 | .4850 | .4854 | .4857 |
| 2.2 | .4861 | .4864 | .4868 | .4871 | .4875 | .4878 | .4881 | .4884 | .4887 | .4890 |
| 2.3 | .4893 | .4896 | .4898 | .4901 | .4904 | .4906 | .4909 | .4911 | .4913 | .4916 |
| 2.4 | .4918 | .4920 | .4922 | .4925 | .4927 | .4929 | .4931 | .4932 | .4934 | .4936 |
| 2.5 | .4938 | .4940 | .4941 | .4943 | .4945 | .4946 | .4948 | .4949 | .4951 | .4952 |
| 2.6 | .4953 | .4955 | .4956 | .4957 | .4959 | .4960 | .4961 | .4962 | .4963 | .4964 |
| 2.7 | .4965 | .4966 | .4967 | .4968 | .4969 | .4970 | .4971 | .4972 | .4973 | .4974 |
| 2.8 | .4974 | .4975 | .4976 | .4977 | .4977 | .4978 | .4979 | .4979 | .4980 | .4981 |
| 2.9 | .4981 | .4982 | .4982 | .4983 | .4984 | .4984 | .4985 | .4985 | .4986 | .4986 |
| 3.0 | .4986 | .4987 | .4987 | .4988 | .4988 | .4989 | .4989 | .4989 | .4990 | .4990 |

## EXHIBIT 3 — t-Distribution

Entries in the table give *t*-values for an area or probability in the upper tail of the *t*-distribution. For example, with 10 degrees of freedom and a .05 area in the upper tail, $t_{.05} = 1.812$.

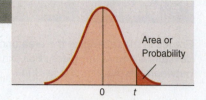

Area or Probability

0   t

| Degrees of Freedom | Area in Upper Tail | | | | |
|---|---|---|---|---|---|
| | .10 | .05 | .025 | .01 | .005 |
| 1 | 3.078 | 6.314 | 12.706 | 31.821 | 63.657 |
| 2 | 1.886 | 2.920 | 4.303 | 6.965 | 9.925 |
| 3 | 1.638 | 2.353 | 3.182 | 4.541 | 5.841 |
| 4 | 1.533 | 2.132 | 2.776 | 3.747 | 4.604 |
| 5 | 1.476 | 2.015 | 2.571 | 3.365 | 4.032 |
| 6 | 1.440 | 1.943 | 2.447 | 3.143 | 3.707 |
| 7 | 1.415 | 1.895 | 2.365 | 2.998 | 3.499 |
| 8 | 1.397 | 1.860 | 2.306 | 2.896 | 3.355 |
| 9 | 1.383 | 1.833 | 2.262 | 2.821 | 3.250 |
| 10 | 1.372 | 1.812 | 2.228 | 2.764 | 3.169 |
| 11 | 1.363 | 1.796 | 2.201 | 2.718 | 3.106 |
| 12 | 1.356 | 1.782 | 2.179 | 2.681 | 3.055 |
| 13 | 1.350 | 1.771 | 2.160 | 2.650 | 3.012 |
| 14 | 1.345 | 1.761 | 2.145 | 2.624 | 2.977 |
| 15 | 1.341 | 1.753 | 2.131 | 2.602 | 2.947 |
| 16 | 1.337 | 1.746 | 2.120 | 2.583 | 2.921 |
| 17 | 1.333 | 1.740 | 2.110 | 2.567 | 2.898 |
| 18 | 1.330 | 1.734 | 2.101 | 2.552 | 2.878 |
| 19 | 1.328 | 1.729 | 2.093 | 2.539 | 2.861 |
| 20 | 1.325 | 1.725 | 2.086 | 2.528 | 2.845 |
| 21 | 1.323 | 1.721 | 2.080 | 2.518 | 2.831 |
| 22 | 1.321 | 1.717 | 2.074 | 2.508 | 2.819 |
| 23 | 1.319 | 1.714 | 2.069 | 2.500 | 2.807 |
| 24 | 1.318 | 1.711 | 2.064 | 2.492 | 2.797 |
| 25 | 1.316 | 1.708 | 2.060 | 2.485 | 2.787 |
| 26 | 1.315 | 1.706 | 2.056 | 2.479 | 2.779 |
| 27 | 1.314 | 1.703 | 2.052 | 2.473 | 2.771 |
| 28 | 1.313 | 1.701 | 2.048 | 2.467 | 2.763 |
| 29 | 1.311 | 1.699 | 2.045 | 2.462 | 2.756 |
| 30 | 1.310 | 1.697 | 2.042 | 2.457 | 2.750 |
| 40 | 1.303 | 1.684 | 2.021 | 2.423 | 2.704 |
| 60 | 1.296 | 1.671 | 2.000 | 2.390 | 2.660 |
| 120 | 1.289 | 1.658 | 1.980 | 2.358 | 2.617 |
| ∞ | 1.282 | 1.645 | 1.960 | 2.326 | 2.576 |

**EXHIBIT 4**  Chi-Square Distribution

Entries in the table give $\chi^2_\alpha$ values, where $\alpha$ is the area or probability in the upper tail of the chi-square distribution. For example, with 10 degrees of freedom and a .01 area in the upper tail, $\chi^2_\alpha$ 23.2093.

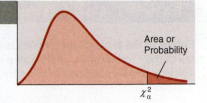

Area or Probability

$\chi^2_\alpha$

| Degrees of Freedom | Area in Upper Tail | | | | | | | | | |
|---|---|---|---|---|---|---|---|---|---|---|
| | .995 | .99 | .975 | .95 | .90 | .10 | .05 | .025 | .01 | .005 |
| 1 | .0000393 | .000157 | .000982 | .000393 | .015709 | 2.70554 | 3.84146 | 5.02389 | 6.63490 | 7.87944 |
| 2 | .0100251 | .0201007 | .0506356 | .102587 | .210720 | 4.60517 | 5.99147 | 7.37776 | 9.21034 | 10.5966 |
| 3 | .0717212 | .114832 | 2.15795 | .351846 | .584375 | 6.25139 | 7.81473 | 9.34840 | 11.3449 | 12.8381 |
| 4 | .206990 | .297110 | .484419 | .710721 | 1.063623 | 7.77944 | 9.48773 | 11.1433 | 13.2767 | 14.8602 |
| 5 | .411740 | .554300 | .831211 | 1.145476 | 1.61031 | 9.23635 | 11.0705 | 12.8325 | 15.0863 | 16.7496 |
| 6 | .675727 | .872085 | 1.237347 | 1.63539 | 2.20413 | 10.6446 | 12.5916 | 14.4494 | 16.8119 | 18.5476 |
| 7 | .989265 | 1.239043 | 1.68987 | 2.16735 | 2.83311 | 12.0170 | 14.0671 | 16.0128 | 18.4753 | 20.2777 |
| 8 | 1.344419 | 1.646482 | 2.17973 | 2.73264 | 3.48954 | 13.3616 | 15.5073 | 17.5346 | 20.0902 | 21.9550 |
| 9 | 1.734926 | 2.087912 | 2.70039 | 3.32511 | 4.16816 | 14.6837 | 16.9190 | 19.0228 | 21.6660 | 23.5893 |
| 10 | 2.15585 | 2.55821 | 3.24697 | 3.94030 | 4.86518 | 15.9871 | 18.3070 | 20.4831 | 23.2093 | 25.1882 |
| 11 | 2.60321 | 3.05347 | 3.81575 | 4.57481 | 5.57779 | 17.2750 | 19.6751 | 21.9200 | 24.7250 | 26.7569 |
| 12 | 3.07382 | 3.57056 | 4.40379 | 5.22603 | 6.30380 | 18.5494 | 21.0261 | 23.3367 | 26.2170 | 28.2995 |
| 13 | 3.56503 | 4.10691 | 5.00874 | 5.89186 | 7.04150 | 19.8119 | 22.3621 | 24.7356 | 27.6883 | 29.8194 |
| 14 | 4.07468 | 4.66043 | 5.62872 | 6.57063 | 7.78953 | 21.0642 | 23.6848 | 26.1190 | 29.1413 | 31.3193 |
| 15 | 4.60094 | 5.22935 | 6.26214 | 7.26094 | 8.54675 | 22.3072 | 24.9958 | 27.4884 | 30.5779 | 32.8013 |
| 16 | 5.14224 | 5.81221 | 6.90766 | 7.96164 | 9.31223 | 23.5418 | 26.2962 | 28.8454 | 31.9999 | 34.2672 |
| 17 | 5.69724 | 6.40776 | 7.56418 | 8.67176 | 10.0852 | 24.7690 | 27.5871 | 30.1910 | 33.4087 | 35.7185 |
| 18 | 6.26481 | 7.01491 | 8.23075 | 9.39046 | 10.8649 | 25.9894 | 28.8693 | 31.5264 | 34.8053 | 37.1564 |
| 19 | 6.84398 | 7.63273 | 8.90655 | 10.1170 | 11.6509 | 27.2036 | 30.1435 | 32.8523 | 36.1908 | 38.5822 |
| 20 | 7.43386 | 8.26040 | 9.59083 | 10.8508 | 12.4426 | 28.4120 | 31.4104 | 34.1696 | 37.5662 | 39.9968 |
| 21 | 8.03366 | 8.89720 | 10.28293 | 11.5913 | 13.2396 | 29.6151 | 32.6705 | 35.4789 | 38.9321 | 41.4010 |
| 22 | 8.64272 | 9.54249 | 10.9823 | 12.3380 | 14.0415 | 30.8133 | 33.9244 | 36.7807 | 40.2894 | 42.7958 |
| 23 | 9.26042 | 10.19567 | 11.6885 | 13.0905 | 14.8479 | 32.0069 | 35.1725 | 38.0757 | 41.6384 | 44.1813 |
| 24 | 9.88623 | 10.8564 | 12.4011 | 13.8484 | 15.6587 | 33.1963 | 36.4151 | 39.3641 | 42.9798 | 45.5585 |
| 25 | 10.5197 | 11.5240 | 13.1197 | 14.6114 | 16.4734 | 34.3816 | 37.6525 | 40.6465 | 44.3141 | 46.9278 |
| 26 | 11.1603 | 12.1981 | 13.8439 | 15.3791 | 17.2919 | 35.5631 | 38.8852 | 41.9232 | 45.6417 | 48.2899 |
| 27 | 11.8076 | 12.8786 | 14.5733 | 16.1513 | 18.1138 | 36.7412 | 40.1133 | 43.1944 | 46.9630 | 49.6449 |
| 28 | 12.4613 | 13.5648 | 15.3079 | 16.9279 | 18.9392 | 37.9159 | 41.3372 | 44.4607 | 48.2782 | 50.9933 |
| 29 | 13.1211 | 14.2565 | 16.0471 | 17.7083 | 19.7677 | 39.0875 | 42.5569 | 45.7222 | 49.5879 | 52.3356 |
| 30 | 13.7867 | 14.9535 | 16.7908 | 18.4926 | 20.5992 | 40.2560 | 43.7729 | 46.9792 | 50.8922 | 53.6720 |
| 40 | 20.765 | 22.1643 | 24.4331 | 26.5093 | 29.0505 | 51.8050 | 55.7585 | 59.3417 | 63.6907 | 66.7659 |
| 50 | 27.9907 | 29.7067 | 32.3574 | 34.7642 | 37.6886 | 63.1671 | 67.5048 | 71.4202 | 76.1539 | 79.4900 |
| 60 | 35.5346 | 37.4848 | 40.4817 | 43.1879 | 46.4589 | 74.3970 | 79.0819 | 83.2976 | 88.3794 | 91.9517 |
| 70 | 43.2752 | 45.4418 | 48.7576 | 51.7393 | 55.3290 | 85.5271 | 90.5312 | 95.0231 | 100.425 | 104.215 |
| 80 | 51.1720 | 53.5400 | 57.1532 | 60.3915 | 64.2778 | 96.5782 | 101.879 | 106.629 | 112.329 | 116.321 |
| 90 | 59.1963 | 61.7541 | 65.6466 | 69.1260 | 73.2912 | 107.565 | 113.145 | 118.136 | 124.116 | 128.299 |
| 100 | 67.3276 | 70.0648 | 74.2219 | 77.9295 | 82.3581 | 118.498 | 124.342 | 129.561 | 135.807 | 140.169 |

| EXHIBIT 5 | *F*-Distribution |
|---|---|

Entries in the table give $F_\alpha$ values, where is the area or probability in the upper tail of the *F*-distribution. For example, with 12 numerator degrees of freedom, 15 denominator degrees of freedom, and a .05 area in the upper tail, $F_{.05} = 2.48$.

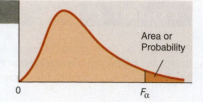

Area or Probability

## Table of $F_{.05}$ Values

### Numerator Degrees of Freedom

| | 1 | 2 | 3 | 4 | 5 | 6 | 7 | 8 | 9 | 10 | 12 | 15 | 20 | 24 | 30 | 40 | 60 | 120 | ∞ |
|---|---|---|---|---|---|---|---|---|---|---|---|---|---|---|---|---|---|---|---|
| 1 | 161.4 | 199.5 | 215.7 | 224.6 | 230.2 | 234.0 | 236.8 | 238.9 | 240.5 | 241.9 | 243.9 | 245.9 | 248.0 | 249.1 | 250.1 | 251.1 | 252.2 | 253.3 | 254.30 |
| 2 | 18.51 | 19.00 | 19.16 | 19.25 | 19.30 | 19.33 | 19.35 | 19.37 | 19.38 | 19.40 | 19.41 | 19.43 | 19.45 | 19.45 | 19.46 | 19.47 | 19.48 | 19.49 | 19.50 |
| 3 | 10.13 | 9.55 | 9.28 | 9.12 | 9.01 | 8.94 | 8.89 | 8.85 | 8.81 | 8.79 | 8.74 | 8.70 | 8.66 | 8.64 | 8.62 | 8.59 | 8.57 | 8.55 | 8.53 |
| 4 | 7.71 | 6.94 | 6.59 | 6.39 | 6.26 | 6.16 | 6.09 | 6.04 | 6.00 | 5.96 | 5.91 | 5.86 | 5.80 | 5.77 | 5.75 | 5.72 | 5.69 | 5.66 | 5.63 |
| 5 | 6.61 | 5.79 | 5.41 | 5.19 | 5.05 | 4.95 | 4.88 | 4.82 | 4.77 | 4.74 | 4.68 | 4.62 | 4.56 | 4.53 | 4.50 | 4.46 | 4.43 | 4.40 | 4.36 |
| 6 | 5.99 | 5.14 | 4.76 | 4.53 | 4.39 | 4.28 | 4.21 | 4.15 | 4.10 | 4.06 | 4.00 | 3.94 | 3.87 | 3.84 | 3.81 | 3.77 | 3.74 | 3.70 | 3.67 |
| 7 | 5.59 | 4.74 | 4.35 | 4.12 | 3.97 | 3.87 | 3.79 | 3.73 | 3.68 | 3.64 | 3.57 | 3.51 | 3.44 | 3.41 | 3.38 | 3.34 | 3.30 | 3.27 | 3.23 |
| 8 | 5.32 | 4.46 | 4.07 | 3.84 | 3.69 | 3.58 | 3.50 | 3.44 | 3.39 | 3.35 | 3.28 | 3.22 | 3.15 | 3.12 | 3.08 | 3.04 | 3.01 | 2.97 | 2.93 |
| 9 | 5.12 | 4.26 | 3.86 | 3.63 | 3.48 | 3.37 | 3.29 | 3.23 | 3.18 | 3.14 | 3.07 | 3.01 | 2.94 | 2.90 | 2.86 | 2.83 | 2.79 | 2.75 | 2.71 |
| 10 | 4.96 | 4.10 | 3.71 | 3.48 | 3.33 | 3.22 | 3.14 | 3.07 | 3.02 | 2.98 | 2.91 | 2.85 | 2.77 | 2.74 | 2.70 | 2.66 | 2.62 | 2.58 | 2.54 |
| 11 | 4.84 | 3.98 | 3.59 | 3.36 | 3.20 | 3.09 | 3.01 | 2.95 | 2.90 | 2.85 | 2.79 | 2.72 | 2.65 | 2.61 | 2.57 | 2.53 | 2.49 | 2.45 | 2.40 |
| 12 | 4.75 | 3.89 | 3.49 | 3.26 | 3.11 | 3.00 | 2.91 | 2.85 | 2.80 | 2.75 | 2.69 | 2.62 | 2.54 | 2.51 | 2.47 | 2.43 | 2.38 | 2.34 | 2.30 |
| 13 | 4.67 | 3.81 | 3.41 | 3.18 | 3.03 | 2.92 | 2.83 | 2.77 | 2.71 | 2.67 | 2.60 | 2.53 | 2.46 | 2.42 | 2.38 | 2.34 | 2.30 | 2.25 | 2.21 |
| 14 | 4.60 | 3.74 | 3.34 | 3.11 | 2.96 | 2.85 | 2.76 | 2.70 | 2.65 | 2.60 | 2.53 | 2.46 | 2.39 | 2.35 | 2.31 | 2.27 | 2.22 | 2.18 | 2.13 |
| 15 | 4.54 | 3.68 | 3.29 | 3.06 | 2.90 | 2.79 | 2.71 | 2.64 | 2.59 | 2.54 | 2.48 | 2.40 | 2.33 | 2.29 | 2.25 | 2.20 | 2.16 | 2.11 | 2.07 |
| 16 | 4.49 | 3.63 | 3.24 | 3.01 | 2.85 | 2.74 | 2.66 | 2.59 | 2.54 | 2.49 | 2.42 | 2.35 | 2.28 | 2.24 | 2.19 | 2.15 | 2.11 | 2.06 | 2.01 |
| 17 | 4.45 | 3.59 | 3.20 | 2.96 | 2.81 | 2.70 | 2.61 | 2.55 | 2.49 | 2.45 | 2.38 | 2.31 | 2.23 | 2.19 | 2.15 | 2.10 | 2.06 | 2.01 | 1.96 |
| 18 | 4.41 | 3.55 | 3.16 | 2.93 | 2.77 | 2.66 | 2.58 | 2.51 | 2.46 | 2.41 | 2.34 | 2.27 | 2.19 | 2.15 | 2.11 | 2.06 | 2.02 | 1.97 | 1.92 |
| 19 | 4.38 | 3.52 | 3.13 | 2.90 | 2.74 | 2.63 | 2.54 | 2.48 | 2.42 | 2.38 | 2.31 | 2.23 | 2.16 | 2.11 | 2.07 | 2.03 | 1.98 | 1.93 | 1.88 |
| 20 | 4.35 | 3.49 | 3.10 | 2.87 | 2.71 | 2.60 | 2.51 | 2.45 | 2.39 | 2.35 | 2.28 | 2.20 | 2.12 | 2.08 | 2.04 | 1.99 | 1.95 | 1.90 | 1.84 |
| 21 | 4.32 | 3.47 | 3.07 | 2.84 | 2.68 | 2.57 | 2.49 | 2.42 | 2.37 | 2.32 | 2.25 | 2.18 | 2.10 | 2.05 | 2.01 | 1.96 | 1.92 | 1.87 | 1.81 |
| 22 | 4.30 | 3.44 | 3.05 | 2.82 | 2.66 | 2.55 | 2.46 | 2.40 | 2.34 | 2.30 | 2.23 | 2.15 | 2.07 | 2.03 | 1.98 | 1.94 | 1.89 | 1.84 | 1.78 |
| 23 | 4.28 | 3.42 | 3.03 | 2.80 | 2.64 | 2.53 | 2.44 | 2.37 | 2.32 | 2.27 | 2.20 | 2.13 | 2.05 | 2.01 | 1.96 | 1.91 | 1.86 | 1.81 | 1.76 |
| 24 | 4.26 | 3.40 | 3.01 | 2.78 | 2.62 | 2.51 | 2.42 | 2.36 | 2.30 | 2.25 | 2.18 | 2.11 | 2.03 | 1.98 | 1.94 | 1.89 | 1.84 | 1.79 | 1.73 |
| 25 | 4.24 | 3.39 | 2.99 | 2.76 | 2.60 | 2.49 | 2.40 | 2.34 | 2.28 | 2.24 | 2.16 | 2.09 | 2.01 | 1.96 | 1.92 | 1.87 | 1.82 | 1.77 | 1.71 |
| 26 | 4.23 | 3.37 | 2.98 | 2.74 | 2.59 | 2.47 | 2.39 | 2.32 | 2.27 | 2.22 | 2.15 | 2.07 | 1.99 | 1.95 | 1.90 | 1.85 | 1.80 | 1.75 | 1.69 |
| 27 | 4.21 | 3.35 | 2.96 | 2.73 | 2.57 | 2.46 | 2.37 | 2.31 | 2.25 | 2.20 | 2.13 | 2.06 | 1.97 | 1.93 | 1.88 | 1.84 | 1.79 | 1.73 | 1.67 |
| 28 | 4.20 | 3.34 | 2.95 | 2.71 | 2.56 | 2.45 | 2.36 | 2.29 | 2.24 | 2.19 | 2.12 | 2.04 | 1.96 | 1.91 | 1.87 | 1.82 | 1.77 | 1.71 | 1.65 |
| 29 | 4.18 | 3.33 | 2.93 | 2.70 | 2.55 | 2.43 | 2.35 | 2.28 | 2.22 | 2.18 | 2.10 | 2.03 | 1.94 | 1.90 | 1.85 | 1.81 | 1.75 | 1.70 | 1.64 |
| 30 | 4.17 | 3.32 | 2.92 | 2.69 | 2.53 | 2.42 | 2.33 | 2.27 | 2.21 | 2.16 | 2.09 | 2.01 | 1.93 | 1.89 | 1.84 | 1.79 | 1.74 | 1.68 | 1.62 |
| 40 | 4.08 | 3.23 | 2.84 | 2.61 | 2.45 | 2.34 | 2.25 | 2.18 | 2.12 | 2.08 | 2.00 | 1.92 | 1.84 | 1.79 | 1.74 | 1.69 | 1.64 | 1.58 | 1.51 |
| 60 | 4.00 | 3.15 | 2.76 | 2.53 | 2.37 | 2.25 | 2.17 | 2.10 | 2.04 | 1.99 | 1.92 | 1.84 | 1.75 | 1.70 | 1.65 | 1.59 | 1.53 | 1.47 | 1.39 |
| 120 | 3.92 | 3.07 | 2.68 | 2.45 | 2.29 | 2.17 | 2.09 | 2.02 | 1.96 | 1.91 | 1.83 | 1.75 | 1.66 | 1.61 | 1.55 | 1.50 | 1.43 | 1.35 | 1.25 |
| ∞ | 3.84 | 3.00 | 2.60 | 2.37 | 2.21 | 2.10 | 2.01 | 1.94 | 1.88 | 1.83 | 1.75 | 1.67 | 1.57 | 1.52 | 1.46 | 1.39 | 1.32 | 1.22 | 1.00 |

## Table of $F_{.05}$ Values

### Numerator Degrees of Freedom

| | 1 | 2 | 3 | 4 | 5 | 6 | 7 | 8 | 9 | 10 | 12 | 15 | 20 | 24 | 30 | 40 | 60 | 120 | $\infty$ |
|---|---|---|---|---|---|---|---|---|---|---|---|---|---|---|---|---|---|---|---|
| 1 | 4052 | 4999.5 | 5403 | 5625 | 5764 | 5859 | 5928 | 5982 | 6022 | 6056 | 6106 | 6157 | 6209 | 6235 | 6261 | 6287 | 6313 | 6339 | 6366 |
| 2 | 98.50 | 99.00 | 99.17 | 99.25 | 99.30 | 99.33 | 99.36 | 99.37 | 99.39 | 99.40 | 99.42 | 99.43 | 99.45 | 99.46 | 99.47 | 99.47 | 99.48 | 99.49 | 99.50 |
| 3 | 34.12 | 30.82 | 29.46 | 28.71 | 28.24 | 27.91 | 27.67 | 27.49 | 27.35 | 27.23 | 27.05 | 26.87 | 26.69 | 26.60 | 26.50 | 26.41 | 26.32 | 26.22 | 26.13 |
| 4 | 21.20 | 18.00 | 16.69 | 15.98 | 15.52 | 51.21 | 14.98 | 14.80 | 14.66 | 14.55 | 14.37 | 14.20 | 14.02 | 13.93 | 13.84 | 13.75 | 13.65 | 13.56 | 13.46 |
| 5 | 16.26 | 13.27 | 12.06 | 11.39 | 10.97 | 10.67 | 10.46 | 10.29 | 10.16 | 10.05 | 9.89 | 9.72 | 9.55 | 9.47 | 9.38 | 9.29 | 9.20 | 9.11 | 9.06 |
| 6 | 13.75 | 10.92 | 9.78 | 9.15 | 8.75 | 8.47 | 8.26 | 8.10 | 7.98 | 7.87 | 7.72 | 7.56 | 7.40 | 7.31 | 7.23 | 7.14 | 7.06 | 6.97 | 6.88 |
| 7 | 12.25 | 9.55 | 8.45 | 7.85 | 7.46 | 7.19 | 6.99 | 6.84 | 6.72 | 6.62 | 6.47 | 6.31 | 6.16 | 6.07 | 5.99 | 5.91 | 5.82 | 5.74 | 5.65 |
| 8 | 11.26 | 8.65 | 7.59 | 7.01 | 6.63 | 6.37 | 6.18 | 6.03 | 5.91 | 5.81 | 5.67 | 5.52 | 5.36 | 5.28 | 5.20 | 5.12 | 5.03 | 4.95 | 4.86 |
| 9 | 10.56 | 8.02 | 6.99 | 6.42 | 6.06 | 5.80 | 5.61 | 5.47 | 5.35 | 5.26 | 5.11 | 4.96 | 4.81 | 4.73 | 4.65 | 4.57 | 4.48 | 4.40 | 4.31 |
| 10 | 10.04 | 7.56 | 6.55 | 5.99 | 5.64 | 5.39 | 5.20 | 5.06 | 4.94 | 4.85 | 4.71 | 4.56 | 4.41 | 4.33 | 4.25 | 4.17 | 4.08 | 4.00 | 3.91 |
| 11 | 9.65 | 7.21 | 6.22 | 5.67 | 5.32 | 5.07 | 4.89 | 4.74 | 4.63 | 4.54 | 4.40 | 4.25 | 4.10 | 4.02 | 3.94 | 3.86 | 3.78 | 3.69 | 3.60 |
| 12 | 9.33 | 6.93 | 5.95 | 5.41 | 5.06 | 4.82 | 4.64 | 4.50 | 4.39 | 4.30 | 4.16 | 4.01 | 3.86 | 3.78 | 3.70 | 3.62 | 3.54 | 3.45 | 3.36 |
| 13 | 9.07 | 6.70 | 5.74 | 5.21 | 4.86 | 4.62 | 4.44 | 4.30 | 4.19 | 4.10 | 3.96 | 3.82 | 3.66 | 3.59 | 3.51 | 3.43 | 3.34 | 3.25 | 3.17 |
| 14 | 8.86 | 6.51 | 5.56 | 5.04 | 4.69 | 4.46 | 4.28 | 4.14 | 4.03 | 3.94 | 3.80 | 3.66 | 3.51 | 3.43 | 3.35 | 3.27 | 3.18 | 3.09 | 3.00 |
| 15 | 8.68 | 6.36 | 5.42 | 4.89 | 4.56 | 4.32 | 4.14 | 4.00 | 3.89 | 3.80 | 3.67 | 3.52 | 3.37 | 3.29 | 3.21 | 3.13 | 3.05 | 2.96 | 2.87 |
| 16 | 8.53 | 6.23 | 5.29 | 4.77 | 4.44 | 4.20 | 4.03 | 3.89 | 3.78 | 3.69 | 3.55 | 3.41 | 3.26 | 3.18 | 3.10 | 3.02 | 2.93 | 2.84 | 2.75 |
| 17 | 8.40 | 6.11 | 5.18 | 4.67 | 4.34 | 4.10 | 3.93 | 3.79 | 3.68 | 3.59 | 3.46 | 3.31 | 3.16 | 3.08 | 3.00 | 2.92 | 2.83 | 2.75 | 2.65 |
| 18 | 8.29 | 6.01 | 5.09 | 4.58 | 4.25 | 4.01 | 3.84 | 3.71 | 3.60 | 3.51 | 3.37 | 3.23 | 3.08 | 3.00 | 2.92 | 2.84 | 2.75 | 2.66 | 2.57 |
| 19 | 8.18 | 5.93 | 5.01 | 4.50 | 4.17 | 3.94 | 3.77 | 3.63 | 3.52 | 3.43 | 3.30 | 3.15 | 3.00 | 2.92 | 2.84 | 2.76 | 2.67 | 2.58 | 2.49 |
| 20 | 8.10 | 5.85 | 4.94 | 4.43 | 4.10 | 3.87 | 3.70 | 3.56 | 3.46 | 3.37 | 3.23 | 3.09 | 2.94 | 2.86 | 2.78 | 2.69 | 2.61 | 2.52 | 2.42 |
| 21 | 8.02 | 5.78 | 4.87 | 4.37 | 4.04 | 3.81 | 3.64 | 3.51 | 3.40 | 3.31 | 3.17 | 3.03 | 2.88 | 2.80 | 2.72 | 2.64 | 2.55 | 2.46 | 2.36 |
| 22 | 7.95 | 5.72 | 4.82 | 4.31 | 3.99 | 3.76 | 3.59 | 3.45 | 3.35 | 3.26 | 3.12 | 2.98 | 2.83 | 2.75 | 2.67 | 2.58 | 2.50 | 2.40 | 2.31 |
| 23 | 7.88 | 5.66 | 4.76 | 4.26 | 3.94 | 3.71 | 3.54 | 3.41 | 3.30 | 3.21 | 3.07 | 2.93 | 2.78 | 2.70 | 2.62 | 2.54 | 2.45 | 2.35 | 2.26 |
| 24 | 7.82 | 5.61 | 4.72 | 4.22 | 3.90 | 3.67 | 3.50 | 3.36 | 3.26 | 3.17 | 3.03 | 2.89 | 2.74 | 2.66 | 2.58 | 2.49 | 2.40 | 2.31 | 2.21 |
| 25 | 7.77 | 5.57 | 4.68 | 4.18 | 3.85 | 3.63 | 3.46 | 3.32 | 3.22 | 3.13 | 2.99 | 2.85 | 2.70 | 2.62 | 2.54 | 2.45 | 2.36 | 2.27 | 2.17 |
| 26 | 7.72 | 5.53 | 4.64 | 4.14 | 3.82 | 3.59 | 3.42 | 3.29 | 3.18 | 3.09 | 2.96 | 2.81 | 2.66 | 2.58 | 2.50 | 2.42 | 2.33 | 2.23 | 2.13 |
| 27 | 7.68 | 5.49 | 4.60 | 4.11 | 3.78 | 3.56 | 3.39 | 3.26 | 3.15 | 3.06 | 2.93 | 2.78 | 2.63 | 2.55 | 2.47 | 2.38 | 2.29 | 2.20 | 2.10 |
| 28 | 7.64 | 5.45 | 4.57 | 4.07 | 3.75 | 3.53 | 3.36 | 3.23 | 3.12 | 3.03 | 2.90 | 2.75 | 2.60 | 2.52 | 2.44 | 2.35 | 2.26 | 2.17 | 2.06 |
| 29 | 7.60 | 5.42 | 4.54 | 4.04 | 3.73 | 3.50 | 3.33 | 3.20 | 3.09 | 3.00 | 2.87 | 2.73 | 2.57 | 2.49 | 2.41 | 2.33 | 2.23 | 2.14 | 2.03 |
| 30 | 7.56 | 5.39 | 4.51 | 4.02 | 3.70 | 3.47 | 3.30 | 3.17 | 3.07 | 2.98 | 2.84 | 2.70 | 2.55 | 2.47 | 2.39 | 2.30 | 2.21 | 2.11 | 2.01 |
| 40 | 7.31 | 5.18 | 4.31 | 3.83 | 3.51 | 3.29 | 3.12 | 2.99 | 2.89 | 2.80 | 2.66 | 2.52 | 2.37 | 2.29 | 2.20 | 2.11 | 2.02 | 1.92 | 1.80 |
| 60 | 7.08 | 4.98 | 4.13 | 3.65 | 3.34 | 3.12 | 2.95 | 2.82 | 2.72 | 2.63 | 2.50 | 2.35 | 2.20 | 2.12 | 2.03 | 1.94 | 1.84 | 1.73 | 1.60 |
| 120 | 6.85 | 4.79 | 3.95 | 3.48 | 3.17 | 2.96 | 2.79 | 2.66 | 2.56 | 2.47 | 2.34 | 2.19 | 2.03 | 1.95 | 1.86 | 1.76 | 1.66 | 1.53 | 1.38 |
| $\infty$ | 6.63 | 4.61 | 3.78 | 3.32 | 3.02 | 2.80 | 2.64 | 2.51 | 2.41 | 2.32 | 2.18 | 2.04 | 1.88 | 1.79 | 1.70 | 1.59 | 1.47 | 1.32 | 1.00 |

# ENDNOTES

## Chapter 1

1. www.marketingpower.com accessed September, 13, 2013.

2. Kris Hudson, "Holiday Inn to Turn Bar into Social Hub," *Wall Street Journal,* October 28, 2010, B10, "Holiday Inn Focuses on Social Hub After Relaunch," http://www .hotelnewsnow.com/Article5874, June 29, 2011.

3. "Invest in Integration: No Matter the Channel, Consumers Want to Buy Easy," *Quirk's Marketing Research Review,* August, 2013, 15–16.

4. http://www.qualtrics.com/blog/bonobos-case-study/March 7, 2013.

5. Stephen E. Brown, Anders Gustafsson and Lars Witell, "Beyond Products," *Wall Street Journal,* June 22, 1009, p. R7.

6. "Unsportsmanlike Conduct: Retailer Ends Era of Many Happy Returns," *Wall Street Journal,* September 16, 2013, A1, A16.

7. "Why Some Customers Are More Equal Than Others," *Fortune*, September 19, 1994, pp. 215–224; and William Wright, "Determinants of Customer Loyalty and Financial Performance," *Journal of Management Accounting Research,* January 2009, pp. 1–12.

8. Sunil Gupta, Donald Lehmann, and Jennifer Ames Stuart, "Valuing Customers," *Journal of Marketing Research*, February 2004, pp. 7–18.

9. "How Current Are your beliefs about Social Media?" *Marketing Research,* Fall 2010, p. 26.

10. Gordon Wyner, "Linked In," *Marketing Insights,* Summer, 2013, 10.

11. "10 Minutes With Gian Fulgoni," *Marketing Insights,* Summer 2013, 22–25.

12. Michael Fielding, "Resorts' email Alerts Revive Flat Business on Slopes," *Marketing News*, March 1, 2005, pp. 17–18.

13. Christine Wright-Isak and David Prensky, "Early Marketing Research: Science and Application," *Marketing Research,* Fall 1993, pp. 16–23.

14. Percival White, *Market Analysis: In Principles and Methods*, 2nd ed. (New York: McGraw-Hill, 1925).

15. Much of this section is taken from David W. Steward, "From Methods and Projects to Systems and Process: The Evolution of Marketing Research Techniques," *Marketing Research,* September 1991, pp. 25–34.

16. "Online Research Still Reigns Supreme," *Quirk's Marketing Research Review,* July 2010, pp. 50–59.

17. "Smartphone Ownership 2013," http://pewinternet.org/Reports/2013/Smartphone-Ownership-2013/Findings.aspx, June 5, 2013.

18. "Only 2 Percent of Americans Can't Get Internet Access, But 20 Percent Choose Not To," www.theverge.com/2013/8/26/4660008

19. "From the Crowd to the Cloud," *Marketing Insights,* summer 2013, 28.

20. Gordon Wyner, "Data, Data Everywhere," *Marketing News,* March 2013, 18.

21. "Big Data: What's Your Plan?" http://www.mckinsey.com/insights/business_technology/big_data_whats_your_plan? April 22, 2013

22. "23.8 Billion – By the Numbers," *Marketing Insights,* Spring 2013, 3.

23. Joseph Rydholm, "Quartz Obsessions Worth Obsessing About", *Quirk's Marketing Research Review,* July 2013, 10.

24. www.google.com/insights/consumersurvey, accessed September 25, 2013; Joseph Rydholm, "Is Google Being Evil With Consumer Surveys Service? *Quirk's Marketing Research Review,* May 2012, 10; Paul McDonald, Matt Mohebbi, and Brett Slatkin, "Company Google Consumer Survey to Existing Probability and Non-Probability Based Internet Samples," www.google.com/insights/consumersurveys/static/357980479559206563/consumer_surveys_whitepaper.pdf.

## Chapter 2

1. Jack Honomichl, "Global Top 25 Report," *Marketing News,* August 2013, p. 20–44 .

2. Ibid.

3. www.commonsenseadvisory.com/default.aspx?contenttype accessed September 26, 2013.

4. "Honomichl Top 50," *Marketing News*, June 2013, pp. 38.

5. Ibid.

6. "Mobile Research … Disruptive but Convenient," *Quirk's Marketing Research Review,* February 2013, p 12,

7. "The Really Smart Phone," *Wall Street Journal,* April 23–24, 2011, C1

8. "Kraft's Miracle Whip Targets Core Consumers with '97 Ads," *Advertising Age,* February 3, 1997, p. 12; also see www.Kraftrecipes.com/MiracleWhip accessed September 11, 2013.

9. Jack Honomichl, "The 2013 Honomichl Top 50 Report," *Marketing News,* June 2013, 26–32.

10. Ibid.

11. Jack Honomichl, "The 2013 Honomichl Global Top 25 Report," *Marketing News,* August 2013, 20–44.

12. Gordon Wyner, "The Practicioner's Dilemma," *Marketing News,'* June 2013, 14–15.

13. These ethical theories are from: Catherine Rainbow, "Descriptions of Ethical Theories and Principles," www.bio.davidson.edu/people/Kabernd/Indep/carainbow.htm, June 22, 2005.

14. "New York State Sues Survey Firm for Allegedly Tricking Students," *Wall Street Journal*, August 30, 2002.

15. Shelby Hunt, Lawrence Chonko, and James Wilcox, "Ethical Problems of Marketing Researchers," *Journal of Marketing Research,* August 1984, p. 314. Reprinted by permission of the American Marketing Association.

16. Terry Grapentine, "You Can't Take the Human Nature out of Black Boxes," *Marketing Research,* Winter 2004, pp. 20–22.

17. "Let Me Help You With That," *Quirk's Marketing Research Review*, October 2008, pp. 30–36.

18. Ibid.

19. "A Web Pioneer Profiles Users by Name, *Wall Street Journal,* October 25, 2010, pp. A1, A16.

20. "Don't Listen Unless Spoken To?" *Quirk's Marketing Research Review,* June 2013, 8.

21. "Professional Researcher Certification," www.mra-net.org, accessed October 11, 2013

22. Mark Goodin, "Clean Up Your Act," *Quirk's Marketing Research Review,* December 2010, pp. 38–43.

23. "Coke Sets Accord over Rigged Test," *International Herald Tribune,* August 4, 2003, p. 10; "Coke Agrees to Pay Burger King $10 Million to Resolve Dispute," *Wall Street Journal,* August 4, 2003, p. B6; "How Coke Officials Beefed Up Results of Marketing Test," *Wall Street Journal,* August 20, 2003, pp. A1, A6; "Coke Fountain Chief Steps Down Amid Furor over Burger King Test," *Wall Street Journal,* August 26, 2003, P. B4.

## Chapter 3

1. Terry H. Grapentine and Dianne Weaver, "Business Goals Are Key to Proper Marketing Research," *Marketing News*, September 15, 2006, pp. 28–31.

2. The hummus story is adapted from "Hummus: The Great American Dip", *Bloomberg Businessweek,* July 22 – July 28, 2013, 16–18.

3. Bonnie Eisenfeld, "Knowing What You Want," *Quirk's Marketing Research Review,* July 2010, pp. 66–70.

4. Todd Wasserman, "K-C Tries Seeing Things From Consumer's POV," *Brandweek*, September 5, 2005, p. 6.

5. Joseph Rydholm, "What Do Clients Want from a Research Firm?" *Marketing Research Review,* October 1995, p. 82.

6. Fred Luthans and Janet K. Larsen, "How Managers Really Communicate," Human Relations 39 (1986), pp. 161–178; and Harry E. Penley and Brian Hawkins, "Studying Interpersonal Communication in Organizations: A Leadership Application," *Academy of Management Journal 28* (1985), pp. 309–326.

7. Rohit Deshpande and Scott Jeffries, "Attitude Affecting the Use of Marketing Research in Decision Making: An Empirical Investigation," in Educators' Conference Proceedings, Series 47, edited by Kenneth L. Bernhardt et al. (Chicago: American Marketing Association, 1981), pp. 1–4.

8. Rohit Deshpande and Gerald Zaltman, "Factors Affecting the Use of Market Information: A Path Analysis," *Journal of Marketing Research 19* (February 1982), pp. 14–31; Rohit Deshpande, "A Comparison of Factors Affecting Researcher and Manager Perceptions of Market Research Use," *Journal of Marketing Research 21* (February 1989), pp. 32–38; Hanjoon Lee, Frank Acito, and Ralph Day, "Evaluation and Use of Marketing Research by Decision Makers: A Behavioral Simulation," *Journal of Marketing Research 24* (May 1987), pp. 187–196; and Michael Hu, "An Experimental Study of Managers' and Researchers' Use of Consumer Market Research," *Journal of the Academy of Marketing Science 14* (Fall 1986), pp. 44–51; and Rohit Deshpande and Gerald Zaltman, "A Comparison of Factors Affecting Use of Marketing Information in Consumer and Industrial Firms," *Journal of Marketing Research 24* (February 1987), pp. 114–118.

9. David Santee, "No More Ammo for Dilbert," *Quirk's Marketing Research Review,* March 2012, 62–68.

10. Joe Cardador and Mark Hunter, "Back to Basics," *Quirk's Marketing Research Review*, March 2009, pp. 46–53.

## Chapter 4

1. http://www.nytimes.com/2012/06/17/technology/acxiom-the-quite-giant-of-consumer-data.marketing.html.

2. Ibid.

3. Ibid.

4. Gordon Plutsky, "Behavioral Targeting: Does It Make Sense For a Company?", www.cmo.com, accessed June 17, 2010.

5. "Exploring Ways to Build a Better Consumer Profile," *Wall Street Journal*, March 15, 2010, B4.

6. "Connect the Thoughts," *Adweek Media*, June 29, 2009, pp. 10–11.

7. Ibid.

8. David White and Nathaniel Rowe, "Go Big or Go Home," Aberdeen Group, September 2012, 2.

9. Michael Minelli, Michele Chambers, and Ambiga Dhiraj, Big Data, Big Analytics (Hoboken: John Wiley & Sons) 2013, 13.

10. "Taking the Good With the Bad," *Quirk's Marketing Research Review*, June 2013, 36.

11. Steven Rosenbush and Clint Boulton, "How the NSA Could Get So Smart So Fast," *Wall Street Journal*, June 13, 2013, A4.

12. Ibid.

13. Ibid.

14. Becky Wu, "Are You (Like Everyone Else) Overwhelmed by Big Data?" *Marketing News*, September, 2013, 20.

15. Gordon Wyner, "Data, Data, Everywhere", *Marketing News*, March 2013, 18–19.

16. "How Much Should People Worry About the Loss on Online Privacy?" *Wall Street Journal*, November 15, 2011, B7-B11.

17. "Sites Feed Personal Details to New Tracking Industry," http://online.wsj.com, July 31, 2010.

18. Ibid.

19. "Tracking Is An Assault On Liberty, With Real Dangers," *Wall Street Journal*, August 7–8, 2010, pp. W1-W2.

20. "Scrapers Dig Deep for Data on Web," *Wall Street Journal*, October 12, 2010, pp. A1, A18.

21. Ibid.

22. Ibid.

23. "Track Me If You Can," *Forbes*, August 12, 2013, 48–57

24. www.westfieldinsurance.com/personal/pg.jsp?page=identify_theft_protection, accessed October 10, 2013.

25. "The Great Data Heist," *Fortune*, May 16, 2005. pp. 66–75.

26. "Choice Point to Exit Non-FCRA. Consumer-Sensitive Data Markets," (www.choicepoint.com), March 4, 2005.

27. "Hackers Aren't Only Threat to Privacy," *Wall Street Journal*, June 23, 2010, p. B5.

28. Ibid.

29. The section on GIS has been updated by Joshua Been, The University of Texas at Arlington.

30. "Turning a Map into a Layer Cake of Information," *New York Times*, January 20, 2000, Thursday, Late Edition—Final, Section G; Page 1, Column 1, Circuits, 2132 words, by Catherine Greenman.

31. Amy Cortese, "Is Your Business in the Right Spot? *Business 2.0*, May 2004, pp. 76–77.

32. Jon Gentner, "Nate Silver: The Data Demystifier," *Fast Company*, June 2013, 70–73, 152–154.

## Chapter 5

1. Projections by the authors. October 2013.

2. Projections by the authors, October 2013.

3. "Motives Are as Important as Words When Group Describes a Product," *Marketing News*, August 28, 1987, p. 49.

4. John Houlahan, "In Defense of the Focus Group," *Quirk's Marketing Research Review*, October 2003, pp. 16, 84.

5. Peter Tuckel, Elaine Leppo, and Barbara Kaplan, "Focus Groups under Scrutiny," *Marketing Research,* June 1992, pp. 12–17; see also "Break These Three Focus Group Rules," *Quirk's Marketing Research Review*, December 1999, pp. 50–53.

6. Naomi Henderson, "Guidelines for Choosing a Moderator," *Marketing Research,* Summer 2012, 24–25.

7. "Qualitative Research Panels: A New Spin on Traditional Focus Groups," *Quirk's Marketing Research Review*, May 2010, pp. 18–20.

8. Kieron Mathews, "Learning From the Enemy," *Quirk's Marketing Research Review*, December 2011, 44–47.

9. "In My Professional Opinion," *Quirk's Marketing Research Review*, May 2009, pp. 52–55.

10. Naomi Henderson, "Art and Science of Effective In-Depth Qualitative Interviews," *Quirk's Marketing Research Review*, December 1998, pp. 24–31; reprinted by permission; "Dangerous Intersections," *Marketing News*, February 28, 2000, p. 18; and "Go In-Depth with Depth Interviews," *Quirk's Marketing Research Review*, April 2000, pp. 36–40.

11. Linda Lynch, "How to Make Good Equal Great," *Quirk's Marketing Research Review,* December 2011, 22–24.

12. "Dealing With the Digresser," *Quirk's Marketing Research Review*, December 2008, pp. 32–35.

13. Patricia Sauerbrey Colton, "Awakening the Dreamer Within," *Quirk's Marketing Research Review,* December 2011, 54–58.

14. The material on analogies is from: Andrew Cutler, "What's the Real Story?" *Quirk's Marketing Research Review*, December 2006, pp. 38–45.

15. The material on personification is from Cutler, "What's the Real Story?" *Quirk's Marketing Research Review*, December 2006, pp. 38–45.

16. Tom Neveril, "I'll Always Go Back to That Hotel," *Quirk's Marketing Research Review*, December 2009, p. 42.

17. Gerald Berstell, "Listen and Learn – and Sell," *Quirk's Marketing Research Review,* December 2011, 48–52.

18. Christina Birkner, "10 Minutes With Ashlee Yingling," *Marketing News,* May 31, 2012, 24–27; also see: http://www.aboutmcdonalds.com/mcd/newsroom/electronic_press_kits/mcdonalds_usa_commitments_to_offer_improved_nutrition_choices/listening_tour.html; and http://www.brandchannel.com/home/post/2012/03/26/mcdonalds-US-Listening-Tour-032612.aspx.

## Chapter 6

1. "Assessing the Representativeness of Public Opinion Surveys," Pew Research Center for the People and the Press, May 15, 2013.

2. Bonnie Eisenfeld, "Pay It Forward," *Quirk's Marketing Research Review,* January 2011, 58–61.

3. http://www.linkin/com/groups/Interview-Length-2202074.S.51690705, accessed October 28, 2013.

4. "Customer Satisfaction," January 2010, http://www.pb.com/docs/US/pdf/Our-Company/Corporate-responsibility/customer-satisfaction.white-paper-2010.pdf; also see: Michael Calderwood, "Satisfaction in Action," *Quirks Marketing Research Review,* April 2011, 30–33.

## Chapter 7

1. "Digital Is Real," *Smart Money,* September 2012, 62–63.

2. "Open Up a Second World: Using B logging for Market Research," October 2, 2013, http://www.greenbook.org/marketing-research/using-blogging-for-market-research.

3. Ibid.

4. "Promising But Not Perfect," *Quirk's Marketing Research Review,* Jnuary 2012, 54–57.

5. Ibid.

6. Ibid.

7. Ibid.

8. "Be True to Your School," *Quirk's Marketing Research Review,* May 2012, 42-

9. "Need Research, Won't Travel?" *Quirks Marketing Research Review,* May 2012, 22–28.

10. Ibid.

11. www.channelM2.com, October 29, 2013.

12. Vauhini Vara, "Researchers Mine Web for Focus Groups," *The Wall Street Journal* (November 17, 2007), p. B3E.

13. "Marrying Phone and Web," *Quirk's Marketing Research Review,* May 2011, 42–46.

14. "Guideposts For a Fresh Path," *Quirk's Marketing Research Review,* May 2013, 48–69.

15. Gregory S. Heist, "Beyond Brand Building," *Quirk's Marketing Research Review* (July/August 2007), pp. 62–67.

16. Ibid.

17. Ibid.

18. "Give'em All Something to Talk About," *Quirk's Marketing Research Review,* April 2012, 40–45.

19. Ibid.

20. Anouk Willems, Tom DeRuyck and Niels Schillewaert, "Three Steps Closer," *Quirk's Marketing Research Review,* April 2013, 38–56.

21. Chris Yalonis, "The Revolution in e-Research," *CASRO Marketing Research Journal* (1999), pp. 131–133; "The Power of On-line Research," *Quirk's Marketing Research Review* (April 2000), pp. 46–48; Bill MacElroy, "The Need for Speed," *Quirk's Marketing Research Review* (July–August 2002), pp. 22–27; Cristina Mititelu, "Internet Surveys: Limits and Beyond Limits," *Quirk's Marketing Research Review* (January 2003), pp. 30–33; Nina Ray, "Cybersurveys Come of Age," *Marketing Research* (Spring 2003), pp. 32–37; "Online Market Research Booming, According to Survey," *Quirk's Marketing Research Review* (January 2005); Roger Gates, "Internet Data Collection So Far," speech given to Kaiser Permanente (May 2005); and Gabe Gelb, "Online Options Change Biz a Little—And a Lot," *Marketing News* (November 1, 2006), pp. 23–24; and "10 Minutes With Bo Mattsson," *Marketing News,* November 30, 2012, 24–30.

22. "What Can Web Do For You?" *Quirk's Marketing Research Review,* January 2011, 28–32

23. Interview with Roger Gates, President DSS Research, October 30, 2013.

24. Lee Smith, "Online Research's Time Has Come as a Proven Methodology," *CASRO Journal* (2002), pp. 45–50.

25. Bill MacElroy, "International Growth of Web Survey Activity," *Quirk's Marketing Research Review* (November 2000), pp. 48–51.

26. "Taking the Reins," *Quirk's Marketing Research Review,* July 2011, 42–47.

27. Ibid.

28. "Tips Offer Better Response Rates, Engaging Surveys," *Marketing News* (April 1, 2007), p. 28.

29. Jamin Brazil, Aaron Jue, Chandra Mulkins, and Jayme Plunkett, "Capture Their Interest," *Quirk's Marketing Research Review* (July/August 2006), pp. 46–54.

30. Ibid.

31. "The New Online Era of Consumer Surveys," *Marketing Research,* Fall 2012, 15–19

32. "Survey Monkey Says," *Fortune,* September 26, 2011, 68.

33. "Innovation Takes Flight," *Business Week,* October 21–27, 2013, S5.

34. "Resistance Is Futile," *Quirk's Marketing Research Review,* July 2013, 52–55.

35. See: "Right Place, Right Time," *Quirk's Marketing Research Review,* July 2013, 56–59.

36. "Why Respondents Suffer if You're Not Mobile Ready," October 2013, www.quirks.com/articles/2013/2013/026-2.aspx.

37. Birgi Martin, "Research-to-Go," *Quirk's Marketing Research Review* (November 2007), pp. 68–72.

38. Kristin Luck, "Involve While You Evolve," *Quirk's Marketing Research Review,* June 2011, 52–58.

39. Ibid.

40. Ibid.

41. Ibid.

42. "Instant Insight," *Quirk's Marketing Research Review,* February 2013, 46–49.

43. "Are You Talking to Me?" *Wall Street Journal,* April 25, 2011, R5.

44. Ibid.

45. Scott Koenig and Wendy Neuman, "There's the Beef," *Quirk's Marketing Research Review,* August 2012, 26–28.

46. Ibid.

47. Ibid.

48. Julie Wittes Schlack, "Character Counts, Characters Count," *Quirk's Marketing Research Review,* July 2013, 48–51.

## Chapter 8

1. "Loose Change, Lotion, and Expired Coupons," *Quirk's Marketing Research Review,* February 2008, p. 20.

2. Author's estimate, November 5, 2013.

3. "The Chocolate War," *Marketing Research,* Winter 2005, p. 4.

4. "Paying More to Get More," *Quirk's Marketing Research Review,* December 2008, p. 44; also see: "The Irreplaceable on-Site Ethnographer," *Quirk's Marketing Research Review,* February 2012, 20–22.

5. "Business Ethnography and the Discipline of Anthropology," *Quirk's Marketing Research Review*, February 2009, pp. 20–27; also see: "Watch Me As I Buy," *Quirk's Marketing Research Review*, February 2010, pp. 32–35.

6. "The Value of Second Sight in Qualitative and Ethnographic Field Work," *Quirk's Marketing Research Review,* February 2011, 16–18.

7. "The Science of Desire," *Business Week*, June 5, 2006, p. 104.

8. Ibid.

9. Ibid.

10. Brian Green, "As the World Works," *Quirk's Marketing Research Review,* November 2011, 31–36.

11. "Trendy Method or Essential Tool?" *Quirk's Marketing Research Review*, February 2009, pp. 34–37.

12. "Mystery Shopper," *Smart Money*, December 2005, p. 98.

13. Randall Brandt, "Improve the Customer Experience," *Quirk's Marketing Research Review*, January 2006, p. 68.

14. "Get Your Restaurant's Data To-Go," *Quirk's Marketing Research Review*, January 2009, p. 66.

15. "Getting the Most Out of Every Shopper," *Business Week*, February 9, 2009, pp. 45–46; "Testing Positive," *Quirk's Marketing Research Review*, March 2009, pp. 20–24; and "A Research Plan You Can Take to the Bank," *Quirk's Marketing Research Review*, January 2010, pp. 50–53.

16. "It's Everywhere You Want to Be," *Quirk's Marketing Research Review,* January 2013, 56–61

17. Adam Penenberg, "They Have Hacked Your Brain," *Fast Company,* September 2011, 84–89, 123–125.

18. Ibid.

19. Ibid.

20. Ibid.

21. Graham Page, "Increasing Our Brainpower," *Quirk's Marketing Research Review,* May 2011, 48–54.

22. Ibid.; also see: "FAQ: Neuromarketing Research," *Quirk's Marketing Research Review,* May 2011, 56–59; Joseph Rydholm, "Advise on How To Approach Neuromarketing Research," *Quirk's Marketing Research Review,* May 2011, 120–121; "Hook-Up, Love Affair or Happy Marriage," *Quirk's Marketing Research Review,* May 2012, 28–32; "Neuromarketing Research – Hardwired to be Different." *Quirk's Marketing Research Review,* August 2013, 12–13.

23. "Tobii Glasses Aim to Make Eye-Tracking More Mobile," *Quirk's Marketing Research Review*, October 2010, p. 14.

24. Cathleen Zapata, "What Caught Their Eye?" *Quirk's Marketing Research Review,* May 2012, 32–37.

25. "Look Your Best," *Quirk's Marketing Research Review*, March 2013, 52–55; also see: "Closing the Gap," *Quirk's Marketing Research Review*, July 2013, 42–46.

26. Zapata, "What Caught …."

27. Zapata, "What Caught …."

28. Andy Rasking, "A Face Any Business Can Trust," *Business 2.0*, December 2003, pp. 58–60.

29. Dan Hill and Aron Levin, "On the Face Of It," *Quirk's Marketing Research Review,* March 2013, 46–52.

30. Rasking, "A Face Any Business…"

31. "Billboards That Can See You," WSJ, September 3, 2010, p. B5; and "Ad Displays Track Age," *Wall Street Journal*, February 3, 2010, p. B5.

32. "Big Brother Has Arrived at a Store Near You," *Bloomberg Businessweek,* December 19–25, 2011, 41–44; also see: "Turning Shoppers Into Heat Maps," *Bloomberg Businessweek,* April 29-May 5, 2013, 36–37

33. Ibid.

34. "Of SKUs, CPUs, and QR Codes," *Quirk's Marketing Research Review,* July 2012, 52–56.

35. Ibid.

36. "Nielsen to Add Data for Mobile Viewing," *Wall Street Journal,* September 20, 2013, B3.

37. "Linking to Thinking," *Quirk's Marketing Research Review,* July 2013, 18.

38. "TV's Next Wave: Tuning In To You," *Wall Street Journal,* March 7, 2011, A1, A12.

39. http://www.iriworldwide.com/SolutionsandServices/Detail.aspx?ProductID=177. Accessed November 8, 2013.

40. "Mac Users See Pricier Hotels on Orbitz," *Wall Street Journal,* June 26, 2012, A1-A2.

41. "The Stalker," *Forbes,* June 10, 2013, 48–50.

42. Ibid.; also see: "Online Ads Can Now Follow You Home," *Wall Street Journal,* April 30, 2013, 134.

43. "Your E-Book is Reading You," *Wall Street Journal,* June 29, 2012, D1, D2.

44. Ibid.

45. Ibid.

46. Jayson DeMers, "The Top 7 Social Media Marketing Trends That Will Dominate 2014," September 24, 2013, http://www.forbes.com/sites/jaysondemers/2013/09/24/the-top-7-social-media-marketing-trends-that-will-dominate-2014/

47. http://tech2.in.com/news/social-networking/facebook-admits-to-tracking-users-as-well-as-nonusers/829922, accessed November 8, 2013.

48. "Conversion Tracking," https://www.facebook.com/help/435189689870514/ accessed November 9, 2013.

49. Ibid.

50. Ibid.

51. http://blogs.wsj.com/cio/2013/10/30/facebook-considers-vast-increase-in-data-collection-tab/print. Accessed November 10, 2013

52. http://www.businessinsider.com/the-potential-of-pinterest-advertising-2013–10

53. http://searchenginewatch.com/article/2273658/Pinterest-Analytics-The-Ultimate-Guide-to-tracking-your-site's-performance-on-pinterest.

54. Ibid.

55. Ibid.

56. http://www.motherjones.com/print/234711. Accessed November 8, 2013.

57. Ibid.

58. http://www.honeytechblog.com/top-50-twitter-tracking-and-analytics-tools/. Accessed November 22, 2013.59. Raymond R. Burke, "Virtual Shopping: Breakthrough in Marketing Research," *Harvard Business Review*, March/April 1996, pp. 120–131.

60. Ellen Byron, "A Virtual View of the Store Aisle," *Wall Street Journal,* October 3, 2007, pp. B1, B12.

61. Ibid.

62. Ibid.; also see "Virtual Shopping, Real Results, *Brandweek*, April 16, 2009, pp. 16–18.

63. Remington Tonar and Jacob Jasperson, "Eat Well and Going Good," *Quirk's Marketing Research Review*, February 2013, 28–32.

## Chapter 9

1. Thomas D. Cook and Donald T. Campbell, *Experimentation: Design Analysis Issues for Field Settings* (Chicago: Rand McNally, 1979).

2. See Claire Selltiz et al., *Research in Social Relations*, rev. ed. (New York: Holt, Rinehart & Winston, 1959), pp. 80–82.

3. A good example of a laboratory experiment is described in Caroll Mohn, "Simulated-Purchase 'Chip' Testing vs. Trade-Off Conjoint Analysis—Coca-Cola's Experience." *Marketing Research* (March 1990), pp. 49–54.

4. A. G. Sawyer, "Demand Artifacts in Laboratory: Experiments in Consumer Research," *Journal of Consumer Research 2* (March 1975), pp. 181–201; and N. Giges, "No Miracle in Small Miracle: Story Behind Failure," *Advertising Age* (August 1989), p. 76.

5. John G. Lynch, "On the External Validity of Experiments in Consumer Research," *Journal of Consumer Research 9* (December 1982), pp. 225–239.

6. For a more detailed discussion of this and other experimental issues, see Thomas D. Cook and Donald T. Campbell, "The Design and Conduct of Quasi-Experiments and True Experiments in Field Settings," in M. Dunnette, ed., *Handbook of Industrial and Organizational Psychology* (Skokie, IL: Rand McNally, 1978).

7. Ibid.

8. Bob Gertsley, "Data Use: The Insidious Top-Box and Its Effects on Measuring Line Share," *Quirk's Marketing Research Review* (August 2008), p. 20.

9. For further discussion of the characteristics of various types of experimental designs, see Donald T. Campbell and Julian C. Stanley, *Experimental and Quasi-Experimental Design for Research* (Chicago: Rand McNally, 1966); see also Richard Bagozzi and Youjar Ti, "On the Use of Structural Equation Models in Experimental Design," *Journal of Marketing Research 26* (August 1989), pp. 225–270.

10. Stefan Althoff, "Does the Survey Sender's Gender Matter?" *Quirk's Marketing Research Review 31*, no. 2 (February 2007), pp. 24, 26.

11. Thomas D. Cook and Donald T. Campbell, *Quasi-Experimentation: Design and Analysis Issues for Field Settings* (Boston: Houghton Mifflin, 1979), p. 56.

12. T. Karger, "Test Marketing as Dress Rehearsals," *Journal of Consumer Marketing 2* (Fall 1985), pp. 49–55; Tim Harris, "Marketing Research Passes Toy Marketer Test," *Advertising Age* (August 24, 1987), pp. 1, 8; John L. Carefoot, "Marketing and Experimental Designs in Marketing Research: Uses and Misuses," *Marketing News* (June 7, 1993), p. 21; and Jim Miller and Sheila Lundy, "Test Marketing Plugs into the Internet," *Consumer Insights* (Spring 2002), p. 23.

13. Joshua Gray, Section G, "McLobsters and Test Marketing." http://uwmktg301. blogspot.com/2010/03/mclobsters-and-test-marketing.html.

14. Mark Sandler and Chris Slane, "Unlocking the Potential," *Quirk's Marketing Research Review* (October 2010), pp. 28-32.

15. Norma Ramage, "Testing, Testing 1–2–3," *Marketing Magazine 110*, no. 25 (July 18, 2005).

16. http://www.cbsnews.com/news/columbus-ohio-test-market-of-the-usa. 2012 CBS Interactive, Inc., June 24, 2012, accessed 2/12/2014.

17. G. A. Churchill & Jr. *Basic Marketing Research*, 4th ed. (Fort Worth, TX: Dryden Press, 2001), pp. 144–145.

18. Melvin, P. "Choosing Simulated Test Marketing Systems." *Marketing Research, 4*, no. 3 (September 1992), pp. 14–16.

19. Ibid.

20. Joseph Rydholm, "To Test or Not to Test," *Quirk's Marketing Research Review* (February 1992), pp. 61–62.

21. "Test Marketing Is Valuable, but It's Often Abused," *Marketing News* (January 2, 1987), p. 40.

22. Deborah L. Vence, "Proper Message, Design in Global Markets Require Tests," *Marketing News* (September 1, 2006), pp. 18–25.

23. "Miller to Test Market Low-Cal Craft Beers in Minneapolis," *Minneapolis-St. Paul Business Journal* (December 14, 2007).

24. Roger Fillion, "Denver Test Market for Beer Ads," *Rocky Mountain News* (July 4, 2006).

25. Jeremiah McWilliams, "Anheuser-Busch Test Markets New Vodka Brand," *St. Louis Post-Dispatch* (November 27, 2007).

26. Dina Berta, "Utah City Turns Out to be Best Test Market for Brazilian Concept," *Nation's Restaurant News* (September 22, 2003).

27. "Simulated Test Marketing Gets Your New Products/Services Off On The Right Foot," posted by Copernicus Marketing Consulting and Research, August 13, 2010. Available at http://www.greenbook.org/marketing-research/simulated-test-marketing-new-product-services. Accessed 2-12-2014.

## Chapter 10

1. F. N. Kerlinger, *Foundations of Behavioral Research*, 3rd ed. (New York: Rinehart and Winston, 1986), p. 403; see also Mel Crask and R. J. Fox, "An Exploration of the Internal Properties of Three Commonly Used Research Scales," *Journal of Marketing Research Society*, October 1987, pp. 317–319.

2. Adapted from Claire Selltiz, Laurence Wrightsman, and Stuart Cook, *Research Methods in Social Relations*, 3rd ed. (New York: Holt Rinehart and Winston, 1976), pp. 164–168.

3. Linda Naiditch, "A More Informed Process," *Quirk's Marketing Research Review*, July 2013, 60–63.

4. Adapted from: William Trochim, *Research Methods Knowledge Base*, www.atomicdog.com/trochim, October 20, 2006.

5. "What Women Want," *Quirk's Marketing Research Review*, October 2013, 14.

## Chapter 11

1. See Brian Sternthal and C. Samuel Craig, *Consumer Behavior: An Information Processing Perspective* (Englewood Cliffs, NJ: Prentice Hall, 1982), pp. 157–162; see also Barbara Loken and Ronald Hoverstad, "Relationships between Information Recall and Subsequent Attitudes: Some Exploratory Findings," *Journal of Consumer Research 12* (September 1985), pp. 155–168.

2. Robert E. Smith and William Swinyard, "Attitude Behavior Consistency: The Impact of Product Trial versus Advertising," *Journal of Marketing Research 20* (August 1983), pp. 257–267.

3. See Richard Lutz, "The Rise of Attitude Theory in Marketing," in Harold Kassarjian and Thomas Robertson, eds., *Perspectives in Consumer Behavior*, 4th ed. (Upper Saddle River, NJ: Prentice Hall, 1991), pp. 317–339.

4. The first five factors are taken from John Mowen and Michael Minor, *Consumer Behavior*, 5th ed. (Upper Saddle River, NJ: Prentice Hall, 1998), p. 263.

5. Linda F. Alwitt and Ida E. Berger, "Understanding the Link between Environmental Attitudes and Consumer Product Usage: Measuring the Moderating Rise of Attitude Strength," in Leigh McAlister and Michael Rothschild, eds., *Advances in Consumer Research 20* (1992), pp. 194–198.

6. Pete Cape, "Slider Scales in Online Surveys," Paper originally presented at the CASRO Panel Conference in New Orleans, LA, February 2009. Available at *http://www.surveysampling.com/sites/all/files/SSI%20Sliders%20White%20Pape.pdf* (accessed March 8, 2011).

7. Gerald Albaum, Catherine Roster, Julie H. Yu, and Robert D. Rogers, "Simple Rating Scale Formats: Exploring Extreme Response," *International Journal of Market Research 49*, no. 5 (2007), pp. 633–649.

8. For an excellent discussion of the semantic differential, see Charles E. Osgood, George Suci, and Percy Tannenbaum, *The Measurement of Meaning* (Urbana: University of Illinois Press, 1957). Also see Karin Braunsberger and Roger Gates (2009), "Developing Inventories for Satisfaction and Likert Scales in a Service Environment," *Journal of Services Marketing, 23*, no. 4, pp. 219–225.

9. Ibid., pp. 140–153, 192, 193; see also William D. Barclay, "The Semantic Differential as an Index of Brand Attitude," *Journal of Advertising Research 4* (March 1964), pp. 30–33.

10. Theodore Clevenger, Jr., and Gilbert A. Lazier, "Measurement of Corporate Images by the Semantic Differential," *Journal of Marketing Research 2* (February 1965), pp. 80–82.

11. Michael J. Etzel, Terrell G. Williams, John C. Rogers, and Douglas J. Lincoln, "The Comparability of Three Stapel Forms in a Marketing Setting," in Ronald F. Bush and Shelby D. Hunt, eds., *Marketing Theory: Philosophy of Science Perspectives* (Chicago: American Marketing Association, 1982), pp. 303–306.

12. An excellent article on purchase intent is: Pierre Chandon, Vicki Morwitz, and Werner Reinartz, "Do Intentions Really Predict Behavior? Self Generated Validity Effects in Survey Research," *Journal of Marketing* (April 2005), pp. 1–14.

13. Albert Bemmaor, "Predicting Behavior from Intention-to-Buy Measures: The Parametric Case," *Journal of Marketing Research* (May 1995), pp. 176–191.

14. We use a more conservative set of weights than those recommended by Linda Jamieson and Frank Bass, "Adjusting Stated Intention Measures to Predict Trial Purchase of New Products: A Comparison of Models and Methods," *Journal of Marketing Research* (August 1989), pp. 336–345.

15. This section on scale conversions is from Rajan Sambandam, "Scale Conversions," *Quirk's Marketing Research Review* (December 2006), pp. 22–28.

16. Fred Reichheld, "The One Number You Need to Grow," *Harvard Business Review,* December 2013, 46–54.

17. RandyHanson, "Life After UPS," *Marketing Research,* Summer 2011, 8–11.

18. "Pardon Our Mistake," *Quirk's Marketing Research Review,* August 2013, 15–16.

19. "The Passives Are Not Passive," *Quirk's Marketing Research Review,* October 2011, 72–78.

20. Ibid.

21. William O. and Richard G. Netemeyer, *Handbook of Marketing Scales*, 2nd ed. (Newbury Park, CA: Sage Publications, 1999), pp. 1–9.

22. Brian Engelland, Bruce Alford, and Ron Taylor, "Cautions and Precautions on the Use of Borrowed Scales in Marketing Research," *Proceedings: Society for Marketing Advances* (November 2001).

23. J. A. Krosnick and L. R. Fabrigar, "Designing Rating Scales for Effective Measurement in Surveys," in L. Lybert, M. Collins, L. Decker, E. Deleeuw, C. Dippo, N. Schwarz, and D. Trewing, eds., *Survey Measurement and Process Quality* (New York: Wiley-Interscience, 1997). Also see Madhubalan Viswanathan, Seymore Sudman, and Michael Johnson, "Maximum Versus Meaningful Discrimination in Scale Response: Implications for Validity Measurement of Consumer Perceptions about Products," *Journal of Business Review* (February 2004), pp. 108–124; also see: Adam Cook, "An Analysis of the Impact of Survey Scales," *Quirk's Marketing Research Review,* November 2013, 22–27.

24. This section is based on James H. Myers and Mark I. Alpert, "Determinant Buying Attitudes: Meaning and Management," *Marketing Management* (Summer 1997), pp. 50–56.

25. William Wells and Leonard Lo Scruto, "Direct Observation of Purchasing Behavior," *Journal of Marketing Research* (August 1996), pp. 42–51.

26. Thomas Hartley, "Improving the Long-Term Prognosis," *Quirk's Marketing Research Review,* October 2013, 60–66.

## Chapter 12

1. Pete Cape, "How to Make Your Questionnaire Mobile-Ready," *Quirk's Marketing Research Review* e-newsletter (April 27, 2013). Retrieved from http://www.quirks.com/articles/2013/20130826-1.

2. Tom Ewing, "Not Just Playing Around – Where Gamification Came From and Why It Could Be Here To Stay," *Quirk's Marketing Research Review* (March 2012) pp. 30-34.

3. Keith Price, "Maximizing Respondent Cooperation," *Quirk's Marketing Research Review 19,* no. 7 (July-August 2005), pp. 78-81.

4. Janet Westergaard, "Your Survey, Our Needs," *Quirk's Marketing Research Review 19,* no. 10 (November 2005), pp. 64-66.

5. R. M. Groves, S. Presser, and S. Dipko, "The Role of Topic Interest in Survey Participation Decisions," *Public Opinion Quarterly 58,* no. 1 (Spring 2004), pp. 2-31.

6. Dan Wiese, "Delivering the Desired Results-Iowa City Finds Mail Survey Fits Its Needs," *Quirk's Marketing Research Review* (November 2011), pp. 36-38.

7. Stephen J. Blumberg, Ph.D., and Julian V. Luke, "Wireless Solution: Early Release of Estimates From the National Health Interview Survey, July-December 2010," National Center for Health Statistics. June 2013. Available from http://www.cdc.gov/nchs/nhis.htm.

8. Adam Berman, "A Moving Target – Tips for Effective Mobile Surveying," *Quirk's Marketing Research Review* (November 2013), pp. 38-41.

9. Ibid. (OR USE: http://www.knotice.com/reports/Knotice_Mobile_Email_Opens_Report_FirstHalf2012.pd. Accessed 6-30-2014.

10. This section is adapted from Naomi Henderson, "The Power of Probing," *Marketing Research,* Winter 2007, pp. 38-39.

11. Ibid.

12. "Intelligent Survey Design," *Quirk's Marketing Research Review* (July 2010), pp. 42-46.

13. "Ask and Your Shall Receive," *Quirk's Marketing Research Review,* October 2010, pp. 66-68.

14. www.CMOR.org, June 15, 2005; also see, "A Playbook for Creating Survey Introductions For Online Panels," *Quirk's Marketing Research Review* (March 24, 2009).

15. Lynn Newmann, "That's a Good Question," *American Demographics,* June 1995, pp. 10-15. Reprinted from *American Demographics* magazine with permission. Copyright© 1995, Cowles Business Media, Ithaca, New York.

16. Tom Cates, "A Beginner's Guide to DIY Research," *Quirk's Marketing Research Review* e-newsletter (August 13, 2012). Retrieved from http://www.quirks.com/articles/2012/20120825-1.

17. Survey Sampling International, "Top 10 Tips for Designing a Mobile-Friendly Questionnaire (April 17, 2013). Available at http://www.surveysampling.com/en/learning-center/mobile-research/10-tips-mobile. Accessed 5-8-2014.

18. Hans Baumgartner and Jan-Benedict E. M. Steenkamp, "Response Styles in Marketing Research: A Cross-National Investigation," *Journal of Marketing Research 38*, no. 2, May 2001, pp. 145-156.

19. Internal company documents supplied to the authors by M/A/R/C, Inc.

20. Internal company documents supplied to the authors by M/A/R/C, Inc.

## Chapter 13

1. For excellent discussions of sampling, see Seymour Sudman, Applied Sampling (New York: Academic Press, 1976), and L. J. Kish, Survey Sampling (New York: John Wiley & Sons, 1965).

2. Jack Baker, Adelamar Alcantara, et al., "A Comparative Evaluation of Error and Bias in Census Tract-Level Age/Sex-Specific Population Estimates: Component I (Net-Migration) vs. Component III (Hamilton-Perry)," *Population Research and Policy Review 32*, Issue 6 (December 2013), pp. 919-942.

3. A. Adimora Adaora, Victor J. Schoenbach, et al., "Driver's License and Voter Registration Lists as Population-Based Sampling Frames for Rural African Americans," *Annals of Epidemiology 11*, no. 60 (August 2001), pp. 385–388.

4. Stephen J. Blumberg, Ph.D., and Julian V. Luke, "Wireless Substitution: Eagerly Release of Estimates From the National Health Interview Survey, July-December 2012," National Center for Health Statistics. June 2013. Available from http://www.cdc.gov/nchs/nhis.htm.

5. Matthijs Visser, "A Choice in the Matter—What Happens When You Let Respondents Choose Their Feedback Method," Quirk's Marketing Research Review (February 2014), p. 24.

6. Martin Filz and Steven Gittelman, "Optimum Blending of Panels and Social Network Respondents," Research Now and Mktg. Incorporated.

7. S. Sudman, *Applied Sampling*, pp. 63–67.

8. G. J. Glasser and G. D. Metzger, "Random-Digit Dialing as a Method of Telephone Sampling," *Journal of Marketing Research 9* (February 1972), pp. 59–64; and S. Roslow and L. Roslow, "Unlisted Phone Subscribers Are Different," *Journal of Advertising 12* (August 1972), pp. 59–64.

9. Charles D. Cowan, "Using Multiple Sample Frames to Improve Survey Coverage, Quality, and Costs," *Marketing Research* (December 1991), pp. 66–69.

10. Blumberg, et al.

11. Survey Sampling International.

12. James McClove and P. George Benson, *Statistics for Business and Economics* (San Francisco: Dellen Publishing, 1988), pp. 184–185; and "Probability Sampling in the Real World," *CATI NEWS* (Summer 1993), pp. 1, 4–6; Susie Sangren, "Survey and Sampling in an Imperfect World," *Quirk's Marketing Research Review* (April 2000), pp. 16, 66–69.

13. R. J. Jaeger, *Sampling in Education and the Social Sciences* (New York: Longman, 1984), pp. 28–35.

14. Lewis C. Winters, "What's New in Telephone Sampling Technology?" *Marketing Research* (March 1990), pp. 80–82; and "A Survey Researcher's Handbook of Industry Terminology and Definitions" (Fairfield, CT: Survey Sampling, 1992), pp. 3–20.

15. Michael A. Fallig and Derek Allen, "An Examination of Strategies for Panel-Blending," *Quirk's Marketing Research Review* (July 2009), p. 50.

16. For an excellent discussion of stratified sampling, see William G. Cochran, *Sampling Techniques*, 2nd ed. (New York: John Wiley & Sons, 1963); and Sangren, "Survey and Sampling in an Imperfect World," pp. 16, 66-69.

17. Sudman, "Applied Science," pp. 110–121.

18. Ibid.

19. Earl R. Babbie, *The Practice of Social Research*, 2nd ed. (Belmont, CA: Wadsworth Publishing, 1979), p. 167.

20. "Convenience Sampling Outpacing Probability Sampling" (Fairfield, CT: Survey Sampling, March 1994), p. 4.

21. Leo A. Goodman, "Snowball Sampling," *Annals of Mathematical Statistics 32* (1961), pp. 148–170.

22. Douglas Rivers, "Fulfilling the Promise of the Web," *Quirk's Marketing Research Review* (February 2000), pp. 34–41.

23. Braunsberger, Karin, Hans Wybenga, and Roger Gates (2007), "A Comparison of Reliability between Telephone and Web based Surveys," *Journal of Business Research*, Vol. 60, No. 7, 758-764.

24. "New Research from Survey Sampling International Suggests Sample Blending Results in Better Data Quality," *Market Research Bulletin* (April 26, 2010). Available at http://marketresearchbulletin.com/?p5537 (accessed March 9, 2011).

## Chapter 14

1. Nat Ives, "The Super Bowl's Real Results: The Brands that Lifted Purchase Consideration Most," *Advertising Age* (February 6, 2014).

2. Tom McGoldrick, David Hyatt, and Lori Laffin, "How Big Is Big Enough?" *Marketing Tools* (May 1998), pp. 54–58.

3. McGoldrick et al., "How Big Is Big Enough?" pp. 54–58.

4. Lafayette Jones, "A Case for Ethnic Sampling," *Promo* (October 1, 2000), p. 12.

5. Erik Mooi and Marko Sarstedt, *A Concise Guide to Market Research*. (Springer Publisher, 2001).

6. M. H. Vivienne, C. J. Lahaut, et al., "Non-Response Bias in a Sample Survey on Alcohol Consumption," *Alcohol & Alcoholism 37*, no. 3 (2002), pp. 256–260.

7. Gang Xu, "Estimating Sample Size for a Descriptive Study in Quantitative Research," *Quirk's Marketing Research Review* (June 1999), pp. 14, 52–53.

8. Susie Sangren, "A Simple Solution to Nagging Questions," *Quirk's Marketing Research Review* (January 1999), pp. 18, 53.

9. Gang Xu, "Estimating Sample Size for a Descriptive Study in Quantitative Research."

10. For discussions of these techniques, see Bill Williams, *A Sampler on Sampling* (New York: John Wiley & Sons, 1978); and Richard Jaeger, *Sampling in Education and the Social Sciences* (New York: Longman, 1984).

11. Peter DePaulo, "Sample Size for Qualitative Research," *Quirks Marketing Research Review* (December 2000).

12. Survey Sampling, "Estimate Sample Size with Precision," *The Frame* (January 1999), p. 1.

**13.** David Anderson, Dennis Sweeney, and Thomas Williams, *Statistics for Business and Economics*, 4th ed. (St. Paul, MN: West Publishing, 1990), pp. 355–357.

## Chapter 15

**1.** DSS Research.

**2.** Joseph Rydholm, "Dealing with Those Pesky Open-Ended Responses," *Quirk's Marketing Research Review* (February 1994), pp. 70–79.

**3.** Raymond Raud and Michael A. Fallig, "Automating the Coding Process with Neural Networks," *Quirk's Marketing Research Review* (May 1993), pp. 14–16, 40–47.

**4.** For information on semiotics, see Paul Cobley, Litza Jansz, and Richard Appignanesi, *Introducing Semiotics* (Melborne, Australia: Totem Books, 1997); Marcel Danesi, *Of Cigarettes, High Heels and Other Interesting Things: An Introduction to Semiotics* (New York: St. Martin's Press, 1998); and Umberto Eco, *Semiotics and the Philosophy of Languages* (Bloomington: Indiana University Press, 1986).

**5.** Eric Weight, "What Can Text Analytics Teach Us?" *Quirk's Marketing Research Review* (August 2011), pp. 58-62.

**6.** Semantria. https://semantria.com.

**7.** Joseph Rydholm, "Scanning the Seas: Scannable Questionnaires Give Princess Cruises Accuracy and Quick Turnaround," *Quirk's Marketing Research Review* (May 1993), pp. 38–42.

**8.** Tim Macer, "Software Review: Q Data Analysis Software," *Quirk's Marketing Research Review* (August 2010), p. 20.

## Chapter 16

**1.** Terry H. Grapentine, "Statistical Significance Revisited," *Quirk's Marketing Research Review* (April 2011), pp. 18-23.

**2.** Stephen J. Hellebusch, "Let's Test Everything," *Quirk's Marketing Research Review* (May 2004), p. 28.

**3.** Dr. Ali Khounsary, "What Is Statistically Significant?" *Ask a Scientist*, Mathematics Archives (1999), Argonne National Laboratory, Department of Energy, at: *www.newton.dep.anl.gov/askasci/math99/math99052.htm.*

**4.** Stephen J. Hellebusch, "One Chi Square Beats Two Z-tests," *Marketing News* (June 4, 2001), p. 11.

**5.** Grapentine, "Statistical Significance Revisited," 18–23.

**6.** Thomas Exter, "What's Behind the Numbers," *Quirk's Marketing Research Review* (March 1997), pp. 53–59.

**7.** Tony Babinec, "How to Think about Your Tables," *Quirk's Marketing Research Review* (January 1991), pp. 10–12. For a discussion of these issues, see Gopal K. Kanji, *100 Statistical Tests*, (London: Sage Publications, 1993), p. 75.

**8.** Michael Latta, Mark Mitchell, Albert J. Taylor and Charles Thrash, "Study Results Guide Enhancements to Myrtle Beach Golf Passport," *Quirk's Marketing Research Review* (October 2012), pp. 34-37.

**9.** Gary M. Mullet, "Correctly Estimating the Variances of Proportions," *Marketing Research* (June 1991), pp. 47–51.

**10.** Richard Armstrong and Anthony Hilton, "The Use of Analysis of Variance (ANOVA) in Applied Microbiology," *Microbiologist* (December 2004), pp. 18–21; available online at: *www.blackwellpublishing. com/Microbiology/pdfs/anova.pdf.* THIS LINK NO LONGER APPEARS TO WORK.

http://www.google.com/url?url=http://dv.fosjc.unesp.br/ivan/downloads/Aulas%252 0em%2520PDF*Armstrong_-__The_use_of_ANOVA_in_applied__microbiology-_ artigo_de__R._A._Armstrong.pdf&rct=j&frm=1&q=&esrc=s&sa=U&ei=pdfjU5HC MfOt8gGr8oGIAg&ved=0CBQQFjAA&usg=AFQjCNGM40d7cwLF8TXzb5YiOA_ awj_Afg - /accessed 8/7/2014

## Chapter 17

1. Joanna Weiss, "Sex Ed from Teen Mom," *The Boston Globe* (January 26, 2014). http://www.bostonglobe.com/opinion/2014/01/26/sex-from-teen-mom/3OJZyNBQ WDWz82w31yzwFN/story.html.

2. *This content was provided by TRC. Visit their website at www.trchome.com.*http://www .greenbook.org/marketing-research/survey-of-analysis-methods-part-i Posted March 2, 2010 by TRC White Paper.

3. Miaofen Yen and Li-Hua Lo, "Examining Test–Retest Reliability: An Intra-Class Correlation Approach," *Nursing Research 51*, no. 1 (January–February 2002), pp. 59–62.

4. Adam DiPaula, "Do Your 'BESD' When Explaining Correlation Results," *Quirk's Marketing Research Review* (November 2000).

5. Pascale de Becker, Johan Roeykens, et al., "Exercise Capacity in Chronic Fatigue Syndrome," *Archives of Internal Medicine 160* (November 27, 2000), pp. 3270–3277.

6. Douglas Kirby et al., "Manifestations of Poverty and Birthrates among Young Teenagers in California Zip Code Areas," *Family Planning Perspectives 33*, no. 2 (March–April 2001), reprinted by the Alan Guttmacher Institute at: *www.guttmacher.org/pubs/ journals/3306301.html. NO LONGER AVAILABLE AT GUTTMACHER Available at http://www.ncbi.nlm.nih.gov/pubmed/11330852. Accessed 5-12-14.*

7. Clayton E. Cramer, "Antigunners Admit Brady Failed," and "Is Gun Control Reducing Murder Rates?" (August 2000), at: *www.claytoncramer.com.*

## Chapter 18

1. Thomas H. Davenport and D.J. Patil, "Data Scientist: The Sexiest Job of the 21st Century," *Harvard Business Review* (October 2012).

2. Ase Dragland, "Big Data—for better or worse," SINTEF. Available at http://www. sintef.no/home/Press-Room/Research-News/Big-Data--for-better-or-worse/.

3. For an excellent and highly understandable presentation of all the multivariate techniques presented in this chapter, see Joseph Hair, Rolph Anderson, Ron Tatham, and William Black, *Multivariate Data Analysis,* 5th ed. (New York: Prentice Hall, 1998); see also Charles J. Schwartz, "A Marketing Research's Guide to Multivariate Analysis," *Quirk's Marketing Research Review* (November 1994), pp. 12–14.

4. Joseph R. Garber, "Deadbeat Repellant," *Forbes* (February 14, 1994), p. 164.

5. Michael Richarme (2007). "Eleven Multivariate Analysis Techniques: Key Tools in Your Marketing Research Survival Kit," [white paper] produced by Decision Analyst. Available at *http://decisionanalyst.com/Downloads/MultivariateAnalysisTechniques.pdf* (accessed April 1, 2011).

6. Jonathan Camhi, "Banks Set Stage For Customer Acquisition with Data Analytics," Bank Systems & Technology (February 10, 2014). Available at http://banktech.com/ business-intelligence/banks-set-stage-for-customer-acquisition/240166009).

7. For a thorough discussion of regression analysis, see Larry D. Schroeder, *Understanding Regression Analysis: An Introductory Guide (Quantitative Applications in the Social Sciences),* (SAGE Publications, 1986).

8. Charlotte H. Mason and William D. Perreault Jr., "Collinear Power and Interpretation of Multiple Regression Analysis," *Journal of Marketing Research* (August 1991), pp. 268–280; Doug Grisaffe, "Appropriate Use of Regression in Customer Satisfaction Analyses: A Response to William McLauchlan," *Quirk's Marketing Review* (February 1993), pp. 10–17; and Terry Clark, "Managing Outliers: Qualitative Issues in the Handling of Extreme Observations in Market Research," *Marketing Research* (June 1989), pp. 31–45.

9. See Hair et al., *Multivariate Data Analysis,* p. 46.

10. William D. Neal, "Using Discriminant Analysis in Marketing Research: Part 1," *Marketing Research* (September 1989), pp. 79–81; William D Neal, "Using Discriminant Analysis in Marketing Research: Part 2," *Marketing Research* (December 1989), pp. 55–60; and Steve Struhl, "Multivariate and Perceptual Mapping with Discriminant Analysis," *Quirk's Marketing Research Review* (March 1993), pp. 10–15, 43.

11. See Girish Punj and David Stewart, "Cluster Analysis in Marketing Research: Review and Suggestions for Application," *Journal of Market Research 20* (May 1983), pp. 134–138; and G. Ray Funkhouser, Anindya Chatterjee, and Richard Parker, "Segmenting Samples," *Marketing Research* (Winter 1994), pp. 40–46.

12. Susie Sangren, "A Survey of Multivariate Methods Useful for Market Research," *Quirk's Marketing Research Review* (May 1999), pp. 16, 63–69.

13. This section is based on material prepared by Glen Jarboe; see also Paul Green, Donald Tull, and Gerald Albaum, *Research for Marketing Decision,* 5th ed. (Englewood Cliffs, NJ: Prentice Hall, 1998), pp. 553–573.

14. Dick Wittink and Phillipe Cattin, "Commercial Use of Conjoint Analysis: An Update," *Journal of Marketing* (July 1989), pp. 91–96; see also Rajeev Kohli, "Assessing Attribute Significance in Conjoint Analysis: Nonparametric Tests and Empirical Validation," *Journal of Marketing Research* (May 1988), pp. 123–133.

15. Examples of current issues and applications are provided in Richard Smallwood, "Using Conjoint Analysis for Price Optimization," *Quirk's Marketing Research Review* (October 1991), pp. 10–13; Paul E. Green, Abba M. Krieger, and Manoj K. Agarwal, "Adaptive Conjoint Analysis: Some Caveats and Suggestions," *Journal of Marketing Research* (May 1991), pp. 215–222; Paul E. Green and V. Srinivasan, "Conjoint Analysis in Marketing: New Developments with Implications for Research and Practice," *Journal of Marketing Research Review* (October 1990), pp. 3–19; Joseph Curry, "Determining Product Feature Price Sensitivities," *Quirk's Marketing Research Review* (November 1990), pp. 14–17; Gordon A. Wyner, "Customer-Based Pricing Research," *Marketing Research* (Spring 1993), pp. 50–52; Steven Struhl, "Discrete Choice Modeling Comes to the PC," *Quirk's Marketing Research Review* (May 1993), pp. 12–15, 36–41: Steven Struhl, "Discrete Choice: Understanding a Better Conjoint . . . ," *Quirk's Marketing Research Review* (June/July 1994), pp. 12–15, 36–39; Bashir A. Datoo, "Measuring Price Elasticity," *Marketing Research* (Spring 1994), pp. 30–34; Gordon A. Wyner, "Uses and Limitations of Conjoint Analysis—Part 1," *Marketing Research* (June 1992), pp. 12–44; and Gordon A. Wyner, "Uses and Limitations of Conjoint Analysis—Part II," *Marketing Research* (September 1992), pp. 46–47; Yilian Yuan and Gang Xu, "Conjoint Analysis in Pharmaceutical Marketing Research," *Quirk's Marketing Research Review* (June 2001), pp. 18, 54–61; and Bryan Orme, "Assessing the Monetary Value of Attribute Levels with Conjoint Analysis: Warnings and Suggestions," *Quirk's Marketing Research Review* (May 2001), pp. 16, 44–47.

16. Mehmed Kantardzic, *Data Mining: Concepts, Models, Methods, and Algorithms* John Wiley & Sons, IBSN 0471228524. OCLC 50055336 (*http://www.worldcat.org/oclc/50055336*); and Y. Peng, G. Kou, Y. Shi, and Z. Chen (2008).

"A Descriptive Framework for the Field of Data Mining and Knowledge Discovery." *International Journal of Information Technology and Decision Making, 7, No.47*:639–682. Doi: 10.1142/S0219622008003204 (http://dx.doi.org/10.1142%2FS0219622008003204).

17. Kashmir Hill, "How Target Figured Out a Teen Girl was Pregnant Before Her Father Did," *Forbes* online, (February 2, 2012). Available at http://www.forbes.com/sites/kashmirhill/2012/02/16/how-target-figured-out-a-teen-girl-was-pregnant-before-her-father-did/.

18. See: Robert Eng, "Is the Market Research Industry Failing Its TQM Clients?" *Quirk's Marketing Research Review* (October f1996), pp. 24, 36-38.

## Chapter 19

1. Piet Levy, "How to Write a Research Report," *Marketing News* (May 30, 2010) Vol 44, No. 7, p.6.

2. Scott Fiaschetti, "More Insights, Less Data – Why Your Research Should Tell A Story," *Quirk's Marketing Research Review e-Newsletter* (September 24, 2012).

3. Gary A. Schmidt, "Take A Risk, Keep It Simple," *Quirk's Marketing Research Review* (April 2007), p. 52.

4. Tim Macer and Sheila Wilson, "Do Something about PowerPoint!" *Quirk's Marketing Research Review* (March 2008), p. 61.

## Chapter 20

1. "Now and for the Future," *Quirk's Marketing Research Review* (August 2010), pp. 52–57.

2. "Industry Study Finds Researchers Struggling, Adapting," *Quirk's Marketing Research Review* (December 2009), pp. 160-161.

3. Joseph Rydholm, "What Do Clients Want from a Research Firm?" *Quirk's Marketing Research Review* (October 1996), p. 80.

4. Michael Rosenberg, "The 10 Commandments of MR Client Management," *Quirk's Marketing Research Review e-Newsletter*, January 2014.

5. "Is Supplier Research Quality Improving?" *Marketing News* (September 30, 2009), pp. 38-39.

6. Joseph Rydholm, "Research 2010: More Work, More Data, Same Budget," *Quirk's Marketing Research Review* (February 2010), pp. 96–97.

7. John Walters and John Colias, "The Simple Secret to Effective Market Research," *CASRO Journal*, 2002, pp. 65–66.

8. Bonnie Eisenfeld, "Managing the Satisfiers and Dissatisfiers," *Quirk's Marketing Research Review* (May 2008), pp. 70–75.

9. Ibid.

10. Colleen Moore Mezler, "Managing Projects with Ease," Marketing Research Association *Alert!* online magazine, January 2011.

11. The material on organizing a supplier firm is from: Michael Mitrano, "Supplier Side: Organizing Your Company – Are Project Teams the Answer?" *Quirk's Marketing Research Review* (April 2002), pp. 20, 68.

12. Joseph Rydholm, "No Margin for Margin of Error," *Quirk's Marketing Research Review* (February 2008), pp. 117–118.

13. Rydholm, "Research 2010…"

14. Susan Greco, "Choose or Lose." Reprinted with permission from *Inc.* magazine (February 2001). Copyright 1998 by Gruner & Jahr USA Publishing.

15. Kathleen Knight, "Finding and Retaining Research Staff: A Perspective," *Quirk's Marketing Research Review* (February 1998), pp. 18, 54. Reprinted by permission.

16. The sections on allocating the research budget, prioritizing projects, and retaining skilled staff are from Diane Schmalensee and A. Dawn Lesh, "Creating Win-Win Relationships," *Marketing Research* (Winter 2007).

17. Ibid.

18. Ibid.

19. Ibid.

20. Bonnie Eisenfeld, "The Quest for the Ideal Marketing Researcher," *Quirk's Marketing Research Review* (August 2009), pp. 56–57.

21. Adapted from Richard Snyder, "Selecting the Right Research Vendor," *Quirk's Marketing Research Review* (November 2002), pp. 62–65.

22. "More for the Money," *Marketing News*, June 30, 2009, pp. 8–10.

23. Ibid.

24. "Newell Rubbermaid Shakes Up CMO Model By Putting Research in Charge," *Advertising Age*, http://adage.com/print/291377. Accessed 2/13/2014. Check citation for style.

25. Allison Enright, "Give 'em What They Need," *Marketing News*, February 1, 2008, p. 30.

26. Ibid.; also see Natalie Jobity and Jeff Scott, "Practices Make Perfect—Improving Research and Consulting Through Collaboration," *CASRO Journal* (2002), pp. 19–24; and Diane Schmalensee and Dawn Lesh, "Show Them and Tell Them," *Quirk's Marketing Research Review* (January 2010), pp. 36–38.

27. Ian Lewis, "A Road Map to Increased Relevance," *Quirk's Marketing Research Review* (January 2010), pp. 28–34.

28. The material on "Achieving Strategic Consultative Relevance," is adapted from: Lewis, "A Road Map."

29. Jennifer Rooney, "Here's What The Marketing Organization Of The Future Should Look Like," *Forbes CMO Network*, October 4, 2013. Check citation for style.

30. The material on "Achieving Strategic Consultative Relevance," is adapted from: Lewis, "A Road Map".

31. Tim Ambler, "Differing Dimensions," *Marketing Research*, Fall 2004, pp. 8–13; also see: "Measure Up," *Marketing News*, May 30, 2009, pp. 8–11.

32. This section of ROI is from A. Dawn Lesh and Diane Schmalensee, "Measuring Returns of Research," *Marketing Research*, Fall 2004, pp. 22–27.

33. Ibid.

34. Brett Hagins, "The ROI On Calculating Researcher's ROI," *Quirk's Marketing Research Review* (May 2010), p. 52.

# GLOSSARY

**after-only with control group design** True experimental design that involves random assignment of subjects or test units to experimental and control groups, but no premeasurement of the dependent variable.

**ad hoc mail surveys** Questionnaires sent to selected names and addresses without prior contact by the researcher; sometimes called *one-shot mail surveys*.

**allowable sampling error** Amount of sampling error the researcher is willing to accept.

**analogy** Drawing a comparison between two items in terms of their similarities.

**analysis of variance (ANOVA)** Test for the differences among the means of two or more independent samples.

**applied research** Research aimed at solving a specific, pragmatic problem—better understanding of the marketplace, determination of why a strategy or tactic failed, or reduction of uncertainty in management decision making.

**attitude** Enduring organization of motivational, emotional, perceptual, and cognitive processes with respect to some aspect of a person's environment.

**balanced scales** Measurement scales that have the same number of positive and negative categories.

**basic, or pure, research** Research aimed at expanding the frontiers of knowledge rather than solving a specific, pragmatic problem.

**before and after with control group design** True experimental design that involves random assignment of subjects or test units to experimental and control groups and pre- and postmeasurements of both groups.

**behavioral targeting** The use of online and offline data to understand a consumer's habits, demographics, and social networks in order to increase the effectiveness of online advertising.

**Big Data** The accumulation and analysis of massive quantities of information.

**bivariate regression analysis** Analysis of the strength of the linear relationship between two variables when one is considered the independent variable and the other the dependent variable.

**bivariate techniques** Statistical methods of analyzing the relationship between two variables.

**call center telephone interviews** Interviews conducted by calling respondents from a centrally located marketing research facility.

**captive outsourcing** When a research firm creates a wholly owned foreign facility for outsourcing.

**cartoon test** Projective test in which the respondent fills in the dialogue of one of two characters in a cartoon.

**case analysis** Reviewing information from situations that are similar to the current one.

**causal research** Research designed to determine whether a change in one variable likely caused an observed change in another.

**causal studies** Research studies that examine whether the value of one variable causes or determines the value of another variable.

**causation** Inference that a change in one variable is responsible for (caused) an observed change in another variable.

**census** Collection of data obtained from or about every member of the population of interest.

**central limit theorem** Idea that a distribution of a large number of sample means or sample proportions will approximate a normal distribution, regardless of the distribution of the population from which they were drawn.

**chance variation** The difference between the sample value and the true value of the population mean.

**chi-square test** Test of the goodness of fit between the observed distribution and the expected distribution of a variable.

**clarity** Achieved by avoiding ambiguous terminology, using reasonable, vernacular language adjusted to the target group, and asking only one question at a time.

**closed-ended questions** Questions that require the respondent to choose from a list of answers.

**closed online panel recruitment** Inviting only prevalidated individuals or those with shared known characteristics to enroll in a research panel.

**cluster analysis** General term for statistical procedures that classify objects or people into some number of mutually exclusive and exhaustive groups on the basis of two or more classification variables.

**cluster sample** Probability sample in which the sampling units are selected from a number of small geographic areas to reduce data collection costs.

**Coding** Process of grouping and assigning numeric codes to the various responses to a question.

**coefficient of determination** Measure of the percentage of the variation in the dependent variable explained by variations in the independent variables.

**coefficient of determination** Percentage of the total variation in the dependent variable explained by the independent variable.

**collinearity** Correlation of independent variables with each other, which can bias estimates of regression coefficients.

**commercial online panels** Group of individuals who have agreed to receive invitations to do online surveys from a particular panel company such as eRewards or SSI. The panel company charges organizations doing surveys for access to the panel. Charges are usually so much per survey depending on survey length and the type of people being sought for the survey. The panel company controls all access to the members of its panel.

**comparative scales** Measurement scales in which one object, concept, or person is compared with another on a scale.

**computer-assisted telephone interviews (CATI)** Call center telephone interviews in which interviewers enter respondents' answers directly into a computer.

**conclusions** Generalizations that answer the questions raised by the research objectives or otherwise satisfy the objectives.

**concomitant variation** The degree to which a presumed cause and a presumed effect occur or vary together.

**concurrent validity** Degree to which another variable, measured at the same point in time as the variable of interest, can be predicted by the measurement instrument.

**confidence interval** Interval that, at the specified confidence level, includes the true population value.

**confidence level** Probability that a particular interval will include true population value; also called *confidence coefficient.*

**conjoint analysis** Multivariate procedure used to quantify the value that consumers associate with different levels of product/service attributes or features.

**constant sum scales** Measurement scales that ask the respondent to divide a given number of points, typically 100, among two or more attributes, based on their importance to him or her.

**constitutive definition** Statement of the meaning of the central idea or concept under study, establishing its boundaries; also known as *theoretical,* or *conceptual, definition.*

**constructs** Specific types of concepts that exist at higher levels of abstraction.

**construct validity** Degree to which a measurement instrument represents and logically connects, via the underlying theory, the observed phenomenon to the construct.

**consumer drawings** Projective technique in which respondents draw what they are feeling or how they perceive an object.

**consumer orientation** The identification of and focus on the people or firms most likely to buy a product and the production of a good or service that will meet their needs most effectively.

**contamination** Inclusion in a test of a group of respondents who are not normally there; for example, buyers

from outside the test market who see an advertisement intended only for those in the test area and enter the area to purchase the product being tested.

**content validity** Representativeness, or sampling adequacy, of the content of the measurement instrument.

**convenience samples** Nonprobability samples based on using people who are easily accessible.

**convergent validity** Degree of correlation among different measurement instruments that purport to measure the same construct.

**conversion** An action that a person takes based on an advertiser's website, such as checking out, registering, adding an item to the shopping cart, or viewing a specific page.

**correlation analysis** Analysis of the degree to which changes in one variable are associated with changes in another.

**cost per impression** The cost to offer potential customers one opportunity to see an advertisement. Often expressed in terms of cost per thousand (CPM).

**creativity** The ability to generate and recognize potentially useful ideas.

**criterion-related validity** Degree to which a measurement instrument can predict a variable that is designated a criterion.

**cross tabulation** Examination of the responses to one question relative to the responses to one or more other questions.

**custom research firms** Companies that carry out customized marketing research to address specific projects for corporate clients.

**data entry** Process of converting information to an electronic format.

**data mining** The use of statistical and other advanced software to discover nonobvious patterns hidden in a database.

**data visualization** The use of picture visualization techniques to illustrate the relationship within data.

**decision rule** Rule or standard used to determine whether to reject or fail to reject the null hypothesis.

**decision support system (DSS)** An interactive, personalized information management system, designed to be

initiated and controlled by individual decision makers.

**degrees of freedom** Number of observations in a statistical problem that are free to vary.

**Delphi Method** Rounds of individual data collection from knowledgeable people. Results are summarized and returned to the "participants for further refinement.

**dependent variable** A symbol or concept expected to be explained or influenced by the independent variable.

**dependent variable** Variable expected to be explained or caused by the independent variable.

**descriptive function** The gathering and presentation of statements of fact.

**descriptive studies** Research studies that answer the questions who, what, when, where, and how.

**design control** Use of the experimental design to control extraneous causal factors.

**determinant attitudes** Those consumer attitudes most closely related to preferences or to actual purchase decisions.

**diagnostic function** The explanation of data or actions.

**dichotomous questions** Closed-ended questions that ask the respondents to choose between two answers.

**discriminant coefficient** Estimate of the discriminatory power of a particular independent variable; also called *discriminant weight.*

**discriminant score** Score that is the basis for predicting to which group a particular object or individual belongs; also called *Z score.*

**discriminant validity** Measure of the lack of association among constructs that are supposed to be different.

**discussion guide** Written outline of topics to be covered during a focus group discussion.

**disguised observation** Process of monitoring people who do not know they are being watched.

**disproportional, or optimal, allocation** Sampling in which the number of elements taken from a given stratum is proportional to the relative size of the stratum and the standard deviation of the characteristic under consideration.

**door-to-door interviews** Interviews conducted face to face with consumers in their homes.

**dummy variables** In regression analysis, a way of representing two-group or dichotomous, nominally scaled independent variables by coding one group as 0 and the other as 1.

**editing** Going through each questionnaire to ensure that skip patterns were followed and the required questions filled out.

**editing** Process of ascertaining that questionnaires were filled out properly and completely.

**electroencephalograph (EEG)** Machine that measures electrical pulses on the scalp and generates a record of electrical activity in the brain.

**equivalent form reliability** Ability of two very similar forms of an instrument to produce closely correlated results.

**error-checking routines** Computer programs that accept instructions from the user to check for logical errors in the data.

**error sum of squares** Variation not explained by the regression.

**ethics** Moral principles or values, generally governing the conduct of an individual or group.

**ethnographic research** Study of human behavior in its natural context, involving observation of behavior and physical setting.

**evaluative research** Research done to assess program performance.

**executive interviews** Industrial equivalent of door-to-door interviewing.

**executive summary** Portion of a research report that explains why the research was done, what was found, what those findings mean, and what action, if any, management should undertake.

**experience surveys** Discussions with knowledgeable individuals, both inside and outside the organization, who may provide insights into the problem.

**experiment** Research approach in which one variable is manipulated and the effect on another variable is observed.

**experimental design** Test in which the researcher has control over and manipulates one or more independent variables.

**experimental effect** Effect of the treatment variable on the dependent variable.

**experiments** Research to measure causality, in which the researcher changes one or more independent variables and observes the effect of the changes on the dependent variable.

**exploratory research** Preliminary research conducted to increase understanding of a concept, to clarify the exact nature of the problem to be solved, or to identify important variables to be studied.

**external validity** Extent to which causal relationships measured in an experiment can be generalized to outside persons, settings, and times.

**face validity** Degree to which a measurement seems to measure what it is supposed to measure.

**factor** A linear combination of variables that are correlated with each other.

**factor analysis** Procedure for simplifying data by reducing a large set of variables to a smaller set of factors or composite variables by identifying underlying dimensions of the data.

**factor loading** Correlation between factor scores and the original variables.

**field experiments** Tests conducted outside the laboratory in an actual environment, such as a marketplace.

**field management companies** Firms that provide such support services as questionnaire formatting, screener writing, and coordination of data collection.

**Field service firms** Companies that only collect survey data for corporate clients or research firms.

**finite population correction factor (FPC)** An adjustment to the required sample size that is made in cases where the sample is expected to be equal to 5 percent or more of the total population.

**focus group** Group of 8 to 12 participants who are led by a moderator in an in-depth discussion on one particular topic or concept.

**focus group facility** Research facility consisting of a conference room or living room setting and a separate observation room with a one-way mirror or live audiovisual feed.

**focus group moderator** Person hired by the client to lead the focus group; this person should have a background in psychology or sociology or, at least, marketing.

**frame error** Error resulting from an inaccurate or incomplete sampling frame.

**F test** Test of the probability that a particular calculated value could have been due to chance.

**galvanic skin response (GSR)** Change in the electric resistance of the skin associated with activation responses; also called *electrodermal response*.

**garbologists** Researchers who sort through people's garbage to analyze household consumption patterns.

**geographic information system (GIS)** Computer-based system that uses secondary and/or primary data to generate maps that visually display various types of data geographically.

**goal orientation** A focus on the accomplishment of corporate goals; a limit set on consumer orientation.

**graphic rating scales** Measurement scales that include a graphic continuum, anchored by two extremes.

**group dynamics** Interaction among people in a group.

**hermeneutic research** Research that focuses on interpretation through conversations.

**history** Intervention, between the beginning and end of an experiment, of outside variables or events that might change the dependent variable.

**hypothesis** An assumption or theory (guess) that a researcher or manager makes about some characteristic of the population being investigated.

**hypothesis** Assumption or theory that a researcher or manager makes about some characteristic of the population under study.

**hypothesis test of proportions** Test to determine whether the difference between proportions is greater than would be expected because of sampling error.

**independence assumption** Assumption that sample elements are drawn independently.

**independent samples** Samples in which measurement of a variable in one population has no effect on measurement of the variable in the other.

**independent variable** A symbol or concept over which the researcher has some control and that is hypothesized to cause or influence the dependent variable.

**independent variable** Variable believed to affect the value of the dependent variable.

**individual depth interviews** One-on-one interviews that probe and elicit detailed answers to questions, often using nondirective techniques to uncover hidden motivations.

**innovation** The successful implementation of creative ideas within an organization.

**input error** Error that results from the incorrect input of information into a computer file or database.

**insight** Newer knowledge that has the potential to create significant marketing impact.

**instant analysis** Moderator debriefing, offering a forum for brainstorming by the moderator and client observers.

**instrument variation** Changes in measurement instruments (e.g., interviewers or observers) that might affect measurements.

**intelligent data entry** Form of data entry in which the information being entered into the data entry device is checked for internal logic.

**internal consistency reliability** Ability of an instrument to produce similar results when used on different samples during the same time period to measure a phenomenon.

**internal database** A collection of related information developed from data within the organization.

**internal validity** Extent to which competing explanations for the experimental results observed can be ruled out.

**interrupted time-series design** Research in which repeated measurement of an effect "interrupts" previous data patterns.

**interval estimate** Interval or range of values within which the true population value is estimated to fall.

**interval scales** Scales that have the characteristics of ordinal scales, plus equal intervals between points to show relative amounts; they may include an arbitrary zero point.

**interviewer error, or interviewer bias** Error that results from the interviewer's influencing—consciously or unconsciously—the answers of the respondent.

**itemized rating scales** Measurement scales in which the respondent selects an answer from a limited number of ordered categories.

**judgment samples** Nonprobability samples in which the selection criteria are based on the researcher's judgment about representativeness of the population under study.

**laboratory experiments** Experiments conducted in a controlled setting.

**Likert scales** Measurement scales in which the respondent specifies a level of agreement or disagreement with statements expressing either a favorable or an unfavorable attitude toward the concept under study.

**logical or machine cleaning of data** Final computerized error check of data.

**longitudinal study** Study in which the same respondents are resampled over time.

**low-ball pricing** Quoting an unrealistically low price to secure a firm's business and then using some means to substantially raise the price.

**mail panels** Precontacted and pre-screened participants who are periodically sent questionnaires.

**mall-intercept interviews** Interviews conducted by intercepting mall shoppers (or shoppers in other high-traffic locations) and interviewing them face to face.

**management decision problem** A statement specifying the type of managerial action required to solve the problem.

**marketing** The process of planning and executing the conception, pricing, promotion, and distribution of ideas, goods, and services to create exchanges that satisfy individual and organizational objectives.

**marketing concept** A business philosophy based on consumer orientation, goal orientation, and systems orientation.

**marketing mix** The unique blend of product/service, pricing, promotion, and distribution strategies designed to meet the needs of a specific target market.

**marketing research** The planning, collection, and analysis of data relevant to marketing decision making and the communication of the results of this analysis to management.

**marketing research objective** A goal statement, defining the specific information needed to solve the marketing research problem.

**marketing research online community (MROC)** Carefully selected group of consumers who agree to participate in an ongoing dialogue with a corporation.

**marketing research problem** A statement specifying the type of information needed by the decision maker to help solve the management decision problem and how that information can be obtained efficiently and effectively.

**marketing strategy** A plan to guide the long-term use of a firm's resources based on its existing and projected internal capabilities and on projected changes in the external environment.

**maturation** Changes in subjects occurring during the experiment that are not related to the experiment but that may affect subjects' response to the treatment factor.

**mean** Sum of the values for all observations of a variable divided by the number of observations.

**measurement** Process of assigning numbers or labels to persons, objects, or events in accordance with specific rules for representing quantities or qualities of attributes.

**measurement error** Systematic error that results from a variation between the information being sought and what is actually obtained by the measurement process.

**measurement instrument bias** Error that results from the design of the questionnaire or measurement instrument; also known as *questionnaire bias*.

**median** Value below which 50 percent of the observations fall.

**metric scale** A type of quantitative that provides the most precise measurement.

**mode** Value that occurs most frequently.

**mortality** Loss of test units or subjects during the course of an experiment, which may result in a nonrepresentativeness.

**multidimensional scales** Scales designed to measure several dimensions of a concept, respondent, or object.

**multiple-choice questions** Closed-ended questions that ask the respondent to choose among several answers; also called *multichotomous questions*.

**multiple discriminant analysis** Procedure for predicting group membership for a (nominal or categorical) dependent variable on the basis of two or more independent variables.

**multiple regression analysis** Procedure for predicting the level or magnitude of a (metric) dependent variable based on the levels of multiple independent variables.

**multiple time-series design** Interrupted time-series design with a control group.

**multistage area sampling** Geographic areas selected for national or regional surveys in progressively smaller population units, such as counties, then residential blocks, then homes.

**multivariate analysis** A general term for statistical procedures that simultaneously analyze multiple measurements on each individual or object under study.

**mystery shoppers** People who pose as consumers and shop at a company's own stores or those of its competitors to collect data about customer–employee interactions and to gather observational data; they may also compare prices, displays, and the like.

**net promoter score** A measure of satisfaction; the percentage of promoters minus the percentage of detractors when answering the question, "Would you recommend this to a friend?"

**neural network** A computer program that mimics the processes of the human brain and thus is capable of learning from examples to find patterns in data.

**Neuromarketing** The process of researching the brain patterns and certain physiological measures of consumers to marketing stimuli.

**nominal or categorical** A type of nonmetric qualitative data scale that only uses numbers to indicate membership in a group (e.g., 1 = male, 2 = female). Most mathematical and statistical procedures cannot be applied to nominal data.

**nominal scales** Scales that partition data into mutually exclusive and collectively exhaustive categories.

**nonbalanced scales** Measurement scales that are weighted toward one end or the other of the scale.

**noncomparative scales** Measurement scales in which judgment is made without reference to another object, concept, or person.

**nonprobability sample** A subset of a population in which the chances of selection for the various elements in the population are unknown.

**nonprobability samples** Samples in which specific elements from the population have been selected in a nonrandom manner.

**nonresponse bias** Error that results from a systematic difference between those who do and those who do not respond to a measurement instrument.

**nonsampling error** All errors other than sampling error; also called *measurement error*.

**normal distribution** Continuous distribution that is bell-shaped and symmetric about the mean; the mean, median, and mode are equal.

**null hypothesis** The hypothesis of status quo, no difference, no effect.

**observation research** Typically, descriptive research that monitors respondents' actions without direct interaction.

**observation research** Systematic process of recording patterns of occurrences or behaviors without normally communicating with the people involved.

**one-group pretest–posttest design** Pre-experimental design with pre- and postmeasurements but no control group.

**one-shot case study design** Pre-experimental design with no pretest observations, no control group, and an after measurement only.

**one-way frequency table** Table showing the number of respondents choosing each answer to a survey question.

**one-way mirror observation** Practice of watching behaviors or activities from behind a one-way mirror.

**open-ended questions** Questions to which the respondent replies in her or his own words.

**open observation** Process of monitoring people who know they are being watched.

**open online panel recruitment** Any person with Internet access can self-select to be in a research panel.

**operational definition** Statement of precisely which observable characteristics will be measured and the process for assigning a value to the concept.

**opportunity identification** Using marketing research to find and evaluate new opportunities.

**ordinal scales** Scales that maintain the labeling characteristics of nominal scales and have the ability to order data.

**outsourcing** Having personnel in another country perform some, or all, of the functions involved in a marketing research project.

**paired comparison scales** Measurement scales that ask the respondent to pick one of two objects in a set, based on some stated criteria.

**Pearson's product–moment correlation** Correlation analysis technique for use with metric data.

**personification** Drawing a comparison between a product and a person.

**photo sort** Projective technique in which a respondent sorts photos of different types of people, identifying those people who she or he feels would use the specified product or service.

**physical control** Holding constant the value or level of extraneous variables throughout the course of an experiment.

**pilot studies** Surveys using a limited number of respondents and often employing less rigorous sampling techniques than are employed in large, quantitative studies.

**point estimate** Particular estimate of a population value.

**population** Entire group of people about whom information is needed; also called *universe* or *population of interest*.

**population distribution** Frequency distribution of all the elements of a population.

**population parameter** A value that accurately portrays or typifies a factor of a complete population, such as average age or income.

**population specification error** Error that results from incorrectly defining the population or universe from which a sample is chosen.

**population standard deviation** Standard deviation of a variable for the entire population.

**predictive function** Specification of how to use descriptive and diagnostic research to predict the results of a planned marketing decision.

**predictive validity** Degree to which a future level of a criterion variable can be forecast by a current measurement scale.

**pre-experimental designs** Designs that offer little or no control over extraneous factors.

**pretest** Trial run of a questionnaire.

**primary data** New data gathered to help solve the problem under investigation.

**probability sample** A subset of a population where every element in the population has a known nonzero chance of being selected.

**probability samples** Samples in which every element of the population has a known, nonzero likelihood of selection.

**profession** Organization whose membership is determined by objective standards, such as an examination.

**professionalism** Quality said to be possessed by a worker with a high level of expertise, the freedom to exercise judgment, and the ability to work independently.

**programmatic research** Research conducted to develop marketing options through market segmentation, market opportunity analyses, or consumer attitude and product usage studies.

**projective test** Technique for tapping respondents' deepest feelings by having them project those feelings into an unstructured situation.

**proportional allocation** Sampling in which the number of elements selected from a stratum is directly proportional to the size of the stratum relative to the size of the population.

**proportional property of the normal distribution** Feature that the number of observations falling between the mean and a given number of standard deviations from the mean is the same for all normal distributions.

**purchase-intent scales** Scales used to measure a respondent's intention to buy or not buy a product.

*P* **value** Exact probability of getting a computed test statistic that is due to chance. The smaller the *p* value, the smaller the probability that the observed result occurred by chance.

**qualitative research** Research whose findings are not subject to quantification or quantitative analysis.

**quantitative research** Research that uses mathematical analysis.

**quasi-experiments** Studies in which the researcher lacks complete control over the scheduling of treatments or must assign respondents to treatments in a nonrandom manner.

**questionnaire** Set of questions designed to generate the data necessary to accomplish the objectives of the research project; also called an *interview schedule* or *survey instrument*.

**quota samples** Nonprobability samples in which quotas, based on demographic or classification factors selected by the researcher, are established for population subgroups.

**random-digit dialing** Method of generating lists of telephone numbers at random.

**random error, or random sampling error** Error that results from chance variation.

**randomization** Random assignment of subjects to treatment conditions to ensure equal representation of subject characteristics.

**rank-order scales** Measurement scales in which the respondent compares two or more items and ranks them.

**ratio scales** Scales that have the characteristics of interval scales, plus a meaningful zero point so that magnitudes can be compared arithmetically.

**recommendations** Conclusions applied to marketing strategies or tactics that focus on a client's achievement of differential advantage.

**refusal rate** Percentage of persons contacted who refused to participate in a survey.

**regression coefficients** Estimates of the effect of individual independent variables on the dependent variable.

**regression to the mean** Tendency of subjects with extreme behavior to move toward the average for that behavior during the course of an experiment.

**related samples** Samples in which measurement of a variable in one population may influence measurement of the variable in the other.

**reliability** Degree to which measures are free from random error and, therefore, provide consistent data.

**request for proposal (RFP)** A solicitation sent to marketing research suppliers inviting them to submit a formal proposal, including a bid.

**research design** The plan to be followed to answer the marketing research objectives.

**research management** Overseeing the development of excellent communication systems, data quality, time schedules, cost controls, client profitability, and staff development.

**research proposal** A document developed, usually in response to an RFP, that presents the research objectives, research design, timeline, and cost of a project.

**research request** An internal document used by large organizations that describes a potential research project, its benefits to the organization, and estimated costs; it must be formally approved before a research project can begin.

**response bias** Error that results from the tendency of people to answer a question incorrectly through either deliberate falsification or unconscious misrepresentation.

**return on quality** Management objective based on the principles that (1) the quality being delivered is at a level desired by the target market and (2) the level of quality must have a positive impact on profitability.

**rule** Guide, method, or command that tells a researcher what to do.

**sample** Subset of all the members of a population of interest.

**sample design error** Systematic error that results from an error in the sample design or sampling procedures.

**sample distribution** Frequency distribution of all the elements of an individual sample.

**sample size** The identified and selected population subset for the survey, chosen because it represents the entire group.

**sampling** Process of obtaining information from a subset of a larger group.

**sampling distribution of the mean** Theoretical frequency distribution of the means of all possible samples of a given size drawn from a particular population; it is normally distributed.

**sampling distribution of the proportion** Relative frequency distribution of the sample proportions of many random samples of a given size drawn from a particular population; it is normally distributed.

**sampling error** Error that occurs because the sample selected is not perfectly representative of the population.

**sampling frame** The list of population elements or members from which units to be sampled are selected.

**sampling frame** List of population elements from which units to be sampled can be selected or a specified procedure for generating such a list.

**scale** Set of symbols or numbers so constructed that the symbols or numbers can be assigned by a rule to the individuals (or their behaviors or attitudes) to whom the scale is applied.

**scaled-response questions** Closed-ended questions in which the response choices are designed to capture the intensity of the respondent's feeling.

**scaling** Procedures for assigning numbers (or other symbols) to properties of an object in order to impart some numerical characteristics to the properties in question.

**scaling of coefficients** A method of directly comparing the magnitudes of the regression coefficients of independent variables by scaling them in the same units or by standardizing the data.

**scanning technology** Form of data entry in which responses on questionnaires are read in automatically by the data entry device.

**scatter diagram** Graphic plot of the data with dependent variable on the $Y$ (vertical) axis and the independent variable on the $X$ (horizontal) axis. Shows the nature of the relationship between the two variables, linear or nonlinear.

**screeners** Questions used to identify appropriate respondents.

**secondary data** Data that have been previously gathered.

**selection bias** Systematic differences between the test group and the control group due to a biased selection process.

**selection error** Error that results from incomplete or improper sample selection procedures or not following appropriate procedures.

**selective research** Research used to test decision alternatives.

**self-administered questionnaires** Questionnaires filled out by respondents with no interviewer present.

**semantic differential scales** Measurement scales that examine the strengths and weaknesses of a concept by having the respondent rank it between dichotomous pairs of words or phrases that could be used to describe it; the means of the responses are then plotted as a profile or image.

**sentence and story completion test** Projective test in which respondents complete sentences or stories in their own words.

**simple random sample** Probability sample selected by assigning a number to every element of the population and then using a table of random numbers to select specific elements for inclusion in the sample.

**situation analysis** Studying the decision-making environment within which the marketing research will take place.

**skip pattern** Sequence in which questions are asked, based on a respondent's answer.

**skip pattern** Sequence in which later questions are asked, based on a respondent's answer to an earlier question or questions.

**snowball samples** Nonprobability samples in which additional respondents are selected based on referrals from initial respondents.

**split-half technique** Method of assessing the reliability of a scale by dividing the total set of measurement items in half and correlating the results.

**spurious association** A relationship between a presumed cause and a presumed effect that occurs as a result of an unexamined variable or set of variables.

**stability** Lack of change in results from test to retest

**standard deviation** Measure of dispersion calculated by subtracting the mean of the series from each value in a series, squaring each result, summing the results, dividing the sum by the number of items minus 1, and taking the square root of this value.

**standard error of the mean** Standard deviation of a distribution of sample means.

**standard normal distribution** Normal distribution with a mean of zero and a standard deviation of one.

**Stapel scales** Measurement scales that require the respondent to rate, on a scale ranging from +5 to –5, how closely and in what direction a descriptor adjective fits a given concept.

**statistical control** Adjusting for the effects of confounded variables by statistically adjusting the value of the dependent variable for each treatment condition.

**statistical power** Probability of not making a type II error.

**statistical significance** A difference that is large enough that it is not likely to have occurred because of chance or sampling error.

**storytelling** Projective technique in which respondents are required to tell stories about their experiences, with a company or product, for example; also known as the *metaphor technique.*

**strategic partnership** An alliance formed by two or more firms with unique skills and resources to offer a new service for clients, provide strategic support for each firm, or in some other manner create mutual benefits.

**stratified sample** Probability sample that is forced to be more representative through simple random sampling of mutually exclusive and exhaustive subsets.

**sum of squares due to regression** Variation explained by the regression.

**supervisor's instructions** Written directions to the field service firm on how to conduct the survey.

**surrogate information error** Error that results from a discrepancy between the information needed to solve a problem and that sought by the researcher.

**survey objectives** Outline of the decision-making information sought through the questionnaire.

**survey research** Research in which an interviewer (except in mail and Internet surveys) interacts with respondents to obtain facts, opinions, and attitudes.

**syndicated service research firms** Companies that collect, package, and sell market research data to many firms.

**systematic error, or bias** Error that results from problems or flaws in the execution of the research design; sometimes called *nonsampling error.*

**systematic sampling** Probability sampling in which the entire population is numbered and elements are selected using a skip interval.

**systems orientation** The creation of systems to monitor the external environment and deliver the desired marketing mix to the target market.

**temporal sequence** An appropriate causal order of events.

**testing effect** Effect that is a by-product of the research process itself.

**test market** Real-world testing of a new product or some element of the marketing mix using an experimental or quasi-experimental design.

**test–retest reliability** Ability of the same instrument to produce consistent results when used a second time under conditions as similar as possible to the original conditions.

**third-person technique** Projective technique in which the interviewer learns about respondents' feelings by asking them to answer for a third party, such as "your neighbor" or "most people."

**treatment variable** Independent variable that is manipulated in an experiment.

**true experimental design** Research using an experimental group and a control group, to which test units are randomly assigned.

**t test** Hypothesis test used for a single mean if the sample is too small to use the $Z$ test.

**type I error ($\alpha$ error)** Rejection of the null hypothesis when, in fact, it is true.

**type II error ($\beta$ error)** Failure to reject the null hypothesis when, in fact, it is false.

**unidimensional scales** Scales designed to measure only one attribute of a concept, respondent, or object.

**unrestricted Internet sample** Self-selected sample group consisting of anyone who wishes to complete an Internet survey.

**utilities** The relative value of attribute levels determined through conjoint analysis.

**validation** Process of ascertaining that interviews actually were conducted as specified.

**validity** The degree to which what the researcher was trying to measure was actually measured.

**variable** A symbol or concept that can assume any one of a set of values.

**word association test** Projective test in which the interviewer says a word and the respondent must mention the first thing that comes to mind.

**Z test** Hypothesis test used for a single mean if the sample is large enough and drawn at random.

**S01.** Which of the following categories best describes your age?

1 Under 18 years **(TERMINATE)**
2 18
3 19
4 20
5 21
6 22 – 24
7 25 – 29
8 30 – 34
9 35 – 39 **(TERMINATE)**
10 40 – 44 **(TERMINATE)**
11 45 – 49 **(TERMINATE)**
12 50 – 54 **(TERMINATE)**
13 55 – 59 **(TERMINATE)**
14 60 – 64 **(TERMINATE)**
15 65 – 69 **(TERMINATE)**
16 70 – 74 **(TERMINATE)**
17 75 or older **(TERMINATE)**

**Q01.** How many times do you eat the following meals on a typical WEEKDAY?

(ALLOW 2 DIGITS FOR EACH MEAL - 0-99)

Breakfast _____
Lunch _____
Dinner _____
Snacks _____

**Q02.** How many times do you eat the following meals on a typical WEEKEND day?

(ALLOW 2 DIGITS FOR EACH MEAL - 0-99)

Breakfast _____
Lunch _____
Dinner _____
Snacks _____

CALCULATE MONTHLY TOTAL FOR EACH MEAL BY MULTIPLYING Q01 RESPONSES BY 22 AND Q02 RESPONSES BY 8. ADD THE TWO PRODUCTS TOGETHER AND INSERT TOTAL (MEAL_PROD) IN TABLE FOR Q06.

**Q03.** A Quick Service Restaurant is one in which you can order a meal and typically have it ready to go immediately or within a few minutes.

When thinking of Quick Service Restaurants, which one comes to mind first? (ALLOW ONE RESPONSE OF 100 CHARACTERS)

**Q04.** Which other Quick Service Restaurants come to your mind? (SHOW 25 TEXT BOXES, EACH ALLOWING 100 CHARACTERS)

**Q05.** You may have already mentioned some of the Quick Service Restaurants shown below, but please select all of the restaurants you have heard of.

a Arby's
b Bojangles'
c Boston Market
d Burger King
e Captain D's
f Carl's Jr.
g Checkers/Rally's
h Chick-fil-A
i Chipotle Mexican Grill
j Church's Chicken
k CiCi's Pizza
l Culver's
m Dairy Queen
n Del Taco
o Domino's Pizza
p El Pollo Loco
q Five Guys Burgers & Fries
r Hardee's
s In-N-Out Burger
t Jack in the Box
u Jason's Deli
v Jimmy John's
w KFC
x Little Caesars
y Long John Silver's
z McDonald's
aa Moe's Southwest Grill
bb Panda Express
cc Panera Bread
dd Papa John's
ee Papa Murphy's
ff Pizza Hut
gg Popeyes Louisiana Kitchen
hh Qdoba Mexican Grill
ii Quiznos

jj Sonic Drive-In
kk Steak 'n Shake
ll Subway
mm Taco Bell
nn Tim Hortons
oo Wendy's

pp Whataburger
qq White Castle
rr Wingstop
ss Zaxby's
zz I have not heard of any of these restaurants (EXCLUSIVE)

Q06. On average, how many times in a month do you eat meals at the following locations?

Show following grid

| | Breakfast (eaten **meal_prod** times per month) | Lunch (eaten **meal_prod** times per month) | Dinner (eaten **meal_prod** times per month) | Snacks (eaten **meal_prod** times per month) |
|---|---|---|---|---|
| Show list of items selected in Q5. | **Allow open end response of 3 digits** | **Allow open end response of 3 digits** | **Allow open end response of 3 digits** | **Allow open end response of 3 digits** |
| Some other restaurant **(ANCHOR)** | | | | |
| At home **(ANCHOR)** | | | | |
| Total | **Total for column must equal meal_prod calculation.** | **Total for column must equal meal_prod calculation.** | **Total for column must equal meal_prod calculation.** | **Total for column must equal meal_prod calculation.** |

**(IF "AT HOME" ROW IS EQUAL TO MEAL_PROD FOR EACH COLUMN, THEN ASK Q07 AND THEN SKIP TO Q18, ELSE SKIP TO Q08)**

Q07. Why have you not visited a Quick Service Restaurant in the past month?

Q08. Using the list below, please indicate which of the following factors is the MOST important for you when deciding on which Quick Service Restaurant to visit.

(RANDOMIZE LIST)

Price
Speed of service
Location
Quality of food
Cleanliness
Menu variety
Nutritional content/healthiness of food
Quantity of food
Ease of getting in and out
Atmosphere
Popularity of restaurant (number of people there)
Friendliness of employees
Number of people in your party

Q09. Which of the following factors is LEAST important in your decision-making process?

Show randomized list from Q08 with the previously chosen response removed.

Q10. Of the remaining factors, which one is MOST important to you?

Show randomized list from Q08 with the previously chosen responses removed.

Q11. Of the remaining factors, which one is LEAST important to you?

Show randomized list from Q08 with the previously chosen responses removed.

Q12. Of the remaining factors, which one is MOST important to you?

Show randomized list from Q08 with the previously chosen responses removed.

Q13. Of the remaining factors, which one is LEAST important to you?

Show randomized list from Q08 with the previously chosen responses removed.

Q14. Of the remaining factors, which one is MOST important to you?

Show randomized list from Q08 with the previously chosen responses removed.

**Q15.** Of the remaining factors, which one is LEAST important to you?

Show randomized list from Q08 with the previously chosen responses removed.

(IF RESPONDENT ONLY GAVE ONE RESPONSE (OR ONE RESPONSE AND ZZ) TO Q05, SKIP TO Q18)

**Q16.** In your opinion, which restaurant performs the BEST in each of these areas?

(INSERT TABLE WITH LIST FROM Q08 RANDOMIZED ACROSS THE TOP (COLUMNS) AND LIST OF RESTAURANTS CHOSEN IN Q05 SHOWN AS THE ROWS. ONLY ALLOW ONE SELECTION FOR EACH COLUMN)

**Q17.** Now, which restaurant performs the WORST in each of these areas?

(INSERT TABLE WITH LIST FROM Q08 RANDOMIZED ACROSS THE TOP (COLUMNS) AND LIST OF RESTAURANTS CHOSEN IN Q05 SHOWN AS THE ROWS. ONLY ALLOW ONE SELECTION FOR EACH COLUMN. DO NOT ALLOW A RESPONDENT TO SELECT A RESTAURANT CHOSEN AS WORST FOR Q17 IF IT WAS CHOSEN AS THE BEST FOR Q16. IF THIS HAPPENS, SHOW POP-UP BOX THAT SAYS "YOU SAID THIS RESTAURANT WAS BEST IN THIS AREA ON THE PREVIOUS QUESTION. PLEASE REVIEW YOUR RESPONSE".)

These last few questions are asked for classification purposes only.

**Q18.** In general, would you say your health is:

5 Excellent
4 Very Good
3 Good
2 Fair
1 Poor
9 Don't know

**Q19.** What is your gender?

1 Male
2 Female

**Q20.** What is the highest level of education that you have completed?

1 Eighth grade or less
2 Some high school, did not graduate
3 High school graduate or GED
4 Some college or 2 year degree

5 4 year college graduate
6 More than 4 year college degree
8 Prefer not to answer

**Q21.** Are you currently enrolled in an educational institution?

1 Yes, I am currently a FULL-TIME student
2 Yes, I am currently a PART-TIME student
3 No, I am not currently a student **(SKIP TO Q24)**

**Q22.** Do you receive any type of financial support from your parents or other family member(s)?

1 Yes

2 No **(SKIP TO Q24)**

**Q23.** How much financial support do you receive on a monthly basis?

Please enter only whole dollars.
(IF THEY ENTER ANYTHING OTHER THAN WHOLE NUMBERS, PLEASE SHOW A POP-UP BOX THAT SAYS "PLEASE ENTER THE NEAREST WHOLE DOLLAR AMOINT, WITHOUT COMMAS OR DECIMALS".)
_____. 00 ALLOW 5 DIGITS

**Q24.** Which one of the following best describes your current employment status?

1 Employed outside the home full-time
2 Employed outside the home part-time
3 Self-employed
4 Not employed outside the home
5 Retired
8 Other
9 Prefer not to answer

**Q25.** Which one of the following best describes your current living situation?

1 I live at home with my parents
2 I live on my own by myself
3 I live on my own with a significant other or roommates
4 Other (SPECIFY) _____

**Q26.** What is your current marital status?

1 Married or living with a partner
2 Single (never married)
3 Widowed
4 Divorced
5 Separated
8 Prefer not to answer

Q27. Including yourself, what is the total number of adults (18 years of age or older) currently living in your household? Please count all adults, whether related to you or not.

1 One
2 Two
3 Three
4 Four
5 Five
6 Six or more
8 Prefer not to answer

Q28. How many children, under the age of 18, currently live in your household?

0 None / Zero
1 One
2 Two
3 Three
4 Four
5 Five or more
8 Prefer not to answer

Q29. Which of the following best describes your racial or ethnic background? You may select more than one response.

a. Black or African-American
b. White or Caucasian
c. Hispanic
d. Asian or Pacific Islander
e. American-Indian or Alaskan native, or
f. Some other background (specify) _____
g. Don't know
h. Prefer not to answer

Q30. Which of the following categories includes your 2013 total household income from all sources before taxes?

1 Less than $10,000
2 $10,000 to less than $15,000
3 $15,000 to less than $25,000
4 $25,000 to less than $35,000
5 $35,000 to less than $50,000
6 $50,000 to less than $75,000
7 $75,000 to less than $100,000
8 $100,000 to less than $150,000
9 $150,000 to less than $200,000
10 $200,000 or more
98 Prefer not to answer

Thank you for your participation.

## TERM LANGUAGE FOR ALL NON-QUALIFIERS:

Thank you for answering these screener questions. Unfortunately, you do not fit the profile of respondents we need for this particular study, so the topic will not be relevant for you. We appreciate your time and interest.

# INDEX

*Note:* Page numbers followed by "t" indicate the entry is in a table, those followed by an "f" indicate the entry is in a figure.

## A

ABS. *See* Address-based sampling (ABS)
Abuse, respondent, 35
Acceptable error, 316
Ace Hardware, 86
ACNielsen, 210, 211. *See also* Nielsen Company
Act utilitarianism, 33
Acxiom, 320
Ad hoc mail surveys, 129–131
Adaptation, questionnaires, 300–301
Address-based sampling (ABS), 315
Administrative error, 318
Advocacy studies, 34
After-only with control group design, 205
Age recognition systems, 180
Alcohol consumption study, 340–341
Alcon, 221
Allowable sampling error, 344
Althoff, Stefan, 203
Amazon.com, 30
American Airlines, 20
Amoroso, Gala, 540
Analogies, 111
Analysis of variance (ANOVA), 425–428, 476
Applied research, 7–8
Appropriate time order of occurrence, 195
Area sampling, 324–325
AT&T wireless, 433–434
Attitude measurement scales. *See* Measurement scales
Attitude strength, 243
Attitudes link with behavior, 242–243
Automated coding systems, 368–369
Availability, secondary data, 75
Awareness data, 217
Axcis Athletic Shoes, 460

## B

Background information, secondary data and, 75
Background knowledge, 35
Balanced scales, 260
Banana Republic, 30
Bar charts, 381–383
Bar codes, 54
Basic research, 7
BBDO Worldwide, 113
Beck, Sarah, 534
Before and after with control group design, 205
Behavior link with attitudes, 242–243
Behavioral targeting, 78
Behavioral tracking, 83
Bias, survey research and, 121
Bids, ethics and, 36–37
Big data, 484
Big data analytics, 79–86
    automated decision making, 81
    data visualization, 81, 81f
    deeper and broader insights, 79
    defining relationships, 79
    NoSQL database, 79–80
    privacy issues and (*see* Consumer privacy)
    ZQ intelligence, 80
Binomial effect size display (BESD), 455–456

Bivariate and multivariate correlation combined, 457
Bivariate correlation and regression
    bivariate analysis of association, 438–439
    bivariate regression, 439–452
    correlation analysis, 452–457
    dependent variables and, 438
    independent variables and, 438
Bivariate regression, 439–452
    coefficient of determination and, 448
    error sum of squares, 449
    example of, 441–444
    hypotheses about regression coefficient, 451–452
    hypotheses concerning overall regression, 450–451
    least-squares estimation procedure, 442–444
    nature of the relationship and, 439–441
    regression line, 446
    scatter diagrams and, 439–440, 440f
    SPSS jump start for, 445–446
    statistical significance of regression results, 448–449
    strength of association and, 446–448
    sum of squares due to regression, 349, 449
Bivariate techniques, 438
Black box branding, 36
Blended sampling, 327
Blockbuster, 174
Blogging, 143–144
British Airways, 5, 103
Budgets. *See also* Costs
    determining sample size and, 331
    research department allocation and, 535–538
    survey method and, 133
Budweiser super bowl, 332
Burger King, 29, 34
Burke, Inc., 22
Buy-one-give-one (B1G1), 190–192

## C

Cablevision targeting, 182
California's Notice of Security Breach Law, 85
Call center telephone interviews, 126–127
Cambridge SoundWorks, 171
Canonical correlation, 467
Captive outsourcing, 531
CardLock service, 208–210
Carnival Cruise Lines, 30
Cartoon tests, 112–113, 112f
Case analysis, 49
Casuist ethical theory, 33
Causal factors, 195
Causal research, 54, 194
Causation, 471
Census, 125, 309
Central limit theorem, 335
Central tendency measures, 383–384
Certification, researcher, 41
Chance variation, 121
Channel M2, 145–146
Chase Manhattan, 86
Children's Online Privacy Protection Act (COPPA), 85
China's transition, 15

Chi-square test
    defined, 409
    of single sample, 411–412
    SPSS jump start for, 414–415
    of two independent samples, 412–416
ChoicePoint, 83
Classification matrix, 472
Clients
    client-side researcher's compensation, 537t
    confidentiality and, 25
    contact with, 24
    determining needs of, 523–525
    difficult, 525
    ethics and, 36–38
    making false promises to, 37
    profitability management and, 532–533
    requesting bids to obtain free advice and methodology, 36–37
    requesting bids when supplier has been predetermined, 36
    requesting proposals without authorization, 37
    retailer ethics, 37–38
Closed online panel recruitment, 155
Close-ended questions, 284–285
Cluster analysis, 473–476
    clustering procedures, 473–475
    K-means cluster analysis, 475
    market segmentation and, 475–476
    techniques and, 467
Cluster sampling, 323–325, 346
Clustered bar chart, 382
Coca-Cola, 188
Coding
    automated coding systems, 368–369
    consolidating responses and, 367
    data analysis and, 366–372
    entering codes, 368
    listing responses and, 367
    process of, 367–368
    questionnaires and, 273–274
    setting codes, 368
Coefficient of determination, 448, 470
Coefficient scaling, 471
Cognitive interview, 231–232
Colias, John, 526
Collinearity, 471
Columbus, Ohio, 211
Commercial online panels. *See* Online panels
Communication, 525–526, 545–546
Community Bank, 330
Comparative scales, 249
Competitive response, 217
Computer-assisted telephone interviews (CATI), 127
ConAgra Foods, 178
Concept of interest, measurement and, 223
Concomitant variation, 55, 194–195
Concomm Telecom, 353–354
Concurrent validity, 237
Confidence interval, 342
Confidence levels, 316, 342
Confidentiality
    client, 25
    outsourcing and, 532t
Confirmit, 26, 531

Confounding variables, 199
Conjoint analysis, 479–484
  example of, 479–480
  features, 480–481
  limitations of, 484
  simulation, 482–484
  techniques and, 467
  utilities, 481–482
Constant sum scales, 250, 251f
Constitutive definition, measurement and, 224
Construct equivalence, 225
Construct validity, 237–238
Constructs, measurement and, 224
Consumer and industrial corporate marketing
  research departments, 25–26
Consumer and industrial goods and services
  producers, 20–22
Consumer drawings, 113, 114f
Consumer involvement, attitude measurement
  and, 242
Consumer orientation, 2
Consumer privacy, 81–85
  behavioral tracking and, 83
  federal laws and, 85
  government actions and, 85
  identity theft and, 83–84
  online trackers, 84f
  state laws and, 85
Consumer Vision System (CVS), 55
Consumer watch suppliers, 26–27
Contact/completion rates, 349
Contamination, experimental research and, 202
Content validity, 235–236
Contrived situations, observation research and,
  166–167
Control groups, experimentation and, 201
Controlled test markets, 210–211
Convenience samples, 325
Convergent validity, 237
Cookies, 183
Corporate marketing research, 28–31
  external clients and, 28–29
  finance departments and, 30
  franchisees and, 29
  human resource managers and, 30
  internal clients and, 29–31
  marketing managers and, 29–30
  top management and, 30
  vendors and, 28–29
Correlation analysis, 452–457
  explaining correlation results, 455–456
  Pearson's product–moment correlation, 456–457
Correspondence analysis, 467
Costs. See also Budgets
  conducting marketing research and, 10
  cost-plus projects, 526
  experimental research and, 201
  management of, 531–532
  online surveys and, 150
  questionnaires and, 302–303
  test marketing and, 212
Coupons, 17
Coyle, Karin, 457
Craigslist, 146
Cramer, Clayton E., 457
Creative problem-solving process, 545t
Creativity, 545
Criterion-related validity, 236–237
Cronbach alpha technique, 234
Cross-assignment of work, 529
Cross-tabulations, 380
Cross-training, 529
Cultural issues, outsourcing and, 532t

Curtis Publishing Company, 11
Custom research firms, 22
Custom Research Incorporated, 532
Customer care research, 108
Customer satisfaction, 4–5, 64–66, 257
Customers
  loyalty of, 68f
  retention of, 5
  return rates and, 66f
Cyber criminals, 84

D
Daboll, Peter, 542
Data analysis
  coding and, 366–372
  data entry and, 372–374
  descriptive statistics and, 383–386
  editing and, 362–366
  graphical representations and, 379–383
  logical cleaning of data and, 374–375
  purpose of, 57
  quality assurance, 360–362
  software for, 379
  tabulation and statistical analysis, 375–379
  validation and, 359–360
Data cleaning, 374–375
Data collection, 56–57
  questionnaire design and, 276–281
  sampling and, 312–313
Data entry
  intelligent entry systems and, 373
  process and, 373
Data graphical representation, 379–383
  bar charts and, 381–383
  line charts and, 380
  pie charts and, 381
Data management, on-line analysis and, 13
Data mining, 77–78
Data quality, survey method and, 133–134, 134t
Data quality management, 529–530
Data scientist job market, 465
Data visualization, 81, 81f
Decision Analyst, 22, 150
Decision makers, motivation to use research
  information, 61–62
Decision rule, hypothesis testing and, 401
Decision support systems (DSS), 87–88
Degrees of freedom, 409
Deliberate falsification, survey research and, 124
Deliverable quality, outsourcing and, 532t
Delphi Method, 110–111
Demographics, test markets and, 208
Deontology, 32
Dependent variables, 54, 438
Descriptive function, marketing research and, 4
Descriptive statistics
  central tendency measures, 383–384
  dispersion measures, 384–386
  mean, 384
  median, 384
  mode, 384
  percentages and statistical tests, 386
Descriptive studies, 54
Design control, extraneous variables and, 199
Determinant attitudes, 261
Di Resta, Ellen, 171
Diagnostic function, marketing research and, 4
Dichotomous questions, 285
Differences and relationships
  analysis of variance and, 425–428
  evaluation of, 395–396
  goodness of fit and, 409–416
  hypotheses about one mean and, 416–420

hypotheses about proportions, 422–424
hypotheses about two means, 421–422
hypothesis testing and, 398–407
P values and significance testing, 428–429
statistical significance and, 396–398
Digital money, 15
Direct observation, 167–168
Direct questioning, determinant attitudes and,
  261–262
Discriminant analysis, 467
Discriminant coefficients, 473
Discriminant score, 473
Discriminant validity, 237
Discussion guide, focus groups and, 99, 100t
Disguised observation, 167
Dispersion measures, 384–386
Disproportional allocation, 322
Dodd, Michelle, 319
Do-it-yourself (DIY) survey research, 298–299
Domain knowledge, outsourcing and, 532t
Domino's Pizza, 86
Door-to-door interviews, 125
Double-barreled question, 288
DoubleClick, 78
Drillman, Paula, 113
Driver's license, as sampling frames, 310–311
DSS Research, 22, 23
Dual questioning, 262
Dummy variables, 470–471
DuPont, 30
Dutch researchers, 341

E
E. & J. Gallo Winery, 30–31
Editing
  data analysis and, 359–366
  questionnaires and, 274
Electroencephalograph (EEG), 176–178
Electronic test markets, 210
Eli Lilly, 179
Elimination of other possible causal factors, 195
Elrick and Lavidge Marketing Research, 22
Employee liability, outsourcing and, 532t
Equivalence, 234
Equivalent form reliability, 233–234
E-readers, 184
Error checking routines, 374
Error minimization, survey research and, 124t
Error sum of squares, 449
Ethics, 32–41
  abusing respondents and, 35
  allowing subjectivity into research, 34–35
  black box branding and, 36
  casuist ethical theory, 33
  client ethics, 36–38
  deontological theory and, 32
  ethical theories, 32–33
  field service ethics, 38
  low-ball pricing and, 33–34
  making false promises and, 37
  professionalism and, 40–41
  requesting bids to obtain free advice and
    methodology, 36–37
  requesting bids when supplier has been
    predetermined, 36
  requesting proposals without authorization, 37
  research supplier ethics, 33–36
  respondents' rights and, 38–41
  retailer ethics, 37–38
  selling unnecessary research and, 35
  using professional respondents and, 38
  utilitarianism and, 33
  violating client confidentiality and, 35

Ethnographic research, 169–174
  advantages of, 169–170
  conducting, 170–172
  focus groups, 173
  focus groups and, 174
  observation, 172
  online survey, 173
  participant documentation, 172
  people interact, 172, 173
  pictures, 173
  triangulation and, 171
  utilization study, 173
  video diaries, 173
Evaluative research, 8
Executive interviews, 125
EXelate Media, 78
Expectations, managing, 528
Experience surveys, 49
Experimental design, 200
Experimental effect, 201
Experimental notation, 196–197
Experimental setting, 195–196
Experimental validity, 196
Experimentation. *See also* Extraneous variables;
    Test markets
  appropriate time order of occurrence, 195
  causal factor elimination and, 195
  concept of, 194
  concomitant variation and, 194–195
  demonstrating causation, 194–195
  experimental design/effect, 200–201
  experimental notation, 196–197
  experimental validity, 196
  extraneous variables, 197–199
  field experiments, 196
  high cost of, 201
  implementation problems, 202
  laboratory experiments, 195–196
  laboratory/field setting, 195–196
  limitations of, 201–202
  pre-experimental designs, 202–203
  quasi-experiments, 205–206
  security issues and, 201
  selected experimental designs, 202–206
  selection bias and gender, 203–204
  treatment variable and, 200
  true experimental designs, 204–205, 204f
  validity and, 196
Exploratory research, 48
External validity, 196
Extraneous variables, 197–199
  design control and, 199
  history, 197
  instrument variation, 198
  maturation, 197
  mortality, 198
  physical control and, 199
  randomization and, 199
  regression to the mean, 199
  selection bias, 198
  statistical control and, 199
  testing effects, 198
Eye tracking, 178–179
Ezekiel, Mordecai, 12

F

*F* test, 427
Face validity, 235
Facebook, 6, 78, 83, 184–185
Facebook Questions, 301–302
Facial action coding system, 179–180
Facilities, focus groups and, 96
Factor analysis, 467, 476–479

factor loadings and, 478
factor scores and, 477–478
naming factors and, 479
number of factors to retain and, 479
Factor loadings, 478
Factor scores, 477–478
Fair Credit Reporting Act (FCRA), 85
False promises, 37
Falsification, survey research and, 124
Federal Express, 25
Federal laws, consumer privacy and, 85
Female Behavioral Insight (FBI) profiles, 240
Field experiments, 196
Field management companies, questionnaires
    and, 296–297
Field service ethics, 38
Field service firms, 24–25
Final questionnaire copy, 294–295
Finance departments, 30
Financial Services Modernization Act, 85
Finite population correction factor, 348
Fisher-Price toys, 176
Flexibility, difficult clients and, 529
Focus groups, 95–105. *See also* Online focus
    groups
  advantages of, 104
  client's role and, 101
  conducting, 96–102, 96f, 97f, 98t, 100t, 101t
  costs of, 109
  disadvantages of, 104–105
  discussion guide and, 99, 100t
  ethnographic research and, 174
  facilities for, 96
  group dynamics and, 95
  instant analysis and, 101
  length and, 99, 101
  marketing professionals as respondents and,
      103–104
  moderators and, 98–99
  online and mobile groups and, 102
  panels and, 102
  participants and, 97–98
  popularity of, 95–96
  report and, 101–102
  response time per question and, 101t
  role of, 49–50
  Rotated Opposed View, 102–103
  sample screening questions for, 98
  setting for, 96–97, 97f
  trends and, 102–104
Follow up, 58, 528
Foote, Nelson, 261
Forced choice, 260
Ford Motor Company, 111
Formatting, research report, 504
Frame error, survey research and, 121
Franchisees, 29
Frito-Lay, 166, 188, 325
Fuller's brewery, 215

G

Gale, Harlow, 11
Galvanic skin response, 178
Garbologists, 167
Gatorade, 30
Gender, selection bias and, 203–204
Gender recognition systems, 180
General Electric (GE), 113, 261
General Mills, 188, 214
General Motors, 180
Geographic information systems (GIS), 86–87
Global Bazaar Segmentation analysis, 432–433
Goal orientation, 2

Gold's Gym, 86
Goodman, John, 259
Goodness of fit, 409–416
  chi-square test of a single sample, 411–412
  chi-square test of two independent samples,
      412–416
Goodyear, 188
Google, 83
Google Consumer Surveys, 18
Gould, Jeffrey B., 457
Government actions, consumer privacy and, 85
Gramm-Leach Bliley Act (Financial Services
    Modernization Act), 85
Graphic rating scales, 244–245, 244f
Graphical representation. *See* Data graphical
    representation
Greenfield Online, 150, 151
Group dynamics, 95

H

Hadoop, 484
Halo effect, 252
Hard-to-reach contacts, online surveys and, 150
Harris Interactive, 150, 211
Health Insurance Portability and Accountability
    Act, 85
Heinz, 178
Hermeneutic research, 109
Hewlett-Packard, 125
Hill, Dan, 180
History variable, experimentation and, 197
Human observation, 169–176
  ethnographic research and, 169–174
  mystery shoppers and, 174–175
  one-way mirror observations, 175–176
Human resource managers, 30
Hypotheses about one mean, 416–420
  *t* test, 417–420
  *Z* test, 416–417
Hypotheses about proportions, 422–424
  proportion in one sample, 422–423
  two proportions in independent samples,
      423–424
Hypotheses about regression coefficient,
    451–452
Hypotheses about two means, 421–422
Hypotheses concerning overall regression, 450–451
Hypothesis test of proportions, 422
Hypothesis testing, 398–407
  calculating value of test statistic, 401
  choosing appropriate statistical test and, 399
  degrees of freedom, 409
  developing decision rule, 401
  error types in, 402–403
  independent *vs.* related samples, 408–409
  null hypothesis and, 399
  one-tailed tests and, 403–404
  significance testing, tips, 404–405
  starting the hypothesis, 399
  stating the conclusion and, 402
  two-tailed tests and, 403–404
  type I error and, 402–403, 402t
  type II error and, 402–403, 402t

I

Iceberg principle, 50
Identity theft, 83–84
IDEO, Inc., 171
Immel, Jeff, 258
Implementation problems, experimental research
    and, 202
IMS Health, 23
Inaccuracy, secondary data and, 76

Incidence rate, 134–135, 349, 530
Independence assumption, 347
Independent samples, 408
Independent variables, 54, 438
Indirect observation, 167–168
Indirect questioning, determinant attitudes
    and, 262
Individual depth interviews, 106–110
    advantages of, 106–107
    applications of, 108
    costs of, 109
    customer care research and, 108
    disadvantages of, 107
    hermeneutics and, 109
    online, 146–147
Infopoll, 152
Information availability, 51–52
Information sources, Internet's impact on, 13
Infrastructure, outsourcing and, 532t
Inner-directed lifestyles, 233t, 234
Innovation, 545
Innovation Focus, Inc., 103
Input error, survey research and, 123
Insight, consumer and market, 543–545
Insourcing, 531
Instant analysis, focus groups and, 101
In-store tracking, 180–181
Instrument variation, experimentation and, 198
Insufficiency, secondary data and, 77
Interactive testing effects, experimentation
    and, 198
Internal consistency reliability, 234
Internal databases, 77–78
    behavioral targeting and, 78
    creation of, 77
    data mining, 77–78
Internal validity, 196
International Restaurant Concepts, 215
Internet. See also Online marketing research
    commercial online panels, 154–159
    mobile Internet research, 157–159
    online survey research, 149–154
    online trackers, 84f
    privacy issues and, 81–85
    questionnaire development and, 297
    sampling and data collection on, 319
    secondary data and, 140–144, 141t–142t
    surveys on, 326–327
Internet. See also Online marketing research
    presentations on, 513
    report dissemination and, 57
Interpretations, research report and, 502–505
Interrupted time-series designs, 206
Interval estimates, 342
Interval scales, 228
Interviewer error, survey research and, 122
Interviewer training, 24
Interviewing status reports, 24
Interviews, 359
In-Touch Survey Systems, Inc., 129
Intraclass correlation, 453
Intranets, 50
Intuitive understanding, 92
Inverse relationships, experimentation, 194–195
Itemized rating scales, 245–248, 246f–247f, 248t

**J**
Jet Blue, 49
Jiffy Lube, 174
Job losses, outsourcing and, 532t
Johnny Jets Drive-Ins, 551–552
Judgment samples, 325–326

**K**
Kellogg, 122, 178
Kendall-Jackson Winery, 30
Ketchum Advertising, 104
Kimberly-Clark, 55, 178, 187
Kiosk-based computer interviewing, 129
Kirby, Douglas, 457
Kiwi Brands, 34
K-means cluster analysis, 475
Knight, Kathleen, 534
Knowledge Based Marketing, 319
KR-20 technique, 234
Kraft Foods, 75

**L**
Laboratory experiments, 195–196
Lambda Networks, 461
Lead country strategy, 217
Leadership, 542–543
Least-squares estimation procedure, 442–444
Levels of confidence, 316
Leverage, 534
Lexus, 5
Likert scales, 245–246, 253–254, 255f
LimeWire, 83
Limited-function research firms, 23
Line charts, 380
Linked-In, 6
Listening, difficult clients and, 524
Logic of statistical (stat) testing, 397–398
Logical or machine cleaning of data, 374–375
Logistic regression analysis, 466–467
Longitudinal study, 129
Lotame, 78
Low-ball pricing, 33–34

**M**
Machine observation, 176–183
    cablevision targeting, 182
    electroencephalograph and, 176–178
    eye tracking and, 178–179
    facial action coding service and, 179–180
    galvanic skin response and, 178
    gender and age recognition systems and, 180
    in-store tracking, 180–181
    neuromarketing, 176–181
    symphony IRI Consumer Network and,
        182–183
    television audience measurement and, 181
    TiVo targeting, 182
Magnetic resonance imaging (MRI), 176
Mail panels, 129
Mail surveys, 129–131, 131t
Main testing effects, experimentation and, 198
Mall-intercept interviews, 125–126
Management
    client profitability management, 532–533
    communication and, 525–526
    converting management to marketing research
        problems, 51–52
    difficult clients and, 525
    managerial significance, 408
    managerially important differences, 396
    marketing managers, 29–30
    marketing research department management,
        535–549
    profitability and, 532–533
    research process management, 527–535
    staff management and development, 533–535
    supplier consolidation and, 525
    supplier management, 523–525

time management, 530–531
Manipulation, experimentation and, 200
Manufacturers, 22
MapInfo, 87
MARC Group, 22
Margin of error, 530
Market Facts, Inc., 22
Market Research Executive Board (MREB), 542
Market research proposal, 69–72
Market segmentation, cluster analysis and,
    475–476
Marketing concept, 2
Marketing mix, 3
Marketing research
    adolescent years: 1920-1950, 11–12
    connected world: 2000-present, 13
    corporate perspective on, 28–31
    decision to conduct, 8–10, 10t
    defined, 4
    descriptive function and, 4
    development of, 11–15
    early growth: 1900-1920, 11
    general categories of organization involved in,
        20–25, 21t
    importance to management, 4–5
    inception: pre-1900, 11
    mature years: 1950-2000, 12
    objectives and, 51
    opportunistic nature of, 2
    predictive function and, 4
    proactive role of, 6–7
    problem specification and, 51
    return on quality and, 5
    situations precluding, 8–10
    understanding marketplace and, 6
    user-generated content and, 6
Marketing research and ethical issues, 495
Marketing Research Association code of
    marketing standards, 41t
Marketing research department management,
    535–549
    budget allocation and, 535–538
    client-side researchers' compensation, 537t
    communicating for impact and, 545–546
    creative problem-solving process, 545t
    creativity and innovation, 545
    customer and market insights and, 543–545
    decision-making role and, 540–546
    leadership and strategic priorities, 542–543
    marketplace impact and, 542
    prioritizing projects and, 536–537
    retaining skilled staff and, 537–538
    return on investment and, 546–549
    soft skills for researchers and, 539
    supplier selection and, 538–540
Marketing research industry
    big data analytic firms, 24
    consumer and industrial goods and services
        producers and, 20–22
    custom research firms, 22
    evolving structure of, 20
    governments and Universities and, 22
    limited-function research firms, 23
    manufacturers and, 22
    marketing research supplier service firms,
        24–25
    media companies and, 22
    online and mobile tracking firms, 23
    organizations involved, 20–25
    period of change, 31–32
    retailers and wholesalers and, 20
    software firms, 25
    specialized service suppliers, 24–25

state of, 31–32
structure of, 20, 21f
syndicated service firms, 22–23, 23t
Marketing research online community (MROC), 147–149
Marketing research process, 53–58, 53f
    causal studies and, 54–55
    client needs and, 523–525
    concomitant variation and, 55
    data analysis and, 57
    data collection and, 56–57
    dependent variables and, 54
    descriptive studies and, 54
    following up and, 58
    independent variables and, 54
    Internet and report dissemination, 57
    management of, 527–535
    nonprobability sample and, 56
    observations and, 55
    probability sample and, 56
    report quality and, 57
    report writing and presentation and, 57
    research design creation, 54–55
    research method choice and, 55–56
    sampling procedure selection and, 56
    spurious association and, 55
    surveys and, 55
    temporal sequence and, 54
    variables and, 54
Marketing research proposal, 59–61
    benefits of, 74t
    elements in, 59–60
    marketing research suppliers and, 61
Marketing research suppliers, 61
MarketingResearchCareers.com, 25
Marketplace understanding, 6
MarketSight, 25, 531
Marriott Hotels, 30, 171
Matching, experimentation and, 198
Mathematical differences, 396
Maturation, experimentation and, 197
McCann-Erickson, 113
McDonald's, 29, 174
McDonald's test marketing, 207
Mean, 343–345, 384
    hypotheses about one mean, 416–420
    hypotheses about two means, 421–422
Measurement
    basic levels of, 226t
    concept of interest and, 223
    constitutive definition and, 224
    construct development and, 224
    construct equivalence and, 225
    error types and, 402–403
    instrument bias and, 123
    interval scales and, 228
    nominal scales and, 226–227
    operational definition and, 224–225
    ordinal scales and, 227–228
    process of, 222, 223f
    questionnaire design, 231–232
    random error and, 229–230
    ratio scales and, 228
    reliability and, 232–233, 238
    role ambiguity and, 225t
    rules and, 222–223
    scale, defined, 226
    survey research and, 121–122
    systematic error and, 229–230
    validity and, 234–238, 235t
Measurement scales, 226–228
    attitude measurement scales, 244–259
    attitudes and behavior, 242–243

balanced vs. nonbalanced scale, 260
comparative scales, 249
constant sum scales, 250, 251f
determinant attitudes, 261
direct questioning and, 261–262
enhancing marketing effectiveness and, 243
forced vs. nonforced choice, 260
graphic rating scales, 244–245, 244f
identifying determinant attitudes and, 262
indirect questioning and, 262
itemized rating scales, 245–248, 246f–247f, 248t
Likert scales, 245–246, 253–254, 255f
long-term prognosis improvement, 266–270
management decision making and, 261–263
multidimensional scales, 243
net promoter score, 258
noncomparative scales, 248
observation and, 262
one-stage format, 248
paired comparison scales, 250, 250f
purchase-intent scales, 254–257, 256t
rank-order scales, 249, 249f
scale categories and, 260
scale conversions, 257–258
scale selection considerations, 259–260
scale type considerations, 259
scaling defined, 243
semantic differential scales, 250–252, 251f
slider scales, 245–246
stapel scales, 252–253, 252f
two-stage format, 248
unidimensional scales, 243
Media companies, 22
Median, 384
Meineke Car Care Centers, 86, 87
Merton, Robert, 12
Miller, Christopher, 103
Miller, Jim, 215
Miller Brewing Company, 215
Miracle Whip, 29
Misrepresentation, unconscious, 124
Mobile Internet research, 157–159
Mobile Web, 14–15
Mode, 384
Moderators, focus groups and, 98–99
Mortality, experimentation and, 198
MSN, 83
Multidimensional scaling (MDS), 243, 467
Multiple discriminant analysis, 472–473
    applications of, 473
    discriminant coefficients and, 473
    discriminant score and, 473
    metric scale and, 472
    nominal or categorical dependent variable and, 472
Multiple regression analysis
    applications of, 469
    causation and, 471
    classification matrix, 472
    coefficient of determination and, 470
    collinearity and, 471
    dummy variables and, 470–471
    measures, 470
    potential use and interpretation problems, 471–472
    regression coefficients and, 470
    sample size and, 472
    scaling of coefficients and, 471
    standardizing regression coefficients, 471–472
    techniques and, 466
Multiple time-series designs, 206
Multiple-choice questions, 285–286

Multiple-row, three-dimensional bar charts, 382–383
Multistage area sampling, 324
Multivariate analysis of variance (MANOVA), 467
Multivariate and bivariate correlation combined, 457
Multivariate data analysis
    big data and Hadoop, 484
    cluster analysis, 473–476
    conjoint analysis, 479–484
    data analysis techniques, 466–467
    factor analysis, 476–479
    multiple discriminant analysis, 472–473
    multiple regression analysis, 468–472
    multivariate software, 466–468
    predictive analytics, 484–487
    procedures, 464–466, 466b
Multivariate software, 466–468
Multivariate techniques, 438
Mystery shoppers, 29, 174–175

**N**

Naming factors, 479
National Cattlemen's Beef Association (NCBA), 160
National Consumer Panel (NCP), 182
Natural situations, observation research and, 166–167
NEC Electronics, 180
Net promoter score (NPS), 258–259
Neuromarketing, 176–181
Neutral networks, 77
Newsgroups, 140–144
Nextel, 179
Nice-to-know syndrome, 52
Nickelodeon, 48–49
Nielsen, A.C., 12
Nielsen Company. See also ACNielsen
    consumer buy and, 27
    consumer watch and, 26–27
    syndicated data and, 23
Nielsen Media Research, 181
Nominal scales, 226–227
Nonbalanced scales, 260
Noncomparative scales, 248
Nonforced choice, 260
Nonprobability samples, 56, 316
Nonprobability sampling methods, 325–326
    convenience samples, 325
    judgment samples, 325–326
    quota samples, 326
    snowball samples, 326
Nonrandomnes, 316
Nonresponse bias, 123, 340–341
Nonsampling errors, 318
Normal distribution, 335–337
    central limit theorem and, 335
    general properties and, 335–336
    proportional property of, 336
    standard deviations and, 337
    standard normal distribution, 336–337
Null hypothesis, 399
Numbers International, 379

**O**

Observation research, 55. See also Human observation; Machine observation
    advantages of, 168
    approaches to, 166
    B1G1, 190–192
    conditions for using, 166
    determinant attitudes and, 262

Observation research (*Continued*)
 direct *vs.* indirect observation, 167–168
 disadvantages of, 168–169
 human observation, 169–176
 human *vs.* machine observers, 167
 machine observation, 176–183
 natural *vs.* contrived situations, 166–167
 nature of, 165–169
 observation situations, 166t
 online tracking, 183–187
 open *vs.* disguised observation, 167
 virtual shopping and, 187–188
Oluwatosin, Olatunji, 83
One-group, pretest-posttest design, 203
One-shot case study design, 202–203
One-stage cluster sample, 323
One-way frequency tables, 375–377
One-way mirror observation, 175–176
Online focus groups, 144–147
 MROC, 147–149
 using Channel M2 and, 145–146
 using Web to find participants in, 146
 virtual groups, 144–145
 webcam groups, 144
Online individual depth interviewing, 146–147
Online marketing research
 blogs and, 143–144
 commercial online panels, 154–159
 focus groups and, 144–147
 individual depth interviewing and, 146–147
 mobile Internet research, 157–159
 newsgroups and, 140–144
 online qualitative research, 144–149
 online survey research, 149–154
 online world, 140
 periodical, newspaper, and book databases, 140
 secondary data and, 140–144, 141t–142t
 sites of interest, 140
 social media, 159–161
Online panels, 154–159
 by-invitation-only, 155
 closed online panel recruitment, 155
 open online panel recruitment, 154
 panel freshness and, 157
 panel management and, 156–157
 panel recruitment and, 154–156
 respondent cooperation and, 156
Online qualitative research, 144–149
Online survey research, 149–154. *See also* Online
  panels
 advantages of, 149–150
 design and, 153
 disadvantages of, 150–151
 gaining survey completions and, 152–154
 maximizing user response and, 276
 unrestricted Internet sample and, 151
 Web hosting sites and, 154
 Web survey software and, 152
Online tracking, 183–187
 cookies and, 183
 digitally agnostic, 183
 e-readers, 184
 Facebook, 184–185
 Pinterest, 185–186
 social media tracking, 184
 Twitter, 186–187
Open observation, 167
Open online panel recruitment, 154
Open-ended questions, 281–284, 366–368
Operational definition, measurement and, 224–
 225, 225t
Operational procedures, selecting sample
 elements and, 316–317

Operational sampling plan, 315t
Opinion Research Corp., 22
Opportunity, conducting marketing research
 and, 9
Opportunity identification, 47
Optimal allocation, 322
Oral presentations, Internet and, 13
Ordinal scales, 227–228
Organization, research report, 501–502
Oscar Mayer, 4
Outsourcing, 531, 532t
Owad, Tom, 82

**P**

*P* values, 428–429
Paired comparison scales, 250, 250f
Panel management, online surveys and, 150
Panels. *See* Online panels
Panels, focus groups and, 102
Papp, Daryl, 542
Participants, focus groups and, 97–98
PatientsLikeMe, 83
Pearson's product-moment correlation, 452–457
 medical statistics and, 456–457
 rethinking of, 453–454
Peisner, Steven, 84
People Reader, 23
Percent of variance accounted for, 455
Percentages and statistical tests, 386
Personalization, online surveys and, 150
Personification, 111–112
P.F. Chang's, 174
Phone numbers, estimating requirements for, 349
Photo sorts, 113
Physical control, extraneous variables and, 199
Pictured Aspirations Technique (PAT), 113
Pie charts, 381
Pilot studies, 48
Pinterest, 185–186
Pitney Bowes Places, 137–138
Pizza Quik, 491–492
Point estimates, 341–342
Point Forward, Inc., 146
Point of view, clients, 524
Population
 parameter, 318
 sample distributions and, 337
 sample size and, 346–349
 sampling and, 309–312, 311t
 specification error, 121
 standard deviation, 334
Positive relationships, experimentation and,
 194–195
Post Cereals, 29
PowerPoint, 513
Predictive analytics, 484–487, 492–493
 applying results, 486–487
 data set, 485
 Gibson's use of, 492–493
 modeling process, 485
 pre-processing data, 485
 privacy concerns and ethics, 487
 results validation, 485–486
 tools and applications, 487
Predictive function, marketing research and, 4
Predictive validity, 237
Pre-experimental designs, 202–203
 one-group pretest–posttest design, 203
 one-shot case study design, 202–203
Presentations, 508–513
Pretesting, questionnaire design and, 294–295
Price sensitivity, 243

Primary data, 73
Privacy. *See* Consumer privacy; Identity theft
Privacy rights, respondents and, 39–40
Probability samples, 56, 316
Probability sampling methods, 318–325
 cluster sampling, 323–325
 simple random sampling, 319–320
 stratified sampling, 321–323
 systematic sampling, 320–321
Probing, questionnaire design and, 282–283
Problem alerts, secondary data and, 75
Problem clarification, secondary data and, 74
Problem definition, 46–52, 47f
 avoiding nice-to-know syndrome, 52
 case analysis and, 49
 completing exploratory research and, 50
 determining if information already exists,
  51–52
 determining information purpose and, 48
 determining question answerability, 52
 experience surveys and, 49
 exploratory research and, 48
 focus groups and, 49–50
 Intranet use and, 50
 management decision problem and, 51
 marketing research objective and, 51
 marketing research problem and, 51
 opportunity identification and, 47
 pilot studies and, 48
 secondary data analysis and, 49
 situation analysis and, 48
 stating research objectives and, 52
 symptom use to clarify problem, 50–51
Problem solution, secondary data and, 74
Problems, looking out for, 528
Problem-solving process, 545t
Procter & Gamble, 9, 20, 21t, 163–164, 166,
 172, 178, 188
Product-specific test market, 215
Professional Researcher Certification program,
 41
Professional respondents, 38
Professionalism, 40–41
 fostering, 40
 researcher certification and, 41
Profitability, 532–533
 marketing research firm and, 532
 questionnaires and, 302–303
Programmatic research, 8
Project manager, communication role and, 526
Project prioritization, 536–537
Projective tests, 110–115
 analogies, 111
 cartoon tests, 112–113, 112f
 consumer drawings and, 113, 114f
 obstacles and, 110–111
 personification and, 112–113
 photo sorts, 113
 sentence and story completion tests, 112
 storytelling, 113–115
 third-person technique, 115
 word association tests, 111
Proportional allocation, 322
Proportional property of the normal distribution,
 336
Proportions, 345–346, 422–424
Proposal tips, 534–535
Proposals, requesting without authorization, 37
Prosumers, 103–104
Psychodrama tests, 111
Purchase data, experimentation and, 217
Purchase-intent scales, 254–257, 256t
Purposeful nonramdomness, 316

## Q

Q data analysis software, 379
Qualitative research. *See also* Online qualitative
 research
 Delphi method, 110–111
 focus groups, 95–105
 future of, 115–116
 individual depth interviews, 106–110
 limitations of, 94
 nature of, 92–94
 popularity of, 93–94
 projective tests, 110–115
 quantitative research *vs.*, 93, 93t
 sample size for, 346–349
Quality, return on, 5
Quality control, 24
Quantitative research, qualitative research *vs.*,
 93, 93t
Quasi-experiments, 205–206
 interrupted time-series designs, 206
 multiple time-series designs, 206
Question answerability, 52
Question response format, 281–286
Question wording, 287–290
 biasing the respondent and, 288
 clarity and, 287–288
 respondent's ability to answer and, 288–289
 respondent's willingness to answer and,
 289–290
Questionnaire design
 approval and, 293–294
 close-ended questions and, 284–285
 cognitive interview, 231–232
 data collection method and, 276–281
 dichotomous questions and, 285
 DIY research, 298–299
 final questionnaire preparation, 294–295
 flow and layout and, 290–292
 information accomplishing objectives
 and, 293
 model closing, 292
 model introduction/opening, 292
 multiple-choice questions and, 285–286
 objectives, resources, and constraints and,
 275–276
 open-ended questions and, 281–284
 organization and, 290t
 pretesting and revising, 294
 probing, and, 282–283
 process, 275–297, 275f
 question length and, 293
 question necessity and, 293
 question response format and, 281–286
 question wording and, 287–290
 questionnaire evaluation and, 293
 scaled-response questions and, 286
 supervisor's instructions and, 295–296
 survey implementation and, 295
Questionnaire flow and layout, 290–292
 general questions and, 291
 getting respondent interest and, 291
 instructions in capital letters, 292
 model closing, 292
 model introduction/opening, 292
 proper introduction and closing and, 292
 questions requiring "work, 291
 screening questions and, 290–291
 sensitive, threatening, and demographic
 question positioning, 292
Questionnaires
 adaptation, 300
 costs and profitability and, 302–303
 criteria for, 272–274
  decision-making information and, 272–273
  editing and coding requirements and,
   273–274
  Facebook as survey research platform,
   301–302
  field management companies and, 296–297
  Internet impact and, 297
  length of, 134
  online surveys and, 276
  respondent and, 273
  role of, 271–272
  sample questionnaire, 363–365
  self-administered, 128–129
  skip patterns and, 274, 274f
  structure of, 135
  survey research and, 123
  tips for writing, 294–295
  understanding buyer behavior and, 305–306
*Quirk's Marketing Research Review*, 25
Quota samples, 326

## R

Random sampling error, 120–121, 229–230,
 318, 529
Random-digit dialing, 314
Random-digit sampling, 126
Randomization
 controlling extraneous variables and, 199
 experimentation and, 198
Rank-order scales, 249, 249f
RapLeaf, 39
Ratio scales, 228
Real-time reporting, online surveys and, 149
Recommendations, research reports and, 504–
 505
Refusal rate, survey research and, 123
Regression, SPSS jump start for, 445–446
Regression coefficients, 470
Regression line, 446
Regression to the mean, 199
Related samples, 408–409
Relevance, secondary data and, 75–76
Reliability, 232–234
 data, 133
 equivalent form reliability, 233–234
 internal consistency reliability, 234
 split-half technique and, 234
 stability and, 233
 test-retest reliability, 233
Reports. *See* Research reports
Request for proposal (RFP), 13, 59
Research design creation, 54–55
Research Group, 329–330
Research information, decision maker
 motivation and, 61–62
Research method choice, 55–56
Research Now, 150, 155
Research objectives, 52–53
Research process management, 58–59, 527–535
 cost management and, 531–532
 data quality management and, 530–531
 outsourcing and insourcing and, 531–532
 request for proposal and, 59
 research request and, 58–59
 supplier firm organization and, 527–529
 time management and, 530–531
Research proposal, 59
Research reports, 57, 499–505
 conclusions and, 502
 data loss, 503–504
 dissemination of, 57
 executive summary and, 502
  findings interpretation and, 502–505
  formatting of, 504
  formulating recommendations and, 504–505
  graphics and, 511f–512f
  guidelines, 505–506
  insights and data, 503–504
  Internet publishing and distribution of, 13
  organization of, 501–502
  presentation and, 505
  quality of, 57
  sample background and objectives, 509f
  sample first page of executive summary, 509f,
   510f
  sample methodology, 510f
  sample table of contents, 507f
  sample title, 507f
Research request, 58–59
Research supplier ethics, 33–36
 abusing respondents and, 35
 allowing subjectivity into research, 34–35
 low-ball pricing and, 33–34
 selling unnecessary research and, 35
 violating client confidentiality and, 35
Research suppliers, 26–27
 consumer buy, 27
 consumer watch, 26–27
 largest marketing research firms, 27t
 organization and, 527–529
 supplier selection, 538–540
Researcher certification, 41
Resources, questionnaire design and, 275–276
Respondents
 online panels and, 156
 professional, 38
 questionnaires and, 273
 recruiters for, 44–45
 survey method and, 133
 telephone interviews, 127–128
Respondents' rights, 38–40
 right to be informed, 39
 right to choose, 38
 right to privacy, 39–40
 right to safety, 38–39
Response bias, survey research and, 124
Response rates, online surveys and, 150
Retail environments, 64–68
Retailer ethics, 37–38
Return on investment (ROI), 535, 546–549
 ROI complete, 547–549
 ROI lite, 546–547
Return on quality, 5
Revision, questionnaire design and, 294
Rich, David, 174
Right to be informed, respondents and, 39
Right to choose, respondents and, 38
Right to safety, respondents and, 38–39
Rite Aid, 174
Role ambiguity, measurement and, 225t
Rolling rollout, 217
Roper Starch Worldwide, 23
Rotated Opposed View (ROV), 102–103
Rotella, Perry, 80
Rule utilitarianism, 33

## S

Sample design error, survey research and, 121
Sample distribution, 337
Sample frames, secondary data and, 75
Sample size
 allowable sampling error and, 344
 budget availability and, 334
 determining, 316

Sample size (*Continued*)
  finite population correction factor and, 348
  general properties and, 335–336
  independence assumption and, 347
  multiple regression analysis and, 472
  normal distribution and, 335–337
  population and sample distributions, 337
  population size and, 346–348
  population standard deviation and, 344
  for probability samples, 331–332
  problems involving means, 343–345
  problems involving proportions, 345–346
  for qualitative research, 346–348
  rule of thumb and, 334
  sample units needed and, 350
  sampling distribution of the mean, 337–343
  sampling units required and, 349–350
  standard normal distribution and, 336–337
  statistical power and, 350–351
  for stratified and cluster samples, 346
  subgroups analyzed and, 334
  traditional statistical methods and, 335
Sampling
  address-based sampling, 315
  blended samples, 327
  definition, 308
  disproportional allocation and, 322
  Internet panels and, 319
  Internet sampling, 326–327
  multistage area sampling, 324
  nonprobability samples, 316
  nonprobability sampling methods, 325–326
  and nonsampling errors, 318
  online samples, 313
  operational sampling plan, 315t
  population and, 309
  population parameter and, 318
  probability samples, 316
  probability sampling methods, 318–325
  proportional allocation and, 322
  random-digit dialing and, 314
  sample *vs.* census, 309
  sampling frames, 310–311, 313–314
  sampling method classification, 314f
  sampling plan development, 309–317, 310f
  screening questions and, 312f
  single online respondent pool, 317
Sampling distribution of the mean, 337–343
  basic concepts and, 338–341
  confidence interval and, 342
  confidence level and, 342
  interval estimate and, 342
  making inferences on single sample, 341
  point and interval estimates, 341–342
  sampling distribution of the proportion, 343
  standard error of the mean, 338
Sampling distribution of the proportion, 343
Sampling errors, 120–121, 318, 404, 407
Sampling firms, 25
Sampling frames, 121, 310–311, 313–314
Sampling plan development, 309–317, 310f
  choosing data-collection method, 312–313
  defining population of interest,
    310–312, 311f
  operational procedure development, 316–317
  operational sampling plan execution, 317
  sample size determination, 316
  sampling frame identification, 313–314
  sampling method selection, 314, 316
Sampling precision, survey method and,
    131–133, 132t
Sara Lee Corporation, 10

Sawtooth CiW, 152
Scale categories, 260
Scale conversions, 257–258
Scaled-response questions, 286
Scaling of coefficients, 471
Scanner test markets, 210
Scanning technology, 374
Scatter diagrams, 439–440, 440f
Schmiege, Paul, 404
Scott, Walter Dill, 11
Scraping, 82
Screening questions, 98, 290–291, 312f, 533
Sechrist, Horace, 12
Secondary data. *See also* Big data analytics
  advantages of, 74–75
  analysis of, 49
  background information and, 75
  inaccuracy and, 76
  insufficiency and, 77
  internal databases and, 77–78
  Internet and, 140–144, 141t–142t
  lack of availability and, 75
  lack of relevance and, 75–76
  limitations of, 75–77
  nature of, 73–77
  potential problem alerts and, 75
  primary data research alternative and, 74
  problem clarification or redefinition and, 74
  problem solution and, 74
  sample frames and, 75
Security issues, experimental research and, 201
Security questions, sampling and, 311
Selection bias, 198, 203–204
Selection error, survey research and, 121
Selective research, 8
Self-administered questionnaires, 128–129
Selling unnecessary research, 35
Sellitsafe Inc., 84
Semantic differential scales, 250–252, 251f
Sensory Logic, 179
Sentence and story completion tests, 112
Settings, focus groups and, 96–97
Set-top boxes, 181
Shriver, Beth, 540
Significance testing, 404–405, 428–429
Silver, Nate, 90–91
Simple random sampling, 319–320
Simulated test market (SMT), 211, 216
Single online respondent pool, 317
Situation analysis, 48
Skip patterns, 274, 274f, 365–366
Slider scales, 245–246
SMT. *See* Simulated test market (SMT)
Snowball samples, 326
Social media, 6, 39, 159–161, 313
  conducting surveys, 161
  Facebook Focus Group, 160
Soft skills, marketing researchers and, 539
Soft-drink description, 455
Software firms, 25
Source of sales, 217
Split-half technique, 234
SPSS Quanquest, 152
Spurious association, causal studies and, 55
SSI Internet panels, 150
Stability, 233
Stacked bar charts, 382
Staff
  management and development, 533–535
  retaining, 537–538
Standard deviation, 336
Standard error of the mean, 338

Stapel scales, 252–253, 252f
Starbucks, 54, 55, 174
Starch, Daniel, 11
State laws, consumer privacy and, 85
Statistical control, extraneous variables and, 199
Statistical power, 350–351
Statistical precision, 407–408
Statistical significance, 396–397
Statistical significance of regression results,
    448–449
Statistical tests and their uses, 400t
Stengel, Jim, 172
Stewart, Joe, 330
Stone, Lewis, 95
Storytelling, 113–115
Strategic partnerships, 28
Stratified sampling, 321–323, 346
Strength of association, bivariate regression and,
    446–448
Strong, E.K., 11
Structural equation modeling (SEM), 467
Subaru America, 86
Subgroups analyzed, sample size and, 334
Subjectivity and research, 34–35
Sum of squares due to regression, 349
Supervisor's instructions, questionnaires and,
    295–296
Suppliers. *See* Research suppliers
Surrogate information error, survey research
    and, 122
Survey completions, online survey research and,
    152–154
Survey objectives, questionnaire design and,
    275–276
Survey research. *See also* Online survey research
  budgets and, 133
  data quality and, 133–134, 134t
  determining survey method, 131–135,
    132t, 134t
  door-to-door interviews, 125
  error minimization strategies and, 124t
  executive interviews, 125
  frame error and, 121
  incidence rate and, 134–135
  input error and, 123
  interviewer error and, 122
  mail surveys, 129–131, 131t
  mall-intercept interviews, 125–126
  measurement error and, 121–122
  measurement instrument bias and, 123
  method determination and, 131–135,
    132t, 134t
  non-Internet forms of, 132t
  nonresponse bias and, 123
  popularity of, 119–120
  population specification error and, 121
  questionnaire length and, 134
  questionnaire structure and, 135
  refusal rate and, 123
  respondent reaction requirements and, 133
  response bias and, 124
  sample design error and, 121
  sampling error and, 120–121
  sampling precision and, 131–133, 132t
  selection error and, 121
  self-administered questionnaires, 128–129
  strengths and weaknesses of, 134t
  surrogate information error and, 122
  systematic error and, 121–124, 124f, 124t
  telephone interviews, 126–127
  time availability and, 135
  types of errors in, 120–124, 120f, 124t

Survey Sampling, Inc., 25, 349
Survey Sampling International (SSI), 315, 327
SurveyGold, 152
Surveys, scannable, 374
Symphony IRI Consumer Network, 182
Symptom use to clarify problems, 50–51
Syndicated data, 23
Syndicated service research firms, 22–23, 23t
Synovate, 36, 211
Systematic error, 121–124, 124f, 229–230
Systematic sampling, 320–321
Systems orientation, 2

**T**

*t* test, 417–420
Taco Bell, 87
Target, 87, 179
Target philosophy, 486–487
TargetPro GIS software, 87
Taste tests, 133
Telephone interviews, 126–127
    call center telephone interviews, 126–127
    computer-assisted telephone interviews, 127
    predictive dialing, 126
Television audience measurement, 181
Temporal sequence, causal studies and, 54
Test groups, experimentation and, 201
Test markets
    basic approach selection and, 213–214
    CardLock service, 208–210
    characteristics of, 207–208
    controlled test markets, 210–211
    costs of, 212
    defining objective and, 213
    demographics and, 208
    indirect costs and, 212
    issues used for, 208
    lead country strategy and, 217
    McDonald's test marketing, 207
    plan execution and, 216–217
    quick scans of, 215
    rolling rollout and, 217
    scanner/electronic test markets, 210
    selection of, 214–215
    simulated test markets, 211, 216
    study steps, 213–217
    test marketing decision and, 212–213
    test procedure development and, 214
    test result analysis and, 217

traditional/standard market, 210
    types of, 210–211
Test units, 197
Testing effects, experimentation and, 198
Test-retest reliability, 233
Texas Instruments, 50, 57
Texas Red soft drinks, 220–221
Text analytics, 372
Thematic Apperception Test (TAT), 111
33across, 78
Third-person technique, 115
Tico Taco, 390
Time availability, survey method and, 135
Time management, 530–531
Tip percentages, 68f
TiVo targeting, 182
Tobii Technology, 178
Top-box measurement tool, 199–200
Total attitude score, 253
TouchWell, 516–521
Toyota, 30
Traditional/standard test market, 210
Treatment variable, 200
Triangulation, 171
True experimental designs, 204–205
    before and after with control group
      design, 205
    after-only with control group design, 205
    examples of, 204f
Twitter, 6, 186–187
Two-stage cluster sample, 323
Type I error, 350, 402–403, 402t
Type II error, 350, 402–403, 402t

**U**

Unconscious misrepresentation, survey research
    and, 124
Unidimensional scaling, 243
Unilever, 103, 178
United Way, 515–516
Unrestricted Internet sample, online survey
    research and, 151
Updates, providing, 544
UPS, 6
U.S. Census, 125
User response, maximizing in online surveys,
    276
User-generated content, 6
Utilitarianism, 33

**V**

Validation, data analysis and, 359–360
Validity, 234–238
    concurrent validity, 237
    construct validity, 237–238
    content validity, 235–236
    convergent validity, 237
    criterion-related validity, 236–237
    data, 133
    discriminant validity, 237
    face validity, 235
    as measurement instrument, 235t
    predictive validity, 237
Vendors, strategic partnerships and, 28–29
Video transmissions, focus groups and, 102
Village Home Builders, 354–355
Virtual shopping, 187–188
Voice-of-the-customer (VOC) data, 257
Voter registration list, as sampling frames,
    310–311
Vovici, 26, 531

**W**

Wal-Mart, 30, 87, 174
Walther, Larry, 550–551
Waters, Emily, 534
Web survey software, 152
Webcam online focus groups, 144
WebSurveyor, 154
Wehling, Robert, 96
Westat, 23
White, Percival, 11
Whole Food Markets, 174
Wholesalers, 20
Willets, Gary, 104
Word association tests, 111
Working phone rate, 349

**Y**

Yahoo, 82
Yen, Miaofen, 453
Yule, G. Udney, 12

**Z**

*Z* test, 416–417
Zaltman, Gerald, 114
Zoomerang, 154